The
Encyclopedia
of the Midwest

by Allan Carpenter

Editorial Assistant
Carl Provorse

Contributor
Randy Lyon

Facts On File
New York • Oxford

The Encyclopedia of the Midwest

copyright © 1989 by Facts On File, Inc.

> Facts On File, Inc.
> 460 Park Avenue South
> New York, New York 10016

Library of Congress Cataloging-in-Publication Data

Carpenter, Allan, 1917-
    The encyclopedia of the Midwest / Allan Carpenter.
      p.   cm.
    Includes index.
    ISBN 0-8160-1660-7
    1. Middle West—Dictionaries and encyclopedias.   I. Title.
F351.C33 1988
977'.003'21—dc19   88-27410
                                          CIP

British CIP data available on request

Printed in the United States of America

10 9 8 7 6 5 4 3 2 1

CONTENTS

iii

ACKNOWLEDGMENTS

The author wishes to thank the following for their very generous assistance in preparation of this work. Those sources which provided illustrations along with other valuable assistance are listed with a page number.

American Airlines, 90
Architect of the U.S. Capitol, 169
Board of Harbor Commissioners, City of Milwaukee, 318
Chicago Convention and Tourism Bureau, 24, 60, 85, 342
Chicago Historical Society, 48, 115, 171, 345, 351, 378, 381, 386, 387, 403, 407
Eisenhower Museum, Abilene, KS, 146
Evanston, Illinois, Public Library
Field Museum of Natural History, 157
Ford Motor Company, 30, 166
Greater Cleveland Growth Association, 99
Green Bay Area Chamber of Commerce, 367
Greenfield Village and Henry Ford Museum, 119
Harry S Truman Nat. Historic Site,
Ill. Dept. of Commerce, 21, 86, 226, 228, 345, 439, 442, 469
Indiana Department of Commerce, 81, 185, 347
Indiana Development Commission, 79, 240, 244, 472
Iowa Development Commission, 11, 15, 54, 124, 135, 250, 374
Jesse Besser Museum
Libraries of Loyola University
Library of Congress
Library, Rand McNally and Co.
Mackinac Island State Park Commission, 38
Mayo Clinic
Michigan Bell Telephone Company, 8, 77, 177, 235, 371
Michigan Dept. of Natural Resources, 212, 315
Michigan Travel Commission, 6, 40, 277, 294, 300
Milwaukee Public Museum, 32
Minneapolis Chamber of Commerce, 200
Minneapolis Convention and Tourism Commission, 321
Minnesota Dept. of Economic Development, 63, 265, 327, 373, 475, 489
Missouri Division of Tourism, 44, 46, 57, 75, 97, 109, 256, 257, 262, 264, 334, 427, 465
National Archives
National Hot Air Championship, 36
National Park Service, 214
National Portrait Gallery 143, 483
New York Historical Society, 65
New York Public Library, 125, 467
Northwestern University Library
Ohio Dept. of Economic Devel., 70, 103, 118, 180, 196, 203, 205, 208, 361, 376, 426
Ohio Historical Society
Owensboro-Daviess County Chamber of Commerce
State of Kentucky Dept. of Public Information, 53
State of Louisiana Office of Tourism,
U.S. Army, 154
U.S. Postal Service, Stamp Division, 127
U.S.D.I., Fish and Wildlife Service, 18
Univ. of Mich., W.L. Clements Library, 106, 397
University of Iowa, 252
Virginia State Library, 96
West Point Museum, 429
Wisconsin Division of Tourism, 151, 258, 287, 296

INTRODUCTION

Methodology

The *Encyclopedia of the Midwest* follows the usual alphabetical arrangement, presenting information of the widest variety, focused on the eight states selected by the author as comprising that region. The states are Illinois, Indiana, Iowa, Michigan, Minnesota, Missouri, Ohio and Wisconsin.

Geographers and historians fail to agree on their selection of Midwest states. The selection here is based on various factors of geography, such as the demarcation of rivers; on economy, particularly of agriculture in the case of the Midwest; and on historical and chronological considerations, among others. The varying interpretations of these factors account for the wide disparity of opinion in the selection of the states which belong in the Midwest.

The encyclopedic format of the work has been expanded to reflect the author's experience, developed over more than fifty years in writing about the states. Retaining its encyclopedic form in every sense, the work is intended also to enhance both the reader-interest and variety of the reference materials by the inclusion of types of information and methods of presentation not usually found in such a work. The addition of incidents, anecdotes and other items of human interest is intended to provide a new dimension to the encyclopedia.

The intent has been not only to present the widest possible body of reference material on the Midwest but also to offer a readable work, one to be dipped into for enjoyment as well as information.

Content

Content of the work is concentrated on the individual region involved. Every entry has been designed to meet this focus and to set the work apart from works which are readily available in general references. The *Encyclopedia of the Midwest* performs as a useful supplement to atlases, gazetteers, almanacs and condensed biographies—reference works which because of space limitations cannot devote broad attention to a particular subject within a specialized field, such as the Midwest.

Such a framework assures a greater volume of entries on the region and permits the inclusion of the more localized subject matter not provided elsewhere.

For example, the article on Jefferson Davis, President of the Confederate States, is not intended as a full-fledged biography such as may be found in more general reference works and in entire volumes dedicated to the subject. Rather, the entry on Davis in this volume is devoted to the period of, and episodes, in his life in the Midwest. Such detail often cannot be included in short general biographies. In this case such coverage can be told briefly but in a way which emphasizes the importance of the biographees in the region.

Through such specialization, the student has access to many lesser-known details about a subject, which may prove rewarding for further investigation.

Treatment of natives of the eight Midwest states is somewhat more detailed, in consideration of their indigeousness.

A word must be said here concerning the tendency of some scholars to equate quality with volume of material. The length of an entry in this work is not intended to indicate that one entry is necessarily either more or less important than a similar entry. Again, the emphasis and length of the content depend on both the relationship of the material to the region and the addition of any unique quality or qualities a given entry is thought to possess, particularly if the information given is not readily available in other references.

Illustrations

The selection of illustrations for this volume has not been based upon iconography alone. While indeed the inclusion of

6

many illustrations has been designed to emphasize the theme or importance of an existing entry, there have been other considerations in selection. Some illustrations do stand alone without reference to any other entries. These have been provided not only for visual variety and interest but also to add subject matter. Any illustration which is not related otherwise to the text will be treated as a separate entry in the caption describing it.

Further dimension is added to the work through the inclusion of archival illustrations. The regional emphasis permits use of lesser-known portraits, paintings, prints and others not generally found outside the region.

Coverage

Content is designed to cover the whole range of subject matter germane to the region, including aspects of:

Geology
Geography
History
Anthropology
Natural History
Economy
Biography
Academic Institutions
Cultural Institutions
Political, Social and Religious Concerns
Government
Education
Tourism

A brief summary of facts and statistics precedes each state entry as well as those of the larger cities of the eight states covered here.

Organization

Entries are in boldface type and are alphabetized after the comma, viz., IOWA STATE UNIVERSITY precedes IOWA, UNIVERSITY OF. Personalities are alphabetized by inverted name—LINCOLN, Abraham. However, institutions named for individuals are not inverted—GEORGE WASHINGTON CARVER NATIONAL MONUMENT. Titled personalities are listed in the manner of most frequent usage, as, La SALLE, Sieur de (Robert Cavelier), not Cavelier, Robert (Sieur de La Salle).

Subjects alluded to in one entry are often covered in more depth or in a different manner in other entries. As a help in directing readers to related entries, these are indicated within the text by the use of small capital letters, as, AGRICULTURE.

As an additional aid, a brief bibliography is included, providing reference to frequently recommended books covering the region in more depth.

Detroit, Michigan, oldest city in the Midwest, is symbollic of the region, its industries, its varied peoples and its culture.

Abolition Movement

ABOLITION MOVEMENT. Organized attempt to outlaw SLAVERY as a legal institution, relying on means ranging from philosophical debate to outright and illegal violence. In the East, protests against slavery began with the Quakers as early as 1688 and reached crusading proportions in the 1830s, about the time that strong anti-slavery sentiment also came into prominence in the Midwest. There, as in the rest of the country, the response was both philosophical and practical. Some believed only in "moral suasion," while others were determined that political action would lead to abolition of slavery; eventually, many turned to violence and lawlessness to win their goals.

A number of Midwest editors, writers, preachers and philosophers supported the moderate movement from the standpoint of morality.

Charles Osborn (1775-1850) published his important *Letters on American Slavery* in RIPLEY Ohio, in 1826. He strongly influenced the thought of the famous Abolitionist William Lloyd Garrison.

One of the earlier political conflicts over slavery resulted in the MISSOURI COMPROMISE (1820-1821). Until that time, the slave and free states were equal in number. The pro- and anti-slavery forces struggled to maintain that balance with a series of proposals and compromises that resulted in admitting Maine as a free state and Missouri as a slave state. One of the compromises required the Missouri constitution to be free of any clause that would abridge the rights of citizens of the United States. Senator Jesse B. Thomas of Illinois was one of the most important figures in the struggle to write the Missouri Compromise.

The murder by pro-slavery forces of Presbyterian minister Elijah P. Lovejoy (1802-37) in ALTON Illinois, where he published the radical Abolitionist paper *Alton Observer*, aroused widespread sympathy for leaders of the movement, both in the Midwest and throughout the North. This concern was greatly increased by the spellbinding oratory of Wendell Phillips (1811-1884) as he made the death of Lovejoy a national cause.

Nevertheless, the Midwest remained divided on the slavery issue and on how it should be addressed. The southern border states of the Midwest, and particularly in the areas nearest the borders, were torn with conflict about Abolition. The conflict was particularly strong in CINCINNATI, the leading border city. In many cases, families were torn apart, some supporting Abolition, others as violently opposed, some wishing to keep the conflict from becoming violent, with others feeling deeply that only action would be effective.

Because the Midwest lay on the line between the slavery of the South and the free states of the North, most of the Midwest states became heavily involved in the UNDERGROUND RAILROAD. In his house on the OHIO RIVER near Cincinnati, John RANKIN sheltered as many as twelve escaped slaves in a single night and personally aided more than 2,000 to escape to safety in Canada. Hundreds of whites and free blacks in the Midwest from, Ohio to Iowa, took part in the Underground Railroad movement.

There had been a fugitive slave law in the federal statutes since 1793, but it had received little attention. However, the increasing effectiveness of the Underground Railroad brought pro-slavery forces to call for urgent action, and Congress passed a tough Fugitive Slave Law as part of the Compromise of 1850. Not only were there stiff penalties for helping slaves to escape, but there also were provisions making it a crime for refusing to assist in the capture of escaped slaves.

This inflamed much of the North, and state laws were passed which appeared to run counter to the federal orders.

One of the most celebrated cases in which the Fugitive Slave Law was involved concerned Abolitionist Sherman M. BOOTH of RACINE, Wisconsin, who aided escaped slave Joshua Glover. The prosecution of Booth for violating the Fugitive Slave Law brought the federal and state courts into a classic disagreement over constitutional law. In 1854 the Wisconsin Supreme Court had declared the Fugitive Slave Law unconstitutional, and Booth was freed. However, in a shattering precedent, the U.S.

Abolition

Michigan's 24 Regiment played a prominent part in the Battle of Gettysburg. Painting by Robert Thom, copyright 1967 Mich. Bell Telephone Co.

Supreme Court on March 7, 1859, denied the right of a state to interfere in a federal case, and upheld the constitutionality of the law. The Wisconsin legislature then adopted a resolution defending state sovereignty, and controversy continued.

The entire Compromise of 1850 generally offended the Abolitionists, since it was designed to give the South equal opportunities in the new territories of the Southwest. This question was addressed in an even more inflamatory way by the Kansas-Nebraska Act of 1854. These territories were given the opportunity to choose between entering the Union as free or slave states. This set the stage for the most dramatic of all the pre-Civil War conflicts between the slavery supporters and the Abolitionists. It was assumed that Nebraska would be a free state, but Kansas was undecided, so both sides sent settlers to Kansas, where such violence erupted that the territory became known as "Bleeding Kansas." The violence continued to mount until Kansas became a free state at the beginning of the CIVIL WAR.

A key figure in the battle for Kansas was one of the most radical of them all, JOHN BROWN, former Cincinnati wool merchant, who had emerged as the symbol of militant opposition to slavery. He trained many of his Abolitionist "troops" at his headquarters at SPRINGDALE and TABOR, Iowa, where he operated stations on the Underground Railroad. His forays into Kansas increased the misery of "bleeding Kansas." His career ended with his capture of the arsenal at Harpers Ferry, then in Virginia, marking a peak of Abolitionist fervor. Cleveland Abolitionists aided in his trial for treason. With his execution, Brown became a martyr to his cause and a symbol of the anti-slavery movement.

The more moderate Abolitionists in Michigan, Wisconsin and Illinois were so dissatisfied with the existing political parties that in 1854-1856 a REPUBLICAN PARTY was established separately in each of those states to oppose the Democrats, who were seen as supporters of slavery. Each state now claims to have been the birthplace of the Republican Party.

With the DRED SCOTT DECISION (1856-1857) by

the U.S. Supreme Court, many Abolitionists concluded that peaceful means were hopeless. However, the Republican Party became the hope of many others, and with the split in the Democratic Party between North and South, in the election of 1860, the Republicans were able to elect Abraham LINCOLN of Illinois, who would become the key figure in the great struggle to follow.

Several women with Midwest associations were significant figures in Abolitionist achievement. Harriet Beecher STOWE had grown to understand and deplore slavery during her years in Cincinnati, Ohio. Her *Uncle Tom's Cabin* (1852) has been cited as one of the major influences in the Abolitionist Movement and in bringing on the Civil War.

Even distant Minnesota produced one of the major Abolitionist voices. Jane Gray SWISSHELM of ST. CLOUD published a widely known newspaper opposing slavery.

Although not a Midwesterner by birth, one of the most remarkable of the Abolitionists, Sojourner TRUTH, made her last home in BATTLE CREEK, Michigan, where she died in 1883. Born in 1797(?) in New York State, she was emancipated with the passage of the New York Emancipation Act in 1827. She became an evangelist, preaching against slavery and for woman suffrage. In the Midwest her voice was heard in Illinois, Indiana and Ohio, all responding to her remarkable power as a preacher.

Historians disagree on the extent to which the Abolitionist movement actually succeeded in bringing about the eventual end of slavery. However, there is little doubt that few political movements have conveyed the high moral purpose and commitment of the Abolitionists, whatever may have been the faults of the methods of some. Their constant and growing pressure eventually made slavery the most important political, social and moral question facing the country. The vigorous Abolitionist actions undoubtedly had hastened the onset of the Civil War. A number of anti-slavery people of the North felt that less hot-blooded action might have led to peaceful settlement of the slavery problem, but slavery might have dragged on for years or even decades without the furor of the Abolitionists. Then, perhaps, war might still have been inevitable.

ACKLEY, Iowa. City (pop. 1,794). About thirty miles west of WATERLOO, Iowa, in the north central part of the state, situated near the meeting of Grundy, Butler, Franklin and Hardin counties, on U.S. highway 20. It is a thriving center of one of the world's best agricultural areas. Known for its various auctions and fairs, the city has become widely prominent for its annual Sauerkraut Day, perhaps the only one of its kind, providing free sauerkraut, sausage and entertainment.

ADAMS, Cuyler. (Canton, IL, Aug. 20, 1852—Duluth, MN, Nov. 29, 1932). Mining engineer, developer of the CUYUNA RANGE, Minnesota. Adams journeyed to Minnesota in 1870 as an employee of the Northern Pacific Railroad. After exploring and developing mining properties in Ontario, Canada, in the latter half of the 19th Century, he returned to Minnesota. There he discoverd the Cuyuna Iron Range, where he began production in 1911. In a sense the range was named for his dog, Una. Cuyler took the first three letters of his first name and added the name of his dog to arrive at Cuyuna. The Cuyuna was the last of the great Minnesota ranges to be discovered and developed.

ADDAMS, Jane. (Cedarville, IL, September 6, 1860—Chicago, IL, May 21, 1935). Settlement worker, founder of Hull House settlement in CHICAGO. After graduation from Rockford College, she attended Woman's Medical College in Philadelphia until failing health caused her to leave in 1882. Visiting Europe to improve her health in 1887-88 she became interested in the British settlement houses and studied settlement work abroad. Inspired by the movement to help the urban poor and with a special interest in the problems of immigrants, Jane Addams returned to Illinois and founded Hull House in Chicago in 1889. There the working poor could leave their children for care and instruction, and adults could come together for study and socialization. Her affection for children, her tact in working with rich and poor alike and her overriding impulse to help soon earned the respect and help of many Chicagoans. She was particularly adept at enlisting the assistance of talented women who worked with her. By 1905 she had built a fine plant and was acknowledged to have created by far the finest facilities and program in the U.S. for working class education and recreation. Her cultural program included the Hull House Players, a music school and a labor museum. Many of Chicago's talented artists, musicians and scholars assisted in her work. Addams made Hull House the most famous settlement house in the world. Her many books helped to bring her work to public attention. The best known of these was *Twenty Years at Hull House* (1910). She later branched out to aid the woman suffrage movement and causes for world peace. A recipient of the Nobel Peace Prize in 1931, Addams was accepted as one of the greatest women of her times, receiving numerous other honors.

ADE, George. (Kentland, IN, February 9, 1866—Brook, IN, May 16, 1944). Playwright and humorist. Ade joined the staff of the Chicago *Record* in 1890. His column, done with John T. MC CUTCHEON , was given the title *Fables in Slang* in 1899. Eleven volumes written by Ade gently pointed out follies and foibles of his peers. Many have considered his work to be master portraits of the common man. He was especially praised for his masterful use of the vernacular. As a playwright Ade once had three plays in New York running simultaneously. He also wrote a number of motion picture scripts. In 1936 Ade wrote the popular book, *The Old Time Saloon*.

ADENA PEOPLE. Prehistoric peoples, remains discovered at Adena Estate, near ADENA, Ohio. In 1901 the Ohio estate of Thomas WORTHINGTON was the scene of an exciting archeological discovery. Workers at Adena were converting it to a museum when they uncovered a log building, apparently used as a tomb by a prehistoric people. Skeletons, ornaments and weapons were found. The culture first discovered at Adena was given the name of the estate. Evidences of Adena Culture have been found in various parts of Ohio and Indiana. Adena culture is characterized by great conical piles of earth often arranged in triangular groups and placed close to streams. As in the FORT ANCIENT CULTURE, there are no sacred enclosures in the Adena culture. However, as in the following HOPEWELL CULTURE, ornaments of mica and copper, beads and skillful weaving have been found along with artistic carvings in stone and bone. The mound at Miamisburg, Ohio, is the largest of the culture yet found. It reaches a height of 68 feet. Some scholars contend that the Adena and Hopewell cultures should be considered as identical. Others have thought them to be two separate groups.

The skeletons of the Adena people add to their mystery. The round skulls were different from the long skulls of other prehistoric people known in the area. They must have been almost a race of giants, with women over six feet tall and men nearly seven feet in height. It is thought they forced their way into the OHIO RIVER Valley from somewhere else about 3000 years ago, but no one is certain of their earlier origin, perhaps from Mexico, where some similar customs were known. One of their greatest achievements was in their effigy mounds. The great SERPENT MOUND near CINCINNATI is one of the premier accomplishments of early peoples anywhere on earth. This earthen mound squirms across the countryside for a quarter of a mile, with a width up to thirty feet. The mouth appears to be swallowing an egg. The engineering skills required to achieve such perfection over such an area would be enough to tax many modern designers, and evidences of other skilled craftsmanship are equally striking. Perhaps about 2,400 years ago the equally mysterious Hopewell People had begun to drive a wedge of settlement into the Adena areas. The Adena culture began to decline and the Hopewell to rise to extraordinary heights.

ADENA STATE MEMORIAL. The estate of Thomas WORTHINGTON, near CHILLICOTHE, Ohio, was donated to the state and restored as Adena State Memorial. In 1803 the estate was the scene of meeting called by Worthington at his handsome new home, Adena. Those assembled beside Worthington included William Creighton, secretary of the new state of Ohio, and the new governor, Edward Tiffin. These men were the leaders of the group that called for statehood. They had many difficult problems to discuss and worked through the night. In early morning the group had agreed on most of the solutions to their problems. When they went out to the terrace, the sun was just rising over Mount Logan to the east. Creighton, as secretary of state, had used his own seal because the state had not adopted one. The group was so impressed with the scene that Creighton proposed to use it for the future Ohio state seal, and that scene is still the one used on the seal today. The estate is open to visitors and provides ample evidence of the good life which could be attained even in early pioneer days.

ADENA, Ohio. Town (pop. 1,062), farming community near CHILLICOTHE. It grew up around Adena, the estate of Thomas WORTHINGTON, in the early 1800s. The town took the estate's name, which is derived from the Hebrew *adena* meaning "a name given to places remarkable for the delightfulness of their situations." This site of the ADENA STATE MEMORIAL preserves the Worthington estate.

ADRIAN, Michigan. City (pop. 21,186), seat of Lenawee County, southeastern Michigan on the Lower Peninsula, southwest of ANN ARBOR. Adrian was founded in 1826 by Addison J. Comstock. With his father, Darius, Comstock built the first railroad west of Schenectady, N. Y., and extended to Adrian between 1832 and 1836. The railroad was first operated with horses until a locomotive was obtained in 1837. Adrian is a prosperous small college town and an agricultural and industrial center. An impressive historical district contains seventy-nine homes of many architectural styles. The homes, privately owned, are open during special tours in September.

AGASSIZ, Lake. Prehistoric lake named in honor of naturalist and glacial expert, Louis Agassiz. Lake Agassiz covered much of present northwest Minnesota, northeast North Dakota and large portions of Canada.

AGRICULTURE. The bounty of food, fiber and livestock flowing from the Midwest equals nearly a third of the entire U.S. total value—a third of the entire agricultural income of the world's leading agricultural nation. In 1984 the total value of U.S. agricultural products was $136,000,000. Of this, the Midwest produced $41,469,000,000.

Although most crops can be, and are, grown in the region, the Midwest concentrates on corn and soybeans, providing the world's greatest production of feed and food materials. This invaluable supply of feed has enabled the Midwest to zero in on livestock, both for market and for dairy products.

For years Iowa led all the other states in value of agricultural production. However, with their high priced specialty products, California and Texas have surpassed Iowa in dollar value.

In total value of agricultural products, in 1984 Iowa dropped to third place behind California and very slightly behind Texas. Illinois is fifth in the nation and Minnesota sixth.

In the Midwest, Iowa's lead is far ahead of second place Illinois, with Minnesota a close third to Illinois. Michigan ranks last among the Midwest agricultural states. Iowa leads the nation and the world in corn production, followed by Illinois, second, and Indiana, third. Missouri produces the least corn of the Midwest states. In 1984 Illinois ranked first in

Farm and city combine in this Iowa scene near Des Moines.

soybeans, leading both the nation and the Midwest in that vastly important category. Iowa was second in 1984 in both the nation and the Midwest, but the two states historically have alternated rank in soybean production. Wisconsin is not ranked in soybean production. Iowa produces two and a half times as many hogs as any other state—far and away the the world leader in production of meat animals. Even in cattle production Iowa ranks fourth in the nation as well as first in the Midwest. Illinois is a distant second in Midwest cattle, with Missouri and Wisconsin third and fourth. However, Wisconsin is by far the U.S. leader in dairy products, with California a distant second. Minnesota is a very distant second to Wisconsin in Midwest dairy production and value. Minnesota ranks second in the U.S. in turkey production, and Indiana holds second place in the nation in production of chickens. Missouri is the only Midwest state to produce cotton, ranking last in the nation in that crop. Although not among the top wheat states, five Midwest states, Illinois, Indiana, Michigan, Minnesota and Ohio, produce substantial volumes of wheat. Only Michigan, Minnesota and Wisconsin are ranked in the production of potatoes.

The Midwest's state's agricultural production (in billions of dollars), with their principal agricultural products (1984):

Iowa—9,312, Hogs, corn, soybeans, dairy products
Illinois—6,738, Corn, soybeans, hogs, cattle
Minnesota—6,242, Dairy products, soybeans, corn, cattle
Wisconsin—5,136, Dairy products, cattle, corn, hogs
Indiana—3,924, Corn, soybeans, hogs, dairy products
Missouri—3,729, Cattle, soybeans, hogs, dairy products
Ohio—3,611, Soybeans, dairy products, corn, hogs
Michigan—2,777, Dairy products, corn, cattle, soybeans

AIR MAIL. First flights. Airmail may be said to have originated in two flights from Iowa. In 1912 pioneer aviator Lincoln Beachy was made a deputy postmaster by the postmaster at DUBUQUE. He took off from the Dubuque fairgrounds, circled over the city and dropped a special sack of mail in front of a local hotel. Two years later another pioneer Iowa aviator, William "Billy" ROBINSON of GRINNELL, was authorized to fly mail from DES MOINES to CHICAGO. He overshot his mark and landed at Kentland, Indiana, which also made a new record for a cross country flight—a total of 362 miles.

AKINS, Zoe. (Humansville, MO, October 30, 1886—Los Angeles, CA, Oct. 29, 1958). Author, poet, U.S. dramatist, screen writer. Akins won the PULITZER PRIZE in 1935 for her play *The Old Maid*. This and several of Akins' non-dramatic works, including *The Morning Glory*, were adapted for audiences. This work also became a motion picture in 1932. She wrote the screenplay based on Edna FERBER's *Showboat*. Her poetry included *Interpretations* (1911) and *The Hills Grow Smaller* (1937).

AKRON, Ohio. City (pop. 227,177), seat of Summit County, situated on the Little Cuyahoga River in northeast Ohio. Suburban communities include CUYAHOGA FALLS and BARBERTON. The city occupies an area of 60.2 square miles. The city name is derived from the Greek word meaning summit, used in the U.S. to indicate a position on a ridge or high point. With capital of $1,000 each from 19 Akron men, Benjamin Franklin GOODRICH established the Goodrich company in 1870. He had discovered a means of strengthening rubber, now called vulcanizing. Much of the success of Akron in the rubber field would be dependent on that process. Other rubber companies followed, and Akron became the world center of the RUBBER industry, producing almost every type of rubber product. These have included the dirigibles *Akron* and *Macon* and the famed Goodyear blimps.

Settlement in the area began slowly about 1807. Akron itself was laid out by Major Minor Spicer in 1825. He and his associates anticipated the coming of the OHIO AND ERIE CANAL in 1827, and the first packet on the canal was launched at Akron that year. The Canal spurred the community's growth, which was further stimulated by Akron's being named the county seat in 1842 and by the coming of the railroads.

Today, in addition to rubber, manufactures include plastics, missiles, fishing tackle, and heavy machinery. In the period from 1970 to 1984 the population declined slightly from 275,000 to 227,000. In racial composition the city's black population is 22.2 percent. Higher education is represented by the University of Akron, and the major industry is enhanced by the work of the Institute of Rubber Research. Community culture is based on a music center, symphony orchestra and an art institute, among other institutions and activities. Abolitionist leader John BROWN lived in the city from 1844 to 1846, and his house there has been preserved as a museum. One of the principal points of interest is the vast dirigible airdock, one of the world's largest structures without internal support. A unique annual event has enlivened city activities. The famous SOAP BOX DERBY's national finals have brought thousands of boys and girls to the specially built sloping track at Derby Downs. Their homemade motorless cars compete in a race for valuable scholarships.

ALBERT LEA, Minnesota. City (pop. 19,190), southeastern Minnesota, west of AUSTIN, one of the early railroad towns on the Southern Minnesota Railroad, major packing and food-processing center. Albert Lea is named for a lieutenant who published a journal and maps of the region based upon his participation on an 1835 expedition into Minnesota. In 1856 many settlers were confronted with one of the worst winters on record. Those who left in the spring, however, were replaced by large numbers of new pioneers who developed one of the most successful agricultural operations of the period. By the 1860s Albert Lea was linked to the MISSISSIPPI RIVER by the Southern Minnesota Railroad. Shipments of wheat could now easily be made to the elevators being built along the tracks. Today the city manufactures road machinery, beverages and dairy products. Albert Lea Lake is the headwaters of the Shell Rock River. On the northeast side of the lake is the Helmer Myre State Park containing 1,500 acres of prairie land and a wooded lake island. The Owen Johnson Interpretative Center, located in the park, has a large collection of Indian artifacts.

ALBERT, Eddie. (Rock Island, IL, April 22, 1908—). Character actor. Albert, whose name was originally Eddie Albert Heimberger, has been noted for playing honest guy roles in motion pictures, radio plays and on the stage. Among his credits are roles in *Brother Rat* (1938), *An Angel from Texas* (1940), *The Wagons Roll at Night* (1941), *Strange Voyage* (1945), *The Longest Day* (1962), *Miracle of the White Stallions* (1965), and a starring role in the television series *Green Acres* from 1965 to 1970. Albert is a frequent guest star and spokesman for conservation groups.

ALBION, Michigan. City (pop. 11,059), in Calhoun County, south-central Michigan on the Lower Peninsula at the forks of the Kalamazoo River. Albion College was founded there in 1835. Albion was incorporated in 1855. An industrial community, it produces wire, heaters, electronic parts, air conditioners and bakery ovens. At Albion Colege the song "Sweetheart of Sigma Chi" was composed in 1911. A century old grist mill has been converted as True Grist Dinner Theater. Festival of the Forks is the community's annual event. The area is noted for its many lakes.

ALEXANDRIA, Minnesota. City (pop. 7,-608), seat of Douglas County in west-central Minnesota, northeast of ST. CLOUD. Alexander and William Kincaid moved to the area along the shores of Lake Agnes in 1858. Other settlers soon followed and a community was formed and named Alexandria in honor of Alexander Kincaid. A townsite company erected a log hotel named the Gregory which became a favorite gathering place for settlers. In 1859 a trail was cut through the woods to connect St. Cloud and BRECKENRIDGE. The present path of Interstate 94 follows this route. With the completion of the trail, Alexandria became a convenient stopping place and has been a popular fishing and resort area. It was incorporated in 1877. The economy is based on light manufacturing, agriculture and tourism. There are 200 lakes in the vicinity. Fort Alexandria Agricultural Museum displays life in the 19th and early 20th centuries. The Runestone Museum contains the KENSINGTON RUNESTONE found on the farm of Olaf Ohman in 1898. Viking implements claimed to be of the 14th century, pioneer and Indian artifacts are displayed.

ALGOMA, Wisconsin. Town (pop. 3,856), situated in Kewaunee County on the shores of Lake MICHIGAN, Algoma is surrounded by hills which taper down to the line of sandy beach. Its name actually comes from the Indian word meaning sandy place. The community was settled in 1818. Algoma is home to the largest hardwood-manufacturing operation in the country. Plywood and veneers are produced there. Dairy products are also important. Visitors enjoy the tour of the Von Stiehl Winery and the Kewaunee County Historical Museum and Old Jail.

ALGONQUIN LANGUAGE GROUP. The Algonquin are the most varied and most widely distributed and perhaps the most historically important of the Indian peoples of North

America. They had dealings with the early European colonists almost as soon as the latter arrived. They were the first Indian peoples to make friends with the French in the north, and the settlers of Jamestown had to deal with the great confederation of King Powhatan, also of the language group. The various tribes extended from coast to coast.

Some version of the Algonquian language is native to nearly 80,000 present day Indians in the United States and Canada. At one time the language had over 50 different tribal variations.

In the Midwest the Algonquin were the most numerous and held the largest part of the territory. In the region, only the Winnebago were neither Algonquian nor Iroquoian in tongue.

Prominent Midwest Algonquin tribes included the MENOMINEE, OTTAWA, POTAWATOMI, OJIBWAY, FOX, SAUK, ILLINI and MIAMI, the latter probably the most numerous in the region.

The Algonquian groups generally sided with the French, and so in many cases were treated more harshly when control of the region finally came to the British. As population of the region increased, they were forced to give up their lands by treaty and were gradually moved to the west. After the BLACK HAWK WAR of 1832, most of the Algonquian tribes had been removed. However, they left a lasting legacy in the language, including such words as hominy, hickory, tomahawk, wigwam, woodchuck, terrapin, moccasin and hundreds of Midwest place names such as Wapsipinicon.

ALLISON, William Boyd. (Perry Township, OH, Mar. 1, 1829—Dubuque, IA, Aug. 4, 1908). U.S. Senator from 1903 to 1908, he had also served earlier terms in the House (1863-1871). Allison was one of the most influential Republican politicians of his time. He missed the nomination for president by only one vote during the Republican convention of 1888. Although a political moderate he was outspoken in promoting the farming interests of the Midwest, especially in opposing tariffs harmful to farmers. He modified the free coinage of silver in the Bland-Allison Act. Allison served Iowa in national politics longer than any other officeholder, from 1863 until his death.

ALLOUEZ, Father Claude. (Saint Didier, Haute Loire, France, June 6, 1622—Niles, MI, Aug. 22, 1689). Priest and missionary. In 1663 Allouez became the vicar general of all Indians and traders in the NORTHWEST TERRITORY. He made a missionary tour of the missions in the

area between 1667-1669 when he traveled among the POTAWATOMI Indians near GREEN BAY, Wisconsin. Allouez served as a missionary to the Outagami tribe in 1670, the year he established St. Mark's Mission and the mission of St. James among the MIAMI and MASCOUTEN tribes. He returned to the Green Bay missions in 1670. Allouez continued to work among the Indians by establishing the Mission of Rapids des Peres (now De Pere, Wisconsin) on the FOX RIVER in 1671 and a mission among the ILLINI Indians around KASKASKIA from 1677 to 1689.

ALMA, Michigan. City (pop. 9,700), Gratiot County, west of SAGINAW on Michigan's Lower Peninsula. Alma College was founded there in 1886. Alma is located near the geographical center of Michigan and hosts an annual Scottish Highland Festival and Games in late May. One of the most nearly complete and authentic of the Scottish games in the U.S., the Alma Festival has brought as many as 300,000 spectators to this small community.

ALPENA, Michigan. City (pop. 12,214), seat of Alpena County, northeastern coast of Michigan's Lower Peninsula on Lake HURON's Thunder Bay. Settled in 1854 at the head of Thunder Bay, Alpena has been known as the home of the world's largest cement plant. The lumber industry prospered until the end of the nineteenth century, and Alpena is now known for its limestone quarries and beverage and paper industries. Near the city are natural sinkholes, some more than 150 feet deep, which are caused by the sinking of the limestone crust into caverns formed by underground streams.

ALTENBURG, Missouri. Village (pop. 280), eastern Missouri in Perry County, southeast of Perryville. It was named by its settlers for Altenburg, Germany. Now a quiet farming community, Altenburg had an interesting history. It is one of six Perry County communities settled in 1839 by Saxon Lutherans. From a communal fund of just over nine thousand dollars, 4,472 acres were purchased. The land had to be cleared of timber by the settlers who, as students or professional men, were unused to hard physical labor. The citizens of Altenburg made their homes of half-timbered, neatly plastered walls covered by roofs of red tile made in local kilns. They established Concordia Seminary, the first evangelical Lutheran seminary west of the Mississippi, in a square, one-story log building dedicated on December 9, 1839.

ALTGELD, John Peter. (Niederselters, Germany, 1847—Joliet, IL, March 12, 1902). Illinois governor. Altgeld, a lawyer, was a county superior court judge from 1886 to 1891, before his election, in 1892, as the first foreign-born Democratic Illinois governor in thirty-six years. His pardon on June 26, 1892, of three men convicted of a bombing during the HAYMARKET RIOT in 1886 was controversial, but his administration, from 1892 to 1896, continued to champion liberal causes. Altgeld supported important labor legislation. Illinois' first legislative session with Altgeld as governor passed a strong factory inspection statute which regulated employment conditions for women and for children under fourteen years of age. Altgeld sponsored an amendment in 1893 which would have given the legislature the right to regulate relations between management and labor. In a referendum the amendment fell short of the necessary majority. On July 5, 1894, Altgeld protested President Cleveland's dispatch of federal troops from FORT SHERIDAN to end the Pullman Strike of the American Railway Union under the leadership of Eugene DEBS. In 1895 Illinois created a state board of arbitration to settle labor disputes. Altgeld's administration provided CHICAGO with better police courts, raised corporate and inheritance taxes, and provided the rights of parole and probation to prisoners. Ambitious for political power, Altgeld dismissed many career executives who had been appointed under Republican governors, replacing them with his own followers. Although he was denounced as a radical in his own day, he later became known as a champion of individual rights against entrenched power.

ALTON, Illinois. City (pop. 34,171), Madison Co., southwestern Illinois, north of East St. Louis, near the MISSISSIPPI RIVER, named for one of the sons of Colonel Rufus Easton, planner of the downtown area. Alton was founded in 1816. Platted in 1818 as a steamboat landing, Alton benefitted from superior quality limestone and outcroppings of coal which added to the value of the nearby land. During the 1830s Alton grew as a steamboat and packing center. Commercially the city competed with St. Louis and hoped to be the western terminal of the NATIONAL ROAD at the Mississippi River. In light balloting in 1834, Alton was nearly chosen the site of the new state capital. As the largest Illinois city on the Mississippi, Alton was the terminus of three railroads. In 1846 railroad workmen at Alton completed the destruction of the original fearsome PIASA BIRD (Thunderbird), painted by unknown prehistoric peoples, when they blasted apart the cliffs on which it had been painted, to provide ballast for the first railroad southwest of CHICAGO. Alton served as a station on the UNDERGROUND RAILROAD before the CIVIL WAR, but witnessed publically the murder, on November 7, 1837, of the early Abolitionist Elijah Lovejoy by a mob whose leaders went unpunished. The community hosted the LINCOLN-DOUGLAS DEBATE of October 15, 1858. In 1890 Alton was one of twenty Illinois cities with a population over ten thousand. Today it is the site of the largest bottle and glass container manufacturing plant in the United States. There also are oil refineries, foundries and flour mills. Limestone quarrying still adds to the economy. The Alton Museum of History and Art features the city's history and river heritage.

AMANA COLONIES. A group of seven communities southwest of CEDAR RAPIDS on the IOWA RIVER. The Amanas were founded by about 800 members of a German religious communal group known as the Community of True

Baking bread in the Amana Colonies.

American Fur Company - Anderson

Inspiration, a name taken from the German *Workzeuge,* "Inspired Prophets." The settlers came from their former colony near Buffalo, New York, and settled in Iowa County, with the first Amana founded in 1855 on the 25,000 acres of Iowa prairie which had been bought by the group. Seven villages developed, each self-supporting, providing an eighth grade education, slaughterhouse, bakery, icehouse, general store, farm department and church, along with selected workshops and factories. Amana was perhaps the most successful of all the many communal groups settled in the U.S. Their farms produced abundantly; their woolen mills and furniture factories continued to manufacture quality goods of wide distribution, and the organization was noted for its cradle-to-grave care of all of its members, who shared according to need in all property and concerns of the group. Housing was assigned by the elders. Meals were prepared in large kitchens and served communally. Each member was given a credit allowance based "according to justice and equity," from which each could purchase at the general store.

Today community ownership has changed to stock interest, but the region continues to prosper with its refrigerators, freezers, air conditioners and other refrigeration products now known all over the world. The business had a modest start in the 1930s when Amanaite George Foerstner was asked to build a beverage cooler. He not only did so but began to build a general business in various fields of refrigeration. In 1936 the Society bought Foerstner's interest. In 1950 the Society sold the business back to him for $1,500,000. Moving into different fields, Foerstner developed the radar range and continued to expand in refrigeration, with marketing and advertising skills developing the company's reputation as one of the best known of its type in the world.

The Amana villages provide probably the greatest single tourist attraction in the state, pulling visitors from both near and abroad, attracted by the noted farm-style food service, the local crafts, wines (especially rhubarb), foodstuffs and finely hand-crafted furniture made of the finest hard woods.

AMERICAN FUR COMPANY. Chartered by John Jacob ASTOR in 1808 to compete with the great fur trading companies of Canada. His early operations around the GREAT LAKES were known as the South West Company, in which Canadian associates took part. In 1821 an alliance with CHOUTEAU interests gave the company a monopoly in the Missouri River region. One of the first of the great trusts, it ruthlessly crushed all opposition. After Astor withdrew in 1834, the name continued. As workers were brought in to the trading posts and as others followed, the posts became the nucleus of many settlements. In this way the company played a significant role in opening up the western Midwestern lands for settlement. One of the most successful representatives of the company was Hercules DOUSMAN, who built VILLA LOUIS in PRAIRIE DU CHIEN, Wisconsin.

AMES, Iowa. City (pop. 45,775). Situated on the SKUNK RIVER in Story County in the center of the state, the city was named for Oakes Ames, a Massachusetts politician-industrialist who had railroad interests in the area. Incorporated in 1870, Ames has an economy largely keyed to the noted IOWA STATE UNIVERSITY. Among the thirty-eight manufacturing plants, there are no major industries. Electronic equipment and water-analysis and water-treatment equipment are the local products. The university is usually considered to be pre-eminent in agricultural education and research. Particularly notable is the Iowa State Center, a complex of four buildings, achieved without any federal or state appropriations. The center includes an auditorium, coliseum, theater and the Brunnier Art Gallery. Another attraction of the university is the Farm House, which may be considered the site of the founding of scientific agriculture under Dean James "Tama Jim" WILSON. It has been restored with period furnishings. The university's notable Horticultural Gardens are a teaching resource. The Grant WOOD murals in Parks Library are considered to be among that artist's finest works. Also of interest at Ames is the Iowa Arboretum. One of the major festivals on a university campus is the Iowa State Veishea Spring Festival, held in early May. There is also a Summerfest in mid July.

ANDERSON, Indiana. City (pop. 64,695), east-central Indiana seat of Madison County, located on the WHITE RIVER, name derived from an English translation of the name of a Delaware chief. Andersonville, as it was originally known, was platted in 1823, but experienced little growth until rumors of its proximity to the Indiana Central Canal encouraged new settlement. The canal never proved economical and it was not until the discovery of pockets of natural gas in the region, in 1865, that Anderson experienced an industrial boom. Today the auto industry is the principal employer. The Guide Lamp Corporation manufactures automobile lights and the Delco-Remy Corporation produces other electrical equipment for General Motors cars.

ANDERSON, Missouri. Town (pop. 1,237), southwestern Missouri in McDonald County, south of JOPLIN. In 1887 Anderson was the scene of gold and silver fever when reports came in that "pay dirt" had been found at Splitlog, a small settlement to the northwest. A group of promoters interested Matthias Splitlog in financing the venture. Splitlog was a Wyandotte Indian who made a fortune in KANSAS CITY land deals, despite being illiterate. The Splitlog Silver Mining Company was established. Assay reports indicated large deposits of gold and silver. Roads were choked with wagons headed for the fields. No one remembers what caused the bubble to burst, but suspicions began to mount. The promoters fled in time to avoid arrest, but Splitlog was ruined. Anderson returned to its former role as a sleepy trading center.

ANDERSON, Sherwood. (Camden, Ohio, Sept. 13, 1876—Panama, Mar. 8, 1941). Author. After a childhood of poverty, Anderson left school at fourteen and took a number of minor jobs, ending in CHICAGO, where he joined the National Guard. He served for a short period in Cuba during the SPANISH-AMERICAN WAR (1898-1899), then returned to Chicago for preparatory studies, became an advertising executive, and went back to Elyria, Ohio, where he opened a paint factory. In another sudden switch, after five years in paint, he went back to Chicago, determined to have a literary life. He associated with the Chicago Circle of writers, including Carl SANDBURG, Ben HECHT, Theodore DREISER and Edgar Lee MASTERS. Anderson's writing included articles in the *Little Review* and other similar magazines. His first novel was *Windy McPherson's Son* (1916), followed by *Marching Men* (1917). His most famous book was a collection of short stories and sketches with interrelated themes, entitled *Winesburg, Ohio,* in 1919, followed by *Poor White* (1920) and *The Triumph of the Egg* (1921). These three are the basis for his continuing fame. His posthumous *Memoirs* appeared in 1942. Anderson "pioneered in psychological naturalism and use of vernacular prose." He dealt with the sterility of the success-oriented machine age that dominates most work and with the conflict of the individual against organized industrial

society. Many critics contend that his short stories contain the best expression of his talent.

ANDREWS' RAID. CIVIL WAR episode. In 1862 James J. Andrews, an aide to Civil War Union General Ormsby M. Mitchel, was directed by Mitchel to lead a raiding party into the South to destroy as many railroads and railroad bridges and capture as much railroad equipment as possible. In civilian clothes, the raiders infiltrated the South, but several of them were captured and, because they were out of uniform, they were executed as spies, including Andrews, who was hanged at Atlanta. However, six of the raiders managed to escape capture and seized a locomotive on April 12, 1862. Pursued by Southerners in another locomotive, the six raiders eventually eluded capture and returned to Ohio. The picturesque nature of the exploit has captured public attention, and it has gone down in history as "The GREAT LOCOMOTIVE CHASE," frequently a subject of fiction and film.

ANDREWS, Roy Chapman. (Beloit, Wis., Jan 26, 1884—Carmel, CA, Mar. 11, 1960). Explorer, scientist. He was one of the best known graduates of BELOIT COLLEGE at BELOIT, Wisconsin (1906). He immediately joined the staff of the American Museum of Natural History in New York, where he specialized in the study of whales. Traveling around the world to study them, he became recognized as the world's top cetologist. In 1914 he became the head of the museum's division of Asian exploration. Discoverer of some of the world's largest fossil fields, from 1914 to 1932 Andrews led scientific expeditions to Alaska, northern Korea, Tibet, southwestern China, Burma, northern China and Outer Mongolia. On his 1919 expedition to Central Asia, he was the discoverer of the first known dinosaur eggs, perfectly preserved. He was first to find evidence of the Baluchitherium, the largest known land animal, as well as other important discoveries of prehistoric life. Andrews was director of the American Museum of Natural History from 1935 to 1942, when he retired. His numerous writings include *The New Conquest of Central Asia* (1933) and *This Amazing Planet* (1940).

ANGEL MOUNDS. Primitive remains of prehistoric man in Vanderburgh County, Indiana. Angel Mounds, the largest group of prehistoric mounds in Indiana, were excavated in 1939-1940 by Glenn A. Black.

ANGOLA, Indiana. Town (pop. 5,486), extreme northeastern Indiana in the state's popular resort area, seat of Steuben County. This quiet college town is home to TRI-STATE UNIVERSITY. The university's athletic facilities are open to the public. In the wooded hills surrounding the community are more than 100 lakes. Steuben County 101 Lakes Festival is held in Angola each June.

ANHEUSER, Eberhard. (St. Louis, MO, May 19, 1880—Sappington, MO, July, 1963). Businessman. Anheuser formed a partnership with Adolphus BUSCH in 1896 and purchased a bankrupt ST. LOUIS brewery. They developed a method of brewing beer without pasteurization and pioneered in bottling beer. Anheuser began serving as chairman of the board in 1950 after many years of directing the marketing of his product.

ANIMAL LIFE IN THE MIDWEST. The largest animal to roam the Midwest during human times was the BUFFALO. This was true despite the general impression that this animal was confined to the western plains. However,

by the time of general settlement in the region, the buffalo had, indeed, moved to the West.

In the Midwest at one time some of the larger cats, such as the cougar and bobcat, were fairly common, and reports still persist of their sighting in certain areas. Deer, which were hunted until they appeared to be on the verge of extinction have made an amazing comeback, to the point of becoming a nuisance in various areas. Moose, largest of the deer family, are mainly represented by the herd on Isle Royale.

Except for the grizzly, most of the original bear family still may be found in the wilder northern areas. Even in the lower Midwest and the earlier settled states a few coyote and a scattering of wolves have been reported. Red fox, muskrat, woodchuck, mink, porcupine and opossum may be found in varying numbers. The wily raccoon thrives in almost every locale and is especially bothersome in many suburbs.

Although the fierce WOLVERINE gives Michigan its nickname, the Wolverine State, probably none of these animals may be found there today, nor are marten, woodland caribou and cougar found there any longer.

The BADGER State, Wisconsin, can still claim

Benjamin Franklin once suggested making the wild turkey the national bird.

some few of its state animal. Wisconsin's wild life animal is the white tailed deer.

Of the several hundred species of birds once common to the Midwest, many are no longer found. One of the saddest chapters in ornithology concerns the PASSENGER PIGEON, a beautiful bird about fifteen inches long, which arrived in much of the upper Midwest in March, in vast-scale migrations from its winter quarters. At one time there were probably more passenger pigeons than any other bird, but constant hunting drove them to extinction. Their migrations blocked out the sun and sometimes continued for hours over a given spot, but there were no conservationists to save them from destruction.

Though still on the endangered list outside of Alaska, America's symbol, the bald eagle, appears to be making a comeback. The Ozarks shelter a number of them, and large numbers can be seen along parts of the MISSISSIPPI FLYWAY. That flyway through the Midwest is one of the world's largest migration routes. Millions of waterfowl follow the flyway, resting at dozens of refuges along the way. The red-tailed hawk gives Iowa its nickname of the Hawkeye State, and many hawks and owls are still found in the Midwest.

Missouri extends far enough south to harbor some of the water birds, such as the green herons in the willow thickets of the Ozarks, the great blue herons and American egrets.

Most of the popular native game birds have been hunted to near extinction in much of the region, although fortunately, the wild TURKEY is making a comeback in some parts. The most popular game bird today is an immigrant, the PHEASANT, imported from China, found today in Iowa more than the other Midwestern states and hunted with zest wherever it is found.

Midwest reptiles are mostly of the "common garden variety." Although a few scattered rattlesnakes and other venomous snakes are reported, they are not found in the numbers of former years.

Few exotic insects are found. Wisconsin's state insect is the common HONEYBEE. Ohio chose the LADYBUG and Illinois the MONARCH BUTTERFLY.

Inland fish are among the Midwest's most valued creatures. At one time a substantial industry was based on Great Lakes trout, until the lamprey eel reduced their numbers. They are now making a comeback in the lakes. Most of the Great Lakes states have now taken to introducing such fish as the coho salmon, which has become a popular game fish both in the Great Lakes and the spawning waters which enter them. Warm water streams produce carp, buffalo fish, sheepshead, channel cat, flathead cat, blue cat, bullheads and many others, some popular with commercial fishermen. The colder waters of the north are popular for their game fish, especially the wide variety of trout. Michigan's state fish is the BROOK TROUT. Minnesota's state fish is the WALLEYED PIKE and Wisconsin's is the mighty MUSKELLUNGE, celebrated in many a local festival.

ANN ARBOR, Michigan. City (pop. 107,-316), seat of Washtenaw county, situated in southeast Michigan on the HURON RIVER. It was incorporated as a city in 1851 and occupies an area of 25 square miles. Lying only about 25 miles west of DETROIT, Ann Arbor is sometimes considered as a suburb of the larger city. It takes its name from the wives of settlers John Allen and Elisha Rumsey. Both women were named Ann. The women were so fond of sitting together under a grape arbor that the men called the town Ann Arbor.

With a substantial number of government and private research facilities, the city is known as a center of research and development. Precision machinery, lasers, computers, scientific instruments, automotive parts and hospital and laboratory equipment are principal products. The hospitals and medical school of the University of MICHIGAN, veterans hospital, community hospital and neuropsychiatric hospital combine to make the city a great center of the health industry.

The University of Michigan began in 1817 and was moved to Ann Arbor in 1837, greatly assisted by the gift of land in the area from the Indians, as one of the provisions of the Treaty of Fort Meigs. On the campus are many attractions for visitors. Among these is the presidential library of Gerald FORD. Indian mounds are found in the vicinity. Among the annual events are the Ya'ssoo Festival in early June and the May Festival. At the latter, internationally renowned symphony orchestras are featured.

ANOKA, Minnesota. City (pop. 15,634), southeastern Minnesota, northwest of MINNEAPOLIS, located at the junction of the Rum and MISSISSIPPI rivers. The first white settlers came to the region in 1844 and traded with Joseph Belanger who established a one-room trading post and with his companions carried two hundred pound packs as far as Mille Lacs to trade with the Indians. Light sandy soil discouraged agriculture and many settlers moved farther west. By 1855 the town had continued to grow and reached a population of three hundred. Trees cut upstream and floated down to Anoka brought a lumber boom and encouraged the belief that this community and not Minneapolis would become the metropolitan center of the state. Eventually the Twin Cities of Minneapolis and ST. PAUL grew faster because of their position as milling and rail centers. Today Anoka is a center of farming communities. Its industries include ammunition and metal products manufacturers. Near the mouth of the Rum River is the Father Hennepin Stone, on which the explorer's name is found, probably cut there by the Franciscan priest himself circa 1680. The annual Halloween Festival has been held there since 1920.

ANSON, Adrian Constantine (Cap). (Marshalltown, Iowa, 1851—Chicago, IL, 1922). American baseball player-manager, one of the most notable sports personalities of his era. Played most of his career with the Chicago Cubs (1876-1897) and was four times National League batting champion. As manager (1879-1897), he led the team to five pennants. He was elected to the National Baseball Hall of Fame in 1939. His father was the founder of MARSHALLTOWN, Iowa. Anson has another claim to fame as the discoverer of William Ashley "Billy" SUNDAY of Iowa as baseball star. Sunday later became a famed evangelist.

ANTIOCH UNIVERSITY. Chartered at YELLOW SPRINGS, Ohio, in 1852 in order to develop not only the intellect but also to influence the entire personality. Special attention was to be given to promoting social consciousness and competence. The first president of the college after it opened in 1853 was Dr. Horace Mann, considered to be one of the greatest persons in the history of education. Dr. Mann worked to organize a college along the lines of his educational philosophy. However, outside pressures to change the goals of the college toward more practical courses were so strong that he ruined his health and died in 1859. Antioch's greatest influence in education came in 1920 when its president, Dr. Arthur E. Morgan revised its curriculum and inaugurated the "Antioch Plan." This work-study system generally requires five years. Each college year is divided between on-campus study and off-campus work, each segment full time. The university is particularly noted for providing students with a voice in college and community

policies, as well as affording their participation in various administrative programs. An elaborate foreign study program ties the college to distinguished universities abroad. The Antioch Plan and its implementation gained wide recognition. Studies in human development are undertaken on campus through the Fels Research Institute. The Charles F. Kettering Research Laboratory offers research opportunities in biological science, and there are other experimental and research centers on campus.

APOSTLE ISLANDS NATIONAL LAKESHORE. Near BAYFIELD, Wisconsin. Twenty picturesque islands and an 11-mile strip of adjacent Bayfield Peninsula along the south shore of Lake SUPERIOR comprise this park, established September 16, 1970.

APPLE BLOSSOM. The apple blossom is the state flower of Michigan, where much of the countryside in spring is a sea of apple blooms.

APPLES. The apple is a member of the vast rose family. It is thought to have originated in the Caucasus Mountains of west Asia, and is the most widely distributed fruit of northern regions. Apples are grown widely throughout the Midwest, commercially most important in Michigan. However, the greatest contribution of the region to apple lovers and the apple industry was the development of the DELICIOUS APPLE, first in Iowa and then in Missouri until it had gained worldwide appeal.

APPLETON, Wisconsin. City (pop. 59,032), seat of Outagamie County, situated in east central Wisconsin on the rapids of the FOX RIVER, near its outlet to Lake WINNEBAGO. Established in 1848, it was first named Grand Chute, but was renamed Appleton for the father-in-law of Amos A. Lawrence one of the founders. Lawrence had donated $10,000 for the establishment of a Methodist college to be situated there because the Methodist Conference was enamored of the beauty of the site.

That site soon attracted industry to its waterpower, including a cabinet factory, flour and woolen mills. With the decline of wheat growing in the area, pulp and paper mills replaced flour milling. The waterpower of the thirty-eight foot drop of the Fox River within the city limits provided the city with national distinction when the first hydroelectric plant in North America was operated there (1882). Another important first for Appleton was the first electric street railway in the state (1886).

Judge J.E. Harriman of Appleton had witnessed the demonstration of the electric streetcar in CHICAGO in 1882. He returned to Appleton and soon had five electric cars operating on Appleton streets.

Today the pulp and paper industry is the city's largest enterprise, and the INSTITUTE OF PAPER CHEMISTRY is located there. LAWRENCE UNIVERSITY was named for Amos Lawrence, and in 1964 it merged with Milwaukee Downer College. The college operates the Worcester Art Center and the Music-Drama Center, including the Cloak Theater, an experimental arena playhouse.

Magician Harry Houdini was born at Appleton in 1874.

Visitors may explore the Dard Hunter Paper Museum of the Institute of Paper Chemistry, which displays early handmade papers, rare books and manuscripts, watermarks and models. Of particular interest is the replica of the hydroelectric power station at Appleton. The New London Public Museum in nearby New London, offers Indian and African artifacts and other exhibits.

ARCADIA WEAVERS. Project of the Works Progress Administration in 1936. Women near Arcadia, Missouri, were encouraged to revive the art of weaving which had once flourished there. Many of the women who had jobs continued their weaving on "off hours" and offered their products for sale. Tourists continue to seek such Missouri crafts for souvenirs.

ARCH ROCK. A scenic rock formation on MACKINAC ISLAND, Michigan. This rock bridge hangs above the eastern shore line, appearing from certain angles to be suspended in midair. Arch Rock rises 149 feet above the lake with a span of 50 feet. Indian lore says that it was created by the Giant Fairies as a gateway to the island, but scientists credit erosion for its formation.

ARCHAIC PEOPLE. In a time frame of perhaps six to seven thousand years ago, a group known to archaeologists as the Archaic People lived in the Midwestern United States, centered, perhaps, in Ohio. Enough has been discovered to verify their existence, but little substantive information is known about them.

ARCHITECTURE. The statement that modern architecture originated in the American Midwest may be open to challenge, but a strong case can be made for such a claim. From the

Sears Tower is the World's tallest.

first use of the common "frame" house to the invention of the skyscraper and its development to date, much of the history of architecture has been written in the region, which also has produced or nurtured some of the world's most notable architects.

The story begins in CHICAGO and much of it continues in that city, still frequently said to be the architectural gem of the world. As early as 1832 George W. Snow of Chicago invented a new method of building small houses and other buildings of wood. Until this time, wooden frames required bulky corner posts of large timbers and much bracing. Snow's simpler method placed smaller studs closely together, held by a sheath under the clapboards. This "balloon frame" construction called for much less wood, was lighter and stronger and became almost universally used. This is the skeleton construction still so familiar today in new housing projects calling for small frame buildings.

In 1883 Major William le Baron JENNEY (1832-1907) revolutionized architecture when he unveiled a building which gave substance to his theory that building height could only be achieved by techniques which he had worked out. When his Home Insurance Building was completed at Chicago in that year, the ten-story structure became known technically as the first SKYSCRAPER. It was the first in which floors and the exterior masonry walls were borne by a skeleton framework of metal. The outer walls were only a "skin" to provide a cover for the building and supported no weight.

The invention of the skyscraper remains Chicago's most significant contribution to modern city life. The first dictionary definition of skyscraper described "A very tall building such as are now being built in Chicago." The Jenney techniques have been adapted all over the world but nowhere more dramatically than in his own Chicago, where the SEARS TOWER reaches 110 stories as the highest in the world, and the Standard Oil and JOHN HANCOCK BUILDING s are the fourth and fifth highest.

Chicago continued to dominate architectural fashion with the outstanding work of Louis SULLIVAN (1856-1924) whose gold and red Transportation Building at the Chicago WORLD'S COLUMBIAN EXPOSITION of 1893 stood out among the white classical buildings surrounding it. "Mixed use" buildings of the modern style began in 1889 with Adler and Sullivan's Auditorium Building, which contained a hotel, office building and two theaters.

A young architect named Frank Lloyd WRIGHT (1867-1959) worked for Adler and Sullivan but soon went out on his own to become perhaps the best known and most controversial architect of his time. His early work was done in Chicago, and his famed houses and buildings in the city and suburbs, particularly OAK PARK, are still pointed out as architectural landmarks. But many of his buildings are also scattered about the Midwest. Wright, a Wisconsin native, made his later headquarters at SPRING GREEN, Wisconsin, where he conducted a school for young architects, who took his ideas around the world.

Chicago next encountered German architect-designer Ludwig MIES VAN DER ROHE (1886-1969), who became director of Armour Institute, now ILLINOIS INSTITUTE OF TECHNOLOGY. His two apartment buildings on Lake Shore Drive (1951-52) were acclaimed as a whole new concept in skyscraper construction, in which superficial siding and facing materials were eliminated and only the essential elements of the building remained. When Mies van der Rohe designed the Seagram Building in New York (1956-1958), the rush was on, and his type of steel and glass buildings was put up around the world.

In Chicago the round towers of Marina City, the pyramidal shapes of the First National Bank Building and the John Hancock Center and the triangular form of Lake Point Tower have all marked major steps in design and construction techniques.

At the UNIVERSITY OF ILLINOIS at Urbana the bowl-shaped Assembly Hall, is another Midwest architectural triumph.

All around the Midwest, the fine private homes and early structures have been preserved, including such gems as VILLA LOUIS at PRAIRIE DU CHIEN, Wisconsin. However, another small Midwestern town has become the most talked about architectural community of its size anywhere. COLUMBUS, Indiana, is known around the world for its invitation to famous architects of many nations who came there at the city's request to design buildings which combine to make the small city a center of modern architecture.

All around the Midwest, structures such as the Roofless Church of NEW HARMONY, Indiana, demonstrate the region's support of architectural advances.

SAINT LOUIS, Missouri, is another Midwest city of many architectural distinctions, but unique among them, and unique in the world, is the nation's tallest monument, the great GATEWAY ARCH designed by Eero Saarinen, a rainbow-shape, soaring into the sky, gleaming with its outer face of stainless steel.

One European architect wrote a telling summary of the architectural distinction of the Midwest: "I came to Chicago expecting to find remarkable architecture and a history of unique architectural accomplishment, and indeed I found all of that, but even more remarkable was the evidence of architectural advance which I found throughout the rest of the Midwest."

ARGONNE NATIONAL LABORATORY. Founded in 1946 near CHICAGO by the Atomic Energy Commission, it also operates testing laboratories at Idaho Falls, Idaho. The laboratory carries on its research with the cooperation of a consortium of universities under the leadership of the UNIVERSITY OF CHICAGO. Its main activities devolve around nuclear research.

ARMSTRONG, Neil Alden. (Wapakoneta, Ohio, Aug. 5, 1930—). Astronaut, first man on the moon. Armstrong's early interest in aviation brought him a pilot's license at the age of sixteen. A naval air cadet at PURDUE UNIVERSITY, he was called to active duty in the Korean War. He received the Air Medal three times for his 78 combat missions. He returned to Purdue, where he graduated in 1955, then became a test pilot for the National Advisory Committee for

Aeronautics. In 1962 he was accepted as a NASA pilot. On his first space flight in March 1966, he commanded *Gemini VIII* and performed the first manual docking maneuver in space. The name Neil Armstrong will long be remembered for his becoming the first man to reach a long-sought goal of mankind. Commanding the Apollo-Saturn 10 flight on *Apollo XI*, beginning July 16, 1969, he headed for the moon. On July 10th, Armstrong landed the lunar landing module on the moon's surface. Armstrong descended to become the first man ever to step on the moon's surface and made one of the notable comments of all time when he declared: "That's one small step for a man, one giant leap for mankind." Armstrong's companion for their 21 hours and 36 seconds on the moon was Edwin E. Aldrin, Jr. They set up experiments on the moon, gathered a quantity of moon material and the next day rocketed back to the command ship in its lunar orbit. President Richard Nixon journeyed to the carrier *Hornet* to congratulate the lunar astronauts after their splashdown in the Pacific. In 1970 Armstrong resigned from the astronaut program but became a NASA administrator. In 1971 he resigned to join the faculty of the University of CINCINNATI.

ARNESS, James. (Minneapolis, MN, May 26, 1923—). Television and movie actor. Arness, originally spelled Aurness, began a movie career after working in advertising. He played minor roles in such movies as *The Thing* in 1952 before creating the role of Marshal Matt Dillon on television's long-running dramatic series, *Gunsmoke* (1955-1975). Arness, six feet seven inches in height, was suggested for the role by John Wayne, the first choice of the producers, who was hesitant to commit himself to a weekly series. From February 12, 1978 to April 23, 1979, Arness played the role of Zeb Macahan in the television series *How the West Was Won.*

ART IN THE MIDWEST. Some of the best known names in American art are associated with the Midwest in various ways. Perhaps most notable were those artists who chose to depict the vast landscape of the region as well as the lives and personalities of the region's sturdy, self-sufficient people. One of the most copied and most often cartooned of all art work is Grant WOOD's "American Gothic" (1930) with its portrayal of a couple who have come to be considered as typical Iowans. Many of Wood's works, including some stunning landscapes,

depict the prairie scene and its life. He has become known as the "Painter of the Soil."

One of the most widely recognized of the "regionalist" painters was Thomas Hart BENTON (1889-1975), whose extensive travels through the Midwest as a boy are reflected in his paintings and murals, in which he created a not always flattering picture of life as he had seen it.

Other Midwest artists chose other themes and other media.

Far more traditional was George YEWELL (1830-1923) of Iowa, whose studies in Europe evoked a theme of European cities and peoples. Among the several modern American families of artists, Illinois claims the Albrights, father and twin sons. Ivan Le Lorraine Albright (1897-) was the best known of these, with his paintings of the ghastly and the macabre.

The Midwest has produced some of the nation's notable sculptors. These include Minnesota's James Earle Fraser (1876-1953), who produced the widely known "End of the Trail." One of the most prominent sculptors of her time, whose works are some of the best, was Wisconsin's Vinnie REAM (1847-1915). She created the only sculpture from life of Abraham LINCOLN and won the first commission for sculpture ever granted by Congress to a woman. Only recently has the quality of her work gained the attention it deserves, according to some art critics. Among the most noted sculptors of his day was Lorado TAFT of Illinois (1860-1936). His monumental "Fountain of Time" has been cited as "moving sculpture into a new dimension, especially in group composition."

The magazine *Urban Sculpture* considers CHICAGO to be the leading center of outdoor sculpture, with the enormous steel "woman" of Picasso, Chagall's half-block long mosaic, Calder's Flamingo and many more.

Cartooning is a specialized form, widely recognized in some art circles and scorned in others. It is, however, an important form in which Midwest artists have truly been preeminent. The imagination of Missouri's Walt DISNEY (1901-1966)has provided entertainment for the world, as he developed an entirely new art concept.

Cartoons of a quite different type won world fame for Iowa's PULITZER PRIZE winner J.N. "Ding" DARLING (1876-1962). His particular interest was conservation, and many of his cartoons called attention to the problems of wildlife management. However, he drew telling cartoon frames on almost every topic of the day. Still different was the work of cartoonist Frank

McKinney (Kin) HUBBARD (1878-1930), who created the rustic philosopher Abe Martin, who illustrated his creator's folk philosophy.

As in other forms of cultural endeavor, many experts consider that the contributions of the Midwest have customarily been undervalued. However, the renewed attention being given to such Midwest artists as Wood, Yewell and Ream emphasizes the true quality of the Midwest artistic product, which goes well beyond its regional scope. For example, Wood, decried in one period, has resurfaced as one of the country's most admired in modern times. A retrospective exhibit of his work has toured leading world museums during the early 1980s. Continuing reevaluation in the art world will certainly lead to other "revivals."

ART INSTITUTE OF CHICAGO. CHICAGO, Illinois, museum noted for its collection of impressionist masters. The Art Institute of Chicago was incorporated in 1879 as the Chicago Academy of Fine Arts. At first a school of instruction, the Institute became a museum. However, the Institute still operates one of the world's largest schools of the arts. Exhibits

Massive lions guard the Art Institute of Chicago.

include almost every master from the 13th century to the present. Many exhibits have been donated by wealthy Chicagoans.

ASHLAND, Ohio. City (pop. 20,326) seat of Ashland County in northern Ohio, incorporated in 1833. Platted by William Montgomery in 1815 and then known as Uniontown, the present name is derived from Henry Clay's estate at Lexington, Kentucky. Industrial development began in 1850 when the introduction of a clover-hulling machine led to the opening of a factory. Machine tools, pumps, spray equipment, rubber products, animal medications, adhesives and machine tools are produced there. In the period between 1970 and 1984, the city's population showed a slight gain, from 19,872 to 20,326. A notorious event in Ashland's history was the 1884 hanging of George Andrew Horn and William Henry Gribben who had murdered a fellow townsman. Although the hanging was supposed to have been private, an unruly crowd of 12,000 arrived to witness the spectacle. A storm of protest over this mob brought about the passage of the Ohio privacy of execution act. In 1915 school children of the area gave their pennies and collected small stones to help in building the city's monument to Johnny Appleseed, who had once been in the region. Ashland College is a denominational coeducational school founded by the Brethren Church for the teaching of ministers and religious workers.

ASHLAND, Wisconsin. City (pop. 16,783), seat of Ashland County, the city is situated in northwestern Wisconsin on CHEQUAMEGON BAY, which is said to be the "Shining Big Sea Water" of Longfellow's *Hiawatha.* The community is named for the presence of forests of ash trees in the area. The city occupies a sunken plain and sweeps in a long semicircle around the southern shore of the bay. The region was first visited in 1659 by Pierre RADISSON and the Sieur de GROSEILIERS, who built a fort near present Ashland. In 1665 Father Claude ALLOUEZ built a chapel of bark near the present city, but the mission was abandoned. Almost 200 years were to pass before Asaph Whittlesey built a cabin on the site of Ashland in 1854. With the coming of the railroad in 1877, Ashland boomed. Brownstone quarries, iron ore deposits increased interest in the area. Now an important port on the Great Lakes, the harbor is the site of imports and exports of COAL, iron ore and other products. The location of the first house built by a white settler in Wisconsin is

Ashley - Associations

marked in Ashland. Visitors find Ashland to be the gateway to the popular APOSTLE ISLANDS to the north. Ashland is the site of Northland College, founded in 1878 to bring higher education to the isolated population of the area. Sigurd Olson Environmental Institute on the campus is an earth-sheltered, solar-heated building. Historic Wheeler Hall of the college was constructed in 1892 of the famed Lake Superior brownstone of the area. Copper Falls State Park provides spectacular scenery.

ASHLEY, William Henry. (Powhatan County, VA, 1778—Boonesville, MO, March 26, 1838). Fur trader. Ashley served the State of Missouri as its lieutenant governor in 1820, as a general in the Missouri Territorial Militia, and as a member of the United States House of Representatives from 1831 to 1837, but it was his fur business for which he gained fame. As one of the principal leaders in the ROCKY MOUNTAIN FUR COMPANY (1824-1826), the successor of the MISSOURI FUR COMPANY, Ashley sent fur trading parties throughout the west. He explored the Green River, Wyoming, area in 1824 and the Great Salt Lake region in 1826.

ASNER, Ed. (Kansas City, MO, November 15, 1929—). Character actor. Asner has usually played tough-guy with heart of gold roles in movies and television. He is probably best known as "Mr. Grant" on the Mary Tyler Moore Show from 1970 to 1972. He later played Lou Grant, a newspaper editor on the television series of the same name. Asner has played in a number of movie roles.

ASSEMBLY-LINE PRODUCTION. Systematic method of production, brought to widespread use and improved by the early auto industry, especially by Henry FORD in his Michigan automobile factories. By 1908 when the Model T Ford was introduced, the Ford Company had developed some assembly line methods. In 1913 the assembly line had been developed by Ford so that the Model T of that year made the first true mass production of AUTOMOBILES a reality. Basic to the assembly line system, a conveyor belt carries parts of the product at a steady speed past various "stations." At each station, workers perform a specific task such as tightening, painting or inspecting. A key element of assembly-line production is the use of interchangeable parts, an idea credited to Eli Whitney, making it possible for unskilled labor and even machines to assemble products. Robot assembly is rapidly being adopted for many operations.

ASSOCIATIONS AND GROUPS. Because of its central location, the Midwest region is a natural choice of headquarters for major associations. As the most-visited convention center in the U.S., CHICAGO and its suburbs have been chosen as national headquarters for many of the nation's largest associations. Among those with the largest memberships are the American Medical Association, the country's largest group of doctors. Among others in the health field are the American Osteopathic Association, the American Dental Association, the American Hospital Association. The field of scholarship is led by the National Congress of Parents and Teachers and the American Library Association, both in Chicago.

In Chicago's classified telephone directory are six pages of other associations of the greater Chicago area, including national Rotary in Evanston; the National Realtors Association; American Bar Association; National Home Furnishings Association; National Housewares Association; National Livestock and Meat Board; National Macaroni Manufacturers Association; National Association of Coin Laundry Operators; National Association of College Admissions Counselors; National Association of Retail Druggists; National Association of Retail Grocers of the U.S.; National Beer Wholesalers' Association and hundreds of others

Among the many Cleveland associations may be found the Association for Management Excellence, the International Platform Association, the International Oxygen Manufacturers Association, the National Association of Collegiate Directors of Athletics, the National Flexible Packaging Association and National Association of Credit Management.

All around the Midwest are other major associations or organizations of special interest and appeal, including American Chiropractic Association, and National Pork Producers Council, DES MOINES, Iowa; American Citizens Concerned for Life, Inc., and International Festivals Association, MINNEAPOLIS, Minnesota; American Ceramic Society, National Food Service Association, and American Cemetery Society, COLUMBUS, Ohio; American Hereford Association, National Agri-Management Association, and National Association of Parliamentarians, KANSAS CITY, Missouri; American Optometric Association, National Hairdressers, International Consumer Credit Association, and Cosmetologists Association, ST. LOUIS, Missouri; American Power Boat Association, St. Clair Shore, Michigan; American School Health Association, Kent, Ohio; American Society for Training and Development and National Association of Advertising Publishers, and International Association of Managing Directors, MADISON, Wisconsin; National Association of College Stores, OBERLIN, Ohio; National Council of Teachers of English, URBANA, Illinois; National Electrical Contractors Association, HAMMOND, Indiana; National Executive Housekeepers Association, Gallipolis, Ohio; National Feed Ingredients Association, West Des Moines, Iowa; National Foster Parents Association, CLAYTON, Missouri; National Funeral Directors Association, MILWAUKEE, Wisconsin; National Guild of Decoupers, GROSSE POINTE, Michigan; National Hearing Aid Society, LIVONIA, Michigan; International Association. of Printing House Craftsmen, CINCINNATI, Ohio; and International Chiropractors Association, DAVENPORT, Iowa.

ASTOR, John Jacob. (Waldorf, Germany, July 17, 1763—New York City, March 29, 1848) Founder of the AMERICAN FUR COMPANY, chartered in 1808 and headquartered at MACKINAC ISLAND, Michigan. Astor came to America in 1784 and established a shop dealing in furs and musical instruments. He went on frequent fur-buying expeditions, and formed several fur trading companies, including one in Oregon. Astor hired many of the most experienced frontiersmen he could find. Charles de LANGLADE, founder of the first permanent settlement in Wisconsin, worked for Astor's American Fur Company. By 1816 Astor's fur company was the most important trading establishment in the Minnesota area. It was perhaps only Manuel LISA 's MISSOURI FUR COMPANY that ever bettered Astor in carving out a trading empire in the Midwest and West. Astor sent his men into unexplored wilderness to set up his posts as far as the Pacific coast. Wherever a trading post was established, development was sure to follow. Other merchants found opportunities, and settlers came in. In Astor's later years he purchased Manhattan real estate, became a leading merchant in trade with China, and built the Park Hotel (later Astor House) in New York City. At his death, Astor was the wealthiest man in the United States.

ATCHISON, David Rice. (Frogtown, KY, August 11, 1807—Clinton County, MO, January 26, 1866). Senator, Democrat from Missouri. Atchison had a long and distinguished career in public service to the state of Missouri. He was a member of the Missouri House of Representatives in 1834 and 1838 before being elected to the United States Senate from Missouri and serving from 1843 to 1855. He was elected president pro tem. from 1846 to 1849 and again from 1852 to 1854. Atchison worked for land grant legislation to assist Missouri railroads. He was pro-slavery and worked for the repeal of the MISSOURI COMPROMISE. He promoted the Kansas-Nebraska bill. After his defeat for the Senate in 1855, he lapsed into obscurity. Atchison County, Missouri, the Atchison, Topeka and Santa Fe Railroad and the City of Atchison in Kansas are named in his honor.

ATHENS, Ohio. City (pop 19,743), county seat of Athens County, situated on a series of hills above the HOCKING RIVER, with some of the bluffs rising as much as seventy feet above the river. The network of streets runs over the town at odd angles. The name, from the Greek city of Athens, is a particular favorite of university towns. It was incorporated as a town in 1811, but not as a city until 1912. Over the years the industries have been diverse, including office equipment, meat packing, dairy products and building materials. The city benefits as a university town and county seat and from the nearby coal fields. When the OHIO COMPANY OF ASSOCIATES purchased the Muskingum Valley lands in 1787, two townships were set aside for "the use of a university." Athens was in the area selected. In 1800 General Rufus PUTNAM surveyed the town and named the village, with its six cabins, Athens, anticipating that the university would make the city a cultural center. OHIO UNIVERSITY was chartered in 1804, and by 1805, with the coming of more settlers, the community was chosen as county seat. Athens' growth came slowly. The Hocking Canal was opened for trade in 1841, and the railroad arrived nine years later. Boring and milling machinery, office systems and shoes are among the manufactures in today's Athens. During the period from 1970 through 1980, the population of Athens declined from 24,168 to 19,743. The city attracts hobby buffs with two national events—the National Jigsaw Puzzle Championship in August and the Quilt National Exhibition in June.

ATOMIC BOMB, DEVELOPMENT.
Weapon, deriving its force from the release of
atomic energy through the process of splitting
(or fusion) of heavy nuclei. Perhaps no other
single project in history changed the world so
completely as the work which was begun on
August 13, 1942. The project was shrouded in
the utmost secrecy. Probably no setting for a
great event could have been more prosaic. Some
of the world's top scientists labored in a
laboratory under the stands at Stagg Field of
the Univeristy of CHICAGO. For many decades
scientists had known that there was great
power in the atom, if somehow it could be
released. The great Italian scientist, Enrico
FERMI, had been placed in charge of a program at
the University to unleash the power of the
atom, working with Nobel scientist Arthur
COMPTON and many others. In what looked like a
large brick oven, the scientists had built a
"pile" consisting of aluminum and graphite in
layers. The secrecy of the work led to some
interesting situations. When they asked the
Goodyear Rubber Company to produce some
"square" balloons, there was a good deal of
laughter. When they felt the time had come, the
distinguished scientists gathered around the
pile. George Weil withdrew the cadmium-plated
control rod and by this action released and
controlled the energy of the atom. This first
chain reaction in nuclear fission was accomplished at 3:25 p.m. on December 2, 1942. The
first bomb was completed in 1945 after three
additional years of research and a cost of two
billion dollars. The first experimental explosion
of an atomic bomb occurred on July 16, 1945,
near Alamogordo, New Mexico. The first
military use of the findings made in CHICAGO
came on August 6, 1945, when an atomic bomb
was dropped on Hiroshima, Japan. The vast
network laboring on the development of atomic
energy later became known to the public as the
"Manhattan Project."

**AU SABLE RIVER WILD AND SCENIC
RIVER SYSTEM.** At Cadillac, Michigan.
This short stretch of river preserves only a
small portion of one of Michigan's most popular
canoeing rivers. The Au Sable also is one of
America's most productive trout fishing
streams. Swiftest river in Michigan's Lower
Peninsula, it flows southward from its source,
Lake Tecon, toward GRAYLING where it begins to
flow southeastward toward its mouth on Lake
HURON and the town of Osconda. Along the
banks of this river, which was once used in
logging, is the Lumberman's Memorial, a
monument to the many people involved in the
history of Michigan's lumber industry.

AUGSBURG COLLEGE. Privately supported religiously affiliated liberal arts college,
founded in 1896. Located on an eighteen acre
campus near the MINNEAPOLIS central district
and the University of MINNESOTA in Minneapolis, Minnesota, Augsburg offers courses leading
to a Bachelor of Arts degree in forty two fields
of study. Religious subjects are required for
graduation. Augsburg maintains a cooperative
academic program in medical technology with
several hospitals where students spend one year
at the hospital for credit. University dormitories provide housing for 850 men and women
and eleven married couples. During the 1985-
1986 academic year Augsburg enrolled 1,802
students. There were 192 faculty members.

AURORA, Illinois. City (pop. 81,293), situated in Kane County on the FOX RIVER, about
thirty miles from central CHICAGO, one of the
"outer ring" of Chicago suburbs. The name
comes from the Roman goddess of dawn. In
Illinois there is an additional connotation
coming from the Iroquoian word *deawendote*,
meaning "constant dawn." The city was
incorporated in 1837. Aurora is the heart of a
farm and industrial complex, with important
railroad yards. Leading products include road
machinery and heavy steel products. There was
a sizeable POTAWATOMI village on the site of
Aurora when the earliest settler, Joseph
McCarty, came there in 1834. Soon after he
established Aurora, McCarty came east to look
at the site of Chicago, but dismissed it as "more
promising for the raising of bullfrogs than
humans." Two towns grew up opposite each
other along the Fox River, and there was
considerable rivalry. Eventually it became
apparent that they would be better off to
cooperate than continue to compete, so a joint
civic center was established on Stolp's Island in
the middle of the river, and the two settlements
were combined as Aurora. The city holds a
permanant place in Illinois history as the first
Illinois community to install electric street
lights, in 1881. These were placed on tall towers
so that each one could illuminate a large area.
Unlike the majority of larger Midwest cities,
Aurora enjoyed a proportionately large increase
in population between 1970 and 1980, from
74,389 to 81,293. Aurora is the seat of Aurora
College. A notable 20-room mansion houses the
local historical society.

AUSTIN, Minnesota. City (pop. 23,020), southeastern Minnesota, east of ALBERT LEA, seat of Mower County; center of food and livestock processing industry; named for Austin R. Nicholas, Austin's first resident. Austin is located on an historic ford in the CEDAR RIVER used for years by Indians and settlers. Nicholas, a fur trapper, settled in the area in 1853. The community developed through the efforts of Chauncey Leverich who established a sawmill and was later criticized for being pompous when he built the town's first frame house. Residents of Austin who served as county commissioners resented the distance they had to travel to Frankfort, the first county seat. They decided that because no courthouse had been constructed in Frankfort the city did not deserve to be the county seat. The Austin commissioners stole the county records and fled toward Austin. When they were arrested and brought to trial, citizens of Austin attended the court proceedings with guns to see that justice was carried out. The commissioners were released and in a county-wide election in 1857 the seat of government was moved to Austin. Memorabilia of Austin's early days may be seen in the Mower County Historical Center. Five miles of self-guided nature trails on which some of Minnesota's most exotic plants may be observed are found at the J. C. Hormel Nature Center.

AUSTIN, Moses. (Durham, Connecticut, Oct. 4, 1761—Louisiana, June 10, 1821). Businessman. In 1789 Austin established the town of Potosi, Missouri, after several years of surveying lead mines in the southeastern part of the state. He assisted in the organization of the Bank of St. Louis in 1816, but when it failed during the depression of 1819, he moved to San Antonio, Texas. In 1821 he successfully applied to the Spanish government for permission to bring three hundred families into Texas. He died before the plans could be carried out.

AUTOMOBILES. Although much of the early development of automobiles occurred in Europe, the Midwest soon became and, despite serious problems, has remained the principal world center in the modern history and commercial development and production of automobiles. The region's first "modern" automobile, constructed by inventor Elwood Haynes, drove along roads in KOKOMO, Indiana, in 1893. Before the turn of the century, American inventors had designed gasoline-electric- and steam-propelled carriages.

Due to what would now be known as "networking," there was a concentration of this automotive experimenting and activity in the DETROIT, Michigan, area. The inventors there apparently had realized that there was great potential in the commercial development of the automobile. As inventor Hiram Maxim noted, these men "began to work on a self-propelled road vehicle at about the same time because it had become apparent that civilization was ready for the mechanical vehicle." The development of the Detroit area as world automotive center was rapidly accelerated because of the increasing concentration of automotive talent there, with most of the future auto tycoons continuing the work they had begun in the Detroit area. Of course, Detroit also was in an especially advantageous location for heavy industry, with Great Lakes TRANSPORTATION available for steel and other supplies and with more than adequate ground transportation, as well. Also, even in the early auto days, Detroit had an unusually talented supply of skilled labor.

The other Midwest centers were by no means disinterested in the auto business. By 1899 the Studebaker Company at SOUTH BEND, Indiana, had turned from buggies to autos. Indiana saw the production of such automobiles as the Cord, Stutz, Overland, Duesenberg, Auburn and Lexington.

Many other midwestern states made cars or were offered an opportunity of developing an automotive industry. Illinois, had no less than nine locally produced automobiles, including one distributed by Deere and Company and another, the Moline, built by the Moline Plow Company.

Such companies enjoyed brief local popularity, but never developed a national outlet for their product.

Costs of production and maintenance kept automobiles out of the financial reach of most people until continuing new developments and manufacturing techniques made cheaper cars possible through greater production. Interchangeable parts, allowing repair of any car of the same model, were developed by Henry M. Leland, president of the Cadillac Automobile Company. Henry FORD (1863-1947) drove his first cars in Detroit in 1896, and he was already thinking of ways to build the least expensive autos.

ASSEMBLY LINE PRODUCTION of automobiles began in Detroit after a huge fire in 1901 at the Olds Motor Works. After the fire, Ransom OLDS (1864-1950) signed contracts with three machine shops to manufacture many of the parts needed at the plant. Parts were brought to the assembly line and wheeled from one worker to another. This scheme allowed Olds to increase production from 425 cars in 1901 to 3,750 cars in 1902, and 5,000 in 1903.

Ford pioneered in improving the assembly line methods of production to lessen expense. His 1908 Model T, costing $850, was still too expensive for most, but was close to Ford's goal of manufacturing cars anyone could purchase. In 1913 Ford's Michigan plant installed a moving assembly line. One year later a car could be produced in one-and one-half hours, down from the previous record time of twelve-and-one-half hours. In 1916 the Model T could be sold at a profit for less than $400. Between 1908 and 1927, approximately fifteen million Ford automobiles were sold, more than one-half of the total number of cars made in the United States.

In the early days of the industry, advances in style, comfort and technology began to be concentrated in the region, especially in the extraordinary improvement of the primitive gasoline engine that took place in Wisconsin and Illinois, and with the perfection of the inflatable tire at Akron. During 1910-1911, Charles F. Kettering (1876-1958), an Ohio inventor, developed the electric starter, which did away with the need for cranking the engine by hand. This advance enabled more women to operate cars and made them more attractive to the market in general. Technical advances continued through such later developments as six- eight- and twelve-cylinder engines, front wheel drive (1937) and the automatic transmission (1939). The early 1950s saw the introduction of power devices designed to make driving easier, such as power steering and power brakes. Engine efficiency was enhanced by such devices as fuel injection, introduced in the late 1950s. There have been an almost endless number of luxuries, such as power windows and seats, coming into more general use in the 1960s. The dramatic developments in streamlining began with the first streamlined Chrysler, shown triumphantly at the 1934 Chicago Century of Progress, promising new speed and fuel economy. More efficient streamlining is still one of the most important goals of auto designers.

Many technological developments sprang from auto racing, which is still dominated by the Midwest. Barney OLDFIELD (1878-1946) won an exhibition as early as 1899, and in 1903 at DAYTON, Ohio, he set a world record at a mile a minute. However, the following year a Ford 999

Arrow Racer achieved 90 miles per hour on a frozen lake. The world-renowned INDIANAPOLIS SPEEDWAY was inaugurated in 1908. The tremendous strains and pressures undergone by racing cars, have always brought out the flaws in construction and technology and have spurred many improvements.

While the improvements of the internal combustion engine from 1900 to 1920 and the improvements in gasoline doomed the steam-powered car, steam had many advantages and for a while seemed to be winning over the gasoline cars. The Stanley twins, Francis (1849-1918) and Freelan (1849-1940), brought out the Stanley Steamer, a simple, effective car that broke the record time for a mile run in 1906, just over 26 seconds (127+ miles per hour). However, the average driver was never quite enough of an "engineer" to manage steam power.

Electricity was a popular power for a number of Detroit cars, including the Detroit Electric. Few Midwest towns lacked the stately elderly ladies with their "electrics." But electric cars were slow running and took a long time for recharging, and they too gave way to internal combustion.

The Midwest continued for many years unchallenged as the world's leading producer of automobiles, accessories and parts, with few worries about competition.

But the Great Depression of 1929 dropped auto production from 4,576,400 units in 1929 to 1,135,491 units in 1932. By 1939 there were only 21 different cars manufactured in the U.S., where there had been almost 2,000 ten years before.

During the four-year period of WORLD WAR II, auto production was halted, as the great automakers turned their talents to war production. At the close of the war, with the old cars falling apart, there was such a pentup demand for cars, that a sellers' market prevailed for several years. The small Studebaker company was the first to bring out a postwar model, with the hood lowered in front and the trunk tilting downward. The new Studebaker had an entirely new look, and the race was on to find other means of achieving a different appearance. Although the Studebaker design had the real advantage of adding streamlined efficiency, other makers often seemed content to extend a line here or put a bulge elsewhere, without much relation to beauty or efficiency, heralding a period of splayed fins, over-done chrome decoration and cumbersome size, all of which sold almost without question.

Automobiles

Henry Ford tries out an early Ford in Detroit, painting by Norman Rockwell.

By the late 1950s even the smaller auto firms that remained were beginning to disappear or to be consolidated. Studebaker and Packard merged but had only a few more years to live. Hudson, Willys and other small makers joined previous makes as historical memories. New efforts such as the Kaiser-Frazer and the Tucker had short lives.

The decline of the smaller makers followed similar trends in other major industries. The consolidation of capital and greater resources available to the larger firms permitted the vast expenditures needed to tool up for new models every one- two- or three-year period. Only the larger firms could commit the necessary funds to experimental research needed in every aspect of the industry from design and comfort through safety. Only the large firms could afford the huge outlays required for international advertising on an almost constant basis. Nor could the smaller firms hold the loyalty of buyers, who feared they might not be able to purchase parts or depend on their warranties.

The Big Three, General Motors, Ford and Chrysler, continued to grow and to dominate the market. Even they sometimes failed in an effort, such as the short-lived Edsel of the Ford company. The 1960s saw the trend to clean, trim low lines pioneered by the Ford Thunderbird in 1957 and such "compacts" as General Motors Skylark, Chevell and Camaro. Station wagons came into large scale production.

However, by 1964, the U.S. world lead had declined to 50 percent of the market, following the growing popularity of European cars, led by the German Volkswagen.

The American decline was hastened by the January 1, 1968 deadline for the incorporation of safety devices in new models, and the difficulties resulting from government regulations on emission control and fuel economy. Foreign makers were able to respond to such regulations with more economy and speed. During the 1970s, American production became more and more challenged by Japanese competition. The Japanese cars were perceived by the buying public as cheaper and of higher quality and resale value.

Sales of American cars dropped so dramatically that giants such as Chrysler were threatened. Other Detroit automakers also were hurt and alarmed. Thousands of auto workers were laid off, given early retirement or fired in auto plants around the Midwest. Estimates place the number between 200,000 and 300,000 in Michigan, alone.

Fewer paychecks meant that restaurants and stores were losing business wherever the auto business suffered. Equipment and parts suppliers closed, with their workers unemployed.

Partially destroyed by the earlier race riots, Detroit feared becoming a ghost town. Between 1970 and 1980 more than 300,000 persons fled that city to find a better life. Nearly 200,000 more had continued to leave in the four year period from 1980 to 1984. Much smaller FLINT lost almost 25% of its population in the period 1970-1984. During the same period, other Midwest auto assembly communities lost population, including KANSAS CITY, Missouri, which lost 45,000 people, and ST. LOUIS, Missouri, almost 200,000. Especially hard hit was KENOSHA, Wisconsin, home of American Motors. Unable to keep up with the giants in technical and cosmetic advances, lacking universal dealerships and adequate advertising funds, American Motors sales dipped most dramatically of all.

Midwest manufacturers of tires and other parts and equipment, such as those at AKRON, Ohio, and SOUTH BEND, Indiana, also lost heavily during the auto crisis.

Chrysler was saved only by the dramatic intervention of the federal government's guarantee of huge loans, finally arranged on December 21, 1979. With improved conditions, Chrysler later paid off the loans entirely. Chrysler and the other automakers were assisted by their unions, which realized the problems of the auto industry and gave up raises and made other concessions which helped the automakers to survive.

Formation and organization of LABOR AND LABOR UNIONS had been slow in the beginning of the industry. In 1935, the United Automobile Workers organized, with headquarters in Detroit. The sitdown strike was the dramatic method used by the UAW to obtain recognition from the auto industry's leading firm, General Motors. When workmen sat down in seventeen GM plants in December, 1936, and January, 1937, Michigan's Governor Frank Murphy refused to drive the strikers out at gunpoint, but used the troops to maintain peace. General Motor's February 11, 1937, recognition of the UAW, spurred auto workers to join the union. Membership mushroomed from 30,000 in the spring of 1936 to 300,000 within fifteen months, eventually going over a million. The Ford

Motor Company held out the longest by offering the workers more than the other companies.

Today, the major auto manufacturers and most of their purveyors are thoroughly unionized. Relations between workers and employers have improved since the invasion of the foreign cars, loss of the American auto markets, government safety and emission regulations and other problems. By the late 1970s the entire automobile community, both labor and management had begun to realize that they must work together or face a very uncertain future. Threats of strikes were based less on long term contracts with annual salary increases and were more concentrated on job security. During the second half of the 1980s, companywide labor agreements were negotiated with the major auto manufacturers, with most of the concessions being made in the form of perquisites, such as retraining and job security, rather than salaries.

Recognizing the need to modernize their operations to meet foreign competition, American producers proceeded to turn to robotics and other modern techniques and made great effort to improve the quality of their product, spending billions on capital improvements, technology and design.

By the mid-1980s the balance had shifted, until such giants as Ford and General Motors could show huge profits and could provide more secure contracts for their plant workers. In the late 1980s the decline of value of the dollar against foreign currencies brought higher prices for imports, again assisting the local manufacturers.

Michigan continues to produce more automobiles than any other area of the world, with Detroit still the leader. Most of the Midwest states produce automobile parts for assembly in Michigan, Wisconsin, Illinois, Missouri and Ohio. Nevertheless, trouble spots continue to plague the industry, with incidents such as the arbitrary closing of of the former American Motors plant at Kenosha in 1988, after it was taken over by Chrysler. The loss of 5,000 jobs there also meant lost jobs for thousands of other workers in support industries.

The decline in jobs was not so widespread in most of the region. Although in 1987-1988 Michigan lost more than 40,000 jobs in the industry, other states of the region picked up most of the slack, so that the net loss of such employment in the Midwest was less than 3,000 jobs in that period. Illinois had the largest gain.

Auto sales in 1987 and in the first part of

Milwaukee Museum diorama shows Aztalan of about 1200 A.D.

1988 continued to climb, and the industry began to regain some of its loss to foreign markets, bringing greater stability to the Midwest economy. Midwest populations also began to stabilize in the late 1980s, slowing the flight to the Sunbelt.

Part of the gain was realized as Midwest automakers regained much of their early lead in technology, with greater attention to aerodynamics, fuel efficiency and safety, all beginning to pay off in Detroit and elsewhere in the Midwest.

During the gasoline crisis of the 1970s, attention again turned to electric power, and substantial developments were made in storage batteries and other technical matters, but with the return of plentiful gasoline, interest ebbed once more.

Today the automobile has been called "the single most important influence on modern society." The Midwest region has, in turn, been the single most important influence on the automobile.

AUTOMOBILES, FIRST RACE. In 1873, Dr. F.W. Carhart of RACINE, Wisconsin, made a steam horseless carriage which he called "The Spark." This pioneering TRANSPORTATION brought on a rage for horseless carriages in Wisconsin, which in some ways was unique. In 1875 the state legislature offered a $10,000 prize to the inventor-builder of the first horseless carriage that could run 100 miles, and which also would be capable of running backward and being guided down the road by the operator. This is probably the only such legislative action ever taken in the U.S. The committee to pick the winner chose to make their choice the winner of a race between GREEN BAY and MADISON, Wisconsin. There were two entrants. The Green Bay car was capable of several speeds forward but was so complicated that it broke down during the race. A steam car from OSHKOSH dashed in at the average speed of six miles per hour. This is claimed to be the first race ever run between automobiles.

AYRES, LEW. (Minneapolis, MN, December 28, 1908—). Screen actor. Ayres was a leading man in films of the 1930s who hurt his career by declaring himself a conscientious objector in WORLD WAR II. His best known film was *All Quiet on the Western Front* (1930). Among his film credits are *Holiday* (1938), *Young Dr. Kildare* (1938), *Advise and Consent* (1961), and *The Carpetbaggers* (1964).

AZTALAN STATE PARK. In south central Wisconsin near Lake Mills, the state has preserved one of the most unusual archeological sites in the United States. When he discovered the terraced pyramid ruins of an ancient people there in 1837, Judge Nathaniel F. Hyer, called the site Aztalan because he thought it might have been a remote outpost of the Mexican Aztecs. Later study indicates that he may indeed have been right. The people seemed to have no relationship to any of their neighbors. Some Aztec peoples had come up the Mississippi Valley, but if Aztalan is Aztec, it marks the northernmost extension of Mexican influence on the continent. Remains of human bones indicate that the people of Aztalan were cannibals. Archeologists now believe that neighboring Indian tribes destroyed the cannibal peoples because they were angered at their slaughter of many Indians for food. The destruction of the community is thought to have occurred at not more than 100 years before the arrival of European explorers. In many ways the people of Aztalan were more advanced than their neighbors. They worked sheet copper, made fine products of shell, bone and stone. They surrounded their community with walls nineteen feet high, constructed differently from any other primitive fortifications of the state.

B

BABCOCK, Stephen Moulton. (Bridgewater, N.Y., 1843—1931). Agricultural chemist. After graduation from Tufts College in 1866, Babcock studied at Cornell, and in 1879 took a Ph.D at the University of Gottingen. He taught at Cornell in 1881 and 1882, then worked for five years as a chemist at the agricultural experiment station at Cornell. He joined the University of Wisconsin faculty in 1887 as Professor of agricultural chemistry and served until he retired in 1913. As director of the Agricultural Experiment Station of the University and of the Wisconsin Agricultural Experiment Station from 1887 to 1913, Babcock made possible some of the most notable advances in his field. In 1890 he invented the still-used method of testing the amount of butterfat in milk. This paved the way for the modern dairy industry and was one of the principal factors in the leadership of Wisconsin in DAIRYING. The tester enabled buyers at markets to determine the quality of the milk they were buying, helping both milk producers and sellers in quality control and avoidance of fraud. As one creamery owner remarked, "This will make farmers more honest than the Ten Commandments ever did." The discovery provided a means of evaluating the production of individual cows, offering insight into breeding for better production. Babcock made extensive studies in the nutritional requirements of animals. This formed the basis for the discovery of vitamin A by E.V. McCollum in 1912. In later life Babcock devoted himself to basic research to determine the relation of matter to energy. He never patented his discoveries, making them available to benefit all.

BABE (The Blue Ox). Legendary companion of the mythical Paul BUNYAN. The tales of Paul Bunyan and his blue ox, Babe, probably began with French loggers, but in Michigan and Minnesota the folklore blossomed. Babe reputedly arose out of Lake Bemidji during a blue snowstorm. According to legend, Babe drank huge quantities of water from the GREAT LAKES at several year intervals, causing significant drops in water levels. Thus he was responsible for the high and low water levels of the lakes that are a serious concern even today. Babe also consumed tremendous quantities of potato peels and hay, and he could haul an entire forest of logs. When Babe needed new shoes, a new mine in Minnesota would have to be opened to provide the iron. The blacksmith sank knee-deep in solid rock while carrying Babe's huge shoes. BRAINERD, Minnesota, considers itself the home of Paul Bunyan and Babe and features the largest animated statue of the two giants ever made. The statue is said to be the nation's most photographed.

BAD AXE, BATTLE OF. Closing battle of the BLACK HAWK WAR, August 1, 1832. In the spring of 1832, the renowned Chief BLACK HAWK

(1767-1838) of the SAC and FOX group had returned to Illinois from exile in Iowa with 400 of his braves and their families. They were determined to live once more in the state of their birth. Not receiving the support he expected from other Indian groups, Black Hawk attempted to drive them out but admitted defeat, but his emissaries of surrender were killed, and the chief went on the warpath in what has become known as the BLACK HAWK WAR, fought during the summer of 1832. After defeating a larger U.S. army in Illinois, the chief and his forces fled into Wisconsin. A masterful retreat brought them to the shores of the Bad Axe River in Wisconsin, and almost to the banks of the MISSISSIPPI RIVER. The exact site is not known, but a marker near Genoa, Wisconsin, indicates the probable place. U.S. General Henry Atkinson had gathered a large force of volunteers, assisted by a group of Sioux warriors. In the battle that followed, the Black Hawk group was trapped, and the chief displayed the white flag of surrender. However, the opposing forces massacred men, women and children as they tried to flee across the Misssissippi. Many of them were killed in mid-river. A few, including Black Hawk, escaped; he was later captured, then freed.

BADGERS (NICKNAME). Nickname for the state of Wisconsin and its people. During the lead mining boom in northeast Iowa and southwest Wisconsin, hundreds of miners flocked into the region. In the early days of the boom, beginning in 1823, some miners worked during the summer and went south for the winter. Others stayed on during the winter and dug shelters into the Wisconsin hillsides. They were said to be imitating the badgers, and the Wisconsin nickname, Badger State, was derived from these early primitive homemakers.

BAILEY, Joseph. (OH, May, 1826 or 1827—Vernon County, MO, Mar. 16, 1867) Civil War hero. Lieutenant Colonel Bailey, of WISCONSIN DELLS, Wisconsin, accomplished one of the most famed engineering feats of the CIVIL WAR and saved Union forces from probable defeat in the Red River campaign in Louisiana. As chief engineer of the Fourth Wisconsin Regiment, he suggested a way to save the Union's river fleet of heavy gunboats which had been trapped by low water in the river near Alexandria, Louisiana. This made the fleet vulnerable to Confederate attacks from shore. Although his suggestion was laughed at, he was given 3,000 troops and told to go ahead. The

colonel's plan was based on his experience in driving timber down the WISCONSIN RIVER, using a procedure called the "lift." He requisitioned the lumberjack boys from the various Wisconsin units, and they hurriedly put together a complete log dam. On May 12, 1864, as soon as the dam raised the water enough to float the heavy Union gunboats, they weighed anchor, crashed into the dam, splintering it, and plunged on into the deeper water below. For his contribution, Bailey received a promotion to brevet brigadier-general and was given a sword and silver bowl, which are still on display at the Wisconsin State Historical Museum. After the war he returned to Wisconsin Dells but left to become a deputy sheriff in Vernon county, Missouri. There he was killed while attempting to arrest two suspects.

BAKER, Newton Diehl. (Martinsburg, WV, Dec. 3, 1871—Shaker Heights, OH, Dec. 25, 1937). Cabinet officer, U.S. Secretary of War 1916-1921. Baker graduated from Johns Hopkins University in 1892. There one of his professors was Woodrow Wilson. He earned his law degree from Washington and Lee University in 1892 and returned to Martinsburg to practice law. Moving to CLEVELAND, he was city soliciter (1902-1912) and Mayor of Cleveland (1912-1916). As mayor he was notable for his tax reform measures. Appointed secretary of war by Woodrow Wilson in March, 1916, he began his service just as Mexican revolutionary Pancho Villa was threatening the U.S border with Mexico, and WORLD WAR I was spreading in Europe. During his first year in office, Baker did little to strengthen U.S. armed forces, despite the growing war threats. Many members of both parties were displeased, and complained about his known pacifist feelings. He was investigated by Congress in 1917 but not removed from office. Baker overcame the early judgments of his administration and ended his service to the War Department with almost universal praise for his mobilization effort. Nevertheless, he remained one of the most ardent advocates of peace and continued to urge U.S. entry into the League of Nations. In 1928 Coolidge appointed him to the Permanent Court of Arbitration at The Hague.

BALANCE ROCK. Unique rock formation. At the Wisconsin Dells on the WISCONSIN RIVER near the community of WISCONSIN DELLS, stands one of the most famous and most publicized rock formations of its type, Balance Rock. On a cliff high above the river, the rock perches on a base which is said to be the smallest of its type in proportion to the mass above. The rock has attracted millions of tourists since it was first described by a geologist in 1847.

BALD KNOBBERS. Band of Missouri vigilantes secretly established at Forsyth in 1884 who turned into a mob of thugs. They were thought to be responsible for many murders, robberies and beatings. Outraged citizens rounded up thirty of the men in 1887. Four were tried for first degree murder and sentenced to hang. During appeals of their sentences three managed to escape. Two of the men were recaptured and the three were hanged on May 10, 1889, ending the terrorism.

BALDWIN, Frank D. (Manchester, MI, June 26, 1842—April 22, 1923.) One of two Michigan natives to win the Congressional Medal of Honor twice. Baldwin served in the Michigan Horse Guards and the Nineteenth Michigan Infantry from 1861 to 1865, rising in rank from second lieutenant to captain. He then enlisted in the regular army and was eventually promoted to brigadier general. Baldwin won the Medal of Honor "for distinguished bravery in the battle of Peach Tree Creek, Georgia, July 20, 1864," and the second time "for distinguished gallantry in action against Indians in Texas, Nov. 8, 1874." He retired from military service on June 26, 1906.

BALDWIN, Michigan. Village (pop. 700), Lake County. west-central portion of Michigan's LOWER PENINSULA, northwest of G R A N D RAPIDS. Baldwin, a former railroad junction, lies near Manistee National Forest. The village is also home to Shrine of the Pines. Created by Raymond Oberholzer, the shrine is a collection of hand-chisled home furnishings made from tree stumps and roots left behind when lumbermen cut the forests in the late 1880s. Especially impressive is a drawered table carved from a seven-hundred-pound stump.

BALL STATE UNIVERSITY. Muncie, Indiana, opened in 1899 as the Eastern Indiana Normal University. It was acquired by the five Ball brothers in 1918. The Ball Brothers were founders at MUNCIE of a glass works which became the world's largest producer of glass containers. They established a foundation and gave the college to Indiana as Ball State Teachers College. Later donations of the Ball foundation were responsible for construction of most of the major buildings on campus. The

institution reached university status in 1965, but education remains as a principal emphasis in the curriculum. The biology department is particularly strong in its field and maintains a noted outdoor laboratory-arboretum. In 1985-1986 Ball State enrolled 17,039 students and had 1,359 faculty members.

BALLOONING, NATIONAL HOT AIR CHAMPIONSHIP. Held every August through 1988, the competition multiplied the population of INDIANOLA, Iowa, as much as eight times, when eighty to a hundred thousand spectators gathered for the National Hot Air Balloon Championship there. The Iowa town became an international center for ballooning. The city is also the site of the National Balloon Museum, sponsored by the Balloon Federation of America and Indianola Ballooners, Inc. The museum features a collection of items related to the lighter-than-cold-air sport. To the consternation of the people of Indianola, the Balloon Federation announced that beginning in 1989 the championship meet would be held at Baton Rouge, Louisiana.

BANKS, Ernie. (Dallas, TX, January 31,-1931—). Baseball star. A graduate of NORTH-WESTERN UNIVERSITY in business, Banks then played with the Kansas City Monarchs of the Negro American League from 1950 to 1953. He joined the Chicago Cubs in 1953, where he was shortstop then first baseman until 1971. Leaving active play, he coached first base and moved into Cubs management. He also founded an automotive sales agency. Banks was the National League home run leader in 1958 and 1960. Selected the Most Valuable Player in the National League in 1958 and again in 1959, Banks' career record stands at 512 home runs. He played in thirteen All-Star games and holds the record for lifetime grand slam home runs. He was elected to the Baseball Hall of Fame in 1987.

BARABOO, Wisconsin. City (pop. 8,081), seat of Sauk County, situated in south central Wisconsin on the Baraboo River not far from its mouth at the WISCONSIN RIVER, the city was named in honor of Jean Baribault, who is supposed to have set up a trading post at the confluence of the rivers. Baraboo was founded in 1830, but its site was not ceded by the WINNEBAGO INDIANS until 1837. The steep bluffs hampered the community's growth, and the regular stage coaches did not reach the town until 1855. Sustained moderate growth fol-

National Hot Air Ballooning Championship, Indianola, Iowa.

lowed. Today the city is a center for the DAIRY processing industry, and more than twenty other small factories operate there. The city is best known as the birthplace of the RINGLING brothers, of circus fame, for the winter headquarters which they established there and for the Circus World Museum, which is housed in the original six buildings of the Ringlings' winter quarters. The community also offers the Sauk County Historical Museum, with pioneer and early history displays, and the Mid-Continent Railway Museum. The railway museum is centered on a restored 1894 depot. The displays emulate a complete railway environment of the 1900 era, with steam locomotives, steam wrecker, snowplows, coaches and other exhibits. An hour-long steam train ride is offered. Nearby Devils Head Lodge and Mirror Lake State Park have splendid recreational facilities. Baraboo celebrates with an annual country music show called Wisconsin Opry, presented nightly from Memorial Day to Labor Day.

BARAJA, Father Frederic. (Dobernig, Austria, June 29, 1797—Marquette, MI, Jan. 19, 1868.) Missionary to the Indians on Michigan's Upper Peninsula. Father Baraja (sometimes spelled "Baraga") was educated in Austria. After receiving his law degree from the University of Vienna, Father Baraja decided to enter the church and was ordained into the priesthood Sept. 21, 1823. Seven years later he was sent as a missionary to the Ottawa village of Arbre Croche, now Harbor Springs, Michigan. Father Baraja was very well-received at his first Indian mission, and in 1833 he began a new mission at the present site of GRAND RAPIDS, Michigan. Here he angered the traders by denouncing their liquor trade with the tribes, and in 1835 was transferred to the far shores of Lake SUPERIOR. There he suffered many hardships in the cold winters. He studied the CHIPPEWA language for years, and wrote a grammar book and dictionary that are still used by Chippewa scholars. He also translated a hymn book and other devotional materials. He is known as "the parish priest of Lake Superior."

BARBERTON, Ohio. City (pop. 29,751) situated in northeast Ohio, a suburb of AKRON. Laid out in 1891 and named for its founder, Ohio Columbus Barber. Founder of the Diamond Match company in 1880, O. C. Barber promoted the town as a site for other industries by generous offers of land. The demand of the early factories for cheap labor brought large numbers of immigrants. Barber's match company covered two city blocks and was one of the largest of its kind. Today the city follows the lead of its larger neighbor and is a major producer of a variety of rubber products, including tires. Because of the flight of industry to the Sun Belt, the population of Barberton declined from 33,052 to 29,751 in the decade beginning in 1970. Barber's nearby Anna Dean Farm is a major attraction of the area. This estate occupied most of Barber's interests after he retired from the match company in 1913. He spent $3,000,000 on the 3,000 acre experimental farm, called Barber's Folly by area residents.

BATAVIA, Illinois. City (12,574), Kane Co., one of the earliest areas of Illinois to be settled following the BLACK HAWK WAR in 1832. Batavia has enjoyed the triple advantage of fertile soil, water power, and surface limestone. By 1850 it had extensively developed its limestone resources to the point that the city was nicknamed Quarry City. Bellevue Place Sanitarium in Batavia was the site of Mary Todd Lincoln's confinement from May 20 to September 10, 1875. The eastern limits of Batavia are near the western boundary of the National Accelerator Laboratory, an experimental facility in the field of atomic research, operated for the Atomic Energy Commission. The laboratory is one of the major employers of the area.

BATES, Frederick. (Belmont, VA, June 23, 1777—Chesterfield, MO, August 4, 1825). Jurist. Bates was appointed one of three judges for the Michigan Territory in 1805. The following year he became secretary of the Louisiana Territory (the original LOUISIANA PURCHASE), and then was made acting governor. In 1808 Bates was responsible for the revised Code of the Louisiana Territory, including much of the western Midwest. His 1808 compilation of the laws of Louisiana was the first book to be published in Missouri. Bates served as governor of Missouri from 1824 to 1825.

BATTLE CREEK, Michigan. City (pop. 35,724), Calhoun County, southwestern portion of Michigan's LOWER PENINSULA at the confluence of Battle Creek, which gives the city its name, and the Kalamazoo River. The name originated from a fight between an early land surveyor and an Indian along the creek's banks in 1825. Battle Creek is widely known as the home of

the Post and Kellogg plants which produce processed breakfast cereals. C.W. POST (1854-1914) and Will Keith KELLOGG (1860-1951) were pioneers in this field, and both of them built their plants in this southern Michigan city. Today the city has other food processers, particularly in pet foods and crackers. Other industries include pumps, valves, farm equipment and trucks. The KELLOGG FOUNDATION, established by W. K. Kellogg, has financed many worthy causes in education and the arts. Another prominent citizen was Sojourner Truth (1797?-1883), an ex-slave noted for her fight against SLAVERY. She carried her crusade for freedom personally to President Abraham LINCOLN. Truth made her home in BATTLE CREEK from 1858 until her death in 1883. She is buried in Oak Hill Cemetery. Battle Creek is the home of a civil defense staff college, training center for U.S. civilian defense directors. Attractions of the city include the seventy-two acre Leila Arboretum with its Kingman Museum of Natural History and planetarium. The W. K. Kellogg Bird Sanctuary is on nearby Wintergreen Lake. The Kellogg Battle Creek plant plays host to an estimated 20,000 visitors annually. One-hour tours explain how farmers' grain is converted into crispy flakes or puffs. John W. Bailey Park hosts national amateur baseball tournaments.

BAY CITY, Michigan. City (pop. 41,593), seat of Bay County, located in the Thumb Country of Michigan's LOWER PENINSULA, a rich sugar beet, potato and melon farming region on Saginaw Bay, an inlet of Lake HURON. The Bay City port receives 850 domestic ships and over 100 foreign ships annually, handling more than seven million tons of cargo. Other industries include shipbuilding, cranes, automobile parts, electronics and petrochemicals. Bay City was incorporated in 1859, including a number of small contiguous communities. A roaring lumber mill town at the turn of the century, its lumber industry was replaced by the shipping and agricultural industries. The stately mansions of lumber barons can still be seen on tree-lined streets. The Defoe Ship Company has been a producer of guided missile destroyers. The nearby SAGINAW RIVER and Saginaw Bay provide recreational activities. The Historical Museum of Bay County traces the history of the area. The city hall is noted for its spectacular woven tapestry depicting the history of the community. St. Stanislaus Polish Festival is held in late June and the Potato Festival in late July.

BAYFIELD, Wisconsin. Village (pop. 778), situated on Lake SUPERIOR in far north central Wisconsin, Bayfield was named for Admiral Henry Bayfield of the British navy who surveyed in the area about 1823. The village was founded in 1857; the railroad came in 1880, and the community became a lumbering center. Today Bayfield is the point of embarkation for the Apostle Islands. The headquarters and visitors' center of APOSTLE ISLANDS NATIONAL LAKESHORE is located at Bayfield. Regular ferry service from April through December connects Bayfield with historic MADELINE ISLAND, most important of the Apostles. Madeline Island Historical Museum operates a replica of a pioneer AMERICAN FUR COMPANY post.

BEARD, Charles Austin. (Knightstown, IN, Nov. 27, 1874—New Haven, CT, Sept. 1, 1948). Historian and political scientist. Graduating from DE PAUW UNIVERSITY in 1898, Beard spent four years abroad, first studying for a year at Oxford. From 1907 to 1917 he taught politics and history at Columbia University. During that time his interests turned from European to American history and economics. *The Supreme Court and the Constitution* (1912) was one of his early important works. He became an intellectual leader of the Progressive movement. Protesting Columbia's suppression of academic freedom, he left Columbia and was named director of the Training School for Public Service in 1917. In 1919 he was one of the founders of the New School for Social Research. He continued to write on political and historical matters and is considered one of America's most influential historians. He did much to encourage Economic Determinism as an approach to the study of history. With his wife Mary, in 1927 Beard began work on a four-part series called *The Rise of American Civilization.* his *A Basic History of the United States* (1944) has continued to be a standard text. Prior to WORLD WAR II Beard became a severe critic of F. D. Roosevelt's foreign policies. Beard's writings include *The Development of Modern Europe* (1907) and *President Roosevelt and the Coming of War, 1941-1948.* His *An Economic Interpretation of the Constitution of the United States* (1913) is considered to have created a whole school of history that is still addressed today, sometimes known as the "New History" of economic theory.

BEAUMONT, William. (CT, Nov. 21, 1785—St. Louis, MO, April 25, 1853). Physician and medical researcher. Educated in Vermont, Beaumont was licensed to practice medicine in 1812. He served in the WAR OF 1812. After practicing privately for four years, he reenlisted and was assigned to be post surgeon at FORT MACKINAC, Michigan, from 1820 to 1825.

William Beaumont treating Alexis St. Martin.

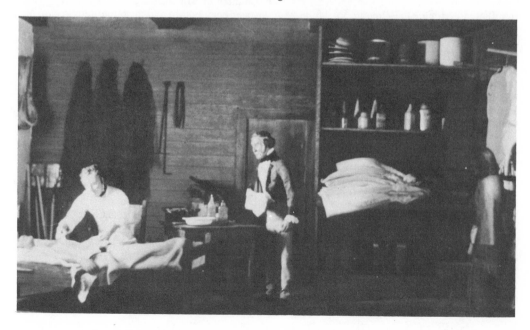

There he began his famous study of the digestive process as he labored to heal a young trapper, Alexis St. Martin. Although he appeared quite healthy, St. Martin had been severely wounded in the abdomen in a gun accident. The wound never completely healed. By studying the opening in St. Martin's abdomen, Dr. Beaumont made many observations about human digestion, and his research became world famous. Beaumont wrote *Experiments and Observations on the Gastric Juice and the Physiology of Digestion* in 1833. After resigning from the Army Medical Corps in 1839, he practiced medicine in ST. LOUIS until his death.

BEAVER ISLAND, Michigan. Largest of the islands comprising the Beaver Archipelago in upper Lake MICHIGAN about 35 miles west of the STRAITS OF MACKINAC. Beaver Island, known as Big Beaver, is 13 miles long and between 3 and 6 miles wide. The east side of the island contains sandy beaches which slope upward to the range of sand dunes on the west side. Seven lakes on it teem with game fish. The island's history is especially interesting, with the unique account of the coming of the MORMONS under "King" Jesse STRANG (1813-1856) in 1847, the conflict of the Mormons with the "Gentiles" and the strange fate of Strang. Today, the quiet island is a favorite of commercial and sports fishermen and other vacationers. Quaint St. James is home to descendants of the early Irish fishermen, whose descendants may still be seen on the streets, along with the descendants of the original OTTAWA and CHIPPEWA Indians.

BECKNELL, William. (Amherst County, VA, 1796—April 30, 1865). Trader and explorer known as "The Father of the SANTA FE TRAIL." In August, 1821, Becknell and seventeen other men left Franklin, Missouri, on a trading mission to the Indians. After days of unsuccessful wandering the party was picked up by a company of Spanish soldiers and escorted to Santa Fe. Instead of facing prison the traders were shocked at the wild enthusiasm with which they were met and with the quick sale of their trading goods. The Mexicans had successfully revolted from Spain and were anxious to trade with the United States. Returning to Missouri with bags of Spanish silver, Becknell had no difficulty in arranging another trading mission. On May 22, 1822, Becknell and a party of twenty-one men and three covered wagons left Arrow Rock in western Missouri. This was the first trade caravan of wheeled vehicles on the Santa Fe Trail. Becknell's party returned to Missouri with huge profits from the sale of their goods. In 1834 he moved to Texas, as part of the pioneering U.S. colony there. He served in the Texas revolutionary forces and later became a Texas Ranger.

BEDFORD, Indiana. City (pop. 14,410), southeastern Indiana, seat of Lawrence Co., center of the Indiana limestone industry. Bedford limestone is a favorite with architects. It has been used in the construction of the Empire State Building in New York City, the ART INSTITUTE OF CHICAGO, and the Mellon Institute in Pittsburgh, among others. In addition to the limestone there are several small industries and a foundry. The town began in the late 1850s when the importance of the limestone became understood, and the city quickly grew with the development of its limestone. In the 1880s a Bedford physician, Dr. Joseph Gardner, bequeathed a portion of land, known as the Red Cross Farm, to the Red Cross, and Clara Barton, founder of the Red Cross, used a building in town as a part-time residence. The city was incorporated in 1889. The Moses Fell Annex Farm, near Bedford, was given to PURDUE UNIVERSITY in 1914 by Moses Fell for experimental work in livestock raising, horticulture, and bee and poultry keeping. Work done at the farm has continued to benefit Indiana farmers interested in scientific farming. Nearby is the Pioneer Mothers' Memorial Forest, renowned for its huge trees and used for ecological studies.

BEE TREES. Prized by pioneers for their honey. Because there was little or no sugar on the frontier, the bee trees (hives of wild bees, filled with honey) were greatly sought after. Both Iowa and Missouri claimed a sizeable tract of land and disputed the location of the border, an area in which the bee trees were particularly numerous. When three men from Missouri came into the section claimed by Iowa and cut down three of the prized trees, the governors of the two states declared "war," and in August, 1839, ragged troops from both sides headed for the disputed territory, carrying an assortment of churn dashers, pitch forks and other armaments. Fortunately the "war" never materialized, and in 1850 the U.S. Supreme Court finally decided the matter in Iowa's favor.

BELLE ISLE. Island, three-fourths of a mile offshore at DETROIT, in Michigan's DETROIT RIVER.

Scotts Fountain, Belle Isle, Detroit, Michigan

In 1845, the island was christened Belle Isle in honor of Isabella, daughter of former governor Lewis CASS. The name was not formally adopted until 1881. In 1780, Lieutenant George McDougall of the English garrison purchased Belle Isle from the Indians for three rolls of tobacco, five barrels of rum, three pounds of red paint, and a belt of wampum, a total of about $970. William Macomb bought the island for 1,594 pounds and sold it in 1817 to Barnabas Campau for $5,000. It was privately owned until 1879 when the city of Detroit purchased it for $200,000. The island then contained 768 acres, but subsequent land reclamation has significantly increased its size. The island is two miles long and has 20 miles of shore and intra-island highways. The entire island is now Belle Isle Park, known for its aquarium, the Belle Isle Nature Center featuring changing exhibits on area wildlife, and the Belle Isle Zoo with its elevated walkways which enable visitors to see animals roaming uncaged in their natural habitat. The Dossin Great Lakes Museum highlights the history of Great Lakes sailing vessels.

BELLEVILLE, Illinois. City (pop. 42,150), county seat of St. Clair Co.; south of East St. Louis; name suggested by John Hay, prominent Canadian in the early years of the state. It is located on the eastern bluffs of the American Bottom, in the heart of the bituminous COAL region. Its factories produce batteries, boilers, castings, dies, beer, enamelled ware and shoes and boots. It is a center of rail and road transport. Belleville also is hub of a substantial agricultural area and is the center for U.S. production of bleached asparagus. French residents of Illinois who were dissatisfied with political conditions at CAHOKIA began to come to the Belleville area, and the first house was built there in 1806. By 1818 Belleville was the northernmost point of mail delivery from the East, and the community was incorporated as a village in 1819. Coal mining grew rapidly, and miners hauled the fuel over the first macadam road in Illinois from Belleville to the Illinois-town ferry. City incorporation was achieved in 1850. By 1890 Belleville was one of twenty Illinois cities with a population in excess of ten thousand. In 1917 one of Illinois' two aviation bases was established in Belleville at Scott Field. The national Shrine of Our Lady of Snows features a replica of the Lourdes Grotto, and a 6,200-seat amphitheater.

BELLOW, Saul. (Lachine, Quebec, June 10, 1915—). Author. After spending his early life in Lachine, Bellow moved to CHICAGO in 1924, where he attended the University of CHICAGO, then graduated from NORTHWESTERN UNIVERSITY in 1937. Working as a biographer in the WPA writers' project, he also taught for about four years at Pestalozzi-Froebel Teachers College in CHICAGO. He taught English at the University of MINNESOTA and Bard College and was a fellow in writing at Yale and Princeton Universities. His first novel, *Dangling Man*, was published in 1944, and he continued with his writing. He became known for his theme of the conflict within the individual, struggling to reconcile his personal needs with the demands of society. Bellow's characters have ranged from the grim in his first novels to the exuberant and comic depicted in what is considered his best fiction. More recent characters are older and more thoughtful. Settings used in his writing range from Chicago to New York City, with its violence and tension. *Herzog* (1964) is his semi-autobiographical novel about the life of a university professor who struggles with his alienation from society. This brought Bellow his second National Book Award. *Mr. Sammler's Planet* (1970) made him the first American author to win three National Book Awards. He won the NOBEL PRIZE for Literature in 1976. He has served on the faculty of the University of Chicago and on its Committee on Social Thought since 1962.

BELLOWS, George Wesley. (Columbus, OH, Aug. 12, 1882—New York, NY, Jan. 8, 1925). Artist and lithographer. After graduating from OHIO STATE UNIVERSITY, he went to New York City in 1904 and studied art, gaining an early mastery of the palette and developing a highly individual style. He became associated with the radical young artists group known as The Eight. As a fine athlete, he was attracted to athletic scenes, tension and action. He frequented Tom Sharkey's boxing gym and painted a series of stark, highly contrasted scenes of the gym. His 1907 painting "Stag at Sharkey's" is one of the best known by a U.S. artist. He was one of the organizers of the famous Armory Show at New York in 1913. He turned to the study of lithography and became one of the experts in that field. He taught from time to time at New York's Art Students League and the ART INSTITUTE OF CHICAGO.

BELMONT, Wisconsin. Village (pop. 826), situated in far southwestern Wisconsin, was the first capital of the Territory of Wisconsin, now called Old Belmont. In 1836 lumber was imported from far off Pittsburgh to this heavily timbered region to build the building which was rented as a capitol. When the capital was moved to MADISON in 1836, Old Belmont became a ghost town. Gradually the ghost gained a few new settlers and matured as the small agricultural community of today. Of particular interest is First Capitol State Park. The Council House and Supreme Court building have been restored by the Lafayette County Historical Society. At Belmont Mound, a tower offers views of four states. The Badger Mine and Museum provides an opportunity to tour the tunnels of a pioneer lead mine.

BELOIT COLLEGE. Soon after a group of New England settlers moved to present BELOIT, in 1837 Wisconsin, they founded a congregational seminary. The founding group included as a part of its charter its determination to encourage art, religion and education. In 1846 the Congregational Church took over the operation as Beloit College. The two professors who were hired were to receive $600 each per year "if available." Almost from the beginning the institution became known for its academic quality, a reputation heightened by an exchange professorship with Harvard. Today it is generally recognized as one of the top small colleges in the United States. One of its specialities, anthropology and archeology, produced the famed alumnus, Roy Chapman ANDREWS, explorer and long time director of New York's American Museum of Natural History. Another prominent alumnus was J.N. (Ding) DARLING, one of the country's most noted cartoonists, whose work was the most widely syndicated of its type at the time. The college operates two noted museums, the Lyman Wright Museum of Art and the Logan Museum of Anthropology. The student body of 1,070 is instructed by a faculty of 112.

BELOIT, Wisconsin. City (pop. 35,207), situated in Rock County in far south central Wisconsin, on the ROCK RIVER at the border with Illinois, the city was named for its site (bel, beautiful) combined with (-oit), borrowed from Detroit, a name said to be fancied by one of the founders. A trading post was established at the site in 1824. Today the city is a center of manufacture of diesel engines, machinery, papermaking equipment, desalinzation equipment, pumps and electrical equipment. In 1837 Dr. Horace White, acting as agent of the New England Emigrating Company, bought a tract in the area, and most of the population of

Colebrook, New Hampshire, moved to the site. Incorporated in 1846, the community endured the names of Turtle Blodgett's Settlement and New Albany before settling on Beloit in 1857. To combat hard times the community encouraged industry by concessions of land and other favors. Builders of heavy machinery moved in, including the company which later became the vast Fairbanks-Morse operation, founded by Charles Hosmer Morse. Today, in addition to manufacturing, the city centers around its acclaimed BELOIT COLLEGE, founded in 1846 by the New England settlers. Two notable early structures of the community are open to visitors—The Hanchetty-Bartlett Homestead and the Rasey House.

BEMIDJI, Minnesota. City (pop. 10,949), northwestern Minnesota, seat of Beltrami County, the city was named for an Indian chief who lived on the southern shore of Lake Bemidji near the site of the present city. The name in Chippewa means, "easy crossing." The area of Bemidji was on the Red Lake Trail, a popular route for fur trappers and early settlers. The earliest settlement, founded in 1866, grew very slowly until 1894 when one of the more unusual episodes in Minnesota history occurred. A homesteader strolling along Lake Bemidji accidentally kicked a piece of stone that shimmered. Bending down he uncovered more of the stones which, by now, he was sure were diamonds. While waiting for the specimens to be analyzed by an expert in New York City, the homesteader formed an association with friends which soon bought all the available land in sure belief they were to become diamond kings of North America. The report from New York must have been a shock. All the stones were quartzite. The aspiring kings were left owners of vast tracts of undeveloped land far from civilization. During 1894 and 1895 promotions brought industry to the region with the beginnings of prosperity for the land owners. The first sawmill in the area was set up on the shore of the lake. In its heyday Bemidji was one of the wildest frontier towns in the far North. The population nearly doubled every ten years from 1900 to 1920. The Bemidji of today is more commercially diversified. TOURISM is the major industry, augmented by boat manufactures and wood products. In the recreational heartland of Minnesota, the city is a few miles north of Itasca State Park and Lake ITASCA, the headwaters of the MISSISSIPPI RIVER. Cass Lake, with its pine-covered Star Island, is a few miles to the east. RED LAKE lies to the north. The

region is nationally known for its fishing. Bemidji claims to be the birthplace of Minnesota's legendary logger, Paul BUNYAN. An eighteen-foot steel and concrete statue of Paul and a fourteen-foot high and eighteen-foot long statue of his blue ox BABE, stand on the shore of Lake Bemidji. The Bunyan House Information Center features a collection of Paul Bunyan tools with amusing descriptions. The Fireplace of the States has stones from every state and Canadian province. Annual events include Paul Bunyan Water Carnival on July 4th weekend with fireworks, water show and a beauty pageant.

BENEFICIATING. Process developed to concentrate the iron content of low-grade ores. The first experimental beneficiating plant was constructed in 1907 by the Oliver Mining Division of the United States Steel Corporation on the shore of Trout Lake near Coleraine, Minnesota. The modern industry, however, came about as a result of the work of Professor E.W. Davis of the University of MINNESOTA who, working over a period of several decades, developed a way of concentrating the thin content of the magnetic TACONITE found in the MESABI RANGE into pellets of sixty percent iron. The process starts as the taconite is crushed and ground to a powder. Magnets are used to separate the useful taconite from the waste rock. The taconite particles are fed into a steel barrel where they are mixed with coal dust and heated to form marble-sized balls. The coal burns away, and the remaining highly concentrated taconite is shipped to foundries for further processing. The first large-scale processing plant for taconite, operated by Reserve Mining Company, opened in Silver Bay, Minnesota, in 1955. Because of the success of the process the iron ore mining industry in Minnesota, which was nearing the end of its supplies of high grade ore, was again promised a profitable future.

BENNARD, George. (Youngstown, Ohio, Feb. 4, 1873— ?). Methodist minister, evangelist, and composer. Bennard is remembered primarily for "The Old Rugged Cross," (copyright 1913) a hymn he composed in ALBION, Michigan. Monuments mark the site of his home and the place where his much-loved hymn was first sung. Bennard published several volumes of songs.

BENTON HARBOR, Michigan. City (pop. 14,707), Berrien County, one of the southwest

Lower Peninsula's "Twin Cities." At its mouth on Lake Michigan, the ST. JOSEPH RIVER separates Benton Harbor from SAINT JOSEPH, but the two cities are virtually one, geographically. In the years after St. Joseph's incorporation in 1836, settlers considered its land prices too high and built their homes east of the river.

These new settlers started manufacturing barrel bungs. They named their community Bronson Harbor after its founder, but St. Joseph's citizens disdainfully called it "Bungtown Harbor." In 1869 the village was incorporated as Benton Harbor. By 1889 Benton Harbor had grown much faster than St. Joseph, and it applied for a city charter.

St. Joseph disputed the location of the boundary between the cities, and the state legislature decided to issue one city charter to include both communities. When a mutually acceptable name could not be found the two cities were finally given separate charters in 1891. As the years passed, Benton Harbor continued to grow in size and importance while St. Joseph lost its standing as a key lake port, and their rivalry and ill feeling grew. Eventually common economic considerations brought the two communities together to discuss ways to enlarge local trade. The animosity between them gradually faded away, and a spirit of friendship and cooperation developed.

In 1903, religious leader Benjamin Franklin PURNELL established a colony of his Israelite HOUSE OF DAVID in Benton Harbor.

The community remained prosperous, with a growing number of manufacturing plants and as a center of AGRICULTURE. The agricultural bounty of the region is still obvious at the Benton Harbor Fruit Market, reputedly the largest cash-to-grower market in the United States.

Unfortunately, the city began to suffer an economic decline, which rapidly accelerated in the 1960s. From a thriving community with over 500 factories within the city limits in 1960, fewer than 100 remain, according to local sources. As the factories found more efficient and less costly sites in the Sunbelt and elsewhere, thousands of Benton Harbor citizens lost their jobs.

Places Rated Almanac ranks the city eighth from the bottom in economic status among the 329 communities surveyed. With an average per capita annual income of $3,766, government figures show 40% of the population below the established poverty level. More than 40% are unemployed. Over 60% of the population receive some form of public assistance.

However, local sources now report a continu-ing modest improvement beginning in mid 1986. New industries are arriving, including an Israeli auto assembly plant. A riverside condo-marina has brightened the waterfront, and the city has been able to obtain loans to pay off its debt to the state.

Cooperation with St. Joseph continues on the administrative level, and the two communities live together peaceably despite the population mix of 95% white in St. Joseph and 85% black in Benton Harbor. Blossomtime Festival is a popular local event in late April. There is a Western Amateur Golf Tournament in July.

BENTON, Thomas Hart. (Hillsboro, N.C., Mar. 14, 1782—Washington, D.C., Apr. 10, 1858). Senator, politician, Democratic Party leader and writer. He spent his early years in Tennessee, then attended the University of North Carolina in 1799. Admitted to the bar in 1806, he practiced law and was elected to the Tennessee legislature in 1809. He served under Andrew Jackson in the WAR of 1812, then moved to frontier ST. LOUIS, Missouri. There he both practiced law and edited the *Missouri Enquirer* (1818-1820). He gained such popularity through his editorials that in 1820 he was elected to the U.S. Senate, where he served for thirty years, becoming the chief spokesman for the Jacksonians in the upper house. As a supporter of sound money, he became known as "Old Bullion." He crusaded for the distribution of public lands to settlers, and one of his proposals later became the basis for the homestead act. He was one of the most prominent promoters of westward expansion. In the 1830s he led a successful fight to dissolve the Bank of the United States, supported hard money (as opposed to uncertain specie) and advocated a federal independent treasury. He continued to be the strong supporter of the free small farmer. Believing that SLAVERY was hindering his beloved western expansion, he turned more and more against slavery. His stand against the Compromise of 1850 led to his defeat for another Senate term, when he announced his belief that it gave too much to the slave states. Still popular, he ran successfully for the United States House of Representatives from Missouri and served from 1853 to 1855. However, he was defeated for reelection and was an unsuccessful candidate for Missouri governor in 1856. Despite his desertion by the party, he continued to support the Democrats, even when the Republicans nominated his son-in-law, John C. Fremont, for the presidency in 1856. He wrote an autobiogra-

Benton - Bethel

Artist Thomas Hart Benton Painted this mural of pioneers and Indians.

phy entitled, *Thirty Years View* (1854-56).

BENTON, Thomas Hart. (Neosho, MO., Apr. 15, 1889—Jan. 19, 1975) Artist. Regionalist painter. Grandnephew of Senator Thomas Hart BENTON. As a boy traveling about the Midwest with his politician father, he became acquainted with much of the country and its traditions and decided to translate his interest into art. After study at the School of the ART INSTITUTE OF CHICAGO in 1906, he spent several years of art study in Paris, and began his career as a professional artist in 1912. Leaving the navy after service in WORLD WAR I, he taught art at Bryn Mawr, Dartmouth and the Art Students League of New York. Extensive travel through the country in the late 1920s and early 30s resulted in his book *An Artist in America* (1937). He gained increasing attention as an artist with his style known as Regionalism, slightly cartoonish in its technique. He specialized in flowing, highly colored, sometimes mythic, portrayals of the dramatic themes of rural American life. Later he dealt with folk themes, as depicted in his painting of Huckleberry Finn. He opposed abstract art, which he felt was contrary to American traditions. He is particularly well known for his large murals, decorating state capitols and the Truman Library at INDEPENDENCE, Missouri.

BERG, Patty. (Minneapolis, MN, 1918—). Professional golfer. In 1946 Berg won the first

U.S. Women's Open ever held. Between 1935 and 1964 she won eighty-three tournaments and served as the first president of the Ladies Professional Golf Association, a group she helped to organize. Chosen by the Associated Press as the Athlete-of-the-Year three times, Berg was elected to the American Golf Hall of Fame in 1972.

BETHEL, Missouri. Village (pop. 402) located in Shelby County in the northeastern part of the state, northeast of Macon. A famous experiment in communal living took place in Bethel in the mid-1800s. Dr. William Keil persuaded five hundred followers from Pennsylvania and Ohio to join him in a new Missouri settlement. They arrived in Bethel in 1845. Title to 3,500 acres was controlled by a few selected leaders. Dr. Keil's word was law; there was no written law or constitution.

The community owned a water mill, tailor shop, glove and shoe factories and a tannery. Each family was given a house. Wives did the housework and made the girls' clothing. The girls worked in the shops and the boys and men ran the business houses or farmed. Members with no families lived in the Big House which served as a dormitory and hotel near the center of town. A brick building served as a church and school; marriages were conducted in the home. Food was distributed on Saturday night, and every spring and fall one individual checked the clothing needs of each person.

The community existed for thirty years in this manner and gained national attention for the quality of its buckskin gloves which won first prize in the New York World's Fair in 1858. With the arrival of "outside" families in the community Dr. Kiel feared spiritual contamination of his group and planned a new community far west of Missouri.

His son William was promised that he could join this group, but he died before final plans were made. To honor his pledge to his son, Dr. Kiel had the body placed in alcohol in an iron casket. When the travelers arrived in Oregon's Willapah Valley, William was buried.

For twenty years Dr. Kiel directed business in Bethel by mail from Oregon. After his death in 1879 the Bethel community broke up. Each man received the amount of his original contribution plus twenty-nine dollars for each year he lived in the community. Women received half this amount. Many of the present residents of Bethel are able to trace their families back to these original citizens. More than thirty of the original buildings remain, and guided walking tours are available. Annual events in Bethel include the Antiques Show and Sale in May, the Mid-American Fiddling Championship the second weekend in June, the World Lamb and Wool Fest on Labor Day weekend, a Harvest Fest on the first weekend in October, and on the first Sunday in December An Old Fashioned Christmas.

BETTENDORF, Iowa. City (pop. 24,381), in Scott County, on the MISSISSIPPI RIVER, formerly known as Gilbert, settled in 1840 and incorporated in 1903, when the name was changed in honor of the prominent Bettendorf family of industrialists, and especially for W. P. Bettendorf and J. W. Bettendorf, president and secretary-treasurer, respectively, of the company which had begun as a manufacturer of axles and wagons and later shifted to railroad cars. During WORLD WAR II the plant turned out tanks and military vehicles and greatly developed the community. Today aluminum manufacture is also important there. Fourteen parks, a bicycle path, band shell and golf course provide recreational facilities. The Bettendorf museum, established by the Bettendorf family, provides displays of local memorabilia. Bettendorf is one of the four Quad Cities, of DAVENPORT, Iowa, ROCK ISLAND and MOLINE in Illinois.

BEVERIDGE, Albert J. (Highland Co., OH, October 6, 1862—Indianapolis, IN, April 27, 1927). Historian and political leader. Beveridge was a successful Republican compromise candidate for the United States Senate in 1899, and he served in the Senate until 1911. As an Indiana senator, Beveridge was the chief spokesmen for United States imperialism. Renominated in 1905 he became increasingly identified with the Progressive wing of the REPUBLICAN PARTY and was a firm supporter of President Theodore Roosevelt's policies concerning the regulation of big business. Beveridge assisted the passage of the Pure Food and Meat Inspection Acts of 1906 and championed child labor legislation. Defeated in 1910 when conservative Republicans withheld their support, Beveridge joined Roosevelt's PROGRESSIVE PARTY and gave the keynote speech in 1912, the same year in which he ran unsuccessfully for the governorship of Indiana. Beveridge rejoined the Republican Party in 1916 and supported the candidacy of Charles Evans Hughes for president. Beveridge was defeated in 1922 in his attempt to return to the Senate from Indiana. Anti-British and nationalistic, Beveridge wrote a book in 1915 sympathizing with the Central Powers. After 1917 he supported the war effort, but opposed United States participation in the League of Nations. An historian, Beveridge wrote, among other works, a four volume biography of Chief Justice John Marshall (1916-1918), and at the time of his death had completed two volumes of a biography of Abraham LINCOLN.

BIG CORMORANT LAKE. Minnesota lake located ten miles south of Lake Park, Minnesota. Three large granite boulders, the so-called "anchor stones," were found on the north shore of this lake. Each boulder has a hole about nine inches deep and one inch wide cut into it. The boulders are located approximately three hundred feet from the present lake on what was an earlier shoreline. Archaeologists and local residents debate the theory that these stones were used to anchor the ships of early Norse EXPLORERS who came here in 1362. These explorers are considered by some to have been the same people who left the famous KENSINGTON RUNESTONE in a field seventy miles south of Cormorant Lake, near Kensington, Minnesota, in Douglas County.

BIG RAPIDS, Michigan. City (pop. 14,361), seat of Mecosta County on the upper MUSKEGON RIVER, the west central Lower Peninsula. The original name of this community was Leonard in honor of an early settler, but authorities

Big Sioux River - Bingham

Big Springs in Missouri, one of the world's largest.

changed the name because mail was frequently addressed to persons "at the big rapids." The first house was built in 1854, and a memorial plaque may be seen at its site on the corner of N. State and W. Bellevue Streets. The early LUMBER industry boomed, and the town grew so rapidly that there was an acute food shortage during the winter of 1857-1858. Fortunately three backwoodsmen, adept at torch hunting at night, were able to supply enough venison to feed the community until spring. After the timber was depleted, Big Rapids, with its twenty nearby lakes, became a year-round vacation resort. In addition there are manufacturers of wood products, machine tools and shoes. Ferris Institute, established in 1855 by Woodbridge N. Ferris, later governor and U.S. Senator from Michigan, is located in Big Rapids. Begun as a privately operated "school for the masses," the Institute was incorporated into the state educational system in 1923 and is known as FERRIS STATE COLLEGE, widely praised for its college of pharmacy.

BIG SIOUX RIVER. Rises in northeastern South Dakota at a height of 1,760 feet, just north of Watertown. It flows southward for 420 miles, through the Coteau des Prairies of southwestern Minnesota and northwestern Iowa. At Sioux Falls, South Dakota, the river drops about 20 feet. Its principal tributary is the ROCK RIVER, which enters the Big Sioux northwest of LE MARS, Iowa. Between Sioux Falls and SIOUX CITY, Iowa, where it meets the MISSOURI RIVER, the Big Sioux forms the border between Iowa and South Dakota. For much of its length the river is considered to be the demarcation line between the corn belt and the prime cattle country to the west.

BIG SPRINGS. Located in Carter County, south central Missouri. It is one of the largest springs in the U.S. with an average daily flow of 600,000,000 gallons. The spring begins beneath a 250-foot limestone cliff, topples over a ledge, then rebounds in a massive spray before coursing to the CURRENT RIVER. It is found at the center of a 4,416-acre state park. The city of VAN BUREN is nearby.

BIG STONE LAKE. Border lake, source of the MINNESOTA RIVER, a narrow body of water lying between Minnesota and South Dakota, at the northeast corner of South Dakota. It was created by a natural dam formed when sediment was deposited across the outlet of the Whetstone River of South Dakota. Big Stone Lake extends nearly thirty miles in length.

BINGHAM, George Caleb. (Augusta County, VA, Mar. 20, 1811—Kansas City, MO, July 7, 1879). Artist. He read law privately, as well as theology, but was attracted to art. Although almost entirely self taught, Bingham was able to open his first studio in Missouri in 1834. At different times he established studios in KANSAS CITY, ST. LOUIS, and JEFFERSON CITY, Missouri. He received his main support from his much-admired portraits, but he preferred to paint pioneer life, river scenes and political events in the MISSOURI RIVER valley. After he visited Germany between 1856 and 1858, he apparently was influenced by the styles of the old masters, and, with the exception of his portraits, his work became less original and less admired. His genre work, however, continues to increase in popularity, and he is known as one of the best artists of the frontier. His "Jolly Flatboatmen," "Raftsmen Playing Cards," " Canvassing for a Vote," and "Emigration of Daniel Boone," all painted between 1840 and 1860, are his best remembered paintings. In later life he became increasingly involved in politics. He was elected to the Missouri Legislature in 1848, served as the state's treasurer from 1862 to 1865 and was adjutant general in 1875.

BISSELL, Richard Pike. (Dubuque, Iowa, June 27, 1913—Dubuque, Iowa, May 4, 1977). Known as the teller of tall tales about the MISSISSIPPI RIVER, Bissell is associated with other writers about the river, but his writing and experience were considerably more varied. He came from a wealthy DUBUQUE family, attended Exeter and Harvard (1933-1937). After work in the Venezuela oil fields and travel as an ordinary seaman, Bissell returned to the Midwest to become a licensed pilot on the Mississippi-Ohio river system. His best known river work is *A Stretch on the River* (1950). His novel *Seven and a Half Cents* (1953) was the basis for the Broadway hit *Pajama Game* (1957), based on his family's clothing manufacturing business. He also wrote the script for the Broadway version and adapted some of his other work for the musical stage.

BISSOT, Francois Marie (Morgane) (Sieur de Vincennes). (Montreal, Canada, June 27, 1700—Memphis, TN, March 25, 1736). Founder of VINCENNES, Indiana. Vincennes was the French commander at Ke-ki-onga, a Miami Indian village on the site of present-day FORT WAYNE, Indiana. He served as a cadet under his father, Jean Baptiste Bissot, Sieur de Vincennes, exploring the Indiana region and working with the MIAMI Indians. After his father's death he continued to work

with the Indians and became a great favorite with them. Upon the request of the French government of Louisiana he had a fort built on the present site of Vincennes in 1732. He assisted in the Indian wars of the period in an attempt to save the Mississippi Valley for France. He was killed by the CHICKASAW Indians. The residents of Vincennes named their community in his memory.

BLACK HAWK (Chief). (Near Rock Island, IL, 1767—Des Moines, Iowa, October 31, 1838). Sauk chief remembered for his struggle against white settlement in Illinois and for the BLACK HAWK WAR (1832). The SAUK and FOX Indians once claimed all the land east of the MISSISSIPPI RIVER and west of the FOX and ILLINOIS rivers. Black Hawk, born near the mouth of the ROCK RIVER and a chief of the Sauk and Fox tribe beginning in 1788, never accepted the fact that five tribal leaders had deeded the land away to the federal government in 1804. The agreement, renewed in 1816, 1822, and 1825, gave the Indians the right to live on the land as long as it belonged to the federal government. The Sauk lived near present-day ROCK ISLAND and the Fox lived nearby along the Mississippi river. Lead miners, stopping off on their way to GALENA, Illinois, began settling in the area. Under a new arrangement the government proposed to compensate the Indians for their land. Led by KEOKUK the Indians began to move across the Mississippi River into Iowa. Black Hawk, less friendly to the settlers, was convinced by the British and their Indian allies, that the $1000 a year annuity was inadequate compensation for his land and announced his intention to remain on his land. Nevertheless, Black Hawk and his followers soon quietly moved into Iowa on June 25, 1831, but in the spring of 1832 they moved back to their homelands, apparently to plant crops. The sight of white farmers plowing sacred Indian burial grounds infuriated the Indians, who began to raid outlying white farms. Alarmed by this "state of actual invasion," Illinois Governor Reynolds called up volunteers under Major Isaiah Stillman. Chief Keokuk, wanted to go to Washington to attempt a peaceful outcome, but he was refused permission by the army. Stillman and his little militia drove the Indians across the Mississippi into Missouri. There they faced famine and their old enemy the SIOUX. In desperation Black Hawk and his most militant followers and their families returned to Illinois. However, Black Hawk failed to find the support he had expected from other Indians and attempted to surrender

Black Hawk Statue - Black Hawk War

and make peace, but his emissaries under a white flag were shot. General Henry Atkinson's (1782-1842) forces attacked but were beaten by Black Hawk in the Battle of Stillman's Run (April, 1832), near Byron in the Rock River valley. However, the Indians could not hold out. With his remaining warriors and their families, Black Hawk fled into Wisconsin and eluded his enemies in a masterful retreat. After they had exhausted themselves in the Wisconsin woods, Black Hawk attempted to lead his followers back across the Mississippi. However, Atkinson's force caught up with them at the mouth of the Bad Axe River on August 2, 1832. Stillman's forces engaged the fleeing Indians in the Battle of BAD AXE. In the debacle that followed, many of the warriors, their wives, and children were slaughtered by the white soldiers. Those attempting to cross the Mississippi to safety were fired upon by a gunboat, with many of the fleeing party killed in midstream. Sioux Indians killed many of those who reached the western shore. Black Hawk was captured and imprisoned at Jefferson Barracks, St. Louis. The agreement known as Scott's Purchase ended the BLACK HAWK WAR. This agreement provided compensation to the Indians for the loss of their lands, which were opened to white settlement. Freed from prison, Black Hawk was taken to Washington, D.C., in 1833. There he was introduced to President Andrew Jackson, as part of the government policy to placate and

impress many of the Indian chiefs by their meeting with the chief executive. Black Hawk returned to Iowa, making several stops in what appeared to be a kind of triumphal tour. In 1833 he wrote *Autobiography of Black Hawk* which presented his side of the issues. This is considered a classic statement of the Indian case against the whites. When Black Hawk died on a reservation near DES MOINES, Iowa, on October 31, 1838, his body was first prepared in an Indian ceremony. Later in a bizarre turn of fate his bones were placed on display in the Historical Society Building in BURLINGTON, Iowa. There they were lost in a fire which destroyed the building.

BLACK HAWK STATUE. An heroic statue, by famed sculptor Lorado TAFT, depicting the Sauk and Fox war chief. The statue looms above a cliff in Lowden State Park overlooking the ROCK RIVER near OREGON, Illinois, along Illinois State Highway 64.

BLACK HAWK WAR. In 1832, last futile attempt of some SAUK INDIANS to remain in their Illinois and Wisconsin homelands. Chief BLACK HAWK was attacked and pushed into Wisconsin by General Henry Atkinson with a force of regulars and militia. In an interesting historical sidelight, among Atkinson's volunteers was young Abraham LINCOLN. The Black Hawk War culminated in the last battle of the war, known

Henry Lewis painted the action at the Battle of Bad Axe.

as the Battle of BAD AXE (August 2, 1832). Large numbers of the tribe—men, women and children—were massacred in that battle. The agreement known as Scott's Purchase ended the war. In this treaty the Indians gave up their remaining lands in Wisconsin and granted permission for white settlement in an area of Iowa. As compensation, the Indians received thirty annual payments of $20,000, forty barrels of salt, blacksmith services, forty barrels of tobacco, and their debts of $40,000 were paid by the government.

BLACK RIVER FALLS, Wisconsin. Town (pop. 3,434), seat of Jackson County, situated on the Black River in west central Wisconsin. In 1819 the wilderness of pine along the Black River was the site of a sawmill, one of the first to be established in Wisconsin. The mill burned, probably through the work of unfriendly Indians. Logging continued for more than two generations until the timber stands gave out, and the community turned to farming and other pursuits. The town was the locale for an unusual encounter. A group of MORMONS, migrating from NAUVOO, Illinois, was among the earliest settlers. Their Elder told his flock that since the property was the Lord's they need not respect any other claims. When Jacob Spaulding found that the Mormons had cut 300 trees from his property, he protested without avail, then brought in his followers, who drove the Mormons off. The Mormons sent to Nauvoo for armed reinforcements. Spaulding threatened to send to PRAIRIE DU CHIEN for government officials, and the Mormons finally departed. In another picturesque incident, forty brawling loggers on a spree, plowed up two blocks of Main Street, then broke into a feed store and sowed the street with oats; then they poured sacks of flour over themselves and went to bed exhausted. Today the community is more serene, trading focus of a farming community and the center for Black River Falls State Forest and a variety of winter sports and deer hunting. The Thunderbird Museum has extensive exhibits of INDIAN LIFE. Twice each year one of the nation's noted Indian festivals, the Winnebago Indian Pow-Wow, is held at the Red Cloud Memorial Pow-Wow Grounds, on the weekends of Memorial Day and Labor Day.

BLACK ROBES. Indian term for Catholic clergy. Impressed by the somber gowns worn by the white religious leaders, the Indians coined the term to describe the churchmen, and some version of the term was used by the Indian tribes almost universally across the continent.

BLACKBURN COLLEGE. CARLINVILLE, Illinois, coeducational college with a liberal arts program. Blackburn College was established by Reverend Gideon Blackburn, a Presbyterian, who bought large tracts of land at the government price of $1.25 an acre and sold them at $2.00. College courses began in 1864. The state legislature authorized its designation as a university in 1869, but it continues to call itself a college. Since 1913, students have been expected to do manual labor thirteen hours per week. Lumpkin Library and the Alumni Hall of Biology were built by students. Blackburn College, with 590 students and 45 staff members, is affiliated with the Presbyterian Church.

BLAIR, Francis Preston, Jr. (Lexington, KY, February 19, 1821—St. Louis, MO, July 9, 1875). Senator. Although a slaveholder himself, he came to dislike SLAVERY, published a Free Soil newspaper and led the Missouri Free Soil movement. He served as a Free-Soiler from Missouri in the United States House of Representatives beginning in 1857. For his second term he was elected as a Republican and served through 1860. He was the chairman of the committee on military defense in 1861. Blair was one of the leaders of the forces that kept Missouri in the Union prior to the CIVIL WAR. If Missouri had fallen, the war's outcome might have been different. During the War he served under Ulysses S. GRANT and William Tecumseh SHERMAN. He defended Abraham LINCOLN's reconstruction plan and, turning to the Democratic Party, was an unsuccessful nominee for United States vice president in 1868. In 1870 Blair helped to overcome the Missouri radicals, then was elected to the legislature, which, in turn, elected him to the United States Senate from Missouri as a Democrat. He served from 1871 to 1873. He helped secure Horace Greeley's nomination for President of the United States in 1872.

BLAND, Richard Parks. (Hartford, KY, August 19, 1835—Lebanon, MO, June 15, 1899). Congressman. Bland came to Missouri from Nevada in 1865. Known as "Silver Dick" Bland for his 16-to-1 coinage stand in 1877, Bland was re-elected to Congress twelve times and became the leader of the Free Silver bloc. He co-authored the Bland-Allison Act which, when passed in 1878, provided for the monthly purchase by the treasury of two to four million dollars in silver as the standard for the circulation of silver certificates. The objective was to increase the circulation of currency which would raise commodity prices. The Act re-established a bi-metallic standard after a five-year lapse. Bland became a leading candidate for the Democratic presidential nomination, but lost when the 1896 convention was swept away by the oratory of William Jennings BRYAN. Bland died on his farm in Lebanon.

BLANKET WEDDING CEREMONY. The MENOMINEE and some of the other Indian groups had an interesting marriage custom. The bride and groom exchanged blankets. If the marriage was not satisfactory, divorce was easy. The unhappy partner, whether husband or wife, simply returned the partner's blanket, and the marriage was dissolved.

BLASHFIELD, Edwin H. (New York, N.Y., Dec. 15, 1848—Cape Cod, Mass., Oct. 12, 1936). American designer and mural painter. After studying in New York and Paris, in 1890 he concentrated on his mural work. He is best known in the Midwest for his capitol murals in Iowa, Minnesota and Wisconsin and for his interior decorations at the Chicago WORLD'S COLUMBIAN EXPOSITION in 1893. His murals generally were of an historical or allegorical nature. He also is well known for his murals in the Library of Congress and Church of St. Matthew in Washington, D. C. He was the author of *Mural Painting in America* (1913).

BLENNERHASSETT, Harman. (Ireland, 1765—Island of Guernsey, UK, 1833). Pioneer leader. A wealthy immigrant to the United States in 1796, where in 1798 he became a pioneer in the OHIO RIVER Valley. Blennerhassett fled to America after he married his beautiful and attractive niece and they were ostracized by family and friends. Blennerhassett bought 170 acres of the large island in the Ohio River near present Parkersburg, West Virginia, which now bears his name. There he built a substantial estate and developed the island as a center of civilization in an as yet unsettled area. There was nothing like it in the "west." Blennerhassett went about the estate in blue broadcloth coat, scarlet knee-breeches, silk stockings and silver buckled shoes. He read constantly and conducted experiments in electricity, played the cello and composed songs. It was said he could recite the *Iliad* from memory. Mrs. Blennerhassett sometimes entertained their guests with informal performances of Shakespeare plays. In

1805, after the fatal duel with Alexander Hamilton, Aaron BURR visited Blennerhassett Island. He returned again later with his beautiful daughter, Theodosia, and Blennerhasset financed Burr's purchase of the Bastrop Grant on the Washita River, where Burr began preparations to take a colony of sixty immigrants to lands in the west. President Jefferson distrusted Burr's motives, thinking he planned to set up an empire of his own west of the MISSISSIPPI. Burr was ordered arrested as a traitor. Blennerhasset left the island with Burr, fleeing down the Ohio but was taken into custody at Natchez, Mississippi, as Burr's accomplice. When Burr was acquited, Blennerhassett was released. For the Blennerhassetts, the so-called conspiracy was the beginning of a long period of flight, ruined hopes and poverty. His plantation was destroyed and his fortune gone. After trying to recoup on a Mississippi plantation, Blennerhassett next tried to practice law in Montreal but returned to England in 1822 and died on the Island of Guernsey. In 1842 Mary Blennerhassett returned to the U.S. and petitioned Congress to compensate her for the destruction of her home on the island. Henry Clay presented her petition sympathetically, but she died in New York before it could be granted.

BLOOMER, Amelia Jenks. (Homer, N.Y., May 17, 1818—Council Bluffs, Iowa, Dec. 30, 1894). American reformer. One of the earliest proponents of women's rights, she published a women's rights and temperance journal called the *Lily,* founded in 1849. This was one of the first journals founded and published by a woman. Her topics included temperance, unjust marriage laws, suffrage and education. Although outstanding for her reform work, she is best known today for her innovation in the dress reform movement, especially for the "Bloomer" costume for which she became notorious. She did not invent bloomers, the "scandalous" trousers, full in the leg and tight at the ankles. They were first devised by Elizabeth Smith Miller, but because Mrs. Bloomer pictured herself in her magazine wearing the short dress over the full trousers, and because she advertised it in the magazine, the trousers of the costume became universally known as bloomers. Popularizing this garment was simply another of her many attempts to call attention to her causes. The costume was adopted by Susan B. Anthony and others interested in her causes. Eventually the billowing trousers were worn by women all over the world, even by the Empress Eugenie. Men called the style brazen and women labeled it scandalous. However, the costume added to Mrs. Bloomer's fame, and the demands on her time for lectures and other work were so great that her health broke. She and her husband, D.C. Bloomer, moved to COUNCIL BLUFFS, Iowa, where she recuperated. When her health improved, she served as president of the Iowa women's suffrage movement. When she was asked why in later years she was never seen wearing the costume, she replied that it had served its purpose of focusing male attention on the problems of American women.

BLOOMFIELD HILLS, Michigan. City (pop. 3,985), residential community on the northwest outskirts of DETROIT. Settlement of the area was begun by Amasa Bagley in 1819 when he followed an Indian trail into the woods and cleared land for a farm on a site that would later become the city's business district. Other settlers arrived, and the new village was called Bagley's Corners. In 1830 Bagley moved to Pontiac, and his village renamed itself Bloomfield Center. When citizens of nearby large cities began to buy estates in the area in the early 1890s, the village was renamed Bloomfield Hills. It was officially incorporated as a village in 1927, and became a city in 1932. Among the prominent Detroit citizens who bought estates in this rural community were the publisher of the Detroit *News*, George G. Booth, and his wife, Ellen Scripps Booth. Their estate, Cranbrook, was named after the village in Kent, England, where Mr. Booth's father was born. The 300-acre estate is a renowned educational and cultural center including science and art museums, a graduate art academy, college preparatory schools, and elaborate gardens. Cranbrook House, an English manor home, designed by Alfred Kahn, is open to the public on designated days. Four of the buildings were designed by architect Eliel Saarinen, and sculptor Carl Milles designed some of the fountains and statuary. The Cranbrook Gardens include forty acres of formal plantings, pine walks, woods, and a lake. Bloomfield Hills is also the home of the annual Maple Syrup Festival, held in mid-March. The Kirk-in-the-Hills Presbyterian Church installed one of the world's largest carillons in 1960. The tower contains seventy-seven bells weighing a total of sixty-six tons. Bloomfield Hills has become one of the celebrated centers of wealth, with many mansions and splendid homes scattered across the hills.

BLOOMINGTON, Illinois. City (pop. 44,-189), McLean County., central Illinois, on Interstate Highways 55 and 74, named from the original Blooming Grove so called because of its abundant flowers. Located in a rich agricultural area, Bloomington grew without the advantage of a navigable river. In 1856 dissatisfied members of many political parties met in Bloomington and formed the REPUBLICAN Party. Although the city is considered by many to be the founding site of the national party, communities in Michigan and Wisconsin also have claimed this honor. At the convention forming the party, Abraham LINCOLN made his famous "lost speech," which spelled out his principles upon which he later was elected president. Between 1860 and 1870 the city grew at a rate faster than Chicago's. Increasingly industrial, Bloomington was, by 1890, one of twenty Illinois cities with a population above ten thousand. Today coal mining, dairying and ironworks are the principal industries. Bloomington is the home of ILLINOIS WESLEYAN COLLEGE. Bloomington hosts an annual Passion Play which claims to be the first of its kind in the United States. Visitors may also see Clover Lawn, the home of former United States Senator and Supreme Court Justice David Davis. The Italianate villa is furnished in the style of 1872. The Ewing Museum of the Nations displays Pre-Columbian art and artifacts as well as examples of art from Africa, Mexico and the Pacific. An annual arts festival the last weekend in September features works of midwestern artists, craft demonstrations and music.

BLOOMINGTON, Indiana. City (pop. 51,-646), major southwestern Indiana city, seat of Monroe Co., about 50 miles southwest of INDIANAPOLIS, name suggested by pioneers who were impressed by the blooming flowers and foliage in the surrounding area. Much of Bloomington's growth the last half century has been due to the employment found in the thirty stone quarries in the area and to its advantages as the home of INDIANA UNIVERSITY, founded in 1820 and the second oldest state university west of the Allegheny Mountains. The city was settled in 1818 but was not incorporated until 1878. In addition to the famed Indiana limestone, the city's industries include electronic and electrical devices and elevators. Indiana University's Art Museum, on the Fine Arts Plaza, was designed by architect I.M. Pei. The museum features art by Millet, Monet, Matisse, Rodin and Warhol. Lilly Library, on the University campus, is noted for its collection of rare books and contains an extensive collection of works on Abraham LINCOLN. A variety of special events awaits the visitor to Bloomington. The late April feature is the "Little 500" bicycle race, central theme of a motion picture distributed in1985. The Fourth Street Festival of the Arts and Crafts is held during the Labor Day weekend. Madigral feasts and a 16th-century festival dominate the social calendar in December. Outdoor recreation opportunities await at Monroe Reservoir, the largest lake in Indiana, ten miles southeast of Bloomington; Hoosier National Forest; and McCormick Creek State Park.

BLOOMINGTON, Minnesota. City, (pop. 81,831), situated in southeastern Minnesota, a suburb to the south of MINNEAPOLIS in Hennepin County. It was incorporated as a city in 1853. The name is said to be descriptive of the locale, perhaps a "blooming town." Of the many industries, electronic equipment, metal products and lawnmowers take the lead. With the intense rivalry between Minneapolis and St. Paul, Bloomington is often chosen as a neutral site for sports and other events. The Bloomington site of Metropolitan Stadium is a good example of a locale which does not favor either metropolis. The stadium is home to the Minnesota Twins baseball team and houses other major groups and events. The Normandale Japanese Garden on the campus of Normandale Community College has two acres of footpaths, handcarved stone lanterns, a Japanese shrine and a lagoon.

BLUE MOUND. Oval-shaped prehistoric mound near Horton, Missouri. Blue Mound has a base area of nearly 150 acres and was connected, by those who built it, to a smaller mound with a large, earthen, wall-like section. Its builders are unknown. The OSAGE INDIANS used Blue Mound within historic times as the burial site for Chief White Hair (1825).

BLUE SPRINGS, Missouri. City (pop. 25,927), Jackson Co., southeast of INDEPEND-ENCE. A major trade center and residential community in a farm and fruit region, it was incorporated in 1904. Manufactures include metal and plastic products. Local AGRICULTURE is devoted mainly to DAIRYING and orchards. *Press Woman* (1937), a journalism magazine, is published here monthly.

BLUEBIRD. The state bird of Missouri. Bluebird is the common name for a migratory bird of the thrush family. The plumage of the male is of vivid blue. The cinnamon red breast is a distinct contrast to the male's blue. The female is of duller color, and she attends to the incubation of eggs. Bluebirds are particularly valued for destroying harmful insects. They usually nest on the edges of woodlands.

BOEPPLE, John F. (Hamburg, Germany—Muscatine, Iowa, January 30, 1912). Manufacturer. Boepple transformed MUSCATINE, Iowa, into the button-making capital of the world. Boepple was by trade a turner, a person who used lathes to cut blanks from a variety of hard substances including ivory and shell. Hearing of a great river west of Chicago where he could obtain the shells he needed, he moved to Muscatine where the shell supply in the MISSISSIPPI RIVER was adequate. Boepple used the shells to make novelties, but when the McKinley tariff of 1890 drove the price of buttons to a penny each, he turned his talents in the direction of button manufacture and invented button making machinery. He opened a successful shop, and soon there were fifty-three button companies in Muscatine and hundreds of cottage operations. Ironically, Boepple died of an infection from cutting his foot on a clam shell.

BOIS de SIOUX RIVER. River flowing on the western border of Minnesota near the common border of North and South Dakota. The Bois de Sioux River continues northward and meets with the OTTER TAIL RIVER at BRECKENRIDGE, Minnesota, to form the RED RIVER OF THE NORTH.

BOLIVAR, Ohio. Village (pop. 989) in southeast Ohio, south of CANTON on Interstate 77, at one time a flourishing center of several counties in the boom times of the OHIO AND ERIE and Sandy and Beaver canals, named for the South American revolutionary hero. After the early railroads and important highways passed it by, it became a peaceful New England style village with one main street. Nearby is the site of the cabin built in 1761 by Christian Frederick Post, a Moravian missionary. It was the first structure ever constructed by a European in Ohio. At Bolivar is Fort Laurens State Park, the only American military post in Ohio during the Revolutionary War. Bolivar dam is a large flood control dam on the MUSKINGUM watershed.

BOND, Carrie Jacobs. (Janesville, WI, 1862—1946). One of the most beloved song writers of her day. A self-taught musician, she wrote both words and music of 175 songs and became wealthy from the income of her work. One of her songs, "I Love You Truly," (1901) remains as probably the most popular of all the songs sung at weddings. Many of her other songs also continue to be popular. Her autobiography *The Roads of Melody* was published in 1927.

BOND, Shadrach. (Frederickstown, MD, November 24, 1773—Kaskaskia, IL, April 12, 1832). First governor of Illinois. In Illinois he founded the Bond Party, but it generally was considered to be affiliated with the Democratic Party. Bond was elected to the Illinois Territorial Legislature in 1806. In 1808 he became the presiding judge of the St. Clair County Court of Common Pleas. He was the first delegate to the U.S. House of Representatives from Illinois and served from 1812 to 1814. In 1813 Bond sponsored a preemption law which permitted the first settlers in a territory to buy the land they occupied, thus making much more desirable a move to new lands, such as Illinois. Bond was elected without opposition as the first governor of Illinois and served from 1818 to 1822.

BOONE, Daniel. (Near Reading, PA, Nov. 2, 1734—Charette, MO., Sept. 26, 1820). Frontiersman and explorer. In 1750 Boone moved with his Quaker parents to the Yadkin River Valley in North Carolina. Following service under Edward Braddock in Pennsylvania in the FRENCH AND INDIAN WAR, Boone returned to the South and began his explorations through the Appalachian ridges. For two years beginning in 1767 Boone and companions, including John Finley, traveled through the Cumberland Gap and explored the lands of present-day Kentucky. In 1775 he founded the Kentucky settlement of Boonesboro. The Daniel Boone of legend first caught the popular imagination during the Revolution, when he was captured by the British, escaped by pretending to cooperate with them, and then rode 160 miles in four days to alert fellow patriots about an imminent attack. True to the image of the uneducated woodsman, he was careless about legal title to lands, and this cost him his own cleared lands in the new territory. Disgusted by this introduction of imperfect law into the wilderness, he moved to the Spanish territory of Missouri. Boone was treated well under the

The John James Audubon painting of Daniel Boone.

Spanish and given a grant of land and a Spanish judgeship. However, with the coming of U.S. control, he was again deprived of land for failing to register his claim. In deference to his service to the country, however, Congress granted him 850 acres in Missouri in 1814. Boone has been a popular figure in American folklore ever since the publication in 1784 of his spectacular autobiography. This was actually a romanticized version of his experiences written by John Filson. Boone's fame had spread to Europe by the time Byron portrayed him as the great natural man in "Don Juan" (1823), and it was increased at home after James Fenimore Cooper made him the prototype of Natty Bumpo in *The Leatherstocking Tales* (1823-1827). Legend aside, Boone is unrivalled as an individual developer of the American frontier, from the East coast to the Midwest. His character was one of his greatest assets. He was loyal to his friend and modest about his vast knowledge of the frontier.

BOONE, Iowa. City (pop. 12,802), seat of Boone County, situated in central Iowa fifteen miles west of AMES. The city was probably named for Nathan Boone, son of Daniel BOONE, who marched through the area with U.S. soldiers on June 23, 1835. One of Nathan's relatives, W. M. Boone, moved there in the 1850s, at the time of the founding of Boonesboro, now part of Boone. The city is a railroad and industrial center. The railroad

Boone and Scenic Valley Railroad.

built a high, double-decked bridge there in 1887. This was the locale of the famed episode of Kate SHELLEY and her heroism, when on July 6, 1881, she stopped a swift passenger train before it reached a washed-out bridge. Boone industry includes plastic sign production and STEEL fabrication. Boonesboro was the first county seat, in 1847, and a steam mill was built there in 1854 on Polecat Slough. When the railroad was projected, payment from Boonesboro was expected. Finding that the money was not forthcoming, the railroad placed its tracks and station half a mile to the east and called the new town Boone. Boonesboro was annexed in 1887. Boone is the site of the Mamie Doud EISENHOWER Birthplace, which has been restored. The Boone and Scenic Valley Railroad is a shortline tourist road, offering a 10+ mile round trip in vintage equipment. Boone celebrates Pufferbilly Days each Labor Day weekend.

BOONVILLE, Missouri. City (pop. 7,090), seat of Cooper Co., located in mid-state on the south bank of the MISSOURI RIVER. Settled in 1810, incorporated in 1839, and chartered a city in 1896, it was named for Daniel BOONE. A n important trading post on the Missouri and on the SANTA FE TRAIL, it was a center of conflict during the CIVIL WAR. Industries include stone quarrying, shoe and veneer manufacture, and bottling. It is the hub of an area of chicken and dairy farms. Boonville is the location of Missouri Training School (1899) and Kemper Academy (1884).

BOOT HEEL. Extreme southeastern region of Missouri lying below the thirty-sixth latitude. This area extends south of the rest of the state between the MISSISSIPPI and ST. FRANCIS rivers,

enveloped on the west and south by northeastern Arkansas. The region is pictured as providing a heel for Missouri's boot. Missouri owes its possession of the land to John Hardeman Walker. Upon hearing that this area in which he lived was not to be part of Missouri, Walker mounted a successful campaign to change the boundary.

BOOTH'S WAR. Wisconsin controversy over the Fugitive Slave Law, beginning in 1854. Sherman M. Booth was the editor of the MILWAUKEE, Wisconsin, *Free Democrat.* As an ardent Abolitionist, Booth made his journal a voice against SLAVERY. When Joshua GLOVER, an escaped slave living in RACINE, Wisconsin, was recaptured by his "owner" in 1854 and taken to jail in Milwaukee, Booth called on the people of Milwaukee to rally at the jail. The crowd broke down the door, rescued Glover, paraded him through the streets and sent him to safety in Canada. Booth was arrested for violating the Fugitive Slave Law and was jailed, but the charges were dismissed by the Wisconsin courts. Then, because the Fugitive Slave Law was a federal act, Booth was fined and jailed by U.S. courts. His friends helped him to escape to RIPON, Wisconsin, where he had many friends who shielded him from the U.S. agents. While free he made many speeches against slavery, and during the month of August, 1860, he played a cat and mouse game, eluding the government men. Finally he was captured by the agents, but he was pardoned by President James Buchanan. Booth was not only responsible for turning much of Wisconsin against slavery, but he also became the symbol for an important legal decision, which established a precedent concerning the relationship between the state and federal courts. The Fugitive Slave Act made it a federal criminal offense to assist a runaway slave. This was declared unconstitutional by the Wisconsin Supreme Court in their decision about Booth, but the federal courts held that a U.S. law could not be negated by a state court. This permanently established the supremacy of U.S. laws over those of the states in certain cases.

BOULDER JUNCTION, Wisconsin. Village (pop. 300) This tiny community in far north central Wisconsin in Vilas County is situated in the northern portion of Northern Highland-American Legion State Forest. Because of the lakes and streams and other outdoor advantages of the area, Boulder Junction's importance as the "gateway to recreation" far outweighs its population. In fact, its registered trademark boldly states that it is "Musky Capital of the World." Opportunities for both winter and summer recreation make it a year-round capital. In mid-August, Boulder Junction hosts its Muskie Jamboree, when local guides contribute many of the great fish to a bake served to vacationers. The Fall Colorama, in late September, features a grand barbecue. Nearby state nurseries cultivate young pines for reforestation.

BOUNDARY DISPUTES. Although the Northwest Ordinance had provided that new states would be created from what is now most of the Midwest, there was great uncertainty as to just where some of the boundaries of these new states would be. One of the most serious disputes concerned the boundary between Ohio and Michigan at the western edge of Lake ERIE. In 1835 this dispute threatened to become a real conflict and was called the "Border War." Finally, Ohio was granted the disputed area, and Michigan was given the vast, almost uninhabited UPPER PENINSULA.

A similar border problem occurred in relation to Illinois and Wisconsin. Until Illinois was ready for statehood in 1818, its northern border was thought to be just parallel with the southernmost point of Lake MICHIGAN. Nathaniel POPE, Illinois delegate to Congress, argued that the new state should be given a short portion of the lakeshore, and he was so persuasive that Congress shifted the border to the north. If this had not been done, the present site of Chicago would have been in Wisconsin, and Illinois would have had no lakeshore.

Another boundary dispute which almost led to a real conflict was called the "HONEY WAR" because the disputed region contained the valued honey trees of the wild bees. In early days of settlement, sweeteners were scarce, and honey was precious. The Iowa border with Missouri was to run westward from the "rapids of the River DES MOINES." Iowans claimed this meant the Des Moines Rapids in the MISSISSIPPI, but Missouri claimed it designated a small rapids in the Des Moines River, thirteen miles farther north. This would have stripped Iowa of 2,600 square miles of territory, containing some of the finest bee trees. In August, 1839, each of the governors mustered a militia of sorts, with makeshift weapons such as pitchforks and the dasher of a churn, and the competing "armies" marched toward the disputed territory. Fortunately the governors cooled down and appointed a committee. However, the matter dragged on

and was not settled until 1850 when the U.S. Supreme Court decided in Iowa's favor.

The international boundary between Canada and the U.S. remained unclear and disputed for most of its length until the Webster-Ashburton Treaty (1842) defined the boundary as far west as the Great Lakes States. Minnesota's unusual northern boundary was not finally determined until 1867. That border takes an abrupt jog into Canada, forming the NORTHWEST ANGLE, cutting through the great LAKE OF THE WOODS, most of which lies in Canada. In a strange twist of geography, the northernmost tip of conterminous United States, a small point of land in the Northwest Angle, cannot be reached by land from the rest of the country.

BOUQUET, Henry. (Switzerland, 1719—Pensacola, FL, 1765). British army officer. Bouquet came to America in 1756, when he joined the British forces there. He was second in command to General John Forbes in the capture of Fort Duquesne (Pittsburgh) in 1758. Using his early experiences on the frontier, Bouquet adapted the British battle techniques to the requirements of frontier fighting. He was the leader of the British troops in the fierce Battle of Bushy Run, near Pittsburgh in 1763. His greatest success came with the agreement made near the town of COSHOCTON, Ohio, in 1764. At Coshocton General Bouquet had gathered a force of 1,500 men, highly trained Scottish Highlanders, Royal Americans and Pennsylvania regulars. The Indians were impressed by the numbers of the British army and by the training given them by Bouquet. The General called for the return of all white prisoners within Indian territory. The informal treaty of Coshocton resulted in the release of 206 captives followed by a short period of uncertain peace.

BOURGMONT, Etienne Venyard, (Sieur de). (Normandy, France, 1680—France, 1730). French administrator, explorer. After coming to America c. 1717, Bourgmont was made acting commander at DETROIT. His harsh treatment of the Indians there caused them to revolt, and Bourgmont deserted his post in 1706, fleeing to the wilderness. He explored much of the lower MISSOURI RIVER valley, reaching the Platte River as early as 1714. In these journeys he dealt fairly with the Indians in contrast to his early actions, and he became very popular among the tribes. In 1720 the French made Bourgmont commandant of the Missouri region. This was the earliest French attempt to control the Missouri River valley. In 1725 Bourgmont returned to France with Chicagou, the chief of the MICHIGAMEA.

BOWERS, Claude. (Hamilton County, IN, Nov. 20, 1878—New York, NY, Jan. 21, 1958). Diplomat, journalist and historian. Bowers performed editorial duties for NEWSPAPERS in INDIANAPOLIS, TERRE HAUTE and FORT WAYNE, Indiana. He delivered the keynote address to the 1928 Democratic convention in Houston, Texas, and was appointed Ambassador to Spain in 1933 by President F.D. Roosevelt. He resigned his position in 1939 when the United States recognized Francisco Franco's regime, but was reappointed to an ambassador's position in Chile where he served until his retirement in 1953. His writings on social, political and economic themes include *The Party Battles of the Jackson Period,* (1922—rep. 1955), *Jefferson and Hamilton* (1925), *The Young Jefferson (1743-1789)* (1945—rep. 1969), *Chile through Embassy Windows* (1958) and others, all of which were well received among historians. Bowers most widely read book was *The Tragic Era, A History of Reconstruction* (1929).

BOWLING GREEN, Missouri. Town (pop. 3,022), seat of Pike County, named for the Kentucky home of many of the town's citizens. A center of diversified farming, Bowling Green was the home of James Beauchamp "Champ" CLARK. Clark served as a member of the United States House of Representatives from 1893 to his death in 1921.

BRADLEY, Omar Nelson. (Clark, MO, Feb. 12, 1893—Fort Bliss, TX, April 8, 1981). American five star general. Two natives of Missouri have reached the highest ranks in the history of the modern U.S. Army. They were John J. PERSHING and Bradley. After graduation from West Point, Bradley served in WORLD WAR I. He filled a number of administrative army posts in the period before WORLD WAR II. In 1943 he took command of the Second Corps and played an important role in the invasions of North Africa and Sicily, under Dwight D. Eisenhower. Eisenhower chose him to lead the Allied invasion of Normandy in 1944. He participated in the planning for that landing and Bradley commanded the First Army in the actual invasion, when he and his men landed on June 6, 1944. Two months later he was placed in command of the Twelfth Army, the largest ever

to be led by a single American field commander, and in 1945 he received the four stars of a full general. Under Eisenhower, he was the principal figure in Allied operations in the battle to take Germany.

After serving as Army Chief of Staff 1948 to 1949, he became the first Chairman of the Joint Chiefs of Staff, serving from 1949 to 1953. In 1950 he was promoted to the five star rank of General of the Army. He retired to a business career in 1953. Among the many commendations earned by Bradley were the Distinguished Service Medal with three oak leaf clusters, Silver Star, Bronze Star, Presidential Medal of Freedom, Grand Cross Legion of Honor, Croix de Guerre with palm (France), Order Kutuzov (Russia), Grand Cross Couronne de Chene, Croix de Guerre (Luxembourg), and the Croix de Guerre with palm (Belgium).

BRAINERD, Minnesota. City (pop. 11,489), north-central Minnesota directly east of FERGUS FALLS, seat of Crow Wing County. Brainerd, platted in 1871 by the Lake Superior and Puget Sound Company, was chosen by the surveyors of the Northern Pacific for that railroad's bridge over the MISSISSIPPI RIVER. The community was named for the maiden name of the wife of the railroad president. The Indians then referred to it as Oski-odena, or "new town." The first train arrived in Brainerd on March 11, 1871, but regular service was not established until September. The LUMBER industry was attracted to the tall stands of pine in the area. Maine and New Brunswick lumbermen settled there, and the city grew quickly until the financial panic of 1873 when the population decreased to less than one-half its peak. The decline in the lumber industry coincided with the first discovery of iron ore in Crow Wing County, and the population climbed once again. Today, still a railroad center, Brainerd continues in lumbering and papermilling. Brainerd's Franklin School, with funds provided by the Carnegie Foundation, was a pioneer in the field of pre-parental education. In an area of approximately five hundred lakes, Brainerd is a popular recreation center with many resorts offering golf, fishing, boating, tennis and archery. The community bills itself as the "Hometown of Paul BUNYAN." In July the men of the Brainerd region grow beards for the annual festival recognizing Paul Bunyan. Competition is held in log-rolling, chopping, sawing and canoe tilting. Paul Bunyon Amusement Center features a forty-foot animated figure of Paul Bunyon that broadcasts recorded stories

Old Matt's Cabin, Branson, Missouri.

of his adventures. Lumbertown, U.S.A. re-creates Minnesota of the 1870s. Crow Wing County Historical Society Museum, once a sheriff's house, displays Indian artifacts and items of everyday use in the 19th century.

BRANSON, Missouri. Town (pop. 2,550). Resort community, southwestern Missouri near the Arkansas border, in the OZARK s, overlooking Lake TANEYCOMO. Branson is a town with access to many of the area's lakes. Its other attractions are more numerous and varied than those of most other communities of its size. The region was the setting for Harold Bell WRIGHT 's novel of the homesteading Matthews family, *Shepherd of the Hills* (1907). In the Shepherd of the Hills country are many reminders of the book's characters, including Old Matt's Cabin, Old Matt's Mill and Old Trail Still. Scenic wonders of the region include Inspirational Point, with its panoramic view of the countryside, where Wright camped while writing his book. MARVEL CAVE is one of the largest limestone caverns in Missouri. Inside the cave is the massive Pike's Peak, a 175 foot rock formation. A complete trip through the ten miles of passages takes nine hours, including such sights as Cathedral

Room, promoted as the highest natural unsupported dome in the world. Sportsmen find many boating and fishing opportunities at Table Rock Lake. Ralph Foster Museum is housed in the SCHOOL OF THE OZARKS. Concerts featuring the 96-bell carillon are given several times daily. Nine miles west is SILVER DOLLAR CITY, a unique amusement area, with a 3,000-seat theater. Silver Dollar City is renowned for its Ozark craftspeople, who feature thirty different skills. Branson's crafts are featured at Mutton Hollow Craft Village, recreating an earlier period. Waltzing Waters show provides impressive displays of lights and motion. Annual Branson events include the Ozark Mountain Crafts Festival from April 30 to May 22 and the Fall National Crafts Festival from September 17 to October 23. Country dancing is demonstrated at the Mountain Clog Dancing Festival from June 17 to 19, and country music rocks the hills during Mountain Folks Music Festival from June 11 to 19. Kewpiesta, honoring artist Rose O'Neill, creator of the Kewpie Doll, is scheduled in mid-April.

BRAZIL, Indiana. City (pop. 7,852), south-western Indiana, seat of Clay County, the community was named by William Stewart in honor of the South American country. Brazil is a principal Indiana coal mining center, noted for its huge open-strip mines. The community also is a manufacturing center producing glazed building brick, conduits, sewer pipe, and tile. Brazil and Harmony, Indiana, were the first cities in the United States linked with an electric interurban line, built in 1893. One of the better known personalities of Brazil was labor leader Jimmy Hoffa

BREADROOT. Midwestern flowering plant. The roots were used as food by the Indians and early Europeans. The psoralea or Indian breadroot may be recognized by its tall blue spike bloom. Once plentiful, the plant is rapidly becoming rare.

BRECKENRIDGE, Minnesota. Town (pop. 3,909), western Minnesota town at the junction of the OTTER TAIL and BOIS de SIOUX RIVER rivers, where they form the RED RIVER OF THE NORTH. In 1859 the Chamber of Commerce of ST. PAUL offered $2,000 to anyone who could establish steamboat service on the Red River. This would provide St. Paul's access to the river traffic by connecting with the existing stage route between Breckenridge and St. Paul. Anson Northrup dismantled his steamer at LITTLE FALLS and with the help of sixty men and thirty-four teams hauled the boat in sections across the state to the Red River. Despite the hardship and success in reassembling the ship, Northrup lost interest in the project and sold the boat to the Minnesota Stage Company. The *Anson Northrop* became one of the several steamers to ply the river during the riverboat period. The steamboat traffic has long been gone, but Breckenridge remains a center of livestock traffic.

BRECKENRIDGE, Missouri. Village (pop. 523), northwestern Missouri, west of Chillicothe, named in honor of John C. Breckenridge who served as Vice-President under Buchanan from 1857 to 1861 and was a candidate for President against Lincoln in 1860. Breckenridge was the site of HAUN'S MILL where, on October 30, 1838, state militia attacked and killed eighteen MORMONS. The event has been commemorated with a millstone in the city park. The mill itself was vandalized and destroyed by those who sought mementos of the Mormons' difficulties in the Midwest.

BRECKINRIDGE, Sophonisba Preston. (Lexington, KY., Apr. 1, 1866—Chicago, Ill.,

July 30, 1948). Educator and social reformer. She was the first woman to be admitted to the bar in Kentucky (1897), and was the first woman to represent the U.S. at an international conference when she was delegate to the Pan-American Conference in Uruguay (1933). A professor at the University of CHICAGO (1925-33), just previously she had been involved with the social work of Chicago's Hull House. For the last four years of her tenure at the U. of Chicago, she was professor of public welfare. Breckinridge was president of the American Association of Schools of Social Work (1934). Her writings include *Public Welfare Administration in an American Community* (1927) and *Women in the Twentieth Century* (1933).

BREWERIES. The Midwest is home for many of the nation's largest bottlers of beer. By 1900 Eberhard ANHEUSER and Adolphus BUSCH had developed a method of brewing beer without requiring pasteurization and had pioneered in bottling beer. Their ST. LOUIS brewery was the world's largest by 1900. In total production of beer, with its many breweries, MILWAUKEE, Wisconsin, became the center of beer production. Today Milwaukee still leads the world in the production of beer, although its leadership has narrowed because of increased competition. Smaller breweries operate in most of the other Midwest states. The only operating brewery in Iowa is Dubuque's Star Brewery. Midwest brewery production results in annual income ranging between three and four billion dollars.

BRIDGER, James (Richmond, VA. Mar. 17, 1804—Kansas City, MO. July 17, 1881). Frontiersman, fur trader and scout, one of the most famed of the western mountain men. He was working as a blacksmith in ST. LOUIS when he joined the William ASHLEY expedition in 1822. Bridger was the first white man to visit Great Salt Lake, in 1824. After years of fur trapping in the region north of the Spanish territories, he became so thoroughly acquainted with the area that he was in great demand as a guide. He served the Jedediah Smith and Marcus Whitman parties in that capacity, among many others. With several partners he established the ROCKY MOUNTAIN FUR COMPANY (1822). With the decline of the fur trade, in 1843 he established Fort Bridger to serve travelers on the OREGON TRAIL. In 1853 he was forced to turn the fort over to the MORMONS. In 1857 Bridger led an expedition to the region now known as Yellowstone Park and became one of the most vocal proponents of the wonders of the park. He continued to guide both private and government parties and became well known for his tall tales of his travels. Modern biographers rank him as one of the most picturesque characters of the frontier.

BRIDGETON, Missouri. City (pop. 18,445), St. Louis County, northwest of ST. LOUIS, Missouri. The community was settled in 1765 and incorporated in 1843. In 1852 the land around Bridgeton was leased to individuals for a term of 999 years at an annual rent of between 10 and 75 cents per acre. Today Bridgeton is largely residential, with some farming and industry. A monthly table tennis magazine has been published here since 1933.

BRITISH IN THE MIDWEST. With their defeat in the FRENCH AND INDIAN WAR, the French were eliminated from control in North America until the retrocession of Louisiana from Spain to France by secret treaty on October 1, 1800. The British, however, did little to bring law and order to the area west of the Appalachians and east of the MISSISSIPPI. In an attempt to control further colonial expansion beyond the eastern seaboard, the British king issued the PROCLAMATION OF 1763 which forbade additional settlement west of the mountains, but this law often was overlooked, and some new settlements developed. A confederation under Chief PONTIAC swept British troops from present-day Indiana until 1777 when Henry HAMILTON, the British commander at DETROIT, sent troops to VINCENNES, Indiana. Indians living in the region sided with the British during the American Revolution and engaged in wanton scalping, encouraged by "Hair Buyer" Hamilton. The British were routed from much of their Midwestern claims by the exploits of George Rogers CLARK who on the Fourth of July, 1778, captured KASKASKIA, Illinois, and then Vincennes in August, 1778. Hamilton recaptured Vincennes in December, 1778, only to have it recaptured by Clark and 170 men in February, 1779, after they had marched through icy water and flooded lowlands to surprise the British defenders. The British were outsmarted by Clark's tactics, with the help of the French citizens who supplied the Americans with needed ammunition. Because he failed to receive supplies and reinforcements from Virginia, Clark was unable to realize his hope to capture Detroit, but his success in the region supported American claims to territory which became Indiana, Ohio, Illinois, Michigan, Wisconsin, and parts of Minnesota. The British treated their defeat in the REVOLUTIONARY WAR as a temporary setback in their planning for the old NORTHWEST TERRITORY. They continued to encourage Indian attacks on American pioneers. The fact that the British supplied guns to the Indians was shown by the British ammunition discovered among the dead at the battle of TIPPECANOE in 1811. When British-American conflict erupted in the WAR of 1812, the British again turned to their Indian allies. Wounded Americans at the Battle of RAISIN RIVER (January, 1813) were left to the Indians who massacred them. British hopes to revive the Indian confederacy died with TECUMSEH, an officer in the British army, at the Battle of Thames in Canada. In the first peace negotiations the British attempted to reserve the Northwest for an Indian reservation. American victories in 1814 put an end to attempts to dictate such terms, and the peace treaty was signed on December 24, 1814, in Ghent, Belgium, ending British conspiracies and all realistic hopes of any British domination south of Canada and east of the Mississippi.

BRITT, Iowa. City, (pop. 2,185), situated in Hancock County, in north central Iowa, between Clear Lake and Algona. This modest farming community can count on international publicity every year. It is the site of the annual NATIONAL HOBO CONVENTION. The convention began with a hoax. The editor of the Britt newspaper announced that hobos from around the continent would gather at Britt in 1900 to celebrate the "Knights of the Road" by choosing their king. Reporters representing most of the press of the time arrived in Britt, only to find they had been hoodwinked. Nevertheless, they published fanciful stories of the supposed event. To everyone's surprise the fabrications brought hobos to Britt in increasing numbers each year after the hoax. Today, real hobos and would-be hobos flock to Britt to cook and enjoy slumgullion, and reminisce about past times. Without fail, national media are assigned to report the colorful and unique meeting. Highlight is the selection of the king and queen of the hobos. The townspeople make the choice.

BROMFIELD, Louis. (Mansfield, Ohio, Dec. 17, 1896—Columbus, Ohio, Mar. 18, 1956). Author. After early life on the farm, in 1914 Bromfield entered Cornell University to study AGRICULTURE, but a year later he began journalism classes at Columbia University. In 1916 as

Porpoises "fly" at Brookfield Zoo.

BROOK TROUT. Official state fish of Michigan. Trout are members of the large fish family known as Salmonidae. The brook belong to the salvelinus branch of the salmon family. In Europe they are known as char. Most varieties of trout will swim to the ocean if there is a cold, freshwater connection. However, in inland areas, such as Michigan, they live and reproduce in a landlocked environment. Michigan brook, or speckled trout, is highly prized by fishermen.

BROOKFIELD ZOO. Illinois pioneer in natural habitat displays. Founded in 1934 this Illinois institution originated the technique of exhibiting animals in their natural settings. Located in the CHICAGO suburb of Brookfield, Illinois, the zoo covers nearly two hundred acres. A childrens' zoo displays baby animals and the Seven Seas Panorama features a porpoise show in a new building said to provide the largest indoor attraction of its kind. The African and Latin American building features the largest reproduction of tropical habitats anywhere. There the animals of the two regions roam freely in separate controlled environments, featuring tropical storms and other simulations of tropical areas.

a volunteer with the American Ambulance Corps in France, he received many decorations. Returning to America he undertook a number of journalistic assignments, while working on his first book. His *Early Autumn* (1926) won the PULITZER PRIZE for 1927. It was part of a tetralogy, including his first book, *The Green Bay Tree* (1924), *Possession* (1925) and *A Good Woman* (1927) described as "a penetrating commentary on the American scene." This work and others depict the industrial life of his home area of MANSFIELD. His novel *The Farm,* written in Paris in 1933, was a nostalgic story of early life in Ohio. After fourteen years abroad, Bromfield returned to Mansfield, and remembering his early interest in agriculture, he bought a thousand-acre farm and became an agricultural experimenter. Named "Malabar" the farm was developed by Bromfield to become a country showplace. The homestead is still used as an agricultural experiment station, and the house is preserved with its original furnishing in Malabar State Park. In later years Bromfield supported the New Deal but decried its farm policies. His later works were not very well received, generally. However, several were bought for the screen, including the well known *The Rains Came* (1937).

BROOKS, Gwendolyn. (Topeka, KS, June 7, 1917—). Poet and playwright. Brooks grew up in CHICAGO and graduated from Wilson Junior College in 1936. Fascinated with poetry from childhood, she had her first poem published when she was thirteen. Working at a variety of jobs, she attended the poetry workshop at the South Side Community Art Center, where her writing technique matured. Brooks often writes portraits in verse of ordinary Chicago Afro-Americans and their lives. Her first appearance in *Poetry Magazine* occurred in 1944. Her 1945 collection, *A Street in Bronzeville* received wide critical acclaim and led to two Guggenheim Fellowships. The 1950 PULITZER PRIZE w a s awarded for her collection *Annie Allen*. She was the first black woman so honored. She has taught poetry at a number of Chicago colleges, and she was chosen the poet laureate of Illinois in 1968. Brooks has sponsored and funded a variety of writing workshops and competitions as well as encouraged neighborhood cultural events for young black Chicago residents. Brooks holds twenty-nine honorary doctorates and the American Academy of Arts and Letters Award. She was elected to the OANational Institute of the Arts in 1960.

Brown County - Brush

BROWN COUNTY INDIANA. Central Indiana county named for Major General Jacob Brown, commander-in-chief of the United States Army from 1821 to 1828. Brown County State Park and Game Preserve contains a total of 15,212 acres. NASHVILLE, Indiana, the county seat and the largest town, is home for many painters and photographers and attracts thousands of tourists who come to the area for its scenery. The Nashville courthouse's lawn features the Liar's Bench. Armless at one end and capable of seating six, the bench rewards anyone able to tell tall tales. The man at the armless end is pushed off as the new "expert" takes a place on the bench. Brown County is prominent for such imaginative community names as Needmore, GNAW BONE, and Bean Blossom. Poplar Tree Monument in Grouch Cemetery marks the burial site of John Allcorn, a man buried in a casket made from the tree which fell and killed him. After his burial, the wood of the casket sprouted and grew into a tree, which became Allcorn's memorial. Abe Martin Lodge in Brown County State Park is named for the popular character created by Indiana cartoonist Kin HUBBARD, and has become known as one of the country's most popular state lodges. Visitors have an unobstructed view of fifteen to twenty miles from Weedpatch Hill, highest hill in southern Indiana. Bumper-to-bumper weekend traffic throughout Brown county in the fall attests that it is one of America's most famous areas for fall leaf color. Similar claims are made for the spring blooming season. Also attractive are the many scenic COVERED BRIDGES.

BROWN'S VALLEY MAN. Remains of PREHISTORIC PEOPLE found in a gravel pit near Brown's Valley in west-central Minnesota near the BOIS DE SIOUX RIVER. Resembling the present-day Eskimo of Greenland, Brown's Valley Man lived in the area west of Morris, Minnesota, nearly twelve thousand years ago.

BROWN, John. (Torrington, CT, 1800—Charles Town, VA, December 2,1859). Abolitionist. He was brought to Hudson, Ohio, in 1805 and spent most of his life in the Midwest. At age 18 he began but soon abandoned study for the ministry. In Ohio he was a surveyor, tanner and sheep farmer, then a wool broker at Richfield and AKRON, Ohio. His business career ended in bankruptcy at Akron in 1842. Later, in his crusade against SLAVERY, Brown drilled his troops at SPRINGDALE and TABOR, Iowa, and had his headquarters at the latter for a time. Many of his raids against slavery and his activities in the UNDERGROUND RAILROAD were based in the Midwest. When Brown went on trial for treason (December, 1859), friends at CLEVELAND, Ohio, sent one of the city's ablest lawyers to defend him. When he was hanged, the city's bells tolled for half an hour. Flags at Akron, his former home town, were hung at half mast. Throughout much of the Midwest "John Brown's Body" was sung at gatherings, and his death brought about much stronger Abolitionist feelings in the region.

BROWN, Joseph Renshaw. (1805—1870). First resident of HASTINGS, Minnesota, when he established a trading post there in 1833. Brown came to Minnesota as a drummer for Colonel Leavenworth in 1819. As a soldier, he discovered Lake MINNETONKA near present MINNEAPOLIS. Later in life Brown built a nineteen-room mansion at Sacred Heart, Minnesota. The house, scene of many elaborate parties, was named Farther and Gay Castle as a pun on the Fotheringay Castle in England where Mary, Queen of Scots, spent her last days. The Brown mansion was destroyed by the SIOUX in 1861. Brown enjoyed careers in politics and journalism. He invented a steam-propelled wagon years before the AUTOMOBILE was established. Samuel Brown, son of Joseph, was an Indian scout at Fort Wadsworth, Dakota Territory, in 1866. On the night of April 19, 1866, Sam Brown rode through the western Minnesota countryside warning the settlers of a Sioux attack. Sam Brown has been called the "Paul Revere of western Minnesota."

BROWNING, Orville Hickman. (Harrison County, KY, 1806—1881) U.S. Secretary of the Interior. Noted as one of the organizers of the REPUBLICAN PARTY, in 1860 he was one of the most instrumental in securing the presidential nomination for his friend Abraham LINCOLN. However, as a U.S. senator he opposed Lincoln's Emancipation Proclamation. After Lincoln's death he opposed the Radical Republicans and supported President Johnson's reconstruction policy. Made secretary of the interior in 1866, he became one of Johnson's best friends and supporters in opposing the president's impeachment. His two-volume diary (published 1927-33) is one of the premiere sources about much of the Lincoln and Johnson administrations.

BRUSH, Charles Francis. (Euclid, OH, Mar. 17, 1849—June 15, 1928). Inventor and manufacturer, Brush perfected the first long lasting electric arc lamp in his CLEVELAND, Ohio, workshop while EDISON was still struggling with the incandescent lamp. In 1879 Brush was the first to provide electric lighting for a major store, Wanamakers in Philadelphia, and in the next year he introduced outdoor electric lighting for the first time, filling Cleveland's Public Square with brilliant white light. By 1881 a central power station had been built and the Brush electric Light and Power Company began to place arc lights throughout the city. In efforts to improve his lighting system, Brush also developed the first practical storage battery and perfected the most efficient electric generator of his time. The Brush company and the company of Thomas Edison were combined to form the giant General Electric Company at Nela Park in EAST CLEVELAND in 1892.

BRYAN, William Jennings. (Salem, IL, March 18, 1860—Miami, FL, July 26, 1925). Political leader, often called "The Great Commoner" because of his advocacy of the common man. He studied law at Union College in CHICAGO and practiced law in JACKSONVILLE, Illinois (1883-87). Moving to Lincoln, Nebraska (1887), he continued to practice law but left the law for politics. Despite the nominally Republican reputation of his district, Democrat Bryan was elected to Congress in 1880 and reelected in 1892. He became a prominent speaker in Congress, where he was particularly known as an advocate for farm interests and for free silver, but he failed in a Senate election bid in 1894. He started a career as a newspaper editor in Omaha, Nebraska, and because of his eloquence became a sought-after speaker at Chautauqua and other gatherings. After his famous "Cross of Gold" speech at the Democratic convention in 1896, Bryan was the Democratic presidential candidate. Although not successful in its outcome his campaign was perhaps the most vigorous and extensive ever seen until that time. He stressed the "sectional struggle between Wall Street and the 'toiling masses.'" He became known for his constant support of silver as the basis for U.S. currency. He was defeated for the presidency by McKinley in 1896, but scarcely 600,000 popular votes separated the two candidates. Nominated again in 1900 he again stressed silver against gold, but spoke even more vigorously on the need for America to expand. He lost to Theodore Roosevelt by a larger margin than in 1896. Nominated by the Democrats again in 1908, he received only 162 electoral votes to 483

for Taft. Bryan's opposition to the candidacy of Missouri Representative James Beauchamp CLARK for President of the United States in 1912 on the Democratic ticket cost Clark the nomination. Bryan then worked to elect Woodrow Wilson and served as Wilson's Secretary of State until 1915, when he resigned because he was bitterly opposed to Wilson's war policies. Nevertheless, he campaigned for Wilson again in 1916. He made his last political appearance at the Democratic convention of 1924, where he supported W. G. McAdoo. His greatest publicity came when he acted for the prosecution at the trial of J.T. Scopes in 1925. Scopes was accused of teaching evolution. Bryan was a bitter foe of evolutionary theory, and he was successful in his clash with Clarence Darrow, defense attorney at the trial. Five days after the trial ended, Bryan died in his sleep. Although the country had constantly rejected him, many of his causes were adopted later. In his own view, his notable service was negotiation of thirty arbitration treaties with foreign states. His memoirs were unfinished, but they were completed by his wife and published in 1925, reprinted 1971.

BUCKEYE. State tree of Ohio. The people of the state have come to be called Buckeyes and their state the Buckeye State. Buckeyes are a variety, generally smaller, of the horse chestnut, but not a true chestnut. Their nut is edible but only after considerable preparation. It was widely used by the Indians. They noted the white spot on the nut and thought it looked like the eye of a buck deer, hence the name. Some people still carry the carefully polished nut as a good luck charm. The soft wood can be used for paper pulp.

BUFFALO. Name given to a large native American animal which zoologists prefer to refer to as a bison. American bison bulls may weigh as much as three thousand pounds. Buffalo cows are much smaller and rarely weigh more than nine hundred pounds. Herds of the animals once roamed from the Appalachian Mountains to the Rockies. With the increasing density of settlement in the Midwest, few were seen in the region after the early 1800s.

BULL BOAT. Tub-shaped boats made by Northern plains Indians by stretching hide over a framework of bent willow branches. Bull boats were light, but clumsy to steer. European visitors to Mandan Indian lodges often commented on the dual servicibility of bull boats.

They frequently would be seen on the roof of the Indian lodges, where they were used to cover the smoke holes during heavy rains.

BULL SHOALS LAKE. Large recreational lake in southwestern Missouri including parts of Ozark and Taney counties and leading into northwestern Arkansas. More than half of the lake's area lies in Arkansas, the location of the Bull Shoals Dam which impounds the waters of the Beaver River. The twisting lake extends in some places for miles up many drowned valleys. The lake reaches as far west as BRANSON, Missouri. The huge expanse of water and multiple points of access provide the kinds of opportunities for lakeside recreation and living never before possible in such areas until lakes such as Bull Shoals were created.

BUNCHE, Ralph. (Detroit, MI, Aug. 7, 1904—Kew Gardens, NY, Dec. 9, 1971). American statesman, first black to win the NOBEL Peace Prize (1950). Bunche was educated at U.C.L.A. and Harvard, earning a Ph.D in 1934. He did post-doctoral study in anthropology and colonial policy at NORTHWESTERN UNIVERSITY, the London School of Economics,

and the University of Capetown, South Africa. He received a Rosenwald fellowship to study in Europe, North and West Africa. A Social Science Research Council fellowship enabled him to take further study in Europe, South and East Africa, Malaya and the Netherlands Indies. Bunche was a member of the political science department of Howard University from 1928 to 1950, rising from instructor to full professor and head of the department. Bunche's diplomatic career began in 1944 when he joined the Department of State. In four years he attended nine international conferences as an adviser or delegate. He helped found the United Nations, and he became director of the division of trusteeships in the U.N. Secretariat in 1946. He served as a U. N. Undersecretary from 1955 to 1971. Bunche received numerous honors in addition to the Nobel Prize, including the Springarn medal by the N.A.A.C.P. in 1949, the Theodore Roosevelt Association Medal of Honor in 1954, Third Order of St. Francis Peace Award in 1954, and the Presidential Medal of Freedom in 1963.

BUNYAN, PAUL. Legendary American lumberjack. This gigantic hero of countless tall

Paul Bunyan dominates Bemidji, Minnesota.

tales could create lakes and flatten vast timberlands with his fist. Known and bantered about in lumber camps across the northern timber country, but particularly in Wisconsin and Minnesota, to Bunyan was ascribed the power to do almost anything, and any fantastic accomplishment was likely to be linked to him. He was said to have ruled his mythical LUMBER kingdom from the year of the blue snow to the spring that came up from China. His great prize was his blue ox, BABE, boasting a width between the horns of 42 ax handles plus a plug of tobacco. Babe was supposed to have come to Paul out of Lake BEMIDJI, Minnesota, during the blue snowstorm. The southern lumber camps had a mythical hero similar to Bunyan, known as Tony Beaver.

BURLINGTON, Iowa. city (pop. 29,529), principal river port on the MISSISSIPPI RIVER in far southeast Iowa. Zebulon PIKE (1779-1813) stopped there in 1805 to raise a flag, and a trading post was built in 1808. A settlement gradually grew in the area, and in 1833 the first store was opened. The next year the town took the name Burlington, from the Vermont town. By 1838 the community had grown to become the temporary capital of the Territory of Wisconsin and was incorporated in that year. Burlington served as capital of Iowa Territory from 1838 to 1841. In 1856, the stream of immigrants entering Iowa at Burlingon reached its peak. In August, alone, 20,000 people crossed the Mississippi by ferry. Railroads made Burlington a bustling railroad center. The river bridge was completed in 1868, and the Chicago Burlington and Quincy Railroad began its operation. At present, MANUFACTURING includes electronic instruments, chemicals, tractors, furniture and other items. The city is a major center of retail trade for three states. This area of Iowa is noted for its GEODES, and Geode State Park is six miles west of Burlington. The annual combined Burlington Steamboat Days and the American Music Festival features a wide variety of events.

BURLINGTON, Wisconsin. City (pop. 8,-385) in Racine County in far southeast Wisconsin on the FOX RIVER. First settled in 1833, the city was named Foxville for the river but was renamed in 1835 by a group of settlers arriving from Burlington, Vermont. Waterpower potential of the WHITE and Fox rivers first lured settlers to the area, and the streams were soon powering a grist mill and a sawmill. As livestock farmers turned to sheep, woolen mills sparked the industrial life of the community. Today the principal activities center on the surrounding DAIRY industry. Burlington has an international reputation as the home of the LIAR'S CLUB. Founded to preserve the rustic traditions of story-telling, the club now presents a prize to the winner each year who tells the whoppingest story. With the publicity, which snowballed each year, the contest became one of the most quoted of all the folk contests. Visitors to Burlington may enjoy a visit to Green Meadows Farm, an operating farm which offers pony and hay rides, guided tours, milking demonstrations and animal exhibits. During the summer, Burlington hosts the Aquaducks Water Ski Show. In 1987 it held a special celebration honoring the city's designation as "Chocolate City."

BURNS HARBOR. At Portage, Indiana. Burns Harbor is the state's largest port on Lake MICHIGAN. Ships are able to navigate from there to the Atlantic Ocean through the lakes and the St. Lawrence Seaway. The opening of the harbor in 1970 was controversial due to environmental concern for the dunes.

BURNSIDE, Ambrose E. (Liberty, IN, May 23, 1824—Bristol, RI, Sept. 13, 1881). Union general in the CIVIL WAR and governor of Rhode Island. Before the Civil War, Burnside operated a factory in Rhode Island. There he produced a breech-loading carbine which he had invented, but the firm became bankrupt in 1857. In 1861, after recruiting a regiment, Burnside commanded the brigade which opened the first battle of Bull Run, July 21, 1861. In November, 1862, he succeeded General George McClellan as commander of the Army of the Potomac, but after being defeated at Fredericksburg in December, 1862, was himself replaced. Burnside continued his military service in Tennessee, Virginia and Ohio. He was successful in stopping General John Hunt MORGAN's cavalry raid into Ohio in 1863. During the Wilderness Campaign, Burnside was blamed for the decisive defeat at Petersburg, June, 1864, and felt compelled to resign from the army. After the Civil War, Burnside entered the railroad business, served as governor of Rhode Island from 1866 to 1869, and was a United States senator from 1875 to 1881, when he died.

BURR CONSPIRACY. Among the Midwesterners involved in the so-called conspiracy of Aaron BURR was Major Davis Floyd, a resident of JEFFERSONVILLE, Indiana. He was persuaded

by former vice-president Aaron Burr to participate in what he thought was a plan to conquer
Mexico. Floyd thought the plan had the
backing of the federal government, so he
recruited volunteers and had a fleet of boats
built near present-day NEW ALBANY, Indiana.
Burr's real plans have never been known. He
may have planned to establish an empire for
himself west of the MISSISSIPPI. In the autumn of
1806 Burr and fellow "conspirators" floated
down the OHIO and the Mississippi to carry out
their schemes. Floyd was arrested along with
Burr and convicted of treason. He was fined
$20.00 and sentenced to three hours in jail. In
1807 Burr was tried for treason, but found not
guilty. A transplanted Ohioan, Harman BLEN-
NERHASSET, was another of the prominent
Midwest men duped by Burr into joining his ill-
fated expedition.

BURR, Aaron. (Newark, N.J., Feb. 6,
1756—Port Richmond, NY, Sept. 14, 1836).
Politician, adventurer. One of the major figures,
and one of the most controversial in the period
of the founding of the U.S. After a career in the
U.S. Senate (1790-1796) Burr ran for the U.S.
vice-presidency. Confusion in the Electoral
College vote ended in a tie of Burr with Thomas
Jefferson, not for the vice presidency but for
the presidency itself. After thirty-five ballots
the House of Representatives selected Jefferson
as president, leaving the vice-presidency to
Burr. Alexander Hamilton was the principal
opponent of Burr in this selection, and he also
was responsible later for Burr's defeat in a bid
for the New York governorship. To avenge
Hamilton's supposed offenses, Burr challenged
him to a duel, resulting in Hamilton's death.
The murder of this popular figure left Burr
almost an outcast. Looking for a change of
scene, he visited the Midwest, and was indeed
profoundly changed by this visit and later
experiences in the Midwest. One day in 1805,
he stopped his elaborate houseboat at the OHIO
RIVER dock of Harman BLENNERHASSETT on
Blennerhassett Island, near Belpre, Ohio. There
he visited with Harman and Mary Blennerhassett at their palatial estate in the Ohio valley
wilderness. Later Burr returned to Blennerhassett with his beautiful daughter, Theodosia.
They probably discussed Burr's mysterious
plans, which resulted in so much trouble for
both of them. Financed by Blennerhassett,
Burr purchased land on the Washita River in
the Arkansas-Oklahoma area of the LOUISIANA
PURCHASE, and with further help of Blennerhassett built fifteen heavy barges, recruited sixty

Aaron Burr, portrait by James Van Dyke.

"settlers," armed the barges excessively and in
1806 set out with his patron, supposedly to
settle on the Washita property. Their exact
plans have never been known, but people of the
Ohio River area looked askance at what they
considered to be a military operation designed
to set up a new country in the west or to attack
Mexican holdings. President Jefferson, an old
enemy of Burr, ordered him held and tried for
treason. He was acquitted in 1808 but never
regained a place in public life. After a fruitless
stay in Europe, he returned to New York City
in 1812, resumed his law practice and remained
out of the spotlight until his death.

BURSTYN, Ellen. (Detroit, MI, Dec. 7,
1932—) American film and television actress
best known for the film *Alice Doesn't Live Here
Anymore,* (1974) for which she won an
Academy Award for Best Actress. She won a
Tony Award for *Same Time Next Year* in 1978.
Burstyn was nominated for an Academy Award
for her acting in *The Exorcist* (1973) and *The
Last Picture Show* (1971).

BURT LAKE. Northern Michigan lake located about one mile southwest of Indian River
on SR 68. On the banks of Burt Lake is the
Indian River Shrine, with its 31-foot high cross
bearing one of the largest figures of Christ ever
made, the work of sculptor Marshall Fredericks.
The 405-acre Burt Lake State Park is a popular

recreational area. Activities include water sports and cross-country skiing.

BUSCH, Adolphus. (Mainz-on-the-Rhine, Germany, July 10, 1839—St. Louis, MO, Oct. 10, 1913). Brewer. Busch and Eberhard ANHEU-SER formed a partnership in 1896 that developed into the world famous Anheuser-Busch Brewing Association of ST. LOUIS. Busch pioneered in brewing without pasteurization, in bottling and in refrigeration methods.

BUSHWACKERS. Bands of Confederate supporters during the CIVIL WAR. They fought behind Union lines. The Bushwackers were organized in response to raids of Jayhawkers from Kansas who attacked border towns in Missouri. Federal troops considered these guerrillas to be outlaws, while southerners thought of them as heroes. Because of its location and support of the guerrillas, NEVADA, Missouri, was called the "Bushwacker Capital." Famous bushwackers from Nevada included Frank JAMES and James A. "Dick" Liddil, a member of the James gang.

BUTLER UNIVERSITY. Privately supported Indiana university founded in 1855. Butler University, in INDIANAPOLIS, offers liberal arts education to undergraduate students in business, music, dance, pre-law, pre-dentistry, drama, pre-med, teacher education, and medical technology. Butler provides a cooperative program with Dow Chemical for chemistry majors. The campus has 286 acres, 18 buildings, an observatory and planetarium. In the 1985-1986 academic year Butler University enrolled 3,741 students and had 347 faculty members.

BUTTERFAT TESTER. Invention of Stephen BABCOCK. The tester provided a reliable means of testing the amount of butterfat in milk and has been called "one of the world's most important discoveries" because of its implications to AGRICULTURE and public health. In 1890, Dr. Babcock of the University of WISCONSIN, discovered this means of testing butterfat which could be used at every DAIRY or farm where cows were milked. Dr. Babcock refused to patent the test and made it available as a public service. It not only helped to assure the quality of milk but also enabled dairies to eliminate cheating in the purchase of milk from farmers, many of whom "watered" milk to increase its volume for sale.

BYRNE, Jane. (Chicago, IL, May 24, 1934—). First woman mayor of CHICAGO, Illinois. Byrne began her political career when appointed by Chicago's Mayor Richard DALEY to the antipoverty program. She was named commissioner of consumer sales in 1968 and continued in that position under Mayor Michael Bilandic, the successor of Richard Daley. In 1979 she was elected mayor of Chicago with 82% of the vote—the highest percentage ever received. A dynamic and popular figure, Mayor Byrne was responsible for creating many of the annual festivals for which Chicago has become known. Although not entirely independent of the Daley machine, she managed to institute a revitalization of public services, repair of streets, collection of garbage, snow removal and other needed changes. She served as mayor of Chicago until 1983 when she was defeated for reelection and again suffered defeat in 1986.

C

CADILLAC, Antoine de la Mothe. (Gascony, France, 1656—Castle Sarrazin, France, Oct. 18, 1730). Founder of DETROIT, Michigan, and governor of Louisiana. Son of a minor nobleman, Cadillac enlisted in the French army in 1677, first as a cadet and then as a lieutenant in the regiment of Clairembault. In 1683 he came to America and established a home at Port Royal, Annapolis Royal, Nova Scotia. In

1687 Cadillac married Marie Therese Guyon, who later became one of the first two European women in Michigan. They lived for a short time on his grant which included the island of Mount Desert in Maine. During his 1689 trip to France, the British sacked and burned his Port Royal home. He won the favor of Count de Frontenac, who called him "a worthy man, good officer, keen witted," and in 1694, Cadillac was

Cadiz - Cahokia

granted the command of the important post at SAINT IGNACE, now in Michigan. In 1697 the post was ordered abandoned, so Cadillac returned to Canada and later to France. In 1699, he outlined his plans for a post on the DETROIT RIVER and was given the title of Lieutenant of the King and received the grant of DETROIT. There he assembled a group of 150 colonists, which included Recollet missionaries, to minister to the Indians. This action angered the Jesuits at Mackinac, who resented their loss of influence with the Indians. By such actions, Cadillac made many enemies, and in 1704 he was arrested, tried, and acquitted in Quebec. His return to Detroit was a triumphant one, and his superiors were pleased with his accomplishments. Although Cadillac planned to spend the rest of his life in Detroit with his family, he was recalled in 1711. His next assignment was the governorship of Louisiana in 1713. He was dissatisfied with this position. During his three years there, he alienated many people, including former governor Bienville and his family. Cadillac also sought great wealth, and he even traveled to Illinois in a futile search for silver mines. In 1716, Cadillac was recalled to France and may have been imprisoned for a brief time in the Bastille. After his release in 1717, he returned to his province where he died. Over 200 years later, his name is mainly remembered as the name of an automobile.

CADIZ, Ohio. City (pop. 4,058), seat of Harrison County, situated on a large hill in far southeastern Ohio on U.S. highway 250 halfway between Ulrichsville and Martins Ferry, Ohio. The name is derived from that of Cadiz, Spain, mentioned often in American newspapers during the War of the Spanish Peninsula, 1808-14, and chosen for communities in both Ohio and Kentucky. Located in the heart of a rich sheep-raising and coal-mining district, Cadiz was laid out in 1803. Early immigrants from the East stayed in the area for a time before moving on. As late as 1830, when Cadiz was made the county seat, there were only 1,000 residents in the entire county. The town grew slowly as the center of a rich farming and trading area; the community has been little affected by depressions and recessions. For decades Cadiz was considered to have the greatest per-capita wealth in Ohio. In 1938, when a Hollywood publicity group put on a campaign to find the American town with a population under 5,000 having the most illustrious roster of noted people, Cadiz won easily. The famed Cadizians included Edwin M. Stanton (1814-1869), Lin-

coln's Secretary of War, and actor Clark Gable (1901-1960), among the eight others submitted by town leaders for consideration in the competition.

CAHOKIA INDIANS. One of six groups of related Indian tribes in early Illinois. The Cahokia, MICHIGAMEA, MOINGWENA, Peoria, TAMAROA and Kaskaskia called themselves "ILLINI" meaning "the men" because they felt themselves superior to the other people living in the area.

CAHOKIA MOUNDS. Important prehistoric site. Dating from 900 A.D., in Cahokia State Park near EAST ST. LOUIS, Illinois. The approximately 85 mounds, often in the shape of EFFIGIES, were built by prehistoric peoples of the Middle Mississippian culture, commonly called "MOUND BUILDERS." At its peak, the area supported a population sometimes estimated at "tens of thousands." Monks mound, a rectangular, flat topped earthwork with a 17-acre base is named for Trappist monks who settled on its top. MONKS MOUND is frequently described as the largest primitive earthwork in the world. Some mounds were burial sites or bases of temples. Now classified as a national historic landmark, the mounds are considered to be the most important prehistoric works found north of the Gulf States and the Southwest. They have been designated a World Heritage Site by UNESCO.

CAHOKIA, Illinois. Town (pop. 18,904), southwestern Illinois, oldest community in Illinois, suburb of EAST ST. LOUIS, Illinois in St. Clair County. Founded in 1699 by French priests, Cahokia was named for the CAHOKIA INDIANS. It was the first permanent European settlement in the Mississippi Valley. After New Orleans was founded in 1718, trade flourished and cargoes of flour, lumber, pork, and lead were shipped by KEEL BOAT to that city. Under British control after 1765 and the Americans after 1778, Cahokia remained almost totally French in culture and continued to be an important center. Cahokia's decline came through the economic rise of St. Louis and East St. Louis, the annual floods of the MISSISSIPPI, and a decline in the influence of the Catholic Church. In 1814 the county seat was moved to Clinton Hill, later called BELLEVILLE. The Cahokia Courthouse State Historic Site preserves the oldest building in Illinois. The Church of the Holy Family is the oldest church in Illinois.

CAIRO, Illinois. City (pop. 5,931), seat of Alexander County, southern Illinois city it lies farther south than Richmond, Virginia. Named for the capital of Egypt, Cairo is located at the junction of the MISSISSIPPI and OHIO rivers on a tongue of land between the two rivers. It was named by a St. Louis merchant who thought the site looked like that in Egypt. Vulnerable to the rivers' floods, the city is protected by levees. The rivers are spanned by several bridges. Cairo was an early site of land speculation based upon its anticipated important location at the meeting of the rivers. Speculators, including Charles Dickens, invested in the Cairo City and Canal Company which promoted the site with elaborate maps of a proposed metropolis. The sponsors began permanent settlement of the city in 1837 under Darius B. Holbrook, who built a levee and opened shops. However, the promoting company failed, and many investors lost their money. The city declined drastically until a federal grant to Illinois in 1850 funded the building of a railroad from Cairo to Dunleith (East Dubuque) with a branch to CHICAGO. The resulting Illinois Central Railroad, 705.5 miles long, was the world's longest when completed in 1856. The railroad brought rapid growth to the community. During the 1850s Cairo's population increased tenfold. It was a strategic river city in the CIVIL WAR. Mound City, eight miles above Cairo on the Ohio River, became the chief naval depot for the Union fleet which split the Confederacy during the Civil War. After the Civil War, Cairo, QUINCY, and ROCK ISLAND were among the river towns from which freed slaves found railroad TRANS-PORTATION throughout the North. Today Cairo is a center of AGRICULTURE and a hub of rail, highway and river traffic. Magnolia Manor, built in 1869, has been restored as a community showplace.

CALUMET. Ceremonial tobacco pipe smoked by Indians of the Mississippi Valley, GREAT LAKES and Great Plains regions of the United States as a sign of friendship and peace. Often called "peace pipes," calumets had a stone bowl attached to a long wooden stem decorated with feathers. The pipe was passed from person to person as it was smoked. The name "calumet" came from French explorers from their word for the reed used as the pipe's stem.

CALUMET SEAPORT. Principal port of Chicago (1968). With the completion of the SAINT LAWRENCE RIVER SYSTEM AND SEAWAY in 1959, CHICAGO and other great lakes cities were able to obtain access to ocean shipping. The Calumet Sag Channel provides access to the port. The port was dredged from portions of Lake Calumet and forms Chicago's principal harbor. Over half of the world's ships are able to travel to Chicago's Calumet Seaport. However, recent years have shown a dramatic decline in the port's business, and studies have been made in an attempt to determine why this happened and what might be done to revitalize the facilities and bring Chicago back to its important port status.

CALUMET, Minnesota. Village (pop. 469), northeastern Minnesota, northeast of GRAND RAPIDS, site of the Hill-Annex Mine, the first to use electricity in its operations; last of the towns constructed in the Canisteo District; named for the French word describing the ceremonial pipe smoked by several Indian tribes. Calumet was platted by the Powers Improvement Company which also constructed a hotel. The Hill-Annex Mine is now inactive except for the one and one-half hour tours which take visitors to the bottom of the five hundred foot deep open pit iron mine.

CAMBRIDGE, Ohio. City (pop. 13,573), incorporated 1837, seat of Guernsey County, situated in central eastern Ohio at the junction of Interstate highways 70 and 77, stretching out along a high ridge overlooking rolling hills to the north and south. The name is derived from Cambridge, Maryland, traced back to Cambridge, Massachusetts and then back to Cambridge, England. First settled in 1798 by immigrants from the Isle of Guernsey, the town was laid out in 1803 by Zacheus Beatty and Jacob Gomber, who named it for their Maryland home town, which was also by that time the former home of many of the other settlers. With the coming of the NATIONAL ROAD in 1826, the community took on an active commercial life. AGRICULTURE, milling and salt-making became important. Manufacturing began in the 1880s when oil and gas were discovered nearby, and coal mining became a large-scale industry in eastern Ohio. A large glass factory was founded in 1901. Clay deposits in the vicinity led to the establishment of several potteries and fire-clay manufactures. A STEEL mill brought employment to nearly 1,000 workers, but the mill closed in the early 1930s. However, the community continues as a manufacturing and trade center, with activity in neighboring coal, gas and clay resources. It gains much support from the a large agricultural and dairying area. The glass museum displays historical glass objects made in the city. Lakes and parks surround the city, and the large Salt Fork State Park is handy.

CAMP LINCOLN. Mankato, Minnesota, site of the largest mass execution ever conducted in the United States. On December 26, 1862, thirty-eight Indians charged with attacking women and/or participating in massacres during the Sioux Uprising were hanged on order of a military court whose proceedings had been reviewed by a commission set up by President Abraham LINCOLN, and finally by the president himself.

CAMP MORTON. Instruction camp at INDIANAPOLIS, Indiana, for Union soldiers and later a prison camp for Confederate soldiers during the CIVIL WAR. Named for the governor of Indiana, Oliver P. MORTON, Camp Morton was actually the converted grounds of the Indiana State Fair. The Confederate prisoners-of-war were treated so well at Camp Morton that they contributed the bronze bust of Colonel Richard Owen, commander of the prison, now placed at the base of the dome in the Indiana capitol.

CAMPUS MARTIUS FORT. Provided protection for MARIETTA, the first settlement in Ohio (1788). The fort was built under the supervision of General Rufus PUTNAM (1738-1824) to protect the settlement at the confluence of the OHIO and MUSKINGUM rivers. It was named by the erudite settlers of the region in honor of the Roman Campus Martius. When General Putnam arrived at the river site with his 48 men, all veterans of Washington's army, his first thought was to put up a strong bulwark that would turn back the Indian raiders. When it was finished, a square standing 180 feet in each direction, Putnam called the fort "the strongest fortification in the Territory of the United States...the handsomest pile of buildings on this side of the Allegheny Mountains." The fort was the seat of government of the area, residence of General Putnam as military leader and of territorial governor Arthur ST. CLAIR (1736-1818), other officials and many of the settlers. It also housed much of the social life of the area and had the first day school and Sunday school in the NORTHWEST TERRITORY throughout the winter of 1788-1789. During the Indian War more than 300 people, some of whom had fled from the various settlements along the MUSKINGUM, were quartered in Campus Martius. The fort survived all the rigor of the

pioneer period, and today, a museum on the site of the old fort displays one of the finest collections of pioneer implements and artifacts.

CANADIAN INSURRECTION. Unsuccessful attempt by American citizens to overthrow the British and create an independent Canadian government. To aid Canadian rebels, these Americans held a mass meeting in DETROIT in 1838 to plan an attack on Canada. They stole arms and ammunition from the Detroit jail, captured the schooner *Ann*, and prepared their attack. Michigan Governor Stevens T. MASON (1811-1843) was compelled to prevent such an invasion of a friendly nation by American citizens, despite his sympathy for their cause. Finally, in December, 1838, a group of American partisans was able to land above Windsor, Ontario, where they were soon killed or captured.

CANAL WINCHESTER, Ohio. Town, (pop. 2,749), situated in south central Ohio on U.S. highway 33, halfway between COLUMBUS to the northwest and LANCASTER to the southeast, named for Winchester, England, and the OHIO AND ERIE CANAL. The town developed around the commerce of the canal. Well known composer and conductor, Oley SPEAKS was born at Canal Winchester. Nearby is the village of Lithopolis a name taken from the Greek meaning Stone City, in honor of the deposits of lithopolis sandstone in the vicinity, which have been quarried for building stone.

CANALS AND CANAL BOATS. One of the most important early factors in the growth of the Midwest was provided by canals in a relatively short period from the early 1830s to the coming of the railroads in the 1840s and 1850s. The Erie Canal, opened in 1825, was not in the Midwest, but it provided TRANSPORTATION to the entire GREAT LAKES region, and vast numbers of settlers and a great volume of commerce flowed into the area and on into other parts of the Midwest.

In the Midwest itself many canals were needed for a number of reasons. From the earliest explorations it was obvious that water commerce from Lake SUPERIOR to Lake HURON was impossible because of the the difference in water level between the two lakes. The rapids of the ST. MARY'S RIVER kept commercial boats from reaching Lake Superior. As early as 1797 the French had built a small canal at the rapids of SAULT SAINTE MARIE, but it was destroyed during the WAR OF 1812.

Canal Boats - Canary

Tourists can still ride canal boats in Ohio.

The first large canal on the St. Mary's was built by the state of Michigan and finished in 1855. The Canadian canal, with one lock, was built in 1895. The American canal was enlarged and reconstructed by the federal government to accommodate larger vessels. Today the popularly called SOO CANALS carry by far the greatest volume of traffic of any canal in the world.

The OHIO AND ERIE CANAL between CLEVELAND on Lake ERIE and PORTSMOUTH on the Ohio River was completed in 1832. It utilized much of the extent of the CUYAHOGA, MUSKINGUM and SCIOTO rivers and had 49 locks. The longest canal on the North American continent was the WABASH AND ERIE, begun in 1836, connecting Lake ERIE with the OHIO RIVER, then by way of its outlet through the MISSISSIPPI RIVER to the Gulf of Mexico. The canal ran for 460 mile cutting through the divide from the MAUMEE RIVER, then along the historic WABASH RIVER to its mouth on the Ohio.

As early as the explorations of MARQUETTE AND JOLLIET, the latter had conceived a waterway connecting Lake MICHIGAN with the Mississippi. The ILLINOIS AND MICHIGAN CANAL was opened in 1836, cutting across the narrow divide separating the CHICAGO RIVER from the tributaries of the Mississippi River and connecting Lake Michigan with the ILLINOIS RIVER at LA SALLE. In 1872 the work of canalizing the lower Illinois River was completed, with lock and dams. In 1900 the water route from Lake Michigan to the Illinois River was vastly enlarged by changing the flow of the Chicago River and utilizing a series of locks at LOCKPORT to carry shipping across the divide, completing the long-dreamed-of all-water route from Lake Michigan to New

Orleans. Completion of the Calumet River and Sag Channal in eastern Illinois in 1922 added another leg to the busy waterway.

By providing relatively cheap water transport, canals helped to open up the Midwest to commerce and settlement. Construction brought in laborers, many from abroad, most of whom took up residence in the areas of their work. Settlements grew quickly; agricultural products and manufactured goods could be shipped to far markets expeditiously, and industries were established and flourished and brought new workers to new jobs. Passenger canal boats provided comparative luxury to travelers, who escaped the jolting stagecoaches.

Some of the most picturesque forms of transportation were provided by the various canal boats. In early days small canal barges were hauled by mules toiling along towpaths beside the canals. Packet boats followed, and then came self-propelled barges.

With the decline of most of the canals due to the railroads, only the major routes remain active today. Some communities have reactivated short stretches of nearby canals and provided historic rides on oldfashioned canal boats.

CANARY, Martha (Calamity Jane). (Princeton, MO, 1852—Deadwood, SD, 1903). Frontierswoman. Canary and her parents moved from Princeton to Virginia City, Montana, in 1864. The parents separated and she was raised in a series of mining camps in Utah and Wyoming where she learned to be an expert with pistol and rifle and became skilled as a horsewoman. She loved to dress in men's clothes and boast of her achievements as an army scout and shotgun on stagecoaches. Her life was hard, and legends concerning the history of her nickname suggest that she warned anyone that to annoy her was to invite calamity. She may have served as a scout for George Armstrong CUSTER and certainly spent some time at such frontier posts as Fort Bridger and Fort Russell in Wyoming. In 1875 Canary moved to Deadwood, South Dakota, during the gold rush. She often was seen drinking in saloons with Wild Bill Hickock, whom she claimed to have married, but there is no other evidence of this. Actually she may have married a man named Burke. She became a heroine by working with the only doctor in Deadwood, treating smallpox victims during the epidemic in 1878. During the following 25 years, she wandered across South Dakota, Wyoming and Montana, being reported in brawls and shooting scrapes. She returned to Deadwood in 1903 where, destitute, she lived in poverty, and the citizens helped to support her and collected money to send her daughter to school in the East. She is buried beside Deadwood Dick in Mt. Moriah Cemetery, Deadwood.

CANNELTON, Indiana. Town (pop. 2,373), southern Indiana, seat of Perry County, located on the OHIO RIVER, named for the beds of cannel COAL found in the region. Cannelton was founded in 1837 by eastern capitalists to exploit coal deposits. It was the first Indiana town touched by Abraham LINCOLN and his family as they moved to Indiana from Kentucky. Cannelton, a thriving river town during the steamboat era, fell from importance as Ohio River traffic and coal deposits in the region disappeared.

CANNON, Joseph Gurney. (New Garden, Guilford County, NC, May 7, 1836—Danville, IL, November 12, 1926). Congressman. Cannon, is considered to have been the most domineering Speaker of the United States House of Representatives in its history.

Cannon was first elected to the house as a Republican in 1872, holding the seat until 1891. He was elected again in 1892. He was defeated for reelection in 1912 but again returned in 1914 and remained until 1923, a total of House service of 46 years. He served as speaker from 1903 to 1911.

As speaker, Cannon began an arbitrary and partisan control of House procedure which became known as "Cannonism." As chairman of the House rules committee, he and his conservative "Old Guard" Republican commi

tee members had the power to block almost any measure they opposed and to carry any measure they approved. Cannon demonstrated his power by such measures as successfully sponsoring a bill to serve navy bean soup every day in the capitol restaurant. This was done in tribute to Michigan beans and is carried on to the present time. However, more importantly, he could block important legislation, such as civil rights. Such overt power displays were not unusual for the man some called "the Hayseed member from Illinois," or "foul-mouthed Joe."

A combination of insurgent Republicans and Democrats managed to pass a resolution placing the power to appoint committees in the hands of the House. This action, stripping Speaker Cannon and those who followed of much power, became known as the "Revolution of 1910." Although one writer claims Cannon was "one of the most important figures in Congressional history," most seem to agree with *Webster's American Biographies*: "In a total of 46 years in the House, Cannon failed to attach his name to a single major legislative measure. He was, however, popular with his colleagues, even after his reign as speaker, and was affectionately referred to as 'Uncle Joe'."

CANTON, Ohio. City (pop. 93,077), seat of Stark County, situated in southeast Ohio, at the junction of three branches of Nimishillen Creek. Incorporated 1822, the city was named by Bezaleel Wells for Canton, the Baltimore estate of his friend Captain John O'Donnel, who had named his home for Canton, China.

Canton's history goes back to the time when the Indians made camp there before going over the Old Portage Trail. In 1784 Chief Turtle Heart deeded the land to unremembered white traders. The year 1793 brought five government land scouts who reported on the high quality of the area for settlement, but settlement did not begin until 1805. In that year six pioneers from New England built homes on the flood plain at the forks of the creek. In 1806 the father of Canton, Bezaleel Wells, and his friend James Leonard, platted the town. Wells had the foresight to insist that the streets be made unusually wide.

In 1827 Joshua Gibbs of Canton perfected an improved metal plow, and Canton soon became one of the most important plow manufacturing centers west of the Alleghenies. The reaper company founded by C. Aultman began operation there in 1851; the railroads arrived in 1853, and the community was incorporated as a city in 1854.

With the availability of fine steel from CLEVELAND, Canton soon became a major center of STEEL manufacturing, attracting a large number of skilled German and Swiss artisans. Henry H. Timken (1831-1909) had perfected and patented in 1877 a tapered roller bearing and set up his plant at Canton. Before long it had become Canton's biggest factory and the world's largest manufacturer of roller bearings.

In 1867 a young major returning from the CIVIL WAR opened his first law practice that year in Canton. This was the future president William MC KINLEY (1843-1901), whose life ended tragically by assassination.

Another Canton martyr was newspaper editor Don Mellett. who campaigned against the gangsters who had almost taken over the city. He was murdered gangland style in 1926, and his death sparked a cleanup of vice and crime.

Canton is still a major manufacturer of steel products, along with heavy office equipment, water softeners and forgings. One especially well known product is the vacuum cleaner, made originally at Canton by Herbert W. Hoover.

As with most major Midwest cities, hard hit by decline in manufacturing and moves to the Sunbelt, Canton's population declined from 110,053 in the 1970 census to 93,077 in 1980, removing the city from its cherished status as one of those in the category of over l00,000 population.

Walsh College operates in suburban North Canton.

One of the country's most impressive memorials is the McKinley Tomb and Monument, a large granite structure begun in 1904 and dedicated in 1907. Operated by the state, it somewhat resembles the Taj Mahal and the tomb of Hadrian. About halfway up the steps is a bronze statue of Mc Kinley. Mr. and Mrs. McKinley and their two daughters are entombed there. Adjacent to the memorial, the Stark County Historical Center contains a Mc Kinley museum.

Another major attraction of the city is the professional FOOTBALL HALL OF FAME, with memorabilia of the game. It pays tribute to more than 170 of the greatest professional football players of all time.

CAPE GIRARDEAU, Missouri. City (pop. 32,400), southeastern Missouri near the MISSISSIPPI RIVER in Cape Girardeau County, named for Jean Baptiste Girardot who traded here in 1733. Spanish promises of inexpensive, tax

exempt land attracted settlers to the area, and a thriving river trade kept the town growing until the CIVIL WAR, when trade suffered a severe decline. With the 1880s and the establishment of new railroad lines, the city again began to grow and remains healthy today. Cape Rock marks the site of Girardot's trading post. Although nothing remains of the building, the view of the Mississippi is spectacular. The Trail of Tears State Park contains a small part of the route the Cherokee Indians were forced to take from their original homes in the South to Oklahoma. Its manufactures include clothing, shoes, and electrical appliances. Cape Girardeau is the home of SOUTHEAST MISSOURI STATE UNIVERSITY.

CAPONE, Alphonse. (Naples, Italy, Jan. 17, 1899—Miami, FL, Jan. 25, 1947). CHICAGO gangster of the 1920s and 1930s. He emigrated from Italy with his family in 1899, grew up in Brooklyn and left school after the fourth grade. He became the bodyguard for the notorious Johnny Torrio. Because of a razor slash across his face, he became known as "Scarface." Torrio moved to Chicago soon after Prohibiton in 1920 and summoned Capone to Chicago to help him gain control of the bootlg whiskey market there. After a series of spectacular clashes with other gang leaders and gangland style murders, in 1925 Torrio was "shot up" and retired. Now in charge, Capone soon controlled prostitution, gambling and dance halls in Chicago, in addition to bootlegging. Grand scale bribery kept him out of police hands. By 1927 his wealth was estimated at $100 million. Blamed for the 1929 St. Valentine's Day Massacre of a rival gang and other killings, Capone was never found guilty of such crimes but was finally convicted of income tax evasion in 1931 and sentenced to eleven years in prison and fined $70,000. He was imprisoned in Atlanta and then on Alcatraz Island, California, before being released in 1939 as a hopeless paretic. He retired to his Miami Beach estate where he died.

CARBON ARC LAMP. Earliest practical electric light. Charles F. BRUSH OF CLEVELAND, Ohio, discovered the means of harnessing the highly luminous and intensely hot discharge of the carbon arc to produce electric light of a more nearly permanent type than had been previously available, by a technique of enclosing it in glass. Soon after Brush discovered the principle in 1878, the arc lamp was first used to light the public square of Cleveland, quickly

Cardiff - Carleton

followed by use in other cities until it was replaced by the incandescent lamp.

CARDIFF GIANT. One of the most famous of all hoaxes, originated in the Midwest at ACKLEY and FORT DODGE, Iowa. As George Hull listened to a sermon at Ackley, the subject brought to his mind prehistoric people and their discovery. He bought a huge block of Fort Dodge's famous gypsum and shipped it to Chicago. There he had a sculptor chisel out a crude but mammoth figure, for which Hull posed. Then they all spent hours hammering holes in the figure with steel needles, to create the "pores." The thing was bathed in sulphuric acid to give it an aged look. Then they shipped the creature to Hull's cousin's farm near Cardiff, New York. On the pretext of drilling a well a year later (1870), the prehistoric monster was "discovered" and soon came to be called the Cardiff Giant, for the nearby town. The owners set up a tent around the thing and the word spread rapidly. Soon they had taken in $20,000 in ten cent admissions. Scientists from around the world came to inspect the creature. Some thought it was a petrified man from ancient times; others declared it to be the work of prehistoric sculptors. Then Galusha Parsons, a lawyer from Fort Dodge, visited the site and uncovered the deception. The perpetrators readily admitted their activity but said there had been no fraud. They had never made any claims for the object. Others had done enough of that. The publicity had been such that the Cardiff Giant continued to be popular. P.T. Barnum even offered to buy it for his show. Today it still is a popular attraction at the Farmers Museum in Cooperstown, New York.

CARDINAL. State bird of several Midwest states, Illinois, Indiana and Ohio. Cardinal or redbird is the familiar name for this North American bird of the worldwide finch family. The male has coloring of the brightest red, the female of a modest brown-tan with patches of red coloration. Both sexes have crests and red bills. Both male and females attend to building the cup-shaped nests, and both help in rearing the young.

CARLETON COLLEGE. Privately supported, non-denominational college established by the General Conference of the Congregational Churches of Minnesota in 1866. Accredited by the North Central Association of Colleges and Schools, Carleton offers a liberal education leading to the bachelor of arts degree.

Harper's Weekly depicts the "discovery" of the Cardiff Giant.

The music department at Carleton is usually ranked among the top five of its type in the United States. An overseas program for more than 150 students in 20 countries is offered as well as urban study, geology field study programs, and academic cooperative programs for engineering students. Carleton is located on a 90-acre campus which includes the Lyman Lakes near Northfield, Minnesota. Adjacent to the campus are the college-owned arboretum and the College Farm totalling 900 acres. Approximately 48% of those applying for admission are accepted and 96% of the freshman class return for the sophomore year. During the 1985-1986 academic year, Carleton enrolled 1,864 students and had 156 staff members.

CARLETON, Will. (Near Hudson, MI, Oct. 21, 1845—Brooklyn, NY, Dec. 18, 1912). Poet. After completing his education at Hillsdale College in Michigan, Carleton worked on NEWSPAPERS in Hillsdale, DETROIT, CHICAGO, Boston, and New York for several years before becoming editor of *Everywhere* magazine in Brooklyn. His "Betsy and I Are Out" appeared in 1871 and established Carleton as the best known "Balladeer of the Simple Life." He gained a reputation as one of the first American poets to read from his poems in public. He said he practiced his lectures on the farm animals, and the horses generally went to sleep. His best known work, "Over the Hills to the Poorhouse" (1873) used Hillsdale as its setting.

CARLINVILLE, Illinois. City (pop. 5,439), Macoupin County, west central Illinois, midway between SPRINGFIELD and EAST ST. LOUIS, located on Illinois 108, named for the governor of the state from 1834 to 1842. Carlinville is known for its Macoupin County Courthouse completed in January, 1870, after repeated bond issues and nearly a triple cost overrun. The city is the home of BLACKBURN COLLEGE and the American Hotel, one of the sites able to boast that Lincoln slept there.

CARMICHAEL, Hoagland (Hoagie). (Bloomington, IN, Nov. 22, 1899—Rancho Mirage, CA, Dec. 27, 1981). Actor and composer. Carmichael first encountered jazz music as a student at the INDIANA UNIVERSITY. One of his songs, "Riverboat Shuffle," was given to Bix Beiderbecke when he visited the campus and became one of his best recordings. Carmichael formed a band of his own, but continued with his legal education and earned his degree in 1926. He practiced law for a time before joining a band and then forming another group of his own. In 1929, after moving to New York City, he wrote one of the most popular songs of all time, "Star Dust," which established him as a composer. "Rockin' Chair" and "Georgia on My Mind" were published in 1930. In 1931 Carmichael assembled for a recording session a band which included Jimmy Dorsey, Benny Goodman, Bix Beiderbecke, and Gene Krupa. The group was called the most impressive jazz ensemble ever gathered together. One of the songs recorded by this group was "Lazy River." Other Carmichael songs include "Two Sleepy People," "Lazybones," and "The Nearness of You." Carmichael's "Lamplighter's Serenade" was the first song recorded by Frank Sinatra. Carmichael appeared in feature films and had a popular radio program and television program in the 1950s. His "In the Cool, Cool, Cool of the Evening" won the 1951 Academy Award after it was played in the movie *Here Comes the Groom*. In 1971 Carmichael was one of the first ten popular composers elected to the Songwriters' Hall of Fame.

CARNATION. Scarlet carnation, state flower of Ohio. The carnation is a member of the pink family, originating in the old world. Carnations have been recorded since before the time of Christ. In England they were known as the gillyflower. About 2,000 varieties of carnations are now known, all descended from the flesh-colored gillyflower.

CARNEGIE, Dale. (Pumpkin Center, MO, Nov. 24, 1888—New York, NY, Nov. 1, 1955). Writer and lecturer. Carnegie was one of the first persons to make a fortune showing other people how to be successful. He graduated from the State Teachers College, in WARRENSBURG, Missouri, at the age of nineteen and worked for a time as a salesman for Armour and Company. He moved to New York in 1911 where he taught public speaking to businessmen and put many of his simple, well-phrased rules into books which have enjoyed unprecedented success in their field. Over ten million copies of his book *How to Win Friends and Influence People* have been sold since its publication in 1936. He also wrote *How to Stop Worrying and Start Living* (1948).

CARSON, Johnny. (Corning, Iowa, Oct. 23, 1925—). Radio and TV comedian and talk show host has been called "the single most observed person in history." Carson often harks back to his Midwest origin, where, in addition to Corning, he lived in RED OAK and Avoca, Iowa, before moving to Nebraska with his family. He attempted to overcome his shyness by entertaining with magic and card tricks and later tried ventriloquism. When he received a Christmas present of a magician's cape bearing the title "The Great Carsoni," he adopted the name for a hoped-for stage career. His WORLD WAR II service took him to duty in the Pacific on the *U.S.S. Pennsylvania*. He often entertained his shipmates with tricks and humor. He graduated from the University of NEBRASKA with a bachlor's degree in radio and drama in 1949, entered radio in Omaha that year and then went to Los Angeles, where, in 1951, he had a comedy show called *Carson's Cellar*. Carson then began writing for the comedy stars, starting with Red Skelton. He made a hit as a substitute on Skelton's show when the star was ill and was offered *The Johnny Carson Show* by CBS in 1955. After that closed he went to New York for a 1957 ABC show, *Who Do You Trust?* which he hosted for five years. A hit as a substitute on the NBC *Tonight Show* in 1958, he became the host of that show, continuing in that post for more than thirty years, to become perhaps the best-known personality in show business.

CARTHAGE, Missouri. City (pop. 11,104), seat of Jasper County, southwestern Missouri, northeast of JOPLIN, named for the ancient commercial center in northern Africa. Platted in 1842, Carthage was burned to the ground July 5, 1861, by Confederate troops in the first major battle of the CIVIL WAR west of the MISSISSIPPI RIVER. Stages of that battle may be seen today as visitors follow markers around the community. What would have doomed other towns failed to stifle Carthage which profited immediately after the war by a lead and zinc mining boom in nearby Joplin, followed by the opening of its noted grey marble quarries in the 1880s. Dairying steadily increased in importance due to the "Missouri Dairy Club" of E.G. Bennett. Two women gave Carthage a nationwide reputation. Myra Belle Shirley, better known as Belle STARR, Confederate spy, member of QUANTRILL'S RAIDERS and leader of a band of outlaws, was born in Carthage in 1846. In 1890 Annie Baxter of Carthage was elected clerk of Jasper County, but was denied her office because she was a woman. Mrs. Baxter took her case to the State Supreme Court. She won and thus was the first woman in the United States to hold elective office. Her fight for equal rights brought such attention to her that she was made a colonel on the governor's staff. Local history is shown in a mural by Lowell Davis in the Courthouse built of Carthage marble in 1894. George Washington CARVER's birthsite is near by. An annual event is the Maple Leaf Festival on the third weekend of October.

CARUTHERSVILLE, Missouri. City (pop. 7,958), seat of Pemiscot County, extreme southeastern Missouri, named for a Madison County lawyer and judge. The first white settlement near present-day Caruthersville was that of a French trading post established by Francois Le Sieur in 1794. John Hardeman Walker and his family moved to the region from Tennessee in 1810 and stayed despite the violent EARTHQUAKE of 1811 in NEW MADRID, Missouri, with aftershocks that rocked the area for several years. In 1818 Walker learned that the proposed southern boundary of Missouri would not include his property. He campaigned vigorously to include all land south to the thirty-sixth parallel between the MISSISSIPPI and ST. FRANCIS rivers. Missouri thus owes its "BOOT HEEL" to the efforts of this early nineteenth-century pioneer. Walker and George W. Bushey platted a town on part of the Walker farm and named it Caruthersville. The town grew slowly until it became the eastern terminus of the St. Louis, Kennett and Southern Railroad. Near Caruthersville stands the largest prehistoric mound in southeastern Missouri. Four hundred feet long, thirty-five feet wide and over two hundred feet tall, the mound was used by early white settlers as a refuge in times of flood.

CARVER, George Washington. (Diamond

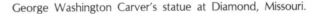

George Washington Carver's statue at Diamond, Missouri.

Grove, MO, 1864?—Tuskeegee, AL, Jan. 5, 1943). Black scientist and educator. Carver was born near Diamond Grove, Missouri. In his youth he and his mother were stolen and taken to Arkansas where his mother was sold and he was traded for a race horse valued at $300.00. He was returned to his former home in Missouri; worked his way through high school in Minneapolis, Kansas; studied art at SIMPSON COLLEGE in INDIANOLA, Iowa; and worked his way through Iowa State College where he graduated in 1894 with the help of "Tama Jim" WILSON. Carver was elected to the faculty of Iowa State, now IOWA STATE UNIVERSITY, where Carver devoted himself to bacterial laboratory work in botany. After gaining his master's degree from Iowa State in 1896, he joined the faculty of Tuskegee Institute at the invitation of its head, Booker T. Washington. There he won international recognition for discoveries of industrial uses for agricultural products, including sweet potatoes and peanuts. Carver's discovery of three hundred by-products for the peanut gave hope to the South as it looked for a new crop to replace cotton which had depleted the soil and was threatened by the boll weevil. Carver was chosen to be a member of the Royal Society of Arts in London in 1916 and in 1923 won the Spingarn medal for distinguished service in the field of agricultural chemistry. In 1935 he was a collaborator in the Bureau of Plant Industry for the United States Department of Agriculture and received the Roosevelt medal in 1939 for his valuable contributions to science. In 1940 he contributed his savings to establish the Carver Foundation, to continue his work in AGRICULTURE. During WORLD WAR II, Carver developed 500 colors of dyes to replace those that no longer could be imported from Europe. January 5 has been designated George Washington Carver Day by the United States Congress. At the Missouri farm on which he was born 210 acres were set aside in 1953 as the GEORGE WASHINGTON CARVER NATIONAL MONUMENT. A visitor's center features an audiovisual program showing his life and work. A self-guided tour explains features of the birthplace site, including the statue of Carver by Robert Amendola, and the Moses Carver house.

CASE WESTERN RESERVE UNIVERSITY. Private university established at CLEVELAND, Ohio, in 1967 with the merger of Western Reserve University, which had been chartered in 1826, and Case Institute of Technology, which had been chartered in 1880. The university has eight professional schools, a

graduate school and two undergraduate colleges: Case Institute of Technology and Western Reserve College. The Frances Payne Bolton School of Nursing was the first offering the N.C. (doctorate in nursing) degree. The university has been rated seventh among the best ten schools for social work (1981), eleventh among the best eleven schools for medicine (1981) and first among the top ten schools for nursing (1981). The student body of 8,261 is instructed by a faculty of 1,465.

CASH REGISTER. In 1879 James Ritty of DAYTON, Ohio, invented the "Mechanical money drawer," but the people of Dayton thought it was a joke, laughing every time the bell rang when the drawer opened. Merchants, however, soon discovered that the drawer was a handy time-saver and the bell a deterrent to thieves in the petty cash. By 1890 the bells of the National Cash Register Company had begun to ring all over the world. Today the company manufactures diverse products, including computers.

CASS LAKE. North-central Minnesota lake southeast of BEMIDJI, on the shores of which are headquarters of the Consolidated Chippewa Indian Agency, borders the Chippewa National Forest. The Indian name for the lake meant "the-place-of-the-red-cedars." The first whites called it Upper Red Cedar Lake. Explorations for the source of the MISSISSIPPI RIER included the Cass Expedition, led by Territorial Governor Lewis CASS of Michigan, who reached the lake in 1820. Henry R. SCHOOLCRAFT, who accompanied Cass, did not agree with Cass that Elk Lake was the source of the Mississippi and returned in 1832 with his own expedition and discovered Lake ITASCA, the true source. Schoolcraft renamed Upper Red Cedar Lake in honor of Cass. Schoolcraft also mapped and described 1,200-acre Star Island, the largest of several islands in six mile long Cass Lake and a popular scenic and recreational spot. Schoolcraft originally called the island "Colcaspi" in honor of its three explorers (Schoolcraft, Cass, and Pike). Lake Windigo, located on Star Island, was the home of Schoolcraft's guide, Chief Yellow Head (Ozawindib), and his tribe of 160.

CASS LAKE, Minnesota. Town (pop. 1,-001), north-central Minnesota. With the organization of Cass County in 1851, lumbermen moved in to harvest the stands of pine, poplar, oak, cedar, spruce, maple and birch. The Cass Lake settlement grew quickly with the arrival of

Lewis Cass explores, by Robert Thom, copyright 1964 by Michigan Bell Telephone Co.

the Great Northern Railroad in 1898. Further growth of the town came with the Minneapolis, St. Paul, and Sault Ste. Marie Railroad (Soo Line) in 1900. While LUMBERING has been a principal industry for years, farming and DAIRYING have been developed in the cutover lands. Cass Lake village was for many years the location of the U.S. Government Nursery, the largest pine nursery in the world.

CASS. Lewis. (Exeter, New Hampshire, Oct. 9, 1782—Detroit, Michigan, June 17, 1866). Senator and territorial governor. As governor of Michigan Territory (1813-1831), Cass was determined to improve the reputation of the region. In 1820 he and a party of explorers traveled great distances in the unexplored land to disprove a government report in 1815 that claimed the land was worthless. His glowing reports and those of geologist Henry SCHOOL-CRAFT attracted new settlers. Cass was only thirty-one when he assumed the office of governor in 1813, but remained in the position for eighteen years. In 1831 he was appointed as United States secretary of war under President Jackson and served in that office for five years, whereupon he was appointed this nation's minister to France. Cass returned to Michigan in 1842 and successfully ran for the United

States Senate as a Democrat. He served in the Senate from 1845 to 1848. As the Democratic nominee for president in 1848, Cass was defeated by Zachary Taylor. He was returned to the Senate (1849-1857). There he favored Texas annexation and supported U.S. claims in Oregon and the Compromise of 1850. Cass was secretary of state from 1857 to 1860 under President Buchanan. During his second period of service in the Senate he developed and proposed the doctrine of popular sovereignty, the concept that territorial residents could decide whether to permit SLAVERY in their territory, an idea later adopted by Stephen DOUGLAS.

CASSVILLE, Wisconsin. Town (pop. 1,270), situated in far southwestern Wisconsin, on the MISSISSIPPI RIVER south of PRAIRIE DU CHIEN. The community was founded in 1831 by Garrett V. Denniston and Lucius Lyon, who had hopes it might be the Wisconsin capital. Nearby is Nelson Dewey State Park. At the park is Stonefield Village, a crossroad village of the 1890s, and the State Farm and Craft Museum with its display of historical agricultural machinery.

CATLIN, George. (Wilkes Barre, PA, 1796—Jersey City, NJ, Dec. 23, 1872). American artist. Catlin practiced law in western Pennsylvania until 1823, then turned to portrait painting in Philadelphia. Here he encountered a group of western Indians and resolved "to use my art and so much of the labors of my future life as might be required in rescuing from oblivion the looks and customs of the vanishing races of native man in America." Catlin has provided some of the earliest impressions of life among the Indians of the upper Mississippi region, as well as those farther west. He spent summers from 1830 to 1836 traveling among the tribes and by 1837 had nearly five hundred portraits and sketches and information on almost fifty tribes. He used his material in an exhibition called "Catlin's Indian Gallery," which traveled to major American and European cities. In Minnesota Catlin was the first white to describe the reddish stone, later called catlinite in his honor, which the Indians used to make the bowls of their ceremonial pipes. His work pictured villages, religious ceremonies, games and occupations as well as his notable series of portraits of Indian leaders. *Catlin's North American Indian Portfolio* appeared in 1845, and he published *Life Among the Indians* in 1867.

CATTLE. The Midwest is the second largest U.S. producer of cattle, both meat and milk. However, the individual states are not leaders in cattle production. Iowa is the largest producer of cattle in the Midwest, with 5,600,000 head (1984), having a value of $1,181,000,000, but Iowa ranks only fourth among all the states, behind Texas, Kansas and Nebraska. Missouri is the second largest cattle state in the Midwest with total herds of 4,850,000, having a value of $778,300,000. Michigan is the Midwest state with the lowest cattle production.

CATTLE PRODUCTION IN THE MID-WEST
Number of cattle on farms (1975)

Iowa 5,600,000
Missouri 4,850,000
Wisconsin 4,440,000
Minnesota 3,550,000
Illinois 2,500,000
Ohio 1,835,000
Indiana 1,670,000
Michigan 1,450,000

CAVE OF THE MOUNDS. Near Blue Mounds, Wisconsin, workers were blasting in 1939 when they suddenly uncovered the entrance to a cavern. Now open to the public, the cave is particularly noted for its rare formation of crystallized white limestone with black stripings, caused by deposits of oxide of manganese. Oxides of iron have caused unusual colored lines of reds, yellows, brown and orange on the peculiar rock formations.

CEDAR FALLS, Iowa. City (pop. 36,322), Black Hawk County, northwest of CEDAR RAPIDS and adjacent to WATERLOO. William Sturgis and his brother-in-law E.D. Adams and their families arrived in March of 1845 and built cabins on the CEDAR RIVER. The new community was called Sturgis Falls. A sawmill was built in 1848 and a gristmill was added in 1850. During the following decade, Cedar Falls used the waterpower of its falls on the Cedar River to become one of Iowa's most important milling centers. Originally selected as the county seat, Cedar Falls lost out in a rivalry with Waterloo in 1855. The arrival of the railroad after the CIVIL WAR helped the city develop into an important commercial and industrial area until much of the industry eventually left the city for nearby Waterloo. However, a number of smaller industries remain. Cedar Falls became a bedroom city of Waterloo and a college community serving the needs of the Iowa State Normal School, now the University of NORTHERN IOWA. The Ice House Museum provides a unique display of ice cutting harvesting, storing equipment and other exhibits relating to the natural ice industry. Sturgis Falls Days Celebration is an annual late-July event.

CEDAR GROVE, Wisconsin. Town (pop. 1,420), situated on Lake MICHIGAN, south of SHEBOYGAN. Cedar Grove was founded in 1848 by Presbyterian minister Peter Zonne, and became one of the first two Dutch Protestant communities in the state. Several Dutch Reformed Churches also were quickly formed to serve the growing Dutch population. Today the community is renowned for its annual Dutch festival.

CEDAR RAPIDS, Iowa. City (pop. 110,200), seat of Linn County, on the CEDAR RIVER, leading manufacturing and distributing center in Iowa. Cedar Rapids has grown from a single cabin in 1838 to a world leader in the manufacturing of cereal products. Quaker Oats enjoys an international reputation and was a pioneer in the field of prepared cereals, beginning in 1873. The city's leadership in avionics is due to Collins

Radio division of Rockwell International, which develops sophisticated electronic mechanisms for the government and private industry. Other industries include milk processing machinery, packaged meats, stock feeds and farm hardware. For years Cedar Rapids had the highest per capita population of Czechoslovakians in the nation. Czech history is preserved in Czech Village. Cedar Rapids was the birthplace of Grant WOOD, one of the nation's most famous artists. The largest collection of Grant Wood art is housed in the Cedar Rapids Museum of Art. Carl Van Vechten (1880-1964), writer, photographer, and critic, was born in Cedar Rapids. His *Nigger Heaven* (1926) was among the first novels written about Harlem and is still considered one of the best. His *The Tattooed Countess* (1924) purports to depict life in a community such as Cedar Rapids. Rhodes scholar and University of Iowa professor Paul ENGLE (1908—) delivered NEWSPAPERS in Cedar Rapids as a child before gaining fame with his poetry. The Masonic Library claims to house the most complete Masonic collection in the United States. Built of Vermont marble, the library contains 100,000 volumes and memorabilia. It was established in 1845 as the first Grand Lodge Masonic library in the United States. Cedar Rapids for years was home of Arthur Collins, who founded Collins Radio, a pioneering company in electronics. Brucemore, the twenty-six acre estate of local manufacturing tycoon Howard Hall, is on the National Trust for Historic Preservation roll and may be toured by the public. Attractions include Cedar Rapids Museum of Art and the Seminole Valley Farm, a restored pioneer farm. Houby Days and Czech Village Festival are annual events celebrating the Czech heritage.

CEDAR RIVER. The Cedar is one of the two Iowa rivers on the U.S. Geological Survey's list of major rivers. It forms in southern Minnesota near Hayfield, then crosses the state line into Iowa at Otranto. It passes CHARLES CITY and WAVERLY, descends the falls which give CEDAR FALLS its name and bisects two major Iowa communities, WATERLOO and CEDAR RAPIDS. F o r about a hundred miles more it passes through quiet Iowa countryside until it reaches the IOWA RIVER. Although the Cedar is the main stream, the merged river continues with the name Iowa River, in tribute to the name of the state. The divide between the Cedar and WAPSIPINICON rivers is so narrow that there are no tributaries between them on either river.

The Cedar River bisects Cedar Rapids, Iowa.

CELERON DE BLAINVILLE, Pierre Joseph. (Ville Marie, Montreal, 1680—Paris, 1768) Governor and colonizer of the vast French claims to Louisiana. He was a midshipman in the royal navy before serving on the 1697 Hudson Bay expedition of his brother, another famed explorer, Pierre le Moyne, Sieur d' Iberville. The next year he again followed his brother on their expedition to the mouth of the MISSISSIPPI. In addition to his nominal control of the French claims in the Midwest, his most interesting connection with that region was his expedition of June, 1749, down the OHIO RIVER to reassert the French claim to the area. Along with his party of 250, Celeron carried a supply of six lead plates. These he buried at strategic locations in the Ohio Valley. They were designed to provide tangible evidence of the French claims to counter the growing influence of the British in the region. Historian Harlan Hatcher calls the expedition the "most diverting episode in the bloody realism of all our early Ohio history." One of the plates was found in modern times by two Ohio boys swimming in the river near MARIETTA, Ohio. Part of the plate had been melted to make bullets before its value was recognized, and it was sold to a museum in Massachusetts.

CENTRAL MISSOURI STATE UNIVERSITY. Publicly supported university located in WARRENSBURG, Missouri. When founded in 1871 the school was called the State Normal School for the Second District. It gained its accreditation as a four-year teachers' college in 1915. The present name was adopted in 1972. Accreditation for the university is provided by the North Central Association of Colleges and Schools, the National Council for Accreditation of Teacher Education and several professional organizations. The school owns one thousand acres of land of which 188 are taken up by the college farm. A cooperative arrangement in engineering is available with several other state institutions. The university offers extensive music programs and a freshman opportunity for the educationally disadvantaged. During the 1985-1986 academic year 8,821 students were enrolled. The university has 445 faculty members.

CENTRALIA, Missouri. Town (pop. 3,537), established in 1857 on the proposed route of the North Missouri Railroad; named for its central location between ST. LOUIS and OTTUMWA, Iowa; east-central Missouri northwest of MEXICO, Missouri. Centralia was the scene of a vicious attack of Confederate guerrillas led by William "Bloody Bill" Anderson on unarmed Federal troops. The attack on September 27, 1864, was later known as the "Centralia Massacre." After robbing a train's passengers and the baggage-car safe, the Confederates lined the twenty-three or twenty-four Union soldiers up and executed them. That afternoon a Union force of 175 men under Major A.V.E. Johnson was led into an ambush by Anderson and all but twelve of the men were killed. Jesse JAMES was said to have been a participant in the killing.

CENTURY OF PROGRESS EXPOSITION. Second CHICAGO world's fair and one of the few to realize a profit. The Exposition opened in Chicago in 1933, one hundred years after the founding of the city, and continued for a second year. Builders of the fair, under the direction of Louis Skidmore, used many money-saving techniques, as Chicago was then suffering from the worldwide depression. Science exhibits operated by the visitors were especially popular. The main feature was a sky ride between two towers called Amos and Andy, named for the two popular radio comedians. Many of the exhibits became part of the Chicago MUSEUM OF SCIENCE AND INDUSTRY.

CHAGRIN RIVER. Originates east of CLEVELAND, Ohio, flows south and west to the community of CHAGRIN FALLS, named for the falls of the river near where its flow turns abruptly north. It courses past Gates Mills and Willoughby and empties into Lake ERIE near the village of Timberlake. The river has an interesting historical significance. Moses CLEAVELAND, founder of Cleveland, and his surveying party followed the river for a number of miles, thinking they had found the CUYAHOGA RIVER, for which they were searching. When they discovered the error, in their embarrassment they named the river Chagrin. However, another explanation of the name contends that it comes from the Indian word *shaguin* or *shagrin*, which means "clear water."

CHAIN OF LAKES. Lake country in northeastern Illinois near the Wisconsin border in Lake and McHenry Counties. The FOX RIVER flows into Grass Lake, the northernmost of three interconnected lakes, including the Fox and Pistakee, to the south. Chain of Lakes State Park includes 960 acres. Hunting and fishing are the principal sports.

CHANUTE FIELD. WORLD WAR II ground school training station at Rantoul, Illinois. Trainees were sent to France. With the end of the war, Chanute Field became a separation center where discharge papers were issued. Now it is the site of a U.S. air force base and the Air Force Technical School.

CHAPMAN, John (Johnny Appleseed). (MA, 1774—near Fort Wayne, IN, Mar., 1845). Frontiersman and folk hero. Chapman left no record of his early life, but he appeared in Pennsylvania about 1800. Gathering seeds from the APPLE orchards and cidar presses of that state, he moved on into Ohio. For about forty years he traveled across Ohio and Indiana, a strange but familiar figure dressed in a coffee sack shirt wearing a pasteboard hat with a peak to keep off the sun, a recognized figure, traveling back and forth over a vast territory of the Midwest.

Chapman became familiarly known to those of his day, and later almost as a legend, as Johnny Appleseed. He told of having been kicked by a horse at the age of twenty-six and then of having a vision of heaven filled with blooming apple trees. From that time on, he said, he had traveled with leather bags full of his precious apple seeds, planting them in carefully considered locations. He always seemed to remember precisely where he had planted them and often returned to prune and care for the trees as they matured. He frequently gave seeds or cuttings to settlers and provided full instructions on the best means of orchard culture.

It was verified that during the WAR OF 1812, he hurried thirty miles to bring troops to MANSFIELD, Ohio, to prevent an Indian threat in the area. Heedless of rattlesnakes, thorns, stones and other impediments, he always walked barefoot. On the several occasions when friendly people gave him shoes, he would give them to poor families. Respected by the Indians as a great medicine man, he was never harmed by them, in fact was treated by them with great kindness and was much beloved by the Indian children.

He was a religious mystic and a disciple of Emanuel Swedenborg. He preached fiery sermons to receptive crowds. He practiced the respect for life later personified by Albert Schweitzer. Chapman refused to harm any living thing. If mosquitoes flew into his campfire, he would put the fire out. Once when he killed a rattlesnake after it bit him, he never forgave himself. If he saw a domestic animal being abused, he would try to buy it and give it to a settler he knew would treat it well.

In the summer of 1845 he stopped at the home of Allen County, Indiana, settlers. They gave him a warm welcome, offered him supper, but he only accepted some milk and bread to eat on the front porch. He preached to the family from the Beatitudes and lay down to sleep on the porch. The next morning the legendary eccentric was found dead where he slept.

His grave attracts many visitors to FORT WAYNE to read the inscription on the simple stone which marks his grave site. His work lierally bore fruit over 100,000 square miles of territory. Some of his orchards are now buried under great cities, but a few still blossom on.

CHARDON, Ohio. City, (pop. 4,434), seat of Geauga County, situated in northeast Ohio, about 25 miles northeast of CLEVELAND, at the junction of U.S. highway six and Ohio 44. Named for Peter Chardon Brooks, first owner of the site, it is renowned as one of the great maple syrup centers. The annual late March or early April Geauga County Maple Festival has drawn thousands of visitors to watch both the modern and the old-fashioned methods of rendering sap and to taste the syrup and sugar fresh from the vats.

CHARITON RIVER. Midwestern river whose source lies near Weldon, Iowa. The stream flows east past Chariton, Iowa, then south-southeast through Iowa's Appanoose County, where it forms Lake Rathbun, then on into Missouri to form the boundary between Missouri's Putnam and Schuyler counties. It continues flowing southward through Adair County and Thousand Hills State Park near KIRKSVILLE. The Chariton begins to flow south-southwest as it moves through Macon and

Grave of "Johnny Appleseed" Chapman.

Chariton counties where its mouth is located at the MISSOURI RIVER near New Frankfort. The Chariton River valley is one of the the most important waterfowl flyways in the central states.

CHARLES CITY, Iowa. City (pop. 8,778). Seat of Floyd County, situated in north-northeast Iowa on the CEDAR RIVER. The name has been variously attributed to Charles HART (1872-1937) and Charles PARR (1869-1941), who invented the tractor there about 1896; to Charles Kelly, son of the community founder, and perhaps more accurately to Charles FLOYD, for whom the county was named. Founded in 1852, it became an industrial city with the invention of the tractor there and the subsequent founding of the Hart-Parr company, with the first tractor being manufactured about 1901. The firm continues as a major manufacturer of farm implements. Charles City was the home of Carrie Chapman Catt (1859-1947), a well-known advocate of women's rights. The city was the birthplace (1861) of C.A. Fullerton nationally known for his pioneering efforts in developing school music training for rural school children. Twelve miles southeast is the famed "LITTLE BROWN CHURCH IN THE VALE". One of the largest events of its kind is the annual Cedar Valley Engine Club Thresher Reunion on Labor Day weekend

CHARLESTON, Illinois. City (pop. 19,355), seat of Coles Co., east central Illinois near

Illinois Highways 16 and 130; home of EASTERN ILLINOIS UNIVERSITY; named for Charles Morton, one of the founders. First settlers in Charleston arrived in 1826. Charleston became the county seat in 1831, a village in 1835 and a city in 1865. Manufactures include electronic equipment, farm buildings, shoes and tools. The city is a rail and trade center. The fourth of the LINCOLN-DOUGLAS DEBATES occurred near the eastern end of the present Coles County Fairgrounds on September 8, 1858. Before a crowd of 12,000 Abraham LINCOLN answered DOUGLAS' charge that he advocated interracial marriage. Lincoln forcibly made Orlando B. Ficklin, a Douglas supporter, admit during the debate that the charges that Lincoln voted against supplies for the army in Mexico were untrue. Near the western end of the fairgrounds is the grave of Dennis Hanks, who claimed to have taught Abraham Lincoln to read. During the CIVIL WAR Charleston was a center for the COPPERHEADS, advocates of a negotiated peace with the South. Lincoln's parents settled there. Lincoln Log Cabin State Historic Site features the reconstructed cabin of Thomas and Sarah Bush Lincoln. Both are buried in the nearby Shiloh Cemetery.

CHASE, William Merritt. (Williamsburg, Indiana, Nov. 1, 1849—Oct. 25, 1916). Artist. Indiana raised and educated in art, Chase specialized in portraits, landscapes, and was even better known for his still-life subjects, among which his fish are considered masterpieces. He was notable for his colorful bravura style of painting, developed between 1872 and 1878 in Munich, Germany, while studying with F. Wagner and Karl von Piloty. He is said to have taught more students than any other American artist, while continuing to produce so many of his own finished works in his "lightning" technique.

CHEESE. The Midwest is the nation's greatest producer of DAIRY PRODUCTS. Most of the Midwest states produce cheese in some quantity. However, Wisconsin is the leading producer of cheese in the U.S. Much of this leadership can be traced to William Hoard of Fort Atkinson, Wisconsin, who promoted the dairy industry in his *Hoard's Dairyman*, a weekly founded in 1885, which gained nationwide circulation and influence. Hoard later became governor of Wisconsin (1889-1891) and continued to promote the dairy industry. Hirum Smith was Wisconsin's first cheesemaker in 1859. Large-scale cheese making in the state

began with Chester Hazen's cheese factory at Ladoga, where it was established in 1864. A few small cheese-making plants continue to use the old-fashioned methods. However, modern Midwest dairies are models of state-of-the-art production. Steam heated stainless steel vats receive the milk which is "started" by the addition of rennet from the membrane of a calf's stomach. After the curds are formed, they are mechanically kneaded into the desired shape, then plunged into icy brine in the first curing process. Seven to eight months of curing are required for some variety of cheeses. The curing cheeses in their icy refrigeration are visited by the cheese scraper, whose sole function is to scrape away traces of green mold from the wheels or blocks of cheese. With Wisconsin far in the lead, the Midwest produces more than a fourth of all the nation's cheese, ranging well over a million pounds annually.

CHEQUAMEGON BAY. Said to be one of the two finest harbors on the GREAT LAKES, the bay extends from the southern shore of Lake SUPERIOR in far northern Wisconsin. Today at the southern end of the bay the city of ASHLAND derives advantage from that harbor. In the seventeenth century the mouth of the bay was closed by a sand spit, later removed.

CHICAGO PORTAGE NATIONAL HISTORIC SITE. Designated an historic site January 3, 1952, near River Forest, Illinois. A portion of the portage discovered by French explorers Jacques MARQUETTE and Louis JOLLIET is preserved here. Used by the pioneers as a link between the GREAT LAKES and the MISSISSIPPI, the portage and subsequent canal linkage were of great economic benefit to CHICAGO.

CHICAGO RIVER. Northeastern Illinois, the direction of flow of which was changed to accommodate a growing CHICAGO. MARQUETTE and JOLLIET established winter headquarters near the river in 1675. They recognized the potential of the river to form a portion of a water route to the MISSISSIPPI RIVER and the Gulf of Mexico. This prospect caused Nathaniel POPE, territorial secretary, acting governor, and member of the United State Congress as Territorial Representative in 1816, to offer an amendment placing the northern Illinois boundary in its present location. This kept Chicago and its river within the boundaries of Illinois. The first canal making the connection opened in 1848 after twelve years of construction. The ILLINOIS and DES PLAINES rivers were canalized and locks were used to lift barges into the Chicago River. When completed in 1900 the SANITARY AND SHIP CANAL, popularly known as the Drainage Canal, served three purposes: it entirely reversed the flow of the river, permitting the pollutants to flow out of and not into Lake MICHIGAN by making the southern branch of the Chicago River much deeper; it served as a link in the Great Lakes-Gulf Waterway and it provided hydroelectric power from a plant built at LOCKPORT, Illinois. For the first time, in 1957, after Chicago's heaviest rainfall of seven inches in twenty-four hours, the river locks at Lake Michigan were opened and the flow of the Chicago River into Lake Michigan resumed for a short time. The river continues as an important link in one of the world's main commerce routes.

CHICAGO ROAD. An important link in the early history of DETROIT, Michigan, and CHICAGO. Completed in 1835, the Chicago Road ran from Detroit through DEARBORN, Ypsilanti, Saline, Jonesville, Coldwater and NILES to Chicago. Now the route of US 12, the Chicago Road section within the city limits of DEARBORN and Detroit is called Michigan Avenue.

CHICAGO SYMPHONY ORCHESTRA
The Chicago Symphony Orchestra was founded, in 1891, by Theodore THOMAS. The orchestra began playing concerts in the Auditorium Theater, but Thomas considered the Auditorium, designed by Henry Louis SULLIVAN (1856-1924) and Dankmar Adler (1844-1900), to be too large for the symphony. He therefore solicited contributions from 8,500 wealthy Chicagoans to build a new home for the symphony. He moved the orchestra to Orchestra Hall in 1905. He lived long enough to conduct only three concerts there. Thomas was succeeded, in 1905, by Frederick STOCK (1872-1942) who directed the symphony for the next thirty-seven seasons. Stock brought the orchestra to international stature through his introduction of the classical music of many of the greatest composers of the first half of the 19th century. Sir Georg SOLTI, who became the musical director and conductor in 1969, was the first to take the orchestra abroad, greatly enhancing its international reputation. *Time* Magazine's evaluation of American symphonies regularly ranks the Chicago Symphony as the finest in the country, and many critics have called it the finest in the world.

CHICAGO, ILLINOIS

Name: Said to be from checagou, Indian for "strong and mighty," probably from the wild onion.

Nickname: The "I Will" City

Area: 200 plus square miles

Elevation: 597 feet

Population:
2,992,472 (1984)
Rank: Third
Percent change: Minus .3%
Density (city): 13,180 per sq. mi.
Metropolitan Population: 8,016,000 (1983)
Percent Change: .3%

Racial and Ethnic makeup:
White: 41%
Black: 39.8%
Hispanic: 14%
Other: 5.2%

Ages:
18 and under: 25%
65 and over: 11.4%

TV Stations: 9

Radio Stations: 31

Hospitals: 123

Sports Teams:
Cubs and Sox (baseball)
Bears (football)
Bulls (basketball)
Sting (soccer)

Further Information: Association of Commerce and Industry 200 N. La Salle, Chicago, IL 60601

CHICAGO, Illinois. Seat of Cook County, situated in northern Illinois near the lower end of Lake MICHIGAN, incorporated as a city in 1837. Chicago is the urban center of communities extending into northwestern Indiana and southern Wisconsin, with western expansion almost to the FOX RIVER Valley, particularly in Du Page County, one of the fastest growing counties in the United states.
Principal suburbs are EVANSTON, WILMETTE, Highland Park, Lake Forest and Waukegan on the north; Skokie, DES PLAINES, Morton Grove,

Chicago

Park Ridge and Arlington Heights on the northwest; Schaumburg, Wheaton, Glen Ellyn, Lombard, Elmhurst, Downers Grove and OAK PARK on the west; Chicago Heights, Harvey and Calumet City on the south, and HAMMOND and GARY in Indiana.

The principal attribute of the city is its extended shoreline on Lake Michigan, stretching along the eastern edge of the city from its southern to its northern extremities. Most of this extraordinary waterfront has been preserved for public use, making it unique among GREAT LAKES cities in this respect.

The CHICAGO RIVER also has been a principal factor in the city's development. One of the major engineering activities of the early 20th Century was the reversal of the Chicago River in 1900 to provide both a sanitary canal and an avenue for barge traffic. This project made a direct connection possible through the ILLINOIS and MISSISSIPPI rivers to the Gulf of Mexico. The resultant barge traffic has become important in the area's economy.

Chicago's major expansion began soon after the opening of the ERIE CANAL in New York in 1825. The city's location as head of water navigation of the entire lower Midwest was further expanded by the opening of the ST. LAWRENCE SEAWAY in 1959, making Chicago an ocean port for ship traffic to and from the Atlantic.

The central location made Chicago an early railroad hub, and the city still leads all others worldwide in volume of railroad traffic.

Of its three major airports, O'HARE INTERNATIONAL maintains its lead by transporting the most passengers of any airport in the nation. O'Hare is undergoing substantial expansion over a ten-year period and recently was connected to the downtown area (The Loop) by rapid transit in 1985. The city is also a hub of trucking and package delivery services.

The metropolitan Chicago area produces the greatest volume of manufactured goods of all major U.S. centers. The 14,000 plus factories of the area hold first or second rank in production of food products, electronic equipment, machinery, railroad equipment, packaging materials, housewares, candy and confections, cosmetics, athletic goods and others.

However, due to labor, high taxes and confused and indifferent city administration, much manufacturing is leaving the central city for other Illinois cities, or for other more attractive and more distant cities. Among the most obvious of these departures was the closing of the famed Chicago Stockyards and

the near extinction of the Chicago meat packing industry. This development obliterated the city's world leadership as a livestock market.

Chicago ranks third among U.S. cities in banking and finance and is headquarters for major insurance companies.

Chicago's site has been occupied since prehistoric times. First community known to history was the Indian village which grew up around the Mission of the Guardian Angel, established by Father Pierre Pinet in 1696, near the junction of the north and south branches of the Chicago River.

During French control for more than 100 years, followed by the British, no settlements were made on the site. After the American Revolution, in 1779, Jean Baptiste Point DU SABLE built a large squared log cabin on the north bank of the river, near the lake. He traded with the Indians and the white traders, who occasionally came into the area. Du Sable then sold this successful operation and departed in 1800.

The U.S. government acquired the region by treaty with the Indians and FORT DEARBORN was established (1803) on the river at the present location of Michigan Avenue bridge. A scattering of cabins was built nearby. During the WAR OF 1812, the fort was evacuated on an ill-considered order from higher authority. A short distance from the fort, about 100 soldiers and residents were massacred by the Indians. Only the KINZIE family escaped. Kinzie had taken over du Sable's operations in 1804, and he became the area leader.

Chicago continued to drowse until the Erie Canal began to bring volume traffic down the lake. In 1833, 20,000 visitors passed through the growing city. In 1838, actor Joseph Jefferson wrote, "The new town of Chicago has just turned from an Indian village into a thriving little place."

The low, muddy, sandy site made sanitary conditions difficult, so in the 1850s the by then substantial city was raised twelve feet in an extraordinary effort of engineering. Many former first floors became basements, due to the operation.

With the growth of farming in the Midwest, vast quantities of grain poured in to Chicago elevators and mills. In 1862 alone, 64,500,000 bushels were shipped in to them.

On October 8, 1871, conductor Theodore THOMAS was leading his symphony orchestra at the Crosby Opera House at about the same time that a fire (FIRE, CHICAGO) was starting to sweep the city. The resulting conflagration wiped out most of the city's business and much of its housing. But almost overnight the city began to build again, and debris from the fire was deposited on the lake shore to form Grant Park, one of the city's major recreational areas.

In 1889, Jane ADDAMS opened Hull House, and President Benjamin HARRISON dedicated the grand new Auditorium Theater. Other architectural history was being made with the world's first steel frame SKYSCRAPER, devised by architect William LeBaron JENNEY in 1885.

Chicago architecture was further enhanced by the extraordinary structures of the WORLD'S COLUMBIAN EXPOSITION of 1893, which also gave the world "The Midway" and the first wheel devised by George Washington Gale FERRIS. Architects Daniel Burnham, Frank Lloyd WRIGHT and Ludwig Mies Van Der Rohe have contributed toward making Chicago the "Architectural Capital of the World."

Notable events of the 20th Century included the Iroquois Theater fire in 1903, costing 575 lives and the 1915 Eastland steamer disaster, which took 812 lives.

In the 1930s, Samuel Insull lost his utility empire, but Chicago triumphed against the Great Depression with another world's fair, the 1933-1934 CENTURY OF PROGRESS, in which a number of future trends were correctly anticipated.

Chicago today has done much to overcome its image as a GANGSTER city, the home of AI CAPONE and the site of the St. Valentine's Day Massacre, but some of the old stigma remains, especially abroad.

During the 1980s, new construction placed Chicago in first or second rank among major U.S. cities. In the 1970s and 1980s, three of the nation's five tallest buildings have been constructed there, including SEARS TOWER, the world's tallest.

Chicago leads the country, and claims world leadership, in the number of conventions and the number of convention visitors each year. Mc Cormick Place, not content with being the largest facility of its kind anywhere, has nearly doubled its capacity with a new annex, completed in 1986. Hotel renovations, including the $150,000,000 reconstruction of the Hilton Hotel chain flagship on Michigan Avenue, and new hotel construction continue to keep up with convention and tourists demands.

State Street remains as a major merchandising center with the largest department stores, including giant Marshall Fields. However, North Michigan Avenue has become the

Chicago and the Chicago River.

Magnificent Mile, encompassing most of the nation's major retail chains, as well as a substantial number of specialty shops, many in such facilities as Water Tower Place, the first of the nation's major mixed-use skyscraper facilities.

A major weekly news publication has ranked the CHICAGO SYMPHONY as the finest in the United States, and it tours the world to nearly uniform acclaim. The Lyric Opera and forty-eight theaters operate within the city limits. *Places Rated Almanac* ranks Chicago second to New York in scope and quality of its cultural activities.

However, the same source rated Chicago 13th among major cities on the overall quality of its educational facilities. This is balanced by the quality of the leading institutions of higher education—University of CHICAGO, LOYOLA, DE PAUL, NORTHWESTERN and ROOSEVELT universities, among the 95 colleges and universities of the city and suburbs.

In health care and environment, Chicago is ranked second. Despite its reputation for crime, Chicago is not included in any of the ratings of the most crime ridden cities.

Chicago holds the record for the largest number of bascule bridges, crossing the main

Unique State of Illinois Building, Chicago.

branch and two side branches of the Chicago River. The main public works program of the era has been the excavation of the deep tunnel water storage system, to eliminate city flooding. Another major government project, completed in 1985, is the State of Illinois Building, one of the most unusual and controversial structures of the day.

Chicago has six major museums and fifteen specialized museums, along with 14 in the suburbs. The FIELD MUSEUM is known for originating the idea of the DIORAMA and has one of the world's largest and best displayed natural history collections. The MUSEUM OF SCIENCE AND INDUSTRY holds the attendance record for museums worldwide and was a pioneer in its specialty.

The ART INSTITUTE OF CHICAGO is generally regarded as being of world rank and operates one of the largest schools of art. The SHEDD AQUARIUM has the world's greatest tank capacity for indoor displays, and new construction in the late 1880s nearly doubled its size. The Chicago Historical Society has one of the country's largest collections of local historical materials. The Oriental Institute of the University of Chicago offers one of the major collections of the ancient civilizations of the Middle East.

Lincoln Park Zoo generates the country's largest zoo attendance, and BROOKFIELD ZOO in the suburbs claims to have been the first to display animals in their natural habitat.

Chicago is one of the two major cities with two major league baseball teams, the Cubs and the Sox. Chicago's National Football League Bears were Super Bowl champions in 1986. The basketball Bulls, the hockey Black Hawks and soccer Sting complete the city's roster of major league sports teams.

The Chicago Temple, a Methodist congregation, claims the world's highest church spire, 570 feet.

Chicago has been ranked among the world's top ten cities for outdoor sculpture. The statue by Picasso, supposedly of a woman, which stands in the City Hall plaza, has become a symbol of Chicago. Other outdoor statuary includes Calder's Flamingo, Chagall's half block-long mosaic, Miro's Chicago, the Batcolumn of Oldenburg, the Sounding Sculpture of Bertoia and many portrait sculptures by other famous sculptors.

A magnet of the Near North side is the Old WATER TOWER, left standing after the great fire.

Visitors generally comment on the dynamic quality of Chicago life, and this is usually considered to be the key to that city's growth and prosperity, along with the determination of the city that insists, "I Will!"

CHICAGO, UNIVERSITY of. Chicago, Illinois, famous for its experiments to improve higher education in the United States and as the birthplace of nuclear energy. The University of Chicago opened for classes on October 1, 1892. Unlike many similar institutions, it began as a full university with facilities for undergraduate and graduate study. The year it opened, the university became the first to establish a department of sociology. Two of its professors, Albion Small and George Vincent, wrote the first sociology textbook, in 1894. Many other internationally recognized experts have served on the faculty. Enrico FERMI (1901-1954) led the team of scientists who at the university conducted the first atomic research near the end of WORLD WAR II. The university has established the Enrico Fermi Institute for research in high energy physics. Among the leading economists who have taught at the university are Thorstein VEBLEN (1857-1929) and Noble Prize winning economist, Milton Friedman. The university laboratory schools in education were established by John Dewey (1859-1952) in 1896. The university operates the ARGONNE NATIONAL LABORATORY for the United States Department of Energy and the YERKES OBSERVATORY in Wisconsin. The University of Chicago continues in the image held for it by its first president, William Rainey Harper (1856-1906), who designed it to be a model university. In 1892 he established the first correspondence course in the nation and the University of Chicago Press, now one of the largest academic publishers. The most noted head of the university was Robert Maynard HUTCHINS (1899-1977), who inaugurated completely revised theories of undergraduate education. The university's school of law has been rated number five of the top ten and its medical school number six of the top eleven. In 1985-1986 the University of Chicago enrolled 9,456 students and had 1,121 faculty members.

"CHIEF WHO NEVER SLEEPS". Name given by the Indians to General Anthony WAYNE.

CHILLICOTHE, Ohio. City (pop. 23,420), seat of Ross County, once the capital of Ohio, situated on the SCIOTO RIVER in the south central part of the state, at the junction of U.S. highways 50, 23, 35 and 36. Incorporated in 1802, its name is possibly derived from the SHAWNEE word meaning village. The city lies in the bent elbow of the extensive river valley, about 45 miles south of the capital of COLUMBUS. Above the valley lies Mt. Logan, engraved on the minds of most Ohioans as the mountain symbol on the state seal.

The city is the trading center for an agricultural area specializing in growing HOGS and raising CATTLE and CORN. Manufactures include aluminum cooking utensils, floor tiles, shoes and large paper mills.

Boat construction for the trade from Chillicothe to New Orleans began to flourish as early as the 1820s. Boats at the yards at the foot of Mulberry Street were loaded with turkeys and pork, grain and other products. Boatmen who finished the hazardous trip usually sold the flatboats for the good Ohio timber and then walked back to Chillicothe. The first paper mill there was established as early as 1812 and PAPER MAKING has continued to be the pride of the city. A steam operated flour mill was grinding flour as early as 1815. The railroad arrived in 1852. At one time the city was one of the busiest and most prosperous in the Midwest, with an extremely wide variety of factory products.

Although Chillicothe had a slight population decline from 1970 to 1980, the varied industrial

and agricultural activities prevented the severe population loss suffered by most Midwest industrial centers during that period.

Nathaniel Massie attempted to colonize the area in 1795 but was driven out by the Shawnee. Beginning in 1798 with Edward TIFFIN and followed by other young men from Virginia, in only five years Chillicothe had become the aristocratic settlement chosen as the capital of the NORTHWEST TERRITORY. Fine houses were built of the local sandstone and patterned after the mansions of Virginia. Most prominent of all was the mansion of Thomas WORTHINGTON (1773-1827), ADENA, planned by Benjamin Latrobe (1764-1820), America's first professional architect, and later architect of the city of Washington.

After 1800, political intrigue was rampant. General Arthur ST. CLAIR, territorial governor, opposed Ohio statehood, which would have removed him from his long-time office. His opponents even threatened him in his home, but Edward Tiffin, his rival, protected the aged governor. When Ohio achieved statehood in 1803, Chillicothe was the capital and Tiffin the governor. However, in 1810, the capital was moved to ZANESVILLE.

During the CIVIL WAR, one moment of excitement came to the city when it was said that Southern raider John Hunt MORGAN (1825-1864) was approaching. Guards at the covered bridge burned it down when they mistook a local search party for Morgan and his men. The foot of water in Paint Creek would hardly have stopped the foolhardy Morgan, but he never appeared.

WORLD WAR I saw the establishment of Camp Sherman, with servicemen often outnumbering the local population three to one. The camp later became a veterans' hospital.

Just outside the city is MOUND CITY GROUP NATIONAL MONUMENT, attracting visitors to the prehistoric remains of ancient peoples. ADENA STATE MEMORIAL preserves the estate of Thomas Worthington, and Ross County Historical Society Museum exhibits pioneer crafts and rifle making. Some of the splendid homes of the early days may still be seen.

The city is the site of a branch of OHIO UNIVERSITY.

CHIPPEWA INDIANS. Tribe, also known as the Objibway, belonging to the ALGONQUIN group that lived around the shores of Lakes HURON and SUPERIOR. A powerful tribe able to hold their land against the IROQUOIS and SIOUX, the Chippewa lived on fish, wild rice, CORN, squash and sugar. Their homes were birch-covered wig-wams. The Chippewa sided with the French in the FRENCH AND INDIAN WAR and joined PONTIAC in the rebellion of 1763. The Chippewa were allies of the British in the WAR OF 1812 and by the Treaty of 1816 ceded all their lands in Ohio. By 1851 the Chippewa, forced to cede the remaining lands east of the Mississippi, were moved west into Indian territory.

CHIROPRACTIC MEDICINE. The modern practice of Chiropractic medicine was developed in the Midwest at DAVENPORT, Iowa, first by D.D. Palmer beginning in 1895, followed by his son B.J. and grandson David. B.J. PALMER had studied European techniques of body manipulation, concentrated mainly on the spine. He told the story of his first patient who had stooped over and heard "something snap" in his neck, followed by severe pain and loss of hearing. On the third day of spinal manipulation by Palmer, the man suddenly cried out, "I can hear, Doc.; I can hear!" The basic tenet of chiropractic is that many problems, some seemingly unrelated, are caused by displaced vertebrae (sublaxation), and that these can be helped by application of various types of pressure to the spine (called adjustment) and further improvement made by massage and treatment by various methods of heat and light. At first not acknowledged by more traditional medical authorities, chiropractic now has legal recognition in the U.S. and other parts of the world, and various aspects of the profession are gaining increased support in the health field. The chiropractors' national association is located in DES MOINES. The PALMER COLLEGE OF CHIROPRACTIC at Davenport, a leader in the field of education for the profession, has graduated more than half of all chiropractic practioners in the country.

CHISHOLM, Minnesota. City (pop. 5,930), northeastern Minnesota, northeast of GRAND RAPIDS and HIBBING, self-proclaimed geographical center of Minnesota. The town, located in the iron ore-rich MESABI RANGE, was platted in 1901 by A.M. Chisholm and a group of explorers and businessmen organized as the Chisholm Improvement Company. Within six years the population had grown to nearly 6,000. The town had a city hall, two banks, an electric-lighting plant, sewers and two weekly NEWSPAPERS. On September 5, 1908, a brush fire swept through the town, destroying almost every structure but killing no one. Rebuilding started immediately

and within a year seventy fireproof brick buildings, a municipal water plant and five miles of mains had been constructed. Chisholm became a city in 1934. The area around Chisholm has supported forty-five mines. The largest is the Godfrey. The Shenango, with a maximum depth of four hundred feet, is the deepest open-pit iron mine in the world. While mining is the principal industry in the region, dairying is also important. Iron Range Interpretive Center, on the edge of Glen open pit mine, offers audiovisual displays of the ethnic and cultural history of the region and exhibits showing the development of the local iron and taconite mining industries. The Minnesota Museum of Mining houses indoor and outdoor exhibits of mining equipment.

CHOLERA EPIDEMICS. Cholera, a disease caused mainly by poor sanitary conditions, is less than 3% fatal today, but in earlier times it brought on fatality rates as high as 90% and was one of the most dreaded of the epidemics. DETROIT suffered one of the country's most severe cholera epidemics in 1832 when a steamer brought soldiers to the port, and before it was discovered that some of them were infected, the disease had spread on shore. Many died, and the doctors were not able to handle the case load. The disease had almost run its course when Father Gabriel RICHARD (1767-1832), one of Detroit's most notable citizens, became infected, and he died on September 13, 1832. His funeral was attended by more than two thousand people, more than the whole population of Detroit at that time. Another Midwest city, ST. LOUIS, suffered a severe epidemic of cholera in 1849; at the same time a fire destroyed fifteen blocks in the heart of the city. Other areas of the Midwest suffered in varying degrees at different times from influxes of cholera. However, throughout the country, the Indians probably suffered the most from cholera, as they did from other diseases imported from Europe, because of their lack of immunity to them. Indian deaths from cholera were uncounted, but they totalled many thousands.

CHOPIN, Kate O'Flaherty. (St. Louis, Mo., Feb. 8, 1851—St. Loius, Mo., Aug. 22, 1904). Author. Of Irish-Creole descent, she married a Louisiana businessman in 1870 and moved to New Orleans. She returned to ST. LOUIS in 1883 after his death and began to write, drawing largely on the life of the bayou which she had experienced in the South. She was considered a representative of the "local color" school of writing of the late Nineteenth Century. The publication of *The Awakening* (1899) was controversial because her use of sensual prose offended the Victorian morality of the time. Her *Bayou Folk* (1894), was also of the same controversial nature.

CHOUTEAU, Pierre. (St. Louis, MO, Jan. 19,1789—St. Louis, MO, Sept. 6, 1865). Frontiersman, businessman. Son of Jean Pierre Chouteau, he began work with the St. Louis Missouri Fur Company in 1809. He became John Jacob ASTOR's western representative and bought out the Astor interests in 1834. He operated the *Yellowstone*, the first steamer on the upper Missouri, and on its second voyage, in 1832, he was a passenger to Fort Pierre, when Pierre, now South Dakota's capital, was organized and named in his honor. He expanded his business empire to iron mining in Missouri, railroading in Illinois and other ventures. For a period he made New York City the headquarters of his operation. One of the wealthiest men of his time, he was known for his generosity to scientific expeditions, artists and missionaries who were interested in the MISSOURI RIVER region. He was especially helpful to the region's Indians.

CHOUTEAU, Pierre Auguste. (St. Louis, MO., May 9, 1786—Fort Gibson, MO., Dec. 25, 1838). Fur trader, son of Rene Auguste CHOUTEAU. An 1806 graduate of the U.S. Military Academy at West Point, N.Y., he served as an aide to General James Wilkinson, governor of Louisiana in 1807, but resigned his army post in that year and two years later became a member of his family's St. Louis Missouri Fur Company. In 1817 he was captured by the Spanish while on a trading expedition to the upper Arkansas River but was released. He later settled in Oklahoma where he traded with the OSAGE INDIANS. Washington Irving was a member of one of Chouteau's expeditions, which is described in Irving's *Tour of the Prairies* (1835).

CHOUTEAU, Rene Auguste (New Orleans, LA, Sept. 7, 1749—St. Louis, MO., Feb. 24, 1829). American frontiersman, merchant. At age 14, he accompanied French merchant Pierre LACLEDE on an expedition authorized by the French government of Louisiana to trade west of the MISSISSIPPI RIVER. In 1764 they established a post that would later become the city of ST. LOUIS. The two men founded a major

fur trading business, which Chouteau assumed with his brother Jean Pierre Chouteau, after Laclede's death. After St. Louis became part of the U.S., he was named in 1804 as a court of common pleas justice in the territory and became president of the first board of trustees of St. Louis in 1809. He also represented the U.S. government in the negotiation of Indian treaties. Chouteau held many other positions of importance and was the most influential person in St. Louis and the Missouri Valley area. However, his greatest contribution to the region was in the financing of much of the expansion of St. Louis and the valley.

CHRISTIANSEN, F. Mellius. (Eidsvold, Norway, Apr. 1, 1871—Northfield, MN, June 1, 1955). Music director. Christiansen was the Director of Music at ST. OLAF COLLEGE in NORTHFIELD, Minnesota, from 1903 to 1943. He was the founder and director of the St. Olaf Lutheran Choir. Christiansen composed a variety of music, including the *St. Olaf Choir Series* (8 volumes). He came to the United States in 1889 and later received the Knight Order of St. Olaf, Class I from the King of Norway and honorary doctorates from OBERLIN COLLEGE, Muhlenberg College and the University of MINNESOTA.

CHURCHILL, Winston. (St. Louis, MO., 1871—1947), Novelist. Although almost entirely contemporary with his famous British namesake, the wartime prime minister, the Missouri Churchill had little in common with the noted leader, except the names and the ability to be best-selling authors. The Missouri Churchill has been called one of the most widely read of his day. He graduated from the naval academy at Annapolis in 1894, but went into a career of writing, which produced such novels as *Richard Carvel* (1899), *The Crisis* (1901) and *The Crossing* (1904). His later works reflected his interests in political, religious and social problems.

CINCINNATI, OHIO

Name: From the "Society of the Cincinnati" which took its name from Cincinnatus the farmer-soldier and official of the Roman Empire.

Nickname: Queen City

Area: 78.1 square miles.

Elevation: 550 feet

Cincinnati

Population:
1984: 370,481

Rank: 38th

Percent change (1980-1984): minus 3.9%

Density (city): 4,491 per sq. mi.

Metropolitan Population: 1,674,000

Percent change (1980-1984): .84%

Racial and Ethnic makeup (1980):
White: 65.2%

Black: 33.9%

Hispanic origin: 3,263 persons

Indian: 567 persons

Asian: 2,332 persons

Other: 736 persons

Age:
18 and under: 25.2%

65 and over: 14.5%

TV Stations: 8

Radio Stations: 25

Hospitals: 30

Sports Teams:
Reds (baseball)

Bengals (football)

Further Information: Cincinnati Chamber of Commerce, 120 West 5th Street, Cincinnati, OH 45202

CINCINNATI, Ohio. City, Seat of Hamilton County, on the OHIO RIVER, at the mouth of the MIAMI RIVER in extreme southwest Ohio, opposite Covington, Kentucky, founded by leading Revolutionary officers at the end of the war. Its name was given to it by Governor Arthur ST. CLAIR of the NORTHWEST TERRITORY in honor of a group known as the Society of Cincinnati, from Cincinnatus, the farmer-general of Rome. The city occupies a land area of 78 square miles. It was incorporated as a city in 1819.

Cincinnati is the center of a large urban area of Ohio, including the suburbs of Norwood and Springdale. Covington, Kentucky, and its suburbs are included in the official metropolitan region.

The city owed its early commercial success to its location on the river, down which poured an ever-increasing flood of settlers and merchandise, at first on FLATBOATS, then on paddle wheel steamers and finally an even greater commerce was carried on barges powered by sturdy tugs.

Almost equally strategic for commerce was the city's location nearly midway between the business centers of North and South.

Today the city is the country's leader in soap and cleaning products, with the two giant companies of the industry located there. In the important field of machine tools, the city has held an imposing lead. Glass making of all kinds has been a leading industry since the first choice Bohemian glass was made there in 1800. Fine, rare colored and milk glass is produced. The city is the leading center of playing card production. Radar equipment, airplane engines, truck bodies, electrical machinery, cosmetics and metal goods also are important products.

In 1788 a small group of settlers, led by Benjamin STITES who had previously explored the land, floated down the Ohio on flatboats, and founded a settlement called Losantiville which grew around FORT WASHINGTON. When the community was chosen as capital of the vast Northwest Territory, the first governor, General Arthur St. Clair changed the name.

As many as 10,000 settlers a year floated down the Ohio, large numbers of them choosing Cincinnati because of its favored location. The coming of the first STEAMBOAT in 1811 vastly increased the city's river income. It became, and has remained, one of the great river ports.

Because of its proximity to the south, Cincinnati was one of the principal stations on the UNDERGROUND RAILROAD, guiding slaves to safety in Canada. After the war, to regain its commerce with the south, the city began to build a railroad, the only U.S. community to undertake such a project. The railroad was completed in 1880. A trend toward poor law enforcement and corrupt politics culminated in the Cincinnati Riot of March, 1884, followed by the rise to power of political boss G. B. Cox, who exercised firm control over the city. Also in 1884 the Ohio River overflowed in one of its worst FLOODS.

To honor its hundredth birthday, Cincinnati celebrated with a Centennial Exposition in 1888. The three-block-long main building was built over a canal, and Italian gondolas provided indoor transportation.

A reform movement in 1924 resulted in a switch to the city manager form of government. The 1937 Ohio River flood was the worst in the city's history, but a series of flood control measures has lestened the flood danger.

Despite its commercial diversity, the city has suffered a substantial loss in population in recent years. In the period 1970 through 1984, population figures plummeted from 450,000 to

River Front Stadium and the Ohio River, Cincinnati.

370,000, making it now 38th among the major U.S. metropolitan centers. The 1980 census figures showed a black population of 33.8 percent and less than one percent of Hispanic background.

As a center of German immigration, and a mecca for other educated European and eastern immigrants, the city's educational and cultural achievements made it known as the Queen City of the West, a reputation it still holds, though no longer of the "West."

For many years the city's music conservatory produced some of America's finest symphonic talent. The Cincinnati Symphony was one of the earliest outside the East. The city is home to the University of CINCINNATI, XAVIER UNIVERSITY, Edgecliff College and a number of other educational institutions.

The Taft Museum is one of the Cincinnati landmarks of the first family of Cincinnati, the Taft dynasty, founded by President and Chief Justice of the United States, William Howard TAFT (1857-1930), and carried on by his son Senator Robert TAFT (1889-1953) and other members of the family.

Eden Park is a notable center, affording the Cincinnati Art Museum, a natural history museum and zoo.

Cincinnati was home to the world's first professional baseball team, the Cincinnati Red Stockings, who won every game of their first season, 1866. The Cincinnati Reds have produced notable baseball record holders, including Cy YOUNG (1867-1955), winningest of all pitchers and Johnny VANDER MEER (1914—), the only pitcher to achieve two no-hit games in succession. The Bengals represent Cincinnati in the American Football Conference.

CINCINNATI, University of. The institution was founded in 1819 as a municipal college, incorporated in 1870 as a municipal university and affiliated with the state university system in 1968. The local College-Conservatory of Music merged with the university in 1962. Affiliated with the university are Hebrew Union College-Jewish Institute of Religion and the Art Academy of Cincinnati. The university was a notable pioneer in cooperative education, starting in 1906, and has an exceptional science program, known especially for its archaeological expeditions. Within its many colleges, the university grants associate, baccalaureate, master, doctoral and specialist degrees. The student body totals 34,666, a faculty of 3,186.

CIRCLEVILLE, Ohio. City, (pop. 11,700), seat of Pickaway County, situated in south central Ohio, on the SCIOTO RIVER, halfway between COLUMBUS and CHILLICOTHE. Incorporated in 1853, the city takes its name from the circular prehistoric earthwork within which it was first built. The city lies at the junction of U.S. highways 22 and 23 and has a stable population of 11,700. This community of unique name and situation was laid out inside the round enclosure made by early peoples who surrounded the enclosure with two walls about 20 feet high, with a deep ditch between them, entered by a single gate. There was also a square enclosure with eight entrances. Each entrance had been defended by a circular mound or platform. Circleville was first settled in 1810, with a round public "square" in the center, from which ran four streets like the spokes of a wheel, extending to the original circular ditch. The ditch existed as late as 1820 and had an average depth of 15 feet. Two streets formed complete circles around the town.

From the beginning the community had been the seat of Pickaway county, a misspelling of the name of the Piqua, a group of SHAWNEE who lived in the region known as Pickaway Plains. The coming of the OHIO AND ERIE CANAL gave the city impetus as an agricultural center, shipping millions of pounds of pork and bacon, lard, CORN, broom corn and wheat.

In 1840 the citizens tired of their "circular" life and "squared" the circle, providing for a more usual street plan at right angles. With pumpkins boasted to be as large as kitchen tables, Circleville inaugurated its extremely popular annual Circleville Pumpkin Show, a fall festival that exhibits the largest pumpkins and best corn and other produce of the region.

CIRCUS WORLD MUSEUM. This unique museum at BARABOO, Wisconsin, helps to recall the days when Wisconsin was center of the circus world, with over 100 circuses headquartered in the state. As boys at Baraboo, the RINGLING BROTHERS began their circus activities in 1882, and as their enterprise grew into the world's largest circus, they established their winter headquarters at Baraboo. Today, the museum spreads over six buildings of that headquarters. There are "big top" circus acts, menagerie, animal acts, daily circus parade, historic circus wagons and caliope and many other reminders of the glory days of circuses.

CITIES, MAJOR. Of the one-hundred largest cities in the United States, eighteen are found in the Midwest, according to 1984 census figures. Ohio has the greatest number of the largest cities, with six. Illinois and Iowa only have one each, and all the other Midwest states boast only of two each. However, Illinois has produced the largest city in the Midwest. CHICAGO, for almost a century was the nation's second city behind New York, but dropped to third rank behind both New York and Los Angeles. Ohio's major six and their rankings are: COLUMBUS, 21; CLEVELAND, 23; CINCINNATI, 38; TOLEDO, 45; AKRON, 74, and DAYTON 82. In Minnesota MINNEAPOLIS is ranked 42, and ST. PAUL 58. Missouri places with KANSAS CITY 29 and ST. LOUIS 30. Wisconsin leaders are MILWAUKEE 18, and MADISON 90. In Indiana INDIANAPOLIS is in 14th place and FORT WAYNE 93rd. Michigan places DETROIT at 6 and GRAND RAPIDS at 80. Iowa's only entry is DES MOINES, ranked 77th. The Urban Institute of Washington, D.C., lists Minneapolis, Minnesota, as the best place in which to live in all of the United States. However, another ranking source, *Places Rated Almanac* of Rand McNally, does not list Minneapolis in any top ranking. Among all metropolitan areas of a million or more population, it rates only four Midwest metropolitan areas among the top twenty: St. Louis, Missouri, 6th; Cincinnati, Ohio, 13th; Chicago, Illinois, 15th, and Cleveland, Ohio, 19th. *Places Rated Almanac* does not list any Midwest metropolitan areas in the top twenty metro areas with a population range of 250,000 to 1,000,000. Among America's twenty best small metro areas, population less than 250,000, the same source lists SOUTH BEND - MISHAWAKA, Indiana, 9th; SPRINGFIELD, Illinois, 13th, and LA CROSSE, Wisconsin, 20th.

CIVIL WAR IN THE MIDWEST. The roots of this conflict form such a complex combination of economic, political, social and psychological factors that historians continue to disagree widely on its causes.

The sectional differences between North and South had continued to grow over the years, particularly after the MISSOURI COMPROMISE of 1820-1821. The North forged ahead in industry, while the South remained agriculturally oriented, seemingly inextricably dependent on black SLAVERY. Almost every political action taken appeared inevitably to favor one side or the other and to drive a deepening wedge between them. The injustice of slavery resulted in the growing moral influence and anti-slavery activity of the Abolitionists, while Harriet Beecher STOWE's *Uncle Tom's Cabin* stirred the

North to an even greater anti-slavery pitch.

By the year 1861, it appeared to both sides that the situation had reached a point where it could not be resolved without physical action, as some historians still contend, "an irrepressible conflict." However, others believe that the war was "criminally stupid, brought on by arrogant extremists and blundering politicians." Whatever the viewpoint as to cause and justification, the result was the most costly conflict in the country's history, particularly in the dreadful loss of life, exceeding even that of WORLD WAR II.

As the southern states seceded, and although war seemed inevitable, neither side was prepared for actual fighting when the first shot of the war was fired on Fort Sumter in Charleston, South Carolina, harbor on April 12, 1861.

During the conflict that followed, the Midwest was in a generally favorable position. With the exception of Missouri, the major battles were fought elsewhere. Except for the southern portions of the border states and portions of Missouri, the Midwest almost universally favored the Union, and the people and energies of the region could be turned quickly toward winning the war.

In the opinion of many authorities, the greatest contribution of the Midwest to the Civil War was found in the two men who led the North to victory, Abraham LINCOLN and Ulysses S. GRANT. Lincoln, who never lived to see his ultimate triumph, was not born in the Midwest, but Illinois claims him as its own. His leadership in the conflict has been the source of innumerable books and ever-continuing analysis.

Grant was a native of POINT PLEASANT, Ohio, and was living there when he went to West Point. He was a resident of GALENA, Illinois, when he rejoined the army in the Civil War. To many, Grant is the first "modern" general because he was the first to devise and fight a "total war."

The general absence of battle in the Midwest assured that most of the resources of the region were available to the war effort. Midwesterners were among the most vociferous proponents of the war and generally provided men and supplies in a share disproportionate to their population.

Untouched for the most part by any destruction, the factories of the Midwest turned toward supplying the needs of war, and the broad expansion of manufacturing in the region not only helped the wartime cause but also contributed greatly to the later growth of the region. Even more important was the region's contribution in AGRICULTURE. From the world's greatest breadbasket, poured the food and fiber required to sustain the Union in the conflict.

While these contributions continued across the region as a whole, the various states of the Midwest were affected by the war in their individual ways.

Some of the Midwest states were the scene of actual battles and forays. All contributed fully equipped and armed units to army and navy service, and many of these took part in key battles of the war. Many of the notable military personalities of the war came from the Midwest. Although most of those in service from the Midwest fought for the northern cause, each of the states counted men and women who fought on the Confederate side. Governors and officials and the majority of civilians of all the Midwest states also made varying but significant contributions to the war. Of these, many Missourians were among the most important.

The only major Midwest battles of the war were fought in Missouri, which also suffered the most from Confederate raids. The loyalty of Missouri was vital to both sides in the Civil War. Governor Hancock Jackson favored the Confederacy, but Francis P. BLAIR and Captain Nathaniel Lyon were for the Union. When the governor refused Lincoln's call for troops, Blair offered his private militia, and Lyon armed them from the ST. LOUIS Arsenal, which he had captured. In the first battles in Missouri, Lyon defeated southern forces which had concentrated near BOONEVILLE and then captured JEFFERSON CITY, the capital.

Union forces then were beaten in the Battle of WILSON'S CREEK on August 10, 1861, near SPRINGFIELD, and General Lyon was killed there. The winner of that battle, General Sterling Price, became the principal Confederate figure in Missouri. Union forces surrendered at LEXINGTON, and deposed governor Jackson assembled another government at NEOSHO, after which Missouri was admitted as the twelfth Confederate State.

Union troops held St. Louis, but Confederates kept most of the rest of Missouri until the spring of 1862, when Union forces drove them below the southern border. Outnumbered Union troops defeated the Confederates in the Battle of Pea Ridge in Arkansas (March 6-7, 1862), and Missouri was saved for the North for the time. However, the attacks of Confederate raiders were probably more frequent and more devastating there than in any other state.

Civil War

In late 1864, General Price once more invaded Missouri. Union forces held them off at PILOT KNOB until forces of the North were mobilized at St. Louis and kept that city from attack. Battles at GLASGOW and Lexington preceded the clash of amost 30,000 troops at WESTPORT on October 23, 1864. The Battle of WESTPORT has been called the Gettysburg of the West because of its bloody losses and the fact that it saved the North from further penetration by the Confederates.

In all, 1,100 battles and skirmishes had taken place in the state.

A total of 149,000 Missourians participated in the war—109,000 in northern armies and 40,000 in Confederate service.

In addition to Missouri, two OHIO RIVER border states, Ohio and Indiana, were the only Midwest states to experience actual attack during the Civil War. In 1862, Confederate General Albert Jenkins swept into Ohio with a small group of men, but did little damage. In 1863 at least forty-nine Ohio towns suffered moderately from the attacks of Confederate raider John Hunt MORGAN.

In July, 1863, Morgan invaded Indiana with 3,000 cavalrymen, temporarily took Paoli and Greenville. At CORYDON, 400 volunteers held off the raiders in the only actual Civil War battle in Indiana.

The regiments and other military units of the Midwest states made notable contributions on the fighting front. Illinois troops played an important part in the plan of Illinois' own U.S. Grant's successful campaign to capture the entire MISSISSIPPI RIVER and cut the Confederacy in two. One of the most daring of the military actions of the war was "Grierson's Raid," when General Benjamin H. Grierson led his Illinois cavalry entirely through the Confederate lines from Tennessee to a meeting with federal troops in distant Baton Rouge, Louisiana (April-May,1863).

Michigan's Cavalry Brigade, led by General George Armstrong CUSTER, played a key part in the Confederate loss at Gettysburg (July 1-3, 1863). Michigan engineers saved the day for Union troops besieged at Chattanooga, Tennessee, by building a pontoon bridge over the Tennessee River, over which supplies could be sent (November, 1863). The eleventh Michigan Infantry Brigade performed one of the most spectacular charges of the war in the Battle of Missionary Ridge, near Chattanooga (November 25, 1863). The fourth Michigan Cavalry captured Confederate President Jefferson DAVIS (May 10, 1865) at the end of the Civil War.

Sherman Marches through Georgia, painting by A. B. Carlin.

Michigan sent 92,000 into wartime service, and 10,000 died.

The Wisconsin "EAGLE" REGIMENT was known not only for its bravery but for possessing perhaps the most celebrated mascot of the war, OLD ABE, their proud and noble bird. Of a population of only 775,881, Wisconsin sent 91,379 troops into service.

One Iowa Civil War regiment is probably unique in military annals. It was made up of men over the legal age of forty-five, most over fifty and several over seventy. Because so many overage men wanted to join up, Governor Samuel J. KIRKWOOD of Iowa received special permission from the war department to create such a group, called the GREYBEARD REGIMENT. The 1,300 men of the regiment were not expected to fight, but the Greybeards escorted trains, guarded railroads and prisoners and performed other necessary duties.

Iowa troops played important roles in the battles of Wilson's Creek (August 10, 1861), IUKA (September 19, 1862), Shiloh (April 6-7, 1862), Corinth, the siege of Vicksburg, ending in July, 1863, and Sherman's March to the Sea (November, 1864). About 80,000 Iowans took part in the war, and more than 12,000 died.

The newborn state of Minnesota was the first to respond when Lincoln called for troops at the start of the war. In the first Battle of Bull run (July 21, 1861), the First Minnesota Regiment had more losses than any other northern regiment and drew high praise from the war department. In a suicidal charge at the Battle of Gettysburg, Minnesota's First Regiment is credited by many war historians with saving that crucial battle for the North. Only 50 men of the 262 who made the charge escaped injury or death. With the smallest population of any of the states, Minnesota contributed over 22,000 troops to Union service.

The war affected Minnesota in a unique way. With so many men away on army duty, the Indians saw an opportunity to regain their lost lands and went on the warpath. The forces of Chief LITTLE CROW were finally decisively defeated by H.H. SIBLEY's troops, who took 2,200 Indian prisoners and released 269 white captives (September 23, 1862).

About 435,000 Ohioans served in the Union army, and six Ohioans received the first CONGRESSIONAL MEDAL OF HONOR, for heroic service during the war. A total of 208,367 from Indiana saw service, and 24,416 lost their lives.

Of the thousands of individual military leaders and heroes of the war, some of the most notable were in service from the Midwest.

One of the earliest casualties of the war occurred shortly after war had been declared in April, 1861. Colonel Elmer E. ELLSWORTH, who had been on Abraham LINCOLN's law staff in SPRINGFIELD, Illinois, was killed on May 14, while heroically trying to haul down a rebel flag flying from an Alexandria, Virginia, hotel. His loss was a great personal blow to the president.

Another Illinois man took an important role early in the fighting. Captain James H. Stokes of CHICAGO, Illinois, went south to St. Louis to try and seize armament from the Armory there. Holding off a howling mob trying to keep the arms from going to Union troops, he and a few recruits removed 10,000 muskets and ammunition to a steamboat, which reached ALTON, Illinois, safely, and women and children helped unload it for Illinois soldiers.

Among other individual heroes of the war were the three Cushing brothers of Wisconsin. William B. CUSHING went from one daring accomplishment to another, including one of the first uses of the torpedo in naval warfare (October, 1864). Another Wisconsin man, Lieutenant Colonel Joseph BAILEY, saved the entire Union Mississippi River fleet by freeing its trapped ships from low water on the Red River.

A Michigan boy, Charles Howard Gardner, entered Civil War service at the age of twelve in order to keep from being separated from his teacher.

Many Midwest state officials, as well as countless civilians, made noteworthy contributions to the war effort.

Among these, perhaps the most notable of all was from the Midwest, Indiana's Governor Oliver P. MORTON. He has been called the nation's strongest Civil War governor. In a move unique in history, the governor supported part of the war effort from funds he had personally borrowed. He is sometimes known as the "Assistant President of the U.S."

Another notable governor was Iowa's Samuel J. Kirkwood, who outfitted the entire First Iowa Regiment at his own expense.

Wisconsin was better prepared for war than most of the other states, thanks to the foresight of Governor Alexander Randall. His successor, Governor Louis P. HARVEY was known as the soldiers' friend. Reports of heavy Wisconsin war casualties led Harvey to call for donations of medical supplies from Wisconsin's people. He set out to take the supplies personally to the front. In attempting to cross from one Tennessee River steamboat to another, he fell into the swift currents of the river, and his body was never recovered.

Many Midwest women took an active part in the war, with hundreds serving as nurses and other hundreds disguising themselves as men and serving bravely in the front lines. Even more daring were those who volunteered as couriers or as spies behind the enemy lines. Countless thousands of women performed such tasks as sewing and preparing bandages and other supplies. Iowa women donated their service to make the uniforms of the First Iowa Regiment, and there were similar devoted home services throughout the region.

Two Midwest women made unique contributions, which in some ways altered traditional warfare.

Cordelia HARVEY, wife of Wisconsin Governor Harvey, was determined to continue the work of her husband in helping service men and women. Hearing that Wisconsin men were dying in Union hospital camps in the South, because of the climate, she took the problem directly to President Lincoln. She finally persuaded a reluctant Lincoln to set up three hospitals in the cool, healthful climate of Wisconsin, and she became known as the "Wisconsin Angel." Annie WITTENMEYER of Iowa organized the famous diet kitchens of the northern forces, probably the first wartime effort to provide suitable food for wounded soldiers.

When the war ended most of the North had been transformed, and this was particularly true in the Midwest. The impetus given to industry and agriculture in the region is thought to have brought about growth at a rate several hundred times that which might have been expected under normal conditions. The tragedy of death and the hardships of the thousands of prisoners of war had invaded every community. But, whereas the South was devastated, little destruction had occurred in the Midwest, and the region experienced new prosperity and even greater progress.

CLARK, George Rogers. (Charlottesville, VA, Nov. 19, 1752—Louisville, KY, Feb. 13, 1818). Army officer, named as "savior of the Midwest" by his commander, Governor Patrick Henry of Virginia. Clark was the organizer and military leader of the American forces created to defend the frontier against British-supported Indian raids between 1776-1777. As a representative of Virginia, which claimed the area, Clark conquered Illinois with supplies from Virginia and captured KASKASKIA (July 4, 1778) CAHOKIA, Illinois (1780) and VINCENNES, Indiana (February 25, 1779) to ensure colonial control. He used his own money to pay and feed his troops, an action which left him penniless. Clark was made a brigadier general in 1780, and from that year until 1782 he engaged in several later battles to protect the NORTHWEST TERRITORY, including conflict with the SHAWNEE and his successful defence of St. Louis against the British. He had hoped to capture Detroit, but received no supplies or reinforcements for the job. Between 1779 and 1783 Clark served on a board of commissioners which supervised the allotment of lands in Illinois. He was a member of a commission making a treaty with Indians in the Northwest and was asked by President Thomas Jefferson to explore the land west of the MISSISSIPPI RIVER. He refused this task which was later carried out by his younger brother, William, of the LEWIS AND CLARK EXPEDITION. George Rogers Clark unsuccessfully attempted to establish a town called Clarksville. He was occupied in several questionable ventures supposedly aimed at western colonization. Clark died in poverty and ill-health partially caused by excessive drinking.

CLARK, James Beauchamp (Champ). (Lawrenceburg, KY., Mar. 7, 1850—Washington, D.C., Mar. 2, 1921). Politician. Clark settled in BOWLING GREEN, Missouri, in 1876, where he began a career as a newspaper editor, city and county prosecuting attorney, Missouri state legislator and member of the U.S. House (1893-95, 1897-1921). A disciple of Democrat and Populist leader William Jennings BRYAN, his philosophy was progressive, representing

George Rogers Clark, by Wesley Jarvis.

the Western and Southern opinion on national matters. As Democratic leader in the House, Clark led a successful fight against the dictatorial control of speaker Joseph G. CANNON. He served as speaker from 1911 to 1919. Clark was the leading candidate for the Democratic presidential nomination in 1912 and was ahead in the first fourteen ballots, until William Jennings Bryan shifted from Clark and threw his support to Woodrow Wilson.

CLARKSVILLE, Indiana. City (pop. 15,-164), southeastern Indiana city in Clark County, founded 1784 on the OHIO RIVER near Louisville, Kentucky; one of three towns in Indiana established by and named by George Rogers CLARK. Clarksville, Louisville, and JEFFERSONVILLE were founded out of a tract of 150,000 acres presented to Clark and his men by the State of Virginia in recognition of their military service in the REVOLUTIONARY WAR. The land was divided into 500-acre lots with 1,000 acres being set aside as a town site called Clarksville. Henry Clay and Humphrey Marshall, both members of the Kentucky legislature, fought a duel near Clarksville in 1808. Each received a flesh wound and declared their honor satisfied. In 1810 near Silver Creek, militiamen captured several boatloads of Aaron BURR's followers on his ill-fated and never explained venture involving the American West. Today the community is involved in soap manufacture.

Clarksville - Clemens

CLARKSVILLE, Missouri. Village (pop. 585), eastern Missouri, near the MISSISSIPPI RIVER in Pike County. "Snake frolics" were favorite pastimes of the residents. The record was held by Miles Price, the constable and justice of the peace in Pike County, who joined with his neighbors to kill nine thousand rattlesnakes on one of their annual spring hunts. The settlement dates from 1816 when it is claimed Territorial Governor William Clark wintered in the area with a company of soldiers.

CLAYTON, Missouri. City (pop. 14,219), seat of St. Louis County, in northeastern Missouri. A residential suburb of ST. LOUIS incorporated in 1919, it also serves as an educational hub of the area, offering many fine educational institutions, including the Concordia Seminary.

CLEAVELAND, Moses. (Canterbury, CT, 1754—1806). After four years of service in the American Revolution (1777-1781), Cleaveland returned to his native city to practice law. In 1787 he began service in the state legislature. His reputation was gained principally from his service to the Connecticut Land Company in 1796, when he led a surveying party to the land purchased by the company in the WESTERN RESERVE section of east central Ohio. They chose a site at the mouth of the CUYAHOGA RIVER as the location of the principal city, which was named Cleaveland in honor of the surveyor. Cleaveland himself predicted, modestly as it turned out, that some day the city would be as large as his small Connecticut birthplace. The story is told that the name was changed to CLEVELAND when a local newspaperman did not have room for the extra "A" in a headline. Cleaveland and his party surveyed and laid out a number of towns and villages in the Western Reserve, including CHAGRIN FALLS. This place was said to have been given its name when the company was embarrassed by mistaking the CHAGRIN RIVER for the Cuyahoga.

CLEMENS, Samuel Langhorn (Mark Twain). (Florida, MO, Nov. 30, 1835 —Redding, CT., Apr. 21, 1910). Novelist, short story writer, and humorist. When he was four years old, Clemens moved with his family to HANNIBAL, Missouri, where he experienced a childhood of harmless adventures, recalled in romantic fashion in *The Adventures of Tom Sawyer* (1876) and its more sophisticated sequel *The Adventures of Huckleberry Finn* (1884). His father died when he was young, and Clemens was employed in a variety of professions from the age of twelve, when he was apprenticed to a printer. Most important to his writing was his experience as a PILOT on Mississippi River steamers in his twenties; his pen name, Mark Twain, was taken from the riverboat term meaning safe water of two fathoms.

When the CIVIL WAR disrupted river traffic, Clemens traveled west to Nevada in 1862, where he was a stringer for several newspapers

Hannibal, Missouri, honors Mark Twain with an annual festival, including Tom Sawyer's fence painting episode.

and established a reputation as a humorist, poking fun at the rugged lifestyles there. He also became a popular lecturer, a trade that he would later pursue on European tours. After moving to San Francisco, California, in 1864, he wrote the "Celebrated Jumping Frog of Calaveras County," published the next year. The modest fame he achieved with that story encouraged him to travel and write about his travels. It was as a journalist that he was sent on a tour of the Holy Land. The result was his first important work, *Innocents Abroad* (1869), a satire on Old World pretensions from the perspective of a commonsense American. This brought him the financial stability required for his marriage to the relatively aristocratic Olivia Langdon. They moved to the East and settled in Connecticut.

Clemens reached his literary peak with *Huckleburry Finn*, the story of a boy and an escaped slave in flight down the MISSISSIPPI RIVER in the pre-Civil War South. It is a touchstone in American literature in both its address to the national trauma surrounding the SLAVERY issue and its essential hostility to social organization of all sorts and desire for the freedom of the frontier. Clemens' important other works include *A Connecticut Yankee in King Arthur's Court* (1889) and *Pudd'nhead Wilson* (1894). In these later years Clemens squandered a fortune on an ill-advised publishing scheme (the C.L. Webster and Company Publishing House), regained it with an enormously popular European lecture tour, and oversaw construction of "Stormfield," his elaborate Connecticut home, now a museum in Redding, Connecticut. His later works, such as *The Man That Corrupted Hadleyburg* (1899), reflect the bitterness and pain that Clemens felt on the deaths of two of his daughters and the long illness and death of his wife.

CLEVELAND, OHIO

Name: Formerly called Cleaveland for Moses Cleaveland, an officer under George Washington and a surveyor of the Western Reserve.

Area: 79 square miles.

Elevation: 680 feet

Population:
1984: 546,543
Rank: 22nd
Percent change (1980-1984): minus 4.8%

Density (city): 4,941 per sq. mi.
Metropolitan Population: 2,788,000
Percent change (1980-1984): minus 1.6%

Racial and Ethnic Makeup (1980):
White: 53.5%
Black: 43.8%
Hispanic origin: 17,896 persons
Indian: 1,282 persons
Asian: 3,372 persons
Other: 8,785 persons

Age:
18 and under: 27.8%
65 and over: 13%

TV Stations: 7

Radio Stations: 53

Hospitals: 19

Sports Teams:
Indians (baseball)
Browns (football)
Cavaliers (basketball)

Further Information: Cleveland Convention Visitor's Bureau, 1301 East 6th Street, Cleveland, OH 44114

CLEVELAND, Ohio. City, seat of Cuyahoga County, port of entry on Lake ERIE at the mouth of the CUYAHOGA RIVER, chartered as a city in 1836. The suburban periphery includes such well-known and elegant communities as Shaker Heights, along with Cleveland Heights, Euclid, Garfield Heights, Maple Heights, Parma and Parma Heights and Brook Park. The city covers an area of 79 square miles.

The prime GREAT LAKES locale, midway between the iron ORE of Minnesota and the COAL and oil of Pennsylvania, very early made the city a leading force in the iron and STEEL industry, the leading ore receiving port of the nation, and, as a consequence, one of the leaders in steel production and iron and steel products. It gained leadership in the petroleum industry with the founding of the Rockefeller dynasty there. In addition to metallurgy and petroleum, Cleveland is a major center of chemical production, food processing, electrical and garment industries. The early 1900s found six leading automobile manufacturers centered in the city, and seventy-four other AUTOMOBILE brand names were produced there over the years. A Cleveland man, Charles B. Shanks, claimed the honor of creating the word automobile itself in an article in the Cleveland *Plain Dealer*. Cleveland remains a leading center of auto bodies and parts production.

The giant General Electric Company, headquartered at Nela Park, has contributed greatly to the area's industry through its huge research facilities and vast operations.

From early times, Connecticut had claimed the region where Cleveland now stands. These "western" lands were given up, but the New England state "reserved" the right to sell or give lands in this WESTERN RESERVE. War claims and the services of Revolutionary veterans were settled with cession of land rights there. So many easterners moved to their claims that the region was known as a second New England. It also is frequently called the Western Reserve.

Moses CLEAVELAND laid out the city in 1796. It took his name with the slight variation in spelling which is said to be due to a newspaper editor who could not fit the extra "A" into his headline. The opening of the Great Lakes by the Erie Canal in 1825, and the OHIO AND ERIE CANAL in 1827, brought trade and new prosperity, as did the first railroad, in 1851.

The city grew with the growth of Standard Oil and the rise of its founder, John D. ROCKEFELLER, and it came to be known as the oil capital of the nation. Pioneer electrical expert, Charles F. BRUSH, who developed automobile ignition processes and who lighted Public Square in Cleveland, joined his Brush Electric Company with that of Thomas A. EDISON to form the giant General Electric Company, making the metropolitan area one of the world's industrial giants.

The opening of the ST. LAWRENCE SEAWAY in 1959 further expanded the importance of the Port of Cleveland

Yet despite its leadership in urban renewal and slum clearance the city could not escape the devastation and unrest of racial disturbances so widespread in the 1960s. Racial unrest, especially in the Hough and Glenville sections, resulted in eleven deaths and extensive destruction of property.

The city suffered also from the kind of decline of importance of its central area which was nearly universal in American urban areas. Even more difficult was the decline in the steel and petroleum industries due to foreign competition in steel as well as the emergence of new materials and the petroleum shortages brought on by the petroleum cartel in the 1970s.

From a population of 751,000 in 1970, the population declined to 547,000 in 1984, one of

Landmark Terminal Tower, Cleveland.

the most drastic of such drops among the nation's major cities. This resulted in loss of its rank of first in population in the state and a decline to 22nd rank in the nation. The city's black population rose to 43.8 percent, and the Hispanic population reached 3.1 percent in 1984.

It is hoped that major investment and construction in the downtown area will result in substantial revival for the city.

Public Square remains at the heart of Cleveland, with its Soldiers and Sailors Monument at the center, honoring Civil War veterans. At one time the 52-story Terminal Tower was the tallest building west of New York City.

The Cleveland Orchestra has long been ranked among the nation's top ten symphonies, having been led by such world-renowned conductors as George Szell, Artur Rodzinski and Lorin Maazel. Its home base is Severance Hall, gift of John L. Severance. Another leading cultural institution is the Cleveland Health Museum, the first of its kind in the country.

The Cleveland Museum of Art and the Fine Arts Garden, the natural history museum with its planetarium, and Rockefeller Park are other outstanding attractions. The latter boasts the Cultural Gardens, unique of their type, as well as the Shakespeare Garden. Gordon Park provides a museum of historical medicine and an aquarium.

Higher education is represented by CASE WESTERN RESERVE UNIVERSITY, John Carroll University, Cleveland State University, St. John College of Cleveland, Notre Dame College, Ursuline College, the Cleveland Institutes of Art and Music and St. Mary Seminary.

The city has long been noted for its sports leadership especially with baseball's Cleveland Indians, which took the nickname from two noted players of Indian birth. In professional football, the Cleveland Browns have been a powerhouse. The Cavaliers have represented Cleveland in the Central Division of the National Basketball Association.

CLIFTY FALLS. Principal attraction of Clifty Falls State Park, a 617-acre recreation area near Hanover, Indiana. Clifty Creek flows over ledges of rock and drops in a shower, ninety feet into a huge stone basin.

COAL. The most plentiful of all the fossil fuels. Illinois is the only Midwest state among the nation's leading five producers, and it continues to hold fifth place. Illinois coal is classified as bituminous, a grade just below semibituminous. It is hampered in the market because it is a "dirty" burner, its smoke producing environmental hazards while burning. With the growing success of processes for overcoming such fumes, the coal of Illinois and other areas with similar problems has been finding a growing market. Coal ranks first in value of the mineral products of both Ohio and Indiana. While coal is produced in some of the other Midwest states, such as Iowa, it is not a principal mineral product in any of them, in dollar value. Minnesota has the largest deposits of peat of any of U.S. state. Peat is a "relative" of coal. New techniques for using peat for smelting iron and STEEL are proving increasingly practical and may herald a large new industry for Minnesota.

CODY, William Frederick (Buffalo Bill). (Le Clair, IA, Feb. 26, 1846—Denver, CO, Jan. 10, 1917). Frontiersman and showman. Son of an Iowa pioneer in Scott County, Cody became the famed scout and frontiersman of the plains. The family moved to Kansas in 1854, and when his father died in 1857, Bill began to earn the family living, working for railroad supply trains, freighting companies, prospecting in the Colorado gold fields and riding the PONY EXPRESS

(1860-1861). During the CIVIL WAR he was a scout and trooper. He gained great fame in the west for killing huge numbers of buffalo to feed the workers on the Kansas Pacific Railroad. Billy Comstock, another buffalo hunter, claimed to be the greatest buffalo hunter on the plains. A match was arranged between the two Bills to see who could kill the most in a given time period. The winner would receive $500 and the title "Buffalo Bill." Cody killed sixty-nine and Comstock only forty-six, so Cody received the name which he made famous. He became chief of scouts for the U.S. cavalry (1868-1872), a position in which the Indian languages he had learned as a young man were particularly important in dealing with the people of the plains. The dime novels of Ned Buntline, which gave Americans stirring tales about Bill's life, made the plainsman so famous that in 1873 Buntline persuaded Bill to go into show business. Buffalo Bill spent the rest of his life in that field, except for a brief period scouting against the SIOUX in 1876. In that year he killed and scalped Indian leader Yellow Hand in a famous duel. Returning to show business, he divided his time between shows and his Nebraska ranch. In 1883 he organized Buffalo Bill's Wild West Show, featuring bands of Indians, cowboys, roughriders, bucking broncos and buffalo. He toured with the show for many years throughout the U.S. and Europe. He even appeared before such notables as Queen Victoria, who loved the "bucking ponies" and gave him a jeweled crest. One of the most popular men of his time, he was given a ranch by the state of Wyoming, on which the town of Cody was laid out. After his sudden death in Denver, he was buried on nearby Lookout Mountain, where his grave continues to attract tourists. His own autobiography (1879) reads almost as excitingly as the dime novels of Buntline and Prentice Ingraham.

COE COLLEGE. A coeducational college in CEDAR RAPIDS, Iowa, established in 1851 by a gift from Daniel Coe of New York, who gave $1,500 with an unusual request for the time: "It is my strong desire that this institute should be made available for the education of females as well as males." The gift was used to purchase an 80-acre Iowa farm, providing the basis for the growth of the school, which was founded as Cedar Rapids Collegiate Institute, then was chartered in 1881 under its present name. Coé is privately controlled but affiliated with the Presbyterian church. Extensive off-campus opportunities include professional work-service programs of one term. The college also offers internships abroad. Enrollment is 1,084, with a faculty of 121,

COEDUCATION. College study of women and men together. Four years after it was founded in 1833, OBERLIN COLLEGE, OBERLIN, Ohio, dropped a bombshell with the announcement that it would accept women students. There was great excitement among the students; most were angry; others may have been pleased, but the tenor of the times did not permit them to show it. In 1841, the first women received their diplomas from Oberlin to become the first of their sex to be graduated from an institution of higher education in the U.S. In another record for the Midwest, the University of MICHIGAN (chartered 1837) was the first major university to admit women.

COFFIN, Levi. (New Garden City, NC, Oct. 28, 1789—Avondale, Cincinnati, OH, Sept. 16, 1877). Abolitionist. Coffin, a conductor on the UNDERGROUND RAILROAD, opened a wholesale free-labor goods store, sponsored by the Quaker Convention in Indiana, in CINCINNATI, Ohio in 1847. In FOUNTAIN CITY, Indiana, his home, known as "Central Union Station of the Underground Railroad," Coffin gave shelter to an estimated two thousand runaway slaves. Coffin was an organizer of the English Freedmen's Aid Society in England in 1864 and a delegate to the International Anti-Slavery Convention in Paris, France, in 1867.

COLES, Edward. (Albemarle County, VA, Dec. 15, l786—-Philadelphia, PA, July 7, l868). Second governor of Illinois. Coles County, Illinois, is named in his honor. President Madison's private secretary from 1809 to 1815, Coles was sent by Madison to Russia in 1816 as a goodwill ambassador. Upon coming to Illinois in 1819, Coles freed his slaves in the middle of the OHIO RIVER, the boundary between free and slave states and, and gave each of them 160 acres of land. His anti-slavery stand was a prominent issue in his political life, but as governor of Illinois (1822-1826), he won the fight to keep SLAVERY out of Illinois. Coles organized the first State Agricultural Society of Illinois in 1819.

COLFAX, Schuyler. (New York, NY, March 23, 1823—Mankato, MN, Jan. 13, 1885). United States vice president. Colfax was responsible for turning the SOUTH BEND, Indiana, *Free Press* into one of the state's leading Whig

publications under the new name of the *St. Joseph Valley Register.* He was a member of the Indiana Constitutional Convention of 1850, and as a Republican member of the United States House of Representatives from Indiana in the 34th through 40th congresses (1854-1869). During his fourteen years in Congress, he served as chairman of the committee on post offices and post roads from 1859-1861 and as speaker from 1863-1869. He was known as a leader in the Radical wing of the party. Elected in 1868 as vice-president under GRANT (1822-1885), Colfax was involved in the Credit Mobilier scandals (1867-1873) which ruined his career. It was later discovered that he had accepted a large campaign contribution from a supplier of government envelopes when he led the House committee on post offices. After leaving the government he became a popular speaker on lecture tours.

COLON, Michigan. Town (pop. 1,190), St. Joseph County, south-central portion of Michigan's LOWER PENINSULA, less than 25 miles from the Indiana border. Colon has been called the "Magic Capital of the World" because so much equipment used by magicians is manufactured there.

COLUMBIA CITY, Indiana. City (pop. 5,091), northeastern Indiana city in Whitley Co., name derived from the feminine form of Columbus, prosperous agricultural and industrial city. Columbia City was the home of Thomas Riley Marshall (1854-1925), Vice-President of the United States for two terms under Woodrow Wilson. Marshall is credited with making the remark, "What this country needs is a good five-cent cigar." Lloyd Cassel Douglas (1877-1951), author of *The Green Light* and *The Magnificent Obsession* was born in the city in 1877. Major industries of the city have been meat-packing, a woolen mill and production of overalls.

COLUMBIA, Missouri. City (pop. 58,804), seat of Boone County, on the MISSOURI RIVER in central Missouri. The original settlement, in 1819, was named Smithton. Growth was stimulated in 1822 with the rerouting through Columbia of Boone's Lick Trail. Incorporated in 1826, the city pledged $117,900 in 1839 to construct the first state university west of the Mississippi, now the University of MISSOURI. Today, with the university, Stephens College and Columbia College, Columbia is a major educational center. The economy is based on education, professional organizations, insurance companies, and some light industry. The state cancer hospital and mental health clinic are located in Columbia.

COLUMBUS, Indiana. City (pop. 30,614), seat of Bartholomew County, situated on the East Fork of the WHITE RIVER in southeast central Indiana. Today the city has become the world capital of modern small town architecture. The movement was spearheaded by J. Irwin Miller of the local Cummins Engine Company, who offered to pay the architects' fees for new buildings if the designs came from distinguished architects. Other Columbus institutions and companies have done the same. Since 1930 more than fifty buildings have been built in Columbus following designs of world-famous architects, such as John Carl Warnecke, Harry Weese, I. M. Pei, Eliot Noyes, Kevin Roche, J. M. Johansen and Eero Saarinen. The famed Saarinen church of 1930 started the international parade of architecture. Columbus was incorporated in 1821. During the CIVIL WAR it was a depot for Union armies. The wartime activities and the railroads brought many industries, some still existing in Columbus today. Products of the city include electric controls, diesel engines, plastic components, automotive parts, metal furniture and castings. Principal tourist attractions are the more than fifty architectural sites which may be visited by bus, auto and walking tours, fanning out from the Visitor Center, which also offers an art museum and gift shop. Also at Columbus is the Otter Creek Golf Course, designed by all-time champion Bobby Jones and rated as one of the top ten public courses in the country.

COLUMBUS, OHIO

Name: From Christoforo Columbo, taking the Anglicized version of his name, Columbus.

Area: 185.8 square miles.

Elevation: 780 feet

Population:
1984: 566,144
Rank: 20th
Percent change (1980-1984): .2%
Density (city): 3,121 per sq. mi.
Metropolitan Population: 1,279,000
Percent change (1980-1984): 2.8%

Racial and Ethnic Makeup (1980):
White: 76.2%
Black: 22.1%
Hispanic origin: 5,300 persons
Indian: 1,024 persons
Asian: 5,410 persons
Other: 1,777 persons

Age:
18 and under: 25.8%
65 and over: 8.9%

TV Stations: 5

Radio Stations: 19

Hospitals: 22

Sports Teams:
Clippers (minor-league baseball)

Further Information: Columbus Chamber of Commerce, P.O. Box 1527, Columbus, OH 43216

COLUMBUS, Ohio. City, capital of Ohio, seat of Franklin County and largest city in the state, situated in central Ohio on the SCIOTO RIVER. The name honors Christoforo Columbo, taking the Anglicized version of his name. The capital covers a land area of 185.8 square miles and was incorporated as a city in 1834.

Its neighboring communities are small suburbs, including Lincoln Village, Grove City, Blacklick Estates and Gahanna. Upper Arlington is governed separately although surrounded by the larger city.

The rich farm region for which it is the center and its location as a focal point of highway, rail and air TRANSPORTATION have contributed to the city's growth as a commercial and industrial hub. Its principal industries are missiles and aircraft, household appliances, foundry and machine shop products, processing equipment, automatic controls, coated fabrics and glass. Commercial growth is enhanced by Battelle Memorial Institute, which contributes intensive industrial research in the fields of graphic arts, metallurgy, ceramic arts and other selected fields.

In 1812 Columbus was laid out as the capital, which was moved there from CHILLICOTHE. Its growth was hastened by the opening of a spur to the OHIO AND ERIE CANAL in 1831, by the coming of the NATIONAL ROAD in 1833 and by the arrival of the first railroad in 1850.

In the period from 1970 through 1984, the

The massive capitol at Columbus, Ohio.

dramatic decline of CLEVELAND 's population and the continued modest growth of Columbus resulted in Columbus' attaining number one rank in Ohio population. The population of Columbus in 1970 was 540,000, in 1984, 566,114. The capital ranks fifth in population among the major cities of the Midwest and 20th in the U.S. Twenty-two percent of the population is black, with less than one percent of Hispanic origin.

The architecture of the massive capitol is unique in the U.S. Its simple lines, with a colonnaded front and an unornamented truncated dome give it a modern look, but the cornerstone was laid in 1839. However, twenty-two years passed before the building was finished in 1861, under the direction of a succession of five different architects and twelve governors. Its foundation walls are twelve to fifteen feet thick. The concept of the interior is also unique. Under the dome, thirteen blocks of marble represent the thirteen original states. Circles of marble stand for the various territories before statehood, as well as the Louisiana Purchase and the territories acquired after the MEXICAN WAR. The outer ring, a circle of 32 points, represents the number of states at the time of Ohio statehood.

The statue on the northwest corner of the capitol grounds has an interesting history. It was part of the Ohio exhibit at the WORLD'S COLUMBIAN EXPOSITION in CHICAGO in 1893. Afterward the people of Ohio took up a subscription to re-erect it at the capitol. The central figure of the Roman mother, Cornelia (whose children were her "jewels"), is surrounded at the base by statues of Ohio's own "jewels," William Tecumseh SHERMAN, Philip H. SHERIDAN, Edwin M. Stanton, Ulysses S. GRANT, James A. GARFIELD, Salmon P. CHASE and Rutherford B. HAYES.

Each year Columbus hosts one of the nation's notable state fairs. A feature of the fairgrounds is a reproduction of the home of President William Henry HARRISON (1773-1841).

One of the country's academic and sports powerhouses is OHIO STATE UNIVERSITY. Capital University, Ohio Dominican College and state schools for the blind and deaf are among the other educational institutions.

The State Archeological and Historical Society houses a fine library and museum. One of the world's largest rose gardens is provided at the American Rose Society's headquarters.

COMPTON, Arthur Holly. (Wooster, OH, Sept. 10, 1892—Berkeley, CA, March 15, 1962). Physicist. From a family of renowned educators, Compton graduated from the College of

Wooster, where his father was a professor. He took his doctorate at Princeton in 1916, then took further work at Cambridge, England. He began an academic career as head of the physics department at WASHINGTON UNIVERSITY, ST. LOUIS, in 1920. In 1923 he moved to the University of CHICAGO, where he remained until the end of WORLD WAR II. At CHICAGO, Compton directed the Metallurgical Division of the Manhattan Project (1942-1945), where he supervised the development of plutonium for the ATOMIC BOMB project. His assignment was to produce enough plutonium for one or more atomic bombs. He served as chancellor of Washington University from 1953 to 1961. Compton won the NOBEL PRIZE in 1927 for his discovery of the change in the wave length of scattered X-rays, the Compton Effect. He also discovered the electrical nature of cosmic rays. Unlike many scientists, Compton was also known for his broad humanitarian interests. In addition to scientific writing he wrote *The Freedom of Man* (1935) and *The Human Meaning of Science* (1940). He served in several governmental advisory positions and lectured widely until his death.

CONCORDIA COLLEGE. Privately supported liberal arts college in MOORHEAD, Minnesota. Accredited with the North Central Association of Colleges and Schools, Concordia had 2,481 students enrolled during the 1985-1986 academic year and 179 faculty members. Extensive music programs are offered. Special programs of the college include May Seminars Overseas to Africa, Europe and Asia, Junior Year in Europe, and Washington Seminar. Religious subjects are required. Concordia is located on 120 acres and has thirty buildings. Dormitory facilities are available for 1,050 men and 1,041 women.

CONE, Marvin. (Cedar Rapids, IA, Oct. 21, 1891—Cedar Rapids, IA, May 18, 1965), Artist and teacher. Cone and artist Grant WOOD were classmates in high school and together they painted scenery for plays and hung paintings at the CEDAR RAPIDS Art Association. After studies at the Ecole des Beaux Arts, Cone spent summers painting—in Paris in 1929 and in Mexico in 1939. His work progressed through such phases as nature, impressionist, still life and haunted houses and ghosts. In 1932 he joined Grant Wood as a teacher at Wood's STONE CITY, Iowa, art center. He was a beloved teacher of art at COE COLLEGE for many years,

and his works hang in many of the prominent Midwest art museums.

CONGRESSIONAL MEDAL OF HONOR. Midwest men had the distinction of being the first to receive the newly created Congressional Medal of Honor, established by joint resolution of Congress July 12, 1862. These were the six Ohio men who returned from the raiding party headed by James J. Andrews, after a strike at southern railroads, which became known popularly as the GREAT LOCOMOTIVE CHASE. Two Michigan men, Thomas W. Custer, brother of famed General George CUSTER, and Frank D. BALDWIN, had the unusual distinction of winning the medal twice. More than three hundred men and women from the Midwest have received the honor since it was inaugurated.

CONNERSVILLE, Indiana. City (pop. 17,-023), east central seat of Fayette County, site of the former manufacture of the Auburn, Cord, and Duesenberg AUTOMOBILES. Connorsville is named for John Connor, founder of the city, who, as a child, was kidnapped and raised by Indians. He was one of the nine commissioners who chose INDIANAPOLIS as the state capital in 1820. The first industrial boom came from the WHITEWATER CANAL. A restored section of the canal was later used by the power company to generate electricity. Today the city manufactures dishwashers, automobile and building supplies. The Whitewater Canoe Race is an annual event in late September.

CONSERVANCY ACT. Pioneer conservation effort. The OHIO RIVER flood of 1913, one of the worst floods in the river's history, sparked a major conservation effort, one of the earliest ever undertaken by a state. In 1914 the Ohio state legislature passed the Conservancy Act, calling for a series of flood-control dams on the various rivers of the Ohio watershed. The system has been studied by flood-control experts from all over the world, and many have praised it as one of the most successful early efforts to keep the rich soil from running off the land. Other Midwest states have established small conservation projects, but at present most of the effort is made in cooperation with U.S. government agencies.

CONTOUR FARMING. The practice of plowing along the contours of hills instead of in straight rows, now almost universally followed in hilly ares as a means of slowing runoff and loss of topsoil. The practice was developed at the tiny village of COON VALLEY, Wisconsin, near LA CROSSE. The hilly area around Coon Valley was judged to be typical of most such regions greatly at risk from soil erosion. The Coon Valley Demonstrational Project, first of its kind in the nation, was begun in 1933 by the U.S. Department of Agriculture, with the cooperation of the University of WISCONSIN, to work out methods of coping with erosion in hilly regions. Over 400 farmers in the Coon Creek Watershed received free technical assistance, and their experiments resulted in many new soil conservation techniques, principal of which was the simple method of contour plowing, which continues to provide dramatic results. On hilly land farmers plow across the terrain, rather than up and down. The plowed soil creates ridges which trap runoff water, thus preventing soil erosion while actually enhancing the ability of the ground to absorb the moisture. The procedure is particularly important on rolling ground in the Midwest.

COOKE, Jay. (Aug. 10, 1821, Sandusky, OH—Elkins Park, PA., Feb. 18, 1905). Financier. After several modest jobs, Cooke joined E. W. Clarks and Company bank at Philadelphia in 1839. Two years later he became a partner. Cooke founded Cooke and Company in 1861. This company marketed the bulk of the Union bonds during the CIVIL WAR, raising over a billion dollars. In 1870 Cooke undertook to raise $100,000,000 to finance the Northern Pacific Railroad, but after the road reached Bismarck, North Dakota, financing faltered. The Cooke company then closed its doors, becoming one of the principal factors in the financial panic of 1871. Undaunted, Cooke was able to raise money on his personal responsibility to invest in western mining stocks. The confidence of his investors was rewarded by his success and his honesty. By 1880 he had managed to pay back all his creditors. Continuing his comeback, Cooke continued his wise investment policies and before the end of the 1880s had recouped his fortune in western mining and other ventures. Earlier, in 1864, Cooke bought Gibralter Island in Lake ERIE north of SANDUSKY, Ohio. There, except for a brief period following the panic when the house was turned over to his creditors, Cooke spent a part of each year, entertaining friends in his large mansion on the island.

COON VALLEY, Wisconsin. Village (pop. 758). Situated southeast of LA CROSSE in Vernon County, it lies scattered among the high bluffs in the valley of the same name. The village has a unique distinction in AGRICULTURE, having been the location for the first experiments investigating the value of contour plowing, now almost universally practiced as a principal means of soil conservation. This plowing technique was one of many pioneering conservation measures undertaken, beginning with work among 315 cooperating farmers in the Coon Valley area. In 1933 the region was chosen because of its steep hills and ideal conditions for all types of erosion study which were carried out there.

COOPER, Kent. (Columbus, IN, March 22, 1880—New York, NY, Jan. 31, 1965). Newspaperman. Cooper was a newspaper reporter in INDIANAPOLIS, Indiana, from 1901 to 1909 when he began working for the Associated Press. Cooper established the Associated Press in South America, Great Britain and Germany as well as the A.P. system of Wirephoto, the wire method of news photo delivery, the first of its kind. Cooper served as the president of the Press Association, 1940-1951, Wide World, 1941-1951, and New York City News Association, 1942-1951. Composer and lyricist of many songs, Cooper established two Kent Cooper Journalism Scholarships for men and two Sally Cooper Journalism Scholarships for women at INDIANA UNIVERSITY.

COOPER, Mildred. (—) Heroine. Captain Braxton Cooper's daughter risked her life to summon help for the outnumbered defenders of Fort Cooper in Missouri. On October 15, 1869, the fort was attacked by a large force of Indians. Help from nearby Fort Hempstead was needed, but no one at the fort could be spared for the dangerous ride to alert the troops. Cooper asked to go, with only the request that she be given a spur. Her sudden appearance at the fort's gate surprised the Indians who were unprepared for her gallant and successful ride, which resulted in the arrival of troops from Fort Hempstead in time to save Fort Cooper.

COPPER CULTURE. The Copper Age in the Midwest. There the Copper Culture peoples began about 6000 years ago to use the plentiful pure maleable copper of Michigan and Wisconsin, pounding it into sheets and producing useful items and jewelry. A typical Copper Culture burying ground was found near OCONTO, Wisconsin. Some of the most interesting traces of these prehistoric people in the Midwest are found on ISLE ROYALE, now part of Michigan, in

University of Michigan displays Copper Culture remains.

Lake SUPERIOR. On the island ten thousand copper-mining pits have been found, with evidence of their working by the primitive people. It would appear that similar cultures were evolving around the world at about the same time, such as the work of the prehistoric copper people of Egypt and Sudan.

COPPER HARBOR, Michigan. Village (pop. 40), Michigan's northernmost community, located on Keweenaw Peninsula on Michigan's UPPER PENINSULA. Copper Harbor, now a small resort community, began as a mining town after the mineral survey of 1840-1843. Exposed lumps of pure copper were found along the bay, and more than a dozen copper mining locations were established shortly after the Indians surrendered the territory. The mineral deposits were soon exhausted, however, and when nearby Fort Wilkins was closed, Copper Harbor lost its vitality. In recent years tourists have discovered the natural beauty of the area. Attractions include boat trips to ISLE ROYALE NATIONAL PARK, the Astor House Museum containing antique dolls, Indian relics and artifacts of local history; Copper Harbor Lighthouse Boat Tour and Museum featuring a 20-minute boat ride and an hour tour of the

lighthouse; and Fort Wilkins State Park's 199 acres containing restored buildings of Fort Wilkins which was established in 1844 and closed in 1870. When no buyer was found for the fort, the government used it as a home for disabled soldiers. In 1921 the fort and surrounding land were purchased by Houghton and Keweenaw Counties and turned over to the State of Michigan. Visitors may see the restored stockade, officers' quarters and other buildings.

COPPERHEADS. Reproachful term for those northerners sympathetic to the South. Before and during the CIVIL WAR the term Copperhead was mostly derogatory, and particularly to those sympathetic to SLAVERY itself. The sentiment was especially strong in Illinois, Indiana and Ohio. While many Democrats held such sympathies, there was a tendency to label all Democrats as Copperheads if they opposed LINCOLN's policies. The Knights of the Golden Circle was an organization formed as a secret society of Copperheads.

CORN. Most valuable crop grown in the United States. The annual value of corn production in the United States, which produces half of the world's total, equals approximately twenty and one-half billion dollars. The United States in 1984 ranked as the world's largest exporter of corn followed by Argentina and People's Republic of China. A large portion of the corn raised in the United States is used for livestock feed. The remainder of the crop is sold for use in cornstarch, plastics and corn syrup. Eight of the top nine corn producing states are in the Midwest. Iowa is the world, national and Midwest leader, followed in rank in the Midwest by Illinois, Indiana, Nebraska and Minnesota. Prices received by the farmers for corn have dropped from a high of $3.25 per bushel in 1983 to $2.42 in 1985, one of the many causes of the poor farm economy in the mid-eighties. Originating as Indian maize, corn was grown in the Midwest long before European exploration. Modern settlers saw its value, and plantings flourished in the rich soils. Iowa became known as the land where the tall corn grows. However, tall corn wasted too much of its growth in stalk. Experimenters began to improve the varieties. Henry A. WALLACE, later secretary of agriculture and vice president, developed hybrid corn in Iowa. Today dozens of producers have created varieties to match almost every need of soil and climate. The hybrid process still requires the labor of thousands of students and others in the field to detassel the corn, preventing its natural fertilization. Sweet corn, popcorn, ornamental corn, all add variety to the corn crop. In the 1984 crop the eight Midwest states produced 4,944,000,000 bushels of corn.

CORN BORER. A serious insect menace to CORN crops in the Midwest. The borer, a larva of a night-flying moth which lays its eggs on the leaves of corn plants in June, feeds on the young leaves and tassels of the plant. As they mature, the larvae feed on the ears and stem. Depending upon the length of the growing season, one or more generations of the borer may appear. Farmers battle the borer by feeding cornstalks to livestock, or by burning or shredding the stalk. Late planting avoids the first flight of the moths. Insecticides are helpful as are varieties of hybrid corn plants that are not affected by the insect.

CORNELL COLLEGE. A coeducational liberal arts school, founded in 1853 at Mount Vernon, Iowa, controlled by the Methodist church. The enrollment is 1,101, with a faculty of 96. The college claims to have been the first west of the MISSISSIPPI RIVER to admit women

students. In another claim to fame, the handsome 100-acre campus is said to be the only campus listed in its entirety in the National Register of Historic Places. An unusual annual feature for a school of this size is the appearance there each year by the CHICAGO SYMPHONY ORCHESTRA in May.

CORNISH SETTLEMENT. The community of MINERAL POINT, Wisconsin, was settled first by migrants from the south, but subsequently miners from Cornwall, England, flocked to the lead mining region. Called "Cousin Jacks," these Cornish lead miners introduced more modern mining methods and built the first permanent homes in the mining boom area. These small houses were truly "permanent" being built from solid blocks of limestone. At dinner time the miners on the opposite hillside could see their homes, and the wives would wave dishcloths out of the window as signal that dinner was ready. Because of this, the community became known as "Shake Rag." Today, the Pendarvis restoration at Mineral Point exhibits some of the restored Cornish homes, still lining Shake Rag Street.

CORNSTALK, Tallest. Known as the "Tall Corn State," Iowa holds the world's record for the tallest cornstalk. Raised in 1946 near WASHINGTON, Iowa, by Don Radda, the monsterous stalk reached 31 feet 3 inches.

CORYDON, Indiana. Town (pop. 2,724), Harrison County, once the seat of Indiana government, scene of the only Indiana battle in the CIVIL WAR. The site of Corydon was originally owned by General William Henry HARRISON from 1804 until he sold it to Harvey Heth who platted the land as the county seat. The courthouse, later the state capitol, was built in 1811-1812. On May 1, 1813, after the NORTHWEST TERRITORY was divided, the Indiana territorial government was transferred from VINCENNES. The Indiana Constitutional Convention met here in 1816 when Corydon was chosen the new state capital, which it remained until 1825 when the government was moved to INDIANAPOLIS. On July 8, 1863, Corydon was attacked by Confederate forces under the command of General John Hunt MORGAN. Three of the four hundred Corydon Home Guards were killed and two were wounded before the defenders surrendered. Morgan and his men remained only a few hours. The Zimmerman Glass Company is the leading industry in this center of AGRICULTURE.

COSHOCTON, Ohio. City (pop. 13,405), seat of Coshocton County, situated in central Ohio on a plateau southeast of the confluence of the Walhonding and TUSCARAWAS rivers, where the MUSKINGUM RIVER is formed, incorporated in 1833. The name is thought to be derived from either of two Indian terms, Cush-og-wenk, which means black bear town, or Goshoch-gung, meaning union of waters, which seems the more logical. A warlike DELAWARE group had a village of the same name on the site. The arrival of the OHIO AND ERIE CANAL in 1830 brought an outlet for its produce; the railroads followed in 1865 and made possible the development of the coal fields in the area. In 1887 J. F. Meek built an advertising novelty plant that became the town's leading industry. Flooding was one of the principal concerns of the community over the years. The worst flood damage occurred in the floods of 1913 and 1935. The dams of the Muskingum Conservancy District were designed to alleviate the flood conditions.

In recent years the population has held stable, with only a slight decline from 13,747 in the 1970 census to 13,405 in 1980. Of interest to tourists is the nearby restored Ohio-Erie Canal town known as Roscoe Village.

COUNCIL BLUFFS, Iowa. City (pop. 56,449); seat of Pottawattamie County; southwestern Iowa across the MISSOURI RIVER from Omaha, Nebraska; name derived from the Indian powwows, or councils, held on the bluffs overlooking the Missouri River. Council Bluffs early in Iowa history gained importance as a railroad center. By 1870 the community was served by eight railroads. Today it is a key trading and busy manufacturing town. In 1852 Grenville M. Dodge came to Council Bluffs to survey the Platte River Valley for a railroad. While staying at Council Bluffs' Pacific House, Dodge answered a battery of questions from a young lawyer, Abraham LINCOLN. It is presumed that Lincoln's chat with Dodge in Council Bluffs led Lincoln as president to choose Council Bluffs for the eastern terminus of the transcontinental railroad, completed to the city in 1869. This fact is commemorated by the Golden Spike Monument shaped like an enormous railroad spike. Council Bluffs has undergone many changes of name. It was originally called Hart's Bluff for a white man who traded in the area before 1824. On June 14, 1846, the first MORMONS arrived and changed the name of the settlement to Kanesville in honor of Thomas L. Kane, a friendly army officer.

The name was changed to Council Bluffs when the last of the Mormons left in the spring of 1852, dropping the city's population from 8,000 to 1,000. In the mid-1850s Council Bluffs became the home of women's rights activist Amelia BLOOMER, who initially shocked the world wearing a new style of clothing to which her name was given. The Dodge residence is a museum today of some of the general's possessions as a Civil War army officer and railroad builder. The bronze sculpture "The Angel of Death" by noted sculptor Daniel Chester French is part of the memorial to Ruth Ann Dodge, wife of the general. French was the sculptor of the seated Lincoln statue in the Lincoln Memorial in Washington, D.C. A stone with a bronze plaque marks the site of Father De Smet's mission among the POTAWATAMI Indians, founded in May, 1838. DeSmet was later sent farther west, becoming known as the "Apostle of the Rockies."

COUNTRY OF THE SIX BULLS. Nickname given to southwestern Missouri as a result of a misunderstanding. According to a story, a hunter, Edmund Jennings, visited this area and was impressed by the great springs he found. He described the region as the country of the "six boils," or springs. His pronunciation of the word "boils" sounded like "bulls" and the term remained as a nickname for this section of Missouri.

COUNTY SEAT RIVALRY. Often desperate attempts of towns and cities to gain designation as the seat of local government. The rivalry between MINNEAPOLIS and ST. PAUL, Minnesota, was described as "incredible." Census takers were kidnapped to prevent one city or the other from appearing ahead in population. NEWSPAPERS often kept the emotions of local residents at a fever pitch. ALBERT LEA, Minnesota, obtained the county seat when its favorite racehorse beat the favorite of Itasca and left the residents of that city so poor they could not advertise their city adequately to win the title. Unfortunately such rivalry prevented cooperation needed to accomplish needed local projects. In many parts of the Midwest, county records were "kidnapped," money was spent for courthouses that were never used, and almost every device known was tried by supporters of the various county seat candidates.

COUREURS DE BOIS. French woodsmen and explorers who were among the first whites to venture into the wilderness of the MISSISSIPPI

Covered bridges are a well-loved memento of history.

and MISSOURI RIVER valleys. Many of them became thoroughly acquainted with wide areas of the Midwest and opened the way for fur trade, trading posts and settlement.

COVERED BRIDGES. Structures built to cross streams while protecting the wood and nails of the flooring from weather. In the early 1800s Timothy Palmer of New England pioneered in the new style of placing a wooden housing over bridges and proved that such a covering was very effective in preserving wooden bridges from rain, snow and frost. His bridges in the east were so successful that during early settlement in the Midwest, that, for bridges experiencing only light traffic, the scheme was copied almost universally, as far west as Iowa. About 600 of these survive nationwide, with perhaps a fourth still found in the Midwest. Indiana has the largest number of covered bridges remaining in the Midwest. Parke County, Indiana, with more than thirty covered bridges, has an annual Covered Bridge Festival in October.

COVERED WAGONS. Sturdy, canvas-covered, carryall used by the American pioneers. Covered wagons went by a variety of names. They were known as "camels of the prairies" or more commonly Conestoga wagons for the name of the town in Pennsylvania where they were first built. Often colorfully painted, the wagons were built higher at both ends than in the middle for structural strength. The canvas roof was high and rounded. The body of the wagon was raised high to ride over tree stumps left in the roadway, and the broad rims of the wheels helped prevent miring down in mud. Wheels were removable, and the wagon body could then be converted to a boat. Teams of four to six horses were used for pulling. In pioneer days in the Midwest, the wagons were the premiere vehicle wherever water TRANSPOR-TATION was not available.

COW WAR. Episode in the history of northwestern Minnesota during the drouth of the 1930s. Ranchers from the Dakotas attempted to drive their CATTLE herds across the border into northwestern Minnesota, which had escaped most of the drouth and had supplies of water. Governor Floyd Olson called out the National Guard to keep the cattle out and prevent violence.

COX, James Middleton. (Butler County, OH, 1870-1957). Newspaper journalist and politician. He started his newspaper career as a cub reporter on the Cincinnati *Enquirer* and later bought the Dayton *Daily News* (1898). He subsequently bought several other NEWSPAPERS in various states. Beginning in 1909, he served two terms in the U.S. House of Representatives, then served two non-consecutive terms as governor, the first 1913-15 and second 1917-21. His principal national prominence to that time had been as a supporter of the political philosophy of President Woodrow Wilson in his liberal policies concerning direct primaries, regulation of utilities and other reform measures. Cox was strongly in favor of Wilson's international policies such as freedom of the seas, arms reduction, freedom of trade and, particularly, some kind of union of nations. In 1920 Cox was nominated for the presidency by the Democratic Party, with F.D. Roosevelt as his running mate. His firm support of the League of Nations is thought to have been a major contributing factor to his defeat by Warren G. HARDING.

COX, Kenyon. (Warren, OH, 1856—1919). American art critic, draftsman, painter. Cox studied art first in CINCINNATI, then at the Pennsylvania Academy of the Fine Arts, before going to Paris for study with Carolus-Duran and Gerome. Working in New York City, he became an influential teacher at the National Academy of Design and the Art Students League. His well known works in the Midwest Region include murals in the capitols of Iowa and Minnesota and the public library of WINONA, Minnesota. Among his best-known murals are those he painted for the Library of Congress. The Metropolitan Museum of New York acquired his well-known portrait of Saint-Gaudens, the sculptor. He was also prominent for his books on art.

COX, Samuel Sullivan. (Zanesville, OH, 1824-1889). Politician, diplomat. Samuel Sullivan Cox began his political career at the exceptionally early age of fourteen, when he served as deputy director of the Muskingum County Court of Common Pleas. He practiced law and was a newspaperman before beginning a term in the U.S. Congress (1857-1865). Moving to New York state, he was elected to the House in 1869, again in 1886. In those three separate periods of congressional service he marked up a total of twenty years. He was secretary to the American legation in Lima, Peru in 1855 and was U.S. minister to Turkey in 1885. One of his best known books was *A Buckeye Abroad* (1852).

CRAFTS. The crafts of the Midwest can be traced back to the ancient peoples who produced jewelry of copper, shells, stone and other available materials, along with many other ornamental and useful objects. Perhaps the most skilled and notable primitive craftsmen were the Indian artists who fashioned the splendid peace pipes from the soft red stone (catlinite) of what is now PIPESTONE NATIONAL MONUMENT in Minnesota.

The paintings of Indian life by early European artists show that Midwest Indians had great skill in creating headdresses and necklaces of the feathers of many birds, particularly the eagles. They had, however, lost many of the skills of some of the prehistoric peoples who preceded them. However, they quickly adapted the beads and metal articles brought in by the European explorers to such articles as fine beaded belts and vests and jewelry of wonderful imagination, worn with pride. Their ability to create beautiful and useful garments from animal skins and other materials has scarcely been recognized. Their light and handsome canoes of birchbark have been ranked with the most effective means of manually powered TRANSPORTATION anywhere.

While the Midwest tribes never developed the giant totems of the West, they did much imaginative work in the wide variety of woods available to them.

As European immigrants began to flock to the Midwest, they brought the crafts of the old countries with them. The Amish were particularly known for their fine handwork, as were the settlers of Amana who founded the AMANA COLONIES in Iowa. Because the early settlers had to create many of their basic necessities, most became skilled in work that has now become "craft." The soap and candle making, the splendid hardwood furniture and many items of past utility are now highly prized and highly priced.

Today, in an age of leisure, a large percentage of the population engages in some form of craft work. The professional craftsmen are legion, and almost every community now has shops specializing in the sale of local crafts, and summer craft fairs are prolific. One of the finest assemblies of Midwest crafts is found in the shops of the seven Amana villages in Iowa. Perhaps the largest display of crafts in the Midwest is the annual Festival of Ozark Crafts, held each year at SILVER DOLLAR CITY near BRANSON, Missouri, where the mountain crafts of the Ozarks are displayed and sold. In many parts of the Midwest, the craftsmen may be seen displaying their works at roadside stands.

CRANBERRIES. Cranberry marshes in the region of WISCONSIN RAPIDS produce the largest volume of the fruit of any inland U.S. region. Wisconsin is one of the three principal cranberry states in the country and ranks second in total production. The native American cranberry has been commercially produced in this country since about 1840, first in New Jersey, then Massachusetts, where it is the chief export crop. Some botanists consider the cranberry to be a relative of the blueberry.

CRAWFORDSVILLE, Indiana. City (pop. 13,325), west central Indiana, named for William Harris Crawford, Virginia statesman and Secretary of the Treasury under President Monroe; known as the "Hoosier Athens;" seat of WABASH COLLEGE. Lew WALLACE (1827-1905), hero of the CIVIL WAR, territorial governor of New Mexico, United States minister to Turkey, and author of *Ben Hur*, moved to Crawfordsville in 1853. The General Lew Wallace Study is located on the grounds of the general's home which was built when he returned from Turkey. The museum houses a collection of his effects. Meredith Nicholson was born in Crawfordsville in 1866 and lived there until he joined the staff of an INDIANAPOLIS newspaper. Nicholson wrote *The Valley of Democracy, The Hoosiers,* and *The House of a Thousand Candles.* Maurice Thompson (1844-1901), author of *Alice of Old Vincennes,* spent most of his life in Crawfordsville. Crawfordsville is the trading center of a large area. Its industries include nail and wire manufacture, printing and binding and plastic and metal products. Popular tourist attractions are the Old Jail Museum with its two-story rotating cylindrical jail block, which could be turned by a crank so the sheriff could keep track of prisoners without leaving his desk. The Henry Lane Home dates from 1845 and was built by the former Governor of Indiana and United States Senator during the Civil War. Annual events include the Sugar Creek Canoe Race held the third weekend in April, the Strawberry Festival in mid-June, and the Jail Breakout at the Old Jail Museum on Labor Day.

CREEL, George Edward (Lafayette Co., MO. Dec. 1, 1876—San Francisco CA, Oct. 2, 1953). Journalist. Beginning his career as a news reporter for the Kansas City *World* (1894), and then on his own newspaper. His Kansas City *Independence* (1899), established Creel's reputation as a dedicated investigative reporter. In 1917, President Woodrow Wilson appointed him head of the U.S. Committee on Public Information. Creel ran unsuccessfully against novelist Upton Sinclair for the Democratic nomination for governor of California in 1934. He published 13 books, including *War Criminals and Punishment* (1944).

CREVE COEUR, Illinois. Village (pop. 6,851), central Illinois residential area near PEORIA, Illinois. Creve Coeur is near the site where LA SALLE and Henri DE TONTI built a temporary fort, in 1680, which they named Creve Coeur, "Broken Heart," after a town in the Netherlands. Three months after the fort was completed it was destroyed by the Indians and never rebuilt by the troops left by La Salle and Tonti. The present village was incorporated in 1921. It is the home of large numbers of people employed in East Peoria. Nearby is Creve Coeur State Park.

CROGHAN, George. (Dublin, Ireland, 1722?—Passyunk, PA, Aug. 31, 1782). Frontiersman and colonial figure. Emigrating to America in 1741, he began trading with the Indians on the colonial frontier. He learned Indian languages and built up a trading empire. His techniques in dealing with the Indians are worth noting.

Typical of his tactic was his expedition of 1751. The MIAMI INDIAN village of PICKAWILLANY (near present Sidney, Ohio) was an important Indian center at the crossroad of the much-used Indian trails in western Ohio. Croghan established a British trading post there and was exceptionally successful in luring the Indian sympathies from the French, with gunpowder, clothes and rum. To counteract British influence, in 1749 the French leader, CELERON DE BLAINVILLE, went to the Miami Valley to try to win back the Indian confidence. Croghan sought to find a means to reassert the British influence. In February, 1751, Croghan returned to Pickawillany with explorer Christopher GIST, who represented the Ohio Land Company, in an effort to win a treaty to promote the colonization of the Ohio Valley from Miami Chief Old Britain. The old chief received them warmly and flew the British flag. In spite of the arrival of a French delegation which brought "two small caggs of brandy" and the claims of France, Chief Old Britain continued his loyalty to the British.

More alarmed than ever by the increasing British presence beyond the Alleghenies, the

French stepped up their attempts to hold the territory. The FRENCH AND INDIAN WAR s began in 1754, and the hostilities wiped out Croghan's business.

Croghan became deputy secretary of Indian affairs under Sir William Johnson. During the war, Croghan was particularly influential in winning many tribes away from the French cause. His greatest success came when he brought about the treaty ending PONTIAC's rebellion (1763-1766). Croghan resigned from his post and tried to establish his claims to large tracts in Illinois, among other areas. During the Revolution he was accused of being a Tory, but he managed to clear himself. He never regained his holdings and died in poverty.

CROGHAN, George. (Louisville, Ky., 1791—1849). Soldier. Nephew of George Rogers CLARK and William Clark, Croghan's claim to fame was his extraordinary defense of FORT STEPHENSON, near present FREMONT, Ohio. On August 2, 1813, during the WAR OF 1812, a large British force of about 1,200 attacked and surrounded the fort, defended by Croghan and only about 150 Americans. Croghan had only one cannon, which he called "Old Betsy." He cleverly shifted Old Betsy from place to place, strafing the British and repulsing each futile charge against the fort until the attackers finally withdrew. Croghan received a congressional citation for his skill and bravery. He also distinguished himself in other battles of the war. Today Soldiers' Monument marks the site of his victory, and his remains were reinterred at the monument in 1906. Old Betsy still guards the grave of the man who commanded her so triumphantly.

CROSS TIMBERS, Missouri. Village (pop. 217), southwestern Missouri, northeast of Bolivar in Hickory County, named for the intersection of two timber-belts. According to legend, the Lost Silver Mine is located three miles southwest of this quiet Missouri community. The mine, originally called Old Brooksie, was producing silver when the CIVIL WAR started and Union troops occupied the area. The operator dammed the Pomme de Terre River and flooded the shaft to hide its location rather than have Federal troops seize his wealth, and the mine has never been rediscovered.

CROWDER, Enoch Herbert (Edinburg, MO, Apr. 11, 1859—Washington, DC, May 7, 1932). Army officer, diplomat. Crowder is best remembered for his competent administration in bringing military justice more in line with equal treatment for all, while serving as Judge Advocate General of the Army. He developed a complex plan for raising a huge army for WORLD WAR I and for this purpose his Selective Service plan was adopted by Congress. As a military officer, Crowder was a commander in campaigns against Geronimo and Sitting Bull. Crowder also served as the first U.S. ambassador to Cuba, beginning in 1923.

CUIVRE RIVER. Eastern Missouri river whose name in French means Copper River, from the belief that copper could be found along its banks. The West Fork of the Cuivre River has its source in Mexico County south of Benton City. This branch flows northeast before turning southeast as it flows past Middletown, Olney and Truxton. The North Fork of the Cuivre River has its source in Pike County south of BOWLING GREEN. This branch flows southwest and then southeast before it meets with the West Fork north of Cuivre River State Park. The river continues to flow southeast before turning northeast to its mouth at the MISSISSIPPI RIVER near Old Monroe.

CULVER MILITARY SCHOOL. Indiana school near the town of Argos. Founded in 1894 by Henry Harrison Culver, a ST. LOUIS stove manufacturer. Culver Military School's military course is four years with an optional two-year junior college course. Annually the school enrolls approximately 550 boys between the ages of thirteen and eighteen. Near the campus, located on the shore of Lake Maxinkinckee, is the one hundred twenty-acre Culver Bird Sanctuary which is used by the military school for studying wildlife.

CUSHING, William Barker. (Gallipolis, OH, Nov. 4, 1842—Washington, DC, Dec. 17, 1874). Soldier. Cushing gained national fame with so many acts of heroism that the secretary of the navy, called him "The Hero of the Civil War." He did not complete work at the Naval Academy, due to his disregard for tradition and discipline. However, he was called to navy service in the Civil War.

He almost singlehandedly saved the ship *Commodore Perry* from capture in 1862. He captured many prize ships, raided the Confederate coast and narrowly escaped capture. His most daring attack occurred on October 27, 1864. With fourteen officers and men on a steam launch, he attacked the Confederate ram *Albemarle.* and sank the ship with a torpedo, probably the first time a major vessel had been put out of commission that way. Cushing and one other man of the raiding party were the only two to escape alive. For this exploit he is credited as a pioneer in torpedo warfare.

William Cushing led a heroic charge in the capture of Fort Fisher at Wilmington, North Carolina, in January, 1865. He continued to take "one prize ship after another." He had been under enemy fire many times, but always escaped without a scratch. After the war he continued with the navy and in 1873 made a daring raid at Santiago, Cuba, to save some American sailors captured there. He was transferred to Washington, where he died.

An imposing granite shaft was erected in 1915, and Cushing Memorial Park was created by the Waukesha, Wisconsin, County Historical Society to honor the heroism of William, along with his brothers Alonzo and Howard Cushing. The Cushings were among the many military brothers who have brought distinction to their states and localities.

Alonzo B. Cushing died a hero in the defense against Pickett's charge in the Battle of Gettysburg. Howard Cushing was named by his junior officer as "the bravest man I ever saw." He was killed during the Indian wars in 1871.

CUSTER, George Armstrong. (New Rumley, OH, Dec. 5, 1839—Little Bighorn, MT, June 25, 1876). Military leader and Indian fighter. Custer was a flamboyant and controversial man who wanted to be a soldier from his youth. He graduated at the bottom of his class from the U.S. Military Academy in 1861, as the CIVIL WAR was beginning. He became a fearless cavalry officer and was promoted to the brevet rank of general at age 23, the youngest general in the Union Army. Custer led the Michigan Cavalry Brigade to victory at the Battle of Gettysburg (July 1-3, 1862). He won many admirers due to his handsome appearance and dashing manner and the boldness with which he led his forces. However, he also made many enemies who considered him to be reckless, headstrong, arrogant and a publicity seeker. After the war he was reduced to his permanent rank of captain. In 1866 he enlisted in the Seventh Cavalry Regiment, subsequently becoming a lieutenant colonel in command and fought Indians in the Southwest and in the Montana and Dakota territories. In 1876, he was assigned to the Sioux Campaign,designed to move the Cheyenne and SIOUX INDIANS onto reservations. As the regiment moved into the Montana Territory, Custer was ordered by his commander, General Alfred H. Terry, to find an Indian village which had been reported by scouts. Custer saw the village from a distance of fifteen miles and estimated that it contained about 1,000 warriors who he was sure could easily be handled by his 650-man regiment. The camp actually contained 2,500 to 5,000 hostile warriors. Without further reconnoitering, Custer divided his forces into three parts and attacked. The resulting Battle of LITTLE BIG HORN (June 25, 1876) has become known as "Custer's Last Stand." The strength, fury and brilliant leadership of the Indians created a no-win situation, which resulted in the death of Custer and his entire command. It remains even today the subject of much controversy concerning the propriety of Custer's actions. In retrospect, Custer was blamed for dividing his forces, for not scouting the enemy, for disregarding the size of the enemy force and for what some have called "reckless abandon." The defeat was the worst of the Indian wars of the period and has become the most famous of all the many battles with the Indians in the West. Custer's brother, Thomas Custer, two-time winner of the CONGRESSIONAL MEDAL OF HONOR was killed with his brother. A nephew and a brother-in-law also perished in the battle.

CUTLER, Manasseh. (Killingly, CT., 1742—1823). American clergyman and scientist, principally responsible for the first American settlement in the Midwest. Cutler studied law and theology, was admitted to the bar in 1767 and was ordained in 1771. He became pastor of the Congregational Church at Hamilton, Massachusetts. This versatile genius also studied and practiced medicine and wrote many scientific papers in his varied branches of science, including the first scientific classification of New England flora. Early in 1786 Cutler called together a distinguished group of New Englanders, including Revolutionary General Rufus PUTNAM, and proposed a plan for settlement in the "West." They gathered at the Bunch of Grapes Tavern in Boston and organized the OHIO COMPANY OF ASSOCIATES. As agent for the Company, he carried on extended negotiations with the Continental Congress, and he not only obtained the land grant for the company but also was particularly influential in obtaining the passage of the famed NORTHWEST ORDINANCE OF 1787, which organized the new American possessions in the West. The Company organized boat builders and surveyors, floated down the OHIO RIVER in FLATBOATS and founded MARIETTA, Ohio's first permanent European settlement. Cutler was influential in the careful selection of the first settlers for their varied skills and abilities. The Rev. Cutler continued his scientific research and also was elected to Congress for the terms 1801-05. He was a member of the American Academy of Arts and Sciences and author of *A Description of Ohio*, 1787. One of the founders of OHIO UNIVERSITY, the Rev. Cutler based its charter on that of Yale University. Because of his efforts on behalf of the university, founded at Marietta in 1809 as the first institution of higher learning in the entire NORTHWEST TERRITORY, the first college building at the university, constructed in 1817, was named Cutler Hall.

CUYAHOGA FALLS, Ohio. City, (pop. 43,710) situated in northeastern Ohio at the great turn of the CUYAHOGA RIVER. The city takes its name from the portion of the river which drops 220 feet in its course through the city, tumbling over a series of falls and rapids. The community was incorporated in 1836. As a suburb of AKRON, Cuyahoga Falls is linked to the larger city by the high level bridge, completed in 1915 as the highest concrete bridge in the United States, 196 feet above the river at its highest point. The city is both a residential and industrial suburb, with the perennial rubber goods, along with machinery, milk processing and metal goods. The population of 49,815 in 1970 had dropped to 43,710 in 1980, due to the decline in number of the industrial jobs as industry moved to the Sunbelt.

CUYAHOGA RIVER. Flowing its entire 130-mile length through northeast Ohio, over Cuyahoga Falls to Lake ERIE, the river gains importance by forming the great port of CLEVELAND. The Cuyahoga originates only a few miles south of Lake Erie near Hartsgrove, Ohio, flows southwest through CUYAHOGA FALLS to the great turn at AKRON, then flows almost directly north to Cleveland and the lake. The Cuyahoga had become one of the country's most polluted streams by the 1960s, a principal contributor to the expected "death" of Lake Erie. However, massive conservation efforts throughout the river basin have done much to restore the water quality of the river and the lake.

CUYAHOGA VALLEY NATIONAL REC-REATION AREA. This recreation area links the urban centers of CLEVELAND and AKRON, preserving the rural character of the CUYAHOGA RIVER Valley and such historic resources as the century-old OHIO AND ERIE CANAL system.

D

DABLON, Father Claude. (Dieppe, France, Feb., 1618 or Jan. 21, 1619—Quebec, Canada, 1697). Missionary and explorer. In 1655, Dablon came as a Jesuit missionary to the Iroquois mission in New France, now Canada. He was co-leader in 1661 of an expedition up the Saguenay River and Lake St. John. In 1668 Dablon accompanied Father Jacques MAR-QUETTE (1637-1675), and the two established the first permanent white settlement in Michigan, and in the Midwest, at SAULT STE. MARIE. Three years later the PAGEANT OF THE SAULT was held there, in an elaborate ceremony to impress the Indians, during which France claimed most of North America as its own. Dablon explored central Wisconsin in 1670, and in 1671 he was appointed superior of Canadian missions. One of his subordinates, Father Claude Jean ALLOUEZ (1622-1689), sent to Dublon the first surviving written reference to the "Island named Michili-mackinac" (the great turtle), now called MACKINAC ISLAND. Father Dublon appointed Father Marquette to accompany Louis JOLLIET on the voyage during which the upper Mississippi was discovered.

DAHL, Arlene. (Minneapolis, MN, August 11, 1928—). Television and movie actress, former model and beauty columnist. Dahl starred in such movies as *My Wild Irish Rose* (1947), *Three Little Words* (1950) and *Inside Straight* (1951). Dahl was already a recognized star when she appeared with Paul Douglas and Hoagy CARMICHAEL (1899-1981) in the Lux Video Theatre adaptation of *Casablanca* in 1954.

DAIRYING AND DAIRY PRODUCTS.

DACOTAH (SIOUX) INDIANS. Henry Lewis painted a Sioux Indian burial.

All the states of the Midwest have notable capability in animal husbandry. The lush prairie grasses, unequalled in capacity for growing animal feeds, and plentiful water supplies pervade the entire region. Many factors, however, have contributed to Wisconsin's world superiority as a dairy center. For example, state experts developed new methods of improving cattle, increasing the amount of milk produced per animal, along with new ways of testing and using milk products. Swiss and other nationality groups early brought to their new homes their best techniques for producing butter, cheese and other dairy products. As a result, in 1919 Wisconsin took the lead in milk and milk products among the states and has been the first-ranking dairy state ever since. Today, Wisconsin annually produces about 23 million pounds of whole milk almost twice as much as second-place California. Furthermore, the Midwest produces more than a third of the entire U.S. supply of milk and milk products, with 51,942,000 pounds annually. The $6,851,000,000 annual value of Midwest whole milk is substantially more than a third of the country's total.

DALEY, Richard J. (Chicago, IL, May 15, 1902—CHICAGO, IL, Dec. 20, 1976). CHICAGO mayor. Daley gained an early understanding of politics in the local political clubs in the "Back of the Yards" district where he grew up. Working in the stockyards, he studied law at night and took his degree in 1933 from LOYOLA UNIVERSITY. After much routine party election work he was elected to the Illinois House of Representatives in 1936, Daley later served in the Illinois Senate. His service in the Illinois legislature totalled ten years. Running for sheriff of Cook County in 1946, he suffered the only defeat of his career in politics, but he was appointed that year as state revenue director and in 1950 as Cook County clerk. His selection as chairman of the Democratic county organization in 1953 brought him a powerful position which he soon massively consolidated. Mayor of Chicago from 1955 until his death, Daley wielded the great power of both offices to command the Democratic political machine he had inherited. He soon gained national political stature, with apparent control of the Illinois Democratic delegates to the party's national conventions. He then became an adviser to Presidents Kennedy and Johnson. He even managed to make some inroads on the city's notorious corruption. Daley's administration reorganized the Chicago scandal-ridden police department, stressed urban renewal, and encouraged construction of major downtown buildings. Scandals during his terms of office—charges of bribery, misappropriated funds and other offenses of other city officials—never involved Daley personally. The notoriety of the 1968 Chicago Democratic convention centered on the harsh measures Daley used to quell the rioters who were protesting the Vietnam War. His delegate slate to the national convention was defeated in 1972, and he became an outsider at that convention. However, he was reelected in 1975 to an unprecedented sixth term as mayor. He died the next year. He was considered the last of America's "big cities bosses."

DANA, Indiana. Town (pop. 804), west central Indiana birthplace of Indiana-born journalist Ernie PYLE (1900-1945), the popular Pulitzer Prize winning newspaper correspondent of WORLD WAR II. Pyle memorabilia are displayed in his farm home which typifies a midwestern home of 1900.

DARLING, J.N. (Ding). (Norwood, MI, Oct. 21, 1876—1962). Political cartoonist and "Father of Conservation." Darling gained fame drawing political cartoons that depicted national events and human weaknesses. He won the PULITZER PRIZE for editorial cartooning twice, in 1923 and 1943. Darling was born Jay Norwood Darling. His nickname "Ding" was a shortened form of his last name. He began his career as a reporter, but turned to cartooning in 1901. In 1906 Darling joined the staff of the Des Moines *Register* where he remained until 1949, except for two years, between 1911-1913, when he worked for the New York *Globe.* His cartoons went into syndication in 1917 and appeared in as many as 135 papers. Darling was also a leader in America's conservation movement. He successfully worked for the establishment of wildlife preservation laws, migratory waterfowl refuges and soil conservation. Among the best collections of his work is the one maintained by the University of IOWA in IOWA CITY.

DASCH, George. (Cincinnati, OH, May 14, 1887—Glenview, IL, Apr. 12, 1955). Conductor, composer. Dasch, a member of the Cincinnati Symphony from 1895 to 1898, joined the Theodore THOMAS Orchestra in CHICAGO in 1898 and continued with its successor, the CHICAGO SYMPHONY ORCHESTRA, until 1923. Before he left the symphony, he served as the assistant conductor of the Chicago Civic Orchestra under Frederick STOCK (1872-1942), which he had founded with Stock. Until 1927 he was the conductor of the Little Symphony Orchestra of Chicago, which he founded in 1923. Until

financial problems caused its closing, the orchestra made successful national tours. Dasch was the first violinist in the George Dasch String Quartet and head of the music department at NORTHWESTERN UNIVERSITY and the conductor of the university's Symphony Orchestra from 1928 to 1945. He resigned from Northwestern and became a member of the music faculty of EVANSVILLE COLLEGE (1946-1955). Dasch was the conductor of the Chicago Business Men's Orchestra, (1936-1955), the WATERLOO, Iowa, Symphony (1936-44) and the Evansville Philharmonic Orchestra in EVANS-VILLE, Indiana (1946-1955).

DAUMONT, Francois (Sieur de St. Lusson). (France — 1674) French explorer. In 1663, Daumont traveled to Canada with Commander Gaudais-Dupont, where he received a grant of land. He acted as agent for Jean Talon who sent Daumont to the Upper GREAT LAKES area (1671) to claim the land for the King and to explore for minerals near Lake SUPERIOR. Daumont, also known by his title, Sieur de St. Lusson, is best remembered for his part in the PAGEANT OF THE SAULT on May 14, 1671. This was his first act in carrying out the commission from the French governor of Canada to make formal claim to most of North America, for King Louis XIV of France.

DAVENPORT, Iowa. City (pop. 103,300), seat of Scott County, largest Iowa city on the MISSISSIPPI RIVER, named for Colonel George Davenport. Davenport is one of the Quad Cities which include BETTENDORF, Iowa; ROCK ISLAND and MOLINE, Illinois. Its economy is based on the production of farm equipment, clothing, and food. The city was founded by Antoine LeClaire and Colonel George Davenport in 1836. The first bridge across the Mississippi was under construction from Rock Island to Davenport between 1853 and 1856, and its opening led to the rapid expansion of the city's population. As a cultural center, Davenport can boast its status as the birthplace or home of many talented men and women. Susan Glaspell (1882-1948) and her husband George Cram Cook (1873-1924) were co-founders, in 1915, of the Provincetown Players which produced Eugene O'Neill's first plays. Glaspell won a PULITZER PRIZE in 1930 for her play *Alison House.* Cook was the author of number of plays, including *Suppresed Desires* (with Glaspell, 1915). Davenport was the hometown of jazz great Leon "Bix" Beiderbecke and Harry Hansen, editor of the *World Almanac* from 1948 to 1965. Davenport was the home of Colonel B.J. PALMER (1881-1961), the father of CHIROPRACTIC treatment and his school of Chiropractic. Long scorned, this method of treatment is gaining gradual recognition for its place in the medical profession. St. Ambrose and Marycrest College are both in Davenport. St. Ambrose College, founded by the Roman Catholics in 1882, enrolled 2,221 students during the 1985-1986 academic year and had 158 faculty members. Marycrest, a Catholic school founded in 1939, enrolled 1,600 students and had 79 faculty members during 1985-1986. A popular annual event is the Bix Beiderbecke Jazz Festival every July. In mid-December the residents of the Village of East Davenport, sixty square blocks of early homes and businesses, don costumes and enact frontier and Victorian Christmas scenes in storefront windows. The village also sponsors the Civil War Muster and Mercantile Exposition in September. During this event Civil War units reenact battles in the riverfront park.

DAVID BERGER NATIONAL MEMO-RIAL. Cleveland Heights, Ohio. This site honors the memory of the eleven Israeli athletes who were assassinated at the 1972 Olympic Games in Munich, Germany. One of these victims was David Berger, who was an American citizen. The site is administered by the Jewish Community Center of Cleveland.

DAVIS, Benjamin Oliver (Washington, DC, July 1, 1877—N. Chicago, IL, Nov 26, 1970). Military officer. After studying at Howard University (1897) Davis became a lieutenant of volunteers in the SPANISH-AMERICAN WAR. In 1899 he enlisted in the regular Army as a private and rose to the rank of lieutenant in the Philippine service. He was military attache in Liberia (1909-12). He taught at several universities until 1938 when he was given his first independent command, 369th New York National Guard infantry regiment. In 1940 Davis became the first black general in the U.S. army. The appointment aroused much criticism, both because of his race and because the appointment was said to be politically motivated. Davis became assistant to the inspector general of the army in 1941. He served in Europe in WORLD WAR II as an adviser on race relation. He retired in 1948. He is the father of retired air force officer Benjamin Oliver Davis, Jr.

DAVIS, Edwin Weyerhaeuser. (Rock Island, IL, June 16, 1895—St. Paul, MN, February 13, 1962). Business executive. As Director of the University of Minnesota Bureau of Mines Experiment Station Davis worked for several decades and finally developed the inexpensive concentration process that made TACONITE mining practical. The process, commercially activated in 1955, is known as BENEFICIATING. This has proved enormously important to the area and to United States industry generally.

DAVIS, Elmer. (Aurora, IN, January 13, 1890—Washington, DC, May 18, 1958). Broadcast journalist, author. Davis, a writer of international note, was a teacher at the Franklin, Indiana High School from 1909 to 1910. He moved to the editorial staff of *Adventure* from 1913 to 1914 from which he moved to the staff of the New York *Times* from 1914 to 1924. Davis was a news analyst for the Columbia Broadcasting System from 1939 to 1942 when he became director of the Office of War Information for the national government, 1942-1945, for which he received the Medal of Merit. He moved to the American Broadcasting Company as a news analyst from 1945 to 1956. Davis wrote *But We Were Born Free* (1953), *Two Minutes Till Midnight* (1955) and various novels.

DAVIS, Jefferson. (Fairview, KY., June 3, 1808—New Orleans, LA, Dec. 6, 1889). The Confederate President had slight but interesting connections with the Midwest. Along with several other young West Point graduates, in the early 1830s Davis was stationed near present PORTAGE, Wisconsin, and was placed in command of building FORT WINNEBAGO. There he helped to raft logs for the fort past the rapids of the WISCONSIN RIVER at what is now WISCONSIN DELLS. At FORT CRAWFORD in Wisconsin, Davis first met his future bride, the daughter of Zachary TAYLOR. In another, stranger, connection, a Wisconsin Civil War regiment shared in the honor of capturing Jefferson Davis (May 10, 1865), as the Confederacy collapsed.

DAYTON, Ohio. City (pop. 178,920). Seat of Montgomery County, spreading over the great flood plain and into the surrounding hills of the MIAMI RIVER valley, 50 miles north of CINCINNATI, it lies at the forks of the Great Miami River, where four streams unite. The others include the Stillwater, the Mad, and Wolf Creek. The city was named for Revolutionary general Jonathan Dayton, who was one of the four proprietors of the Ohio lands where the city is now established. With its multiple rivers, the

Gemini III space capsule, Air Force Museum, Dayton. p 119 Henry Ford Museum, Dearborn.

city has both a number of bridges and floods. The flood of 1805 inspired the beginning of levees which grew higher from time to time but did not prevent loss of 361 lives in the disastrous flood of 1913.

Dayton was founded in 1796. As a river port, Dayton soon became a center of commerce. Manufacturing took on added impetus when James Ritty invented the cash register, which is still manufactured at Dayton, and industry was further strengthened when Charles Kettering (1876-1958) invented and began to manufacture the self starter for AUTOMOBILES. Automobile parts and air conditioners are other modern products.

The efforts of the local Wright Brothers began the process which resulted in the location at Dayton of WRIGHT-PATTERSON AIR FORCE BASE, with its great research facilities, the Air Force Institute of Technology and the vast Air Force Museum, said to be the most comprehensive military aviation museum in the world.

In 1913 Dayton was the first city in the nation to adopt the city-manager plan of government. Dayton is the site of the University of DAYTON, and WRIGHT STATE UNIVERSITY.

Poet Paul Laurence DUNBAR (1872-1906), another prominent Daytonian, is remembered by Dunbar State Memorial, which preserves his birthplace. Other points of interest include Carillon Park, with historical displays, Na-

tional Aviation Hall of Fame, and Wright Brothers Memorial. Annual events include River Festival, Dayton Horse Show and Dayton Hydroglobe.

DAYTON, University of. The University of Dayton was founded at the Ohio city in 1850 as St. Mary's Institute. It boasted four students and two teachers. It is particularly known for its instruction in engineering. Today the coeducational Catholic institution has an enrollment of 10,287 with a faculty of 707.

DE PAUL UNIVERSITY, CHICAGO, Illinois Coeducational Roman Catholic university. De Paul was founded, in 1898, as St. Vincent's College by the Vincentian Fathers. The university is now administered by a board of trustees. De Paul grants bachelor's, master's, and doctor's degrees. Lincoln Park Campus and the Frank J. Lewis Center are the university's two campuses. There are colleges of commerce, sciences, music, law, liberal arts and education. The School of Special Learning offers programs leading to the bachelor's degree for anyone twenty-four years of age or older. DePaul College offers a general education program. According to the university, twenty-one percent of the attorneys practicing in Chicago are graduates of De Paul University's College of Law. During the 1985-86 academic year the university enrolled 12,836 students and employed 709 staff members.

DE PAUW UNIVERSITY. Indiana university near GREENCASTLE. Founded in 1836 by the Methodist Episcopal Church and originally called Indiana Asbury University, De Pauw was renamed in 1884 to honor Washington C. De Pauw, a New Albany glass manufacturer who saved the school from closing by making a large donation. The university includes a College of Liberal Arts and a School of Music. Among prominent alumni are Willis Van Devanter, U.S. Supreme Court Justice; Albert BEVERIDGE (1862-1927), U.S. Senator; and Charles A. BEARD (1874-1948), historian. The university is particularly well known for its music college. In 1985-86 the university enrolled 2,393 students and had 201 faculty members.

DE PRIEST, Oscar. (Florence, AL, Mar. 9, 1871—Chicago, IL, May 12, 1951). Congressman. De Priest, a resident of CHICAGO, Illinois, was the first black elected to the United States House of Representatives from the North. De Priest's election in 1929, as a member of the REPUBLICAN PARTY, gave him the opportunity to vote against F.D. Roosevelt's New Deal concepts—a fact which eventually cost him his seat in 1934. His most notable victory was his amendment to the bill creating the Civilian Conservation Corps barring discrimination because of race, color, or creed. He called upon the government to live up to its promises to the Indians and introduced a measure to have the government pay a pension to an estimated one hundred thousand ex-slaves.

DE TONTI, Henri. (Gaeta, Italy, 1650—Mobile, AL, 1704). Considered the true founder of Illinois. De Tonti, known as "Iron Hand" to the Indians, enlisted under LA SALLE in 1678. Together they built FORT CREVE COEUR on Lake Peoria during the winter of 1679-80. When La Salle left the fort, De Tonti assumed command, but Iroquois raids and desertion of men caused him to evacuate the fort. De Tonti rejoined La Salle in the construction of Fort St. Louis on the ILLINOIS RIVER. De Tonti brought settlers, supplies and missionaries from Canada to Illinois until 1700. He was respected by both the French and the Indians.

DEARBORN, Michigan. City (pop. 90,700), eastern Wayne County on Michigan's LOWER PENINSULA on the River Rouge; named to honor General Henry Dearborn, Secretary of War

Henry Ford Museum, Dearborn.

under President Andrew Jackson. Dearborn is the home of the Ford Motor Company. As a city, Dearborn was created by the merger of two towns, Fordson, formerly Springwells, and Dearborn, and incorporated in 1929. The cities of Dearborn and DETROIT have spread out so closely together that only occasional signs indicate where one begins and the other ends.

The first white residents (1795) were probably A. J. Bucklin and the Thomas brothers from Ohio, former army scouts whose property is now part of the Ford estate. Large migration to the area after the WAR OF 1812 led to the creation of Pekin, Springwells, and Greenfield Townships, now all part of Dearborn.

In 1818 one of the first Protestant churches was built on the River Rouge which meanders through the present city. The nickname of Michigan as the WOLVERINE STATE may have originated in this area around 1824. In 1832 Congress removed the Detroit arsenal to Dearborn as a munitions depot for militia and military posts. The area further benefitted from the construction of the CHICAGO ROAD with the help of Father Gabriel RICHARD (1767-1832), one of the few Catholic priests chosen as a delegate to Congress. The Michigan Central Railroad was built through Dearborn in 1837 and a settlement was established in Springwells Township between Detroit and Dearborn. Detroit annexed the eastern and northern sections of this population center. Springwells, renamed Fordson, and Dearborn were merged in 1928.

Between 1920 and 1930 the Ford Motor Company experienced intensive development and the population of Dearborn increased 2,000 percent, making the city the fastest-growing community in Michigan. The drop in population from 104,199 in 1970 to 90,700 in 1984 reflects the slowdown in the auto and other industries and the loss of jobs and income.

Today Dearborn overflows with places for visitors to see. Among the most popular sites is GREENFIELD VILLAGE, a 240-acre historical site with buildings moved here by Henry FORD (1863-1947) from across the United States. The Henry Ford Museum covers fourteen acres. Exhibits focus on TRANSPORTATION, AGRICULTURE, home appliances, musical instruments and furniture. There is also a fine collection of firearms.

DEATH'S DOOR STRAIT. Porte des Mortes (Death's Door) was the name given by the early French VOYAGEURS to the passage in Lake MICHIGAN between WASHINGTON ISLAND and the Door Peninsula of Wisconsin. Indian canoists had a longtime knowledge of the treacherous nature of this half-mile-wide passage. Undercurrents swell up without warning and are are so swift that in 1871, alone, nearly a hundred ships of various sizes were wrecked trying to get in or out of GREEN BAY through this deadly strait. LA SALLE 's (1643-1687) famous ship, the *GRIFFON*, which sailed out of Washington Island (1679), was never seen again in one of the great mysteries of ships at "sea." Many historians now feel it was swallowed up by the treacherous passage.

DEBS, Eugene. (Terre Haute, IN, November 5, 1855—Elmhurst, IL, October 20, 1926). Labor leader, Socialist Party presidential candidate. Debs worked in railroad shops in TERRE HAUTE, Indiana, and became a locomotive fireman. In 1875 he helped establish the first local lodge of the Brotherhood of Locomotive Firemen. Between 1880 and 1884 he was city clerk of Terre Haute and in 1885 a member of the lower house of the Indiana legislature. Debs soon came to criticize social conditions and began to view labor's problem as one of the factions destroying group solidarity. He opposed unionization along craft lines, resigned his position with the Locomotive Firemen, and formed the American Railway Union, an organization open to all railroad workers. An

April 1894 victory against the Great Northern Railroad encouraged the union to strike the Pullman Company. Violence in CHICAGO and federal intervention resulted in the jailing of Debs and several associates for six months on contempt of court charges. The union was destroyed. Debs later claimed that the term in jail, with time to read, led him to socialism. In 1896 Debs supported William Jennings BRYAN for president, but organized the Social Democratic Party of America the next year. In 1901 Debs' followers joined with a faction of the Socialist Labor Party to form the Socialist Party of America. Debs was to be the socialist candidate for president five times, successively between 1900 and 1912, and again in 1920, while in jail. In 1912 he received six percent of the total vote, the highest total ever gained by a socialist. Debs was indicted under the Espionage Act in 1918, for his opposition to entry of the United States into WORLD WAR I. Sentenced to ten years in prison, he was pardoned in 1921 by President HARDING. Debs had remained a socialist when the communists broke with the party in 1919. He was occasionally to criticize American communists in the years to come, and in 1924 he supported the unsuccessful Socialist presidential candidacy of Senator Robert LA FOLLETTE.

DECATUR, Illinois. City (pop. 93,939), seat of Macon County, situated on the SANGAMON RIVER, which has been dammed there to form Lake Decatur. The city was incorporated in 1839, named in honor of Stephen F. Decatur, distinguished commodore of the U.S. Navy during the WAR OF 1812 and later against the Barbary pirates.

In 1829 Macon County chose as its county seat an entirely vacant stretch of prairie without even a road or footpath. This area was named Decatur. Soon James Renshaw erected the first cabin in the area set aside for the coming city. By the following year, when Abraham LINCOLN (1809-1865) came through the settlement to live with his family on a nearby farm, a few other buildings had been erected. Lincoln worked for farmers in the area, practiced his famous rail-splitting, borrowed books from a county offical and otherwise worked, studied and matured. He made his first public speech in what is now Lincoln Park in Decatur.

Most commercial development was based on the surrounding farming region. RAILROADS, arriving in 1854, stimulated manufacturing, followed by increased production during the

CIVIL WAR. In 1874 the first coal mines of the area brought new activities.

One of the leaders of the region was James Millikin, who made a fortune as a banker and industrialist. Part of his wealth was used to endow a university at Decatur which now bears his name and was dedicated by President Theodore Roosevelt in 1903.

In 1923, in order to provide an adequate water supply, the city built a dam which formed the present Lake Decatur with its twelve-mile shoreline.

WORLD WAR II caused a great expansion in Decatur's manufacturing, including a federal government factory which worked on an atomic bomb part. The tremendous expansion of soybean growing brought an entirely new industry of bean milling and processing. The city prefers to be called the world's soybean capital.

There is a substantial railroad repair shop operation, and manufactures include tires and other automobile equipment, tractors and machinery.

Among attractions for visitors, the location where the Lincoln family first settled in Illinois is now maintained as LINCOLN TRAIL HOMESTEAD PARK. The Lincoln Log Cabin Courthouse, where Lincoln practiced law, was once in the heart of the city but now has been moved to Fairview Park.

Meeting in Fairview Park in 1860, the State Republican Convention selected Lincoln as its favorite son and sent its delegates to the national convention at CHICAGO. Other Lincoln memories are preserved in the collection of the Decatur library.

DECORAH, Iowa. (pop. 7,237) Seat of Winneshiek County, the town named for Waukon-Decorah, a chief of the WINNEBAGO and descendant of Sabrevoir de Carrie, an officer in the French colonial army who married a Winnebago woman. The town is situated in northeast Iowa on the Upper Iowa River in a picturesque area between springs and limestone spires. It is the trading hub of a rich agricultural area and has some small industries. With the great influx of Norwegian settlers, Luther college was founded in 1866. Decorah has been called "a center of Norwegian culture in the U.S." It is noted particularly for its Norwegian-American Museum, Besterheim, founded in 1877 by Luther College to collect and conserve the cultural and historical interests of Norwegian pioneers. It is said to be the largest museum in the U.S. devoted to one ethnic

group. The collections include a Norwegian boat that crossed the Atlantic, an immigrant's house, firearms, Indian relics and Norwegian costumes among many others. At nearby SPILLVILLE is the unique Bily Clocks collection of hand carved clocks made by the Bily family over a period of many years. The collection is housed in a building once occupied by famed composer Czech Antonin DVORAK, and there is a Dvorak memorial at Spillville.

DEERE, John. (Rutland, VT, Feb. 7, 1804—Moline, IL, May 17, 1886). Inventor and manufacturer. Deere, a Vermont-born blacksmith, opened a very successful shop in Grand Detour, Ogle County, Illinois, in 1837. Finding the style of plows used in the East unsuitable for the heavy soils of the prairies, Deere experimented with plows of various forms and materials and finally developed one with an iron landslide and moldboard and steel share. Deere's "Grand Detour Plow" proved very successful. Deere started a new company in MOLINE, Illinois, because of its superior transportation facilities. By 1857 Deere's new company was producing 10,000 plows annually. The business was incorporated as Deere and Company in 1868 and moved into manufacturing other agricultural implements. Deere remained the president of the company for the rest of his life.

DEFIANCE, Ohio. City (pop. 16,810), in northwest Ohio, situated on a bluff at the confluence of the MAUMEE and Auglaize rivers. The name comes from FORT DEFIANCE, constructed at the site by General Anthony WAYNE, who defied the English, the Indians and all the devils in hell to take it. It was incorporated as a city in 1836 and is the center of a farming community with manufactures including food products, machinery and fabricated metal. Before European settlement, the area was heavily populated by the Indians, with their mud houses and fields of CORN and tobacco extending for miles along the local rivers. As early as 1760, the French were trading with the Indians there. White settlement began in the area in 1790. The coming of more and more white settlers made the Indians uneasy. General Wayne arrived at Defiance on August 6, 1794, and referred to the place as "the grand emporium of the hostile Indians of the West." After the Indian troubles and the WAR OF 1812 were over, the community began to grow, especially after the coming of the MIAMI AND ERIE and WABASH AND ERIE canals, which joined nearby. In modern times, the community has "defied" recent trends in population decline, and in the period of 1970-80 the population grew very slightly from 16,281 to 16,810. Defiance is the site of Defiance College, and the name is also perpetuated in Fort Defiance City Park, site of the early fort, as well as in the name of Fort Defiance State Park, a narrow strip of forest along the Maumee River. Nearby is the site of the birthplace of famed Chief PONTIAC (1720?-1769), thought to have been on the north bank of the Maumee, opposite the site of Fort Defiance.

DELAVAN, Wisconsin. City (pop. 5,684), situated in Walworth County, in far southeast Wisconsin, the city was named for Edward Cornelius Delavan. The founders of the town in 1836, Henry and Samuel Phoenix, gave their new community its name in honor of the New York temperance leader they admired. In fact, the brothers planned their community as a temperance colony, and all deeds contained a clause forbidding the sale of intoxicants. Ed and Jerry Mabie of New York established their circus headquarters at Delavan, and by 1850 almost everyone in Delavan had some connection with circuses. Some built the wagons; others cared for or trained the animals; some became performers. Nearby farmers provided horses and supplies. William C. Coup organized the famed P.T. Barnum circus at Delavan in 1870-1871. Between 1847 and 1894 Delavan boasted the headquarters of 28 different circuses. Today, the town's cemeteries are the "last lot" for over a hundred members of the 19th-century circus colony.

DELAWARE INDIANS. A group of three closely related tribes living in Delaware, New Jersey and Pennsylvania. Originally living in the Northwest, the Delaware who moved to the east were friendly to the whites and successfully traded with the Dutch. Defeated in an Indian war of 1720 by the IROQUOIS tribes of the Six Nations, the Delaware were forced to move to Ohio. They sided with the French during the FRENCH AND INDIAN WAR and were finally removed westward to Indian Territory.

DELAWARE, Ohio. City (pop. 18,780), seat of Delaware County, situated in south west-central Ohio, on a rolling site on the west side of the Olentangy River, it takes its name from the DELAWARE INDIANS, whose English name was derived in turn from Delaware Bay and from the state of Delaware. The bay was named by

Captain Samuel Argall, who discovered it in 1610, in honor of Thomas West, Lord de la Warr. Mingo Indians had a town on the Ohio site, named Pluggy's Town. The Delaware also had a village there, which gave the present town its name. Both groups were attracted to the mineral springs nearby, which they called Medicine Waters. In 1804 Moses Byxbe laid out a town on the east side of the Olentangy, but it was soon abandoned. In 1807 Joseph Barber built the first European-style house on the present site and opened a tavern. In 1833 a company was formed to exploit the mineral springs. A large stone structure called the Mansion house was built in 1834 as a health resort. When it failed, the Methodist Episcopal church acquired it. Named Elliot Hall, it became the first building for OHIO WESLEYAN UNIVERSITY, chartered in 1842, around which much of the community activities have centered ever since. However, there is modest manufacturing, and the city is the commercial center of a prosperous farming and livestock area. Delaware was also the birthplace of President Rutherford B. HAYES (1822-1893). Perkins Observatory, operated by Ohio Wesleyan and OHIO STATE universities, the Delaware County Historical Society Museum and Alum Creek State Park are attractions of the area. Olentangy Caverns, south of the city, offers visitors the only three-level cave in Ohio.

DELICIOUS APPLES. The worldwide distribution and international fame of the delicious apple was due to a most unusual combination of circumstances, originating in the Midwest and beginning in 1881. The history of the apple began with a very ordinary tree on the Jesse Hiatt farm near PERU, Iowa. His yellow belleflower apple tree had been destroyed by storms, but new shoots grew from the mangled top. When apples finally appeared from the new shoots, they were strangely formed, elongated with a row of peculiar nubs on the bottom. The Hiatts thought the fruit was defective, and the tree was about to be destroyed when they and their neighbors tried the apples, and all thought they were "delicious." Hiatt rooted cuttings from the modified tree and improved the fruit for twelve years, marketing his apple and calling it the Hawkeye, in honor of the Hawkeye state. In 1894 he sold the rights to the fruit to Stark Brothers Nurseries and Orchards in Missouri. They took out a trademark for the Delicious Apple. Tama Jim WILSON (1836-1920), Secretary of Agriculture, an Iowan, declared the apple to be a

Densmore - Des Moines

"promising new fruit." That promise exceeded all expectations, with the delicious having become probably the most widely distributed of any single apple species.

DENSMORE, Frances. (Red Wing, MN, May 21, 1867—Red Wing, MN, June 5, 1957). Music historian. Densmore made a career of preserving the American Indian heritage. Although in the early 1900s she made many photographs of Indians doing everyday tasks, Densmore was better known as a music historian. She began studying the music of American Indians in 1893 and made special researches into American INDIAN MUSIC for the Bureau of American Ethnology, beginning in 1907. The Smithsonian-Densmore Collection contains sound recordings of American Indian music made between 1941 and 1943. Densmore was the author of *American Indians and their Music* (1926), *Teton Sioux Music* (1918) and many other books on the various tribes and groups. In 1940, Densmore received the National Association of American Composers and Conductors award for service to American music.

DES MOINES RIVER. River rising in southwestern Minnesota, and traveling 535 miles, generally southeast, to meet the MISSISSIPPI RIVER. It flows through Algona, FORT DODGE, DES MOINES, and Ottumwa in Iowa and forms the short river border between Iowa and Missouri. Several flood control projects are found along the Des Moines. Most important of these is Red Rock Dam, which forms Red Rock Lake, southeast of Des Moines.

DES MOINES, IOWA

Name: From the Des Moines River, from the French and Indian languages.

Area: 66.1 square miles.

Elevation: 963 feet

Population:
1984: 190,832
Rank: 77th
Percent change (1980-1984): minus .1%
Density (city): 2,890 per sq. mi.
Metropolitan Population: 377,000
Percent change (1980-1984): 2.5%

Racial and Ethnic Makeup (1980):
White: 90.4%
Black: 6.8%
Hispanic origin: 3,523 persons
Indian: 556 persons
Asian: 1,596 persons

Age:
18 and under: 25.9%
65 and over: 12.5%

TV Stations: 5

Radio Stations: 18

Hospitals: 8

Sports Teams:
Cubs (minor-league baseball)

Further Information: Chamber of Commerce, 8th & High Streets, Des Moines, IA 50309

DES MOINES, Iowa. City, capital of Iowa and seat of Polk County, situated at the junction of the RACCOON RIVER with the DES MOINES RIVER, chartered as Des Moines in 1857.

Few cities have generated so much speculation about the origin of their names. The Indian word moingona means "river of the mounds." The French name "Riviere des Moines," meaning "River of the Monks," was said to have been used because Catholic missionaries explored the river. Perhaps the most logical, but least accepted, is the French "De Moyen," thought to describe the middle or principal river between the Missouri and Mississippi rivers.

Far from any large body of water and almost in the exact center of the conterminous states, Des Moines, not unexpectedly, has a continental climate, with rather long cold winters, hot summers and short springs and falls. Normal average temperatures range from 19 in January to 76 in July.

The city is the commercial center of the greatest food producing region of the world, and much of its manufacture is concerned with food processing. As home to more than 50 insurance companies, it ranks second in the country in that field, after Hartford, Connecticut, often being called the Hartford of the West. Despite its insular location, the city is a major center of publishing. Among many other publishers, one of the major publishers of magazines and books, a Fortune 500 company, Meredith Publishing Company is headquartered there.

In other communications areas, the Des

The gold-domed capitol, Des Moines.

Moines *Register* is read statewide, and cable television purveyor Heritage Communications is one of the largest in its field.

Principal manufactured products include concrete blocks, dental equipment and plastics.

FORT DES MOINES was begun in 1843. The city of Fort Des Moines was incorporated in 1851 and became a center for homesteaders in the 1850s. The town was selected as state capital in 1856. In 1857, when it took its present name, the seat of state government was moved there from IOWA CITY, because of its more central location.

The decline in population in the period from 1970 through 1984 was less than might have been expected, due to the serious problems of the farm country of which the city is the center. In 1970 the population stood at 201,000, at 191,000 in 1984.

Des Moines is the home of DRAKE UNIVERSITY, one of the state's largest private centers of higher education. The university has national renown as the sponsor of the Drake Relays, one of the major annual track events. The College of Osteopathic Medicine and Surgery and Open Bible College are other higher education institutions.

On its hilltop situation, the capitol with its gleaming gold-leaf dome, can be seen for miles across the countryside. The building is considered one of the most handsome of all state capitols. Begun in 1871, it was not completed until thirteen years later. Because there were no granite quarries in the state, the region was combed for large granite boulders, left by the glaciers. Most of the stone for the exterior walls was cut from these great rocks. The capitol interior is particularly renowned and features the great mural *Westward* by Edwin H. BLASHFIELD, representing various groups of Iowa settlers.

The 93-acre capitol grounds have been

described as the "largest and most beautiful setting for a state capitol."

The state historical society and museum is housed in a large new center for which private funds were solicited and which was completed in 1987. The governor's home is a distinguished old mansion.

Des Moines' museums are remarkable for a city of its size. The art center has been enlarged several times with the assistance of noted architects. Its collection contains works of most of the masters, including a particularly noteworthy statue by Henry Moore. There is a fine Center of Science and Industry.

During the 1980s the city concentrated on renewal of the downtown area, with new SKYSCRAPERS, enclosed shopping malls and enclosed elevated walkways and bridges connecting central city buildings.

The most comprehensive and authoritative of its type is the collection of Living History Farms, just outside Des Moines. These include reproductions of farms of the various periods in the nation's premier farming state, as well as demonstrations and contests in farm activities.

Annual Des Moines events include Two Rivers Festival in late June.

DES PLAINES RIVER. Source in southeastern Wisconsin, approximately 150 miles long, the Des Plaines flows south to join with the KANKAKEE RIVER to form the ILLINOIS RIVER. The Des Plaines passes close to CHICAGO and flows through several of its suburbs, including JOLIET, Illinois. Louis JOLLIET (1645-1700) was the first to suggest creating a canal between the Chicago and Des Plaines rivers. In 1900 this dream was realized with the opening of the SANITARY AND SHIP CANAL. The south branch of the Chicago River had been deepened, a canal had been dug between the Chicago and Des Plaines rivers, and locks installed. The locks keep Lake MICHIGAN from flowing too quickly into the new river system that reversed the flow of the Chicago river and enabled boats to travel from the GREAT LAKES to the MISSISSIPPI RIVER by way of the Des Plaines and Illinois rivers.

DES PLAINES, Illinois. City (pop. 53,568), Cook Co., suburb of CHICAGO, Illinois, directly north of O'HARE INTERNATIONAL AIRPORT, the city named for the presence of a species of maple called "plaine" by the French. Des Plaines' population explosion, from 8,798 people in 1939, began in the 1950s when businesses recognized the advantages of locating near Chicago and its transportation facilities. Des

Plaines, founded in 1835 by New Englanders who called their community Rand, saw builders in the 1960s invest heavily in office buildings that were easily accessible to Chicago businesses and professional people. Des Plaines houses the national office of the General Association of Regular Baptist Churches and is the western end of the Chicago terminal district for railroad transportation. According to industry figures, every third railroad carload in the United States originates, moves through, or ends in this area.

DESOTA BEND NATIONAL WILDLIFE REFUGE. On the Iowa side of one of the largest bends of the MISSOURI RIVER, n e a r Missouri Valley, Iowa, and about fifteen miles north of COUNCIL BLUFFS, Iowa, and Omaha, Nebraska. This 7,823 acre heart of the Missouri River flyway, provides a secure resting place for as many as 200,000 snow geese and 175,000 mallard ducks on their annual migrations, along with a total of millions of other migrating fowl, as well as local wildlife which make their homes there. In 1981 a visitors' center was established, including a museum. In addition to the wildlife displays and exhibits, the museum includes relics salvaged from the CIVIL WAR era river steamship *Bertrand,* which sank nearby and was buried in silt.

DETROIT LAKES, Minnesota. City (pop. 7,106), northwest Minnesota, resort and fishing center. The first settlers to the area came in 1868. According to a local story the settlement was first called "Detroit" because a French priest was to have said, "See the beautiful

detroit" when referring with a French word to a narrows created in the lake by a sandbar. Tourism is a major source of revenue. The Becker County Historical Society Museum offers a fine collection of Indian, Viking and pioneer artifacts. Fort Detroit is the largest deer park in Minnesota with nearly one hundred tame deer ready to be hand-fed. Stagecoach and pony rides are available.

DETROIT RIVER. Although only thirty-one miles long, the Detroit River forms an integral part of the Great Lakes shipping lane. It joins lakes HURON and ST. CLAIR. The ST. CLAIR RIVER provides the linkage from that lake to Lake Huron. Together they connect Superior, the other GREAT LAKES and the sea.

DETROIT, MICHIGAN

Name: From the French Ville d'estrait, meaning "city of the strait," due to its situation on the strait known as the Detroit River, between Lake Erie and Lake St. Clair.

Nickname: Motor City or Motown

Area: 135.6 square miles

Elevation: 685 feet

Population:
1984: 1,088,973
Rank: 6th
Percent change (1980-1984): minus 9.5%
Density (city): 8,848 per sq. mi.

Detroit, Michigan, from an 1834 lithograph.

Detroit

Metropolitan Population: 4,577,000

Percent change (1980-1984): minus 3.7%

Racial and Ethnic Makeup (1980):

White: 34.9%

Black: 63%

Hispanic origin: 28,466 persons

Indian: 3,846 persons

Asian: 7,614 persons

Other: 12,882 persons

Age:

18 and under: 30.3%

65 and over: 11.7%

TV Stations: 9

Radio Stations: 37

Hospitals: 28

Sports Teams:

Detroit Tigers (baseball)

Detroit Lions (football)

Detroit Pistons (basketball)

Detroit Spirits (minor-league basketball)

Detroit Red Wings (hockey)

Further Information: Detroit Chamber
of Commerce, 150 Michigan Avenue, Detroit, MI 48226

DETROIT, Michigan. City, seat of Wayne County. The name is derived from the French word meaning "strait," due to its situation between Lake ERIE and Lake ST. CLAIR. On the DETROIT RIVER (which is really a strait), at the border with Canada, Detroit is a port of entry and a major center of GREAT LAKES shipping and rail center. It was incorporated in 1815.

Its immediate suburbs are Wyandotte, Lincoln Park, Allen Park, DEARBORN and Dearborn Heights on the south and southwest; Southfield, Oak Park, Ferndale, WARREN, East Detroit, Harper Woods and Grosse Point Woods on the north. GROSSE POINTE, an elegant enclave on Lake St. Clair, now is part of the city.

Other suburbs include STERLING HEIGHTS, Troy, Royal Oak, Farmington, LIVONIA and Garden City. The area of BLOOMFIELD HILLS on the northwest has attracted some of the city's wealthy residents and boasts some of the finest modern homes of the area.

During the nineteenth century, Detroit assumed significance as a shipping and manu-facturing center, laying the basis for its later industrial growth. Its substantial carriage manufacturing industry provided a base for the development of the automobile industry. Despite many setbacks, this industry continues to place the city first in the world in production of motor vehicles.

The city ranks first in production of grey iron foundry products, machine tools and metal stampings. Other important products are paint and wire goods.

A French fort and trading settlement was founded by Antoine de la Mothe CADILLAC in 1701. Called Ville d'etroit, it was to be the first major city founded in the Midwest region. The British captured the town in 1760. In 1763 Indian Chief PONTIAC laid siege to the city. Lasting for 175 days, this was the longest Indian siege of a city. Pontiac failed and was forced to make peace.

Jay's Treaty of 1796 resulted in American control, which was contested by the British, who seized the city during the WAR OF 1812, but American General William Henry HARRISON (1773-1841) regained it in 1813. One of the major disasters of the period was the FIRE which destroyed almost every building in 1805, but new plans were laid by famed city planner Pierre l'Enfant, and rebuilding began.

The city was the capital of Michigan from 1805 to 1847. An epidemic of CHOLERA swept the city in 1832. A few years later a foreign visitor described the city with its "...lofty buildings, enormous steamers, noisy port and busy streets..."

The capital was moved to LANSING in 1848, but the city continued to grow and prosper. Detroit Mayor Hazen S. PINGREE was elected governor in 1897. He kept both positions until, forced by the state supreme court to give up one, he resigned as mayor. The early nineteen hundreds saw the beginning of the automobile industry. According to historian Raymond C. Miller, Detroit "...remade America with the automobile. Henry FORD (1863-1947) and the Ford Motor Company, Ransom OLDS (1864-1950) and his Oldsmobile, the General Motors Corporation, and Chrysler Motors of Walter P. CHRYSLER (1875-1940) brought the city its leadership in the field."

During WORLD WAR I, the city was considered a center for German spy activity. After the war William B. STOUT produced the FORD TRIMOTOR, which gave commercial aviation its early impetus. The Depression of 1929 was particularly difficult for Detroit because of the drop in auto sales. In WORLD WAR II, Detroit surpassed all other cities in war production. The Ford Willow Run plant could produce a B-24 bomber every hour.

Beginning in 1930, Frank Murphy was one of the city's notable mayors. The opening in 1959 of the ST. LAWRENCE SEAWAY gave the port of Detroit access to the world's shipping.

The race riots of 1967 caused property damage of $150,000,000. Much of the downtown area was destroyed, but developments such as the Renaissance Center and Cobo Hall, one of the largest of the nation's convention centers, have helped to restore the central city, but the city still has failed to recover its once-robust central core, due to the loss of jobs and income.

Recessions in the 1970s and the competition of Japanese and other foreign auto makers have brought unemployment, but in the 1980s the industry was able to rebound substantially. However, problems continue, with the increase in unemployment proceeding in the period 1980 through 1984, 12.44% of Detroit jobs were lost. Of 329 metropolitan areas studied in *Places Rated Almanac*, Detroit was ranked 312th in its economy.

In 1984 Detroit population ranked sixth among U.S. cities, with a population of 1,088,973, down almost 200,000 in the four years following the 1980 census of 1,203,339. However, the city still ranks second in population in the Midwest. Population of the metropolitan region, extending as far as ANNE ARBOR, was placed at 4,577,000 in 1984.

The black population of the city in the 1980 census had grown to 758,468, almost twice the white population of 420,529.

In sports Detroit teams have won many national championships. Professional teams include the football Lions, the hockey Red Wings, basketball Pistons and baseball Tigers. The entire city went wild when the Tigers won the World's Series in 1984.

Another principal tourist attraction of the city is its proximity to Canada, connected with the northern nation by tunnel and the world's longest international suspension bridge, Ambassador International.

Cultural institutions include the Detroit Symphony, organized in 1914, the Detroit Institute of Arts, the University of DETROIT and WAYNE STATE UNIVERSITY. One of the outstanding museum complexes was founded at Dearborn by Henry Ford. The vast Ford museum has one of the largest collections of transportation displays, and GREENFIELD VILLAGE includes homes and workshops of famous Americans brought there from various parts of the country.

A major park among cities is BELLE ISLE, in the Detroit River, with its gardens, children's zoo, conservatory and aquarium.

DETROIT, UNIVERSITY OF. Catholic institution directed by the Jesuit Fathers. The University of Detroit was founded in 1877 and reorganized in 1911. The seventy-acre campus is in the northwest residential section of DETROIT and has thirty-nine buildings. The university includes the Colleges of Business Administration, Education and Human Services, Arts, Engineering and Science and the Schools of Law, Dentistry, Architecture, Graduate School and the Evening College of Administration and Business. The institution is accredited by the North Central Association of Colleges and Schools. The university enrolled 6,157 students and employed 430 faculty members during the 1985-1986 academic year.

DEVIL'S ELBOW. Weekend recreation spot on a bend of the BIG PINEY RIVER northeast of Waynesville, Missouri, near the Gasconade Division of the Mark Twain National Forest, named by lumberjacks who feared the annual logjams that formed at the river's bend. The region abounds in legend of lost treasure and outlaws. One story claims that a wealthy California gold-miner buried $60,000 in gold in the hills. Jesse JAMES and his gang supposedly used the area for a hideout. Portuguese Point, a high elevation, is a favorite for artists and photographers. The valley nearby was settled by Portuguese farmers who raised CATTLE and sheep.

DEWEY, Thomas Edmund. (Owosso, MI, Mar. 24, 1902—New York, NY, Mar. 16, 1971). Crime fighter and governor. He graduated from the University of Michigan in 1923, took a law degree from Columbia in 1925 and began to practice law in New York City. Dewey gained national fame as the special prosecutor during the investigation of organized crime in New York from 1935 to 1937. He was elected the district attorney of New York County in 1937 and was the Republican candidate for governor of New York in 1938. Dewey was elected then and reelected every election through 1950. As governor he took the stand of a Moderate Republican on most issues, but was renowned for his opposition to the New Deal of President F.D. Roosevelt. Dewey was the unsuccessful Republican nominee for President of the United States in 1944 and again in 1948. Dewey was the author of *The Case Against the New Deal* (1940), *Journey to the Far Pacific* (1952), and *Thomas E. Dewey on the Two Party System* (1966).

DEWITT, Missouri. Village, located in northwest Missouri's Carroll County, became a hot-bed of controversy when MORMONS from FAR WEST, Missouri, began to purchase property in the community. The Mormons let their gentile neighbors know of their hope to change the town into a Mormon springboard for other settlements. Friction between the Mormons and non-Mormons flared into conflict. A Carroll County delegation on September 10, 1838, gave the Mormons ten days to leave the area. Troops from Howard, Clay, Saline and Ray counties prepared for conflict when the Mormons indicated they would resist the order. On the day before battle William F. Dunnica and Judge James Earickson of Glasgow, Missouri, obtained a promise from the Mormons that they would leave Carroll County the following morning. Bloodshed was avoided with only hours to spare.

DIORAMAS. Exhibits of modeled figures or objects in front of a modeled or painted background. Dioramas, in their present form, are thought to have originated in the FIELD MUSEUM in CHICAGO, Illinois. For perspective, models become smaller toward the back of the exhibit, finally blending with the background to create lifelike scenes. Dioramas generally use curved backgrounds to give the feeling of distance in outdoor scenes. They show animals and plants in their natural surroundings, historical events, and industrial methods. The word "Diorama" was first used by Louis Daguerre, a French inventor, in 1822 to name transparent paintings he exhibited and a theater he opened.

DIRIGIBLES. Cigar-shaped, steerable, helium or hydrogen-filled airships powered by engines. Control is achieved with vertical fins and a rudder. Although midwesterners might have seen their first dirigible hovering about the capitol dome in DES MOINES, Iowa, in 1906, the first dirigible meet in the country, was held in ST. LOUIS, Missouri, in 1908. AKRON, Ohio, became the U.S. dirigible capital, the U.S. *Akron* and *Macon* were built there and housed in the gigantic hanger at the airport. The city is still the center of U.S. blimp production.

DISASTERS, NATURAL. The Midwest has had its share of natural disasters. The worst fortunately occurred during a period and in an area where there was little settlement. This was in 1811 when the greatest EARTHQUAKE ever experienced on the North American continent was centered at NEW MADRID, Missouri, and was felt throughout much of the eastern portion of the entire continent. New lakes were formed; rivers changed course; islands disappeared, and heavy quakes continued for almost a year. Experts say that such a quake could occur at any time, and they feel that if one occurred today in the same place, cities such as ST. LOUIS might be almost entirely destroyed. The Midwest continues to experience earthquakes, such as the one registering 5.0 on the Richter Scale which rattled central Illinois and was felt as far as CHICAGO in 1987.

In terms of loss of life and property, the fires which on October 8, 1871, swept almost simultaneously through Chicago, the area of PESHTIGO, Wisconsin, and around HOLLAND, Michigan, were the worst in total effect in the Midwest. Lives lost in Chicago were 250 and 1,182 in Wisconsin. In the Holland fire 18,000 were left homeless. Chicago's fire caused $196,000,000 in property damage, which would be many billions in today's dollars. St. Louis and DETROIT also suffered disastrous fires.

The Midwest is "tornado territory." All the states of the region have suffered tornado damage. The deaths and damage of the TORNADOES which swept Missouri, Illinois and Indiana on March 18, 1925, took the record toll of dead, with 689 losing their lives.

With some of the nation's largest rivers bordering much of the region, the Midwest is always subject to severe FLOODS. The worst floods in U.S. history occurred in the OHIO and MISSISSIPPI RIVER valleys in 1937, when 250 people lost their lives. The Mississippi is particularly noted for changing its course and devouring cities or parts of cities, in disasters such as the 1805 flood which swept away historic KASKASKIA, Illinois, and left a part of Illinois on the west side of the river. The river has also taken its toll in sinkings of ships. Among the worst was the wrecking, during a storm, of a steamer, in 1890, with a loss of 98 lives.

The most prolonged natural disaster in the region occurred in the 1930s when the worst DROUTH on record continued until much of the Midwest was swept by winds carrying suffocating clouds of dust, picked up from the parched prairies, and crops were devastated. In 1988 most of the Midwest suffered from a drouth described as "the second worst in history."

DISNEY, Walter E. (Chicago, IL, Dec. 5, 1901—Los Angeles, CA, Dec. 15, 1966). Motion picture and amusement park innovator. Disney spent much of his childhood in MARCELINE, Missouri. There he drew cartoons with tar on his grandfather's barn door and later was responsible for taking the field of animated cartooning to heights never dreamed possible. He was too young for armed service during WORLD WAR I but insisted on taking part by driving a Red Cross ambulance. As a cartoonist in KANSAS CITY, beginning in 1926, he experimented with animation. His third cartoon short, featuring Mickey Mouse, brought him wide attention, and he progressed quickly in the field. In 1937 *Snow White and the Seven Dwarfs* was the first animated feature film. It received the Academy of Motion Picture Arts and Sciences award in 1938 and continues to be revived for new audiences. *Fantasia* (1940), considered one of Disney's finest efforts, earned him a plaque from the Dowling Foundation, a scroll from New York Critics, and a medal from the New York School of Music. He won France's highest artistic honor, Officier d'Academie, in 1956 for his series called *True Adventure*. He then began to branch out into other types of entertainment. Disney founded Disneyland as a base for television programming in 1954. During his career he received thirty-nine awards from the Academy of Motion Picture Arts and Sciences, four Emmy awards and hundreds of other awards and decorations. The most popular of all his enterprises, Disney World, in Florida, was planned by Disney but not realized during his lifetime. He was directing its construction at the time of his death.

DISSECTED TILL PLAINS. Region in the southwestern corner of Minnesota where glaciers left a deep deposit of soil-forming clay, gravel and sand known as till. The few level places in the area make excellent farmland, while streams have cut up or dissected much of the land.

DIVIDES. Watersheds. The great divides which separate the waters of continents are usually only thought of as vast mountain ranges, such as the Rockies, where the Continental Divide snakes from north to south, for the most part along the crests of the highest ranges. In the Midwest the divides are far less

dramatic but nonetheless real and important. As early as the explorations of Father MARQUETTE (1637-1675) and Louis JOLLIET (1645-1700), most of the Midwest divides were known.

When they carried their canoes across the short distance between the DES PLAINES RIVER to the CHICAGO RIVER, Jolliet and Marquette were well aware that they had crossed the divide which separated waters flowing into the GREAT LAKES from those flowing eventually into the MISSISSIPPI RIVER and the Gulf of Mexico. Even at that early date, Jolliet realized that a short canal across the divide would open a water route between the Great Lakes and the Gulf.

In their entirety the Great Lakes have a relatively shallow watershed, particularly along the U.S. side. In Ohio, roughly less than a third of the state sends its rivers to the Great Lakes. In Indiana the divide occupies a much smaller percentage of the state. Surrounded by the Great Lakes, Michigan is the major exception. All its rivers flow into the lakes. However, Michigan also has more divides than the others. These separate the waters which flow into Lake MICHIGAN from those which flow into lakes HURON and ERIE in the LOWER PENINSULA and in the UPPER PENINSULA separate those flowing into Lake Michigan from those emptying into Lake Superior.

Technically, Illinois lies entirely within the Mississippi watershed, due to the engineers' reversal of the Chicago River, which once flowed into Lake Michigan. Wisconsin's northern rivers flowing into Superior and the eastern ones into Lake Michigan are relatively short.

Minnesota is the only state which discharges its waters to the north into Hudson Bay, east into the Great Lakes-ST. LAWRENCE RIVER SYSTEM and south to the Gulf through the Mississippi. Both the Mississippi and the St. Lawrence originate in Minnesota. Most of the rivers of the Midwest empty into the Mississippi River system through the Ohio and Missouri rivers. This system constitutes one of the world's greatest watersheds. Iowa and Missouri lie entirely inside its divides. Most of Ohio and Indiana drain into the Ohio, and the largest part of both Minnesota and Wisconsin follows the same pattern, as they drain into the Mississippi.

"DIXIE." Song. The great rallying song of the Confederacy, "Dixie", was actually the product of a Midwest composer, Daniel Decatur EMMETT of MOUNT VERNON, Ohio. One morning while he was playing with Bryant's Minstrels, Emmett was asked to compose an ensemble number on very short notice. The resultant song was "Dixie" (1859). It was played in New Orleans in the spring of 1861, where it brought down the house and was soon adopted by the Confederacy. Eventually most of the U.S. South became known as Dixie. Despite its use by the South, the song was never entirely repudiated by the North, and President Abraham LINCOLN (1809-1865) is said to have loved it.

DODGE, Henry. (Vincennes, IN, 1782—1867). One of the most colorful characters in the Midwest during the early 1800s, Henry Dodge came to the area under a cloud of suspicion. He had been indicted as one of the co-conspirators of Aaron BURR. During his trial he had physically beaten nine of the jurors and yet was acquitted. Arriving in present Wisconsin in 1827, he settled illegally on Indian land. When Chief BLACK HAWK appeared to be a threat, Dodge organized his militia known as the Rangers. Black Hawk, who called Dodge "Hairy Face," claimed that Dodge was most responsible for the defeat and massacre of his tribesmen at the Battle of BAD AXE, August 2, 1832. After the BLACK HAWK WAR, Wisconsin Territory was organized in 1836, combining all of present Iowa, Wisconsin, Minnesota and parts of the Dakotas. Henry Dodge was named governor of the territory. Conservative Midwesterners were horrified by his language, and some were terrified by the Bowie knife he always carried with him. Dodge lost his governorship in 1841 but was reappointed later. When Wisconsin became a state in 1848, Democrat Dodge was appointed as one of the first two senators and served in the U.S. Senate until 1857, when he retired. His son, Augustus Caesar Dodge (1812-1883) was Iowa's first U.S. senator (1848-55) and was minister to Spain from 1855 to 1859.

DODGE BROTHERS, Horace E. (Niles, MI, May 17, 1868—Dec. 10, 1920), John (Niles, MI, Oct. 25, 1864—Jan. 14, 1920). Automobile manufacturers. Horace Dodge and his older brother, John, began their careers making bicycles and stove parts. Soon they were manufacturing engines and auto parts for Ford Motor Company and Olds Motor Works. On November 14, 1914, the first Dodge automobile was produced, and the brothers stopped working for other companies and started their own auto manufacturing business. They built one of the first all-steel American cars. Horace Dodge invented many improvements for the industry, including an oven for baking enamel on steel car bodies. Both of the Dodge brothers died in 1920, and their company was taken over by the Chrysler Corporation in 1928.

DOGWOOD. The state tree of Missouri. Flowering dogwood is native to eastern America. The so-called flowers are a small inconspicuous part of what actually appears to be a flower. The white or pink outer part surrounding the true flower is actually made up of bracts, generally mistaken for petals. The flowering dogwoods grow wild throughout the southern areas of the Midwest. The cultivated variety is popular wherever it can be grown, and the cultivated "flower" is much larger and more showy. The wood is hard and used for machinery bearings and tool handles. The bark has been used as a substitute for quinine, and it also is rich in tannin.

DONIPHAN, Alexander William. (Maysville, KY, July 9, 1808—Richmond, MO, August 8, 1887). Lawyer and army officer. Doniphan refused to carry out the subsequently revoked court martial sentence of death ordered by the state of Missouri for Joseph SMITH, and other MORMON leaders arrested in FAR WEST, Missouri. Doniphan began his legal career in Missouri in 1830 and became a leading attorney, specializing in criminal cases. He served in the Missouri legislature in 1836, 1840 and 1856. In 1838 he was commanding a brigade against the Mormons when he received his order from General Samuel D. Lucas to execute the Mormon leaders, a command which he ignored and termed pure murder. Doniphan later commanded a regiment of Missourians on a march from Valverde, New Mexico, to Chihuahua, Mexico, during the MEXICAN WAR. This is considered one of the most brilliant long marches ever made. Before the CIVIL WAR he advocated Missouri neutrality and opposed secession. Doniphan was a Missouri delegate to the Washington, D.C. Peace Conference in 1861, the same year in which he was a major general in command of the Missouri militia.

DOOR COUNTY. Named by some travel experts as one of the ten most interesting tourist counties in the United States. Door County occupies most of the "Thumb" of Wisconsin, that peninsula which stretches out into Lake MICHIGAN in east central Wisconsin and separates the waters of Green Bay from the lake proper. The largest town of the area and jumping off place for the peninsula is GREEN BAY at the inland end of the bay. However, the actual "gateway" to Door county is the city of STURGEON BAY, at the head of its own narrow bay, which extends for almost 1,000 feet into the narrowest part of the peninsula. A region of fabulous fishing, picturesque villages, such as EGG HARBOR, FISH CREEK and Sister Bay, and year-round recreation, Door County provides summer, fall, winter and spring activity. The spring display of thousands of acres of apple and cherry orchards provides one of the country's major blossom festivals. By contrast, the presence of hundreds of shipwrecks lying in treacherous DEATH'S DOOR STRAIT has become one of the most unusual lures for scuba divers. Fall colors are among the most spectacular anywhere, and the roads which bring the visitors to this colorful display are transformed into cross-country ski routes in winter. Door County Summer theater and concert series are world renowned, as are the boutiques and art galleries, most featuring work of the large number of local artists. Perhaps most famous of all are the nearly legendary fish boils, featuring local trout, whitefish and many types of vegetables, all cooked in cauldrons over open fires. When the "stew" is ready, kerosene is poured into the cauldron, and the resulting fire burns away unwanted fish oils, leaving a perfectly cooked delicacy.

DOS PASSOS, John Roderigo. Chicago, IL, Jan. 14, 1896—Baltimore, MD, Sept. 28, 1970). Author. After graduating from Harvard in 1916, he traveled in Spain, expecting to become a student of architecture. WORLD WAR I intervened, and he volunteered for the French ambulance corps, later becoming a private in the U.S. Army medical corps. His first two books were derived from his war experiences—*One Man's Initiation—1917* (1920) and *Three Soldiers* (1921), bitterly portraying the effects of war on the three main characters. By 1925 in his *Manhattan Transfer*, he had developed a unique style combining naturalism and stream-of-consciousness. His major work was a fuller expression of his radical approach to life. This was the trilogy U.S.A., which included *The 42nd Parallel* (1930), *1919* (1932) and *The Big Money* (1936). These traced the first three decades of the 1900s in what he found to be the absurdity, deterioration and helplessness of the lives of his varied characters. In these works he incorporated background fragments of newspaper headlines, advertisements, songs of the era and other insertions. Lives of lesser figures were highlighted against the biographies of promi-

nent Americans. His later work became more conservative and he eventually expressed disillusion with liberal and radical movements. Later novels included *The Great Days* (1958) and *Midcentury* (1961). His works included books on travel, history and biography.

DOTY, James Duane. (Salem, NY, 1799—Salt Lake City, UT, 1865). Politician, lawyer, speculator. In 1819 he moved to Detroit from the East. In late October, 1823, the twenty-three-year-old lawyer from the East arrived at GREEN BAY Wisconsin, to take his post as federal judge of much of what was then the Northwest. Losing his judgeship in 1832, Doty traveled across the Wisconsin wilderness, shrewdly purchasing prime tracts of land at negligible prices. Among these tracts was a 1,200-acre site in the Four Lakes region in central Wisconsin. To further his interests, he became the Wisconsin delegate to Congress and governor. As the "stormy petrel of early Wisconsin politics," Doty carefully lobbied the legislature to select his wilderness acreage as the site of the new Wisconsin capital, although not one person lived in the area permanently at the time. Doty had already named the proposed town MADISON, and of course it became the present capital of Wisconsin.

DOUGLAS, Stephen Arnold. (Brandon, VT, Apr. 23, 1813—Chicago, IL, June 3, 1861). Politician, U.S. senator, lawyer. He began to study law but finding little opportunity in the East he journeyed to Illinois in 1833, becoming a schoolmaster at Winchester. He received his Illinois license to practice law at JACKSONVILLE in 1834. In less than a year he was elected as state's attorney for the first judicial district. He helped to fashion the Democratic political machine in Illinois and was greatly assisted by it.

He served in various state posts, including secretary of state (1840). He continued to work for party candidates and was himself chosen for the U.S. Senate in 1847. In that year he also took up residence in Chicago.

As chairman of the committee on territories, the Democratic U.S. Senator was one of the most powerful in that body. The issue of SLAVERY in the territories was the most crucial facing the Congress. Because his wife had inherited 150 slaves, some critics thought Douglas leaned toward slavery. However, he created the Doctrine of Popular Sovereignty, which he hoped would help unite the Democrats of North and South. He also was the author of the KANSAS-NEBRASKA ACT which authorized the citizens in the two territories to choose between their being slave or free states. But in an effort not to alienate the South,he spoke in favor of the Fugitive Slave Act.

Instead of promoting popular sovereignty in a peaceful solution of the problem, pro- and anti-slavery forces moved in to create a "bloody Kansas." This conflict alienated Douglas' supporters on both sides.

In his famous debates with Abraham LINCOLN, the noted orator proclaimed his views throughout Illinois. Although the Republicans won a majority of the Illinois popular vote in 1858, Douglas was reelected to the Senate by the state legislature. However, he was removed from his chairmanship, and his influence declined. With the Democratic party split in the 1860 election, Douglas, as candidate of the northern Democrats, lost to Lincoln.

The campaign was the first occasion when two major presidential candidates came from the same state. After the election Douglas supported Lincoln and worked so tirelessly to try and reconcile the North and South that his health broke, and he died of typhoid fever early in the war. Although Douglas' reputation has suffered by comparison with that of Lincoln, some authorities claim that he was the first American to have a truly "national vision."

DOUGLAS, William Orville. (Maine, MN, October 16, 1898—Goose Prairie, WA, January 19, 1980). Associate justice of the United States Supreme Court. Educated at Whitman College, with a law degree from Columbia University Law School in 1925, he became a member of the Columbia faculty (1925-1928). He served in various federal posts and was made chairman of the Securities and Exchange Commission in 1937. Douglas was appointed to the Supreme Court in 1939. His career on the court was marked by his strong defense of individual liberties, and he was one of the most controversial figures in recent history of the court. Although generally considered a liberal, he wrote several dissents on anti-trust cases, contending that American law tended to support monopoly. He retired from the court in November, 1975, but continued in active public life, always championing the have-nots of society. An aggressive outdoorsman, Douglas wrote several books on wilderness areas, including *Of Men and Mountains* (1950), and *A Wilderness Bill of Rights* (1965). He also was the author of *Points of Rebellion* (1969), *Holocaust or Hemisphere Cooperation* (1971),

An Almanac of Liberty (1954) and *The Bible and the Schools* (1966).

DOUSMAN, Hercules. (—). One of John Jacob Astor's most successful agents, Dousman amassed a fortune from the fur trade in the Midwest before it declined in favor of the far West. He is considered to have been the first millionaire in vast Wisconsin Territory. With headquarters at PRAIRIE DU CHIEN, Wisconsin, Dousman built one of the most extraordinary estates of its day, especially in view of its location away from the centers of eastern "civilization." His mansion, called VILLA LOUIS, was begun in 1843. He developed the estate with a private racetrack, featuring purebred horses. The speed of the track was enhanced by its imported cork surface. Stocked ponds provided assured fishing for the guests of the estate, who were invited to play pool on the table inlaid with ivory. Madam Dousman played for their guests on one of the first pianos imported into the entire region. Today, visitors may visit the mansion and its outbuildings, restored and furnished to look much as it did in its heyday.

DOW, Herbert H. (Belleville, Ontario, Canada, 1866—Rochester, MN, Oct. 15, 1930). Chemist and industrialist. His college thesis at Case School of Applied Science (1888) concerned the study of extracting minerals from the brines underlying much of Ohio. Encouraged by his teachers, Dow studied the vast undeground resources of brines also found in nearby states, presenting his studies at a meeting of the American Association for the Advancement of Science in 1888. In 1889 he discovered and patented an inexpensive method of extracting bromine, chromium and lithium from brine by electrolysis. Moving to Midland, Michigan, he founded the Dow Chemical Company in 1897. With his single-minded dedication to the resources from brine, Dow built one of the major industrial enterprises of the day. Dow Chemical was the first company in the United States to manufacture indigo and phenol, a compound used in explosives. During WORLD WAR I the company manufactured mustard gas for troops in Europe. The company has continued as a producer of a very wide variety of chemicals, including bleaches, insecticides, iodine, salicylates, magnesium and many others.

DOWLING, Michael John. (Huntington, MA, February 17, 1866—Olivia, MN, April 25,

1921). Banker. Dowling, a dealer in real estate, served as the president of the Olivia State Bank and as the secretary of the National Republican League from 1895 to 1897. In 1901 he was the speaker of the Minnesota house of representatives. Dowling accomplished all this despite a severe handicap. As a boy, Dowling lost both legs, one hand and part of another hand during a blizzard. He dedicated much of his time to encouraging others afflicted with physical handicaps.

DRAKE UNIVERSITY. In DES MOINES, Iowa, on the northwest side of the city, established in 1881 by the Disciples of Christ and named for Iowa governor, Francis M. Drake. The University's nine colleges and schools instruct an enrollment of 5,502, with a faculty of 306. One of the largest private schools in the state, the university has achieved international fame for its annual Drake Relays, one of the oldest and most popular of such track and field events in the country. It is especially well known for its music school. In the academic year 1986-1987 the student body of 5,537 was instructed by a faculty of 263

DRED SCOTT DECISION. Decision by the U.S. Supreme Court, written in 1857 by Chief Justice Roger Taney, a member of the Court's Southern majority. It stated that (1) moving a slave to "free" territory did not result in freedom for that slave; (2) Congress had no power to exclude slaves from territories; and (3) Negroes could not be citizens. This ruling added much fuel to the growing antagonism between supporters of the slavery system and Abolitionists, prior to the outbreak of the CIVIL WAR. The decision involved Dred Scott, a Missouri slave who was taken by his master to reside in Illinois, a free state. From Illinois he was taken to the free territory of Wisconsin before returning to Missouri. The Dred Scott Decision, in which Scott was declared still a slave, was one of the major factors that further inflamed the tensions leading to the Civil War.

DREISER, Theodore. (Terre Haute, IN, August 27, 1871—Hollywood, CA, December 28, 1945). Journalist and author. Growing up in a poor family of tendency to religious fanaticism, Drieser managed a year at the INDIANA UNIVERSITY before becoming a newspaper reporter in several cities until he settled in New York City. It may have been his impoverished childhood that caused him to believe in the difference between the promise and reality of

life in the United States. This realization deeply influenced Dreiser who is considered the principal American writer of a somber and pessimistic form of realism known as the naturalism movement. Characters in Dreiser's work fall victim to seemingly meaningless incidents which cause stress the characters are neither able to control or understand. In such works as his first novel, *Sister Carrie* (1900), and *An American Tragedy* (1925), he condemned the society that produces villains. *Sister Carrie,* was reluctantly published, although the wife of the president at Doubleday, Page, and Company objected to the morals of the primary character. Dreiser held the company to its contract, but the book was released without advertising or efforts made to distribute it. The conflict so disturbed Dreiser that he suffered a nervous breakdown and gave up writing and worked as an editor for several years. With the novel *Jennie Gerhardt* (1911) he was more seriously received, and his reputation was assured with the publication of *The Financier* in 1912. Dreiser meant for this to be the first of a trilogy, but the second volume, *The Titan* (1914), was a failure and the third, *The Stoic*, remained unpublished until two years after Dreiser's death. Dreiser is best remembered for *An American Tragedy.*

DRESSER, Paul. (Terre Haute, IN, April 21, 1857—Brooklyn, NY, January 30, 1906). Songwriter. Dresser, brother of novelist Theodore Dreiser, left home in 1873 and changed his name to enter a medicine show. He joined the Billy Rice Ministrels in 1884 and formed Howley, Haviland and Dresser, song publishers, in 1901. Dresser's songs include "On the Banks of the Wabash, Far Away" (1897, the official song of Indiana), and "My Gal Sal" (1905).

DRIFTLESS AREAS. Unglaciated regions. Areas such as those in northeastern Iowa, southeastern Minnesota and southwest Wisconsin along the MISSISSIPPI RIVER never touched by the four great glaciers. The areas are often exceedingly rough, with deep valleys cut by swift-flowing streams.

DROUTH. The most devastating and widespread drouth of modern times in the U.S. occurred in the 1930s when rainfall diminished sharply over a long period. This drouth was the most severe in the Great Plains, but its effect was strongly felt in the Midwest. Winds from the west picked up the dry dust of the more westerly states and filled the skies, sometimes crossing almost all of the region, of course, diminishing to the east. However, although the effects of the 30s drouth were heavily felt in the Midwest, especially on the western edge, that region has never had a crop failure as such. More damaging in the Midwest, particularly from the standpoint of the economy, was the drouth of 1962, when most of the Eastern United States suffered the worst drouth in fifty years, including most of the Midwest breadbasket. The drouth of 1988 has been called "the second worst in the history of the country," and it hit the Midwest with great severity, reducing CORN by as much as half and SOYBEANS up to thirty percent.

DU QUOIN, Illinois. City (pop. 6,594), mining community in southern Illinois. Du Quoin was named for Jean Baptiste du Quoigne, of French-Indian parents and a chief of the KASKASKIA tribe. Although COAL is a dominant industry of the region, farming is profitable. West of Du Quoin is one of the largest strip mining operations in the United States. The city is a shipping point for grain, livestock and fruit as well as coal. The Hambletonian harness races are held in Du Quoin every August.

DU SABLE, Jean Baptiste. (Haiti, 1745—St. Charles, MO, August 28, 1818). Frontier trader and settler, first permanent non-Indian resident of the "Eschecagou" (CHICAGO), Illinois, area. Du Sable, of French and African parentage, at the age of twenty went to New Orleans as an agent of a Haitian mercantile firm. When the city came under Spanish control in 1762-1763, Du Sable moved north along the MISSISSIPPI RIVER to ST. LOUIS. As French influence continued to retreat, Du Sable moved farther north until, by the 1770s, he was living in the present area of PEORIA, Illinois, where he married a POTAWATOMI woman. His trade with Indians flourished and he established a post on Lake MICHIGAN at the mouth of the CHICAGO RIVER. In 1779 Du Sable was arrested by the British who distrusted his French manner. He was taken to MACKINAC, but because of his reputation among the Indians was soon released and made the superintendent, from 1780 to 1784, of Lieutenant Governor Patrick Sinclair's business, the Pinery, on the ST. CLAIR RIVER. He returned to "Eschecagou" (an Indian word meaning "skunk" or "wild onion") and continued his trading business, which along with a large farm, made him very wealthy. In

1800 he sold his interests to Jean Lalime and moved to ST. CHARLES, Missouri, where he died.

DUBLIN, Indiana. Town (pop. 979), historic rural community in eastern Indiana, a stagecoach stop on the NATIONAL ROAD. "The Maples," largest of the remaining early buildings, was built of handmade brick in 1825. It was then, as now, a tavern. Dublin was the home of Amanda Way, organizer of the first woman's suffrage group in Indiana. In 1852 the Women's Rights Society, formed soon after an 1851 meeting in Dublin, filed a petition on women's suffrage with the Indiana General Assembly. The committee to which the petition was referred found it "inexpedient at this time," a status it retained until the passage of the Nineteenth Amendment in 1919.

DUBUQUE, Iowa. City (pop. 93,745), seat of Dubuque County, situated in northeast Iowa, built partly on the flood plain of the MISSISSIPPI RIVER, with the larger part of the city perched on the picturesque bluffs above the river. The community grew up around the trading and smelting post of pioneer settler Julien DUBUQUE, from whom it takes its name. The Black Hawk Treaty of 1833 at the conclusion of the BLACK HAWK WAR (1767-1838) ended the Indian control of the area, and settlers began to pour in. The city was not chartered until 1841 but nevertheless is considered the oldest European-style settlement in Iowa. During the 1830s Father Charles MAZZUCHELLI (1806-1864), a Catholic priest, came to Dubuque, designed St. Raphael's Church there and helped to build it with his own hands. He gained the great respect of the community and was one of the most influential figures in the growth there of the Catholic Church, still the most prominent religious group in the region. The See of Dubuque was created in 1837, and Bishop Mathias Loras took over Mazzuchelli's diocese which even in that early day consisted of thirty-one hundred members. The Dubuque *Visitor* was started in 1836 and is the oldest newspaper in the state. It is now known as the *Telegraph Herald*. From lead processing the community went on to lumbering and milling. Today Dubuque is one of the major manufacturing centers of Iowa, with shipyards, railroad shops, chemicals, cast iron and sheet metals, and brewery. The city is the site of Loras College, University of Dubuque and Clarke College. Points of interest for visitors include the Cathedral and the incline railroad up the bluff. Eagle Point Park overlooking the locks and dam of the Mississippi, the oldest log cabin in the state, the numerous old mansions and picturesquely located houses, nearby Crystal Lake Cave, Bixby State Park and, to the west, Melleray Abbey, are other attractions for visitors in the vicinity.

DUBUQUE, Julien. (St. Pierre Les Brecquets, Que, Can., Jan. 10, 1762—Dubuque, IA, Mar. 24, 1810). Iowa's pioneer settler, first European to settle in what is now the state, Dubuque came to the area of PRAIRIE DU CHIEN, Wisconsin, in 1785 as a fur hunter and trader, when the region was still part of Spanish Louisiana. Detecting rich resources of lead near present DUBUQUE, in 1788 Dubuque worked out an oral agreement with Chief Kettle of the FOX Indians to mine lead ore south of Dubuque. He moved into the chief's camp, built a cabin and constructed a furnace to smelt the lead for the ST. LOUIS market. His workers were French Canadian settlers and local Indians. Their product was finished lead bars. He also continued in the fur trade. He received a land grant from Baron Carondolet, the Spanish governor, strengthening his hold on the land around Catfish Creek. This grant extended for 21 miles along the MISSISSIPPI RIVER and inland for as much as nine miles. During his twenty-two years in the area, he traded away about half of his grant for goods bought in St. Louis. When he died in 1810, the Fox Indians gave him a burial befitting a chief. However, with the Louisiana Purchase and United States control of the area, the question of legality of Spanish grants was decided unfavorably by the U.S. Supreme Court. A stone tower on the bluff overlooking the Mississippi marks his burial site, near the junction of Catfish Creek with the Mississippi. The city of Dubuque, which began to grow up around his holdings, is named in his honor.

DULUTH, Lake. Huge prehistoric glacial lake which once covered much of present-day Minnesota.

DULUTH, Minnesota. City (pop. 92,811), northeastern Minnesota on the shore of Lake SUPERIOR, nicknamed Minnesota's "air-conditioned city." Duluth is located in a narrow band of lowland stretching from the mouth of the ST. LOUIS RIVER for twenty-five miles along the shore of Lake Superior. The city has earned its nickname because of its dependence on the lake-created weather system which brings cool breezes off the lake on hot summer days.

Mississippi waterfront, Dubuque, Iowa.

Among the earliest explorers of the region were Pierre Esprit RADISSON (1636-1710) and Medart Chouart GROSEILLIERS (1618?-1690), who visited there between 1654 and 1660.

One of the earliest settlements was an OJIBWAY village named Fond du Lac, meaning "head of the lake." In 1679 Daniel Greysolon, Sieur Du Lhut (DULUTH, 1636-1710), visited the area and attempted to bring peace to the warring SIOUX and Ojibway to protect the prosperous FUR TRADE. The future city was named for him.

Fond du Lac became a gateway to the lakes and streams of the region as traders made their passage up the St. Louis to the portage at Big Sandy Lake where they crossed to the MISSISSIPPI RIVER. Fond du Lac and several other small towns continued to grow, but only slowly, despite rumors in 1854 that copper and ore were being found on the North Shore. In 1857 much of the village shut down as a result of the national monetary panic. In 1858 the few remaining residents were struck by a SCARLET FEVER epidemic. The year 1865 marked the lowest point of Duluth's fortunes.

In 1869 the Lake Superior and Mississippi Railroad was near completion from ST. PAUL to Duluth. By 1870 when travelers could reach Duluth from St. Paul in only sixteen hours the population leaped. This was the same year Jay COOKE (1821-1905), an eastern financier, decided to support the construction of the Northern Pacific Railroad from Duluth to the Pacific.

The city also decided to cut a channel through Minnesota Point, saving boats from a seven-mile trip to the natural opening at Superior Cut. News that the town of SUPERIOR, Wisconsin, was seeking an injunction to block construction caused a furious weekend of shoveling by nearly every citizen of Duluth to complete work before the order could be served.

In 1873 Duluth suffered a severe setback when the financial empire of Cooke collapsed. The population of the city shrank from 5,000 to 2,000; the city council was dissolved, and the city returned to a village status. But in five years the disaster was forgotten. Farms in the RED RIVER Valley began shipping wheat to Duluth on the Northern Pacific. Grain elevators were built along with sawmills to handle the lumber business. In 1893 the Duluth, Missabe, and Northern Railroad began carrying loads of iron ore from the newly discovered Mesabi Iron Range. Docks were constructed. In the 1900s Duluth prospered even more. United States Steel came to town and purchased 1,000 acres for a steel plant. Portland Cement moved to Duluth in 1916.

The city was threatened again in the 1950s with the news that the iron ore would be depleted. This situation was ameliorated when a process of removing low grade ore and forming it into TACONITE pellets was developed by Professor Henry DAVIS from the University of MINNESOTA.

With the opening of the ST. LAWRENCE SEAWAY, Duluth's position as a leading inland port was assured. Today, in addition to the huge shipping industry of the port and to steel and cement, manufactures include textiles, electrical equipment, prepared foods, metal and wood products.

Duluth's waterfront location has encouraged the growth of recreational areas. Boating access points dot the Western Waterfront Trail, a five mile-path along the St. Louis River. In winter the trail is a favorite spot for cross-country skiing. Summer events include the Lake Superior Music Festival and Old-Time Fiddle Contest, Grandma's Marathon, and the Point Park Invitational Art Fair in June and the NI-MI-WIN Ojibway Indian Festival in August. Glensheen, the estate of attorney, entrepreneur, and state legislator Chester A. Congdon includes formal gardens and a lake view. The home, a Jacobean-style mansion, features unusual lighting fixtures, custom furniture and stained glass. The Depot, the St. Louis County Heritage and Arts Center, is a renovated railroad station from 1892, with four levels of historical displays including an antique doll and toy collection and displays of 200 years of styles in clothing. Dioramas illustrate the life of early French explorers, missionaries and traders.

Duluth of 1910 is re-created in Depot Square with 24 oldtime stores. The immigration room through which many settlers passed is retained in its original state. A collection of railroad cars and locomotives includes the first engine used in Minnesota. An annual event is the International Folk Festival on the first Saturday of August.

DULUTH or Du Lhut, Sieur (Daniel Greysolon). (St. Germain-en-Laye, France, 1636—Montreal, Canada, Feb. 27, 1710), Explorer. In 1678 he journeyed westward in the Lake SUPERIOR region, under orders of Count de Frontenac, the governor of Canada, to explore the lake and routes west. He made extensive explorations in the upper GREAT LAKES and in 1679 was probably the first European to visit present Minnesota. In that year he claimed the entire Great Lakes region and all of the lands west of the ALLEGHENY MOUNTAINS in the name of France. He successfuly negotiated treaties of peace between the SIOUX and the CHIPPEWA in 1679 and made alliance with the Sioux. It was Duluth who rescued three explorers, Accault, Du Gray and Father Louis HENNEPIN from the Sioux in 1680. In later years he was often called upon to settle Indian disputes. The city of DULUTH, Minnesota, is named in his honor.

DULUTH-SUPERIOR HARBOR. The finest natural harbor on the GREAT LAKES and one of the best in the world. The Duluth-Superior Harbor covers an area of nineteen square miles. There are ninety-nine docks, seventeen miles of dredged channels and twenty grain elevators with a total capacity in excess of forty-six million bushels. The coal docks are among the largest in the world. The natural breakwater for the harbor is formed by MINNESOTA POINT, with a width of about two city blocks, which was created after the last glacier melted, and the action of the ST. LOUIS RIVER and Lake SUPERIOR caused a nine-mile-long deposition of sand and gravel between the north and south shores of the lake. There are two entries. The Superior Ship Canal was cut naturally by the St. Louis River. The second entry is the man-made Duluth Ship Canal.

DUNBAR, Paul Laurence. (Dayton, OH, 1872—Dayton, OH, Feb. 10, 1906). Poet and novelist, long acclaimed as one of the outstanding American poets and one of the country's first black poets to gain international fame. Growing up as a poor boy, supported in early life by his mother, who took in washing, by the time he reached high school, Dunbar had been chosen president of the school literary society and editor of the school newspaper, although he was the only black in his class. His first poems were published in DAYTON newspapers. His first volume of verse, *Oak and Ivy*, was published (1893) in a small edition by the United brethren publishing House at Dayton. He won wide recognition for his *Lyrics of a Lowly Life* (1896), a collection of poems taken from his earlier work. This brought him wide readership, speaking engagements and a trip to England in 1897. Returning to Dayton after the London trip, despite his fame and frail health, Dunbar felt obligated to "work himself to death" to support his mother and himself by running a Dayton elevator while keeping up a frenzied course of writing in his meager spare time. For the last seven years of his short life, he did not even take time out to treat the tuberculosis which took him at the age of 34. His output included seven volumes of poetry, two volumes of short stories and two novels. According to William Dean HOWELLS (1837-1929), Dunbar was "the only man of pure African blood and of American civilization to feel the Negro life aesthetically and express it lyrically." The *Ohio State Guide* declared, "Dunbar became the idol of his race and an artist admired by many other Americans, establishing a tradition that un-doubtedly encouraged...Countee Cullen, Claude McKaye and Langston Hughes. His most popular poems are those in dialect..." His mother lived on in their home in Dayton until her death in 1934. She cherished a collection of his poems and memorabilia and did a great deal to keep her son's memory alive. She may have influenced modern critics who have treated the poet with much more consideration than did most of his contemporaries. Among other tributes, a 10-cent U.S. stamp honoring him was issued in the American Poets series, and his house in Dayton has been preserved as a state museum (1938), displaying his manuscripts and mementoes.

DUNDAS, Minnesota. Town (pop. 422); southeastern Minnesota; south of NORTHFIELD; railway town platted in 1857 and named by two millers, John and Edward Archibald, emigrants from Dundas, Ontario. Dundas was the wheat milling center for Minnesota during the 1850s after the Archibald brothers built a mill along the Cannon River. When milled, spring wheat was full of chaff and had a dark color that caused it to spoil quickly. Edmond N. La Croix of Dundas created a new method of making a whiter, finer flour by using sifters, and silk sieves, which removed the undesired "middlings" and became known as the MIDLINGS PURIFIER. The complex "middlings purifier"

Paul Laurence Dunbar

American poet

10 cents U.S. postage

U.S. stamp honors Paul L. Dunbar.

method was so popular that farmers traveled long distances to the Archibald's mill. Gradually the process became the accepted standard for the Minneapolis mills, and Dundas' importance faded.

DUNES. Hills or mounds of sand created by wind drift, commonly found in sandy regions, including deserts, lake shores, and other coastal areas. Large dunes may be hundreds of feet tall, while most are much smaller. Dunes may travel as one side loses sand to the other side by the action of the wind. Singing dunes make sounds as the sand grains rub against each other as they are blown in the wind. In the Midwest, the south and east shores of Lake MICHIGAN in Indiana and Michigan offer some of the world's most spectacular dunes, including SLEEPING BEAR DUNES NATIONAL LAKESHORE, INDIANA DUNES NATIONAL LAKESHORE and INDIANA DUNES STATE PARK. These areas are unlike any others in the world.

DVORAK, Antonin. (Nelahozeves near Prague, Czechoslovakia, Sept. 18, 1841—Prague, May 1, 1904). The famed Czech composer was in the Midwest for only a short while, but the summer visit and the rest from conducting and social obligations in the eastern

U.S. greatly enriched his creative powers and provided him with native and folk melodies of the Midwest and West on which some of his future compositions were partially based. In New York City in June, 1893, Dvorak packed up his wife, six children and their maid and arrived in the quiet northeast Iowa village of SPILLVILLE. There he made important changes in his "Symphony in E minor, From the New World," and finished a "String Quintet in E flat." On a visit to MINNEHAHA FALLS in Minnesota, when he was unable to find a piece of paper, he jotted down some notes on his stiff shirt cuff. The story is told that the shirt was sent to be laundered and the composer's wife was only just able to save the precious notes from the suds. The resultant music from the shirt cuff was the famous "Opus 100, The Indian Maiden." When "Papa" Dvorak found that his oldest daughter was planning to elope with a local boy, he packed up the family again and moved back to New York at the end of the summer.

DYERSVILLE, Iowa. Town (pop. 3,825), situated in east central Iowa about thirty miles west of DUBUQUE, the community was named for James J. Dyer, Jr., leader of the English settlers in the area, who developed the town. Dyersville has gained distinction for two notable features unusual for a community of its size. The most prominent of these is the Basilica of St. Francis Xavier. This grand Catholic "Cathedral of the Plains" can be seen for miles with its two dramatic spires piercing the Iowa skies. The

other distinction belongs to Dyersville's Ertl Toy company, founded by Fred Ertl and his family. The Ertls began to make cast aluminum toys by melting aluminum pistons in their furnace. The business expanded to a multi-million dollar operation, with branches even in China but firmly based in Dyersville. Ertl believes "small industry belongs in small towns and this town had everything we wanted...good people, good transportation, and room to grow." The town's economy is also fueled by the wealthy surrounding farm country.

DYLAN, Bob. (Duluth, MN, May 24, 1941—). American folk singer and composer. His real name was Robert Zimmerman, but he adopted the given name of Dylan Thomas, the Welsh poet. He began to teach himself guitar and other instruments at the age of ten. His turbulent early life included running away from home several times until he left for good and rode freight trains around the country, doing odd jobs and writing songs, many inspired by Woody Guthrie. In New York City in 1961, his occasional coffee-house appearances soon gained a reputation, and his first record album was released later that year. Dylan is considered the musical symbol of protest by Americans who began to develop their social conscience in the 1960s. His best-known works including "Blowin' in the Wind" (1962), "The Times They Are A-Changin'" (1963), and "Like a Rolling Stone" (1965), focused on social injustice.

EADS, James Buchanan (Lawrenceburg, IN., May 23, 1820—Nassau, Bahama Islands, Mar. 8, 1887). Engineer and inventor. Self-educated, Eads invented a diving bell which he began to use in 1842 to salvage sunken steamboats from rivers. Three years later he opened a glassworks in ST. LOUIS, Missouri, but it failed in 1848. Returning to the salvage business, he made another fortune. In 1861, President Abraham LINCOLN requested him to devise a plan to protect the MISSISSIPPI RIVER and its tributaries from Confederate power during the CIVIL WAR. His plan called for seven steam-

driven armored artillery ships. He had devised a number of ingenious designs for armor plating the ships and for the mounting of firepower. He completed the contract in 100 days. His best-known achievement is the Eads Bridge, constructed of steel and masonry (1867-74), across the Mississippi at St. Louis. Twenty-six trained experts had said no bridge could be built at that location. Eads solved the problems of the length of the span across the river and of the height that was required to let boats pass beneath the bridge. He designed and constructed a series of jetties and water sluices which maintained deep water at the Mississippi's main outlet to the gulf, the South Pass of the river, successfully completed in 1879. This eliminated the need for continual costly dredging and gave New Orleans access to deep water shipping. Eads was unsuccessful in persuading Congress to accept his plan to build a railway for ships as a less costly alternative to the Panama Canal.

EAGLE EFFIGY MOUND. One of the unique records of prehistoric civilization. Built by the advanced HOPEWELL People, perhaps the only one of its kind, this effigy is preserved in Mound Builders State Park, at NEWARK, Ohio. As seen from above, the eagle shape is easily recognizable. However, since it seems obvious that the builders did not have an opportunity to view their creation from the same vantage point, their ability to lay out a figure of such perfect form and large size is even more remarkable. The figure was formed on a sixty-acre tract within a circle mound built up by earthworks.

EAGLE HARBOR, Michigan. Tiny resort village on the Keweenaw Peninsula and Lake SUPERIOR, about 30 miles north and slightly east of HOUGHTON. In the copper country of Michigan, the area is renowned for the prehistoric copper mines of the area. After the rich copper deposits were surveyed by Dr. Douglass HOUGHTON, beginning in 1840 thousands of claims were filed and millions of pounds of copper had been mined in the area. With the depletion of the copper deposits, the area lost population and settled down to the life of a tourist community. The most notable landmark of the region is much-photographed Eagle Harbor Lighthouse, on the west side of the Lake Superior harbor. The area is also known as the site where the rituals were written for the Order of Knights of Pythias by Justus H. Rathbone, a schoolteacher there from 1858 to 1861. During the long winters of northern Michigan, Rathbone offered theatrical presentations in his school, including one based on the friendship of Damon and Pythias. The small school building later became a Knights of Pythias Shrine.

EAGLE MOUNTAIN. Highest point in Minnesota at 2,301 feet, the crest of the Misquah Hills in Cook County.

EAGLE REGIMENT. Eighth Wisconsin CIVIL WAR Infantry. As the Civil War was beginning, the boys of Company C of the Eighth scraped together five dollars and bought a bald eagle. Before long OLD ABE, the eagle, had become so well known and such a favorite that his troop was named the Eagle Regiment. Chicago newspapers gave the Eagle Regiment added publicity and praise because of their mascot. At the battle of Corinth, his first battle, Old Able flew among his boys, encouraging them. He was never hurt as the regiment took part in forty-one battles or skirmishes. The regiment was one of the most decorated of the war, and a number of the soldiers proudly said they took their courage and pride from the example of the eagle that gave them their name.

EAGLE RIVER, Wisconsin. City (pop. 1,326), seat of Vilas County, situated on the Eagle River in northeast Wisconsin. The community takes its name from the bald eagles, which used to be so abundant and which still may be seen occasionally in the area. Eagle River is a very popular resort area, especially for the winter sports, and it is one of the Midwest's major ski centers, with every kind of skiing activity. Eagle River pioneered in winter activities, with one of the first ski jumps, together with toboggan slide, and indoor ice hockey. The Eagle Lake chain of twenty-seven sparkling bodies of water provides the longest stretch of connected freshwater lakes in the world and offers the single greatest tourist attraction of the area in all seasons. Trees for Tomorrow Natural Resources Education Center at Eagle River provides demonstrations and tours on outdoor conservation and skills. The annual World Championship Snowmobile Derby is held at Eagle River the third weekend of January. The first weekend of October finds the community celebrating the local crop with its Cranberry Fest.

EARTHQUAKES. The Midwest is generally considered to be a stable center of the country. Yet the worst earthquake ever to strike North America occurred in 1811 in the Midwest, centered at NEW MADRID, Missouri. Although the modern instruments for measuring earthquakes were not then available, the New Madrid quake is considered to have surpassed in strength the Alaska earthquake of 1964. The New Madrid quake changed the course of rivers, created lakes and was felt over a vast area. Very heavy aftershocks troubled the area for almost a year. It has been pointed out that quakes in the Midwest spread their shock waves farther because of the nature of the surface and the underground composition. Fortunately for life and property, the New Madrid quake occurred in a very sparsely settled region. If such a shock were to occur today, most of the Midwest's major cities would suffer damage from extremely severe to severe to moderate, even at such limits as MINNEAPOLIS and CLEVELAND. S T . LOUIS would be in great peril, and experts consider that such a quake could occur in the region, within a few years, or, perhaps, not for` centuries. Much of the Midwest was reminded of that possibility in June of 1987, when a quake in central Illinois, reaching 5.0 on the Richter scale, caused damage to be reported as far north as CHICAGO. Other moderate earthquakes have shaken the Midwest over the past forty years.

EAST CLEVELAND, Ohio. City (pop. 36,957), a suburb of CLEVELAND, situated in northeast Ohio, on Lake ERIE,. The present city has no connection with the former East Cleveland, which was annexed by the larger city in 1872. The name disappeared from the map until 1892 when neighboring Collamer, with other land to the east, became East Cleveland Hamlet. East Cleveland was incorporated as a city in 1911. The city is mostly residential. However, it has a major industry, the General Electric lamp factory and research institute in the company's large holding, Nela Park, landscaped acres overlooking Lake Erie. Forrest Hill is the former estate of industrialist John D. ROCKEFELLER, an area of natural ravines and woodland, bought in 1870 following his early success in the oil industry. Later, much of the estate was donated to East Cleveland for public parks.

EAST LANSING, Michigan. City (pop. 48,300), Ingham County, south-central Michigan on the Lower Peninsula. Although East Lansing appears to be part of its larger neighbor, the state capital of LANSING, the two cities are politically separate. The first settler in what is now East Lansing was D. Robert Burcham, who came in 1852 and purchased a large tract of land. In 1855 Michigan authorized the first agricultural college in the U.S. under the name of Michigan Agricultural College and located it there. The college opened in 1857, and soon thereafter Joel Harrison built the first rooming house for students in East Lansing. From this humble beginning, this college, now known as MICHIGAN STATE UNIVERSITY, has grown from three buildings in a field to comprise 5,320 acres and one of the nation's largest enrollments. Another educational institution was the Michigan Female College, founded by two spinster sisters in 1855. About 1,000 young women attended this school before it closed in June, 1869, after the death of one of the sisters. During the 1890s, the temperance movement was very evident as the deeds for many city properties contained a clause prohibiting the sale of alcoholic beverages on the premises. When East Lansing received its city charter from the legislature on May 8, 1907, it was the smallest city in Michigan. There were several suggestions for the city's name, including College Park, but the Post Office made the final decision by calling the city East Lansing because all mail came through the Lansing Post Office.

EAST ST. LOUIS, Illinois. City (pop. 55,200), St. Clair Co., important part of the southwestern Illinois-ST. LOUIS, Missouri, industrial complex, located on the MISSISSIPPI RIVER. East St. Louis, platted in 1859, across the river from the Missouri city, benefitted from the westward movement of pioneers, the rise of steamboat commerce on the Mississippi, rich deposits of coal nearby, and the construction of the Eads Bridge to St. Louis in 1874. During the late 1800s East St. Louis declined as a river town, while it grew as an industrial center. Swift and Company, Hunter Packing Company, and Royal Packing Company all built plants in East St. Louis. Three large agrichemical producers and three major fertilizer plants are now important to the economy. The National Stock Yards, called the Hog Capital of the Nation, flourish in a separately organized village called National City. Cahokia Downs, host of the annual St. Louis Derby, brings many Midwest three-year-old racehorses to compete in the mile and one-sixteenth event. East St. Louis remains an important loading depot due to its location on Interstates 55 and 70 and five other United States highways. CAHOKIA MOUNDS State Historic Site is a 1,300 acre area with many prehistoric mounds, evidence of a Mississippian culture which flourished from 900 to 1300 A.D.

EASTERN ILLINOIS UNIVERSITY. CHARLESTON, Illinois, founded May 22, 1863, as a state normal school. It became a college in 1921 and a university in 1957. The university offers bachelor's, master's, and specialist's degrees in education and was one of the first in Illinois to offer Afro-American studies. During the 1985-86 academic year the university enrolled 9,926 students and had 549 faculty. It occupies 35 buildings on 316 acres and operates Robert G.

Buzard Elementary School as a laboratory for teachers.

EASTERN MICHIGAN UNIVERSITY. Publically supported institution, with its main campus on 275 acres on the northern edge of YPSILANTI. There are an additional 182 acres with intercollegiate and intramural athletic facilities, a field laboratory and housing for married students. Founded in 1849, the school attained university status in 1959. Eastern Michigan consists of the Colleges of Health and Human Services, Technology, Business, Education, Arts and Sciences, and the Graduate School. A number of special programs are offered, including Music Therapy, Historical Preservation, Language and International Trade, Arts Management, and Radio-Television-Film. During the 1985-1986 academic year 20,166 students were enrolled in the university and 838 were on the faculty.

EATON RAPIDS, Michigan. Town (pop. 4,510), Eaton County, south-central portion of Michigan's LOWER PENINSULA. Located on the GRAND RIVER which has provided power for local woolen mills, Eaton Rapids is the center of Michigan's largest sheep-raising region and is also the national headquarters of the Veterans of Foreign Wars. A city itself in size, the veterans' facility has a 640-acre site, home for several hundred widows and orphans of veterans.

EAU CLAIRE, Wisconsin. City (pop. 51,-509), seat of Eau Claire County, situated at the junction of the EAU CLAIRE and CHIPPEWA Rivers, the community was named for the sparkling clear quality of those waters. As early as 1784 a trapper named Le Duc made his home on the site, living among the SIOUX INDIANS. By 1822 logging had begun along the Chippewa, but the county and city were not organized until 1856, with word of the coming of a railroad. In the heart of the lumber country, Eau Claire engaged in constant battles with neighboring CHIPPEWA FALLS for rights to build dams and for other exploitation of the valuable timber. By 1870, when the railroad arrived, there were twenty-two sawmills operating in Eau Claire. As traditional logging declined, pulp for paper and paper mills continued to bring prosperity. Industries of various types also came in, and today the city manufactures kitchen equipment, defense items, tires and dairy goods, in addition to paper products. The University of WISCONSIN has a branch at Eau Claire, and there

is a state fish hatchery. Paul Bunyan Logging Camp is restored to recreate the life of a camp, with cook's shanty, smithy, bunkhouse and demonstration of lumbering techniques. Dells Mills Museum demonstrates the activities of the five-story water-powered flour and grist mill built in 1864 of hand-hewn timbers, held together with wooden pegs. The Chippewa Valley Museum exhibits prehistoric and historic items, street scenes, period rooms and other exhibits and offers an old-fashioned ice cream parlor. April finds the community celebrating with its annual Dixieland Jazz Festival, and June brings Sawdust Days.

ECONOMIC STATUS. The Midwest today is clearly the economic giant of the U.S. In the value of all goods and services produced, the region accounts for a fourth of the national total, including thirty percent of the income from agriculture and twenty-eight per cent of the income from manufacturing. This is true despite the fact that no individual Midwest state leads the nation in any one of the major economic categories. However, the region as a whole possesses a concentration of states so important in so many economic areas that, combined, they give the region its preeminent status.

In other regions, each boasts one leading state, New York, Texas, California and Florida, with the other states of their regions lagging behind in most of the important economic categories. Whereas, in the Midwest, a majority of the states rank among the leaders in most of these categories.

In AGRICULTURE the Midwest holds seven of the top ten rankings. In MANUFACTURING the Midwest produces more than a fourth of the entire nation's income. In the three primary production areas, the Midwest loses first place only in MINERAL production, where it ranks fourth. In view of the region's central location, its leadership in numbers of rail and air passengers and rail and truck carloadings it seems almost obvious that it leads in TRANSPORTATION of all types except oceangoing.

The Midwest leadership is illustrated by other selected categories.

In the vital area of exports, the region leads in ten of the nineteen most important categories, including two of the three top-dollar categories, food and kindred products and transportation equipment. In the extremely important and rapidly growing area of services, the Midwest ranks a close second only to the six East Central states.

Edina - Edison

The Midwest leads all others in total individual net worth. The region's annual total personal income amounts to 23% of the national total.

In a state-by-state summary, Illinois remains the Midwest's most prosperous in manufacturing receipts, followed by Ohio and Michigan. Minnesota is the least productive manufacturing state in the region. The nation's single largest industry is the production of AUTOMOBILES, in which the region is the leader. Illinois, again, leads in the service industries, followed, once more, by Ohio and Michigan. Iowa is the leader in agriculture, third in the U.S. in dollar value and first in total volume of production. Illinois ranks next in agriculture, followed by Minnesota. Ohio's agricultural income lags behind that of the other Midwestern states. Illinois leads the region in tourist income, with Wisconsin close behind, followed by Ohio and Michigan. Minnesota attracts the fewest tourist dollars in the Midwest. Illinois, once again, heads the list, this time in mining revenue, followed closely by Michigan and Ohio. Wisconsin's mining income is the lowest in the Midwest.

MIDWEST
ECONOMIC STATUS IN THE U.S.
(1984)
(billions of $)

	U.S. Total	Midwest	Percent
Agriculture	136,260	41,472	30.04
Manufacturing	1,960,206	548,859	28.00
Service	426,982	80,558	18.86
Exports	252,865	40,210	15.90
Minerals	168,778	11,723	6.90
Total of goods and services	2,945,091	722,822	24.54

THE MIDWEST ECONOMY—1984

Total of all goods and services, in billions of dollars
Illinois 166,986
Ohio 152,123
Michigan 128,854
Indiana 84,027
Wisconsin 72,394
Missouri 58,731
Iowa 55,736
Minnesota 50,718

EDINA, Minnesota. City, (pop. 44,046) situated in Hennepin County in southeastern Minnesota, a suburb of MINNEAPOLIS at the southwest corner of the larger city. The city derives its name from the Edina Flour Mill there, which name was taken in turn from that of Edinburgh, Scotland, from which place the early settlers came. The city is crossed by two branches of Interstate 169, with Interstate 494 passing along the southern boundary. Electronic and computer equipment are the major industries of this mainly residential community, which is noted for its many parks and for the recreation provided by the more than 60 lakes within its boundaries. The 1970 population of 46,073 was slightly reduced in the 1980 census, which placed the number of persons at 44,046.

EDISON, Thomas Alva. (Milan, Ohio, February 11, 1847—West Orange, New Jersey, October 18, 1931). Inventor. Edison's only formal schooling, at PORT HURON, Michigan, lasted only three months. Yet he later became the most prolific inventor of all time, with hundreds of inventions, ranging from such modest improvements as the megaphone to inventions that helped to revolutionize many aspects of living, such memorable and essential items as the phonograph (1877), the incandescent lamp (1879), motion pictures (1891).

Even as a boy at Port Huron, Edison developed an electric battery. After working as a railroad newsboy, in 1863 he became a railroad telegrapher. Working the telegraph turned his mind to electricity. He was granted his first patent in 1869 for an electrical vote recorder. In that year he moved to New York City and managed a stock-ticker company, at which time he also was a partner in an electrical engineering firm. When the firm was sold, Edison began his first research and development company from which many inventions poured. He opened his Menlo Park, New Jersey, laboratory in 1876, and its first major device was the phonograph. The development of a practical method of distributing electricity for its multiple uses was perhaps the most important of all his contributions. His one scientific discovery, the Edison Effect, led to the later development of the electron tube. He became the major stockholder in the giant General Electric Company in 1892. He had moved his laboratory to West Orange, New Jersey, in 1887, where four years later he patented the first motion picture machine. When Henry FORD built GREENFIELD VILLAGE, as a

Education

Edison demonstrates his phonograph, by A.A. Anderson.

tribute to American men of genius, he felt special attention should be given to Edison. Edison was the first prominent person to encourage Ford's development of the automobile. In Greenfield Village Edison's workshop is reproduced exactly as it was the day Edison left it.

EDUCATIONAL ACCOMPLISHMENTS.

The Midwest region has made notable contributions both to educational philosophy and practice, in some instances pioneering in areas of controversy, such as COEDUCATION and early advancement. Other pioneering has included the establishment of state sponsored higher education, the first teaching of scientific agriculture, the first public high school, first kindergarten and first accredited school of nursing. Many of the Midwest accomplishments have come from the minds of some of the world's leading educators.

What was perhaps the most far-reaching change in education was instituted in Ohio when OBERLIN COLLEGE became coeducational in 1841, the first institution of higher education in the United States to do so.

Another pioneering effort occurred in Michigan. Higher education in Europe had long counted on government support. However, a Midwest institution took the first step in that direction in the U.S. when the University of MICHIGAN became the nation's first state-operated college of higher education at its opening at ANN ARBOR in 1817. It also is noted

for having the first hospital of any state university.

MICHIGAN STATE UNIVERSITY, at EAST LANSING, opened in 1857 and was the world's first university to boast a college of scientific agriculture.

What was considered a drastic departure at the time was the pioneering effort of one of the world's most distinguished centers of higher education, the University of CHICAGO. Chicago became the center of controversy among educational philosophers when it inaugurated its pioneering educational experiment in 1929, a policy of accepting any student of whatever age who could pass the entrance examination. Over the years this practice has become more and more widely accepted.

In the important area of the organization of educational systems, Indiana pioneered in 1816 as the first state to provide in its constitution for a graduated system of schooling from primary district schools through the university, open to all for free instruction.

Another notable educational first, the country's first KINDERGARTEN, was opened at WATERTOWN, Wisconsin, by Mrs. Carl Schurz, who brought the concept from Germany in 1856.

Also in that year Chicago established what is considered to be the first truly public high school, known then as Chicago High.

Perhaps the greatest accomplishment of the region in regard to elementary/high school education is the Midwest's preeminence in literacy. Iowa has long led all the states in percentage of those who can read and write, and the other Midwest states are not far behind.

The Midwest has enjoyed outstanding educational leadership in the person of some of the most distinguished individuals in their field.

Unique among educators was William Holmes MC GUFFEY (1800-1873), whose McGuffey readers have been among the most widely read of all books ever printed. That world renowned series of reading books is being used increasingly again today. McGuffey taught in CINCINNATI at both MIAMI UNIVERSITY and CINCINNATI UNIVERSITY and was also president of OHIO UNIVERSITY at ATHENS.

Another internationally famed educator was Horace MANN (1796-1859). Dr. Mann reorganized the school system of Massachusetts in such a way as to "profoundly affect educational practices throughout the nation." His *Common School Journal* was widely read as were his annual reports. Salaries of educators in Massachusetts set the standard for the rest of the nation, among his other innovations. Dr. Mann brought his educational expertise to the Midwest as president of ANTIOCH COLLEGE in YELLOW SPRINGS, Ohio.

At the age of 29 as president of the University of Chicago, Robert Maynard HUTCHINS (1899-1977) was said to have "turned the educational world upside down," with his ideas of early-age entrance for college students and many other educational novelties.

E.F. LINDQUIST (1901-1978) of the University of IOWA, became the leading authority on educational testing, and Paul ENGLE (1908-) of that university is recognized as a principal authority on the teaching of writing. James "Tama Jim" WILSON of IOWA STATE UNIVERSITY (1836-1920) was the nation's pioneer in agricultural education theory and methodology.

Knute ROCKNE of NOTRE DAME is usually said to be the outstanding football coach of all time, providing a master educational touch in his methods of teaching young men how to work together and in providing for the emotional development and maturity of his "boys."

A different educational service was provided by the pioneering work in medical education instituted by the MAYO family and associates at ROCHESTER, Minnesota. This included their unusually fine post-MD work with young doctors, and the school of nursing established at Rochester in 1909, the first ever to be fully accredited.

Harry Steenbock of the University of WISCONSIN was a pioneer in the study and teaching of nutrition.

Many of the Midwest's colleges and universities are noted for their accomplishments in a variety of specialties. The University of MISSOURI, the oldest state university west of the Mississippi (1839), is particularly renowned for its college of journalism, often named the finest anywhere, and also for the most powerful reactor on a university campus. The University of Wisconsin is ranked by the Association of Research Libraries as first among all U.S. universities in its program of graduate studies. The University of IOWA is noted for the extraordinary success of its program of teaching writing and for one of the finest colleges of medicine, especially in its pioneering work in orthopedic surgery.

A small town in Minnesota has a unique educational distinction as being the only community of its size with two colleges, both listed frequently in rank among the top ten small colleges. NORTHFIELD is home to both NORTHFIELD COLLEGE and ST. OLAF COLLEGE.

The School of the ART INSTITUTE at Chicago is said to be the world's largest of its kind.

A less formal but nonetheless widely acknowledged educational influence was found in the concepts expounded by the scientists and philosophers of the colony of NEW HARMONY, Indiana. They are known to have had a strong affect on educational policy, far beyond the Midwest.

Although the Midwest lacks the prestige in formal education enjoyed by the Ivy League institutions and others of the east and west coasts, the region which continually teaches more of its citizens to read, which brought higher education to women and pioneered from the kindergarten to become the leader in graduate education—such a region can truly be said to have made distinctive accomplishments in the field.

EEL RIVER. Either of two Indiana Rivers. The southwestern Indiana Eel River begins in Whitley County and flows into the east fork of the WHITE RIVER near WORTHINGTON, Indiana. This is the Eel River called Shakamak, meaning snakefish or eel, by the DELAWARE INDIANS. This stream still contains eels. The Eel River of northeastern Indiana has its source north of FORT WAYNE and flows into the WABASH RIVER at LOGANSPORT. Famous chief LITTLE TURTLE of the MIAMI INDIANS had his village near its mouth. The Miami called this Eel River Kenapocomoco, also meaning snakefish. The northeastern Indiana Eel River flows past North Manchester, Indiana, and was a favorite hunting area for the Indian tribes in the region, where some even panned for gold.

EFFIGY MOUNDS. While prehistoric mounds of many types, built for many varied purposes, are widely found in the United States, the Midwest has perhaps the largest number and variety of those known as effigy mounds. Such mounds usually have only one purpose, and that is to portray some figure, generally a bird or animal, and formed by piling up mounds of dirt on flat ground in the shape of the intended figure. Ohio boasts some of the largest and finest effigy mounds, in the shape of eagles, snakes and other figures. Perhaps the most famous anywhere is the great SERPENT MOUND near HILLSBORO, Ohio, which winds for 1,330 feet through long dramatic curves, ending in a mouth which seems to be swallowing a gigantic egg. It is the largest effigy mound in the country. The best way to observe such mounds, and sometimes the only way, is from the air. Since the prehistoric builders had no way of observing their work from a suitable distance above their art, their skill in forming such outstanding figures is even more remarkable. The only such mound group to be named a national preserve is EFFIGY MOUNDS NATIONAL MONUMENT in northeastern Iowa. One of the effigies is in the form of an enormous bear, 137 feet long and 70 feet wide across the shoulders. Most gigantic and perhaps most spectacular of the effigy mounds is the enormous human figure, MAN MOUND near BARABOO, Wisconsin. It is 150 feet tall and fifty feet broad at the shoulders. Other Wisconsin effigies are formed to represent turtles, serpents and other animal figures. Illinois is the best represented of all the states in mounds of various kinds, including, perhaps, the largest number of effigies of varying shapes and sizes.

EFFIGY MOUNDS NATIONAL MONU- MENT. Near McGregor, Iowa. This monument contains outstanding examples of prehistoric burial mounds and EFFIGY MOUNDS, some in the shapes of birds and bears. It became a national site in 1962.

EGG HARBOR, Wisconsin. Village (pop. 283), situated on the eastern shore of GREEN BAY in DOOR COUNTY, the village is particularly notable because of its name. A group of prominent Wisconsinites had spent some time in the area; in high spirits they began to pelt each other with hardtack; when that ran out they turned to the picnic eggs. One of the women wrote later, "I crawled under the tarpaulin, where I was comparatively safe, although an occasional egg would strike me on the head....The next morning the scene of battle presented a strange appearance, strewn as it was with egg shells...and the place was formally christened Egg Harbor." Today the community is a popular resort. It features the Chief Oshkosh Indian Museum and the prominent annual month-long Birch Creek Music concerts, held in a barn from mid-June to mid-July.

EGGLESTON, Edward. (Vevay, IN, Dec. 10, 1837—Lake George, NY, Sept. 4, 1902). Novelist, religious leader and historian. Eggleston, a writer of midwestern fiction and history, is credited with influencing American literature toward realism. He grew up on what was then the frontier, became a Bible agent in 1855 and a year later a Methodist circuit rider. He went to Minnesota in 1858, where he held a number of pastorates. Moving to Evanston, Illinois, in 1866, he edited juvenile papers and published children's books. His first novel, *The Hoosier Schoolmaster* (1871), established his literary reputation. His thirteen historical articles in the *Century* Magazine, and his school histories and biographical publications, were all parts of an ambitious plan to write a history of life in the United States. Eggleston lived to complete two volumes, *The Beginnings of a Nation* (1896) and *The Transit of Civilization* (1900). His view that history was ideally a record of a people's culture and not simply a record of events did much to shape the work of succeeding historians. In 1900 he was elected president of the American Historical Association.

EISENHOWER, Mamie Doud. (Boone, IA, Nov. 14. 1896—Washington, DC, Nov. l, 1979) The wife of President Dwight David Eisenhower, was born in BOONE, Iowa, but the wealthy family soon moved to Denver where Mamie lived and from where she traveled with her family. On one of those travels she met young Lieutenant Eisenhower at Fort Sam Houston, Texas, in October, 1915, and they were married in 1916. Mrs. Eisenhower did not retain any close associations with the Midwest after leaving Iowa. However, her birthplace at Boone has been restored to the style of the family's residence there, with period furnishings, including the original bedroom furniture and other memorabilia in a museum.

Mamie Eisenhower with husband Dwight.

ELECTRIC POWER. APPLETON, Wisconsin, was the site of the first plant in the world to produce hydroelectric power (1882). The claim has also been made that the plant at Appleton was the first community power plant of any type. Of course, the Midwest has continued to remain in the forefront of electric generating techniques, with atomic power added to that of water and fossil fuels. In 1987 the ARGONNE LABORATORY, near CHICAGO, announced its discoveries (in cooperation with others) of techniques for high speed transmission of electric power with almost no loss of energy.

ELEPHANT ROCKS. Huge, eroded, picturesque red granite boulders with an estimated age of 1.2 billion years. The rocks are the featured attraction in the Elephant Rocks State Park southeast of POTOSI, Missouri, in Iron County. The park's name comes from Elephant Rock standing twenty-seven feet tall and weighing an estimated 680 tons.

ELEVEN POINT RIVER NATIONAL WILD AND SCENIC RIVER SYSTEM. At ROLLA, Missouri. This spring-fed stream meanders past the limestone bluffs and the crystal clear springs in Missouri's OZARK hills.

ELGIN, Illinois. City (pop. 63,798), in Kane County, situated in northeast Illinois on the FOX RIVER. It was incorporated in 1854. Named by James T. Gifford, probably from a Scottish hymn of that name, but also possibly for the community of Elgin, Scotland, or for a Lord Elgin, holder of a Scottish title. Elgin is a railroad, trade and industrial city, producing an

increasing variety of products, including gaskets, paper products, household appliances, electric and electronic equipment, machinery and watches. During much of the late 18th and early 19th centuries, in the United States the name Elgin was almost synonymous with watches, due to the famed Elgin watch factory there. At one time Elgin was the center of much of the dairying industry of the Midwest, and its markets established the price of butter and cheese over a wide area. After the end of the BLACK HAWK WAR, James and Hezekiah Gifford settled along the Fox River in 1835. When Gifford plotted a road to BELVIDERE, his wife joked "Anyone would think that you expected this farm to become a city, with stagecoaches going through." Before the year ended two stages came by each week, with a flurry of horns, and the city of Elgin gradually took form. Several small industries, including dairying and the establishment of the Elgin National Watch Company in 1866, brought prosperity. The population growth of Elgin in the period of 1970 through 1980 was proportionally larger than that of most of the principal cities of the Midwest, increasing from 55,691 to 63,668. Judson College is located there. Fox River Trolley Museum has much historic and antique railway equipment, including the oldest trolley car in the U.S. There is an annual Electric Railroad Fair in late June and an Ethnic Fest at about the same time.

ELIZA. The famed fictional escaped slave of Harriet Beecher STOWE 's *Uncle Tom's Cabin* (1852) is said to be based on a real Eliza who fled across the OHIO RIVER on the ice, carrying her baby in her arms and sheltered in the Underground Railroad station home of John RANKIN on the banks of the Ohio near CINCINNATI.

ELKHART, Indiana. City (pop. 41,305), major northern Indiana city, community of bridges, located at the confluence of the St. Joseph and Elkhart Rivers and Christiana Creek. Founded in 1832 and named for a small island in the ST. JOSEPH RIVER thought to resemble an elk's heart, Elkhart is considered the musical instrument capital of the United States. Fifteen musical instrument factories produce fifty percent of the wind and percussion instruments made in the country. However, Elkhart also is a city of diversified industry, with 500 other factories producing mobile homes, pharmaceuticals, electronic components and many others. Located on three waterways, it is almost impossible to move from one of the city's sections into another without using one of Elkhart's ten bridges. A permanent collection of American art, including representative works of Norman Rockwell, Alexander Calder and Grandma Moses is housed in the Midwest Museum of American Art. The Ruthmere Museum is a restored Beaux-Arts mansion built in 1908 by A.R. Beardsley, a founder of Miles Laboratories.

ELLSWORTH, Elmer Ephraim. (Malta, NY, April 11, 1837—Alexandria, VA, May 24, 1861). Soldier. Ellsworth served as a law student in Abraham LINCOLN's law office in SPRINGFIELD, Illinois, prior to the start of the CIVIL WAR. Colonel Ellsworth led troops from the capital of Washington on May 24, 1861, to meet the enemy. Victorious in battle, he was killed while attempting to retrieve a Confederate flag. Because of his connection with Lincoln and the president's grief over his loss, the death of Ellsworth became widely known, and the words, "Remember Ellsworth" served as a rallying cry throughout the North and especially in the Midwest.

ELY, Minnesota. Village (pop. 4,820), northeastern Minnesota, located on the shore of Shagawa Lake. Once known as the "Capital of the Vermilion Range." Ely lies within the 3.7-million-acre Superior National Forest, a short distance from the Boundary Waters Canoe Area. Now the supply point for those wishing to outfit themselves to explore the surrounding countryside, Ely was once a thriving mining community. Ore was discovered at Ely in 1886 at the Chandler Mine. The town was named for Arthur Ely, an Ohio businessman. Hundreds of tourists visit the town to be outfitted and supplied for their travel to the nearby one-million-acre wilderness known as the Boundary Waters Canoe Area. The All-American Championship Sled Dog Races are held the third weekend in January with "Wilderness Trek," cross country ski races in February.

EMMETT, Daniel Decatur. (Mount Vernon, Ohio, Oct. 29, 1815—Mt. Vernon, Ohio, June 28, 1904). Composer, entertainer. Very early in life Emmett acquired an interest in music from his mother. At the age of sixteen he composed "Old Dan Tucker" (1831). A year later he joined the army as a fifer and continued to study music in every spare moment. Discharged in 1835, he joined a traveling circus. In 1842-1843 he organized the Virginia Minstrels,

probably the first of the blackface groups which became especially popular in the mid-nineteenth century. They made their first professional appearance in New York City in February of 1843. A great success, they traveled to other cities and to England. Emmett eventually disbanded the group and joined Bryant's Minstrels. Because they had no really rousing song for a close, on a September day in New York in 1859, Emmett composed one of the national treasures, "DIXIE". The song was an almost instant hit, one of the most sensational successes in U.S. musical history. It was played for the inauguration of Jefferson DAVIS as president of the Confederacy in 1861 and became the marching song of the Confederacy, even then not despised in the north and later recognized almost everywhere. This first success was followed by Emmett's composition and popularizing of several other famous songs.

ENGLE, Paul. (Cedar Rapids, IA, Oct. 12, 1908—). One of the world's most distinguished educators in the field of writing, Engle attended COE COLLEGE at CEDAR RAPIDS, Iowa, and the University of IOWA, where his thesis, *Worn Earth* won the prestigious Yale Series of Younger Poets Award in 1932. His further education included work at Columbia University and a Rhodes scholarship. Meanwhile, he gained increasing recognition as a poet. Joining the English department of the University of Iowa in 1936, Engle was convinced that there were more effective ways of teaching writing. He was instrumental in founding the world-famous Iowa Writers' Workshop, where a personal relationship with and among young writers of promise, a kind of "family feeling," has provided pools of talent, sending many of its students to fame. In 1967 Engle and his wife, Aualing Nieh Engle, founded the International Writing Program, funded by the University of Iowa and several corporations, foundations and individuals. This organization brings together writers of varying age and experiences to Iowa City for intensive work with their renowned associates, the Engles.

ERIE CANAL. While not itself in the Midwest, the Erie Canal was one of the primary factors in the development of the entire region. With the opening of the canal in 1825, the vast shores of the GREAT LAKES and the prairie lands beyond them at last lay within comparatively easy reach of the east coast, and especially handy to New York City, where the hosts of European immigrants had begun to swarm in, looking for the streets of gold in the New World. Before this time there was no easy way to the west. Now by way of the Hudson River and the Erie Canal and the Great Lakes the Midwest lay open as never before.

ERIE INDIANS. At about the time Europeans first became acquainted with the Midwest, the Erie Indians lived in northeastern Ohio. After long and bitter fighting, in 1656 the Erie were almost exterminated by the IROQUOIS but not before they had given their name to Lake ERIE. The few remaining were adopted or enslaved in the Iroquois confederacy.

ERIE, Lake. Fourth largest of the GREAT LAKES, more than half of Lake Erie's shoreline touches the Midwest states of Ohio and Michigan. The first European known to have seen the lake was Louis JOLLIET, in 1669. Roughly in the center of the lake, between the lake's north and south shorelines, runs the boundary between the U.S. and Canada.

Lake Erie's surface is 572 feet above sea level, and it has a maximum depth of only 210 feet. The shallowest of the Great Lakes, it is the only one with a "floor" above sea level.

Lake Erie is part of the ST. LAWRENCE SEAWAY chain which opens the entire Great Lakes region to international shipping. The lake has the reputation of being the most dangerous of the Great Lakes, with sudden storms buffeting and often sinking smaller vessels. Because the lake moderates the climate, the islands and shoreline area provide the longest growing season in Ohio.

North of SANDUSKY, Ohio, lie twenty islands of varying size, Pelee and KELLEYS having several thousand acres each. On the American side are Kelleys, Green, Rattlesnake, Ballast, Sugar, Starve, Gibraltar, Mouse and the three Bass islands.

French missionary Gabriel Segard is said to have discovered the islands before 1632. Several small rivers enter the lake from the Midwest, including the CUYAHOGA, MAUMEE and SANDUSKY. Pollution from DETROIT, CLEVELAND and other industrial cities posed a serious danger to the lake, which was thought to be almost dead and beyond recovery. More strict provisions for eliminating pollution had a substantial effect, however, and the lake appears to have recovered substantially.

At one time the western end of Lake Erie provided some of the finest commercial fishing in U.S. fresh waters, until it was almost eliminated by the pollution. However, with the improvement of lake water quality, and introduction of new species, fishing has again improved. Major midwest ports are Cleveland and TOLEDO.

ESCANABA, Michigan. Town (pop. 3,100), seat of Delta County, important iron-ore shipping port on Michigan's UPPER PENINSULA, only ore port on Lake MICHIGAN. Escanaba was first developed by lumbermen who came to the region as early as 1830, anxious to take advantage of the huge stands of timber on the Upper Peninsula. When the lumber industry faded and mining increased, the miners began to notice the fine deep-water harbor at the mouth of the Escanaba River on Little Bay de Noc. Railroadmen, interested in a deep-water shipping port on Lake Michigan, constructed the first dock in 1863. The town continued to flourish as a shipping point of iron-ore. The harbor also served to attract commercial fisherman who were soon marketing more than two million pounds of fish annually. Today the second stand of timber is again furnishing a valuable resource for the region. Ninety-five percent of the world's supply of bird's-eye pine has grown within a two-hundred mile radius of the community. In 1936 Escanaba lumbermen furnished 100,000 square feet of this wood for the construction of the Cunard line's S.S. *Queen Mary*. The location of the town on Lake Michigan has given it further opportunities in the tourist business. The season has traditionally begun during the first week of April with the annual Smelt Fishing Jamboree, three days of festivities associated with the smelt runs in the Ford and Escanaba rivers. A busy season of watersports has been capped by the Venetian Night Program in August. The end of the season is marked by the Upper Peninsula State Fair during the third week of August. Activities during the fair have included a national log-birling contest.

ESTHERVILLE, Iowa. City (pop. 7,518), seat of Emmet County, located near the northern border of the state in the central western portion of Iowa, on the west branch of the DES MOINES RIVER, about twelve miles east of Spirit Lake, the city was named for Esther A. Ridley, wife of one of the founders. In 1879, Estherville was the site of one of the more notable astronomical phenomena of the period. The peaceful afternoon calm was shattered by a hiss and roar which rattled dishes, broke windows and shook the town and the whole region for fifty miles around. One of the major

METEORS to survive earth's atmosphere in that era had shattered into three major pieces over Estherville. Estherville hosts a Winter Sports Festival in the first weekend of February, featuring snow sculpture and cross country skiing as well as indoor displays and activities. The Holiday Mountain Ski Area is nearby. The area was the site of Fort Defiance, built during the CIVIL WAR for protection against the Indians. The area is now a state park, notable for fishing, hiking, snowmobiling and bridal trails.

EVANS, John. (Waynesville, OH, March 9, 1814—Denver, CO, July 3, 1897). Physician, city builder, founder of universities. As a doctor in ATTICA, Indiana, he was financially successful, and he engaged in several reform movements. He was principally responsible for the establishment of Indiana's first state hospital for the mentally ill in 1845. He went to INDIANAPOLIS that year to become the hospital superintendent. John Evans had predicted even greater success for himself—that he would become wealthy, build a city, establish a college, govern a state, and become a United States Senator. Moving to Illinois, he became professor of obstetrics at Rush Medical College at CHICAGO. He also invested in Chicago real estate and became a director and part builder of the Fort Wayne and Chicago Railroad. He then gained new prominence as one of the founders of NORTHWESTERN UNIVERSITY (1851) at EVANSTON, Illinois. The Chicago suburb was named EVANSTON in his honor. On March 26, 1862, Evans was appointed the territorial governor of Colorado, and he became one of the most influential persons in the region. He had more than lived up to all his predictions except for a U.S. Senate post. The acting Colorado legislature elected him to the Senate in 1865, but Colorado failed to achieve statehood at that time, and he never took his seat. He remained in the area and assisted in the establishment of the University of Denver and railroad lines, ensuring Denver's growth. He gave generously to many charitable causes. Evans achieved one honor which he had not predicted. In 1895 Mt. Evans was named in his honor.

EVANSTON, Illinois. City (pop.73,706), first of the residential cities to develop north of CHICAGO on Lake MICHIGAN, named for Dr. John EVANS, one of the three organizers of NORTHWESTERN UNIVERSITY in 1851. Evanston, incorporated in 1863, thrives as a cultural center, the main seat of Northwestern University, and a retail sales location for many of Chicago's fashionable stores. The city became the headquarters of the National Woman's Christian Temperance Union as well as hundreds of other national organizations. The home of Charles G. Dawes, Vice President of the United States under Calvin Coolidge, now a museum, displays Indian objects, ceramics, coins and furniture. The Temperance Union headquarters stands at the rear of the former home of Frances Willard, organizer of the association. Tours of the home are by appointment. Northwestern University offers the Deering Library's collection of rare books and art exhibits for the visitor as well as the Lindheimer Astronomical Research Center. The Evanston branch of the TERRA MUSEUM of American Art contains examples of American art from the 18th to the 20th centuries.

EVANSVILLE, Indiana. City (pop. 130,-496), situated in extreme southwest Indiana on a great bend of the OHIO RIVER, seat of Vanderburgh County, incorporated in 1819 and named for Robert Evans, who platted the townsite. It occupies an area of 37.4 square miles. Its principal neighbor is the city of Henderson on the Kentucky side of the Ohio River. As a major port on the river and a center of a substantial farming and coal mining region, the city is a shipping and commercial hub and offers substantial educational facilities. Excavating machinery, fabricated metals, air conditioning equipment, aluminum and pharamaceuticals are major industries. During the period between 1970 and 1984 the city declined in population from 139,000 to 130,496, due to the loss of jobs, as industries departed for the Sunbelt. A campus of INDIANA STATE UNIVERSITY, the University of EVANSVILLE and several technical colleges are centered at Evansville. Angel Mounds State Park is a memorial to the PREHISTORIC PEOPLES whose relics have been found there. The city also recalls the life of James Bethel Gresham, one of the first three Americans to lose their lives during WORLD WAR I. There is a museum of arts and science and a zoo. The Evansville Philharmonic gained great stature with the coming of famed conductor George DASCH as its director. During the 1960s, the city was one of the first to convert its downtown area into a shopping plaza, featuring a winding walkway.

EVANSVILLE, UNIVERSITY OF. Privately supported Indiana university founded in 1854 and moved to EVANSVILLE in 1919. Course work leads to degrees in teacher education, business administration, fine arts, and health services. The university, located in the fourth largest city in the state and the largest in southern Indiana, has a 75-acre campus. There is a cooperative education program for engineering, physics, and computer science with alternating work and class periods. During the 1985-1986 academic year the university enrolled 4,033 students and had 272 faculty members.

EVELETH, Minnesota. City (pop. 5,042), northeastern Minnesota; south of VIRGINIA; mining community; known as the "Hill Top City," named for Erwin Eveleth, a lumberman. Eveleth came to the region in 1883 to purchase forest lands for lumbering. The discovery of iron ore deposits there caused the town to be platted the same year. Finds of rich deposits of iron ore beneath the community itself caused all the buildings to be moved one mile in 1895. Several sites had to be tested before the residents were able to find a place to relocate their dead. Two miles to the east, on US 53, is the Hockey Hall of Fame where films, pictures and equipment tell the story of the development of the sport in the United States.

EXCELSIOR SPRINGS, Missouri. City (pop. 10,400), northwest Missouri, northeast of KANSAS CITY in Clay County. Health spa. Ten natural mineral waters in four groups—soda, iron manganese, saline, and calcium—are responsible for the reputation of Excelsior Springs as a health resort. Bath departments for men and women are operated by the city at the Hall of Waters. A Hall of Springs dispenses water for drinking, and more is bottled at a modern bottling plant. Near Excelsior Springs is the Watkins Woolen Mill State Historic Site. This is a nonoperating, but fully equipped, woolen mill with spinners, twisters and looms.

EXPERIMENTAL AIRCRAFT ASSO-CIATION. Headquartered at OSHKOSH, Wisconsin, the association has encouraged individuals to design and construct, or simply to construct, their own airplanes. They especially urge anyone with a good idea to try it out in a full-size working plane. The association maintains an Air Museum at Oshkosh, featuring home built-aircraft, as well as examples of types of planes from gliders and ultralights through rotary-winged craft. Its International Fly-in Convention at Oshkosh in late July and early August is said to be the largest and most significant aviation event in the world, attracting thousands of aircraft of all kinds from

around the world and featuring such attractions as the Blue Angels. The 1987 show attracted 15,000 aircraft and more than 900,000 spectators.

EXPLORATION AND EXPLORERS IN THE MIDWEST. Exploration laid the foundation for the expansion of geographic knowledge, understanding of the INDIAN TRIBES, the growth of european populations and economic development of the region. The intrepid explorers provided the basis for the colonial claims throughout the region and in the earliest cases offered insight into the enormous expanses that were still completely unknown to Europeans.

The concept of a vast expanse of land, covered with lakes, rivers mountains and forests, leading to unknown seas and perhaps unconquerable peoples is so divorced from today's reality that few people can imagine the trepidation, the suspense, the excitement that must have been felt by those from Europe who in the early 1600s stood on the edge of wilderness North America and proposed to solve its mysteries.

However, those European explorers were latecomers. Non-European peoples had earlier been moving across the Americas for at least 40,000 years, according to the best recent authority. So, of course, the earliest Midwest explorers actually were the PREHISTORIC PEOPLES, and there is abundant evidence of their presence throughout the Midwest, although there is no agreement among experts as to when the earliest peoples arrived in the region. Estimates range from 30,000 to 10,000 years ago.

Over the millenia, they reached from the land bridge of the ice ages into present Alaska and on to the farthest reaches of the continent. In what is now the Midwest, some of the more advanced peoples apparently had explored the routes to such far places as Mexico and carried on trade there.

Conventional wisdom contends, of course, that modern exploration of the Western Hemisphere began with Columbus in 1492. However, more and more scholars appear to concur that European explorers from the north had reached North America generations before Columbus.

Considerable evidence has been gathered to indicate that those explorers may have reached farther inland than originally thought, perhaps as far inland as Minnesota as early as 1362, as indicated by the controversial KENSINGTON

Marquette and Jolliet enter the Mississippi, 1673.

RUNESTONE, found near Kensington, Minnesota, in 1898. Such apparent physical evidence of Scandinavian or Welsh explorers, also extends from the OHIO RIVER to Oklahoma and continues to produce theories of early inland incursions of pre-Columbians. Perhaps most persuasive of all is the conviction of experts, such as Gloria Farley and Dr. John Denmark, of the genuineness of the Heavener Runestone in Heavener Runestone Oklahoma State Park and other relics found in nearby communities.

Almost as much confusion exists as to the exact dates when later European explorers reached what is now the Midwest. Some accounts say that Hernando de Soto's expedition may have touched southern Missouri in 1541. Francisco Vasquez de Coronado may have reached Missouri in August, 1541, after his long trek across the Southwest. At the least, these early contacts gave the great powers of Europe some idea of the extent of the continent beyond the eastern and southwestern fringes.

By the early 1600s, footholds had been gouged out by Europeans on the east coast and for very short distances inland, but the interior of the continent was *terra incognita*.

True, the Indians had been masters of the continent for centuries, but they generally did not roam very far. Tribal lore told of distant lands visited by prehistoric peoples, and most of the tribal wisemen knew of great lakes and mountains to the West, but their descriptions and diagrams were vague.

It was all yet to be discovered and, more particularly, to be recorded. What kind of a person was ready and anxious to go westward into the wilderness? Samuel de CHAMPLAIN of France was just such a bold adventurer. By the time he founded Montreal in 1611 he had explored most of the coast and offshore islands of what is now the northeastern U.S. and southeastern Canada, along with much of the

St. Lawrence River. Historian Charles Slocum contends that Champlain reached as far west as present FORT WAYNE, Indiana, in 1614, but that seems doubtful. Nevertheless, he laid the basis for far-reaching French claims and brought the French to a realization that New France might be claimed to extend for thousands of miles to the west and that the chain of enormous lakes drained by the St. Lawrence would provide an easy route for further exploration.

For the British, farther to the south, there was to be no such easy route over the mountains, and they would remain far behind the French in the race to explore and claim the vast back country.

Being first was very important, because legal claim to new territory was most often based on the right of discovery—what nation's representatives had reached an area first? Conflicting claims of the right of discovery and the overwhelming drive for sovereignty in North America were among the many causes of the almost constant rivalry and warfare between and among England, France and Spain. First sighting of a disputed area was not only the basis of legal claims, but it also generally opened the way for practical control and later settlement of the region. Exploration laid the foundation for expansion of geographic knowledge, understanding of the Indian tribes, preceding the growth of European populations and economic development of the region.

As French settlement progressed in the coastal northeast and as British settlement began to the south in the early 1600s, of course, the long standing rivalries of the two powers carried over into the New World.

The French had the advantage in turning to the West, because the GREAT LAKES and the Mississippi and Ohio rivers provided the easiest means of access to the interior. If Champlain did not reach the region in 1614, then another

Exploration

French explorer, Etienne BRULE, was probably the first to do so. He is known to have explored as far as the western Great Lakes area between 1618 and 1622, when he discovered Lake SUPERIOR. He touched Michigan and probably other Midwest Great Lakes states on those explorations.

Perhaps the most picturesque of the very early explorers to reach the Midwest was Jean NICOLET. Searching for the fabled route to the Orient, Nicolet arrived at the Indian village of Red Bank near present GREEN BAY, Wisconsin, in 1634, where he thought at first that he had reached China.

In 1671, the French governor of Canada sent Francois DAUMONT, Sieur de St. Lusson, to claim the entire continent in the name of the King of France. French missionaries had already opened a mission on the banks of the ST. MARYS RIVER, where SAULT STE. MARIE stands today. On June 14, 1671, Daumont led a procession out of the mission, and held an elaborate ceremony to impress the Indians. In this performance (now known as the PAGEANT OF THE SAULT), he formally claimed the lands to the west in the king's name. Thus the French hoped to establish even more clearly their legal precedence around the GREAT LAKES and to the south and west.

Even more important for the legal claims of the French were the events two years later. The portage across a mile and a half of land at what is now PORTAGE, Wisconsin, was all that was required to complete the water route from the Great Lakes to the Mississippi Valley. In 1763 the famed French explorers MARQUETTE (1637-1675) and JOLLIET (1645-1700) discovered the upper Mississipi by following this route over the short portage in the early part of their notable exploration. On the Mississippi, they passed the present Midwest states of Iowa and Missouri and then made the first recorded passage through central Illinois by way of the now-connected rivers—ILLINOIS, DES PLAINES and CHICAGO. This exploration greatly enhanced the French claim of the entire upper Mississippi valley.

The most important move for de facto French control of the continent came with the Midwest explorations and establishment of a string of fort/settlements by Robert Cavelier, Sieur de LA SALLE, and his associate, Henri DE TONTI. La Salle made his first visit to the Midwest in 1679, and in that year he established FORT MIAMI, at present ST. JOSEPH, Michigan, the first of the forts occupied by the French until 1763. These forts extended diagonally from Michigan to present Louisiana.

Daniel Greysolon, Sieur du Lhut (DULUTH, 1636-1710), also traveled for the French king. He visited what is now Minnesota in 1679 to discourage the wars between the SIOUX and CHIPPEWA and to impress the tribes with the power of the French. In 1680 Father Louis HENNEPIN discovered the Falls of ST. ANTHONY at present MINNEAPOLIS, Minnesota. French nobleman La Verendrye and his sons and nephew opened the canoe route from Lake Superior to Lake Winnipeg and were the first Europeans to visit the RED RIVER valley. They established a trading post, Fort St. Charles, on the NORTH-WEST ANGLE in 1732.

Also important for the French cause, were the French VOYAGEURS and trappers, who were not far behind the first explorers. By the early 1700s these fearless businessmen had been over most of the Midwest and had become familiar with almost every lake and stream throughout the region. Their explorations were, perhaps, more important in revealing the character of the land and its peoples than those of the more formal explorations.

Despite the many European footsteps now criss-crossing the land, settlement of the region followed only slowly and sporadically, and the land long remained almost entirely in Indian hands, although still claimed by both France and England.

Beginning in 1689 the interminable warfare between the French and English proceeded in earnest, and, of course, almost immediately spread to North America. In the beginning, this warfare was mostly confined to the east coast, but it inevitably gained momentum beyond the Alleghenies and along the Great Lakes.

To re-substantiate their legal claims in the Midwest, in 1749 the French sent explorer CELORON de Blainville to bury a series of lead plates at six points on the Ohio River, as physical proof of their sovereignty. The English paid no attention and sent noted explorer Christopher GIST for their first real exploration of the Ohio River valley (1750-1751). Gist made remarkable progress in turning the loyalty of the Indians toward the English.

By this time the wars between the two nations had spread westward into the Midwest region. The long and bloody war was over only when the victorious British drove the French from the continent with the signing of the Treaty of Paris in 1763. However almost constant conflict continued with the Indians, who favored the French, and then during the Revolutionary War, when many of the tribes fought on the side of the British.

Fairmont - Fallen Timbers

By the end of the Revolutionary War, most of the Midwest east of the Mississippi had not only been thoroughly traversed but also was generally well charted. Nevertheless, some important Midwest explorations were still to be undertaken.

In 1820, Lewis CASS (1782-1866), governor of Michigan Territory, traveled west to explore for minerals and to find the long-sought source of the Mississippi River, which he failed to do, but his expedition was particularly successful in locating the rich mineral deposits in parts of the region. Discovery of the Mississippi source was left to Henry R. SCHOOLCRAFT (1793-1864), who in 1832, named Lake ITASCA in Minnesota as the source.

Perhaps the greatest exploration in U.S. times was begun in the Midwest by LEWIS AND CLARK at ST. LOUIS , Missouri, on May 14, 1804. They and their party journeyed up the MISSOURI RIVER , paused on the Iowa shores and left the Midwest, returning two years later. The last major expedition to explore the Midwest was led by Zebulon PIKE (1779-1813) in 1805. Much of his route was well known, but he hoped to find the long-sought source of the Mississippi. He failed in this, but was able to convince many of the Indians of the region to turn their allegiance to the U.S., as the new owners of Louisiana Territory.

As settlers moved into the western and northwestern portions of the Midwest in the 1840s and 1850s, many minor discoveries were made about the land and its people, but few unknown areas remained on Midwest maps.

FAIRMONT, Minnesota. City (pop. 11,506), south-central Minnesota, west of ALBERT LEA, originally called Fair Mount because of the height which provided a view of Lake Sisseton. Fairmont is located on a north-south chain of eighteen lakes which were deeply eroded valleys before being filled by glacier waters. Despite harsh weather, Fairmont and the county grew rapidly between 1856 and 1862, when a severe winter was followed by spring floods and the Sioux Uprising. Settlers fled the area so quickly tables were found set and household items left as if the residents had simply stepped outside for a moment. By 1873 the town had returned to normal and an English farming colony settled there. Many of the group were Oxford and Cambridge graduates with titles but no hopes of inheritance in England. The timing of the colony was very poor. In June, 1873, Rocky Mountain locusts invaded the region, destroyed gardens and nearly ruined the colony's attempt to make Fairmont a "bean" capital. Many of the English settlers left the colony, but those who remained established an organization which became known throughout the state as the Fairmont Sportsmen, developers of an active fox-hunting club, boat club, and English-style football team. Today, many well-known firms have branches at Fairmont, including 3-M Company, American Western, Armour and Company, Weigh-Tronix and Fairmont Railway Motors. Annual events include the Heritage Acres Bluegrass Festival on July 4th and King Korn Days in mid-September.

FALLEN TIMBERS, BATTLE OF. Decisive American victory over the Indians. The battle took place on August 20, 1794, just southwest of present TOLEDO, Ohio. Opposing forces were an Indian confederation under the general direction of Chief LITTLE TURTLE and American troops commanded by General Anthony WAYNE. Wayne recognized that a clear-cut victory in battle was needed before the Indians could be removed as a serious threat to American settlement in the territory. He drilled his men for a year and then marched into Indian country and built Forts Greenville, Defiance and Recovery. Hostile Indians watched and waited for an opportunity to strike. Chief LITTLE TURTLE recognized that defeating Wayne's army would be difficult. He repeatedly counseled his people to accept Wayne's offers of peace, but the MIAMI were defiant under the spell of their victories against Josiah HARMAR and Arthur ST. CLAIR and the encouragement they received from the British. The counsel of Little Turtle was overruled, and the Indians decided to ambush Wayne in a dense forest setting, littered with fallen trees.

Battle of Fallen Timbers

Wayne's men approached the Indian forces and used their bayonets and close-rifle fire to drive the Indians from their positions and scatter them in disarray. In a forty minute battle between 1,500 and 2,000 Indians were defeated. The allies of the Miami were convinced that further battles were useless and left for their homes. Wayne destroyed all the property in the area, both British and Indian, along with the Indian crops. On a march to the MAUMEE RIVER he continued to destroy whatever he found in a manner later seen in the SHERMAN march to the sea during the CIVIL WAR. At the meeting of the ST. MARYS and ST. JOSEPH rivers Wayne built FORT WAYNE and then returned with his army to winter quarters in GREENVILLE. Deprived of shelter and food, the Indians survived the winter on British charity. One by one the chiefs visited Wayne and promised peace. In August, 1795, the TREATY OF GREEN VILLE was signed by the Indians who ceded much of what is now Ohio to the settlers. A narrow strip of eastern Indiana was opened to settlement. The Indians promised to cease their raiding, and British agents withdrew to Canada.

FAR WEST, Missouri. Former MORMON stronghold in Missouri and one time county seat of Caldwell County. Within months of the Missouri legislature's establishment of Caldwell County in December, 1836, hundreds of Saints (Mormons) chose to move to the area where the settlements of SALEM and Far West were founded. Far West was chosen as the county seat. A temple square 396 feet cross and four

main streets, each 100 feet wide, were platted. Side streets in this magnificent city were designed to be 82 1/2 feet wide. Among the famous Mormons working on the site were Brigham YOUNG and Joseph SMITH. Disputes with gentile neighbors led to violence, and the Saints were declared dangerous to the public good. After the Mormons of Far West surrendered to the state militia, the Mormon leaders were court martialed and ordered executed. The order to shoot the Mormons was disobeyed by Alexander DONIPHAN, and the prisoners were taken to jail in Independence. Later, on the way to Columbia, most of the prisoners escaped and fled to Illinois. The houses of Far West were torn down, but the community remained the county seat until Kingston was platted in 1843. Today nothing remains of this once thriving Missouri community.

FARIBAULT, Minnesota. City (pop. 16,-241), seat of Rice County, southeastern Minnesota, northeast of MANKATO, incorporated 1872. The city is noted for its peony farms. Its manufactures include food products, electrical equipment and metal products. Faribault Woolen Mill has been manufacturing "Faribo" blankets there since 1865. The community is located in a year-round vacation area known as "Hiawathaland." Faribault was founded in 1826 by fur trader Alexander Fairibault. It was a center of trapping in the early history of Minnesota. Faribault's trading post supplied most of the commerce of the area until the 1850s when milling and wheat farming grew in importance. The Cannon and Straight rivers provided power for the town's grist and sawmills. Enough settlers gathered ginseng root to report that in 1859 six tons were brought to Faribault for export in one week. The former home of Alexander Faribault is restored and open for visitors. Other sites include the Cathedral of Our Merciful Savior which was begun in 1862 by Bishop Henry Whipple. One stained glass window shows a peace pipe superimposed over a broken tomahawk, indicating the Indians' appreciation of Whipple's efforts in protecting their rights.

FARMER-LABOR PARTY OF MINNESOTA. A Third Party offshoot of the National Partisan League, organized after the Minnesota members of the league failed to gain control of the Minnesota Republican Party in 1918 and 1920 elections. In 1922, they entered a state Farmer-Labor Party, elected Henrik Shipstead to the U.S. Senate and sent three of their members to Congress. The party continued to gain strength in Minnesota, becoming dominant in the state after electing Floyd B. Olson as governor in 1930. He served for three two-year terms. After his death in 1936, he was followed as governor by two other members of the party. Supporting F.D. Roosevelt in 1932 and 1936, the party carried Minnesota for him. Modified forms of the Farmer-Labor platform were carried out in the Roosevelt New Deal. These included tax reform, Social Security and, particularly, aid to farmers, who were burdened with debt. Also in 1936, the Farmer-Labor Party gained control of the lower house of the Minnesota legislature, both Senate seats and a majority of the Congressional positions. A merger of the Democratic Party and the Minnesota Farmer-Labor party was brought about in 1944 by Hubert H. HUMPHREY, later a U.S. senator and vice president. This Democratic-Farmer-Labor Party grew in power from the 1950s through the early 1970s when the state's Republican Party changed its name to the Independent-Republicans of Minnesota and recaptured many elective offices.

FATHER MARQUETTE NATIONAL MEMORIAL. At LANSING, Michigan. The memorial pays tribute to the life and work of Father Jacques MARQUETTE, French priest and explorer. It is located in Straits State Park near ST. IGNACE, Michigan, where Marquette founded a Jesuit mission in 1671 and was buried in 1678.

FERBER, Edna. (Kalamazoo, MI, Aug. 15, 1885—New York City, Apr. 16, 1968). Author. She grew up in KALAMAZOO and APPLETON, Wisconsin, where she graduated from high school and worked for a local newspaper as a reporter. She served in newspaper posts in MILWAUKEE and CHICAGO until 1911, when she devoted herself to writing. Her first novel, *Dawn O'Hara* (1911) encouraged her to take up writing full time. She was a prolific producer of very popular magazine stories. These were gathered together in several book collections. With the publication of *So Big* in 1924, she gained a firm place on best-seller lists and also won the PULITZER PRIZE. As a keen observer of American life and times, she was noted for her characterizations and choice of settings for her novels. The ever popular *Show Boat* was published in 1926 and formed the basis for musicals and motion pictures. Ferber was the author of many other famous novels including *Giant* (1952), and *Saratoga Trunk* (1941). With

George S. Kaufman. She co-authored several plays, including the perennial *Dinner at Eight* (1932). Although she was dismissed as a light romantic by many critics, others have praised Ferber's serious approach to her many themes. She wrote two autobiographical works, *A Peculiar Treasure* (1930) and *A Kind of Magic* (1963).

FERGUS FALLS, Minnesota. City (pop. 12,519), northwestern Minnesota, southeast of MOORHEAD. Fergus Falls was named for James Fergus, who loaned the founder a dog team. It was established by Joseph Whitford in 1857 near a falls on the OTTER TAIL RIVER. A log cabin served as the first post office in the community. The German postmaster could not read English and emptied the mail sack on the floor. He let people sift through the letters to find those addressed to them. In 1873 the citizens formed the Red River Slack Water Navigation Company to ship goods up the Otter Tail River to the Perham railroad station, but the endeavor was hopeless in dry months, and the idea was eventually dropped. In 1879 the Northern Pacific Railroad arrived. A devastating TORNADO struck and destroyed much of the community in 1919 and killed sixty people. Today's industry includes packaged meats, dairy products, cabinets and clothing. Within the city itself are five hundred acres of parkland. Phelps Mill Park along the Otter Tail River offers a look at a non-operational mill. Inspiration Peak State Park is noted for the second highest point in the state, and Maplewood State Park is known for its scenic beauty. Otter Tail County Historical Society Museum displays life in the early 1900s.

FERMI NATIONAL ACCELERATOR LABORATORY. Physics research laboratory, commonly called Fermilab, near BATAVIA, Illinois. It was named in honor of Enrico FERMI, the physicist who produced the first nuclear chain reaction. Fermilab contains one of the world's largest particle accelerators, also known as atom smashers. Within a circular underground tunnel one and one-third miles in diameter, protons are accelerated almost to the speed of light. The protons are directed at a target and the result of the collision is studied. Fermilab is managed by Universities Research Association, Incorporated, a consortium of fifty-three universities reporting to the United States Department of Energy.

FERMI, Enrico. (Rome, Italy, Sept. 29,

1901—Chicago, IL, Nov. 28, 1954). Nuclear physicist. After graduating from the University of Pisa with a doctorate, in 1922, Fermi lectured in physics at several notable European universities. He was on the staff of the University of Rome for eleven years. His research on the theory of atomic physics encouraged him to feel that further experiments in the field might bring results. His careful procedures led him to a reaction of uranium, which he found puzzling. Although scientists generally agreed that a such a reaction of uranium was impossible, Fermi's discoveries indicated that the scientists had been wrong. If his discovery was indeed accurate, it could lead to the the realization of nuclear fission. Not willing at the time to go against established scientific opinion, Fermi did not pursue the matter further at the time, not realizing at the time that he had discovered the secret of unlocking the atom. Disgusted with the Fascist government of Italy and fearful for his wife, Laura, who was Jewish, he planned to leave Italy. His opportunity came when he was awarded the NOBEL PRIZE for Physics in 1938 and went to Stockholm to receive the award. Afterward he went directly to the United States. In 1939 German scientists reproduced Fermi's experiments and found that they did actually lead to fission. Fermi joined with Albert Einstein and other scientists in persuading President F.D. Roosevelt of the importance of nuclear energy and convinced the president of the prospect that the Germans might find and use it first. With the U.S. finally embarked on one of the most costly and dramatic endeavors of history (the Manhattan Project), Fermi was chosen to lead the project in a crash program to achieve sustained nuclear reaction. He designed the first atomic pile, which produced the first nuclear reaction, at CHICAGO, in 1942. Fermi then went to the super-secret installation at Los Alamos, New Mexico, where the first atomic bomb was exploded on July 16, 1945. In 1946 he received the Congressional Medal of Merit for his work. Returning to the University of CHICAGO, he headed a program later named the Enrico Fermi Institute for Nuclear Studies. He was the first person to receive the Atomic Energy Commission's prize, later called the Fermi Prize. He died shortly after receiving the award.

FERRIS STATE UNIVERSITY. Publically supported institution founded in 1884 in BIG RAPIDS, Michigan. The college is located on a 443-acre campus on the MUSKEGON RIVER. The goal of the college is to provide vocationally and occupationally centered programs emphasizing business, health sciences, optometry, pharmacy, and technical and applied arts. No freshman may bring a motor vehicle to the university or the Big Rapids area. Accreditation comes from the North Central Association of Colleges and Schools and the appropriate educational and professional organizations. During the 1985-1986 academic year 10,909 students were enrolled, and the college employed 650 faculty members.

FERRIS, George Washington Gale. (Galesburg, IL, Feb. 14, 1859—Pittsburgh, PA, Nov. 22, 1896). Mechanical engineer. After graduating from Rensselaer Polytechnic Institute in 1881, Ferris was involved with a number of construction companies, particularly in constructing bridges. In 1892 Ferris responded to an appeal by Daniel H. Burnham, planner of Chicago's WORLD'S COLUMBIAN EXPOSITION. Burnham wanted the fair to boast an engineering marvel, such as the Eiffel Tower in Paris. Responding, Ferris designed a great upright wheel, which would revolve and soar 250 feet above the fairgrounds. Despite the skeptics, the plan was accepted and the first Ferris Wheel became a marvel of the fair. It could carry 40 people in each of 36 cars as large as a streetcar. It operated with precision and perfect safety throughout the fair in 1893. The wheel also was used in 1904 at the St. Louis exhibition and then sold for scrap. Today the name of Ferris is carried all over the world on smaller models of the amusement device he pioneered.

FIELD MUSEUM OF NATURAL HISTORY. CHICAGO, Illinois, noted for its interrelated functions of research, education and exhibition. The museum was founded in 1893 following the WORLD'S COLUMBIAN EXPOSITION from which it received many exhibits. The museum made a breakthrough in display techniques by creating the first of the modern-style DIORAMAS, three-dimensional objects combined with painted background to heighten the effect of realism. Many wealthy patrons contributed to the museum, led by Marshall FIELD I who initially gave one million dollars, adding four hundred thousand dollars more during his life and eight million dollars at his death through his will. Until the present building was opened in 1921, exhibits were housed in the Palace of Fine Arts of the Exposition. Special exhibits, demonstrations and educational programs supplement the regular collections. Some authori-

Field Museum displays world's largest mounted elephants.

ties contend that this museum is the finest of its type in the world.

FIELD, Eugene. (St. Louis, MO, Sept. 23, 1850—Chicago, IL, Nov. 4, 1895). Author and journalist. He held editorial positions with NEWSPAPERS in ST. JOSEPH, KANSAS CITY and ST. LOUIS, Missouri. He then produced columns for CHICAGO newspapers, under the title of "Sharps and Flats," beginning 1883. He was a pioneer in the field of the newspaper personal column. His columns were wide ranging, from critcism of the rich Chicago meat packers to poems and recollections of childhood. His work was urbane and witty and set the tone for many of the columnists who followed him. As a working journalist he aided many young writers and was one of the important figures in early Chicago literary history. He also was noted for his ingenuity in practical jokes. Most of his books were collections of his newspaper work. Typical was his *A Little Book of Western Verse* (1889). He was the author of many poems including "Lovers Lane, St. Joe," the lullaby "Wynken,

Blynken and Nod" and the universally beloved "Little Boy Blue," all appearing first in his columns.

FIELD, Marshall. (Conway, MA, Aug. 18, 1834—Chicago, IL, Jan. 16, 1906). Merchant. Field left school at the age of 16 to work as a clerk. When he moved to CHICAGO in 1856 he became a traveling salesman and clerk in a major wholesale firm, rising to a position of partner in 1862. Field and his partner, Levi Z. Leiter, joined Potter PALMER to form Field, Palmer and Leiter in 1865. This became Field, Leiter and Company after Palmer left in 1867. The firm survived the Chicago FIRE, the depression of 1873 and another fire in 1877. In 1881 Field bought out his partners and established Marshall Field and Company. Field introduced new merchandising policies, including marking prices on the product and allowing customers to return items if they were dissatisfied. Making a special effort to attract the woman shopper, Field created the slogan, "Give the Lady What She Wants." Marshall Field's was the first store to sell goods in a bargain basement and was a leader in advertising and window displays. Field was renowned for his ability to forecast trends in merchandising. Field contributed ten acres as a location for the UNIVERSITY OF CHICAGO and nearly nine million dollars to establish the FIELD MUSEUM OF NATURAL HISTORY in Chicago, among many other contributions. Among his descendants, Marshall Field III established newspaper and other publishing and broadcasting enterprises and was succeeded by Marshall Field IV.

FIGHTING MC COOKS. The wartime record of the McCook family seems to have been unique in American military history. Daniel McCook and John McCook were Ohio brothers. Early in the CIVIL WAR Daniel enlisted with his eight living sons. The five sons of John also served in the Union forces. All fourteen took an active part in the war. They became known as "The Tribe of Dan" and "The Tribe of John." Dan's tribe produced three major generals, two brigadier generals, one colonel, two majors and a private. John's tribe produced a major general, a brigadier general, two lieutenants, a chaplain and a navy lieutenant. Daniel McCook and three of his sons died in the war. General Anson McCook, Colonel George McCook and Captain Francis McCook are buried in Union Cemetery, STEUBENVILLE, Ohio. The latter was the maternal grandfather of Woodrow Wilson.

FIRE, CHICAGO. One of the worst such disasters in the country's history. Known as the "Gem of the Prairie," or the "Queen City," CHICAGO, in 1871, was a city with thousands of wooden structures, wooden sidewalks, and streets paved with wooden blocks. During the summer of 1871 only five inches of rain had fallen on Chicago between July and October. According to legend, the fire began on October 8, 1871, when a cow, belonging to Mrs. Patrick O'Leary supposedly kicked over a lantern in a barn behind the O'Leary home on DeKoven Street. Many of the first firemen to arrive had fought a huge fire on the West Side of Chicago just the day before. They recruited volunteers who soon fled, precluding the last opportunity to contain the fire. The watchman on duty on the Courthouse roof gave incorrect instructions to other firemen who had to search for the fire's location. As valuable time was wasted, winds blew the flames toward downtown Chicago. Thousands were forced to flee and others were overwhelmed without notice. Hundreds of people waded into Lake MICHIGAN to escape the heat and flying sparks. The heat was so intense it could be felt in Michigan, 100 miles east across Lake Michigan. In Chicago it caused coins, bottles, tumblers, and other glass objects to melt into lumps such as are now shown in the Chicago Historical Society Museum in Lincoln Park. Over seventeen thousand buildings were destroyed in twenty-four hours. An estimated two hundred fifty people perished. Fifty-six insurance companies in ten states went bankrupt as a result of claims against them. Reconstruction began immediately with supplies and money from across the country and from Europe. Debris was dumped into Lake Michigan and became subsoil for Grant Park. Until the 1930s, the Relic House, a beer garden built with salvaged materials from the Great Fire and owned by the father of movie star Gloria Swanson, stood across the street from Lincoln Park.

FIRE, DETROIT. When General William Hull, the first governor of Michigan Territory, arrived in DETROIT, the capital, on July 1, 1805, he found the fort and small village had just been destroyed by fire. The resulting demand for lumber to rebuild created the first important commercial lumbering in the state. The 1805 fire destroyed all evidence of French and English architecture, a style marked by logs placed horizontally and chinked with clay. The fire was not without its benefits. The original houses had scarcely been habitable and had

been built with no plan in mind as to streets or size of property. Rebuilding the city was done under a plan designed by Judge Augustus B. WOODWARD, who used L'Enfant's plan for Washington, D.C., with its radial street concept and little parks. Progress was slow, but eventually a great city emerged.

FIRE, SAINT LOUIS. In 1849 a tremendous fire began on the levee at ST. LOUIS and wreaked havoc over much of this MISSISSIPPI RIVER port. By eyewitness accounts the fire began sometime before 10:00 p.m. on May 17, 1849. The steamboat *White Cloud* is cited as the source of the first flames. An attempt to set the boat adrift and away from the other ships was foiled. An offshore breeze jostled her back into port, setting twenty-two other ships ablaze. The fiery holocaust eventually spread to the city and consumed fifteen blocks with a resulting property damage estimated at $5,500,000.

FIRST RUN. To encourage steamboat captains to attempt the journey up the MISSISSIPPI RIVER to reach ST. PAUL as early in the spring as possible, a large cash prize was offered by commercial interests along the river. This was done because as soon as the river was opened, shipping could commence. This prize went to the first captain to get his vessel through the dangerous ice jams. The winner of the $1000 prize in 1857 was a legendary pilot of the river, Captain Stephen B. Hanks, cousin of Abraham LINCOLN.

FISH AND FISHING. The MISSISSIPPI RIVER and the GREAT LAKES, along with the many other larger rivers, provide for major inland fisheries in the United States. Annually inland waters produce an estimated 266 million pounds of fish for the commercial market.

Most of the freshwater fish are caught with nets or traps. The Midwest's freshwater catch, accounting for three percent of the United States total, is valued in excess of $907 million annually. Fishing for profit is carried on in all of the Midwest states, principally in the GREAT LAKES and the major rivers.

Fish of importance to inland commercial fishermen include carp, catfish and chub. Protecting commercial and sport fishing has been the responsibility of such state agencies as Michigan's Bureau of Fisheries Research. Such agencies are often involved in the artificial propagation of fish in lakes and streams as well as investigating stream improvement and the effects of erosion and pollution on streams.

Fishing

"Fishing on the Sault," by George Catlin, a time-honored tradition.

States such as Michigan have had to take drastic actions to save their fishing industries. Michigan grayling, once native to most streams in the Lower Peninsula, declined sharply during the logging era of the late 1800s. Eastern brook trout, introduced after the grayling disappeared, could not withstand the intensive fishing brought about by the expansion of highways in Michigan and increased use of the automobile. The numbers of whitefish and Mackinaw trout were so reduced by the 1940s as to threaten their very role in the commercial fishing industry.

The fishing industry of Illinois centers on the Mississippi and ILLINOIS rivers, which together produce two-thirds of the catch, in addition to that of Lake MICHIGAN. Lake trout, once an important part of the Illinois fishing industry, were almost entirely wiped out by lamprey eels, first seen in Lake Michigan in 1921, until measures were taken to control the eels and restock the trout.

Salmon have also been introduced to several of the Great Lakes and are now an important part of the annual catch.

As early as 1889 the Great Lakes were producing 117 million pounds of fish annually. In that year eleven million pounds of lake trout and sixteen million pounds of whitefish were caught. By the 1950s the catch had dwindled to two million pounds of each, although the Great Lakes as a whole were still producing as much as 81 million pounds total in that period.

As the lakes became more and more polluted by city and industrial sewage, the Great Lakes began to "die." Commercial fishing almost died as well. With more careful conservation measures the lakes are making a comeback. The latest figures show a gradual return to an average of about 70 million pounds caught in the Great Lakes each year, with a total dollar value of about eleven million.

In 1908 commercial fishing in the Mississippi River and its tributaries reached a high mark of 148 million pounds. Today's annual catch in the Midwest rivers averages about 95 million pounds, with an annual value now averaging about thirty million dollars.

Some fish farms (raising fish for sale in farm ponds) are found in the Midwest, but they have not become as popular as in the Southern states.

Sport fishing is also an important facet of the fishing industry. The sale of tackle, licenses, and the resort business all bring profit to Midwestern states, which offer anglers opportunities at places like Lake ST. CLAIR, Michigan, to catch MUSKELLUNGE weighing up to forty pounds, or varieties of feisty panfish like smallmouth and largemouth bass, trout, crappie, walleye, or northern pike.

New breeds of fish like the tiger muskie, a cross of the popular northern pike and the muskie, promise a fast-growing aggressive game fish and demonstrate that states like Iowa, which stocked that fish in the late 1970s, are looking forward to years of revenue raised from out-of-state and resident sportsmen.

Winter is no obstacle to Midwestern fishermen. Fishing "houses" with no floors are dragged onto the ice in such numbers that addresses and street signs are needed to locate them. Fishermen may pursue their sport in warmth while waiting for a fish to strike at their lure dangling inches below them in a hole augered mechanically through the several feet of ice found on northern lakes in midwinter.

FISH CREEK, Wisconsin. Village (pop 250, est.), situated in DOOR COUNTY near the mouth of GREEN BAY, the community took its name from the abundance of fish and good fishing. First settler, in 1844, was the notorious Increase Claflin who had also lived at STURGEON BAY nearby. Claflin plied the Indians with liquor and cheated them at every opportunity. At one time Chief Silver Band and a group of his men leaped from some shrubbery and overpowered Claflin, who suggested they confer over a keg of whiskey. When the Indians agreed, Claflin produced a keg, took off the top, told the Indians it was full of gunpowder, and held a lighted torch over the barrel, threatening to blow them all up. The Indians hurriedly departed. Today, Fish Creek is a picturesque resort village, noted for its many interesting shops. During Peninsula Days Festival in early June a parade of yachts and a show of arts and crafts are featured.

FITZGERALD, F(rancis) S(cott). (St. Paul, MN, Sept. 24, 1896—Hollywood, CA, December 21, 1940). Leading author of America's "Jazz Age." Although not a member of the wealthy set, his elite education in private elementary and secondary schools provided insight into the life of the wealthy. His college education began at Princeton, but he resigned before graduating and joined the army in 1917. While in the army he began his first book, which was published in 1920 as *This Side of Paradise*. His success with the book brought him into the wealthy class for a while. After publication of *Tales of the Jazz Age* (1922), he was credited with coining the term "Jazz Age" to describe his era. In 1924 Fitzgerald went to Europe where he lived for six years. There he produced the book for which he is best known, *The Great Gatsby* (1925). Fitzgerald's early success appeared to lead to his spiritual and physical downfall, which he described in an essay entitled, "The Crack-Up" (1936). The mental illness of his wife, Zelda Sayre Fitzger-

ald, and his bouts with alcohol hampered his literary production and left him in a difficult financial position. *Tender Is the Night* (1934) was a financial failure. Turning to scriptwriting for Hollywood in 1936, Fitzgerald rediscovered his energy and literary talent. However, before his *The Last Tycoon* was finished he died from a heart attack. Fitzgerald both described and participated in the age of excess known today as the "Roaring Twenties." As an observer, he captured the perceived moral emptiness of the wealthy in American society. His novels gave him lasting stature as an author. Ironically, his death occurred a few years before his work achieved the recognition and the fame he had craved throughout life.

FIVE-HUNDRED-MILE-RACE. Annual racing event held on Memorial Day in INDIANAPOLIS, Indiana. As many as seventy percent of all automotive innovations have been tested on the Five Hundred Mile's course. The oval track, two and one-half miles long, is lined with grandstands capable of seating 238,000 spectators. Two straightaways are each 3,300 feet long and two short ones are each 660 feet in length. Each of the four sweeping curves is 1,320 feet long. The track, fifty feet wide on the stretches, is wider on the turns. A month-long festival precedes the race, with events including the Queen's Ball, Mechanic's Recognition Party, Memorial Parade, and Memorial Service. In 1986 the winner of the race, Bobby Rahal, averaged 170.722 miles per hour. Among the multiple winners of the Indianapolis 500 have been Bobby Unser, A.J. Foyt, Al Unser, and Johnny Rutherford.

FLANDRAU, Charles E. (New York, NY, July 15, 1828—St. Paul, MN, 1903). Lawyer. Flandrau began his practice of law in ST. PAUL in 1853. He served as a member of the Territorial Council and the constitutional convention of 1857. Flandrau was an associate supreme court justice in both Minnesota Territory and State from 1857 to 1864. During the Sioux Uprising he served as the commander-in-chief of the volunteer forces which defeated the Indians at NEW ULM on August 18, 1862, in a battle which lasted forty hours. He resigned from the supreme court in 1864 and moved temporarily to Carson City, Nevada, and then ST. LOUIS before returning to Minnesota. Flandrau was the city attorney for MINNEAPOLIS and was the first president of the Minneapolis Board of Trade. He served as chairman of the State Democratic Executive Committee (1868—1869.)

FLATBOATS. Large, raft-like barges used extensively to float passengers and freight down major inland waterways during the first decades of the 1800s. Flatboats, benefitting from their flat-bottom, could be used in shallow water and were moved by the current of the stream and large oars which were mainly used for steering. For the early years of settlement, flatboats on the OHIO RIVER were the principal means of moving settlers and their goods to Ohio, Indiana and Illinois. They were widely used to float produce from the Midwest down the river systems as far as New Orleans, where the boats were broken up for timber.

FLINT, Michigan. City, (pop. 159,611) seat of Genessee County, situated in east central Michigan on the Flint River, sixty miles northwest of DETROIT, it is the fourth largest city in the state. Incorporated in 1855, it occupies an area of 32.7 square miles. Founded on the base of a large carriage manufacturing business, in 1902 Flint became one of the major U.S. centers of automobile manufacture and still ranks second to Detroit in that field. Chevrolet and Buick were there when they were incorporated into mammoth General Motors, founded at Flint in 1908. Many other automobiles, some now gone but all well known in their time, were manufactured there. They included Nash, Champion and Chrysler.

The American auto industry's decline in the 1970s hit Flint hardest of all the automobile communities. During the 1970s, Flint suffered a population loss of seventeen percent, with many of those residents leaving for the suburbs. In the period 1970 through 1980, the population declined from 193,000 to 143,000 and then began a gradual rise to the present mark of nearly 160,000.

The 1982 unemployment rate in the city was 22 percent, highest in the nation. High unemployment was followed by an increasing rate of crime, third worst in the nation. By the mid 1980s, the brighter outlook for U.S. auto production brought increasing signs of recovery to Flint.

Flint began in 1819 as a fur-trading post. As the quantity of furs declined, the vast forests provided a lumber boom. When lumber faded, the manufacture of carts and horse-drawn vehicles took over, followed by automobiles. One of the more dramatic events in the city's history was the damaging tornado of 1953.

Flint is the site of a branch of the University of MICHIGAN. General Motors operates an automotive institute there, and the state provides a school for the deaf. The city offers visitors an art museum, planetarium and nature preserve. Water Street Pavilion is a downtown retail and restaurant center.

FLOAT TRIPS. Many Midwestern streams are known for the much-heralded one-day or multi-day float trips available on them. In Missouri such excursions, called "john-boat forays," are offered on such streams as the WHITE, BLACK, CURRENT, GASCONADE, Big or Little Piney, and NIANGUA rivers. "Striking blue water" in such streams means that quiet pools have been reached, where fishing may prove to be excellent. Guides often act as hosts at a shore lunch they prepare over a roaring fire. In Iowa such streams as the Upper Iowa and the WAPSIPINICON are especially popular in the fall with the radiant leaf color along the river banks. For those of an adventurous spirit the AU SABLE RIVER in Michigan offers a chance to participate in the annual canoe carnival in August in which as many as one hundred canoes race fifty miles. A more leisurely trip is possible throughout the summer. One of the popular streams in Minnesota is the ST. CROIX. Canoeists can choose between a thirty-mile trip from HINCKLEY to a toll bridge or, by camping out and spending one more day, cover an additional forty miles to Taylor Falls. Fishing for smallmouth bass is excellent and many of the tributaries of the St. Croix offer fine trout fishing. In Illinois, floaters may choose between their own craft and a one-hour trip offered on the SANGAMON RIVER at New Salem State park, aboard a replica of the stern-wheeler *Talisman*, the first steamboat to venture along the Sangamon in Abraham LINCOLN's time.

FLOODS. The major rivers of the Midwest, MISSISSIPPI, OHIO and MISSOURI, flood to some extent almost every spring as ice and snow melt in their watersheds, making the region the most vulnerable of all American regions to heavy river flooding. The most disastrous river floods in Midwest history occurred on the MIAMI and Ohio Rivers in 1913, on the Ohio in 1937 and on the Mississippi in 1927 and 1973. A series of dams on the Ohio and dams and levees on the Mississippi are designed to lessen the possibility of flood damage. Low lying areas of ST. LOUIS are among the most liable to flooding among major cities of the Midwest. With the unprecedented rise of the water levels of the GREAT LAKES in the 1980s, a somewhat unexpected flood threat posed a problem for the lake states and especially for the cities. One form of flood occurs when strong winds cause a constant pressure toward the windward side of a lake, a condition known as a surge. A surge at CHICAGO, Illinois, in early 1987 flooded many portions of the city's lakefront which had never before been under water, and considerable damage was done. More surges were expected at other major cities in the Midwest. Extreme damage was predicted along the Great Lakes if the rise in water level continued or did not subside. Many lakeside homes and other property have already been destroyed by the high water levels. However, by late 1988 the Great Lakes water level had subsided by almost three feet.

FLORIDA, Missouri. Village in eastern Missouri's Monroe County, notable mainly for its association with the Clemens family. Florida was the birthplace of Samuel Langhorne CLEMENS (Mark Twain). The Clemens family moved to Florida in 1835 at the suggestion of James Quarles, a relative of Mrs. Clemens and one of the wealthiest men in the four-year-old community. "Uncle James" was later portrayed by Twain as Colonel Mulberry Sellers in *The Gilded Age* (1873). The senior Clemens formed a partnership with Quarles as optimism grew for the new town which had three mills, a pottery, a hemp factory, five distilleries, and in 1837 the Florida Academy. The Quarles-Clemens partnership dissolved in 1837 or 1838 and Clemens opened his own store while maintaining his law practice and serving as Justice of the Peace. After the death of their daughter Margaret the Clemens family moved to HANNIBAL, Missouri. Florida never lived up to its early promise, and other cities soon surpassed it. Despite his family's move to Hannibal, Sam Clemens often returned to Florida for summer vacation and spent part of his short service as a Confederate volunteer during 1861 in the same community. MARK TWAIN STATE PARK preserves the birthplace of Samuel Clemens in a steel, glass and stone building. A handwritten manuscript of *Tom Sawyer* and memorabilia of Twain's life are displayed.

FLORISSANT, Missouri. City (pop. 55,400), eastern Missouri, suburb of ST. LOUIS. French settlers founded the fleurissant, or "flowering," valley in 1786. Florissant still shows a strong French and Spanish influence. Traders passed through the area many times before the French finally developed it into a settlement in 1785. Spaniards changed the city's name to St. Ferdinand, after the church built there (1821)

but the name reverted to its original in 1839. Today it is a mainly residential city. St. Ferdinand's Shrine, constructed in 1820, is the oldest Catholic church between the MISSISSIPPI RIVER and the Rocky Mountains. The twenty-three room mansion known as the Taille de Noyer House in Florissant is thought to be one of the oldest residences in St. Louis County. Before many renovations, the home was a fur-trading post in 1790. Tours of Florissant's many historic homes take place annually during the Valley of Flowers Festival in early May.

FLOUR MILLING. An early industry in most of the Midwest and increasingly important industry in Minnesota, the principal Midwest milling state. Of course, smaller milling operations had developed throughout the other Midwest states which had been settled earlier. Finding a suitable mill site on a river or stream almost inevitably led to founding of a mill and subsequent settlement at almost every suitable location. The first milling operation in Minnesota was established by Lemuel Boles in 1845. It is claimed that he had to use part of his wife's dress in one of the sifting processes. Spring wheat, the main type grown in the state, was so hard that a great amount of husk or "middlings" was left in the flour. This undesirable material gave the flour a dark color and hastened the spoilage, but a Frenchman, Edmond N. La Croix, working at the Archibald mill at DUNDAS, Minnesota, introduced a secret new method of milling hard wheat. By 1870 the "middlings purifier" method of rollers, vibrators, silk sieves and other processes had revolutionized milling. With the plentiful supply of hard wheat in the vast areas to the north and west, MINNEAPOLIS became the "Flour Capital of the World." Until other power sources were available, water power continued to be important, and Minneapolis had the advantage of the Falls of ST. ANTHONY at its doorstep. Today Minneapolis ranks third among U.S. cities in total grain milling, but it remains the headquarters for the world's five largest milling companies. The process of improving the milling of flour continues. In 1960 General Mills introduced a new method they called "Air Spun" which reputedly results in whiter flour of uniform quality.

FLOYD, Charles. (—Sioux City, IA, Aug. 21, 1804) Sergeant Floyd was the only member of the LEWIS AND CLARK EXPEDITION to die during the rough and dangerous journey and the first white man to be buried in present-day Iowa. He died in 1804 of appendicitis as the party moved up the MISSOURI RIVER. He was buried on August 21, 1804, on the bluffs near present-day SIOUX CITY, Iowa. The 100 foot stone obelisk marking his grave was the first national historical landmark in the United States.

FLUORITE. Illinois state gem. The crystalized mineral called fluorite or fluorspar, is found widely in other countries, but in the U.S. principally in Illinois. Its main use is as a metal flux, but it also is used in production of hydrofluoric acid and in the manufacture of opal glass and enamel.

FOND DU LAC, Wisconsin. City (pop. 35,863), seat of Fond du Lac County, situated in southeast Wisconsin at the "Lower End of the Lake" in its French translation. The city lies in that position on Lake WINNEBAGO. The area was visited by French explorers, traders and trappers in the 1600s, but it was not settled until 1835. It gained prominence as a lumbering and railroad center. The railroad did not come easily, as told in some of the quaint lore of the state. Twenty miles of track were laid from the city in 1853, but they made no connections with other railroads. The only approach to the city at the time was by plank road. The owners of the road refused to transport the locomotive, saying the road was available only to horse-drawn vehicles. Disregarding the road proprietors, the railroad men hitched up a team of twenty horses and hauled the locomotive over the plank highway. During the celebration over its arrival, the train was wrecked by running into an ox on a trestle. However, the railroad did begin to operate. The city became an industrial center, now manufacturing snowmobiles, engines, leather goods and machine tools, among others. Several historic homes are available to visitors, including Octagon House, with its hidden room and secret passageways and underground tunnel; historic Galloway House and Village of twenty-two buildings, and Silver Wheel Manor, a farmhouse of thirty rooms, furnished as in the 1860s. St. Paul's Cathedral possesses rare ecclesiastical artifacts. Marian College has an ornithological collection. An Ice Age Interpretive Center features an unusual facility for the study of the great prehistoric glaciers. Fond du Lac is "fond" of annual celebrations, which include: Lakeside Winter Celebration, last weekend of January; Walleye Weekend Festival and National Walleye Tournament, second weekend of June; International Aerobatic Championship, with pilots worldwide competing in August, and the Fall Flyway Tours and Harvest Dinner.

FORD FOUNDATION. World's wealthiest philanthropic organization, established by Henry FORD and his son, Edsel. The organization seeks to promote human welfare through grants for educational purposes. In its early years the foundation money went to educational and charitable agencies in Michigan. In 1950 the foundation became national and since that time the scope has broadened to an international scene. The foundation has awarded or pledged nearly $4.8 billion since its establishment in 1936. The money has gone to ninety-five countries outside the United States and to 7,100 organizations within the United States. Ford Foundation money supports programs in the fields of education and research, the arts, national affairs, international affairs, communications, and resources and environment. Foundation money helped establish the Public Broadcasting Service.

FORD PEACE SHIP. Vessel used by Henry FORD on his peace mission to Europe. On December 4, 1915, Henry Ford and 150 men and women left New York City on the ship privately chartered by Ford for a peace mission to Europe. Ford's object was to organize a conference of peace advocates who would then attempt to influence the warring governments to come to terms early in WORLD WAR I. Ford returned home after reaching Christiania, Norway, but the rest of the mission continued on through Stockholm, Sweden, to Copenhagen, Denmark, and through Germany and back to The Hague. Ford's mission was not sponsored by the United States government and despite the best intentions of those who visited with many prominent Europeans, no peace was achieved.

FORD TRIMOTOR. Airplane developed under the auspices of Henry FORD. Ford, generally remembered for his role in the automobile industry, did a great deal to promote the aircraft industry. With William B. STOUT (1880-1956), Ford developed the famous Trimotor plane based on Stout's first all-metal airplane, which Ford bought in 1925. With Stout's help Ford developed the single engine plane into one of three engines, still all-metal. The Trimotor had a great influence in the development of the commercial air travel industry. Many of Ford's planes were still in service fifty years after being built.

FORD, Edsel Bryant. (Detroit, MI, Nov. 6, 1898—Dearborn, MI, May 26, 1943). Automotive executive, son of Henry FORD. In 1919 he succeeded his father in 1919 as President and Treasurer of the Ford Motor Company, when the elder Ford decided to retire. However, industry opinion held that Edsel's authority was almost entirely nominal and that he merely carried out his father's wishes. Henry Ford resumed the presidency when Edsel died in 1943. Together the Fords established the FORD FOUNDATION. Edsel's name is perhaps best remembered in the ill-fated Edsel car which proved to be ahead of its time and now is in great demand as a classic car.

FORD, Gerald Rudolph. (Omaha, NE, July 14, 1913—). Thirty-eighth President of the United States. Christened Leslie King at birth. Ford's parents divorced about two years after his birth and his mother took him from his birthplace in Omaha, Nebraska, to GRAND RAPIDS, Michigan, where she had friends. In 1916 she married Gerald Rudolph Ford who adopted the boy and gave him his name. Ford grew up in Grand Rapids and entered the University of MICHIGAN where he played center on the undefeated Michigan football teams of 1932 and 1933.

Although offered professional football contracts with the Detroit Lions and the Green Bay Packers, Ford chose to study law and accepted a job coaching football at Yale, from 1935 until 1938, when he was accepted at the law school.

As a Republican, Ford successfully ran for Congress in 1948 and was re-elected by the citizens of Michigan's Fifth Congressional District twelve straight times. His generally moderate opinions made him a popular figure on both the Republican and Democratic sides of the House. In 1965 Ford became the House minority leader and served in that position for eight years. He attracted national attention when, with Senate Minority Leader Everett M. Dirksen, he appeared in a series of televised Republican press conferences dubbed by reporters the "Ev and Jerry Show."

Ford reversed his support of the Johnson Administration's policies in Vietnam and became a vocal opponent, also managing to unite Republicans and Southern Democrats in opposition to Johnson social programs. In 1970 Ford led an effort to impeach Justice William O. Douglas for what some considered to be his misuse of his position on the Supreme Court. This matter ended with the House deciding

there was insufficient evidence to support the impeachment proceedings.

In early 1972 federal investigators found that Vice President Spiro Agnew had accepted bribes when he had been a Baltimore County Executive and then as governor of Maryland and Vice President. Agnew resigned and President Richard Nixon nominated Ford to become Vice President. The Senate approved the nomination by a vote of 92 to 3 on November 27. The House approved by a vote of 387 to 35 on December 6th. With this overwhelming support of Congress, Ford was sworn in as the 40th Vice-President later that day. Ford became the first appointed Vice-President in the history of the United States.

Shortly before Ford became Vice-President, the House of Representatives began impeachment proceedings against President Richard Nixon feeling he was withholding evidence related to the Watergate crisis. Ford went on a forty-state speaking tour in support of the President, as the evidence continued to mount. In July, 1974, the House Judiciary Committee recommended that Nixon be impeached. Nixon resigned on the morning of August 9th.

At noon that day Ford took the oath of office as the 38th President of the United States. Ford then became the only American to assume the presidency who had not been elected vice-president or president.

A variety of problems faced the new president. According to many historians, his ability to handle domestic problems was severely hurt by his pardon of Richard Nixon on September 8, 1974, for any crimes he may have committed while President of the United States. Ford claimed to take the action to end divisions within the country.

Ford attempted to deal with draft violence by granting amnesty to draft dodgers and deserters of the Vietnam War period if the offenders would work in a public service job for up to two years. Twenty-two thousand of the estimated 106,000 eligible men applied for the amnesty while the others objected to the work requirement.

Most observers agreed that the condition of the economy was the most important problem facing the new president. On the economic front, Ford declared inflation to be the nation's major problem and launched the "WIN," Whip Inflation Now, campaign. Nevertheless, inflation continued a steady rise during his term. Labor leaders disputed Ford's inflation priorities. They called for economic stimulation. Liberals opposed Ford's suggested tax increases.

Because unemployment had risen drastically from 5,156,000 persons in 1974 to 7,929,000 in 1975, labor called for a program to create new jobs. Although unemployment dropped even more dramatically by over a million persons in 1977, the change did little help the president's image.

During Ford's partial term many events of interest occurred. The president conferred in Tokyo with the prime minister and the emperor of Japan (November 19, 1974). Nelson A. Rockefeller became vice president on December 19, 1974. The government of South Vietnam unconditionally surrendered to the Vietcong (April 30, 1975). President Ford visited China on December 1, 1975). The Mariana Islands become a commonwealth (February 24, 1976). Also, during Ford's term, the first women were enrolled in a national service academy (Air Force, June 28, 1976). On July 4, 1976, during the Ford administration, the nation celebrated the bicentennial of the signing of the Declartion of Independence.

Ford survived two assassination attempts. The first occurred on September 5, 1975, when Lynette Fromme pointed a loaded pistol at him near the capitol in Sacramento, California. On September 22, 1975, Sara Jane Moore fired a single shot at the president in front of the St. Francis Hotel in San Francisco but missed him by five feet. She was quickly disarmed.

In the 1976 election Ford and California governor Ronald REAGAN fought a bitter contest for the nomination, eventually won by Ford. The Democratic nominee, Jimmy Carter, charged that Ford had mismanaged the economy, despite the substantial rise in employment just then being experienced, the combination of inflation and recession being experienced baffled the best economic minds. The second series of televised debates in history occurred during the campaign, in which Ford failed to shine.

As the campaign continuied, Carter made much of the economic situation without providing any clear blueprints about what should be done. He played on the nation's disenchantment with Washington politicians and their ineptitude during the Vietnamese era.

Carter defeated Ford by fewer than two million votes out of 81 1/2 million cast. Ford carried twenty-seven states while Carter carried 23 states and the District of Columbia, but Carter received 297 electoral votes compared to Ford's 240. Reagan received one electoral vote.

Ford left office to enter the political scene as a retired president and frequently requested speaker.

Ford donated to the federal government his historical materials and documents, accumulted in congress, as vice president and president. He was the first president to do so while still in office. He would not accept any tax exemption for the gift. The material is now located at the Gerald R. Ford Library on the campus of the University of MICHIGAN at ANN ARBOR.

Gerald Rudolph Ford began life as Leslie Lynch King, Jr. and had seven half-brothers and sisters through the two marriages of his mother, Dorothy Ayer Gardner King Ford. On October 15, 1948, at the age of 35, Ford married Elizabeth (Betty) Bloomer Warren Ford at GRAND RAPIDS, Michigan. They had three children.

FORD, Henry. (Dearborn Township, Wayne County, MI, July 30, 1863—Dearborn, MI, April 7, 1947). Automobile manufacturer. Ford became a machinist in DETROIT and began experimenting with engines about 1890. He worked as the chief engineer at the Edison Illuminating Company and completed his first gasoline engine in 1893. The first Ford automobile was completed in 1896. The crude-looking machine had a single seat, a steering tiller, and an electric bell on the front. The engine's cylinder was made from an exhaust pipe from a steam engine.

While others scoffed, Thomas EDISON encouraged the young Ford, who organized the Ford Motor Company in 1903. His belief that every man, regardless of financial condition, should be able to have a car led to the development of the Model T, beginning in 1908. Ford managed to reduce the price of the Model T until it was almost within reach of everyone. The car brought fame and fortune to Ford who responded by announcing that the company would share its profits with its employees; the work-day would be cut from nine to eight hours, and the minimum wage would go from the industry standard of $1.00 a day to $5.00.

Stockholders in the company wanted the profits paid to them as dividends so Ford bought them all out to avoid complaints and to expand the business. From 1919 to 1956 the Ford family had sole control of the company.

Ford paid the expenses of a "peace trip" to Europe in 1915 for 150 men and women. The trip was not authorized by the United States government and ended in failure.

While opposed to the entry of the United States into World War I and II, Ford quickly made his plants available for the manufacture of war materials. The WILLOW RUN, Michigan,

Forest Park - Forest Products

Henry Ford at work, painted by Norman Rockwell, (C) Ford Motor Co.

plant was the largest aircraft assembly plant in the world and fulfilled a pledge of Ford's that he would construct a plant capable of building a bomber each hour. During WORLD WAR II the Willow Run plant manufactured B-24 BOMBERS until the end of the conflict.

Ford developed the V-8 engine in 1932 and gradually took a less active role in the company. He established GREENFIELD VILLAGE and the Ford Museum in DEARBORN, Michigan. With Edsel, his son, Ford established the Ford Foundation. Ford passed the presidency of the company to his son Edsel in 1919 and then resumed the office when Edsel died in 1943. In 1945 Henry Ford again relinquished the company presidency, turning it over to Edsel's son, Henry Ford II.

FOREST PARK. Second largest city park in the United States. Located in St. LOUIS, Missouri, Forest Park covers 1,293 acres and was the site of most of the LOUISIANA PURCHASE EXPOSITION in 1904. Forest Park contains the outstanding St. Louis Zoo which is noted for the training and exhibits of many animals. Within the 83-acre complex are more than 2,000 animals in a close to natural habitat. If tired, a visitor can catch the Zooline Railroad to the next stop. Special

exhibits include Big Cat Country and the Children's Zoo. An outstanding conservatory in the park is called the Jewel Box. Unique flower and plant displays are featured there along with holiday exhibits of lilies at Easter and poinsettias during Christmas. McDonnell Planetarium ranks as one of the nation's foremost astronomical facilities. Exhibits on physics, astronomy, and daily sky shows are among its features. The planetarium also boasts a Foucault pendulum and holography exhibits. One of the annual events of Forest Park is the Muny Opera in a 12,000-seat outdoor theater during mid-June through August.

FOREST PRODUCTS LABORATORY. The laboratory was established in 1910 at the University of WISCONSIN, MADISON, and is operated by the United States Forest Service in cooperation with the university. In 1932 it acquired its own distinctive building designed by famed architectural firm Holabird and Root. For many years the laboratory was the only institution of its kind doing research on wood and its potential uses. Every type of equipment needed to investigate wood, from the raw state through plastics, cellulose, paper, lignin and other forms, is used by the laboratory. There are experimental sawmills, paper-making machinery, kilns, gluing presses and machinery, chemical conversion equipment and other facilities for every type of wood experiment or analysis. The laboratory receives thousands of samples of woods from around the world and makes hundreds of thousands of mechanical, chemical and other tests. Its experiments in boxing and crating alone save the TRANSPORTATION and packaging industries millions of dollars every year. It has made a reputation in crime analyses, such as the tests on the wooden ladder used in the Lindbergh kidnapping case.

FORT ANCIENT CULTURE. Seven miles southeast of LEBANON, Ohio, on route 350 stands the Fort Ancient State Memorial Museum, displaying implements and ornaments that tell of the area's PREHISTORIC PEOPLE. Some of these objects are thought to date to a period known as that of the HOPEWELL CULTURE. However, other items found seem to belong to a later period. The period of the people who left these later effects has been described as that of the Fort Ancient Culture. Some authorities believe the Fort Ancient people may have lived in the area as late as 1650, considerably after the east coast of North America had been occupied by Europeans. The exact relationship of the Fort Ancients to the Hopewell and other prehistoric peoples has not yet been established. These prehistoric people once lived mainly in present-day Indiana and Ohio. Fort Ancient sites show a great deal of habitation near mounds which were used as burial sites. Large amounts of debris indicate that the people lived in one area for long periods of time and imply that they were agricultural. Pottery is distinctive to those trained in its identification. The Fort Ancient people worked in bone, made flaking tools, awls, and needles. They made few stone tools. The most obvious feature of their culture is the string of forts found along the Ohio River.

FORT ATKINSON, Iowa. Town (pop. 336), in northeast Iowa, near SPILLEVILLE and about twelve miles southwest of DECORAH, on Iowa highway 24. The site was the location of a fort unique in American history. It was constructed by the government in 1840 to protect the WINNEBAGO Indians of the area from the SIOUX, the only fort ever erected for a similar purpose. In 1849, after the Winnebago were moved to Minnesota, the fort was abandoned. In 1958, reconstruction of the stockade, block houses and offices was started as an historical monument. There visitors may enjoy the historic structures, fashioned from the nearby gray limestone, just as they may have appeared to the original occupants.

FORT BEAUHARNOIS. French post built on the MISSISSIPPI RIVER in 1727. Located in present-day Minnesota's Goodhue County south of Frontenac and north of Lake City, Fort Beauharnois was built to serve as a permanent base from which to explore. It contained a Jesuit mission and Minnesota's first church. Flooding and continual fighting between the FOX and SIOUX Indians caused the French to abandon the post in 1729. An attempt was made to rebuild the fort in 1750, and trade with the Indians was carried on for several years before the French troops at the fort were recalled to fight the British in the FRENCH AND INDIAN WAR.

FORT BENJAMIN HARRISON. United States Army post established in 1903 near INDIANAPOLIS, Indiana. The fort, a 2,030 acre base which includes Schoen Field airport, was built to receive as many as 8,000 troops. The base has been used as an induction center from which recruits are transferred throughout the United States.

FORT CRAWFORD. Pioneer fort built by the American government at PRAIRIE DU CHIEN, Wisconsin, to succeed previous Fort McKay burned to the ground by the British at the end of the WAR OF 1812. Fort Crawford was begun in 1816 by Brigadier General Thomas A. Smith, who led several U.S. army companies stationed there. Earlier Indian leaders who were sympathetic to the British were treated harshly, and the Indians were almost unmanageable until they signed the treaty of 1825. The fort was moved to higher ground in 1829, due to water damage. Colonel Zachary TAYLOR (1784-1850) became the commander in 1829, and Lieutenant Jefferson DAVIS (1808-1889), then one of his assistants, fell in love with Taylor's daughter Sarah, whom he married in 1835, despite her fathers protests. The presence together of the future presidents of the United States and of the Confederacy is one of the unusual accidents of history. The fort was abandoned in 1856, used temporarily during the CIVIL WAR and dismantled in 1865. Dr. William BEAUMONT performed some of his famous experiments on the digestive system at Fort Crawford, and the site is occupied today by the Fort Crawford Medical Museum, dedicated to Beaumont's honor.

FORT DAVIDSON. Military post constructed near PILOT KNOB, Missouri, by Union troops during the CIVIL WAR to protect the mineral deposits of Pilot Knob and IRON MOUNTAIN. During the War the heroic stand of General Thomas Ewing and one thousand men in August, 1861, held off Confederate General Sterling Price and a force of 12,000 to 20,000 soldiers long enough to permit ST. LOUIS to reinforce itself. By the time Price reached St. Louis, he found the city so well protected he dared not attack.

FORT DE CHARTRES STATE PARK. Historic Illinois site, near Prairie du Rocher. Fort de Chartres was once the largest and most formidible fort on the North American continent. It was constructed by the French beginning in 1718. New eighteen-foot-high walls covering four acres replaced the original wooden fort in 1756. On October 10, 1765, the English took the fort and on December 6, 1768, the first court with English jurisdiction was held within its walls. The fort, partially undermined by the MISSISSIPPI RIVER, was abandoned by the English in 1772. In 1915 the state of Illinois acquired the site as a park. The foundations were repaired, a museum constructed and the reproductions of several structures completed.

FORT DEARBORN. Early frontier military post on the future site of CHICAGO, Illinois. Fort Dearborn was named after Thomas Jefferson's Secretary of War, Henry Dearborn. The fort, built under the leadership of Captain John Whistler, was abandoned under foolish government orders in 1812. Records of the Dearborn Massacre recount the slaughter of residents of the fort for whom obeying the order to abandon Dearborn was a death sentence at the hands of hostile WINNEBAGO. The fort was burned by the Indians and not rebuilt until 1816 when troops were sent to pacify the Winnebagos. During the BLACK HAWK WAR, in 1831, Fort Dearborn served as a refuge for settlers. Today, the site is marked only by bronze inserts on the sidewalk to the south of the present Michigan Avenue bridge, where the fort once stood.

FORT DEFIANCE. Built in 1791 to defy the Indians. In 1791 the governor of the NORTHWEST TERRITORY, General Arthur ST. CLAIR (1736-1818), fell into an ambush laid by Chief LITTLE TURTLE at a point where Celina, Ohio, now stands. Nine hundred of his men were killed, but St. Clair escaped, carrying away eight bullet holes in his

clothing. Alarmed at the situation in the west, George Washington sent one of his top generals, Anthony, "Mad Anthony," WAYNE to quell the Indians. General Wayne spent much time in drilling his troops and building fortifications. One of these was a fort built on a bluff at the confluence of the Auglaize and MAUMEE rivers, site of present DEFIANCE, Ohio. The general named the strong point Fort Defiance, saying, "I defy the English, the Indians, and all the devils in hell to take it." The fort proved to be one of the strong points in the conflict with the Indians.

FORT DES MOINES. Originally established in 1843 at the fork of the RACCOON and DES MOINES Rivers with an appropriation by Congress of $129,000 and the gift of 400 acres of land by the citizens of the area. A town grew up around the fort and the fort was abandoned as a cavalry post in 1857, when the word "fort" was removed and DES MOINES became the capital of Iowa.

FORT DODGE, Iowa. City (pop. 29,423), seat of Webster County, situated on the DES MOINES RIVER in the near-northwestern part of the state. The community was settled in 1846, and in 1850 a strong point was built and named Fort Clarke but renamed Fort Dodge, for General Henry Dodge, the following year. The fort was abandoned in 1853, but the town was laid out in 1854 and incorporated in 1869. The city lies in a region of forty square miles of gypsum, the mineral used for plaster. This mineral resource is considered the largest of its kind in the country. Gypsum mills were an early industry. The gypsum industry in this area continues as one of the leaders in its field. The city is a center of a rich agricultural region and prospers on the processing and distribution of farm products. It supports Fort Dodge Community College. The Fort Dodge Historical Museum is housed in a replica of the old fort.

FORT MACKINAC. Original fortification in the NORTHWEST TERRITORY on MACKINAC ISLAND, Michigan. Built by the British in 1780, the fort's walls are constructed of local limestone. The post was later occupied by the Americans in 1813. The fourteen buildings present today are all original. Costumed guides conduct hourly tours, and dioramas, murals and life-sized period settings show the history of the fort. Inside the fort is the Beaumont Memorial, dedicated to William BEAUMONT, an American surgeon at Fort Mackinac who, in 1822, made

Fort Madison - Fort Miami

Old Fort Mackinac, painted by Seth Eastman.

important studies of the digestive process while treating a patient there. The role of Fort Mackinac in the FUR TRADE of the region is explained in the Stuart House Museum of the Astor Fur Post. This was the original headquarters for the AMERICAN FUR COMPANY. Records of the fur company, the agent's house, and furniture of the period are among the many relics on display. Three vaults were originally built into the warehouse to store ammunition, money and whiskey.

FORT MADISON, Iowa. City (pop 13,520), seat of Lee County, situated on the MISSISSIPPI RIVER at the northeastern end of the Iowa "peninsula." This is the extension of land between the IOWA and MISSISSIPI rivers, which forms the southeastern point of the state. Incorporated in 1848. The fort, built in 1808, was the first U.S. post west of the Mississippi and was named for James Madison, then president. The fort was burned by the Indians and abandoned in 1813 during the WAR OF 1812. Resettlement began in 1833. The city is a river port for barge traffic, an agricultural, rail, commercial and industrial center. W. H. SHAEFFER, who developed the fountain pen, began the manufacture of fountain pens at Fort Madison, and the company continues as one of the world's largest manufacturers of writing instruments. Other products are chemicals, fertilzers, van trailers, paints and paper products, decorative and protective finishes and ammunition containers. The Iowa State Penitentiary at Fort Madison is the oldest west of the Mississippi. The largest railroad bridge of its kind in the world is the swing-span bridge with double track and double deck, which crosses the Mississippi at Fort Madison. The Lee County Courthouse (1841) is the oldest structure of its kind still in use in Iowa. The Tri-State Championship Rodeo at Fort Madison is ranked as one of the ten best in the world.

FORT MEIGS. Built near present MAUMEE, Ohio, by General William Henry HARRISON in February, 1813, during the mcWAR OF 1812. Throughout the spring and summer of 1813, the fort continued to hold out against the British and their Indian allies. It became so strong that it was known as the Gibralter of the Northwest. At present, a 61-foot shaft marks the site of the old stronghold, now known as Fort Meigs State Park, with adjacent Fort Meigs Cemetery, burial place of the soldiers slain in the Dudley Massacre. In the spring of 1813, During the WAR OF 1812, Colonel Dudley had been sent to relieve Fort Meigs. He made the mistake of leaving the fort to pursue the English, and 660 men were slain in an ambush.

FORT MIAMI (Michigan). Military post constructed in 1679 under the supervision of famous French explorer, LA SALLE. The post, named Fort Miami after a local Indian tribe, became a thriving trading post. It was the original settlement on the site of present-day ST. JOSEPH, Michigan.

FORT MIAMI (Ohio). In 1680, the French built a fort at the location of present MAUMEE, Ohio. Destroyed by the Indians, the fort was rebuilt in 1693, then deserted until 1764 when the British built Fort Miami there after the continent was forfeited by the French. Given up by the British after the Revolution, it was reoccupied by them after the BATTLE OF FALLEN TIMBERS in 1794 and again during the WAR OF 1812.

FORT MICHILIMACKINAC. Restored early Michigan fortification. Visitors may view one of the most complete restorations of an early Midwest fort. Today it nestles near the south end of the great MACKINAC BRIDGE. The French trading post there was converted to a fort in 1715. British occupied this post in 1761. In 1763 it was captured by the Indians during PONTIAC's uprising, but reoccupied by the British in 1764. It was abandoned and a new fort was built on MACKINAC ISLAND in 1780-1781.

FORT OF THE MIAMI. One of the first permanent European outposts in Indiana, begun between 1682 and 1686. Forts Miami, OUIATENON (1720), and VINCENNES (1732-1733) were established by the French to protect their traders from English competition, under the direction of LA SALLE. The advantage of the location of the fort, where the ST. MARY and ST. JOSEPH rivers meet to form the MAUMEE RIVER, was the principal factor leading to the growth of FORT WAYNE, Indiana, seat of Allen County and one of the largest cities in the state.

FORT OUIATENON. Early European settlement built near present-day LA FAYETTE, Indiana, in 1720. The area was then the site of five contiguous Indian villages with over one thousand residents. Because grants of land were not made to settlers, Ouiatenon had a small white population. The French considered it important to their control of the Ohio Valley, but they lost it to the British in the FRENCH AND INDIAN WAR. In June, 1763, during Pontiac's War, the English garrison was captured by Indians and by 1767 Ouiatenon was primarily an Indian rendezvous. General Charles Scott, under orders in 1791 to stop Indian attacks on settlers, destroyed much of Ouiatenon, which was attacked a second time the same year. It was never rebuilt.

FORT RECOVERY. In 1791, near the present village of Celina, Ohio, the governor of the NORTHWEST TERRITORY, Arthur ST. CLAIR, was defeated by the Indians under Chief LITTLE TURTLE, losing 900 men in one of the worst defeats ever suffered by an American army. To save the new American territory, George Washington sent General Anthony "Mad Anthony" WAYNE, who trained his soldiers well, built a fort on the site of the battle and called it

Fort Recovery, hoping the stronghold would help recover the region. Encouraged by the British, the Indians attacked the fort but were repulsed and later defeated at the BATTLE OF FALLEN TIMBERS (1794). In later years the fort was rebuilt as Fort Recovery State Park, under the direction of the Ohio State Archaeological Society. The fort was built entirely of wood, even to the pegs and hinges. A log house was constructed as Fort Recovery Museum and houses articles recovered from the old well—boots, silver forks, bones and other relics.

FORT RIDGELY. Minnesota military post built in 1853. Located near NEW ULM, Fort Ridgley was built to protect settlers in the MINNESOTA RIVER Valley and control the SIOUX who were transferred to a reservation in the area. The protection given by the fort encouraged white settlement and stimulated steamboat traffic. Indians hoped to capture the fort and control the entire Minnesota Valley. They attacked the fort twice during the Sioux Uprising (1862) and were decisively defeated with a loss of nearly one hundred warriors. Over two hundred fifty settlers who left their homes for the protection of the fort were saved.

FORT SHERIDAN. Military post twenty-seven miles from CHICAGO, established, November, 1888, on the west shore of Lake MICHIGAN, named for Civil War General Philip SHERIDAN (1831-1888). Labor strikes and violence of the late 1880s concerned the Chicago business establishment which successfully supported passage of a law in SPRINGFIELD allowing the federal government to build Fort Sheridan and thus have troops available, if necessary, to restore law and order. During WORLD WAR I, Fort Sheridan served as an officers' training camp for nine thousand servicemen and women. Before World War I ended, Fort Sheridan became a general hospital. In WORLD WAR II, Fort Sheridan was the first induction center for the army and later served in the discharge of thousands of war-weary soldiers. The continuation of the fort is in doubt, and controversy over its future has not yet been resolved.

FORT SNELLING. United States military post established at the meeting of the MINNESOTA and MISSISSIPPI rivers. Following the LOUISIANA PURCHASE in 1803 the United States government determined there was a need for a post to block British influence and expansion in the West. Land was purchased in 1805 from Chief LITTLE CROW, a SIOUX Indian, for sixty

Fort Snelling, c. 1849, painted by Henry Lewis.

gallons of whiskey and the promise of $2,000 in merchandise or cash. The site of the fort was originally chosen by Zebulon PIKE in 1805. The first to command the area was Colonel Henry LEAVENWORTH in charge of the fort and the one hundred soldiers there in 1819. He was succeeded by Colonel Josiah SNELLING, who had the permanent stone fort built. The cornerstone was laid on September 10, 1820. Construction of the walls and buildings was completed in 1823. Fort St. Anthony, later renamed Fort Snelling, remained the most northwesterly army post and was the only one in Minnesota from 1820 to 1850. After the removal of the British threat in the West, troops from Snelling attempted to keep whites from intruding on Indian reservations as far south as the Iowa border. As other posts were built closer to the frontier, Fort Snelling lost much of its importance and was used only as a supply post. With the outbreak of the CIVIL WAR, Fort Snelling became a training camp. It was the only Minnesota post to remain in military service through the Spanish-American War and both world wars.

FORT STEPHENSON. Site of an heroic American defense. On August 2, 1813, during the WAR OF 1812, Fort Stephenson, at present-day FREMONT, Ohio, was attacked by a large British force under the command of Colonel Henry PROCTOR, who surrounded the fort and demanded its surrender (August 2, 1813). The American commander, youthful Major George CROGHAN (1791-1849), with only 160 defenders, refused. During the siege he kept shifting his single cannon, called Old Betsy, from place to place, confusing the enemy and repulsing their advances until they withdrew in fatigue and frustration. Old Betsy was placed at the foot of Soldier's Monument in Fremont, where the remains of Major Croghan were reinterred.

FORT VINCENNES. An early French outpost in Indiana, now the city of VINCENNES, built in 1732 or 1733 to protect French traders. The fort was constructed under the leadership of Francois Morgane, Sieur de VINCENNES, post commander for several years at FORT OUIATENON. It remained an important French trading post until 1763 when it was ceded to England. Following the capture of Fort Sackville by George Rogers CLARK, on February 25, 1779, Fort Vincennes fell into American hands. Vincennes was named as the seat of government when Indiana became a territory in 1800.

FORT WASHINGTON. Early guardian of CINCINNATI and much of the NORTHWEST TERRITORY. In 1789 the U.S. Army had begun construction of a small fort, named in honor of George Washington, in present-day Ohio, at the mouth of the MIAMI RIVER on the OHIO RIVER. A tiny community already on the site was named Losantiville. When General Arthur ST. CLAIR (1736-1818), governor of the Northwest Territory arrived at Losantiville to make the fort his headquarters, he changed the name of the village to CINCINNATI. For the next five years, Fort Washington was the base of the entire area for operations against the Indians. From there, both generals St. Clair and Josiah HARMAR

Fort Wayne

(1753-1813) went out on expeditions against the Indians and came back defeated. In 1792 the commander, General Anthony "Mad Anthony" WAYNE (1745-1796) took over at the fort, drilled his raw militiamen beside a prehistoric mound at the waterfront and then went out to break the resistance of the Ohio Indians. The location of the old fort became lost among the streets and buildings of Cincinnati, although the plans of the fort were still available. During excavation for a new building, the powder magazine of the old fort was found, almost intact. Now it is possible to trace the outline of Fort Washington, and a bronze marker on an insurance building shows where the old powder magazine was discovered.

FORT WAYNE. Michigan military post authorized by Congress in 1841 and named for General Anthony WAYNE (1745-1796). The fort, built on a bluff overlooking the DETROIT RIVER, was constructed under the supervision of Lieutenant M.C. Meigs. It was square and had a moat and earth embankments. Brick-vaulted tunnels led to emplacements and loopholes for gunfire. The brick-faced walls and stone barracks were restored in 1937, financed by a three-million-dollar Works Progress Administration fund. Michigan troops were stationed there during the CIVIL WAR. The fort was heavily garrisoned during WORLD WAR I. Fort Wayne, now part of DETROIT, Michigan, was never attacked by enemy troops. Murals depicting military scenes were the subjects of Frank Cassara who produced the displays as part of the Michigan Art Project of the W.P.A. Fort Wayne is considered the best-preserved pre-Civil War military post in the United States.

FORT WAYNE, Indiana. City (pop. 178,-269) seat of Allen County, situated in northeast Indiana at the ST. JOSEPH and ST. MARYS rivers where they join to form the MAUMEE RIVER. Incorporated in 1840, the city occupies an area of 51.9 square miles. It was named in honor of General Anthony "Mad Anthony" WAYNE (1745-1796) and is now the second largest city in the state.

A major industrial and shipping point, the city is the world leader in production of diamond cutting tools, as well as the world center of gasoline-pump manufacture. The latter had its inception in the invention of Sylvanus F. Bowser of a self-measuring tank for kerosene, which developed into the modern filling station pump. Today there also are large automotive and electronics industries.

By way of the Maumee River and the ST. LAWRENCE SEAWAY, the city has direct access to the world's ocean commerce. Along with ample railroad and highway connections, substantial commerce quickly developed, and the city now serves as trading center for a large agricultural area.

According to historian Dr. Charles Slocum, the region may have been explored by Samuel de CHAMPLAIN (1567?-1635) as early as 1614. Father Jacques MARQUETTE (1637-1675) and Father Claude ALLOUEZ (1622-1689) may have reached the region separately in 1673, but that is not certain. Also not certain is the exact date of the founding of Fort Wayne. Some authorities say that the French founded a trading post in 1680 at the principal Miami Indian village of Kekionga, for which the Indians had selected this stragetic site, the location of the present city. Others contend that the FORT OF THE MIAMIS was built there as early as 1700. Still others assert that the fort was not begun intil 1714.

With the end of French control in 1763, the region came nominally into British hands, then, also nominally, to the Americans after the Revolution. Alarmed at the loss of their lands, American control was disputed by the Indians until they were defeated on the banks of the Maumee in Ohio in the BATTLE OF FALLEN TIMBERS. In 1794, the victor in that battle, General Anthony WAYNE, built the fort that bears his name on the site of old Fort Miami.

Indian troubles continued, encouraged by the British, and Fort Wayne was besieged but managed to hold out during the WAR OF 1812. After the war, the city began a steady growth, based on a flourishing FUR TRADE. Commerce was encouraged by the start of work on the WABASH AND ERIE CANAL in 1832. After twenty years in construction, the canal was opened for a length of 460 miles and became noted as the longest in the world. By this time the railroads also had arrived, reducing the usefulness of the canal but further boosting the city as a commercial center.

During the pre-Civil War period, Fort Wayne was a principal station on the UNDERGROUND RAILROAD, protecting slaves on their way from masters in the South to freedom in Canada. During the CIVIL WAR, Hugh McCulloch of Fort Wayne was secretary of the treasury under Lincoln and then in the same post under President Johnson. Later, momentary fame was gained when the city was the site of the first night baseball game in history, June 2, 1883.

The several institutions of higher education include the Indiana Institute of Technology, a branch of PURDUE UNIVERSITY, Concordia Senior College, St. Francis College and a Roman Catholic seminary.

Among the many differing attractions, the Lincoln Museum at Fort Wayne claims to have the largest collection of literature ever assembled in one place dealing with the Great Emancipator. The combined city and county historical museum attracts visitors to Swinney Park. The Johnny Appleseed Memorial Park honors that almost legendary, but very real and eccentric personality, John CHAPMAN. The restored pioneer portion of the city is known as The Landing.

FORT WINNEBAGO. The fort was built in 1828 near present PORTAGE, Wisconsin, to protect the white settlers in the region from Indian attacks. Even before the fort was completed, Red Bird, Chief of the WINNEBAGOS, had surrendered on the site. One of the young officers who floated logs down the WISCONSIN RIVER to build the fort was Jefferson DAVIS, future President of the Confederate States of America. He was in direct command of the construction.

FOUNTAIN CITY, Indiana. Town (pop. 800), located in eastern Indiana northeast of RICHMOND, named for the discovery of an underground lake from which water rises automatically to the surface through pipes. Fountain City was a Quaker settlement in which most of the residents were ABOLITIONISTS active in the UNDERGROUND RAILROAD. Fountain City was the Indiana meeting point of three lines of the underground railroad running from CINCINNATI, MADISON and JEFFERSONVILLE to Fountain City. Prominent abolitionists active in the underground railroad were Levi and Catharine COFFIN, North Carolina Quakers upon whom Simeon and Rachel Halliday of *Uncle Tom's Cabin* were patterned. The Levi Coffin home, a Federal-style house known as the "Grand Central Station of the Underground Railroad," temporarily sheltered over two thousand slaves between 1827 and 1847 when the Coffins lived in Fountain City. The home, now a museum, features furnishings typical of the period prior to 1847.

FOX INDIANS. Algonguian tribe, closely related to the SAUK. The Fox lived near Lake WINNEBAGO, Wisconsin, when the French, whom they opposed, arrived. The Fox called themselves Meskwakihug, or Meskwakie, meaning "people of the red earth." The Fox were divided into fourteen clans. Each person inherited his clan through his father. Clan members were forbidden to marry within the clan. The Fox believed in many spirits or manitou. The most important spirit was Wisaka who created the earth and men and lived in lands of the north.

Important festivals included the green corn feast and the beginning of the harvest and the adoption ceremony. When a person died, the body was placed on a scaffold or buried in a sitting position. Warriors who died in battle if possible were buried sitting on an enemy. A person of the same sex and approximate age was adopted by the deceased person's family. The adopted person took over the duties and privileges of the deceased.

According to traditions of the Fox, their original homeland was along the southern shore of Lake SUPERIOR. They may also have lived with the Sauk around Saginaw Bay in eastern Michigan. By 1640 the Fox had settled in the GREEN BAY area where they became a nuisance to French traders by requiring a tool from anyone passing along the FOX RIVER. The French responded by arming enemies of the Fox, the SIOUX and OJIBWAY.

Between 1712 and 1737 the Fox and French fought bitterly, with the Fox being close to complete defeat on several occasions. Gradually the combined Sauk and Fox were driven southward by the French and Ojibway and occupied lands once controlled by the Illinois tribes.

By 1780 the Sauk and Fox were living on the MISSISSIPPI RIVER near the ROCK RIVER. In 1804 a band of the Sauk ceded all lands east of the Mississippi River to the United States. After the defeat of BLACK HAWK, the Fox moved across the Mississippi River where they were joined by the remaining Sauk.

Whites attempted to keep the Sauk and Fox separated from the SIOUX by creating a buffer zone in 1825. This "Neutral Ground," a forty-mile-wide strip of land in Iowa running along the Upper Iowa River, marked the farthest point north the Sauk and Fox were to move. The Sioux remained in the north.

Lead mines owned by the Fox near DUBUQUE were illegally seized. In 1842 the Sauk and Fox sold their remaining lands in Iowa and moved to a reservation in Kansas.

Between 1856 and 1859, after a dispute with the Sauk, most of the Fox returned to Iowa and settled near TAMA, where they eventually purchased three thousand acres, creating a unique Indian-owned homeland rather than a reservation.

FOX RIVER (Wisconsin). This river is one of two of the same name which rise in Wisconsin. The one which flows its entire length within Wisconsin rises in the south central Wisconsin lake district and flows past OSHKOSH into Lake WINNEBAGO, for which it is also the outlet. Continuing its northeasterly flow beyond the lake, it bisects the city of GREEN BAY, Wisconsin, and enters Lake MICHIGAN at Green Bay, after traversing a course of 176 miles.

FOX RIVER (Wisconsin-Illinois). This Fox is one of the two of the same name which rise in Wisconsin. Originating at Big Bend, Wisconsin, near MENOMONEE FALLS, west of MILWAUKEE, the southbound Fox flows through WAUKESHA and BURLINGTON in Wisconsin before crossing the Illinois border and entering the CHAIN OF LAKES, including Fox Lake. The river provided excellent sites for founding of Illinois communities, including Carpentersville, Dundee, ELGIN, St. Charles, Geneva and BATAVIA. After leaving Batavia, it flows through peaceful farming country before it joins the ILLINOIS RIVER near OTTAWA.

FRANKENMUTH, Michigan. Town (pop. 3,800); Tusola County; southeast portion of Michigan's Lower Peninsula; southeast of SAGINAW ; name translates from German to mean, "courage of the Franconians." Concern for the religious life of Germans who had moved to America, as well as an interest in doing missionary work among the Indians, prompted fifteen Franconians from Bavaria to come to Saginaw Valley in 1845. Later settlers were refugees from the unsuccessful German revolution of 1848. The Indian mission moved, but the German influence remained in the isolated wilderness setting. For years German was the principal language. The European influence is still observed in the architecture and the merry Bavarian Festival in mid-June. Murals depicting education at the turn of the century may be seen in School Haus Square, once the St. Lorenz Lutheran School. Frankenmuth Historical Museum houses permanent and changing exhibits showing life from pioneer days to the present. Michigan's Own Military and Space Museum honors the military heroes of Michigan, Medal of Honor winners, and state governors. Among the displays are the flight-suits and uniforms of Michigan astronauts Brewster Shaw, James McDivitt, Al Worden and Jack Lousma. Daily at 11, noon, and every three hours beginning at 3:00 p.m. the 35-bell

carillon in the Bavarian Inn's Glockenspiel Tower plays three melodies followed by a presentation of three carved figures showing the legend of the Pied Piper of Hamlin. Regionally the town was known for its Frankenmuth beer and its chicken dinners, served harvester style. Guided tours at Carling National Breweries show the process of malt beverage manufacture.

FRANKFORT, Michigan. Town (pop. 1,-603), northeast shore of Michigan's LOWER PENINSULA and Lake MICHIGAN, Benzie County. A popular resort, it attracts boaters and fishermen with a full facility, 40-slip marina. Frankfort has an international reputation as a glider-soaring site. Many world's gliding records have been set with the aid of ideal winds and other conditions. Near Frankfort, along thirty-three miles of the Lower Peninsula's shoreline with Lake Michigan is the SLEEPING BEAR DUNES NATIONAL LAKESHORE.

FRANKLIN, John Hope. (Rentiesville, OK, Jan. 2, 1915—). Educator, historian. A graduate of Fisk University in 1925, with a 1941 Ph.D from Harvard, Franklin taught on several college faculties, including Fisk, (1936) St. Augustine College (1939) and North Carolina College (1943). In 1947 he joined the Howard University staff and was the Fulbright Scholarship (1954) and William Pitt Scholarship student (1962), both at Cambridge University. His principal connection with the Midwest has been at the University of CHICAGO, beginning in 1964, where he became chairman of the history department in 1969. Chicago University named Franklin the John Matthews Manly Distinguished Service professor of history (1969-1982). Franklin was a trustee of the CHICAGO SYMPHONY from 1976 to 1980. He is considered one of the foremost historians of his time. He emphasized social, political and cultural history and biography in his writings and teachings. His writings include *From Slavery to Freedom: A History of Negro Americans*, (1947), *The Militant South* (1956), *Reconstruction After the Civil War*, (1961), *The Emancipation Proclamation* (1963). Franklin was named to the Oklahoma Hall of Fame in 1978.

FRASER, James Earle. (Winona, MN, Nov. 4, 1876—Westport, CT, Oct. 11, 1953). Sculptor. The work of this Minnesota native has attained world rank. He studied art at the ART INSTITUTE OF CHICAGO in 1894 and later moved to Paris to study at the Ecole des Beaux-Arts. His most famous work was completed early in his career, when in 1896 he finished "The End of the Trail." This sculpture drew on his early experiences on the prairie and depicts an exhausted Indian on horseback, symbolizing, perhaps, the lot of the American Indian of the period. In 1898 he became the student-assistant of famed sculptor Augustus St. Gaudens. The success of his work may be measured by the number of awards it brought to the artist and by the many galleries and public buildings in which it is displayed. As an artist, Fraser was the recipient of hundreds of awards, including first prize for best work in sculpture by the American Art Association in 1898, first prize competitive medal for design, the Edison medal in 1906, decorated Knight Order of Vasa (Sweden), gold medal from the National Institute of Arts and Letters, the Century Association medal and the National Sculpture Society Medal of Honor in 1917. Principal works of Fraser include a bust of Theodore Roosevelt on display in the Senate Chamber, two heroic figures, "Justice" and "Law" before the Supreme Court Building, statues of Albert Gallatin and Alexander Hamilton for the Treasury Building, and the "Flaming Sword" for the 2nd Division Memorial, all in Washington, D.C.; the Buffalo nickel; monuments to Thomas EDISON for the Edison Institute in DEARBORN, Michigan; MAYO brothers for ROCHESTER, Minnesota, and two groups—"Discoverers" and "Pioneers"—for the Michigan Avenue Memorial Bridge in CHICAGO, Illinois.

FREE, J. N. (1828—1906), Known as "The Immortal J.N." Free became one of the best-known American eccentrics. He spent his boyhood in TIFFIN, Ohio, studied law, and then went to California where he made a fortune in the gold rush. However, he was swindled out of his money, became critically ill, and his mind was shattered. Calling Tiffin home and visiting there often, for the rest of his life, Free traveled across the country, refusing to pay for anything. He took all the necessities of life as his due, relying on others wherever he went for clothing, meals, hotel accommodations and all his other needs. His eccentricities soon became known, and people went along with him. When asked to pay, he would proclaim, "I am the immortal J.N." Hotel men urged him to stay with them because of the publicity. By the time of his death he had received lifetime passes from almost every railroad in the country and had gained worldwide notoriety.

FREEPORT, Illinois. City (pop. 26,406), seat of Stephenson County, shipping center for dairy and field products, industrial city with headquarters of major farm insurance companies, name first given to the home of a generous settler and then applied to the town, first settled in 1838. Early settlers in Freeport included miners from GALENA, Illinois, and Pennsylvania Germans. The first railroad to reach Freeport, in 1853, was the Galena and Chicago Union. Freeport was the host to the second LINCOLN-DOUGLAS DEBATE on August 27, 1858. One of the first Illinois monuments to the CIVIL WAR dead was erected on the Courthouse square in 1869. The Stephenson County Historical Society is housed in a two-story stone house called "Bohemiana." Trees surrounding the house were brought to the community by covered wagon and the furnishings in the house came from the Jane Addams home in Cedarville.

FREMONT, Ohio. City (pop. 17,834), seat of Sandusky County, situated in north east-central Ohio, about ten miles from SANDUSKY BAY of Lake ERIE, lying in the eroded sandstone valley of the SANDUSKY RIVER. Residential areas perch on small hills and nestle in intimate valleys throughout the city. As early as 1650 the WYANDOTTE Indians built two villages at the site, both of which were destroyed by the British. On the main path between Pittsburgh and DETROIT, the site was visited by many historic personages.

In 1782 the British built an outpost there in the same year that James Whitaker and his wife established a home near the present town. They are generally said to be the first European settlers in Ohio. The TREATY OF GREEN VILLE in 1795 turned the site over to the Americans, who built FORT STEPHENSON there in 1812 and successfully defended it under the skillful leadership of Major George CROGHAN (1791-1849) during the WAR OF 1812.

After the war, two towns were started, Croghansville, named for the major, and Lower Sandusky. With the coming of lake boats and more commerce, the settlements grew. They united in 1829 under the name Lower Sandusky, but the name was changed to Fremont in 1849, in honor of the explorer-statesman. Railroads arrived in 1853, and the second national bank in Ohio was established there in 1863, attracting new industries. These now include products as diverse as dry cell batteries, razor blades, castings, fabric for automobiles, dyes and supplies for hunting and trapping.

In 1970 the population stood at 18,490. By

1980 it had dropped to 17,834 as industries and jobs moved to the Sun Belt.

A monument to Croghan and the Battle of Fort Stephanson marks the burial site of the hero. In front of it stands Old Betsy, the single cannon of the fort, which played a critical part in the victory. At SPIEGEL GROVE State Park is the estate of President Rutherford B. HAYES, (1822-1893) a parklike wooded acreage of lakes and brooks, turned over to the state in honor of the president, who began his law practice at Fremont and who returned to his beautiful home after leaving the presidency. The home was built in typical Victorian style in 1859. Near the house are the graves of President and Lucy Hayes, and not far off are granite boulders commemorating Hayes' favorite horses. The Hayes memorial preserves letters, diary, pamphlets and memorabilia relating to Hayes.

FRENCH AND INDIAN WAR. The phase of the Seven Years' War fought in America from 1754 through 1763 between England and France and their Indian allies. During the first two years of that war in America, the British seemed to move from one defeat to another. However, when William Pitt became prime minister in 1758, British fortunes began to improve. Pitt recognized the enormous value of French Canada as well as the the lands beyond the Alleghenies to the MISSISSIPPI RIVER and around the GREAT LAKES, now comprising much of the Midwest. He moved at once to strengthen the British forces in America. England claimed all the land inland from its coastal settlements. France claimed all the land drained by the rivers it had explored. In this area, in addition to the European forces, Indian tribes were recruited as allies and most sided with the French. However, actual warfare in what is now the Midwest was confined to skirmishes and attacks by both sides on British and French settlements and on the villages of their Indians allies. The great British victories came in the northeastern U.S. and in French Canada, which was decisively defeated. By 1763, after more than 75 years of bitter struggle, the French had been expelled and British controlled all of continental North America east of the Mississippi.

FRUITS. A large part of the Midwest could grow the popular fruits, and each Midwest state does produce large quantities of most of the common fruits. However, most of the Midwest concentrates on its dominance in the growing of grains and raising of livestock, leaving fruit production, generally, to the highly specialized areas. Michigan leads the nation in the production of cherries and holds third rank in apples, and in plums and prunes. Wisconsin is the nation's second largest producer of CRANBERRIES. While many of the Midwest states are producing increasing quantities of grapes for a growing Midwest wine industry, that growth has not yet managed to mount a significant challenge to the ranking producers in other regions.

FULBRIGHT, James William. (Sumner, MO, Apr. 9, 1905—). U.S. senator, educator. A Rhodes scholar who earned his law degree at George Washington University, Fulbright rose to prominence in Arkansas politics. He became president of the University of ARKANSAS (1939-1941), and was elected as a Democrat to the U.S. House of Representatives (1943-45) and to the U.S. Senate (1945-75). He was author of the Fulbright Act (1946) which established an international educational exchange program. In 1959 he became chairman of the powerful Senate Foreign Relations Committee. During the administrations of Lyndon B. Johnson and Richard Nixon, he earned a reputation as the most formidable opponent of the Vietnam war. One of his most important books was *The Arrogance of Power* (1964). He retired in 1974 after his surprising failure to be renominated.

FULTON, Missouri. City (pop. 11,000), seat of Callaway County; originally named Volney for Count Constantin Volney, French scientist; re-named Fulton to honor Robert Fulton, American scientist, marine engineer, and artist. Its industries include printing and factories producing farm equipment. In 1824 fifty acres of land for the city were donated by George Nichols, one of the first settlers in the region. The State Lunatic Asylum, the first hospital for mental patients west of the Mississippi, was established in Fulton in 1847 and opened in 1849. Its administrative building, designed by Solomon Jenkins, was completed in 1851. The State School for the Deaf was founded in Fulton in 1851. Fulton is also the home of William Woods and WESTMINSTER colleges. It was at Westminister College that Winston Churchill delivered his "IRON CURTAIN" speech on March 5, 1946. The bombed ruins of Christopher Wren's 17th-century Church of St. Mary, Aldermanbury, were moved from London to Westminister College in 1966 and the building now houses a collection of Churchill memorabilia. Fulton was the birthplace of poet, musician,

Painter Robert Thom depicts a fur trading scene, (C) 1966 by Mich. Bell Telephone Co.

novelist and reviewer Henry Bellamann. Bella-mann published seven novels and three books of poetry between 1920 and 1945.

FUR TRADE. The earliest source of Euro-pean-style commerce in what is now the Midwest. Almost as soon as the early explorers reached an area, French business men were buying furs from the Indians in exchange for knives, utensils and other necessities along with beads, other trinkets, and alcohol, regrettable, as well. These operations were formalized by such great organizations as the Hudson's Bay Company during the British occupation of the various regions. After the LOUISIANA PURCHASE, trading companies of New Orleans, such as those of the CHOUTEAU family, established trading posts up the MISSOURI RIVER Valley, and these were swallowed up by the enormous AMERICAN FUR COMPANY of John Jacob ASTOR, the first of the country's ruthless monopolies. As increased settlement cut off the homes of the beaver and other fur animals in the Midwest, the fur trade moved on westward, dealing with the western tribes.

FURNITURE. The wonderful hardwoods of the Midwest are particularly suitable for furniture making, especially those of Michigan. The plentiful maple, oak, beech and other woods around GRAND RAPIDS attracted a number of furniture makers, many of whose names became famous in the industry. These included William Haldane, George Widdicomb, George W. Gay and the Berkey brothers, Julius and William—all bringing with them exceptional skills as cabinet makers. The exhibition of Grand Rapids furniture at the Centennial Exposition in Philadelphia in 1876 made that industry famous, Haldane's chairs are still valued as antiques. Other furniture makers appeared, including some of the country's largest, until Grand Rapids became known as the national center of the furniture industry. On a smaller scale, the furniture makers of the AMANAS in Iowa also became well known for their handsomely simple designs, the extraordinary quality of their hand workmanship and the supurb finishes. Furniture making remains one of the principal attractions of the Amanas.

FURROW, LONGEST CONTINUOUS. Marked the first road in Iowa, and it had an interesting history. Travelers on the prairie, where there were few landmarks, often lost their way. Determined to help them, DUBUQUE merchant Lyman Dillon hitched his five oxen to a heavy plow and plowed a deep, straight furrow all the way to IOWA CITY. Although it has not made its way into the Guiness record books, it is considered to have been the longest continuous furrow ever plowed—stretching the 89 miles between the two communities. Soon the tracks of wagons produced a well defined road, beside the furrow, and today a concrete highway follows almost the same route.

GABRILOWITSCH, Ossip. (St. Petersburg, Russia, Feb. 7, 1878—Detroit, MI, Sept. 14, 1936). Orchestra conductor, pianist. Gabrilowitsch brought worldwide fame to the Detroit Symphony Orchestra which had been established in 1914. He had gained a reputation in Europe as a brilliant concert pianist and conductor of several European orchestras. After many tours in the United States playing recitals and directing leading orchestras, Gabrilowitsch settled in DETROIT in 1918. Under such a renowned conductor, contributions to the symphony came in so quickly that within six years the orchestra had a new building for a permanent home and a regular membership of ninety musicians.

GALE, Zona. (Portage, WI, 1874—1938). Winner of the PULITZER PRIZE in 1921 for the dramatization of her novel *Miss Lulu Bett,* Zona Gale had gained a national reputation previously for her novels, beginning with *Friendship Village* in 1908. Her novels were said always to deal with humble, undistinguished people set in her "ordinary" kind of town, treated with a kind of "gentle irony." Her Pulitzer winner revealed characters more sharply as petty and bigoted. Critic Carl Van Doren wrote that she "varied the same device; that of showing how childlike children are...how motherly are mothers...how lovely are lovers of whatever age, sex, color, or condition." Her *Borgia,* 1928, was different from the earlier works in showing a person possessed "with a sense of her own evil because of the disasters which overtake those who associate with her."

GALENA (lead). Galena (or lead glance) is the official mineral of both Wisconsin and Missouri. It is a blue-grey metal of lustrous quality, the principal ore of lead. Missouri is the world leader in lead production. Since galena often contains silver, it is frequently processed for that metal as well as the lead. Older people will remember the crystal radio set in which the crystal was a small inset of galena, by means of which the set was "tuned."

GALENA, Illinois. City (pop. 3,876), historic western Illinois lead mining community in Jo Daviess Co., on the Galena River, twenty miles east of DUBUQUE, Iowa, on U.S. Highway 20, named for the lead ore. Galena was once the most important, the best known, and the largest city north of ST. LOUIS, Missouri. The first of the "western style" mining booms in the United States occurred in a triangular section of the Midwest bordered by Dubuque, Iowa; Galena, Illinois; and Schullsburg, Wisconsin. The boom in lead mining started in 1823 when the first group of miners accompanied Moses Meeker into the future area of Galena. Meeker was the first person to obtain a lease from the federal government to mine in the region. The number of miners annually moving to Illinois resembled, to some observers, the habits of a species of fish called the sucker. This may have led to the nickname "Sucker State" which has been applied to Illinois.

Despite the boom economy, Galena never developed the wild and lawless reputation of other later mining communities. In 1827, the Fever River was renamed the Galena river. The *Miners Journal,* the first newspaper in Illinois outside of the southern counties, was started in 1828.

Hard times began with an unfavorable tariff, in 1829, combined with over-production and then depletion of the best lead sources. In the 1831-1840 decade farming became as profitable as mining in Jo Daviess County. Miners left Galena to hunt for strikes in the West, and others found better salaries working for the rapidly proliferating railroads. Reachable only by steep roads, Galena was poorly situated for a commercial center.

Galesburg - Galloway

Railroads were thought to offer economic benefit to Galena, and when the railroad came, the Chicago markets were opened to the town. Nevertheless, after its heyday, Galena settled down to become for several decades just another small Midwest town.

Galena's most famous resident was Ulysses S. GRANT, who worked for his father in a leather-goods store before leaving to fight in the CIVIL WAR. After the war, Grant was given a house costing $16,000 as a gift from his hometown neighbors. That structure became one of the many tourist destinations which have galvanized modern Galena.

The fine old houses, the history and the beauty of the community attracted wealthy Chicagoans and others. Most of the fine homes were restored. The nearby ski resort attracted sport lovers. As a result, Galena is now one of the principal tourist attractions in the Midwest. Semi-annual architectural tours feature the many styles in the city. Most of its historic commercial structures, including the Desoto Hotel, also have been restored. The Dowling House (ca. 1826) is reputedly the oldest house in Galena. The stately Belvedere House was constructed in 1857 by J. Russell Jones, a steamboat owner and Ambassador to Belgium. The 22-room mansion features period furniture and decorations.

Old Market House State Historic Site is one of the oldest remaining market houses in the Midwest. The Turney House is the restored living quarters and office of John Turney, Galena's first attorney. The Ulysses S. Grant Home State Historic Site preserves the house where the general lived until 1867 when he became the Secretary of War. The house features many of Grant's possessions.

The Galena Gazette Museum and Printery displays operating presses and a pictorial documentary of Galena's history and newspaper. The nearby Vinegar Hill Lead Mine was founded by John Furlong, an Irish soldier impressed into the British military who escaped and came to the Midwest to mine lead. Guided tours of the mine are available.

GALESBURG, Illinois. City (pop. 35,305); seat of Knox County, northwestern Illinois; south of MOLINE and northwest of PEORIA; named for its founder, Reverend George Washington Gale. Galesburg is the only site of LINCOLN-DOUGLAS DEBATES that still retains the original setting. On October 7, 1858, Abraham LINCOLN and Stephen A. DOUGLAS held the fifth of their debates in Old Main on the campus of KNOX

COLLEGE. The building was preserved with Civil War-period furniture. Gale planned the community in Oneida, New York, in 1835, where he studied reports of available land in Indiana and Illinois. Fifty families invested more than twenty thousand dollars with which land was purchased. Upon arriving in their new settlement, families immediately began building permanent homes as there were to be no crude shelters in Galesburg. Gale planned that the hardworking farmers would so improve their land that prices would go up, the farms could be sold and the money used to endow a college for ministers. As a result, Knox College was founded in 1837. Establishment of Galesburg as a division point for the Chicago, Burlington and Quincy railroad led to the ballooning of its population from 882 in 1850 to nearly 4,000 in 1856. Anti-slavery feeling made the community an important stop on the UNDERGROUND RAILROAD before the CIVIL WAR. Galesburg boasts many famous people as former residents. One of America's literary giants, Carl SANDBURG, was born in Galesburg on January 6, 1878. His home, only twenty feet square, was purchased in 1946 and restored by the Carl Sandburg Association. Remembrance Rock, located behind the house, is his gravesite. Two residents who gained fame in journalism were Samuel S. McClure and John H. Finley. McClure founded a magazine he named for himself and in 1897 began publishing inquiries into political abuses. His writers, including Lincoln Steffens, were called muckrakers. Finley was the Commissioner of Education of New York State from 1913 to 1921 when he joined the New York *Times*. He later became its editor-in-chief.

GALLOWAY, William (Bill). (Traer, IA, 1877—Waterloo, IA, 1952). Industrialist-catalog marketer. As he sold pencils, to work his way through college, Bill Galloway was acquiring a knowledge of human nature and sales skills which enabled him to to become one of the first of the mass marketers through catalog solicitation. With his brother James, he started the Galloway Company at WATERLOO, Iowa, to produce farm machinery. Bill Galloway pioneered in marketing through catalog display and selective direct mailings. The firm produced a complete line of farm machinery, developing such devices as the mechanical manure spreader; for a short time they even produced the Galloway, an automobile, all designed by their brilliant inventor-relative, D.K. Wilson. As the business grew, their manufacturing operations expanded to encom-

James A. Garfield.

pass a line of buildings almost a mile long. Internal disputes among management eventually resulted in the Galloway Brothers' departure from their successful business, which soon dwindled without their business touch. They eventually began another business in nearby CEDAR FALLS, Iowa, which pioneered in the manufacture and distribution of automatic humidifiers for furnaces, also invented by D.K. Wilson. Galloway Park in Waterloo pays tribute to the pioneer Iowa Galloway industrialists.

GANGSTERS. Organized criminals. During the 1920s CHICAGO, Illinois, gained a worldwide reputation as a haven for criminals. Unchecked syndicated crime in Chicago between 1926 and 1929 left an estimated two hundred men killed in gang warfare. Gangsters grew powerful because of their ruthlessness and their adoption of the efficient organizational structures of legitimate business. Al CAPONE (1897-1947) was one of the most notorious. Territories of neighborhood gangs often expanded to become national networks. Reformers were unable to make progress in controlling crime because many politicians tolerated the mob in exchange for money and votes. Rural residents were unconcerned because they saw crime as an urban problem. The middle class was convinced the struggle was hopeless. Over the years the gangs have changed the basis of their operations from liquor to gambling to drugs and many other rackets, but they continue to thrive. However, recent efforts in Chicago, New York and elsewhere, seem to be producing a

reduction in the old-style gang power as law enforcement agencies successfully indict gang leaders for a variety of criminal activities. However, the influx of illicit drugs has caused the expansion of new-style drug gangs, and Chicago continues to be regarded by much of the world as gangland territory.

GARDEN OF THE GODS. Section of SHAWNEE NATIONAL FOREST in southern Illinois, noted for its rock formations and some of the most colorful and rugged scenery between the Appalachians and the Missouri OZARKS. Shawnee National Forest was acquired by the Forest Service of the United States Department of Agriculture in 1933.

GARFIELD, James Abram. (near Orange, OH, Nov. 19, 1831—Elberon, NJ, Sept. 19 1881). U.S. president. Born in poverty, he worked as a carpenter, farmer and canal boatman. Through this effort and with the help of his widowed mother, Elizabeth Ballou Garfield, he obtained a good education. After he graduated from Williams College in 1856, he became a teacher and also a lay preacher of the Disciples of Christ. His early interest in politics led to his election as a Republican state senator, who soon gained a wide reputation as an effective speaker and an anti-slavery man.

He helped to raise the 42nd Ohio Volunteer Infantry in 1861 and commanded it capably at the start of the CIVIL WAR. Made brigade commander, Garfield won a victory at Middle Creek, Kentucky, in 1862. With other successes, he rose to the rank of major general of volunteers in the Union Army.

Elected to Congress in 1863, he served there until 1880 and had many leading roles.

He was elected to the Senate in 1880 but never took his seat. Garfield had gained little national prominence before the election of 1880. However, the Republican nominating convention was deadlocked. On the first ballot, Garfield did not receive a single vote. By the sixth ballot he had received two votes. After the thirteenth ballot Garfield dropped from the running. A Pennsylvania delegate voted for Garfield again on the nineteenth ballot. His votes then doubled, but by the thirty-third ballot he had dropped back to one vote. On the thirty-fifth he received fifty votes, and on the thirty-sixth he took 399. This brought him over the top. After 36 ballots Garfield at last received the Republican nomination.

Gafield had studied Latin, Greek and German at Williams College, and his knowledge of German helped to gain the large German vote. This may have been particularly important because out of nine million votes cast, Garfield received a plurality of only 9,454 votes. However, he garnered 214 electoral votes, compared with 155 for his Democratic opponent, W.S. Hancock, and so won the election.

Garfield holds a unique place in American history. On November 2, 1880, Garfield was a member of the U.S. House of Representatives, was Senator-elect and President-elect. He surrendered his seat in the Senate and resigned from the House.

He took the oath of office in a heavy snowstorm. He was the first president to review an inaugural parade from a grandstand in front of the White House. His mother, Elizabeth Ballou Garfield, was the first mother of a president to attend her son's inauguration. A principal feature of his inaugural ball at the Smithsonian Institution was a single electric lamp.

The party was severely split, and he made many political enemies; he was constantly harrassed by office seekers. One disappointed office seeker, Charles J. Guiteau, shot him while he waited for a train at the Washington, D.C., Potomac Railroad station, on July 2, 1881. He lingered on for 80 days. On September 6, 1881, he was taken to Elberon, New Jersey. A thousand volunteers built a spur track from the main railroad to his seashore cottage, so the president could be moved there comfortably. For a while he seemed to be improving, and he wrote to his mother, "Don't be distrubed by conflicting reports about my condition. It is true I am still weak and on my back, but I am gaining every day..." However, he developed blood poisoning and died on September 19.

Garfield was a brilliant speaker and a man of many talents with a popular personality, but his short term in office gave no opportunity for him to demonstrate his ability as president.

His wife, Lucretia "Crete" Rudolph Garfield was the nation's first lady for less than seven months. She survived the president for 36 years and died at age 85. Garfield was the fifth child in a family of five. He and his wife had seven children. Six states have recognized Garfield with cities named for him.

GARLAND, Hamlin. (West Salem, WI, Sept. 14, 1860— Mar. 4, 1940). Author of bitter novels about the Midwest farm region where he grew up, stories mainly dealing with the difficult lives of the farmers there. Garland's early stories and sketches were gathered in his 1891 collection as *Main-Travelled Roads*. This was followed by his first novel in 1893, called *Prairie Folks. Wayside Courtships* (1897) was said to "portray in vivid detail the ugliness and despair of Western farm life." His first autobiographical novel, a nostalgic work, was *A Son of the Middle Border* (1917). He won the PULITZER PRIZE in 1922 for his second autobiographical novel *A Daughter of the Middle Border*. Garland was a part of the succession of Pulitzer winning authors of the Midwest dealing with similar Midwestern subjects, Zona GALE in 1921 and Margaret WILSON in 1923. He also published a number of politically oriented works, collections of essays and verse. He moved to Los Angeles in 1929 and lived there until his death.

GARLAND, Judy. (Grand Rapids, MI, June 10, 1922— London, June 22, 1969). Actress and singer. Born Frances Gumm, Garland was a preschooler when she became a singer in her father's theater in GRAND RAPIDS. She became a stage actress and toured the United States until 1935, when she went under contract to Metro-Goldwyn-Mayer at the age of thirteen and remained at MGM until 1950. As a singing actress, Garland appeared in many pictures between 1936 and 1962, but perhaps the one she is most remembered for is *The Wizard of Oz* in 1939. She received a special Academy Award that year for "her outstanding performance as a screen juvenile." The tensions and demands of movie acting and the pressures of her star status proved a heavy burden and led to difficulties with directors and producers and the cancellation of her MGM contract. Then she began a series of singing tours in the U.S. and Europe. She returned to the screen in 1954 with one of her greatest successes, *A Star Is Born*. Garland continued to make concert tours, attaining the status of a cult figure. Her illnesses and frequent failures to appear on schedule only seemed to intensify the support of her public, for whom she remained one of the few truly great of the entertainment world.

GARRISON, Iowa. Village, (pop. 400), situated in east central Iowa, in Benton County, near VINTON and about halfway between WATERLOO and CEDAR RAPIDS, this tiny farm-center community has the unusual distinction of also being a center of Midwest theater art. Artistic director Tom Johnson built the Old Creamery Theater Company into an acting phenomenon. Housed in a remodeled creamery, the company has performed a wide variety of plays, attracting as many as 30,000 to 40,000 in annual attendance, bringing extraordinary crowds to the small community and touring to reach out to another 75,000.

GARY, Indiana. City (pop. 151,953), situated on Lake MICHIGAN in the northwest corner of Indiana, in Lake County. It was named for Elbert H. Gary chairman of the board of U.S. Steel, which founded the city and incorporated it in 1906. It occupies 39.4 square miles of territory. Nearby communities are HAMMOND and East Chicago, Highland and Munster on the west, Hobart and Merrillville on the south and Portage on the east.

The normally continental climate of the region is modified both winter and summer by Lake Michigan. The lake also is responsible for lake effect snows which sometimes sweep across the length of the lake, piling snow high on its southern end.

In the early 1900s the site of Gary was sparsely occupied but an ideal location for certain industries, particularly iron and STEEL. At the foot of Lake Michigan, where great ore boats could bring the ore from Minnesota, within easy distance of the coal and limestone needed for smelting, the site appeared to be one of the best in the country to Judge Elbert Gary and the board of U.S. Steel.

The city sprang up almost full-fledged around the great steel operation. Gary is the largest city in the United States to have been founded in the Twentieth Century. The steel works sparked related industries and attracted others. Nearby WHITING is a leading center of oil refining.

Steel workers at Gary have always been active in the LABOR movement, especially in the nationwide steel strike of 1919, when federal troops occupied the city for several months. With the decline in demand for this country's steel, that industry became one of the most depressed in the country. Widespread closedowns and layoffs in the 1980s brought financial distress to much of Gary. U.S. Steel workers began the longest strike in their history, which only ended in early 1987, and limited operations were resumed at Gary. However, the continuing economic difficulties of the city cost longtime mayor Richard G. Hatcher his post, which he had held since 1967.

GASCONADE RIVER. Major waterway having its source in southern Missouri in the OZARK MOUNTAINS. The river passes east of SPRINGFIELD and travels 265 miles northeast to the MISSOURI RIVER. During early settlement days, lumber camps were established along the river to take advantage of the dense pine woods. On its path through Missouri the river flows near Fort Leonard Wood, Waynesville, and ROLLA, Missouri. The Gasconade is noted for its fishing.

GATES, John Warne. (near Turner Junction, IL, May 8, 1855—Paris, France, Aug. 9, 1911). Financier, speculator and industrialist. "Bet a million" Gates, as he was called, was born in what is now West Chicago, Illinois. He rose from work in a hardware store and as a traveling barbed wire salesman to become founder of many notable industries and one of the wealthiest men of his day. His career was based on a brilliant scheme to demonstrate the barbed wire fencing he was selling as a young man. At San Antonio, Texas, he built a barbed wire corral, filled it with rambunctious longhorns and proved the value of barbed wire to Texas cattlemen. He took so many orders he left his employer and started a company of his own at ST. LOUIS, Missouri. His career proceeded through a series of mergers, consolidations, watering of stock of holding companies and other activities, until he gained a huge fortune. His daring and boldness in attempting to manipulate the markets brought about his nickname. However, he was unsuccessful in an attempt to manipulate his partner, J.P. Morgan, and he retired to Port Arthur, Texas. He was prominent in developing the Port Arthur area, where he continued to wheel and deal on a much smaller scale.

GATLING, Richard Jordan. (Hertford County, NC, Sept. 12, 1818—New York, NY, Feb. 26, 1903). Inventor. Gatling had been interested since 1839 in improving agricultural implements. He set up factories in ST. LOUIS, Missouri; SPRINGFIELD, Ohio; and INDIANAPOLIS, Indiana. He continued to invent new agricultural implements for his factories, including a hemp decorticating machine and a steam plow. When he contracted smallpox and could not find medical care, he entered medical school and graduated in 1850, although he never practiced. He contented himself with the knowledge that he was qualified to treat himself and his family. On November 4, 1862, Gatling received patent number 36,836 for a rapid-fire gun, the "Gatling gun" for which he gained worldwide fame. The first gun, capable of firing 250 shots per minute, was manufactured in Indianapolis. The CIVIL WAR was over before the machine gun could be used extensively, but it was adopted by the army in 1866 and played a role in the western Indian wars. Gatling continued to experiment with different gun designs and improvements and served for six years as the president of the American Association of Inventors and Manufacturers. He continued to experiment with machinery until his death.

GENEVA, Indiana. Town (pop. 1,400), central Indiana, in Shelby County, southeast of INDIANAPOLIS, Indiana. Geneva was the home of Indiana author Gene Stratton PORTER. Limberlost State Historic Site includes the original two-story, fourteen-room Limberlost Cabin which served as the Porter home for eighteen years. Built of white cedar logs and redwood shingles to blend into the surroundings, the cabin houses some of Porter's personal belongings and photographs.

GENTRY, Mrs. Richard. (—) One of the first women in the United States to receive an appointment as postmistress. Mrs. Gentry's husband, the second postmaster, was killed in the Seminole wars in Florida. Through the influence of Senator Thomas Hart BENTON, Mrs. Gentry assumed her husband's job in COLUMBIA, Missouri, and kept it for thirty years.

GEODE. The geode is the official state rock of Iowa, where collectors often find prize specimens along and near the MISSISSIPI RIVER in southern Iowa. Geodes are round stonelike objects of various sizes. When broken or cut open, they generally have a layer of quartz and a hollow inside, surrounding which have grown crystals of varying colors, often of spectacular nature. The creation of geodes is a long and complicated process, involving inward and outward migrations of chemical bearing waters and crystalization and expansion pressures, among other forces.

GEOGRAPHY. The geography of the Midwest, as defined in this volume, covers a region crudely outlined as a triangle with a long, fairly straight side on the west, a far from straight border on the southeast. The northeastern limitations of the region must be marked by a purely hypothetical line from the northeast corner of Ohio to the northwest corner of Minnesota, through lakes ERIE, HURON and SUPERIOR.

Starting with the RED RIVER OF THE NORTH, much of the western border follows natural lines, including the BIG SIOUX and MISSOURI Rivers to KANSAS CITY, then south on a manmade line to the southwestern corner of Missouri and across that state's southern border, with a dip where the BOOT HEEL follows the ST. FRANCIS RIVER, then cuts straight across to the MISSISSIPPI RIVER.

After a short stretch northward on that river, the southeastern regional border follows the OHIO RIVER to the Pennsylvania border.

Across the region, from the northeast boundary of Ohio to the northwest corner of Iowa the distance is 919 miles. From the jog of the NORTHWEST ANGLE in northern Minnesota southward to the jog of the Boot Heel in southeast Missouri, the distance is 914 miles. The region's triangle would fit in a square roughly 920 miles long and 920 miles wide.

Internal borders of the western tier of five states north and south are almost entirely defined by the Mississippi River along with a small stretch of the ST. CROIX RIVER, north of which is the only artificial boundary dividing those states.

The borders between Minnesota and Iowa and Iowa and Missouri are manmade except for the small section between Iowa and Missouri on the DES MOINES RIVER.

The southern borders of Illinois, Indiana and Ohio follow the winding course of the Ohio River. Ohio's border with Pennsylvania is manmade, as are the borders between Michigan and Indiana, Michigan and Ohio and Ohio with Indiana.

The region provides the sources of three of the major river systems of the continent, the vast ST. LAWRENCE RIVER drainage system, the Red River of the North a part of the great Nelson River system, and the Mississippi River system.

The Mississippi becomes one of the two major internal rivers of Minnesota as it leaves its source in Lake ITASCA, winds north then east then south before it forms the Minnesota border with Wisconsin. The other major internal river in Minnesota is its namesake river.

The Des Moines, CEDAR and IOWA are the major internal Iowa rivers, as are the ILLINOIS and ROCK rivers in Illinois. Wisconsin's major river is also its namesake. The WABASH is Indiana's major river, celebrated in song. By contrast, Ohio and Michigan have no internal rivers of the first class.

The only Midwest mountains, in less than the strict sense of that classification, are the OZARKS, striding across Missouri, with a lower cluster extending into Illinois, and the MESABI

RANGE, stretching across eastern Minnesota.

Topographically, the higher reaches in eastern Ohio are the foothills of the Allegheny Mountains to the east. These highlands extend east and west across much of the north central portion of Ohio, forming a watershed, or DIVIDE, between Lake Erie and the Ohio River. Michigan's LOWER PENINSULA also has such a divide, formed by substantially higher ground running north and south through most of that area. The UPPER PENINSULA is even more rugged, with several modest ranges such as the Gogebic. Higher land in eastern Indiana continues to decline westward toward the predominately flat prairielands of Illinois, which state has its highest elevations to the west, running north from the Ozark extension, parallel with the Mississippi.

Except for the small, rugged unglaciated area of the southwest, Wisconsin is relatively flat in the south, extending to highlands in the north, east-northeast, not quite reaching mountain status at Timms Peak in Price County, 1952 feet. Missouri is the most "mountainous" state in the region, with its Ozarks having TAUM SAUK MOUNTAIN as the highest peak. To the north, Missouri's level lands blend into generally flat Iowa, relieved only by the bluffs of the Mississippi, Missouri and other major rivers. However, Iowa rises gradually to its greatest height in the northwest.

Minnesota also gradually ascends, but from south to northeast, where there are a number of modest ranges, such as the MESABI. From the Red River Valley, Minnesota rises gradually to meet the Plains region.

Not surprisingly, the GREAT LAKES must be considered the most distinctive natural feature of the region. The Midwest surrounds Lake Michigan, the only one wholly within U.S. borders. With the exception of Lake Ontario, all of the U.S. Great Lakes borders are within the Midwest, from the farthest tip of Lake Erie to the westernmost point of Lake Superior. These great bodies of water may be considered, in one sense, the most valuable natural resource in the country. They contain the largest volume of fresh water in the world. Other natural lakes are modest in the Midwest, except in Minnesota, and the larger artificial lakes are mostly confined to southern Missouri.

Climate of the region finds the average annual range of precipitation extending moderately from about 30 in. to slightly over 40 in. Extreme temperatures in the region range from the 151 degrees of Indiana to the 173 degrees in the Minnesota northland.

GEOLOGY (Geomorphology). Every force of nature has been at work in forming the landscape of the Midwest and its underlayment. Fantastic subsurface forces raised and lowered the surface several times. As the surface subsided, shallow seas washed in, then dried up while the surface was raised once more. Successive layers of sand and shell were buried to form the sandstone and limestone, also covering the successive layers of plant and animal life to form the coal, peat and petroleum.

As the temperatures changed, the region varied from tropical to temperate to frigid. Much later, the various ice ages scraped, gouged, deposited and watered much of the surface. Perhaps the greatest legacy of the GLACIERS to the Midwest is the vast water treasure of the GREAT LAKES

During the early Cambrian period, the land surface seems to have been quite similar to the present. Then the Ordovician period found almost the entire area under shallow seas, with much the same during the Silurian period, except for highlands throughout most of Minnesota. In the Devonian period, the Midwest Basin covered much of region except for the outer edges. The carboniferous period found the Equator cutting across northwestern Minnesota, south of which there were parallel rows of low mountains, jutting up from the seas. The Permian period found all of the region again above water, except for a basin in southern Missouri and Illinois. Most of the region remained above water during the Mesozoic Era, ending with the Cretaceous period, when much of the rest of the country was under water. By the Cenozoic Era, the region had generally stabilized, with the Ancestral Mississippi following much of the course of the present MISSOURI and the High Plains rising to the west.

During the Quaternary Ice Age, the great glaciers covered all of Michigan, most of Minnesota, much of Iowa and Wisconsin, more than half of Indiana and Ohio and much of northern Illinois. Notable exceptions to the ice cover were the rugged glacierless areas of northeast Iowa and southwest Wisconsin.

Today's Midwest land surface mirrors few changes from the time of the last ice age glacier, estimated about 10,000 years ago. However, the few unglaciated areas represent periods of time vastly earlier than that of the glaciers. The copper bearing rocks of Michigan's UPPER PENINSULA are considered to be among the oldest on the earth's surface.

By far the largest area of the Midwest is presently included in the geological classifications of the early and late Paleozoic period of sedimentary rocks. Most of Ohio, all of Michigan's LOWER PENINSULA, more than half of Indiana, most of Illinois and more than half of Missouri and Iowa represent the late period. A quarter of Ohio and of Indiana, the small northern portion of Illinois, two-thirds of Wisconsin, small segments of northeast Iowa and southeast Minnesota and about half of Missouri are found from the early Paleozoic period. The Pre-Cambrian period of Igneous (intrusive and metamorphic) rocks covers the western half of Michigan's Upper Peninsula, northern Wisconsin and most of northern Minnesota. Northwestern and southwestern Minnesota and much of northwest-central Iowa are the Midwest's only representatives of the Mesozoic Period of Sedimentary Rocks. Far southeast Missouri, including the BOOT HEEL, and the tiniest tip of southern Illinois, represent the Midwest's only Cenozoic Region of Sedimentary Rocks.

GEORGE ROGERS CLARK NATIONAL HISTORICAL PARK.

Indiana memorial in VINCENNES on the site of old Fort Sackville. The memorial, ninety feet in diameter and eighty-two feet high, contains a bronze statue of CLARK by the sculptor Hermon A. MacNeil and seven large murals by Ezra Winter illustrating important scenes in the history of the NORTH-WEST TERRITORY and Clark's seizure of Fort Sackville February 27, 1779. Carved in stone above the murals are Clark's words to Patrick Henry: "Great things have been effected by a few men well conducted—our cause is just—our country will be grateful."

GEORGE WASHINGTON CARVER NATIONAL MONUMENT.

Birthplace at DIAMOND, Missouri, and childhood home of George Washington CARVER, the famous black agronomist. The national site includes the Carver family cemetery and the locale of Carver's birth.

GEORGETOWN, Ohio.

City (pop 3.478), seat of Brown County, situated in southeastern Ohio in the valley of White Oak Creek about seven miles north of the mouth of the creek on the OHIO RIVER. It was surveyed in 1819 and named for Georgetown, Kentucky, which was named for George Washington. The town became an important tobacco distribution center. Small manufacturing and the trade of

Clark National Historic Site.

the farming community contribute to the economy. Ulysses S. GRANT was brought to Georgetown as an infant by his father, Jesse Grant, who built a two-story home there. Grant went to school in a building erected at FREMONT in 1804. In 1899 the Grant Memorial Association converted the school into a repository for Grant memorabilia, including an original drawing of West Point done in 1840 and signed by Grant. Today the principal city manufactures are shoes.

GHOST TOWNS.

In the Midwest, when mining or lumbering gave out, most communities had AGRICULTURE or manufacturing to turn to, and almost none became the classic ghost town of the far west. Illinois has two typical examples of communities which almost but not quite became ghosts. At one time GALENA's lead mining boom made it the largest and most influential city in Illinois. As the lead supply diminished, Galena faded from thousands to a few hundred population but persists today as a farming center and host to hordes of tourists lured by the restored attractions of a bygone age.

NAUVOO, also, at one time was the largest and most influential city in the state, due to the great influx of MORMON settlers and their astonishing temple and other accomplishments. With the desperate departure of the Mormons, the town faded almost to nothing until the ICARIANS brought a new influx with their wine industry. That too faded, but the community continued until today, with the agricultural economy and the gradual restoration of the Mormon structures and their lure to tourists, the smaller community prospers.

KASKASKIA, Illinois, represents another kind of community fate. the one-time capital of Illinois was wiped off the map when the MISSISSIPPI RIVER cut through the narrow neck of land occupied by the town and washed away its historic buildings. Today the river covers most of the place where the capital once stood. The island left by the river is now the only part of Illinois lying "west of the Missisippi." It is now occupied by Kaskasia Memorial Park.

The community of Buckingam, Iowa, illustrates another very common type of community disappearance, through "misplacement". When the railroad bypassed the tiny community, most of the merchants and homeowners put their structures on rollers, moved to the nearest section of the railroad and called their new town TRAER in honor of an itinerant wanderer. The former site of Buckingham village is now Buckingham cemetery, a ghost town in a different sense. Similar dislocations occurred hundreds of times across the country.

Many Missouri communities also faded when minerals gave out or other economic or historic problems brought about their decline. The Missouri town of FAR WEST suffered the worst fate. Settled by the Mormons, with broad streets and plans for many fine buildings, Far West was leveled to the ground when the Mormons were driven out.

GIANT CITY STATE PARK. Illinois state park south of CARBONDALE, Illinois, on Highway 51. Established in 1927, the park contains 1,675 acres of hills, forests, and unique rock formations. During the CIVIL WAR the area was a headquarters of the KNIGHTS OF THE GOLDEN CIRCLE, a secret society of Southern sympathizers, who carried on espionage behind Union lines and encouraged draft resistance. Included in the park is the Old Stone Fort, believed to be one of seven known Indian BUFFALO traps. The park is named for streetlike passages between blocks of sandstone which resemble the walls of a city or castle.

GIBAULT, Pierre. (Montreal, Canada, April, 1737—New Madrid, Spanish Territory, 1804). Roman Catholic clergyman. Gibault was an ally of George Rogers CLARK in his campaign to gain control of the West for the Americans during the REVOLUTIONARY WAR. Gibault, vicar-general of the Illinois mission territory, was instrumental in securing the allegiance of the French residents at VINCENNES, Indiana. After he heard that Clark had captured KASKASKIA, Illinois, Gibault rang a bell, later known as the "Little Liberty Bell," to call the people to their church to pledge their allegiance and sign an oath to support the Americans. Gibault later recruited French volunteers for the expedition to recapture Vincennes from the British. For his

valuable help, Gibault received the thanks of the Virginia Assembly, but was denied the small claim of $1,500 and two acres of land.

GILBERT, Cass. (Zanesville, OH, Nov. 1859—Brockenhurst, England, May 17, 1934). Architect. Gilbert studied architecture at the Massachusetts Institute of Technology (1878-1879). After travel in Europe and service in architectural firms, he set up a practice of his own in ST. PAUL, Minnesota. Gilbert's early fame was gained when he was commissioned in 1896 to design the striking capitol of Minnesota at St. Paul. For many years the world's tallest and most talked-about skyscraper was his Woolworth Building (1913) in New York City. He was one of the notable developers of skyscraper construction techniques. In a change of pace, Gilbert was the consulting architect of the George Washington Bridge. His most famous building is the Supreme Court Building in Washington, D.C. His designs have been used in the Federal Reserve Bank of MINNEAPOLIS and for the general plan of the Universities of MINNESOTA and Texas His St. Louis Louisiana Purchase Exposition Art Building now houses that city's art museum. He was awarded the gold medal by the Academy of Arts and Sciences and was a past-president of the National Institute of Arts and Letters. The quantity and quality of Gilbert's output continue to amaze experts in the field.

GILMORE, Patrick Sarsfield. (County Galway, Ireland, Dec. 25, 1829—St. Louis, MO, Sept. 24, 1892). Bandleader and composer. He was noted for creating enormous performances of music. These reached a climax in the 1872 concert of Boston's World Peace Jubilee in which he led 20,000 choristers, 2,000 instrumentalists, including performers with church bells, cannon fire and one hundred Boston firemen pounding on real anvils in the "Anvil Chorus." Considered the leading U.S. bandmaster of the 19th century, Gilmore is credited with composing "When Johnny Comes Marching Home" (1863). He died suddenly in the midst of conducting his band.

GIST, Christopher. (MD, 1706—Cherokee country, 1759). The American frontiersman was commissioned by the Ohio Company to explore their western lands in 1750. He penetrated the Kentucky region eighteen years before the more celebrated Daniel BOONE arrived there. He then reached the WYANDOTTE village near present COSHOCTON, Ohio, on the MUSKIN-

GUM RIVER, where George CROGHAN had established a trading post. There on Christmas day, Gist was snowbound and spent the time reading the Bible aloud. The Indians were so taken with the translation of the Christmas story that they became friendly to the English for the first time. The next season Gist more carefully mapped the OHIO RIVER watershed and with George Croghan arrived at the MIAMI INDIAN village of PICKAWILANY, near present Sidney, Ohio. The Miami chief was much impressed with the visit and its accompanying gifts and said, "brother, we have heard what you have said to us....You may depend upon sincere and true friendship towards you as long as we have strength." Gist's visits with the SHAWNEE and the Miami gave the British a stronger hold on the western region, but the French soon struck back. Gist returned to New England with his reports to his parent company. He kept a careful diary and his records form one of the best early accounts of the areas in which he traveled. In 1753-54, Gist went with George WASHINGTON on his mission from the Virginia governor to win the Indians from the French. He is credited with twice saving the young Washington's life. On another similar mission to the Cherokee nation, Gist took smallpox and died.

GLACIERS. Huge masses of ice and snow which move slowly across land. Downward pressure from the ice, which may reach hundreds of feet in thickness, gradually softens the lower part of the ice which then acts like a thickly viscous liquid, permitting the great mass to slide slowly downward. During the Great Ice Age, beginning approximately one million years ago, glaciers advanced and retreated four times in North America. The last of the ice sheets retreated only about 10,000 years ago.

The first two glaciers spread the farthest and reached almost the same extremes. The earliest, known as the Nebraskan, is recognized from the drift it deposited which was entirely covered by later deposits. Drift of the Second ice sheet, the Kansan, forms much of the Midwest land surface from the driftless areas of Iowa and Wisconsin as far west as Kansas.

The exposure of this drift to erosion has caused it to lose almost all of its characteristics. MORAINES have completely disappeared and stream valleys have carved the areas sufficiently to provide effective drainage and there are none of the swamps, lakes, and waterlogged areas typical of newer glacial deposits. The drift of

the third glacier, the Illinoian, which occurred approximately 150,000 years ago, is exposed over half of Illinois, southern Indiana and a narrow strip of Ohio. Nearly half of the original drift has been cut away to form narrow valleys up to one hundred feet deep.

Land between the valleys is extremely flat as most of the ice-formed irregularities have been eroded. It is in the Wisconsin glacier, the last ice sheet, that moved into Illinois 70,000 years ago and began to recede 57,000 years ago, that the work of glaciers in the Midwest is most obvious. In the relatively short period of time since the retreat of this glacier, ending about 10,000 years ago, little change has occurred in the land. Features of the glacier are sharply defined. Parallel scratches, or striae, may be seen where rocks carried along by the glacier scratched the bedrock as they passed over. Some scratches are so delicate that they may only be seen after the rock is brushed clean and dampened. One example of heavy grooving may be seen on the limestone of KELLEY'S ISLAND, near the western end of Lake ERIE in Glacial Grooves State Park.

In the Midwest the farthest advance of the ice sheets can be seen on the edges of the nonglaciated regions of southeastern Ohio, part of southern Indiana, the extreme southern tip of Illinois and an island-shaped region including southwestern Wisconsin, northeastern Iowa and northwestern Illinois.

A listing of the dramatic effects glaciers caused in the Midwest would begin with the obliteration of a great river which once flowed from the mountains of North Carolina in an arc across northern Indiana and into an arm of the Gulf of Mexico near ST. LOUIS. The headwaters of this ancient river, called the Teays for a town standing by it in West Virginia, remains as the present-day New River. Parts of its original valley now carry segments of the ILLINOIS RIVER near Beardstown and the SCIOTO below CHILLICOTHE. The rest of its valley has been filled in with glacial drift and lake-bottom sediment. The course of the MISSISSIPPI RIVER was changed south of ROCK ISLAND, Illinois. The river, in preglacial times, had met the Teays near the present city of LINCOLN, Illinois. A lobe of glacial ice blocked this path, forcing the channel farther west.

The glaciers remodeled the GREAT LAKES, which existed as only minor water-holding basins prior to the Ice Age. One of the pre-Ice Age valleys changed by the ice ran through the STRAITS OF MACKINAC.

At one time, Lakes MICHIGAN, SUPERIOR, and

HURON were one large body of water called Lake Nipissing. As the glaciers melted, the land rose again. Lake Superior became separated from Lake Huron except for the channel of the ST. MARYS RIVER.

The DIVIDE between the drainage basins of the St. Lawrence and the Mississippi, however, remained so low that during recorded history Indians could push their canoes across it in high water rather than portage.

The most remarkable effect of the glaciation was not the erosion, but the deposit of layer upon layer of drift for thousands of square miles. Drift deposited and left in one place has been called "till" by geologists. Thoroughly decomposed glacial till is shown by the Iowa soil known as "gumbo" which appears slick and sticky when wet, but dries like concrete. "Gumbo" soils have developed in Illinoian drift, but never occur in deposits as young as those of the Wisconsin.

Geologists estimate that over the Great Lakes region the drift averages forty feet deep. In Iowa the average depth of drift is two hundred feet. One buried valley in Ohio lies under nearly eight hundred feet and a record was set just south of CADILLAC, Michigan, with 1,189 feet.

The greater part of glacial drift originated very near from where it now lies. An exception to that rule was the discovery of eleven pebble-sized, high quality diamonds in drift which originated in an area between Lake Superior and Hudson Bay.

Glaciers have also left low, stream-lined hills called drumlins. How these hills were formed is still a subject of debate. One of the famous drumlin fields, located in southeastern Wisconsin, contains nearly five thousand hills.

Near LANSING, Michigan, and in northeastern parts of Minnesota, eskers, often miles long, may be found. These long, winding ridges are thought to be the bottom deposits of streams which flowed through tunnels under the ice.

The extreme edges of a glacier are marked by moraines, a chaotic accumulation of rock. The largest moraines are located where two major ice lobes converged. Areas displaying such ridges of stone include southeastern Wisconsin in a strip running from Door Peninsula beyond the Illinois border. Moraines in Illinois and Indiana are named for the cities built upon them; the Shelbyville, Marsailles, BLOOMINGTON and VALPARAISO.

Faint arcs may be seen on the flat land southwest of Lake Erie, Lake Michigan, and Saginaw Bay.

Fine sediment, destined to be enriched by prairie grasses to become particularly suitable for mechanical cultivation, created by the glaciers often dried and then became wind-driven. This silt, or loess, is over one hundred feet thick near the Mississippi River in Illinois. This loess blanket thins farther away from the rivers. It also becomes finer in texture.

Rivers of the Ice Age bear little comparison with their weaker decendants. Valleys of these great rivers which carried mighty torrents of rushing melt water, cut sharply into the generally flat ground. Wide, U-shaped troughs with steep sides and flat bottoms mark the path of Ice Age rivers. Remnants of these grand rivers include the WABASH, ILLINOIS, ROCK and ST. CROIX.

GLASGOW, Missouri. Town (pop. 1,336); north-central Missouri; north of BOONVILLE in Howard County; named for James Glasgow, a ST. LOUIS merchant. Glasgow was platted in 1836 after three earlier unsuccessful attempts to establish a river port in the area. The town was the scene of fierce warfare during the CIVIL WAR including the torture of Colonel Benjamin Lewis by men under the command of William "Bloody Bill" Anderson. Construction of the Chicago and Alton Railroad Bridge in 1878-1879, the first all-steel bridge in the world, marked an end to the river traffic that had brought Glasgow its early prosperity.

GLENN, John Herschel, Jr. (Cambridge, OH, July 18, 1921--). The first American astronaut to orbit the earth, the third man to do so, following two Russian astronauts. After marine flight training, Glenn flew 59 Marine missions in the WORLD WAR II Pacific theater during 1944 and 1945. He won two Distinguished Flying Crosses, along with eight Air Medals. In Korea he flew 90 missions and won more awards for his service. After completing test-pilot training in 1954, he transferred to the Naval Air Test Center. As a test pilot he made the first transcontinental supersonic flight in 1957. In 1959 he became one of the first seven men in U.S. astronaut training on the Project Mercury program. After three years of rigorous training, on February 20, 1962, in four hours thirty-six minutes, Glenn circled the earth three times, covering a distance of about 81,000 miles. After his descent, Glenn was recovered from the Atlantic Ocean near the Bahamas. In his Mercury space capsule, *Friendship*, the astronaut reached a maximum altitude of 187.75 miles and a maximum velocity of 17,545 miles per hour. Greeted by President Kennedy on his arrival at Cape Canaveral and given one of New York's largest ticker-tape celebrations, Glenn became a national hero. His native state of Ohio elected him to the Senate in 1974. He was reelected in 1980 and 1986. In the 1984 presidential primaries, he explored his potential for election to that office.

GLENWOOD, Minnesota. City (pop. 2,523), west-central Minnesota, east of Morris, popular vacation city. Glenwood was platted in 1866 and named for the wooded valley occupied by Lake Minnewaska. The lake, thirteenth largest in Minnesota, is named for an Indian princess believed buried in one of the many Indian mounds bordering the lake's northern edge. The view from Mount Lookout reveals the action of glaciers eleven thousand years ago. Rocks and sand forming the hills around the lake were deposited as the glacier receded to the northwest. The basin of the lake was created when part of the glacier split off from the ice sheet. The city is site of the State Fisheries Headquarters. Indian and pioneer relics may be seen in the Pope County Historical Museum which includes a reconstructed trapper's cabin, blacksmith shop and Indian camp. A popular annual event is Waterama, held the last weekend in July.

"GLORIOUS GATE." PORTAGE between the MAUMEE and Little Wabash rivers, used by early explorers in present-day Indiana and named because it offered such a "glorious" passage from the GREAT LAKES to the watershed of the MISSISSIPPI RIVER.

GLOVER, Joshua. (—). The experience of Joshua Glover, an escaped slave, was one of the most inflamatory events leading to the CIVIL WAR. In 1854 Glover was recaptured where he was living, at RACINE, Wisconsin, by his master, who turned him over to federal agents. He was taken to federal jail at MILWAUKEE. Sherman BOOTH, editor of the Abolitionist Milwaukee newspaper, the *Daily Free Democrat,* published an account of Glover's troubles and then circulated through Milwaukee streets, urging the people to storm the jail and free Glover. They did just that, breaking down the jail doors, and parading Glover through the downtown area singing "Glory, Hallelujah!" Glover quickly disappeared, taken to freedom in Canada. Booth was then jailed for violation of the federal Fugitive Slave Act. There followed a bitter seven-year period in which the conflict

over slavery in the area became even more severe.

GNADENHUTTEN, Ohio. Town (pop. 1,-320), situated in east central Ohio on the TUSCARAWAS RIVER on U.S. route 36, between COSHOCTON and Uhrichsville. Near the town is Gnadenhutten Memorial State Park, where a monument commemorates ninety-six Christian Indians massacred in 1782 by white men. They are buried in the mound inside the park. They had been converted to Christianity at David Zeisberger's Moravian mission at SCHOENBRUNN and, under the leadership of Joshua, a Mohican elder, in 1772, they founded Gnadenhutten, which means in German "tents of grace." The nearby Indian groups were hostile to them, and they were disliked also by the many renegade settlers in the area. They held on at Gnadenhutten until 1781 when they were forced to leave by a white renegade, named Elliott, and several DELAWARE INDIAN chiefs. They spent a difficult winter on the Sandusky plains and returned to the Tuscarawas valley in February of the following year after their supplies ran low. On March 7 an expedition led by Captain David Williamson arrived at Gnadenhutten. They disarmed the men and herded them into one building, with the women and children in another. While the Indians prayed, the soldiers drank. They held mock trials and declared that the innocent victims should be executed. At dawn the merciless killings began. One militiaman alone killed fourteen. Despite being scalped, two Indian boys escaped to Schoenbrunn to warn their fellow Christians. Gnadenhutten was pillaged and burned. This uncivilized massacre understandably further aroused the Indians against the Americans.

GODFROY, Francis. (—Peru, IN, 1840) Last of the MIAMI war chiefs. Godfroy led his tribe in their last battle on the Mississinewa when General William Henry HARRISON destroyed the Miami villages to prevent Indian assistance to the British during the WAR OF 1812. Godfroy retired from warfare and established a trading post from which he became very wealthy. He was extraordinarily large, weighing nearly four hundred pounds. He died in 1840 and was buried near PERU, Indiana, in a family cemetery. His last name was that of a Frenchman who married the daughter of one of the Miami chiefs.

GOGEBIC RANGE. East-west range, extending for about eighty miles across the western tip of Michigan's UPPER PENINSULA and into northern Wisconsin. Its width varies from half a mile to a mile. From the crest the view covers vast expanses of treetops broken by small lakes. Lake Gogebic, in Michigan, is the largest in the vast area. The western end of the range is known as Penokee. Surveyor Charles Whittlesey called this region Pewabie, the Indian name for iron, but the map maker misread the name, and called it Penokie, which also might mean wild potato ground in Indian language. Iron deposits were discovered as early as 1848. The first iron ore was shipped out of the range in that year, and then millions of tons of ore poured into the shipping ports of ASHLAND, Wisconsin, and DULUTH-SUPERIOR, Wisconsin-Minnesota. The high grade ore was extracted from some of the world's deepest mines. When the high quality iron-oxide deposits were depleted after WORLD WAR II, the region began to suffer, but methods of utilizing the vast quantities of low-grade iron ore, known as TACONITE, slowly revitalized the mining communities, beginning in 1956. The great forests covering the Gobebic Range also provided a flourishing LUMBER industry until they too were wiped out. HURLEY and IRONWOOD, Wisconsin, were typical of the lawless mining-timber communities which seemed to spring up overnight. Soon after the operations began, Hurley was populated by hundreds of transient lumberjacks and miners. It was said in the region that the world's four toughest places were Cumberland, Hayward, Hurley and Hell, and that Hurley was the toughest of all.

GOLDFINCH. The state bird of Iowa. The eastern goldfinch is often called the wild canary. The finches are the world's largest family of birds, found in various forms almost everywhere. Goldfinches are found throughout most of the U.S., but there is a western variety. They are known for their meticulous nests which they maintain the year round. The goldfinch was adopted by the 45th Iowa general assembly on March 22, 1933.

GOODRICH, Benjamin Franklin. (Ripley, NY, Nov. 4, 1841— Manitou Springs, CO, Aug. 3, 1888). In 1870 Dr. Goodrich moved to AKRON, Ohio, with the theory that great things could be done with the new process of vulcanization of rubber. Vulcanization made rubber harder and stronger so that it could be used in many ways not possible before. Goodrich was able to persuade 19 Akron men to invest $1,000 each in a new plant for manufacturing vulcanized fire

hose, wringer rolls and beverage tubing. The Goodrich company went on to make the first solid rubber tires and the first pneumatic tires. Other rubber manufacturers joined the Goodrich pioneers to make Akron the rubber capital of the world.

GOSHEN COLLEGE. Coeducational Mennonite institution in GOSHEN, Indiana. Goshen College evolved from the Elkhart Academy, founded in 1894. In 1903, with $10,000 offered by the city for building, the academy was reorganized as a junior college. A four-year curriculum was adopted in 1909 and after organizational problems in the 1920s, during which Goshen College closed for one year, the school was reorganized. Goshen College is the only four-year college of the Mennonite Church in the United States. Courses are offered in theology, teacher training, and liberal arts.

GOSHEN, Indiana. City (pop. 19,665), northern Indiana city southeast of ELKHART in Elkhart County, prosperous agricultural community with a large Mennonite population. Goshen occupies the site of Fort Beane, early refuge for white settlers. Amish settlers arrived in 1841. Mennonites came to the area in 1843. In recent years many of the younger generation Amish have converted to the more liberal Mennonite faith. In 1894 the Mennonites founded an institution which was to become GOSHEN COLLEGE.

GOVERNMENT. The Midwest has generally but not always lived up to its reputation for conservatism in its state governments and the constitutions and laws under which each of its states operates. However, Wisconsin, with its WISCONSIN IDEA, propounded by Governor Robert LA FOLLETTE, has been perhaps the most forward-looking and most imitated of all the states in the U.S. in the reform of state government. Two Midwest states still operate under their original constitutions—Wisconsin, 1848, and Minnesota, 1858. Illinois, current constitution 1970, and Michigan, current in 1963, have each been governed under four constitutions. All the Midwest states have bicameral legislative bodies. Four states call these bodies the "General Assembly," while three call them the "Legislature." Each state has four principal elected officials, governor, lieutenant governor, secretary of state and attorney general. All, too, have a supreme court with a chief justice. General among the Midwest states, as well, are varied independent and semi-independent state commissions and other regulatory agencies, serving a very wide diversity of functions. All Midwest states also cooperate to one degree or another with the various applicable interstate councils, agencies and commissions and in the varied programs of interstate relations. One of the most effective of these activities was the cooperation of the Midwest states in efforts to save the GREAT LAKES from pollution, which proved to be far more effective than expected. Another successul cooperative effort for the Great Lakes was the planting of coho salmon in the small streams draining into Lake MICHIGAN. The salmon population has thrived, and fishermen find their catches are good. All Midwest states also provide varying degrees of support for local agencies, such as in education and mental health, and all participate to some degree in conservation activities. Ohio was one of the earliest in the country to voice legislative concern about conservation of all natural resources. The Midwest states all operate to some degree in the regulation of utilities, railroads and banks. Licensing of professionals is another usual state governmental function.

GRAHAM CAVE NATIONAL HISTORIC LANDMARK. Site of important finds of early humans in the Midwest. Located in Montgomery County, Missouri, Graham Cave sheltered its first inhabitants at least 10,000 years ago. Because of the number of stone tools, weapons and other important artifacts found there, the site was chosen for historic landmark status.

GRAIN BUNDLING KNOTTER. As a young man in Wisconsin, John APPLEBY (1840-1917) knew the difficulties of bundling grain by hand in the field. In the northern wheat country of Minnesota and Wisconsin and later the Dakotas, hired help was scarce, and large quantities of grain were wasted in the field. Appleby was binding sheaves on a farm in 1859 when he conceived the idea that grain could be bundled by machine. After working on the project off and on for seventeen years, Appleby patented his knotter and binder in 1878-1879. This equipment turned out bound bundles of grain as the reaper moved through the field and helped to revolutionize farming methods throughout the world.

GRAND ARMY OF THE REPUBLIC. Civil War veterans organization. The Grand Army of the Republic (G.A.R.) was founded in DECATUR, Illinois, on April 6, 1866, on recom-

mendations by Dr. Benjamin STEPHENSON, an Illinois regimental surgeon. The first national encampment was held at INDIANAPOLIS, Indiana, November 20, 1866, with ten states and the District of Columbia represented.

GRAND PORTAGE NATIONAL MONUMENT. One mile east of the village of GRAND PORTAGE, the first European settlement in Minnesota, is the beginning of a nine-mile portage to the Pigeon River on the Canadian border, used for hundreds of years by Indians who traveled from Lake SUPERIOR to the interior. The first verified Europeans to use the portage were Pierre La VERENDRYE, his sons, and fifty soldiers who arrived at Grand Portage Bay in August of 1731. VOYAGEURS used the trail to transfer trade goods from Lake Superior to the border-lake canoe routes. Trappers moving furs from the northwest to eastern markets also used the trail. Based upon archaeological excavations, the Grand Portage post of the NORTHWEST FUR COMPANY has been reconstructed. The atmosphere of two centuries ago is captured by the the warehouse, stockade, "Great Hall," and kitchen.

GRAND RAPIDS, MICHIGAN

Name: Grand Rapids takes its name from the many rapids in the Grand River which runs through the city.

Nickname: The Rapids.

Area: 44.9 square miles

Elevation: 785 feet

Population:
1984: 183,000
Rank: 80th
Percent change (1980-1984): .6%
Density (city): 4,217per sq. mi.
Metropolitan Population: 601,680
Percent change (1980-1984): .9%

Racial and Ethnic makeup (1980):
White: 80.9%
Black: 5.3%
Hispanic origin: 5,752 persons
Indian: 1,260 persons
Asian: 1,130 persons

Age:
18 and under: 27.4%
65 and over: 13.4%

TV Stations: 6

Radio Stations: 20

Hospitals: 12

Further Information: Chamber of Commerce, 17 Fountain Street, NW, Grand Rapids, MI 49503

GRAND RAPIDS, Michigan. City, seat of Kent County, situated on the GRAND RIVER, in central southwest Michigan at the site of many rapids on the river, from which it takes its name. Locally, the city is often known as "The Rapids." It was incorporated in 1850 and occupies an area of 43.4 square miles.

The city is bisected by the Grand, largest river in Michigan. It nestles in the valley 30 miles east of Lake MICHIGAN, surrounded by tall bluffs and hills on all sides, towering above the valley. The climate is often influenced by Lake Michigan. Cooled in the spring by the lake, the growing season is delayed until frost danger has passed. The warming effect of the lake in summer generally retards the frost until crops have been harvested. The snowy and cold winters usually do not include prolonged spells of severe cold. The average monthly mean temperature in January is 23.2 degrees, in July 71.5.

Michigan hardwoods have been particularly suitable for FURNITURE making. In 1836, William Haldane, a cabinet maker, became the first of many furniture manufactuers in Grand Rapids. His black walnut chairs are still in great demand at high prices. The display by Grand Rapids furniture manufacturers at the 1876 Philadelphia Centennial Exposition generated a flood of orders for the fine furniture of the city, and since that time Grand Rapids has frequently been called the "Furniture Capital of the U.S."

Today the more than 1,500 manufacturing plants provide a diverse economy, which during recent recessions has left the city in better position than many other major Michigan communities. In addition to furniture, Grand Rapids products include carpet sweepers (The Bissell company is the largest in the world of its type.) office supplies, jet avionics, and pollution control equipment. Steelcase Incorporated is the world's principal office furniture and offices systems manufacturer, employing over 7,500. Its new headquarters building is one of the city's most important. Other major employers include such internationally known names as Amway and Kelvinator.

Since it is the center of a major fruit growing area, processing of fruit is also important. A horticultural experiment station gives particular attention to care and improvement of the area fruit crops.

The city also is rapidly becoming a center of specialized health care, with hospitals praised for such specialities as burn, special surgery and poison control centers.

Despite its rugged economy, during the period of 1970 to 1984 the population continued a steady drop from 198,000 to 183,000.

In 1826 Louis Campeau established a post on the site for trading with the Indians. Population grew, and the city was incorporated in 1850.

The city is home to Calvin College, Aquinas College and Grand Rapids Baptist Bible College and Seminary.

As the boyhood home of Gerald FORD and as the base of his political activities, the city honors Michigan's only president with its Gerald Ford Museum. In another field, the Furniture Museum, a tribute to the city's pioneer industry, is the only one of its kind. There is also an art gallery, and the city supports a symphony orchestra.

GRAND RAPIDS, Minnesota. City (pop. 7,934), northeastern Minnesota, southwest of HIBBING and northwest of DULUTH, Itasca County, at the head of navigation on the MISSISSIPPI RIVER, named for nearby waters. Grand Rapids was one of the important lumbering centers in Minnesota. The LUMBER industry in this area was established by Leonard Day and his sons who arrived in 1870. As many as 600 men were hired to cut timber. The railroad reached the city in 1890 and brought enough new settlers to support incorporation in the following year. In 1894 the Pokegama Hotel boasted of having the first electric lights in the city. In 1902 a paper mill was built. Today the city is a principal tourist hub. In addition to four lakes within the city, Grand Rapids provides access to Chippewa National Forest's 1,321 lakes. A prehistoric turtle mound, found in the park, is one of the features of Turtle Mound Trail. Central School Heritage and Arts Center is located in a school built in 1895. Collections of regional arts and crafts are displayed in the building, offices, a museum and restaurant. Man's relationship to the forest is depicted at the Forest History Center. Changing exhibits illustrate forest history. Visitors are also able to observe a 1934 forest ranger cabin, a logging camp of the early

1900s, and a Modern Forest Management exhibit of genetically improved trees. There are two miles of trails for self-guided tours or cross-country skiing. Annual events include the Mississippi Melodie Showboat featuring amateur musicals and variety programs on the last three weekends of July. Tall Timber Days annually recall the lumber era and feature the U.S. Lumberjack Championships during the last weekend of July and first week of August.

GRAND RIVER (Michigan). Rising in south central Michigan only 100 miles from Lake MICHIGAN, the Grand takes such a winding course that it flows for 260 miles before emptying into the lake at Grand Haven. It is navigable from Lake Michigan for about forty miles. Waterpower from the falls at GRAND RAPIDS was responsible for the founding of that city, now one of the state's major manufacturing centers.

GRANDFATHER FALLS. This falls of the WISCONSIN RIVER above Merrill, Wisconsin, is known in history as the site of the biggest LOG JAM on record.

GRANDVIEW, Missouri. City (pop. 24,502), Jackson County, in western Missouri south of KANSAS CITY. A residential suburb of Kansas City, Grandview, incorporated in 1929, also lies in a farm region, producing corn and wheat. Richards-Gebaur Air Force Base is nearby.

GRANGE, The. Historically one of the most important farmers' organizations in the United States. The Patrons of Husbandry, popularly known as the Grange, was founded in ST. PAUL, Minnesota, in 1867 by a government clerk, Oliver Hudson Kelley, and six associates. Kelley believed struggling farmers would be attracted by a fraternal order which would give them a chance to learn advanced farming methods. Kelley organized the movement in Minnesota. By 1875 there were 850,000 members in 21,000 granges nationwide. The movement was especially strong in the Midwest, offering educational, social and legislative programs. They were successful in founding and managing of mills, stores and grain elevators but did not succeed in the manufacture of farm machines. Through their political activities, they succeeded in putting through Granger laws in Illinois, Iowa, Minnesota and Wisconsin. These laws established governmental regulations over many farm-related industries. The laws were upheld by the U.S. Supreme Court, but other organizations and parties began to take over the farmers' causes, and the Grange reverted to its original social and educational functions, gradually fading out in much of the country.

GRANITE (red). Red granite is the state rock of Wisconsin. WAUSAU, Wisconsin, is the granite quarrying center of the state. The city lies at the foot of RIB MOUNTAIN a 1,940 foot mountain of solid granite. Large deposits of red granite are also found in Missouri.

GRANITEVILLE, Missouri. Village in southeastern Missouri's Iron County. Graniteville was established as a company-owned town of the A.J. Sheahan Granite Company. Many of the buildings are made of the red granite found locally in quarries established in 1868 by B.G. Brown, governor of Missouri from 1870-1872, and Thomas Allen, founder of the St. Louis and Iron Mountain Railroad Company. North of Graniteville and reached by a short footpath, are the famous ELEPHANT ROCKS, huge masses of stone eroded by wind and water, located in Elephant Rocks State Park.

GRANT BIRTHPLACE STATE MEMORIAL. POINT PLEASANT, Ohio, Dedicated as a state memorial October 4, 1936. The log cabin section of the birthplace of general and president, Ulysses S. GRANT, had been on exhibition at the State fair grounds in COLUMBUS, Ohio, since 1895. It was returned to Point Pleasant, Grant's birthplace, southeast of CINCINNATI, in 1936, when the house was restored to its original form. A number of belongings of the general are displayed there. The Grant Memorial Church, a modest native stone building, is a part of the memorial.

GRANT, Ulysses Simpson. (Point Pleasant, OH, April 27, 1822—Mt. McGregor, NY, July 23, 1885). Union general in the CIVIL WAR and 18th President of the United States. The son of a tanner, Grant was named Hiram Ulysses at birth but dropped the first name upon muster at West Point in 1839. Graduated from the U.S. Military Academy in 1843, he served with Zachary TAYLOR in the MEXICAN WAR but was requested to resign from the armed forces in 1854 because of his drinking. At the outbreak of the Civil War he was a failed businessman of no immediate interest to the draft boards formed by President Abraham LINCOLN, but was finally enlisted in 1861 in the 21st Illinois Volunteers by a Union Army desperate for trained officers.

Ulysses S. Grant.

Grant was a relatively inarticulate tactician whose uncanny brilliance at VICKSBURG, and CHATTANOOGA brought him the appointment as Supreme Commander of the Union Army in October of 1863. A shabby man in personal appearance, he presided with systematic authority and unflinching calculation over a Union campaign that brought him the surrender of Gen. Robert E. Lee at Appomattox Court House on April 9, 1865.

Nominated for Secretary of State by President Andrew Johnson after the war, Grant was never approved by Congress for this office. He later parted ways with Johnson but was nevertheless elected President on the Republican ticket of 1868 and then reelected in 1872. Both administrations were marred by the ravages of Reconstruction and by corruption, although Grant himself never benefitted by any of the graft that was rampant during his tenure in office. At the end of his life he was financially ruined, writing his memoirs for the future benefit of his family and petitioning the military for a resumption of his resigned commission for the pension it would bring his heirs. *The Personal Memoirs of U.S. Grant* were finished only a few days before he died. Published (1895-1896) by his friend Mark Twain, they brought much needed funds to his family and are considered to rank as a principal work of autobiography.

GRAVES, Peter. (Minneapolis, MN, March 18, 1926—). Leading man and brother of James ARNESS. Graves is best remembered as the leader of the *Mission Impossible* team on the popular television series running from 1967 to 1972. Other television series in which Graves starred include *Fury* from 1955 to 1959 and the short-lived *Whiplash* of 1960. Graves has had roles in such movies as *Rogue River* (1950), *Beneath the Twelve-Mile Reef* (1953), and *Wolf Larsen* (1959). He hosted the television science program *Discovery* which has been placed in syndication.

GRAY, Hanna Holborn. (Heidelberg, Germany, October 5, 1930—) University president. Gray served as an assistant professor at the University of CHICAGO from 1961 to 1964 and as an associate professor from 1964 to 1972. From 1972 to 1974 she was a dean and professor at NORTHWESTERN UNIVERSITY, EVANSTON, Illinois. Gray became president and professor of history at the University of Chicago in 1978. She soon was frequently named as one of the most influential women in U.S. public life. Gray was co-editor of *Journal of Modern History* from 1965 to 1970.

GRAYLING, Michigan. Town (pop. 1,792), seat of Crawford County, north-central portion of Michigan's Lower Peninsula, named for the nearly extinct fish, the Michigan grayling. Grayling is a leading recreation center of its area. The town is a hub for such sports as trout fishing on the AU SABLE RIVER, as well as for canoeing, and hunting. The area has been the site of the world's longest toboggan run, sweeping contestants down 3,000 feet at speeds of nearly one hundred miles per hour. A popular summer event is the World Championship Au Sable Canoe Marathon in late July from Grayling to Osconda on Lake HURON. Birdwatchers must obtain permission to participate in guided tours of a restricted area northeast of Grayling where the rare Kirtland warbler nests after its migration from the Bahamas.

GREAT LAKES. Group of five major bodies of water, four shared by the United States and Canada. Lakes Ontario, ERIE, HURON, MICHIGAN and SUPERIOR combine to form the largest body of fresh water in the world, covering an area of 95,000 square miles. All of the Midwest states except Iowa and Missouri have direct access to the Great Lakes. Michigan has shore lines on all but one, Lake Ontario. Michigan's area includes nearly half the area of lakes Michigan,

Superior and Huron, defined by boundaries located in those lakes, and also including a small portion of lake Erie. The international boundary with Canada passes through the approximate center of all the Great Lakes except Michigan, so that Ohio and Michigan have borders with Canada, although they do not touch on land. The lakes are connected to each other by rivers, short straits and CANALS. From the elevation of Lake Superior above sea level at 602 feet, the surface level drops to 246 feet on Lake Ontario. Niagara Falls provides the largest single drop in lake levels. All the lake bottoms are below sea level except that of Lake Erie, which is the shallowest. The lake basins were gouged out by the force of the great GLACIERS of the ice age. When the glaciers melted, vast bodies of water were left. These drained to form the present lakes. The entire region south of the lakes was the scene of endless struggle between the French and English for control of the rich FUR TRADE, a conflict finally won by the British in 1763, partially won by the U.S. after the Revolution and finally decided in America's victory in the WAR OF 1812. The coming of sail and then steam power on the lakes was hastened by the opening of the ERIE CANAL in 1825. The SOO CANAL and the canalization of the ST. LAWRENCE WATERWAY, completed in 1959, opened the Great Lakes to ocean commerce through to the far ends of lakes Superior and Michigan. Canals between the lakes and Midwest rivers also opened water routes to the Gulf of Mexico.

GREAT LOCOMOTIVE CHASE. The southern railroads were a particular target of the North during the CIVIL WAR. If the railroads in the deep south could be disrupted, the economy would be further damaged. Operating from CINCINNATI, General Ormsby M. Mitchel directed a group of Ohio men in 1862 to infiltrate the South and destroy as many railroad facilities as possible. Led by James J. Andrews, the group filtered south, but before they could accomplish much, some, including Andrews, were captured, tried and executed as spies because they were not in uniform. A part of the group escaped, stole a locomotive and raced back toward the north. Southern forces commandeered another locomotive and pursued the Union men up the tracks. After many stirring incidents, the remaining northern raiders managed to get back to Ohio. Several movie and TV versions of the story have made it a popularized episode of the war.

GREEN BAY, Wisconsin. City (pop. 87,-899), Bayfield County, situated at the mouth of the FOX RIVER, at the head of the narrow bay of Lake MICHIGAN, from which it takes its name. The French called the lake extension La Baie Verte, for the color of the water. Green Bay's continental climate is somewhat modified by Lake SUPERIOR to the north and by Lake MICHIGAN and the bay to the east. The pleasant summer days are followed by cool evenings. Long and cold winters are relieved to some extent by the moderate amount of snow for its latitude. January monthly mean temperature is 15.4 degrees, July, 69.2 degrees.

With most of the precipitation falling during the summer. With the modest temperature variation, dairy farming flourishes in the Green Bay area, along with extensive plantings of vegetables, grown for canning. Nearby cherry and APPLE orchards provide for fruit canning, and potatoes are grown in areas slightly to the west.

The harbor is one of the best on the GREAT LAKES, and the city transfers water commerce to the RAILROADS for which it is a major hub. Food and dairy processing, papermaking and machinery manufacture are among the varied industries. The recorded history of Green Bay commences in 1634 with the arrival of French explorer Jean NICOLET at the WINNEBAGO INDIAN village of RED BANKS, near the present city. Nicolet had expected to land from Lake Michigan on the shores of China. To the wonderment of the Indian people gathered to watch, he came ashore wearing embroidered Mandarin robes and firing pistols in the air with both hands.

Much better known explorers, MARQUETTE and JOLLIET, took off from the Green Bay area for their journey across Wisconsin and along the MISSISSIPPI RIVER in 1673. Although missionaries had labored in the Green Bay area and trapping and trading had been carried on there for 111 years, the area had no settlement until Green Bay was founded in 1764 as the first permanent European settlement in future Wisconsin. The founder was Charles de LANGLADE, employed by John Jacob ASTOR's AMERICAN FUR COMPANY.

Green Bay's steady growth has made it the third largest city in the state. Unlike the sharp population decline of most major Midwest cities, during the decade of the seventies, the population of Green Bay showed a very modest increase from 87,809 to 87,899.

Most cities of such size do not boast giant football stadia and professional football teams, bringing mammoth crowds and almost doubling the population for some games. However, that is the boast of Green Bay. With its Packers team, the city is the smallest to support a major league franchise, and they can also claim the victory in the first Super Bowl, in 1967.

Other visitors are attracted to the first city in Wisconsin for its historical memories. The Tank cottage (1776) is the oldest building still standing in the state. The National Railroad Museum displays a wide range of locomotives and equipment and offers passenger rides in old-time coaches pulled by steam engines.

Beckoning at the head of the Green Bay region, the city welcomes visitors to one of the Midwest's major summer playgrounds, the cool attractions of nearby DOOR COUNTY.

GREEN VILLE, TREATY of. Treaty, signed at the site of the present Ohio community of Greenville [sic] by an Indian confederacy of OTTAWA, CHIPPEWA, SHAWNEE, and POTTAWATOMI tribes and the United States government in 1795, which marked an end to twenty years of war in the old Northwest. After their severe defeat at the Battle of FALLEN TIMBERS, the Indians ceded the southeastern corner of the NORTHWEST TERRITORY and sixteen settlements including the sites of CHICAGO, VINCENNES and DETROIT in return for annuities of nearly $10,000.

GREENCASTLE, Indiana. City (pop. 8,-403), seat of Putnam County, west central Indiana city west of INDIANAPOLIS; founded in 1823; named for Greencastle, Pennsylvania. The city is a center of dairy farming and lumbering, with industry at neighboring limestone quarries. Greencastle is the location of the state's oldest Methodist church, on the campus of DE PAUW UNIVERSITY, founded 1837, and the campus is the home of the Indiana Journalism Hall of Fame.

GREENFIELD VILLAGE. One-of-a-kind assemblage of notable original residences and worksites from across the United States. Greenfield Village is a 240-acre outdoor museum in DEARBORN, Michigan. Many of the structures are famous or historic buildings brought together there by Henry FORD. Others are reconstructions. The intended effect has been carried out to recreate an authentic looking small New England community. Ford placed special emphasis on the Industrial Revolution. Workshops and laboratories associated with Thomas EDISON, including Edison's Menlo Park, New Jersey, laboratory, commemorate the greatness of this American. Authenticity was heightened by bringing in the actual earth from around the original workshop. Ford had a special fondness for Edison who encouraged the young car manufacturer in his work. Among many other buildings are the 1850 Eagle Tavern, where Abraham LINCOLN often gathered during his law practice, and the homes of Noah Webster and the WRIGHT brothers. Seasonal events are held throughout the year,

Treaty of Green Ville, by Howard Chandler Christy

including the Autumn Harvest Festival in early October.

GREENFIELD, Indiana. City (pop. 11,439), central Indiana city, east of INDIANAPOLIS, seat of Hancock County, named for the green fields in the area. Greenfield is a tomato-canning center in late summer and early fall. James Whitcomb RILEY, the Indiana poet, was born here on October 7, 1849. Thousands of animals are kept at the Eli Lilly Company Biological Laboratories there for experiments in the development of pharmaceuticals. The annual James Whitcomb Riley Festival is held on or close to Riley's birthday, October 7th.

GREY, Zane. (Zanesville, OH, Jan. 31, 1875—Altadena, CA, Oct. 23, 1939). While a pupil in the ZANESVILLE public schools, Zane Grey used a cave back of his home as a studio in which to write a romantic tale about his great-great grandfather, Ebenezer ZANE, founder of Zanesville. Grey loved the outdoor life and the region around Zanesville, where his family was still very prominent. After graduating from the University of Pennsvylvania in 1896, a top athlete, Grey made a try at professional baseball but gave it up and went into dentistry. Next he tried writing. He had to pay for the publication of his first novel, *Betty Zane* (1904), based on the life of another of his relatives. Going west, Zane absorbed the sights and sounds of the late frontier and turned his attention to stories of the West. With the publication of his *Riders of the Purple Sage* in 1912, and subsequent novels, he became in his time the foremost American author of adventure stories. "Riders" sold the then unheard of number of 2,000,000 copies. Altogether, during his lifetime, over 30 million copies of his books were sold, and they continue to sell. Grey was on the best-seller list every year from 1917 to 1926, making him one of the most widely read authors of the century. His work set the tone for most of the "western fiction" of the era. His lone-wolf gunfighter characters became typical of most of the heroes of western movies and television. When he died at his home in Altadena, California, he left more than twenty manuscripts to be published over the next period of years.

GREYBEARD REGIMENT. Perhaps unique in the annals of U.S. war service, an Iowa regiment of men over the legal army age of 45 was specially authorized by the secretary of war. As the CIVIL WAR advanced into 1863, so many Iowa men, too old legally to fight, were clamoring to serve, that Iowa governor, Samuel KIRKWOOD, obtained permission to form an entire regiment, which came to be known as the Greybeards. The regiment was quickly formed, outfitted and mustered for ST. LOUIS. Although many of the men were over seventy years of age, and most were over fifty, the snappy step and smart appearance of the regiment was much appreciated when they paraded in St. Louis. Not expected to take part in actual fighting, the regiment was assigned essential duties such as guarding the railroads, escorting trains and guarding prisoners of war. Before the war ended, the Greybeards had supervised more than 160,000 prisoners. One supply train they guarded was fired on near Memphis, and two Greybeards were killed in the only actual "combat" they experienced. Their unique service was recognized when they were honorably discharged at DAVENPORT in 1865, the first group of three-year men to be disbanded.

GRIFFON (boat). First recorded large ship to sail on the GREAT LAKES. The *Griffon* was built by LA SALLE and his men to carry furs to market. Anchored in Detroit Harbor on WASHINGTON ISLAND, off the tip of DOOR COUNTY, Wisconsin. Hundreds of Indians brought canoe loads of their furs to barter. Filled with its valuable fur cargo, the ship set sail one day in 1679 and was never seen again. It is presumed to have been sunk in treacherous DEATH'S DOOR STRAIT, graveyard of countless other ships.

GRINDSTONE CITY, Michigan. Village. Located on the tip of lower Michigan's "Thumb," Grindstone City in Huron County provided the United States and the world with some of its finest abrasive stones and almost monopolized the industry for nearly one hundred years. Two factories operated until WORLD WAR I when the development of carborundum made grindstone quarrying unprofitable and drove the community out of the business.

GRINNELL COLLEGE. Founded on a gift of land from Josiah GRINNELL in 1856 as Grinnell University, it was merged in 1859 with the College of Davenport, a Congregationalist school founded in 1848, and the merged body took the present name in 1909. Although retaining some denominational ties, the college is now non-sectarian. Its academic excellence is recognized by its almost constant inclusion in the various lists of the ten best small liberal arts colleges in the United States. Its student body averages about 1,250, and the faculty numbers 118.

GRINNELL, Josiah Bushnell. (New Haven, VT, Dec. 22, 1821-Marshalltown, IA, March 31, 1891). "Go West, young man, go West!" That phrase has become a familiar and often quoted admonition. It was first coined by famed newspaperman Horace Greeley who was asked for career advice by young Congregational minister Josiah GRINNELL. The young minister, an ardent Abolitionist had preached a sensational sermon against SLAVERY in his church, the First Congregational at Washington, D.C. When the sermon cost him his job, he turned to the most outspoken of all the Abolitionists, Horace Greeley. Grinnell took Greeley's counsel seriously. The last phrase of the quotation is usually omitted. It goes, "...and grow up with the country." That is exactly what Grinnell did. He went to Iowa, where in 1854 he founded the city of GRINNELL, named in his honor, and in 1859 founded GRINNELL COLLEGE, also named for him, for his gift of the land on which the college was founded. During his lifetime, he also founded four other towns. Retiring from the ministry, he became a wool grower, continued his promotion of the Abolitionst cause, helped with the UNDERGROUND RAILROAD, helped with the founding of the REPUBLICAN PARTY and served Iowa in the U.S. Congress for two terms. He was active in promoting RAILROADS in the Midwest and worked for the development of AGRICULTURE, with particular emphasis on promoting new breeds.

GRINNELL, Iowa. City (pop. 8,868), in central Iowa's Jasper County, about thirty miles east of DES MOINES. In March, 1854, three men chose the site of this community on what was then the bare treeless prairie about halfway between the DES MOINES and SKUNK Rivers. Leading the group was the young Congregational minister, Josiah Bushnell GRINNELL, accompanied by Dr. Thomas Holyoke and the Rev. Homer Hamlin. Together they founded the community, with the stipulation that there would be no liquor sold in the town, and property would be set aside for a college. Property deeds carried the penalty of reverting back to the Grinnell estate if liquor were sold. The community is still dry. GRINNELL COLLEGE was founded only a year later. Today the town thrives with its college, almost universally designated as one of the country's ten best small schools. Small manufacturing also flourishes with more than twenty factories, many of them processing the produce of one of the country's richest agricultural areas.

GROSEILLIERS, Sieur de. (1618?—1690). Medard Chouart, Sieur de Groseilliers, and his brother-in-law Pierre Esprit RADISSON, were the first Europeans to venture into the northern Wisconsin region. In 1659 they reached the area of CHEQUAMEGON BAY, where they were portaged by the Indians across the spit that then blocked the entrance to the bay. They built a crude fort out of branches and stakes, which is supposed to have been located at the mouth of Whittlesey Creek. In the fall of 1661 the two explorers paddled up the ST. LOUIS RIVER and next year camped on the present site of SUPERIOR, Wisconsin. In their extensive travels over much of the GREAT LAKES, the two explorers may have reached as far west as present Minnesota, but that has not been proven.

GROSSE POINTE, Michigan. Village (pop. 5,901), one of the finest residential areas in the United States, fronting on Lake ST. CLAIR near DETROIT, Michigan. Grosse Pointe is comprised of four communities: Grosse Pointe Shores, Grosse Pointe Farms, Grosse Point Park and Grosse Pointe. A fifth community, Lochmoor, is also considered part of the development and was incorporated under the name of Grosse Pointe Woods in 1939. The communities developed from very narrow ribbon farms which extended back a mile or more from Lake St. Clair. Wealthy Detroit residents began building in the area during the late 1840s. The lake front became popular as a site for summer homes. Grosse Pointe Shores was incorporated as a village in 1911. There is no business section in this area. The larger homes and estates are all constructed along Lake Shore Road. Grosse Pointe Shores boasts the 85-acre estate of Edsel FORD and the Grosse Pointe Yacht Club, home port of some of the finest yachts on the GREAT LAKES. The clubhouse was completed in 1929 on fill-dirt poured 1,200 feet into Lake St. Clair. Grosse Pointe Farms, incorporated as a village in 1879, is the oldest and most developed section. Alger House was a gift of the Russell A. Alger family to the City of Detroit for the Gross Pointe branch of the Detroit Institute of Arts. Of Italian Villa architecture, the residence became the home of a permanent collection of Renaissance sculpture, painting and tapestries. The Country Club of Detroit, founded in 1897, is thought to be the oldest golf and country club in Michigan. The City of Grosse Pointe has a width of less than three-fourths of a mile. Grosse Point Park blends the hurry and noise of the busy city of Detroit with the quiet elegance of the other Grosse Pointe areas. Grosse Pointe Woods is the newest addition to the Grosse Pointe development.

GUERIN, Jules. (St. Louis, MO, Nov. 18, 1866—Neptune, NJ, June 13, 1946) Painter and illustrator. Guerin painted murals for important public and private buildings. He is best known for his murals in the Lincoln Memorial, Washington, D.C. Other buildings with his murals include the Federal Reserve Bank of San Francisco, Illinois Merchant's Bank in CHICAGO, and Louisiana's capitol in Baton Rouge.

GUERRILLA WARFARE. Style of hit-and-run warfare. In the Midwest it was practiced widely, but primarily in Missouri during the CIVIL WAR. The sentiments against the Union grew when the Federal Government authorized the formation of volunteer Kansas companies to weed out Confederate activity in southwest Missouri. These companies, known as JAYHAWK-ERS, Kansas FREEBOOTERS or Gallant Knights, raided and looted with a free hand. In retaliation and for defense, guerrilla bands were formed, but never had sufficient strength to attempt to overthrow Federal control. The history of the guerrilla is one of violent excess. On August 21, 1863, William QUANTRILL captured Lawrence, Kansas, burned 185 buildings and killed approximately 150 people. Guerrilla battles took place at such sites as Lone Tree, INDEPENDENCE, and CENTRALIA in Missouri. Frequently the forays turned into mass killings, like the Lawrence raid of Quantrill or the Centralia execution of twenty-three or twenty-four Union soldiers by William Anderson. Many of the West's infamous outlaws, including the JAMES and YOUNGER brothers, a peculiar Missouri raider named Sam Hildebrand, and the notorious BELLE STARR, began their criminal careers as guerrillas. Realization that their guardians were as bad as the Northerners they feared turned southern sympathizers against the guerrillas. Clay County residents at LIBERTY, Missouri, declared the guerrillas were "ravenous monsters of society." The relatives of one guerrilla, Jesse James, were banished from their county, and by 1880 most of the guerilla activity in the Midwest had died away.

GUEST, Edgar Albert. (Birmingham, England, Aug. 20, 1881—Detroit, MI, Aug. 5, 1959). W----. Guest, one of the world's most popular

poets, was brought to the United States in 1891 and entered in the DETROIT schools. He was associated with the Detroit *Free Press* where he wrote a column of verse and humorous sketches of everyday situations, which was probably the most widely syndicated of its kind. Serious critics deplored his light verse, but he became, perhaps, the most widely read verse writer of the day.

GUSTAVUS ADOLPHUS COLLEGE. Privately supported liberal arts college located in ST. PETER, Minnesota, founded 1862, which was originally supported by the Minnesota Conference of the Augustana Lutheran Church beginning in 1962 by the Lutheran Church in America, now no longer in existence. One of the oldest educational institutions in Minnesota. The college offers extensive music programs as well as overseas programs, including the Institute for European Studies and programs in Japan and Sweden. Religious subjects are required. A Scandinanian Studies major is offered. During the 1985-1986 academic year Gustavus Adolphus College enrolled 2,210 students and had 199 faculty.

GUTHRIE CENTER, Iowa. City (pop. 1,713), seat of Guthrie County, perched on a hillside overlooking the South Branch of the RACCOON RIVER in the southwest quadrant of the state, it was named for Edwin Guthrie, an army officer killed during the MEXICAN WAR. Despite its small size, the city is a thriving center of trade for a large segment of central-western Iowa. An outstanding attraction just to the west is Sheeder Prairie, a state preserve, conserving one of the last segments of VIRGIN PRAIRIE which once covered most of the state. Here the state has set aside for study and appreciation the remnants of the enormous reaches of shoulder-high grasses, wildflowers and wildlife which have succumbed to civilization elsewhere. To the north of Guthrie Center is Springbrook State Park and conservation center.

GUTHRIE, Sir (William) Tyrone. (1900—1971). English stage director, playwright and writer. First appearing on the London stage in 1924, Guthrie soon turned to writing and directing, in such famed theatrical groups as the Old Vic, the Festival Theatre, the Scottish National Theatre and the Sadler's Wells Company. He later directed both theater and opera in many parts of the world but is most noted in America and the Midwest for

Guthrie Theater, Minneapolis, honors sir Tyrone Guthrie.

creating the famed GUTHRIE THEATER at MINNEAP-OLIS, Minnesota. In a flower garden setting, this ultra-modern theater has become a theatrical leader, a place where prominent actors very willingly appear. Guthrie was also noted as being one of the first to write plays for radio.

HALL, Charles Martin. (Thompson, OH, Dec. 6, 1863—Daytona Beach, FL, Dec. 27, 1914). Chemist, manufacturer. While studying at OBERLIN COLLEGE, Hall became interested in the problem of separating pure aluminum from the basic ore, in commercial quantities. The matter had defied experienced scientists for more than forty year, most of whom tried heat methods of eliminating the inert materials from the aluminum. They had succeeded in producing an aluminum which was not entirely pure. After graduating, Hall addressed himself to the problem. Within only a few months of work in his house at 64 E. College Street in OBERLIN, Ohio, Hall had discovered the electrolytic process of making aluminum, independently of French inventor P.L.T. Heroult. Hall concluded his experiments on February 23, 1886, and produced a batch of pure aluminum. Although aluminum is the most abundant of all the minerals, it does not occur uncombined and free of other minerals. Hall's process made the widespread production and use of aluminum practical. He patented the process in 1889, but Heroult contested the claim, saying he had succeeded first. However, the matter was decided in Hall's favor in 1893. Heroult and Hall later became friends and collaborated in refining the techniques in what has come to be called the Hall-Heroult process, now in general use. Hall's discovery transformed the industrial, architectural and domestic worlds and paved the way for commercial aviation. The Aluminum Company of America (Alcoa) was founded by Hall in 1888 as the Pittsburgh Reduction Company, and he made a fortune from his discovery. At Oberlin, Hall had been motivated in his aluminum experiments by a lecture of his professor, Frank P. Jewett. He left the college a third of his large estate.

HALL, James Norman. (Colfax, IA, Apr. 22,

1887—Papeete, Tahiti, July 6, 1951). Author. Hall graduated from GRINNELL COLLEGE in 1910, and was a fighter pilot in 1914 in WORLD WAR I. His works include essays, stories, travel articles, poems and historical fiction. In 1920 Hall and Charles Nordhoff went to Tahiti, where they collaborated and lived for three decades. There they developed the famous trilogy, *Mutiny on the Bounty* (1932), *Men Against the Sea* (1934) and *Pitcairn's Island* (1934). Of his native state from which he had so long been a voluntary exile, Hall wrote, "Iowa for all the years I have been away from it, has always been and still is home to me."

HALL, Joyce Clyde. (David City, NE, Aug. 29, 1891—Leaward, KY, Oct. 29, 1982) U.S. manufacturer, greeting card pioneer. While still in high school, Hall began to sell postcards. After graduating, he moved to KANSAS CITY, Missouri, and with his brother started a wholesale business in postcards. In 1913, Hall became convinced that standard greetings could be printed to fit almost every occasion, and the greeting card company he and his brother founded at Kansas City in 1916 provided the business pattern followed almost universally since. They created an entire new industry. Hall devised marketing practices, such as the independent display rack. He invented the special occasion card, with appropriate cards for several hundred special occasions and events. Hallmark became the biggest name in the field and entered other related and unrelated businesses. As sponsors of quality radio and TV drama, Hall's company was also a pioneer. He conceived and carried out the plans for a mixed-use center at Kansas City which contributed to the revitalization of the city.

HAMILTON, Henry. (England —1796). Hamilton served in the British army in the West Indies and Canada during the FRENCH AND INDIAN WAR. He was appointed lieutenant governor of DETROIT in 1775, where he commanded the British forces in much of the present Midwest during the Revolutionary War. Hamilton was given the nickname "Hair Buyer" because he encouraged the Indians in their attacks on American settlers and paid for scalps. He therefore became one of the most hated men in the history of the region. Hamilton was captured by George Rogers CLARK at VINCENNES, Indiana, in 1770. Exchanged to the British, Hamilton held imperial administrative posts until his death.

HAMMOND, Indiana. City (Pop. 93,714), situated in Lake County on Lake MICHIGAN at the extreme northwest corner of the state. It was named for George H. Hammond, early industrialist there. East Chicago and WHITING lie to the north. Highland and Munster are south, and GARY is on the east. On the border with Illinois, Hammond is flanked by Calumet City on the west and by its largest neighbor, CHICAGO, on the northwest. The Little Calumet River forms part of the border, and the city is traversed by the Grand Calumet River. It was incorporated in 1884. With its location on Lake Michigan and easy access to the harbor of Chicago, Hammond would appear to have every commercial advantage of its larger neighbor, and many of these advantages have been realized. The first industry to develop was the meat packing plant established by George Hammond in 1869. Hammond was also the inventor of the refrigerated freight car, which he used to ship his meat products, encouraging the growth of the city as a rail center. When the meat packing plant burned in 1901, the city turned to other industries. As a highly industrialized center of the Calumet area, Hammond has developed a large business in steel founderies, petroleum products and publishing. Its other products include hospital and surgical supplies, forgings and railroad equipment, soaps and toilet articles.

PURDUE UNIVERSITY operates a campus at Hammond. The city holds its Little Red Schoolhouse Festival every year in late June and its annual International Culture Festival in September.

HANBY, Benjamin Russell. (Rushville, OH, 1833—Otterbein, OH, 1867). Hanby prepared for the ministry at OTTERBEIN College but became, instead, a school teacher. Helping his father operate a "station," a refuge for slaves on the UNDERGROUND RAILROAD, Hanby became interested in the plight of slaves. He was especially interested in the story of Joe SELBY, a slave who died during a desperate flight to freedom across Ohio. On his deathbed Selby spoke of his lost sweetheart, Nellie Gray. Stirred by the story, Hanby turned the account into a song and sent it to a music publisher. The resulting "Darling Nellie Gray" (1861) became an instant hit. Even in modern times it has been listed as one of the ten most popular songs of the past. It played such an important roll in the campaign against SLAVERY that it has become known as "The Uncle Tom's Cabin of Song." When Hanby wrote to his publisher inquiring about his royalties, the publisher replied, "Dear Sir: Your favor received. Nellie Gray is sung on both sides of the Atlantic. We have made the money and you the fame—that balances the account." Hanby went on to write a total of sixty-eight songs. Many of these were popular in their day, and some are still popular. The Hanby home at WESTERVILLE, Ohio, has been restored and preserves remembrances of the Hanby family, with a large collection of Hanby songs.

HANCOCK, Michigan. City (pop. 5,100), Houghton County, northern region of Michigan's UPPER PENINSULA near Lake SUPERIOR, named for John Hancock. The copper boom of the 1880s in the UPPER PENINSULA brought Finnish farmers and Cornish miners to America. Many settled near Hancock. A tasty reminder today of their presence is the pasty, a meat pie miners carried to work for lunch. Suomi College in Hancock, founded 1896, is the only college established by Americans of Finnish descent. Students and faculty celebrate FinnFest in late July. To benefit commerce, residents dredged Portage Lake and cut a canal to Lake SUPERIOR. Shippers are now able to avoid the dangerous waters off Keweenaw Point. Arcadian Copper Mine no longer operates, but provides a quarter-mile guided walking tour. The Quincy Mine Hoist is exhibited on US 41 north of town. This hoist is reputed to be the largest steam-powered hoist ever constructed. In operation the hoist could lift ten tons of ore at a rate of 3,200 feet per minute.

HANNIBAL, Missouri. City (pop. 18,811), Marion and Rolls Counties, in northeastern Missouri on the MISSISSIPPI RIVER. As the boyhood home of Mark Twain, Samuel CLEMENS, many of the local attractions celebrate the writer. Twain's name appears on a bridge, lighthouse, museum, and statue. Each July, Tom Sawyer Days provides a Mark Twain fence painting contest. Hannibal was also the birthplace of Admiral Robert E. Coontz and portrait painter Carroll Beckwith. The site for this industrial city was granted in 1818. The community grew slowly until the railroad came in 1856. Present industries include the manufacture of shoes, STEEL, cement, and lumber products. There are also grain and dairy farms. Hannibal-LaGrange College is found here. Attractions include the Mark Twain Museum and Boyhood Home, Becky Thatcher House, Mark Twain Cave and the Tom and Huck

Statue. The Adventures of Tom Sawyer Diorama Museum offers three-dimensional miniature scenes from the book. There is an Historic Crafts Festival the first weekend of November.

HANOVER COLLEGE. A privately supported liberal arts college in Hanover, Indiana. Hanover was founded in 1827 by the Presbyterians as a manual labor college. It is the oldest of the four-year private colleges in Indiana and grants the bachelor's degree. There are 31 buildings on a 600-acre campus. During the 1985-1986 academic year, the college enrolled 1,007 students and employed 73 faculty members.

HARDING, Warren Gamaliel. (Blooming Grove now Corsica, OH, Nov. 2, 1865—San Francisco, CA, Aug. 2, 1923). Twenty-ninth President of the United States. Harding studied at Ohio Central College, moved with his family to MARION, Ohio, and began a journalistic career which brought him a place in the journalism hall of fame of OHIO STATE UNIVERSITY. He bought the Marion *Star* and built a strong Republican political base in Ohio. In 1899 he went to the state legislature and in 1904 became lieutenant governor of Ohio. He lost a bid for the governorship but continued to rise politically. At the Republican national convention in 1912, he was chosen to present the nomination of William Howard TAFT of Ohio. In 1914 he was elected to the U.S. Senate, where he had an undistinguished term. One observer said his term was reminiscent of the Gilbert and Sullivan quotation, "He always voted at his party's call and never voted for himself at all." However, a group of his fellow Republican senators proposed his name for president at the Republican convention of 1920. When the convention became deadlocked, Harding was thought of as an ideal compromise candidate. He received the nomination on the tenth ballot and ran against Democrat James Cox, also of Ohio. According to the New Columbi Encyclopedia, "His vague pronouncements, his ambivalence about the League of Nations and lack of commitment to specifics helped him win the election."

The election was marked by a strange coincidence. Both Harding and Cox were newspaper men. The Single Tax Party ran Robert C. Macauley, a reporter from Philadelphia, so that all three of the 1920 candidates had newspaper connections.

The election of Harding was the first to be

Warren G. Harding

reported by radio, when Leo H. Rosenberg of Pittsburgh's KDKA broadcast the news of Harding's election.

Harding had promised to form a cabinet of only the "best minds." In many instances Harding chose his administrative team well, but he also chose others with little civic responsibility.

Another source had the most succinct comment about the president. "The administration that followed was marked by one achievement, the Washington (naval) Conference (1921-1922)."

In August, 1923, Harding became the first president to visit Alaska. It is thought that on this trip he received some notice of scandals in his administration which had been kept from him until that time. On his way home, at San Francisco Harding died unexpectedly under circumstances still not entirely explained. So he was not troubled by the humiliating scandals which plagued the administration he left behind, including but not limited to, the Teapot Dome scandal, involving his secretary of the interior, Albert B. Fall, and attorney general, Harry M. Daugherty.

Warren G. Harding was the oldest of eight children. When he was 25 years of age, on July 8, 1891, he married Florence Kling De Wolfe at Marion, Ohio. She was five years older, divorced, and had one son. The Hardings were married for 31 years, and they had no children. Mrs. Harding survived her husband for only about a year.

On December 20, 1927, their bodies were removed from a vault in Marion, Ohio,

Cemetery to a grand new memorial. Dedicated on June 16, 1931, by President Herbert HOOVER and Governor George White of Ohio. The Harding Memorial at Marion, Ohio, has been called the most beautiful in the state. In the center of the monument are the sarchophagi of the Hardings, covered by two slabs of emerald pearl Labrador granite.

HARMAR, Josiah. (Philadelphia, PA, Nov. 10, 1753—Philadelphia, PA, Aug. 20, 1813). Army officer. Harmar's military career included service in the Third and Sixth Pennsylvania Regiments in 1776-1777 before joining the Continental Army under George WASHINGTON from 1778 to 1780 and Greene in the South from 1781 to 1782. In 1784 he was placed in command of the army. In 1790 he led a campaign against the MIAMI Indians in the Ohio country, attempting to put down the Indian menace. He was defeated by Chief LITTLE TURTLE. Harmar's troops were poorly trained and lacked discipline. Harmer felt it would be almost impossible to win against the Indians until better trained troops were available in the back country. He attempted to point out that more trouble would come, but the new commander, Arthur ST. CLAIR (1736-1818), did nothing to remedy the situation. Harmar retired to Pennsylvania. When St. Clair was defeated by Little Turtle in 1791 in one of the worst setbacks in the army's history, Harmar's warning proved to be all too true.

HARRIS, Charles K. (Poughkeepsie, NY, 1865—New York, NY, 1930). Songwriter. The Milwaukee composer of the 1890s is listed by the state's promotion agency as one of the "Hundred Great Wisconsin People." He gained world fame and became one of the wealthiest in his field with the publication of his song "After the Ball Is Over" (1892). Of his many other tunes, one of the most popular was "Break the News to Mother" (1897).

HARRIS, Julie. (Gross Pointe Park, MI, Dec. 2, 1925—). American stage actress now best known for such films as *The Member of the Wedding* (1950), *Forty Carats* (Tony Award, 1969) and *The Belle of Amherst* (Tony Award, 1976).

HARRIS, William Torrey. (North Killingly, CT, Sept. 10, 1835—Washington, DC. 1909). Philosopher and educator, United States Commissioner of Education. Harris rose from a teaching position at ST. LOUIS to become school superintendent. He was instrumental in founding one of the first public school kindergartens in the United States, established in St. Louis in 1873. Harris began an intensive study of philosophy, founding the *Journal of Speculative Philosophy*. This journal published many articles on the philosophy of Georg Hegl, Charles S. Peirce, William James and John Dewey. In 1880 he resigned from the St. Louis schools to help Bronson Alcott found the Concord School of Philosophy at Concord, Massachusetts. He was U.S. commissioner of Education from 1889 to 1906. Credited with writing 479 books, Harris had a major influence on educational practice in this country through the widespread dissemination of his educational philosophy, as expressed in his books, lectures and articles. His annual reports as superintendent at St. Louis were considered models for other superintendents. He was editor-in-chief of *Webster's International Dictionary*, beginning in 1900. Considered to be the most important of his hundreds of books is *Introduction to the Study of Philosophy* (1889).

HARRISON, Benjamin. (North Bend, OH, Aug. 20, 1833—Indianapolis, IN, Mar. 13, 1901). Twenty-third U.S. President of the U.S., lawyer. Grandson of William Henry HARRISON, Benjamin graduated from MIAMI UNIVERSITY in Ohio in 1852. He moved to INDIANAPOLIS, Indiana, practiced law, advanced in Indiana Republican politics and then became a brigadier general in the CIVIL WAR.

Returning to law practice in Indianapolis after the war, he enjoyed a steady rise in both his profession and politics. He supported the Radical Reconstruction after the war. Although failing in two attempts at the Indiana governorship, in the latter (1876), he gained such national publicity that he was considered as a likely nominee for president at the ninth Republican Party Convention. Meeting in Chicago's Civic Auditorium June 9-23, 1888, the convention nominated Harrison on the eighth ballot. His campaign has been called the country's most corrupt for that high office. Although his opponent, Grover Cleveland, garnered a slightly larger popular vote, Harrison was chosen the winner by the Electoral College. Harrison is the only president in U.S. history to have been both preceeded in the presidency and followed in the presidency by the same man, Grover Cleveland. Harrison also was the only president who was the grandson of a president, William Henry Harrison.

He was inaugurated March 4, 1889, on the east portico of the capitol during a torrential rain storm. Despite the rains and high winds, he had ridden to the capitol in an open carriage and had delivered his inaugural address. Twelve-thousand people attended his inaugural ball.

His presidency included some new approaches to international relations through his capable secretary of state, James G. Blaine. Harrison presided at a unique point in American history. More states were admitted to the Union during his presidency than that of any other president. These included North and South Dakota, Montana, Washington, Idaho, and Wyoming. The economy also reached a turning point in the Harrison era. The Congress during his term was the first ever to appropriate a budget of a billion dollars.

Harrison's domestic politics were generally unpopular because of the Silver Purchase Act, the McKinley Tariff, the excesses of the Veterans Bureau and, particularly, because of Harrison's financial and labor policies. His presidency ended with one term, in 1893, with the succession of Cleveland for his second term.

Harrison returned to his Indianapolis law practice. In 1901 his *Views of an Ex-President* was published.

Benjamin Harrison was the fifth of his father's thirteen children, the second of ten children of a second marriage. Benjamin first married Caroline Lavinia Scott Harrison on October 20, 1853. They had two children, were married for 39 years, and she died October 25, 1892. The president survived her for eight years.

After his term in the White House, on April 6, 1896, Benjamin Harrison married Mary Scott Lord Dimmick Harrison. She was the niece of the first Mrs. Harrison and had lived in the White House for six years, helping with the care of her aunt, who had become an invalid, but she was never mistress of the White House. Mary and Benjamin Harrison had a daughter, born February 21, 1897. She was younger than the president's four grandchildren. Mary Harrison survived the president for almost 47 years. The president and both of his wives are buried in Indianapolis.

HARRISON, William Henry. (Charles City Co., VA, Feb. 9, 1773—Washington, DC, Apr. 4, 1841). Ninth President of the United States. He was a WAR OF 1812 general and served the shortest term of any president. Although not a Midwest native, he is usually considered as a Midwesterner for his association with the region in Ohio and Indiana. Son of a wealthy and politically prominent father, he attended Hampden-Sydney College, then (1790) studied medicine under famed Dr. Benjamin Rush.

After joining the army in 1791 he was sent to the old NORTHWEST TERRITORY where most of his life in public service was centered.

After serving as an aide to General Anthony WAYNE, he led several campaigns against the Indians, including the decisive Battle of FALLEN TIMBERS (1794).

Resigning from the army, Harrison was made secretary of the territory in 1799. He became governor of Indiana Territory in 1800, holding the position until 1812.

He gained fame in the wars against the Indians. Best remembered of his successes was the battle with the Indians on the shores of the TIPPECANOE RIVER for which he gained national fame. He was perhaps more influential than anyone else in opening Ohio and Indiana to settlement through treaties with and wartime successes over the Indians.

During the WAR OF 1812, he secured final control over much of the old Northwest Territory by his victories over the Indians and the British. He led the victorious American forces in the crucial battle with the British and Indians at Thames, Ontario, Canada, in October, 1813. In 1814, Harrison resigned from the army and in the same year oversaw the final peace treaty with the Indians in the area.

He moved to NORTH BEND, Ohio, in 1815. His public service continued in the U.S. House, the Ohio House and Senate (1819 to 1828). After being out of the public eye for several years, he headed the party of dissident Whigs but lost to Martin Van Buren in the presidential election of 1836.

In 1840 at the Whig Party Convention in Zion Lutheran Church, Harrisburg, Pennsylvania, he won the nomination and conducted a brilliant campaign for the presidency. Harrison is credited with being the first politician to use public relations in political campaigning. Although his victory at Tippecanoe was relatively minor, he linked that victory with his vice presidential candidate John Tyler in the oft-quoted slogan "Tippecanoe and Tyler Too." Publicity of the log cabin and hard cider campaign (reminders of his conquests on the frontier) transformed the aristocratic Harrison into a tough frontiersman and brought fame to Tyler as well, and Harrison achieved the presidency. Media hoopla in presidential campaigns has grown ever since.

On inauguration day, at the age of 68,

William Henry Harrison.

Harrison rode to the capitol in an open carriage, refusing to wear either hat or coat in spite of the cold and stormy weather. He read the longest inaugural address on record, 8,578 words, extending over an hour and forty-five minutes. After the ceremony he led the inaugural parade to the White House, then attended three inaugural balls. Sadly, the rigors of the campaign were so overwhelming and the inaugural day was so taxing that, after only 31 days in office, Harrison died of a respiratory ailment, the first president to die in office and the first to lie in state in the White House.

His death occurred before what appeared to be a brilliant government organization could take effect.

William Henry Harrison was the youngest of seven children. He married Anna Tuthill Symmes Harrison at North Bend, Ohio, on November 25, 1795. They were married for 45 years and had ten children. She was only two years younger than the president, but she survived him for almost twenty-three years. The Harrison home, Grouseland, at VINCENNES, Indiana, has been preserved and refurnished as an historic shrine.

HARRISONVILLE, Missouri. City (pop. 6,372), seat of Cass County in west-central Missouri thirty miles south of INDEPENDENCE. Harrisonville, centered in prosperous farm country, was the home town of the YOUNGERS, outlaw brothers who rode with Jesse JAMES. Colonel William Henry Younger once owned a large farm in the area before moving to town where he owned an interest in two large stores and had a contract with the United States Government to carry mail. The outlaw career of the three Youngers was provoked by a terrorism campaign by some Union army officers which resulted in the death of the senior Younger and destruction of the Younger homes in the area. Today the city is a thriving livestock hub.

HARRY S TRUMAN NATIONAL HISTORIC SITE.

At INDEPENDENCE, Missouri. Harry S (no period) TRUMAN (1884-1972), the 33rd President, called this Victorian structure home from 1919 until his death in 1972. Constructed by Mrs. Truman's grandfather, it was known as the "Summer White House" from 1945 to 1953 and was the only home ever owned by the Trumans.

HART, Charles W.

(Charles City, IA, July 6, 1872—Missoula, MT, Mar. 14, 1937). Co-inventor of the tractor. At the University of WISCONSIN, Hart met Charles H. PARR of I O W A CITY. Upon graduation in 1896, they established a shop at MADISON, Wisconsin. In 1898 they moved to CHARLES CITY, Iowa, where they produced a new type of farm equipment, an oil-cooled engine incorporated in a stationary platform. Realizing that a mobile farm machine, which could actually go into the fields and perform a variety of functions, would be invaluable in agriculture, the two men experimented with a means of adding "traction" to their machine. When they perfected a new traction vehicle, they called the resulting machine a "tractor," and the term they invented has been in use ever since. By 1910 10,000 tractors had already been sold, demonstrating the value of their invention. They founded the Hart-Parr Company, a leading producer of farm implements at Charles City.

HARVEY FAMILY.

Louis P. Harvey and his wife were prominent Midwesterners in the CIVIL WAR. Louis Harvey was Wisconsin's "seventy-three-day governor." He received this name as a result of his concern for Wisconsin troops in battle. In 1862, when reports from the front told of the needs for medical supplies for Wisconsin soldiers at the front, Governor Harvey called on his state to provide medicines and other needed items. He volunteered to visit the war front to deliver those generously provided necessities. Tragically, he fell into the Tennessee River while trying to get from one boat to another, and his body was recovered sixty-three miles downstream. He had been in office only seventy-three days. His wife, Cordelia, felt it was her duty to carry on her husband's good work in whatever way she could. She found that servicemen were dying because of poor conditions in army hospitals, especially where Union troops were fighting in the hot and humid South. She managed to have three appointments with President Abraham LINCOLN, who was not pleased with the lady's interference. However, he finally issued an order establishing army hospitals in the more healthful climate of Wisconsin. Three such hospitals were established in that state, one named in honor of the late governor. His wife came to be called the "Angel of Wisconsin." When the war was over, Cordelia Harvey was responsible for the conversion of the Harvey Hospital into a home for war orphans.

HASTINGS, Minnesota.

City (pop. 12,827), seat of Dakota County, east-central Minnesota; southeast of ST. PAUL ; located at the convergence of the MISSISSIPPI, ST. CROIX, and VERMILLION rivers; an important agricultural center in Minnesota, with light manufacturing. White settlement began in 1831 when Joseph R. Brown moved to the area and raised wheat. Alexis Bailly, Sr., began the first permanent settlement in 1850. The small settlement was called Oliver's Grove, named for Lt. William Oliver whose supply boat for the construction of FORT SNELLING became stuck in the ice there in 1819. By 1853 the settlement had grown and was renamed Hastings, for the middle name of Henry Hastings SIBLEY, Minnesota's first governor. Water power for mills helped establish Hastings as one of the important wheat markets of the Northwest. Remains of Ramsey Mill, the first flour mill in the state, built by Alexander Ramsey in 1857, are visible today near Hastings. The U.S. Army Corps of Engineers' Lock and Dam No. 2 has created a large lake there, used for recreation. An observation tower provides a view of boats and barges passing through the 600-foot lock which lifts vessels twelve feet. The Carpenter-St. Croix Valley Nature Center, near the ST. CROIX RIVER, provides fifteen miles of trails for cross-country skiing or snowshoeing. Rivertown Days, celebrated the last weekend in July, includes town tours, an arts and crafts fair and theater performances. A highlight of the weekend is Flotilla Frolic, a boat parade accompanied by music and fireworks. Hastings, one of five Minnesota "Main Street" towns on the National Register of Historic Buildings, has sixty buildings of historical significance.

HAUN'S MILL.

Site of a MORMON massacre in Missouri on October 30, 1838, near present BRECKENRIDGE, Missouri. Public officials in

Missouri had declared that the Mormons were a threat to the public good. When an estimated two hundred militia came upon a small group of Mormons near Breckenridge, in a brief fight eighteen Mormons were killed. These included women and children, according to the Mormons. The remaining Mormons were denied permission to bury the bodies which were thrown down a well by the militia. Statewide opposition to the Mormons resulted in their flight from Missouri, ending in 1839 when all had left. Since the massacre, visiting Mormons have carried off all traces of the mill which had become a Mormon shrine. Today the site is marked by a millstone in the corner of the Breckenridge, Missouri, park.

HAWTHORN BLOSSOM. Missouri state flower. The hawthorn tree, surprisingly, is a member of the vast rose family, so in a sense Missouri's state flower might be called a kind of rose. The trees are widely distributed in most temperate climates, particularly in North America. The clusters of white flowers in the spring gradually mature to colorful fall fruit, resembling tiny apples, and some can be used in jellies. The very hard hawthorn wood is used for tool handles and other small items.

HAY. Wild and cultivated grasses and other plants mown and dried for use as animal fodder. Principal hay crop in the Midwest now is alfalfa. Annual hay production in the Midwest exceeds 50 million tons, about one third of the nation's total. Wisconsin far exceeds the other Midwest states in hay production, with Michigan next in the region, followed by Iowa. Indiana has the lowest hay production in the region. Because of its use as fodder, hay production predominately fluctuates along with livestock production for meat and diary products.

HAY, John. (Salem, IN, Oct. 8, 1838—Newburg, NH, July 1, 1905). United States secretary of state (1898-1905) under Presidents MC KINLEY and Theodore Roosevelt. Hay practiced law in SPRINGFIELD, Illinois, next door to Abraham LINCOLN, and served as a private secretary to Lincoln until the assassination. He held a variety of diplomatic and private posts before becoming the first assistant secretary of state from 1879 to 1881. As secretary, Hay was responsible for the Open Door Policy with China and negotiated treaties with Colombia, England and Panama which, latter, led to the construction of the Panama Canal. Although he is best remembered as a diplomat, Hay was a notable poet and writer. His poems were published in an 1871 volume entitled *Pike County Ballads and Other Pieces*. His record of impressions of and travels in Spain resulted in *Castilian Days*, also in 1871.

HAY, Merle. (Glidden, IA, July 20, 1896—Artois, France, Nov. 3, 1917). Private Hay gained unhappy prominence as one of the first three members of the American Expeditionary force to be killed during WORLD WAR I. In recognition, Iowa has honored the name in several ways. The legislature designated the road from DES MOINES to Camp Dodge as Merle Hay Memorial Highway, on which a large shopping center now carries his name. The body was returned to Glidden, where memorials were erected.

HAYES, Rutherford Birchard. (Delaware, OH, Oct. 4, 1822—Fremont, OH, Jan. 17, 1893), Nineteenth President of the United States. Hayes graduated from KENYON COLLEGE in 1843 and Harvard Law School in 1845. He practiced law in CINCINNATI and was made city soliciter in 1858. Volunteering in the CIVIL WAR, he was wounded several times and left the service as a major general of volunteers. Without campaigning, he was elected to Congress by Ohio Republicans of his district while still in war service but refused to take his seat until he left the army in 1865.

Hayes was a three-time governor of Ohio, first from 1867 to 1873. Due to the precedent of limiting service to two terms for governor, Hayes did not seek reelection. However, he was dismayed by Democratic gains in Ohio and regained the governor's chair in 1875. The national attention given his campaign aided his plans to run for president. He was also aided in this quest by the selection of Cincinnati's Exposition Hall as the site of the Republican Party national convention of 1876. There he was nominated for president on the seventh ballot. During the campaign, he managed to unify the old guard and reform wings of the party.

At the time of that famous election, reconstruction from the Civil War was still going on in the South. The chaotic conditions brought contested elections in several southern states. Hayes' Democratic opponent, Samuel Tilden, appeared to have won, but the Republicans contested the election in Oregon, Louisiana, Florida and South Carolina. An electoral commission was created by Congress. With eight Republicans and seven democrats,

Rutherford B. Hayes.

the commission voted strictly along party lines and gave enough of the disputed votes to Hayes to provide a margin of one vote in the electoral college. In the meantime, Southern Democrats agreed to go along with Hayes' election in exchange for the withdrawal of all federal troops from Louisiana and South Carolina. The decision was made only three days before the date set for the inauguration.

Because of the attendant confusion, Hayes took the oath of office on Saturday, March 3, 1877 in the Red Room of the White House, the first time such a ceremony had been held in the mansion. There was a torchlight parade on Monday night, followed by a reception, but there was no inaugural parade or ball.

The close election and the partisan vote turned many politicians away from Hayes and made his administration difficult. Hayes' first important step was to carry out the compromise which won him the commission's support. That was to remove all federal troops from the South, giving the states of the region autonomy for the first time since the Civil War. Northern hardliners thought Hayes was "soft" on the South, but through Hayes' effort, much of the conflict disappeared, and some prosperity returned to the Southern states. Hayes worked to promote civil service, managed to fire corrupt officials and improve the currency situation, in which specie payments were resumed and coinage of silver also began once more. As his administrative ability and honesty became apparent, public admiration for him grew. However, from the beginning, Hayes had declared that one term presidencies were the best for the country. He kept a vow not to seek a second term and retired from the presidency after only one term.

He wrote, "Nobody ever left the Presidency with less regret, less disappointment, fewer heartburnings, or more general content with the result of his term...than I do."

In retirement he gave his support to several worthy causes. His diary, containing a record of the activities of every day of his presidency, is one of the most important documents of the period. It is now in the possession of the Hayes Memorial at FREMONT, where Hayes and his wife are buried.

Rutherford B. Hayes was the youngest in a family of five children. At the age of 30 he married Lucy Ware Webb Hayes at Cincinnati, Ohio, on December 30, 1852. They had eight children and were married for 40 years before her death on June 25, 1889. The president survived her by three years.

The Hayes property, SPIEGEL GROVE, was turned over to the state in 1915, and the house and memorial are open to the public.

HAYMARKET RIOT. Violent incident in CHICAGO, Illinois, arising from the eight-hour day movement in the 1880s. Attempts to establish the eight-hour day continued throughout the last half of the nineteenth century. Trade unions and "eight hour leagues" often resorted to strikes and demonstrations. At one such demonstration, in Chicago, several strikers were shot and killed. On May 4, 1886, a meeting of labor leaders, newspaper editors, Mayor Carter Harrison and over one hundred police was scheduled in Haymarket Square, Chicago. After the mayor left, the crowd was ordered to disperse, but a bomb was thrown by an unknown person. The explosion killed seven policemen and injured 60 spectators. Eight anarchists were arrested and convicted of conspiracy. In 1887 four were hanged. One committed suicide. In 1893, Governor John ALTGELD pardoned the other three because he considered their trials had been unfair. As a result of the bombing, the eight-hour day movement received a setback for a generation.

HAYNES, Elwood. (Portland, IN, Oct. 14, 1857—Kokomo, IN, April 13, 1925). Inventor. Elwood Haynes was one of the pioneers in development of American AUTOMOBILES. In 1893-1894 he designed and constructed a horseless carriage, the oldest American automobile in existence and now on exhibit at the Smithsonian Institution. He was the first to use aluminum in automobile engines and was the inventor and builder of a rotary engine in 1903. Haynes discovered tungsten chrome steel and developed an alloy of cobalt and chromium for making cutting tools. The Haynes Stellite Company manufactured tools from 1912 to 1920 and developed "stainless steel" which was patented in 1919.

HAYWARD, Wisconsin. City (pop. 1,698), seat of Sawyer County, situated in northwest Wisconsin on the Namekagon River, was named in honor of Anthony Judson Hayward, a local sawmill owner. Once the center of important lumbering operations, Hayward refused to become a ghost town, as had so many others, when the vast forests were reduced. Instead, the community turned to its extraordinary opportunities for summer recreation. It became what was soon called an "elastic town." During the summer months the population swelled to five or six times its normal size, transformed into a bustling resort. At the center of one of the many Wisconsin lake regions, headquarters of the great Chequamegon National Forest, Hayward's summer theme is forest recreation. Historyland exhibits an old-time logging camp and Indian museums. The Lumberjack World Championships are held at Historyland in late July. Logrolling, climbing, chopping, sawing and other related events bring enthusiastic crowds each year. Hayward also offers the National Fresh Water Fishing Hall of Fame. The main building is built to resemble a giant muskie, 143 feet long and four stories high, with the mouth forming an observation deck. World record catches and other fishing "tall tales" are explained in exhibits, along with angling artifacts and outboard motor historical exhibits in four other museum buildings. The National Musky Festival is held at Hayward every June.

HEARST, George. (Franklin County, MO, Sept. 3, 1820—Washington, DC, Feb. 28, 1891). Prospector, mine owner and senator. Hearst accumulated great wealth through mineral discoveries in the American West. His holdings included the Homestake Mine in South Dakota, the Anaconda Mine in Montana, and the Ophir Mine in Nevada. He served as a member of the California Assembly from 1865 to 1866 and acquired the San Francisco *Daily Examiner* in 1880. He turned the management of the newspaper over to his son, William Randolph Hearst in order to give his own attention to politics. In 1883 George ran unsuccessfully for a seat in the United States Senate from California, but in 1886 he was appointed to an unexpired senate term. With the support of the

Examiner, he was elected to a full term in 1888 and served until his death. George Hearst founded family and publishing dynasties which continue to the present time.

HECHT, Ben. (New York, NY, Feb. 28, 1893—New York, NY, Apr. 18, 1964). The controversial American writer grew up in Wisconsin and gained his fame in CHICAGO. He began working for Chicago NEWSPAPERS while still in his teens. Between 1918 and 1920 he was a correspondent in Germany and Russia for the Chicago *Daily News*. With Charles MacArthur he produced his most famous work, the play *The Front Page* (1928), which reflected his newspaper experiences. Hecht became more and more involved in the Chicago literary scene, including among his friends many of the future great writers of the day. In 1923 he founded and edited for two years the Chicago *Literary Times*. In addition to plays, he produced novels and collections of short stories and directed and produced many motion pictures. Other well-known works include *Twentieth Century* (1933), again with MacArthur, and his autobiography *A Child of the Century* (1954). *The Scoundrel* screenplay won Hecht and MacArthur the Academy Award in 1935. Hecht was active in the support of Jewish refugees, and his later books reflected that interest.

HEMINGWAY, Ernest. (Oak Park, IL, July 21, 1898—Ketchum, ID, July 2, 1961). Author. Hemingway was one of the most famous American writers of the century. After high school, he became a reporter in KANSAS CITY. During WORLD WAR I he joined a volunteer ambulance unit in Italy where he was wounded, supposedly severely. Staying on in Europe, he became a part of the literary scene in France, including association with many famous American expatriates. His World War I experiences inspired *A Farewell to Arms* (1929), assuring his reputation. His writings reflected his many interests, including bullfighting and African big game and the Civil War in Spain, which brought him to write one of his best-known works, *For Whom the Bell Tolls* (1940). His WORLD WAR II reporting took him on many of the major campaigns in Europe and led to his *Across the River and into the Trees* (1950). He won the PULITZER PRIZE in 1953 for his novel *The Old Man and the Sea*. He received the 1954 NOBEL PRIZE for literature. Hemingway developed a type of male character who typically faced violence and destruction with courage. The

"Hemingway code" called for unemotional behavior at dangerous times. He died of a self-inflicted gunshot wound at his Ketcham home. Early Paris sketches of his life were collected and appeared posthumously with the title *A Moveable Feast* (1964).

HENNEPIN, Louis. (Ath, Belgium, April 7, 1640—1701). Clergyman and explorer. As a companion of LA SALLE (1643-1687), Hennepin explored much of the Illinois country. Perhaps more importantly, Hennepin was one of the first white explorers of the upper Midwest. In 1680 he joined the expedition of Michel Aco on the upper MISSISSIPPI at the request of LA SALLE. He and two companions were captured by the SIOUX INDIANS somewhere near Lake PEPIN. They then wandered about much of the Minnesota countryside, accompanying the Indians on hunting expeditions. The three were rescued by the Sieur DULUTH on July 25, 1680. During his captivity Hennepin discovered the falls at the future site of MINNEAPOLIS and named them ST. ANTHONY FALLS after his patron saint, Anthony of Padua. He went to France in 1682, but was expelled for unknown reasons in 1690. Hennepin was unable to return to the New World, despite his pleas to both England and France, and he made his way to Rome. No records of him exist after 1701. He was the author of a book entitled *New Discovery of a Very Great Region Situated in America* published safely in 1697 after La Salle's death, in which he claimed credit for many of LaSalle's discoveries.

HERBERT HOOVER NATIONAL HISTORIC SITE. At WEST BRANCH, Iowa. The birthplace, home and boyhood neighborhood of the 31st President. The gravesite of President and Mrs. HOOVER and the Hoover Presidential Library and Museum are within the park. The library and museum are administered by the National Archives and Records Service.

HERMANN, Missouri. Town (pop. 2,695), eastern Missouri, in Gasconade County near the MISSOURI RIVER. Hermann was established in 1837 as a colony of the German Settlement Society of Philadelphia, Pennsylvania. The members in Philadelphia were concerned that their children would lose their German heritage among so many other nationalities in the eastern part of the United States. Scouts were sent to Indiana, Missouri, and Illinois in search of a remote area for a settlement where they could enjoy the advantages of America without losing their uniqueness. Missouri was chosen

because it was the home of Paul Follenius, a leader of the Settlement Society of Giessen which hoped to found a German State within the Union. The settlers soon found the control from Philadelphia too remote and they separated from the society in 1839. Growth in the settlement before the CIVIL WAR was rapid. A grape-growing culture developed so successfully that a Hermann resident won the New York State Fair award in 1853 for the best Catawba wine made west of the MISSISSIPPI RIVER. Fortunes were made in river trade. Today German is still taught extensively, and wine-making has been revived. Toys, shoes and metalworking provide industry. Several of the old German homes have been restored for visitors. Grape Stomping Festival in August and Winefest-Octoberfest are annual events.

HERSCHER, Illinois. City (pop. 1,214), Kankakee County, southwest of Kankakee, Ill. Site of the largest underground storage field for natural gas in the United States.

HEWITT, Charles Nathaniel. (Vergennes, VT, June 3, 1835—Red Wing, MN, 1910). Physician. Hewitt's most important contribution to health was his work with Louis Pasteur in Paris in the discovery of a cure for rabies, announced by Pasteur in 1885. Until this time rabies had meant certain death. Hewitt was the secretary and executive officer of the Minnesota State Board of Health from 1872 to 1897 and president of the Minnesota State Medical Society from 1881 to 1882. He served in the United States Army from 1861 to 1865 and was assistant surgeon and surgeon of the 50th New York Regiment and surgeon-in-chief of the engineering brigade of the Army of the Potomac. He moved to RED WING, Minnesota, in 1866 and served as professor of public health at the University of MINNESOTA starting in 1873.

HIBBING, Minnesota. City (pop. 21,193), northeastern Minnesota, southwest of CHISHOLM, site of the HULL-RUST-MAHONING MINE, largest open-pit iron-ore mine in the world. Hibbing was named for the Frank Hibbing, the miner who first discovered iron-ore in its vicinity and who founded the town with much of its early facilities. The town grew as a combination of mining and lumber interests attracted people from all over the United States and Europe. At one time there were more saloons than stores. The Hull-Rust-Mahoning Mine became one of the richest iron-ore sources in the world. In 1910 it became obvious that the town of Hibbing, itself, was located over rich deposits of ore. A site one mile south, called Alice, was chosen to relocate the town. Buildings were dismantled in 1919 and moved. Mining prospered until during WORLD WAR II the mine was delivering a third of the iron ore produced in the U.S. After the top grade ore was exhausted, the area turned to TACONITE production. The Hulls-Rust-Mahoning Mine site is now inactive; tourists may use an observation tower to view one of the largest man-made holes in the world. Hull-Rust Mine covers 1,600 acres and is 5 miles long, 2 miles wide, and 535 feet deep. The Minnesota Museum of Mining records 70 years of the industry. Nearby Paulucci Space Theatre presents programs on astronomy, space exploration and the environment, with the aid of state-of-the-art projection instruments, including a 40-foot diameter dome screen and special effects equipment. Annual festivities include the Last Chance Curling Bonspiel, an international competition, and Ethnic Days, a twelve-day ethnic celebration with each day celebrating a different nationality.

HILL, E. Gurney. (Rochdale, Lancaster, England, Sept. 11, 1847—Richmond, IN, Nov. 27, 1933). Rose hybridizer. With his father and sister, Hill formed the E.G. Hill and Company florists in 1881 in RICHMOND, Indiana, and he eventually became president of the company. Hill received over fifty medals, including the gold medal in Paris for his efforts in creating new rose types.

HILL, Edwin C. (Aurora, IN, April 23, 1884—New York, NY, Feb. 12, 1957). Author and radio commentator. From 1904 to 1923 Hill worked as a reporter for the New York *Sun*. He was director of the Fox News Reel from 1923 to 1924 and scenario editor for the Fox Film Corporation in 1925 to 1926. Hill was a feature writer for the *Sun* from 1927 to 1932 when he became a syndicate feature writer and radio broadcaster with "Human Side of the News."

HILL, James J. (Guelph, Ontario, Sept. 16, 1838—St. Paul, MN, May 29, 1916). Railroad president. Hill was one of America's principal builders of RAILROADS. In 1870 he established the Red River Transportation Company which was the first to open communication between Winnipeg and ST. PAUL. He then organized a syndicate which gained control of the St. Paul and Pacific Railroad. This railroad became the Great Northern System in 1890. Hill later

realized his dream of extending the Great Northern from the GREAT LAKES to the Pacific coast with northern and southern branches and steamship connections to Japan and China. Because he did so much to create the new "empire" of the American Northwest, he came to be known as the "Empire Builder." Hill was the owner of one the world's finest collections of modern French paintings.

HILLSBORO, Ohio. City (pop. 6,356), seat of Highland County, situated in southwestern Ohio on a high level plateau. The name is derived from British Lord Hillsborough, member of the board which administered the king's western domain. The site was surveyed and platted in 1807, and settlers from New Jersey, Maryland, Virginia and Pennsylvania followed the next year. Woolen mills, brickyards, tanneries and grist mills provided early commercial activities. The city is a center of a large rural trading area. In 1874 the town gained national attention when a group of women there formed the Women's Temperance Crusade. They went from tavern to tavern calling on the owners to stop selling liquor and were so successful that all but one place in town, a drugstore, did so. The women then set up a tent in front of the store, and the owner sued and won $5 damages for trespassing. Ironically, when state liquor stores were established, the Hillsboro liquor store occupied the same drug store building.

HINCKLEY, Minnesota. Town (pop. 963), northeastern Minnesota. Hinckley grew as an important relay station on the stage road between ST. PAUL, Minnesota, and SUPERIOR, Wisconsin. In 1870 the Lake Superior and Mississippi Railroad was built through Hinckley. Carloads of lumberjacks moved into town. Many stayed at the huge Depot Hotel which had two dining rooms with seating capacity for five hundred. Hinckley continued to grow as a railroad division point and as a supplier to the logging and milling industries of the area, until a great fire occurred in 1894. In that year a persistent drouth dried up many of the rivers and left the forests tinder-dry. A small fire began September 1st at a village called Mission Creek. Fanned by strong winds, the flames roared through the dry forests littered with debris left by the lumberjacks. A train rushed from Sandstone, Minnesota and rescued three hundred residents. The train's engineer, Jim Root, was unable to turn the train around and had to back through a wall of flame. Five minutes after backing across the Grindstone Bridge it collapsed and it was a race to see whether or not the train would beat the flames to the Kettle River. Root suffered burned hands from holding the hot metal throttle. Four hundred people perished before the fire burned out. Hinckley's economy never recovered. The tragic fire is memorialized in the Hinckley Fire Museum, a renovated railroad depot. Newspaper accounts and pictures are on display and a slide-show is presented. An annual event is the Korn and Klover Karnival for two days in mid-July.

HIRAM COLLEGE. Organized at Hiram, Ohio, in 1850, by the Disciples of Christ, the college was known as Western Reserve Eclectic Institute until 1867, when it received its present name. Hiram achieved national recognition in 1934 when it inaugurated its new style study plan. A student devoted most of a nine-week period to a single subject, then transferred to another subject for a similar period. During each semester a student would complete two intensive courses and part of a continuing course. The plan was supposed to eliminate the customary examination period and permit concentration of effort. The college has also been known for its distinguished graduates. President James A. GARFIELD (1831-1881) entered the school in 1851 and worked as a janitor. When he graduated two years later he was class valedictorian, and he began to teach in the English department. Poet Vachel LINDSAY (1879-1931) attended Hiram College before beginning his wanderings on which he traded rhymes for bread. The student body of 1,082 is instructed by a faculty of 86.

HOCKING HILLS. About fourteen miles southwest of LOGAN, Ohio, lies one of the most notable scenic areas of the Midwest. Six Ohio state parks preserve a wide variety of scenery within a circumference of about fifteen miles. Hocking State Park offers a wilderness canyon almost as awesome as many in the West. Rock House State Park is centered on a cave carved into a sheer sandstone cliff. The vaulted ceiling rises to an almost perfect gothic arch. The facade is pierced by five massive sandstone pillars. The interior recalls old-world cathedrals. The other area parks are noted for scenery, recreation and a hermit's cave.

HOGS. Iowa, alone, produces more hogs than the next four Midwest states combined. The annual Iowa hog production is more than 15,000,000 animals, followed in the Midwest by Illinois, Minnesota, Indiana, Missouri, Ohio, Wisconsin and Michigan.

HOLLAND, Michigan. City (pop. 26,281). Situated in southwest Michigan in Ottawa County, at the mouth of the BLACK RIVER at Lake

Michigan's Hollanders celebrate Tulip Time.

Macatawa, only a few miles from Lake MICHIGAN, Holland was named for the country of origin of the first settlers, who have given it an atmosphere of the mother country which has been encouraged to this day. It was founded in 1847 by Dutch settlers and incorporated in 1867. The Holland furnace company has produced heating equipment since 1906. Boats and furniture are other products. The growing of tulips has been an important commercial activity since the founding of the community. The Dutch Reformed Church operates Hope College and Western Theological Seminary in Holland. The city's resorts extend around the shores of Lake Macatawa and over to Lake Michigan. The city considers itself the center of Dutch culture in America, and its annual TULIP FESTIVAL is one of the country's major annual events. The Dutch Village reproduces a typical village of that country, with canals, windmills, tulips, Dutch dancing and wooden shoe carving. Netherlands Museum, Baker Furniture Museum and Poll Museum of Transportation provide historical perspective. Windmill Island has the only operating imported Dutch windmill in the country, relocated by special permission of the Dutch government. It continues to grind flour today. De Graaf Forsythe Galleries, Hope College, Holland State Park and an industrial tour of the wooden shoe factory are other attractions.

HONEYBEE. Official state insect of Wisconsin. Honeybees are a species of the social bees, which number about 400 species.

HONEY WAR. One of the many BOUNDARY DISPUTES between and among states, this argument appeared to be well on the way to actual combat before tempers cooled. When Iowa became a state in 1846, Congress had placed the boundary between Missouri and Iowa westward from the "rapids of the River DES MOINES." Each state interpreted this differently, since each could make a case for a different rapids. The area in question was important to the early settlers because it contained a great number of bee trees, hollow trees where the bees deposited honey, the only sweetening available in many pioneer areas. Armed with pitchforks and other "weapons," helter-skelter armies from both sides began to march into the disputed area. One Iowa "captain" brought six wagon loads of supplies, five of them filled with liquor. Fortunately, the two governors appointed a committee to settle the dispute. However, a final decision was not reached until that by the

U.S. Supreme Court in 1850, favoring Iowa's claim, covering 2,600 square miles of territory.

HOOVER, Herbert Clark. (West Branch, Cedar County, IA, Aug. 10, 1874—New York, NY, Oct. 20, 1964). President of the United States, 1929-33. Son of Jesse Clark Hoover, a blacksmith, and Hulda Randal Minthoren. Student leader, graduate of Stanford in geology in 1895.

Hoover remarked that on his graduation he had "40 dollars in my pocket and no debts." His first work was pushing an ore cart in a California mine. After a rapid rise in the engineering profession, he went to Australia, where he introduced new engineering techniques. From Australia, he proposed by cable to Lou Henry, and returned for their marriage at Monterey, California, on February 10, 1899. They went immediately to China, where he quickly learned the language(s), which enhanced his success there.

During the next five years, he and the growing family, who were with him most of the time, circled the world five times, troubleshooting mining problems. Opening his own engineering firm, Hoover practiced in 14 countries.

Caught in London at the beginning of WORLD WAR I, he headed the Commission for Relief in Belgium. Then as Chairman of the American Relief Commission, he collected a billion dollars and fed more than 11 million people in Belgium and Northern France. When Hoover refused a Belgian decoration because he felt that an American should not accept foreign honors, the King created the Order of Friend of the Belgian People for him, alone.

Upon the U.S. entry into the war, Hoover became U.S. food Administrator, coordinating the food conservation program and the efforts to increase production. At the end of the war, he took the posts of Chairman of the American Relief Commission and Director of the European Relief and Reconstruction Commission.

Under his direction, American relief became a major source of food for 300 million people in 21 countries of Europe and the Middle East. His determination to include Germany in relief efforts was responsible for saving thousands from starvation there. In 1921, Hoover was in charge of much of the relief work during the Russian famine.

As Secretary of Commerce, 1921-28, he brought his engineering training to efficiency management, standardization and elimination

Hoover Birthplace, Hoover National Historic Site

of waste, making the department more efficient. He was determined that the department would be a service agency to serve all the people.

Hoover overhauled the Bureau of Foreign and Domestic Commerce to make it competitive in foreign markets and recruited a new breed of commercial attaches. He established the principle that the radio airwaves were public property, and radio stations increased from two in 1921 to 300 a year later. In 1927, he participated in the first demonstration of television.

Overhauling the Bureau of Fisheries, he instituted strict measures to eliminate fish pirates and protect spawning grounds, also promoted other wide-scale conservation programs. He called the first aviation conference in 1922, and the next year, assembled the first National Conference on Street and Highway Safety. He promoted standardization in manufacturing and served as president of the American Child Health Association.

Both major parties sought him for the presidential nomination in 1928, but he was elected President on the Republican ticket, with Charles Curtis as vice president. He had pledged reforms in business and social life, but he had hardly begun his programs when the stock market crash of 1929 brought a world economic crisis. Hoover believed strongly that

federal action should be channeled through local government. However, Congress passed a number of banking and other acts calling for growing federal intervention. Disclosures about problems in one of these, the Reconstruction Finance Corporation, brought about a run on banks that caused widespread foreclosures.

During the presidential campaign with F.D. Roosevelt in 1932, business almost came to a standstill, awaiting the outcome.

After his landslide defeat, Hoover took a short retirement from public affairs, then resumed his familiar habit of food relief during the early phases of WORLD WAR II, until the U.S. became involved.

After the war, President Harry TRUMAN, a great admirer of Hoover, asked him to advise on the world food situation. At the age of 71, Hoover then traveled 51,000 miles through 38 countries, to locate the areas of most urgent need, and millions were again saved from starvation.

Hoover headed two commissions to study methods of reducing the ever-increasing scope of government, 1947-49 under Truman, and 1953-55 under Eisenhower. Several recommendations were carried out, but the KOREAN WAR brought an end to most of the earlier gains.

For his efforts as engineer, statesman, humanitarian and public servant, Hoover received 468 medals and citations, along with a record number of 66 honorary degrees worldwide, and honorary citizenship in 24 countries.

In 1962, Hoover helped to dedicate the Herbert Hoover Presidential Library in his native town. In his speech on the occasion, he called for a "new council of free nations."

Hoover's last official duty was to serve as special U.S. Representative to the Brussels World's Fair in 1958, where his wartime service to Belgium was again acclaimed.

Upon his death in the Waldorf Astoria in New York at the age of 90, Hoover received full military honors in Washington, D.C., and 80,000 mourners descended on the small town of West Branch, Iowa, for his funeral services.

The Hoovers had two children, Herbert, Jr., (1903-69) and Allan (1907-). Mrs. Hoover died in 1944.

Commenting on his unpopular standing after his presidency, Hoover wrote, "Depressions are not new in human history. All of them are preceded by wars, or inflations, or booms with sprees of speculative greed. When they are worldwide, that makes them worse. No government can legislate away the 'morning after,' any more than it can legislate away the effects of a tornado—not even the New Deal."

Historians are generally reevaluating Hoover's presidency and giving substantially greater credit to his accomplishment in the White House and worldwide.

Among Hoover's published works are his translation (with Mrs. Hoover) of Agricola's *De re Metallica* (1912), *The Challenge of Liberty* (1934), the *Ordeal of Woodrow Wilson* (1958), and *An American Epic* (3 vol., 1959-61).

HOPE, Bob. (Eltham, England, May 19, 1903—), entertainer and world personality. Born Leslie Townes Hope, at the age of four Bob came with his family to CLEVELAND, Ohio, which he considered his real home. After a stint as a comedian, noted for his rapid-fire delivery, he became one of the most popular weekly entertainers on radio and was able to move his performance to an equally popular weekly TV format, beginning in 1950. He gained world renown for his "Road" films (1940-1953) with Bing Crosby and Dorothy Lamour, making over 50 films in all. One of the most charitable figures in the performing arts, from 1940 through 1970, Hope made annual trips overseas to entertain the troops. Giving every evidence of agelessness, he continued to work in commercials and perform in special TV programs in his eighties. Occasionally he even

resumed his visits to entertain the troops. Hope was awarded the Presidential Medal of Freedom in 1969, as well as the Hersholt Award, an Emmy, and an honorary Oscar.

HOPEWELL PEOPLE. Accomplished prehistoric society found in much of the Midwest. The culture began to form about 2,500 years ago, reached its zenith about the beginning of the Christian era and disappeared about 1,500 years later. Their origins are mysterious. Some experts believe they came from the northeast. In any event, they began to impinge on the earlier ADENA Culture, and their first known homeland was the Scioto Valley of South Central Ohio. From there they expanded their outreach and extraordinary culture over a millenium. They extended their sway to the Gulf Coast, perhaps as far east as eastern Pennsylvania, west into central Kansas and probably as far north as the UPPER PENINSULA of Michigan. Throughout this period they dominated this vast area from their Ohio center and built an extraordinary civilization. They were able to clothe themselves in fine furs and robes of well tanned skins and woven cloth. Finely crafted ornaments of copper, bone, mica and shell were worn by both men and women.

The Hopewell took advantage all of the rivers fanning out from the Ohio area, as well as the GREAT LAKES, to cover their enormously extended trading routes. Water traffic was carried on with oak log canoes, some large enough for six paddlers and a leader. From the spreading trade routes came Rocky Mountain obsidian, tobacco from the east, in addition to shark teeth and other ocean products from which to make ornaments, copper from the northern woodlands and mica from North Carolina and Arkansas, as well as many other resources not found in the Midwest. The Hopewell were experienced pearl fishers, plumbing the Scioto River for hundreds of thousands of the precious objects. A single mound in the Turner mound group of Hamilton County, Ohio, produced 12,000 pearls, 35,000 pearl beads and 20,000 shell beads, along with meteoric iron, nuggets of copper and silver and sheets of hammered gold and copper. As *Reader's Digest* noted, "There is an attractive vigor about all this fondness for excess and flamboyance. To envelop a corpse from head to feet in pearls, to weight it down in pounds of copper, to surround it with masterpieces of sculpture and pottery, to bury everything under tons of earth shows a kind of cultural energy for which there is no previous parallel in prehistoric North America."

Horlick - Houdini

Museum diorama depicts the Hopewell culture.

The Hopewells are thought to have been highly developed socially, a well-organized people with an elite upper class, perhaps even having developed unions of various craftsmen and carvers. They were able to form enormous mounds of earth as burial places or for other purposes. Their wide boulevards and geometrical earthworks, all showed their ability to organize many workers at tasks which must have required extraordinary human labor.

No authority has been found for their decline, perhaps due to some agricultural failure, famine, plague, civil war or invasion of fierce uncivilized tribes. No outward trace of them was found among the Indians who occupied the region when Europeans first explored.

HORLICK, William. (Ruardean, England, Feb. 23, 1846—Sept. 25, 1936). Manufacturer. William Horlick came to the U.S. in 1869, settled in RACINE, Wisconsin, in 1876. He and his brother James began manufacturing food products at Racine in 1877. They devoted much attention to developing new products. One of these new products took their business around the world and captivated whole generations of lovers of sweets. In 1877 William Horlick combined two of Wisconsin's most basic products, milk and malt, and invented malted milk. He was president of the company until his death. The company continues as one of the largest operations of its kind. The building which the Horlicks built for their operations was an interesting oddity in itself. Its design was based on a medieval castle in Tudor Gothic architecture, with square castellated towers. The prominence of the family in Racine is demonstrated by the school, park and hospital bearing their name. William (Sir William) went to England and established a branch firm there. He was knighted by the King.

HORSE, PREHISTORIC. The modern horse evolved from ancestors found through much of the present Great Plains area, as well as much of the western Midwest and particularly in Minnesota where many fossils have been found. As time passed, the average horse increased in size and could still be found in North American when the first humans arrived. For some reason still unknown horses disappeared in North America at about the period of the close of the last ice age around 10,000 years ago. Horses were not seen again in the hemisphere until their reintroduction by the Spanish explorers.

HOUDINI, Harry. (Budapest, Hungary, Mar. 24, 1874—Detroit, MI, Oct. 31, 1926). Known as the super star of magicians. Houdini was born Ehrich Weiss but changed his name in honor of the French magician Houdin. Soon after his birth, his parents brought him to APPLETON, Wisconsin. He took up magic as a boy, but in 1882 he went to New York City as a trapeze artist to earn money for the family. After his family joined him there, he began a magic act with his brother. On a trip to England, he mystified Scotland Yard with an escape and earned a wide reputation. He was particularly noted for his ability to escape from almost any seemingly impossible situation such as being handcuffed in a straitjacket or locked in a box under water. However, he has apparently failed in his greatest "escape" trick—escaping death itself. He left instructions that after death he would return to CHICAGO, Illinois, on a specific bridge in Jackson Park on a particular day, and his followers have faithfully kept their vigil there on that day each year, without result.

Houdini was one of the most effective of all those attempting to uncover fraud in seances and other so-called spiritist activities. He left his library of magic to the Library of Congress, and it is considered to be the most nearly complete of its type.

HOUGH, Emerson. (Newton, IA, June 28, 1857—Evanston, IL, Apr. 30, 1923). Author. Hough was educated in law but developed a career on midwestern NEWSPAPERS. His interest in the outdoors and conservation was heightened by work on the magazine *Field and Stream.* Hough was the author of short stories and juvenile fiction, but he is best known for his novel *The Covered Wagon* (1922). The work was one of the most popular of the period and gained even greater fame as a large-scale motion picture. Another popular novel was his *Mississippi Bubble* (1902). Much of his work dealt with life in the West, and he wrote many novels on the theme. Later he wrote outdoor adventure juvenile books, such as *The Young Alaskans on the Trail* (1914).

HOUGHTON, Douglass. (Troy, NY, Sept. 21, 1809—Lake Superior Oct. 13, 1845). Geologist and mayor of DETROIT. Houghton served as a surgeon and botanist on H.R. SCHOOLCRAFT's expedition in 1831 to find the source of the MISSISSIPPI RIVER. Houghton became a practicing physician and surgeon in Detroit from 1832 to 1837 before becoming a professor of geology and mineralogy at the University of MICHIGAN from 1838 to 1845. It was during his years at the university that Houghton also served, from 1842 to 1845, as mayor of DETROIT, Michigan. On another voyage of discovery in the latter year Dr. Houghton lost his life in a storm on Lake Superior.

HOUGHTON, LAKE. Largest lake wholly within the boundaries of Michigan and source of the MUSKEGON RIVER. The 112 square-mile lake is a favorite feeding ground for waterfowl and a favorite fishing spot for sportsmen. The continuous rows of structures give the appearance of one long village along Houghton Lake's southern shore. Resort development has grown to the extent that one resort blends into another.

HOUGHTON, Michigan. City (pop. 7,512), seat of Houghton County, chief shipping and distribution point of the Keweenaw Peninsula, named for Douglass HOUGHTON. Founded in 1852, the city is the oldest incorporated settlement on the Keweenaw Peninsula, the "Treasure Chest of Michigan" or more commonly "Copper Country." The city owes its existence to the copper industry and the boom in the price of the metal between 1875 and WORLD WAR I. Between 1855 and 1870 more than 200 locations were prospected. The shafts dug for copper in this region are the deepest of their type in the world. The architecture of the city is of particular interest because of its use of redstone in either the complete construction of the building or in sandstone trim, an unusual feature in Michigan communities. Houghton is the mainland headquarters for the ISLE ROYALE NATIONAL PARK. Boat service provides two round trips to the island from Houghton weekly during the summer. Exhibits of copper and silver, native to the UPPER PENINSULA, and a re-created iron-manganese cave may be found in the A.E. Seaman Mineralogical Museum at the Michigan Technological University.

HOUSE OF DAVID. Religious cult community established by Benjamin Franklin PURNELL in BENTON HARBOR, Michigan, in 1903. "King Ben" ordered his followers not to smoke, drink, or eat meat. New members gave all their worldly goods to the general fund, and they received enough for their daily needs in exchange for communal work. After Purnell's death in 1927, the colony of six hundred split into two factions, one led by Purnell's widow Mary and the other by Judge Harry T. Dewhirst. "Queen Mary's" group established a new settlement near the original one, and both groups flourished. They were known for their long-bearded baseball teams whose members played bare-handed.

HOUSE RAISINGS. A social event of the early pioneers who willingly participated in helping with the construction of a neighbor's home. After this essential labor, the participants indulged in one of the few opportunities for relaxation on the frontier. They ate a bountiful meal and then sang, danced, or played games.

HOWARD, Roy. (Cincinnati, OH, Jan. 1, 1883—New York, NY, Nov. 20, 1964). Newspaperman. Howard began his news career as a reporter for the Indianapolis *News* in 1902. He moved on to NEWSPAPERS in ST. LOUIS, CINCINNATI, and New York. He became the New York manager of United Press International Association in 1907. He was the president and general manager by 1912, chairman of the board from 1921 to 1936, and president from 1936 to 1952. In 1925 he became chairman of the Scripps-McRae newspaper chain, which became Scripps-Howard, building it into a leading newspaper conglomerate with over 30 papers. Howard negotiated the purchase of three New York City papers which combined to form the New York *World-Telegram and Sun*, of which he was the editor until 1960 and the president until 1962.

HOWE MILITARY SCHOOL. Preparatory school for boys near Howe, Indiana. John B. Howe, a leading citizen of Howe, provided money through his will for the school. Founded in 1884, it offers grammar school and college preparatory curricula for boys from 8-14 years of age. There are fourteen buildings grouped around a parade ground on a forty-acre campus.

HOWELLS, William Dean. (Martins Ferry, OH, Mar. 1, 1837—New York, NY, May 10, 1920). Author, "Dean of American Letters." Howells' education was gained mostly from working in his father's print shop, beginning at the age of nine, and as a writer and editor on small Ohio NEWSPAPERS in HAMILTON, DAYTON, COLUMBUS, ASHTABULA and JEFFERSON. In the tight election of 1860 Howell wrote a winning biography of Abraham LINCOLN and was awarded by appointment as U.S. consul in Venice, Italy. Most of the leading literary figures of the East had become acquainted with Howells, so when he returned from Italy, he had no trouble in joining the *Nation* and contributed to other publications as well. Producing nearly 100 volumes of widely differing nature, Howells came to be known as the father of the realistic American novel. Samuel CLEMENS (1835-1910), Stephen CRANE (1871-1900), Hamlin GARLAND (1860-1940) and Thorstein VEBLEN (1857-1929) considered him their literary mentor. His realistic novels brought him to the top rank of American fiction, particularly *Rise of Silas Lapham* (1885) which several generations of American school children were at one time required to read, but the vogue for his writing has greatly diminished. He wrote a number of works based on his experiences in Ohio and about Ohio characters, some of them very eccentric. From 1900 until his death he wrote the "Easy Chair," a column for *Harpers*

and added dramas, sketches and biography to his list of writings.

HUBBARD, Frank McKinney. (Bellefontaine, OH, 1868—Indianapolis, IN, Dec. 26, 1930). Caricaturist. Hubbard, known as "Kin Hubbard," was employed almost continuously, from 1891, as a caricaturist for the Indianapolis *News*. He wrote "Abe Martin's Sayings" as a very widely syndicated column which was also published annually as a book.

HUDSON, Joseph Lowthian. (Newcastle-on-Tyne, England, Oct. 17, 1846—Detroit, MI, July 15, 1912). Merchant. Hudson and his father began a business at Ionia, Michigan, in 1866 that lasted until 1877. He moved to DETROIT in that year and entered the clothing business with C.R. Mabley for four years. He founded J. L. Hudson and Company, Michigan's largest department store, in Detroit in 1897 and also served as chairman of the board of the Hudson Motor Car Company.

HUGHES, Harold E. (Ida Grove, IA, Feb. 10, 1922—). Governor of Iowa, U.S. Senator. After service in WORLD WAR II, Hughes became the operator of the Iowa Better Trucking Bureau, then served as chairman of the Iowa Commerce Commission. Elected governor in 1962 and reelected in 1964, he then served as a Democrat from Iowa in the U.S. Senate. His liberal views in the Senate and his identification with the popular causes of the day increased his national image to the point where he was considered as a possible nominee for president. However, in a rare act of humanitarian service, Hughes resigned to enter religious life. In one of his few public activities since, during President Carter's term, Hughes served as head of a Commission on Alcoholism.

HUGHES, Howard Robard (Lancaster, MO, Sept. 9, 1869—Houston, TX, Jan., 14, 1924). Inventor and industrialist. After working in the oil drilling business, Hughes invented a revolutionary coneshaped drill bit (1908). He later founded the very successful Hughes Tool Company, which manufactured his bits and other related tools. He was the father of millionaire recluse Howard Hughes, who carried on the company business, gaining great wealth and notoriety for his eccentricities.

HUGHES, Langston. (Joplin, MO, Feb. 1, 1902—New York, NY, May 22, 1967). Author. The product of a broken home, Hughes had already dropped out of Columbia University, shipped out on a vessel for Africa, and traveled in Europe by the time his verse was discovered by Vachel Lindsay in 1925. Lindsey immediately arranged for publication of the work. Hughes was then working as a busboy in Washington, D.C., but the subsequent praise for his work brought him a scholarship, enabling him to graduate from Lincoln University in Pennsylvania in 1929. He worked in New York City as a prominent member of the Harlem literary revival. His free-verse poetry is especially noted for its colloquial rhythms, as in "The Negro Speaks of Rivers" (1926) and "Weary Blues" (1926). His writings include novels and autobiographical works.

HUGHES, Rupert. (Lancaster, MO, Jan. 31, 1872—Los Angeles, CA, Sept. 9, 1956). Author. After graduating from what is now CASE WESTERN RESERVE UNIVERSITY, he earned his Ph.D. from Yale in 1899. His published works include a three-volume biography of George WASHINGTON (1926-30) and the novel *What Will People Say?* (1914).

HULL-RUST-MAHONING MINE. Largest open-pit mine in the world. The mine, located near HIBBING, Minnesota, on the MESABI RANGE, covers 1,600 acres and is five miles long, two miles wide and five hundred thirty-five feet deep. Over one billion tons of ore-bearing rock have been removed from the site in the years since its founding around 1889. A viewing stand to observe the mine is open daily.

HUMPHREY, Hubert Horatio, Jr. (Wallace, SD, May 27, 1911—Washington, DC Jan. 13, 1978). Senator and vice-president. He studied pharamcy at the Denver College of Pharmacy (1932-1933), worked as a pharmacist for a time before graduating from the University of MINNESOTA in 1939, then taking an M.A. from Louisiana state University in 1940. There he also taught political science. After a number of different jobs he became state campaign director for F.D. Roosevelt's 1944 presidential campaign and became an ardent supporter of the New Deal. He was instrumental in the merger of the Democratic and Farmer-Labor parties in Minnesota. In 1945 he was elected mayor of Minneapolis on a fusion ticket. Humphrey served as a U.S. senator from 1948 to 1964 and again from 1971 to 1978. He was principal U.S. delegate to the United Nations in 1956. Unsuccessful in his 1960 bid for the

Democratic presidential nomination, he became assistant majority leader of the Senate in 1961. As manager of the 1964 Civil Rights Bill in the Senate, he raised strong bipartisan support, overcame a three-month filibuster of the bill and obtained enough votes for the passage of what has been called. "The single most important congressional action of the century."

At the Democratic national convention of 1964, Lyndon B. Johnson (1908-1973) selected Humphrey as his vice presidential running mate. After campaigning brilliantly for the ticket, he shared Johnson's landslide victory and served as vice-president under Johnson from 1965 to 1969. After the assassination of Senator Robert Kennedy, Humphrey became the favorite for the Democratic presidential nomination, which he won at the chaotic Chicago convention in 1968. However, he could not escape his role as a national leader during the Vietnam War and lost the election to Richard Nixon by a narrow margin.

Elected to the Senate in 1970 and 1976, Humphrey became the "elder statesman of liberalism." Humphrey received numerous awards during his life and was the author of several books on the American scene.

HUNTINGTON, Indiana. City (pop.16,202), seat of Huntington County in northeastern Indiana, southwest of FORT WAYNE. Originally called Wepecheange, "place of flints," named for Samuel Huntington, a member of the first Continental Congress. It was incorporated in 1848. Today Huntingon is the center of agricultural trade and of growing industry, including manufacture of machinery and automotive parts. It is the seat of Huntington College. The city was the home of John R. Kissinger, a volunteer in Dr. Walter Reed's yellow fever experiments. Kissinger developed a case from which he never fully recovered. Reed is supposed have said that nothing showed more moral courage in the annals of the United States Army than Kissinger's willingness to undergo these experiments. Huntington has also had a bridge over the Little Wabash River which held an entire block of shops, suspended over the river. This bridge has been claimed to be the only bridge of its type in the United States. During the CIVIL WAR a Huntington resident, Lambdin P. Milligan, was one of the most active members of the KNIGHTS OF THE GOLDEN CIRCLE, an organization of men who practiced subversive activity behind Union lines. Accused of treason, Milligan and two other Knights were to be hanged, until the

Supreme Court ruled, in one of its most important cases, that a military court had no jurisdiction except in cases where martial law prevailed and that an emergency does not create additional power to cope with that emergency. A popular annual event is the Forks of the Wabash Pioneer Festival held the last weekend in September.

HURLEY, Wisconsin. Town (pop. 2,015), County Seat of Iron County, in north central Wisconsin on the border with the tip of Michigan's UPPER PENINSULA, named for mining official M. N. Hurley. Perched on the hills overlooking the Montreal River, Hurley looks across the river to its twin, IRONWOOD, in Michigan. The twins were born in 1884 as the center of the iron mining boom in the lengthy GOGEBIC ore range. Hurley was also a hub of the great lumber boom at about the same time. Almost as soon as it was founded, Hurley had a transient population of 7,000 miners and lumbermen and the lusty reputation of all such mining frontier settlements. In fact, local people said that Hurley and Hell were the two toughest places, and Hurley was tougher than Hell. As timber and iron faded, Ironwood forged ahead and left Hurley with little more than memories of its gaudy and booming past. However, TACONITE ore is still shipped from the local mines. Edna FERBER (1887-1968) chose Hurley as the setting for her novel *Come and Get It* (1936), and the principal character was said to be based on the life of Lotta Morgan, a dance hall girl at the old Central Gardens. Ferber's book recounts the true story of how her character was found back of the dance hall one morning with her head split by an ax. Today Hurley is one of the major winter sports areas of the Midwest. Whitecap Mountain Ski area eight miles out of town provides every skiing facility and service known to the sport, including a 5,000-foot run with a vertical drop of 400 feet as well as nineteen miles of double-track cross-country trails. Each year the Red Light Snowmobile Rally is a USSA sanctioned event which also features a radar run and dog races, from December 9 through 13. Another annual event is the Paavo Nurmi Marathon, with its related activities, over the second weekend of August. A local attraction is Iron County Historical Museum, featuring the county's iron mining past.

HURON INDIANS (WYANDOTTE). Samuel de Champlain first observed the Hurons in 1615 in Canada. The Hurons accepted mission-aries and quickly won the favor of the Europeans. In March, 1649, Mohawk and Seneca war parties attacked the unsuspecting Hurons, who fled into the winter. More starved or died of exposure to the cold than in the actual battle. Some Hurons fled as far west as Michigan, Ohio and Wisconsin where they changed their name to Wendat, the name of their earlier confederacy. In white literature the name became Wyandotte. However, the Huron name lives on in several place names and geographic designations.

HURON RIVER (Michigan). The Huron River rises in Portage Lake in southeast Michigan, flows south to Dexter, past ANN ARBOR and Belleville, before emptying into Lake ERIE.

HURON RIVER (Ohio). The Huron River rises in central Huron County, Ohio, near the town of Fitchville, Ohio. It flows northeast, past North Fairfield, Milan and Huron, before entering Lake ERIE.

HURON, LAKE. One of the five GREAT LAKES. Michigan and Ontario, Canada, share a common boundary which runs roughly through the center of Lake Huron from one end to the other. Lake Huron is named for the HURON INDIANS (Wyandotte) who once lived along its shores. Lake Huron lies between Lake ERIE and Lake MICHIGAN. Lakes Huron and Michigan are connected by the STRAITS OF MACKINAC. Huron and SUPERIOR are connected by the ST. MARYS RIVER while the DETROIT RIVER, Lake ST. CLAIR and the ST. CLAIR RIVER link Lake Huron with Lake Erie. That lake extends for nearly 206 miles and forms a part of the boundary between the United States and Canada. At its greatest width, Huron stretches 183 miles. Huron's greatest depth is 750 feet. Two important islands in Lake Huron are MACKINAC ISLAND, in Michigan, and Manitoulin Island, in Ontario, Canada. Between December and May, violent storms make Lake Huron very dangerous for shipping.

HURST. Fannie. (Hamilton, OH, 1889—Feb. 23, 1968). Author of sentimental novels, including *Back Street* (1930), perhaps her best-known, Hurst was even better known for her many short stories. Her other works include *Imitation of Life* (1933), *Lummox* (1923) and *Fool—Be Still* (1964). She also wrote plays and screenplays.

HUTCHINS, Robert Maynard. (Brooklyn,

NY, Jan. 17, 1899—Santa Barbara, CA, May 14, 1977). Educator. In 1929, at the age of 30, he was appointed president of the University of CHICAGO, the youngest president of a major university. At Chicago, Hutchins reorganized the graduate school and established the "Chicago Plan," a four-year junior college and a liberal arts curriculum separate from the professional schools, which permitted students to advance at their own rate of development. His abolishment of Big Ten sports was one of his many controversial acts. He remained at the university until 1951, with the title of chancellor for the last six years. He advocated adult education and wrote *Higher Learning in America* (1936). Hutchins served as associate director of the Ford Foundation from 1951 to 1954 and was president of the Fund for the Republic from 1954 to 1969. The Fund established the Center for the Study of Democratic institutions, of which Hutchins became president, then chairman in 1969. His later writings stressed nonconformity and protest.

HUTCHINSON, Minnesota. City (pop. 1,-090), south-central Minnesota, west of MINNEAPOLIS. Founded by Asa, Judson and John Hutchinson, members of a family of singers who sang Abolitionist songs from 1841 until the end of the CIVIL WAR. Prior to the Civil War the Hutchisons accompanied other settlers leaving Minneapolis to explore areas farther west, and they settled at Hutchinson. Residents who braved a severe first winter began farming, providing the foundation for economic growth. The Hutchinson brothers dictated the politics of the community in a document called the Hutchison Constitution. This advocated complete abolition of SLAVERY, equal rights for women, no gambling, and establishment of the "Humanities Church." Each woman received one of the hundred lots that were divided among the settlers. Many of the residents were killed in the Sioux Uprising led by Chief LITTLE CROW, but the residents did not panic. Citizens built a stockade and saved their crops, although many of the children died in the cold fall and winter from illness that could not be treated without medicine. Hutchinson served as a military post for several years following the Indian scare. In 1863 Little Crow, was killed five miles west of the town while picking berries, decapitated by a soldier, and the skull was retained by the local Historical Society. The white who shot Little Crow was given $75, the bounty for an Indian scalp. Gopher Campfire is a nature preserve for geese, ducks, deer and antelope.

HUTTON, Betty. (Battle Creek, MI, Feb. 26, 1921—). Blonde leading lady in many singing/dancing light films of the 1940s. Hutton, born Betty Jan Thornsburg, had roles in *Red Hot and Blue* (1949), *Incendiary Blond* (1943) and *Annie Get Your Gun* (1950).

ICARIANS. Utopian communal group who settled in NAUVOO, Illinois, after the MORMONS moved from there to Utah. The Icarians came to Nauvoo from Texas in 1849. In an effort to establish a wine industry, they began grape culture. In actively attempting to convert Illinois settlers to their beliefs, they distributed material printed in French, German and English. The colony soon developed financial difficulties, split into factions and, in 1856, expelled their leader, Etienne Cabet. The movement died out, leaving Nauvoo nearly a GHOST TOWN.

ICE AGE NATIONAL SCIENTIFIC RE-SERVE. This 32,500-acre preserve was the first national scientific reserve. It contains widely significant features of continental glaciation. The reserve is headquartered at MADISON, Wisconsin and is scattered throughout various parts of the state in nine different segments.

ICE CAVE. Near DECORAH, Iowa. Innumerable fissures in the limestone in and about the cave retain cold winter temperature far into the summer months. The moisture laden air of spring and summer enters the cave, condensing and forming a coating of crystalline, transparent ice several inches thick on the cave's inner walls. Strangely, by late summer enough warmer air has entered the cave to melt the ice, and the grotto is ice-free in early winter. In the region of the cave, the Pleistocene snail is found, a rarity discovered nowhere else in the world. Also in the area the golden saxifrage may be seen. This plant is found mostly in Iowa. Widespread during the ice age, these curiosities persist in a climate relatively like that of their earlier period.

ICE CREAM CONE. This treat is said to have originated at the LOUISIANA PURCHASE EXPOSITION in ST. LOUIS, Missouri, in 1904. From there it spread around the world gaining almost universal popularity.

ILLINI INDIANS. This confederacy of Algonquin language tribes consisted of the MOINGWENA, Peoria, Kaskaskia, CAHOKIA, MICHIGA-MEA and TAMAROA. The name Illini means "the men," and the peoples of the Illini considered themselves to be superior men and women. By the middle 1600s they were living in what is now southern Wisconsin, most of Illinois and parts of Iowa and Missouri. Jacques MARQUETTE and Louis JOLLIET are thought to have been the first Europeans to travel through their territory, at which time they may have numbered some 6,500. Father Claude Jean ALLOUEZ ministered to them for many years. Wars with other tribes, especially after the assassination of Chief PONTIAC in 1769, continued to reduce their number until by 1800 there were not more than 150 Illini living. Their descendants now occupy reservation lands in northeast Oklahoma, shared with the Wea and Piankasahw groups.

ILLINOIS. State. situated in the south-central portion of the Midwest Region. Illinois has the greatest north-south extent of any state in the region. Its length of 381 miles places CHICAGO almost as far north as Boston, while CAIRO at its southernmost tip is almost as far south as Norfolk, Virginia. Nearly two-thirds of the Illinois borders are formed by rivers, the MISSISSIPPI RIVER forming the entire western boundary, the OHIO forming the southern border and the WABASH occupying nearly half of the southeast and eastern boundary. The other water boundary is formed by Lake MICHIGAN, where the Illinois shore stretches from the border of Indiana on the south to that of Wisconsin on the north.

This lake boundary has a strange history. The original northern border of Illinois was intended to reach only to the southernmost tip of Lake Michigan. This would have placed the area of Chicago in Wisconsin. Fortunately for Illinois, the boundary was changed to give the state its relatively short but enormously important access to the GREAT LAKES and through them to the sea.

Five states border Illinois, Missouri and Iowa to the west, Wisconsin on the north, Indiana to the east, and Kentucky to the south. Technically, also, Illinois, Indiana and Michigan have a common border where their boundary lines come together in Lake Michigan, but this fact is seldom illustrated on maps.

In addition to the boundary rivers, the ILLINOIS RIVER is the most important in the state. The first European explorers known to have reached the area made their way up the Illinois and Des Plaines rivers and realized that a very short portage would connect the Illinois River with the GREAT LAKES, and thus to the sea. Other streams with major classification are the KASKASKIA, EMBARRASS, KANKAKEE, SANGAMON, SPOON and ROCK.

With an area of 56,345 square miles, Illinois ranks 24th in area in the nation and fifth in size in the Midwest Region, just behind Iowa in size. In 1842 famed writer Charles Dickens described the area as, "A vast expanse of level ground; unbroken save by one thin line of trees...A tranquil sea or lake without water...It was lonely and wild but oppressive in its barren monotony." To those easterners and foreigners accustomed to scenery broken by mountains and high hills, the vast prairies did appear dreary.

The mostly level prairies are broken in the south by an offshoot of the OZARK MOUNTAINS. On the northeast, a high elevation known as TERRAPIN RIDGE, east of GALENA, provides some of the most beautiful scenic views in the Midwest.

The Pleistocene GLACIERS were the geologic forces responsible for most of the present surface features of the state. Only a small portion of the northwest Illinois was untouched by the glaciers. A modest area across the north and an even smaller area of the south are early Paleazoic. The main body of the state is Late Paleozoic. The southernmost tip of Illinois just touches the farthest northern reaches of the Cenozoic region.

Before the coming of the glaciers, there were no great bodies of water in the region; Lake Michigan and the other Great Lakes are products of the glaciers.

In modern times meteorologists have classi-fied the climate as "temperate," but bitter winters and hot summers seem to call that classification into question. The hottest temperature ever recorded in the state was 117 degrees, at EAST ST. LOUIS. Mt. Carroll recorded the state's coldest temperature of 35 below zero. This is a temperature spread of 152 degrees.

Contrary to the opinion of early visitors, the flat prairie lands would prove to be one of the most valuable natural assets of any state in the nation, providing the fourth largest annual agricultural income of all the states.

It could be argued, however, that the fertile soils are not the premier asset of Illinois. Valid claims could be made for another aspect of the state's geography—its strategic location. Illinois has long been known as the Crossroads of North America. At the head of the Great Lakes, the state is accessible to ocean traffic, through the ST. LAWRENCE SEAWAY and by the Illinois Waterway from Chicago its goods can reach the Gulf coast through the Chicago, Illinois and Mississippi rivers.

This central location in the nation and, in some respects, the world, has made Illinois a natural hub of TRANSPORTATION, with the greatest total concentrated combination of rail lines, air traffic, superhighway links and barge routes anywhere. In many respects, Illinois deserves to be called the transportation center of the world.

Strategic location has been one of the most important factors in its leadership as an exporting state, often holding first rank among all the states in this very important arena.

In manufacturing, Illinois has fallen to fourth rank among the states, having, perhaps temporarily, lost third place to Massachusetts. Total value of the state's annual manufacture varied in the middle 1980s from 121 billion to 126 billion dollars. The Chicago area, however, has continued to maintain its rank as the nation's leading manufacturing center. Principal state products are machinery (except electrical), food and electrical equipment.

From the beginning of its settlement, Illinois has taken wealth from its thick deposit of fertile soil, the legacy of the glaciers. Only Iowa, among the states, has more such fertile land. In recent times, AGRICULTURE annually has contributed from eight to ten billion dollars in income to the state. Major agricultural products are CORN, SOYBEANS, HOGS and CATTLE, ranked in that order.

One of the nation's major economic changes has been particularly notable in Illinois, where service industries now far outstrip every other source of income except manufacturing. In 1985 service industries accounted for 21 billion dollars of the state's annual receipts.

In TOURISM, Illinois' income ranks only slightly below that of agriculture.

Although minerals have lost some of their importance, they still bring in annual income of more than three billion. As Illinois oil was depleted, oil income dropped, but during the oil shortage of the 1970s, new ways were found to bring more petroleum from old wells, and oil production made a modest comeback in the state. Illinois COAL also had fallen out of favor because of the high quantity of smoke it produces, but it, too, has begun a comeback, due to new lower-smoking processing techniques.

In 1985 the population of Illinois stood at 11,535,000. Population figures have shown only a slight but continuing gain since the 1980 census. The state's longtime rank of 5th in population was threatened by Florida in 1986 when estimates indicated that Florida had taken over 5th place, dropping Illinois to 6th.

Population projections to the year 2000 show a gradual decline of Illinois population totalling 2.7 percent.

Illinois continues to have one of the most diverse ethnic and racial mixes of all the states. Chicago alone claims more Scandianvian, Lithuanian, Dutch, Polish and Greek residents than any other city in the United States. In fact, Chicago is said to have larger Polish and Greek populations than any other city in the world, not excluding the homelands.

More recent years have seen very substantial Hispanic population increases, with influxes from Mexico and Puerto Rico leading the numbers. Chicago also has experienced a substantial influx of residents from the Philippines.

In the 1980 census the black population of Illinois stood at 1,675,000. As early as 1885 the Illinois General Assembly enacted a civil rights law which outlawed racial discrimination on streetcars and railroads and in hotels, restaurants, theaters and other public places.

The work of PREHISTORIC PEOPLES in Illinois was obvious even to the earliest explorers. MARQUETTE and JOLLIET were the first Europeans known to have seen one of the most remarkable and mysterious of all ancient PICTOGRPHS. This huge colored representation of a bird was painted high on the cliffs near present ALTON by some still unknown civilization. Later, the figure was named the PIASA BIRD or Thunderbird, after similar European works.

Almost equally obvious were the great heaps of earth laboriously piled up by the MOUND BUILDERS. MONKS MOUND, near CAHOKIA has been called the largest remaining primitive earth-

Illinois

Counties and County Seats

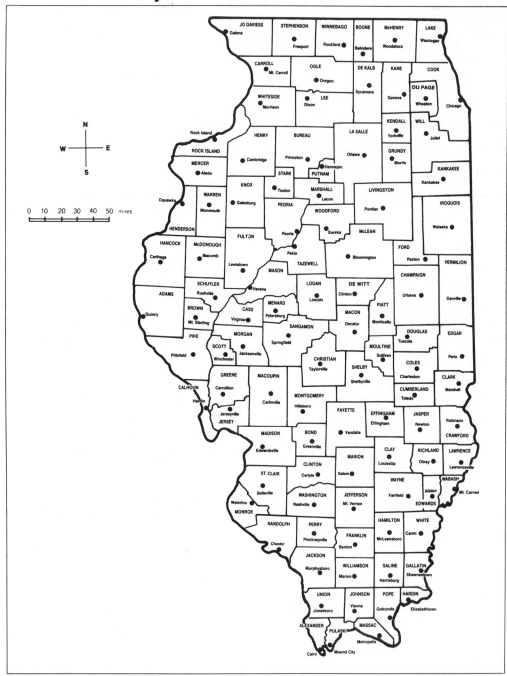

Illinois

STATE OF ILLINOIS

Name: From Illini Indians "perfect and accomplished men." the French Called them the Illini and added -ois to denote tribe.

Nickname: Prairie State

Capital: Springfield

Motto: State Sovereignty, National Union

Symbols and Emblems:
Bird: Cardinal
Fish: Bluegill
Flower: Native Violet
Tree: White oak
Mineral: Fluorite
Song: "Illinois"

Population:
1985: 11,535,000 (1985)
Rank: 5th
Gain or Loss (1970-80): 317,000
Projection (1980-2000): -239,000
Density: 207 per sq. mi. of land (1984)
Percent urban: 83.3 (1980)

Racial Makeup (1980):
White: 80.8
Black: 14.7
Hispanic: 635,525 persons
Indian: 16,300 persons
Others: 501,500 Persons

Largest City:
Chicago (2,992,000-1984)

Other Cities:

Rockford (137,000-1984)
Peoria (117,000-1984)
Springfield (102,000-1984)
Decatur (94,081-1980)
Aurora (81,293-1980)
Joliet (77,956-1980)
Arlington Heights (68,266-1984)

Area: 56,345 sq. mi.
Rank: 24th

Highest Point: 1,235 ft. (377 meters), Charles Mound

Lowest Point: 279 ft. (85 meters) Mississippi River

H.S. Completed: 66.5% (1980)

Four Yrs. College Completed: 16.2% (1980)

STATE GOVERNMENT

ELECTED STATE OFFICIALS (4-year terms, expiring Jan. 1991):
GOVERNOR: $58,000 (1985)
LT. GOV.: $45,500 (1985)
SEC. OF STATE: $50,500 (1985)

GENERAL ASSEMBLY:
Meetings: Biannually in Springfield
Salary: $30,250 per annum (1985)
Senate: 59 members
House: 118 members
Congressional Representatives
Senate: Terms expire 1991, 1993
House of Representatives: 22 Members

Illinois capitol, springfield, exterior, left, rotunda, right.

work in the world. With more than 10,000 mounds, both large and small, Illinois may encompass more works of these primitive people than any other state. Lacking any modern methods of earthmoving, these people, it is thought, carried the earth in baskets to build up the enormous hummocks.

The mounds apparently served several purposes. Skeletons indicate that some were used for burial. Others, of pyramidal shape, apparently were topped by structures, used, perhaps, for religious purposes.

The remains of earlier peoples in Illinois show that they had considerably more skill than the native peoples found by the early explorers. The first groups known to Europeans in the state were six related peoples known collectively as the ILLINI, translated as "The Men." They used this name because they considered themselves superior to other groups. The Illini confederation consisted of the KASKASKIA, Peoria, Tamaroa, MOINGWENA, C A -HOKIA and MICHIGAMEA.

As the fierce IROQUOIS Indians were driven from their homes in the East by white settlement, most of the Illini were killed or driven out by them. For a considerable period, there were no real resident Indian groups in the

state. Then during the period of early European settlement, the confederated SAUK and F O X, Piankeshaw, CHIPPEWA, OTTAWA, MASCOUTEN and POTAWATOMI had homes in what is now Illinois. The latter were the last to leave Illinois as tribal groups. The present Illinois population of native Americans is about 16,000.

French priest, Jacques Marquette, and young French explorer, Louis Jolliet, were the first known Europeans in present Illinois. Their famed canoe journey took them down the Mississippi past future Illinois borders, then returning up the Illinois River, cutting through the center of the present state. They turned into the Des Plaines River at its mouth and made an important discovery. A short overland portage would take them to the Chicago River and Lake Michigan, for their return trip. This easy portage eventually became an international travel route.

The journeys of Marquette and Jolliet, the Sieur de LA SALLE and other French explorers strengthened French claims to the region. La Salle and his associate, DE TONTI, set up forts and established FUR TRADE, as did many who followed them. The town of CAHOKIA was founded by French priests in 1699. KASKASKIA, founded in 1703, became the most important French settlement in the region. FORT DE CHARTRES was known as the strongest on the entire continent.

With the loss of the continent by the French, the English took over. Only a few descendants of the French settlers remain. Remote Illinois was not very important to the British, but George Rogers CLARK was sent to protect their interests there. With the Revolution, Clark's allegiance changed. He and his small group captured Kaskaskia and claimed all of Illinois in the name of the governor of Virginia.

Saved by Clark, Illinois continued as American territory until that ownership was challenged by the British during the WAR OF 1812. The settlers of FORT DEARBORN (Chicago) were massacred by the Indians during the war.

After the war, settlers came mostly by way of the Ohio River, until in 1825 the ERIE CANAL opened the Great Lakes to trade and settlement from the East. Hundreds, then thousands, then hundreds of thousands came to Illinois. As early as 1818 the population warranted statehood, which came on December 3rd.

The displaced Indians made a last futile attempt to reclaim their lands under Chief BLACK HAWK, in the BLACK HAWK WAR, 1832.

NAUVOO, populated by the MORMONS, and GALENA, overwhelmed by the influx of lead miners, were the major cities, years before the little village of Chicago overtook and far surpassed them, due to its location on Lake Michigan and the coming of the RAILROADS.

Prior to the CIVIL WAR, Illinois gained fame as the site of the LINCOLN-DOUGLAS DEBATES and in 1860 when the Republican convention at Chicago nominated Abraham LINCOLN. Senator Stephen A. DOUGLAS was nominated by the Democrats, making the election the first and one of only two in which two major opponents were from the same state. Douglas, the loser, later gave great support to Lincoln and the cause of the Civil War.

Unprepared for the Civil War, the state soon made up for lost time, and Ulysses S. GRANT from Illinois became the Union hero of the war. Illinois troops played an important part in Grant's campaign on the Mississippi River, as well as at Murfreesboro and the Battle of Atlanta.

In 1869, Grant became the second president from Illinois. The Chicago FIRE of 1871, the HAYMARKET RIOT of 1886, in which eight Chicago policemen were killed, and the WORLD'S COLUMBIAN EXPOSITION at Chicago in 1893, were major Illinois events of the late 19th Century. The world's fair has been considered the finest event of its kind.

The new century opened with one of the great engineering achievements of all time, the completion of the reversal of the Chicago River, to form the SANITARY AND SHIP CANAL, with its accompanying locks, canals and channels, which permitted sewage control, much needed by Chicago, and also opened a major waterway between the Great Lakes and the Gulf of Mexico. Another world-altering event was the development of the SKYSCRAPER in Chicago.

Great Lakes Naval Training Station, Camp Grant and FORT SHERIDAN were major centers of WORLD WAR I activity. Illinois was one of the major production centers of both materiel and food for the war effort.

After the war, Chicago gained an unwanted reputation as world headquarters for gangland operations, with such notorious leaders as Al CAPONE. A better reputation was gained for the city through its success with the CENTURY OF PROGRESS EXPOSITION in 1933 and 1934.

Nearly a million men and women from Illinois served in WORLD WAR II, and 27,000 lost their lives.

One of history's most earthshaking events, occurred in Chicago in 1942 when the power of the atom was first harnessed at the University of CHICAGO on December 2nd.

The opening of the ST. LAWRENCE WATERWAY in 1959, with the visit of the Queen of England to Chicago, and the gift of a great statue by artist Pablo Picasso to Chicago, preceded the far less happy event of the 1968 riots during the Democratic National Convention at Chicago.

The 1970s witnessed the adoption of a new state constitution, the opening of the National Accelerator Laboratory at BATAVIA, and the completion of the world's tallest building, the SEARS TOWER. Chicago was saddened by the death in 1976 of its longtime mayor, Richard J. DALEY.

In 1983 Chicago elected its first black mayor, Harold WASHINGTON; in 1987 his second term in office was threatened by the election campaigning of some of his political enemies, but he won reelection, only to die suddenly in 1987.

Chicago and Illinois have distinction in bringing to the fore other black leaders in various fields, including Jean Baptiste Pointe DU SABLE (1745?-1818), founder of Chicago; John W. E. Thomas, Pulitzer Prize winning poet and Illinois Poet Laureate Gwendolyn BROOKS (1917—); scientist Percy JULIAN (1899-1975); renowned singer Mahalia JACKSON (1911-1972); publisher John JOHNSON (1918-); United Nations delegate Archibald Carey; baseball star Ernie BANKS (1931-) and many others.

Illinois has called itself "Land of Lincoln"

Abraham Lincoln's tomb, Springfield.

with good reason since Abraham Lincoln (1809-1865), the great liberator-president, grew to maturity in the state, gained his national fame there, went on to greatness and was returned there to his tomb, mourned by much of the entire world.

The other Illinois president, Ulysses S. GRANT (1822-1885), was far more fortunate as the victor of the Civil War than he was as President of the United States, in a term marred by charges of ineptitude and scandal.

Like Lincoln, Stephen A. DOUGLAS (1813-1861) came to Illinois as a young man. He took his seat in the U.S. Senate in 1847, gained further fame in debating Lincoln but as a presidential candidate was doomed by the split in the Democratic Party over SLAVERY. Despite his disappointment, he supported Lincoln and did much to rally Illinois in support of the Civil War.

Another disappointed office seeker was Adlai E. STEVENSON (1900-1965), 31st governor of Illinois, who was twice defeated for the presidency by Dwight D. Eisenhower. Stevenson, was, however, one of the country's most effective Ambassadors at the United Nations. In a more recent success, Governor James

THOMPSON (1936-)was elected in 1986 to an unprecedented fourth term in that office.

Illinois has produced more pioneers in merchandising and business than any other state, including department store innovator Marshall FIELD, mail order kings Richard SEARS (1863-1914) and A. Montgomery WARD (1843-1913). George PULLMAN (1831-1897) with his Pullman Car Company and its model town for workers, Cyrus H. MC CORMICK (1809-1884), who built a manufacturing empire around his invention of the reaper and John DEERE (1804-1886), who did the same for his invention of the steel plow must rank among the world's industrial great.

Nobel Prize winner, Jane ADDAMS (1860-1935), became world renowned through her social work at Hull House in Chicago.

Cultural leaders include Theodore THOMAS (1835-1905), founder of the CHICAGO SYMPHONY ORCHESTRA, Nobel Prize winning author Ernest HEMINGWAY (1899-1961) of OAK PARK, famed Chicago poet Carl SANDBURG (1868-1967), and world renowned architect Frank Lloyd WRIGHT (1867-1959).

Chicago is no longer Second City in population, but it ranks high among world cities in attractions. Its leading museums, the FIELD MUSEUM OF NATURAL HISTORY, the MUSEUM OF SCIENCE AND INDUSTRY and the ART INSTITUTE are acknowledged as being among the world's best. The SHEDD AQUARIUM is considered the largest in the world under roof.

For other Chicago attractions, see the section on Chicago.

Although neglected by some in favor of Chicago, downstate Illinois has many attractions of its own. The various kinds of attractions devoted to Lincoln have given Illinois the distinction of what is probably the most complete statewide coverage of a single individual in such a manner. These tributes include the LINCOLN NATIONAL MEMORIAL HIGHWAY; the LINCOLN TRAIL HOMESTEAD; LINCOLN LOG CABIN STATE PARK; the MOORE HOME STATE MEMORIAL, home of Lincoln's stepmother; the Thomas LINCOLN Cemetery, and the many memories of the statesman in SPRINGFIELD, including his mammoth tomb and his home, completely restored in 1988.

Particularly impressive is NEW SALEM STATE PARK, where the site of Lincoln's maturing years has been restored as probably the only tribute of its kind to a single individual.

The nearly 100 state parks, including the extraordinary prehistoric earthworks at CAHOKIA MOUNDS PARK, and the Kaskaskia Bell State

Park, are of particular interest. The latter recalls Illinois' first settlement, the site of which now is almost entirely washed away by the Mississippi River. At the memorial building there is "THE LIBERTY BELL OF THE WEST" which pealed when George Rogers Clark captured Kaskaskia from the British.

The Illinois State Fair at Springfield provides one of the nation's outstanding annual attractions.

ILLINOIS AND MICHIGAN CANAL NATIONAL HERITAGE CORRIDOR. Preservation, restoration and recreation are the special interests in commemorating the system of canals linking the GREAT LAKES with the Mississippi Valley, designated a national preserve on August 24, 1984.

ILLINOIS INSTITUTE OF TECHNOLOGY. Chicago, Illinois, school founded in 1940. The Institute was formed with the merging of Armour Institute and Lewis Institute. Ludwig Mies Van Der Rohe, whose innovative ideas were responsible for changes in the construction of skyscrapers and whose presence in CHICAGO gave the city even more renown as a leading center of ARCHITECTURE, added distinction to the staff. As early as the 1920s, in Berlin, Mies had designed tall, glass-covered buildings. The style became known as Miesian. One of the most influential architects of his time, he entirely designed the Promonitory Apartments and Crown Hall of Illinois Tech. The Institute is usually given a place among the top ten U.S. schools of its kind.

ILLINOIS RIVER. Major Illinois waterway. Formed by the junction of the DES PLAINES and KANKAKEE rivers south of JOLIET, Illinois, the river flows almost due west past LA SALLE, OTTAWA and STARVED ROCK STATE PARK. Turning south, it forms the natural Lake Peoria, passes the city of PEORIA and flows south, almost cutting off the entire western bulge of the state. The Illinois River enters the MISSISSIPPI RIVER only a few miles north of ST. LOUIS' northern suburbs. The Illinois River was traversed for its whole length in 1675 by MARQUETTE and JOLLIET on their return voyage to the GREAT LAKES, helping to establish the French claims to the area. The Illinois and Michigan Canal opened on April 23, 1848. With the reversing of the CHICAGO RIVER, locks at Lockport and extensive work on the river, by the early 1900s the Illinois River was providing a water route from the Great Lakes to the Gulf of Mexico. Only the ST.

LAWRENCE SEAWAY equals this combination of river and canal as a major U.S. waterway.

ILLINOIS WESLEYAN UNIVERSITY. BLOOMINGTON, Illinois, Methodist university. Founded in 1850 when it was proposed by members of the Illinois Methodist Episcopal Conference, Illinois Wesleyan's first classes were held in the basement of the Methodist church. Financial problems caused the school to close between 1855 and 1857 when it was reopened through intensive fund-raising activities and with a new president, Reverend Oliver Munsell. In association with Brokaw Hospital, the university maintains the Brokaw Collegiate School of Nursing. Independent study, leading to opportunity for individual advancement according to ability, has been implemented. The university has 33 buildings. During the 1985-1986 academic year the university had an enrollment of 1,647 and 161 faculty members.

ILLINOIS, UNIVERSITY OF. State-supported, chartered in 1867 and opened in 1868. The University of Illinois, originally the Illinois Industrial University, pioneered in the first engineering experimental station, built in 1903, and the first betatron, a machine to accelerate electrons for nuclear physics experiments, built in 1940. The Morrow Plots, established in 1876 at the URBANA -Champaign campus, are the oldest cultivated soil experimental fields in the nation and the oldest corn experimental area in the world. The University of Illinois' campus at Chicago Circle and the Medical Center have been combined as the University of Illinois at Chicago. In 1985-1986 the enrollment of this part of the university was 24,767 with 1,238 faculty members. The University of Illinois at Urbana-Champaign, Illinois, in 1985-1986, had an enrollment of 35,997 students with 2,561 faculty.

INDEPENDENCE, Iowa. City (pop. 6,392), seat of Buchanan County, situated in northeast Iowa on the WAPSIPINICON RIVER about thirty miles east of WATERLOO. It was founded near the time of Fourth of July and took its name from Independence Day. Now a bustling but quiet center of AGRICULTURE and commerce, at one time Independence was internationally celebrated. Its fame began with creamery owner Charles W. WILLIAMS in 1885 when he bought two mares. When each produced a colt he called them Axtell and Allerton. With patient training, they both showed promise of racing ability. However, as yearlings they might have been bought for $300 apiece. Then as a two-year-old Axtell established a new record for his class. At three years he set the world trotting record for stallions of any age. Williams sold him to a syndicate for $105,000. Williams established a racing newspaper at Independence, *The American Trotter* which had world circulation. Soon racing buffs from everywhere were descending on Independence to stay in the elegant three-story hotel, combined with an opera house, which Williams had built in 1892. They traveled over the $40,000 electric trolley line Williams also had built from downtown to his wonderful new track at Rush Park. Called the "racing wonder of its day," the track was shaped like a kite and was said to be several seconds faster than any other. In two weeks, more trotting records fell at Independence than at all the other tracks in the world in the same period. Meanwhile, Allerton had been conquering most of the world's trotting champions, with the one exception of the great mare, the even more famous Nancy Hanks. When the depression of 1893 arrived, Williams left Independence, and today only a decrepit barn remains as a reminder of the faded glory.

INDEPENDENCE, Missouri. City (pop. 111,806), seat of Jackson County, in western Missouri, just east of KANSAS CITY. The area was settled in 1827, with the county named for Andrew Jackson and the city for his love of independence. Incorporated in 1849, the city was a starting point for the SANTA FE, OREGON, and California trails, and later became a rendezvous point for WAGON TRAINS heading for the California gold mines. President Harry S (no period) TRUMAN (1884-1972) was born here and a library and museum bearing his name house his private papers and momentoes. Outlaws such as Frank JAMES were once held in the county jail, built in 1859 and now restored as a museum. The world headquarters of the REORGANIZED CHURCH OF JESUS CHRIST OF LATTER DAY SAINTS (Mormon) is located here. The city has a balanced manufacturing and agricultural economy. Present manufactures include farm machinery, cement, plastics, stoves, and furnaces.

INDIAN LANGUAGES. Until Europeans reached the area, most of the region between the Allegheny and the Great Plains was covered with great forests, the hardwoods of the eastern area and the evergreens of the north and west. In these forest areas of what is now the Midwest, with two exceptions, the Indian

peoples spoke some dialect of Algonquian, the most widespread linguistic family on the continent. There were minor differences among such Algonquian tribes as the POTAWATOMI, MENOMINEE, OJIBWAY, FOX, SAUK, ILLINI and MIAMI, but they all had similar cultures, and differences in dialect were understood. Many Algonquian words have come into American speech, including hickory, moccasin, succotash, tomahawk, totem, terrapin, wigwam and hominy. The WINNEBAGOS of some areas of the north spoke the Siouan language, but in many areas, they got along well with their Algonquian-speaking neighbors, despite the language differences. Indians of the western portion of Missouri, Iowa and Minnesota spoke the Siouian language also, and this included the OSAGE. As the IROQUOIS moved westward, driven away by European settlement, the Iroquoian language also invaded the Midwest. The Indians did not depend entirely on spoken language. Most of them understood sign language, at least to some degree, particularly where they had to come in contact with other language groups. However, sign language could only communicate the simplest kind of exchange.

INDIAN LIFE AND CUSTOMS. When early European explorers and settlers began to reach the Midwest, they were struck by the similarity of the major tribes of that region. There were only minor differences among the MIAMI, MENOMINEE, POTAWATOMI, OJIBWAY, OTTAWA, SAUK, FOX and ILLINI. Even the WINNEBAGO were quite similar to their Algonquian neighbors, except for their Siouan language.

The general uniformity of the region in its geography, climate and resources was the principal factor influencing the similarity of Midwest Indian customs and government, of their religion and rituals and their way of life in general.

All of these tribes were semi-nomadic, but they seldom wandered more than 100 miles from their home base. Everyday life was quite similar throughout the region, except for the minor variations of each tribe and the demands of its particular location. Almost without exception, there was a home village. Outside the home village were the cleared fields, where in the summer the women grew corn, squash, tobacco and whatever local crops were common. The men fished and hunted for small game in the neighboring forests.

Daily diet depended, of course, on what was

immediately available or what could be stored. Because food in the Midwest was relatively plentiful, there was little need to consume ants, grasshoppers and other seemingly less desirable creatures, as some tribes in less fertile regions were forced to do. Nothing was ever wasted, however. Every edible plant, flower, root and berry was used for food, along with the animals brought home from the hunt. Every part of the animal was used, skin for blankets or clothing, sinews for thread or cord and all edible parts.

In many tribes, especially those of the northern and western Midwest, buffalo tongue was considered a delicacy, and the hump behind the shoulders was also choice. When the meat of animals killed could not be eaten at once, it was made into PEMMICAN.

Dried blueberries or other berries provided the equivalent of today's raisins. Flour was often pounded from dried berries, such as the bearberry, and used to thicken gravies. Celery, bulrush and other roots, tree sap, and even mosses, provided food or materials needed to enhance foods. The Indians knew how to use the sap of the maple trees for syrup and sugar. In the northern swampy and shallow lake areas, WILD RICE was the most important food. Indian women gathered the grain into their canoes, and the men would stamp out the chaff.

Housing arrangements varied from tribe to tribe, but permanent winter homes differed little except in size, with some being very large. In general their structures were dome-shaped wigwams, made by covering poles with birch-bark sheets or mats woven of reeds or grass. These could be disassembled for a permanent move, and reassembled at the new site. Away from home on hunts or temporary journeys, the lighter teepee was carried and set up.

Indian clothing was generally made from rabbit fur, deer skin or other animal hides. Moccasins made of hides were almost universal but varied in style. The Chippewa had soft soled moccasins gathered or puckered at the top. The Chippewa were also known as the Ojibway. The word "Ojibway" means "puckered," and the alternate name probably comes from their puckered moccasins.

As European customs became better known and filtered into the most remote areas, Indian dress changed notably. Many chiefs adopted a combination of Indian and European style clothing, perhaps a fantastic and colorful headdress and a necklace of three-inch bear's claws, worn with something resembling a business suit. For most, however, everyday clothing was a blanket over a shirt for men and a long combination dress and blouse for women. Many of the leather garments were handsomely painted. As decorative materials became available through trading, beaded designs, beaded belts and other decorations were added to the feathers, shells, local gemstones and other older-style items of ornamentation.

While many members of different tribes exhibited almost identical face and body paintings, others in the same tribes were permitted to be more imaginative, varying the designs or coming up with novel ones.

Much of Indian life revolved around their rituals and ceremonies, most based on their religious beliefs. Summer was the time for religious festivals. The rituals at these festivals were designed to honor Manitou. Manitou represented the forces present in all things, both inanimate and animate, which were responsible for mankind's destiny. Generally, these forces were kindly, but they could be easily offended and had to be placated with fasting or feasting, dancing and supplication and other ceremonies.

Within the tribes, various kinds of societies were organized to perform the rituals. An early 1600s development was the Midewiwin movement, called the Grand Medicine Society, a secret organization which claimed that its rites cured sickness and brought eternal life, making its membership the most widely sought after of all the societies. Most spectacular of the Midewiwin ceremonies was the Grand Medicine Dance, where the dancers worked themselves into a frenzy and often went into a trance. Other rituals were private and silent.

Most pervasive were the rituals surrounding tobacco, believed to be a gift of the spirits. These evolved to cover almost all activities, from peace to war. Craftsmen from far and wide gathered at the PIPESTONE quarries in Minnesota to make their pipes, many of which showed great artistry. When smoked for peace, the pipes were passed around a circle, beginning with the first chief. If the quest for peace was particularly important, the pipe would make another round. Until tobacco became known to most of the Indians, dried dogwood leaves, called KINNIKINNICK, were smoked.

Most lengthy and elaborate of the rituals concerned warfare. Wars among the tribes were common enough, but not carried on in such a large scale as was customary farther west. Causes for war varied, but most were carried on to avenge some real or imagined wrong. Some came about because one tribe had stolen property from another. Most were simply the

Indian Life

Alfred Jacob Miller illustrates an Indian trading scene.

continuation of long feuds, where one defeat or one capture called for revenge, which in turn brought about vengeance from the other side.

On the night before a battle, each warrior gathered his personal good luck "medicine," wrapped the items in a bundle and brought the bundle to the council house. The medicine man carried these bundles into battle with the expectation that they would bring victory.

Often the women of a tribe would accompany the men part way to the battlefield, singing a plaintive song about the possiblity of death. They returned home still singing, "taking up the burden of loneliness which is woman's share in war," according to Indian authority Frances DENSMORE (1867-1957).

If victory came, each of the victors claimed his medicine and the bundles were opened while the victory was celebrated. As the ceremony began, each successful warrior would solemnly present to the chief the scalps he had collected. Even more important than the scalp was the daring of a warrior who could dart through the foe performing some feat of bravery (known as a coup), such as touching a warrior or chief of the other side.

After the scalps were collected, the war dance began. Each warrior would circle the lodge, lifting his voice in a chant that recounted his feats on the battlefield. The custom of a war dance was pervasive among the various Indian peoples. Most such dances contained the same general elements. While women drummed out the rhythm, the men danced in a rather close knit group, in a style not unlike some of the modern partnerless dances.

Many of the Midwest tribes subscribed to a custom generally thought confined to the U.S. northwest, where it is called potlach. This consisted in giving away items of value at ceremonial parties. The person giving away the most was the most highly regarded.

Early European travelers were treated with great respect. MARQUETTE and JOLLIET recorded their first fearful meeting with the Indians in present Iowa. These were probably members of the ILLINI tribe. The Indians prepared a great feast of dog meat and other delicacies. As a sign of honor, the hosts insisted on placing the bites of food in the mouths of their guests, much to the discomfort of the visitors.

Burial customs varied somewhat, but in general the more easterly tribes were quite similar. These customs ranged from interment in the ground to rituals very strange to Europeans. Some tribes simply placed the body in the fork of a tree. The more elaborate burial ceremonies were generally carried on by the more westerly groups.

The Dacotah (SIOUX) burials were perhaps the

most unusual. Six poles about fifteen feet high were placed in a rough square about twelve feet across. Near the tops of the poles a platform was lashed. The body and useful objects belonging to the dead, such as SNOWSHOES, were placed on the platform. The mourners gathered around the base of the platform.

In some tribes the death of a chief required special attention. He was dressed in his finest robes and most decorative moccasins. The number of eagle feathers in his hair indicated the number of braves he had killed in battle. Some tribes buried their chiefs in a sitting position.

Government within the tribes was quite similar and seemed to be very simple. Smaller tribes, of course, had no need for an elaborate bureaucracy. They usually required only one or two chiefs, generally, but not always, men. As in modern societies, however, the larger tribes required more elaborate organization to preserve social order. In addition there were intricacies of custom and religion which had to be observed, and these made actual administration more complex. The number and nature of these varied duties determined the number and types of leaders required and the division of activities assigned to them.

Larger tribes, such as the Miami, had four chiefs, a man and woman for war along with one of each sex as the civil leaders.

In most cases the chiefs had rather limited powers. While democratic organization in the Midwest was not as formal as in some of the eastern tribes, popular opinion was usually given serious consideration. Most tribes had councils, and larger groups had both war councils and peace councils. These councils assisted in determining regulations and procedures and often performed judicial functions.

Other leaders were the INDIAN MEDICINE men or women. They depended not only upon their real knowledge of herbs and drugs, but they cultivated the superstitions of their fellows to increase their power and respect. Most religious matters were in their hands. Among the most important of these were the puberty rites. On reaching that period, both boys and girls generally were taken to isolated locations, where each fasted alone and hoped for a vision. Boys might fast for as long as four days. They sought a visitation by a guardian spirit, who might even endow them with extraordinary powers. That spirit stayed with the man for the rest of his life. During their isolation period, girls called on divine aid in finding a good husband, for health and for many children.

Wedding ceremonies were generally extremely simple. For the Menominee, a wedding ritual consisted only of a solemn exchange of blankets. If either partner found the marriage unsatisfactory, the dissatisfied partner had only to return the blanket, and the marriage was dissolved.

The place of women in the Midwest tribes was not as exalted as in some eastern tribes, where in every facet of life except for war, the women were in charge and descent of property was often matrilineal. This was not generally the case in the Midwest. The Midwestern Indian women were held in greater esteem, however, than were those of the tribes farther to the west.

Perhaps the most difficult time for women was during the menstrual period, when women were segregated from the rest of the tribe because it was thought that misfortune might come if women mingled during those times.

The OSAGE, who lived the farthest south of all the Midwest tribes, had many customs that were similar to their northern fellows, but their lives were also very different in many ways. They lived in southern Missouri and farther south and have been considered by some to be the most remarkable of the indigenous Americans in what is now the U.S. Their villages were more substantial, built on high land or a terrace, with rectangular houses formed in a circle. The larger house of the chief was placed inside the circle. The Osage were unique in their ability to disregard alcohol, which was often the downfall of most other tribes. They held many European ways in contempt and considered the white man the slave of his way of life.

Of course, as in other societies, Indian customs changed and evolved with time. The new insights acquired from European associations and the new material possessions they made possible brought many changes, often not for the better, as in the case of alcohol. The Indian ways also changed as they were driven ever farther west.

In the region today there are scattered Indian populations in many of the urban areas, and there are fifteen Indian reservations in Wisconsin, fourteen in Minnesota, five in Michigan and one in Iowa. In these there is a growing effort to maintain and recapture much of the best of the old ways and customs.

INDIAN MEDICINE. Every Indian tribe had persons with a gift for healing or prophecy—the medicine men or women. There were many differing personalities and activities. Some wrapped up in blankets like mummies, while they prayed for healing for their patients. Others had stones or other objects with magical powers. Such powers were supposed to locate game, missing objects or lost people. Of even higher rank in some tribes were the holy people, the seers, keepers of tradition and directors of the great rituals. The Indians of many tribes had a surprising knowledge of medicinal herbs, roots and other plant substances. Some authorities today find that they can still learn from the collective medical knowledge of the Indian peoples. A wide variety of plant substances was used both externally and internally to combat diseases, staunch the flow of blood and to speed up healing processes. Some medicine men had an exceptional knowledge of human anatomy and could set broken bones. Some were aware of herbs which could induce abortion, but these were used only when it appeared to be absolutely essential. In some tribes women also became healers, and many were prized as midwives.

INDIAN MUSIC. Many Indian activities were accompanied by music. There were ceremonial songs, war and powwow songs, lullabies for infants and funeral dirges for the dead. After Europeans arrived, their composers often came from far places to hear and learn the Indian songs and to incorporate them in the white man's music. Antonin DVORAK, for example, spent some time in northern Iowa and went into Minnesota to jot down Indian melodies and words of songs. Several of his classical compositions are based on or derived from Indian sources. Flutes often were played by young Indian men in courtship. Some tribes of the western Midwest carved their flutes in the shape of bird's heads and decorated them with a picture of a horse, after the horse had been introduced by the Europeans. Lovers had their own secret tunes, which might be heard at night floating through the still air. In addition to flutes there might be notched sticks, rattles and bull roarers. Then, of course, there were the drums. One old Indian said "The throbbing of the drum is the Indian's heartbeat." Even crude fiddles might be created, fashioned after ones brought by the early Europeans.

INDIAN TRIBES IN THE MIDWEST. In about the year 1500 AD, experts have determined that, in the Midwest, tribes included the ERIE in far northeast Ohio, The Cheyenne and MIAMI in much of Indiana and Illinois and parts

of Michigan; MENOMINEE, WINNEBAGO, FOX and POTAWATOMI in northern Michigan and most of Wisconsin; the IOWAY and OTO in all but the northwest portion of present Iowa; the SIOUX (Dacotah) in northwest Iowa and most of Minnesota, and the Hidatsa in far northeast Minnesota. No one is quite willing to guarantee the complete accuracy of such an assessment.

Most of these peoples were nomadic and moved from place to place. Vast areas of the Midwest were not used as permanent areas of residence but rather for visits to hunt and fish. As European settlements grew in the East, Indian groups of the East began to migrate west. Many of the feared IROQUOIS gradually moved westward, displacing large numbers of the Midwestern tribes, who moved onward little by little.

In Ohio at the time of greater exploration and early settlement, the most numerous groups were the WYANDOT (Huron), DELAWARE, MIAMI and SHAWNEE. Actual Indian settlement in present Indiana did not begin much before the first Europeans arrived. The Miami and Potawatomi were the most important. Others were the WEA, KICKAPOO, Piankashaw, CHIPPEWA, ILLINI, OTTAWA, Wyandot and Shawnee.

Illinois' Indian peoples were dominated by a confederation known as the Illini, made up of six related groups, MICHIGAMEA, MOINGWENA, Peoria, Tamaroa, CAHOKIA and Kaskaskia. As Indian migration continued, many Miami moved to the CHICAGO area, and the Shawnee appeared in southern Illinois. Somewhat later the confederated SAUK and FOX came to Illinois from Wisconsin, then later moved to Iowa. Other Illinois groups included the Chippewa (Ojibway), OTTAWA, Mascouten and Piankeshaw. The Potawatomi, who had moved to northeastern Illinois, were the last Indians to leave the state.

Some of the most important groups in present Michigan in early European times were the Chippewa (Ojibway), Ottawa, Potawatomi, Miami and Menominee. Later the Wyandot (Huron) came in.

In Wisconsin, explorer NICOLET was greeted by the Winnebago, a branch of the Sioux. By 1654 several Algonquian groups, Kickapoo, Mascouten, Potawatomi, Sauk, Chippewa, Fox, Huron, Ottawa and Miami, had established their villages in Wisconsin. One of the most important of these was the Menominee.

The Ioway, OSAGE, Winnebago, Missouri, Omaha, Ponca, Wahpeton, and Sisseton tribes were among the Plains Indians found in Iowa. Woodland tribes included the Illini, Fox, Sauk,

Indiana

Life in a Michigamea village, by Robert Thom, (C) 1966 Michigan Bell Telephone Co.

Chippewa (Ojibway), Potawatomi, Ottawa and Miami.

Ioway, to the north, Missouri to the west and south and Osage to the south, were the principal Indian groups in Missouri at the time of early European exploration. Of these, the Osage were by far the most important.

As the Iroquois moved west and as European settlement expanded in the Midwest, the tribes moved farther west of their own accord, or they ceded their lands to the government and were moved by the government or they died out, sadly, mostly due to the white man's diseases over which they had no immunity.

INDIANA. State. Situated in the East Central section of the Midwest Region. Two-thirds of its borders are man-made. The natural borders include the small fifty-one mile long shoreline on Lake MICHIGAN in the northeast, the southern portion of the southwest boundary formed by the WABASH RIVER and the entire southern border following the winding course of the great OHIO RIVER.

Its longest border with a neighboring state separates Ohio and Indiana. Michigan lies to the north, Illinois to the west, and the border with Kentucky follows the middle of the Ohio

River. The state's river system is confused by the two rivers both bearing the name ST. JOSEPH. The TIPPECANOE, WHITE, Muncie, MISSISSINEWA, Iroquois, KANKAKEE and WHITEWATER are the other larger rivers. Of unusual interest is the LOST RIVER. It takes its name from the fact that for much of its length it flows underground, coming often to the surface and then frequently disappearing for a total underground length of twenty-two miles.

Most of Indiana's nearly thirteen hundred lakes are in the northeast quadrant. Largest in the state is Lake WAWASEE, southeast of Goshen. Lake Maxinkuckee and Lake James are second and third in size. Largest body of water within the state is artificial Monroe Reservoir.

With an area of 36,185 square miles, Indiana is the smallest of the Midwest states. North of the Wabash the lakes and other natural features are typical of a glaciated area, with its rich soil of glacial drift. To the south the balance of the state has shallower soil. The bottomlands are broken by ridges, knolls and modest gorges and valleys. WYANDOTTE CAVE is typical of the limestone cave formations. The state is noted for its mineral springs, especially FRENCH LICK and West Baden.

A small section of the north and two-thirds

Indiana

Counties and County Seats

Indiana

STATE OF INDIANA

Name: Latin form of "Indian" meaning "land of the Indians."

Nickname: Hoosier State

Capital: Indianapolis

Motto: The Crossroads of America

Symbols and Emblems:
Bird: Cardinal
Flower: Peony
Tree: Tulip Poplar
Stone: Limestone
Song: "On the Banks of the Wabash, Far Away"

Population:
1985: 5,499,000 (1985)
Rank: 14th
Gain or Loss (1970-80): + 295,000
Projection (1980-2000): + 189,000
Density: 153 per sq. mi. of land (1984)
Percent urban: 64.2% (1980)

Racial Makeup (1980):
White: 91.14%
Black: 7.5%
Hispanic: 87,020 persons
Indian: 7,800 persons
Others: 63,200 persons

Largest City:
Indianapolis (710,000 - 1984)

Other Cities:
Fort Wayne (165,000 - 1984)
Gary (143,000 - 1984)

Evansville (130,000 - 1984)
South Bend (107,000 - 1984)
Hammond (93,714 - 1980)
Muncie (77,216 - 1980)

Area: 36,185 sq. mi.
Rank: 38th

Highest Point: 1,257 ft.

Lowest Point: 320 ft., Ohio River

H.S. Completed: 66.4% (1980)

Four Yrs. College Completed: 12.5% (1980)

STATE GOVERNMENT

ELECTED OFFICIALS (4 year terms, expiring Jan. 1989):

GOVERNOR: $66,000 plus discretionary expenses (1986)

LT. GOV.: $51,000 plus discretionary expenses (1986)

SEC. OF STATE: $46,000 (1986)

GENERAL ASSEMBLY:

Meetings: Annually in Indianapolis
Salary: $11,600 per annum plus $75 a day while in session and $15 a day when not in session (1986)
Senate: 50 members
House: 100 members

Congressional Representatives

Senate: Terms expire 1989, 1993

House of Representatives: Ten members

of the state's western segment are Early Paleazoic; the eastern third, with a small finger extending to the northwest corner, belongs to the Late Paleozoic period. Beginning with the Permian period, Indiana's geology was little changed through Tertiary times.

Meteorologists classify the state's climate as moderate, with four distinct seasons. Considering the lowest recorded temperature at minus 35 degrees and the highest at 116 degrees, some Indianans might quarrel with the "temperate" classification.

The outstanding physical feature of Indiana is its Lake Michigan shoreline, with its cherished sand dunes. This area is said to be, in a number of ways, unlike any other in the world, with its unique topography and several unique plant types. The lakeshore also provides Indiana with its invaluable toehold on the GREAT LAKES, offering access to the world's oceans by way of the ST. LAWRENCE SEAWAY.

The soils above the surface and the minerals below combine to form the most substantial natural assets of the state. Indiana ranks eleventh among the states in total income from farm products, fifth in the Midwest in farm income. The state usually holds third rank in CORN production, its principal crop. SOYBEANS, HOGS and dairy products are the other ranking agricultural products.

Until the 20th Century, northwest Indiana seemed a nearly worthless swampy wasteland. Then, with the coming of the steel mills at GARY, the area quickly became one of the world's leading production centers. While steel production in the U.S. in general has faltered, Indiana continues to be the country's second most important producer of steel and steel products. The northwest sector is also a leader in petroleum processing, with major refineries of several of the largest oil companies.

Indiana also holds leadership among the states in the production of musical instruments, biological products and prefabricated buildings. ELKHART, band instrument capital of the world, produces almost a third of the woodwind, brass and percussion instruments manufactured in the United States. Miles Laboratories, also at Elkhart, is a major U.S. producer of pharmaceuticals.

Indiana firms were pioneers in automobile production, beginning in 1899 with the Studebaker car, and continuing with such once-well-known names as Duesenburg, Cord, Stutz, Auburn and Overland. The automobile industry continues with important centers producing equipment and supplies, including the world's largest manufacturer of auto lighting equipment.

Famed Indiana limestone provides the most important mineral industry. Bedford limestone is particularly cherished for its ability to take fine carving, as well as for its sturdy building qualities. The Bedford-Bloomington region produces over eighty percent of the country's dimensional, or building, limestone, being the material of such structures as the Empire State Building and the ART INSTITUTE OF CHICAGO.

Despite the prominence of limestone, however, COAL is still the leading mineral product of the state, followed by petroleum and natural gas.

River traffic on the Ohio and several internal rivers, and shipbuilding are important transportation factors. VINCENNES and TERRE HAUTE are leading river ports, and barge traffic continues to increase on the Ohio. The new Lake Michigan port of BURNS HARBOR added to the state's ability to absorb lake and ocean traffic by way of the St. Lawrence Seaway, as well as the other Great Lakes. Indianapolis plays an increasing role as a leading interior transportation center and is the largest U.S. city not on navigable water.

Indiana's population of 5,499,000 in 1985 showed an increase of only 9,000 over the figures for the 1980 census, but the small increase followed a three-year drop in population. Projections for the year 2000 are placed at 5,679,000.

The population of Indiana is predominately white, of European origin. The black population of slightly over 400,000 represents less than one percent of the total.

Most of the information about prehistoric Indiana comes from the mounds found in the state. MOUNDS STATE PARK preserves what is left of one of the more interesting of them. These mounds served different purposes, as sites for temples, burial places and fortifications. Most common of the mounds are the refuse dumps, called kitchen middens. From the other mounds have come copper work, polished stone, textiles, basketry, evidences of the use of bow and arrow and domestication of animals. Remains of the cultures of the HOPEWELL, ADENA and FORT ANCIENT have been found, but all of these appear to have died off before European incursion.

By the time European settlements were appearing in the American East, Indiana seems to have been almost bereft of human inhabitants. Vagrant tribes profited from the fine hunting and fishing in the unpopulated area. However, by the time white explorers reached the area, a number of tribes had settled. The POTAWATAMI and MIAMI were most important in numbers. Other groups included the WYANDOT, SHAWNEE, OTTAWA, CHIPPEWA, Piankashaw, WEA, KICKAPOO and ILLINI.

The Miami had a relatively high degree of organization, operating with a man and woman war chief and a different man and woman civil chief for each tribal group. Principal evidence of the Indian presence today is found only in such names as KOKOMO, Kankakee, Wawausee and, of course, the name of the state itself.

Legends tell of Scandinavian explorers in the area as early as 1200 A.D., resulting in a fabled race of "white" Indians. Some of the Indian languages are said to have words resembling those in the Welsh language. Another discounted claim is that Samuel de CHAMPLAIN (1567-1635) came inland as far as the site of FORT WAYNE. Other French explorers probably touched present Indiana, but firm records tell of the arrival, first, of Robert Cavalier, Sieur de LA SALLE (1643-1687), at the mouth of the St. Joseph River in 1679. He reached the present site of SOUTH BEND on December 3rd. He and his men portaged across to the Kankakee River and sailed down it out of present Indiana.

At a great council with the Indians at South Bend two years later, La Salle reached agreement with the Indian leaders on setting up trading posts and fortifications. However, the first fort, FORT OF THE MIAMIS at present Fort Wayne, was not built until 1700, some say as late as 1714.

Sometime in the period 1727-1732, VINCENNES was started by Francois Morgane de VINCENNES (1700-1736). The coming of several families to Vincennes soon after the fort was established supports its claim as the first permanent European settlement in Indiana (1732-1733). Along with FORT OUIATENON and several others, these forts were designed to protect the French trade routes from Canada to New Orleans.

Paddling down the Maumee River, licensed travelers called VOYAGEURS, crossed the Fort Miami portage, launched into the Little Wabash and from there had a water passage to the mouth of the Mississippi. The Indians traded their furs for ammunition, utensils, blankets, hatchets and glittering trinkets. The French settlers around the fort treated the Indians as equals and always got along well with them.

Into this establishment more and more British traders were intruding. When the French had to give up their entire North American holdings in 1763, the British took over. The king forbade further settlement east of the APPALACHIANS in order to preserve the wilderness for fur bearing. However, the stricture was mostly ignored.

Because the British treated the Indians badly, Chief PONTIAC (1720?-1769) roused his people to fight back, captured Fort Miami and drove the British forces out of the region, until they returned in 1777, during the Revolution. They were soon driven out again by the tiny force of American Revolutionaries under the brilliant direction of George Rogers CLARK (1752-1818), who captured Vincennes from the cruel British leader, Henry HAMILTON (-1796).

The end of the Revolution did not end British hopes to hold the region. They encouraged their Indian allies to resist all American attempts to settle the area. Nevertheless, in 1783-84 Clark was able to establish CLARKSVILLE as the first American settlement in Indiana.

When the eastern states gave up their claims to areas east of the Mississippi, Indiana came under the famed NORTHWEST ORDINANCE, which established the right of territories to become states when certain conditions had been reached.

As more and more of their lands were taken, the Miami formed a confederacy under Chief LITTLE TURTLE (1752-1812) and made several successful attacks. They finally were defeated by General "Mad" Anthony WAYNE (!745-1796) in the BATTLE OF FALLEN TIMBERS (1794), waged just east of the Indiana border.

General Wayne then established Fort Wayne and forced the Indians to sign the Treaty of GREENE VILLE (1794),which opened much of Indiana to settlement. Indiana Territory, a much larger area than the present state, was established under Governor William Henry HARRISON.

However, still more trouble with the Indians was ahead. Led by the renowned Chief TECUMSEH (1768-1813), he and his Indian confederates tried to organize all the western Indians to oppose white advances. Governor Harrison defeated them in the minor Battle of TIPPECANOE (1811), but much more trouble was to follow during the WAR OF 1812, with sieges at forts Harrison and Wayne and a massacre at Pigeon's Roost. The end of the war brought most Indian dangers to a close, and Indiana was made a state on December 11, 1816.

In 1820 the site of Indianapolis, then with only two white settlers, was chosen as the state capital. Settlement continued, with such striking new communities as Harmonie, founded as

The Indiana Capitol, Indianapolis.

At the Republican nominating convention in CHICAGO in 1860, the Indiana delegation gave Abraham LINCOLN all of its 26 votes on the first ballot, which may have assured his nomination.

Under Governor Oliver P. MORTON, the contributions of Indiana to the CIVIL WAR were said to rank with those of states many times its size. Several small battles were fought in southern Indiana, and Indiana troops fought in 308 engagements of the war elsewhere.

During and after the war, Indiana prospered, building particularly from the contributions of the flood of immigrants from England, Scotland, Hungary, Poland, Russia, Italy, Austria, France and, most importantly, Canada. The present capitol was completed in 1878, and WABASH became the world's first city to be lighted with electricity, in 1880.

WORLD WAR I was brought home to Indiana with the death of James Gresham of EVANSVILLE, one of the first three Americans to be lost in the war. Altogether 130,670 Indianans participated in the war.

The short success of the Ku Klux Klan in Indiana after the war and the worst Ohio River FLOOD in history in 1937 were hallmarks of the post-war decades.

WORLD WAR II brought another burst of prosperity but cost the lives of 10,000 from Indiana. Some 338,000 men and women from Indiana served in that war.

Burns Harbor opened for shipping in 1970. Large portions of the valuable Lake Michigan dunes area were preserved as INDIANA DUNES NATIONAL LAKESHORE, and the area was expanded in 1976. In the election of 1984, Ronald REAGAN easily won the Indiana vote, and Robert Orr was returned to the governor's chair in 1986.

Some authorities have stated that Indiana has been the birthplace of or had substantial influence on more prominent Americans than any other state. Abraham LINCOLN (1809-1865) spent his formative years there, maturing for fourteen years in the Little Pigeon Creek region. The family began its life in Indiana in a lean-to shelter and moved on to slightly more comfortable but still rugged pioneer life.

During that time Lincoln's mother, Nancy Hanks Lincoln, died of "milk sick" poisoning, an affliction brought on by drinking milk from cows which have eaten white snakeroot. Abraham's father soon married Sarah Bush Johnson. The new stepmother gave great encouragement to Lincoln's fierce desire for an education, although his father did not approve. In Indiana, Lincoln's experience included jobs as carpenter, cabinetmaker, ploughman, baby

a model religious community by the Rappites under the leadership of George RAPP (1757-1847). Ten years later the settlement was sold to Robert OWEN (1801-1877), who converted it into an even more unusual community called NEW HARMONY. In 1826, Owen brought in a group of artists, scientists, educators and philosophers who floated down the Ohio River to their new home on a flatboat called the Boatload of Knowledge. Their efforts in setting up trade schools, infant school, public libraries, science clubs and women's clubs gave Harmony a reputation as one of the world villages which have made history.

New roads and RAILROADS, canal building, a new state constitution (1851) and other improvements continued to enhance the growth of the state.

SLAVERY in Indiana had disappeared by 1843. From that time on, the people grew more and more opposed to slavery, playing a leading part in the UNDERGROUND RAILROAD, among other anti-slavery roles.

sitter and ferryman. When the family left Indiana in 1830, Lincoln was ready for greater things.

Lincoln was one of three presidents associated with Indiana, although none of these was born in the state. William Henry HARRISON (1773-1841) gained much of his fame while governing the area, and his grandson, Benjamin HARRISON, began the practice of law in Indiana in 1854, was a Civil War general, was a U.S. senator from Indiana, was elected to the presidency from the state in 1888 and returned to live there until he died in 1901.

One of the neglected figures of American history is Civil War Governor Oliver P. MORTON (1823-1877), called "...the Gibraltar of the government" by historian Thomas Beveridge. He "held aloft the hands of Lincoln until victory came. So far as deeds and facts could make it so, Morton was deputy president of the United States in active charge of the Ohio Valley. No man can tell what the results would have been had not some man like our Morton been what and where our Morton was." In 1867 Morton resigned as governor to serve in the U.S. Senate and was active there until he died in 1877.

Unsuccessful 1940 presidential candidate Wendell Lewis Wilkie, was a native of ELWOOD, where he accepted the Republican nomination.

Few Indian leaders achieved the reputation of Chief Tecumseh, an honorable and vastly able man, whose first interest in life was to preserve his native soil for his people. He organized great confederations of Indians and might have been far more successful except for the inevitabiliity of the white man's advance. His half-brother, Tenskwatawa, called the PROPHET (1770-1834) (1866-1944), was also a person of great energy and ability, but he tended to be erratic and undependable. He gained great fame when he pretended to make the sun stand still during the eclipse of June 16, 1806. Chief Tecumseh's life ended in Canada while he was fighting as a British officer in the War of 1812.

Indiana may well hold the record among the states for producing prominent literary figures. From his birth in a log cabin at GREENFIELD, Hoosier Poet James Whitcomb RILEY (1849-1916) went on to international fame. The books of Gene Stratton PORTER (1863-1924) were the best sellers of her day. A native of TERRE HAUTE, Theodore DREISER ((1871-1945) was known for his sketches of Indiana boyhood as well as for his best-known work, *An American Tragedy* (1925). Pultizer Prize winning Albert J.

BEVERIDGE (1862-1927), who was also a U.S. senator, George ADE (1866-1944), Charles Austin BEARD 1874-1948), and his wife Mary were all prominent in the literary scene.

One of America's most controversial authors was Lew WALLACE (1827-1905), who was a Civil War general, general in the Mexican army, territorial governor of New Mexico, Crawfordsville lawyer, and Ambassador to Turkey. While in New Mexico, Wallace wrote the novel *Ben Hur* (1880), which has been recreated many times on stage and in movies and has become one of the best known works of all time.

Famed journalist Ernie PYLE, cartoonists Kin HUBBARD (1868-1930) and John T. MC CUTCHEON (1870-1949), composers Cole PORTER (1893-1964) and Hoagland J. (Hoagy) CARMICHAEL (1899-1981) and lesser known songwriters Thomas Paine Westendorf and Albert von Tilzer were all creative Hoosiers.

Industrialists Charles G. Conn, who founded a major musical instrument company, and Dr. Franklin Miles, founder of the pharmaceutical company, Miles Laboratories, the five BALL brothers who founded a vast glassmaking operation, carriage and automobile manufacturers Henry and Clement Studebaker (1831-1901) and farm implement magnate James Oliver all contributed to the economic growth of Indiana. Most spectacular of all, perhaps, in that aspect of achievement was Elbert GARY (1846-1927), instigator of the great industrial area of northwest Indiana and founder of GARY.

Inventor Elwood HAYNES (1857-1925) was a pioneer in the development of gasoline engine-powered automobiles. George H. Hammmond, originated the idea of refrigerated freight cars and developed a meat-packing operation at HAMMOND, which bears his name. In a different field, Ben Wallace of Peru became one of the world's best-known circus showmen.

Among Indiana attractions, the Indianapolis 500 auto race has gained world renown and continues to rank among the nation's top ten annual attractions. The city itself is centered around the striking Soldiers and Sailors monument which gives its name to imposing Monument Circle. The area is thought to be the first anywhere to be dedicated to the memory of enlisted personnel. The central shaft rises 284 feet. Not far from Monument Circle is the imposing capitol. Another outstanding Indianapolis feature is World War Memorial Plaza, dedicated to the memory of those who died in the two world wars. The Childrens Museum is still another unique attraction.

One of the most popular tourist attractions in the region is BROWN COUNTY , where, in the season of autumn color, all highways are blocked for miles by tourists' cars. Center of the county is quaint and attractive NASHVILLE , home of many artists, whose work is displayed in dozens of galleries. This crossroads village now also houses gift and antique shops and restaurants of great variety. Also adding to the attraction of Brown County are the towns of GNAW BONE and BEAN BLOSSOM .

To the east of Brown County is COLUMBUS , where local boosters encouraged and supported the work of many world-renowned architects, with the result that the city has more remarkable works of modern ARCHITECTURE than any other of its size.

New Harmony has its own unique architecture in the Roofless Church. Much of the original community is associated both with its religious and cultural foundations, and many visitors are attracted to a town which is perhaps the most complete restoration of an early planned community.

PERU has been labeled "Circus City," building on the memories of circus-great Ben Wallace. An entirely different personality is remembered at Johnny Appleseed (CHAPMAN , 1774-1845) Memorial Park at Fort Wayne.

Three Indiana cities are especially notable for universities. NOTRE DAME , SOUTH BEND , built a reputation on its athletic teams, but its academic reputation has kept pace. INDIANA UNIVERSITY , with headquarters in BLOOMINGTON , and PURDUE UNIVERSITY at LAFAYETTE are especially noted for their music departments and great music halls, but they also maintain high academic standards.

INDIANA CENTRAL UNIVERSITY. Privately supported university in INDIANAPOLIS , Indiana. Established in 1902, Indiana Central grants associate, bachelor's, and master's degrees. It maintains a cooperative plan with Duke University in forestry, Methodist Hospital, Indianapolis, in medical technology, and PURDUE UNIVERSITY in engineering. The campus is located on sixty acres and has thirteen buildings. During the 1985-1986 academic year the university enrolled 2,995 students and had 347 faculty members.

INDIANA DUNES NATIONAL LAKE-SHORE. Magnificent dunes rise as high as 180 feet above Lake MICHIGAN 's southern shore. Other natural features include beaches, bogs,

marshes, swamps and prairie remnants; historic sites include an 1822 homestead and 1900 family farm, both partially restored.

INDIANA DUNES STATE PARK. Three and one-half square miles on the southern shore of Lake MICHIGAN midway between GARY and MICHIGAN CITY, Indiana. Nine trails allow visitors access through sandhills, marshes, and forests to unique and valuable regions.

INDIANA STATE UNIVERSITY. Publicly supported, founded in 1865 and located in TERRE HAUTE, Indiana. Undergraduate and graduate programs are available as well as practical arts programs which are specialized, but may not lead to a degree. Degree programs are offered in the sciences, humanities, and teacher education. In 1985-1986 the university enrolled 11,491 students and employed 806 faculty members.

INDIANA UNIVERSITY. Publicly supported, in BLOOMINGTON, Indiana. Founded in 1820, Indiana University has a two-thousand-acre main campus. The Indiana University Medical Center is located fifty miles away in INDIANAPOLIS. The tenth largest university in the nation, Indiana University offers a state-wide system of higher education, including: College of Arts and Sciences, Schools of Dentistry, Law, Medicine, Education, Business, Nursing, Public and Environmental Affairs, Social Work, and Physical Education. In 1985-1986 the university enrolled 30,579 students and had 1,615 faculty members.

INDIANAPOLIS, INDIANA

Name: From the latinized word Indiana meaning "land of the Indians" and the Greek word *polis*, "city."

Nickname: none

Area: 375.2 square miles.

Elevation: 840 feet

Population:
1984: 710,280
Rank: 13th
Percent change (1980-1984): 1.4%
Density (city): 1,893 per sq. mi.
Metropolitan Population: 1,195,000
Percent change (1980-1984): 2.4%

Race and Ethnic (1980):
White: 77%

Black: 21.8%

Hispanic origin: 6,430 persons

Indian: 1,356 persons

Asian: 4,539 persons

Other: 1,738 persons

Age:

18 and under: 29.6%

65 and over: 9.8%

TV Stations: 7

Radio Stations: 27

Hospitals: 17

Sports Teams:

Indians (minor-league baseball)

Colts (football)

Pacers (basketball)

Checkers (minor-league hockey)

Further Information: Indianapolis Chamber of Commerce, 320 North Meridian Street, Indianapolis, IN 46204

INDIANAPOLIS, Indiana. City, capital of Indiana and seat of Marion County, situated on the WHITE RIVER in the central part of the state, the only major U.S. city not on a navigable waterway, occupying a land area of 375.2 square miles. The name is the Latinized form of Indian with the added *polis* being the Greek name for city. The surrounding areas are largely small unincorporated communities; there are no major suburbs.

The city's growth has been due mainly to its location as the principal center of a rich agricultural region and to the varied transportation facilities of which it is the hub. At one time the city held first rank in electric interurban transport, with over 400 trains per day. With the coming of superhighways and air travel, this form of transportation has almost died out completely across the country. Early travelers passed the city on the first major U.S. highway, the great NATIONAL ROAD. As many as twelve STAGECOACHES a day might thunder up for fresh horses while the travelers refreshed themselves and caught up with the news. Today Indianapolis has the greatest concentration of Interstate highways in the nation, the intersection of seven of those major routes. The international airport and six RAILROADS add to the city's dominance as a transportation center.

Indianapolis is a major grain center and a processor of grains and other agricultural

products. Its principal manufactures are automotive and aircraft parts, pharmaceuticals, roadbuilding machinery, telephone and electronic equipment.

Other Indiana cities were flourishing before Indianapolis was founded in 1821. The legislature had decided that as a capital city CORYDON in south-central Indiana was not a suitable location, and the capital should be removed to a rolling woodland site in the central part of the state, although there were a few Indian settlements and only two white settlers. This was the future capital city.

In the bitter times preceding the CIVIL WAR, Indianapolis was a principal station on the UNDERGROUND RAILROAD. During the Civil War itself the city was sometimes known as the second U.S. capital because of the support given President Abraham LINCOLN by Governor Oliver P. MORTON (1823-1877), sometimes called the Assistant President.

The state capitol was built during the decade of 1878-88. In 1902 one of the world's notable memorials was dedicated. The Soldiers and Sailors Monument is said to be the only one dedicated to the memory of enlisted soldiers and seamen.

As with most other major cities of the Midwest, the population of Indianapolis declined from 737,000 in the 1970 census to 710,280 in 1984, a smaller percentage of decline than that of most other cities of the Midwest area. Indianapolis ranks 13th in population among the nation's cities and holds 3rd rank among Midwest metropolises. With no major suburbs, the city drops to 32nd rank in total metropolitan population. Black residents make up 21.8 percent of the population, with Hispanic peoples about one percent.

The six colleges and universities in the city include the Indianapolis campuses of PURDUE UNIVERSITY and INDIANA UNIVERSITY, with many units of the latter, including the Herron School of Art and the notable medical center. Other institutions of higher education are BUTLER UNIVERSITY, Marion College, Indiana Central College and Christian Theological Seminary.

Among the notable institutions of the city, perhaps the best known is the American Legion, with its national headquarters in the World War Memorial Plaza. Extending for five blocks, the plaza includes the Indiana World War Memorial, with its Altar Room. This room is dedicated as a shrine to the American flag. The largest bronze casting ever made in the United States is the giant *Pro Patria* standing outside the World War Memorial. Another notable feature of the plaza is its 100-foot granite obelisk and cenotaph, where James Bethel Gresham is memorialized as one of the first three Americans to die in WORLD WAR I.

The 284-foot high shaft of Soldiers and Sailors Monument, surrounded by heroic sculptures and many fountains, forms the central circle of the city and one of the favored spots for promenades.

Perhaps the only major U.S. public building to be built within its cost estimates, the splendid capitol features grand halls running the full length of the building on each floor, centered by a 234-foot-high dome. Due to his kindness to them, Civil War prisoners from the South contributed the massive bronze bust of Colonel Richard Owen on the main floor at the base of the dome.

The Central Library has been called a "masterpiece of architecture," while the Indiana State Library and Historical Building is said to rival it as an architectural treasure. Another major architectural attraction is the great Scottish Rite Cathedral. Among historic structures are Fort Benjamin Harrison, the homes of Benjamin HARRISON (1833-1901), and of writers James Whitcomb RILEY (1849-1916) and Booth TARKINGTON (1869-1946).

The Childrens Museum, with its 25,000 displays of particular interest to young people, is a unique institution of the city. Another notable cultural entry is the Indianapolis Symphony, housed at Clowes Hall, yet another outstanding architectural attraction.

Indianapolis is home of one of the five major U.S. sporting events and the world's most notable motor classic, the 500 Automobile Race, considered one of the best attended of all American annual sporting events. It takes its name from the 500 mile course on the outstanding track, where speed trials are held over a long period, and speed records have been consistently broken.

Basketball's Indiana Pacers and professional football's Indianapolis eastern division American conference teams are the city's only representatives in major professional sports. There is a large sports center west of the circle, built to attract as many important sports meets as possible.

INDIANOLA, Iowa. City (pop. 10,843), seat of Warren County, situated in south central Iowa, about twenty miles south of DES MOINES. The name is derived from the word Indian plus the CHOCTAW word "ola," which means "this side of." As an agricultural hub, the city is known for its grain elevators. Indianola is the site of

Indianapolis Speedway, site of the Indy 500.

SIMPSON COLLEGE. It also has hosted each year the National Hot Air Balloon Championship, in which several dozen balloons race for the prize of the best flight. The event attracted from 80,000 to 100,000 to the modest city, but in 1988 the sponsors announced the festival would be transferred to Baton Rouge, Louisiana.

INSCRIPTION ROCK. On KELLEY'S ISLAND in Lake ERIE, north of SANDUSKY, Ohio, this thirty-two foot long rock rises eleven feet above the water on the south shore of the island. The limestone ledge forming the rock is said to bear some of the finest petroglyphs in the United States. In 1851 a Colonel Eastman of the U.S. Army made drawings of the inscriptions, and an Indian interpreted them as the history of an Indian tribe in the region, probably the ERIE.

INSTITUTE FOR ATOMIC RESEARCH. The distinguished atomic research of F. H. SPEDDING (1902-1984) and other scientists associated with him at IOWA STATE UNIVERSITY at AMES during WORLD WAR II resulted in the establishment of the Institute for Atomic Research at the University, now the Iowa laboratory of the U.S. Atomic Energy Commission. The Institute gained further impetus with the operation of a $4,500,000 research reactor, opened in 1963.

INSTITUTE OF PAPER CHEMISTRY. Management of the pulp and paper industry, so important in the timber states of the Midwest and particularly in Wisconsin, has been greatly assisted by this institute, established in 1929 at LAWRENCE COLLEGE, APPLETON, Wisconsin. At the time study of paper chemistry was started as a training ground for graduate students in the discipline, the subject was almost unexplored. Four Wisconsin paper-mill companies sponsored the Institute for carrying on research and development in their field, but sponsorship soon expanded to include companies from all the country's important paper-making states. Among the major courses taught are those in wood technology and pulp and paper chemistry and technology.

INTERLOCHEN, Michigan. Village southwest of TRAVERSE CITY on Michigan's LOWER PENINSULA. Activities of Interlochen are centered around the 1,200-acre campus of the Interlochen Center for the Arts, including the NATIONAL MUSIC CAMP and Interlochen Arts Academy. Nearly 1,600 talented students in music, drama and dance attend the camp for eight weeks each summer. The summer session coincides with the Interlochen Arts Festival during which over four hundred concerts and dramatic productions are performed. During the winter, as well, four hundred students participate in fine arts and academics at the center.

INTERNATIONAL FALLS, Minnesota. City (pop. 5,611), extreme north-central Minnesota, near the Canadian border, named for a thirty-five foot falls in the RAINY RIVER n o w submerged by a reservoir above a dam used for hydroelectric power. The city provides a port of entry into Canada through Fort Frances, Ontario. The principal industry of International Falls has been the conversion of trees and wood chips into wood pulp products. The city is also the entry point to VOYAGEURS NATIONAL PARK, a popular sports area of 219,400 acres for those who enjoy canoeing, boating, fishing or winter sports. Tours of the Boise Cascade Mill are available. Annual events include Ice Box Days, lasting a week in late January. Festival activities include ice sculpture, ice-fishing contests, the Freeze Yer Gizzard Blizzard Run, and ice cream pail curling contests.

IOWA. state, situated in the western segment of the Midwest, near the center of the conterminous United States. Its entire eastern border follows the MISSISSIPPI RIVER. The southern two-thirds of the western border is delineated by the MISSOURI RIVER. The balance of the western border is formed by the BIG SIOUX RIVER, which joins the Missouri where Iowa meets its two western neighbor states, South Dakota and Nebraska. A very small portion of South Dakota lies north of Iowa, and the balance of the northern Iowa border touches Minnesota. Wisconsin and Illinois are the Mississippi River neighbors to the east, and Missouri is the southern neighbor.

Iowa has a total of 600 miles of boundary rivers. Most of the Mississippi border consists of steep, high bluffs. The bluffs on the Missouri banks are more moundlike.

The state is well watered, with streams of the eastern two-thirds flowing eastward to the Mississippi, and the western third draining to the Missouri. Principal internal rivers are the CEDAR, IOWA and DES MOINES.

With an area of 56,276 square miles, Iowa is fourth in size among the Midwest states. Its surface is gently rolling, except for the unglaciated area of the northeast and somewhat steeper hills in the northwest.

Iowa

Counties and County Seats

N E S W

0 10 20 30 40 50 miles

LYON
Rock Rapids

OSCEOLA
Sibley

DICKINSON
Spirit Lake

EMMET
Estherville

KOSSUTH

WINNEBAGO
Forest City

WORTH
Northwood

MITCHELL
Osage

HOWARD
Cresco

WINNESHIEK
Decorah

ALLAMAKEE
Waukon

SIOUX
Orange City

O'BRIEN
Primghar

CLAY
Spencer

PALO ALTO
Emmetsburg

HANCOCK
Garner

CERRO GORDO
Mason City

FLOYD
Charles City

CHICKASAW
New Hampton

FAYETTE
West Union

CLAYTON
Elkader

PLYMOUTH
Le Mars

CHEROKEE
Cherokee

BUENA VISTA
Storm Lake

POCAHONTAS
Pocahontas

HUMBOLDT
Dakota City

WRIGHT
Clarion

FRANKLIN
Hampton

BUTLER
Allison

BREMER
Waverly

BLACK HAWK
Waterloo

BUCHANAN
Independence

DELAWARE
Manchester

DUBUQUE
Dubuque

WOODBURY
Sioux City

IDA
Ida Grove

SAC
Sac City

CALHOUN
Rockwell City

WEBSTER
Ft. Dodge

HAMILTON
Webster City

HARDIN
Eldora

GRUNDY
Grundy Center

TAMA
Toledo

BENTON
Vinton

LINN
Cedar Rapids

JONES
Anamosa

JACKSON
Maquoketa

CLINTON
Clinton

MONONA
Onawa

CRAWFORD
Denison

CARROLL
Carroll

GREENE
Jefferson

BOONE
Boone

STORY
Nevada

MARSHALL
Marshalltown

IOWA
Marengo

JOHNSON
Iowa City

CEDAR
Tipton

SCOTT
Davenport

MUSCATINE
Muscatine

HARRISON
Logan

SHELBY
Harlan

AUDUBON
Audubon

GUTHRIE
Guthrie Center

DALLAS
Adel

POLK
Des Moines

JASPER
Newton

POWESHIEK
Montezuma

KEOKUK
Sigourney

WASHINGTON
Washington

LOUISA
Wapello

DES MOINES
Burlington

POTTAWATTAMIE
Council Bluffs

CASS
Atlantic

ADAIR
Greenfield

MADISON
Winterset

WARREN
Indianola

MARION
Knoxville

MAHASKA
Oskaloosa

JEFFERSON
Fairfield

HENRY
Mt. Pleasant

LEE
Ft. Madison

MILLS
Glenwood

MONTGOMERY
Red Oak

ADAMS
Corning

UNION
Creston

CLARKE
Osceola

LUCAS
Chariton

MONROE
Albia

WAPELLO
Ottumwa

VAN BUREN
Keosauqua

FREMONT
Sidney

PAGE
Clarinda

TAYLOR
Bedford

RINGGOLD
Mt. Ayr

DECATUR
Leon

WAYNE
Corydon

APPANOOSE
Centerville

DAVIS
Bloomfield

© Facts On File, Inc. 1984

Iowa

STATE OF IOWA

Name: Iowa, for Ioway Indians

Nickname: The Hawkeye State

Motto: Our liberties we prize and our rights we will maintain

Capital: Des Moines

Symbols and Emblems:
Bird: Eastern goldfinch
Flower: Wild rose
Tree: Oak
Stone: Geode
Song: Song of Iowa

Population:
1984: 2,910,000
Rank: 29th
Gain or loss (1970-80): +77,000
Projection (1980-2000): +59,000
Density: 52 per sq. mi.
Percent urban: 58.6

Racial Makeup (1984):
White: 97.4%
Black: 1.4%
Hispanic: 25,536 persons
Indian: 700 persons
Others: 32,882 persons

Largest City:
Des Moines (919,003)

Other Cities:
Cedar Rapids (110,243)
Davenport (103,264)
Sioux City (82,003)
Waterloo (75,985)
Dubuque (62,231)
Council Bluffs (56,449)
Iowa City (50,508)
Ames (45,774)

Area: 65,275 square miles
Rank: 25th

Highest Point: 1,670 feet

Lowest Point: 509 feet

H.S. Completed: 71.5%

Four Yrs. College Completed: 13.9%

STATE GOVERNMENT

Elected Officials (4-year terms, expiring Jan., 1991):
Governor: $64,000, plus $5,724 expenses
Lt. Gov.: $21,900, plus personal expenses, travel allowance at same rates as for General Assembly
Sec. of State: $41,000
Treasurer: $41,000

General Assembly: (Annual, Jan.) Des Moines:
Salary annually $14,600, plus maximum expense allowance of $40 per day for first 120 days of first session, and first 100 days of second session
Mileage Expense 24 cents per mile
Senate: 50 members
House: 100 members

Congressional Representatives

Senate: Terms expire 1991 and 1993

House of Representatives: Six Member

The most dramatic physical characteristic of the state is the rugged section of the northeast, known as LITTLE SWITZERLAND. The rise in that area, called PIKES PEAK, was named for Zebulon PIKE (1779-1813), after he explored the upper Mississippi in 1805. The name is older than that of the more famous Pikes Peak in Colorado.

Geologically, Iowa is divided almost evenly between the mesozoic area of the northwest and the late paleozoic of the east and south. The latter is broken by the early paleozoic region in the northeast corner.

Before settlement, the Iowa surface was a gently rolling prairie covered with grasses higher than the wheels of the pioneers' wagons. A few examples of the virgin prairies have been maintained as preserves. The virgin woodlands were cut, and most of the hardwood timbered areas along rivers and streams now consist of second and third growth.

The rich soils deposited over most of the state by the four GLACIERS have provided a growing surface unparalleled in any other area of the same size. Iowa has 25 percent of the "grade A" land in the United States. This has proven to be the principal economic resource of the state. Revenues from Iowa AGRICULTURE are surpassed only by those of California and Texas. However, the bulk of actual foodstuffs grown in Iowa far exceeds that of any other state. The state produces 10 percent of the nation's food.

Iowa almost always ranks first in CORN production, generally first, sometimes second, in SOYBEANS, oats and popcorn. Iowa HOG feeders produce almost twice the hog output of the next two states combined. Iowa agronomists claim that each Iowa farmer produces enough to foodstuff to feed 279 people. This is three times the national average.

Iowa industry is generally associated with its agriculture. With the crisis in agriculture in the mid-1980s, Iowa farmers were hard hit, and many lost their property, but generally, Iowa agriculturists fared better than those of other states, and the upturn in agriculture there has been dramatic. The great drouth of 1988 brought renewed hardship, with an estimated 40% reduction in corn and 20% in soybeans.

For some years, the value of manufacture has exceeded that of agriculture. Quaker Oats, of CEDAR RAPIDS, has been a dominant factor in the introduction and manufacture of cereal products.

Iowa also dominates the tractor field. The John Deere tractor plant at WATERLOO is considered the largest of its kind in the world.

The tractor itself originated in Iowa through the efforts of Charles W. HART (1872-1937) and Charles PARR (1869-1941), of CHARLES CITY. After perfecting a "traction device," they called it a tractor, and the word has been in use ever since. The Hart-Parr Company became a leader in tractor production.

The modern washing machine originated with Frederick L. MAYTAG (1857-1937), and the Maytag plant continues in NEWTON. W.A. SHEAFFER (1867-1946) was a pioneer in the fountain pen industry, and the Sheaffer plant has remained at FORT MADISON.

The Lennox Company, at MARSHALLTOWN, has been a leader in the field of warm air heating equipment.

The products of the AMANA Colonies in the refrigeration field are well known. The seven Amana communities are no longer operating on a communal basis as the Amana Church Society, but they were recognized as one of the few successful organizations of their type.

The climate is continental, with an extreme range of 165 degrees. The highest temperature ever recorded in the state was 118 degrees, the lowest, 47 degrees below zero. Average rainfall is 31 inches, with most of the precipitation coming in the summer.

During the decade of the 1970s, Iowa's population increased by only about 84,000. The 1984 population was estimated at 2,910,000. This showed the beginning of a slight decline, due to the farm problems of that period. However, projections of population to the year 2000 indicate a very moderate general increase.

The population is predominantly white, with other races making up less than 4 percent.

The first settlers came from the eastern U.S., but after Iowa Territory was organized in 1838, they were quickly followed by Germans, Czechs, Dutch and Scandinavians, who brought their agricultural skills and their own customs.

The hilly area west and south of Cedar Rapids has a substantial Czech population. The PELLA region has a concentration of people of Dutch descent, and their annual tulip celebration maintains the Dutch traditions. The TRAER area was settled mainly by Scottish pioneers.

When in about 1857 the MESQUAKIE INDIANS returned to Iowa from Kansas, where they had been banished to reservations, they gradually bought land for their present reservation near TAMA. About 700 of them occupy the reservation today, where they have a democratic tribal government.

The IOWAY Indians gave the state its name, according to most authorities, but the tribe was never very large. WINNEBAGO, PONCA, Omaha, Wahpeton and OSAGE were the plains tribes. CHIPPEWA, ILLINI, FOX, SAUK, POTAWATOMI, MIAMI and OTTAWA were the woodland tribes. Most of the woodland groups had been driven west from homes in the east. In 1848, the government removed the 2,800 members of the Winnebago tribe to Minnesota, and most of the other tribespeople died or were removed.

EFFIGY MOUNDS NATIONAL MONUMENT preserves some of the relics of the six known PREHISTORIC PEOPLES who inhabited the Iowa region.

The first known Europeans to visit Iowa were Father Jacques MARQUETTE (1637-1675) and Louis JOLLIET (1645-1700), in 1673. It is probable that they first touched Iowa near present Oakville. Robert Cavelier Sieur de LA SALLE ((1643-1687), Nicholas PERROT (1644-1717), William Des Lisle and Joseph Des Noyelles were a few of the Europeans who followed, but for more than 125 years the region remained much as it was at the time of the first exploration. This was most of the period of the nominal rule of France, Spain, and France again.

In 1796, Julien DUBUQUE (1762-1810) leased land from the Indians and obtained Spanish permission as the first permanent white settler in Iowa. The town of DUBUQUE grew up on his leasehold, beginning about 1833, and becoming the first permanent white settlement in the state.

After the LOUISIANA PURCHASE, the LEWIS AND CLARK EXPEDITION (1770-1838) party passed up the Missouri shores in 1804. The only death among the expedition party occurred at present SIOUX CITY.

Meanwhile, the government attempted to keep most of the land for the Indians, but a rush of frontiersmen, followed by European immigrants, forced the Indians out. Iowa was part of Missouri, Michigan, Wisconsin and Iowa territories before becoming a state in 1846, with IOWA CITY as the capital, and Ansel Briggs as first governor. In 1857, the capital was moved to Des Moines. That year also brought an Indian massacre at SPIRIT LAKE.

Iowa was active in the UNDERGROUND RAILROAD and participated strongly in the CIVIL WAR, particularly in the battles of WILSON'S CREEK (August 10, 1861) and IUKA (September 19, 1862). Because of the number of volunteers, the draft was never needed in Iowa.

By 1856, the Mississippi had been bridged, and Iowa was connected by rail with the East. By 1867, the state had been crossed by railroad, and two years later the first transcontinental railroad linked the state with both coasts.

Hard times of the 1870s saw considerable unrest among the farmers, and agrarian movements had substantial appeal. However, times improved, partly with the help of such organizations as the GRANGE, Farm Bureau and 4-H Clubs. James "Tama Jim" WILSON (1836-1920), from Iowa, was Secretary of Agriculture and provided innovative assistance through a wide variety of new techniques that he developed in the department.

Except for the depression and severe drought of the 1930s, Iowa agriculture has flourished. However, the 1980s have brought some of the worst problems ever to face Iowa farmers—falling prices, vastly increased expenses, falling land values and over-extended debt. Problems have been exacerbated by consolidation of farms and absentee ownership. Again, unrest was spreading, but slow improvement began in the late 1980s.

Iowa has participated in sports in some unusual ways. During the 1890s the small city of INDEPENDENCE became one of the horse-racing centers of the world, with one of the best known tracks and a number of record-breaking performances. In other fields of sport, the University of IOWA at Iowa City and GRINNELL COLLEGE of GRINNELL played the first intercollegiate football game west of the Mississippi (1892), and IOWA STATE at AMES became one of the early football powerhouses.

Grinnell College is consistently rated as one of the ten best institutions of its class in the United States. Iowa State University of Science and Technology at Ames is one of the leading LAND GRANT COLLEGE S. DRAKE UNIVERSITY at Des Moines and CORNELL COLLEGE, MT. VERNON, are other well-known centers of learning. In another aspect of education, Iowa has continued over many years to hold the nation's highest literacy rate.

Iowa politics have garnered nationwide attention in recent years because of the early Iowa caucuses. Jimmy Carter was one of the first to gain substantially from the exposure of his early showing in Iowa, although he did not take the state in the election. In earlier days, the REPUBLICAN PARTY captured the state in 1856, and Abraham LINCOLN received the state vote in 1860. Iowans were consistently Republican until the Great Depression, when, in 1932, Democratic control became complete. Eisenhower turned the tide for the Republicans in 1952, but Johnson captured the state in 1964. Iowa returned to the Republican fold with Nixon in 1968, and Republican candidates for

Des Moines Civic Center.

President have kept the state vote since.

Herbert Clark HOOVER 1874-1964), native of WEST BRANCH, is the best known political figure from the state and was the first president born west of the Mississippi. He and Mrs. Hoover are buried on the grounds of the HOOVER PRESIDENTIAL LIBRARY at West Branch.

Among prominent national families, Iowa has produced the Wallaces, including Henry WALLACE, agricultural scientist and journalist, his son Henry C. WALLACE, Secretary of Agriculture, and Henry A. WALLACE (1888-1965), Secretary of Agriculture and Vice President of the United States.

Tama Jim Wilson holds the all-time record for service in presidential cabinets, serving as secretary of agriculture for 16 years under William MC KINLEY (1843-1901), William Howard TAFT (1857-1930) and Theodore Roosevelt (1858-1919), a seemingly impossible task because of the very different natures of those chief executives.

Artist Grant WOOD (1881-1942) gained international fame for his depiction of Iowa scenes and personalities. His "American Gothic" has become one of the best-known paintings of modern times. Iowa scenes and personalities were also the theme of Margaret WILSON (1882-1976), who won the PULITZER PRIZE for her portrait of a pioneer Iowa family. Hamlin GARLAND (1860-1940), Ruth Suckow, Phil STONG (1899-1957) and MacKinlay KANTOR (1904-1977) are other Iowa authors. Composer Antonin DVORAK (1841-1904) spent some well-publicized months in Iowa, gathering Indian and other local melodies. Composer Meredith WILLSON (1902-1984), of MASON CITY, made his home town famous with his popular *Music Man* (1957).

Black scientist George Washington CARVER (1864?-1943) was sponsored by Tama Jim Wilson at Iowa State and received his education there. Scientist Dr. James VAN ALLEN (1914)

gained immortality with his discovery of the radiation belts, which were named in his honor.

Stage personality Lillian RUSSELL (1861-1922) was born at CLINTON, and Mamie EISENHOWER (1896-1979) was a native of BOONE.

Showman William "Buffalo Bill" CODY (1846-1917) was born near DAVENPORT.

The state's oldest city, Dubuque, has many points of interest, including the view across the Mississippi Valley from the river bluffs. The rugged area on the river to the north is picturesque. Effigy Mounds National Monument, near MC GREGOR, and the Hoover birthplace, the Dutch folk festivals at Pella and the Nordic Fest, DECORAH, are attractions of the state.

The best-known attraction, perhaps, is the cluster of Amana villages. Historic reproductions of aspects of this exceptional commune, handmade products, including furniture, and the several restaurants renowned for their home cooking, as well as the local wines—all add to the interest of the area for the visitor, and all add to the pleasure of a visit to Iowa.

Iowa's most famous church is not a great cathedral but a small wooden building near NASHUA. The building came about as a result of a song by Dr. William PITTS, the *LITTLE BROWN CHURCH IN THE VALE*. After seeing the site, Dr. Pitts wrote the song, which became famous, and the church was built to the song's specifications. It has become world renowned as a site for weddings and other services.

The name of the Iowa capital might seem to have a religious connotation, but it does not mean City of the Monks. Most authorities now feel the name came from the Indian moin or moingona, meaning river or river of the mounds.

The capitol is considered one of the most handsome in the nation, with particular attention given to the large murals. Most of the stone was cut from glacial boulders from the surface of the area, and the 24 carat gold dome shines as a beacon beckoning visitors to the state and the city.

IOWA CITY, Iowa. City (pop. 50,508), seat of Johnson County, situated in east-southcentral Iowa in the broad valley of the IOWA RIVER and occupying both sides of the river, the city was founded in 1839 as the capital of Iowa Territory and incorporated in 1853. The name comes from that of the state, originally thought to have been derived from the name of the IOWAY INDIANS. Although a substantial center of industry and commerce, it remains chiefly a university city, as principal site of the University of IOWA, founded in 1855 and noted particularly for its health facilities, ranked as one of the top ten centers of medical treatment and research in the nation. From time to time the university also surfaces as a leading center of college athletics, with some of its Big Ten teams winning trips to the Rose Bowl and basketball teams often of high rank. The city's greatest growth began with the coming of the RAILROADS in 1855, when it became an important center for the outfitting of the western trails. Today its products include dentifrices, foam rubber, coated papers, toilet goods, food products and animal feed. Unlike most large Midwest cities, the population of Iowa City grew from 46,850 in 1970 to 50,508 in 1980. The widespread campus with its stadium, medical buildings and other facilities provides much of the city's interest for visitors. The old state capitol, now headquarters for the university administration, was built in 1840 and is considered one of the most attractive structures in the state. Not far from Iowa City are the AMANAS, the Herbert Hoover (1874-1964) birthplace and library complex and Coralville dam and reservoir. The Old Capitol Criterium Bicycle Race in April each year is one of the most prestigious in the Midwest.

IOWA RIVER. The river rises in two branches from small lakes in north central Iowa, the west branch and the east branch which join near Belmond to form the main river. It courses over the rapids which give Iowa Falls its name, then passes MARSHALLTOWN and IOWA CITY before joining the CEDAR RIVER. The Cedar is the principal stream, but the continuing river is called the Iowa, probably in recognition of the namesake state. Near OAKVILLE the river makes a great loop to the north and enters the MISSISSIPPI RIVER.

IOWA STATE FAIR. Frequently called the most outstanding of all state fairs, the Iowa fair had a modest beginning at Fairfield in 1854, where the major prize was $150 for the best rider of the eleven girls who competed bareback on horses. Visitors to that fair paid an admission of twenty-five cents. Between 1871 and 1879, the fair had moved among eight other Iowa cities before settling at the Iowa state capital of DES MOINES in 1879. It was established there on grounds bought partly by a $50,000 appropriation by the state legislature on condition that Des Moines would raise an equal sum for site improvements. One of the oldest and largest of the state fairs, Iowa's exposition came to symbolize them all with the 1932 publication of author Phil STONG's (1899-1957) best-selling book *State Fair* and the making of the book into two popular movies. It features the largest annual exhibition of farm machinery and equipment as well as some of the largest displays of farm products and livestock. The state's largest art show, with 600 exhibitors, is held there, and, among other attractions, there are five stages providing entertainment.

IOWA STATE UNIVERSITY OF SCIENCE AND TECHNOLOGY. Recognized almost universally as the leading institution in agricultural education and research, the university, at AMES, Iowa, was chartered in 1858 and opened ten years later as an agricultural college called Iowa State College of Agriculture and Mechanic Arts until 1959, when the name was changed. Some authorities conclude that modern scientific agriculture began in the 1890s at Iowa State when Iowan James "Tama Jim" WILSON (1836-1920) took over as Dean of the College of Agriculture. Tama Jim's theories and practices of agriculture as a science led not only to the university's pre-eminence in that field but also took him to Washington where he was the nation's most successful Secretary of Agriculture. His life is memorialized in the Tama Jim Wilson collection at the University library. The university provided the scientific education for noted black scientist George Washington CARVER (1864?-1943), who progressed under the personal tutelage of Tama Jim. Today the University has become an acknowledged leader in many other fields of science, particularly in atomic fields, with the Institute of Atomic Research of the Atomic Energy Commission. Its campus has been described as one of the most beautiful in the country, benefitting from some of the finest minds in arboriculture and landscape engineering. In its historic past, the university was once the nation's leading football power. When the Iowa State team amazingly beat the then powerful NORTHWESTERN UNIVERSITY team, the Chicago *Tribune* said a "cyclone" had come to town, and the team has been called the Cyclones ever since. The university was one of the first to teach home economics and remains a leader in that field. The modern university enrolls 26,529 graduate and undergraduate students, instructed by a faculty of 2,137.

IOWA TESTS. The American College Testing Program, Iowa Tests of Basic Development and

Old State House, Iowa City.

Iowa Tests of Basic Skills, are among the best known standard tests in educational measurement. All were developed at the University of IOWA. The basic skills test was developed by Dr. E.F. LINDQUIST (1901-1978) for testing elementary school children. Dr. Lindquist later developed a scoring machine for the tests. He produced the educational development tests for high school students in 1942. In 1960 he established the Iowa Educational Information Center, a data bank for teachers, designed to reduce paper work and provide information for educational research. The college testing program was produced to round out the university's examination program from elementary through higher education. The tests have been probably the most widely used of any in their fields.

IOWA, UNIVERSITY OF. Chartered in 1847, the university opened in 1855 at IOWA CITY. It is renowned for its vast medical center, where many medical breakthroughs have occurred, such as the pioneer work of Dr. Arthur STEINDLER (1878-1959) in orthopedics. The university has a reputation for studies in the creative arts, especially its internationally renowned Iowa Writers Workshop. Prominent "graduates" of the workshop include novelists Flannery O'Connor, *Wise Blood* (1952) and John Irving *The World According to Garp* (1978) and Pulitzer Prize winning poets W. D. Snodgrass and Donald Justice. The university science department has produced such recognized authorities as Dr. James VAN ALLEN (1914) for whom the Van Allen belts are named. The products of its testing program are considered to be the most widely used of all standard tests. The university operates the Lakeside Laboratory for the biological sciences and a hydraulic

research institute. The faculty numbers 1,800, the student body 29,651.

IOWAY INDIANS. The Ioway occupied much of central to southeastern portions of the present state of Iowa, which probably received its name from them, and portions of northern Missouri. Of Siouan language stock, they probably never numbered more than two thousand. Although they were strong warriors, most of the fighting men were killed in wars with the SAUK and FOX. After making treaties with the government, they were removed to Oklahoma.

IRON CURTAIN SPEECH. Famous speech delivered by Winston Churchill in FULTON, Missouri, (1946) on the campus of WESTMINISTER COLLEGE. In the speech, entitled "Sinews of Peace," Churchill described an "iron curtain" that ran from Stettin in the Baltic to Trieste in the Adriatic that divided the free and communist world. This was the origin of the phrase to denote the imaginary line between the two opposite factions of the free and the Communist world.

ISHPEMING, Michigan. City (pop. 7,538), Marquette County, Michigan's UPPER PENINSULA southwest of MARQUETTE, name is thought to mean "high grounds." Rich iron-ore deposits were discovered near Ishpeming in 1844. The second active mine in Michigan was opened when the community was still nothing more than a camp. By 1857 the Iron Mountain Railroad between Ishpeming and MARQUETTE had been completed. Mining operations were conducted by the Cleveland Cliffs Iron Company and the Oliver Mining Company. Organized skiing began in 1887 when several Norwegians formed the Norden Ski Club. In 1905 the club took a leading role in forming a national ski association. Annual ski jumping championships are held here in February. The jump, built in 1925, had a gap of seventy-eight feet between the take-off and landing hill which earned its nickname "Suicide Hill." The gap was filled in to prevent accidents. Ishpeming is home of the National Ski Hall of Fame which displays trophies, photographs and equipment from the past.

ISLE ROYALE NATIONAL PARK. This forested island, the largest in Lake SUPERIOR, is distinguished by its wilderness character, timber wolves, moose herd and pre-Columbian copper mines.

ITASCA, LAKE. Source of the MISSISSIPPI RIVER, this lake in north-central Minnesota was called "Mushkos" or elk by the OJIBWAY. Henry SCHOOLCRAFT, on at last finding the source of the Mississippi there in 1832, wanted a better name and combined the latin words "veritas" meaning truth and "caput" meaning head, dropped three letters from the front and back of the combination and arrived at Itasca, the new name. When the river leaves the lake, it is less than two feet deep and ten feet wide. Visitors delight in saying that they have walked across the Mississippi on stepping stones. In 1888 and 1889 Jacob V. Browser made careful topographical and hydrographic surveys of the Itasca basin. He later persuaded the Minnesota legislature to establish Itasca State Park. Containing nearly 32,000 acres and 157 lakes, the park offers exhibits of every flower and animal native to Minnesota.

IUKA, BATTLE OF. On September 19, 1862, a victory by General Sterling Price and his Confederate force at Iuka, Mississippi, might have weakened the Union forces sufficiently to lay the groundwork for a successul Confederate capture of much of the West. However, the success of Midwest troops, particularly of Iowa, was said to "have made Iowa famous in war annals." The Fifth Iowa Infantry, under Colonel Mathies, was thrown across the road directly in front of Price's main charge. A noted historian, S.H.M. Byers, who fought with the Iowa fifth, has contributed one of the most stirring accounts of CIVIL WAR battles in describing this encounter: "We fixed our swords bayonets and our good Whitney rifles and sat down to wait the coming foe. Nearer they come. We hear their very tramp. We think of Iowa. She shall not be dishonored; rather every man at Iuka die than that. The Texans, Louisianians and the Missisisipians, veterans of bloody fields, find that out and falter in the blast from our guns. Blood crimsons the grass and leaves. Poor Shelby of Jasper fell first. We only close up, touch elbows and with grim faces fire and fire until we in turn shall drop in the leaves and blood of that afternoon. No man of the Fifth yields a foot of ground. a big red-shirted Alabamian breaks through the ranks and attempts to seize the colors of the Fifth but is bayoneted. At the range of but a few feet, the lines fire volleys in each other's faces. So the regiment fought until the sun went down; darkness settled on the battlefield, and Price prepared to bury the dead and retreat before the dawn of the morrow." Later General Price wrote, "It was the hardest fought battle I ever witnessed."

Lake Itasca, birthplace of the Mississippi by Seth Eastman

J

J.C. PENNEY MISSOURI FARMS. Birthplace of James Cash PENNEY (1875-1971), founder of the J.C. Penney Company and a large-scale horse breeding operation in Missouri. J.C. Penney Farms, near BRECKENRIDGE, Missouri, have specialized in horse breeding. Among the breeds raised and trained by experts are Belgian and Percheron draft horses, champion jacks, and saddle and thoroughbred stallions. The work of the farms is considered to have been among the most effective in developing the breeds.

JACKSON, Jesse Louis (Greenville, NC, Oct. 8, 1941—). Civil rights leader, politician. He was raised in the poor black section of Greenville. When his mother married Charles H. Jackson, Jesse took the surname of the stepfather. He starred on the basketball, football and baseball teams of all-black Sterling High School. Upon graduation, he refused a contract to play baseball with the Chicago White Sox because they paid black athletes lower salaries than whites.

He accepted an athletic scholarship at the University of Illinois, but transferred to Agricultural and Technical College of North Carolina at Greensboro when he found that blacks were not then allowed to play quarterback on Illinois university football teams. He became not only the college quarterback but also an honor student. As early as 1963, while still a student, he led the student protest which resulted in the integration of Greensboro theaters and restaurants.

Graduating in 1964, Jackson entered Chicago Theological Seminary in 1965. From that time onward, Chicago remained the general base of his operations. That year he joined Dr. Martin Luther King in his civil rights actions in Selma, Alabama. He became a close associate of King and was named head of the Chicago branch of Operation Breadbasket, becoming national director in 1967. With his threat of black boycotts, Jackson had considerable success in forcing retail merchants to employ more blacks.

When Dr. King was assassination on April 4, 1968, many analysts expected Jackson to assume the mantle of Dr. King. However, it was said he refused to do so on the basis that it would eventually make him too dependent on white support.

He was ordained a Baptist minister on June 30, 1968. His power in the Chicago area grew and extended considerably beyond the Chicago black community. With a command of the press amounting almost to genius, Jackson continued to gain national prominence. After a break with the Southern Christian leadership Conference (SCLC) in 1971, Jackson founded the similar Operation Push (People United to Save Humanity).

By this time he had achieved national prominence and a national black following. In 1984 he launched a campaign to win the Democratic presidential nomination, said by some observers to be a test of the waters for the 1988 campaign. Although not considered a serious contender in 1984, he gained valuable support and experience in the field of politics.

In the 1988 campaign for the nomination, Jackson received a measure of support which many observers considered astonishing, especially because of the white vote he received. During the primaries, he garnered a delegate contingent which was the third largest at the party's 1984 convention in Atlanta, Georgia. However, Michael Dukakis remained far in the forefront of delegates.

At the convention, Jesse Jackson and his family were recognized with substantial appearances on the platform and received widespread press attention. Despite his disappointment at not being the nominee, Jackson nevertheless pledged his support to the party ticket.

JACKSON, Mahalia. (New Orleans, LA, Oct., 26, 1911—Evergreen Park, IL, Jan. 27, 1972). Gospel singer. Jackson's career began as leader of a quartet which sang in churches. She began making records in 1934, and went on many concert tours in Europe and the U.S., including Carnegie Hall and Newport Jazz Festivals. She sang for President Dwight Eisenhower on his birthday in 1959 and at John F. Kennedy's inauguration. During the

1960s she became associated with the civil rights movement and became a symbol of black protest. She made eight records that sold over a million copies each.

JACKSON, Michigan. City (pop. 39,700), Seat of Jackson County, southeastern portion of Michigan's LOWER PENINSULA on the GRAND RIVER. It was founded in 1829. As early as 1836 the community promoted a "Make your home in Jackson" movement. Jackson is considered by its supporters to be the birthplace of the REPUBLICAN PARTY (July 6, 1854). The 5,000 Michigan electors who founded the party had to meet out of doors due to a lack of a suitable hall.

During pioneer days, Jackson economy benefitted from its location at the intersection of the GRAND RIVER and an Indian trail. Lumbering became the first industry. Gristmills followed, and the community became a trade center. The Michigan Central Railroad reached Jackson in 1841, and in 1871 the railroad shops gave Jackson its first industrial enterprise.

The city grew as a production center for carriages. As the need for carriages gave way to an interest in AUTOMOBILES, Jackson established plants for manufacturing the Cutting, Jackson, Imperial, Clark-Carter, Briscoe and Earl automobiles. Companies were merged or moved away, but many of the satellite industries of the automotive industry remained.

Other current products include sheet metal, electronic equipment, metal toys and aircraft parts and accessories.

Jackson, once called "Prison City" because of the presence of the State Prison of Southern Michigan, is now nicknamed the "Rose Capital." A distinctive blossom called the Jackson Rose was developed. The annual Rose Festival, is held in late May. Jackson might also be known as "the City of Cascades." Cascades at Sparks Foundation County Park is a 465-acre area containing illuminated cascades, fifteen waterfalls and six fountains, over which water flows in changing patterns. Ella Sharp Memorial Park's museum gives a glimpse of 19th-century farm life. Included are a log cabin, barn, country store and one-room schoolhouse. The Michigan Space Center is housed in a golden geodesic dome. Inside is the Apollo 9 command module, a lunar surveyor, a moon rock and many multimedia presentations.

JACKSON, Missouri. City (pop. 7,827), seat of Cape Girardeau County, eastern Missouri, northwest of CAPE GIRARDEAU, named for President Andrew Jackson. Jackson grew quickly as the political and commercial center of the county because the rival community of Cape Girardeau was entangled in clearing land titles of its first settlers and was unable to handle county business. Jackson was incorporated in 1819. A cholera epidemic struck in 1849, causing many to flee to other cities. Military forces of both sides occupied the city during the CIVIL WAR and disrupted the commerce. Good times returned with an end to the fighting. Jackson became a milling and trading center for a wide farming area.

JACKSONVILLE, Illinois. City (pop. 20,284), county seat of Morgan Co., located 35 miles west of SPRINGFIELD in central Illinois. Founded in 1825 and named for Andrew Jackson, Jacksonville was first settled by southerners. By the 1830s it had attracted so many northerners that the city was the most like New England in character of any town in the state. Illinois College, founded in 1829, and MacMurray College, founded in 1849, are located in Jacksonville. A famous graduate of Illinois College was William Jennings BRYAN (1860-1925). Jacksonville is the home of three long-established state institutions. The Illinois School for the Deaf, founded in Jacksonville in 1843, began with two pupils. The Illinois Braille and Sightsaving School was opened in 1847. Frank Hall, one of the first teachers at the school, invented the braille writer. The Jacksonville State Hospital's first patient arrived in 1851. The Eli Bridge Company of Jacksonville is the nation's only manufacturer of ferris wheels for carnivals. The J. Capps and Sons, Ltd. is one of the oldest clothing manufacturers in the United States. The company once employed "Buffalo Bill" CODY to endorse the Indian blankets it marketed throughout the West.

JAMES A. GARFIELD NATIONAL HISTORIC SITE. Near Lawnfield, Ohio. This site preserves property associated with the life of the 20th President (1831-1881). The site is currently managed by a private organization and is open to the public.

JAMES, Jesse Woodson (Kearney, MO, Sept. 5, 1847—St. Joseph, MO, Apr. 3, 1882). Outlaw. As a teenager, James fought unofficially with "Bloody" Bill ANDERSON's Confederate guerrilla band during the CIVIL WAR. Later with his brother, Frank JAMES, he fought with Col. W. C. QUANTRILL's band. Badly injured by Union troops at the end of the war, he turned to

Janesville - Jefferson City

Jesse James mural, Thomas Hart Benton.

crime. He was declared an outlaw in 1866, and remained a fugitive for 15 years. An expert marksman, he organized the James gang (1867), which committed murders and robberies, most notably, train robberies. A pathological killer, James, with his gang, was the first ever to wreck and rob a train. His gang committed the first train robbery on the evening of July 21, 1873, near Adair in the southwestern part of Iowa. He expected to find $75,000 in gold, but captured only $2,000 and whatever could be taken from the luckless passengers. In September, 1876, the James gang attempted one of their last bank robberies at NORTHFIELD, Minnesota. For a time in 1868 Jesse James lived in ST. JOSEPH, Missouri, under the name of Thomas Howard and joined the Baptist Church. He was shot in the back of the head by Robert Ford, a former member of the gang. Ford found the temptation of the $10,000 reward offered by the governor of Missouri for Jesse's arrest or death too much to resist. James was mourned as something of a western "Robin Hood," due to turn-of-the-century pulp novels from such companies as Beadle and Adams, who turned the exploits of many Old West killers into adventures of fearless giants of the plains.

JANESVILLE, Wisconsin. City (pop. 53,-545), seat of Rock County on the ROCK RIVER in south central Wisconsin, the community took its name from Henry E. Janes, who arrived in 1836 and immediately carved his name on a tree at what is now the intersection of Main

and Milwaukee. After Jane had started a tavern on the river's east bank and almost as soon as he began to run a ferry across the river, the town was named in his honor, and he became postmaster. Always restless, Jane soon left and went west to found two more Janesvilles and moved on to the Pacific coast where he was stalled by the ocean. With stagecoaches routed through the new community and ever-increasing river traffic, the town grew rapidly. The first large riverboats were FLATBOATS propelled over the shallow riverbed by horses on treadmills. Soon shallow-draft STEAMBOATS were arriving with passengers and freight. The community continued to grow with the coming of sawmills processing the logs, harvested above and floated down the river. In 1919 General Motors built a tractor factory there. Industry continues with such products as auto bodies, electrical and electronic equipment and fountain pens. The city still provides a center for products of the surrounding dairy, grain and tobacco growers. The restoration of the Talman House mansion is said to place it among the top ten of the country's remaining structures of its type dating from the CIVIL WAR period. The hexagonal Milton House has become a museum, still connected to the original log cabin. The municipal riverside parks provide many opportunities for water sports and activities. Tours of the General Motors plant are available. Two Labor Day events are held each year, the Waterski show at Traxler Park and the Rock River Threesheree, demonstrations of old-time threshers and farm machinery.

JEFFERSON CITY, Missouri. City (pop. 33,619), capital of the state and seat of Cole County, on the MISSOURI RIVER near the center of the state. The land for a state capital was donated by an Act of Congress in 1821, with the stipulation that it be located within forty miles of the mouth of the OSAGE RIVER. The city was named for President Thomas Jefferson, designed by Daniel M. BOONE, son of the Kentucky pioneer, and incorporated in 1825. During the CIVIL WAR, the city chose to remain a part of the Union, although loyalties were divided between the Union and Confederate sides. The Missouri state prison was constructed there in 1833, but public works allocation led state officials to place the state university elsewhere. Surrounded by farmlands, the city serves as an agricultural trading center. Diversified industries include the manufacture of shoes, cosmetics, small electrical appliances, and printing materials. The capitol, constructed of Carthage

The capitol, Jefferson City.

marble during 1911-1918, features murals by the American artist Thomas Hart BENTON (1889-1975). LINCOLN UNIVERSITY, was founded there in 1866 by black federal army veterans.

JEFFERSON NATIONAL EXPANSION MEMORIAL NATIONAL HISTORIC SITE. At ST. LOUIS, Missouri. This park on the city's MISSISIPPI RIVER memorializes Thomas Jefferson and others who directed territorial expansion of the United States. Eero Saarinen's prize-winning, stainless steel Gateway Arch (1966) commemorates westward pioneers. Visitors may ascend by a train-like lift inside the 630-foot-high arch. In the nearby courthouse DRED SCOTT sued for freedom in the historic SLAVERY case (1856-1857). There is a museum featuring the theme of western expansion, and a theater showing films on the same subject.

JEFFERSONVILLE, Indiana. City (pop. 21,220), seat of Clark County, located in southeastern Indiana, one of the state's oldest cities. Jeffersonville, named for Thomas Jefferson, was laid out on the north bank of the OHIO RIVER, using plans of Thomas Jefferson, and was christened in 1802 by William Henry HARRISON (1773-1841). It lies opposite Louisville, Kentucky. Jeffersonville's shipyards once produced many of the early MISSISSIPPI RIVER packets and

some of the first large ships to steam up the Yukon River in Alaska. It is the terminal for one of the largest river transportation companies in the world. Dairy products, strawberries, tobacco and grain of the surrounding area help to fuel the economy. Louisville Slugger baseball bats are presently Jeffersonville's most famous industry. The Hillerich and Bradsby Company, founded in 1859 and manufacturer of the Slugger and PowerBilt golf clubs, maintains a museum of famous players' bats. Jeffersonville's role in shipbuilding is celebrated each year with an annual Steamboat Days Festival held the first weekend in September. Models of riverboats and artifacts from the Howard Shipyards (1834-1941) are housed in the Howard Steamboat Museum. The museum, in a Victorian mansion dating from 1890, also contains original Howard family furnishings. The Colgate clock on the Colgate-Palmolive plant is said to be the second largest in the world. Near Jeffersonville lies one of the world's few exposed coral formations from the Devonian era, a time when land animals were evolving from marine creatures. The fossil bed at the FALLS OF THE OHIO Conservation Area, bordering Louisville, Kentucky, can best be viewed from the Indiana shore along Riverside Drive near McAlpine Dam.

JENNY, William Le Baron. (Fairhaven, MA, Sept. 25, 1832—Chicago, IL, 1907). Considered the "father of the skyscraper." In 1868 Jenny located in CHICAGO, Illinois, as an architect. He served as a landscape engineer for the West Chicago Parks from 1870 to 1871. Jenny designed a framework of steel beams to hold the weight of buildings. Until that time the height of buildings was limited by the strength of their supporting walls. With Jenney's new design, the walls were simply an outer covering of the building, and the height could, theoretically, be limited only by the ability to raise the supporting steel work. this concept of Jenny's remains the basis of skyscraper construction. The building renowned as the "first" skyscraper was Jenny's Home Insurance building in Chicago (1884-1885). That notable structure was destroyed before the historic preservation movement had been fully organized. Jenny was the architect of the Horticultural Building at the WORLD'S COLUMBIAN EXPOSITION in Chicago (1893).

JOGUES, ISAAC. (Orleans, France, Jan. 10, 1607—Ossernenon, NY, Oct. 18, 1646). Missionary. In 1641 Father Jogues and his

companion, Father Charles Raymbault, named the rapids in the river flowing between Lakes SUPERIOR and HURON. The name chosen was SAULT de SAINTE MARIE. Father Jogues was at this time working among the SIOUX INDIANS living beyond Lake Superior. He was captured by the Mohawk-Iroquois tribe who mutilated and tortured him. Rescued by the Dutch at Fort Orange, Father Jogues returned to France from 1644 until 1646 when he returned to Canada. In attempting to bring Christianity to the Mohawks, he was killed.

JOHN HANCOCK BUILDING. World's tallest residential building, in CHICAGO, Illinois. At 100 stories the Hancock Building is also the fifth tallest building in the world. Chicago boasts three of the world's highest buildings: SEARS TOWER, world's tallest and fourth-ranking Standard Oil Building, followed by the Hancock, only a few feet lower. The Hancock Building, completed in 1969, was a pioneer in mixed use SKYSCRAPERS, combining a department store and other retail businesses, with six floors of garage, thirty-one stories of offices, over 700 condominium apartments with full grocery, service, pool and health facilities, observatory, plus radio and TV broadcast facilities and a ninety-fifth floor restaurant, along with several other restaurant facilities. The condominium section pioneered in the organization of individual condominium ownership of air rights

above the ground floor without ownership of the land below.

JOHN HARDEMAN'S GARDEN. Established in the 1830s as perhaps the first garden and plant experiment station in the Mississippi Valley. The garden consisted of ten acres near Old Franklin, Missouri, with a center maze, ornamental beds, shell-lined paths, and pools.

JOHNSON WAX BUILDING AND RE-SEARCH TOWER. High on most lists of outstanding industrial buildings is this structure designed by famed architect Frank Lloyd WRIGHT (1867-1959) for the Johnson Wax Company at RACINE, Wisconsin. Wright was said to be experimenting with changes in the plans even as construction was in process. The wing-shaped penthouse in streamlined form spans a built-in driveway. Glass bands circle the main structure, continually admitting light. The roof is almost entirely of glass. Tee columns, larger at top than at the bottom, support most of the structure. Wiring is carried through the hollow cores of the columns. The striking research tower, with its rounded corners, dominates the area. Completed in 1950, the building's many features have become standard in modern construction and design.

JOHNSON, John. (Arkansas City, AR, January 19, 1918—). Publisher. A loan of five

Johnson Wax Research Tower, by Frank Lloyd Wright.

hundred dollars from his mother started Johnson toward a Chicago-based publishing empire directed at black readers who, he felt, would respond positively to stories of black achievements. The first of the Johnson publications was begun in 1942 with the title *NEGRO DIGEST*. In 1970 the title was changed to *BLACK WORLD*. Other Johnson magazines include *Ebony* (1945), *Jet* (1951), *Black Stars* (1971) and *Ebony, Jr.* (1973). Johnson was named Publisher of the Year in 1972, the year the Johnson Publishing Company ranked second nationally in earnings among black enterprises. It now has gained first rank.

JOLIET, Illinois. City (pop. 77,956), seat of Will County, situated in northeast Illinois on the DES PLAINES RIVER, incorporated in 1857. It takes its name from explorer Louis JOLLIET, being shortened by the elimination of one "L." The city is one of the principal industrial centers of the state. It holds national leadership in the production of wallpaper. There are over 1,000 other manufactured products, including earth-moving equipment, oil refineries, processing of the limestone brought in from the nearby quarries, chemicals and electronic parts, radio and television parts, paper, as well as steel products such as the substantial quantities of wire manufactured there. Barges carry much traffic on the important Illinois waterway, and railway traffic is also important. Charles Reed, the first settler, founded Joliet in 1831, but the settlement was soon abandoned until after the BLACK HAWK WAR in 1832. First called Juliet because of the nearby town named Romeo (now Romeoville), the name was changed to Joliet in 1845. The arrival of the first boat on the ILLINOIS AND MICHIGAN CANAL in April, 1848, was wildly hailed, and canal traffic brought an early industrial boom to the town. This was enhanced by the coming of the first railroad in 1852, with five additional railroads coming soon after. Steel manufacturing also sprang up. One wallpaper manufacturing plant was followed by another until the six plants of the Joliet region were producing a third of all the wallpaper made in the country. In the decade between the census of 1970 and that of 1980, the population showed a slight decline, from 78,827 to 77,956, but the general economic decline of most major Midwest cities was not experienced. The state penitentiary is located there, and, by contrast, the city is the seat of the College of St. Francis.

JOLLIET, LOUIS. (Beaupre, Quebec, Canada, Sept. 21, 1645—Quebec, Canada, May, 1700). French-Canadian explorer and mapmaker. After studying for the priesthood, Jolliet left the seminary in 1667 to study hydrography in France. He returned to Canada in 1668. Jolliet, one of the first white explorers of much of the Midwest, searched for copper near Lake SUPERIOR in 1669. His party was the first to pass through the GREAT LAKES by way of the DETROIT RIVER. He explored much of the Great Lakes region for the government of New France from 1669 to 1671 during which time he established a fur-trading post at SAULT SAINTE MARIE, where knives and guns were traded to Indian trappers for beaver pelts, which earned large profits when sold in France. Because of his knowledge of the Great Lakes region and his studies in hydrography, Jolliet was chosen by New France intendant Jean Talon to explore and map the then almost unknown MISSISSIPPI RIVER. The Mississippi was even then described as a great waterway flowing to the sea, but few details were known about it. The French felt this sea might be the Pacific Ocean. Jolliet's group of seven included Jesuit missionary Father Jacques MARQUETTE (1637-1675), noted for his knowledge of and ability to deal with the Indians. The party set out from St. Ignace across Lake MICHIGAN on May 17, 1673. They traveled by canoe up the FOX RIVER in Wisconsin, portaged on foot to the WISCONSIN RIVER, which they followed to its mouth at the Mississippi. On June 17, they became the first known Europeans to discover the upper reaches of the Mississippi. They soon decided that the great river flowed south and not west as they had thought and probably emptied into the Gulf of Mexico. At the mouth of the Arkansas River the expedition met hostile Indians and heard of white men living further south who they believed were probably Spanish. Fearing attack from either the Indians or the Spanish, the men turned north on the long return journey. They reached Lake Michigan after traveling through Illinois on the ILLINOIS and DES PLAINES rivers, then passing the future site of CHICAGO and back up Lake Michigan. Jolliet's canoe containing all the maps and records of the journey capsized later in the St. Lawrence River. He was able, however, to reconstruct some of the lost maps from memory. The entire expedition had lasted five months. As a reward for his service, he was given Anticosti Island in the Gulf of St. Lawrence. Jolliet later explored Hudson Bay and charted the Labrador coast. Jolliet was honored by the French government, with his appointment as royal hydrographer of New France (1697), having headquarters in Quebec.

He later taught navigation at a Jesuit college.

JONES ISLAND. A unique enclave in the harbor at MILWAUKEE, Wisconsin. Jones Island developed with the settlement of squatters after the CIVIL WAR. This quasi-legal population finally reached a peak of more than 3,000. Lovers of gourmet seafood flocked to the island's taverns and eating houses for the seafood dinners, supplied by the Polish and German fishermen, who at one time annually caught over six million pounds of fish for the community. The island evolved its own informal government, with law enforcement led by a Polish fisherman named Jacob Muza. It was said that the police of Milwaukee did not dare to venture onto the island. At length the city bought the island, turned it into a peninsula by dumping landfill and built a sewage disposal plant there. The last of the squatters did not give up their claims until 1943.

JONESBORO, Illinois. Town (pop. 1,842), seat of Union County in extreme southwest Illinois, site of the third LINCOLN-DOUGLAS DEBATE. Jonesboro was laid out in 1816 and named for a physician. Jonesboro was on the route taken by federal troops who forcibly removed Cherokee Indians from their traditional homelands in the East. The route was called the "TRAIL OF TEARS" because of the number of Indians who died and the hardships of those who survived. Jonesboro was a Democratic stronghold on September 15, 1858, when one of the LINCOLN-DOUGLAS DEBATES was held there. Consequently, most Jonesboro people became even more anti-Lincoln when Stephen Douglas labeled him an Abolitionist.

JOPLIN, Missouri. City (pop. 38,893), Jasper and Newton Counties, in southwestern Missouri. The leading city of the OZARK region, Joplin was first settled in 1838 and incorporated as a city in 1873. It is most noted as a mining community, producing lead and zinc. Manufactures include chemicals, missiles, leather goods, alcohol, insulation, and furniture. It is the home of Missouri Southern State College. The Museum Complex consists of the Tri-State Mineral Museum and the Dorothea B. Hoover Historical Museum. The Municipal Building is known for its Thomas Hart BENTON

mural. Nearby is GEORGE WASHINGTON CARVER NATIONAL MONUMENT, established July 14, 1943.

JULIAN, Percy Lavon. (Montgomery, AL, Apr. 11, 1899—Waukegan, IL, Apr. 1, 1975). Chemist. A graduate of DePauw University at the head of his class in 1920, he taught chemistry at Fisk University, then in 1922 was awarded a fellowship at Harvard. Although he qualified for a teaching appointment at Harvard, he could not receive it because blacks were not permitted such an appointment. From 1927 to 1929 he therefore taught chemistry at Howard University. Then Julian attended the University of Vienna where he received a Ph.D. in 1931. He next held various professorships until 1935. In that year he synthesized the glaucoma drug physostigmine. In 1936 he became director of research at the Glidden corporation in Chicago. His discoveries in soya chemistry led to less expensive treatments for several human ailments and provided a number of commercial opportunities. He left Glidden in 1953 to found Julian Laboratories. He served on many boards and received many awards, including the 1947 Spingarn Medal of the NAACP.

JUNEAU, Solomon. (Montreal, Canada, 1793—Milwaukee, WI., 1856), founder of the city of MILWAUKEE, Wisconsin, Juneau came to the area in 1818 as the agent for the AMERICAN FUR COMPANY. Branching out on his own, he soon amassed a fortune trading with his good friends the Indians, who had become very fond of him. He often was called on to settle problems between the Indians and the growing number of white settlers. Juneau obtained land between the MILWAUKEE RIVER and Lake MICHIGAN, began building with the first store and tavern and called the place Juneautown. Later, he built the community's first courthouse. In the early days Juneau acquired other properties in the area and started such communities as Theresa, named for his daughter. He became an American citizen in 1831, became Milwaukee's first postmaster in 1835 and first president of the village in 1837. Although he lost much of his fortune in the panic of 1837, Juneau continued to have influence in the area and became Milwaukee's first mayor in 1846.

KALAMAZOO, Michigan. City (pop. 79,-722), seat of Kalamazoo County, name derived from the Indian word Ke-Kalamazoo meaning, "where the water boils in the pot," referring to the fact that Indians found hundreds of bubbling springs in the Kalamazoo River. Kalamazoo is often referred to as "Celery City" because it was the birthplace of America's celery production. The first attempts to raise the plant were the work of a Scottish immigrant, James Taylor, who raised celery seeds imported from England. In 1856 celery was part of the banquet menu at Kalamazoo's Burdick Hotel. Celery's first reception was not positive. Celery's similarity to the poisonous hemlock plant made it difficult to convince skeptics that it was edible. A celery proponent, Marinus De Bruin, began raising the plant and sent his children out to sell it door to door. De Bruin's method proved effective, and by 1870 Dutch immigrants began converting mosquito-filled swamps into profitable farms.

Pansies are grown commercially as an alternate crop to celery. Kalamazoo is also at the center of the commercial cultivation of peppermint. The city is one of the largest producers of oil of peppermint in the United States. It has long been a center of the paper industry, as well as more than 100 other products, including guitars.

A trading post was set up on the banks of the river in 1823. Settlement began in 1838, and a group of Dutch settlers arrived in 1847, refugees from persecution in Holland. In 1918 Kalamazoo was the first Michigan city to adopt the commission-manager form of government.

Dr. William E. Upjohn, a civic leader in Kalamazoo at the time it adopted the commission-manager form, started a small pill-producing business in Kalamazoo which became Upjohn Company, one of the largest pharmaceutical companies in the world. A famous native of Kalamazoo was author Edna FERBER (1887-1968).

WESTERN MICHIGAN UNIVERSITY and Kalamazoo College are found there.

Annual events include Snowflakes and Spirits Festival in February, Maple Sugaring Weekend in March and Michigan Inernational Air Show and Trade Exposition in June. The natural history of the Kalamazoo area is displayed in the Kalamazoo Nature Center, a five hundred acre preserve which includes a pioneer homestead, interpretative center and nature trails. Tours of the Upjohn Company are available by reservation.

KALONA, Iowa. City (pop. 1,568), situated in Washington County, about fifteen miles southwest of IOWA CITY. Kalona is the heart of the largest Amish and Mennonite settlement west of the MISSISSIPPI RIVER. The community has gained a wide reputation as a center in the revival of interest in old-fashioned quilting. Quilt making is a cottage industry there, with many quilters working in their homes. Shops at Kalona offer everything from supplies and finished quilts for sale, to repair service, and quilts are sent from all parts of the country to be repaired or finished. The quilting auctions at Kolona attract bidders worldwide, prepared to bid from $500 to many thousands for some of the finest new work in the field. Woodin Wheel Antiques in Kalona, operated by Marylin Woodin, is said to be the largest retail outlet anywhere for modern and antique quilts. Quilters contribute some of their finest work to the benefit of Mennonite missions around the world.

KANKAKEE RIVER. Indiana and northeastern Illinois river which begins near SOUTH BEND, Indiana, and enters the Great Lakes Plain region of Illinois. The Kankakee River flows past Momence, Illinois, which has been one of the nation's largest producers of gladiolus flowers and bulbs, and past the cities of KANKAKEE and Bourbonnais before it joins the DES PLAINES RIVER to form the ILLINOIS RIVER.

KANSAS CITY, MISSOURI

Name: Kansa from the old Siouan language "people of the south wind" with "s" added by the French to represent the plural, original settlement called Kansas (1838), then Town of Kansas (1839), City of

Kansas City

Kansas (1853) and finally Kansas City in 1889.

Area: 316.3 square miles

Elevation: 1,014 feet

Population:

1984: 443,075
Rank: 28th
Percent change (1980-1984): minus 1.1%
Density (city): 1,401 per sq. mi.
Metropolitan Population: 1,237,020
Percent change (1980-1984): .7%

Racial and Ethnic makeup (1980):

White: 69.8%
Black: 27.4%
Hispanic origin: 14,643 persons
Indian: 2,115 persons
Asian: 3,519 persons
Other: 6,277 persons

Age:

18 and under: 26.5%
65 and over: 12.3%

TV Stations: 6

Radio Stations: 32

Hospitals: 41

Sports Teams:

(baseball) Royals
(football) Chiefs
(basketball) Kings
(soccer) Spurs

Further Information: Chamber of Commerce, 600 Charterbank Center, 920 Main Street, Kansas City, MO 64105

KANSAS CITY, Missouri. City, Clay, Cass, Jackson, and Platte Counties, at the confluence of the MISSOURI and Kansas Rivers in central western Missouri. Today the largest city in Missouri, having surpassed ST. LOUIS in 1984. Kansas City was first settled in 1821 by French fur traders and served as a supply depot. The town grew rapidly as an outfitting point for expeditions, because the two great trails, SANTA FE and OREGON, ran through the town. Trade for the year 1848 to 1849 was estimated at $5

Nichols Fountain, Country Club Plaza, Kansas City

Kantor - Keel Boats

million for the outfitting of 900 wagons and 2,000 travelers. Kansas City's commercial success suffered from a cholera epidemic in the mid-1800s that halved its population, and from the CIVIL WAR, which brought conflict within the town and disrupted its trade. In 1864 Union and Confederate troops engaged in the Battle of WESTPORT (October 23, 1864), on the outskirts of the town. This battle has been called the "Gettysburg of the West" because of its importance to the Union cause. The town was incorporated as the City of Kansas on Feb. 22, 1853.

The arrival of the railroad in 1865 and a bridge constructed across the Missouri River in 1869 assured the commercial future of the city. Stockyards were built and packing houses were opened in the 1870s. By 1884 overhead trolley cars appeared, having been invented by John C. Henry of Kansas City. Influential in the development of the city was the editor and founder of the Kansas City *Star*, William Rockhill Nelson (1841-1915). He absorbed other local newspapers and began a crusade for civic improvement to make Kansas City as attractive as it was prosperous. Much of the community planning and culture evident today is the result of his interest.

In the early 1900s auto assembly plants opened, and during WORLD WAR I business in cattle and horses reached new heights. Often called the world's food capital, Kansas City today is first in the nation in farm equipment and the distribution and marketing of winter wheat. It is also a leader in production of AUTOMOBILES and greeting cards, and is a center of frozen food storage and distribution.

Along with the University of MISSOURI at Kansas City, it is the site of 19 other colleges and universities. The city's hilly terrain contains over 100 parks, one of which is the 1,300-acre Swope Park. Numerous historical and cultural sites dot the city, including the Nelson Gallery and Atkins Museum. There is a citizen-supported Philharmonic Orchestra and a Civic Orchestra that is an affiliate of the Conservatory of Music at the state university.

Kansas City is also the site of the American Royal Livestock and Horse Show and the annual convention of the Future Farmers of America. The metropolitan area includes Kansas City, Kansas; the two cities are separated only by the state line.

KANTOR, MacKinlay. (Webster City, IA, Feb. 4, 1904—Sarasota, FL, Oct. 11, 1977). Author of novels and motion picture scripts,

along with other works. In the Midwest he was particularly known for his description of the SPIRIT LAKE MASSACRE, which actually took place at West OKIBOJI LAKE, not Spirit Lake. His other works include the one for which he is generally most noted, *Andersonville*, for which he won the PULITZER PRIZE in 1956, as well as *Long Remember* (1934), *Gentle Annie* (1942) and others. He also served as a war correspondent in Korea. From 1951 to 1953 Kantor served as technical consultant to the U.S. Air Force.

KASKASKIA RIVER. Southeastern Illinois river which flows southwest toward the MISSISSIPPI RIVER. The source of the river lies southwest of Champaign, Illinois. It flows through the Shelbyville Wildlife Management Area, Hidden Springs State Forest, past VANDALIA, Illinois, and forms artificial Lake Carlyle before continuing to its mouth north of Chester, Illinois, on the Mississippi.

KASKASKIA, Illinois. Village (pop. 79), first capital of Illinois. In 1703 Kaskaskia was founded by the French and became the largest and most important of the French villages of the area. It was lost to the French after their defeat in the FRENCH AND INDIAN WAR in 1763. During the REVOLUTIONARY WAR, Kaskaskia was captured by George Rogers CLARK (1752-1818) from the British with the aid of Virginia's governor, Patrick Henry. The *Herald*, the first newspaper printed in Illinois, was first published in Kaskaskia in 1814. Kaskaskia opened the first Masonic Lodge in Illinois and counted among its members Shadrach BOND (1773-1832), later governor of the state. With statehood on December 3, 1818, Kaskaskia became the Illinois capital for two years, until the capital was moved to VANDALIA, founded in 1819. In a flood, the MISSISSIPPI RIVER cut through Kaskaskia and washed away many of its historic buildings. Today most of the first capital of Illinois lies under water. The remnant village of Kaskaskia is located on Kaskaskia Island, the only part of Illinois west of the Mississippi. Kaskaskia State Memorial, a small brick building located in the village, contains the bell of the Church of the Immaculate Conception, known as the LIBERTY BELL OF THE WEST. George Rogers Clark rang this bell, from old Kaskaskia, on July 4, 1778, to announce that France had joined the American War of Independence.

KEEL BOATS. These flat-bottomed boats were an important factor in river TRANSPORTATION and in the settlement of the Midwest. They

Keel boats provided early river transportation.

were built upriver on the OHIO and other rivers at points near established settlements, from which they would be floated down river, carrying settlers and their goods. Ohio's first settlers floated down the Ohio River in such boats, which they said looked like "a barn on a raft." Because there was no way to get the boat back up river, it was either kept and used to carry passengers or commerce farther downstream or broken up·for its lumber. Beginning in 1788 with the first 47 settlers of the Ohio Company of Associates, tens of thousands of settlers reached the Midwest in this way. Keel boats also were used for commerce. Abraham LINCOLN and his two stepbrothers helped build a keelboat on the SANGAMON RIVER in Illinois in 1831. On the way down the river with a load of produce, the boat stuck on the mill dam at NEW SALEM. It tilted upward and took on water. The ever resourceful Lincoln took out cargo to lighten the boat. When the stern lifted above the water, he borrowed an augur from well-wishers on shore, drilled a hole to let the water out, then filled the hole with a plug, and they got the boat over the dam. As was usual with flatboats, the Lincoln boat was sold at New Orleans for its lumber, and Lincoln walked back to New Salem. For Lincoln and many others, such trips were their introduction to life beyond the frontier.

KELLEY'S ISLAND. A shield-shaped island of 2,888 acres, seven miles across at its widest point, the island lies in Lake ERIE north of SANDUSKY. Its circumference is eighteen miles,

and it rises significantly in the center. In 1833 Ira and Datus Kelley acquired it, settled there, and began to exploit its resources, including its forests of red cedar. Wine was made in 1850, and a year later the first wine cellar north of CINCINNATI was built there. Quarrying began in the 1860s. Summer tourists flock to the island today, but it is isolated and almost self-sufficient in the winter. On the south shore, INSCRIPTION ROCK is one of the country's finest examples of petroglyphs. Another remarkable rock is found in Kelley's Island State Park. This has been called one of the "best examples of glacial action in the world." The story of millions of years of glacial action has been carved into grooves in the rock, making it easy for geologists to "read" the record of glacial action like a book.

KELLOGG, Frank Billings. (Potsdam, NY, Dec. 22, 1856—St. Paul, MN, Dec. 21, 1937). Diplomat, senator, secretary of state. Kellogg served as a United States Senator from Minnesota from 1917 to 1923. He served as the secretary of state in the cabinet of President Calvin Coolidge from March 4, 1925, until March 4, 1929. Kellogg received public notice as special counsel for the United States in the case against Standard Oil. He was also the special counsel for the Interstate Commerce Commission in its investigation of the Harriman railroads and for the United States in its action to dissolve the Union Pacific-Southern Pacific merger. From 1930 until 1935 Kellogg was also a judge of the Permanent Court of International Justice. His most notable achievement was the Kellogg Briand Peace Pact, an unsuccessful attempt at curbing war, for which he received the Nobel Peace Prize in 1929.

KELLOGG, Will Keith. (Battle Creek, MI, Apr. 7, 1860—Battle Creek, MI, Oct. 6, 1951). Manufacturer of food products, philanthropist. Kellogg became known as "the king of the flakes" as the founder of the Kellogg Company with plants in BATTLE CREEK, Michigan, and Omaha, Nebraska. The role of a master salesman was very different from that of the first half of Kellogg's life, which was spent in obscurity. At fourteen he began to sell brooms for his father. In 1864 he went to work for his brother who operated the Battle Creek Sanitarium. The brothers soon began experimenting with prepared cereal products of different kinds. When they hit on a method of rolling mushed-cooked wheat into flakes, they began selling the product by mail to health food users.

In 1906 Will Kellogg began the Kellogg business in cereals. He is credited with creating a new way of life in America, initiating what now may be considered the prepared foods era. He retired from active participation in the firm in 1929 and established the W. K. Kellogg Foundation in Battle Creek. Quietly Kellogg invested most of his fortune in the foundation, supporting endeavors he judged to be helpful. He also made substantial gifts to his home city. He remained chairman of the board of the company until his death.

KENOSHA, Wisconsin. City (pop. 123,132), seat of Kenosha County, situated in extreme southeast Wisconsin on Lake MICHIGAN, near the border with Illinois. The city was incorporated in 1850. The name was derived from a Potawatomi Indian word meaning pike or pickerel. Both fish were found in numbers in the area. An industrial center and lake port, the city was prominent as headquarters for American Motors for many years until it merged with Chrysler. The announcement in 1988 that Chrysler would close the plant, placing more than 5,000 jobs in jeopardy, aroused the city, and a few concessions were made, but the economy was expected to take a severe decline. Other industries include clothing, metal products and electrical equipment. In Wisconsin history, Kenosha boasts the first public school

in the state, begun there in 1849. The University of Wisconsin-Parkside attracts visitors with its unique campus. Campus buildings are interconnected by glass enclosed corridors radiating out from the Wyllie Library Learning Center. Carthage College, founded in 1847, and a technical school are located in the city. Visitors find particular interest in the Kenosha library, designed by famed architect Daniel Burnham (1846-1912). Unlike most of the major GREAT LAKES communities, the city owns almost all of the Lake Michigan frontage, which has been substantially devoted to parks. The Civic center includes the county courthouse, historical museum and art museum. Kenosha receives much publicity as international headquarters for the Society for Preservation and Encouragement of Barber Shop Quartet Singing in America.

KENSINGTON RUNESTONE. Highly controversial artifact discovered in 1898, bearing inscriptions indicating that Norsemen penetrated the Minnesota-Great Lakes frontier via Greenland and perhaps Hudson Bay nearly a century before Columbus arrived in the New World. Belief in the authenticity of the stone runs deep in many Scandinavian-Americans. They contend that the stone corroborates other evidence, such as bits of Norse legend and literature, as proof that Norse sailors were

Kensington Runestone replica at Alexandria, Minnesota.

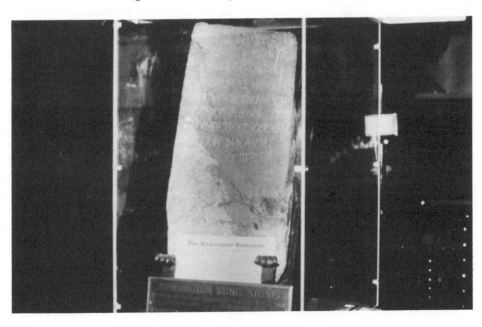

capable of such a navigational feat. But doubts of the stone's authenticity arose almost immediately. Critics believed it was part of a Scandanivan-American plot to discredit an 1888 assertion by Norwegian historian Dr. Gustav Storm that Norsemen had never touched United States soil. These critics find it more than a coincidence that the stone was discovered only five years after the successful voyage of a replica of a Viking ship from Bergen, Norway, to the New World. Other critics point to more historical fact. According to the original story, the stone was found under the roots of a seventy-year-old poplar tree on the farm of Olof Ohman in 1898. Drawings made of the tree by Ohman indicate a much younger tree and questions arise as to why such an historic find was never announced to the world until five months after its discovery when it was shown to a local realtor. The stone was sent to O.J. Breda, professor of Scandanivan languages at the University of Minnesota, who doubted its genuineness. Three professors of Christiania (Oslo) University called the stone a forgery based upon copies of the inscription mailed to them. The stone was returned to Ohman who did nothing more with it until 1907 when Hjalmar Rued HOLAND visited him while researching a book on Norwegian settlements. Holand left with the stone which became a major feature in his book. Holand toured Europe with the stone before attempting to sell it to the Minnesota Historical Society for $5000. The Society endorsed the stone despite the fact that it was unable to get any of numerous European or American specialists to accept the value of the stone. Linguistic and runological sections of the Society's report were the work of the stone's principal supporter, Holand. Holand defended the stone in lectures, articles and interviews. Critics have continued to claim that much of the stone's text came from a popular reference of the period entitled, *The Well-Informed Schoolmaster* by Carl Roslander. Despite the controversy, the stone has been displayed at the Smithsonian Institution. In 1951, a Runestone Memorial Park was inaugurated at ALEXANDRIA, Minnesota, at which time a giant replica of the stone was unveiled at public ceremony. The Kensington Stone's discoverer, Olof Ohman, died without ever claiming it was genuine.

KENYON COLLEGE. The college was founded in 1824 at Gambier, Ohio, on a wooded plateau above the Kokosing River. The Gothic style buildings remind visitors of Oxford in England. Old Kenyon (1827), oldest building on the campus, is a massive sandstone structure, surmounted by a 100-foot bell tower. Kenyon was one of the earliest in higher education to institute a division of aeronautics. There also is a well known divinity school. The *Kenyon Review* is a notable literary periodical. Among the graduates one of the most prominent is President Rutherford B. HAYES (1822-1893), along with many judges, congressmen and other distinguished figures. The student body of 1,485 is instructed by a faculty of 111.

KEOKUK (chief). (Saukenuk, not far from Rock Island, IL, 1788?—Sauk Agency, Franklin Co., KS, Apr. 1848?). Called Watchful Eye (a shortened version of He Who Moves Around Alert), the SAUK and FOX leader refused to join Chief BLACK HAWK in his support for the British in the WAR OF 1812. His support for the U.S. was rewarded by a grant of land for his people near KEOKUK, Iowa, after the BLACK HAWK WAR (1832). He visited Washington, D.C., in 1833 and 1837. In Washington he helped conclude a peace treaty between his tribe and the SIOUX. Making further accommodations with the U.S. government he moved with his tribe to reservations in Kansas. His body was returned to Keokuk from a Kansas reservation. In Rand Park there, the chief's resting place is marked by an imposing monument, topped by his statue.

KEOKUK, Iowa. City (pop 13,536). Seat of Lee County, situated at the southeasternmost tip of Iowa on the MISSISSIPPI RIVER, near its junction with the DES MOINES RIVER, at the foot of the rapids of the latter river. Incorporated in 1847, it takes its name from Chief KEOKUK of the SAUK and FOX, the name "He Who Moves Around Alert." Power for Keokuk's industries is furnished by the gravity dam and power plant completed in 1913. Manufactured products include corrugated cartons, sponge rubber, metal products and processed food products. The first cabin was built at Keokuk in 1820, and a trading post began operations in 1829. The Mississippi River brought substantial traffic. Five army hospitals at Keokuk tended the wounded during the CIVIL WAR. Those who died are buried in the national cemetery there. Tourists find much to interest them in the largest of all the locks on the Mississippi, the massive monument to Chief KEOKUK (1788?-1848?) and his grave, the unknown soldier monument in the national cemetery and the relics of Mark Twain at the public library. Twain worked in Keokuk as a printer in his brother's shop. He set the type for the first city directory. An outdoor attraction is the lake, formed by the dam, which stretches as far as BURLINGTON, Iowa.

KEWADIN, Michigan. Village located northeast of TRAVERSE CITY on Elk Lake in Antrim County on Michigan's LOWER PENINSULA, named for Chief Kewaydin who formerly lived there. Kewadin was the site of the discovery of a copper kettle three feet in diameter of undetermined age, found in the care of an Indian named Mamagona. The kettle was fashioned with great skill from a single sheet of copper. A stone with which the kettle was fashioned was found inside the vessel with flakes of copper embedded in it. This unique artifact has attracted much speculation.

KICKAPOO INDIANS. In the late 1600s this Algonquin language group occupied southwest Wisconsin. They lived in much the same way as the Eastern Woodland groups. However, in addition, they hunted BUFFALO, an activity adapted from their neighbors on the plains. After the ILLINI Indians were massacred by the Kickpoo and their allies, the Kickpoo moved southward into present south central Illinois, numbering altogether about 3,000. Siding with the British in the Revolution and the WAR OF 1812, and with TECUMSEH in his move to drive out the white settlers, they were forced in 1819 to cede all their lands in Illinois to the U.S. Despite this, they remained on and sided with BLACK HAWK in the BLACK HAWK WAR and after the war were forced to move to Missouri. At about the same time, a dissatisfied group moved to Mexico and became known as the Mexican Kickapoo. Today some of the Kickapoo descendants live on a reservation in Chihuahua, Mexico, and others live on reservations in Oklahoma and Kansas; the latter number about 1,000 persons.

KICKAPOO STATE PARK. Site of early salt wells used by the Indians and pioneers near Danville, Illinois. The park, with 1,539 acres, was developed on land abandoned after stripmining. Hundreds of ponds there are stocked with fish. The first land was acquired by the state in 1939 after Clinton C. Tilton, a retired newspaperman, raised $15,000 in donations. The grave of John Cox, Indian fighter after the American Revolution and scout in the BLACK HAWK WAR, is located in the park. An evaporating kettle used by the pioneers at the salt springs is located in a small memorial one-half mile from the entrance to the park.

KINDERGARTEN, First in the U.S. Mrs. Karl (Margarethe) Schurz, wife of the famed German reformer who fled to WATERTOWN, Wisconsin, after the ill-fated revolution of 1848, gained her own international fame by starting at Watertown the first kindergarten in the United States (1856). She had been familiar with the operation of kindergartens in Germany and was sure that such education would also be useful in America. Based on the German experience, she was convinced that earlier formal schooling resulted in quicker advancement in later education. Her pioneering venture was soon picked up at MILWAUKEE. The building housing the first kindergarten is the 57-room octagonal mansion in Watertown, completed in 1854 by John Richards, open for viewing by visitors.

KING, Karl Laurence. (Paintersville, OH, Feb. 21, 1891—Fort Dodge, IA, Mar. 32, 1971). Composer. Said by some to have inherited the mantle of John Philip Sousa as the nation's march king, Laurence composed some of the most popular marches of the day. Although he had almost no instruction in composing, at the age of seventeen he sold two of his marches. After joining the band of the Barnum and Bailey Circus in 1913, he composed the famous "Barnum and Bailey's Favorite" march, dedicated to the circus's conductor, Ned Brill. After composing numerous other circus marches, he settled in FORT DODGE, Iowa, where he conducted the Fort Dodge band and the Iowa State Fair band for forty years. His "Home Town Boy" (1957) was written in honor of Iowan Meredith WILLSON (1902-1984) when the latter's *Music Man* had its motion picture premiere. In later years, King composed the school marches for many universities, including IOWA, MINNESOTA and ILLINOIS.

KINNICK, Nile. (Adel, IA, July 9, 1919—at sea, June 2, 1943). Athlete and aviator. In the late 1930s the football team of the University of IOWA gained national fame as the Iron Men. A student of law at the university, Kinnick was the most prominent player on that team. Iron Man Kinnick won the Heisman trophy in 1939 as one of college football's all-time greats. He died during WORLD WAR II in the crash of his USNR plane in the Caribbean.

KINNIKINNICK. Dried dogwood leaves

smoked by Midwestern Indians until the more prized tobacco was introduced.

KINZIE, John. (Quebec, Canada, Dec. 3, 1763—Chicago, IL, Jan. 6, 1828). Trader. Kinzie came to the CHICAGO area in 1804 and took over the trading post Jean la Lime had purchased from Jean Baptiste DU SABLE. In 1810 Kinzie was responsible for the removal of Captain John Whistler (father of the famous painter) from the command of FORT DEARBORN. Whistler had attempted to stop the sale of liquor to the Indians. Kinzie was hired by John Jacob ASTOR to barter with the Indians for furs. In 1812 Kinzie and La Lime had a violent quarrel in which La Lime shot Kinzie in the neck before being fatally wounded. During the FORT DEARBORN massacre (August 15, 1812), an event Kinzie attempted to prevent by warning the soldiers to hold the fort instead of evacuating, Kinzie saved his family by putting them on a boat. He returned to the region in 1816 and lived to assist Chicago as it started its rise to commercial power.

KIRKSVILLE, Missouri. City (pop. 17,167), seat of Adair County; one of the largest cities in northeastern Missouri; named, according to legend, for the Kirk family who wined and dined the county commissioners to persuade them to name the town in their honor. Kirksville was founded in 1841 as the county seat. During the CIVIL WAR the Battle of Kirksville was fought on August 6, 1862. Federal troops routed the Confederates in what was to be the only battle of any importance in the region. The city manufactures shoes, hospital equipment and machinery. Kirksville has a long, proud history in the field of education, beginning in 1857 with the establishment of the state's first normal school. John R. Kirk, president of the school for twenty-six years, pioneered rural school development and established experimental schools to test theories. He championed music education, consolidated schools, and worked to secure better physical equipment. Today the NORTHEAST MISSOURI STATE UNIVERSITY continues the normal school's tradition of training teachers. The Kirksville College of Osteopathic Medicine, founded in 1892, was the first of its kind in the world. The college was established by Dr. Andrew Taylor STILL (1828-1917) who came to Missouri as a boy and later moved to Kansas where he developed his new theory of healing. Still returned to Missouri and spent the rest of his life practicing and teaching his ideas. The

institution he founded is now the Kirksville College of Medicine.

KIRKWOOD, Missouri. City (pop. 27,987), St. Louis Co., in east central Missouri. It was settled with the development of the railroad in 1852, incorporated in 1865, and named for the railroad's chief engineer, James P. Kirkwood. Today it is an industrial and residential suburb of ST. LOUIS.

KIRKWOOD, Samuel Jordan. (Hartford County, MD, Dec. 20, 1813—Iowa City, IA, Sept., 1894). Kirkwood, who served two terms as Iowa governor during the CIVIL WAR, was noted as one of the principal supporters of the war among Northern governors. He outfitted the FIRST IOWA REGIMENT at his own expense, and he served a part of a term as U.S. senator (1866-1867). Although he preferred going back to the Senate, state Republicans drafted him again as governor (1876-1877). He did return to the Senate in 1877, then served as secretary of interior (1881-82). He was the only Iowa official to have served the state as governor, U.S. senator and as a member of a presidential cabinet.

KIRTLAND, Ohio. City (pop. 5,969), situated in northeast Ohio in Lake County. The name is derived from Turhand Kirtland, an agent of the Connecticut Land Company, which owned portions of the land. It is a suburban CLEVELAND residential community on a hill overlooking the East Branch of the CHAGRIN RIVER. In 1831 Joseph SMITH (1805-1844), founder of the MORMON faith, came to Kirtland. The Mormon faith grew rapidly there. Some estimates place the number at Kirtland as high as 20,000, but the depression of 1837 brought a collapse to Kirtland, and Smith and most of his followers left for Missouri. They left behind many reminders of their unique presence, including the striking temple. This was built by the followers and included stucco in which Mormon women mixed their shattered glassware to provide the glitter. The building was sold to satisfy a judgment. For twenty years a normal school operated in it. When the Mormon church divided, most of the Mormons in Kirtland went to the REORGANIZED CHURCH OF LATER DAY SAINTS, and, after long litigation, the reorganized group gained control of the temple.

KOEHLER, Robert. (Hamburg, Germany, 1850—Minneapolis, MN, 1917). Artist, art teacher. Brought to MILWAUKEE, Wisconsin, at the age of four, Koehler later began to study art in Milwaukee. After going to Munich in 1873 to study art, Koehler studied and maintained an art school there until 1892. Returning to America at New York, he joined the New York Art Students' League. Much of his work emphasizes his social consciousness. He became the director of the Minneapolis School of Fine Arts in 1893 and continued there until his death. He is noted as a pioneer in the Midwest in techniques of art instruction.

KOHLER, Wisconsin. Town (pop. 1,651), situated in southeast Wisconsin as a suburb of SHEBOYGAN, the community was founded in 1873 by the Kohler family, founders and developers of the Kohler Company, premier manufacturers of bathroom fixtures and other plumbing and heating products. Walter Kohler (1875-1940) was a controversial governor of Wisconsin (1928-1930). Although the company and town were noted for their paternal policies to workers and their families, the company has been over the years one of the worst hit by labor disputes, beginning with Walter Kohler's opposition to unions. The original community consisted of 450 cottages, carefully planned in their placement around the extensive factory grounds. The community has been particularly noted for its landscaping. Under the direction of Ruth and Marie Kohler, the Kohler Foundation carried out the restoration of the famed WADE HOUSE at Sheboygan, among the foundation's other activities.

KOKOMO, Indiana. City (pop. 47,808), seat of Howard County, north central Indiana industrial city north of INDIANAPOLIS and east of LAFAYETTE. Kokomo, named for the Miami chief, Kokomoko, grew as a result of the arrival of the railroad in 1853 and the discovery of natural gas in 1886. Among the products of Kokomo are iron, STEEL, brass, farm machinery, automobile parts and furnaces. Points of interest in Kokomo include taxidermically preserved "Old Ben," the largest steer ever raised in Indiana, which weighed 4,470 pounds, stood six feet four

inches tall and measured over 16 feet from the tip of its tail to its nose. Distinguished residents of the city have included Elwood HAYNES (1857-1925), the builder of the first mechanically successful spark-ignition automobile and developer of stainless steel, and stellite. The Elwood Haynes Museum contains exhibits relating to the inventor's life, while a statue east of the city marks the first road test, on July 4, 1894, of Haynes' automobile. An antique car competition, known as the Haynes-Apperson Festival, is held on the Fourth of July weekend. Grissom Air Force Base, fifteen miles north of Kokomo, houses a fine collection of vintage planes.

KRESGE FOUNDATION. Nonprofit corporation established in 1924 through a donation by Sebastian S. KRESGE (1867-1966) of DETROIT, Michigan, founder of the Kresge stores. The foundation awards grants to institutions working in the arts, health, conservation, four-year college education and the care of the young and aged. Most grants are used for major equipment and construction. The foundation has made more than 2,000 grants with a total worth of approximately $230 million. Money has been used in forty-eight of the states; eleven nations; Puerto Rico and Washington, D.C.

KRESGE, Sebastian S. (Bald Mount, PA, July 31, 1867—Detroit, MI, Oct. 18, 1966). Merchant. Kresge founded the huge Kresge variety store chain. He started in a 5 & 10 cent store with J. G. McCrory in Memphis, Tennessee, in 1897 before moving to DETROIT, Michigan, and starting Kresge and Wilson in 1899. Kresge and Wilson became S.S. Kresge and was incorporated under the name S. S. Kresge and Company in 1912. Kresge was the founder and sole donor of the KRESGE FOUNDATION. Its support was given mainly to colleges and universities and religious institutions. After 1960, its gifts were mainly for the construction of new buildings and facilities in educational institutions, with less emphasis on religious organizations.

L

LABOR AND LABOR UNIONS (MID-WEST HIGHLIGHTS). From its earliest settlement until the early Twentieth Century, the Midwest has been a land of laborers, generally independent farmers, with, perhaps, a "hired hand." It is said that traditionally Midwesterners have had a better appreciation of labor's worth because of their own labor. This is certainly the case with the Midwest's own Abraham LINCOLN, who had been a laborer as a youth. In an 1847 lecture Lincoln made one of the most important statements on the value of labor, stating, "...if we except the light and the air of heaven, no good thing has been or can be enjoyed by us without having first cost labor. And insamuch as most good things are produced by labor, it follows that all such things of right belong to those whose labor has produced them. But it has so happened, in all ages of the world, that some have labored, and others have without labor enjoyed a large proportion of the fruits. This is wrong and should not continue. To secure to each laborer the whole product of his labor or as nearly as possible, is a worthy object of any good government."

It was with the hope of securing a greater share of the "product" of labor that the first labor organizations began. By the beginning of the 1800s, the East was well on its way to industrialization, and in New York City workers had organized as early as 1778. Meanwhile, the sparsely populated Midwest was almost entirely rural, inhabited mainly by fiercely independent farmers, who hired few laborers. "For the pioneers there were no classes and no workers." Yet some of the earliest labor legislation and early stirring of workers occurred in the Midwest.

In 1813 the Michigan territorial legislature passed the mechanics lein law, which safeguarded the collection of money owed to laborers who had no contracts. This covered a very large territory, because at that time Michigan Territory extended as far west as Iowa. By 1813 the Midwest had its first craft organization in Ohio, the DAYTON Mechanics' Society. Five years later, in 1818, a group of workers organized the DETROIT Mechanics' society. A year later, mechanics in Detroit were earning from $1.00 to $2.25 per day, while unorganized labor in Philadelphia was averaging only twelve cents a day.

By 1831 one of the nation's first labor newspapers, the *Workingman's Shield*, was being published at CINCINNATI, Ohio. The Michigan printers organized in 1835, and a year later the region had what is probably its first strike, when the Cincinnati Harnessmakers Union left their jobs for increased wages and a ten-hour day.

The great depression of 1837 drove most workers' organizations out of the field. Nevertheless, of the nine U.S. strikes recorded that year, four occurred in the Midwest, where the full effects of the financial panic had not yet been felt. The Detroit *Daily Advertiser* of April 4, 1837, noted that "Yesterday our streets were paraded by a large company of respectable looking journeymen carpenters, carrying standards bearing this pithy couplet: 'Ten hours a day, And two dollars for pay.'"

By 1855 the Mechanics Union in Illinois was successful in leading the fight for free public schools. In the period before the CIVIL WAR, union organizing continued in the Midwest and even during the war, when the Brotherhood of Locomotive Engineers was organized in Detroit in 1863.

After the war, the rising prices and costs and the mechanization of trades brought widespread unrest among industrial workers.

Formed in 1869, the Knights of Labor became the first labor group to be organized throughout most of the country. Any worker could join, except, perhaps ironically, for lawyers.

There are no accurate estimates of the impact of the group in the Midwest. The editors of *Michigan* of the Michigan Writers Project note that, "Probably the Knight's membership in Michigan was never more than 10,000, though newspaper reports credited it with 25,000 members in 1886." On the other hand, the Ohio Writers Project editors asserted, "By 1885 it had an Ohio membership of tens of thousands, notably in Cincinnati, where approximately 25,000 workers were members." In Illinois the "Knights of Labor formed a hundred new lodges throughout the state each week early in 1886." Even in rural Iowa, at the peak of the organization's membership, there were estimates of 25,000 members. In Wisconsin the organization was said to be "the largest union of the time."

However, the depression of 1873 interrupted labor's gains when union membership declined by 85%, and wages were cut in half.

Nevertheless, some legislators were giving thought to workers and especially to working conditions. In 1872 Illinois passed the first law dealing with working conditions in mines. Other Midwest states soon followed with similar laws.

July, 1877, found the nation involved in a strike of railroad men, called the "first large national strike," and noted to have been "hell on wheels." Ohio was particularly hard hit by this strike, which reached much of the Midwest.

The period 1880 to 1900 has been called "one of the most turbulent in labor history." The turmoil referred to included such events as the 1881 lumber strike at EAU CLAIRE, Wisconsin, and the coal strike in Ohio. After almost two years of bitter attempts of government and management to break their union, on August 30, 1884, workers of the Ohio Miners' Amalgamated Association at Straitsville, Ohio, sent five burning cars into a mine. The strike was settled the next spring, but the resulting fire burned for fifty years.

Perhaps the most notorious labor disturbance during the period was the so-called HAYMARKET RIOT at CHICAGO, Illinois, May 4, 1886. A bomb was thrown; seven policemen were killed, along with four civilians. Eight "anarchists" were tried and convicted without any proof that they had thrown the bomb. The incident was used by foes of organized labor as they contested with the Knights of Labor, which lost much of its influence following the event. However, individual state federations of labor then rose in influence.

A key point in labor history was reached on December 10, 1886, at COLUMBUS, Ohio, when the American Federation of Labor was formed, with Samuel Gompers as president. Whereas the Knights of Labor attempted to form a single giant union, embracing all types of work, the Federation formed a decentralized association of the local labor organizations, recognizing the autonomy of the various members. This provided a powerful national body without jeopardizing the local interests of labor.

Meanwhile, Midwest legislators continued to pass laws regulating the use of labor. Michigan

passed the ten-hour day in 1885; in 1890 an Iowa law required automatic couplers on railroad cars, greatly reducing rail deaths, and serving as a model for national legislation; between 1872 and 1877, child labor laws were passed in Illinois.

The most dramatic and widely publicized labor struggle occurred in the Midwest in 1894. On May 11, workers of the Pullman Palace Car Company at Chicago struck to protest wage cuts and firing of union representatives. The American Railway Union under Eugene V. DEBS (1853-1926) came to their aid on June 26, with a boycott of all Pullman railway cars, and within days 50,000 rail workers had heeded the call. On July 2 the federal government obtained a court injunction, and two days later President Grover Cleveland sent troops to Chicago. After much rioting and bloodshed, the strike was broken and the boycott collapsed. Debs was jailed for violating the injunction.

Quite different was the action of Jacob S. Coxey, who organized "Coxey's Army" at Massillon, Ohio, to march on Washington, D.C., seeking government action to help the workers in distress from the depression of 1893. About 100 men left Massillon on Easter Sunday, 1894. They were widely hailed on the route, where they expected to recruit thousands more, but only about 500 reached Washington, and the movement ended in an anticlimax, when the leaders were arrested for walking on the capitol lawn.

In his election to the presidency in 1896, William MC KINLEY (1843-1901) won much labor support by his slogan calling for a "full dinner pail."

However, early in his term he appeared to be conciliatory to "businessmen," and the growing calls for war with Spain kept him from working on this labor pledge.

In the early 1900s, the Industrial Workers of the World (IWW), organized in Chicago in 1905, was the most radical of all the union endeavors, but by 1930 its membership had declined from 30,000 to about 10,000. Because of its radical nature, it was particularly lacking in success in the Midwest.

Under Robert LA FOLLETTE (1855-1925), Wisconsin was one of the leaders in labor legislation. In 1911 the state passed seven labor laws, concerning workmen's compensation, child labor, apprenticeship, hours of work for women and fraudulent advertising. These helped to set a national pattern.

WORLD WAR I brought a period of labor peace, as the country turned to producing the needs of

Labor

war. The war brought new techniques of manufacture and a vast increase in the use of automatic machinery and methods, which required far fewer workers. The United Auto, Aircraft and Vehicles Union attempted to keep workers jobs, but their efforts failed in the depression of 1921. During 1926-1927 the American Federation of Labor sought to organize the AUTOMOBILE workers, but the FORD changeover from Model T to Model A brought a shutdown which threw 100,000 Ford employees out of work, and the organizing effort was unsuccessful.

The Great Depression of 1929 soon threw a third of all workers out of their jobs, and employers called for workers to "stretch out, speed up and find new efficiency." Despite the perils of the times, strikes continued.

The strikes at Hormel in AUSTIN, Minnesota, in 1933 and the strike at J.I. Case in RACINE, Wisconsin, have each been labeled the "first sitdown strike." This is the type of strike where the workers occupy key parts of the company itself.

The year 1934 saw the strike which began at the Toledo Auto-Lite plant spread to become the first major strike in the automobile industry and drew national attention.

Meanwhile, labor was counting on F.D. Roosevelt's New Deal for help, and Congress came through with many measures helpful to the working man, particularly the Wagner Labor Relations Act of 1935. An important aspect of this act was its provision protecting the worker from being fired for forming or participating in a union. In 1935 this spurred the founding of the Committee for Industrial Organization, later the Congress for Industrial Organization, (CIO). The CIO was organized to become a nationwide union of all labor, rather than an association of individual unions as in the AFL. The CIO drives for members, especially in auto and steel, were spectacularly successful. By 1955 when it merged with the AFL, the CIO had acquired 32 international unions and had 5,000,000 members.

Of the CIO group, one of the most successful was the United Automobile Workers of America, UAW, growing from 30,000 members in 1936 to 400,000 only a year later. In 1937 a wave of sit-down strikes hit the automakers.

That year also found the CIO's steelworkers involved in one of the most difficult strike situations in the nation's history. In 1937 the South Chicago plant of Republic Steel was hit by a strike. Men were killed and maimed by the Chicago police, and the incident is often described as a massacre. The public indignation led most of the nation's steel companies to bargain with the CIO union.

The nationwide 1937 auto strike of the CIO, in which the Midwest was hardest hit because of its central position in the industry, has been described as the " first great triumph of the CIO."

Labor historian Leslie F. Orear calls the January 26, 1946 national strike against all major meat packers, "One of the four or five most important since the 1930s." Due to the centralization of the industry in the Midwest, the region was the hardest hit at such leaders as Armour, Swift, Wilson, Cudahy, John Morrell and Rath. The latter, at WATERLOO, Iowa, was the largest of the independent packers. The strike ended with President Harry S Truman's seizure of the struck plants and award of hourly wage increases.

An important turning point in labor relations occurred on December 5, 1955, when the AF of L and the CIO merged to form the AFL-CIO, which merged organization then included 85% of all U.S. union membership. Midwest membership was said to be about the same as the national percentage.

The labor related laws and actions and the labor strife from this period on generally involved the Midwest in about the same manner as the rest of the country, with few labor highlights in the region.

In the 1960s and 1970s the relationship between employers and labor changed significantly, particularly in the Midwest. As jobs were lost in the Midwest due to the obsolescence of factories, high labor costs and transfer of plants to the Sunbelt, by the 1970s labor relations were generally peaceful in the region. By 1976 the unemployment rate in the region was the highest it had been in several decades. By 1982 Flint had an unemployment rate of 22%, highest in the nation. In view of these lasting problems, and particularly the loss of jobs, by 1978 the number of striking workers in the Midwest had reached the lowest point in ten years. Union workers cooperated with employers to assist in such depressed industries as automobile production and related suppliers. As agricultural equipment, steel and automobiles gradually began to improve, the unions continued to cooperate with employers, seeking non-wage-related benefits. The September 20, 1987, contract of Ford with the UAW was hailed as a model, providing job security and other benefits. The other makers soon followed the Ford model.

La Crosse - La Follette

273

During the decade of 1970-1980, the decline of labor union membership in the Midwest had not been as dramatic as had been the case nationwide, only about 3%, overall. In the region, Illinois had the largest number of organized workers, 1,487,000, with Iowa the smallest, 244,000. The percentage of employed laborers who belong to unions ranged from .08% in Iowa to 14.2% in Michigan. Total union membership in the Midwest as of the Department of Labor figures for 1980 was 6,606,000.

Since the 1970s only a few labor actions have been highlighted in the Midwest. The Chicago *Tribune* strike, beginning in 1986 was settled in 1988. The Chicago teachers strike of 1987 was the longest and most costly in the region, and the National Football League strike in 1987, occupied the Midwest teams in a clash between wealthy players and wealthy owners.

Looking ahead to the prospects for labor in the Midwest, in 1988 the secretary of labor summarized labors prospects, predicting drastic changes in the economy. However, the working men and women were said to be still the principal driving force. Record numbers of new jobs were predicted. But workers were warned that in the coming years they would face unprecedented economic competition on a global scale.

"But this new economic environment also will offer unprecedented opportuinties for American workers and the businesses that employ them. To take advantage of these opportunities, we must build a skilled flexible workforce that makes full use of our most precious asset—our human resources."

LA CROSSE, Wisconsin. City (pop. 48,347), seat of La Crosse County, situated in western Wisconsin on the MISSISSIPPI RIVER at the mouths of the BLACK and LA CROSSE rivers, the city was named for the Indian game called lacrosse by the French. Lacrosse was the most popular sport among the Indians of the area, and the city was located on their favorite playing fields. From Granddad Bluff, looking down on the city from a height of 570 feet, the highest of all the city's outlooks over the Mississippi, parts of two other states, Iowa and Minnesota, can also be seen. The community began in the late 1700s as a French trading post. In 1842, nineteen-year-old Nathan Myrick built the first log hut and trading post of the present city. The trickle of early settlers continued to trade with the Indians. The early 1850s saw growing settlement, and the community became the county

seat in 1851. German and Norwegian immigrants fled the revolutions at home to provide skilled craftsmen for the community and brought many of their native customs with them. The city charter came in 1856. During the CIVIL WAR, a local editor, Mark M. Pomeroy, strongly supported the southern cause. When LINCOLN was assassinated, a mob started for the paper to lynch Pomeroy, but they stopped at the nearest bar and forgot to go on. La Crosse became the most important commercial center between DUBUQUE and MINNEAPOLIS-ST. PAUL. The first railroad bridge carried trains across the Mississippi in 1876, greatly expanding the city's commerce. Lumbering was important from 1880 to 1905. Today the leading products are rubber footwear, air conditioning equipment, metal products, clothing and well-drilling equipment. Riverside USA offers an extensive exposition of river commerce and wildlife. Hixon House and Swarthout Museum have interesting displays and exhibits. Granddad Bluff remains one of the most popular viewing places on the Mississippi. During the summer the steamboat *La Crosse Queen* provides sightseeing cruises on the Mississippi. Mt. La Crosse Ski Area makes its own snow for a wide variety of skiing activities. Industrial tours include the Christina Wine Cellars and the G. Heileman Brewing Company. Riverfest in early July, La Crosse Interstate Fair in late July and Oktoberfest in late October are annual events of interest.

LA FOLLETTE, Robert Marion. (Primrose, WI, Feb. 6, 1855—Washington, DC, June 18, 1925). Graduating in law from the University of WISCONSIN in 1879, Robert M. LaFollette, was admitted to the bar the next year and elected district attorney of Dane County, despite opposition by the ruling Republican machine. For most of his life La Follette was a member of the "loyal opposition" in the Republican party.

He was known for championing the "little guy" against wealthy and entrenched interests. He was elected to the House of Representatives as a Republican (1885-1891).

After he lost his seat due to the general reaction against the 1890 tariff, he began to crystallize a reform program, including: direct-primary nominations protected by law; the equalization of taxation of corporate property with that of other property; the regulation of railroad charges, and the erection of commissions of experts to regulate railroads. These programs somewhat anticipated the Progressive movement and were partly reminiscent of Populism.

Although he lost the Republican nomination for governor in 1896 and 1898, he was nominated in 1900 by the Republican Party. In 1901, supported by the constituency he had won to his programs, he became the first native Wisconsinite to serve as governor of the state.

He immediately began to revise and expand his reform program. However, his liberal reform policies had alienated many of the more conservative party leaders, and his programs failed in a Republican legislature.

Winning the governorship again in the election of 1902, he gained a friendly legislature, and over a period from 1903 to 1905 many of his reforms were adopted. The nation's first statewide primary election law of 1904 gave the people of the state the opportunity to select their own candidates. Other measures provided for pensions for the blind, old age assistance, laws governing working conditions of children and unemployment compensation. These all proceeded from ideas first formulated by La Follette. Such reforms were copied throughout much of the country as the "WISCONSIN IDEA". As governor, LaFollete was one of the first to call on economic and other experts as government consultants, using many of the professors from the University of Wisconsin. This idea was also widely adopted and served to change many of the concepts of government.

As a Republican member of the U.S. Senate from Wisconsin (1906-1924), he became one of the most influential men in the Senate. In 1908 at the Republican convention, his name was placed in nomination for president. However, because he had alienated many key Republicans by his progressive ideas, he lost the nomination to William Howard TAFT (1847-1930). In 1909 LaFollette organized the National Progressive Republican League, gaining many liberal Republican followers. However, LaFollette's health failed temporarily in 1912 so that he could not promote his policies, and Theodore Roosevelt (1858-1919) took advantage of this disability, adopting many of LaFollette's ideas for his new Bull Moose party. This attracted many LaFollete supporters and split the liberal Republicans in the election of 1912. LaFollette never forgave Roosevelt for what he considered a betrayal and for the party schism which brought Woodrow Wilson to the presidency.

As a senator, La Follette opposed American entry into WORLD WAR I but during the war, he supported most of Wilson's policies, although he continued to believe that U.S. entry into the war was a mistake. La Follette broke with Wilson to oppose the League of Nations and the World Court, and his power in the Senate was a key factor in the rejection of the League and Court.

On the domestic front, Senator LaFollette supported Wilson's programs for railroad legislation and for regulation of conditions of maritime employment. In 1913 he advocated the 17th Amendment to the U.S. constitution, providing for direct popular election of U.S. Senators. After the war he fought U.S. postwar deflation policy. In 1924 he ran unsuccessfully for president on the PROGRESSIVE PARTY ticket. Nevertheless, he polled five million votes. However, the strain of campaigning helped to bring on his death in 1925.

LA SALLE, Illinois. City (pop. 10,347), once an important steamboat port and southern terminus of the ILLINOIS AND MICHIGAN CANAL. L a Salle is named for Robert Cavelier (Sieur de LA SALLE) (1643-1687), the French explorer who traversed the ILLINOIS RIVER in 1679. The community was first settled in 1830 and incorporated in 1852. When the Illinois and Michigan Canal was completed in 1848, it took 22 hours to cover the distance between CHICAGO and La Salle, a much shorter time than by overland travel. Within four years La Salle experienced a boom economy. However, the canal was soon made obsolete by RAILROADS, lack of coordination between river and canal vessels, and the irregularity of steamboat service. The economy continued to grow as La Salle became a coal mining community. In 1863, strikes by coal miners led to the La Salle Black Law, enforced for twenty years with fines and imprisonment, which prohibited anyone from preventing any person from working or from unionizing. Today LaSalle is a center for mining and cement and zinc products, electronic and electrical equipment and motors and is known as the home of Big Ben clocks. Matthiessen State Park Nature Area contains canyon trails, waterfalls, a stockade and a pioneer blockhouse. Not far from LaSalle, also, is famed STARVED ROCK STATE PARK, where LaSalle and his associate, Henri de DE TONTI (1650-1704) built a fort in 1680.

LA SALLE, Sieur de (Robert Cavelier). (Rouen, France, Nov. 22, 1643—Brazos River, TX, March 19, 1687). Explorer. La Salle, an early French explorer of the Midwest, claimed to have discovered the OHIO RIVER as early as 1669. He returned to France in 1673, obtained a patent of nobility, a monopoly of Indian trade, and an extensive tract of land around Fort Frontenac (now Kingston, Ontario, Canada) which he then commanded. In 1678 he set out to reinforce French claims on the GREAT LAKES and the MISSISSIPPI. In 1679, he built FT. MIAMI on the site of present ST. JOSEPH, Michigan, and Fort Creve Coeur, near presemt PEORIA, Illinois, in 1680. These were part of a long string of forts built by La Salle and his aide Henri DE TONTI reaching to French Louisiana. These were designed to protect the French interests in the entire area east of the Mississippi. These activities resulted in substantial discoveries in the middle and lower Mississippi valley, and he named the entire vast territory Louisiana and claimed it for Louis XIV, the King of France. In 1684 La Salle was made viceroy of North America, with command from the Great Lakes to the Spanish borders and the Gulf of Mexico. The first explorer to trace the Mississippi River to its mouth, he went on into the gulf areas, exploring and claiming land, and was killed by one of his own men in what is now Texas.

LACLEDE, Pierre Ligueste. (Bedous, France, c. 1724—near the mouth of the Arkansas River, AR, June 20, 1778). French fur trader and frontiersman. Working in the FUR TRADE in New Orleans during the 1750s, Laclede allied himself with his stepson Rene Auguste CHOUTEAU and co-founded the trading post that later became ST. LOUIS, Missouri. (1764).

LADYBUG. The Ohio ladybug is the official insect of Ohio. Also called the ladybird beetle, it is a member of the large beetle family. Ladybugs have been valued since early times because both the larvae and adult insects eat a variety of harmful aphids and other plant-eating insects. The name ladybug apparently started in the middle ages when the helpful insects were named for the Virgin Mary.

LADYSLIPPER. The pink and white ladyslipper is the state flower of Minnesota, where it is known as the "shoe of Venus, the queen," *Cypripedium reginae*, its scientific name; it also sometimes is called the moçcasin. The flower is one of the vast orchid family. It once was fairly common in parts of Minnesota but now is rare there, due in part to the fact that the plant grows so slowly, requiring ten to twenty years before it can bear blossoms. It may live to an age of fifty years. In order to grow, the ladyslipper must have the presence of a small fungus which is required to allow the plant's roots to take nourishment from the soil. Because of its many unusual qualities, the ladyslipper is truly unique among the state flowers.

LAFAYETTE, Indiana. City (pop. 44,955), Seat of Tippecanoe county, major northwestern Indiana city northwest of INDIANAPOLIS, shipping and trade center on the WABASH RIVER. Lafayette was named in 1824 by the founder of the city, William Digby, for the Marquis de LaFayette. Digby bought the town site for $1.25 an acre and sold it a year later to Samuel Sargent for a total of $240. Sargent's heirs gave the remainder of the land to the county, with the provision that Lafayette become the permanent county seat. The city is home to a wide diversity of manufactures, including pharmaceuticals, automotive gears and supplies and electrical equipment. It is the center for a broad farm region, with cattle and dairy farms. PURDUE UNIVERSITY is a hub of education and culture. Lafayette's Springvale Cemetery is the burial site of Helen Mar Jackson Gougar, suffragette, temperance leader, and the first woman lawyer in Indiana to appear before the state supreme court when she sued the election board for her right to vote. The Greater Lafayette Museum of Art houses collections of historical and current Indiana artwork. In early October, the Feast of the Hunters' Moon includes a reenactment at rebuilt FORT OUIATENON of the historic gathering, over two hundred fifty years ago, of Canadian traders, trappers, Indians and soldiers to celebrate the fall season. Another popular annual event is the Iron Horse Festival, said to be the only railroad festival of its kind in the United States. The festivities are organized around the restored Vandalia railroad station. Twelve miles north is the Tippecanoe Battlefield State Historic Site commemorating the 1811 battle between General William Henry HARRISON (1773-1841) and Indians led by TECUMSEH's brother, the PROPHET (1770-1834). The 90-acre park contains a museum.

LAKE ERIE, Battle of. During the WAR OF 1812 Oliver Hazard PERRY (1785-1809) was given a command on Lake ERIE in March, 1813. By the summer he and skilled experts had built a fleet of nine fully stocked warships, constructed from the lakeside forests near Erie, Pennsylvania. He sailed his fleet to Bass Island north of SANDUSKY, Ohio, where in August, 1813, they "put in" the harbor there, which has been called PUT-IN-BAY ever since. On September 10, sighting the British fleet of six strong warships, Perry sailed out northwest, toward the Sister Islands, to meet them. The British had 63 guns, four howitzers and two swivel guns. The Americans had 54 guns and two swivels. Perry's command ship, the *Lawrence*, pushed ahead of his other ships, which were becalmed. The full power of the British force was unleashed against the command ship, pounding her guns into silence. Perry abandoned her and rowed to the *Niagara*, which had finally managed to come up with the other American ships. He then led the fleet into a fierce battle, and at 3 o'clock in the afternoon the British surrendered. The message which Perry sent to General William Henry HARRISON has become famous; it read, "Dear General—We have met the enemy, and they are ours. Two ships, two brigs, one schooner, and one sloop. Yours with great respect and esteem, O.H.Perry." Perry's victory gave the Americans control of the GREAT LAKES and permitted Harrison to invade Canada, ending the war in the area. The Battle of Lake Erie has been considered to be one of the important battles of world history, a turning point in the struggle between the British and Americans for control of much of the New World.

LAKE GENEVA, Wisconsin. City (pop. 5,612), situated in southeastern Wisconsin near the Illinois border on the beautiful lake of the same name, the community was named in honor of Geneva, New York. Because it was only a day's drive by carriage from CHICAGO, beginning in about 1870, wealthy Chicagoans began to buy property on the lake and build magnificent mansions, creating what some called a "second Newport," referring to the elegant Rhode Island community. During the great Chicago FIRE (1871) most of the wealthy Chicagoans, including the mayor, hurried their families to Lake Geneva. Eventually almost every great name in Chicago society was represented in the fine estates which were so secluded that they could only be glimpsed from the lake itself. Today the community still boasts many of the fine homes and estates, but the air of exclusivity has almost disappeared, and the community is a popular resort without reference to social standing. For those who don't own their own boats, a popular summer activity is riding the excursion boats, some providing meals. Boating still offers about the only means of glimpsing establishments of current or bygone glamor along the shores. The year-round resort is a popular center for skiing

and other winter sports. Some of the first ice fishing in the area was enjoyed on the lake when jerry-built huts were put up to catch the big ones through the ice. The annual Venetian Festival at Flatiron Park in the third weekend of August is a popular feature. The community offers some of the finest specialty shops.

LAMAR, Missouri. Town (pop. 4,053); seat of Barton County; southwest Missouri; northeast of JOPLIN ; founded in 1856 and named for Mirabeau B. Lamar, President of the Texas Republic from 1838 to 1841. Lamar is best remembered as the birthplace of U.S. President Harry S [sic] TRUMAN. The HARRY S TRUMAN NATIONAL HISTORIC SITE features the restored home with furniture of the period donated by the United Automobile Workers. An annual event is the Harry S Truman Arts and Crafts Show in May.

LANCASTER, Ohio. City (pop. 34,953), seat of Fairfield County, in south central Ohio, situated on the HOCKING RIVER in a livestock and dairy area. The river valley walls rise swiftly up Main Street Hill. The city was named for Lancaster, Pennsylvania, which took its name from Lancaster, Lancashire, England. In 1797 Zane's Trace passed by the sandstone heights called Mount Pleasant, or Standing Stone by the Indians. The government gave Ebenezer ZANE three sections of land to pay him for his completion of the road. In 1800 he founded the town and called it New Lancaster because of the settlers there from Pennsylvania's Lancaster. As early 1806, while there were only a few cabins in the town, it was named as county seat. In 1831 it was incorporated as the village of Lancaster. The town began to boom with the OHIO AND ERIE CANAL in 1836, and the RAILROADS added to the prosperity, which continued with the discovery of natural gas in 1887. In 1890 the town bought its own gas distribution system, one of the few to be owned by a municipality at the time. Today, still an agricultural center, Lancaster has a varied industry producing automotive parts, shoes and glassware. The Anchor Hocking Glass Company was created in 1938 through the merger of the Hocking and Anchor glass companies. The brothers, General William Tecumseh SHERMAN (1820-1891) and Senator John Sherman (1823-1900), were born at Lancaster, and the birthplace has been preserved. John Sherman was also a prominent secretary of the treasury (1870-1879). The Lancaster region is an area of several covered bridges. Mount Pleasant landmark rises to 250 feet overlooking the city. It was a favorite observation point for Indians and early settlers.

LANGLADE, Charles Michel de. (Mackinac, MI, 1729—Green Bay, WI, 1801) Soldier. Son of Augustin Monet de Langlade, who arrived at GREEN BAY in 1745, seeking a better opportunity in the FUR TRADE. Honest and kindly to the Indians and with a fine knowledge of INDIAN LANGUAGES, Langlade soon achieved a virtual monopoly of the fur trade in the area, with the help of his son Charles, his sons-in-law, and other family members. Their good government in the area made them almost independent of the distant French government and the even more distant French king. Charles de Langlade, whose mother was a member of the OTTAWA tribe, had great influence with the Indians. He organized and led Indian troops in the FRENCH AND INDIAN WAR, helping in the defeat of British General Edward Braddock in 1755, and took part in the campaign at Quebec in 1759. After the French defeat, despite his opposition to the British, he became a British citizen and lived like a patriarch at Green Bay, site of his trading post. During the REVOLUTIONARY WAR he led Indian forces against the colonies. The Langlede family became so wealthy and influential, and Charles Langlede had such widespread experience and influence in the area that he is known as "The Father of Wisconsin." He entered his first battle at the age of ten and claimed to have fought in ninety-nine battles. In his old age, he said he wished to fight one more battle to make his record an even one hundred.

LANSING, Michigan. City (pop. 130,414), capital of Michigan, situated in Ingham County in the south central portion of the state at the confluence of the GRAND and Red Cedar rivers. The community was incorporated as a city in 1859 and occupies an area of 35.3 square miles. The name is derived from a village in New York which only survived from 1801 to 1814 and which took the name of Revolutionary hero John Lansing who became a popular New York legislator.

Along with government, the principal industries are automobile manufacture, started in 1897, and manufacture of automobile parts. The industrial development was spurred by the coming of the RAILROAD in 1870.

Ransom E. OLDS (1864-1950), founder of Oldsmobile, was driving a three-wheel steam car around Lansing as early as 1887. He was a pioneer in the mass production of AUTOMOBILES.

Capitol at Lansing, Michigan.

Until the 1840s Detroit had served as state capital, but the legislators were determined that the capital must be more centrally placed. In 1847 they therefore decided to start with a fresh new site where only one log house and a sawmill represented civilization. The seat of government was moved to this "Capital in the Wilderness" in 1848, while the new capitol was still being completed. It was constructed from the great walnut trees of the area.

The present capitol was dedicated in 1879 and was technically much ahead of its time, with gas lights operated by electric switches and a steam operated elevator among other advances. It is notable for its Tiffany chandeliers. The building was constructed of the local limestone; its rotunda is the center of grand staircases rising on either side.

MICHIGAN STATE UNIVERSITY was founded at Lansing in 1855, as the nation's first agricultural college. It is noted for its beautifully landscaped campus, and visitors are welcome at the Abrams Planetarium there. Other Lansing attractions include the Michigan Historical Museum, Brenke River Sculpture and Fish Ladder, Carl G. Fenner Arboretum, Woldumar Nature Center, Impression 5 Science Museum, R. E. Olds Museum, Williamston, "Antique Capital of America," and The Ledges of the Grand River. Annual events include the Mint Festival and Riverfest.

LAWRENCE UNIVERSITY. Chartered in 1847, Lawrence College became the nucleus for the growth of the community of APPLETON, Wisconsin. Money to found the Methodist college was provided by Boston businessman Amos Lawrence. The college is generally found on most lists of the best ten colleges of its class in the country. In 1929 Lawrence College created the INSTITUTE OF PAPER CHEMISTRY to provide postgraduate instruction and research in Appleton's most important field, that of pulp and PAPERMAKING, then a relatively unexplored research field. In 1964 Lawrence acquired Milwaukee-Downer College and became a university. Among visitor attractions, the university provides Worcester Art Center and a Music-Drama Center, including Cloak Theater, an experimental arena playhouse. For a good many years, the university has been known as "the cradle of university presidents," having provided presidents for Harvard, Duke and Brown universities, among others. A student body of 1,036 is instructed by a faculty of 108.

LE MARS, Iowa. City (pop. 8,276), seat of Plymouth County, situated on the Floyd River in northwest Iowa about twenty miles north-northeast of SIOUX CITY. The city has one of the most unusual origins of its name. A railroad official invited a group to visit the new townsite, and the name was taken from the initial letters of the surnames of the women. Two wealthy English brothers, James and Fred Close, bought 30,000 acres of land near Le Mars. They were successful in luring other wealthy English settlers to the small town which was founded in 1869 and soon became a center of landed British culture in Iowa. Their wealth provided a life entirely remote from that of most prairie pioneers. Their large land holdings were worked by hired hands while the owners lived the life of country gentlemen. According to a newspaper of the period, the men "carried the latest agony in canes," and the women sallied forth "in the most coquettish of bonnets." However, the day after their arrival, most of them donned their tweeds and began supervision of their properties. They were liked and respected by their neighbors. They introduced the game of cricket, played polo on the prairies and haunted the "House of Lords," a typical English pub. The community became well known in England and was advertised as a place where "second sons" of wealthy and titled families could study and practice AGRICULTURE. Gradually the community was integrated with the coming of immigrants

of other nationalities, and the English no longer form a distinct group, but they left behind a unique legacy of cosmopolitan culture on the prairie. The community is still the hub of a rich agricultural community and has a number of small industries. Westmar College, started in 1890, is located at Le Mars.

LE SUEUR, Minnesota. Town (pop. 3,800), seat of Le Center County, south-central Minnesota; north of MANKATO ; early milling center, founded after the Indians surrendered the land in 1851; named for Pierre Charles Le Sueur, a 17th-century explorer of the MINNESOTA RIVER Valley. County seat rivalry caused citizens of nearby Cleveland to attempt a raid on the county government in Le Sueur in 1859 with the hope of kidnapping the records. Government officials in Le Sueur hid the records and loaded their guns. The Cleveland mob saved face by running off with several maps, some legal papers and a desk. The city is the home of the multi-million dollar Green Giant Company, one of the world's largest vegetable processing and canning plants. In addition to Green Giant, a foundry and cheese plant are found there. Le Sueur's most famous citizen was Dr. William W. MAYO (1819-1911), who practiced as a local physician in the area between 1858 and 1863. His home with its nine by ten foot office on the second floor is preserved for visitors. Nearby Traverse des Sioux Park was the site in 1851 of the signing of the Treaty of Traverse des Sioux in which the Indians ceded over twenty-four million acres to the Federal government for a little more than twelve cents an acre to be paid over fifty years. Anger over the terms and handling of the treaty is thought to have been one of the principal causes of the Sioux Uprising of 1862.

LEAVENWORTH, Henry. (New Haven, CT, Dec. 10, 1783—Camp Smith, KS, July 21, 1834). Army officer. Leavenworth was sent in 1819 to build a fort on land where the MINNESOTA and MISSISSIPPI rivers join. To pacify the Indians who had never received payment for the land they had sold to Zebulon PIKE, Leavenworth's party gave them two thousand dollars worth of blankets, tobacco, guns and powder. Log buildings were established near MENDOTA and the group survived a harsh winter with the unusual benefit of the companionship of their wives who accompanied the soldiers on the mission. Leavenworth continued a distinguished military career in later years by building Fort Leavenworth (1827), now Leavenworth, Kansas, and being placed in command of the entire the South Western Frontier in 1834, shortly before his death.

LEWIS AND CLARK EXPEDITION. The greatest EXPLORATION in America's history began in the Midwest. On May 14, 1804, Captain Meriwether LEWIS (1774-1809) and his former army superior, William CLARK (1770-1838), left ST. LOUIS, Missouri, under Lewis' leadership. President Thomas Jefferson had instructed them to follow the course of the MISSOURI RIVER to its source and then proceed across the Rocky Mountains to the Pacific Ocean. This was to be done to find out as much as possible about the countryside, the peoples, and the natural history of the vast region acquired by the U.S. in the LOUISIANA PURCHASE of 1803.

The early portion of the journey, the lower Missouri, was already well known, and the party kept diaries describing the beauty and richness of Missouri. On the second day out, the explorers almost lost their leader. Lewis slipped while climbing a river bluff, but fell only twenty feet before catching himself. At the foot of the bluff the party examined the writings of early travelers who had carved their names in the walls of a cave, and they also found prehistoric PICTOGRAPHS.

At what was to become WESTPORT LANDING, one of the men was given fifty lashes for stealing whiskey and another 100 lashes for being drunk. The party fired a cannon to celebrate the Fourth of July at what was to become ST. JOSEPH, Missouri, where one of the men was bitten by a rattlesnake. Another of the men suffered a sunstroke in the fierce summer heat.

At the mouth of the NODAWAY RIVER they left Missouri and spent thirty-three days passing along the borders of the present state of Iowa. The only death among the party on the entire two-year journey was that of Sergeant Charles FLOYD, who died at present SIOUX CITY, Iowa, of what is thought to have been acute appendicitis. He was buried there, and a large monument marks his grave.

The party then passed out of the Midwest on the far journey to the Pacific. With no important problems coming back, they made a triumphant return, following the Missouri back along its Iowa banks and through Missouri back to the St. Louis starting point in September, 1806. Both Lewis and Clark kept careful records of their journey. Clark was a renowned expert on Indian affairs and relations, and his work in making friends with Indian leaders

helped to keep peace among the Indians of the northwest for many years after their visit. The maps they made, their discovery of the source of the Missouri River, the scientific information they gathered concerning the flora, fauna and other resources of the region—all contributed to a new knowledge of the vast portion of the continent which was previously unknown to most Americans.

LEWIS, Meriwether. (Albermarle Co., VA, Aug. 18, 1774—Nashville, TN, Oct. 11, 1809). Military officer and explorer. An army captain in 1801, he was invited by President Thomas Jefferson to become his private secretary. Two years later Jefferson asked Lewis to undertake the EXPLORATION of much of the territory recently obtained in the LOUISIANA PURCHASE. Beginning in May, 1804, Lewis and William CLARK (1770-1838), his former army superior, traveled thousands of miles, returning in 1806 with priceless diaries and maps that cleared up many misconceptions about what is now the American Northwest and bolstered American claims to the region. The LEWIS AND CLARK EXPEDITION also returned with animals, plants, and minerals, which yielded valuable scientific information. Jefferson appointed Lewis governor of the LOUISIANA TERRITORY in 1806. In 1809, on his way to Washington, he was supposedly murdered in a tavern outside of what is now Nashville, Tennessee. Some historians say he took his own life, which was beset by personal problems and the strains of his governorship.

LEWIS, Sinclair. (Sauk Centre, MN, Feb. 7, 1884—Rome, Italy, Jan. 10, 1951). Author. Lewis graduated from Yale in 1908 and began his writing career as a reporter for NEWSPAPERS in New Haven and San Francisco. He later worked for the Associated Press. He published a novel for juveniles in 1912. In 1920 he published his first major work, *Main Street*. *Babbitt* appeared two years later. These works gained immediate fame for the author as well as almost lifelong controversy for his debunking of much of the life he observed in the U.S. "Babbitt" and "Babbittry" became standard terms to describe the complacency and conformity Lewis hated and described so well. He refused to accept the 1926 Pulitzer Prize for his *Arrowsmith*, published the year before. Residents of his hometown of SAUK CENTRE resented his depiction of smalltown life and only after his winning of the NOBEL PRIZE for literature in 1930 did they again accept him. As a principal American voice between the World Wars, Lewis remained in this country rather than becoming an expatriate in Europe as so many other prominent Americans had done. Despite his gloomy characterizations, Lewis continued to voice an underlying optimism. His most notable later work was *It Can't Happen Here* (1935), his description of a Nazi takeover of the U.S. at some future time. He wrote plays such as *Dodsworth* (1934) and the 1936 stage version of *It Can't Happen Here*. His total output was twenty-two novels and three plays.

LEXINGTON, Missouri. City (pop. 5,063), western Missouri, on the MISSOURI RIVER in Lafayette County. Lexington was the site of the CIVIL WAR battle described as the "Battle of the Hemp Bales." The battle was named for the movable barricades used by Confederate troops under the command of Major General Sterling Price. The battle, on September 18-20, 1861, saw the defeat of Union troops commanded by Colonel James A. Mulligan. Today the city is center of coal mines and rock quarrying. The scene of the fighting is now part of the Battle of Lexington State Historic Site. Overlooking the battlefield is the Anderson House. Built in 1853, the home was used as a field hospital and changed hands many times over the two days of fighting. The building has been preserved with its original furnishings and serves as a museum of Civil War relics. Other Civil War memorabilia may be found at the Lexington Historical Museum. Built as a church in 1846, the museum also houses steamboat models, PONY EXPRESS items and early photographs of the city.

LIARS' CLUB. BURLINGTON, Wisconsin, has gained fame as the home of the LIARS' CLUB, a group founded there "to preserve a little bit of Americana which vanished with the old-time grocery store when our granddads used to gather and spin their wonderfully concocted yarns." Each year since its founding the club has provided a prize to the best of all the thousands of tall yarns, which now come from around the world to compete. The reputation of the club and its award spread rapidly after a 1934 national radio network broadcast a program of award-winning selections. The awards have never ceased to attract exceptional media attention. Typical of the prize winners is one of the first, awarded in 1934 for the story, "My grandfather had a clock that was so old that the shadow from the pendulum swinging back and forth had worn a hole in the back of it."

LIBERAL, Missouri. Village (pop. 709), southwestern Missouri in Barton County, northwest of LAMAR. Liberal was founded in 1880 on land purchased by G. H. Walser, a disciple of Robert C. Ingersoll. The settlement prided itself as a community of Free Thinkers, allowing no church, no priests, no saloon, no devil, no debauchery and no drunkenness. Despite local and national opposition, Walser expanded the community by constructing the Universal Mental Liberty Hall, where anyone could speak on any topic, and the Liberal Normal School in 1884. A semimonthly magazine, The *Orthodoedian,* was published until 1900. H. H. Waggoner founded an addition to Liberal in 1881 and invited only orthodox Christians to take up residence. The residents of Liberal built a barbed wire fence between the two communities and in 1883 bought the Christian suburb to rid themselves of their neighbors. Walser later became interested in spirtualism, and seances were regularly held until 1899 when a fire exposed the "spirits" as fakes. With the death of Walser in 1910, the community lost much of its original character.

"LIBERTY BELL OF THE WEST." Bell rung by George Rogers CLARK (1752-1818) when he captured KASKASKIA, Illinois, on July 4, 1778, his first victory during the REVOLUTIONARY WAR campaign to drive the British from the NORTHWEST TERRITORY. The bell, older than the Liberty Bell in Philadelphia, Pennsylvania, now hangs in the Kaskaskia Memorial Building.

LIEURANCE, Thurlow. (Oskaloosa, IA, Mar. 21, 1878—Wichita, KS, Oct. 9, 1963). Composer. He spent twenty years researching and recording the music of American Indians and became the recognized authority on INDIAN MUSIC. Many of his songs were based on Indian themes or reflected Indian melodic lines. He published *Nine Indian Songs* (1919) and *Songs of the North American Indian* (1921), among other works. Lieurance's most popular work was the song, "By the Waters of Minnetonka." Lieurance was dean and dean emeritus of the University of Wichita, Kansas.

LINCOLN BOYHOOD NATIONAL ME-MORIAL. Site, south of LINCOLN CITY, Indiana, of the farm where Abraham LINCOLN (1809-1865) lived from 1816 to 1830. The two hundred acre park includes the Lincoln's reconstructed homestead and the burial site of Lincoln's mother, Nancy Hanks Lincoln, who died of "milk sickness" when Lincoln was nine years old. A Living Historical Farm, including log buildings, restored fields and a garden in a corner of the original Thomas LINCOLN farm recreates the kind of rural environment Abraham Lincoln would have experienced. The Memorial Visitors Center, built of native wood and stone, features halls honoring the lives of Abraham and Nancy Hanks Lincoln. Exterior sculptured panels illustrate important periods in Abraham Lincoln's life. A film and museum show Lincoln's life in Indiana.

LINCOLN HOME NATIONAL HISTORICAL SITE.

SPRINGFIELD, Illinois, residence of Abraham LINCOLN (1809-1865). The only home ever owned by him, he purchased from Rev. Charles Dresser for $1,500. Lincoln lived there with his family from 1844 until he left for Washington for his inauguration as president on February 7, 1861. Lincoln added a brick wall and picket fence in 1850, raised the roof in 1857 and added a second story at a cost of $2,400. While president, Lincoln rented the house to Lucien Tilton of the Great Western Railroad for $300 a year. After 1887 the house became Illinois' first state memorial after another renter, Osborn H. Oldroyd, persuaded Robert Todd LINCOLN (1843-1926) to give Lincoln's home to the State of Illinois. The house, which remained open to the public, deteriorated until a thorough restoration was made between 1950 and 1952. In 1971 President Nixon signed an Act of Congress making the home a National Historical Site. The Act also provided that a four-block area around the home be restored to its condition during Lincoln's life. The National Park Service was given jurisdiction over the project, and another thorough restoration was completed in 1988.

LINCOLN TOMB.

Burial site, in Oak Ridge Cemetery in SPRINGFIELD, Illinois, of Abraham LINCOLN, his wife, and their sons, Edward, William, and Thomas. Abraham Lincoln's body arrived on May 4, 1865. It was placed in a temporary vault, while a National Lincoln Monument Association was formed to raise money for a suitable monument. Larkin Mead, of Brattleboro, Vermont, designed the tomb. Construction, which was to cost one hundred eighty thousand dollars, began in 1869. The monument was dedicated on October 15, 1874, and the tomb was given to the State in 1875. Reconstruction was begun in 1901 with interior remodeling in 1931, the same year the monu-

ment was rededicated by President Herbert C. HOOVER (1874-1964).

LINCOLN UNIVERSITY.

State-supported, comprehensive coed institution located in the Missouri state capital of JEFFERSON CITY, Lincoln University was founded in 1866 as a college for Negroes, but over the years the student body has become predominantly white. The school offers liberal arts, teacher education, and professional training programs. Most degrees are conferred in business and management, education, social sciences, public affairs and services, and engineering. Missouri provides 69% of the students, and 18% pursue full-time graduate or professional study immediately after graduating. Faculty: 189. Enrollment: 2,657 total graduate and undergraduate.

LINCOLN, Abraham.

(Near Hodgenville, KY., Feb. 12, 1809—Washington, DC, Apr. 15, 1865). Sixteenth President of the United States. As Lincoln himself wrote, "I was born February 12, 1809, in then Hardin County, Kentucky, at a point within the now recently formed county of Larue, a mile, or a mile and a half from where Hodginsville sic now is," wrote Abraham Lincoln, as he recalled his birthplace.

Son of Thomas and Nancy Hanks LINCOLN, Abraham was seven in 1816 when the family crossed the OHIO RIVER to Indiana on a makeshift raft. "Old Minerva, a colored slave, who had been attracted to the scene, seeing the condition of the children, went back into the house and came back immediately with a plate heaped with slices of homemade bread covered with butter, a pitcher of milk and some cups," according to an eyewitness.

Conditions for the family were scarcely better in Indiana, where they lived through a bitter winter in a lean-to and then barely managed to subsist. As Lincoln matured he had only about a year of formal school, but he read everything he could find and worked hard at odd jobs, removing brush and cutting grain for neighbors, becoming skilled at carpentry and cabinet making.

His father frequently hired him out at twenty-five cents a day as hostler, wood chopper, ploughman, carpenter, even babysitter. He also operated the ferry at ANDERSON, Indiana. In a revealing minor episode, at the age of eighteen Lincoln was charged with a ferry violation. He served as his own attorney and was acquitted.

When the family moved to Illinois in 1830, Lincoln was a mature twenty-one. In his

Abraham Lincoln as a young man.

untanned skin moccasins, he towered six feet four inches as he led the oxteam drawing one of the wagons. Not generally remembered is the fact that he had a small stock of peddler's goods and sold knives, thread, needles, buttons and other items to occasional settlers and other travelers along the way. When they reached DECATUR, relative John Hanks had selected a homesite for them. Clearing ten acres of land and making rail fences, Lincoln acquired his nickname, the Railsplitter.

In 1831 Abraham and his two stepbrothers helped build a flatboat and piloted its load of produce down the MISSISSIPPI RIVER all the way to New Orleans. On the way down the SANGAMON RIVER, their flatboat stuck on the milldam at NEW SALEM, where the bow turned up toward the sky, and water began to flow in. While spectators gave a number of suggestions about getting the boat free, Lincoln calmly took off some of the cargo and borrowed an auger. After he drilled a hole in the bow and let the water out, he filled the hole with a plug, and they were able to float the boat off the dam and continue the journey.

Such a trip must have given this brilliant young man a new idea of what life could be like beyond the rough pioneer country which was all he had known up to this time. The trip had

been the idea of Denton Offut, noted for his many ideas but hardly ever able to make them succeed. When Lincoln came back north, Offut hired him to run a store he had established at the town of NEW SALEM, Illinois, then only two years old.

At the store, Lincoln served his customers with great conscientiousness and charm and became well liked. Every spare moment found him lying outside the store on his back under a tree reading grammar books and anything else he could find to "improve his mind."

Frontier amusements were rough and ready—cock fighting, horse racing and wrestling. Denton Offut had bragged so much about his new clerk's great strength that the boys from Clary's Grove came over to New Salem with their champion, Jack Armstrong, and challenged Lincoln to a wrestling match. Just when Armstrong was about to give in, his friends rushed in to help him, and the enraged Lincoln flung out a challenge to any of them to wrestle, but no one dared. Later Lincoln and Armstrong became friends.

When the Offut store closed in 1832, Lincoln volunteered to serve in the BLACK HAWK WAR and was promptly elected captain of the local militia. After duty in several outfits, he wrote about the experience, "...I had a good many bloody struggles with the musquetoes, and I can truly say I was often hungry."

Returning to New Salem he went into partnership in another store, which failed and left him in debt. His appointment as postmaster did not give him enough income, and he took up surveying. Defeated in a try for the state legislature in 1832, Lincoln tried again in 1834 and won, then was reelected in 1836, 1838 and 1840, becoming a power in the minority Whig Party. His service in the legislature increased his interest in the law. One of his most important contributions in the legislature was his work with eight other tall legislators, known as the Long Nine, which resulted in the move of the state capital to SPRINGFIELD. He continued his law studies with the help of his friend John T. Stuart of Springfield. In 1837 Abraham lincoln was admitted to the bar. In New Salem he borrowed a horse, stuffed his few belongings into his saddlebags and began life in Springfield. His six years in New Salem are generally considered to have been the turning point of his life.

After serving in two partnerships, Lincoln was able to found his own law firm, taking William H. Herndon for a junior partner, and this firm continued until Lincoln's death. In

Lincoln

1842, Lincoln married Mary Todd, a rather aristocratic girl from Kentucky whom he had met when she was visiting her sister in Springfield. The first of their sons, Robert Todd LINCOLN, was born in 1843.

By this time Abraham Lincoln was ranked among the best lawyers of Illinois. The eighth Illinois judicial circuit had been organized in 1839. The judges went from one county seat to another holding court in a circuit. Most lawyers stayed in their own and adjoining counties, but Lincoln loved to travel and went all over the eighth circuit gaining a wide reputation in courthouses at Mt. Pulaski, Metamora Courthouse, Postville Courthouse and many others. He also came to know thousands of people and the problems they faced. In twenty-four years of practice, Lincoln represented clients in hundreds of law cases. Many of these were famous and important cases, such as the Rock Island-Davenport bridge case, in which he opposed Mississippi shipping interests and saved the bridge from being torn down. Others are remembered for their human interest.

In 1846 Lincoln was elected for his first and only term in the U.S House of Representatives, the only Whig from Illinois in the House. He generally supported the party line and worked for Zachary TAYLOR (1784-1850) for president in 1848. He made little impression on the capital at Washington, and his opposition to the war with Mexico brought him into temporary disfavor with the voters of his district, who refused to return him to Congress.

When Taylor failed to appoint Lincoln as Commissioner of the General Land Office, he retired from politics and returned to practice law. By this time, the backwoods Illinois lawyer had been admitted to practice law before the Supreme Court of the United States, in 1849.

Lincoln's growing prominence brought him an offer from President Taylor, to become the secretary of the newly formed Oregon Territory and later the position of governor, but he refused both appointments, which would have taken him far from the life and career he enjoyed.

One of the saddest days for the Lincolns came in 1850 when their second son, Edward BAKER, aged four, died after fifty-two days of illness. It is said that neither of the Lincolns was ever quite the same after this loss. However, there was the happiness of the birth of their third son, William WALLACE in the same year as Edward's death.

The prairie lawyer was again caught up in politics when he fought the policy of Stephen A. DOUGLAS (1813-1861) over slavery. Lincoln particularly opposed the Kansas-Nebraska Act (May 30, 1854). The Lincoln speeches at Springfield and Peoria attacked the policy of slavery in the territories and harked back to the Declaration of Independence and attracted great attention. Despite his growing popularity, Lincoln failed to be elected as a Whig to the U.S. Senate in 1854. He soon found himself pulling away from the Whig Party, and joined the new Republican Party in 1856. His leadership ability soon brought him prominence in the party, and he was nominated as the Republican candidate for the Senate in 1858. He engaged in the famed debates with Douglas, the Democratic candidate. They met seven times before excited crowds at OTTAWA, FREEPORT, JONESBORO, CHARLESTON, GALESBURG, QUINCY and ALTON, all in Illinois, between August 21 and October 15, 1858. Lincoln declared over and over that it was time to decide if SLAVERY was to be permitted to encroach on free soil. Lincoln would have won the popular vote, but in the time when state legislatures selected U.S. senators, the Illinois legislature selected Douglas.

Although he had lost the election, Lincoln had become popular and well known throughout the country. He was even mentioned as a presidential candidate. The second national convention of the new REPUBLICAN PARTY was held in CHICAGO in May of 1860. The city had built a large new convention hall, called the Wigwam, especially for the important event. When the convention was called to order for the third day, May 18, 1860, American history reached a turning point. The maneuvering among the candidates was fierce and heated. On the third ballot Lincoln was selected as the party's presidential candidate, and "the city was wild with delight." The nominee had not even come to the convention and was officially notified by a delegation sent to Springfield.

Douglas was the candidate of the Northern Democrats. Here were two of Illinois' most famous sons competing against one another, as they had on other occasions—this time for the highest office in the land. Although Lincoln stayed in Springfield and took no active part in the campaign, his positions had become well known nationally through the debates with Douglas and his widely acclaimed 1860 speech at the Cooper Union in New York. Lincoln's stands on the issues of slavery were stressed. Much was made of the paradox of Douglas' favoring "popular sovereignty" while at the same time opposing certain implications of the

Lincoln, Illinois

Dred Scott case. The fact that Douglas avoided taking a position on the moral aspects of slavery became a significant emphasis of the campaign. Lincoln was pictured not as an Abolitionist but as one who regarded slavery as unjust and evil. He unalterably opposed its extension.

Lincoln, of course, was the winner in an election made heartbreaking by the growing rift between North and South, and he took the oath of office on March 4, 1861. On becoming president, Lincoln tried to conciliate the South. When this failed, he assumed broad executive powers, such as suspending habeas corpus, blockading southern ports and making unauthorized expenditures. Later, these were ratified by Congress. After the early battle losses, he changed military leaders with a rapidly growing insight of war operations. As the Republican Party became more radical, Lincoln found means of conciliating them such as the Emancipation Proclamation.

After an 1863 New Years morning reception, Lincoln called several of his closest advisers together and ceremoniously signed a document which was to become one of the most momentous in U.S. history. The document soon became known as the Emancipation Proclamation. Many Northerners felt it went too far, while others complained that Lincoln had "freed" slaves where he had no control and had left them in slavery in areas where he could have freed them. Nevertheless, history has supported Lincoln and supplied his most important nickname, "The Great Emancipator."

In his Gettysburg Address (November 19, 1863) Lincoln reasserted the American faith. Although his 1864 reelection prospects looked dim due to wartime losses of the North, the war situation quickly improved, and Lincoln received a large majority in the electoral college, although his popular majority was slim. In his second term he turned his attention to conciliation, calling for moderation and patience in dealing with the South. He managed to push the Thirteenth Amendment through Congress and continued to develop his Reconstruction program, opposing the radical reconstruction plans of Congress. Most experts feel that had Lincoln lived, he might have faced many of the problems encountered by his successor.

Only a few of the highlights of his tenure can be added here. These include his highly controversial call for 75,000 volunteers on April 15, 1861. First Battle of Bull Run (July 21, 1861) was dramatic proof that the war would not be won easily. On March 11, 1862, Lincoln assumed command of the army and navy to give more direction to the floundering Union commanders. On the domestic front, the department of agriculture was established on May 15, 1862, and the homestead act was approved May 20, of that year. West Virginia was admitted as 35th state on June 19, 1863. The great turning point of the war, the Battle of Gettysburg took its heavy toll from July 1 to 3, 1863. Nevada was admitted as 36th state on October 31, 1864. General W.T. SHERMAN captured Atlanta on September 2, 1864. The Thirteenth Amendment passed, prohibiting slavery (January 31, 1865). The Confederate capital of Richmond was evacuated April 3, 1865, preparing the way for the surrender of General Robert E. Lee to General U.S. GRANT at Appomatox Courthouse, Virginia, (April 9, 1865).

Many tragedies came to the Lincolns during his terms as president. Among the worst was the death in the White House on February 20, 1862, of William Wallace, just eleven years old. There were also the defeats in battle, the bitter words of people who did not like his actions and the treachery of several friends and associates. Among the worst of these troubles was the unfounded rumor that Mrs. Lincoln was a Confederate spy.

But through all defeats and adversity the quiet man from Illinois dominated—"The gaunt figure of one man stands above all the rest. The prairie son gave his life so that 'government of the people, by the people, for the people, shall not perish from the earth.' The bullet which silenced his words could not silence the spirit of them—'with malice toward none; with charity for all.'"

The return of Lincoln's body to Springfield by train resulted in one of the most unusual tributes ever paid to a hero, as the multitudes greeted the train at every station. This culminated in the burial ceremonies at Springfield, where the body lies today in the great memorial tomb.

LINCOLN, Illinois. City (pop. 16,327), only city named for Abraham LINCOLN (1809-1865) while he was alive, seat of Logan County, between SPRINGFIELD and BLOOMINGTON, Illinois, on Interstate 55. It was founded in 1853 and incorporated in 1865. As the lawyer for the founders of the community, Abraham Lincoln protested that he "never knew anything named Lincoln that amounted to anything," but finally agreed to the honor and became master of ceremonies at the dedication. Humorously he dedicated the site with watermelon juice and then served a feast for the occasion—more watermelon—an entire wagon load. The city today is a center of shipping and small industry.

LINCOLN, Robert Todd. (Springfield, IL, Aug. 1, 1843—Manchester, VT, July 26, 1926). Secretary of War and Minister to England. Lincoln was the eldest son of Abraham and Mary (Todd) LINCOLN. Given every educational advantage denied his father, Lincoln graduated from Harvard, and on September 24, 1868, married the daughter of Iowa Senator James Harlan. He studied law in CHICAGO and was admitted to the bar in 1867. A charter member of the Chicago Bar Association, Lincoln avoided politics, but became secretary of war 1881-1885). Lincoln resumed his law practice until recalled by President Benjamin HARRISON (1833-1901) as Minister to England (1889-1893). His government service was not considered noteworty. Again resuming his law practice, he was retained by many railroad and corporate clients, including the Pullman Company. When George PULLMAN died, Lincoln was made first the company's acting executive and then its president. Failing health made him resign in 1911, but he retained a company connection by remaining the chairman of the board of directors. In 1912 he moved to Washington, D.C., where he continued his interest in astronomy and solving algebraic problems.

LINCOLN, Thomas. (Linville Creek, Rockingham County, VA, Jan. 6, 1778—Jan. 17, 1851). Father of Abraham LINCOLN. Thomas Lincoln, described as a thick-set man with dark eyes, coarse black hair, and a round face, never realized the hopes that brought him to Indiana and Illinois. A plain man, Thomas Lincoln held claim to many more acres than he ever farmed, choosing instead to help his neighbors with tasks they found for him around their farms. In 1816, when his son Abraham was seven years old, Thomas moved his family from Hardin County, Kentucky, to Spencer County, Indiana. The family moved in the fall, which proved to be poor timing as winter set in before a cabin could be built. The Lincolns lived in a three-sided shelter open on the south and heated by an open fireplace. The second year saw the death of his wife, Nancy. For a year the family struggled on before Thomas left for Kentucky and returned a few weeks later with a new wife, Sarah Johnston Lincoln and her three children. It was Sarah who encouraged Abraham in his studies, time his father thought would have been better used with chores. Poor land in Spencer County and another attack of "milksick" which had killed his first wife caused Thomas to move his family in 1830 to Illinois, where he died, with very little in common with his soon-to-become-famous son.

LINCOLN-DOUGLAS DEBATES. Series of confrontations with Stephen A. DOUGLAS in 1858, which propelled Abraham LINCOLN to national attention. In 1858 Lincoln was nominated by the REPUBLICAN PARTY to run for the United States Senate seat from Illinois held by Douglas. Lincoln challenged Douglas to a series of seven debates. The first occurred on August 21, 1858, in OTTAWA, Illinois. The second took place in northern Illinois in FREEPORT on August 27th. The third debate, and the one with the smallest attendance, took place on September 15th in JONESBORO, Illinois. Three days later the candidates met in CHARLESTON, Illinois, and on October 7th the fifth debate was hosted by GALESBURG, Illinois. QUINCY, Illinois, on the MISSISSIPPI RIVER was the scene of the sixth debate, on October 13th, and the last occurred in ALTON, Illinois, on October 15, 1858. Douglas defended the policy of the Kansas-Nebraska Act which he called "popular sovereignty." He denied Lincoln's charge that the DRED SCOTT DECISION of the United States Supreme Court had opened SLAVERY to all territories. He claimed that the people of any territory could keep slavery out simply by refusing to pass laws protecting it. Douglas' position became known as the "Freeport Doctrine." Lincoln emphasized slavery as a moral issue, opposed popular sovereignty and insisted that slavery should not be extended further. Newspapers gave the debaters national attention. In the election, Lincoln candidates for the legislature received more votes, but the division of the state into districts gave Douglas supporters a majority of the seats. Douglas was re-elected by a vote of 54 to 46 in the Illinois legislature, in the period when United States Senators were elected by the state legislatures.

LINDBERGH, Charles Augustus, Sr. (Sweden, Jan. 20, 1860—Little Falls, MN, May 25, 1924). Congressman. Lindbergh served Minnesota as a member of the 60th to 64th Congresses from the 6th Minnesota District. He was the author of *Banking and Currency* (1913) and *Why Is Your Country at War* (1917). His son, Charles A. LINDBERGH, was the world famous aviator. Lindbergh Sr. practiced law in LITTLE FALLS, but lost popularity by his stand in opposition to the United States entering WORLD WAR I. He was defeated for a seat in the United States Senate in 1917 and lost an election for governor of Minnesota in 1918.

LINDBERGH, Charles Augustus, Jr. (Detroit, MI, Feb 4, 1902—Kipahulu, Maui, HI, Aug. 26, 1974). Aviator, the "Lone Eagle." Lindbergh made the first solo nonstop trans-Atlantic flight, New York-Paris in 1927. Overnight he became one of the world's great heroes. After attending the University of Wisconsin (1920-1922), Lindbergh enrolled at the flying school in Lincoln, Nebraska. In 1923 he purchased his first plane, a WORLD WAR I surplus Curtiss "Jenny," then soloed and barnstormed. After army flying school at Brooks Field, Texas, he received a captain's commission in the U.S. Air Service in 1924. Tempted by the $25,000 prize for the first non-stop solo flight across the Atlantic, Lindbergh bought a Ryan monoplane and flew the plane from San Diego to Long Island in a record cross-continental flight. On May 20, 1927, he left Long Island's Roosevelt field with the plane so weighted with gasoline some of his helpers thought it would not get off the ground. Thirty-three and a half hours and 3,600 miles later he arrived in Paris to a tumultuous welcome. His ticker tape reception in New York City was the largest up to that time. He made other prominent appearances, married Anne Morrow in 1929, and they made many flights together. Their infant son was kidnapped and murdered in 1932 in one of the most sensational of all such cases. Living in Europe from 1935 to 1939, Lindbergh was able to assess German air power and made reports to the U.S. government. He became a spokesman for American isolationism in 1939 and lost popular favor but flew combat missions in the Pacific during WORLD WAR II. Lindbergh became a brigadier general in the Air Force Reserve in 1954 and was a consultant to the Defense Department. He was awarded the PULITZER PRIZE in 1953 for his autobiography, *The Spirit of St. Louis,* named for his famed plane. An earlier autobiographical book was *We* (1927). His wife was also a prominent author and one of the most important figures in the conservation movement.

LINDQUIST. E.F. (Gowrie, IA, June 4, 1901—Iowa City, IA, May 3, 1978). Educator. As director of the testing program at the University of IOWA, Lindquist developed the program until its products and services became among the best known and most universally used of their kind. The three major IOWA TESTS

of Skills and Educational Development are standard in elementary through college grades. Lindquist also invented a scoring machine for the tests and originated the Iowa Educational Information Center, with its data bank for public schools, resulting in reduced paper work for teachers and providing a valuable educational research tool. He was the author of several books on testing and measurement.

LISA, Manuel (New Orleans, LA, Sept. 8, 1772—St. Louis, MO, Aug. 12, 1820). Fur trader and pioneer. Of Spanish descent, he became an American citizen when Louisiana was purchased in 1803. He was one of the leading fur traders on the upper MISSISSIPPI RIVER, and although he was granted the monopoly of trade with the OSAGE INDIANS in 1802, he lost it with the transfer of national domination in 1804. He led a number of expeditions and was considered a major factor in opening the MISSOURI RIVER area to white traders and settlers. He established two forts: Fort Raymond, later Manuel's Fort, at the mouth of the Bighorn River; and Fort Lisa, near Omaha, Nebraska. He was a U.S. Indian subagent for tribes in the Missouri River region from 1814 to 1820.

LITTLE BEAVER CREEK WILD AND SCENIC RIVER SYSTEM. This stream system and surrounding valley near the Pennsylvania border contain some of Ohio's wildest lands.

LITTLE BROWN CHURCH IN THE VALE. At NASHUA, Iowa. The church came about as a result of a popular song of the same name composed by Dr. William Potter when he came to the area in 1857 to visit his fiancee. He was impressed by the "vale" at Bradford, near Nashua, and composed the song. Later the church was built as described in the song and became, perhaps, the best-known small church in the country. It has been the site of countless weddings and is still booked far in advance for weddings, repetition of wedding vows and other ceremonies.

LITTLE CROW. (1803—near Hutchinson, MN, July 23, 1863) Chief of the Kaposia band of the Mdewakanton SIOUX who lived near the present site of ST. PAUL, Minnesota. Little Crow was the first Indian to sign the Treaty of Mendota on August 5, 1851, which completed the sale of the Sioux homeland to the United States. The area was bordered by the MISSISSIPPI

RIVER below FORT SNELLING on the east and the Blue Earth and MINNESOTA rivers on the west. The Indians were removed to a reservation twenty miles wide and sixty miles long on either side of the Minnesota River between the mouths of the Little Rock and Yellow Medicine rivers. Little Crow's tribe received ninety thousand dollars. Restricted movement on the reservation, a crop failure which left many Indians close to starvation, and the appointment of an Indian agent who seemed to have no understanding of Indian problems, caused unrest. The mistaken belief that the government could not fight both a CIVIL WAR and an Indian uprising led Little Crow to feel it was time to act to recover their lands. Therefore, on August 18, 1862, a large band of Sioux attacked the Redwood, or Lower Sioux, Agency, killing the traders and burning the buildings. An appeal from Governor Ramsey to the few soldiers at FORT RIDGELY brought reenforcements before August 20th when Little Crow attacked the fort. Unable to defeat the soldiers, the Sioux withdrew and regrouped. On August 22nd they attacked again and were decisively defeated with a loss of one hundred warriors. Battles at NEW ULM and Fort Ridgely thoroughly frightened most of the settlers who often deserted their homes in such haste that meals were left uneaten on the table. On September 23, 1862, the Sioux were decisively defeated at the Battle of Wood Lake. Little Crow escaped after the battle but was shot and killed on July 23, 1863, while picking berries with his son. The deed was done by two deer hunters who did not even recognize him.

LITTLE FALLS, Minnesota. City (pop. 7,250), seat of Morrison County, central Minnesota, northwest of ST. CLOUD, named for the falls, boyhood home of Charles LINDBERGH, JR. The area of Little Falls was first explored by Zebulon PIKE in 1805 and later Henry SCHOOLCRAFT in 1832, during his successful expedition to locate the source of the MISSISSIPPI RIVER. James Green moved there in 1849 and built the first dam and sawmill across the Mississippi. Rapid growth followed. In 1856 the Little Falls Manufacturing Company incorporated and produced LUMBER and flour. The Pine Lumber Company occupied over fifty acres. The rapid growth of the town drew many lawless men who, by the late 1850s, seemed in control of the town. When a group of these men beat the town constable, R.L. Barnum, in his home, the law-abiding citizens formed a vigilante committee and ran the criminals out of town. New

elections put the law-and-order forces back in charge. The boyhood home of Charles Lindbergh is now part of a 294-acre state park. His father, Charles A. LINDBERGH SR. had practiced law in the community beginning in 1883. The Charles A. Lindbergh House and Interpretative Center features the boyhood home of the famous aviator and contains exhibits from three Lindbergh generations. A representative home of the style built in the 19th century is the Charles A. Weyerhaeuser Memorial Museum. The Camp Ripley Interpretative Center shows the history of the National Guard training camp.

LITTLE MIAMI RIVER WILD AND SCENIC RIVER SYSTEM. Flowing through a deep gorge, wooded bluffs and rolling farmlands, the popular Ohio stream is easily reached from CINCINNATI or DAYTON.

LITTLE NORWAY. Not an incorporated community, little Norway, near MADISON, Wisconsin, in the foothills of the BLUE MOUNDS, was founded in 1926 by Isak Dahle, a Norse-American businessman of CHICAGO. He set a crew of Norwegian artisans and craftsmen to work to recreate the feeling of a Norwegian village. The Norway building of the 1893 WORLD'S COLUMBIAN EXPOSITION at Chicago was moved there as a fine example of ancient Norse church architecture. Dahle added to the atmosphere with hewn-oak houses with sod roofs and bright blue window casements. He brought in an extensive collection of Norwegiana, all attracting large numbers of tourists.

Wisconsin Chapel, Little Norway.

LITTLE SIOUX RIVER. Rising just north of the Iowa border in southwest Minnesota, the Little Sioux flows generally south, southwest for 221 miles through western Iowa until it reaches the MISSIOURI RIVER on the south-central secton of Iowa's western border. It passes SPENCER, Iowa, where it turns east for a few miles, then proceeds south past Cherokee and several smaller towns. The river is used substantially for irrigation in the rich AGRICULTURE of its valley. The four dams of the Nepper Watershed project, near Smithland, were completed in 1948. Severe floods of 1953 and 1954 led to further flood control and soil conservation programs in the valley.

LITTLE TURTLE. (Eel River northwest of Ft. Wayne, IN, 1752—Ft. Wayne, IN, 1812). Indian leader. Little Turtle, also known as Meshekinnoquah, was a chief of the MIAMI INDIANS in the present states of Ohio and Indiana. Little Turtle led Indians in victories over General Josiah HARMER (1743-1813) in 1790 and General Arthur ST. CLAIR in 1791. It was once believed that he led the Indian forces defeated at the Battle of FALLEN TIMBERS, but this is now questioned by some historians. In 1795, Little Turtle was one of several Indian leaders who signed a treaty opening southern Ohio to white settlement. He is credited with preventing the Miami Indians from aligning with Tecumseh's confederacy.

LIVONIA, Michigan. City (pop. 104,814). Western suburb of DETROIT, Livonia was named for a Livonia in New York, which was named for Livonia, Estonia, now a province of Russia. It was founded in 1835 and incorporated in 1850. Its manufactures include paint, auto bodies and parts and tools and dies. It is the seat of Madonna College, and hosts the Detroit race track.

LOESS SOIL. A type of silt that forms fertile topsoil. Loess consists of wind driven mineral particles finer than sand, but coarser than clay. Most of the world's loess originated in the area once covered by GLACIERS or in the great deserts of Asia. Topsoils containing loess are located in northwestern and central sections of the United States, central and eastern Europe, and eastern China. In the Midwest, a major loess region is the 3,000-square-mile portion of southeast Minnesota, known as a driftless area because none of the four major glaciers covered it. Smaller loess deposits are found along the MISSISSIPPI RIVER and some of its tributaries.

LOGAN, James (Indian leader). (Sundbury, PA, 1725—1780). Son of famed Chief Shikellamy, Logan was long noted for his friendliness to Europeans, a leader of the Mingo tribe, but never a chief. Logan's trust was rewarded by the murder of his family. He revenged himself with savage attacks on settlers and was a leader in those tribes opposed to Lord Dunmore, the British commander. In 1774 he refused to meet Dunmore in a council with other chiefs. Dunmore sent trader John Gibson to bring him to the council. Logan led the young trader to the woods where there was a great elm tree. He made a remarkable speech to Gibson, who translated and read it to the council. This is one of the few examples of the wisdom and humanity of American Indian leaders which have been preserved relatively intact. Thomas Jefferson included it in his Notes on the State of Virginia. Logan is reported to have said, "I appeal to any white man to say, if ever he entered Logan's cabin hungry and I gave him not meat; if ever he came cold or naked and I gave him not clothing. During the course of the last long bloody war, Logan remained in his tent an advocate for peace. Nay, such was my love for the whites, that those of my own country pointed at me as they passed by and said, 'Logan is the friend of the white men.' I had even thought to live with you, but for the injuries of one man. Colonel Cresap, last spring, in cold blood, and unprovoked, cut off all the relatives of Logan; not sparing even my women and children. There runs not a drop of my blood in the veins of any human creature. This called on me for revenge. I have sought it. I have killed many. I have fully glutted my vengeance. For my country, I rejoice at the beams of peace. Yet, do not harbor the thought that mine is the joy of fear. Logan never felt fear. He will not turn on his heel to save his life. Who is there to mourn for Logan? Not one." This speech was published in newspapers throughout the American colonies. It was reprinted in the literary journals of Great Britain and translated into several languages. Schoolboys repeated it in speech contests. Near CIRCLEVILLE, Ohio, the tree under which Logan made his speech was preserved as Logan's Elm. Logan then continued to ravage settlers until his death. While aiding the British during the Revolution, he was killed by one of his tribesmen.

LOGAN, Ohio. City (pop. 6,557), seat of Hocking County, situated in southeast Ohio, on the HOCKING RIVER. The origin of its name is disputed. One source asserts that the name comes from Benjamin F. Logan, Virginia soldier, patriot and Indian fighter, associated with Kentucky. He was active in the area during the American Revolution. Another reliable source claims the name was derived from James LOGAN, a leader of the Mingo Indians. Logan was founded in 1816 by Governor Thomas WORTHINGTON, who purchased a level tract near the Hocking Falls, platted the town and set up mills. The Hocking Canal opened to Logan in 1840; a stagecoach line linked the town to the OHIO RIVER, and the Hocking Valley Railroad reached Logan in 1869, all important milestones in the town's history. Coal mining languished when the New Straitsville coal fields caught fire. Then oil and gas wells rejuvenated the region, until they too diminished. As the center of its commercial region and with several small manufacturing operations, the city has continued on a fairly even keel. Hocking Hills Indian Run is an annual event in the third weekend of September.

LOGANSPORT, Indiana. City (pop. 17,-899), seat of Cass County, located at the confluence of the WABASH and EEL Rivers in north-central Indiana, northwest of KOKOMO, early trading post in Indiana. Logansport, called "The City of Bridges" because all entrances to the city must be made by crossing water, was named for James John LOGAN, a Mingo leader. Colonel John B. Duret won the right to name the town by winning a marksmanship contest. Logan was founded in 1838. Today its industries include electrical goods, transportation equipment, fabricated metals, building materials, precision equipment, beverage and processed metals. Logansport was the home of Frederick Landis, Indiana writer, lecturer, and congressman and brother of Kenesaw Mountain LANDIS, "czar" of baseball.

LOGGING AND LOGGERS. Led by legendary but beloved Paul BUNYAN, logging was a colorful rough and tough occupation once almost universal in the upper Midwest. In early logging days, the modern techniques had not been acquired and most of the cutting and hauling was done by muscle and by heavy carts. As soon as the ice melted on the rivers in spring in the lumber regions of the northern Midwest, the log drives began. Timber that had been cut previously and moved to the nearest stream was floated downstream in tremendous masses. The

lumberjacks could nimbly jump from log to log, twirling them with their feet to keep their balance. Often logs piled together in massive LOG JAMS. Sometimes if the "key" log were pulled loose, the whole log jam would break up, often catching and drowning the lumberjacks in spite of all their skill. Sometimes lumber was tied together in rafts to be floated downstream. Many times whole families would gather on a raft and picnic as their craft floated along. As the great Midwestern forests of the north were cut off, old-fashioned lumber operations declined. Now, with reforestation and planned cutting, modern lumbering methods have done away with much that was picturesque in the early days. Those days are recalled by old-time lumber festivals in several cities. The Lumberman's Memorial on the AU SABLE RIVER in Iosco County, Michigan, is the monument to the many people who worked in the industry.

LOMBARD, Carol. (Fort Wayne, IN, Oct. 6, 1908—Jan. 16, 1942). Actress. Lombard, wife of William Powell and then Clark Gable, began in motion pictures with Fox Studios in 1926. Lombard gained fame for her beauty and her roles in "screwball" comedies. She appeared in such movies as *No Man of her Own* (1932),*My Man Godfrey* (1936) and *They Knew What They Wanted* (1940). She died tragically in a plane crash in Tennessee.

LONE JACK BATTLEFIELD AND SOLDIERS CEMETERY. Located near Lone Jack, Missouri, southeast of KANSAS CITY in Jackson County. Lone Jack was named for a single blackjack tree growing near a spring which served as a prairie landmark. On August 15, 1862, Union Major Emory S. Foster marched into town to prevent Confederates from recruiting. Confederate troops and irregulars, including the YOUNGER and JAMES brothers, attacked on August 16th in a fierce house to house battle. The Union forces were defeated and forced to retreat. Union and Confederate dead were buried in separate trenches in the Soldiers Cemetery. The dead were left unidentified. The Confederate dead are marked by a twenty-six foot tall marble shaft. The Union dead were removed in 1867 to Leavenworth, Kansas.

LOON. State bird of Minnesota. Loon is the name given to any of several types of water birds that dive beneath the water's surface for food. The Minnesota state bird is the common loon. Also known as the great northern diver, the common loon may be found from the northern United States to the Arctic. Loons are approximately thirty-six inches long with black wings and have a black back covered with white spots. The head and neck are black and green, and the neck has white streaks. The lonely cry of loons is frequently heard on northern lakes. It's weird call gives rise to the expression "crazy as a loon." Loons live primarily on fish. When they take off to fly, they patter their feet along the water for a considerable distance before they are airborne.

LORAIN, Ohio. City (pop. 75,416), seat of Elyria County, located about twelve miles west of CLEVELAND, situated at the mouth of the BLACK RIVER on one of the finest harbors on the south shore of Lake ERIE. Lorain was named for Lorraine, France, but had earlier been named Charleston. Incorporated in 1834, Lorain has become an important ore receiving port, with shipyards, steelworks, automobile assembly plants and commercial fisheries. The community's history extends back to 1787, when a band of Moravian missionaries and their Indian converts camped at the mouth of the river, but the DELAWARE INDIANS ordered them to move on. In 1807 Nathan Perry and the Azariah Beebes established a trading post there, and a permanent settlement arose. Shipbuilding began in 1819, as the first of the major industries. The city boomed and was incorporated in 1836 as Charleston. When the railroad and OHIO AND ERIE CANAL both bypassed Lorain, the town went into decline, but it revived with the coming of the Cleveland, Lorain and Wheeling Railroad in 1872. The name was changed in 1876 to avoid conflict with another Ohio Charleston. In 1894 Tom L. Johnson moved his steel plant from Pennsylvania to South Lorain, attracting many laborers to wages which were high for their time. On June 29, 1924, a terrible TORNADO killed 79 people, injured 1,000 more and destroyed hundreds of homes, seventeen businesses and 298 other buildings. Lorain was left with a gigantic task of rebuilding damage totalling twenty-five million dollars, a huge sum for the time. Lorain was the birthplace of Admiral Ernest J. King of WORLD WAR II fame. The city has long boasted of its assimilation of ethnic and racial groups. To celebrate, it holds a three-day annual International Festival at the Sheffield Shopping Center, in the last week in June.

LORD DUNMORE'S WAR. John Murray, Scottish Earl of Dunmore, was governor of Virginia during Indian wars in Ohio and West Virginia. In 1774 he sent Andrews Lewis by way of the Kanawha River valley to put an end to the war in that area. Dunmore, himself, led the northern column of 2,500 men, a huge force in those days. Dunmore built a stockade called Fort Gower at the site of present Hockinport, Ohio, on the Hocking River. They proceeded up the Hocking valley and established Camp Charlotte. This large army and the new fortifications succeeded in restoring the peace in that large area. Meanwhile James LOGAN (1725?-1780), leader of the Mingo, and Chief Cornstalk (Keigh-tugh-qua) of the SHAWNEE commanded a federation of Indian tribes in attacking Lewis at Point Pleasant, West Virginia. The outnumbered Indians were forced to retreat, but they were so skillfully led by Cornstalk that they escaped with only 40 killed. Cornstalk wanted to continue the war, but the others decided the odds were against them. All except Logan went to Camp Charlotte and signed a peace treaty, accepting the OHIO RIVER as their southern boundary. However, when the REVOLUTIONARY WAR broke out the next year, the Indians went back to their frontier forays.

LOST RIVER. Rising in Martin County, Indiana, and flowing through Orange and Washington counties, the elusive Lost River disappears below the surface and rises at intervals, accounting for its name. In a course of more than 100 miles, it flows underground for a total of twenty-two miles. It makes its principal aboveground appearance at Orangeville, Orange County, Indiana.

LOUISIANA PURCHASE. The largest and most important annexation to the original 13 states, purchased from France in 1803. The vaguely-defined area, which had been known as Louisiana, was first claimed by France when LA SALLE (1643-1687) reached the mouth of the MISSISSIPPI RIVER in 1682. He claimed all the land around the river and its tributaries, and named the area after Louis XIV. In 1762 the area was ceded to Spain in exchange for territory in Italy. Despite foreign sovereignty, much of the territory was settled by American colonists, particularly the Ohio River valley. The Mississippi River as a means of shipping goods was vital to the economy of the new settlements.

In 1795 Spain had granted the United States the right to use the river and to ship goods from the mouth of the river without paying duty. This right was revoked by Spain in 1802 and the port of New Orleans was closed to

Americans. Although the port was soon reopened, the need to acquire New Orleans became apparent to President Thomas Jefferson. The Spanish were still thought to be in control in Louisiana, but it became known in 1801 that they had secretly ceded the territory back to France. In 1803 Jefferson began negotiations to purchase Louisiana.

Because of the impending war with Britain, France was more interested in her international situation than she was interested in retaining Louisiana. Jefferson, who still considered Britain an enemy, saw the necessity of obtaining the territory so that it would not fall into British hands.

Robert Livingston, the U.S. minister to France, and James Monroe, who had previous diplomatic dealings with France, were instructed by Jefferson to purchase New Orleans and Florida for $2 million. Negotiations opened in France in April, 1803. Charles Talleyrand, Napoleon's representative, surprised Livingston and Monroe by asking what the United States would pay for all of Louisiana, not just the intended American purchase. Talleyrand's proposal to sell all of Louisiana was probably a result of Napoleon's concern that an Anglo-American alliance might take place because of French possession of the Mississippi, and because France needed funds for its impending war with England.

Bargaining began and by April 29 terms were agreed upon. The United States would pay France $15 million, and the treaty, dated April 30, 1803, was signed several days later. Congress ratified the treaty on October 21, 1803. Although the boundaries for the new territory were controversial and not settled for several years, the United States had doubled its area. In the Midwest, all of present-day Missouri and Iowa were included, along with all of southern Minnesota and portions of the present north central and southwestern sections of the state. The undefined boundaries were settled by treaties with Britain in 1818 and with Spain in 1819.

LOUISIANA PURCHASE EXPOSITION. World's Fair celebration held in ST. LOUIS, Missouri, in 1904 to commemorate the 100th anniversary of the purchase of the LOUISIANA TERRITORY by the United States from France. Fifty-three nations and forty-two states took part in the festivities. Among the many innovations introduced at the Exposition was said to be the ice cream cone. The St. Louis Art Museum was originally the art building of the Exposition. The museum now features European and American paintings. The Missouri mining exhibit assigned to the University of MISSOURI at ROLLA for the Exposition is now housed in the university's Minerals Museum. The fair gained immortality through the Judy GARLAND (1922-1969) movie *Meet Me in St. Louis* (1944).

LOWDEN, Frank O. (Sunrise, MN, Jan. 26, 1861—Tucson, AZ, Mar. 20, 1943). Illinois governor. Lowden achieved wealth as a corporation lawyer in CHICAGO, Illinois. In 1896 He married George PULLMAN 's daughter Florence and established Sinissippi Farm near Oregon, Illinois, where improved methods of agricultural production were demonstrated and where his campaign for the governorship was later based. In 1906 he was elected to the U.S. House holding the seat until 1911. He sponsored several measures to promote agriculture. Elected as Illinois governor in 1917, he served until 1921. When President Wilson broke diplomatic relations with Germany, Governor "Win the War" Lowden issued a statement that loyalty was a solemn duty of all Americans. He obtained a pledge of the legislature to back the national administration, a politically courageous act for a Republican in Illinois which had more German and Austrian-born residents than any other state. Lowden helped establish the State Council of Defense which cooperated with all other wartime agencies. In 1918 he supported a sixty-million dollar bond issue to improve Illinois roads. Routes were graded and bridges started, but only two miles of pavement were laid, at Bates, Illinois, because bonds were not sold by Governor Lowden, who felt that cement prices had risen too rapidly, making the project too expensive. He gained national stature as an outstanding governor, and his career peaked at the Republican national Convention of 1920, when he was a favored candidate for president, but he lost the nomination to Warren G. Harding (1865-1923). He was offered the Republican vice-presidential nomination at the 1924 convention, but refused. He could not muster support for a presidential campaign in 1928. In his later years he worked for farmer welfare during the depression, and the Domestic Allotment Act of 1936 was based on his proposal of 1929.

LOWER PENINSULA. Geographically the larger "half" of Michigan. Not until the year 1669 did any Europeans venture into the Lower Peninsula. This was many years after explorers had visited the UPPER PENINSULA region. The first European to enter the Lower Peninsula area is thought to have been Adrien Jolliet, older brother of Louis JOLLIET (1645-1700), the famous explorer.

The surface of the Lower Peninsula is generally low-lying with an occasional hill and two large upland areas. A ridge of glacial deposit seldom rising above 1,500 feet bisects the northern half of the peninsula from MACKINAC to central Michigan. Running parallel to the lake shores are ranges of hills that mark the shore lines of the GREAT LAKES in ancient times. River systems developed from glacial action. Streams are short and generally flow gently over well-worn beds.

The climate in the Lower Peninsula benefits from its location between lakes MICHIGAN and HURON. Winds blowing into the Lower Peninsula are cooler in summer and milder in winter, allowing farmers to develop a fruit industry in a belt forty miles wide from the Grand Traverse region southward to the border of Indiana. Warmth from the deeper waters of Lake MICHIGAN warms the cold prevailing winds in winter causing heavy snows, but rarely excessively low temperatures. Cool winds in spring retard the budding of fruit trees until most danger of freezing is past. The mean annual temperature is 48 degrees F. The temperature range is 120 degrees from winter to summer, ten degrees less than in the Upper Peninsula.

The forests of the southern portions of the Lower Peninsula are primarily made up of hardwood trees. Moving farther north, the trees become primarily coniferous until at the northernmost part of the Lower Peninsula white birch and jack pines predominate.

Swift flowing streams in the northern parts of the Lower Peninsula are favorites of rainbow, brook and brown trout. Pike are found in the larger rivers. Panfish are common in the lakes. Lower Peninsula residents turn the annual smelt runs on the east shore of Lake Michigan into festive occasions.

LOWER SAINT CROIX NATIONAL SCENIC RIVERWAY.

At ST. CROIX FALLS, Wisconsin. Recreational opportunities for much of the upper Midwest are provided here along this 27-mile segment of the ST. CROIX RIVER, a component of the Wild and Scenic Rivers System. There are limited Federal facilities.

LOYOLA UNIVERSITY.

Roman Catholic, coeducational university in CHICAGO, Illinois.

Founded by the Jesuits in 1870, Loyola University grants bachelor's, master's, and doctor's degrees. It has three campuses in the Chicago area and one in Rome, Italy. Included in the university are colleges of arts and sciences, a graduate school and professional schools of dentistry, business administration, law, medicine, nursing, and social work. There are divisions of continuing education and part-time study. During the 1985-1986 academic year, the university, with a faculty of 1,332, had a student enrollment of 15,197.

LUDINGTON, Michigan. City (pop. 8,937). Seat of Mason County; central-northwest Michigan's LOWER PENINSULA; named for the community's founder, James Ludington. Ludington was originally called Marquette in honor of the French missionary who died there in 1675. Located on a knoll in Pere Marquette Park is a boulder marking his first grave. Two years after his death his Indian friends carried the body to the Roman Catholic mission at ST. IGNACE for reburial. Later these remains were moved to MARQUETTE UNIVERSITY in MILWAUKEE, Wisconsin. A solemn Pere Marquette Memorial Pageant has been held annually for three nights in August. Located at the mouth of the PERE MARQUETTE RIVER, Ludington has been one of Michigan's important shipping ports on Lake MICHIGAN. Pere Marquette Lake provides safe harbor for car ferries and lake freighters. Ludington is also a popular fishing spot. Coho salmon are caught in the Pere Marquette River and Lake Michigan. Exhibits showing life in the logging industry are found in Historic White Pine Village, a reconstructed community of nineteen buildings.

LUMBER AND LUMBERING. The northern Midwest states have been among the leaders in the production of lumber. Beginning in the northeast, the vast forests were exhausted, and so production steadily moved to the West, starting in Michigan in the 1840s and moving, again, steadily westward, until, as in the East, the supply of marketable trees had been almost exhausted. Today the replanting of millions of trees in cutover patches, along with planned growth and cutting, have brought substantial timbers back to the northern Midwest, where much of the output is used as pulp for paper, pressed woods, plywood and other subsidiary products. In 1980 Michigan's 19,370,000 acres of forest land, gave the state second rank among all states east of Texas and Colorado. In the Midwest. Minnesota is second, with 16,709,000 acres. Although all the Midwest states have some commercial timber, with Wisconsin third. Iowa, not surprisingly has the smallest Midwest acreage, 1,561,000 acres. Another surprise is the total growth on over six million acres in long-settled Ohio. A rather modern trend is the increasing acreage of small farm woodlots throughout the area, where farmers are turning to long-term investment in trees best suited to their region.

MACALESTER COLLEGE. Privately supported liberal arts college of the United Presbyterian Church. Founded in 1873 as a college for men, Macalester became coeducational in 1881. The school is located on a forty-four acre campus midway between MINNEAPOLIS and ST. PAUL. ST. LOUIS UNIVERSITY offers a cooperative program with Macalester for students studying engineering. Rush Medical College and Macalester offer cooperative programs for students of nursing. More than thirty-five percent of the graduates have participated in one of the thirty exchange programs with overseas universities. Enrollment is presently equally divided with approximately eight hundred men and eight hundred women.

MACKINAC BRIDGE, (BIG MAC). Bridge connecting the LOWER PENINSULA of Michigan at MACKINAW CITY to the UPPER PENINSULA at ST. IGNACE. The five-mile bridge, now one of Upper Michigan's major tourist attractions, has a distance of 8,614 feet between cable anchorages, making it the fourth-longest suspension bridge in the world. It cost one hundred million dollars to construct, much higher than estimates in the 1940s of thirty-two million dollars. It was opened in 1957 and eliminated such nightmares as miles-long lines of cars waiting for ferry service across the STRAITS OF MACKINAC. Governor G. Mennen Williams referred to it as "another Northwest Passage." An annual Mackinac Bridge Walk is held every Labor Day. As many as forty thousand people participate. Artifacts and memorabilia from the construction of the bridge are housed in the Mackinac Bridge Museum. A film on the history of the bridge is presented continuously.

MACKINAC ISLAND. Important island located between Lakes HURON and MICHIGAN. Mackinac Island was originally called Michilimackinac, or "great turtle" by the Indians because of its shape. The island is three miles long and two miles wide with high cliffs, ravines, natural bridges and strange rock formations. Its strategic importance in the control of the STRAITS OF MACKINAC was recognized by every country attempting to control the region. The island was first seen by white men when Jean NICOLET (1598-1642) canoed through the straits in 1634. The first written reference to the island was made by Father Claude Jean ALLOUEZ (1622-1689) in a letter to his superior, Father Claude DABLON (1618-1697). It is known that the island was visited by Father Jacques MARQUETTE (1637-1675) and Robert Cavelier, Sieur de LA SALLE (1643-1687), who passed it in 1679 on the GRIFFON. At the conclusion of the FRENCH AND INDIAN WAR, t h e British moved their garrison to the island. In 1781, at the end of the American Revolution, Mackinac was ceded to the United States, but it was not until the signing of the Jay Treaty (1794) that the British gave up their military position on the island. The British captured Fort Michilimackinac and the island on July 17, 1812, from the Americans without a shot being fired because the United States government had forgotten to notify its frontier posts that the WAR OF 1812 had been declared. Despite repeated attempts, the Americans were never able to achieve by force what the Treaty of Ghent in 1814 ending the fighting gave them—control of the island. The war's conclusion gave America a monopoly on the fur trade in this region. Realizing the potential, John Jacob ASTOR (1763-1848) centered his AMERICAN FUR COMPANY at Mackinac Island in 1817. The peak of the fur industry occurred in 1822 when pelts valued at three million dollars were checked through the Mackinac post. Astor closed the office on Mackinac in 1830. The island's population then diminished to only a few whites and Indians. New money came in when it was promoted as a resort area. Wealthy southerners built summer homes on its shores

Mackinaw City - Maddy

"Big Mac," Mackinac Bridge connects Upper and Lower Michigan.

until the CIVIL WAR left these wealthy people financially ruined. Wealthy Chicagoans then moved to the island, and the resort industry revived. Carriage routes were laid out during the 1860s and the grounds were landscaped. Locals built carriages to take visitors to the historic military post. Students of architecture found the Officers' Headquarters Building one of the few examples of British Colonial style left in the state. New England Colonial design could be seen in the Agent's House, built in 1822. In 1875 Mackinac was made a national military reservation. Ferry service began in 1881. The island became a supply point for the fishing and lumber industries and was so popular that the huge Grand Hotel was constructed for wealthy tourists and other visitors. It is said to be the largest summer hotel anywhere, with the world's longest front porch. The last garrison was removed from FORT MACKINAC in 1894 and the post was then turned over to the state. In 1895 ninety-five percent of the island was declared a state park. Once on the island, visitors have the choice of transportation by foot, bicycle, carriage or horse. There are no motorized vehicles allowed except for an ambulance, fire truck and public utilities truck. The one state highway circling the island is perhaps the only one in the nation on which no motor vehicle accident has ever occurred. Carriage tours continue to carry tourists past many of the island's scenic and historic points. Old Fort Mackinac is preserved as a museum. The history of the original fourteen buildings is shown through dioramas and murals. Costumed guides conduct tours and demonstrate musket and cannon firing. At the old fort is a memorial to Dr. William BEAUMONT (1785-1853), illustrious figure in Michigan's medical history. Biddle House is reputedly the oldest house on the island. An Indian museum with working 1840 kitchen is located in the Indian Dormitory at the base of the fort. The Stuart House

Museum was the original headquarters for the American Fur Company.

MACKINAW CITY, Michigan. Village (pop. 820), northernmost tip of Michigan's LOWER PENINSULA. FORT MICHILACKINAC stood on the site of Mackinaw City in 1760 when it was abandoned by the French. The British occupied the post for a few years before it was attacked by Indians involved in the PONTIAC (1720?-1769) Conspiracy (1762). The English reoccupied the fort in 1764 before moving the garrison to MACKINAC ISLAND. Mackinaw City sits at the southern end of the MACKINAC BRIDGE, the toll bridge across the straits. Each Labor Day nearly forty thousand people participate in the Mackinac Bridge Walk from Mackinaw to ST. IGNACE. Memorabilia from the building of the bridge is contained in the Mackinac Bridge Museum. Other relics of the past may be seen in the Old Mill Creek State Historic Park, site of an 18th-century industrial complex thought to be the oldest in northern Michigan. The remains of the sawmill which supplied lumber for the construction of Fort Mackinac was found in 1872 by a CHEBOYGAN high school history teacher. Archaeological work is still going on.

MADDY, Joseph Edgar. (Wellington, KS, Oct. 14, 1891—Interlochen, MI, April 18, 1966). Musician, music educator. Maddy founded the NATIONAL MUSIC CAMP at INTERLOCHEN, Michigan in 1928. Talented musicians from all over the United States study with prominent teachers and have the opportunity to meet and study music with equally talented youth at a camp in a beautiful woodland setting. Maddy had a long history of improving music opportunities for this nation's youth. He organized the first national high school orchestra in DETROIT in 1926. The second national high school orchestra was organized for a convention of school superintendents in 1927. He served as chairman of the committee on instrumental affairs in charge of the development of school band and orchestra contests in the United States for the Music Education National Conference from 1926 to 1934. As a professor of music at the University of MICHIGAN, beginnining in 1924, Maddy originated radio music instruction from the university and conducted music lessons over the radio for the National Broadcasting Corporation from 1935 to 1939. He served as the chairman of the Michigan Commission on Radio Education in 1945 and led the fight to free educational broadcasts from union controls. He also invented the aluminum violin and string bass., beginning in 1924.

MADELINE ISLAND. Historic Madeline Island, fourteen miles long, is the largest of the twenty APOSTLE ISLANDS lying north of the entrance to CHEQUAMEGON BAY in Lake SUPERIOR in northern Wisconsin. It is the only one of the islands not a part of the APOSTLE ISLANDS NATIONAL LAKESHORE and the only one of the group with roads, villages and other evidences of settlement. La Pointe is an historic village at the southwest tip of the island. It is connected with BAYFIELD by ferry. Fort La Pointe was built there by 1718. It was established to maintain peace among the Indian tribes of the region. Beginning in 1727, Louis Denis, Sieur de La Ronde, garrisoned the fort and began development of the island, with a dock, perhaps a mill, and some agriculture. After the FRENCH AND INDIAN WAR, English fur trader Alexander Henry revived trading activity on the island. A Protestant mission was built in 1832, and it was the site of the signing of the treaty which in 1854 established reservations for the CHIPPEWA Indians on it. Today the island has 45 miles of roads and tourist facilities. Madeline Island Historical Museum is located on the site of the AMERICAN FUR COMPANY post, combining four log structures. Local crafts are well established and are sold in a shop on the island.

MADISON, Indiana. City (pop. 12,472), seat of Jefferson County, located in southeastern Indiana near the OHIO RIVER. It is a major center of tobacco marketing, and its manufactures include organs, machinery, metal products and electric motors. The Madison area, first settled in 1805, was sold in 1809 to John Paul, a Revolutionary War soldier, who platted the town and named it for President James Madison. As the nearest port for interior Indiana, Madison grew quickly and between

1850 and 1855 was the largest city in Indiana until more direct routes were established to the East from Louisville and CINCINNATI. Madison shipyards built a Union gunboat during the CIVIL WAR and, in the 1880s and 1890s, constructed many of the packets for Ohio River commerce. Captain Charles Lewis Shrewsbury of Madison accumulated a fortune with a fleet of Ohio River boats. Another resident of Madison, James F. D. LANIER, advanced nearly one million dollars as an unsecured loan when Indiana, without money or credit, funds needed to equip soldiers for the Civil War. The homes of both men have been opened to the public. Madison also boasted the first public library in the NORTHWEST TERRITORY. Alexander Meek and a group of Easterners met there in 1811 to form the Madison Society Library. Twenty-four subscribers each paid five dollars for borrowing privileges. The library soon outgrew its first quarters in an inn and after the Civil War became a county operation. The annual tour of historic homes at Madison, held the last weekend in September, is one of the best known in the country. Also one of the premiere examples of its type is the Regatta and Governor's Cup Race for hydroplanes competing on the Ohio River. Near Madison is CLIFTY FALLS State Park.

MADISON, WISCONSIN

Name: From James Madison the fourth President of the United States.

Area: 53.9 square miles

Elevation: 846 feet

Population:
1984: 170,745
Rank: 90th
Percent change (1980-1984): .1%
Density (city): 3,071 per sq. mi.
Metropolitan Population: 333,000
Percent change (1980-1984): .7%

Racial and Ethnic makeup (1980):
White: 94.33%
Black: 2.7%
Hispanic origin: 2,242 persons
Indian: 425 persons
Asian: 2,688 persons

Age:
18 and under: 20.5%
65 and over: 8.7%

Madison

TV Stations: 4

Radio Stations: 7

Hospitals: 2

Sports Teams:
(baseball) Muskies

Further Information: Madison Chamber of Commerce, 615 East Washington, Post Office Box 71, Madison, Wisconsin 53701

MADISON, Wisconsin. City, capital of Wisconsin and seat of Dane County, situated in south central Wisconsin on the narrow strip of land forming an isthmus between lakes MEN-DOTA and Monona, also spreading out to the northeast and southwest of the lakes. It takes its name from the fourth President of the United States, James Madison (1751-1836). It was incorporated in 1856.

The climate is typical of continental North America, with a wide temperature range. Average of winter temperatures is 20 degrees, with the summer average at 68. Polar air masses are most common in the city. The city lakes are apt to be frozen from mid-December to early April. Most precipitation arrives during summer months. It occupies 55.6 square miles of territory.

In recent years, the city has added a broader commercial base to its primary concerns, state government and education. As the center of a thriving agricultural and dairy area, much of the manufacturing is agriculturally based, including dairying machinery. Other major products are medical equipment and batteries.

The city was founded in 1836 to be the territorial capital, before any settlement was made in the site. Judge James Duane DOTY (1799-1865) was mainly responsible for selection. Because he owned substantial property in the area, there was some suggestion that he had bribed the legislature, but no action was taken. The location has provided a beautiful setting for one of the nation's most attractive capital cities.

In 1842 the territorial capitol was the scene of a murder. In an argument between two legislators, Charles Arndt and James R. Vineyard, Vineyard shot Arndt to death, was tried more than a year later but freed.

With Wisconsin statehood in 1848, the city became the state capital. The University of WISCONSIN was also chartered in 1848 and began operations the next year. A new capitol was finished in 1869 and enlarged in 1882, but that

The capitol, Madison, Wisconsin.

capitol was destroyed by fire in 1904. The present building was completed in 1917. Its Greek cross plan is unique among U.S. capitals. The four identical wings radiate from the rotunda underneath the dome. The construction is notable for its use of thirty-six varieties of granite and marble. Strangely, there are no records of either a cornerstone or dedication ceremony.

By contrast to many cities of the Midwest, during the period of 1970 to 1984, Madison's population remained almost stable. More than 97 percent of the population consists of persons of European descent. The city ranks third in per capita income among U.S. cities of over 100,000 population. In 1984 its employment rate ranked 12th highest in the nation. The city holds high rank in spending for police and fire protection, public schools and libraries. It has a history of good government, well financed.

In addition to government, the principal activity centers around the vast main campus of the University of Wisconson. The university is often a serious contender in various college sports. A university arboretum is a popular tourist mecca, especially during the blooming of its lilac plantation. Also interesting is the wildlife preserve. In academic fields, the university's doctoral programs are ranked first in the nation by the Association of Research Libraries. The university is particularly notable for its scientfic research, including the work of vitamin D pioneer Dr. Harry Steenbock. Funds from research benefit the unique ALUMNI RESEARCH FOUNDATION.

Much valuable research benefitting the great

forests and pulp mills of the state comes from the U.S. FOREST PRODUCTS LABORATORY at Madison.

The collections, research and publications of the State Historical Society have been called the finest of their type in the country. Its museum collection is outstanding, including the largest collection of guns in the world.

The Unitarian church, designed by famed architect Frank Lloyd WRIGHT, and the zoo in Vilas Park are other attractions.The Jazz Festival is a notable event each spring.

MALARIA. Although somewhat common in the southern United States, malaria is occasionally found in some form in most of the Midwest, generally brought from some more tropical area. With the draining of swamps and other breeding places of the malarial mosquitoes, new cases in the Midwest are not numerous. However, the Midwest has a special place in treatment of the disease. Dr. John SAPPINGTON (1776-1856) of ARROW ROCK, Missouri, was a pioneer in use of quinine in the treatment of malaria. He also was an internationally recognized authority on treatments of many other fevers.

MAMMOTH. Prehistoric animal related to the modern elephant. Huge, lumbering beasts, mammoths were more than fourteen feet tall and had tusks and trunks. Tusks, often thirteen feet long, curved down from the lower jaw and then upward to cross in front of the trunk. Some types of mammoths were covered with long hair. Studies indicate that mammoths reached North America from Eurasia nearly 500,000 years ago and were hunted by prehistoric man for food. Remains of mammoths are commonly found as fossils in Midwestern states as far north as Minnesota.

MAN MOUND. One of the most famous of the thousands of mounds built up by PREHISTORIC PEOPLES in many part of the United States is found near BARABOO, Wisconsin. This is one of the effigy mounds, which generally take animal form, snakes, turtles, birds and others. The Baraboo mound is perhaps unique in its form, that of a man 150 feet from head to toe and 50 feet broad at the shoulders. Substantial ability was required to pile up dirt to form a figure as perfectly shaped and proportioned as this, especially since it probably was not possible for the ancient architects to have looked down from some height to examine their work.

MANISTEE, Michigan. City (pop. 7,566), seat of Manistee County, northwest portion Michigan's LOWER PENINSULA, north of LUDINGTON on the shore of Lake MICHIGAN, name derived from an Indian word meaning, "spirit of the woods" and the name of a Chippewa town. Manistee lies at the mouth of the Manistee River as it enters Lake Michigan. Manistee was once the center of a thriving lumber industry. It is here that the "round forty" plan of timber is thought to have originated. A lumberman purchased forty acres of timber and then began cutting the trees on his own land and the land around it as quickly as possible. The original forty acres became the center of a cut area that included land owned by other people unsuspecting of what was happening. The lumber industry gradually faded in importance. The river was dredged and the harbor gained as increased trade passed through the city on its way to GREAT LAKES markets. Nearby brine deposits made Manistee a major salt producing region and the salt's reputed medicinal properties encouraged its use in health bath immersion treatments. Manistee was partially destroyed by the great forest FIRE in 1871 which also destroyed HOLLAND, Michigan. At the turn of the century, lumber baron T.J. Ramsdell built one of the largest opera houses of the world of the time, in Manistee. The building is now used for summer theater.

MANITOWOC, Wisconsin. City (pop. 32,-547), seat of Manitowoc County, situated in central eastern Wisconsin on Lake MICHIGAN at the mouth of the Manitowoc River. It takes its name from the Indian word meaning "land of the spirit," possibly of the evil spirit. In the early 1800s the site of the present city was a stopover for travelers on the lake on the route between GREEN BAY and CHICAGO. Manitowoc and its twin city, TWO RIVERS, were begun in 1836. Manitowoc grew through stages as a lumber camp, fishing town and shipbuilding center. Its shipbuilding dates from 1847. During WORLD WAR II, over a hundred navy vessels were built there, including submarines, wooden minesweepers and sub chasers. Today the fine harbor encourages international trade through the ST. LAWRENCE SEAWAY. One of the largest manufacturers of aluminum ware operates at Manitowoc, and the city is one of the state's leaders in the canning industry. A fur trading post was built on the site in 1795 by the Northwest Company. The city is the home of Silver Lake College of the Holy Family. Among other Manitowoc attractions is its Maritime Museum, depicting 150 years of maritime history. Nearby is the International Submariners Memorial, based on a submarine docked permanently in the river and designated as a National Landmark. The Rahr-West Museum is a Victorian house with period rooms. Pine Crest Historical Village offers fifteen authentic buildings of the last half of the nineteenth century, brought to the site from various parts of the city. Nearby is Hidden Valley Ski Area.

MANKATO, Minnesota. City (pop.28,642), seat of Blue Earth County, south-central Minnesota; northwest of ALBERT LEA at the junction of the Blue Earth and Minnesota. The name comes from a SIOUX word meaning "blue earth," from the colored clay found along the shore of the Blue Earth River. A leading city of its area and a natural trading center for nearby northern Iowa, its influence extends even into eastern South Dakota. The trade developed with a prosperous steamboat traffic. Today it is the flourishing center of dairy products and their processing. Quarrying of the prominent Mankato stone has been carried on for more than 100 years. Settlers were protected from Indians when Fort Ridgely was constructed up the river in 1853. The city was incorported in 1865. Blue Earth County Historical Society Museum is housed in an 18-room mansion erected in 1871. Special exhibits include a restored log cabin built in 1873, barber and cobbler shops, and Victorian gardens near the mansion. A wind-driven grist mill built in 1864 may be seen in Minneopa State Park. A botanical garden and picnic grounds are part of the 100-acre Sibley Park adjacent to the Blue Earth and Minnesota rivers.

MANN, Horace. (Franklin, MA, May 4, 1796—Yellow Springs, OH, Aug. 2, 1859. Much of Mann's career was devoted to duties outside the Midwest. In the East he had become one of the leading proponents of better education and helped to bring about many educational improvements and established a public school system in Massachusetts which became a model for the nation. After running unsuccessfully for governor of Massachusetts in 1852, he became the first president of ANTIOCH COLLEGE, at YELLOW SPRINGS, in 1853. While there he promoted and demonstrated the value of coeducation and brought the college to a high academic level. He continued to promote his support of wider public education, substantive conferences for educators in all fields, as well as better salaries for all educators. He is considered to have been one of the most influential of American educators.

MANSFIELD, Ohio. City (pop. 53,927), seat of Richland County, situated in north central Ohio, in a hilly region of rich farms, it was named for Richard Mansfield, surveyor general of the United States, who was directed by President Jefferson to inspect the area and under whose direction it was laid out in 1808. The ridge on which it is located is encircled by the last foothills of the Appalachian Mountains. During the WAR OF 1812, Johnny Appleseed CHAPMAN (1774-1845) made a speedy journey of 30 miles to bring troops to the community, preventing a possible Indian massacre. Modern growth began in 1846 when the first railroad arrived. The town was an important station on the UNDERGROUND RAILROAD prior to the CIVIL WAR. A political group there was one of the first to endorse Abraham LINCOLN (1809-1865) for president. After the war the firm of Aultman and Taylor became one of the largest makers of threshing machines. The Ohio State Reformatory was located there in 1885, and the Ohio Brass Company was founded there in 1888. Mansfield Tire and Rubber, Tappan Stove Company and a Westinghouse electric plant added to the industrial prosperity. The city was one of the few which continued its boom during the depression of 1929, thanks mainly to its electrical industry. Much of the early industry remains in this busy industrial center. Pulitzer Prize winning author, Louis BROMFIELD (1896-1956), was a Mansfield native. Many of his novels are identified with the Mansfield of his early years. Leaving Paris in 1930 after fourteen years of residence in France, Bromfield returned to Ohio to purchase a Richland County farm, where he conducted agricultural research. Malabar Farm State Park preserves Bromfield's home with the original furnishings, and the land is still used as an agricultural experiment farm. A fine view of Mansfield is had from Ashland Hill across the Rocky Fork Valley. Kingwood Center and Gardens, Pleasant Hill Lake Park, Richland County Museum and Mansfield Art Center are visitor attractions. Another attraction is the annual Ohio Ski Carnival at Snow Trails Ski Resort, and the Richland County Fair is held there.

MANSHIP, Paul. (St. Paul, MN, Dec. 25, 1885—Gloucester, MA, Jan. 31, 1966). Sculptor. Manship earned an international reputation in the field of art and was recognized for his contributions with such awards as the international award for sculpture San Luca, Florence, Italy, in 1961 and decoration of chevalier Legion of Honor (France). He was an honorary president of the National Sculpture Society and was past president of the American Academy of Arts and Letters. Manship's works stand in galleries and museums around the world.

MAPLE. The sugar maple is the state tree of Minnesota and Wisconsin. The hard wood of the sugar maple has often been used for shipbuilding, as well as in aircraft construction and for floors and fuel. All the maples have the characteristic winged seeds. The sugar maple and black maple are the only ones used for maple syrup.

MAQUOKETA RIVER. Rising in northeast Iowa, the Maquoketa River flows through the Iowa towns of Manchester, Monticello and MAQUOKETA before being joined by its North Fork. It empties into the MISSISSIPPI RIVER near the town of Green Island.

MARIETTA, Ohio. City (pop. 16,467), seat of Washington County, situated on the OHIO RIVER, at the mouth of the MUSKINGUM RIVER, in far southeast Ohio, the community was named for Queen Marie Antoinette by General Rufus PUTNAM in recognition of her assistance during the American Revolution. The city was the first permanent European town west of the Alleghenies, so also, of course, the first in Ohio.

Today it is a pleasant residential city of tree-lined streets.

Hundreds, perhaps thousands, of years before, the city was the site of prehistoric settlement, evidenced by well-preserved earthworks and other relics.

After the Ordinance of 1787 was passed, legal purchase and settlement of lands in the old NORTHWEST TERRITORY was permitted. A group of New Englanders, headed by Manasseh CUTLER (1742-1823) and Revolutionary General Rufus Putnam organized the OHIO COMPANY OF ASSOCIATES to buy 1,500,000 acres of land and settle in the west. They sent twenty-two boat builders to the Youghiogheny River in western Pennsylvania. With 2 flatboats and five pirogues, the company started down river on April 1, 1788. They arrived on April 7th at the mouth of the Muskingum, and almost immediately began building on the east bank, first calling the settlement Muskingum, later calling it Marietta.

The first cabins were built along what is now Front Street, and a stockade, called Picketed Point, later a fort called CAMPUS MARTIUS, was made for protection. Since General Putnam also had built the fortress of West Point, it must be assumed that Marietta was well protected, and a contemporary called it "the strongest fortification in the Territory of the United States."

Of the settlement, George WASHINGTON said, "...I know many of the settlers personally and there never were men better calculated to promote the welfare of a community."

Marietta celebrated the sesquicentennial of its founding on April 7, 1938, when a party of modern pioneers reenacted the journey of Putnam and his followers and their arrival in the city in vessels duplicating the originals. On July 8, 1938, President F. D. Roosevelt dedicated a memorial in Muskingum Park, commemorating 150 years of civil government in the Northwest territory.

Soon after its founding, Marietta became an important shipbuilding center, then went on to become one of the most important ports along the Ohio in the steamboating days. Brickmaking was the earliest industry, and many of the pioneer homes were made of brick. Before 1900 a rich oil field was developed. There is now a wide variety of manufacturing, including alloys, plastics, office equipment and paints.

Marietta College was founded there in 1835. The well-educated founders of Marietta clearly understood the importance of the prehistoric mounds around which they settled and immediately made plans to preserve them in local parks. Perhaps the most interesting is in Mound Cemetery, where a thirty-foot mound is surrounded by graves of twenty-four Revolutionary War officers.

Rufus Putnam's house is now Campus Martius Museum, preserving mementoes of the early days. Another point of interest is Ohio River Museum State Memorial, with its exhibits and displays of the history of inland waterways. During the summer months, river cruises are available on a sternwheeler. Labor Day weekend finds countless visitors for the annual Ohio River Stern-wheel festival, where such boats from all over the nation have an exciting race. September brings the annual Indian Summer Arts and Crafts Festival. During the summer and fall the showboat *Becky Thatcher* is docked for varied performances.

MARQUETTE UNIVERSITY. Chartered as a Jesuit University in 1864, the institution had its beginnings in 1857 when two Jesuit priests founded St. Aloysius Academy at MILWAUKEE, Wisconsin. Marquette College opened in Milwaukee in 1881 and became a university in 1907. It was named in honor of the famed Jesuit explorer Father Jacques MARQUETTE (1637-1675). It is known for its medical and dental instruction and for its School of Journalism. A striking structure on the campus is St. Joan of Arc Chapel, a fifteenth-century structure from France brought to Marquette in 1964. The 48 bells of Marquette Hall carillon form one of the largest "musical instruments" of its kind in the country. Haggery Museum of Art houses a notable collection of more than 5,000 works. The student body of 11,442 is instructed by a faculty of 959.

MARQUETTE, Jacques. (Laon, France, June 1, 1637—near Ludington, MI, May 18, 1675). Explorer and missionary. A Jesuit priest, Marquette went to Quebec, Canada, in 1666 to study Indian languages and was appointed to work with the OTTAWA Indians on the shore of Lake HURON. He established missions at SAULT STE. MARIE and later at what is now ST. IGNACE, Michigan. In 1672-73, with Louis JOLLIET (1645-1700), he set forth to explore what the Indians referred to as the "great river"—the MISSISSIPPI. From Lake MICHIGAN they entered GREEN BAY in present Wisconsin, paddled up the FOX RIVER and made the easy portage across to the WISCONSIN RIVER, down which they drifted into the Mississippi, becoming the first Europeans known to have been in the upper reaches of that river. When they reached the mouth of the Arkansas River, they were told that the Mississippi emptied into the Gulf of Mexico. In

Father Marquette guards Fort Mackinac.

order to avoid the Spanish rulers there, the party turned northward, entered the ILLINOIS RIVER, crossing northeast along the course of that river over much of the present state. They then made another important portage from the DES PLAINES to the CHICAGO RIVER. They wintered in the area of present CHICAGO, then journeyed back north. Marquette had promised the ILLINI INDIANS to return to them and teach them about Christanity, and he started back to Illinois, but his health failed, and he died on the journey. His journal of the exploration with Jolliet, along with maps and other data, was instrumental in later explorations and settlements in the area.

MARSHALL, Michigan. City (pop. 7,200), Calhoun County, southwestern portion of Michigan's LOWER PENINSULA. Founded in 1830, the town grew quietly attracting numerous well-to-do residents who built fine houses, many before the CIVIL WAR. Between 1835 and 1847 the community hoped to be designated the state capital, but lost the honor to LANSING. Today Marshall has been described as a living museum of fine ARCHITECTURE, including Gothic Revival, Queen Anne, and Italianate. The homes have been preserved because the great plans for its expansion never came about, and the cherished buildings were never destroyed, so they remain today in fine condition. It was in Marshall that the groundwork for the Fugitive Slave Act of 1850 was laid. In 1846 Adam Crosswhite, a citizen of Marshall, was seized by men working for the slaveowner who had owned him two years before. The residents of Marshall, however, rushed to Crosswhite's aid and sent the agents of the slaveholder home without their prize and then aided Crosswhite and his family to escape into Canada. The southern slaveholder sued the citizens of Marshall and won. The Crosswhite case led to the 1850 passage of the Fugitive Slave Law, dealing with runaway slaves which, in turn, was one of many causes for the Civil War. A self-guided tour brings the visitor to most of the splendid homes and buildings. Among the unique attractions is the Honolulu House Museum, built by a U.S. consul to the Sandwich Islands (Hawaii), with many period furnishings and artifacts. This building houses the Marshall Historical Society.

MARSHALLTOWN, Iowa. City (pop. 26,-938). Seat of Marshall County, situated in central Iowa on the IOWA RIVER, about thirty miles northeast of DES MOINES. It takes its name from Marshall, Michigan, was named by the founder, Harry Anson, and was incorporated in 1863. An agricultural and industrial center, its earliest industries were woolen goods, wagon and carriage factories and an iron foundry. Billy SUNDAY (1862-1935), the famed evangelist, spent much time trying to rid the town of its 22 saloons. When William Fisher, local superintendent of the water department, was trying to keep up water pressure during a disastrous fire (May 2, 1872) in Marshalltown, he conceived the idea for his constant pressure pump governor, and in 1880 he started one of the city's major industries, the Fisher Controls Company, now a division of the Monsanto company. Even better known is the Lennox Company, one of the world's largest manufacturers of warm-air heating equipment. Because of its industries, the city is sometimes known as "Little Pittsburgh." Unlike many Midwest industrial cities, Marshalltown's population has remained relatively stable, rising slightly in the decade of 1970-1980.

MARTINSVILLE, Indiana. City (pop. 11,-311), central Indiana city southwest of INDIANAPOLIS, called the "Artesian City" because of its therapeutic artesian waters discovered years ago by prospectors drilling for natural gas. It became the site of many sanitoriums for arthritis, and related illnesses. The curative powers of the water were discovered, according to residents, when a retired racehorse drank some of the water and returned to its former winning ways at the track. The annual Fall Foliage Festival features sporting events, shows and handicrafts.

MASON CITY, Iowa. City (pop. 30,144). Seat of Cerro Gordo County, situated in north, northeast Iowa, on the Winnebago River, it takes its name from the Masonic Lodge of which there were many early members in the town, also from the large brick and tile industry of the area which required many masons. The city is still headquarters for a large manufacturing industry producing brick and tile and other clayware. At one time the Mason City area also produced a fifth of all the nation's cement. The Iowa cement industry is still centered there. The city gained considerable fame as the model for the fictional town created by renowned composer Meredith WILLSON (1902-1984) for his hit musical, *The Music Man* (1957). Keeping up its musical reputation, the city's annual North Iowa Band Festival is known as one of the outstanding events of its kind.

MASON, Stevens Thomson. (Loudoun County, VA, Oct. 27, 1811—Jan. 4, 1843). Governor of Michigan. Mason was appointed the secretary of Michigan Territory in 1831 by President Andrew Jackson and served until 1834 when he became the acting governor upon the death of Governor George B. Porter. Mason, at the age of nineteen, is believed to have been the youngest person ever to hold the office of governor. The people of Michigan were very upset to have such a young executive, but he proved to be an effective administrator and promised to listen to the counsel of older and more experienced men. Mason, the only governor for the Territory of Michigan, became the first governor of the State of Michigan in 1836 when he was twenty-four. He served until 1838. During his term as governor Mason had a difficult time restraining Americans who wanted to help those in Canada attempting to revolt from the British. After two years as governor, Mason announced he would not seek a second term. He entered a self-imposed exile in the East where he died. His body was returned to Michigan in 1905. A memorial to him stands in DETROIT.

MASSACRE OF PIGEON ROOST. Indiana Indian massacre in 1812. A wandering band of SHAWNEE and DELAWARE Indians attacked Pigeon Roost, a three-year-old settlement, on September 3, 1812. In an hour three men, five women, and sixteen children were killed, scalped and mutilated. Only the home of William Collings, an expert marksman who kept the Indians away and allowed several settlers to escape, was spared. Reasons for the massacre include resentment over the Battle of TIPPECANOE (November 7, 1811) but may have also involved theft of Indian property, cheating of Indians in a horse trade, and whiskey dealing with the Indians. A memorial of Indiana limestone stands at the site near Scottsburg, Indiana.

MASTODONS. Prehistoric species of animal resembling an elephant that lived in the Midwest millions of years ago. Mastodon remains have been found throughout the Midwest. The remains of mastodons and humans were found together in 1838 in the Bourbeuse River region of Missouri, indicating that they co-existed. This discovery was the first of its kind in the Americas and came only two years after similar discoveries were made in Europe.

MATTOON, Illinois. City (pop. 19,787).

Named for William Mattoon, railroad engineer and landowner, and founded in 1848. The city is the center of broom corn production in Illinois. Broom corn, grown in the area around Mattoon, is made into brooms in PARIS, Illinois, the site of the largest broom factory in the world. Mattoon produces goods ranging from heavy machinery to dresses.

MAUMEE RIVER. Indiana river formed by the meeting of the ST. JOSEPH and ST. MARYS rivers at FORT WAYNE, Indiana. The Maumee flows almost directly east, a rare occurrence among Midwest rivers. General Anthony WAYNE defeated Indians along the Maumee at the BATTLE OF FALLEN TIMBERS.

MAYO CLINIC. Noted medical facility started at ROCHESTER, Minnesota, in 1889 and now one of the largest and most widely recognized medical centers in the world. The clinic was founded by William Worrall MAYO (1819-1911) and his two sons to care for surgical patients, and gradually more physicians were added to the staff. The function of the facility was changed to a general medical center by the Mayo brothers just before WORLD WAR I. Over two hundred thousand patients are treated at the Mayo Clinic annually. Since its founding, an estimated three million patients have come to the clinic for help.

MAYO FOUNDATION FOR MEDICAL EDUCATION. Nonprofit charitable organization that supports medical research and education and provides the primary financial support for the Mayo Medical School and Graduate School of Medicine in ROCHESTER, Minnesota. The foundation was established in 1919 by doctors William J. MAYO (1861-1939) and Charles H. MAYO (1865-1939) as a means of returning the net earnings of the MAYO CLINIC to mankind through education.

MAYO, Charles Horace. (Rochester, MN, July 19, 1865—Rochester, MN, May 26, 1939). Surgeon, son of William Worrell MAYO. Mayo began his "medical" career at the age of nine, standing on a box to administer ether while his father operated. Beginning in 1888, he practiced medicine in ROCHESTER. In addition to the $2,800,000 donation to establish the MAYO FOUNDATION FOR MEDICAL EDUCATION AND RESEARCH (1919) at Rochester, Mayo and his brother, William J. MAYO (1861-1939), founded the Mayo Properties Association as a trust to hold all funds, endowments, and properties of the Mayo

Clinic to ensure the permanency of the institution for public service. Mayo was honored personally for his devotion to medicine by President Franklin Roosevelt in 1934, with a commemorative plaque.

MAYO, William J. (Le Seur, MN, June 29, 1861—Rochester, MN, July 28, 1939). Surgeon, son of William Worrell MAYO. Mayo and his brother, Charles Horace MAYO (1865-1939), donated $2,800,000 to establish the MAYO FOUNDATION FOR MEDICAL EDUCATION AND RESEARCH at ROCHESTER in affiliation with the University of MINNESOTA.

MAYO, William Worrell. (Manchester, England (1819—1911). Pioneering doctor. Mayo was the leading physician and surgeon in Minnesota in the late 1800s. He was one of the first doctors to use a microscope to diagnosis disease. When a tornado struck ROCHESTER, Minnesota, in 1883, Mayo was placed in charge of the emergency hospital. He was assisted by the Sisters of St. Francis who were so impressed by his work that they offered to build a hospital if he would direct its work. In 1889 Mayo and his two sons, William James (1861-1939) and Charles Horace (1865-1939), started the now famed MAYO CLINIC at St. Mary's Hospital. Much of their success came about through Dr. William Mayo's unusual administrative ability, his ability to attract the best young doctors to his practice and his never-ending zeal in keeping up with everything new in the health sciences.

MAYTAG, Frederick Lewis. (Elgin, IL, July 14, 1857—Newton, IA, Mar. 26, 1937). Manufacturer. At one time NEWTON, Iowa, produced half of all the washing machines manufacturered in the U.S. The city still calls itself the "Washing Machine Capital of the World." Frederick L., the senior Maytag, converted his implement business into a factory in 1907 to manufacture hand operated washing machines, designed by Howard Snyder. Four years later the men attached a motor to their machine, introducing the motorized washing machine. With the invention by Snyder of the aluminum tub in 1922, the company took a position of leadership in the industry. Frederick's son took over the company management in 1926 and continued its research and promotion. In 1948 the company produced the first automatic washer and continued to be a leading manufacturer of major appliances.

MAZZUCHELLI, Samuel Charles. (Milan, Italy, Nov. 4, 1806—Dubuque, IA, Feb. 23, 1864). Italian missionary and architect. The Dominican priest was ordered to MACKINAC ISLAND as the sole permanant priest in the upper GREAT LAKES region. At GREEN BAY, Wisconsin, he founded the only Catholic school in Wisconsin and continued his mission work among the Indians. Moving to GALENA, Illinois, about 1835, he founded more than twenty churches, including those at Galena, BURLINGTON and DAVENPORT in Iowa. As an architect, he designed all his churches, including St. Raphael's Church at DUBUQUE, Iowa, and helped to lay the mortar for the latter with his own hands. It is thought that he drew the plans for the territorial capitol at IOWA CITY, which is now used as the administration building for the University of IOWA. This structure is considered among the most handsome in the state. In 1864 he died of pneumonia, brought on by overwork in caring for the sick.

MC CORMICK PLACE. A complex of three enormous connected halls, McCormick Place on the lakeshore at CHICAGO, Illinois, offers the country's largest indoor exhibit area, with a total of more than 1,600,000 square feet of exhibit space, along with a wide variety of other halls on eight levels. The complex includes restaurants of many sizes and types to accommodate a total number of visitors and exhibitors, the largest anywhere. There are seventy-six meeting halls of varying sizes, all fully equipped for meetings of a wide variety. The complex also boasts one of the country's largest theaters and several theaters of smaller size.

MC CORMICK, Cyrus Hall. (Rockbridge Co., VA, Feb. 15,1809—Chicago, IL, May 13, 1884). Inventor and philanthropist. He developed the first successful mechanical reaper (1831), which became the basis of all grain harvesting machines that followed. He set up his first factory in CHICAGO in 1847 under the management of his brothers. McCormick also gave liberally to McCormick Theological Seminary (Presbyterian school founded in 1829 at Hanover, Indiana, and moved to Chicago in 1859). It took his name after his death. McCormick engaged in real estate, mining, and railroading. The McCormick Company and the Deering Company combined in 1902 to form International Harvester, under McCormick's son, Cyrus, Jr.

MC CUTCHEON, John T. (South Raub, Tippecanoe County, IN, May 6, 1870—Lake Forest, IL; June 10, 1949). Cartoonist. McCutcheon's first political cartoon work occurred in the presidential campaign of 1896. He went to the Chicago *Tribune* in 1903. Through the rest of his career he traveled the world, in peace visiting the Gobi, the Amazon valley and other exotic spots and in war covering the Boer conflict and the Mexican revolution of 1914 among others. He also attempted to cover many events personally, such as the Atlantic crossing of the *Graf Zepplin* in 1935. His cartoons reflected his extraordinary background. McCutcheon won the Pulitzer prize for cartoons in 1931. He wrote *Cartoons by McCutcheon* (1903), *Bird Center Cartoons* (1904), *The Mysterious Stranger and Other Cartoons* (1905). The *Tribune* has continued to reprint McCutcheon's "Indian Summer" cartoon on an annual basis, believing it to be typical of the Midwest heritage.

MC GUFFEY, William Holmes. (Claysville, PA, Sept. 23, 1800— Charlottesville, VA, May 4, 1873). Educator, author. While active in Ohio education, Mc Guffey began to write a series of books which have probably sold more copies than those of any other author. His six-volume *Eclectic Readers* are estimated to have sold 122,000,000 copies and are still being sold and used in the schools. They were the standard reading texts in almost every school in the country during the last half of the nineteenth century, shaping the minds of three generations of school children. While attending Washington and Jefferson College at Washington, Pennsylvania, McGuffey taught in rural schools. Upon graduating in 1826, he became professor of languages at MIAMI UNIVERSITY, OXFORD, Ohio. He then became president of Cincinnati College in 1836, when his first and second readers were published. From 1839 to 1843 he served as president of OHIO UNIVERSITY at ATHENS, then as professor of philosophy at Woodward College in CINCINNATI, by which time five of the readers had been published. His last reader was published in 1857 when he was professor of moral philosophy at the University of Virginia. He was instrumental in the formation of the Ohio public school system. His home at Oxford, Ohio, has been restored as the Mc Guffey Museum.

MC INTYRE, Oscar Odd. (Plattsburg, MO, Feb. 18, 1884—New York, NY, Feb. 14, 1938). McIntyre was one of the nation's most noted

Mc Kinley

columnists. His "New York Day by Day" was syndicated in 550 newspapers. McIntyre began his career in journalism as a feature writer for the East Liverpool, Missouri, *Tribune* from 1904 to 1905. He became a political writer and then managing editor of the DAYTON, Ohio, *Herald* in 1906. He was the telegraph editor, city editor and assistant manager for the CINCINNATI *Post* for four years, beginning in 1907, then went to New York, where his column "brought Broadway to Main Street."

MC KINLEY, William. (Niles, OH, Jan. 29, 1843—Sept. 14, 1901), twenty-fifth President of the United States. McKinley was educated at Poland, Ohio, seminary and at Allegheny College, Meadville, Pennsylvania. He served with distinction in the CIVIL WAR and returned to Ohio, practicing law at CANTON. He was elected to the House of Representative as a Republican in 1876 and served there until 1891, except for a part of a term when his election was disputed by a Democratic House.

McKinley was in favor of protective tariffs, which he considered good policy for the country. As the chairman of the House Ways and Means Committee, McKinley was largely responsible for the tariff act which carried his name—the McKinley Tariff Act of 1890. The high tariffs proved unpopular and an Ohio backlash cost him his seat in the House of Representatives.

However, he had meanwhile attracted the attention of the Ohio political power Marcus Hanna, and under his guidance McKinley was elected governor of Ohio in 1891 and 1893.

At a specially built auditorium in ST. LOUIS,

William Mc Kinley.

Missouri, June 16-18, 1896, the Republican convention met to pick a candidate. Hanna's masterful handling of the Republican nomination resulted in McKinley's selection as the presidential candidate on the first ballot. Hanna's equally masterful campaign and some division in the Democratic party helped put McKinley in the White House. His quiet campaign was conducted from his home in Canton and was called the "front porch campaign." McKinley was the first candidate for president to use the telephone in his campaign. From Canton he made calls to thirty-eight of his campaign managers in their respective states, on matters concerning the handling of the campaign.

The early part of his presidency was relatively uneventful, but many domestic programs were overshadowed by the growing popular concern over Spanish actions in Cuba and elsewhere. McKinley tried to avoid the war pressures but finally turned the matter over to a Congress enthusiastic for war.

However, McKinley proved to be an able war president during the SPANISH AMERICAN WAR (1898). The war was brief, and Mc Kinley found his country at the threshold of world power. Recognizing this fact, he was the architect of the policies which acquired and governed the new territories coming under U.S. jurisdiction. On July 7, 1898, he signed the bill annexing Hawaii. The Treaty of Paris, signed December 10, 1898, freed Cuba and ceded Guam, Puerto Rico and the Philippines to the U.S. Spain was paid $20,000,000 for the Philippines. Two months later Filipino insurgents began their guerrilla warfare against the U.S., in an unsuccessful campaign to win their independence. On December 2, 1899, American Samoa was acquired by treaty, completing the American "empire." In another foreign relations field, McKinley supported the open door policy in China, taking every advantage of U.S. interests.

Reelected in 1900, his term had scarcely begun when he went to Buffalo, New York, to open the world's fair there. After his speech at the opening ceremonies on September 6, 1901, he stood in a reception line and was holding out his hand to a man wearing a bandage on his hand, when the man shot the president from a gun hidden beneath the bandage. The assassin was anarchist Leon Czolgosz. Czolgosz was tried by the New York Supreme Court, convicted and electrocuted on October 29, 1901.

The president lingered for nine days and died on the fourteenth of the month. McKinley had been greatly admired for his quiet efficiency, for his integrity and faultless private life. He was greatly mourned.

McKinley was the seventh child in a family of nine children. At the age of thirty, on January 25, 1871, he married Ida Saxton McKinley, a native of Canton. They had two children and were married 30 years, until his death. Ida McKinley had been an invalid for many years, suffering from epileptic seizures. The president was well known for his affection for his wife and for the tender care he gave her. She survived him for more than five years.

In 1907 a splendid memorial to McKinley was dedicated at Canton. A bronze statue of the president shows him as he was making his last speech, at Buffalo. The funds for the memorial were raised by public subscription.

MC MANUS, George. (St. Louis, MO, Jan. 23, 1884—Beverly Hills, CA, Oct. 22, 1954). Cartoonist. McManus created the famous comic strip "Bringing Up Father," featuring Maggie and Jiggs. His comic series included "Let George Do It," "The Newly Weds and Their Baby, Snookums," and "Bringing Up Father." The "Bringing Up Father" strip, featuring his two most famous characters, appeared in over seven hundred papers around the world in twenty-seven langues. McManus was awarded an honorary tribute in the *Congressional Record* of January 26, 1932, and received the Award of Honor from the National Father's Day Committee in 1940.

MENASHA, Wisconsin. City (pop. 54,952). One of the twin cities always linked closely together as Neenah-Menasha. They lie on each side of the two channels through which Lake WINNEBAGO drains into the FOX RIVER of the north, in east central Wisconsin. The name Menasha is Indian and probably means "island." The two cities were settled at about the same time, but they are substantially different. Menasha has been traditionally the community of small neat homes of Irish, Scandinavian and Polish factory workers. Neenah is a city of more substantial wealth. The region was occupied by the MENOMINEE, FOX and WINNEBAGO Indians when the first missionaries and traders arrived. Doty Island, in the lake between the towns, was the home of the noted Indian woman Ho-po-ko-ekaw (Glory of the Morning), who was the heroine of W. E. Leonard's poetic drama *Glory of the Morning*. The island is divided between the two cities. In 1843 Harrison Reed bought land on which the two communities now stand. After a quarrel with his partner, Reed was ousted from Neenah and founded Menasha. He was awarded the water power rights, and Menasha became the industrialized twin. A wooden pail factory was established in 1849 and the city was noted as the best market for hardwood in the area. Pulp and paper products came to the region about 1870, and today the region is one of the world's largest producers of a vast array of paper-based materials. Smith Park features a monument to Jean NICOLET (1598-1642) who came to the area in 1634, trying to arrange peace among the Indian tribes

MENDOTA, Lake. One of the two lakes which bisect MADISON, Wisconsin, and provide for the state's capital a unique location among American capitals. On the shores of sparkling Lake Mendota, most prominent is the main campus of the vast University of WISCONSIN. Across a wing of the lake to the north is Governor Nelson State Park. Farther along the shore is Mendota Mental Health Center. On the east bank is the governor's mansion and the community of Maple Bluff. Between the two lakes is the Civic Center and downtown Madison.

MENDOTA, Minnesota. Town (pop. 219), suburb of MINNEAPOLIS-ST. PAUL, Dacotah word for "where the waters mingle," place where the MISSISSIPPI RIVER is joined by the MINNESOTA, site of the first permanent white settlement in Minnesota. Mendota, known until 1837 as St. Peter's, offered a gathering spot for trappers and traders and in 1834 became the headquarters for Henry H. SIBLEY (1811-1891) of the AMERICAN FUR COMPANY. Sibley, known as the "Squire of Mendota," built the first stone house west of the Mississippi in Mendota in 1836. The home, known as the "Mount Vernon of Minnesota," was the place where Alexander Ramsey issued the proclamation which officially recognized Minnesota as a territory. St. Peter's Catholic Church, built in 1853, is the oldest church in continuous use in Minnesota. The importance of the town declined with the end of the fur trade. The Sibley House has been restored and outfitted with period furnishings. Faribault House is next door and offers displays of Indian relics.

MENOMINEE INDIANS. Tribe of Indians who lived in UPPER MICHIGAN and Wisconsin. Once in possession of over nine million acres, the Menominee lived by hunting and gathering wild plants. The term menominee means, "wild rice people." The Menominee gathered wild rice by shaking the ripe grain into their canoes. Treaties between the Indians and the United States government limited the Menominee to a reservation of 235,000 acres. In 1953 the government began a policy called termination in which federal support and protection of certain reservation Indians was ended. The Menominee reservation was eliminated in 1961. Termination caused economic hardship and the Menominee campaigned to have the policy reversed. In 1973 tribal rights and status were returned and the reservation was re-established in 1975.

MERAMEC RIVER (Missouri). Waterway originating in south central Missouri, just east of SALEM. It flows north, northeast, and southeast for 210 miles to empty into the MISSISSIPPI RIVER, about 20 miles south of ST. LOUIS.

MERCHANDISING. Midwest merchants must rank among the most original and numerous anywhere. The modern concept of the department store developed in CHICAGO, Illinois, through the pioneering work of Marshall FIELD (1834-1906). Field promoted the idea of a single giant store where merchandise of almost every type would be sold in departments. He insisted that his store should "Give the Lady What She Wants," and if the buyer was not satisfied, the merchandise could be returned with the money refunded, a novel idea for the time. Pioneers in the great mail order business included A. Montgomery WARD (1843-1913), and Richard SEARS (1863-1914) of Chicago, and William "Bill" GALLOWAY (1877-1952) of WATER-LOO, Iowa. Michigan contributed Joseph L. HUDSON (1846-1912), who founded the state's largest department store, and Harry Gordon SELFRIDGE (1857?-1947). Selfridge gave American merchants an international flavor by founding London's largest department store. George Nelson Dayton built his giant department store operation in MINNEAPOLIS. The Dayton and Hudson operations were merged in recent years to form another giant Midwest merchandising complex. The GIMBEL FAMILY began merchandising in VINCENNES, Indiana, in 1889, spread to MILWAUKEE, Wisconsin, then rapidly expanded until in 1930 Gimbel Brothers was the world's largest department store chain. It has since undergone several consolidations.

MEREDITH, Edwin Thomas, Sr. (Avoca, IA, Dec. 23, 1876—Des Moines, IA, June 17, 1928). Founder of the Meredith Publishing

Company of DES MOINES, Meredith started in the publishing business with a wedding gift from his grandfather of the magazine *The Farmer's Tribune.* He sold it and bought another magazine, *Successful Farming* (1902). His well-established policies to "provide useful information to farmers in the form of articles that help them farm better, earn more and live a happier life" set the tone of the publishing operation. To this he added his jingle, "No piffle, no passion, no fiction, no fashion." By 1914 *Successful Farming* had become the most successful of all farm journals. In 1922, Meredith began to publish *Fruit, Garden, and Home,* which became Better Homes and Gardens. Meredith served as Secretary of Agriculture from 1913 to 1920 in President Wilson's cabinet and also was president of the Associated Advertising Clubs of the World. The company he founded has expanded to include other magazine titles, radio, television, very substantial book publishing and other fields. It is one of the few publishing houses on the *Fortune* 500 list.

MESABI RANGE. When discovered, held the largest concentration of iron ore deposits in the world. As early as the 1700s the early missionaries and explorers traveling through Minnesota may have suspected the presence of iron ore. Gold and copper were the pursuits of these men, however. The region was drawn on Joseph Nicollet's 1741 map and labeled "Missabay Heights." "Missabay" was an OJIBWAY word meaning "giant" or "big man hills" referring to a ridge of land that divides the drainage between Hudson Bay and Lake SUPERIOR. The first iron deposits were discovered at Lake Vermilion in 1865 by Leonidas MERRITT and his six brothers after twenty years of searching. Red earth into which their wagon sank one day was analyzed and found to be sixty-four percent pure iron. Unlike the deep veins that required vertical shafts to be mined, the Mesabi deposits were layered horizontally near the surface enabling them to be mined in huge open pits. Ore taken from this location tested fifty percent iron. The financial panic of 1893 destroyed the Merritts, and by 1900 control of the mineral deposits in the Mesabi Range passed into the hands of the giant steel companies. In the 1940s the Mesabi mines supplied one-third of the world's iron ore. Now depleted of its rich deposits, the area supplies TACONITE, a low-grade iron of twenty to thirty percent purity.

METEOR, (Estherville, Iowa). One of the

largest and most spectacular meteors of the time exploded in the air near ESTHERVILLE, Iowa, in 1879. Buildings shook and glass broke for miles around. The explosion created three major pieces. The largest rammed into the earth, gouging a depression fifteen feet deep and twelve feet wide at the top. This piece, weighing several hundred pounds, was retrieved and sold to the British Museum of Natural History. The University of MINNESOTA museum bought the second largest piece, weighing about 150 pounds. The third is no longer accounted for. Thousands of smaller pieces were scattered over the landscape, and hundreds of souvenir hunters held "meteor picnics," looking for the scraps. A local metalsmith was kept busy making rings from the metallic scrap.

METZ, Christian. (Neuwied, Prussia, Dec. 30, 1794—Amana, IA, July 27, 1867). Leader of the Community of True Inspiration. Metz and his followers from New York State settled in Iowa on 26,000 acres in 1854 and founded the AMANA Colonies. Metz had been a leader of the Community of True Inspiration in Prussia from 1823 to 1842. He believed God wanted the Inspirationists to move westward to find a home in America. In 1842 he came to America with a group and after three months of searching organized an Inspiration community near Buffalo, New York, that lasted from 1842 to 1854. Lack of sufficient land brought Metz and three men westward again. In 1854 they chose the Iowa site near the IOWA RIVER in present-day Iowa County. A good supply of timber along the waterways, and substantial stands of walnut, promised sufficient building and fuel supplies. Limestone, sandstone, and clay for bricks were natural resources in addition to the rich Iowa black soil. The Amana colonies became the most successful of all such communal experiments in the U.S., and today these communities provide one of the leading tourist attractions among the smaller cities of the Midwest.

MEXICAN WAR. Much of the Midwest was still unsettled frontier when the United States went to war with Mexico in 1846. Frontiersmen are generally daring and love excitement, so the Midwest sent volunteers to the war in numbers far beyond the percentage of population of the various Midwest states, especially those from the western section of the region. One of America's most interesting warriors received his baptism of fire when he began military service at the age of nineteen and fought in Mexico. This was Indiana's Lew WALLACE (1827-1905), who enjoyed four wholly different careers, including that of a general in the CIVIL WAR and of being one of the best-known writers. Missourians made up most of the Army of the West. Missouri's Alexander William DONIPHAN (1808-1887) organized the Missouri Mounted Volunteers, then led them on what many authorities have considered one of the most brilliant long marches in military history. During the course of twelve months they covered 3,600 miles by land and 2,000 miles by water. Doniphan and his forces subdued the area of Santa Fe, New Mexico, then went on to conquer Chihuahua in Mexico. They marched back and forth across Mexico, winning many skirmishes. When their enlistment term was over, they sailed down the Rio Grande River and went home, completing one of the nation's most famous military expeditions.

MIAMI AND ERIE CANAL. Extending from CINCINNATI to DAYTON, Ohio, and extended later to TOLEDO. The canal was begun in the summer of 1825 with elaborate ceremonies and was partially opened in 1827. It was completed in 1845. The 813 miles of canal gave agriculture and the infant industries of Ohio many markets, attracted thousands of immigrants to the state, tremendously increased all kinds of traffic, connected interior Ohio with New York and the Atlantic coast markets and the markets of the deep South, and through all these channels reached foreign trading centers. For almost thirty years the canal system carried freight in line-boats and passengers in packets. With a crew of a captain, two drivers for the animals on the banks, two steersmen and a cook, the packets proceeded at a leisurely three miles per hour. Passengers slept on shelves three feet wide, on straw-stuffed mattresses and pillows. When the packets were crowded, many were forced to sleep on tables or floor. Sometimes the heavily laden barges would race each other, with the drivers spurring on the mules along the tow paths. With the coming of the RAILROADS, the canal was used less and less and gradually was deserted for other quicker means of transportation.

MIAMI CONFEDERACY. Miami Indians and allied tribes which fought against U.S. troops in the Ohio Valley Indian wars of the 1790s. Led by LITTLE TURTLE (1752-1812) the Indians won many battles, but were defeated by General Anthony WAYNE at the Battle of FALLEN TIMBERS in 1794.

MIAMI INDIANS. Algonquian tribe which moved from the GREEN BAY, Wisconsin, area in the mid-17th century to much of the Midwest area south of the GREAT LAKES. The Miami were divided into bands called the WEA, Piankashaw, Pepicokia, Atchatchakangouen, Kilatika and Mengakonkia. The latter three combined and were known as the Miami proper, or Crane Band. The Pepicokia were absorbed by the Wea and Piankashaw or acted as separate tribes and had their own tribal councils by 1818. The political structure of the Miami was well organized and based on the clan system. Each person inherited his clan through his father, and marriage within a clan was forbidden. A village chief was elected from a council of chiefs of each of the clans. Delegates from the village council attended the band council which sent delegates to the tribal council. Clan, village, band and tribal chiefs were chosen on the basis of merit and enjoyed great respect and authority. Meetings were held in a council house. Houses were constructed of poles covered by rush mats. The Miami believed in many spirits called manito. The sun was considered the supreme deity. The Miami had a Midewiwin or Grand Medicine Society made up of priests with special magical powers for curing. There were lesser shamans who cured with medicinal herbs and roots. The two most important festivals were held in honor of the fall harvest and the return from the winter hunt. Festivals called for games, feasting, dancing and music. Burial customs included entombment in hollowed out logs, on scaffolds or in sealed log cabins. Village life was stable, based primarily on agriculture. The Miami were recognized for growing a superior type of corn. They also grew pumpkins, squash and melons. About 1650 the Miami fled beyond the MISSISSIPPI to escape IROQUOIS war parties. Conflict with the SIOUX soon brought them back to Wisconsin. By 1669 some of the Miami were settled at the mouth of the ST. JOSEPH RIVER in southwestern Michigan. The Miami entered into a loose trade alliance with the French by 1683. The French negotiated a peace treaty between the Miami and Iroquois in 1701. By 1712 the Miami in Michigan moved to the headwaters of the MAUMEE in Ohio to escape the POTAWATOMI. The Miami fought to prevent the flood of whites from entering the Ohio Valley, but by 1763 had given up most of their Ohio lands and moved to Indiana. In 1790-1791 the Miami and allied tribes inflicted several defeats on the Americans, but the defeat at the Battle of FALLEN TIMBERS in 1794 crushed their resist-

ance. By 1827 most of their lands had been taken from them and some members were beginning to move to Kansas. After the CIVIL WAR the various bands in Kansas were moved to the Quapaw Reservation in Indian Territory, now Oklahoma.

MIAMI RIVER (or Greater Miami). Begins near Indian Lake in northwest Ohio and flows for 160 miles, past Sidney, PIQUA, Troy, DAYTON and Hamilton, to empty into the OHIO RIVER at the border with Indiana. The MIAMI AND ERIE CANAL connected the upper Miami with Lake ERIE at TOLEDO and provided one of the great early transportation links. In later years a series of dams offered large-scale flood control. With a length of 95 miles, the Little Miami River rises southeast of SPRINGFIELD and generally flows parallel to the Miami, until it reaches the Ohio River at CINCINNATI.

MIAMI UNIVERSITY. The establishment of Miami university at OXFORD, Ohio, was ordered by the state legislature in 1809. Joel Collins, a surveyor, guided the committee in selection of the site, and the university opened formally in the fall of 1824. Dormitory room rent was five dollars per year, including a servant. Robert Bishop, the first president, a Scot, thought a bell was a sinful extravagance, so the hours were marked by the notes of a bugle. Many influential people have been connected with the university. William Holmes MC GUFFEY (1800-1873) compiled his first *Eclectic Readers* there, and the Confederate Mc Guffey Societies long convened at Oxford every year. Three national fraternities, Beta Theta Pi, Phi Delta Theta and Sigma Chi had their beginnings at the university. The Oxford College for Women flourished for eighty years before it was absorbed by the university. Today's student body of 15,466 is instructed by a faculty of 824.

MICHIGAMEA INDIANS. One of the six related groups living in present Illinois, who were known collectively as ILLINI and who gave the state its name. The Michigamea were found generally in southern Illinois and in Missouri.

MICHIGAN. State, situated as the most northeasterly of the Midwest states. Its borders are among the more complex. As the only state touching four of the five GREAT LAKES, Michigan has water boundaries with five states and one nation. It has no land connection with neighbors Illinois and Minnesota nor with neighboring Canada. The Illinois border is found toward the middle of Lake MICHIGAN, while the Minnesota border rests in the waters of Lake SUPERIOR.

The tortuous border with Canada begins with the outlet of the DETROIT RIVER in Lake ERIE, then wanders through Lake ST. CLAIR, and then through the ST. CLAIR RIVER to Lake HURON which it also shares with Canada. Then it passes up the ST. MARYS RIVER and canal into vast Lake SUPERIOR, where it bends far enough north to enclose ISLE ROYALE before reaching the end of the border with Canada at the water border with Minnesota. Michigan's longest borders with Wisconsin are placed within lakes Michigan and Superior. It shares the western tip of Lake Erie with Ohio.

Short land borders separate Michigan from Ohio and Indiana to the south, while the tip of the UPPER PENINSULA has a southern land boundary with Wisconsin. The Upper and Lower peninsulas are entirely separated by water, making it the only state with such a division. Until Alaska became a state, Michigan had the longest shoreline of all the states. Now it ranks second, with Great Lakes shores stretching for 3,121 miles.

More than 11,000 lakes are found in interior Michigan. The St. Clair and St. Marys are really straits, although they bear the names of rivers. Michigan has no major interior rivers, but among other rivers are the SAGINAW, BLACK, ST. JOSEPH and Tahquamenon.

Michigan's peculiar geography also provides many individual eccentricities. PORT HURON, Michigan, lies as far to the east as Greenville, South Carolina. The distance across Michigan from DETROIT to HOUGHTON is greater than from Detroit to "far off" Baltimore. Parts of the "northern neighbor," Canada lie to the south of most of Michigan.

If its exterior water areas in the Great Lakes are considered, Michigan is the largest state east of the MISSISSIPPI RIVER. Including the exterior water, Michigan has a total area of 96,791 square miles. Land area, alone, totals 57,022 square miles. Considering land area only, Michigan is second in size to Minnesota, in the Midwest region.

Of course, the vast extent of its exterior and interior fresh water is the outstanding physical characteristic of Michigan. The proportion of water to land is the greatest for any similar area anywhere.

Weather-wise, each of the four well-defined seasons is tempered by the Great Lakes. Minimum January temperatures in the Upper Peninsula average from zero to ten above, ten to twenty in the lower. In the Upper Peninsula, maximum average temperatures never exceed 80 degrees, 90 in most of the Lower.

In geology the westernmost Upper Peninsula is classified as Pre-cambrian, the rest of the state as Late Paleozoic. The glacial ages enveloped almost the entire area of the present state. However, the copper-bearing rocks near HOUGHTON are considered to rank among the oldest of all the world's rock formations, unchanged almost from the beginning of time. Throughout the rest of the state, the lakes and the Great Lakes are legacies of the glaciers.

The rugged shoreline of the Upper Peninsula and its vast forest cover contrast sharply with the lake-covered flatlands and the rounded dune shores of most of the rest of the state.

The water resources of the state are followed closely by minerals and forests as natural assets. The resources of iron ore and copper have proven to be invaluable, while the supplies of salt could meet the entire world's requirements for centuries. MANISTEE is the world's largest salt producer, and Dow Chemical Company is one of the largest processors of a variety of chemicals from salt brines.

At one time, Michigan produced more timber than any other state, until the supplies of the best woods were almost exhausted. By that time, Michigan forests had produced more wealth than all the gold of California. The lumbering industry has made a comeback due to careful conservation, and the state still produces about 43 million board feet each year.

Michigan is one of the world's manufacturing giants, still leading the world in automobile production, furniture manufacture and processed breakfast foods. The state ranks fourth among the states in income from manufacturing and holds the same rank in export of manufactured products. BATTLE CREEK rules the breakfast world with both of the largest breakfast food processors, one started by W. Keith KELLOGG (1860-1951) and the other by C. W. POST (1854-1914).

In addition to automobiles, Michigan produces the most automobile parts and leads the states as well in engines, trailers, boats, office equipment and refrigerators. Stove and furnace production is also important. ALPENA boasts the largest cement manufacturing plant in the world, and GRINDSTONE CITY continues its near monopoly of natural grindstone production. In a more exotic field, COLON is the world center of magic products manufacture. Baby food, booster rockets, guided-missile destroyers, com-

Michigan

Counties and County Seats

© Facts On File, Inc. 1984

Michigan

STATE OF MICHIGAN

Name: Indian words Michi Gama, meaning Great Lake

Nickname: Wolverine State

Capital: Lansing

Motto: Si Quaeris Peninsulam Amoenam Circumspice (If you Seek a Pleasant Peninsula, Look About You)

Symbols and Emblems:
Bird: Robin
Flower: Apple Blossom
Tree: White Pine
Stone: Petoskey Stone
Fish: Trout
Song: "Michigan, My Michigan"

Population:
1985: 9,088,000
Rank: 8th
Density: 160 per sq. mi. of land
Percent Urban: 70.7% (1980)
Gain or Loss (1970-80): + 308,000
Projection (1980-2000): -50,000

Racial and Ethnic makeup (1980):
White: 85%
Black: 13%
Hispanic: 162,000 persons
Indian: 40,000 persons
Others: 150,800 persons

Largest City:
Detroit (1,089,000 - 1984)

Other Cities:
Grand Rapids (183,000 - 1984)
Warren (152,000 - 1984)
Flint (149,000 - 1984)
Lansing (128,000 - 1984)
Sterling Heights (109,000 - 1984)
Ann Arbor (104,000 - 1984)

Area: 58,216 Sq. mi.
Rank: 23rd

Highest Point: 1,979 Ft. Mount Arvon

Lowest Point: 527 ft. Lake Erie

H.S. Completed: 68% (1980)

Four Yrs. College Completed: 14.3% (1980)

STATE GOVERNMENT

ELECTED OFFICIALS (4 year terms, expiring Jan. 1991):
GOVERNOR: $81,900 (1985)
LT. GOV.: $56,175 (1985)
SEC. OF STATE: $75,000 (1985)

GENERAL ASSEMBLY:
Meetings: Annually at Lansing
Salary: $34,860 per annum plus $6,700 expense allowance (1985)
Senate: 38 members
House: 110 members

Congressional REPRESENTATIVES
U.S. Senate: Terms expire 1989, 1991
U.S. House of Representatives: Eighteen

puter and avionic products are among the 2,200 different manufactures of the state.

Steam-driven automobiles appeared in Michigan as early as 1884. A gasoline car was driven in Detroit by Charles G. King as early as 1896. Henry FORD (1863-1947) was one of the first Michigan men to successfully manufacture an auto in Detroit, and of course he went on to become one of the world's most notable industrialists, beginning most successfully with the first Model T in 1906. Even before this, Ransom E. OLDS (1864-1950) had produced 5,000 Oldsmobiles in 1904. The giant General Motors Corporation was formed in 1908. It was not until 1925 that Walter P. CHRYSLER (1875-1940) put together the third of the giant automakers, vastly enlarged a short time later by takeover of the successful Dodge company after the death of the DODGE brothers (John Francis, 1864-1920, and Horace Elgin, 1868-1920). Despite some dispersion of the industry, Michigan still produces more than eighty percent of the automobiles made in the United States.

Other aspects of transportation also have a dramatic history in Michigan. The first canal at the SOO was built in 1797. A major canal was opened there "in the wilderness" in 1855. Today the locks can handle 700-foot freighters, and the canal carries more traffic than any other canal in the world. The Detroit River is the busiest waterway of its type anywhere, and the ST. LAWRENCE SEAWAY opened Michigan ports to ocean traffic in 1959.

In spite of its leadership in manufacturing, world competition has brought major headaches to Michigan auto makers. The consequent slump in the economy produced a drop in population from the peak of 9,266,000 in 1979 to 9,088,000 in 1985. Population projections for the year 2000 indicate a population of 9,208,-000.

Black residents make up about twelve percent of the total population. Other races, including the American Indian, make up less than one percent.

About the time that workers of ancient Egypt and Sudan were fashioning copper objects, ancient peoples of present Michigan also were producing objects from that metal, their work found in the 10,000 prehistoric copper mining pits on Isle Royale. Little is known about these people, nor have many archeological discoveries been made in the state concerning earlier or later people of prehistoric times.

By the time European explorers reached present Michigan, the native peoples had regressed to the stone age, working exclusively with stone instruments. These peoples then included the OTTAWA, OJIBWAY (or Chippewa), POTAWATOMI, MENOMINEE and MIAMI. Somewhat later came the HURON. As the IROQUOIS Indians were driven from their eastern homes by European settlement, they in turn drove out most of the resident groups of Indians from the Lower Peninsula.

The earliest explorers came from French Canada to the east. Etienne BRULE (1592?-1632?) and his companion, Grenoble, apparently were the first Europeans to reach present Michigan, perhaps as early as 1618, no later than 1622. In 1634 explorer Jean NICOLET (1598-1642) may have reached and passed Michigan on his way to Green Bay. Other explorers, fur traders and Catholic missionaries followed. In 1668 famed missionary explorer, Father Jacques MARQUETTE (1637-1675), founded the first permanent European settlement in the entire Midwest on the banks of the Soo.

French trappers, called "COUREURS DU BOIS" and boatmen, known as "VOYAGEURS," along with missionaries attempting to convert the Indians, continued in the French territories, but few settlers came in. As early as 1689 British settlements along the coast had a population of more than 300,000, while scarcely more than 20,000 peopled all the French holdings in North America west of the East Coast.

Finally alarmed at this disparity, the French took some action. The famed exploration of Marquette and JOLLIET (1645-1700) began at ST. IGNACE, and ended back in Michigan. Father Marquette died near LUDINGTON on another trip. Explorer-colonizer LA SALLE (1643-1687) built the first French fort in Michigan at what is now ST. JOSEPH and called it FORT MIAMI. FORT ST. JOSEPH was next, started near present PORT HURON in 1686 by Daniel Greysolon (DULUTH) (1636-1710).

Most notable of all was the action in 1701 of Antoine de la Mothe CADILLAC (1658-1730), who founded Detroit in that year. Cadillac was a notable colonizer who deserves greater fame than having a car carrying his name. Detroit became the first major city to have been founded in the entire Midwest.

As more British began to poach in French preserves, the French continued to protest, setting up FORT MICHILIMACKINAC in 1715 in an effort to hold on to their claims. Periods of war and peace followed, until the French were driven from the continent in 1763. The Indians, disturbed by losing their French friends, attacked Detroit later that year, under their notable leader Chief PONTIAC (1720?-1769). The

175-day siege of Detroit was the longest in Indian warfare. Detroit did not fall, but every other fort in Michigan did capitulate to the Indians, in the period of their greatest success.

Nevertheless, the overwhelming white power finally won out; Pontiac made peace, and British control was secure for a short time. Then that control was threatened by the American Revolution. Lieutenant Governor Henry HAMILTON (-1796), the British commander at Detroit, was despised by settlers because he paid the Indians to bring back American scalps. He became known as the "Hair Buyer." Although the Treaty of Paris of 1783 ended the Revolution and gave the Americans nominal control of Michigan, the British continued to occupy Detroit for another thirteen years. Brilliant Revolutionary general, "Mad" Anthony WAYNE finally captured the western lands, which at last came under American control in 1794. General Wayne was hailed as a hero when he went to Detroit in 1796. He is widely remembered in Michigan with place names and names of institutions.

In one of history's memorable statutes, the NORTHWEST ORDINANCE, the infant America set up rules for governing new territories and guiding them toward statehood. Michigan became part of the NORTHWEST TERRITORY of Ohio, Indiana, Illinois, Wisconsin and portions of Minnesota.

In 1805 part of present Michigan became a separate territory, with a capital at Detroit. In that same year the capital city was almost entirely destroyed by FIRE. However, the new governor drew up plans for a larger and better city, based on the plans for Washington, D.C., and the city began the task of rebuilding.

Still not willing to give up the rich territory, during the WAR OF 1812 the British captured Detroit. After Oliver Hazard PERRY's (1785-1839) victory on Lake Erie in 1813, the Americans were able to retake Detroit in September of that year, but the British burned the public buildings before retreating.

Territorial governor, Lewis CASS (1782-1866), did much to promote the area, and with the coming of the first steamboat to Detroit in 1818, the region was set for surprising growth, as freight and passengers poured into Michigan ports. This traffic was encouraged by the opening of the Erie Canal in 1825, giving settlers and commercial interests an easy route to the entire Great Lakes region.

Before Michigan could become a state, a border quarrel with Ohio had to be settled. When Michigan gave up the disputed land, it settled for a much larger area of "worthless"

land, the Upper Peninsula. In the end Michigan gained greatly by losing this Border War.

Michigan was admitted as a state in January of 1837, being paired with Arkansas in order to keep the balance between free and slave states. As more settlers came in, various groups added diversity. The MORMON settlers on BEAVER ISLAND were led by "King" James Jesse STRANG (1813-1856), who ruled the island as an absolute monarch until assassinated in 1856. A far more peaceable group were the Dutch settlers who created a new HOLLAND in Michigan in 1847. In that same year the desolate area of LANSING was chosen as the new capital, the Capital in the Forest.

The slavery question brought strong Abolitionist sentiment to Michigan. At JACKSON, in 1854, an anti-slavery group founded a new political party attended by so many people that its convention had to be held outdoors in "The Convention Under the Oaks." This meeting has been called the founding of the Republican Party, but the claim is disputed.

Twenty-one Michigan regiments were formed during the first year of the CIVIL WAR. The Michigan cavalry brigade under General George Armstrong CUSTER (1839-1876) played a leading part in the victory at Gettysburg. At the end of the war, the Fourth Michigan Cavalry captured Confederate President Jefferson DAVIS (1808-1889). Of the small Michigan population, 15,000 lost their lives in battle and 10,000 died of disease as a result of the war.

The year 1871 was notable in Michigan for the same reason that it was notable in Illinois. However, the terrible fire that swept across parts of southwest Michigan on the same day as the great Chicago FIRE received little attention, although more people were killed in Michigan than in Chicago.

In 1885 Michigan workers won the fight for a ten-hour day, and this achievement may have helped to spur the growth of manufacturing which came about with the success of the automobile giants.

Before the U.S. entered WORLD WAR I, Michigan was known as a center of spy activity because of its location on the international border. As members of the 42nd Division, Michigan troops were among the first Americans to set foot on German soil during the war.

Michigan industry mushroomed during and after the war, but the state was one of the hardest hit during the depression beginning in 1929. That depression ended when Michigan factories began to build war supplies and equipment in anticipation of WORLD WAR II.

Altogether, Michigan produced one-eighth of all the country's war equipment, leading all the states by far. The Ford Motor Willow Run plant was able to produce a great B-24 bomber every hour. Because of its strategic importance, the security around SAULT STE. MARIE was the heaviest in the country

Michigan also contributed 673,000 men and women to armed services during the war. Michigan's Red Arrow Division became the first to meet the Japanese in World War II; its combat record of 654 days still stands.

In 1950, the first American unit to see action in the Korean War (1950-1953) was the Michigan National Guard.

In 1957 the divided state of Michigan was finally united with the completion of the great bridge, known affectionately as "Big Mac," over the STRAITS OF MACKINAC. Two years later, traffic from the oceans of the world began to flow under the bridge with the opening of the ST. LAWRENCE SEAWAY.

Much of central Detroit was destroyed by fire in the riots of 1967, but the city has done much rebuilding, including the massive Renaissance Center, a complex of hotel, offices and stores. However, Detroit and the whole state have suffered due to the increasing competition in the auto industry by the Japanese automakers. But the worst decline in auto sales during 1975 has been followed by considerable recovery.

On October 12, 1973, Michigan's own Gerald Rudolph FORD (1913-)became President of the United States. Ford received the majority Michigan vote in 1976 but lost to Jimmy Carter. Ronald REAGAN (1911-)captured the Michigan vote in the elections of 1980 and 1984, but Democratic Governor James J. Blanchard was elected in 1986.

One of America's most notable Americans has received little attention in general histories. Father Gabriel RICHARD (1767-1832) perhaps contributed more to the growth and well being of Detroit than any other single person in any other American city. His extraordinary devotion and activities carried him into every field of human endeavor. He died caring for the sick during the terrible epidemic of CHOLERA in 1832 and became known as "The Patron Saint of Detroit."

Another lesser known Michigan leader also deserves more fame. At the age of nineteen, Stevens T. MASON (1811-1843) became acting governor of Michigan Territory, the youngest in such a post in U.S. history. In 1835, Michigan elected him governor of the state when he was twenty-four, but he did not actually take that

office until two years later when Congress recognized Michigan as a state.

Another Michigan man to gain fame at an early age was George Armstrong Custer, who became the youngest general of the Civil War at age twenty-three.

Owosso native Thomas E. DEWEY (1902-1971) gained fame as Governor of New York and was twice defeated for the presidency, as the Republican candidate.

Michigan can probably claim more dominant personalities in business and industry than any other state. Merchandising magnates Sebastian S. KRESGE (1867-1966) of Detroit, Aaron Montgomery WARD (1843-1913) of NILES, Harry Gordon SELFRIDGE (1857?-1947) of Jackson, all founded great retail empires of widely varying types.

The names and histories of the automobile barons are known around the world. Henry Ford was the most prominent of all. His ideas completely changed American industry. He modernized the moving assembly line, paid his workers unbelievable wages for the time and was the first to develop the modern ideas of mass markets. He was so opposed to war that he fitted out a "Peace Ship" to travel to Europe in a vain hope of ending World War I. His philanthropies continue through the mammoth FORD FOUNDATION.

One of America's greatest popular heroes, Charles A. LINDBERGH (1902-1974), was born in Detroit. His solo flight to France in 1927 gave him vast world renown and acclaim. Another aviation pioneer was William B. STOUT (1880-1956), the great promoter of commercial aviation.

Michigan has been home to an unusual number of prominent entertainers, including Danny THOMAS (1914-), Stevie WONDER (1950-), Diana ROSS (1944-), Lily TOMLIN (1939-), Betty HUTTON (1920-) and Gilda Radner.

Michigan's greatest tourist attraction is its vast outdoors. The lofty dunes of the Lake Michigan shore are unique in the world, and ISLE ROYALE NATIONAL PARK is also the only one of its kind. The Upper Peninsula provides a wonderful wilderness area for exploration and relaxation.

The many lakes and streams provide contrast to the manufacturing cities.

In addition to the Renaissance Center, Detroit is noted for its Children's Museum, the International Institute of Folk art, Historical Museum and Institute of Arts. BELLE ISLE park is notable among the country's city parks.

DEARBORN has become a world center of

museums and restorations. The Henry Ford Museum provides one of the great concentrations of transportation displays. Nearby, in GREENFIELD VILLAGE, Henry Ford created a unique community. He acquired and installed in his village such attractions as the Edison Institute and Menlo Park compound of Thomas EDISON (1847-1931), along with more than a hundred other historic structures, brought in from around the country. The activities of an earlier period also are demonstrated at Greenfield Village.

Holland, Michigan, provides one of the major annual events of the country with its Tulip Festival, including pageants, floral parades and a collection of tulips not found outside of the mother country of Holland. Another Michigan floral attraction is the Leila Arboretum at BATTLE CREEK, ranked among the world's finest. Also at Battle Creek is the country's largest bird sanctuary, named for its founder W. K. Kellogg.

When the great capitol at Lansing was dedicated in 1879, it was one of the most advanced of its time, with a steam operated elevator and gas lights lit by electric switches.

GRAND RAPIDS, home city of President Gerald Ford is also home to the Gerald Ford Museum as well as the Public Museum, with the only collection of its kind dedicated to the world's furniture. MANISTEE boasts its great opera house, built by lumber baron T. J. Ramsdell. It is now used as a summer theater.

A tourist attraction in its own right, Big Mac bridge looms over another attraction, the restoration of old Fort Michilimackinac. On nearby MACKINAC ISLAND, old FORT MACKINAC still keeps guard. The island retains its country charm by banning motor vehicles and also boasts the world's largest summer hotel.

On the Upper Peninsula, the canal and locks of Sault Ste. Marie are major attractions, where tourists watch the greatest volume of shipping of any canal worldwide. Skiing is another attraction of the Upper Peninsula, and Porcupine Mountains State Park is the nation's largest recreational state park.

MICHIGAN CITY, Indiana.

City (pop. 36,850), northern Indiana resort city in the sand dune country on the southern edge of Lake MICHIGAN. Founded in 1823 as the northern terminal of the Michigan Road, Michigan City was once a greater lake port than CHICAGO, Illinois. The lumber industry peaked in 1884, but Michigan City continues to produce hats,

The Michigan Capitol at Lansing.

metal furniture, cough drops, and clothing. Visitors come to the area every summer on vacation. Charter boats are in peak demand as sportsmen from across the country seek prize catches of abundant coho and chinook salmon, steelhead, brown and lake trout from Lake Michigan. Barker Civic Center was the estate of John H. Barker, the founder of the Haskel-Barker Car Company. The charm of the 38-room mansion comes from its hand-carved marble fireplace, baroque ceilings, mirrored ballroom and Italianate garden. Band concerts are given on Thursday evenings in Washington Park and stage productions by a semiprofessional resident company may be seen at the Canterbury Theater.

MICHIGAN STATE FAIR. Detroit. Established in 1849, the Michigan State Fair is the oldest in the United States. The event is held annually in late August.

MICHIGAN STATE UNIVERSITY. Publically supported institution in EAST LANSING, Michigan. Founded in 1855 as a state institution, the first state agricultural college and one of the earliest of the Land Grant colleges, the university is located on 2,010 acres and has 386 buildings. It boasts the world's most precise cyclotron which is joined with a superconducting cyclotron constructed to work in tandem. The Beaumont Tower is said to mark the site of the first building in the country where agriculture was taught as a science. The Wharton Center for the Performing Arts was completed in 1982 at a cost of 20.1 million dollars. One of the largest and finest-equipped conference centers in the United States is located in the Kellogg Center for Continuing Education. University libraries contain three million volumes. During the 1985-1986 academic year the university enrolled 41,032 students and employed 2,622 faculty members.

MICHIGAN, LAKE. Covering 22,178 square miles, it is the third largest of the GREAT LAKES, the largest body of fresh water and the only one of the Great Lakes to lie wholly within the United States. The upper part of Lake Michigan separates most of the upper and lower peninsulas of Michigan. Illinois and Wisconsin form the western border and a small portion of Indiana touches the southern shore of the lake. Michigan lies along most of the eastern shore. Lake Michigan is connected to the MISSISSIPPI RIVER by the CHICAGO SANITARY AND SHIP CANAL and the ILLINOIS and CHICAGO rivers and to the Atlantic Ocean by way of the ST. LAWRENCE SEAWAY. Important ports on Lake Michigan include MILWAUKEE, GREEN BAY, and Port Washington, Wisconsin; GARY, Indiana; CHICAGO a n d WAUKEGAN, Illinois; and MUSKEGON, Michigan. Lake Michigan is the heir to the vast prehistoric Lake Chicago, formed by the melting glaciers. The prehistoric lake has left shelves of level land to mark its former shores.

MICHIGAN, UNIVERSITY OF. Publically supported institution established in 1817 by a legislative act sponsored by residents of Detroit. The university is said to be the first in the U.S. to be supported by a state. The present name has been used since 1921. The original campus was located on forty acres given to the university in ANN ARBOR. There are 200 major buildings on the 2,608-acre campus there. Over six million volumes are housed in the library system. The Dearborn Campus is located on 210 acres with six buildings on the former Fair Lane estate of Henry FORD. Undergraduate business administration and engineering students must participate in unpaid professional internships or the cooperative education plan. During the 1985-1986 academic year the Ann Arbor campus enrolled 34,340 students and employed 2,768 faculty members. The Flint

campus enrolled 5,672 students and employed 263 faculty members. The Dearborn campus enrolled 5,525 students and employed 311 faculty members.

MIDLAND, Michigan. City (pop. 73,578), seat of Midland County, northeast Michigan on the LOWER PENINSULA near Saginaw Bay. Midland is the home of the Dow Chemical Company. Midland could have become just another ex-lumber town had it not been for the experiments of Dr. Herbert H. DOW (1866-1930) who found ways of extracting bromine and other chemicals from the salt brine so plentiful there and in other regions of Michigan. Dow organized the Midland Chemical Company in 1890 which became Dow Chemical. Records of geologists involved in brine well drillings were used by scientists of the oil industry to uncover deposits of petroleum. The first oil was produced locally in 1928, further adding to the prosperity of the region. Midland Center for the Arts has historical exhibits, musicals and films. The sciences and arts are represented in hands-on displays in the Hall of Ideas. Other hands-on exhibits may be found at the Chippewa Nature Center, 1000 acres of woods, fields, and riverfront property. A museum contains a restored 1870 farm and a maple sugarhouse.

MILAN, Ohio. City, (pop. 1,659), situated in north central Ohio on the HURON RIVER, about ten miles south of Lake ERIE, Milan was once one of the great grain ports of the country. As early as 1787, David Zeisberger and his Indian followers made a temporary settlement at Milan. In 1804 a Moravian pastor established an Indian village there, called Pequotting. As more white settlers came in, the town was laid out in 1816 by Ebenezer Merry. In what might have seemed an overly ambitious move for a town of 280 residents, the community decided to build a canal to the Huron River three miles away. Started in 1832, the canal brought its first boat to the village in 1839. That boat heralded the beginning of the success of Milan as a wheat shipping center, at its peak one of the greatest in the world. The success of Milan drove the lake port of Huron into decline. As many as 365 wagonloads of grain arrived in a day from the farms of eighteen neighboring counties in the upper half of Ohio. They might unload as many as 40,000 bushels of grain daily into the mile-long string of warehouses. Ships as heavy as 250 tons could make their way to the docks. Grain dealers commonly advertised for "100,000 bushels of wheat before the close of navigation." Shipyards sprang up along the river, and shipbuilding flourished. Six revenue cutters were built for the U.S. government. Some of the largest and finest Great Lakes ships came from Milan yards. Not wanting to risk the success of the port, Milan refused a right of way to the first railroad, which bypassed the town. Grain receipts then declined year upon year. Deforestation in the area brought a lowering of the river water level. Lake boats could no longer navigate to Milan; wharves and warehouses lay empty; hotels closed; ships rotted at the wharves. By the 1880s, the canal was no longer useable. The great days never came back. Today Milan is best known as the birthplace of America's greatest inventor, Thomas A. EDISON (1847-1931). He later recalled, "My recollections of Milan are somewhat scanty as I left the town when I was not quite seven years old. I remember that wheat elevators on the canals, and Gay Shipyard; also the launching of new boats, on which occasion the piece of land called the Hogback would be filled with what seemed to me to be the entire population of the town who came to witness the launching. I also recall a public square filled at times with farmers' teams, and also what seemed to me to be an immense number of teams that came to town bringing oak staves for barrels." The Thomas A. Edison Birthplace Museum is open to visitors and contains some original furnishings and memorabilia. Milan Historical Museum occupies the home of Edison's doctor, Lehman Galpin. Half a mile east of Milan is Galpin Wildlife and Bird Sanctuary. Milan holds an annual Melon Festival on Labor Day weekend.

MILWAUKEE, WISCONSIN

Name: From the Algonquian language believed to mean "a good spot or place."

Area: 95.8 square miles.

Elevation: 581 feet

Population:

1984: 620,811

Rank: 17th

Percent change (1980-1984): minus 2.4%

Density (city): 6,627 per sq. mi.

Metropolitan Population: 1,568,000

Percent change (1980-1984): minus .13%

Racial and Ethnic makeup (1980):

White: 73.3%

Black: 23.1%

Hispanic origin: 26,487 persons

Indian: 5,348 persons

Asian: 4,451 persons

Other: 11,294 persons

Age:

18 and under: 27%

65 and over: 12.5%

TV Stations: 7

Radio Stations: 31

Hospitals: 27

Sports Teams:

Brewers (baseball)

Bucks (basketball)

Admirals (minor-league hockey)

Further Information: Milwaukee Association of Commerce, 756 North Milwaukee Street, Milwaukee, WI 53202

MILWAUKEE, Wisconsin. City, seat of Milwaukee County, situated in southeast Wisconsin on Lake MICHIGAN at the outlet of the MENOMONEE , Kinnikinic and MILWAUKEE rivers, taking its name from the Algonquin Indian word malma-waukee sape thought to mean "a gathering place by the river" or simply a good place or location. The city was incorporated in 1846. It occupies a land area of 95.8 square miles.

One of the major GREAT LAKES ports, Milwaukee's leadership in heavy machinery and other massive freight shipments was greatly enhanced by the opening of the ST. LAWRENCE SEAWAY (1959), bringing ocean liners to one of the most modern and efficient of the world's ports. At one time the city was one of the world's major grain ports. As grain production declined in the region, lumber became a major export.

The city has long been known as the nation's brewing capital, with many of the principal brewers operating there. Even more important to the economy is the manufacturing of heavy electrical generating equipment and equipment for transmitting and distributing electric power. Milwaukee holds world rank in production of tractors, diesel and gasoline engines. Electronic products and refrigeration equipment also are important.

Recent years have seen the departure of many industries, particularly among the brew-

Milwaukee

Aerial view of Milwaukee, Wisconsin.

eries, bringing high unemployment. However, a shift to more diversified products in manufacturing is expected to aid the city. This is demonstrated by its recent rise to first rank in the nation in industrial controls and X-ray apparatus.

When Father Jacques MARQUETTE (1637-1675) and Louis JOLLIET (1645-1700) reached the site in 1673, it was even then an Indian trading center. The NORTH WEST COMPANY's fur trading post, established there in 1795, was the first European-style business in the area. The arrival of trader Solomon JUNEAU (1793-1856) in 1818 added to the fur business, and he is credited with founding the city in that year. By 1838 there were several small communities which merged to form Milwaukee.

In 1851 the first railroad in Wisconsin began operation between Milwaukee and WAUKESHA. In time, Milwaukee benefitted greatly from the main northern transcontinental rail lines.

After 1848 German refugees arrived in such large numbers that Milwaukee became known as second Berlin. Their skills contributed to the brewing and other industries. The meat packing industry was growing in importance, along with Great Lakes shipping.

After the CIVIL WAR , the founding of the Knights of St. Crispin marked the beginning of a strong labor movement in the city. Socialist Victor Berger was a prominent Milwaukee leader, as was Mayor Daniel W. Hoan, whose efficient administration made Milwaukee a model for other cities of the period.

The approach of WORLD WAR I caused consider-able apprehension about the attitude of the city's large German population. It was expected that many would be in sympathy with the mother country, but this did not prove to be the case at any time during U.S. participation in the war.

More recently, one of the major events was the 1959 celebration of the opening of the ST. LAWRENCE SEAWAY, with its implications for Milwaukee commerce. The celebration was enhanced by the presence of Queen Elizabeth and Prince Philip of Britain.

As with so many other Midwest cities, Milwaukee's population declined, from 717,000 to 621,000 in the period 1970 through 1984, due largely to the decline in manufacturing. In addition to the still large German and Scandi-navian population, the black population is placed at 23.1 percent with Hispanics at 4.1 per cent.

Major sports arrived at Milwaukee in 1953 in the presence of the baseball Braves. When the Braves won the 1957 World Series, the city went wild. The Milwaukee Bucks represent the National Basketball Association. Although the Green Bay Packers team is headquartered a long distance away, Milwaukee football fans claim them as their very own.

A major center of higher education, Milwau-kee boasts MARQUETTE UNIVERSITY , the substan-tial Milwaukee campus of the University of WISCONSIN, Cardinal Stritch College, Alverno College and Layton School of Art.

The breweries, with the sampling tours, remain one of the major tourist attractions of the city, along with a large number of German restaurants, serving food said to equal that specialty anywhere else in the world.

The modern natural history museum has developed some of the most dramatic display techniques of any institution of its type. The conservatory at Mitchell Park is noted not only for its fine displays but also for the unusual geodesic domes which have become something of a landmark for the city. Summerfest, the Great Circus Parade, several ethnic festivals, Wisonsin State Fair and Holiday Folk Fair are notable annual events of the city.

MILWAUKEE RIVER. The Milwaukee is one of the three rivers which converge to form the great harbor of MILWAUKEE, Wisconsin, and which cause so many problems in bridging together the various segments of the city. The Milwaukee River rises near the town of Eden, southwest of FOND DU LAC. At WEST BEND it takes the turn at the big bend which gives the town its name, flowing east, then north, then beginning to flow south at Waubeka. Its generally southward course takes it parallel to and only a few miles west of Lake MICHIGAN, until it crosses the city line of Milwaukee near the community of Brown Deer. In the heart of the city it meets the MENOMINEE RIVER from the west and the Kinnickinic from the south, and they roughly quadrisect the city. Over the years, improvement of the rivers and harbor have been of primary importance in the city's development.

MINERAL POINT, Wisconsin. City (pop. 1,159), one of the historic communities of the Midwest, situated in southwest Wisconsin, the city takes its name from the minerals and mineral activity of which it was the hub. Its settlement began in 1828, after Nat Morris, a roving prospector, in that year discovered the great deposits of lead, or galena, in the area. The rush of miners followed quickly, first by New Englanders and Southerners, the latter coming up the MISSISSIPI RIVER. However, the large numbers of miners from Cornwall, England, who flocked in beginning in 1833, brought with them a superior knowledge of mining methods. Many of the points of interest in Mineral Point today date to the arrival of these Cornish miners. They built the first permanent houses, of cut limestone blocks. Most of the earlier miners simply burrowed into the hillside like badgers, giving the Badger State its nickname. Working the mine on a hill opposite the town, the Cornish miners could see

their wives come out of the houses and wave a towel, signalling that dinner was ready, so the town was called Shake Rag for some time, and Shake Rag Street still offers a modern-day restoration of the old homes of the mining period. Zinc also became important before the lead was almost worked out. Instead of becoming a ghost town, Mineral Point turned to serving the surrounding agricultural area and later a host of tourists. The Pendarvis Cornish Restoration provides visitors with an opportunity to study the early life of the community and early lead mining methods. Other historical mementoes may be found at the Gundry House. The Looms museum is an old stone brewery with museum displays of antique handweaving equipment. Shake Rag Alley has a collection of shops. The many other historic buildings may be seen on a riding tour following maps provided by the Chamber of Commerce.

MINNEAPOLIS, MINNESOTA

Name: From the Siouan word *Minnehaha* meaning "waterfall" or "laughing water" and the Greek word *polis* meaning city.

Nickname: Twin Cities (along with St. Paul)

Area: 55.1 square miles.

Elevation: 945 feet

Population:
1984: 358,335
Rank: 41st
Percent change (1980-1984): minus 3.4%
Density (city): 6,744 per sq. mi.
Metropolitan Population: 2,231,000
Percent change: (1980-1984) 4.4%

Racial and Ethnic makeup (1980):
White: 87.2%
Black: 7.7%
Hispanic origin: 4,762 persons
Indian: 9,198 persons
Asian: 5,358 persons
Other: 2,511 persons

Age:
18 and under: 20%
65 and over: 15.4%

TV Stations: 6

Radio Stations: 39

Hospitals: 14

Sports Teams:

Minnesota Twins (baseball)
Minnesota Vikings (football)
Minnesota North Stars (hockey)
Minnesota Monarchs (volleyball)
Minnesota Kicks (soccer)

Further Information: Minneapolis
Chamber of Commerce, 15 south 5th
Street, Minneapolis, MN 55402

MINNEAPOLIS, Minnesota. City, seat of
Hennepin County. Situated in central southeast Minnesota, at ST. ANTHONY FALLS , which
marks the head of navigation from downstream
on the MISSISSIPPI RIVER. The city was incorporated in 1856, and is the state's largest city and
a port of entry, occupying a land area of 55.1
square miles.

With adjacent ST. PAUL , the two communities
are known as the Twin Cities. Minneapolis
suburbs include Richfield, Bloomington, Edina,
St. Louis Park, Hopkins, Minnetonka, Plymouth, Golden Valley, New Hope, Crystal,
Brooklyn Center and Brooklyn Park.

The hub of a vast region producing grain and
cattle, as a consequence, it grew as a processing
and trade center. It is a world center of flour
milling, with four of the five largest milling
companies in the world headquartered there,
including General Mills and Pillsbury. Cargill,
Inc., with annual sales of $12.6 billion is the
nation's largest privately owned company and
the world's largest grain trader.

Minneapolis is known for its technical skills,
with such giants as Minnesota Mining and
Manufacturing, the developer of audio and
video tapes and innovator in the field of self-
adhesive products and copying machines.
Minneapolis-Honeywell produced the first
home thermostats and now leads in the
production of a wide variety of automatic
controls. The Twin Cities hold high rank in
production of electronic equipment. Garments,
machinery, fabricated metals and graphic arts
equipment are other major Minneapolis products.

The city is a leading center in transportation.
Northwest Orient Airline is a major carrier
headquartered at Chamberlain Field. Most of
the northern rail routes were planned and
financed from Minneapolis by several of the
leading rail tycoons. A large volume of barge
traffic on the Mississippi debarks for the
metropolitan area and beyond.

St. Anthony Falls apparently was first visited
by a white man in the person of Louis HENNEPIN
in 1683. However, western settlement did not
develop until much later. The founding of FORT
SNELLING in 1819 helped assure the safety of
settlers, and by 1821 the falls were providing
power for a sawmill. In 1839 the village of St.
Anthony was settled. Minneapolis was founded
about 1847, and it annexed St. Anthony in
1872.

The seemingly inexhaustible supply of timber
in the north made Minneapolis the country's
premier lumbering center. But as lumbering
waned, the plains began to produce wheat in
vast quantities, and the new railroads were
available to move grain to Minneapolis, where
the fifty-foot drop of the falls provided ample
power. The city then became the nation's
leading grain center. As wheat production
declined in the immediate area, Minneapolis
dropped to third place in wheat milling.

The important river trade developed rapidly
after the coming of the first paddle wheel
steamboat in 1823. The population in 1984 was
358,000, a significant drop from the 1970
census of 434,000. The city ranks 41st in the
nation in population, eighth in the Midwest.
The metropolitan population of the Twin Cities
and their suburbs is 2,231,000, making this the
seventeenth largest in the country.

Minneapolis has been rated by several
organizations for its high quality of life. The
Urban Institute of Washington, D.C., gave the
Twin Cities first place in the nation for overall
livability. One writer remarked, "This is a city
whose Chamber of Commerce never has to tell
lies, because it comes very close to being the
Utopia of the Upper Midwest.

"This is a city of clean government,
spectacular architetcure, classy cultural resources, freedom from blight, and other wonders that put the town near the top of every
nationwide survey rating the quality of urban
life."

One of the major factors in the approval of
the city is the high level of cultural activity.
Minneapolis has come to be regarded as one of
the nation's principal centers of culture. The
Minnesota Symphony was founded there in
1903. The world-famed GUTHRIE THEATER and the
renowned Children's Theater, the American
Swedish Institute and other museums and
galleries, all add to this reputation.

For many years the University of MINNESOTA ,

at Minneapolis, led all others in the country in enrollment. It remains as one of the leading state universities. Augsburg College and the Minnesota College of Art and Design add academic distinction.

The city was laid out with wide attractive streets; it boasts 22 lakes within its boundaries, along with 153 parks. The Stephens House, in Minnehaha Park, is the oldest European-style building remaining in the state.

Sport fever runs high in Minneapolis, in professional baseball with the Minnesota Twins, in hockey, the Minnesota North Stars, and with the football Vikings.

Much of the city's modern charm originated in the early 1960s when a ten-block mall was created within the main shopping district and lined with flowers and trees. The city reacted to its bitter winter cold weather by building a system of walkways connecting buildings for many blocks by overhead bridges, providing a unique experience in winter foot travel. Renaissance Festival held at a reproduction of a 16th-century village, Victorian Christmas and Aquatennial Festival are annual Minneapolis events. During the summer, an authentic showboat provides play presented by University Theater Productions.

MINNEHAHA CREEK AND FALLS. Minneapolis, Minnesota, mecca for thousands of tourists annually who come to see the fifty-three foot Minnehaha Falls popularized in 1855 by Henry Wadsworth Longfellow's epic poem, "Song of Hiawatha."

MINNESOTA. State, situated in the northwest corner of the Midwest region, Minnesota's geography is highlighted as the birthplace of three of the great river systems of North America, which flow to three different points of the compass. Most extensive of all, the MISSISSIPPI , originates in tiny Lake ITASCA. The farthest reach of the great ST. LAWRENCE RIVER SYSTEM AND SEAWAY is officialy considered to be at the source of the ST. LOUIS RIVER , rising in St. Louis County 160 miles from its mouth in DULUTH.. The RED RIVER OF THE NORTH is formed by the confluence of the OTTER TAIL and BOIS DE SIOUX rivers near BRECKENRIDGE.

Two SIOUX Indian words meaning "sky blue water" have been combined to form the state's name, and it could hardly be more appropriate. It has almost 5,000 more lakes than its often-boasted "Land of Ten Thousand Lakes." There are 25,000 miles of rivers and streams.

About two-thirds of the state borders are

Metrodome and downtown Minneapolis.

formed by rivers or lakes. Lake SUPERIOR lies on the northeast, from Duluth to the Canadian border. Most of the eastern border with Wisconsin is formed by the ST. CROIX and Mississippi rivers. The Bois de Sioux and the Red River of the North account for most of the western border with the Dakotas, North and South. Most of the northern border with Canada follows through a complex of rivers and lakes.

One of the nation's most unusual boundaries is formed by the watery finger of Minnesota which points north into the LAKE OF THE WOODS in Canada. This is known as the NORTHWEST ANGLE. An artificial boundary delineates the Angle's west limits. The north and west manmade boundaries have been drawn through the mighty Lake of the Woods. In a quirk of political geography, the northwest portion of this region cannot be reached by land from the United States.

The longest artificial boundaries separate Minnesota from Iowa on the South and South Dakota on the west. Another short manmade boundary separates central Minnesota from Wisconsin.

With its source in BIG STONE LAKE , the MINNESOTA RIVER is the only major state namesake river in the country to flow its entire distance within the state. It is the most northerly principal tributary of the Mississippi.

Minnesota boundaries include over two thousand square miles of Lake SUPERIOR, providing some of the clearest cleanest water anywhere. The largest internal water body in

Minnesota

Counties and County Seats

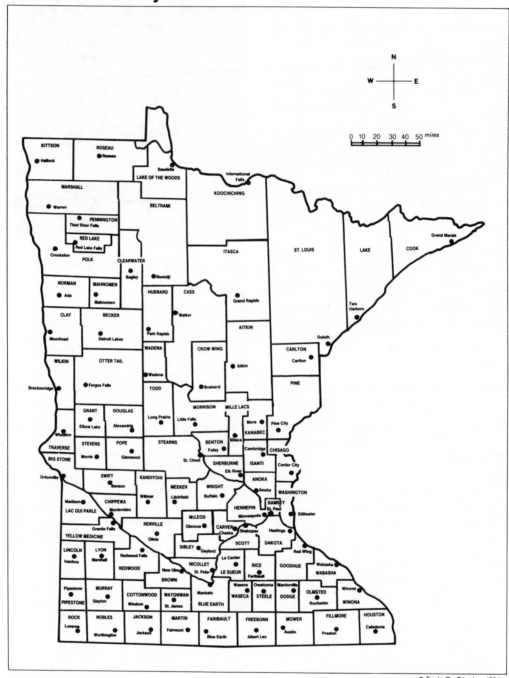

© Facts On File, Inc. 1984

Minnesota

STATE OF MINNESOTA

Name: "Minne sota" Indian words for "sky-tinted water"

Nicknames: North Star State; Gopher State

Capital: Saint Paul

Motto: L'Etoile du Nord (The Star of the North)

Symbols and Emblems:
Bird: Common Loon
Flower: Pink and White   Lady's Slipper
Tree: Red Pine
Gemstone: Lake Superior Agate
Fish: Walleye
Song: "Hail! Minnesota"

Population: 4,193,000 (1985)
Rank: 21st
Gain or Loss (1970-80): +270,000
Projection (1980-2000): +412,000
Density: 52 per sq. mi. of land
Percent urban: 66.9% (1980)

Racial and Ethnic makeup (1980):
White: 96.6%
Black: 1.3%
Hispanic: 32,000 persons
Indian: 35,000 persons
Others: 51,900 persons

Largest City:
Minneapolis (358,000 - 1984)

Other Cities:
St. Paul (266,000 - 1984)

Duluth (92,811 - 1980)
Bloomington (81,831 - 1980)
Rochester (57,890 - 1980)
Edina (46,073 - 1980)

Area: 84,402 sq. mi.
Rank: 12th

Highest Point: 2,301 ft. (702 meters) Eagle Mt.

Lowest Point: 602 ft. (184 meters) Lake Superior

H.S. Completed: 73.1% (1980)

Four Yrs. College Completed: 17.4% (1980)

STATE GOVERNMENT

ELECTED OFFICIALS (4 year terms, expiring Jan. 1991):
GOVERNOR: $84,560 (1985)
LT. GOV.: $46,510 (1985)
SEC. OF STATE: $46,510 (1985)

GENERAL ASSEMBLY:
Meets 120 days within a two-year period at St. Paul

Salary: $18,500 plus expense allowance (1985)
Senate: 67 Members
House: 134 Members
Congressional Representatives

Senate: Terms expire 1989, 1991

House of Representatives: Eight Members

Minnesota is RED LAKE. The much larger Lake of the Woods is shared with Canada. However, the Minnesota portion is the second largest body of water within the state. Unusual among natural lakes is Lake PEPIN, formed by a natural dam across the Mississippi. This is created by sand dumped by the CHIPPEWA RIVER.

With an area of 79,548 square miles, Minnesota is the largest of the Midwest states. All four of the great prehistoric glaciers covered most of the present state, leaving their usual legacy of huge prehistoric lakes, such as Lake DULUTH, Lake AGASSIZ and Lake AITKIN. As it shrank, Lake Duluth became present day Lake Superior. Most of the smaller lakes of today are also products of the glaciers. Not all of the soil of the state resulted from glacial deposits. The LOESS SOIL of the southeast was laid down by wind forces.

Topography of the southwest is marked by deep river valleys and rolling plains. The northeast encompasses deep lakes and rocky ridges, while to the northwest lie the flat plains. Covering almost half the state is the central hill and lake region.

Much of the northern section lies in the climatic region of the moist Great Lakes storm belt. The semi-arid Great Plains region impinges on the western border. With a record extreme high temperature of 114 degrees and a record low of minus 59 degrees, Minnesota has an unenviable temperature range of 173 degrees. Heavy snows and bitter cold are the hallmark of Minneapolis and St. Paul, as well as much of the rest of the state.

Agriculture, forests and minerals have been the principal sources of natural wealth of the state. For several generations, iron ore was practically a trademark of Minnesota, making it at one time the world's most important source of the single most important raw material. Then, over the years, most of the better ore was worked out. However, as new and better methods of extraction have been developed, the great resources of TACONITE (low grade iron ore) have become more important and promise even greater future use. Also important are the country's largest sources of manganese and peat, a low grade coal.

Almost the entire eastern half of the state once was forest covered. The forests were quickly exploited, and by 1890 Minnesota led the states in timber production. When the forests were exhausted, the great timber boom evaporated. The state still maintains about 20,000,000 acres of timber, most of it now harvested as pulp for paper.

In agriculture, the state is a leader in oats, sweet corn, butter, honey and dressed turkeys. Minnesota has relinquished the national leadership it once held in wheat, but wheat is still important.

Wheat milling and the manufacturing of wheat products is a leading industry, with two of the giants in the field in the Minneapolis area. Another international giant is Minnesota Mining and Manufacturing Company, pioneer in plastic adhesive products, copying machines and audio and video cassettes. Minneapolis-Honewell developed the home thermostat in 1885 and continues as a leader in automatic control mechanisms. St. Paul is home to the world's largest manufacturer of calendars. Many state mills continue to process the plentiful wood pulp into paper.

The RED RIVER OX CARTS provided pioneer transportation in Minnesota, carrying furs and other merchandise. The wheels were never greased, and the passage of a train of 600 of these sometimes would cause church services to be dismissed because of the constant squeaking noise. Steamboats on the Red River and the Mississippi provided another early means of transportation, and barge traffic today moves more tonnage than ever before.

Even more important has been the traffic on the Great Lakes, carrying the iron ore and grains for processing elsewhere. Although far in the interior, the port of Duluth-Superior ranks fourth or fifth among all U.S. ports. Minnesota's railroad tycoons brought transcontinental railroading to the state and long-distance bus lines originated there with the Greyhound Company. Northwest Orient Airlines is headquartered at the Minneapolis-St. Paul International Airport.

During the decade through 1985, Minnesota showed a very small but constant increase in population. Projections indicate that this should continue through the year 2000. The state is particularly known for its population of Scandinavian descent, and often is nicknamed Little Scandinavia. It boasts substantial representation from all the northwestern European countries. The non-European population makes up less than one percent of the total.

The prehistoric skeleton known as MINNESOTA MAN represents one of the earliest peoples found in the nation. Discovered in Browns Valley, another skeleton from a period about 12,000 years ago was named BROWNS VALLEY MAN. Mounds left by prehistoric peoples of various periods total more than 10,000 in Minnesota. Some early peoples built stone dams, portions of which still remain. Pictographs from early periods have been well preserved in various areas.

The Dacotah Indians were the earliest Minnesota inhabitants known to history, now more commonly called the SIOUX. European settlement forced the eastern OJIBWAY (Chippewa) Indians into the area. Because they had guns acquired from trading with Europeans, the Chippewa were able to push the Sioux from their hunting grounds. The Sioux were people of the plains. The Chippewa were originally forest people.

The important wild rice was harvested from the swampy areas by the women and husked by the barefoot men, the only work they would deign to do. The marvelous birch canoes of the Chippewa have been called "one of mankind's most efficient devices." The Sioux used a more awkward round craft, the buffalo skin BULL BOAT. The Sioux pulled cargoes on trailers of sticks (TRAVOIS), first using dogs, then horses, for towing, after they were introduced by Europeans.

When Olaf Ohman, a Minnesota farmer, found a slab of stone near the village of Kensington, he noted some kind of writing carved on it. This KENSINGTON RUNE STONE (found 1898) has been identified by some as proof of Viking visitors to the area. as early as 1100 A.D. Others have called the carved stone a hoax. If it is a hoax it was a remarkable piece of work in a little-developed area.

Daniel Greysolon, who took the name Sieur du Lhut, or DULUTH (1636-1710), is the first European known to have visited present Minnesota. He came to the Sioux and Chippewa as representative of the French king and tried to persuade them to stop fighting. Father Louis HENNEPIN (1626-1701?) was another early French visitor. He discovered the Falls of St. Anthony.

For many years VOYAGEURS, French traders, traveled the wilderness exchanging blankets, knives and other goods for the valuable furs collected by the Indians. Travel routes were established to enlarge the communications with French headquarters in Canada. In the early 1700s trading posts were built by such noted frontiersmen as Pierre Gaultier de Varennes, the Sieur de La Verendry,e and his sons Francois and Louis-Joseph. Then in 1768 the trading post at GRAND PORTAGE was founded by the NORTHWEST COMPANY. It became the most important in the region, dealing for goods within a range reaching 1,500 miles. Grand Portage became a metropolis in the wilderness,

with shops boasting French fashions, a police force, many saloons and a harbor accommodating 150 canoes.

The Minnesota region went from French to British hands in 1763 and became part of the U.S. after the Revolution. Most of it was included in the NORTHWEST TERRITORY established in 1787. With the purchase of the LOUISIANA TERRITORY, American claims were reinforced, but the northern boundary had not been established.

In 1805 Lieutenant Zebulon PIKE (1779-1813) explored the upper Mississippi for the U.S., dealing with the Indians and helping assure U.S. control. However, the British continued strong in much of the area, even after the WAR OF 1812. John Jacob Astor's (1763-1848) AMERICAN FUR COMPANY gradually took over the fur trade. In 1820 Colonel Josiah SNELLING (1782-1828) began to build Fort Saint Anthony at the junction of the Minnesota and Mississippi rivers. This again enhanced American control. and settlers began to come in.

By 1825 the first steamboat had arrived, bringing an era of easier transportation to open up the adjoining country. In June of 1832, scientist Henry R. SCHOOLCRAFT (1793-1864) discovered the long-sought source of the Mississippi in little Lake Itasca. The present northern state boundary was established by the Webster-Ashburton Treaty in 1842.

With treaties giving up the Indian lands, settlement became rapid in the 1850s. Statehood came on May 11, 1858, with Henry H. SIBLEY (1811-1891) as first governor. Three years later the new state was among the first to respond to calls for CIVIL WAR volunteers. Minnesota troops had critical roles in many battles, including Gettysburg. With the homefront weakened by absence of 22,000 Civil War soldiers, the Indians attacked. Sioux bands killed and took captives. With most supplies going to the Civil War, the state had few resources to battle the Indians, but H.H. Sibley trained inexperienced troops, defeated the Indians under LITTLE CROW at Wood Lake, took 2,000 Indians prisoner and affected the release of 269 white captives.

Rivalry among the towns and cities, a scourge of grasshoppers in 1873, settling of the Lake of the Woods boundaries in 1876, the building of dams and flood control projects of the 1880s, all were events of the period. The great capitol was dedicated at St. Paul in 1905. WORLD WAR I called 123,325 Minnesotans into service. The rise of the FARMER-LABOR PARTY was significant in the 1920s. Depression, dust storms and drought were the hallmarks of the 1930s. Six thousand Minnesotans lost their lives in WORLD WAR II.

Opening of the St. Lawrence Seaway in 1959 brought ocean commerce to the ports of Minnesota. Important development of the state's taconite took place in the l970s. In 1977 Walter F. MONDALE (1928-) became Vice President of the United States, and Hubert HUMPHREY (born 1911) died in 1978. In the election of 1976 and 1980 Jimmy Carter won the state's vote. Four years later favorite son Walter Mondale edged out Ronald REAGAN (1911-) for the state's vote, placing Minnesota on the losing side in three elections. Democrat Rudy Perpich won the governor's chair in 1986.

Beginning in the mid-1850s a Minnesota doctor started a practice which was to make his name and the name of his city known worldwide. Dr. William Worrell MAYO's (1819-1911) reputation as physician and surgeon grew until it brought more and more doctors to the hospital in ROCHESTER, including Dr. Mayo's sons William J. (1861-1939) and Charles (1865-1939). Based originally on the organizing skills of the Mayo family, the MAYO CLINIC has became a vast medical industry, treating world figures and advancing medical research.

Other prominent Minnesota medical men included Sioux practitioner Dr. Charles A. Eastman, Dr. Justus Ohage, Dr. C. Walton Lillehie and Dr. Charles N. HEWITT (1835-1910). Dr. Hewitt made a dramatic breakthrough when he developed a treatment for rabies. Dr. Lillehie was an open-heart surgery pioneer.

NOBEL PRIZE winner, Sinclair LEWIS (1865-1951), in 1930 was the first American to win that coveted literary honor. His novel *Main Street* was based on his boyhood home at SAUK CENTRE. Ole Edvart ROLVAAG, Thorstein VEBLEN (1857-1929) and F. Scott FITZGERALD (1896-1940) were other notable Minnesota authors.

The world-renowned ST. OLAF COLLEGE choir was developed by musician-composer Dr. F. Melius CHRISTIANSEN (1871-1955).

Industrial pioneers include James J. HILL (1838-1916), "Empire Builder" of railroads and real estate; mining tycoon A. M. Chisholm; department store pioneer George Nelson Dayton; lumber baron Frederick WEYERHAUSER (1834-1914), and food processing magnate John Sargent PILLSBURY (1842-1899).

Among public figures, one of the world's most notable was Charles Augustus LINDBERGH, Jr. (1902-1974), whose solo Atlantic flight made him a popular hero. The Nobel Prize for peace went to Frank Billings KELLOGG (1856-1937), U.S. Senator, ambassador and secretary of state, for his part in the Kellogg-Briand Peace Pact. Both Walter F. Mondale and Hubert Horatio Humphrey won the vice presidency, but the presidency eluded them. William O. DOUGLAS (1898-1980) made a reputation as one of the most controversial members of the U.S. Supreme court. Eugenie Anderson served as the first woman ambassador from the United States.

Of the dozens of "twin cities" around the world, in the United States that term usually means only one thing—Minneapolis and St. Paul. Their metroplitan area has the unique distinction of being ranked as the most desirable place in the country to make a home. The ranking is based on high standings in such important matters as housing, shopping, job opportunities, education and quality and variety of cultural opportunities.

In the latter, the metropolitan areas are particularly outstanding. The Minnesota Symphony, famed Childrens theater, Tyrone GUTHRIE THEATER, one of the nation's most modern libraries, and free summer concerts are only a few of the many attractions. Founded in 1886, the Winter Carnival at St Paul is known as one of the country's ten leading annual festivals. The great ice castle, King Boreas and Queen of the Snows and the "500" snowmobile race are some of the festival attractions. The magnificent capitol at St. Paul by renowned architect Cass GILBERT (1859-1934) is especially notable for its great gilded sculpture of Prosperity, driving four horses. Noted sculptor Daniel Chester FRENCH (1850-1931) provided much of the rest of the capitol's sculpture.

Both the cities are noted for pioneering with their miles of covered walkways, providing access to dozens of stores and restaurants and keeping out the bitter cold.

The mammoth St. Paul city hall features a four-story lobby housing the enormous Indian statue by noted sculptor Carl Milles, called the Peace Memorial Statue. The Cathedral of St. Paul is one of the nation's largest churches.

Other attractions of the metropolitan area are the Minnesota Twins baseball team, restored Fort Snelling, Minnehaha Falls and the State Fair. St. Anthony Falls is an interesting scenic landmark. Its stone underpinning is so soft that the edge of the falls has moved back four miles during historic times.

Perhaps the greatest Minnesota attraction of all is the great outdoors, where legendary Hiawatha went "forth upon the Gitche Gumee, on the shining Big-Sea-Water, with his fishing line of cedar." The state boasts the longest and

Minnesota capitol dominates St. Paul.

greatest wilderness canoe streams. The wilderness areas of the north are among the few where automobiles and other traces of civilization cannot be seen for thousands of square miles. The powdery snow of winter provides the best skiing and snowmobiling.

Unique among all the national monuments is PIPESTONE. In this prehistoric quarry, Indians and their predecessors over thousands of years cut out the beautiful red stone to make their PEACE PIPES, as well as splendid works of jewelry. For generations the quarry was neutral ground where people of all tribes could work their craft in peace. From the stone, found nowhere else, have come some of the finest items of primitive art. Many of the peace pipes are magnificent. The material is reserved today exclusively for use of the Indian people, who continue to make their fine articles there.

Because of its name, the city of MONTEVIDEO remembers its South American namesake with an annual Spanish Festival of substantial merit.

A landmark of the entire Mississippi Valley is Sugar Loaf Monolith at WINONA, rising 500 feet above the Father of Waters. Hundreds of visitors make the trek to Lake Itasca to step across the narrow outlet of that lake which marks the beginning of the mighty Mississippi.

Visitors to the city of Rochester are not looking for scenery. Most have come to find the cause and cure for health afflictions, both common and extremely rare, for which the Mayo Clinic has a world reputation in providing relief. Kings, queens and commoners have been helped there.

Duluth is known as the City in a Rock Garden, perched high on the bluffs above majestic Lake Superior. A sandbar known as Minnesota Point provides a natural breakwater for one of the world's great harbors. Skyline Parkway offers spectacular views of the area, especially in the winter when the ice breaks up, with great frigid sheets shifting, turning, tumbling and forming huge ice sculptures. With this breakup, ships can come into the harbor once more, marking the beginning of another season.

HIBBING calls itself the "Iron Ore Capital of the World" as it shows off the manmade canyons of the open pit mines, carved into the MESABI RANGE. At CHISHOLM, nearby, the Minnesota Museum of mining features the outstanding exhibit of the varied features of iron mining.

The Superior-Quetico primitive region is maintained as nearly as possible in that condition by both the U.S. and Canada, with canoe and hydroplane the only transporation beyond foot travel. The Lake of the Woods region is another vast unspoiled area.

At the vacation city of BEMIDJI stands the statue of mythical Paul BUNYAN and his blue ox BABE, said to be among the most photographed sculptures anywhere. Even larger is the Paul Bunyan statue at the Bunyan Center in BRAINARD, acclaimed as the world's largest animated figure. A model lumbering center has been built there.

At Itasca State Park, as visitors thrill to the opportunity of crossing the Mississippi on stepping stones, they are reminded that the greatest watercourse in half a world has its tiny beginning there, and it progresses, as did the state of Minnesota, from humble beginnings to greatness.

"MINNESOTA MAN." Eleven-thousand-year-old skeleton of a woman (ironically) found under nine feet of silt laid down by a prehistoric glacier in Minnesota. Discovered in 1931 near Pelican Rapids, Minnesota, the skeleton was the first proof that prehistoric humans lived in this area of North America and that these people might have used the land bridge between Asia and North America to enter this continent. Near the remains were an elk antler knife and a conch shell. The shell indicates to anthropologists that these people had contact with other humans living in southern regions, as the Gulf of Mexico is the nearest source of such shells.

MINNESOTA RIVER. Principal tributary of the MISSISSIPPI RIVER in Minnesota. The Minnesota River has the distinction of being the only river in the United States bearing the name of a state through which it flows for its entire length. The source of the river is BIG STONE LAKE. At the junction of the Mississippi and Minnesota rivers Zebulon PIKE signed the first American treaty with Indians ever written in Minnesota. In 1820 Colonel Josiah SNELLING (1782-1828) chose a site in the area for a fort. The scenic Minnesota River Valley was carved in prehistoric times by the enormous prehistoric Warren River which tumbled and churned out of prehistoric Lake AGASSIZ.

MINNESOTA, UNIVERSITY OF. Publicly-supported state university offering programs on five campuses. For many decades the University of Minnesota had the nation's largest enrollment. The university began as a preparatory school and was chartered in 1851, seven years before the Territory of Minnesota became a state. The university's central administration and most of the colleges and schools are on the Twin Cities Campus—MINNEAPOLIS -ST. PAUL. Other campuses are located in Crookston, DULUTH , Waseca and MORRIS. T h e

university is accredited by the North Central Association of Colleges and Schools and by the respective professional and educational organizations in a wide range of subject areas. The university has one of the ten largest university research library systems in the United States. University dormitories house 4,555 students, and 1,720 married students are provided housing by the university. Fraternities and sororities provide housing for an additional 1,200 students. During the 1985-1986 academic year, the university at all of its campuses enrolled 53,791 students and had 5,946 faculty members.

MINNETONKA, Lake. Considered the most beautiful lake in Minnesota and one of the major tourist spots in the United States. The lake, formed along the receding edge of glaciers more than eleven thousand years ago, has over 114 miles of shoreline. Glacial debris and irregular melting of the ice created the numerous bays and channels. The lake, a favorite of the Indians, was not discovered by non-Indians until 1822 when it was located accidentally by a seventeen year-old drummer boy from FORT SNELLING. The lake country was explored by Governor Ramsey who gave the lake its name meaning, "Big Water." As early as the 1890s the lake featured multi-deck steamers. One boat, the "Belle of Minnetonka," was equipped to carry 3,500 passengers. Today the shoreline is heavily developed.

MISSISSIPPI MAN. Name given the most recent group of PREHISTORIC PEOPLES who lived in the central Midwest. Mississippi Man was preceded by Early Man, ARCHAIC PEOPLE , and WOODLAND MAN.

MISSISSIPPI RIVER. Principal river of the U.S. Named "Great Water" or "Father of Waters" by the OJIBWAY INDIANS (*mis*, "great"; *isipi*, "river") Approximately 2,348 miles in length, the river is deserving of its name, considering its role in the development of this country and the vast extent of territory which it drains. Along with its two major tributaries, the MISSOURI and the OHIO rivers, the Mississippi drains 1,243,700 square miles (an area equal to one-eighth of the entire country), a large part of this in the Midwest. It empties approximately 600,000 cubic feet of water per second into the Gulf of Mexico—water from 32 states and 2 Canadian provinces.

In the Midwest, major tributaries from the west in addition to the Missouri are the

MINNESOTA, DES MOINES and IOWA. From the east it is joined by the ST. CROIX, ILLINOIS and OHIO in the Midwest.

The first European to discover the great stream was Hernando de Soto, in the spring of 1541, not far from the site of Helena, Arkansas. Its source at Lake ITASCA in Minnesota was not known until discovered by Henry Rowe SCHOOLCRAFT (1793-1864) in 1832.

During the early years of American colonization, the river posed a barrier to western expansion which actually benefitted the early colonies by unifying them. Settlement of the Mississippi River area was also impeded by the contest between France and Great Britain for sovereignty over the region from the mouth of the St. Lawrence to the Gulf of Mexico.

The Mississippi Territory was created by an act of Congress in 1798, and this, followed by the LOUISIANA PURCHASE in 1803, opened the river and Western lands for settlment.

The geographical importance and advantages of the river were first recognized by the early French trappers who had long used the river to transport their furs. With the territory fast becoming a corn, cotton and wheat belt, the river became essential to Midwestern life, providing transportation to market from remote areas. It is estimated that in 1840 nearly half of all commercial vessels in the country were employed on the river system. With the development of the steamboat, river travel took on an air of opulence in passenger travel during the middle years of the 19th century.

With the outbreak of the CIVIL WAR, the river was vital to both sides. After the fall of Vicksburg, July 4, 1863, Union forces took control of the river, cutting off the western Confederate States, in one of the major blows to the life of the Confederacy.

With the coming of the railroads, river traffic declined until the diesel tug and the great barges brought new life to commerce on the Mississippi system, and much of the bulk cargo of the region is now carried on the waterways.

The memories of early river life have been preserved by Mark Twain in his *Life on the Mississippi* (1883).

The river is navigable from the FALLS OF ST. ANTHONY in the north to its mouth in the Gulf of Mexico. Upstream from the falls the river drops 700 feet in a distance of 500 miles. In its lower region the river flows over land of its own making for nearly 1,000 miles and is subject to disastrous flooding.

The great willful river was never easily navigable. Until partially "tamed," it frequently changed its channels overnight, and presented snagged tree roots and innumerable other obstacles to early shipping. In 1879 the federal government established the Mississippi River Commission, a seven-member group of engineers concerned with flood control construction and navigational improvement. The first federal flood control acts were passed in 1917, and after the crippling flood of 1927, new legislation poured hundreds of millions of dollars annually into widespread projects. Floodways, cutoffs and channels were constructed, and there are now twenty-seven federal dams and locks between MINEAPOLIS and the Gulf of Mexico. Despite the improvements, unexpected flooding continues today as the river can still suddenly change its course and carve out new channels.

The reverse was true in 1988 when the great drouth brought the river levels to their lowest point in recorded history. Hundreds of thousands of tons of cargo were stranded when the water level dropped so low that tugs and barges were stalled until they could be rescued by dredging new channels.

In the Midwest, on the river's west banks are the states of Minnesota (also the only state to possess internal sections of the Mississippi), Iowa and Missouri. On the east banks are Wisconsin and Illinois. Major Midwest cities on the river include MINNEAPOLIS, Minnesota, and ST. LOUIS, Missouri.

MISSOURI. State. In the southwest region of the Midwest. Missouri is on the west bank of the MISSISSIPPI RIVER, which separates it from Illinois over most of its eastern border and from Kentucky and Tennessee in the southeast. Missouri borders Iowa to the north and Arkansas to the south across a boundery that is broken in the southeast by the southern BOOT HEEL projection of Missouri. Its longest western border is with Kansas, across a land boundary and the MISSOURI RIVER, but there are short borders with Nebraska in the northwest and Oklahoma in the southwest.

Located at the center of the Mississippi River division of the U.S., and bisected by its largest western tributary, the Missouri River, Missouri has a special historical status as the gateway to the American West. In the 19th century, particularly after the California gold rush in 1849, Missouri's western cities of ST. JOSEPH and INDEPENDENCE were the departure points for pioneers who arrived by steamboat and departed to the northwest over the OREGON TRAIL and to the southwest over the SANTA FE TRAIL. This is the heritage that is commemo

Missouri

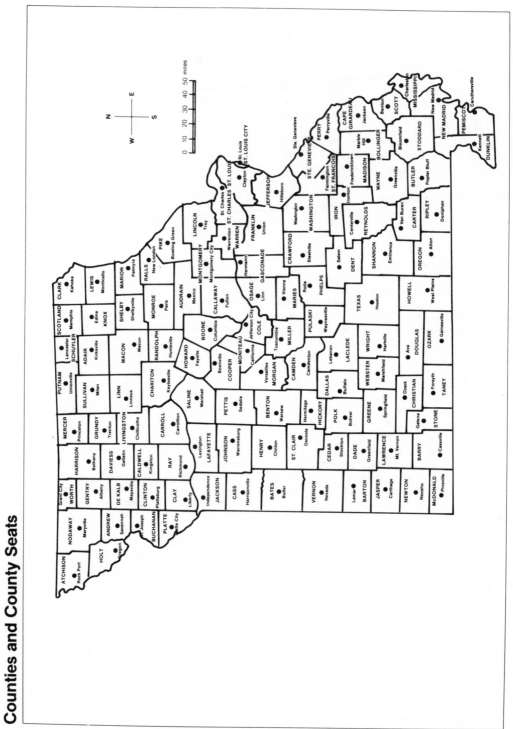

Counties and County Seats

Missouri

STATE OF MISSOURI

Name: Missouri from the Missouri River which got its name from the Indians tribe of that name which lived in the area near the river's mouth

Nickname: The Show Me State

Capital: Jefferson City

Motto: Salus Populi Suprema Les Esto (The Welfare of the People Shall Be the Supreme Law)

Symbols and Emblems:
Bird: Bluebird
Flower: Hawthorn
Tree: Dogwood
Stone: Mozarkite
Song: "Missouri Waltz"

Population:
1985: 5,029,000 (1985)
Rank: 15th
Gain or Loss (1970-80): +239,000
Projection (1980-2000): +163,000
Density: 73 per sq. mi. of land
Percent urban: 68.1% (1980)

Racial and Ethnic makeup (1980):
White: 87.4%
Black: 10.5%
Hispanic: 52,000 persons
Indian: 12,300 persons
Others: 44,500 persons

Largest City:
Kansas City (443,000 - 1984)

Other Cities:
St. Louis (429,000 - 1984)
Springfield (137,000 - 1984)
Independence (112,000 - 1984)
Columbia (62,061 - 1980)
Florissant (55,372 - 1980)

Area: 69,697 Sq. mi. (180,516 Sq. km.)
Rank: 19th

Highest Point: 1,772 ft. (540 meters) Taum Sauk Mt.

Lowest Point: 230 ft. (70 meters) St. Francis River

H.S. Completed: 63.5% (1980)

Four Yrs. College Completed: 13.9% (1980)

STATE GOVERNMENT

ELECTED OFFICIALS (4-year terms, expiring Jan. 1989):
GOVERNOR: $75,000 (1985)
LT. GOV.: $45,000 (1985)
SEC. OF STATE: $60,000 (1985)

GENERAL ASSEMBLY:
Meets annually in Jefferson City

Salary: $18,078 annually (1985)
Senate: 34 members
House: 163 members
Congressional Representatives
Senate: Terms expire 1989, 1993

House of Representatives: Nine members

rated by the 630-foot Gateway Arch, properly called the JEFFERSON NATIONAL EXPANSION MEMORIAL, which now towers over the St. Louis waterfront along the Mississippi River.

In the past century Missouri's growth was most remarkable in regard to population: with fewer than 20,000 residents in 1810, it had more than 3 million by 1900. In the present century population growth has slowed, but Missouri has emerged as an economic power. Manufacturing encourages urbanization, and Missouri includes two important U.S. metropolitan areas: St. Louis on the Mississippi River and KANSAS CITY located 230 miles across the state on the western Kansas border. The visible character of the state, however, is a product of its agricultural economy, for fully 70% of Missouri's lands remain devoted to agriculture.

Most of them lie within two large topographical areas of roughly equal size, the Central Lowland plains in the north and the Ozark Plateau in the south. The plains north of the Missouri River, which crosses the state from west to east and isolates an upper third of its land area, are part of the DISSECTED TILL PLAINS that extend south from Iowa. Between the Missouri and the OSAGE RIVER, which meet near the central capital of JEFFERSON CITY, western Missouri includes a portion of Osage Plains that are related to the topography of Kansas. The OZARK region includes nearly all of the state area south of the Osage and Missouri Rivers. This rugged and scenic plateau is characterized by ridges cut by steep canyons and deep creek beds. It is also notable for springs, caves, and sinkholes created by groundwater dissolving underground limestone. The high point in the state lies in the southeast of the Ozark region at TAUM SAUK MOUNTAIN (1,772 feet). The extreme southeast of the state, including the Boot Heel, is a portion of Mississippi alluvial land isolated by the Ozark Escarpment. Orginally swampy, it has been drained to create some of the most valuable farmland in Missouri.

The original inhabitants of the state were the MISSOURI and OSAGE Indians, tribes based along the banks of the Mississippi and Missouri Rivers. The early exploration of the region was conducted by the French moving south from Canada along the Mississippi River. Louis JOLLIET (1645-1700) and Jacques MARQUETTE (1637-1675) sailed down the river past present-day Missouri in 1673, and they were followed in 1682 by Sieur de LA SALLE (1643-1687), who claimed the region for the French and named it Louisiana after King Louis XIV. The French began to establish trapping outposts and missionary settlements within the current state boundaries by 1699, but these were abandoned after a few years. The first permanent settlement in Missouri was established by the French in 1735 at STE. GENEVIEVE on the Mississippi about 45 miles downstream from St. Louis. St. Louis itself was founded in 1764 by Pierre LACLEDE (1724?-1778) and Rene Auguste CHOUTEAU (1749-1829) as a headquarters for fur trading. In that same year, however, the French ceded their claims east of the Mississippi to England and their Louisiana claim, including Missouri, to Spain.

Despite the Spanish title to the lands of Missouri, most of the effective settlement at the end of the 18th century was accomplished by Americans moving west from Kentucky and Tennessee and by French Canadians moving west from Illinois. By 1800 the American influence had become predominant, and its origin in southern states and terriories led to the importation of slavery into Missouri. In 1800 the Spanish agreed to cede Louisiana to the French. Complicated negotiations resulted in the purchase of Louisiana by the U.S. from France in 1803. The Missouri Territory was set off from Louisiana in 1804, initiating an era of pioneer immigration to the Missouri and Mississippi River settlements that more than tripled the population between 1810 and 1820 to bring it past the 66,000 mark.

Population growth brought with it plans for statehood, with the territory first applying for admission to the Union in 1818. This became a national issue because of the delicate balance in federal politics between Northern and Southern interests. The ensuing debate resulted in the MISSOURI COMPROMISE of 1820, by which the territory would be admitted without a ban on slavery but slavery would be prohibited in the rest of the Louisiana Territory north of 36 degrees 30 minutes latitude, which marks the southern border of Missouri. After a protracted controversy concerning the status of free black persons, who were ultimately permitted to immigrate to the state, Missouri was admitted to the Union as the 24th state on August 10, 1821.

In the early years of statehood, settlement activity extended past the river settlements into the northern plains of Missouri. This was largely accomplished by emigrants from Kentucky, and it included the Platte Purchase of 1836 that extended the western border to the Missouri River. This new population was agricultural in occupation, and it strengthened the links between Missouri and the Southern,

Missouri, Commerce

slave-holding states. For a time, however, this political affiliation was obscured by the boom of westward economic activities and pioneer settlement throughout the state. The ROCKY MOUNTAIN FUR COMPANY expanded traffic on the Missouri River and established St. Louis as a warehouse and shipping center. In 1821 William BECKNELL (1796?-1865) initiated the overland route to Santa Fe via mule and ox teams. Steamboat traffic along the Missouri also expanded in this era, and the commercial routes soon became highways for daily expeditions bound for the Southwest, for California, and for the Northwest.

Political controversies returned to the foreground in the decade before the CIVIL WAR. In 1851, Senator Thomas Hart BENTON (1782-1858), a moderate on the slavery issue, was defeated by Henry Sheffie Dyer, a Whig. In 1854 the Missouri Compromise was repealed by the KANSAS-NEBRASKA ACT, which empowered local legislatures to decide the legality of slavery within their borders, and groups of Missourians crossed the western border into Bleeding Kansas to sway it toward slavery. In 1860 the moderate Stephen A. DOUGLAS carried Missouri's presidential vote; Abraham LINCOLN's call for troops for the Union Army in 1861 forced Missouri to choose between North and South. Governor Claiborne F. Jackson chose the South and engineered the passage of an ordinance of secession in November of 1861. Gen. Nathaniel LYON, however, chose the North, and he occupied JEFFERSON CITY with volunteers and expelled the Jackson legislature from the capital. In 1862 the Union Army defeated the Confederates at Pea Ridge in Arkansas, thus helping to preserve northern control of Missouri for the duration of the war. This permitted the rise of the Radical Unionists to control the state legislature before the Confederate surrender in 1865, and the Unionist control through the Reconstruction era was preserved by enforcement of ironclad oaths that prevented Southern sympathizers from holding political office or voting in elections. The Democratic Party nevertheless regained its traditional control of the state in 1870, and the new constitution it passed in 1875 eliminated many of the evils of Reconstruction while preserving segregation in public schools.

By the end of the 19th century the foundations for Missouri's modern economic stature had been laid. Although supplanted by CHICAGO as the principal railroad link between East and West for passengers, St. Louis established itself as a commercial rail center

after it was linked to the younger town of Kansas City across the state. The state's farmers organized groups such as the Farmer's Alliance and the Grange to protect their own interests and involve commercial banks in the state transition from small subsistence farms to large cash-crop ones. By 1900 Missouri was the fifth most populous state in the U.S. as well as an agricultural and industrial leader.

The most recent change in the character of the state came in the years following WORLD WAR II, when its own Senator Harry S (no period) TRUMAN (1884-1972) became President of the United States. The wartime economy had expanded the state's heavy industries, and these successfully shifted to peacetime production. Urbanization accompanied heavy industry, and the proportion of the state population living in metropolitan areas rose from 51% in 1930 to 70% in 1970. Air travel and highways supplanted railroads, but both Kansas City and St. Louis managed to increase their importance as transportation centers in this new era. Finally, moderate interests prevailed in the transition to integrated schools following the Supreme Court ruling in 1954, and Missouri was spared the racial trauma common to many other states to the south in that decade and into the 1960s.

Today Kansas City and St. Louis remain the population and manufacturing centers in the state. Kansas City has surpassed St. Louis in population. However, St. Louis far outstrips the K.C. metropolitan population. The St. Louis metropolitan area extends from Missouri into Illinois and included 2.398,000 residents in 1984; the Kansas City metropolitan area extends from Missouri into Kansas and included 1,477,000 residents in that year. The statewide population recorded only an insignificant increase in urbanization in the 1980s, a decade during which it grew at a rate lower than the national average and recorded a slight population decrease from net migration movements. The largest urban areas other than St. Louis and Kansas City are SPRINGFIELD in the southern Ozark region and ST. JOSEPH in the northwest plains region.

Manufacturing now generates five times the income of agriculture in Missouri. St. Louis, an automobile, aircraft, and brewery center, and Kansas City, a meat packing and grain processing center, are the principal manufacturing cities for the Great Plains region to the north and west. The state farmlands lie between the corn belt to the north and the cotton belt to the south, and soybeans now

Missouri capitol, Jefferson City.

exceed both of these crops in value to the Missouri economy. Livestock, however, generates slightly more farm income than crops, with cattle and hog production based in the area north of the Missouri River. Missouri also is first in the U.S. in lead production, and it ranks high in cement and stone. It has a relatively high mineral value for a state without fuel reserves. Tourists to the state spent $3.9 billion in 1980, most of it in the scenic Ozark region of southern Missouri and in urban attractions such as St. Louis and Independence.

MISSOURI, USS (battleship). Scene of the Japanese signing of the surrender papers which marked the end of WORLD WAR II on September 2, 1945, in Tokyo harbor. The original papers and a selection of the silver service from the Missouri are now displayed in the Truman Library in INDEPENDENCE, Missouri. In an effort to restore American naval strength, the _Missouri_ was re-outfitted and reactivated in 1986.

MISSOURI COMPROMISE. Acts of Congress passed in 1820-21, which temporarily settled the question of extension of slavery west of the MISSISSIPPI RIVER. The acts allowed Missouri to be admitted to the Union as a slave state, but also stated that slavery could not be established in the remaining Louisiana Territory north of latitude 36° 30'.

When Missouri requested admission to the Union in December, 1818, the balance of slave

and free states was 11 each. The Missouri statehood bill reached the House of Representatives on February 13, 1819, and James Tallmadge, a New York congressman, introduced an amendment that prohibited slavery in the new state. Although the amendment was passed by the House, there was strong opposition to it by Southerners, and it was not passed by the Senate.

The issue was put off until Congress reconvened in December, 1819. On January 3, 1820, the House voted to admit Maine (which had separated from Massachusetts) as a free state. The Senate amended the bill to include Missouri (without the Tallmadge amendment restricting slavery), thus maintaining equality between free and slave states. The bill was further amended by the Senate to exclude slavery forever in the remaining Louisiana Territory north of latitude 36° 30'. This compromise bill was rejected by the House, but the bills were separated and Maine was accepted as a free state in March, 1820. Missouri was instructed to draw up a new constitution that permitted slavery. The new constitution, however, included a provision that prohibited the immigration of mulattoes and free Negroes into Missouri. This provision necessitated what is sometimes referred to as the second Missouri Compromise. Missouri was forced to delete this restriction and to pledge not to impair the rights of citizens. Only then was Missouri admitted to the Union, in August,

1821. Speaker of the House Henry Clay, a representative from Kentucky, was so instrumental in the passage of the Missouri Compromise bills that he is often regarded as their author.

Although the compromise temporarily settled the slavery controversy, it also brought up the question of whether or not Congress could impose restrictions on new states when it didn't impose restrictions on existing states. Because of the proviso which prohibited slavery only north of 36° 30', the Union was committed to admitting Texas as a slave state, which it did in 1845. In 1854 the Missouri Compromise was repealed by the Kansas-Nebraska Act, which added fuel to the impending CIVIL WAR.

MISSOURI INDIANS. People having "dugout canoes" or people having wooden canoes. Tribe of Siouan linguistic stock that lived on the south bank of the MISSOURI RIVER near the mouth of the GRAND RIVER. They gave their name to the river and to the state itself. They were nearly destroyed in 1798 in attacks by the FOX and SAUK Indians and later suffered another tragic defeat by the OSAGE.

MISSOURI MULES. One of the first Missouri products for which the state was famed. As early as 1830, the success of local residents in breeding mules had reached the attention of newspapers. Missouri breeders were soon raising more mules than needed. Exports of the animals to southern states began by steamboat or overland drives to INDEPENDENCE and ST. JOSEPH. "Sugar mules" were bred for use in the Louisiana sugar fields; "cotton mules" were shipped to southern cotton plantations, and others were used on wagon trains. Soon the expression "Missouri mule" had meaning internationally. England purchased a large supply of mules during the Boer War and later during WORLD WAR I, but it was the showing of Missouri mules at the St. Louis world's fair in 1904 that proved their supremacy. Callaway County has been the leading mule producing county in the state. During WORLD WAR II, large numbers of Missouri mules were shipped as far away as Burma, for work on the Burma road.

MISSOURI RIVER. The longest tributary of the MISSISSIPPI (2,465 miles), it rises in southwest Montana and flows north, then east, then southeast to ST. LOUIS, Missouri. Its first point of contact in the Midwest is at the border of Iowa at SIOUX CITY. It follows the southwestern border of Iowa and the northwestern border of

Missouri to KANSAS CITY, where it crosses the state in a generally easterly direction. It was an important transportation route for the Indians. The LEWIS AND CLARK EXPEDITION (1804-1806) was instrumental in opening the route to settlers. Because its drainage area is nearly three times that of the Mississippi, opinions have been expressed that perhaps the Mississippi should be considered the tributary and the entire course from Montana to the Gulf of Mexico should be called the Missouri (if this were so, it would become the longest river in the world).

MISSOURI, UNIVERSITY OF. Land-grant coed institution, main institution of the state university system, the first state university founded west of the MISSISSIPPI RIVER. The University of Missouri began in 1839 at COLUMBIA, a community 125 miles west of ST. LOUIS. In addition to its original Columbia location, the university has three other campuses at ROLLA, KANSAS CITY and ST. LOUIS. T h e four branches together offer about 500 major programs. Columbia has fourteen colleges and schools and 290 programs. Particularly noteworthy is the school of journalism, often rated as the finest of its kind in the United States. The four campuses enroll over 50,000 students and have a combined faculty numbering over 2,400.

MOLINE, Illinois. City (pop. 45,709), MISSISSIPPI RIVER city, founded 1848, grouped with East Moline, Illinois; ROCK ISLAND, Illinois; and DAVENPORT, Iowa to form the "Quad Cities," Midwest manufacturing center of farm implements. The name comes from a Spanish word meaning "hill." Plows manufactured by John DEERE provided the start of Moline's climb to become the capital of the farm implement industry. Deere and Company Administrative Center, designed by Eero Saarinen, in Moline, is the company headquarters. By 1890 the city was one of only twenty in Illinois which had reached a population of over ten thousand people. Deere produced its own automobiles in 1906 and 1907. Nine other local automobile manufacturers, including the Moline Plow Company, which produced the Moline in 1904, all enjoyed a brief local popularity, but failed to achieve a nationwide market. With the outbreak of WORLD WAR II, Moline was one of several Illinois cities to welcome large industrial plants operated by corporations with government contracts. Twenty miles north of Moline, is the Quad Cities Nuclear Generating Station, the principal source of power in the area and the ten-state Mid-Continent Area Power Planners (MAPP) System. The power station is a joint project of Commonwealth Edison Company of Chicago, Illinois, and Iowa-Illinois Gas and Electric Company. Past and present Deere products, as well as a collage illustrating American agriculture from 1837 to 1918, are displayed in the Deere and Company Administrative Center. An elaborate collection of animals is maintained at the Niabi Zoo.

MONDALE, Walter E. (Ceylon, MN, Jan. 5, 1928—). Vice President of the United States. Educated at Macalester College and the University of Minnesota, Mondale graduated from the latter in 1951. When his service in the army was completed, he graduated from Minnesota Law School in 1956 and practiced law from 1958 to 1960. Mondale served as attorney general of Minnesota from 1960 to 1964. He was active in the Democratic-Farmer-Labor Party of Minnesota. He gained national attention in 1963 when he supported the cause of free legal counsel for indigent defendants in a Florida law case, *Gideon v. Wainwright*. In 1964 when the seat of his long-time political advisor, Hubert H. HUMPHREY (1907-1978), was vacated, Mondale was appointed to his seat and was elected on his own in 1972. In 1976, Jimmy Carter chose Mondale as the Democratic nominee for vice president, and he shared the narrow victory won by Carter. He served as Vice President of the United States from 1977 to 1981, when he was succeeded by George Bush. Mondale was the Democratic candidate for president in 1984, but lost in the landslide re-election of Ronald REAGAN (1911-).

MONKS MOUND. World's largest primitive earthwork, near CAHOKIA , Illinois. The mound, built by the Middle Mississippian culture which flourished in the Cahokia area about 900 A.D., covers seventeen acres and is 100 feet high, 710 feet wide, and 1,080 feet long. Eighty-four other mounds once stood around it, showing that large numbers of people lived in the area for long periods of time. The name, Monks Mound, came from the use of the mound from 1803 to 1813 as the site of a monastery for a group of Trappist monks. Coming to America under the direction of Father Urbain Guillet, the monks were encouraged to come to Cahokia by Nicholas Jarrott, a wealthy Frenchman. The Trappists returned to France in 1813.

MONMOUTH COLLEGE. Privately supported liberal arts institution in MONMOUTH ,

Illinois. Accredited with the North Central Association of Colleges and Schools and the American Chemical Society, Monmouth College was founded in 1853 by Presbyterians of Scottish descent as a preparatory school for ministers of the Associated Reformed Presbyterian Church and is now part of the main Presbyterian body. Monmouth was one of the first colleges in the United States to operate as a coeducational institution. It is the birthplace of the nation's first two sororities, Pi Beta Phi and Kappa Kappa Gamma. Monmouth was one of the first colleges in the Midwest to be accredited for preparation of chemists. The campus is located on thirty acres and has thirty-eight buildings. Study overseas is directed through the Associated Colleges of the Midwest. During the 1985-1986 academic year Monmouth College enrolled 700 students and had 73 faculty members.

MONMOUTH, Illinois. City (pop. 10,706), seat of Warren County, located in western Illinois, west of GALESBURG , Illinois, on U.S. Highway 34, home of MONMOUTH COLLEGE. Monmouth named to commemorate the Revolutionary War battle of Monmouth, New Jersey, was founded in 1831. Early roads were so bad that flatboats on wheels, drawn by horses, carried people and merchandise. Construction of surfaced roads did not start until 1891. Monmouth was the birthplace of famous western marshall, Wyatt EARP (1848-1929).

MONONA, Lake. One of the two bodies of water which divide the city of MADISON, Wisconsin, and distinguish the capital city from other capitals. Monona is smaller than MENDOTA , the other lake. Much of Monona's northwestern shore is occupied by downtown Madison, including the massive Capitol building and the City-County building. Dane County Coliseum and Exposition Center dominates the southern shore of the lake. On the east is the community of Monona. Lake Monona is connected by channel with Lake Waubesa to the south.

MONROE, Harriet. Chicago, IL, Dec. 23, 1860—Arequipa, Peru, Sept. 26, 1936). Poet, editor, publisher. One of the most influential figures in the publication and development of modern poetry, Harriet Monroe was educated in CHICAGO and Georgetown, D.C., where she graduated from the Convent of the Visitation in 1879. She was encouraged in her desire to write by such eminent figures as Robert Louis Stevenson and William Dean HOWELLS ((1837-1920), and her first poetic work, *Valeria and Other Poems*, appeared in 1892. She became the art and drama critic for various Chicago newspapers, and published verse in national magazines. Her most important work and greatest fame came with the establishment and brilliant conduct of *Poetry: A Magazine of Verse*. Founded in 1912, that magazine, according to one biographer, "...quickly became the leading poetry journal in the English-speaking world." Its contributors included almost every poet of the period, many of whose reputations were made through appearance in the magazine. Monroe was particularly successful in her effort to include the widest variety of poetical forms, despite her own preference for Imagist expression. During her leadership, the magazine never settled into a particular "literary groove." She published several volumes of her own work and, with Alice Henderson, she edited *New Poetry: An Anthology of Twentieth-Century Verse in English*, published in 1917, revised and edited in 1923 and 1932. Her death came while she attended a poetry conference in Arequipa, Peru. Her magazine continues today with substantial but lessened influence.

MONROE, Michigan. City (pop. 23,531), seat of Monroe County, southeast Michigan on the LOWER PENINSULA near Lake ERIE. The site of the future Monroe was the scene of a massacre during the WAR OF 1812. In 1813 healthy American prisoners were marched off with their British captors while the wounded were left behind to be killed by the Indian allies of the British in the RAISIN RIVER MASSACRE (January, 1813). The site of Monroe was originally settled by the French in 1780. The settlement was called Frenchtown until renamed by Governor Lewis CASS (1782-1866)in honor of the expected visit of President James Monroe. Monroe was the center of the "Toledo War," a bloodless dispute between the governments of Ohio and Michigan over a strip of land. The matter was settled when Congress refused to allow Michigan statehood unless it gave up claim to the land in favor of Ohio. To help Michigan accept the deal, Congress offered the UPPER PENINSULA to Michigan. Michigan gained financially in the years to come from the trade. One of Monroe's first industries was glass manufacturing. A heavy layer of silica sand and sandstone provided the raw materials as early as 1836, when a glass making plant was opened at Monroe. At one time the Monroe plant produced most of the glass used in the Midwest. Papermaking is a major industry. One of Monroe's most famous residents was George Armstrong CUSTER (1839-1876), who lived there in his youth before his military service. Exhibits of Custer memorabilia may be found in the Monroe County Historical Museum.

MONROE, Wisconsin. City (pop. 10,027), seat of Green County beginning in 1839. Situated in far south central Wisconsin, the city was named for President James Monroe. The coming of the railroad in 1857 hastened the community's growth. The many dairy farms and abundance of milk lured European immigrants, especially the Swiss. Cheese making soon became the principal industry, and by 1883 in Green County alone there were 75 cheese factories, specializing in Swiss and limburger cheeses. Monroe became a center for receiving shipments of cheese from other areas as well. Children held their noses as wagons of limburger lumbered by. Fortunately, the town council turned down a motion to forbid the product from the streets. The first cheese day was held in 1914 and drew a crowd of 50,000 to the tiny community. The celebration was stimulated by a "sniffing duel" between the mayor of Monroe and an Iowa postmaster to decide whether the odor of limburger was a perfume or a stench. It was generally agreed that the strong cheese could hold its own against all comers. As many as 300 cheese factories have contributed to the area industry, and today Monroe remains the center of production of its two cheeses, often called "The Swiss Cheese Center of America." The community is noted for the county courthouse with its 120-foot clock tower, and several Monroe homes are on the National Register of Historic places. The Green County Historical museum is housed in the historic former Universalist Church. Nearby is Yellowstone Lake State Park. Cheesemaking is demonstrated in several industrial tours.

MOORE, Marianne. (St. Louis, MO, Nov. 15, 1887—New York, NY, Feb. 5, 1972). Poet and editor. When her father abandoned the family, Moore moved with her mother to Pennsylvania in 1894. There she graduated from Bryn Mawr College in 1909, studied at Carlisle Commercial College, and taught at the Carlisle Indian School (1911-15). Her first verses were published in 1915 and 1916 in innovative literary journals such as The *Egoist* and *Poetry*. In all of her work she experimented with language that was essentially prose but broken into complexly patterned verse stanzas. Her verse carried a bitter irony along with her sharp wit, but she never discarded her obvious sympathy for human responsibility. She was awarded the Bollingen Prize, the National Book Award, and the Pulitzer prize for *Collected Poems* (1951). Her later works included *To Be a Dragon (1959) and the Arctic Ox* (1964), as well as essays such as *Predilections* (1955), and she translated *Fables of La Fontaine* (1954).

MOORHEAD, Minnesota. City (pop. 29,-998), northwestern Minnesota commercial center, on the east bank of the RED RIVER OF THE NORTH, across from FARGO , North Dakota. Founded in 1871, the community became a shipping and processing point for agricultural products. The principal industries of Moorhead are sugar refining, from sugar beets produced in the surrounding area, and grain malting. Local attractions include the home of Solomon G. Comstock, Moorhead politician and founder of Moorhead State University in the city. Concordia College is also locted there. The Plains Art Museum exhibits both historic and contemporary American art. Supporters of the belief that Vikings explored as far west as Minnesota will find the Viking stones in nearby Hawley worth a visit. Measuring several feet in thickness, length and width the stones are embedded in a hill at what once was the highest water line of a lake, where supporters say they anchored Viking craft.

MOOSE LAKE, Minnesota. Town (pop. 1,408), northeastern Minnesota, southwest of DULUTH. Scene of tragic fire in 1918. Logging was the principal industry during the first years, but with the decline of the lumber industry in the late 1800s Scandinavian immigrants farmers arrived and began to clear the land for crops. The town continued to grow, but after a long, dry autumn in 1918 a number of forest fires broke out across St. Louis and Carlton counties. Sixty-mile-per-hour winds fanned the flames. Cloquet, Carlton, Moose Lake and other smaller villages were destroyed with 453 people killed. As a result of these fires, legislation was passed requiring permits to burn outdoors and for mandatory spark protection from train locomotives. The cemetery in Moose Lake contains a 28-foot granite spire to commemorate those who perished in the flames.

MORGAN, John Hunt. (Huntsville, AL, June 1, 1825—Greenville, TN, Sept. 4, 1864). Confederate officer. In July, 1863, Morgan led two thousand men on an unauthorized raid through Indiana and Ohio which went deeper into Union territory than any other force during the CIVIL WAR. While of some psychological value to the South, the raid accomplished little. Most of Morgan's men surrendered at Buffington Island on the OHIO RIVER. Morgan escaped a Union prison and resumed his raids which generally aimed at interrupting communication lines, destroying railroads and equipment, and burning Union supplies. Under investigation and about to lose his command, Morgan planned one more raid on Knoxville, Tennessee. He was surprised and killed by federal troops at Greenville.

MORMONS. Officially, Church of Jesus Christ of Latter-Day-Saints. Joseph SMITH (1805-1844), founder of the Mormon faith, was not very successful in promoting the movement in New York State and planned to move. He sent scouts west to find new land in Missouri. They paused at Mentor, Ohio, at the home of Sidney Rigdon. Rigdon was "visited by an angel" and converted to the Mormon religion. Within a few weeks there were 127 converts in the area.

When this news reached Smith, he had one of his many "revelations." Commanded by God to go to Ohio, Smith and a few of his followers arrived at KIRTLAND, Ohio, in January, 1831. Most of the male members of the group did missionary work; new converts arrived from the east, and by midyear there were more than a thousand Mormons in the area. Although Smith and Rigdon were tarred by a mob who opposed them, the church bought land. Streets were laid out and houses built. Industries rose on the flat below Temple Hill. The prophet himself started a tannery, a sawmill and a general store.

Between 1833 and 1836 each male Mormon gave one seventh of his time toward the building of the temple. In one of Smith's revelations, he declared that God spoke: "It is meet that my servant Joseph Smith, jun., should have a house built in which to live and translate." The house was built. He made his father the patriarch of the church and then said that God wanted the senior Smith to have a salary of ten dollars per week and expenses. Smith claimed to have had seventy-five revelations while at Kirtland.

A Mormon convert, Brigham YOUNG (1801-1877), went to England and converted thou sands, many of whom came to Ohio. The church was completely organized with its Presidents, Apostles, High Priests, Bishops and Stake Presidents. Missionaries were sent to Canada and the East to win more converts.

However, the depression of 1837, brought financial difficulties. Smith was convicted of violating Ohio law but appealed his case. When the Kirtland bank failed, another warrant was issued for Smith, and he moved with many of his followers to Missouri. Smith announced that God had told him to establish the church at INDEPENDENCE.

Within a year more than 1,200 Mormons had arrived in the region. Their distrustful neighbors drove them out. In 1836 the Missouri state legislature designated Caldwell County as a Mormon refuge. There the Mormons established SALEM and FAR WEST. Far West was laid out with magnificent proportions, and within a year there were 4,000 Mormons in Far West.

As Mormon power grew, the neighbors again began to quarrel with them. Eighteen Mormons were massacred at HAUN'S MILL. The governor ordered the group to leave, but the Mormon leaders were being held, and General Samuel D. Lucas ordered General A. W. DONIPHAN (1808-1887) to execute them. Doniphan replied, "It is cold blooded murder. I will not execute your order."

By 1839 the Mormons had left the state for Illinois. There they had astounding success, and their new city, NAUVOO, became the largest in Illinois of the time. Smith became a powerful leader in Illinois politics. It was said that he even planned to run for president.

However, once again the other members of the community and nearby areas were so disturbed by Mormon success and what they feared were immoral practices that they brought charges. Smith and his brother were jailed and murdered at Carthage, Illinois on June 17, 1844, by a mob of non-Mormons.

Control of the church went to Brigham Young who led his followers out of Nauvoo, which became a GHOST TOWN. In 1846 they began to move across Iowa. They created the Mormon trail across the territory, established settlements and supply stations and helped greatly in opening up the western part of Iowa. By the winter of 1846, 4,000 Mormons had reached their winter camp near present COUNCIL BLUFFS. Almost overnight a new city, called Winter Quarters, was built there. Five hundred thirty log houses and eighty-three sod houses were built by skilled craftsmen under Young's energetic direction.

In April, 1847, the first groups began to move onward toward their final settlement in Utah. However, for many years Mormon immigrants plodded across the Midwest to reach their promised land.

Another Midwest state, Michigan, also had a part in Mormon history. A Mormon group settled on BEAVER ISLAND in Lake MICHIGAN in 1846. Their leader on Beaver Island, James Jesse STRANG (1813-1856), ruled as "king" of the island, making it an absolute monarchy.

Disturbed by a strange religion and a so-called king, other Beaver Island settlers had a battle with the Mormons in 1854, but they stayed on. Two years later, a mob from the mainland assassinated Strang, forced the Mormons from the island and took over their property.

MORRISON, William. (—)Fur trader of early nineteenth century Minnesota who claimed he discovered the headwaters of the MISSISSIPPI RIVER in 1804, long before Henry SCHOOLCRAFT (1793-1864) reported Lake ITASCA as the source of the mighty river. Although Morrison waited until 1856 to make his claim, a letter he had written his brother years earlier accurately describes five small feeder streams of Lake Itasca. His report seems to have a firm foundation.

MORTON, Oliver P. (Salisbury, IN, Aug. 4, 1823—Indianapolis, IN, Nov. 1, 1877). Senator and governor of Indiana. Morton practiced law in Centerville, Indiana, from 1847 to 1860. Originally a Democrat, he broke with the party over the Kansas-Nebraska Act (May 30, 1854). His political fortunes rose rapidly with the new Republican Party, and he served as the lieutenant governor of Indiana from 1860 to 1861, then governor from 1861 to 1867. A vitally active supporter of Abraham LINCOLN (1809-1865) and the CIVIL WAR efforts, Morton dissolved the Indiana legislature after Peace Democrats won control in 1862, then ran the state without the legislature from 1863 to 1865. He was sometimes known as the "assistant President" because of his wartime influence. He borrowed large sums on his own credit to finance Indiana's part in the war. Morton was a delegate to the Republican National Convention in 1872 and 1876 and was elected to the United States Senate from Indiana and served from 1867 to 1877. Morton was a radical reconstructionist in the Senate and was largely responsible for ratification of the 15th Amendment prohibiting laws against suffrage because of race.

MOUND BUILDERS AND MOUNDS.

North American archaeologists use the simplified term Mound Builders to describe the various peoples who built hummocks of earth in large numbers from the GREAT LAKES to the Gulf of Mexico and from the Appalachians to the MISSISSIPPI RIVER and slightly beyond. The largest number of these mounds is found in what is now the Midwest, concentrated mainly in the valleys of the Mississipi and OHIO rivers. Most authorities believe that the builders represented different cultures and prehistoric periods. Some probably were the ancestors of the present Indians, and they lived in permanent homes in villages. This permitted them to stay in one place while they worked on vast numbers of mounds of a variety of shapes, conical, pyramidal, elongated, wall-like and a separate type known as EFFIGY MOUNDS.

Illinois, alone, has more than 10,000 mounds of various sizes. The mounds served a variety of purposes, but each was generally restricted to a single purpose, mostly for burial, but also for the site of palaces or ceremonial structures, as dumping sites and, in the case of the effigies, perhaps some religious or cultural rite or simply as art, sometimes of a very high order.

In size they range from 100 feet across to the enormous Illinois MONKS MOUND, 1,000 feet from north to south, 700 feet from east to west and 100 feet high. In the CAHOKIA mound group, this is considered to be the largest primitive earthwork ever created. The difficulty of transporting such huge quantities of material by hand can scarcely be imagined.

The mounds include many materials not found locally and indicate that the builders traded with remote peoples. The FORT ANCIENT site in Ohio is a good example of a prehistoric fortress. This and others have been preserved as state and national preserves, and those in the Midwest have been intensively studied by experts.

Most impressive are the effigy mounds, such as the great SERPENT in Ohio, the hundred-foot long MAN MOUND in Wisconsin and the birds and other figures at EFFIGY MOUNDS NATIONAL MONUMENT in Iowa. The ability of these early people to depict figures realistically on such a large scale is surprising, particularly since they had none of the modern methods of viewing their work from an elevation to see how accurate it was.

The mounds vary in age from the early sixth century to some made after European exploration had begun.

MOUND CITY GROUP NATIONAL MONUMENT. Near CHILLICOTHE, Ohio.

Twenty-three burial mounds of HOPEWELL peoples (200 BC-AD 500) yielded copper breastplates, tools, obsidian blades, shells, ornaments of grizzly bear teeth, and stone pipes carved as birds and animals. These provide insights into the ceremonial customs of these prehistoric people.

MOUNT PLEASANT, Iowa.

City (pop. 7,322), seat of Henry County, situated in southeast Iowa twenty-six miles west of BURLINGTON, the city took its name as a promotion for its pleasant site. The community was settled in 1834 and boasts the oldest courthouse in Iowa, built in 1839. One of the first roads in Iowa was the plank toll road (two cents per mile for horse and wagon) between Mt. Pleasant and Burlington. The city is the seat of Iowa Wesleyan college, with its Lincoln Museum. There is a Museum of Repertoire Americana, featuring memorabilia of early tent, folk and repertoire theater. The city is best known for its annual Midwest Old Settlers and Threshers Steam Show, held five days and ending on Labor Day. The Mount Pleasant Midwest Old Settlers and Thresher's Association of Iowa was formed in 1950 to preserve the vanishing remnants of old time grain threshing operations. The organization's museum has probably the largest collection of threshers and related equipment in the nation. At the annual celebration, seventy steam engines parade and perform for the visitors, threshing grain, sawing lumber and grinding wheat into flour. The history and descriptions of each machine are provided. Thresher meals are served by church organizations, in tents on the grounds.

MOUNT PLEASANT, Ohio.

Village (pop. 616), situated in far east-central Ohio, in Belmont County, dating from the early nineteenth century. As early as 1817, the Quaker community was a refuge for fugitive slaves from the South and in time became one of the leading stations on the UNDERGROUND RAILROAD in Ohio. The first abolitionist newspaper in the United States, the *Philanthropist,* was published there in September, 1817, by Charles Osborn. Later, Benjamin Lundy published his *Genius of Universal Emancipation* there. In 1837 the community was the site of Ohio's first Abolitionist convention. After the 25-acre tract of mulberry trees planted by Thomas White in 1841 began to mature, Mount Pleasant became one of the first communities in the U.S. to produce silk worms and manufacture silk products, including hat plush, dress silks, ribbons and velvet. After three years, the mill was moved to West Virginia, where it failed. The Quaker Meeting House State Memorial pays tribute to the two-story red brick building erected in 1816, which was the first Quaker meeting house west of the Allegheny Mountains. It had an amazing capacity and some very unusual features for the time. The large partition that divided the auditorium into two equal parts was raised or lowered through the operation of a mechanism in the attic known as a Spanish windlass.

MOUNT VERNON, Ohio. City (pop. 14,-323), seat of Knox County, situated in central Ohio on the Walhonding River, the town was laid out in 1805 by Benjamin Butler, Thomas Patterson and Joseph Walker, all of whom had some responsibility for the community development of Mount Vernon, an agricultural and mineral producing center. It was named in honor of George Washington's home. The beloved eccentric, Johnny Appleseed (CHAPMAN) (1774-1845), once owned three lots in the town. In a document dated 1828 he recorded a deed which read in part: "...I Johnny Appleseed, (by occupation a gatherer and planter of apple seeds), residing in Richland County, for the sum of thirty dollars, honest money, do hereby grant to said Jesse B. Thomas...a lot in the village of Mt. Vernon, State of Ohio." Knox County is the largest sheep raising county east of the MISSISSIPPI RIVER, and one of the state's biggest weekly livestock auctions is held at Mount Vernon. It is a center of limestone and oil and gas production, and the state headquarters of the Seventh-Day Adventists are situated there. Daniel Decatur EMMETT (1815-1904), author and composer of *Dixie*, was born there. The Greek Revival architecture of the city is presented in a walking tour offered by the Chamber of Commerce.

MOZARKITE. State rock of Missouri, where it is apparently unique. Mozarkite given its official designation in 1967 by the seventy-fourth general assembly. Avidly sought by collectors from all over the world, mozarkite is a variety of chert, or the commonly known flintrock. It is plentiful in the Ozarks, particularly in Benton County, Missouri. It is found in a variety of colors, primarily in red, purple, green and reddish brown. Its beauty is greatly enhanced by cutting and polishing into ornamental shapes for jewelry.

MUHAMMAD, Elijah (Elijah Poole). (Sandersville, GA, Oct. 10, 1897—Chicago, IL, Feb. 25, 1975). Black Muslim leader. One of 13 children of an itinerant Baptist minister, his education was stopped at the fifth grade. Moving to DETROIT with his family to find work (1923), he experienced unemployment and welfare (1929-31) at first hand and developed a bitter hostility to public assistance that was later reflected in Muslim policies. In 1931 Poole met Wali Farad, founder of the Nation of Islam, who named him Muhammad. Upon Farad's disappearance in 1934, Muhammad was named Messenger of Allah, and, under his leadership, the Muslims began a period of slow growth which accelerated enormously after WORLD WAR II. Since his death, the leadership has been continued by his son, Wallace.

MUIR, John. (Dunbar, Scotland, Apr. 21, 1838—Los Angeles, CA, Dec. 24, 1914). One of the most notable figures in conservation and known as the father of the national park system, Muir was brought as a boy to Columbia County, Wisconsin. His autobiography *The Story of My Boyhood and Youth* describes his boyhood on the crude Wisconsin farm where he grew up. He recounts how his visits to the prairies, swamps and forests around PORTAGE, Wisconsin, awakened his lifelong love of nature. That heritage was further strengthened by Muir's studies at the University of WISCONSIN. There he also continued work on some of his "inventions," and a clock he made at the university is still on display. While he taught at a rural school near Oregon, Wisconsin, he let his inventive imagination fly, creating a clock that would tip him out of bed at his chosen time as well as another that would start the school fire an hour ahead of class time. His later travels along the U.S. west coast as far north as Alaska resulted in many important discoveries in natural history, including Muir Glacier. His traveling studies took him as far afield as Russia, Australia and India. As early as 1866, he had offered to buy a tract of the Columbia County (Wisconsin) prairie meadow, in the area where he grew up, as an early trial in saving such a rapidly vanishing natural treasure. However, the offer was refused. In recognition of Muir's efforts as a crusader for conservation and the creation of natural wonders, Muir Woods National Monument in California was named for him

MUNCIE, Indiana. City (pop. 77,216), seat of Delaware County, major northeastern Indiana city, southwest of FORT WAYNE , named for a subtribe of the DELAWARE Indians who formerly lived in central Indiana. Platted in 1827, the community originally was called "Munsey-town" for the Munsee Indians whose settlement it occupied after the Indians were removed by the Treaty of St. Mary's in 1818. Its present name dates from 1845. Natural gas was discovered in 1876, but was not developed for ten years, an event which then caused many industries to choose Muncie as a site. Housing failed to keep pace with the rate of settlement and an undeveloped section within the city limits soon displayed ramshackle dwellings of board, paper and sheet-iron, causing the spot to be called "Shedtown." Among the new industries to come to Muncie was a glass products plant owned by the Ball brothers of Buffalo, New York, who invested heavily in other local industries. They also revived Eastern Indiana Normal University and, after it had become Ball State Teachers College, donated funds for most of the buildings on campus. The Ball Corporation still maintains its international headquarters in Muncie. Other industries include gear making, steel and wire and transformers. Muncie gained unusual fame when Robert and Helen Lynd, made it the subject of their sociological studies of a small city which they considered typical. The studies resulted in *Middletown* (1929) and *Middletown in Transition* (1937), two of the most famous works in their field. Of interest to visitors to BALL STATE UNIVERSITY are the art gallery, planetarium and observatory and Christy Woods, an outdoor laboratory and arboretum. Visitors also enjoy the Muncie Children's Museum and the Ball Corporation Museum, with displays of glass products. The Indiana Renaissance Fair is held there June 21 and 22. There is a Glass Days Festival in late July, and a well-known track, International Dragway, holds seasonal racing events.

MUNDELEIN COLLEGE. Roman Catholic college founded originally and maintained for years as a college for women in CHICAGO , Illinois. Founded in 1879, Mundelein College had an enrollment in 1985-1986 of 1,182 and had a staff of 89. Its modern library on the shores of Lake Michigan was so much state-of-the-library-art, that its methods and practices were widely followed by other college libraries. In later years the college has become coeducational.

MUSCATINE, Iowa. City (pop. 23,467). Seat of Muscatine County, situated in southeast Iowa, on the MISSISSIPPI RIVER in the great bend where the river turns abruptly south. The name was derived from the MASCOUTEN tribe of the POTAWATOMI INDIANS , their name thought to mean "burning island." Muscatine was incorporated in 1851 and was an early center of river traffic and lumbering. It continues as a shipping and processing center of a rich agricultural region, processing food products and grain. Other products include industrial alcohol, vitamins and machinery for making buttons. In 1891, John F. BOEPPLE opened a plant to manufacture pearl buttons from the clam shells in the Mississippi, after inventing the first machines to process the shells. The industry grew until it was the largest of its kind, with fleets of clammers operating in the river. Sometimes a lucky clammer might even find a pearl. When the clam supply dwindled, the industry almost died out, but the machinery making continued. Attractions for visitors include the Musser home at Muscatine, which houses the Laura Musser Art Gallery and Museum. Another Muscatine museum offers thirty-nine rooms of exhibits, which are designed to become a major collection of old steamboating days on the Mississippi. Nearby Wildcat Den State Park provides an early gristmill and scenic views.

MUSEUM OF SCIENCE AND INDUS-TRY. CHICAGO, Illinois museum considered by many to house the most comprehensive collection of mechanical and scientific exhibits ever assembled. The museum, with nearly five million visitors annually, is thought to hold the attendance record for museums worldwide. Full-sized exhibits include a reproduction of a coal mine in actual operation and the German submarine U 505. Colleen Moore's Doll House

Museum of Science and Industry.

is a major attraction. Fourteen acres of permanent displays are supplemented by seasonal features and displays by various governmental agencies. The newest attraction is the Omnimax Theater (1986).

MUSKEGON RIVER. At 227 miles in length one of the longest rivers in Michigan. The river flows from HOUGHTON LAKE, forms Muskegon Lake, then empties into Lake MICHIGAN at the city of MUSKEGON. Its swift current attracts canoers.

MUSKEGON, Michigan. City (pop. 40,823); seat of Muskegon County; southwestern portion of Michigan on the LOWER PENINSULA; northwest of GRAND RAPIDS at the mouth of the MUSKEGKON RIVER ; name comes from an Indian word muskego meaning, "river-with-marshes." Muskegon was once known as the "Lumber Queen of the World." In one year, 1888, the Muskegon area produced eight hundred million board feet of lumber. Forty-seven sawmills processed the timber in the community during the 1880s. Muskegon owed its early development to the deep river, which allowed transportation into the heart of the fur-trading regions of the state. The height and quantity of the timber first attracted Jean NICOLET (1598-1642) in 1634, but it was not until 1812 that the first permanent trading post was established by Baptiste Recollet, a French trader. The city's greatest benefactor was C. H. Hackley, a man who made a fortune in the lumber business and supported many struggling industries which tried to develop after the timber was gone. A bonus fund of $100,000 was established to bring new industries to town. Promoters focused on the advantages of Lake Michigan shipping, the fine harbor, and the sheltering dunes to attract new business. Muskegon is now the largest city on the eastern shore of Lake Michigan. Displays of Muskegon's lumber industry days

may be seen in the Muskegon County Museum. Hackley House shows the style of life of the lumber barons. The Muskegon Museum of Art features such American artists as Homer, Whistler and Wyeth. In a local cemetery is the grave of Jonathan Walker, the "man with the branded hand" in the writings of John Greenleaf Whittier.

MUSKELLUNGE. The muskellunge (muskie) is the official state fish of Wisconsin. The prized fish is a member of the pike family, a small group of food and game fish popular in Europe, Asia and North America. The muskellunge is the largest of the North American pikes. The name comes from the American Indians; it grows from two to seven feet long and has been known to weigh as much as sixty pounds. It feeds on fish, frogs, snakes and may even devour the young of aquatic mammals.

MUSKINGUM RIVER. Originating at COSHOCTON in central southeastern Ohio at the confluence of the Walhonding and TUSCARAWAS rivers, the Muskingum flows for 112 miles, south past Dresden, the head of navigation, past ZANESVILLE, to enter the OHIO RIVER at MARIETTA. The town of Duncan Falls, south of Zanesville, took part of its name from the Falls of the Muskingum, obliterated by a dam constructed more than 150 years ago. The house of artist-illustrator Howard Chandler (1873-1952), the Barracks, overlooked the wooded river valley from a high rocky bluff not far from Duncan Falls. There he once entertained poet James Whitcomb Riley, who celebrated the river and its valley in a poem, *The Muskingum Valley:* "Where the hills sloped as soft as the dawn down to noon, and the river runs by like an old fiddle tune..." The river is the center of a widespread conservancy district.

NAPERVILLE, Illinois. City (pop.42,330), located west of CHICAGO, Illinois, near the East-West Tollway, Du Page County. Naperville, named for Joseph Naper who platted the town and built the first sawmill in 1832, was chosen the first county seat of Du Page County,

Illinois. In 1867, when the voters of the county decided to move the county government, Naperville officials refused to recognize the vote as legal. In 1868 a wagonload of men had to steal the county records and move them to Wheaton, Illinois, the new county seat. Naperville is the home of the Kroehler Furniture Manufacturing Company, established in 1887. It also has the Du Page Boiler Works, the Du Page Precision Products, Inc., and the Standard Oil Research Laboratories. The city is the center of the vast development of Du Page County, which during the 1980s made it the fastest growing county in the nation. Naper Settlement, a museum in the center of old Naperville, features eleven acres of reconstructed buildings from the period 1831 to 1900. Included in the village are a fort, print shop, chapel, one-room schoolhouse, blacksmith and an Italianate mansion. Guides in costume conduct tours. A brick sidewalk, called Riverwalk, complete with fountains and covered bridges, links Naper Settlement with Naperville's old quarries. The path follows the Du Page River for several miles.

NASHUA, Iowa. City (pop. 1,846). Situated in northeast Iowa in Chickasaw County on the CEDAR RIVER south of CHARLES CITY. The name is probably derived from an Indian tribe, the Nashaways, meaning "beautiful river with a pebbly bottom." The name was used in New Hampshire and Massachusetts, and adopted in several states farther west. The community is best known for the "LITTLE BROWN CHURCH IN THE VALE," internationally famed as a site for weddings.

NASHVILLE, Indiana. Town (pop. 705), central Indiana seat of BROWN COUNTY, near GNAW BONE and west of COLUMBUS. Picturesque countryside makes this Indiana community popular with photographers and artists. The courthouse lawn sports the Liars' Bench which is armless at one end. A person gains a seat if able to tell a tale better than the last person to sit down. Since the bench is capable of holding only six people, the person at the armless end is pushed off. The Brown County Art Gallery Association is one of the oldest art associations in the Midwest. There is a permanent display as a memorial to Glen Cooper Henshaw, the gallery also changes exhibits devoted to the work of member artists. Art work of other local and regional artists is displayed in the historic Minor House by the Brown County Art Guild. Nashville's Brown County Winter Festival, held the first weekend of February, features ski workshops, races and a fishing contest. The arrival of spring is welcomed by the annual Beanblossom Bluegrass Festival held in Beanblossom, north of Nashville, in mid-June. Nashville's shops of great variety, the art

galleries, quaint restaurants, the resident artists and many other attractions make Nashville one of the country's important tourist villages, especially in the fall color season and at Christmas. Many other attractions of BROWN COUNTY are centered in Nashville.

NATIONAL COLLEGE OF EDUCATION. Privately supported liberal arts college in EVANSTON, Illinois. Founded in 1886 to meet the demand for teachers in newly developed kindergarten classes in Chicago, the school has three campuses, in Evanston, the Urban Campus in CHICAGO and the Lombard, Illinois, Campus. The college offers undergraduate and graduate programs in liberal arts, teacher education, and human services. Credit is given for some courses by examination, for previous training and experience. Accredited with the North Central Association of Colleges and Schools, the college uses the quarter system with three-month summer sessions. During the 1985-1986 academic year, the college enrolled 2,350 students and had 118 faculty members.

NATIONAL HOBO CONVENTION. Each year newspaper, radio and television reporters, some from abroad, flock to the small community of BRITT, Iowa, to bring to an international audience the doings of hundreds of hobos, former hobos, and once-a-year hobos. This unique and colorful gathering is highlighted annually by the selection of a king and queen of the hobos, chosen by the people of the town.

NATIONAL ROAD. First long interstate highway built with federal funds and popularly named the Cumberland Road. For years its extension beyond Virginia was held up over serious questions of the constitutional issue of federal appropriations for internal improvements. But appropriations finally were made, and the last appropriation of Congress was made in 1838, bringing the road to its terminus at VANDALIA, Illinois. As it was completed, each section was turned over to the state in which it lay. In the Midwest the National Road followed the route of present-day U.S. Route 40 through such towns and cities CAMBRIDGE, ZANESVILLE, COLUMBUS, and SPRINGFIELD in Ohio, RICHMOND, INDIANAPOLIS, BRAZIL and TERRE HAUTE, all in Indiana; and Casey, Greenup, Montrose, Teutopolis, and Vandalia, all in Illinois.

NATIONAL SKI HALL OF FAME. Place of honor for the greats of American skiing. Located in ISHPEMING, Michigan, the hall contains photographs, historic equipment and trophies. One of the exhibits has been the oldest known ski and pole dating back more than 4,000 years. The hall is operated by the United States Ski Association. The museum was dedicated in 1954.

NAUVOO, Illinois. City (pop. 1,133), Hancock Co., located on the east bank of the MISSISSIPPI RIVER, northeast of KEOKUK, Iowa, name created by Joseph SMITH (1805-1844), based on a Hebrew root, "nawa," interpreted to mean,"beautiful place." Nauvoo was founded in 1839 by Smith, founder and Prophet of the Church of Jesus Christ of Latter-day Saints (MORMON).

Smith planned to build a refuge for his followers who had been expelled from several other states after conflicts with other settlers. In the early 1840s Nauvoo was the largest city in Illinois. Four-acre blocks were divided into four lots. Each family had space for gardens, trees and domesticated animals.

In politically divided Illinois, both parties courted the Mormon vote to the extent that, in 1840, the residents of Nauvoo were given a charter granting almost complete home rule.

City officials had the authority to do anything not expressly forbidden by the state or federal constitutions. The court system had extraordinary powers. The Nauvoo Legion, an independent part of the state militia, received cannon and small arms from SPRINGFIELD, Illinois. As a military force, the Mormon militia was second in size in Illinois only to the United States Army.

Smith became the mayor, chief magistrate, lieutenant general, newspaper editor and real estate promoter. But the town never became a trading center for the surrounding territory. Real estate sales were the chief business, with most of the leaders becoming speculators. The community's wealth came from the money contributed by converts.

With the murder of Smith, the Mormons lost their political power and their charter, leaving the city without government. In 1846 Brigham YOUNG led the first hundred families across the MISSISSIPPI RIVER in what became their epic march to Utah. The remaining Mormons founded a new Mormon denomination called the REORGANIZED CHURCH OF JESUS CHRIST OF LATTER-DAY SAINTS.

In 1849, an ICARIAN group, a society of utopian

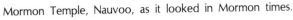

Mormon Temple, Nauvoo, as it looked in Mormon times.

communists from France, moved into Nauvoo from Texas and introduced a grape culture to establish a wine industry. Despite an active attempt to gain converts, the colony failed. The Mormon temple burned and Nauvoo became just one of the many German settlements in Illinois.

In 1920, Nauvoo was the largest town in Illinois without a depot on a rail line.

Today Nauvoo is a tourist attraction with many of the original structures preserved and archaeological excavations in progress. The two Mormon organizations, the Church organized in Utah and the Reorganized Church, are working together to restore the town to its former grandeur.

The Jonathan Browning House is a reconstruction of the home of the famous inventor of several kinds of repeating firearms. The Brigham Young Home is the restored residence of the second president of the Church of Jesus Christ of Latter-day Saints. Meetings to plan the westward migration of the Mormons were held in the office in this house.

The Mansion House has been restored to the appearance it had while it was the permanent residence of Joseph Smith. Smith's Red Brick Store, built in 1842, is the reconstructed general merchandise store he operated and used as church headquarters.

Seventies Hall was the training center for laymen interested in improving their missionary skills. The first floor was used for classes, while the second floor held the community's library. Midwest Federalist-style architecture with arch bricks over the windows is shown in the home of Wilford Woodruff, fourth president of the Mormon Church. Nauvoo Historic Society Museum features a room for each period of the city's history: Indian, Mormon, Icarian, and pioneer.

NEENAH, Wisconsin. City (pop. 22,432), situated on the south bank of the FOX RIVER outlet of Lake WINNEBAGO in east central Wisconsin; the name comes from the Indian meaning running water. Neenah and its sister city MENASHA, across the river, are almost always referred to as one, Neenah-Menasha. Doty Island, in the lake between the two communities, is shared by them. The city was founded in 1843 by Harrison Reed and his partner Harvey Jones. When the partners quarreled, Jones removed Reed from the business, and he went across the river and founded Menasha. The area had a long record of Indian occupation, of French missionaries and of traders. The first

sawmill and gristmill were built on the Neenah side in 1849, but Menasha became the more industrialized, with Neenah the financial center and home of the well-to-do. Today the twin cities are among the world leaders in the production of paper and paper products. Neenah attractions include Doty Grand Loggery, in Doty Park, formerly the home of territorial governor James Duane Doty. South of town is High Cliff State Park, which features High Cliff General Store, a museum showing life in the last half of the 1800s. Both communities benefit from the year-round recreational activities of Lake Winnebago.

NEVADA, Iowa. City (pop. 5,912). Seat of Story County, situated in central Iowa, just east of AMES. The name was chosen by Joseph M. Thrift, a returned forty-niner, who named it for the Sierra Nevada range. The city is best known as the birthplace of famed evangelist William Ashley (Billy) SUNDAY (1862-1935), who as a major league baseball player invented the bunt before leaving professional sports to become a religious figure.

NEW ALBANY, Indiana. City (pop.37,107), southern Indiana, on the OHIO RIVER opposite Louisville, Kentucky; seat of Floyd Co.; named for Albany, New York. New Albany, an important Ohio River city, was the largest community in Indiana from its founding in 1813 to the end of the early river traffic era. From four to seven shipbuilders added to the city's reputation as a shipbuilding center in the period from 1830 to 1860. Two record-setting steamboats manufactured in New Albany shipyards were the *Eclipse* and the *Robert E. Lee*. After railroads put an end to the paddlewheel riverboat era, New Albany came back into prosperity with the growth of the glass industry, developed by John Ford and W.A. De Pauw. The third major industry in New Albany was the fabrication of plywood which benefitted from large amounts of hardwood nearby, favorable climatic conditions for aging the veneer, and low transportation costs. The Culbertson Mansion State Historic Site preserves a French Second Empire-style mansion erected in 1869 for the entrepreneur and philanthropist William S. Culbertson. Among the furnishings are a three-story mahogany and rosewood staircase, a hand-painted ceiling, an Italian marble fireplace and many antiques.

NEW CASTLE, Indiana. City (pop. 20,056), seat of Henry County, eastern Indiana city east of INDIANAPOLIS. New Castle was the birthplace of Wilbur WRIGHT, co-inventor of the airplane. The Wilbur Wright State Historical Site provides a replica of the pioneer aviator's birthplace. The original was destroyed by fire in 1884. Among the thirty-six industries of New Castle are the plants of Chrysler Motors, Mohawk Container, Modernfold, Allegheny Ludlum Steel, American Standard and Avesta Steel.

NEW GLARUS, Wisconsin. Town (pop. 1,763), situated in south central Wisconsin on the Sugar River. Founded in August, 1845, New Glarus took its name from the Swiss canton of Glarus. The story of the picturesque community begins in 1844 in Glarus, Switzerland, where hard times had been brought on by a partial crop failure. The Canton appropriated $600 and private contributions raised $2,000 more to form an emigration society. The society sent Judge Nicholas Duerst and Fridolin Streiff to America to find and purchase land in a locality as similar as possible to Glarus in soil, climate and other features. Each subscriber was to have twenty acres. After traveling across the Midwest for two months, the scouts purchased 1,200 acres of farmland in an oval valley in Wisconsin, along with 92 acres of timber. On April 16, 1845, 193 pioneers set sail for America in a 49-day crossing. Arriving on the MISSISSIPPI, they could not find Duerst or Fridolin. By the time Duerst arrived and directed them to the new land, there were only 106 remaining. Some had gone back to the homeland, and some had died. Settling their land in 1845, they lived poorly for about twenty years until they turned to dairying, as in the old country, and then they became prosperous. Today the community proudly harks back to its Swiss heritage. Every effort is made to keep the impression of a Swiss village. Replicas of the first buildings erected include blacksmith shops, cheese factory, schoolhouse and print shop in the Swiss Historical Village. Original furnishings and tools are seen. The Chalet of the Golden Fleece is an authentic replica of a Swiss chalet, with more then 3,000 Swiss items. The Swiss motif is maintained in three annual festivals which attract thousands of visitors. Heidi Festival is a drama, also providing a crafts fair in late June. Swiss Volkfest in early August features yodeling and dancing and honors the founding of Switzerland in 1291. William Tell Festival on Labor Day weekend presents Schiller's *Wilhelm Tell* in German. There are also Swiss entertainment and a fine arts show.

Roofless Church, New Harmony.

NEW HARMONY, Indiana. Town (pop. 945), situated in Posey County, the most southwesterly county in Indiana. Headed by George RAPP (1757-1847), a religious leader whose followers were called Rappites, a group of German settlers came to the present site in 1815 to found a communal colony which they called Harmonie. The discipline was harsh, but they accomplished near miracles on their 30,000 acres of land, draining swamps, clearing land, constructing large brick houses and public buildings, some still standing in good condition.

Their success spawned wonder and envy in nearby communities. The deeply religious settlers practiced celibacy and constantly prepared for the second coming of Christ. When this did not happen, and many of the disciples became dissatisfied with conditions, in 1825 the remaining members moved back to Pennsylvania, and the community was sold to another remarkable man, Robert OWEN (1771-1858), who called the town New Harmony.

Owen had a dream of establishing a perfect society, also of communal nature, where there would be no inequity; each person would have his own skills and abilities and would contribute those to the good of the community. With the assistance of his four sons, Owen set out to bring to New Harmony a choice collection of creative, scientific and cultural leaders of all sorts. In this they were amazingly successful. One of the first groups floated down the Ohio River on a flatboat dubbed the "Boatload of Knowledge."

Very shortly a large number of other scientists, educators, writers, scholars and others of worldwide reputation had come to New Harmony. The communal nature of the place soon gave way, due mainly to the fact that Owen was away much of the time, but the intellectual group stayed on to make New Harmony such a success that it has been listed among the "world villages that have made history."

Pioneer work in education from infant school and kindergarten upward, with equal opportunity for both boys and girls, free library, scientific experimentation, the initial U.S. geological survey and many other notable achievements were made at New Harmony. It is said that the concept of the Smithsonian Institution was developed there.

Today New Harmony has become one of the principal tourist attractions of Indiana. Visitors may still stay at the old inn and dine in much the same style as yesteryear. The old architecture remains in much of the community but has been blended with the new. One of the most remarkable and controversial structures of the century is the modern Roofless Church, designed by Philip Johnson. Its multifaceted roof forms a most unusual dome, under which stands the famed Jacques Lipchitz' sculpture, "Descent of the Holy Spirit."

Among the original structures still standing, some open to the public, are Macluria Double-log Cabin, Solomon Wolf House, Second Harmonist Cooper Shop, John Beal House (with early European daub and wattle pugging and exhibits of early scientists and educators), Owen House, George Keppler House, Lichtenberger Building and its exhibit of the Maximilian-Bodmer expedition, including Bodmer's prints, the Robert Henry Fauntleroy House, Thrall Opera House and Theater Complex, and the Workingmen's Institute, one of the first free public libraries in America. The labyrinth of hedges, designed to symbolize the twists and turns of life, still confuses visitors. Nearby is Harmonie State park, a popular recreational area.

NEW MADRID, Missouri. Town (pop. 3,204), seat of New Madrid County in southeastern Missouri. The original settlement was founded in 1783 by Francois and Joseph Le Sieur, Canadian trappers and traders. The land passed into Spanish control and with the close of the American Revolution the Spanish territory and the American claims became adjoining. To prevent further American expansion, the Spanish authorities devised a buffer colony. American settlers were given large land grants, religious freedom and local self-government. A port of entry was created, eliminating

the need for Americans to transport goods to New Orleans. The project, under the control of Colonel George Morgan, failed, however, because it conflicted with plans of General James Wilkinson of Kentucky and Estevan Miro, the governor of Louisiana who together had plans for a Spanish Mississippi Valley empire. Miro ended Morgan's project, but confirmed the land grants. New Madrid continued as an agricultural and trade center for the area. Prosperity ended on December 16, 1811, when the citizens awoke to find their houses creaking and furniture falling in an earthquake. The first quake was the worst in North American history and is known as the New Madrid EARTHQUAKE because the town was believed to be at the quake's epicenter. The first shock wave was followed by a series of earthquakes which shook the region every day for almost two years. Some areas sank as much as twenty-five feet. The shock waves churned the Mississippi and sent boats washing into the shore. The disturbance chilled any interest in settlement, as many of the residents left for safety. In 1816 Congress granted residents of New Madrid land in other parts of the state, but only twenty moved. Shifts in the river channel caused New Madrid to relocate three or four times before the CIVIL WAR. Its strategic position was first recognized by the Confederates who constructed fortifications on Island No. 10 to block Union control of the river. The Confederate position was captured by General Albert A Pope and New Madrid returned to life as a county seat in a farming region. Exhibits of the town's earthquakes, Civil War relics and Indian artifacts are housed in the New Madrid Historical Museum. The Hunter-Dawson State Historic Site is the restored fifteen-room mansion of William Hunter, a local merchant. The Greek Revival and Italinate-styled home is furnished as it might have been in the mid-19th century.

NEW MELLERAY ABBEY. The large abbey of the Trappist Monks presents a surprising picture to travelers crossing the prairies of Iowa west of DUBUQUE. The white stone walls, arched windows, buttresses, spires and ornamental chimneys provide an unexpected Gothic touch on the Iowa countryside. Founded in 1849 by groups of monks from Ireland, the abbey consists of four large structures with gabled wings, enclosing a rectangular court. About 130 monks, averaging thirty-five years in age, occupy the abbey and begin their day with prayers at 2:15 A.M. The picturesque robes of the choir monks and the contrasting drab robes of the lay brothers add to the other-worldly quality of the scene. Having taken vows of silence, the members of the abbey communicate in sign language. The extensive woodlands and pastures provide for about 300 beef cattle. Other enterprises include poultry, hogs, wine and honey, as well as articles for religious use, including candles, incense and Eucharistic breads.

NEW PHILADELPHIA, Ohio. City (pop. 16,883), seat of Tuscarawas county, situated in eastern Ohio on the TUSCARAWAS RIVER, the community was founded by John Knisely in 1804, and was named as county seat four years later. It was incorporated in 1833. New Philadelphia is located in an area of coal and clay and produces pottery, machinery and foundry products. The influence of the early Swiss-German settlers is still found in some of the architecture. Two historic early communities are nearby. Zoar Village State Memorial has been restored to preserve some of the flavor of the communal settlement of the ZOAR Society, which lasted for eighty years (1818-1898). SCHOENBRUNN VILLAGE State Memorial is a partial reconstruction of the first Ohio town built by Christian Indians, who were killed in a senseless massacre. Not far away is Laurens State Memorial, only American fort in Ohio during the Revolutionary War. It was built in 1778 as a defense against the British and named in honor of Henry Laurens, president of the Continental Congress. Each year the Zoar Harvest Festival is held on the first two days of August. Another Annual event is the Swiss Festival, on the fourth Friday after Labor Day.

NEW SALEM, Illinois. Village (pop. 170), restoration of a community to its appearance in the lifetime of Abraham LINCOLN. New Salem was founded on the hope it would prosper from river traffic on the SANGAMON RIVER, but the river was not adequate for extensive commercial use. Never having more than one hundred residents, New Salem lasted only ten years. The years Abraham Lincoln spent at New Salem are often considered to be the turning point in his life. He worked there as a laborer, storekeeper, surveyor, soldier, postmaster, and legislator and also began his study of law in the tiny town. Restoration of New Salem includes thirteen cabins, six stores, and the Rutledge Tavern. Only one of the original buildings, the Onstot cooperage shop, remains standing.

NEW ULM, Minnesota. City (pop. 13,755),

seat of Brown County, south-central Minnesota, northwest of MANKATO, located at the meeting of the Cottonwood and MINNESOTA rivers, founded in 1854 by members of the German Land Society, named after the town of Ulm in Wurttemberg, Germany. New Ulm is located on land which was once an island in a glacial river. New Ulm struggled for several years before its residents merged with another group from CINCINNATI, Ohio. This merged group was then known as the German Land Association of Minnesota. Commerce in the town centered on farming, banking, brewing, and various crafts. In 1860 the population included 653 Germans who retained their native language and customs. During the SIOUX Uprising (1862) an important battle was fought at New Ulm on August 23, 1862. Eight hundred Indians under the leadership of LITTLE CROW repeatedly attacked the residents who fought under the leadership of Charles Flandrau, a St. Peter judge. Before retreating, the Indians managed to burn much of New Ulm and kill twenty-six whites. Many of the wounded were treated by Dr. William MAYO of Le Seur. Until danger passed, the entire community of 1,200 was evacuated thirty miles to better safety in Mankato. The work of Wanda Gag, author and illustrator is exhibited in local libraries and museums. Gag was born in New Ulm in 1893. Schonlau Park Plaza displays a rare carillon clock, cast in the Netherlands. The clock's 37 bells weigh nearly three tons. Sliding doors in the tower reveal animated figures that illustrate the history of the community. Bits of native prairie are found along the Cottonwood River in Flandrau State Park. Relics of pioneer and Indian life are exhibited in the Brown County Historical Museum. Harkin General Store is a restored 1870s post office and country store. In July residents of New Ulm celebrate Heritagefest, featuring local and West German entertainers. Each evening an outdoor drama, "Hermannstraum," illustrates the struggles of the German warrior Hermann and of the German immigrants to the New World. Citizens of New Ulm also annually celebrate two German events. Fasching, the weekend before Ash Wednesday, features a masquerade ball, bonfire and parade. Octoberfest is held in mid-October.

NEWARK, Ohio. City (pop. 41,200, 1980), seat of Licking County (1808), situated near the geographic center of Ohio, 35 miles east of COLUMBUS, in a valley where the North and South forks of the Licking River come together to form the river itself. The city is laid out in an attractive rambling valley. Newark was incorporated in 1826, and the name is derived from Newark, New Jersey, and ultimately from Newark, Nottinghamshire, England. The city is a hub of farm trade and processing of farm products, an industrial center and a railroad concentration point. General William Schenck platted the settlement in 1802, close to the ancient mounds of a vanished people, and a few miles from Flint Ridge, an Indian weapons quarry. With ample ideas for his community Schenk laid out a public square and "crazy wide" streets. When it was selected as county seat, the meager population put together a one-room log cabin as county courthouse. With the coming of a charcoal furnace in 1816, the area began to produce iron ingots. With the opening of the OHIO AND ERIE CANAL in 1832, Newark became Ohio's canal capital, and ornate packet-cabins and plain canal barges brought substantial commerce. Two epidemics of CHOLERA, the first railroad in 1854, a destructive fire in 1856, the coming of iron and glass industries, along with stove companies and production of modern lighting fixtures—all were highlights of the city's history. The coming of the Owen-Corning Fiberglass operations in 1933 helped to dull the desperate conditions of economic depression of the period. The Newark Earthworks State Memorials combine to preserve some of the most unusual and impressive prehistoric mounds in the nation, including the famed EAGLE EFFIGY MOUND. Trained observers noted that on June 11, the rays of the rising sun cross the horizon virtually on a line with the axis of the octagon and circle mounds, perhaps an indication of the astronomical standing of the builders. The Museum of Ohio Indian Art is there as well as a division of OHIO STATE UNIVERSITY.

NEWSPAPERS. The *Sentinel of the Northwest Territory* was started in Ohio in 1793 and was the first newspaper to be published north of the OHIO RIVER. The first newspaper published west of the MISSISSIPPI RIVER was the Missouri *Gazette,* which began publication at ST. LOUIS in 1808. Illinois followed soon after, with the *Herald* at KASKASKIA in 1814. Today there are more than 75 daily newspapers in Illinois, led by the CHICAGO *Tribune,* with the Midwest's largest circulation. Ohio has the largest number of dailies, with nearly 100; Indiana, 75; Missouri, 60; Michigan, 54; Iowa, 50; Minnesota, 31, and Wisconsin 22. Iowa has a number of newspaper distinctions. The DES MOINES

Register is unique in serving an entire state, as distinct from serving only an individual metropolitan area. Under the direction of the pioneering Taylor family of journalists, the tiny TRAER, Iowa, *Star-Clipper* has won more national awards for weekly journalism than any other of its class.

NEWTON, Iowa. City (pop. 15,292). Seat of Jasper County, situated in southeast Iowa, about twenty miles east of DES MOINES, the name comes from Revolutionary War hero John Newton, who rescued several patriots from execution by the British. It is an industrial city, incorporated, in 1857, known worldwide as the birthplace of the modern washing machine, nicknamed "The Home Appliance Center of the World." F.L. MAYTAG (1857-1937) and his associate Howard Snyder produced the first hand-powered machine, then the first motorized machine, and their Maytag Company eventually introduced the first automatic washing machine, and more than thirty other home appliances followed. The Jasper County Museum features historical washing products, along with other historical displays, farm implements and tools.

NIAGARA CAVE. Largest cave in the Midwest. Located near Harmony, Minnesota, the cave was discovered accidentally by a farmer who continually lost pigs in a field. Upon investigation, he heard squealing coming from a hole in the ground. He discovered not only his animals but also a cave featuring stalactites, stalagmites and a sixty-foot waterfall 150 feet underground.

NICOLET, Jean. (Cherbourg, France, 1598—Drowned on the St. Lawrence River, Nov. 1, 1642). Explorer. In 1634 Nicolet was the first white man to discover Lake MICHIGAN and present Wisconsin. Nicolet came to New France with Samuel de CHAMPLAIN in 1618. He lived among various Indian tribes and hoped to find the long-sought route to the Orient and its Chinese riches. Nicolet carried a beautiful silk robe decorated with gold braid and jewels, which was given to him by the French governor of Canada who wanted Nicolet dressed properly to meet the Chinese emperor. In the fall of 1634, when he came ashore at the WINNEBAGO village of RED BANKS near present GREEN BAY, Wisconsin, Nicolet wore the robe, brandishing a pistol in each hand. The natives were suitably impressed, but they most certainly were not Chinese. Among the Indians, Nicolet was

Jean Nicolet arrives in "China."

known as Manitou-iriniou, the "wonderful man." He was probably the first white man to see MACKINAC ISLAND, in 1634.

NILES, Michigan. City (pop. 13,115), Cass County, southwestern Michigan on the LOWER PENINSULA, at the St. Joseph River west of Sturgis near the Indiana border, known as the "Four Flags City." During the American Revolution, a party of Spaniards captured the fort at Niles and held it for several days. Because of this even the Spanish flag technically may be added to the French, British, and American flags which have flown over Michigan. A frontier outpost beginning in 1697, the modern city was founded in 1827. On the stagecoach route between Detroit and Chicago, Niles experienced steady growth to become a commercial and industrial center. It claims Aaron Montgomery WARD, originator of the modern mail-order business, the writer Ring Lardner and the two Dodge brothers of automotive fame who grew up there. The Fort St. Joseph Museum is said to contain one of the leading exhibits of the SIOUX Indian nation. Niles Raft Race is an annual event in July.

NILES, Ohio. City (pop. 23,088), situated in Trumbull County in northeast Ohio, on the MAHONING RIVER between WARREN and YOUNGS-

TOWN, the community takes its name from Hezekiah Niles, author of several books on American government. Niles was begun in 1806 by James Heaton, who built the first gristmill and blast furnace in the area, and it was named for Heaton. In 1834 the name was changed to Nilestown for the Baltimore newspaper editor and author whom Heaton admired. The post office later shortened the name. The community is known as the birthplace of President William MC KINLEY, born there January 29, 1843. The president is commemorated at McKinley Memorial Park, with its great colonnaded memorial structure and McKinley statue.

NORMAL, Illinois. City (pop. 35,672), central Illinois city often considered together with BLOOMINGTON, located on Interstates 74 and 55, home of ILLINOIS STATE UNIVERSITY. It was named Normal because it was the seat of what was then the State Normal School. Normal, Illinois, was one of several Illinois cities which began as stations on the Illinois Central Railway. Illinois State University, situated on fifty-six acres, was expanded from a teacher training school into a liberal arts institution at the turn of the century. After the college was founded in 1857, the community grew and was incorporated in 1865. Much of the city's prosperity is based on the university, but it is a center of a prosperous farming community, noted especially for its nursery stock and fruits. Hospital facilities in Bloomington and Normal have made this the health center for central Illinois.

NORTH BEND, Ohio. Village (pop. 546), situated on the northernmost bend of the OHIO RIVER in far southwestern Ohio. The village was founded by John Cleve Symmes in 1789. The fourth settlement in Ohio, it lagged far behind its close neighbor to the east, Losantiville, which became CINCINNATI. North Bend's principal claim to fame is as the site of the birth place of Benjamin HARRISON (1833-1901). The president could boast that he was born in a log house, perhaps not mentioning that the place had thirteen rooms. It was the home of his grandfather, William Henry HARRISON (1773-1841), who lived there until he went to Washington as president. However, Benjamin Harrison spent most of his younger life in his parents' home nearby. On a hilly site, called Mount Nebo, overlooking the river is the William Henry Harrison Tomb State Memorial, a sandstone shaft seventy-five feet high. The shaft is of solid stone except for a passage at its base which leads to the tomb directly back of the monument, in which the ninth president is is buried. A beacon light on top was established as a guide to Ohio River pilots.

NORTHEAST MISSOURI STATE UNIVERSITY. Publicly supported liberal arts and teachers university in KIRKSVILLE, Missouri. The university was founded in 1867 as a normal school and commercial college. Teacher education continues to be a primary emphasis. The university grants certificates, bachelor, specialist and master's degrees. Correspondence courses and cooperative education programs are available in business administration, law enforcement, social science and preparation for the state teaching certificate. The 120-acre campus has thirty-nine buildings. During the 1985-1986 academic year the university enrolled 6,515 students, 291 faculty.

NORTHEASTERN ILLINOIS UNIVERSITY. Founded in 1961 at CHICAGO as the Illinois Teachers College, Chicago North. Control of the institution passed from the Chicago Board of Education to Illinois' Board of Governors of State Colleges in 1965. Special classes are offered for the disadvantaged. In the 1985-1986 academic year, the enrollment of the university was 10,081. There were 498 faculty members.

NORTHERN ILLINOIS UNIVERSITY. Founded in 1899 at DE KALB, Illinois, as a normal school with a two-year course for training teachers. Northern Illinois University continued as a teacher training institution until 1955 when it was granted the authority to give baccalaureate degrees in the arts and sciences. It has developed a graduate program. In 1985-1986 this coeducational institution had a student enrollment of 24,311 with 1,261 faculty members.

NORTHERN IOWA, University of. Established at CEDAR FALLS in 1876, as a state normal college, it later became Iowa State Teachers College and was frequently ranked with Teachers College of Columbia University as a teacher-training institution. With university status, the institution broadened its curriculum and now offers a complete range of studies but continues to be a leader in research and teaching in education. There are 11,514 students and a faculty of 735.

NORTHFIELD, Minnesota. City (pop. 12,-562), southeastern Minnesota, south of MINNEAPOLIS -ST. PAUL, named for John W. North an 1849 settler in St. Anthony, Minnesota, who helped organize the REPUBLICAN PARTY in the state, as well as Northfield, in 1856. Northfield was the scene of a daring bank robbery attempt by Jesse JAMES and his gang. The city is home of two well-respected private liberal arts colleges—CARLETON and ST. OLAF and is a commercial center of food-processing and packaging. Every year on the weekend after Labor Day thousands attend Defeat of Jesse James Days, the retelling the Jesse James-Cole Younger robbery attempt on September 7, 1876. The bungled robbery left two citizens dead and with all the robbers, except for Frank and Jesse James, either captured or killed. Younger claimed the Northfield bank was targeted because it was owned by former Union generals Butler and Ames, both despised by Confederate guerrillas now turned outlaw. The festivities last four days and include an arts fair, parade and reenactment of the raid. Outdoor sports and leisure activities are enjoyed in nearby Nerstrand Woods State Park.

NORTHWEST ANGLE. Most northerly point of the conterminous forty-eight states of the United States. The U.S. land portion juts into the LAKE OF THE WOODS and can only be reached on land by way of approaches through Canada. The Lake of the Woods was important in boundary disputes between the United States and England, as some of the first trading posts in the west were located on its shores. According to the peace treaty ending the Revolutionary War the boundary between the United States and Canada was to run from the northwest angle of the lake west to the MISSISSIPPI RIVER. Later expeditions placed the source of the river one hundred miles further south, so the treaty's provision was meaningless, and the boundary had to be re-negotiated. The unique thrust of United States land into Canada came about through agreement at the Convention of London in 1818.

NORTHWEST COMPANY. Fur-trading company organized by Joseph Frobisher and Simon Mc Tavish in 1790 with a field of operations from the Mandan country to the Pacific and from Hudson Bay territory to Louisiana. In the height of its power the Northwest Company employed two thousand men. In 1768 it established the greatest of all Minnesota fur-trading posts at GRAND PORTAGE. In addition to trading posts, the company equipped expeditions to trade with the Indians in the more important Indian camps. The close proximity of the regions worked by the Hudson's Bay Company and the Northwest Company threw the two organizations into conflict. Competition for furs in the Midwest led the two to employ such devious measures as excessive use of whiskey in trading, stealing furs and inciting the Indians to warfare against the rival company. By 1821 the Northwest Company was absorbed by the Hudson's Bay Company.

NORTHWEST MISSOURI STATE UNIVERSITY. Publicly supported liberal arts and teachers university founded in 1905 in MARYSVILLE, Missouri. The university served as a normal school until 1919, then as a teachers college until 1945. The primary emphasis of the university continues to be preparation of students to be teachers. Cooperative programs with engineering schools in the Midwest are available. The university is situated on a 325-acre campus with seventeen buildings. During the 1985-1986 academic year 4,969 students were enrolled and the university had 236 faculty members.

NORTHWEST ORDINANCE OF 1787. The Ordinance, one of the most far-reaching in American history, set precedent for admitting new states. Territories would petition to be admitted to enter the Union upon attaining a population of 60,000. The law abolished slavery in the territories, established guarantees of civil liberties, and set aside land for the support of public education. The ordinance stated that a minumum of three and a maximum of five states should be created out of the NORTHWEST TERRITORY, which included most of the present Midwest. It was one of the few successful accomplishments of the united colonies under the Articles of Confederation.

NORTHWEST TERRITORY. Land lying west of the Allegheny Mountains, and between the MISSISSIPPI RIVER, the OHIO RIVER, the GREAT LAKES as well as portions of present Minnesota. This territory was ceded to the United States after the American Revolution by Britain and by the various states which had previously claimed the land under colonial charters. The area was organized under the Articles of Confederation and the Northwest Ordinances of 1784, 1785 and 1787. Eventually the states of Michigan, Indiana, Illinois, Ohio, Wisconsin and part of Minnesota were created from the region.

NORTHWESTERN UNIVERSITY. Private coeducational institution located in EVANSTON, Illinois, founded as a Methodist school in 1851. The Chicago campus opened in 1926 and is the center for professional studies. McGaw Medical Center, one of the largest private medical centers in the world, is located there. The Chicago campus also houses the dental and medical schools, law school and evening divisions. The main campus in Evanston has colleges of arts and sciences, education, journalism, speech, music, a graduate school and a graduate school of management. Northwestern has achieved many "firsts" in its history. It was the first university in the nation to establish a school of speech, in which it has been exceptionally successful. This school has trained many actors and other theatrical luminaries. The university also sponsored a children's theater. The law school was the first to organize a scientific detection laboratory. Northwestern was the first university in the U.S. to establish a program in African studies. Its Centers of Urban Affairs, Teaching Professions, and Transportation enjoy national recognition. In 1985-1986 Northwestern had an enrollment of 15,951 and 1,600 faculty.

NOTRE DAME DU LAC, UNIVERSITY OF. Coeducational Roman Catholic school founded near SOUTH BEND, Indiana, in 1842, more generally and familiarly known simply as Notre Dame. The campus, set on 1,250 acres, has ninety buildings, twin lakes and wooded areas and is considered to be one of the most beautiful in the country. The university offers master's degrees in thirty-two departments. Notre Dame's law school, the first of its kind in a Roman Catholic university in the United States, grants the Doctor of Laws degree. Research is carried out by the Medieval Institute which studies the culture, life and thought of the Middle Ages; the Laboratories of

Bacteriology, Lobund Institute, which studies diseases in animals; the Jacques Maritain Center and its philosophical research; and the radiation laboratory built by the U.S. Atomic Energy Commission. The university's international reputation has been founded mainly on its sports. Under football coach Knute ROCKNE its teams revolutionized the game and have continued to rank high in college competition. Its basketball teams are also frequent championship contenders. During the 1985-1986 academic year Notre Dame enrolled 9,500 students and had 947 faculty members.

O'HARE INTERNATIONAL AIRPORT. Located in the northwest corner of CHICAGO, Illinois. It was opened to commercial traffic in 1955 and dedicated formally by President John F. Kennedy in 1963. Except for a brief nod to Atlanta's airport in 1987, O'Hare has been ranked as the busiest commercial airport in the world. For almost a year it shared that honor with the Atlanta airport, with Atlanta having more flights and O'Hare serving more passengers. However, O'Hare regained the overall lead in 1988. Over seven hundred thousand commercial flights carrying an estimated number of more than forty million passengers take off and land at O'Hare every year.

OAK. White oak, state tree of Illinois. Member of the large beech family, with about 300 different types, found mainly in the north temperate zone. Commonly divided into two main groups, black (or red) and white. The white oak is the most important of the family for timber. The wood is valued for its hardness and attractive grain and is used for shipbuilding, furniture, tool handles and veneer. North American Indians valued the acorns as food; they were ground, leached to remove the bitter taste, then cooked. The oak has always stood as a symbol of strength.

OAK PARK, Illinois. Village (pop. 54,887). Residential community directly west of the CHICAGO Loop, birthplace of Ernest HEMINGWAY (1899-1961), named for the many oak trees in the area. Oak Park was first settled in 1833 by Joseph Kettlestrings. Despite its population, the community has retained its village status

and has not sought incoporation as a city. For fifty years civic leaders attempted to obtain a local option so that saloons might be legally barred. This was done in 1907. Deeds to much of the land within the corporate limits contain anti-saloon clauses inserted by the original owners. Architect Frank Lloyd WRIGHT (1867-1959), whose first family home and studio are now open to the public, was another famous resident. Many other examples of Wright's architecture exist in the community. Oak Park's rich architectural heritage may be observed in the Frank Lloyd Wright Prairie School of Architecture National Historic District, which contains 120 buildings of this style and 25 by Wright. His Unity Temple is an example of his use of poured concrete. The Frank Lloyd Wright Home and Studio were built between 1889 and 1898 and remodeled constantly until 1911 as he experimented with different designs. Many architectural tours leave from the Oak Park Visitors Center which provides information on the 125 years of architectural heritage in the community. The Wright Plus Housewalk features the interiors of eleven homes. The Village Art Fair on the Sunday after Labor Day is one of the largest and most prestigious of the outdoor fairs of its type.

OAKLAND UNIVERSITY. Publically supported liberal arts institution in ROCHESTER, Michigan. The university includes the School of Engineering, Computer Science, Nursing, Arts and Sciences, Economics and Management and Human and Educational Services. Non-credit courses are available through the

Division of Continuing Education. The 1,600-acre campus has 21 buildings. The school is accredited by the North Central Association of Colleges and Schools. During the 1985-1986 academic year the university enrolled 12,586 students and employed 575 faculty members.

OAKLEY, Annie. (North Star, OH, Aug. 13, 1860—Greenville, OH, Nov. 3, 1926). Phoebe Annie Oakley Mozee was born in a weather-boarded log cabin. As a child she became skilled in markmanship, killing enough game before she was fourteen to pay the mortgage on her mother's farm. At the age of fifteen, she won a shooting contest against famed vaudeville marksman Frank E. Butler. A few years later they married, and he became her manager. She was a hit with Buffalo Bill's Wild West Show and gave private shooting exhibitions at the invitation of crowned heads in Europe. The German Kaiser insisted that she shoot a cigarette from his lips, and she did. At thirty paces she could slice a playing card with the thin edge toward her. If a card were tossed into the air, she could hit it several times before it reached the ground. From this feat came the term "Annie Oakley"—complimentary passes filled with punch marks. Injured in a train accident in 1901, she was partially paralyzed and could not continue with Buffalo Bill. However, she continued to give some exhibitions and entertained soldiers with exhibitions of her marksmanship during WORLD WAR I.

OAKVILLE, Iowa. Village (pop. 445). Situated in Louisa County, on the IOWA RIVER, near its outlet to the MISSISSIPPI RIVER. On June 25, 1673, the famed exploring party of MARQUETTE (1637-1675) and JOLLIET (1645-1700) made their first landing in what is now Iowa. Although sometimes disputed, this event is considered to have been accomplished on the present site of tiny Oakville. The explorers were very much afraid of hostile intentions of the Indians, but at this landing the native people treated the visitors with great respect. They prepared a feast of dog meat and offered further honor by placing the morsels in the mouths of their guests, a gesture endured by but not appreciated by the Europeans.

OBERLIN COLLEGE. In 1832 Oberlin College and the community of OBERLIN, Ohio, were created together. John L. Shipherd, a Presbyterian minister and Philo P. Steward, a missionary to the Indians, made plans to found a college where both men and women might be educated. In December of the next year Oberlin Collegiate Institute opened with 29 men and 15 women students. The latter were eligible only for the preparatory course. In 1837 four uncertain females applied to the college for admittance and were accepted. Oberlin thus became the world's first coeducational institution of higher education. The college also is said to have been the first in the U.S. to adopt a policy against discrimination because of race, color or creed. The name was changed to Oberlin College in 1850. The Conservatory of Music at Oberlin College is usually ranked among the top three or four of its type in the country. It now occupies a complex of buildings dating from 1964, designed by the architect Minoru Yamasaki. The Kettering Hall of Science was named for inventor Charles F. Kettering (1876-1958). The college enrolls 2,809 students, who are instructed by a faculty of 230.

OBERLIN, Ohio. City, (pop. 8,660), situated in Lorain County in north central Ohio, founded in 1832 and named for Jean Frederic Oberlin, French clergyman, teacher and philanthropist. Among Oberlin's many claims to fame are OBERLIN COLLEGE and one of its graduates, Charles Martin HALL (1863-1914). Hall was inspired by an Oberlin professor, Frank P. Jewett, to invent the modern electrolytic method of processing aluminum, a process which has transformed the world in many ways. Another attraction is Allen Memorial Art Museum, a major college art collection with over 10,000 works, including Dutch paintings of the seventeenth century, later important European works and Japanese art.

OCHEYEDAN, Iowa. Town (pop. 599). Located in Osceola county in western Iowa about ten miles from the border with Minnesota. The town takes its name from nearby Ocheyedan Mound, name derived from the SIOUX meaning "mourning" or a place to mourn a dead relative. The name supposedly stems from a war in the area between Indian tribes in which two boys were killed. The Ocheyeden River originates in Minnesota and flows near the town and on to the LITTLE SIOUX RIVER. At one time the Iowa mound was unique in the country. It was the only prehistoric site which also was considered the highest point in a state. Sadly for this record, a site a few miles northwest, nearer the Minnesota border, was discovered by a recent survey to be a few feet higher, depriving the mound of its record.

ODEBOLDT, Iowa. city (pop. 1,299). Situated in Sac County in west central Iowa, the name was taken from the French trapper, Odebeau, who lived in the area about 1855. Iowa usually ranks first or second in production of corn for popping. As the heart of the state's popcorn region, Odeboldt is nicknamed "The Popcorn Center of the World."

OGDEN, William Butler. (Walton, NY, June 15, 1805—New York, NY, Aug. 3, 1887). First mayor of CHICAGO, Illinois. With the death of his father in 1820, Ogden's hope of a law career faded. He then took over the management of the family estate and in 1835 moved to pioneering Chicago to manage the estate's property there. Over a period of many years Ogden managed to nearly double the value of the estate, becoming the wealthiest man in the region. He was one of the most enthusiastic boosters of Chicago and after being elected mayor in 1837 threw himself into many civic improvements. Ogden insisted that Chicago merchants honor business obligations to insure continued goodwill of the rural traders and credit sources in New York. After his term was over, he devoted himself to railroad development. With his political support, the first successful railroad in Illinois, the Illinois Central, ran westward to GALENA from Chicago. Ogden frustrated eastern capitalists, who hoped the line would fail, by selling stock to farmers who were anxious for a rail access to the Chicago grain and livestock market. To gain commerce from Minnesota and part of Wisconsin, Ogden built the Chicago, St. Paul, and Fond du Lac Railway which became the Chicago and North Western, the name adopted in 1859. He served as president of the North Western Railroad (1859-1868). Chicago's businesses recovered quickly from the Panic of 1857 by following Ogden's policy of accepting, at par, the bills of country banks in Illinois and Wisconsin. Merchants in the smaller towns were able to settle old debts and open new businesses in Chicago. Ogden became president of the Union Pacific railroad in 1862. He left Chicago in 1867, built a home in Fordham Heights outside of New York City and lived there until he died.

OGLESBY, Richard J. (Oldham County, KY, July 25, 1824—Elkhart, IL, Apr. 24, 1899). Illinois governor. Oglesby practiced law and, as a Republican, was Illinois governor from 1865 to 1869, in 1873, and again from 1885-1889. Under Oglesby's leadership, Illinois was the first state to ratify the Thirteenth Amendment to the United States Constitution, which abolished slavery. He played an important role in the founding of the GRAND ARMY OF THE REPUBLIC (G.A.R.), and the charter for the first post was issued April 6, 1866, to DECATUR, Illinois, the governor's hometown. He led also in the creation of a home for the children of deceased soldiers, a school for the feebleminded, location of the Illinois industrial college at URBANA, and the construction of a southern Illinois penitentiary. Between 1873 and 1879 Oglesby served as a United States Senator. During his term he championed soldiers' interests as a member of the pension committee. During his third term as governor and following the HAYMARKET RIOT (May 4, 1886) Governor Oglesby commuted to life imprisonment the sentences of two of those jailed, reflecting the belief of some important conservatives who questioned the death sentence imposed by the court. Laws were passed providing for a soldiers' and sailors' home, a home for juvenile delinquents, and the creation of several pension funds.

OHIO. State, situated as the most easterly of the Midwest Region, Ohio has more natural borders than artificial. Two thirds of the northern border is formed by Lake ERIE. The OHIO RIVER delineates the southeast and southern borders, wandering for over 450 miles and separating Ohio from West Virginia on the southeast and from Kentucky on the south. The eastern border with Pennsylvania, the western border with Indiana and the northern border with Michigan are all pefectly straight.

Originating at DEFIANCE, the MAUMEE RIVER empties into the Ohio at DAYTON. The CUYAHOGA originates near Lake Erie, flows a short semicircular course to empty into the lake at CLEVELAND. Other small rivers flow into Lake Erie. The northern rivers are separated from the waters to the south by a low divide, which forms the shallow watershed of Lake Erie. Major rivers to the south are the MUSKINGUM, SCIOTO and MIAMI, joined at Dayton by the Mad River. The 500 lakes are relatively small and mostly artificial.

With a land area of 41,004 square miles, Ohio is the second smallest in size in the Midwest, just ahead of its Indiana neighbor. The relatively flat surface extends from the sand dunes of Lake Erie to the gorge plateau cut by the Ohio River. The rugged hills of the southeast increase in height as they approach the mountains of neighboring West Virginia.

Only about the western quarter of the state is represented by the Early Paleozoic period. The eastern section is Late Paleozoic. The glacial period brought ice cover to most of the present state. The grooves carved into the rocks at KELLEY'S ISLAND State Park provide dramatic proof of the land-altering forces of the great glaciers.

The official designation of Ohio climate is "temperate but varied and subject to much precipitation." Some Ohioans might quarrel with the "temperate" classification. Temperatures have ranged from a high of 113 degrees near GALLIPOLIS to a low at Milligan of 39 degrees below zero, making a spread of 152 degrees.

The generally open character of the state is its single most striking geographic feature, providing travelers who crossed the rugged Appalachians with a gateway to the west and resulting in one of the nicknames for Ohio, the Gateway State. Almost the entire western half of the state is classified as cropland. Much of the northeast is considered crop and grazing land, while a large part of the Ohio River area is classified as mostly woodland and forest, with some crop and pasture areas.

Early Ohio settlers found that farming was relatively easy and profitable in most parts of the state. Today, six of the eight Midwest states garner more agricultural income than Ohio, but agricultural income in Ohio continues to reach about four billion dollars annually, with soybeans, dairy products, corn and hogs as principal products.

As with all states without exception, manufacturing is the principal source of Ohio income. Ohio is fifth among the states in value of manufactured products, with annual income reaching over 122 billion. Principal products are transportation equipment, machinery except electrical, and fabricated metal. Manufacturing is particularly notable for its even spread across the state. AKRON is the world's rubber capital and CINCINNATI an international center for soap production, including the famous Ivory floating soap, which was discovered by accident. Ohio is also a major world center of glass production.

In the 1980 census, Ohio ranked sixth in population. By 1987 Ohio had slipped to eighth rank among the states in population, this in spite of a small continuing growth of Ohio in total population. Projections for the year 2000 place Ohio population at 10,357,000, Ohio's black population is about eleven percent of the total, with other races less than one percent.

Traces of the earliest people have been found in Ohio, with no indications of pottery or other skills except for a few chipped flints. Traces of the little known ARCHAIC PEOPLE of six or seven thousand years ago have been found, but little is known about them. At the Thomas WORTHINGTON estate of ADENA a log tomb, skeletons, ornaments and weapons were found in 1901, and the civilization discovered was designated as Adena.

The most famous of all Midwest prehistoric civilizations has been called HOPEWELL because the first traces of it were found in the mounds on the farm of a man named Hopewell, in Ross County. These people left pottery and other indications of a rather advanced civilization. Some articles must have resulted from trade with civilizations as remote as Mexico. Among the most striking Hopewell remains are the EFFIGY MOUNDS, built up with earth to represent snakes, eagles and other figures. FORT ANCIENT State Memorial has been preserved as a tribute.

No one knows why the Hopewells disappeared and less capable people took their places. The latter also built many of Ohio's 10,000 mounds. By the time Europeans had arrived, all of these had disappeared, and an Indian group known as the ERIE were found in the northern areas of the state. The Erie were driven out by the IROQUOIS. Later groups included HURON, DELAWARE, SHAWNEE and MIAMI, among others.

On his famous expedition of 1669-1670, Robert Cavelier, Sieur de LA SALLE (1643-1687), was the first European known to have visited the area of present-day Ohio. His travels formed the basis for the French-Canadian claim to the vast region west of the Appalachians. To dispute this claim, England sent explorers and traders into the region. Trader George CROGHAN (1720?-1782) was particularly generous to the Indians and helped to win them to the English side.

French emissary, CELERON DE BLAINVILLE (1680-1768), attempted to counter the English gains by traveling down the Ohio River with 250 men, burying six lead plates at different places, incised with the French claims. At least part of one of these plates can still be seen in a museum in Massachusetts.

The British gave a grant of 200,000 acres of land to the OHIO COMPANY OF VIRGINIA. The company sent George GIST (1706?-1759) on a famed exploration of the Ohio valley. Gist was successful in turning many of the Indian leaders in favor of the British. British victory in the FRENCH AND INDIAN WAR established British supremacy in the area after 1763.

Ohio

Counties and County Seats

Ohio

STATE OF OHIO

Name: Ohio from the Ohio River which the Iroquoian Indians called ohion-hiio "Beautiful River" the Wyandots called it o, he, zu for "Great, grand, fair to look upon."

Nickname: The Buckeye State

Capital: Columbus

Motto: With God, All Things Are Possible

Symbols and Emblems:
Bird: Cardinal

**Flower: Scarlet Carnation
Tree: Buckeye
Stone: Ohio Flint
Beverage: Tomato Juice
Song: "Beautiful Ohio"**

Population:
10,744,000 (1985)

**Rank: 7th
Gain or Loss (1970-80): +141,-000
Projection (1980-2000): -440,000
Density: 262 per sq. mi. of land
Percent urban: 73.3% (1980)**

Racial Makeup (1980):
White: 88.9%

**Black: 10%
Hispanic: 119,880 persons
Indian: 12,200 persons
Others: 111,200 persons**

Largest City:
Columbus (566,000 - 1984)

Other Cities:
Cleveland (547,000 -1984)

**Cincinnati (370,000 -1984)
Toledo (344,000 - 1984)
Akron (227,000 - 1984)
Dayton (181,000 - 1984)
Youngstown (108,000 - 1984)**

Area: 41,330 sq. mi. (107,044 sq. km.)
Rank: 35th

Highest Point: 1,550 ft. Campbell hill

Lowest Point: 433 ft. Ohio River

H.S. Completed: 67% (1980)

Four Yrs. College Completed: 13.7% (1980)

STATE GOVERNMENT

ELECTED OFFICIALS (4 year terms, expiring 1991):
GOVERNOR: $65,000 (1985)
LT. GOV.: $35,000 (1985)
SEC. OF STATE: $50,000 (1985)

GENERAL ASSEMBLY:
Meets at Columbus for 2 sessions every other year, with certain exceptions

Salary: $30,152 per annum (1985)
Senate: 33 members
House: 99 members
Congressional Representatives
Senate: terms expire 1989, 1993

House of Representatives: Twenty-one members

Ohio, Personalities

The British king tried to keep the land west of the Appalachians as an Indian preserve, but settlers continued to flock in, bringing on almost constant trouble with the native Americans. Chief PONTIAC (1720?-1769) led a confederation in a desperate and futile attempt to hold Indian lands. A short peace followed until the Indians struck under Chief Pontiac, were beaten by 2,500 troops under Lord Dunmore, and a new treaty was signed in 1774.

During the Revolution no battles were fought in Ohio, but the Indians continued to kill and scalp and take prisoners. At the end of the war, the "western" lands became territories of the various original colonies, some of which claimed land extending to the Pacific Ocean. To arrange for these areas to advance toward statehood in a peaceful manner, the NORTHWEST TERRITORY was formed, including present Ohio. Virginia and Connecticut agreed to give up claims to large parts of Ohio in exchange for title to large sections. The land "reserved" for Connecticut, including present CLEVELAND, i s called the WESTERN RESERVE. Many New Englanders were given land there for their Revolutionary service. Virginia also gave its reserved land to Revolutionary veterans, including George WASHINGTON (1732-1799), who was given 70,000 acres.

The OHIO COMPANY OF ASSOCIATES was formed to settle land along the Muskingum River, and in 1788, 47 settlers floated down the Ohio River on two flatboats. They built a town at the mouth of the Muskingum which they called MARIETTA. The settlers were well chosen and had ample resources. A smaller group settled farther down river and called their location Losantiville. This was the beginning of CINCINNATI. These pioneers were followed later in 1788 and 1789 by 10,000 others, mostly arriving over the Ohio River route, and they faced great peril from Indians and pirates.

Alarmed at losing their land, the Indians attacked more and more frequently. Governor Arthur ST. CLAIR (1736-1818) was ambushed and lost 900 American soldiers. Although the Indians assembled perhaps the largest native force in American history, they were defeated by General "Mad" Anthony WAYNE (1745-1796) in the critical FALLEN TIMBERS (August 20, 1794). The Indians were forced to agree to the Treaty of GREEN VILLE (August, 1795), giving up three-fourths of their territory.

In just fifteen years, the Ohio population had risen to 70,000, and in 1803, Ohio became the second state west of the mountains to enter the Union.

With the coming of the first steamboat in 1811, Cincinnati's commerce began to flourish, until it became known as the Queen City of the West. Most progress halted with the WAR OF 1812. The Indians assisted the British in such attacks as the Battle of FORT MEIGS (spring, 1813). The famed Indian leader, Chief TECUMSEH (1768-1813), took part in the warfare and held the rank of major in the British army.

One of the decisive battles of world history was fought off Ohio shores in Lake Erie. American commander, Oliver Hazard PERRY (1785-1819), built 50 ships in record time, and in September, 1813, he defeated the English fleet in the Battle of PUT-IN-BAY at the end of which he made his famous announcement: "We have met the enemy, and they are ours."

A different type of war was the "Border War" of 1835, with Michigan. Both sides claimed a section of land lying between them. The matter was settled in Ohio's favor. The election of Ohio favorite William Henry HARRISON (1773-1841) as president and his death after a month in office, the coming of the first railroad in 1848 and the decline of the canals were among the important events of that era.

In the decade of the 1850s slavery was the overriding question. Ohioans were particularly active in the UNDERGROUND RAILROAD, helping slaves escape to Canada. With the advent of the CIVIL WAR, Ohio troops fought in the first land battle at Philippi, now West Virginia. By 1862 Ohio was threatened with invasion. However, several Confederate raids marked the only actual fighting within the Ohio boundaries. A total of 345,000 Ohioans played their part in the armed services.

The founding of the Cincinnati Red Stockings in 1866 created the world's first professional baseball team. The rise of great industries such as Standard Oil Company of John D. ROCKEFELLER and National Cash Register Company of James RITTY, were all hallmarks of general progress. The worst Ohio River flood to the time caused devastation in 1913. WORLD WAR I called 200,000 Ohioans into service. An even worse flood, worst in Ohio River history, occurred in 1937.

WORLD WAR II called 840,000 Ohioans into uniform, and the state's great industries responded with a record quantity of war materials. The decades which followed saw the 1959 opening of the state to world oceans through the ST. LAWRENCE SEAWAY, and Ohioan Neil ARMSTRONG (1930-) became the first man on the moon. In 1974 another Ohio astronaut, John GLENN (1921-), was elected to the U.S.

Senate. In 1984 Glenn lost his bid for the Democratic presidential nomination. In that year, also, Ronald REAGAN (1911-) again won Ohio's vote for president, but Democrat Richard F. Celeste became governor in 1969.

Ohio claims seven native U.S. presidents. Three of these, Ulysses S. GRANT (1822-1885), Rutherford B. HAYES (1822-1893) and James A. GARFIELD (1831-1881), followed each other in order as president. Grant was born at POINT PLEASANT ; he was unsuccessful until later life brought him fame as the Civil War conqueror, but his fame dwindled in an unsuccessful presidency.

Hayes, who was born in DELAWARE, Ohio, also had Civil War rank as a general. His contested election to the presidency was not settled until three days before the inauguration.

Another Union Civil War general, Garfield, was born near Cleveland. He became the second president to be assassinated. Ohio claims President William Henry HARRISON (1773-1841) because of his close association with the state. His grandson, Benjamin HARRISON (1833-1901), was born near NORTH BEND, but he left the state before becoming president. William MC KINLEY (1843-1901), native of NILES, was governor of the state before becoming the 25th president. His assassination marked another sad record for Ohio.

The Taft family has played a prominent role in Ohio history. Cincinnati native William Howard TAFT (1857-1930) is the only American to have been both president and Chief Justice of the United States. His son, Senator Robert A. TAFT (1889-1953, became known as "Mr. Republican," but he died in 1953 without reaching his hoped-for presidency.

Ohio's most recent president, Warren Gamaliel HARDING (1865-1923), died in office, and his administration became a victim of scandals.

To the title Mother of Presidents, Ohio also adds the title of Mother of generals. In addition to Grant, the state cherishes the names of Philip SHERIDAN (1831-1888) and William Tecumseh SHERMAN (1820-1891). William Tecumseh Sherman was born at LANCASTER. His march through Georgia became one of the most famous campaigns of all time. Philip H. Sheridan of SOMERSET played an important part in Union Civil War success. In all, fifty-one commanding generals in the Civil War were from Ohio.

Another military hero was Eddie RICKENBACKER (1890-1973), native of Columbus, who became America's premier flying ace of World War I.

Ohio's massive capitol, Columbus.

Renowned Ohio inventors include Thomas A. EDISON (1847-1931), MILAN native, Charles KETTERING (1876-1958), who invented the electric starter, and Charles Martin HALL (1863-1914), who developed the method for processing aluminum.

Best known of Ohio's black writers was poet Paul Laurence DUNBAR (1872-1906) of Dayton. Zane GREY (1875-1939) gained fame for his western novels, and works of a far different kind made William Holmes MC GUFFEY (1800-1873) one of the most widely read authors of all time. His McGuffey Readers have taught millions of school children how to read. Other creative Ohioans include composers Benjamin R. HANBY and Oley SPEAKS.

Ohio has paid tribute to its presidents by preserving homes and other places associated with them, scattered around the state, generally near their birthplaces. These historic sites are among the most widely visited attractions of the state.

Cleveland boasts of its renowned symphony, the Cleveland Health Museum, a pioneer of its type and Rockefeller Park with its unique Cultural Gardens. At Columbus the massive capitol appears too modern to have been started in 1839. Cincinnati remains a center of musical culture. Its Museum of Natural History and Cincinnati Art Museum are outstanding, as is the Cincinnati Zoo.

OHIO AND ERIE CANAL. Because most interior Ohio rivers were not navigable, farmers of the state who did not have access to either the OHIO RIVER or Lake ERIE were hampered in reaching markets for their produce. With the success of the Erie Canal in New York in 1825, farmers clamored for canals in Ohio. The legislature approved plans for several canals, including the Ohio and Erie Canal, which was to run from CLEVELAND on Lake Erie to PORTSMOUTH on the Ohio River. Many communities competed for the canal. AKRON became a modern city because of it. Cleveland was chosen as the Lake Erie canal port through the work of attorney Alfred Kelley. After the first section was completed between Cleveland and Akron in 1827, Cleveland seemed to explode with prosperity. From 1825 to 1830, Cleveland's population doubled and in the next ten years increased 464 percent. More than 1,000 ships entered the port of Cleveland in 1836 alone. Land prices boomed along the canal route. The canal passed a few miles east of COLUMBUS, but that city was connected by a feeder canal, and it too was soon booming. NEWARK became Ohio's canal capital. PORTSMOUTH, on the Ohio River, was already a busy port, but with the coming of the canal in October, 1832, with the mule drawn canal boats making the trip to Columbus in 24 hours, the city became the southern outlet for the entire valley, transferring the canal traffic to river steamboats. The life of canals was short, however, and most of them soon became obsolete with the coming of the RAILROADS.

OHIO COMPANY OF ASSOCIATES. The association was formed early in 1786 for the purpose of buying land and making a settlement in Ohio. A group of New England leaders was assembled by Manasseh CUTLER (1742-1823), who was the most enthusiastic about the plan, and General Rufus PUTNAM (1738-1824), a Revolutionary leader who had been on Washington's staff. They gathered at the Bunch of Grapes Tavern in Boston and organized the Ohio Company of Associates. They negotiated with Congress for the purchase, and preliminary terms were agreed upon. However, land purchases in the Ohio area were not legal until the ORDINANCE OF 1787 was enacted, providing for the administration of the NORTHWEST TERRITORY, including Ohio. The Associates purchased 1,500,000 acres in what is now southeastern

Ohio. They made careful preparations to assemble a group of settlers who were able and qualified to settle in a frontier country and who had the skills needed for the various jobs to be done. They sent twenty boatbuilders to the community which is now West Newton in Pennsylvania, where they built two flatboats and five pirogues. Joined by the others, under Putnam's command they floated down the Monongahela and OHIO rivers and reached their new property on April 7, 1788. This group was responsible for the first permanent European type settlement in Ohio, MARIETTA, and in much of the rest of the Northwest Territory. George WASHINGTON wrote, "No colony in America was ever settled under such favorable auspices."

OHIO COMPANY OF VIRGINIA. During the mid-1700s, the struggle between the French and British for control of the interior of North America was intense. In 1749 a group of Virginians received a royal British charter for settling on 200,000 acres in an area of present Ohio. The plan was opposed by Pennsylvania, which also had claims in the area. The French seized the opportunity of the clash between the colonies to redouble their efforts in the west. They gained many Indian allies. In 1750 the Ohio Company sent noted frontiersman Christopher GIST (1706?-1759) to explore the area of their proposed settlement and to regain the friendship of the Indians. He was quite successful in this, but the frontier remained so volatile that the Ohio Land Company never managed their objective. After several British defeats, in the East as well as the West, the British leaders determined to take strong action, and the FRENCH AND INDIAN WAR ended with the loss by the French of the entire continent in 1763.

OHIO FLINT. Official gem of Ohio. Flint differs from stone because it can be chipped and shaped with ease when freshly dug. Flint was especially important to the prehistoric people of the area, who chipped flint to form spears and arrowheads.

OHIO RIVER. Major commercial waterway in the United States which flows generally southwestward from its beginning in Pittsburgh, Pennsylvania, where it is formed by the meeting of the Monongahela and Allegheny rivers. It creates the northern boundaries of West Virginia and Kentucky and the southern boundaries of Illinois, Ohio, and Indiana. It flows into the MISSISSIPPI RIVER at CAIRO, Illinois.

Major tributaries of the Ohio River include the Tennessee, SCIOTO, Big Sandy, Cumberland, Kanawha, MIAMI, WABASH and Kentucky rivers. As a commercial river the Ohio has as ports along its 981 miles such cities as Pittsburgh, Pennsylvania; CINCINNATI, Ohio; and Louisville, Kentucky. Coal makes up almost half of the total freight shipped on it every year. The first white explorer to see the Ohio River was LA SALLE (1643-1687) in 1669. Traders used the Ohio during the 1700s to explore the entire river valley. After the NORTHWEST TERRITORY was opened in 1787 most settlers used the Ohio River on their way west. Steamboats, active on the river in the early 1800s, were replaced in the 1900s by tugboats and heavy barges. Some of the country's worst FLOODS have occurred on the river. Flooding has now been generally controlled by means of nineteen federally supported dam-canal structures.

OHIO RIVER, FALLS OF. Near present NEW ALBANY, Indiana, and Louisville, Kentucky, the Falls of the Ohio, a series of rapids with a total twenty-four foot drop, presented an obstacle to navigation, which otherwise would have been opened to traffic as far as the Ohio's source at Pittsburgh, Pennsylvania. A two-and-a-quarter mile bypass canal was opened at Louisville in 1803, and the 1955 system of modern locks now provides passage.

OHIO STATE UNIVERSITY. The school was opened at COLUMBUS, Ohio, as Ohio Agricultural and Mechanical College in 1873 with seventeen students enrolled. It was operated by the state as one of the LAND GRANT COLLEGES. In 1878 it was given its present name. While its academic classes are of a high order, most Americans think of Ohio State as one of the great collegiate football powerhouses, particularly the teams under the direction of the late Woody Hayes. The student enrollment of 57,725 makes the university one of the larger state institutions. There are nineteen colleges with more than 130 departments, a graduate school, medical center and branches in four other Ohio cities. The faculty numbers more than 3,200. In addition to the vast stadium, visitors may see the Ohio State University Galleries, exhibiting both traditional and contemporary art. Cooperating with Ohio Wesleyan University Ohio State operates the Perkins Observatory near DELAWARE, Ohio, and the Perkins telescope near Flagstaff, Arizona.

OHIO TURNPIKE. Opened in 1955, the Ohio Turnpike was one of the pioneers in modern toll road operation. Covering a distance of 241 miles across northern Ohio, to the east it links with the grandfather of all the modern tollroads, the Pennsylvania Turnpike, on the west with the Indiana Turnpike, to form what was at the time the first link of superhighways between Chicago and New York. Today the turnpike is one of the major links in the great Interstate Highway system, from coast to coast and from border to border. Within Ohio, the turnpike skirts the fringes of TOLEDO, CLEVELAND and YOUNGSTOWN before entering Pennsylvania. The Ohio Turnpike's fifteen interchanges connect it with all the major cities of the state, as well as many historical and recreational areas.

OHIO UNIVERSITY. At ATHENS, Ohio, the university is the first institution of higher education to be founded in the old NORTHWEST TERRITORY, including most of the present Midwest. Chartered in 1804, it was opened in 1809 as an academy with three students and a two-room building. By 1822 it had reached classification as a college. It has been a coeducational institution since 1869 and is supported by the state. One of the university's most distinguished presidents was William Holmes MC GUFFEY, who gained his greatest fame for his *McGuffey's Eclectic Reader* series, perhaps the most widely used instructional materials ever produced. These are gaining considerable use again in modern times. Current enrollment exceeds 15,000, and there are nearly 800 faculty.

OHIO WESLEYAN UNIVERSITY. Founded at DELAWARE, Ohio, in 1840 by the North Ohio Conference of the Methodist Episcopal Church, the institution was initially financed by public subscription and private donations, together with the selling of scholarships. In 1877 the school united with Ohio Wesleyan Female College. In 1892-93 financial problems almost caused the school to close, but zealous alumni saved it and brought it back to a position of leadership. In cooperation with OHIO STATE UNIVERSITY, Ohio Wesleyan operates the Perkins Observatory at DELAWARE, an important center for astronomical research, along with the Perkins Telescope at Flagstaff, Arizona. The student body of 1,494 is instructed by 154 faculty.

OJIBWAY INDIANS. Members of the ALGONQUIN language group, the Ojibway occupied the northern areas of Minnesota, Wisconsin and Michigan, typical north woods country. With woodland caribou, moose, bear and countless smaller animals, the Ojibway managed to find sufficient hunting to keep them alive during the rough winters of the North. During the winter, men of the tribes traveled long distances on the hunt, leaving the women and children behind. The women often fished through the ice to add to the family winter food supply. They obtained most of the materials needed for wigwams, snowshoes, cooking pots and other items from the bark, wood and roots of the trees. In most other ways the Ojibway were very similar to the INDIAN LIFE AND CUSTOMS of other tribes of the Midwest.

OKIBOJI LAKES. The name comes from the Okiboji Indians. The lakes form a chain in western Iowa, reaching almost to the border of Minnesota. West Okiboji is the largest, with a shore line of about 60 miles. The *National Geographic* Magazine once named it the third most beautiful lake in the world. The largest lake in Iowa, the sparkling body of water provides much of the state's water related activities, including lake steamer rides. There is also an amusement park. East Okiboji Lake is scarcely more than a bay of its larger body.

OLD ABE (eagle). Perhaps the only individual bald eagle to gain fame on behalf of the official American bird, Old Abe was captured by an Indian in the spring of 1861 in the wilds of the FLAMBEAU RIVER in Wisconsin. Dan McCann purchased the bird for a bushel of corn and played army music to him on his violin. He hoped to sell the eagle to an army group being formed for the CIVIL WAR. The boys of company C of the Eighth Wisconsin Battery at EAU CLAIRE, Wisconsin, managed to collect five dollars and bought the great bird, naming him Old Abe in honor of Abraham LINCOLN. Everywhere the army group went, the bird attracted attention. Before long they had been nicknamed the EAGLE REGIMENT. Old Abe perched proudly on the fancy red white and blue shield his boys had carved for him. On their way to the war front, the regiment paraded in several cities. The music and noise at MADISON, Wisconsin, excited Abe so much that he flew from his perch, grabbed a corner of the American flag and carried it the rest of the parade route. The Chicago *Tribune* admired the bird and predicted that "No doubt the Eau Claire Eagles and their pet bird will be heard of

again." In the parade at ST. LOUIS, Old Abe broke loose, soared high and broke up the march while everyone tried to recapture him. A favorite pastime of the mascot was to steal chickens from the disgruntled cook. Abe's first battle, Corinth, found him in the thick of the fight. Altogether he took part in 42 battles but was never wounded. After the war he was presented to the state of Wisconsin, making his home in a large cage in the capitol basement at MADISON. Pictures, pamphlets of his war experiences and feathers were sold for charity. His authentic feathers brought as much as $400 each. He was exhibited to excited crowds at the Philadelphia World's Fair in 1876. A fire in the capitol destroyed his health and he died on March 28, 1881. Stuffed, he "lived" on in the capitol museum until it, too, was destroyed by fire. A marker near the supposed place of his capture, commemorates his unique achievements. Another stuffed eagle in the Wisconsin capitol also preserves his memory.

OLD COPPER CULTURE PEOPLE. Prehistoric people who lived in the area of Michigan. Remains of this group of people have been found on ISLE ROYALE in Lake SUPERIOR. Ten thousand copper-mining pits have been discovered, suggesting that these people were skilled in working the metal at approximately the same time ancient peoples in Sudan and Egypt were fashioning the same metal in their homelands. For unknown reasons, the skill of working copper was not passed down to succeeding cultures. By the arrival of the white man in Michigan the natives were working exclusively in stone and other non-metals.

OLD DRUM. Old Drum, a noted hunting dog, became the center of the famous Missouri "Dog Trial" after he was killed by the jealous owner of a rival dog. The man who killed Old Drum was brought to court by the owner of the dog, a Charles Burden. The case was twice reversed and twice appealed. George G. VEST, attorney for the owner of the dog, delivered his now famous "Eulogy to the Dog" and won the case. Attorneys involved in the case went on to fame and fortune in such diverse fields as civil service and railroading.

OLD MISSION PENINSULA. Narrow body of land seventeen miles long extending out into Michigan's Grand Traverse Bay creating the West and East Arms of Grand Traverse Bay. The peninsula has claimed the highest concentration of cherry trees of any place in the

United States, 20,000 trees to the square mile. An annual Blessing to the Blossoms has been held to start the Traverse City Cherry Festival.

OLD FRANKLIN, Missouri. Once known as the "metropolis of the West," Old Franklin was platted on the banks of the MISSOURI RIVER i n 1816 and soon found itself at the head of the SANTA FE TRAIL established by a Franklin resident, William BECKNELL. Such famous Missouri residents as Nathaniel Beverly Tucker, Meredith M. Marmaduke, and Dr. John SAPPINGTON contributed to the extraordinary social life of the community at the time. When the rise of cheap steamboat transportation promoted the establishment of towns farther up the Missouri, Franklin's promise began to fade, and in 1823 the county seat was moved to FAYETTE. Today the once thriving community is but a memory in fields now plowed and planted.

OLD VILLAGE. Modern name given to the large prehistoric metropolitan community on the site now occupied by ST. LOUIS, Missouri, and EAST ST. LOUIS, Illinois. Old Village was the center of a civilization of people who lived in the area over one thousand years ago. Archeologists comment on the coincidence of the great prehistoric metropolis having been sited where the modern metropolis now stands. A similar coincidence marks present KANSAS CITY, where the same civilization had built another large metropolis.

OLDFIELD, Barney. (Wauseon, OH, Jan. 29, 1878—Beverely Hills, CA, Oct. 4, 1946). Pioneer racing immortal, got his start in "Old 999" by winning an exhibition race at DAYTON, Ohio, in 1899. In 1903 he won everlasting fame as the first person ever to travel a mile a minute. In his youth Oldfield was a bicycle racer, then met Henry Ford who wanted a driver for his 999, which had no safety devices of any kind. He won many races and endured many crackups for 15 years. His world speed record of 131.724 miles per hour, set in 1910, endured until after WORLD WAR I. He continued to be linked with speed and daring until his name came to stand for any daredevil driver.

OLDS, Ransom Eli. (Geneva, OH, June 3, 1864—Lansing, MI, Aug. 26, 1950). Automobile inventor and manufacturer. Olds is considered the founder of the automobile industry. He constructed the first automobile factory and developed the concept of mass-produced cars. As a pioneer, he built the first three-wheeled horseless carriage in 1886 when experimenting in his father's machine shop in LANSING, Michigan. Olds developed a practical steam-driven four-wheeled automobile in 1893. This was the first U.S. automobile sold abroad. Olds' first gasoline-powered car was built in 1896. In 1899 he founded the Olds Motor Works in DETROIT, Michigan. By 1901 his plant was mass-producing one-cylinder, lightweight and, at $650, low-cost model automobiles. Olds left his company in 1904 to organize a new enterprise to make trucks and automobiles. Olds served as the president of the Reo (his initials) Motor Car Company from 1904 to 1924 and then as its chairman of the board until 1936. Among his philanthropic works was the donation of the Science Hall to Kalamazoo College and an engineering building to MICHIGAN STATE COLLEGE. Two automobiles, the Oldsmobile and Reo, have been named in his honor.

OLIVER, James. (Whitebaugh, Scotland, August 28, 1823—South Bend, Indiana, 1908). Inventor. In 1855 Oliver began manufacturing plows in Indiana and by 1864 had developed a method of hardening steel by chilling which permitted the use of a steel moldboard on plows, keeping them sharp longer. His company, in SOUTH BEND, became very successful, and Oliver acquired great wealth.

ONTONAGON BOULDER. A huge chunk of copper seen by many Indians and several European explorers. Julius Eldred traveled up the ONTONAGON RIVER in 1843 and used a block and tackle to lift the boulder and built a small railroad to the river to get the boulder out. His hopes of displaying the find and earning money from visitors were dashed when the United States government seized it because Eldred did not have permission to remove the boulder from its site. The officials took the rock to Washington, D.C. where it is on display at the Natural History Building of the Smithsonian.

OPEN-PIT MINING. One of the principal methods of mining a variety of minerals, including iron ore. Open-pit mining is used when mineral strata are located near the surface. A thin layer of soil and overbearing material is stripped away to reveal the mineral. Powerful shovels dig out the mineral and often dump it directly into railroad cars or trucks. The huge holes left in the ground are the open-pits. Most iron ore mined in the Lake SUPERIOR region lies close to the surface and is mined by the open-pit method. The largest open-pit mine in the world is the HULL-RUST-MAHONING MINE near HIBBING, Minnesota. This open-pit mine is so huge that an elaborate system of railroad tracks is laid in the pit to facilitate the shipment of ore to refining plants. Open-pit coal mining is another common practice in much of the Midwest. Conservationists have become increasingly concerned about the destruction of the surface, the removal of wildlife habitat and the contamination of areas, due to open-pit operations. Smaller and shallower operations generally associated with open-pit coal mining have increasingly turned to methods intended to diminish conservation problems. In many areas, particularly in Illinois, abandoned coal fields have been filled and restored to parklike surroundings. Such measures are not practical for the deep cuts of larger scale operations, but those operators are increasingly concerned with minimizing the environmental problems.

ORANGE, Ohio. City, (pop. 2,376), situated in northeast Ohio, a southeast suburb of CLEVELAND in Cuyahoga County, Orange was the birthplace of James A. GARFIELD (1831-1881), on a nearby frontier farm. He spent his early years in poverty in Orange.

OREGON TRAIL. Route from the MISSOURI RIVER to the Columbia River. Originally traveled by fur trappers and traders, the route, by 1842, became the "highway" for pioneers to the Oregon Country. From many starting points in Missouri, travelers and traders were outfitted to undertake the long and hazardous journey leaving the Midwest and crossing the Central West and Northwest of the continent to the territory of Oregon.

ORTONVILLE, Minnesota. Town (pop. 2,548), southwestern Minnesota, on the southern shore of BIG STONE LAKE, southwest of MORRIS. Ortonville was platted as a townsite in 1872 by Cornelius Orton. The site, long an important trading center for French and English traders and the Indians, developed further as a major general trade center, although the nearest railroad was forty miles away at Benson, Minnesota. Grain was shipped along the twenty-five-mile-long BIG STONE LAKE on steampowered barges. An Ortonville canning plant was the originator and patent holder of equipment used in canning whole kernel corn. A red granite, quarried in the area for years, supplied the stone for buildings including the City Hall in Minneapolis.

OSAGE INDIANS. Tribe of Siouan linguistic stock that lived on the OSAGE RIVER in Missouri. In addition to giving their name to the river, they also gave it to numerous cities and counties in Missouri and neighboring states, and to the OSAGE ORANGE, a wood favored for making bows for archery. Frequently at war with neighboring tribes, the Osage finally ceded their lands to Missouri and Arkansas (1808), eventually moving to Oklahoma.

The Osage were similar to the other Midwest Indians in many ways (INDIAN LIFE AND CUSTOMS) but were remarkably dissimilar in others. The Osage were considered by some to be the most remarkable of the indigenous Americans in what is now the U.S. Many of the men were over seven feet tall. Many Osage athletes could walk sixty miles a day.

They built their villages on high land or a terrace, with rectangular houses formed in a circle. The larger house of the chief was placed inside the circle. During the hunting season, the permanent villages were deserted except by those unable to go on the hunt, and the others lived in temporary villages. In addition to gathering edible foods, nuts, persimmons and water-lily roots, the Osage cultivated crops, corn, beans, squash or pumpkin.

At the beginning of every day, the girls had the part in their hair painted red, symbolizing the path of the sun as it crossed the day, hopefully providing long life.

The Osage were familiar with many facts of astronomy and were remarkable in their use of medicinal bark, roots, leaves and other natural health products. Chiefdom was hereditary, but warriors were always consulted in tribal council before important decisions were made. the Osage were unique in their ability to disregard alcohol, which was often the downfall of most other tribes. They held many European ways in contempt and considered the white man to be the slave of his way of life.

OSAGE ORANGE TREE. Tree with principal stands in Missouri. The wood is prized for the manufacture of archery bows and takes its name from the OSAGE INDIANS.

OSAGE RIVER. One of the Missouri's major rivers, formed by the confluence of the MARAIS DES CYGNES and Little Osage Rivers in western Missouri. Flowing generally northeast for approximately 250 miles, its course is impounded by Bagnell Dam in Central Missouri, creating the LAKE OF THE OZARKS. It empties into the MISSOURI RIVER near JEFFERSON CITY.

OSHKOSH (chief). (1795—?). The MEN-OMINEE Wisconsin chief, grandson of Cha-kau-cho-ka-ma (Old King), had a remarkable record in his relationship with the white intruders in his land. He is said never to have lifted his hand against them in warfare. However, he fought valorously against other Indian groups under famed Chief Tomah and the even more famous TECUMSEH (1768-1813). In 1927 his bones were removed from his grave at Keshena, Wisconsin, and buried with ceremony in Menominee Park, OSHKOSH, Wisconsin, his namesake city. His statue was placed over the grave in the park. He is best known today by the portrait painted by Wisconsin artist Samuel Brookes.

OSHKOSH, Wisconsin. City (pop. 49,620), seat of Winnebago County, situated in southeastern Wisconsin, on the west shore of Lake WINNEBAGO where the northern FOX RIVER enters the lake. The city was named for OSHKOSH (1795-?), famed chief of the area, whose body rests in Menominee Park in the city. The city's diverse industries began with lumbering, and for a while the community was called "The Sawdust City."

Today's products include transportation equipment, candle making and the garment which has made the city's name famous around the world. Originated in the city, the overalls which bear the slogan "Oshkosh, b'gosh" have been popularized almost everywhere and periodically enjoy revivals of interest. They are still manufactured there.

European settlement did not begin until 1818, when Augustin Grignon and Jacques Porlier established a trading post nearby. The next step, in 1833, was the trading post of George Johnson where the Algoma Street bridge was later built. Two small communities emerged, Algoma and Athens, rivals for the next decade. When Athens was renamed Oshkosh to please the Indians, it forged ahead. Oshkosh was incorporated as a city in 1853, and it absorbed the village of Algoma.

Steamboats on the lake and the new railroad stimulated trade, with boat building an important industry. One of the oldest yacht clubs in the Midwest was founded at Oshkosh in 1870. This period saw the lumber industry hit its peak in the region. The fire of 1875 was the worst of several that had swept the city, wiping out most of the wooden buildings of the business district along with many factories. Reconstruction was mostly of stone and brick.

The Oshkosh Public Museum, housed in a

Chief Oshkosh of the Menominee.

Tudor mansion, has very eclectic exhibits. Another Tudor-style house is the focus of the Paine Art Center and Arboretum. The University of WISCONSIN has a large Oshokosh branch. Lake Winnebago boasts Wisconsin's largest paddleboat for cruising on the lake and the Fox River. The many annual events include International Museums Day, mid-May; Museum Art Fair, early July; Sawdust Daze, commemorating lumbering activities, early July; Waterfest, in mid July.

By far the most important is the (EAA) International Fly-in Convention. This has been called the world's largest and most significant aviation event. More than 500 seminars, workshops and other discussion groups are held. A host of exhibitors, thousands of aircraft of every shape, size and description and exciting daily air shows highlight the period of July 31 through August 7 each year. Some of the most peculiar, unusual and sometimes laughable aircraft have been exhibited, but they all fly in one way or another. Among other Oshkosh attractions are the ninety aircraft on exhibit at the EAA Air Museum.

OSTENSORIUM OF FATHER NOUVEL. The most cherished relic of early-day Wisconsin history. In 1686 the silver ostensorium was given to Father Henri Nouvel, head of the ST. FRANCIS XAVIER MISSION at De Pere, now GREEN BAY, by Nicholas PERROT (1644-1717), military commandant of the Green Bay region. In 1687 the mission burned, but Father Nouvel's Indian friend, Flying Bird, rescued the treasure, although he died of burns suffered in the attempt. The subsequent history of the ostensorium is not known. However, in 1802 a Green Bay resident found it while digging a foundation for a home. The relic, earliest of the French regime, is now a cherished exhibit at the Neville Public Museum at Green Bay.

OTHER DAY, John. Christian Indian who protected sixty-two white refugees in an old building and then led them to safety during the Sioux Uprising in Minnesota in 1862. For his heroic act Other Day was awarded $2,500 by Congress.

OTTAWA INDIANS. ALGONQUIN tribe which lived on Manitoulin Island and the shores of Lake HURON in the early 17th century. The Ottawa spoke a dialect of the OJIBWAY language of the Algonquian linguistic family, and their name was derived from the Algonquian word adawe, meaning "to trade." The Ottawa truly were great traders, often traveling hundreds of miles and often acting as middlemen between the HURON INDIANS and the tribes of the West.

By the 17th century, the Ottawa were divided into many autonomous groups, each with its own chief or chiefs. These groups were further divided into local bands or villages, each having its own leadership. The Ottawa believed that the Great Hare created the world and that everything was controlled by a supreme being called the Master of Life. There were countless spirits, both good and evil, called manito. Shamans could intercede with the manito and seek their assistance in curing illness.

During puberty, both boys and girls fasted in secluded places to acquire guardian spirits through visions. The dead were buried, placed on scaffolds or cremated. Feasts honoring the dead were held every few years.

Ottawa villages were permanent. Longhouses were made of overlapping sheets of bark on a frame of poles. Palisades were sometimes constructed around villages for protection. On hunting trips, mat-covered conical lodges were used.

The Ottawa economy was based on hunting and gathering. The men hunted and trapped beaver, deer, birds and small game and fished the rivers of the upper Midwest with nets. In winter the Indians split up into small hunting groups and then regrouped in spring to plant corn, beans and squash and collect maple sap for syrup. The women collected berries and other plant food.

Crafts included objects from birchbark and leather. Elaborate tattooing and face and body painting were used for adornment.

The IROQUOIS drove the Ottawa west to the STRAITS OF MACKINAC and GREEN BAY in 1649. Some bands of Ottawa settled on Keweenaw Bay and CHEQUAMEGON BAY on Lake SUPERIOR. One group settled at Lake PEPIN, but was driven out by the SIOUX. In the 18th century the Ottawa founded settlements along Lake MICHIGAN and Lake HURON, the GRAND and ST. JOSEPH rivers in Michigan, and on the present sites of MILWAUKEE, CHICAGO and DETROIT.

By the 19th century, the Ottawa were forced out of lower Michigan by treaties with the whites. Some went to Kansas, others settled on Manitoulin and Drummond islands, and a third group settled on reservations in Michigan.

OTTAWA, Illinois. City (pop. 18,166), seat of La Salle County, industrial and distribution center, founded 1830. "Ottawa," an Indian word meaning trade, was incorporated in 1853. It had been the county seat since 1831. Ottawa was the site of the first LINCOLN-DOUGLAS DEBATE, held on August 21, 1858. A publisher, William D. Boyce, organized the Boy Scouts of America there in 1911. Some of the largest industries in glass production use the silica found locally. Historic buildings in the city include the Caton House, built by John Dean Caton, and The Oaks, completed in 1860, home of CIVIL WAR General W.H.L. Wallace, killed at the Battle of Shiloh (April 6-7, 1862). Railroad hobbyists visit Ottawa to see the exhibit of steam locomotive 4978 with its tender and caboose. Seven miles from Ottawa, STARVED ROCK STATE PARK attracts many visitors. The Illinois Waterway Visitor Center provides an excellent view of the locking-through process at Starved Rock Lock and Dam. Audio-visual displays feature the lock operation and the Illinois' Waterway's relationship to other navigable inland and coastal waterways.

OTTER TAIL RIVER. Minnesota river whose source is Otter Tail Lake in central Otter Tail County in west central Minnesota. The river flows west and then south before turning west again to join with the BOIS DE SIOUX RIVER at BRECKENRIDGE in western Minnesota. The two streams unite to form the RED RIVER OF THE NORTH.

OUTBOARD MOTORS. Midwest invention. A vast and growing industry as well as perhaps the largest group of participating sportsmen worldwide have a Midwest man to thank for a device which now has almost universal use. Ole Evenirude of Wisconsin wondered for some time how he might enjoy the speed of motorized water travel without buying an expensive inboard motorboat. After considerable experimentation, Evenirude came up with a simple mechanical device to attach to the back of a boat to propel it forward, and in 1909 he put it on the market. From that time on, boating was revolutionized. The outboard motor had arrived, and lumbering rowboats could be mechanized. Propulsion was by propeller at first and later by jet. Electric motors made possible attachment even to fragile canoes, and gasoline engines evolved to gigantic size, now used all over the world in such far reaches as the Moroni River in the Guianas, where the outboard boatmen are considered the best in the world as they push their forty-foot dugouts up the swift rapids. Ole Evinrude put a few small ads in *Popular Mechanics* Magazine, and boating enthusiasts responded. The Evinrude outboards are still manufactured in MILWAUKEE today, and other makes are produced in other locations around the globe. Ole Evinrude really started a multi-billion dollar sporting extravaganza.

OWATONNA, Minnesota. City (pop. 18,-632), seat of Steele County, southeastern Minnesota, south of MINNEAPOLIS -ST. PAUL. The name, meaning "straight" in the Sioux language, was applied to the Owatonna River, which held a straight course there. Incorporated in 1854, the city grew near where the "Straight River" and Maple Creek join. The arrival in 1866 of the Minnesota Central Railway and the St. Peter and Winona line assured the city of its place as an important agricultural and trade center. Today it is a center of dairy and truck farming, with a tannery, and manufacturing including agricultural machinery and tools. One of Minnesota's most interesting buildings is Owatonna's Northwestern National Bank, erected in 1908 and designed by Louis SULLIVAN (1856-1924), a nationally-known architect. The Village of Yesteryear includes a schoolhouse, two log cabins, a church, a mansion and a museum. Regional and local artists display their work at the Owatonna Arts Center and

Sculpture Garden. Railroad historians come to see "Old No. 201," the locomotive driven by the very real Casey Jones, whose railroad exploits have reached legendary proportions. Annual events include Straight River Days in early June, September Fest in mid-September, and Pumpkin Festival for three days in late October.

OWEN FAMILY. Robert Owen, founder of NEW HARMONY, Indiana and his sons. In giving the welfare of his workers so much attention, Robert Owen (Newtown, Wales, May 14, 1771—November 17, 1858) gained an international reputation. Owen believed a society could improve itself through careful planning and efforts of men of good will. His New Harmony experiment was designed to show that by working together properly people could establish a perfect society. While his experiment at New Harmony failed to achieve his expectations, the people Owen attracted to the Indiana wilderness did ground-breaking work in such areas as infant education, women's clubs, geology, and public libraries. One of Owen's sons, David Dale Owen (New Lanark Scotland, June 24, 1807—New Harmony, Indiana, November 13, 1860) was appointed the state geologist of Indiana in 1860. As a geologist, David Owen was the first to point out the rich mineral nature of lands in Iowa and Wisconsin. Another son, Robert Dale Owen (Glasgow, Scotland, November 9, 1801—Lake George, New York, June 24, 1877) became a reformer and congressman. Robert Dale Owen edited the New Harmony *Gazette* and then became a founder in New York of the Association for Protection of Industry and for Promotion of National Education. He served in the Indiana legislature from 1836 to 1838 and the United States House of Representatives from 1843 to 1847 where he introduced a bill establishing the Smithsonian Institution. Robert Dale Owen served in the Indiana Constitutional Convention in 1850 and as charge d'affaires in Naples, Italy, from 1853 to 1858. New Harmony was one of the most successful and influential of the many "experimental" villages founded in the U.S. in the 1800s.

OWOSSO, Michigan. City (16,455), Shiawassee County, southeastern portion of Michigan's LOWER PENINSULA, west of FLINT, named for Chief Wosso of the OJIBWAY, who is buried in the city. Owosso was the birthplace of two-time presidential candidate Thomas E. DEWEY (1902-1971). It was also the birthplace of writer James

Oliver Curwood, who wrote many stories about the Canadian North. Curwood's studio, resembling a Norman fortress, is open to the public. Owosso is today a trading and industrial center. Curwood Festival annually features raft, bed and canoe races, art show, foot races and entertainment.

OXFORD, Ohio. City (pop. 17,655), situated in southwest Ohio in Butler County near the Indiana line, it was named for Oxford University and Oxford, the borough, Oxfordshire, England. A quiet university town and residential community, Oxford was laid out in 1810 and chartered in 1831. Early Oxford had small factories making buggies, wagons, brooms and organs, along with a distillery, but much of the industry died out, leaving the city to depend mostly on higher education. MIAMI UNIVERSITY was authorized by the state legislature in 1809. The university opened formally in the fall of 1824. One of its prominent graduates was Benjamin HARRISON (1833-1901), later to become president of the U.S. Today Oxford is noted for its annual National Archery Tournament, held in early August at Cook Field of the University. The university offers an art museum and natural history museum. William Holmes MC GUFFEY (1800-1873), at one time on the university staff, the famed author of the six McGuffey Readers, is honored by the McGuffey Museum on the campus, which occupies the professor's home and houses a collection of his books and other memorabilia. Nearby Heston Woods State Park features Pioneer Farm and House Museum, with 1835 period furniture, clothing and toys, and offers demonstrations of apple butter making.

OZARK MOUNTAINS. Area of rugged highlands also referred to as the Ozark Plateau stretching from ST. LOUIS, Missouri, to the ARKANSAS RIVER. Covering nearly 50,000 square miles, they are mainly in Missouri and Arkansas, but portions extend into Illinois, Oklahoma, and Kansas. Primarily of limestone, their highest peak in Missouri is TAUM SAUK in Iron County (1,772 feet). In the southern regions near the WHITE and Arkansas rivers, elevations occasionally reach 2,000 feet in the Boston Mountains area. The Ozarks are noted commercially for lead and zinc mines. Though sparsely populated and with numerous areas of extreme poverty in rural regions, the mountains have a substantial summer tourist trade, particularly at two state parks in Missouri: Big Spring and Lake of the OZARKS. The largest lakes in the Ozarks include Lake of the Ozarks, TABLE ROCK Reservoir, BULL SHOALS, and Beaver.

OZARK NATIONAL SCENIC RIVERWAYS. Near VAN BUREN, Missouri. For about 134 miles the CURRENT and Jacks Fork rivers flow through the OZARK MOUNTAINS. Notable features include huge freshwater springs and numerous caves.

OZARKS, LAKE OF THE. Located in central Missouri, it is the largest lake in the state and is one of the largest artificial lakes in the U.S. Spanning several counties, this 16,529-acre reservoir was designed by the U.S. Army Corps of Engineers, and was created by impounding the OSAGE RIVER with the BAGNELL DAM, in order to provide flood control and the recreation for which it has become famous. The lake is 130 miles long and has a shoreline of almost 1,400 miles.

P

PAGEANT OF THE SAULT (SOO). Ceremony at SAULT STE. MARIE, Michigan, on June 14, 1671, in which the French claimed most of North America as their territory. The official in charge was Francois DAUMONT (-1674), known sometimes by his title Sieur de St. Lusson. Daumont was sent by the French governor of Canada to make a formal claim in the name of the King of France. Realizing that the Indians would be impressed by formality, Daumont arranged for representatives of fourteen tribes to be present. Daumont himself appeared in a procession of European missionaries, interpreters, and attendants, all dressed in their finest clothing, embroidered with gold, with armor shining, the missionaries in their most impressive robes. Muskets were fired as the land was claimed for the king who was described to the Indians as having fantastic powers of destruction.

Pageant of the Sault, by Robert Thom (C) 1966 by Michigan Bell Telephone Co.

PALMER COLLEGE OF CHIROPRACTIC. A DAVENPORT, Iowa, institution developed in the 1920s by D. D. Palmer as the Palmer School of Chiropractic, and very largely promoted by his son B. J. PALMER (1881-1961). The senior Palmer had studied European practices of body manipulation with the hands. The school became the center for U.S. study and practice of chiropractic medicine, a status which it still holds.

PALMER, Bartlett Joshua. (What Cheer, Iowa, Sept. 10, 1881—Sarasota, Fla., May 27, 1961). The practice of chiropractic medicine was introduced to the United States by D.D. Palmer, father of B.J., in 1895. The word chiropractic is from the Greek meaning "done by hand." The early practitioners were sometimes called charlatans because they believed there was some psychic transmission of healing through their hands. B. J. Palmer was the foremost promoter of chiropractic treatment, opening the PALMER COLLEGE OF CHIROPRACTIC at DAVENPORT, Iowa. With only a meager education, the son took over the school after his father died in 1913. One of the pioneers of radio broadcasting, Palmer promoted himself and his school over his major radio station at Davenport. His son, David Palmer, became president and made further changes and developments, including entrance into television with a station which has developed to become one of Iowa's most important outlets.

PALMER, Bertha. (Louisville, KY, May 22, 1849—Osprey, FL, May 5, 1918). Social leader. Wife of Potter PALMER, she gained a position of social leadership in CHICAGO, nationally and in Europe and was chosen president of the Board of Lady Managers of the WORLD'S COLUMBIAN EXPOSITION (1893). The social connections Palmer made in Europe, while promoting the Exposition, remained important throughout her life. Due to her efforts, the women's department of the fair was given serious consideration. Women's exhibits had space in each state building, and many royal women were convinced to lend exhibits. In 1892 Palmer was made a trustee of NORTHWESTERN UNIVERSITY. In 1900 President MC KINLEY (1843-1901) appointed Palmer as a member of the committee to the Paris Exposition. In her later years, she managed the estate left to her upon the death of her husband. She also gave her leadership experience to the management of the charity ball of Chicago which became increasingly important as a social event and as a way of collecting funds.

PALMER, Potter. (Albany County, NY, May

20, 1826—Chicago, IL, May 4, 1902). Merchant, urban developer. In 1852, with his father, Palmer opened a dry-goods store on Lake Street, in CHICAGO, Illinois, then the center of Chicago's commercial district. His revolutionary business methods included allowing customers to inspect the merchandise in their own homes before purchase and to exchange purchases for other merchandise or a return of their money. This retailing concept became known as the "Palmer system." Palmer stressed advertising and attractive displays of goods for sale. With failing health, he retired in 1867 and turned the business over to his partners who included Marshall FIELD. After three years of rest and travel, Palmer returned to Chicago and became interested in real estate development. He built the first Palmer House along with thirty-two other businesses. When the fire of 1871 destroyed much of his holdings, he built larger and more nearly permanent structures, including the second Palmer House which gained international attention. Palmer spent vast sums developing waste lands along the lake into avenues and building sites. He was a vice-president of the first board of local directors of the WORLD'S COLUMBIAN EXPOSITION (1893), the first president of the Chicago Baseball Club, and one of the original incorporators of the Chicago Association of Commerce and the Chicago Board of Trade.

PANA, Illinois. City (pop. 6,040). One of the early stations on the Illinois Central Railway; located in central Illinois south of DECATUR, name, a corruption of Pani, a small tribe of Indiana Indians. Peabody Coal Company's mine No. 17, near Pana, is the second largest producer of coal in Illinois and the sixth largest in the United States. The coal supplies the steam heat necessary to warm sixty acres of greenhouses used locally to grow flowers, one of the largest concentrations of its kind. Millions of roses are shipped annually.

PAPERMAKING AND PAPER PRODUCTS. Wisconsin leads the nation in production of papers of all kinds. Papermaking began in Wisconsin about 1870, when such communities as NEENAH turned to it after lumbering declined. At Neenah the first paper factories used straw as a basic material. Much of the timber now cut in Wisconsin and the other Midwest states is converted to pulp for paper. Wisconsin's paper industry started in the Neenah-MENASHA region. Paper making and manufacture of paper products is the third largest industry in Wisconsin, surprisingly ranking ahead of dairying. The industry is also important in Minnesota, where more than twenty manufacturers turn pulp into paper and other paper products.

PARIS, Illinois. City (pop. 9,885), seat of Edgar County, eastern Illinois, named after Paris, Kentucky, platted in 1853. In 1856 Abraham LINCOLN (1809-1865) spoke in the community in support of presidential candidate John C. Fremont. Paris has the largest broom factory in the world. Other industries include the manufacture of buses, trucks, automobile and airplane parts.

PARR, Charles Henry. (Wyoming Twp., Iowa County, WI, Mar. 18, 1869—Los Angeles, CA, June 10, 1941). Inventor, manufacturer. Two young undergraduates of the University of WISCONSIN (Charles Parr and Charles W. HART) met at the university and began to work together on some projects on the development of farm equipment. After graduation in 1896, they carried on their experiment, first in MADISON, then moved their establishment to CHARLES CITY, Iowa. There they adapted their stationary, gas-engine-powered farm implement to a vehicle which moved with its own traction. So in 1904 they coined the word tractor to describe their new invention, and the word has stuck ever since. The Hart-Parr company continued to be a power in the developing world of the tractor and added other farm implements to its line, as well. Charles City was named for the two Charles's.

PASSENGER PIGEONS. The beautiful passenger pigeon, about 15 inches long, always migrated to the upper Midwest from its winter quarters in the south sometime in March. Experts feel that at one time there were more passenger pigeons than any other bird. As they migrated, the sky was darkened, sometimes for hours, as their enormous flocks continued to pass over. When one of the flocks roosted near PETOSKEY, Michigan, on March 18, 1878, the branches of the beech trees gave way with the weight, and the snapping of branches could be heard throughout the forest. During the one roosting, more than a million were killed by hunters at that one time. They were so popular with hunters that they continued to be killed by the millions. The unsuspecting birds were an easy prey. Hunters would tie a captured live bird to a stool, which innocently lured the other birds by twisting about and flapping its wings.

The term stool pigeon originated from this practice. The relentless killings continued until the last of the millions had been killed, and the wonderful passenger pigeon became extinct when the last known survivor died at the CINCINNATI, Ohio, Zoo in 1914.

PEACE PIPES. Ceremonial tobacco pipes, also called CALUMETS.

PEAT. Soil material consisting of partially decayed and compressed organic matter, mostly of aquatic plants, the earliest stage of transition from compressed plant growth to the formation of coal. The fuel is found in greatest quantity in the Midwest. Minnesota contains almost unlimited supplies of peat, the largest such reserves in the country, and Michigan counts a total of more than a billion tons. Due to the greater heating value of coal, peat has not been extensively utilized, but it remains as one of the great untapped resources of organic fuels. Some new techniques of using peat as fuel for smelting and other purposes may lead the way to many additional uses for the peat of the Midwest.

PECK, George W.. (Henderson, NY, 1840—Milwaukee, WI, 1916) Humorist, journalist. Moved with his family to Wisconsin, where he was raised. He was a rare combination of politician-humorist, publisher of the newspaper *Peck's Sun*, at LA CROSSE, Wisconsin. His best known and very popular work was the series called *Peck's Bad Boy*, published from 1882 through 1900. In it he recounted the tales of a mischievous young man and his rascally father. Peck served as mayor of MILWAUKEE, Wisconsin, was elected governor of the state as a Democrat in 1890 and continued his humorous writings while governor, serving in the post until 1895.

PECULIAR, Missouri. Town (pop. 1,571), western Missouri in Cass County, south of KANSAS CITY. The naming of the town is said to have occurred when a group of spiritualists came to Cass County. When Mrs. Jane Hawkins, leader of the group, first saw the valley she supposedly said, "That's peculiar," because it reminded her of a place she had seen in a vision in Connecticut. The spiritualists bought a farm and platted the town in 1868. Another version of the name contends that the postmaster submitted a name for the town. A letter from the postal department complained that the name he had suggested was "peculiar,"

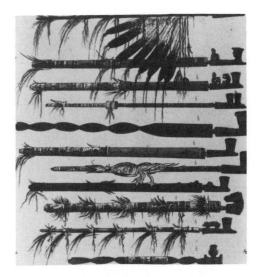

Peace pipes, painted by George Catlin.

so he considered he had been instructed to give the community that name.

PELLA, Iowa. City (pop. 8,349). In southeast Iowa, in Marian County, Pella was named for Pella, the ancient Greek city, the name applied by Dutch immigrants who were seeking refuge from religious intolerance at home. The leader of the 700 pilgrims was their minister, Dominie SCHOLTE (1805-1868). A wealthy group, they took a leisurely trip across country to their new home in Iowa, traveling by rail, canal boat and steamboat and resting for a while in ST. LOUIS, Missouri, before going on to Pella by stagecoach. They arrived in Iowa in 1847, and Mrs. Scholte found all but six pieces of her fine delft china had been broken, so she lined the path between their temporary log cabin and their new house under construction with the broken china pieces. Later the Scholtes donated land for a college and a city park. He was the first president of the theological school known today as Central University of Iowa. The Scholtes also donated a church and a library. Based on the wealth of the settlers and the good Dutch thrift and industry, the community has continued to prosper. Today, it is known across the country as the site of one of the major ethnic festivals, Tulip Time in Pella. The community celebrates when the acres of colorful blossoms are in full bloom, and Dutch costumes and festivities enliven the community. Another attraction for visitors is the Scholte home, preserving many of their possessions, including their rare collection of ancient books.

Tulip Time, Pella, Iowa.

PELLAGRA. A deficiency disease most common in countries where the diet consists almost entirely of corn. Pellagra was one of the diseases conquered through the researches of the WISCONSIN ALUMNI RESEARCH FOUNDATION (WARF) of the University of WISCONSIN, one of the most successful health research organizations in the history of science. Studies there indicated that the disease was caused by lack of nicotinic acid (niacin), plentiful in many foods but almost completely lacking in corn. With this understanding, it was possible for WARF to develop nicotinic acid as a cure for pellagra.

PEMMICAN. Dried, compressed meat prepared by American Indians. Pemmican was prepared by cutting meat into fine pieces and boiling it. The boiled meat was placed in a bag of buffalo skin which lined a hole in the ground. Indians pounded the meat as tightly as possible into the bag and then hot buffalo fat was poured into the sack, tightly sealing the meat from the air. Sewed tight, the sacks kept the meat fresh for long periods of time, even years. Some experts consider this traditional food to be among the most nourishing ever produced,

PENDARVIS CORNISH RESTORATION. One of the principal restorations of early settlement and mining booms in the Midwest, Pendarvis harks back to the days of settlement of miners from Cornwall in the 1820s and 1830s. These skilled miners brought new techniques to the lead (galena) mines of northwest Illinois and southwest Wisconsin. They settled at MINERAL POINT, Wisconsin, where they built some of the first stone homes in the area, duplicating the rock houses of their Cornish homeland. Pendarvis, at Mineral Point, restores some of the log and brick residences of the mining boom period. Also shown are abandoned "badger" holes. These

were the temporary caves cut into the side of hills which the earlier miners used for housing, giving the state its Badger State nickname. The forty-acre area includes a nature walk and the opportunity to visit a pioneer mine shaft.

PENNEY, James Cash. (Breckenridge, MO, Sept. 16, 1875—New York, NY, Feb. 12, 1971). Merchant. Penney, one of twelve children, was born near BRECKENRIDGE, Missouri. He began his business career at the age of twenty as a clerk in a store in Hamilton, Missouri. In failed health he moved to Denver, Colorado, and later Kemmer, Wyoming, where he was employed to manage a store. His employer, T.M. Callahan, allowed him to purchase a one-third interest in the store. This so impressed Penney, that he pioneered in the business principle of participation of his key employees in his business profits. His first wholly-owned store, opened in 1904, located in a building 25 by 40 feet. Four years later he bought two stores from Callahan and began developing one of the nation's largest merchandising chains. An exceptional businessman, Penney took a five-thousand dollar investment and made a profit of over eight thousand dollars the first year. For his 500th store, in 1924 Penney returned to his first workplace, Hamilton, Missouri. By 1937 Penney stores were located in forty-four states. At the time of his death in 1971, the Penney stores were a four billion dollar a year business. Penney served as the president of the company until 1917 and chairman of the board from 1917 to 1958 and a director from 1958 until 1971. Penney was named to the Hall of Fame in Distribution at the State University of Oklahoma; he received the Tobe award for distinguished contributions to American retailing in 1953 and the Horatio Alger award from the American Schools and Colleges Association. He wrote *Fifty Years With the Golden Rule* (1950).

PEONY. State flower of Indiana. Sometimes called piney, the hardy bushy perennials die back each year. The flowers, either single or double, usually bloom in early spring and range in color from white and pink to dark red. The roots have been used as a medicine for convulsions.

PEORIA, Illinois. City (pop. 117,000) seat of Peoria County, situated in central Illinois on the ILLINOIS RIVER where it forms Peoria Lake, a natural expansion of the river. Just to the north is Upper Peoria Lake. The community was incorporated as a city in 1845. Neighboring communities are West Peoria, East Peoria, across the river, and Peoria Heights on the north. For a long period it was the second largest city in Illinois; now ranks third in population. The city covers an area of 42.1 square miles.

The name is derived from the tribe of ILLINI Indians, anglicized from the French *peouarea*, possibly meaning "carriers" or "ones who are carrying packs."

From the river, the topography rises gently, extending to a level tableland. Centered in one of the finest of all agricultural areas as well as in a region of coal, the city quickly became a commercial center and a busy port of entry on the Illinois waterway between CHICAGO and New Orleans. The city was first reached by steamboat in 1828. Most river traffic now is carried by barge.

Grain of the region supplies one of the nation's largest centers of whiskey distilleries, including the world's largest maker of bourbon.

Caterpillar company has been typical of the heavy industry of the area. Many of the agricultural products of the region are processed and shipped from Peoria.

With the financial difficulties of Caterpillar in the 1980s, the city experienced severe economic problems, somewhat alleviated by partial recovery of the giant manufacturer.

Father Jacques MARQUETTE (1637-1675) preached to and baptized the Peoria Indians of the area in 1673. LA SALLE (Robert Cavelier) (1643-1687) and Henri DE TONTI (1650-1704) visited the Peoria region in 1680 and established Fort Crevecoeur (Fort Heartbreak) about two miles south of Peoria Lake, but the fort was abandoned because of Indian pressure.

In 1691 de Tonti established Fort Pimiteoui at Peoria. The name means "Fat Lake," descriptive of the bulge in the river which forms Peoria Lake. Although this might be considered the first permanent European community in Illinois, as Peoria claims, settlement around Fort Pimeteoui was not entirely continuous after 1691 and the community was almost deserted during the American Revolution. However, Peoria certainly can claim the earliest establishment of a major Illinois city.

During the WAR OF 1812, Indian disturbances brought Governor Ninian Edwards to the area, where he destroyed the Indian village of Au Pee on the site of Peoria. This was a tragic mistake. Edwards apparently did not know that Chief Black Partridge of Au Pee had been aiding the Americans in ransoming the captives from the FORT DEARBORN massacre.

Modern Peoria had its beginnings in 1813 when the Americans built Fort Clark where the village of Au Pee had stood. Peoria County was established in 1825, and the community which had grown up around Fort Clark was named as the county seat, with the French name restored. The community grew quickly with establishment of meat packing and whiskey distilling.

Four years before their famous debates, both Stephen A. DOUGLAS (1813-1861) and Abraham LINCOLN (1809-1865) spoke at Peoria in 1854. In his speech, Lincoln, for the first time, publicly denounced slavery.

In 1865 an attempt was made to move the state capital from SPRINGFIELD to Peoria, but nothing came of it.

In the period from 1970 through 1984 the population of Peoria declined significantly from 127,000 to 117,000, following the general decline in manufacturing and agricultural revenues throughout the Midwest.

Bradley University and a research laboratory of the U.S. Department of Agriculture are the major academic facilities.

Lakeview Center for the Arts and Sciences provides for visitors features of recreation, education, fine arts and science. There is a museum, art gallery, auditorium and a museum shop, with a planetarium nearby. Metamora Court House State Memorial recalls Lincoln's circuit days. The original building and chapel of one of Illinois' first colleges are preserved in the nearby Jubilee College State memorial.

PEPIN, Lake. Minnesota lake. The sand and silt deposited across the MISSISSIPPI River by the CHIPPEWA RIVER formed a unique natural dam which backed up the great river for thirty miles, forming the lake. The earliest settlement on the lake was established in 1686 and was called Fort St. Antoine by its founder, Nicholas PERROT (1644-1717). The length of ST. PAUL's shipping season was determined by the freezing and thawing of the lake. In addition to its importance for shipping, Lake Pepin had a prosperous clamming industry. Valuable freshwater pearls were found, supplying two button factories at WINONA, Minnesota, which did a brisk business in the first two decades of the twentieth century.

PERCY, Charles. (Pensacola, FL, September 27, 1919—). Illinois senator. Percy rose from sales trainee in 1938 to chairman of the board of Bell and Howell, from 1963 to 1966. He was a Republican senator from Illinois from 1967 through 1973. Percy has been chairman of the

Perry victory monument, Put-in-Bay, Ohio.

Fund for Adult Education, FORD FOUNDATION director, trustee of the University of CHICAGO, and director of the National Recreation and Park Association. He is the author of *Growing Old in the Country of the Young* (1974), and *I Want to Know about the United States Senate* (1976).

PERE MARQUETTE RIVER WILD AND SCENIC RIVER SYSTEM. The portion of this Michigan river classified in this way. The wild and scenic section wanders gently through overhanging bluffs and across the grassy floodplains of central Michigan. This section of the river is considered one of the finest trout resources of the Midwest. The river's source lies in Lake County near Reed City. On its westward course toward Lake MICHIGAN, the Pere Marquette flows through Scottville and LUDINGTON, Michigan, the latter at the river's mouth.

PERROT, Nicolas. (1644—c.1718). French explorer in Canada and the Midwest. Coming to Canada as a boy, he learned the Indian languages, helped the Jesuit missionaries and engaged in the fur trade around GREEN BAY, Wisconsin, gaining considerable influence over the Indians. He helped the French authorities in controlling the incoming IROQUOIS and was made commandant of the area around Green Bay. In 1689 he formally claimed possession of the upper Mississippi region in the name of

New France (Canada). His explorations took him as far as southwestern Wisconsin and northwestern Illinois, where he discovered the lead resources of the area, and on into eastern portions of Iowa.

PERRY'S VICTORY AND INTERNATIONAL PEACE MEMORIAL. At PUT-IN-BAY, Ohio. Commodore Oliver H. PERRY won the greatest naval battle of the WAR OF 1812 on Lake ERIE. The memorial—the world's most massive Doric column—was constructed 1912-15 "to inculcate the lessons of international peace by arbitration and disarmament." It was designed by Joseph Freedlander and was constructed with funds from the Federal government and 9 states.

PERRY, Oliver Hazard. (South Kingston, RI, Aug. 20, 1785—Trinidad, Aug. 23, 1819), Naval captain. Appointed a midshipman in 1799, he served in the war with Tripoli and was appointed a lieutenant in 1807. He was commissioned to build a fleet of boats on Lake ERIE at the tiny town of Erie, Pennsylvania, then of 400 population. Skilled workers and supplies had to be brought 400 miles, across an area of wilderness. Trees growing in the morning often became planks in a ship before evening. One of the workers on the scene said of Perry, "The public never knew the worth of that man. They have known him only as the victor over the English fleet on Lake Erie, and yet this was far his smallest merit. Hundreds might have fought that battle as well as he did....But to appreciate his character, a person must have seen him, as I did, fitting out a fleet of six new vessels of war,...at some hundreds of miles from the sea coast...not one single article necessary for the equipment of a vessel...was not subject to land transportations of some 120 to 400 miles through roads nearly impassable. I have seen him, when almost abandoned by his country, with less than a hundred sailors under his command, and half of those on the sick list, toiling to fit out his fleet...evincing a courage far greater than what was required to fight the battle of the 10th of September." Preliminary work was begun in September, 1812. The bulk of the building of a complete fleet of ships was done in the incredibly short period of ninety days by men who had to begin the work by making their own tools from iron sheets and bars. After the fleet was built, in the summer of 1813, Perry sailed his new fleet to a small inlet on South Bass Island north and west of present SANDUSKY, Ohio. Because they "put in" there, the place has been known as Put-in-Bay ever since. Sighting the enemy on September 10, he sailed northwest toward the Sister Islands and won a great victory in the Battle of LAKE ERIE. This victory gave the Americans control of the GREAT LAKES and made possible William Henry HARRISON 's invasion of Canada in which Perry took part. The victory not only made Perry a national hero, but it also was considered by many to be one of the major military turning points in history. After the war, Perry served as a captain in the Mediterranean. Then, on a mission in the Caribbean, he took yellow fever and died in Trinidad. His body was brought to Newport, Rhode Island, where a monument was erected to him. However, the major monument in his tribute is the tallest Doric column in the world, the 342-foot granite shaft rising at Put-in-Bay at what is now PERRY'S VICTORY AND INTERNATIONAL PEACE MEMORIAL.

PERSHING, John Joseph (Laclede, MO, Sept. 13, 1860—Washington, DC July 15, 1948). General of the Armies. Graduating from the Military Academy at West Point, N.Y. in 1886, he served in many Indian wars and in the SPANISH-AMERICAN WAR. He served as adjutant general in the Philippine Islands (1906-13), and was commander of the raid against Mexican revolutionary Pancho Villa (1916): A military instructor at the University of Nebraska and at West Point, he was selected by President Woodrow Wilson to command the American troops in Europe during WORLD WAR I. Two months after his appointment, he submitted the "General Organization Report" in which he recommended an army of one million men by 1918 and 3 million by 1919. Despite U.S. concerns for such an expenditure, his recommendations were followed. Although adamant in opposition, he was forced to amalgamate small units of his troops with European soldiers. His army was never totally self-sufficient, but he returned home with a sound reputation. Known as "Black Jack" Pershing, he became General of the Armies in 1919, the only person ever to hold the rank, which had been created for General George Washington, but never bestowed. Later Pershing became chief-of-staff (1921-24). He won the Pulitzer Prize for his memoirs *My Experiences in the World War* (1931). Pershing State Park near Laclede is named in the general's honor.

PERU, Indiana. City (pop. 13,764), seat of Miami County, northern Indiana city north of KOKOMO and east of LOGANSPORT, located at the confluence of the MISSISSINEWA and WABASH rivers, named for the South American country. It was incorporated in 1847 and became known (despite other claims) as the "Circus City of the World," due, in part, to the activities in 1883 of Ben Wallace and James Anderson who formed the Hagenbeck-Wallace Circus and used Peru as the site of their first exhibition. Today it is a rail and processing center, with plastics, furniture and electrical equipment among its manufactures. Near Peru the American Circus Corporation has provided winter quarters for many of America's leading circuses. A vast collection of circus memorabilia may be found at the Circus City Museum which features circus posters and costumes of famous circus performers. Other circus relics and over 40,000 items of local historical importance are found in the Miami County Historical Museum. The circus atmosphere of the city is renewed in mid-July during Peru's Circus City Festival which includes an amateur circus, a parade and many rides. Along the Slocum Trail, named for Frances SLOCUM (1773-1847), the "White Rose of the Miamis," is the home of Cole PORTER (1893-1964), internationally known song writer, who was born here in 1893.

PESHTIGO, Wisconsin. City (pop. 2,807), situated in northeastern Wisconsin on the Peshtigo River above its mouth on GREEN BAY. The name is taken from an Indian word with a completely unknown meaning. The community is best known for its devastating forest fire of 1871, perhaps the most destructive in U.S. history. Estimates of the fire death loss range as high as 1,200, and those deaths went virtually unpublicized because, by a strange coincidence, the great Chicago FIRE was raging at exactly the same time. Adding to the strange coincidence, another forest fire was destroying HOLLAND, Michigan, at the same time. At Peshtigo the summer of 1871 had been extremely dry. Several small fires had burned nearby. Then on September 8 the Peshtigo region seemed to explode with fire. Only two houses remained in the town, and 600 residents were killed. The fire swept on, missing Marinette, consuming part of MENOMINEE, across the border in Michigan, and within four hours had swept a path forty miles long and ten miles wide along the western bay shore. After the fire, Peshtigo was rebuilt with carefully planned wide streets and new businesses and homes. Lumbering has been the traditional industry, and the city is now a thriving manufacturing center, where industrial tours are available at the Badger

Paper Mills. A monument to the fire-dead stands in the Peshtigo Fire Cemetery. The Peshtigo Fire Museum explains the fire and exhibits mementoes.

PHALANX. One of the many communal experiments so common in America in the mid-1800s, Phalanx was founded by the followers of the French socialist Francois Charles Maric Fourier. The members arrived at RIPON, Wisconsin, in 1844, and settled to the south and west of the city. As was usual with such groups, all property was held in common in the name of the society. More unusual was the fact that the entire community lived in one long house and ate at the same table. Most unusual of all was the financial success of the colony. In a few years so much had been accumulated that its members divided the profits and disbanded.

PHEASANTS. Popular oriental game bird introduced to North America in the 1890s. The ring-necked pheasant, originating in China, has became probably the most popular single game object in the country, especially in the Midwest where it flourishes. In Iowa, alone, a million and a half birds are bagged each year, especially in east central and southwestern Iowa, where more shelter still remains for the birds. Most of the 250,000 hunters who seek the quarry in Iowa annually ask permission to hunt on private land. In the off season, male and female pheasants, often with offspring, may be seen by the side of the road, or whirring off in their peculiar low flying pattern.

PIASA BIRD. Remarkable PICTOGRAPH of huge size created by unknown prehistoric artists, near present ALTON, Illinois. Now one of the world's most famous pictographs, it was first noted by the explorers MARQUETTE (1637-1675) and JOLLIET (1645-1700). Father Marquette himself described the discovery, "Passing the mouth of the ILLINOIS RIVER we soon fell into the shadow of a tall promontory and with great astonishment beheld representations of two monsters painted on the lofty limestone front...They are painted red, green, and black and are an object of Indian Worship." A later explorer said the figures seemed to be about thirty feet tall, twelve feet long, and resembled a bat. Famed German artist Henry Lewis visited the area and made a painting of the figures, known as the PIASA BIRDS, making one look like a devil and the other a winged lizard. Experts are at a loss to ascribe an origin to these figures, since they resemble nothing else that is known. Unfortunately, they were used as targets by boatmen on the river and finally were blasted away for railroad ballast in 1846 and 1847. The nearby community of Alton has painted a supposed reproduction of one of the figures on the remaining cliff face.

PICKAWILLANY. MIAMI Indian village. Coming into Indiana and Ohio from Canada, the Miami built a village called Pickawillany where Loramie Creek flows into the MIAMI RIVER, near present PIQUA, Ohio. The town became a center for trade with the English. This enraged the French, who claimed the area. When the

Famed artist Henry Lewis painted the Piasa Bird, Alton, Illinois.

French discovered that the Miami were hiding French army deserters and when they heard that the Miami were said to have killed fifteen French traders, the French sent Charles LANGLEDE with an army of their Indian friends. On June 21, 1752, the Miami were unprepared. The gates of their stockade were open. Warriors were out hunting, and the women were tending the crops. More than a dozen English traders were in the town. As the Langlede forces approached, some of the traders and Miami men and boys managed to close the gates. After several hours of siege, the Miami agreed to surrender the traders, providing they would not be harmed. When the gates were opened the attackers leaped upon a wounded trader, tore off his scalp, cut out his heart and ate it. Old Britain, chief of the Miami, was boiled and eaten. Pickawillany was burned to the ground and the powerful Miami were reduced in respect and authority.

PICTOGRAPHS. The paintings, inscriptions and markings of prehistoric peoples on rocks. One of the world's most famous and mysterious pictographs was painted on the cliffs near present ALTON, Illinois, discovered by MARQUETTE (1637-1675) and JOLLIET (1645-1700) in 1673, and later named the PIASA BIRD for a nearby river. With the exception of the Piasa, in general the pictographs of the Midwest are scanty and of less importance than those of the West and Southwest. Some scattered paintings are found in Iowa. Minnesota has some pictographs, particularly in the Superior National Forest. On a cliff overlooking Hegman Lake in Minnesota, a striking pictograph shows a man, moose, puma and canoes. Portions of some pictographs have been chipped away by chemists who hoped to analyze the content to see how the colors could last so long. The Hegman Lake pictographs were made with red pigment of finely ground iron ore called hematite, mixed with a binder of vegetable oils, blood or egg white. Pictographs in GRAHAM CAVE NATIONAL HISTORIC LANDMARK in present Montgomery County, Missouri, show evidence of a people who could trade with distant sources for ochre and other coloring matter not available in the region.

PICTURED ROCKS NATIONAL LAKE-SHORE. Near Munising, Michigan. Multicolored sandstone cliffs, broad beaches, sand bars, dunes, waterfalls, inland lakes, ponds, marshes, hardwood and coniferous forest and numerous birds and animals comprise this scenic area on lake Superior. This was the first national lakeshore, authorized October 15, 1966.

PIKE, Zebulon Montgomery. (Lamberton, NJ, Jan. 5, 1779—York, Canada, Apr. 27, 1813). Military officer. He entered the military as a boy and became a second lieutenant by age 20. His major achievement in the Midwest came when he served as the leader of an expedition to explore the source of the MISSISSIPPI RIVER, starting from ST. LOUIS, Missouri, in 1805. He raised the first U.S. flag in eastern Iowa and gave his name to a bluff near MC GREGOR, Iowa. That Iowa Pike's Peak is scarcely a mound compared to the Pike's Peak in Colorado, but it is still a notable landmark on the Mississippi. One of his assignments was to win the friendship of the Indians on the route, as well as to locate suitable sites for future fortifications. By the time he had reached present Minnesota, the winter had brought great hardship. The cold was so severe that even the ink froze. Although Pike thought he had reached the headwaters of the Misssissipi at the Upper Red Cedar Lake, now called CASS LAKE, he was mistaken. At Leech lake, site of a trading post, Pike gathered the Indians in powwow and in an imposing ceremony raised the American flag for the first time in what is now Minnesota. This dramatic demonstration was designed to show the Indian groups and whatever white traders and settlers there might be in the area that British claims in the region were no longer valid. Pike returned back down the Mississipi, unaware that he was not the discoverer of the long-sought source of the mighty Mississippi. Most of Pike's fame came from his expedition to the West in 1806.

PILLSBURY, Charles Alfred. (Warner, NH, Dec 3, 1842—Minneapolis, MN, Sept. 17, 1899). Milling tycoon. After graduating from Dartmouth, Pillsbury joined his uncle, John Sargent Pillsbury, in Minneapolis, and they bought a share in a small flour mill there. Charles Pillsbury realized the value of a new method of processing the region's hard wheat, a method invented by Edmond La Croix and George T. Smith. He persuaded Smith to install the new equipment in his mill. The business grew rapidly until by 1889 it had become the world's largest flour mill. He died only ten years later, after selling the mill. His uncle, John Sargent, became one of Minnesota's business leaders as a partner in Charles A. Pillsbury and Company and went on to be active in politics and philanthropy. He served as a regent of the

University of MINNESOTA in 1863, and as a state senator from 1864 to 1876 and was elected governor of Minnesota in 1876, serving until 1882. He presented a science hall to the University of Minnesota in 1889 and by legislative act was made a life regent of the school in 1897.

PIONEER LIFE. As the frontier moved across the Midwest, pioneer life remained about the same wherever the first settlers began to arrive. When seven-year-old Abraham LINCOLN (1809-1865) arrived at Buffaloville, Indiana, with his family, they found only a "wild region with bears and other wild animals still in the woods. The clearing away of surplus wood was the great task ahead," Lincoln wrote later.

Pioneers were overwhelmed by the "ceaseless forests." "We lived the same as Indians 'ceptin we took an interest in politics and religion," wrote Lincoln's cousin, Dennis Hanks. As did many other pioneer families, the Lincoln family spent the first winter in a wilderness "half-faced" camp. A cross-pole was supported by two Y-shaped poles. Lighter poles were angled from this center pole to the ground and then this makeshift "roof" was covered with a thick layer of brush. The front was entirely open to the cold, and a fire was kept going all the time for warmth and cooking.

One of the few occasions which brought the pioneers together provided an opportunity to turn work into play. When a new neighbor needed a house, all the others in the area came round to help. When the crude log structure was completed, they ate a big meal, danced, ran races, and sang songs. When fields were to be cleared, log rolling parties gave the neighbors another chance to get together for work and a little play, helping to clear timber from a tract of land.

Though they were more luxurious than the half-faced camps, most "first" log houses were very primitive, as well. One pioneer recalled, "We children slept in crude lofts over the main room of the cabin. The lofts were reached by a peg 'ladder' driven into the log wall. Many a winter morning I remember waking as the fine snow filtered through the cracks above, caressing my face and drifting over the coverlet."

Most women could claim only one iron skillet for all the cooking chores. The possessor of an iron kettle was called an "aristocrat." Even more aristocratic were those who had such luxuries as bedding, spinning wheel, clock or chest of drawers.

Beds were made by putting one post in the floor, which was simply the hard pressed dirt under foot. Bed rails were supported by the post and to the walls on either side. Rope was wound back and forth for a bedspring and the matteress was a burlap bag stuffed with straw. Slabs of logs with legs became benches and stools.

Gradually, when more settlers came and farm produce brought commerce, conditions improved. Farmers found the soil grew excellent corn. Tales of twenty-foot stalks and one pound ears encouraged migration. Corn was cut and shocked when ripe and husked in the field in cold weather. Sometimes the corn was pulled and neighbors invited to a husking bee in the barn. Practically every farmer made whiskey, and traded it at the local store. When the government taxed whiskey, juries of farmers often refused to indict moonshiners for something they did themselves.

Besides the still, all houses had a collection of outbuildings. The woodshed was used to render lard, boil soap, and for some types of butchering. The smokehouse was used to prepare smoked meat as well as a storage place for salted meat. Behind the smokehouse was the ash hopper where wood ash was accumulated through the winter from which lye to make the family's soap and hominy was made. Clothes, like the soap, were homemade with little attempt to follow fashion. Linen was still spun and woven, but the use of cotton, boosted by Eli Whitney's cotton gin, cut down on the use of linen for shirts and sheets.

Pioneer transport in the Midwest was picturesque. Conestoga wagons were driven by a hard-drinking group of men who enjoyed dancing in the taverns at night and smoking four-for-a cent thin cigars originally called Conestogas, but soon shortened to "stogies." Poor travelers camped along the roads while the more affluent stayed in inns. Guests paid a flat fee and ate their fill at dinner. Manners were as scarce as the tableware.

The people of the Midwest at first settled in clusters of similar origin, but isolation and mutual problems soon broke down the social barriers. Everyone developed an excited interest in politics by which westerners could get the cheap land and RAILROADS they needed. Camp religious meetings lasting a week or more developed in Cane Ridge, Kentucky, in 1801 and spread throughout the Northwest Territory. As many as twenty thousand came to hear relays of ministers, most of them Methodist, preach by day and night. Evangelists moved their audiences to hysteria, violence, and physical collapse, but seldom to brotherhood and mercy. One of these preachers was Crazy Dow, a skinny and filthy man with shoulder-length red hair who hypnotized crowds and sold huge quantities of Dow's Family Medicine.

The towns the preachers visited were often located at the crossroads of the paths running north-south and east-west in straight lines six miles apart following township lines.

Money in these towns was often first nothing more than personal promissory notes. Groups of prosperous men often started private banks which issued their own notes down to fractions of a dollar. The lapse of the charter of the Bank of the United States in 1811 and the refusal of many banks to redeem notes they had issued led to financial collapse in 1819. A second Bank of the United States, chartered in 1816, and some restrictions placed on private banks, offered some calm, but financial panics continued every twenty years or so.

The NORTHWEST TERRITORY, far from the temptations of civilization, led leaders of visionary groups like the Shakers who settled in Ohio, the Rappists who settled on the Wabash in 1814, and Robert OWEN and the people of NEW HARMONY to move to the area as a refuge. As the frontier moved westward, the end of pioneer life in the Northwest Territory was heralded by the coming of ever larger numbers of settlers, which then required the policy of Indian removal to lands west of the Mississippi and heralded the coming of "civilization."

PIPESTONE NATIONAL MONUMENT.

One-fifth of a Sioux Indian reservation in Minnesota which remains sacred ground for all tribes of the Great Plains who have gone there over a period of hundreds of years to quarry the reddish stone they carved into ceremonial pipes. The sacred place was neutral ground where all Indian peoples could gather in peace. The stone is called catlinite for American artist George CATLIN who first described it in his paintings and who painted water colors of the finest and most interesting of the pipes. The deposits vary in thickness from approximately two inches to a foot. The area was declared a national monument in 1937 to protect the remaining catlinite and preserve it for the use of Indians of all tribes, who are the only persons permitted to use it. Principal features of the monument include Leaping Rock used by ancient tribes as a test of strength of their young men who attempted to jump to it from a ridge eleven feet away, and Nicolet Marker, an inscription on a rock noting the 1638 visit of NICOLET (1598-1642) who carved his name and the initials of the members of his expedition. A visitors center contains exhibits and pipe-making demonstrations. The Upper Midwest Indian Cultural Center features craft displays.

PIPESTONE, Minnesota. City (pop. 4,887), seat of Pipestone County, southwestern Minnesota, gateway to PIPESTONE NATIONAL MONUMENT, from which the name comes. Annually a Song of Hiawatha Pageant, an outdoor performance, is held the last two weekends of July through the first weekend in August.

Pipestone quarry, painted by George Catlin.

PIQUA, Ohio. City, (pop. 20,480), situated in Miami county, in west central Ohio, on the MIAMI RIVER, formerly known as Washington, Piqua's name is thought to come from a Shawnee subtribe of which TECUMSEH (1768-1813) was the most famous member. The name means "A man rising out of the ashes." The city is an industrial center, producing steel and iron, airplane and automotive parts, aluminum, paper and wood and metal products. Fort Piqua was built by the French, three miles from the present city, in 1752, after they had destroyed the Miami Indian headquarters of PICKAWILLANY there. Later the SHAWNEE made their headquarters near the fort in a town they called Upper Piqua. Lower Piqua was a smaller Shawnee village on the site of present Piqua. George Rogers CLARK (1752-1818) and his colonial soldiers destroyed Lower Piqua in 1780. Simon Kenton destroyed the partially restored village in 1782. The white village was settled in 1797, and the Shawnee continued to return to their favorite site and marvel at the changes there. Early Piqua thrived by building flatboats and sending the produce of the area to New Orleans. With widespread flax growing, Piqua became the largest flax center in the country. Strawboard was another product. The MIAMI AND ERIE CANAL came in 1836 and was completed in 1847, adding to the city's growth. By mid-1800s, Piqua had more than a hundred factories. The coming of the railroad further stimulated growth. By 1890, the population had tripled, and the modern industrial city developed. Near Piqua is the famed Piqua Historical Area, preserving the notable memories of the area's Indians and including an Historic Indian Museum as well as the John Johnston Home, a restored Dutch colonial farmhouse, and interesting outbuildings. At Piqua a mid-19th-century canal boat takes visitors on the remains of the Miami and Erie Canal. The annual Heritage Festival on Labor Day weekend harks back to the heroic history of the area.

PITTS, William Savage. (Brooklyn, NY, Aug. 18, 1830—Brooklyn, NY, Sept. 25, 1918). Choirmaster, music teacher and composer, Dr. Pitts is best known for one song, "The Little Brown Church in the Vale" (1857). The church did not even exist when Dr. Pitts became enchanted with the site which he passed on leaving Bradford, Iowa, where he taught, on his way to Fredericksburg to visit a girl friend. He remembered the site and visualized a small frame church in the beautiful glade. As he imagined it, the structure would be painted brown, an unusual color for a church. The song was first sung in a church at Bradford, where Pitts led the choir. The song became so popular that the church of Pitts' imagination was actually constructed on the site, near present NASHUA, Iowa. Over the years thousands of wedding and other ceremonies have been conducted in the church, which still averages 1,800 weddings a year. It must be considered the best known church of its size in the country.

PLAINFIELD, Indiana. City (pop. 9,191), central Indiana in Hendricks Co., southwest of INDIANAPOLIS. Plainfield, headquarters for the Society of Friends (Quakers) in western Indiana and eastern Illinois, is remembered for an incident in which former United States President Martin Van Buren was dumped into a mudhole while preparing to enter the 1844 election. Van Buren, as president, had vetoed a bill providing for improvement of the NATIONAL ROAD. Tradition holds that residents gave a silk hat to the driver who overturned the stage at just the right moment for a crowd to be present to witness the event, designed as a lesson for the president's lack of interest in good roads.

PLAINS INDIANS. Few, if any, of the Plains Indians in the western Midwest could trace their ancestry back more than several hundred years. By 1200 A.D. drouth had removed most of the original settlers from the plains, leaving them nearly uninhabited. In the centuries just before European penetration, other Indian groups moved in and out. In Iowa and Missouri during the time of East Coast settlement, these were mostly members of the Algonquian language family, the QUAPAW, OSAGE, MISSOURI, KANSA, OTO, IOWA, PONCA and OMAHA, and, in Minnesota the Dakota SIOUX and Hidatsa. After European settlement in the East, the westward migration was heightened. Most of these groups had made their living from agriculture, but as horses were introduced, many of the tribesmen became skilled horsemen, adopting a nomadic life. European settlement in the East forced the eastern Indians to move west. Because they were better armed than the native tribes, the natives were constantly being forced to move, introducing new tribes to the plains, in their turn.

PLATTEVILLE, Wisconsin. City (pop. 9,-580), situated in Grant County in southwestern Wisconsin, Platteville takes its name from the nearby Platte River in Wisconsin, the name in turn from the French platte, meaning flat or shallow. Platteville has become the largest of the towns which mushroomed in southwestern Wisconsin and northwestern Illinois during the lead mining boom of the 1830s. The community was founded by Major John H. Rountree, whose home is displayed with many of the original furnishings. Today, Platteville is a center of recreation furnished by the many fine fishing streams of the area and the good hunting. The Wisconsin Institute of Technology was founded in 1907 and now is a part of the University of WISCONSIN at Platteville. University students were responsible for Platteville's most noticeable attraction. In 1936 the mining engineering students set out to create the world's largest letter on the slopes of Platteville Mound. They claim to have succeeded with the gigantic "M" which is lighted every year for the university homecoming. The development of lead and zinc mining is traced at the Mining Museum. The Ann and Wilson Cunningham Museum displays the history of the county, and the Rollo Jamison Museum holds the large collection of everyday items collected by Jamison. The Wisconsin Shakespeare Festival held at the University from early July through early August is one of the outstanding annual events of its type.

POINT DOUGLAS. Point of land formed by the meeting of the MISSISSIPPI RIVER with the ST. CROIX RIVER where the Mississippi begins to form the boundary between Wisconsin and Minnesota.

POINT PLEASANT, Ohio. Village, (pop. 75), named for its pleasant site, on the OHIO RIVER about twenty miles southeast of CINCINNATI, the village is known as the birthplace of general and president, Ulysses S. GRANT (1822-1885), where the 1817 cottage has been restored, now part of Grant Birthplace State Memorial. During the record Ohio River flood of 1937, the entire population of the village took refuge in three houses on high ground and in the Grant Memorial Church. The Grant Museum was under several feet of water, but the contents had been saved. A huge boulder was placed on top of the cottage to keep it from floating away.

POKAGON, (Chief) Simon. Last chief of the POTAWATOMI Indians in Indiana. Pokagon was considered the best educated Indian of his day. He attended NOTRE DAME UNIVERSITY and OBERLIN COLLEGE. In 1888 Pokagon collected $150,000

the Federal Government promised to his tribe as part of the price his father had negotiated in 1833 for the southern half of Steuben County and an additional one million acres, including the ground now occupied by CHICAGO, Illinois. Pokagon divided the late payment equally among the members of his tribe. Indiana's Pokagon State Park is named in his honor.

POLAND, Ohio. Town, (pop. 3,084), situated in northeastern Ohio, a suburb of YOUNGSTOWN, it was originally named Fowlers for Jonathan Fowler, who settled in 1799. In the early days the Sparrow Tavern at Poland was an important stop on the Pittsburgh-Cleveland stagecoach run. When William MC KINLEY (1843-1901) was a student at the Poland Union Seminary, he enlisted in the Union Army in April, 1861. Ohio's steel industry got its start at Poland when the Hopewell furnace began operations near there in 1804.

PONCA INDIANS. A tribe of the Shegiha group of the SIOUX linguistic family, the Ponca migrated from the upper Midwest through Minnesota and Iowa, settling from place to place until pushed farther westward, residing for short periods in Minnesota, Nebraska and South Dakota. The government moved them to Oklahoma in 1877. A small tribe, they number approximately 1,000. One of their best known members, whose name was Bright Eyes, became a writer of reputation and was especially prominent for successful intervention with the government on behalf of the Indians.

PONTIAC (Chief). (Maumee River, 1720?—Illinois 1769). Indian chief. PONTIAC, Michigan, is named for this famous Indian. Much of what we believe we know about Pontiac is considered to be fiction. He was probably not responsible for the uprising given his name nor was he necessarily a chief of the Ottawa Indians in 1763 during the siege of the British fort at DETROIT for 175 days, the longest siege in the history of Indian warfare. He made peace with the British and abided by the treaty. His death is a mystery, but it is believed he was killed in Illinois by an Indian who was revenging the death of his brother.

PONY EXPRESS. Short lived but renowned postal delivery system that served the West. Starting in April, 1860, letters were dispatched from ST. JOSEPH, Missouri, to Sacramento, California, a distance of more than 2,000 miles, via men on horseback. They traveled through great stretches of wilderness, where there were stops to change horses and riders at special posts set up along the route every ten to 15 miles. The journey took eight days in each direction, but this was found to be much faster than the former transit of letters by ships or stagecoaches and wagon trains. The service was discontinued soon after the first telegram to California was transmitted from ST. LOUIS on Oct. 24, 1861. But the fame of the Pony Express and its riders lives on in books and motion pictures.

POPE, Nathaniel. (Louisville, KY, Jan. 5, 1784—St. Louis, MO, Jan. 22, 1850). Illinois statesman. Pope moved to KASKASKIA, Illinois, and in 1809, through the influence of his brother John and Henry Clay, was appointed secretary of the Illinois Territory. Pope organized the territory, reestablished certain counties, and appointed the necessary officials when the appointed governor and his cousin, Ninian Edwards, were detained in Kentucky. In the fall of 1816 Pope was elected territorial delegate to Congress. In 1818, when Illinois applied for admission as a state, he drew up the necessary resolution. Pope's influence caused the northern boundary of Illinois to be changed from an east-west line through the foot of Lake MICHIGAN to its present position, giving Illinois an outlet on Lake Michigan and control of the area of present CHICAGO. Pope successfully obtained funding for education in the Illinois Act by setting aside three percent of the sale of public lands for the encouragement of learning. Two percent was earmarked for road construction.

POPLAR BLUFF, Missouri. City (pop. 17,139), seat of Butler County, on the outer edge of the Ozark Highlands in southeastern Missouri, named for a grove of poplar trees near the BLACK RIVER. Poplar Bluff was founded in 1850 by a commission charged with finding a county seat. The town's slow growth was almost halted by guerrilla warfare during the CIVIL WAR, but resumed in 1873 when the Iron Mountain Railroad encouraged the development of the lumber business. Poplar Bluff became a site of manufacturing of wood products. Concern about its one-industry status encouraged the city fathers to look toward agriculture as a second commercial venture. Land cleared of trees was planted, and storage and shipping facilities for the farmers were constructed. A second railroad through the community and the development of the highway system has

benefitted Poplar Bluff by making it a wholesale and retail center for southeastern Missouri and northeast Arkansas. Local sites include the A. L. Hinrichs Totem Poles, depicting histories and carved by the artist with a pocketknife and several homemade tools. There are an estimated 1,800 prehistoric mounds in the region. Northwest of Poplar Bluff is one of the eight sections of the Mark Twain National Forest, established after a bitter court fight with the owners of the mountainous tract who resented the invasion of their isolated way of life.

PORCUPINE MOUNTAINS. Location of the highest point in Michigan, 2,023-foot high Mt. Porcupine, in northwestern Michigan near Lake SUPERIOR in Ontonagon County. The hills were named by the CHIPPEWA Indians who noticed a resemblance between the outline of the range and a crouching porcupine. No permanent settlements have been made. Today Porcupine State Park is the largest recreational state park in the United States. It covers 58,000 acres.

PORT HURON, Michigan. City (pop. 33,-981), eastern Michigan's LOWER PENINSULA; linked to Sarnia, Ontario by the Blue Water International Bridge where Lake HURON empties into the ST. CLAIR RIVER. Port Huron is one of the oldest settlements in the state of Michigan. In 1686 Du Lhut (DULUTH, 1636-1710)) built FORT ST. JOSEPH on the location to guard against British interference with the French fur trade. The first permanent colony was established in 1790. The city seems to have a special relationship with electricity. Thomas Alva EDISON (1847-1931) invented an electric battery while spending his boyhood in Port Huron. The city continued its electrical "connections," when in 1908 it built the first electrified underwater tunnel beneath the St. Clair River. Three hundred years of local history can be traced at the Museum of Arts and History. A popular annual event is the Blue Water Festival held in mid-July.

PORTAGE RIVER. In northwestern Ohio, the five branches of the Portage drain a wide section of the area. The main river begins at Pemberville, where the North Branch joins the water of the other branches. The Middle Branch is the longest and meets the East Branch near New Rochester. The East Branch rises south of Fosteria and flows through that city. The South Branch flows through Arcadia and enters the east branch. The main river

Portage - Porter

flows into Lake ERIE, where it has a wide estuary, with Port Clinton on its west boundary.

PORTAGE, Wisconsin. City (pop. 7,896), seat of Columbia County, situated on the WISCONSIN RIVER in south central Wisconsin, the city takes its name and draws its greatest fame from the historic portage between the upper FOX RIVER and the Wisconsin. At Portage the rivers are only about a mile and a half apart. This small extent of land is the only barrier to a complete water route from the Great Lakes to the Mississippi, an inconsequential land gap separating the GREAT LAKES from the Gulf of Mexico by way of the Fox, Wisconsin and MISSISSIPPI. Indians, of course, had known of this route for centuries. Undoubtedly MARQUETTE (1637-1675) and JOLLIET (1645-1700) had been told by their Indian guides about the portage before they made the historic journey portaging their canoes across the strip of land on June 14, 1673, to become the first known Europeans to complete the passage as they went on their way to the discovery of the upper Mississippi. Later, a plank road was built between the two rivers, and ox teams hauled wagons with passengers and supplies at fifty cents per hundred pounds. The Portage Canal eventually completed the water route. The community of Portage grew around the activities of travel and commerce. Today Portage is a thriving center of a rich agricultural area. Pulitzer Prize author Zona GALE (1874-1938) of Portage used the community as background for several works, and her home is preserved there. The Old Indian Agency House is another restored attraction. It was the home of pioneer agent John KINZIE (1763-1828). Before the city came into being, FORT WINNEBAGO had guarded the area, and the Surgeons' Quarters at the fort have been restored, with many souvenirs of the period. Old French Days at Portage is a two-day annual event harking back to the early times.

PORTAGES. Water routes have offered the easiest means of travel for peoples from the earliest prehistoric times. However, lakes were often not interconnected and river routes were sometimes divided by long weary stretches of land. Fortunately, there are some strategically located areas which bring water routes close to each other, separated only by a short expanse of land. Canoes and packs can easily be carried across the minor land barriers. These portages have held a prominent place in exploration everywhere. Some of the most important in the Midwest have been widely scattered. MARQUETTE (1637-1675) and JOLLIET (1645-1700) made two important portages, the first up and out of the northern FOX RIVER in present Wisconsin. The explorers had only to carry their canoes and luggage for a mile and a half to reach the WISCONSIN RIVER, where PORTAGE, Wisconsin, stands as a reminder of the route. This one short portage provided a water connection for all of the region of the GREAT LAKES with the far shores of the Gulf of Mexico and everything between. An even more important portage for the present day was found by Marquette and Jolliet in Illinois, when they carried their canoes and belongings over the short stretch of land which separated the DES PLAINES RIVER, flowing ultimately into the MISSISSIPPI and the Gulf, with the CHICAGO RIVER, which connected with all of the GREAT LAKES. Jolliet was able to foresee that a canal connecting the two would join two great areas of the continent, as was later done. Indiana boasted several important portages. From Lake ERIE travelers could paddle up the MAUMEE RIVER from present Ohio to present Indiana, with a short portage connecting with the Little Wabash River, giving another route from the Great Lakes to the Gulf. This was known as "The Great Gate" because it provided a relatively easy passage for communication and early commerce. There was another important portage in Indiana between the ST. JOSEPH and KANKAKEE rivers. Wherever two lakes were close together or the upper portions of rivers where separated by narrow watersheds, travelers managed to portage with ease, as in much of the wilderness area of Minnesota, where portages are still the only means of connecting water travel.

PORTER, Cole. (Peru, IN, June 9, 1893—Santa Monica, CA, Oct. 15, 1964). Composer and lyricist. His first song, "The Bobolink Waltz" was published when he was ten. Graduating from Yale in 1913, he already had written the football song "Bulldog." Porter's career began in musical comedies with "See America First" in 1916. He continued composing songs for Broadway and motion pictures until 1958. Among the productions using Porter songs were *Kiss Me Kate* (1948), his finest artistic and greatest financial success. The song for which he is generally best remember is "Begin the Beguine" (1936). He wrote hundreds of songs, many of which remain as classics. After he was kicked by a horse in 1937, he was confined to a wheelchair but continued his career undaunted.

PORTER, Gene Stratton. (Wabash County, IN, 1868—Los Angeles, CA, Dec. 6, 1924). Author and illustrator. Porter was the editor for the camera department of *Recreation* for two years, on the staff of *Outing* for two years, and spent four years as a specialist in natural history photography for *Photographic Times Annual Almanac.* She was the illustrator and author of *A Girl of the Limberlost* (1907) and other tales of the swampy region near her home.

In terms of sale of her books, Porter was the most successful writer of her day. She died as a result of an automobile accident.

PORTSMOUTH, Ohio. City (pop. 25,943), seat of Scioto County, Portsmouth is situated in south central Ohio, at the mouth of the SCIOTO RIVER, where it empties into the OHIO RIVER. Portsmouth was named for Portsmouth, Hampshire, England, and the name means, appropriately, the mouth of the port or harbor. It lies across the Ohio from South Portsmouth, Kentucky, and was connected with that Kentucky city in 1927 by a million-dollar suspension bridge.

The city is the leading Ohio center of two very different products, shoelaces and firebrick. It is an important home of other industries and a railroad center, with railroad shops. It provides the southern gateway to the rich Scioto Valley and Central Ohio. In 1952 Portsmouth was chosen as the site for the Portsmouth Area Project, an Atomic energy Commission plant producing fissionable material.

Portsmouth was founded in 1803 by Virginia land speculator Major Henry Massie. It was incorporated in 1815, with 50 houses and 300 population. Fur trading, lumbering and tanning were the early enterprises, but the first steamboat in 1811 brought the start of Portsmouth as a leading port and steamboat building center. With the coming of the OHIO AND ERIE CANAL in 1832, the town became the busy southern outlet for the entire valley, where produce and merchandise were transferred to river boats bound for southern ports.

Discovery of iron ore in the area turned Portsmouth into a leading STEEL center. Reese Thomas found the value of the local fire clay in 1836, and the refractories industry has been a leading factor in Portsmouth prosperity. Great quantities of building stone have also been quarried nearby.

As the railroads took over much of the river business, Portsmouth was so well located that it continued to be a center of commerce. In 1937,

the worst flood in history up to that time pounded at the Portsmouth floodwall, extending three miles along the Ohio River to the Scioto River. The wall was designed to head off a flood stage of sixty-two feet, which had never been reached. The wall held out for days, but finally was overwhelmed by the seventy-one foot crest of the river, and there was heavy damage.

Boneyfiddle Historic District in downtown Portsmouth offers many interesting shops, including those in the Brewery Arcade, a restored brewery. The Southern Ohio Museum and Cultural Center features visual and performing arts and workshops. The 1810 House is an original homestead, built by hand, and open to the public. Horseshoe Mound was excavated in 1915. Its relics included a curved deer horn with the incisor of a beaver inlaid in its surface and a highly polished and symmetrical specimen of translucent jade, among other objects of importance. Seven miles southwest is Shawnee State Forest, with six lakes, grouse, squirrel and deer hunting in season.

POST, Charles William. (Springfield, IL, Oct. 26, 1854—Washington, DC, May 9, 1914). Food processor. An originator of prepared food techniques. Post, originally a commercial traveler and a partner in a hardware business, broke down from overwork in 1884 and sought treatment at the BATTLE CREEK Sanitarium in 1891. It was at the sanitarium that he became convinced that cereals were the key to health. Upon release, Post established La Vita Inn where he served Postum, a warm cereal drink, which he invented in 1894. He was so successful that by 1905 his company was one the biggest advertisers in the United States and had branched into many other cereal products.

Metea, chief of the Potawatomi.

POTAWATOMI INDIANS. One of the last Indian tribes to leave Illinois. The Potawatomi Indians lived in the CHICAGO area after the MIAMI Indians left the region about 1700. A member of the Algonquin language group of eastern forest tribes, the Potawatomi were closely allied with the OTTAWA and CHIPPEWA. The three tribes were known as the confederacy of "The Three Fires." The Potawatomi raised corn and hunted, lived in bark-covered lodges, and were allies of the French until the end of the FRENCH AND INDIAN WAR. The Potawatomi fought the Americans in the Revolutionary War and ambushed the occupants evacuating FORT DEARBORN (Chicago) in August, 1812. They ceded their lands to the Americans in the 1830s and moved west of the MISSISSIPPI.

POTOSI, Missouri. Town (pop. 2,528), seat of Washington County, southeastern Missouri, northwest of FARMINGTON, named for the Mexican silver mining city of San Luis Potosi. Potosi was formerly a lead-mining town and then became the largest barite source in the United States. Lead was discovered in the area about 1773. Moses AUSTIN (1761-1821) visited the region in 1797 and found mining carried on only part time after the harvest in August. Austin built the first reverberatory furnace west of the Alleghenies, a shot tower, a plant for making lead sheet, a sawmill, a flour mill and a store. By 1804 he estimated that the Potosi mine earned over half of the entire profit realized from lead mining in the state. Lead mining gradually declined in importance in Washington County just as the discoveries were made for the uses of barite. Old lead mines were reopened and new shafts developed. The grave of Moses Austin, Missouri's first industrialist, is located in the Presbyterian cemetery.

Austin's son, Stephen, carried out his father's dream of bringing the first American settlement to Texas after the senior Austin had died before carrying out his plans for Texas.

POULTRY AND POULTRY PRODUCTS. The Midwest generally turns its agricultural talents away from poultry. Of the total almost ten billion chickens, broilers and chicks produced annually in the U.S., the Midwest produces only 102,820,000. However, the Midwest produces about 40% of all the U.S. turkeys raised, and Minnesota ranks second among all the states in turkey production. Missouri produces the second largest number of turkeys in the Midwest. Minnesota holds the Midwest ranking for most chickens, broilers and chicks, far ahead of second-place Indiana. Illinois has the smallest annual poultry industry in the Midwest.

PRAIRIE DU CHIEN, Wisconsin. City (pop. 5,859), seat of Crawford County, second oldest city in Wisconsin, situated on the MISSISSIPPI RIVER in southwest Wisconsin, the name means "prairie of the dog" in French. It comes from the prominent Indian chief Alim, whose Indian name means dog.

Fur traders soon followed MARQUETTE (1637-1675 and JOLLIET (1645-1700) after their voyage past the site in 1673. In 1685 Nicholas PERROT (1644-1717) probably built Fort St. Nicholas near the present site. By the time the first Europeans began to settle in 1781, there was a village of several hundred Indian families. Friol Island was the scene of frenzied trading activity. Resident traders appeared in silk and velvet costumes, and military officers arrived in full uniform to review the products for sale, brought up from centers downriver.

Henry Lewis captured a view of early Prairie du Chien.

American forces built Fort Shelby in 1814, but the British seized it in the WAR OF 1812. They called it FORT MC KAY and at the end of the war evacuated and burned it to the ground. U.S. forces constructed FORT CRAWFORD in 1816. A second was built on higher ground, where, later, St. Mary's College was located. It was at Fort Crawford that Jefferson DAVIS, future President of the Confederate States, met his bride.

When the fort was abandoned, Hercules DOUSMAN, who had made a fortune in the fur trade, bought the site and built VILLA LOUIS, one of the most distinctive estates of the Midwest. The restored mansion is a major attraction of the area today.

Fort Crawford Medical Museum displays health related items of early days and recalls the work of Dr. William BEAUMONT (1785-1873) in studying human digestion. The largest caverns in Wisconsin, used for shelter by the Indians over the centuries, are now known as Kickapoo Indian Caverns and Native American Museum.

PRAIRIE ISLAND. The largest island in the entire length of the MISSISSIPPI RIVER. Prairie Island is located south of HASTINGS, Minnesota.

PREHISTORIC PEOPLES. Experts disagree widely on the earliest arrival of the first human beings on the North American continent. Estimates range from as high as 40,000 years ago to as low as 15,000. There is even greater disagreement as to the first appearance of people in what is now the Midwest. Some experts on Missouri contend they have evidence indicating that human beings lived in that area as long ago as 30,000 years. However, some Midwest discoveries have permitted rather more accurate estimates. A prehistoric woman found in Minnesota (ironically called MINNESOTA MAN), is thought to have lived about 20,000 years ago. The period of BROWNS VALLEY MAN in Minnesota is placed at about 12,000. EARLY MAN, a Missouri group, is considered to have arrived about 10,000 years in the past. The talented people of Wisconsin's COPPER CULTURE may have begun their stay about 7,000 years ago. Beginnings of human life in Ohio probably came about 10,000 to 12,000 years in the past, but there is no certainty of this. The most dramatic evidence left by the early people was the variety of mounds they created, and now most of the prehistoric groups are known by the general term MOUND BUILDERS.

The ARCHAIC PEOPLE of Ohio are fairly well established as having been active in the region 7,000 years ago. About the first century A.D. large areas of the region were occupied by the most talented and advanced of the early Midwest peoples, known as the HOPEWELL. Their wide range of habitation extended from central and southern Ohio through northern Indiana, central Illinois and Wisconsin, as far west as parts of Iowa and as far south as central Missouri and portions of Louisiana. Many of the recognized Hopewell sites are scattered along the MISSISSIPPI RIVER. Their sites have been identified by the special features found among their remains. These include the unique decoration on the pottery, their custom of cremating the dead and their construction of connected mounds. FORT ANCIENT in Ohio is one of the largest and best preserved Hopewell centers. Their culture apparently collapsed about 500 years ago.

The ADENA were late contemporaries of the Hopewell. They did not trade extensively out of their area, as did the Hopewell, but they used native materials in their highly decorated ware. They did trade for copper, apparently from the North, which they used for tools and jewelry.

The most recent group of mound builders, chronologically, were called the MISSISSIPI, with subcultures known as the Upper and Middle Mississippi. Neither group existed before 1400 A.D., and some sites were inhabited at the arrival of white explorers in the late sixteenth century.

The Middle Mississippi culture extended from the mouth of the Arkansas river to the MISSOURI and OHIO river valleys. The Upper Mississippi Culture extended north as far as Minnesota and Wisconsin. The people of the Mississippi Culture had apparently dropped back to stone age life, and were far less advanced than the Hopewell, but no one is certain as to why this came about.

The prehistoric peoples of the Midwest were not all of one race, according to the differences in skeletal structure, but were the ancestors of certain of the Indians found when the white men arrived.

PRESIDENTS OF THE UNITED STATES. The Midwest has nurtured thirteen presidents of the United States. Ohio considers itself as "The Mother of Presidents," claiming eight, although one was not a native of the state. William Henry HARRISON (1773-1841) was not born in Ohio, but is usually thought of in connection with that state. The Ohio natives include Ulysses Simpson GRANT (1822-1885), Rutherford B. HAYES (1822-1893), James A.

GARFIELD (1831-1888), Benjamin HARRISON (1833-1911), William MC KINLEY (1843-1901), William Howard TAFT (1857-1931) and Warren Gamaliel HARDING (1865-1922). Five of Ohio's presidents were generals in the CIVIL WAR, and three of them, Grant, Hayes and Garfield, provided a three-man succession as, 18th, 19th and 20th presidents. Although Abraham LIN-COLN (1809-1865)was not a Midwest native, his boyhood was spent in Indiana, and he matured in Illinois, which claims him as her own. The first president to be born west of the Mississippi was Iowan Herbert HOOVER (1874-1964). Harry S TRUMAN (1884-1972) was born in Missouri. Gerald FORD (1913-)was born just "across" from the Midwest in Omaha, Nebraska, but at the age of two he moved with his mother to Michigan, which claims him as its own. Ronald REAGAN (1911-) was born in Illinois.

PRESQUE ISLE, Michigan. Town (pop. 1,300), Presque Isle County, northeastern portion of Michigan's LOWER PENINSULA, north of ALPENA. Its French name means "almost an island," that is, a peninsula. Presque Isle is the site of the world's largest limestone quarry. Nearby is Presque Isle Harbor, an active lumber port in the 1800s. The first dock was constructed there in 1841 when the harbor was called Burnham's Bay. The Presque Isle lighthouse, second on the GREAT LAKES, was built in 1819. The present lighthouse was constructed in 1870. The lightkeeper's house and tower have been restored.

PRICE, Florence Beatrice Smith. (Little Rock, AR, Apr. 9, 1888—Chicago, IL, June 3, 1953). Composer. Graduating from the New England Conservatory in 1906, she taught at Shorter College (1906-10) and at Clark University (1910-12). After further study at Chicago Musical College and the American Conservatory, she won several competitions, including the Wanamaker Prize (1931-32), and in 1933 premiered her Symphony in E Minor with the CHICAGO SYMPHONY ORCHESTRA, the first by a black woman with a major orchestra. Price's works drew on black spirituals and other tunes, avoided jazz, and kept in the mainstream of late European romanticism. Her songs were popularized by Marian Anderson and others.

PRICE, Vincent. (St. Louis, MO, May 27, 1911—). Character actor, usually associated with horror films, well-known art expert, gourmet cook and cook book author. Price has made an indelible mark on the horror film, often creating characters of larger-than-life cruelty and cunning. Some of his best-known movies are based on Edgar Allan Poe stories such as *The Fall of the House of Usher* and *The Pit and the Pendulum.*

PRIMARY ELECTION LAW. Wisconsin was the first state in the nation to pass a statewide primary election law. This 1904 legislation provided for direct selection by the voters of nominees for office. The pioneering legislation led eventually to adoption of similar laws by most of the other states.

PRINCETON, Missouri. Town (pop. 1,264); Mercer County; northern Missouri; north of TRENTON; named for General Hugh Mercer, colleague of George Washington in the Battle of Princeton, New Jersey. Princeton was the birthplace of Martha CANARY (1825?-1903) who served as a scout for the United States Army during its Indian campaigns in the Black Hills in 1872 and earned the nickname of "Calamity Jane." Princeton was also the home of Ira Hyde, a member of Congress from 1872 to 1874 and his son Arthur Mastick Hyde, governor of Missouri from 1921 to 1925 and Secretary of Agriculture from 1929 to 1933.

PROCLAMATION OF 1763. British parliamentary law organizing the government of the provinces of Quebec, East Florida and West Florida, and establishing the policy to be followed in dealing with the Indians and with western lands, including much of the present Midwest. Indian trade was placed under royal control. Traders were licensed, and colonial governors were prohibited from granting patents for lands beyond the sources of rivers flowing into the Atlantic Ocean. There were to be no private purchases of Indian land or settlement beyond the river sources. The proclamation was strongly opposed by the colonists who resented the prohibitions against westward movement. Veterans of the FRENCH AND INDIAN WAR, who had been promised western lands, were angered at the removal from public sale of these regions. Many powerful colonists opposed the limitation of trade. In general the proclamation had little practical effect in the areas it supposedly governed.

PROGRESSIVE PARTY. The name given to three different groups especially active in the Midwest. The first was partially organized by prominent Wisconsin politician Senator Robert

Progressivism

LA FOLLETTE (1855-1925), who was dissatisfied with President William Howard TAFT (1857-1930), and, with others, formed the National Progressive Republican League in 1911, with La Follette as their candidate for president in 1912. However, when Taft was nominated for a second term by the Republicans and Theodore Roosevelt split away from the party, La Follette was bypassed and the Progressive Party supported Roosevelt's Bull Moose Party. The 1912 platform called for a host of social reforms which have subsequently generally been made, including direct election of U.S. senators, vote for women, initiative and referendum, among others. However, with the vote split, the Democrats won in 1912. When Theodore Roosevelt refused to run in 1916, most Progressive Party members voted Republican, and the national party, did not have the strength to continue. In the election of 1924, a new Progressive Party unsuccessfully ran La Follette for president. The La Follette family kept their Progressive Party in power in Wisconsin until 1938, and that party, as a whole dissolved itself in 1946. The third party to be called "progressive" also had distinctly Midwestern roots. In the election of 1948 the new Progressive Party nominated former vice president Henry A. WALLACE (1888-1965) of Iowa. In the election they won no electoral votes and fewer than a million popular votes.

PROGRESSIVISM. Broadly based reform movement in U.S. history, reaching its peak in the Midwest in the early 1900s, where it was especially effective in Wisconsin.

After the CIVIL WAR, growth of railroads and rapid expansion of industry brought about substantial upheaval of social life, especially in the older urban areas, where slums spread across the poorer parts of many cities, and the working poor were often in desperate condition. The Progressive Movement began as a protest to the effects of these changes.

The "muckraking" newspapers noted the various problems of expansion and industrialization, such as the sweatshop and child labor, the corruption of local and state politics, the monopolistic abuses of the trusts, the rate-fixing of the railroads and the indifference of manufacturers to the purity of foods and drugs. Throughout the country, and particularly in the Midwest, reformers began to spring up to work toward ending these and other abuses.

Their movement differed substantially from that of the Populists, whose political party was formed mainly to express the agrarian protest of the late 19th century, to try and end the many abuses suffered by farmers. They failed to join with the Progressives in making an effective rural-urban coalition to address the needs of both farm and city.

The early evidence of Progressive progress came at the local level. This most practical phase of the progressive movement was led by such dedicated social workers as Jane ADDAMS (1860-1935). These devoted workers, mostly women, went into the slums, established settlement houses and struggled in every way available to them to improve the life of the workers through education and self-help.

Other reformers devoted their activities to attacking corruption in local government, with efforts such as creating non-partisan leagues aimed at removing corrupt municipal officials. Reform mayors were elected, such as Samuel Jones in TOLEDO, Ohio, and Hazen Pingree of DETROIT, Michigan. These promised such local government reforms as municipal ownership of utilities, better city services, better building codes and measures to assure better maintenance of tenements.

Frustrated by state governments dominated by vested interests, the reformers turned their attention to statewide reform. Progressivism reached its high point with the election of Robert LA FOLLETTE (1855-1925) as governor of Wisconsin. He served from 1901 through 1906 and won from the state legislature many of the changes in government he and other Progressives had sponsored over the years. In Wisconsin anti-lobbying laws were passed, railroads and utilities regulated, and corporate taxes raised. Child labor, minimum wage and widows' pension laws carried out the ideas of Progressivism. In Wisconsin, these acts have come to be known as the WISCONSIN IDEA. Over the years they have been widely imitated in various forms by a large percentage of the states.

Next the progressive reformers turned their attention to the national government, in an attempt to have their programs enacted in nationwide laws, and some of these were passed under Theodore Roosevelt. The National Progressive Republican League was formed to block the nomination in 1908 of President William Howard TAFT (1857-1930), an opponent of Progressivism. After Taft was elected, many Progressives joined with Theodore Roosevelt when he broke from the REPUBLICAN PARTY and formed the PROGRESSIVE PARTY for the election of 1912. Because the 1912 vote was split three ways, Woodrow Wilson, the Democratic Candidate, squeaked through to win, but the

Progressive Party fared better than the traditional Republican Party, with Roosevelt receiving over 4,000,000 popular votes and 88 electoral votes. During Wilson's terms he sponsored many of the programs of Progressivism.

The Progressive Party maintained its organization until 1916. Then, after Roosevelt refused to run again, most Progressives voted the Republican ticket for the losing Charles Evans Hughes, and Wilson became the WORLD WAR I president.

After such losses, the Progressive Movement had little formal organization, but most of its programs became a national reality as the years went by.

The Conference for Progressive Political Action in 1922 prompted a revival of Progressivism. In 1924 a new Progressive Party ran Robert LaFollete for president and Burton K. Wheeler for Vice President. Although the Republican Party won by a landslide, the LaFollette ticket won an impressive 5,000,000-plus popular votes. This Progressive Party dissolved itself in 1946.

In the election of 1948, the group headed by Henry A. WALLACE (1888-1965) called itself the Progressive Party and had only a brief revival when Wallace lost his 1948 election bid.

Today, the legacy of the Progressive Movement is enjoyed by most Americans, who are generally unaware of their debt to it.

PROPHET, The. (Mad River, near Springfield, Ohio, Circa 1770—place unknown, possibly Kansas, 1834). Spiritual leader of many of the Indians throughout the Midwest. The Prophet, sometimes known as Tenskwatawa, "man with the loud voice," urged a return to a simple life by preaching against drunkenness, witches and all forms of "civilization" borrowed from the whites. The Prophet, possessing a keen mind and dramatic leadership ability, derived much of his power by his claim that he could foretell an eclipse of the sun on June 16, 1806. Of course, he knew the date, but his followers were greatly impressed. The Prophet's brother, TECUMSEH (1768-1813), planned an Indian confederacy to include all tribes between the GREAT LAKES, the Gulf, the ALLEGHENY MOUNTAINS and the Rockies. A spiritual revival became a political movement among the Indians as both The Prophet and Tecumseh established their headquarters at PROPHETS-TOWN, a village on the WABASH RIVER at the mouth of TIPPECANOE RIVER. When President Madison gave Governor William Henry HARRISON (1773-

1841) permission to destroy the community, The Prophet made the mistake of promising his warriors immunity from wound or death and attacked Harrison without the skillful leadership of his brother. Prophetstown was destroyed, and The Prophet lost much of the spell he had held among his people. The Prophet blamed his wife for the defeat at Tippecanoe, saying that she had touched the pot in which he had brewed charms for his warriors. The Prophet continued to stir up frontier trouble as he wandered through the lands of the KICKAPOO and POTAWATOMI. Indian raids, beginning in 1812, resulted in swift retaliation by Governor Harrison. With the British surrender of DETROIT, the last safe place for Indian raiders, and the death of Tecumseh at the Battle of Thames, the Indian wars were ended for the time in much of the Midwest. The Prophet received a pension from the British government until his death in 1834.

PROPHETSTOWN. Indiana capital of an Indian confederacy in the early 1800s, assembly point for discontented Indians of many tribes. Prophetstown, located near the present city of LA FAYETTE, was built on the north bank of the WABASH at the mouth of TIPPECANOE RIVER by The PROPHET (1770-1834) and TECUMSEH (1768-1813). Liquor was prohibited and crops were planted. It became a center for British influence in the region and a safe place from which to launch raids against settlers, Prophetstown was ordered destroyed by President Madison. Governor William Henry HARRISON (1773-1841) led the campaign which ended in the Indian defeat at the Battle of TIPPECANOE on November 7, 1811, when Prophetstown was destroyed. This victory over the Indians did not ensure peace on the frontier, but it did contribute to the prestige of General Harrison who used his troops' victory thirty years later in his presidential campaign slogan of "Tippecanoe and Tyler Too." Tecumseh returned to the site and, with The Prophet, rebuilt the community.

PROTAR, Fedor. (1838—Beaver Island, MI, Mar. 4, 1925). Russian immigrant and medical doctor. This Russian count was known for his social consciousness and "radical" ideas. He was exiled by the Czar of Russia in the nineteenth century because he performed the unheard of service of freeing his serfs. Living on BEAVER ISLAND, Michigan, off the shores of Lake MICHIGAN, Dr. Protor treated the island's residents without ever charging them a fee. His grave is marked on the island,

PULITZER, Joseph (Mako, Hungary, April 10, 1847—Charleston, SC, Oct. 29, 1911). Newspaper editor and publisher. Raised in Budapest, he tried unsuccessfully many times to enter the military until 1864, when he was inducted as a U.S. agent in Hamburg to emigrate to America and become a Union Army soldier in the CIVIL WAR. Following the war's end, he moved to ST. LOUIS, Missouri, where he did various menial jobs until he accepted a reporter's position on a German-language daily newspaper. In 1871 he bought a share of the newspaper but soon resold it and, in 1874, bought the Staats-Zeitung and sold its Associated Press franchise to the St. Louis *Globe.* He took control of the St. Louis *Dispatch* and The *Post* in 1878 and combined them into what was to become the major evening newspaper in the city. In 1883 Pulitzer acquired the New York newspaper, The *World,* and added an afternoon edition, The *Evening World* in 1887. Having gained major political power through his publications, he was considered responsible, along with fellow publisher William Randolph Hearst, for the promotion of the SPANISH-AMERICAN WAR (1898). He endowed the Columbia University School of Journalism, which opened in 1912. He also established the PULITZER PRIZES, awarded annually since 1917 for outstanding work in biography, drama, fiction, history, music, and various categories of newspaper work.

PULLMAN, George. (Brocton, NY, Mar. 31, 1831—Chicago, IL, Oct. 19, 1897). Inventor and industrialist. Pullman's career began, in 1858, by his contracting with the Chicago and Alton Railroad to remodel two day-coaches into sleeping cars. He built a third car in 1859. Although the designs were popular, the railroad companies did not adopt them. Pullman left Chicago for Colorado where, from 1859 to 1863, he ran a general store while working on plans for his sleeping car. With a partner, Pullman applied for a patent on April 5, 1864, and began construction of his first car, the Pioneer. The Pioneer's size prevented it from passing under many bridges and past station platforms, but its popularity caused one company after another to make the necessary changes in their structures and take on the new cars. In 1867 the Pullman Palace Car Company was organized and grew to be the greatest railroad car building organization in the world. Pullman developed the combined sleeping and restaurant car in 1867, the dining car in 1868, the chair car in 1875, and the vestibule car in 1887. Beginning with

the initial agreement with the Chicago and Alton Railroad, Pullman developed nationwide use of his cars. In 1894 the company suffered one of the bloodiest and unrequited strikes in labor history, when with the use of troops the strike was broken and the the boycott collapsed. The once independent town of Pullman, on the prairie south of Chicago is now a part of the city. Formation of the town was an attempt by Pullman, to create a model town. The town permitted neither home-ownership nor local self-government. Today the community is no longer company owned. A hard-headed businessman, Pullman collected rents twenty-five percent higher than in Chicago. Despite the depression of 1893, George Pullman continued to expect a six percent profit from all his investments, including the town. He was the owner of the Eagleton Wire Works and president of the Metropolitan Elevated Railroad in New York City.

PUMPKIN CENTER, Missouri. Village. Located in Nodaway County in northwest Missouri near Oregon. The international expert on how to win friends and influence people, Dale CARNEGIE (1888-1955), was born and lived on a farm near here.

PURDUE UNIVERSITY. West Lafayette, Indiana, institution offering courses in science, home economics, pharmacy, agriculture and engineering. Founded in 1874, Purdue was named for John Purdue, a local businessman who, with other Tippecanoe residents, offered a total of two hundred thousand dollars to establish the school on its present site. University holdings have included 2,665 acres of farm and forest land used in instruction and experimental agricultural work; an airport, the first university airport in the nation and the one which equipped Amelia Earhart's 'Flying Laboratory' plane; and a housing project. In 1985-1986 Purdue enrolled 31,987 students and had 3,100 faculty members.

PURNELL, Benjamin. (Mayville, KY, Mar. 27, 1861—Dec. 16, 1927). Religious leader. Purnell established the House of David in BENTON HARBOR, Michigan, in 1903. In 1895 Purnell, declaring himself to be the Seventh Messenger and younger brother of Christ, preached that the Millennium was to begin. He predicted that he would arise on the third day after his death and forbade all sexual relations among his followers, including those who were married. In establishing the House of David,

Purnell abandoned the life of an itinerant evangelist he had followed from 1895. Today the House of David is remembered for fielding a long-bearded baseball team.

PUT-IN-BAY, BATTLE OF. In 1813, during the WAR OF 1812, Oliver Hazard PERRY (1785-1819) maneuvered his fleet of six warships to "put in" to the small harbor of Bass Island in Lake ERIE, north of present SANDUSKY, Ohio. Ever since, the harbor has been known as Put-in-Bay. Sighting the British fleet on the morning of September 10, Perry ordered his fleet out to meet them, but changing winds kept the rest of the fleet from keeping up with Perry's flagship, the *Lawrence*. The lead ship was caught in heavy shelling and began to sink. Perry merely salvaged the ship's American flag, which he wrapped around himself, jumped into a ship's boat and was rowed off to the other American ships which had finally caught up. Aboard the *Niagara* Perry continued to lead the battle, and by mid-afternoon the British surrendered. Perry's report of the victory to General William Henry HARRISON (1773-1841) has become one of the best-known quotations of modern times. He wrote, "Dear General—We have met the enemy, and they are ours. Two ships, two brigs, one schooner, and one sloop. Yours with great respect and esteem, O.H.Perry." Control of Lake Erie assured American control of the entire GREAT LAKES and was a major turning point in the War of 1812. The battle is generally considered one of the most important in world history.

PUTNAM, Rufus. (Sutton, MA, 1738—1824), Revolutionary general and statesman. Putnam joined the British army in 1757, during the wars between the French and English, and had a brilliant military career with American forces in the Revolution, including design and construction of the fortress at West Point. Becoming involved with the OHIO COMPANY OF ASSOCIATES, Putnam helped to bring about the ORDINANCE OF 1787, which laid Ohio and the other parts of the NORTHWEST TERRITORY open to settlement. One of the prime movers in the Ohio association, he helped organize the construction of boats, led the party of settlers down the OHIO RIVER, was instrumental in the selection of the site at the mouth of the MUSKINGUM RIVER and had a strong voice in calling the new settlement MARIETTA. Putnam designed the fort, called CAMPUS MARTIUS, which not only served for protection from the Indians but housed most of the early settlment, including the newly arrived governor of the territory, Arthur ST. CLAIR (1736-1818). The fort was considered one of the strongest in the country, and the selection of settlers was said to have provided one of the best groups ever to pioneer in the American West. In 1790 Putnam was appointed judge of the Northwest Territory and later was U.S. surveyor general.

PYLE, Ernie. (near Dana, IN, Aug. 3, 1900—Ie Shima, Apr. 18, 1945). Newspaperman. Pyle began his distinguished newspaper career as a reporter for the LA PORTE (Indiana) *Herald*. He moved on to a variety of positions with newspapers in Washington, D.C. and New York City, including managing editor for the Washington D.C. *Daily News* from 1932 to 1935. He became a roving reporter and widely syndicated columnist in 1935 and served as a war correspondent from 1942 until his death, from Japanese machine-gun fire, in 1945. His syndicated newspaper column was among the most widely distributed of the time. The column brought Pyle an enormous readership, those who appreciated his sympathy for the "little guy" in the news. His wartime reports, concentrated on the ordinary soldier, made him a national hero and brought him the PULITZER PRIZE in 1944. In the Pacific he reported the Iwo Jima and Okinawa campaigns and was shot down by enemy fire on Ie Shima Island.

QUANTRILL, William Clarke. (Canal Dover, OH, 1837—Louisville, KY, jail, 1865). Confederate guerrilla leader, sometimes known as the bloodiest man in American history. Quantrill moved to Kansas from Ohio and became a farmer in 1857. This lasted only one year as he left on a wagon train for the West and the life of a gambler. In 1859 Quantrill returned to Kansas to teach school, but was soon accused of stealing cattle and horses, as well as murder. He escaped arrest and formed a band of guerrillas just as the CIVIL WAR began. Quantrill organized his guerrillas and concentrated his raids in Kansas and Missouri on townsmen and farmers who favored the North. In August, 1862, he was mustered in as a Confederate captain and continued his ruthless and indiscriminate killing. The worst of his raids was that on Lawrence, Kansas on Augusat 21, 1863, when the town was burned and 150 townspeople massacred. Members of his band included Frank and Jesse James from Missouri. Quantrill was wounded and captured by Union forces near Taylorville, Kentucky on May 10, 1865. He died in a Louisville, Kentucky, jail on June 6.

QUINCY, Illinois. City (pop. 42,352), seat of Adams county, both city and county named for President John Quincy Adams, western Illinois on the MISSISSIPPI RIVER. MARQUETTE (1637-1675) and JOLLIET (1645-1700) reported Indians living in the present area of Quincy, when they explored the Mississippi in 1673. John Wood and Williard Keyes established claims on the site in 1822. Their cabins, with those of several other pioneers, made up the settlement called "The Bluffs." John Woods, filling the unexpired term of Governor William Bissell, who died in office, petitioned the legislature to create Adams County in 1825. Willard Keyes persuaded the commissioners empowered to choose a site for the county seat to select "The Bluffs." Quincy was incorporated as a town in 1834 and as a city in 1840. During the 19th century Quincy became the second largest city in Illinois. It fell from this position as other industrial cities surpassed it in the post-Civil War years. While its commerce declined with a decrease in steamboat traffic, it became an important center for railroads. Its industries produce broadcasting equipment, truck bodies, bricks and flour. It is a processing and distributing center for crops and livestock. Quincy College was founded there in 1860. In 1858, Quincy was one of the seven Illinois cities to host the LINCOLN-DOUGLAS DEBATES of 1858. Quincy offers wide architectural diversity. Among the residences of interest are the Governor John Wood Mansion, headquarters of the Historical Society of Quincy and Adams County; the Warfield House; Villa Katherine; the Huffman House, and the Newcomb House.

R

RACCOON RIVER. Three main branches combine about thirty miles west of DES MOINES, Iowa, to form the main river. The principal branch, the North Branch, originates in Buena Vista County, near the town of Marathon. The Middle Branch begins near Carroll, Iowa, and the South Branch near Coon Rapids, Iowa. All of the branches originate east of the narrow divide which separates the MISSOURI RIVER watershed from that of the waters flowing to other tributaries of the MISSISSIPPI RIVER. The main river empties into the DES MOINES RIVER at DES MOINES.

RACINE, Wisconsin. City (85,725), seat of Racine County, situated at the mouth of the Root River at Lake MICHIGAN and incorporated in 1848. The Root River was given its name because there were so many roots protruding from its banks that boats could hardly navigate. The name Racine is derived from the French translation of the POTAWATOMI Indian word for root, ot-chee-beek.

The city is a port of entry, and the more than 300 varied industries include machine tools, heavy construction equipment, farm machinery, automobile parts and electrical equipment. Racine is sometimes called the polishing center of the world, for its Johnson Wax headquarters, with its famous research tower designed by architect Frank Lloyd WRIGHT (1867-1959). Another industrial first was the invention of malted milk by William HORLICK (1846-1936) who established the Horlick plant to produce the tasty product.

A permanent settlement was first established on the site in 1834. Today the city claims to have the nation's largest concentration of people of Danish descent. Improvement of the port in 1844 and the railroad's arrival in 1855 made the city more attractive to industries.

In addition to the Johnson research tower, visitors to Racine may see two other Racine buildings designed by Wright. Famed sculptor Carl Milles executed the reliefs on the county courthouse. The city is the home of the College of Racine. Annual events include Salmon-A-Rama, Safari Day and Old Main Street Octoberfest.

RADIO STATION WHA. Claimed as the world's oldest, the station was developed in the laboratories of the department of physics of the University of WISCONSIN at MADISON. The station started broadcast service in 1915, and clear broadcasting signals were received as far away as Great Lakes Naval Station in northern Illinois. In 1922 WHA received a federal license to broadcast and is considered to be the world's oldest continuously operated radio station. When it first went on the air its tubes were hand blown by local glassmakers and fitted for broadcast by local craftsmen. The station was the first educational radio station and broadcast the first music appreciation program to be sent across the airwaves.

RADISSON, Pierre Esprit. (c.1636, probably Paris, France—somewhere in the New World," c.1710). Before reaching present United States territory. Pierre Radisson explored Hudson Bay. In 1654 Radisson and Medard Chouart, Sieur du GROSEILLIERS (1618?-1690), reached GREEN BAY in Wisconsin on a fur trading expedition and penetrated the wilderness to Lake SUPERIOR to the north, opening up this vast territory to the fur trade. About the region Radisson wrote much later, "I liked noe country as I have that wherein we wintered Washington Island, Wisconsin; for whatever a man could desire was to be had in great plenty; viz. staggs, fishes in abundance, and all sort of meat, corne enough." In 1659 Radisson and Chouart visited present ASHLAND, Wisconsin. Radisson is considered to be the founder of what later became the great Hudson's Bay Company, formed in 1670. He later retired to what one biographer called "the quiet of an English cottage," where some biographers say he wrote his memoirs, rediscovered in 1880 in the Bodleian Library at Oxford and published in 1885. There is, however, much confusion about both his later life and about the *Memoirs*.

RAGBRAI. The acronym stands for the Des Moines (Iowa) *Register's* "Annual Great Bicycle Ride Across Iowa." This is one of the most popular and said to be the largest of the rapidly growing number of bicycle tours. When the event was started, the promoters expected "a couple of dozen people," and they were surprised by 300, of whom 114 completed the 420-mile distance from SIOUX CITY, Iowa, to DAVENPORT. Today, thousands are turned away after the 7,500 participant limit has been reached. Riders include both the experienced and inexperienced; some take the trip every year over the different routes which are chosen, through towns and villages such as Pisgah, Soldier, Ute, Schleswig, LAMONI, Bonaparte and Tingley. The different routes provide wide variety for the participants. Large equipped semi-trailer trucks haul up to 60 tons of baggage to supplement the facilities of the towns and provide facilities along the way. Each of the towns greets participants with free food, entertainment and hospitality which the riders find "unforgettable." As one teen-ager said, "It's wonderful how people let us use their showers, feed us, and are so good to us." At the start of the trip, riders usually dip their wheels in the MISSOURI RIVER and end by a baptism of the bike in the waters of the MISSISSIPPI.

RAILROADS. The opening and development of the Midwest depended on transportation more than any other single factor. The great water routes and easy PORTAGES were in place as a part of the natural setting. These were augmented by CANALS and primitive roads. Railroads came last but were by far the most important in bringing in settlers and in providing a means of carrying the commerce of the region.

Railroads reached the Midwest more than twenty years after the first such roads were chartered in the East. The delay was due mainly to the fact that the Midwest population was still small and that water routes were serving most of the populated areas of the region. The route from New York by way of the Erie Canal (1825) and the GREAT LAKES provided an easy water way to much of the Midwest, and the OHIO RIVER offered another comparatively easy water route to the southern edge of the Midwest. The success of the Erie Canal spawned many other CANALS in the Midwest, taking time and funds from development of other means of transportation. The NATIONAL ROAD, cutting across Ohio, Indiana and Illinois also competed in the transportation field.

However, by the early 1840s, it became apparent that railroads would be the transportation wave of the future. The first small railroad in the Midwest operated in 1834 near SHELBYVILLE, Indiana, with a horse drawn carriage on a one-mile track. The first steam rail operation in the Midwest was begun at MADISON, Indiana, in 1838. It reached COLUMBUS,

Indiana, in 1844, and INDIANAPOLIS in 1847. A year later, the Galena and Chicago Union Railroad opened in Illinois, and the road between DAYTON and SANDUSKY, Ohio, also started in 1848.

The next year the first national railroad convention was held in ST. LOUIS, Missouri, with about a thousand delegates. There Thomas Hart BENTON (1782-1858) urged quick building of a transcontinental railroad.

Iowa became a railroad state on January 1, 1856, when the first fifty miles of road spanned the distance from DAVENPORT to IOWA CITY. By 1856 the Mississippi bridge was built at ROCK ISLAND -DAVENPORT, and the interior of Iowa was opened to eastern railroads.

When the CIVIL WAR broke out, Ohio had greater railroad mileage than any other state, and railroads provided transportation to almost every part of the region. This meant that troops and supplies could be moved about quickly anywhere in the North, and the railroads became one of the crucial advantages of the North over the South. The railroads of the South were in disarray, and new rolling stock and parts were unavailable because 96% of railroad equipment and replacement parts were manufactured in the North.

After the Civil War, The railroad building boom continued in the eastern part of the region but accelerated in the western portion. By 1867 the NorthWestern Railroad had reached COUNCIL BLUFFS, Iowa, on the MISSOURI RIVER, and two years later the first great cross-continental railroad was completed from Council Bluffs to the Pacific. For the first time the goods and people of the nation and the world could flow freely and quickly from coast to coast.

In the northwest portion of the region, Minnesota received its first train on June 22, 1862, and after the war, the railroad tycoons rushed to push the rails across the north to the Pacific. The St. Paul and Pacific Railroad had attempted to span the continent but went bankrupt. James J. HILL (1838-1916) acquired the road, and devoted his skills to the operation of the railroad from its ST. PAUL headquarters. His efforts resulted in extending the line over much of Minnesota, and it reached Seattle, Washington, in 1893.

The period 1900 to post-WORLD WAR II marked the high point of railroad importance, with more than a fourth of all carloadings passing through Midwest rail centers.

After the war, however, a series of circumstances caused decline, especially in passenger business. One of these problems was strikes. The railroads were among the earliest enterprises to be unionized, and there were strikes in 1877 and 1894. Years of comparative labor calm were followed just after World War II by the crippling strike of 1946. In the 1960s several nationwide strikes crippled the industry, and caused loss of business.

The vast increase in long-haul trucking along Interstate and other highways, all paid for by the public, was an important factor in railroad decline. The costs of maintaining their own right-of-ways and other increasing costs were other factors, dramatically illustrated by the decrease in railroad mileage during the period 1970 to 1984, from 206,000 miles to 161,000 miles.

This loss of service was especially harmful to the small towns of the Midwest. The feeder lines serving them were no longer profitable, and thousands of miles of such lines were closed.

Claiming that they were losing money on passenger travel, by 1970 more than 100 of the 500 individual passenger rail lines had petitioned the Interstate Commerce Commission to leave the passenger business. In 1970 Congress passed the National Railroad Passenger Corporation Act, creating A.M.T.R.A.K. Now most of the interstate passenger traffic is handled by AMTRAK, which leases its lines from the existing railroads.

Freight, too, had declined by ten million carloads in the period 1960 to 1984.

However, the principal Midwest products carried by railroads had increased during that period by more than six million carloads annually; because of this continuing business, the percentage of rails lost in the Midwest was 30% lower than the national average.

Despite the general railroad losses, the Midwest continues to claim to be "the railroad hub of the world." The start of Chicago's first railroad in 1848 heralded the beginning of CHICAGO as the railroad "Crossroads of the Nation," a position which it still holds. ST. LOUIS and KANSAS CITY, Missouri, continue to be principal railroad centers. Soon after the first railroad reached Indianapolis in 1847, that city became a another Midwest world railroad center in its own right, particularly important because it is the only major U.S. city not on a principal waterway. Indianapolis, also, at one time had the unique distinction of being the center for more interurban electric railroads than any other community. These were popular throughout most of the Midwest, with electric rail networks making local connections between cities. These died out with the construction of better highways, and only a few remain.

Despite the inroads of trucking and air transport, the railroads in the Midwest remain the principal means of bringing the raw materials of mine and farm to the manufacturing centers and distributing the products of those centers throughout the world. The Great Lakes and the principal trade waterways are unique assets to the region's economy and add greatly to its transportation potential, but they could not function effectively without the rail networks as connecting links.

RAINY LAKE. One of Minnesota's great international lakes. Rainy Lake has a 360 square mile area and lies across the border of Minnesota and the Canadian province of Ontario. Rainy Lake is the source of the RAINY RIVER. Catholic missionaries came to the Indians of the Rainy Lake region as early as 1818. In 1829 Presbyterian missionaries arrived, and they were followed by Methodists and Congregationalists.

RAINY RIVER. Stream that forms part of the United States-Canada border with Minnesota. From its source in RAINY LAKE, Rainy River passes INTERNATIONAL FALLS, Minnesota, and flows between Ontario and Minnesota for approximately eighty miles before emptying into Lake of the Woods.

RAISIN RIVER. Rising in southern Michigan near Somerset, the Raisin takes an erratic course slightly east, then north, then east, then south, then northeast, then east to empty into Lake ERIE at MONROE, Michigan. American soldiers were massacred at Frenchtown, now Monroe, during the WAR OF 1812 in what has been called the RAISIN RIVER MASSACRE.

RAISIN RIVER MASSACRE. Massacre of American troops during the WAR OF 1812 on the RAISIN RIVER near present MONROE, Michigan. In January, 1813, American troops were defeated by a combined force of British soldiers and Indians. The healthy Americans were taken captive by the British and marched away. The injured, left with the Indians, were savagely murdered.

RALLS, Daniel. (1785—St. Louis, MO, Oct. 30, 1820). Representative of Pike County in 1820 who was instrumental in the election of Thomas Hart BENTON (1872-1858) as one of Missouri's first two senators. Benton was in a hotly contested election (settled in those days in the state legislatures), and the votes were very close. When Ralls, seriously ill at his boarding house, heard of Benton's plight, he had four men carry him to the assembly hall so he could vote. Ralls died in Benton's ST. LOUIS home.

RAMSEY, Alexander. (Harrisburg, PA,

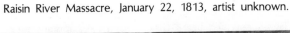

Raisin River Massacre, January 22, 1813, artist unknown.

Sept. 8, 1815—St. Paul, MN, 1903). United States senator and former governor of Minnesota. Ramsey served as the first governor of Minnesota Territory from 1849 to 1853. He opened up large portions of present Minnesota to settlement through numerous treaties with the Indians. He was the mayor of ST. PAUL from 1855 to 1857 before being elected as a Republican to be the first governor of the State of Minnesota in 1859. Ramsey was the first governor to respond to Abraham Lincoln's call for troops to fight in the CIVIL WAR and was responsible for Minnesota's continuing contributions to the war, which were considered to have been well above the state's percentage of population. Ramsey was elected United States senator in 1863 and served until 1875. In the Senate he made significant contributions to postal reform. He was the United States secretary of war from 1879 to 1881. Returning to private life, Ramsey became president of the Germania Bank in St. Paul in 1889.

RANKIN HOUSE. The home of the Rev. John Rankin at RIPLEY, Ohio, the house was one of the most important stations on the UNDERGROUND RAILROAD. A lantern in the window of the house, set on a height above the OHIO RIVER, could be seen for miles across the river and was a guide for escaping slaves. As many as twelve slaves in one night found refuge with Rankin. Local legend told of the slave ELIZA fleeing across the river on the floating ice from the Kentucky shore and finding refuge at the Rankin home. Harriet Beecher STOWE (1811-1896), who lived in CINCINNATI at the time, had visited the Rankin House and had heard the story. Her famed *Uncle Tom's Cabin* (1852) recounted the legend and was one of the most potent forces in bringing about the CIVIL WAR. In 1937 the state purchased the property which is now the John Rankin House State Monument.

RAPP, George. (Iptingen, Oberamt Maulbronn, Wurttemberg, Germany, Nov. 1, 1757—Economy, PA, Aug. 7, 1847). Religious leader. Rapp was the leader of a group who migrated to the United States from Germany in 1803, fleeing petty persecution. They bought land in Butler County, Pennsylvania, and established the town of Harmonie, Pennsylvania in 1804. Rapp founded the Harmonie Society, a communistic theocracy, in 1805. He established and developed Harmonie, Indiana, between 1814 and 1824. His sect became known as Harmonists. Under Rapp's firm direction, the hard-working German people accomplished

a miracle in the Indiana wilderness, clearing land, draining swamps and constructing large brick houses and public buildings. However, after ten years, the people became tired of Rapp's harsh discipline, and they sold their Harmonie holdings to Robert OWEN (1801-1877), who renamed the community NEW HARMONY.

REAGAN, Ronald Wilson. (Tampico, IL, Feb 6, 1911—). Fortieth President of the United States, son of John Edward and Nellie Wilson Reagan. The family moved to Dixon, Illinois, while Ronald was a boy. Following participation in football at Eureka, Illinois, College, he graduated there in 1932. His very successful career as a sportscaster at Radio Station WHO in DES MOINES, Iowa, coupled with his handsome good looks, attracted Hollywood, where he had a successful career as a star of something less than the first magnitude.

His most-remembered movie was *Knute Rockne—All American* (1940). He served in WORLD WAR II as an Air Force captain.

He began a successful administrative career in 1947 as president of the Screen Actors Guild, serving until 1952 and again in 1959. He kept his name before the public in television programs, and was a widely heard radio commentator. Changing from a liberal Democrat to a moderate Republican in 1962, he took an interest in politics, beginning with the unsuccessful campaign of Barry Goldwater for president in 1964. Two years later, after a meteoric rise in politics, Ronald Reagan was elected governor of California. Soon to become the most populous state in the Union, California provided an important opportunity for an aspiring politician. Reagan was reelected in 1970.

His successes in meeting California's budget, reducing the bureaucracy, eliminating the state deficit and reducing social services, were the most noted aspects of his administrations.

Retiring as governor in 1974, he began to put his extraordinary administrative and public relations experience to work in a run for the presidency. He made a strong bid in 1976, but lost the Republican nomination to Gerald FORD. Nominated in 1980, Reagan won a landslide victory over Jimmy Carter, opposing all the Carter liberal policies and accusing him of gross ineptitude.

Minutes after Reagan was inaugurated, on January 20, 1981, the 52 Americans who had been held hostage in Iran for 444 days were flown to freedom, following an agreement to return a portion of the frozen Iranian assets. On March 30, the president was shot in the chest by John Hinckley, Jr., as he walked to his car after an address at the Washington Hilton. On August 5th, in one of his boldest strokes, he fired the striking air traffic controllers, who defied his back-to-work order. His dispatch of a task force to lead the invasion of Grenada in 1983 greatly increased his general popularity. On the domestic front, the administration was dominated by so-called "Reganomics." This economic program called for substantial tax cuts and reduced spending for domestic programs. With the help of a bipartisan coalition in Congress, he succeeded in programs to cut the budget and reform Social Security. His economic policies and their successes were credited by many economists with reducing inflation, and Reagan remained a firm believer in his economic theories. He also was ever vigilant in his program to build up the armed forces, which he felt had been dangerously weakened during the Carter administration.

In 1984 Reagan and Vice President George Bush were nominated by the Republicans and won a landslide victory over Walter MONDALE (1928-). At 73 Reagan became the oldest person ever to hold the office of president. Surgery in 1985 and 1987 was followed by swift recovery, remarkable for a man of his age.

During most of his first term, Reagan had referred to the Soviet Union as an "evil empire." He was a firm advocate of U.S. support for arming Europe in defense of that empire. However, during his second term, he apparently concluded that his military program had brought the Russian leaders to a change of heart, and the administration began arms control discussions.

Reagan's summit meeting with Soviet leader Gorbachev in November, 1985, failed to reach general agreement, but the Reagan-Gorbachev meeting in early 1988 resulted in a draft treaty to reduce nuclear arms in Europe. Later that year in Moscow, the two leaders signed the treaty, which was ratified by the appropriate legislatures in each country.

During the early part of his second term, the president received some of the highest popularity ratings in the history of the office, spurred by low unemployment, strong economy and low interest rates. He continued to be strong in support of the Central American countries, providing help to El Salvador against the insurgents there and successfully promoting support of the Contra rebels in Nicaragua.

That support was undercut by the actions of some of his administrators in selling arms to Iran, moneys for which were diverted to aid for the Contras. This Contra scandal substantially lessened his national support and international stature, making the balance of his second term a period of uncertain accomplishment.

His support of the Contras was further threatened by the refusal of Congress to vote added funds in February, 1988.

In September, 1988, he released funds which had been withheld from the United Nations as a protest against UN policies, providing support for the growing peacemaking successes of the international body.

On January 20, 1940, Ronald Reagan married movie star Jane Wyman. Maureen and Michael (adopted) were the children of that marriage, which was followed by divorce in 1948. In 1951 he married Nancy Davis, and their children are Patricia and Ronald. Nancy Reagan has been a very popular but sometimes controversial first lady.

REAM, Vinney. (Madison, WI, 1847—1915). Said to be the nation's most notable woman sculptor because of the important commissions she received and the finished quality of her work. The Wisconsin native soon left the state for Missouri and then Washington D.C. where she entered a competition for a statue of Abraham LINCOLN (1809-1965). Her life-size model won her a $10,000 commission to complete the statue. Traveling in Europe provided new insight into the classical style for which she was becoming famous and brought her into contact with much of the continent's art colony, as well as such notables as the Queen of Rumania. One of her most notable sculptures is that of Admiral Farragut at Washington. Her sculptures *The West* and *Spirit of the Carnival* may be seen at MADISON.

RED LAKE RIVER. Stream whose source is Lower Red Lake in Minnesota. The 196-mile-long river flows west out of the lake before turning southwest to empty into the RED RIVER OF THE NORTH opposite Grand Forks, North Dakota.

RED LAKE. The largest lake wholly within Minnesota. One of the remaining fragments of prehistoric Lake AGASSIZ, Red Lake, in north-central Minnesota, covers 430 square miles.

RED OAK, Iowa. City (pop. 6,810). Seat of Montgomery County, situated in southwest Iowa on the East Nishnabotha River. It takes its name from the red oak trees of the neighborhood. The industrial and commercial center of its very large area, the city is particularly known for several publishing and printing enterprises, including the Murphy calendar company, one of the largest, and sometimes claimed to be the largest, in the world. The city gave its name to the Red Oak stove, at one time almost synonymous with the pot bellied heater. The city was the home of Darwin R. Merritt, Annapolis graduate, an assistant engineer on the Battleship *Maine,* who was killed in the sinking of the ship, an event which spawned the SPANISH-AMERICAN WAR (1898). Iowa resentment reached fever peak over the slaughter of a young favorite officer. When the battleship was raised after the war, Merritt's personal property, a bunch of mouldy keys, an old watch case and the rusted hilt of a sword were found in his locker and preserved at the Iowa Historical Library.

RED RIVER OF THE NORTH. Given that longer name because of the Red River which empties into the southern MISSISSIPPI RIVER, the northern river is formed at the confluence of the BOIS DE SIOUX and OTTER TAIL rivers, which meet at BRECKENRIDGE, Minnesota. Flowing north, the river forms the border between North Dakota and Minnesota, flowing past Kent, Wolverton, Morehead, Halsted, Grand Forks, Oslo, St. Vincent and Noyes before crossing over into Manitoba, Canada. Chief tributaries joining the Red in the U.S. are the St. Jean, Baptiste, Morris, St. Vital, Winnipeg and Selkirk.

RED RIVER OX CARTS. Sturdy but crude wooden carts drawn by oxen, which transported furs from the wilderness to civilization and brought supplies back to the frontier. The Red River cart trade reached a peak near 1858, after which the combined boat and stage traffic gradually replaced it. The cart traffic began in 1844 with as few as six carts running the trails between the RED RIVER settlements and ST. PAUL. In 1858 the traffic had grown to nearly six hundred carts. One year's worth of goods transported to St. Paul had an estimated value in excess of $180,000. Most furs and hides transported to St. Paul were either buffalo, muskrat, beaver or raccoon. Traders usually spent their money in St. Paul for supplies which were loaded on the empty carts and taken back north. The Red River trails over which the carts moved were Minnesota's earliest roads. Thirty to forty days were needed to make the trek between Pembina by way of

Fort Abercrombie and ST. CLOUD or Crow Wing and Otter Tail Lake. The screeching sound of the carts has gone down in the history of the north. One witness stated that the sound of wooden wheels rubbing on wooden axles without grease was like a group of swine whose lunch was overdue. The squeaking of long cart trains could sometimes be heard for miles.

RED ROCK LAKE. Iowa's largest lake is formed by the Red Rock Dam, also the state's largest, on the DES MOINES RIVER between PELLA and KNOXVILLE. Construction was started in 1960. Built mainly for flood protection, with many secondary recreational and other values, the lake extends for about thirty-three miles upstream, reaching almost to DES MOINES. The site has become popular for summer homes, boating, fishing and swimming. A large waterfowl refuge accommodates numbers of Canadian geese on their annual migrations.

RED WING, Minnesota. City (pop. 13,736), seat of Goodhue County, southeastern Minnesota along the MISSISSIPPI RIVER. The name comes from an Indian word Koo-poo-hoo-sha, meaning "wing of the wild swan dyed scarlet." Early explorers found an Indian village there in 1836. The first white settlement was established in 1849. Erik Norelius, a Swedish immigrant, started a Lutheran community in 1855, which gained religious and political power. By 1873 the area was a leading national grain and wheat market. After becoming the county seat in 1893, Red Wing added to its commercial stature as a stop for steamboats which made the community a center for trade. Many of the old homes and businesses have been restored. An ususual double Indian trail running along the top of the bluff was noted in 1861 by Henry Thoreau as he journeyed up the Mississippi. Frontenac State Park on the north end of Lake PEPIN contains a fur-trading post, Indian burial grounds, scenic overlooks and opportunities to observe thousands of migratory birds. Paddlewheel excursions between Red Wing and Lake Pepin are available.

RENVILLE, Joseph. (1779—1846). Self-styled "king" of Minnesota. Renville, a half-breed and COUREUR DE BOIS, literally "woods runner." He was one of the traders licensed by the French government to trade with the Indians. In the early 1830s he built a stockade overlooking Lac qui Parle, site of the present Minnesota city and county seat of that name. He lived in feudal style with retainers constantly ready to serve him. He had served in the British army during the WAR OF 1812, with the rank of captain. The stockade served as the site of a mission, built in 1835 under the supervision of Reverend Thomas S. Williamson. Assisted by Renville and Reverend Gideon Pond, Williamson translated the Gospels and several hymns into the SIOUX language. Renville assisted Williamson, Gideon and Samuel Pond, and Reverend Stephen Riggs in compiling the first Sioux grammar and dictionary, which was published by the Smithsonian Institution in 1832.

REORGANIZED CHURCH OF JESUS CHRIST OF LATTER DAY SAINTS.
Organization separated from the original Church of Jesus Christ of Latter Day Saints (MORMON). The reorganized church rejected the doctrine of polygamy and maintained that Joseph SMITH (1805-1844), Jr., founder of the church, did not practice or teach the concept. The reorganized church claims succession from the original church started by Smith in 1830. The reorganization began in the 1850s. Joseph Smith III, son of the founder, served as the president from 1860 to 1914. The teachings of the reorganized church are based on the Bible, the Book of Mormon, and modern revelation as published in the Book of Doctrine and Covenants. The ideals of Christian community and stewardship are stressed and members tithe, giving one-tenth of their income, annually. The church claims a membership of 200,000 world-wide with congregations in Asia, Africa, Europe, North and South America and the Pacific Islands. The headquarters of the church are in INDEPENDENCE, Missouri.

REPUBLICAN CONVENTION OF 1860.
First national convention of the Republican Party, held in CHICAGO, Illinois, on May 16-18, 1860. The meeting was held in a temporary frame structure two stories tall, called The Wigwam, at what is now the southeast corner of Lake Street and Wacker Drive. Principal contenders for the presidential nomination were William H. Seward of New York, Abraham LINCOLN (1809-1865) of Illinois, Simon Cameron of Pennsylvania and Salmon P. Chase of Ohio. Seward's positions seemed quite similar to Lincoln's. He assailed the Dred Scott decision of 1857 and supported Kansas' admission as a free state. However, unlike Lincoln, he considered a civil war inevitable. Cameron was nominated as the favorite son of Pennsylvania, with policies much like Lincoln's. After the

promise of a cabinet post, at the convention, Cameron turned his support to Lincoln. Only later did Lincoln learn of the promise made by his campaign leaders and reluctantly named Cameron secretary of war. Chase, also supported many of the same goals as Lincoln but was much more radical. He was known as "attorney general for runaway Negroes." Failing to win the 1860 nomination, he was elected to the Senate from Ohio, but deserted that post to become Lincoln's secretary of the treasury. After fierce and long bargaining in back rooms, Lincoln was nominated on the third ballot amid charges (later proven true) that his managers had won the nomination by making unauthorized promises of jobs, although the candidate had not even come to the convention. The platform in Chicago indicated that the Republican Party was no longer a party of one idea, the anti-slavery party, but was also a party of the North, supporting northern interests. Settlers were promised a free quarter-section of public land and Henry Clay's "American system" of internal improvements and protective tariff was revived. There was to be no more slavery in the territories and no interference with slavery in the states, an idea which was condemned by the Abolitionists. The careful construction of the platform identified the Republican Party as having moved from the control of zealots into the hands of seasoned politicians.

REPUBLICAN PARTY.
The Midwest rightfully claims to be the birthplace of the REPUBLICAN PARTY, but historians still dispute exactly where the party was started. Michigan has, perhaps, the strongest claim. On July 6, 1854, a group of Michigan anti-slavery people held a meeting known as the "Convention Under the Oaks," at JACKSON. They organized a political party and called it the Republican Party. Michigan's claim is further strengthened by the election of 1854, which the new Michigan Republican Party won, electing the first Republican governor in any state. Michigan Republicans won three of the four U.S. house seats, as well as both houses of the state legislature. The meeting of a Wisconsin group which chose the name Republican Party was earlier than that in Michigan. The new Republicans met at RIPON, Wisconsin, on March 20, 1854, because they were dissatisfied with the existing parties. Wisconsin did not elect a Republican governor until 1856. Because of its slightly earlier meeting, Ripon claims to be the birthplace of the party. Perhaps least valid of the claims is that of Illinois, which held its

Republican meeting in 1856 at BLOOMINGTON, calling for land reforms, internal improvements, protective tariffs and asserting that there should be no more slavery in the territories. Its claim as the founding site of the party is enhanced by the adoption generally of its positions by the party convention of 1860 and by the fact that it sent the first Republican president (Abraham LINCOLN) to the White House in the election of 1860. In the Midwest the Republicans swept the elections of 1872, 1908, 1920, 1928, 1952 and 1972. The Republicans have not won a complete sweep of the Midwest since 1972, coming within one state of a sweep with Ronald REAGAN (1911-) in 1984. The Midwest states have voted entirely Democratic only in 1932 and 1964.

REUTHER, Walter Philip. (Wheeling, WV, Sept. 1, 1907—Detroit, MI, May 9, 1970). Labor leader. Reuther worked as a tool and die maker and then foreman in the Ford Motor automobile plant in DETROIT, Michigan, from 1927 to 1932. He was fired for attempting to organize the workers. Reuther traveled through Europe and China between 1932 and 1935 before returning to the United States and joining the C.I.O. in organizing the automobile industry. As director of the General Motors Department of the United Automobile Workers of America, Reuther was physically assaulted and hospitalized while picketing the Ford plant in 1940. He became vice president of the C.I.O. in 1946 after leading the 113-day strike against General Motors in which wage increases and improved working conditions were won. In the merger of the C.I.O with the AFL in 1955, Reuther was a major figure. His "far-seeing policies" brought strength to the union cause. He advocated civil rights, consumer protection, government participation in medical care and health insurance and had considerable force in American foreign policy. Reuther was strongly pro-American and designed a plan to convert peacetime industry to war materiel production in 1941. He led a movement to expel communists from the U.A.W. and C.I.O. and was a strong supporter of the New Deal. After a 1960s confrontation with AFL-CIO president George Meany, Reuther led the United Auto Workers out of that organization in 1968, and the next year formed the Alliance for Labor Action with the Teamsters Union. He was selected for many government and philanthropic boards and took an active part in Detroit civic affairs. Among his writings were

Selected papers of Walter Reuther (1961) and *Education and the Public Good* (1963). He died in an airplane crash near Pellston, Michigan, on May 9, 1970.

REVOLUTIONARY WAR. Many of the complaints of the colonies against British rule had little effect in the remote Midwest. However, many colonists and would-be colonists resented the Act of 1763 which recognized the Indians as the owners of the lands and prohibited settlement west of the Appalachian Mountains. Despite the small population of what is now the Midwest, the revolutionary leaders realized that even if they won in the East, British control of the back country would be disastrous.

Most of the eastern states had claims in the west, some extending to the Pacific Ocean. Virginia had the largest claims, including most of the southern Midwest. Virginia governor Patrick Henry sent George Rogers CLARK (1752-1818) with a small expedition to attempt to wrest the region from British control. In 1778 Clark and 175 men marched into Illinois country and captured KASKASKIA, Illinois, on July 4th, then marched on into Indiana to take VINCENNES and other French villages.

The British, under Henry HAMILTON (-1796), recaptured Vincennes in December of 1778. Hamilton felt sure that Clark would not attack until spring and therefore kept only a small force on hand and dismissed the rest for the winter. Clark knew that if the Americans waited for warm weather his small force could not hope to win, so he led one of the most audacious counterattacks in American history.

In February, with 170 riflemen, called "Long Knives," Clark began a 200 mile march through flooded river bottoms and swamps to reach Vincennes. Often forced to march through icy water up to their shoulders, Clark's men camped at night without fires for fear of betraying their presence. They ran out of food after two weeks and ate only one meal in five days. The attack on Vincennes, on February 25, 1779, caught the British defenders completely off guard. Multiple American flags, moved from place to place by Clark's handful of men, gave the British the idea that they were being attacked by a superior force. French people escaped from Vincennes in the night and just as the Americans were running out of ammunition they showed the Americans where some supplies had been secretly stored. In the morning, a group of Indians arrived with American scalps to collect "Hair Buyer"

Hamilton's bounty. Clark had four of them shot as an example.

Hamilton surrendered and was taken captive. Clark had plans to capture DETROIT, but did not have enough resources to attack that city. Nevertheless, his success in retaining much of the rest of the Midwest for the American cause was one of the turning points of the Revolution. Clark gave the Americans a legitimate claim to the area which would become Ohio, Illinois, Wisconsin, Michigan, Indiana and parts of Minnesota. His capture of this NORTHWEST TERRITORY also caused the British to lessen their attack upon American settlers farther East.

By the Treaty of Paris on September 3, 1783, the Revolutionary War was formally ended. In the terms of the treaty, England surrendered its claims to all the land lying between the Appalachian Mountains and the MISSISSIPPI RIVER.

However, they did not give up their hope of some day regaining their western lands, and frontier fighting continued for many years, as the British urged the Indians to resist the American encroachment on their traditional lands.

RHINELANDER, Wisconsin. City (pop. 7,873), seat of Oneida County in north central Wisconsin, on the upper WISCONSIN RIVER. The community was named for R. H. Rhinelander, president of the Milwaukee, Lakeshore and Western railroad. One of the great northern tourist centers, Rhinelander claims the title of "Gateway to the World's Most Concentrated Lake Region." This is supported by the 232 lakes a short distance away, and the region's fishing excellence is enhanced by two rivers and eleven trout streams. The community began as a lumbering center and went on to manufacture paper and wood products, becoming pre-eminent in production of wax paper. The nickname, the Hodag City, came about as a result of a famous hoax by a local man, Eugene S. Shepard. The hodag was a mythical beast of the area, part of the Paul BUNYAN legend. Shepard contended that the beast still existed. One day he arrived in town with a monster of bulging eyes, hooked claws and daggar-sharp teeth. It had a row of jagged spikes down its back. The monster caused a sensation until Shepard confessed he had put it together himself.

RIB MOUNTAIN. At 1,940 feet, Rib Mountain is the highest point in Wisconsin. The ancient granite outcropping was so tough that during the glacial ages, the glaciers were forced to split and go around, leaving the famed unglaciated areas of southwestern Wisconsin and northeastern Iowa. Legend says that the enormous logger, Paul BUNYAN, jumped from the top of Rib Mountain into the WISCONSIN RIVER, and the splash formed all of Wisconsin's lakes.

RICHARD, Gabriel. (Saintes, France, Oct. 15, 1767—Detroit, MI, Sept. 13, 1832). Missionary and educator. Father Gabriel Richard was the type of person who could see opportunity in nearly every event. In 1802 the city of DETROIT was burned to the ground. Father Richard, then the only clergyman in Michigan, surveyed the damage and said, "We hope for better things; it will arise from its

"Rice gatherers," by Seth Eastman. Indians harvest wild rice.

ashes." Those words have been used in the present seal of the city of Detroit. Father Richard was the Catholic vicar-general of the Detroit area and quickly moved into the field of education. Under his guidance six primary schools and two academies were established. In 1809, he also established the first printing press in the Illinois Territory and in that year began the *Essai du Michigan ou Observateur Impartial,* the first paper printed in Detroit. He edited and published a child's spelling text, devotional books, the laws of Michigan, and a Bible for the Indians. When Father Richard was made prisoner by the British during the WAR OF 1812, his release was demanded by TECUMSEH (1768-1813) and quickly granted. In 1817 Father Richard founded the Catholepistemiad or University of Michigania, a forerunner of the state university, founded the next year. In 1821 he was chosen as a delegate to the United States Congress from Michigan Territory and served from 1823 to 1825. In Congress he presented petitions for school grants, streets in Detroit, and western roads. Father Richard was a charter member of the Michigan Historical Society. He has been called "an empire builder" and the "Patron Saint of Detroit." During the terrible cholera epidemic of 1832, Father Richard "might be seen clothed in the robes of his high calling, pale and emaciated, with spectacles on his forehead and prayer book in his hand, going from house to house to visit his parishioners, encouraging the well and administering spiritual consolation to the sick and dying." Just as the epidemic was ending, an exhausted Father Richard took the disease and succumbed. A crowd of over 2,000, more than the entire population of Detroit, attended his funeral services. The bells tolled all day for the beloved clergyman.

RICHMOND, Indiana. City (pop. 41,349), east central Indiana industrial trade and distribution center, seat of Wayne County., founded in 1805 by soldiers who served with George Rogers CLARK (1752-1818) at VINCENNES. The fertile land around Richmond assured a flourishing community in the early 1800s. Quakers moved to the region and in 1847 gave the community Earlham College which counts among its alumni Joseph CANNON (1836-1926), Speaker of the House of Representatives for ten years; William Penn Nixon, managing editor for many years of the Chicago Inter-Ocean; and Achilles Unthank, civil engineer of many public works in South America and Asia. In challeng-

ing Henry Clay to free his slaves, the Quakers in Richmond contributed to the political troubles leading to the CIVIL WAR. Clay's handling of a petition presented to him during a speech at Richmond may have cost him the election won by Polk. Among its notable residents was E. Gurney Hill, noted for his introduction of new roses in America. He developed the Richmond Rose and established the Hill Floral Products Company, operating one of the largest greenhouses in the United States. Richmond continues to be one of the largest commercial rose-growing centers in the country. More than seventy-three varieties are found in the Hill Memorial Rose Garden in Glen Miller Park. The Hayes Regional Arboretum is a 355-acre preserve for trees and plants native to the Whitewater Region of Indiana and Ohio. Richmond hosts an annual Rose Festival during the third week of June, a Rock and Gem Show in April and an Oktoberfest the first weekend in October. The Old Richmond Historic District, covering more than 250 acres, offers self-guided tours of a rich collection of Federal, Victorian and Greek Revival homes. Other views of pioneer life may be seen in the Wayne County Historical Museum. Pioneer rooms include an 1823 log cabin, a loom house and cobbler and an apothecary shops. The Indiana Football Hall of Fame houses a vast collection of statistics, displays and memorabilia of Indiana teams and players at the high school, college and professional levels of the game.

RICKENBACKER, Edward Vernon (Eddie). (Columbus, OH, Oct. 8, 1890—July 23, 1973). Aviator, business executive. At the age of sixteen, young Rickenbacker was a well-known auto racer, setting several speed records. Volunteering for the American air force, he became the most celebrated aviation ace in WORLD WAR I, setting the record by destroying twenty-six German aircraft. He received the Congressional Medal of Honor. Gaining experience as an executive of several commercial airline companies, he became president of Eastern Airlines (1938), which he built into one of the most important in the country. In 1942 he was appointed special representative of the secretary of war to inspect air bases in the Pacific theater of war, and his B-17 was shot down while on an observation tour in the Pacific during WORLD WAR II. Rickenbacker survived on a raft for twenty-two days and wrote about this experience in his book *Seven Came Through* (1943).

RILEY, James Whitcomb. (Greenfield, IN, 1853—Indianapolis, IN, July 22, 1916). The "Hoosier Poet." He re-created Indiana's past and its people in his writings. He gained his first fame in a hoax, writing a poem, named "Leonainie" (1877), in the style of Edgar Allan Poe. Riley was denounced for his prank, but was remembered for his ability. Many of his poems were written in the Hoosier dialect. Newspapers carried such poems as "The Raggedy Man." His first book collection was published in 1883, entitled *The Old Swimmin' Hole and 'Leven More Poems.* This included "When the Frost Is on the Punkin," perhaps his best-known poem. His output totaled ten more collections of poems. Indiana's children contributed pennies for a statue to Riley in RICHMOND, Indiana.

RINGLING BROTHERS. Circus owners. Sons of a German harnessmaker, while living at MC GREGOR, Iowa, two of the seven brothers became hooked on circus life by the shows presented on a circus boat in the MISSISSIPPI RIVER. Those two, Charles (1863-1926) and John (1866-1936), moved to BARABOO, Wisconsin, to join their brothers Albert (1852-1916), Otto (1858-1911) and Alfred (1861-1919) to form the Classic and Comic Concert Company song-and-dance troop, which began performing in 1882 with moderate success. By 1884 they had organized a ragtag circus. Al's juggling act resulted in the breakage of most of his mother's plates, and their menagerie began with an assortment of chickens, a billy goat, rabbits, a horse named Zachary, bought from a war veteran for $8.42 and their key act, a bear. Nevertheless, they got an act together, and John Ringling set out as the advance man to arrange for locations for this circus. When one owner of a lot agreed, John proved his business acumen by pulling out a formal contract in which, among other provisions, they guaranteed to keep the trees from harm. The owner was even more surprised when the boys arrived in a wagon pulled by their only horse, carrying ther "menagerie" and supplied with tents and pennants. They then carefully roped off the trees. From the beginning their circus operations grew until in 1907 they bought the P.T. Barnum circus and became "The Greatest Show on Earth," Ringling Brothers and Barnum and Bailey. The circus had its headquarters in Baraboo until 1918. Winter headquarters was moved to Sarasota, Florida. Charles continued the active management until he died. Then John Ringling took the circus leadership and bought the Circus Corporation of America in 1929. Altogether the Ringlings had purchased eleven major circuses, eliminating almost all competition and employing 5,000 people, with a main tent seating 10,000. The circus continues a regular circuit each year. Today the Circus World Museum maintains the relics of the great circus days at Baraboo.

RIPLEY, Ohio. Town (pop. 2,174), situated on the OHIO RIVER in Brown County, the town was named for Eleazar Wheelock Ripley, general in the WAR OF 1812, serving in Canada and as an Indian fighter. It was laid out in 1812 by James Poage of Virginia. In early days, Ripley was a center for steamboat building and by some strange twist, also of piano manufacture. It has been a commercial hub of rich Brown County. The city suffered severely from Ohio River floods and was almost wiped out by the great flood of 1937. The city was the home of the Reverend John Rankin, one of the major figures in the Abolition movement. He sheltered hundreds of runaway slaves in his house overlooking the river. The house is now a state monument.

RIPON, Wisconsin. City (pop. 7,111), situated in south central Wisconsin, the city was named for Ripon in Yorkshire, England. It was first settled by followers of socialist Francois Charles Marie Fourier, who influenced Horace Greeley in his ideas on settlement of the western areas. In the pre-Civil War period the community was a hotbed of the Abolition movement, particularly known for sheltering wanted Abolitionist Sherman M. Booth. On March 20, 1854 a group was formed at a political meeting. The claim that this meeting was the beginning of the Republican Party is among the most valid among the several vying for that honor. Today the Little White Schoolhouse where the meeting was held is open to the public as the birthplace of the Republican Party. Ripon is the site of Ripon College.

ROARING RIVER. Originating in one of the largest springs in southern Missouri, the Roaring River begins with the flow of 20,000,000 gallons of spring water and plunges over twin waterfalls, then rushes through the hills with the roar which gives it its name. It is said to be one of the most picturesque of the scenic rivers of the Midwest.

ROBIN. State bird of Michigan and Wisconsin. Robin or robin redbreast, is the common name for a migratory bird of the large thrush family. Noted for its song, the robin is the largest of the thrush family and is readily identified by its "red breast."

ROBINSON, William (Billy). (Redfield, SD, Sept. 24, 1884—Grinnell, IA, Mar. 11, 1916). Pioneer aviator and aircraft experimenter of GRINNELL, Iowa. Robinson developed one of the first radial air-cooled airplane engines. Receiving permission to fly mail from DES MOINES to CHICAGO, he began the first authorized air mail flight in 1914. When he overshot Chicago, possibly on purpose, he landed in KENTLAND, Indiana, breaking the nonstop flying distance record, as well, with a flight of 390 miles in four hours and forty-four minutes. He lost his life in another attempt to break an aviation record. He had previously reached altitudes of over 14,000 feet, but in attempting to surpass the old record of 17,000 feet, he lost control, the exact reason never known, and plummeted to his death.

ROCHESTER, Minnesota. City (pop. 57,-855), seat of Olmsted County, situated in southeastern Minnesota. It was incorporated as a city in 1858. Rochester in Minnesota was named for Rochester, New York, which took its name from Nathaniel Rochester who owned much of the land on which the New York community was platted. In the area of commerce, the city is a farm and trade center, with the processing of foodstuffs, electronic and electrical equipment, plastics, metals, woods and medical equipment. The latter springs from the principal activity of the city, the MAYO CLINIC, founded in 1889 by Dr. William Worrell MAYO (1819-1911) and his two sons, William J. (1861-1939) and Charles (1865-1939). Succeeding the private practice of the Mayos, the clinic received its start when the Catholic Sisters of St. Francis built a hospital with the senior Dr. Mayo, then seventy years of age, in charge. Through the genius and enterprise of the Mayos, the clinic attracted leading medical personnel from around the world, and with its growth over the years has made Rochester one of the most sought-after health centers worldwide. The growth has in large part been based on the unusual ability of the Mayos in organizing and guiding large enterprises. Today, more than 200 physicians, many of them top specialists in their field, lead the unique medical unit which employs more than 11,000. There is another health institution in

Rochester, this one devoted to the mentally ill. For the more than 200,000 persons each year who visit the clinic, as well as for others, the city provides a symphony orchestra, museums of history, antique museums and other displays. French, Spanish, English and American antiques may be observed at Mayowood, the former residence of Dr. Charles H. Mayo. Visitors are welcomed to the Mayo Medical Museum with its many exhibits and life-sized anatomical models of the human body. The 56 bell Rochester Carillon is dedicated to the American soldier.

ROCK FORMATION (world's oldest). Copper-bearing rocks near HOUGHTON, on Michigan's UPPER PENINSULA, are believed to be among the oldest rock formations in the world, existing there with apparently no change since the beginning of time.

ROCK ISLAND, Illinois. City (pop. 47,036), seat of Rock County, one of the Midwest's "Quad Cities." The city of Rock Island is named after the nearby island in the MISSISSIPPI RIVER owned by the United States Government and site of the Rock Island Arsenal. On May 10, 1816, Colonel William Lawrence arrived to establish a fort there, later called Fort Armstrong. George Davenport and Russell Farnham bought land and established a trader's store. By an act of the Illinois General Assembly in 1831, the County of Rock Island, including the island, was carved out of Jo Daviess County. The first settlement on the south bank of the Mississippi was called Farnhamsburg and then Stephenson. It was platted and incorporated on October 21, 1837. In 1841 the town received its charter as a city and was named Rock Island and the seat of Rock Island County. From 1850 to 1890 Rock Island was the most active river port in Illinois. The arrival of the Chicago and Rock Island Railroad on February 22, 1854, made Rock Island a departure point for thousands of immigrants moving on west. The Army evacuated Fort Armstrong in 1836. It served as a base of operations for the SAUK and FOX Indian agent and in 1840-1845 as a government armory. In July, 1863, a stockade and wooden shelters were built as part of a prison for Confederate soldiers. From 1863 through 1865, 1,960 of the 12,215 prisoners kept there died, 500 from smallpox. In 1864 the government erected the first permanent building for the Rock Island Arsenal. This is now the headquarters of the Army Weapons Command and the Rock Island District of the U.S. Army Corps of Engineers.

Rock Island, Illinois, c. 1849, by William Lewis.

Rock Island, MOLINE, and East Moline today make up the center of the farm implement manufacturing industry in the United States. Together with BETTENDORF, Iowa, these cities make up the "Quad Cities." The "Quint Cities" includes Rock Island, Moline, East Moline, Illinois, with Bettendorf and DAVENPORT, Iowa. Quad City Downs provides harness racing, and all day river trips are available on the Mississippi to DUBUQUE. Black Hawk State Historic Site displays Indian relics. An Indian powow is held there on Labor Day weekend. The Rock Island Arsenal welcomes visitors. Also open is the restored home of Colonel Davenport, a reconstruction of the Fort Armstrong Blockhouse, and the John M. Browning Museum of antique and modern firearms.

ROCK RIVER. Northwestern Illinois river, deepened and improved as part of the state's canal system. The river's source is said to be the notable Horicon Marsh just south of FOND DU LAC, Wisconsin. The river flows south and west to meet the MISSISSIPPI RIVER below ROCK ISLAND. Near this area the seventy-five mile long Illinois and Mississippi Canal, also known as the Hennepin Canal, joined the Rock River by way of a feeder canal between the Illinois and Mississippi rivers below Rock Island. The main canal was closed in 1951 when it no longer proved able to handle its navigation demands and appeared too expensive to upgrade. Over its 285 miles the Rock River flows through JANESVILLE and BELOIT, Wisconsin, ROCKFORD, Byron, Oregon, Dixon, Rock Falls, Erie and Milan, Illinois.

ROCKEFELLER, John Davison. (Rich- ford, NY, July 9, 1839—May 23, 1937). Rockefeller moved with his family to CLEVELAND, Ohio, in 1853 and at the age of sixteen went to work as a bookkeeper. Frugally saving his money, in 1859 he was able to enter a partnership in the produce commission business. Four years later, along with his brother William, he invested in a Cleveland oil refining firm, and by 1865 had gained a controlling interest. In 1867 he joined his interests to those of H.M. Flagler and S.V. Harkness, and in 1870 they incorporated their firm as the Standard Oil Company. Rockefeller was ruthless in cutting out his less able competitors and a genius in making agreements with competent competing operators. He displayed an amazing ability for organization and an uncanny talent for predicting fluctuations in the market price of oil. By organizing vertically—acquiring businesses which controlled all stages of production—by guaranteeing large and regular shipments to railroads in exchange for lower rates, by absorbing competitors and by forcing others into bankruptcy, Standard Oil soon became the largest petroleum concern in the nation. By 1890, Standard Oil controlled more than seventy-five percent of the nation's oil refining capacity. In 1896 Rockefeller retired from personal control of the company, although keeping the presidency, in order to devote himself to his philanthropic interest. In 1892 he had been the principal factor in the founding of the University of CHICAGO. In 1901 he gave half a billion dollars (a vast fortune in those days and an almost unimaginable one by today's values) to establish the Rockefeller Institute for Medical Research at New York City. By 1911 he began to turn over management of his philanthropies to his son, John Davison, Jr.

Although the great family fortune was earned in the Midwest, the Rockefeller interests turned mainly to the East.

ROCKFORD, Illinois. City (pop. 139,712) seat of Winnebago County, situated in North Central Illinois on the ROCK RIVER, formed by the merger of two settlements on either side of the river and incorporated in 1839, now covering an area of 40.7 square miles. The name comes from the rocky ford in the river. Belvidere is often considered a suburb.

Frequent cloudiness keeps the winter climate somewhat more mild than that of cities slightly to the west. Distant Lake Michigan sometimes moderates the usually hot but not oppressive summers. The cold winters bring snowcover from late December through February.

Now the second largest city in Illinois, Rockford is an industrial center and the processing, shipping hub of the rich agricultural region. Its manufacuturing includes a long leadership in screws and fasteners, along with substantial production of airplane and automobile parts. The first completely automatic hosiery producing machinery was made in Rockford and has helped that city maintain its lead as a producer in that field.

The route between well-established GALENA and growing CHICAGO was interrupted by a major river. When a shallow part of the Rock River with a hard rocky bed was found, travel concentrated there, and the city of the rocky ford began to grow. Germanicus Kent established a sawmill to take advantage of the waterpower.

Winnebago County was formed in 1836, and Rockford became the county seat in 1839. The Chicago and Galena Union Railroad arrived in the 1850s, and more waterpower industry grew.

In an interesting sidelight, hitting its peak in 1870, the Rockford baseball team was powerful enough to join the newly formed National League, and for a time the city had major league baseball, until supplanted by Chicago. Adrian "Pop" ANSON (1851-1922), later famos as a Chicago player-manager, was a member of the Rockford team.

In the period of 1970 to 1984, Rockford has shown a decline of nearly ten percent in population, from 147,000 to 137,000, due mostly to the farm crisis and the nearly region-wide reduction in manufacturing. However, unemployment remained at a relatively low rate, and personal income increased by almost a third. The black population is about 14 percent, with Hispanics at about 3 percent.

Rockford College and a junior college are the higher education facilities of the city.

Rockford's Scandinavian background is commemorated each year with the Scandinavian Midsummer Festival in Sinnissippi Park. The labor Day weekend features the Midwestern States Championship Powerboat regatta on the Rock river. The home built at Rockford by Robert Tinker in 1865 in the style of a Swiss chalet, and furnished with art objects he collected throughout the world, is now open as Tinker Swiss Cottage. Burpee Gallery of Art displays the art collection of the Rockford Art Associaton. There is a Natural History Museum, and the Erlander Home Museum recalls early Rockford history. The Rock River region is particularly noted for its brilliant fall foliage.

ROCKHURST COLLEGE. Privately supported college for men and women in KANSAS CITY, Missouri. Accredited by the North Central Association of Colleges and Schools, Rockhurst was founded and directed by the Society of Jesus, an affiliate of the Roman Catholic Church. It grants Associate and Bachelor degrees. Religious subjects are a requirement. During the 1985-1986 academic year Rockhurst enrolled 2,885 students and had 195 faculty members.

ROCKNE, Knute. (Voss, Norway, Mar. 4, 1888—KS, Mar. 31, 1931). Football coach. Rockne excelled in football as a student at NOTRE DAME UNIVERSITY, winning a crucial game with Army in 1913 through the then unused forward pass, said to be a turning point in football strategy. After graduation in 1914, he became a chemistry instructor and assistant football coach at Notre Dame, and head coach in 1918. As head coach for 13 years he led his teams in winning 105 games with only 12 losses and 5 ties and made Notre Dame the leading football center of the United States. He revolutionized football theory, stressed offense, developed the precision backfield, called the "Notre Dame shift," perfected line play and other strategy. Among the famous stars he developed were the "Four Horsemen of Notre Dame," the most famous of all backfields. He was noted for his ability to exemplify values and ideals and inculcate qualities of leadership among his "boys." He died tragically in an airplane crash. One of his several books on football was *Coaching, the Way of the Winner* (1905).

ROCKY MOUNTAIN FUR COMPANY.

Successor of the Missouri Fur Company. Succession in the fur business of the 1800s meant that many of the same men active in the previous company were employed by the next. The principal leaders of the Rocky Mountain Fur Company were Andrew Henry, who operated in the field, and William H. ASHLEY (1778-1838), manager of the financial affairs of the company from its headquarters in ST. LOUIS. The first expedition of the Rocky Mountain Fur Company began in 1822 and included such renowned trappers and frontiersmen as Hugh Glass, Jedediah Strong Smith, and Jim BRIDGER (1804-1881).

ROGERS, Ginger. (Independence, MO, July 16, 1911—). Character actress, comedienne and dancer, born Virginia Katherine McMath. Rogers is best remembered for her dancing in 1930s musicals with Fred Astaire. After a brief career as a band singer and some experience on Broadway, Rogers was taken to Hollywood. She appeared in such pictures as *Flying Down to Rio* (1933), *Top Hat* (1935) and *Shall We Dance?* (1937). She won an Academy Award for best actress in 1940 for *Kitty Foyle*.

ROLLA, Missouri. City (pop. 13,300), seat of Phelps County, south-central Missouri, southwest of Sullivan in Phelps County. The origin of the name is a subject of much speculation but no certainty. Rolla was founded in 1855 when railroad contractors built several warehouses and an office near the farm of John Webber. In six months six hundred people moved to the site, hoping to profit from the railroad. Webber wanted the town to be called Hardscrabble. A railroad official suggested the name Phelps. A homesick man from North Carolina suggested the name Raleigh, but the resulting name was spelled the way he pronounced it, according to one version of the naming of the town. Rolla is the headquarters of the Mid-Continent Mapping Center of the United States Geological Survey. The patron saint of engineers, St. Patrick, is honored annually by the students of the University of MISSOURI at Rolla. Graduates are made "knights" in the "Order of St. Patrick." The campus of the university features a partial replica of Stonehenge, the ancient configuration of stones found in England. The replica indicates the date by the position of the sun's rays. The North Star can also be located using the model. Memoryville, U.S.A. is a museum of restored cars from 1907 to 1937 and storefronts from Rolla from the early 20th century.

ROLVAAG, Ole Edvart. (Rolvaag, Helgeland, Norway, Apr. 22, 1876—Northfield, MN, Nov. 5, 1931). Educator and author. Rolvaag is best remembered for *Giants in the Earth* (1927), an epic of early life on South Dakota prairies. This was the first of a trilogy completed in 1931. Rolvaag was educated at ST. OLAF COLLEGE in NORTHFIELD, Minnesota, where he later returned to serve as professor and head of the department of Norwegian language and literature. He resigned in August, 1931, to write full time but died only a few months later.

ROOSEVELT UNIVERSITY. Coeducational institution in CHICAGO, Illinois. Roosevelt University, named for President F.D. Roosevelt, was founded in 1945. Privately controlled, Roosevelt University has colleges in arts and sciences, business administration, education, a graduate division, a division of labor education, and the Chicago Musical College. Bachelor's and master's degrees are offered. During the 1985-1986 academic year 6,400 students were enrolled and there were 481 faculty members. Soon after it was founded, the university bought the famed Auditorium Building, designed by Louis SULLIVAN (1856-1924), in which its main operations are housed.

ROOT, George F. (Sheffield, MA, Aug. 30, 1820—Chicago, IL, Aug. 6, 1895). Composer. Root, an accomplished instructor of music teachers, moved to Chicago, in 1859, and became a partner with his brother in a music store. Root began composing to provide music for the pupils in his classes, under the pen name of "Wurzel" before openly acknowledging his work. Between 1853 and 1855 he composed "The Shining Shore" which has been the best known of his sacred songs. Root's first Civil War song, "The First Gun is Fired," was unsuccessful, but his second song of that war, "The Battle Cry of Freedom," was sung throughout the North. "Tramp, Tramp, Tramp, the Boys are Marching" was almost as popular. Root composed sentimental songs relating to wartime incidents such as "Just Before the Battle, Mother" and "The Vacant Chair." He composed over two hundred individual songs and compiled more than seventy song collections, musical entertainments for schools, and educational works on music.

ROOT, Jim. (—) Engineer for the Northern Pacific Railroad who rescued 50 residents of HINCKLEY, Minnesota, when a forest fire threatened the town on September 1, 1894. Root drove a train into Hinckley from nearby Sandstone, loaded up as many citizens as he could and then found he was unable to turn the train around. To escape the roaring flames Root had to back the train down the track to safety. Upon escaping the fire it was found that Root's hands were seared to the throttle by the incredible heat of the forest fire.

ROOT, John Wellborn. (Lumpkin, GA, Jan. 10, 1850—Chicago, IL, Jan. 15, 1891). Architect. Educated in England, he earned a degree in civil engineering at New York University (1869). Root was a leader of the "Chicago School" promoting contemporary architecture. He broke with traditional design and evolved approaches based more on function and geometric form. Among his designs was the Monadnock Building in Chicago (1891). He was one of the principal planners of the WORLD'S COLUMBIAN EXPOSITION in Chicago in 1893, responsible for the selection of the site and production of the basic plan, but his untimely death did not permit him to see the fair he had planned.

ROSS, Diana. (Detroit, MI, Mar. 26, 1944—   ). Singer, with some film credits. Ross began her singing career as the lead performer with a group called "The Supremes." The original Supremes were Jean Terrell, Diana Ross, and Florence Ballard of DETROIT, Michigan. By 1964 the group had received seven gold records in less than two years. It was the first group to have five consecutive records reach the top of the best-selling charts. As her fame grew the group's name changed to "Diana Ross and the Supremes." She eventually decided to do solo work and continued her successful career. Ross starred in such motion pictures as *Lady Sings the Blues* (1972), *Mahogany* (1974) and *The Wiz* (1984). She has been the recipient of a certificate from then Vice President Hubert HUMPHREY for her efforts on behalf of President Johnson's Youth Opportunity Program and citations from Mrs. Martin Luther King and Reverend Abernathy for contributions to the Southern Christian Leadership Conference. Ross won a Grammy award as the Top Female Singer in 1972 and has been named Female Entertainer of the Year and Image award for Best Actress by the N.A.A.C.P.

ROYAL ENGLISH RANGERS. British troops under the command of Major Robert Rogers during the FRENCH AND INDIAN WAR (1754-

1763). With two hundred Rangers, Rogers occupied DETROIT in 1760. Orders given by Rogers to his troops on how to conduct guerrilla warfare have served as a model for irregular troops to the present day.

RUBBER. In 1870 Dr. Benjamin Franklin GOODRICH was lured to AKRON, Ohio, by a local booster pamphlet. He had been looking for a suitable spot to build a business manufacturing rubber products. He planned to use the system of hardening rubber called vulcanization, which had been patented in 1844 by Charles Goodyear, who had carried on his research in the face of poverty and debt. Dr. Goodrich found nineteen ventursome Akronites who were willing to invest a thousand dollars each in his enterprise. The original plan was to make fire hose, wringer rolls and beverage tubing. In 1879, with business far from booming, the Goodrich plant was reorganized, and the backers were given the choice of continuing or being bought out. They opted for the latter and soon bitterly regretted that move, because the age of wheels was just developing. In 1892 the famed trotting horse Nancy Hanks had shattered the world record, pulling a sulky equipped with pneumatic tires. Soon bicycle and buggy owners were clamoring for such tires. Also, the auto industry was stirring and about to become the largest market for tires. Akron had the head start, and others soon followed Goodrich at Akron—Firestone, Diamond, Swinehart, Star, Seiberling and others. Seiberling organized Goodyear in 1898, taking the inventor's name. A $10,000 stock purchase made at the time Goodyear was organized was worth $1,000,000 twenty-five years later. Akron was well on its way to becoming the Rubber Capital of the World, a position it holds today, despite the defection of Firestone Tire and Rubber to CHICAGO as well as some loss of business due to lessened auto production. Akron accounts for about a fourth of the country's fourteen billion dollar a year income from rubber products.

RURAL FREE DELIVERY. One of the most important factors in the quality of rural life in early days, the delivery of mail to farmers and others outside town and city limits, originated with a Wisconsin man, William F. Vilas, when he was Postmaster General of the United States. Delivery started in 1900. Vilas had a distinguished career in many fields of public and private service.

RUSHVILLE, Indiana. City (pop. 6,113),

seat of Rush County, east central Indiana, city southeast of INDIANAPOLIS. Rushville is named for Benjamin F. Rush, physician, philanthropist, Revolutionary War soldier, and signer of the Declaration of Independence. Rushville was the home of James E. Watson, a powerful figure in Indiana politics for thirty-five years and author of *As I Knew Them,* published in 1933.

RUSK, Jeremiah. (1830—1893), three-term governor of Wisconsin, first official appointee as U.S. Secretary of Agriculture. Rusk came to Wisconsin in 1853 and settled in the area of present Viroqua. He served for six years as Republican congressman in Washington and then started his first term as governor in 1882. One of his most important social contributions became a landmark in the handling of labor disputes. When the Chicago, Portage and Superior Railroad failed, the company left a crew of 1,700 stranded without any resources in a remote region. Nearby property owners called for the national guard, but the governor replied, "These men need bread, not bayonets!" He refused to release the existing assets of the road until the men had been paid their full wages, and the dispute was settled without violence.

RUSSELL, Jane. (Bemidji, MN, June 21, 1921—). Movie actress. Russell became a movie star when an agent sent her picture to Howard Hughes. *The Outlaw,* Hughes' first picture, starring Russell, was held up for three years with censor trouble until 1947. Russell's career continued with roles in *The Young Widow* (1947), *The Paleface* (1948), *Montana Belle* (1951), *Gentlemen Prefer Blondes* (1953), *Gentlemen Marry Brunettes* (1955), *Hot Blood* (1956), *The Tall Men* (1956), *The Revolt of Mamie Stover* (1957), and *The Fuzzy Pink Nightgown* (1957).

RUSSELL, Lillian. (Clinton, IA, Dec 4, 1861—Pittsburgh, PA, June 6, 1922). Singer and actress whose real name was Helen Louise Leonard. Lillian Russell became an international celebrity for her notorious affair with the equally flambouyant Diamond Jim Brady. The relationship of the two dynamic personalities developed into a legend. She first appeared in light opera in 1879. Her career was dramatically advanced with her appearance at Tony Pastor's famed casino in New York City (1880), where she became known as the "American Beauty." She sang with the McCaull Opera Company and subsequently organized her own company. In later years she played straight comedy parts. She loved jewelry and her flaming jewels became a particular trademark.

RUTHERFORD, Joseph Franklin. (Morgan Co., MO, Nov. 8, 1869—San Diego, CA, Jan. 8, 1942). Religious leader. He was the second president of the Jehovah's Witnesses (1916), having become a member of the sect in 1894 while a lawyer in Booneville, Ky. He remained president until his death, and under his leadership the group grew from 3,000 to 50,000 members.

SAGANAGA, Lake. Deepest Minnesota lake, at 240 feet, shared with Canada.

SAGINAW RIVER. Michigan, formed by the junction of several rivers in the southern area of the city of SAGINAW in Saginaw County and flowing through Saginaw into Saginaw Bay of Lake HURON.

SAGINAW, Michigan. City (pop. 77,508), seat of Saginaw County, located in the eastern portion of Michigan's LOWER PENINSULA, on the SAGINAW RIVER. Saginaw was once described as the "Timber Capital of the World." Today the Saginaw-Bay City region, known as "The Thumb," is recognized as an important agricultural area. The earliest white settlers were from Canada. Louis Campau built a fur-trading post in the area of present-day Saginaw in 1816. Campau later built a council house there at the request of Governor Cass and helped negotiate a treaty with the CHIPPEWA. Fort Saginaw was built in 1819. The severity of the winter, terrible spring floods and a summer epidemic of "intermittent fever" made the camp commander write the War Department of his doubts that anything but Indians, muskrats or bullfrogs could long live in such a place. The withdrawal of the troops and the hostility of the Indians prevented further settlement, to the delight of the trappers who liked the situation as it had been for years. By the 1840s timber scouts were buying forested land for $1.50 an acre. Fourteen steam sawmills were operating on the Saginaw River by 1857. When the lumber industry faded, discoveries of coal fueled the economy. Today there are twelve plants of General Motors in Saginaw, and the city is a leader in grey iron and malleable castings and an agricultural marketer of beans, sugar beets and brans. The rivalry between East and West Saginaw, areas divided by the river, was ended in 1889 when the two communities were united. An art museum, historical museum, children's zoo and two notable gardens add to the city's attraction. The annual Big Sam Raft Race is held the last Saturday of June.

SAINT ANTHONY, FALLS OF. Forty-nine foot drop in the MISSISSIPPI RIVER in MINNEAPOLIS. The falls were discovered by Father Louis HENNEPIN (1640-1701) in 1680 and were named for his patron saint, Anthony of Padua. The falls became important as a site for sawmills and grain milling companies. A barrier to upstream river traffic, the falls marked the starting point for smaller craft which navigated the water northwards to Sauk Rapids and Little Falls. As a barrier to northwards navigation the lower falls were an important factor in the rise of ST. PAUL as a commercial city which served as a transfer point and storage location for goods brought as far north as the falls by water. A long history of commercial use of the falls was threatened twice, in October, 1869, and April, 1870, after an unsuccessful attempt to tunnel under Hennepin Island caused several huge chunks of stone to break away, destroying some of the mills.

SAINT ANTHONY, Minnesota. Predecessor of MINNEAPOLIS, early Minnesota community founded near the Falls of ST. ANTHONY. The first sawmill to harness the power of the falls was constructed in 1821 by the military which used the lumber it produced to build FORT SNELLING. In 1823 a grist mill was built. The obvious value of the falls soon created a center of civilization on the east bank of the MISSISSIPPI RIVER as settlers moved to the region. Franklin Steele appears to have been the first of the pioneers to recognize the commercial potential of the falls. He may have had a cabin at the falls as early as 1838 and by 1845 had purchased all the land in the region. By 1850 lumber from the mills was used to manufacture pails and tubs. Increased wheat farming soon made flour milling profitable. The uniting of St. Anthony and Minneapolis in 1872 was a definite benefit to the latter community, which then grew rapidly.

SAINT BENEDICT, College of. Privately supported Roman Catholic liberal arts college for women. Located in ST. JOSEPH, Minnesota, Saint Benedict has an academic exchange program with ST. JOHN'S University for Men in Collegeville, Minnesota. St. Benedict, accredited with the North Central Association of Colleges and Schools, accepts qualified students of all religious faiths and sponsors semesters of study in France, Austria, Greece, Italy, Spain, England and Ireland. Year long exchanges are available with Sophia University in Tokyo, Japan. The college is located on a seven hundred-acre campus, seventy-five miles from MINNEAPOLIS -ST. PAUL and ten miles west of ST. CLOUD. During the 1985-1986 academic year 1,765 students were enrolled and the college had 128 faculty members.

SAINT CATHERINE COLLEGE. Privately supported Roman Catholic liberal arts college for women. Located in ST. PAUL, Minnesota, on a campus covering more than one hundred acres. The college offers a four-year undergraduate program and a Master of Arts in Theology. The school is accredited with the North Central Association of Colleges and Schools. Study programs abroad are available throughout the year. A member of the Associated Colleges of the Twin Cities, a consortium of five private colleges, St. Catherine offers students the opportunity of registering for courses at the other schools. Cooperative academic programs are also available with WASHINGTON UNIVERSITY in ST. LOUIS and the University of MINNESOTA, f o r engineering students. During the 1985-1986 academic year the college enrolled 2,484 students and had 209 faculty members.

SAINT CHARLES, Missouri. City (pop. 37,379), seat of St. Charles County, on the MISSOURI RIVER north of ST. LOUIS. Settled by French traders in 1769 and incorporated as a town in 1809, it is the earliest permanent settlement on the river and served as the state capital in 1826. There is diversified farming, producing corn, oats, and wheat. Mineral production includes coal, gravel, and sand deposits. Railroad cars, steel dies, and soda water also are produced. Lindenwood College (1827) and Sacred Heart Convent (1838) are found there. The first Missouri state capitol has been preserved as a historic site in the St. Charles Historic District, and the Lewis and Clark Center provides a unique museum of the expedition. Festival of the Little Hills is held each third weekend in August.

SAINT CLAIR RIVER. Boundary river between Canada and Michigan. Beginning at PORT HURON, Michigan, the river links Lake HURON with Lake ST. CLAIR and through the DETROIT RIVER to Lake ERIE. These rivers are really straits rather than true rivers. Because they provide the link to the sea, by way of the ST. LAWRENCE WATERWAY for the upper GREAT LAKES, SUPERIOR, HURON and MICHIGAN, these waterways must be ranked among the world's most important.

SAINT CLAIR, Arthur. (Thurso, Aithness County, Scotland, Apr. 3, 1737—Ligonier, PA, Aug. 31, 1818). Army officer, territorial governor, president of the Continental Congress. St. Clair, the first governor of the NORTHWEST TERRITORY, from 1787 to 1802, served with Washington in the battles of Trenton and Princeton in 1776-1777, and was ordered to defend Fort Ticonderoga in 1777. He evacuated the post, but was cleared by a court martial in 1778. As a delegate from Pennsylvania, St. Clair attended the Continental Congress from 1785 to 1787 and served as its president in 1787. In 1791 as a major general in the United States Army he was defeated by Indians in Ohio under Chief LITTLE TURTLE (1752-1812) in one of the greatest defeats ever suffered by United States forces. St. Clair's attempt to build a chain of military posts from FORT WASHINGTON, near the mouth of the MIAMI RIVER, to the MAUMEE RIVER was poorly planned and carried out. He resigned his commission in 1792. Because he wanted to retain his post as governor of the Northwest Territory, headquartered at CINCINNATI, Ohio, he opposed statehood for the territory and attempted to divide the region into small territories to prevent statehood indefinitely. However, because of the strong call for Ohio statehood, he was thwarted in this plan. He died at his home, "Hermitage."

SAINT CLAIR, Lake. Large lake lying between Canada and the United States in the area of DETROIT, Michigan, and Windsor, Ontario, Canada. Waters from Lake HURON flow into Lake St. Clair and then on to Lake ERIE.

SAINT CLOUD, Minnesota. City (pop. 42,566), central Minnesota, northwest of MINNEAPOLIS, named for the city Napoleon built for the Empress Josephine. John Wilson, an admirer of Napoleon, laid out the town and named it. St. Cloud flourished with the fur trade after 1855 when the famous RED RIVER CARTS began coming to St. Cloud rather than Sauk Rapids. Steamboats shortened the trip further by hauling goods to ST. PAUL. Early St. Cloud was divided into three parts—Upper, Middle, and Lower. Upper Town was organized by a Southerner, General Sylvanus Lowry. Lowry and many of his fellow citizens held slaves. After editorials about slavery, the Abolitionist (1815-1884) newspaper of feminist Jane Grey SWISSHELM (1815-1884) was attacked. Swisshelm's press was destroyed and expensive type scattered. With the outbreak of the CIVIL WAR, the Southerners and their slaves soon left the region. Middle Town was settled by Easterners, and Lower Town was populated by Germans. The communities were combined and incorporated in 1856. The granite of the region is prized nationwide. And quarrying, an important industry, began in 1868. Stone from the region has been used in the state capitol and many other buildings across the United States. St. Cloud is known as "The Granite City." Dairying and railroad shops add to the industry. St. Cloud State University, Saint John's Abbey University and Preparatory School and College of St. Benedict are found there.

SAINT CROIX RIVER. The majestic St. Croix rises in the St. Croix flowage, where the three branches of the river converge in northwestern Wisconsin. It flows southwesterly to meet the Minnesota border, and becomes one of the major border rivers of the Midwest, separating the two states until it reaches the MISSISSIPPI RIVER below ST. PAUL-MINNEAPOLIS. The Canyon of the St. Croix is known as the Switzerland of America and includes such features as the Potholes, Devil's Chair and Devil's Pulpit. Interstate State Park lies on both sides of the river and is jointly operated by both states. Nearby is St. Croix Falls. The lower segment of the river is a National Scenic Riverway.

SAINT CROIX NATIONAL SCENIC RIVERWAY. About 200 miles of the beautiful ST. CROIX RIVER and its Namekagon tributary make up this area, one of the original National Wild and Scenic Rivers System selections. It is headquartered at St. Croix Falls, Wisconsin.

SAINT FRANCIS RIVER. Midwestern river whose source lies in Missouri to the north of Mt. TAUM SAUK in the ST. FRANCOIS MOUNTAINS of east-central Missouri. Approximately 475 miles long, the St. Francis initially flows northeast, then south and south-southeast through the Clark National Forest. It forms the boundary between Stoddard and Butler counties and as it continues south makes up fifty miles of the border between Arkansas and Missouri. The St. Francis turns westward as it enters Arkansas and winds its way south, joining the MISSISIPPI RIVER below Memphis, Tennessee.

SAINT FRANCOIS MOUNTAINS. Missouri mountain range found on the east side of the Salem Plateau, between the Big and ST. FRANCIS rivers. It is not a continuous chain but consists of clusters of peaks, composed mostly of granite. The mountains cover roughly 70 square miles and are the highest and most rugged hilltop region in Missouri. TAUM SAUK MOUNTAIN, the highest in the state, is in the range, and Lake Wappapello is nearby.

SAINT IGNACE, Michigan. City (pop.2,-632), seat of Mackinac County, named for St. Ignace of Loyola, located at the southernmost tip of Hiawatha National Forest on Michigan's UPPER PENINSULA. St. Ignace is the second oldest settlement in Michigan. First seen by explorer Jean NICOLET (1598-1642) in 1634, it was not until 1671 that a mission was built on the site by Father Jacques MARQUETTE (1637-1675), who left it two years later for his famed exploration of the Mississippi valley. The last priest, feeling there was little to accomplish in such a lonely place, left after he burned the chapel to the ground rather than have it desecrated. In 1834 the Jesuits built a new church. Ferry service across the straits was begun in 1881. With RAILROADS, came iron smelting furnaces and the beginning of the lumber industry. St. Ignace became the county seat in 1882 and one year later was incorporated as a city. Despite the decline of the smelting of ore and of the lumber industry, St. Ignace has remained steady in its growth due to its position as the entry port to the UPPER PENINSULA by way of the MACKINAC BRIDGE. St. Ignace is base for one of the world's largest icebreakers, the *Chief Wawatam*. The city is also the northern starting point for the annual Labor Day Mackinac Bridge Walk.

SAINT JOHN'S UNIVERSITY. Private, Benedictine, liberal arts college for men including a school of divinity, an institute for advanced ecumenical studies and a graduate school in theological studies. Saint John's University is located in Collegeville, Minnesota, about ninety miles northwest of MINNEAPOLIS-ST. PAUL. Cooperative arrangements between St. John's University and the College of SAINT BENEDICT allow students to pursue studies offered on either campus. Accredited by the North Central Association of Colleges and Schools and professionally by the National Council for the Accreditation for Teacher Education and Association of Theological Schools, St. John's University maintains a student enrollment of over 1,952, with a faculty of 154. The University offers overseas programs in Ireland, Japan, Greece, France, Italy, Austria, England and, Middle East Archaeological and Bible Study in Jerusalem. Religious studies are required.

SAINT JOHNS, Michigan. City (pop. 7,376) seat of Clinton County, located in the south-central portion of Michigan's LOWER PENINSULA, west of FLINT. Saint Johns is the center of Michigan's peppermint industry. Mint is harvested like hay and allowed to dry in the sun for thirty-six hours, then hauled to the still where the oil is extracted.

SAINT JOSEPH RIVER. Source in Hillsdale County in southern Michigan. It flows west northwest across southern Michigan, then curves south and west into northeast Indiana, flowing through ELKHART and SOUTH BEND before turning northwest into Lake MICHIGAN at ST. JOSEPH, Michigan, in west Berrien County. The 210 mile long river is navigable for a short distance from its mouth. The first European exploration of Indiana started in late 1679 when Robert Cavalier, Sieur de LA SALLE, entered the mouth of the Saint Joseph River. Another Saint Joseph flows southeastward from the northwest corner of Ohio before turning southwestward into the northeast corner of Indiana. It meets with the ST. MARYS RIVER to form the MAUMEE.

SAINT JOSEPH, Michigan. City (pop. 9,622), Berrien County, southwestern portion of Michigan's Lower Peninsula. Saint Joseph has been a major tourist stop for those who enjoy the beach and seek the promise of health from its mineral springs. Often mistaken as part of BENTON HARBOR, St. Joseph is nearer Lake MICHIGAN and has the better harbor. It has been a resort of the wealthy. The first settlement in the area was named Newburyport. Founded in

1831, the prosperous community was buried by shifting sand despite valiant attempts by the citizens to erect barriers against the dunes. Giving up, the people moved to higher ground and established St. Joseph. Incorporated in 1836, the settlement was reduced when new settlers found the land prices too high and moved some distance away to establish their homes. That new community gradually developed into Benton Harbor. Rivalry between the two communities continued for many years, but has now been replaced by cooperation aimed at a better quality of living for all, with special attention to the economic problems of Benton Harbor, one of the country's most depressed communities.

SAINT JOSEPH, Missouri. City (pop. 76,691), seat of Buchanan County, in the northwest part of the state, 55 miles northwest of KANSAS CITY on the MISSOURI RIVER. It was settled in 1826 by Joseph Ribidoux, who established a trading post here. In 1836 the town was part of the Platte Purchase in which several Indian tribes sold land to Missouri. The town was named by Ribidoux after his patron saint. Incorporated as a city in 1845, St. Joseph prospered by equipping prospectors during the gold rush years, and the arrival of the railroad in the mid-1800s opened the city to expanded trade. The city became the eastern teminus of the famed PONY EXPRESS, connecting the railhead at St. Joseph with the Pacific coast for the express's short span of a part of 1860 and 1861. Located in a rich agricultural area, the city produces bluegrass, corn, fruit, and grains. Industries include the manufacture of textiles, candy, dairy products, and machine goods, and there are extensive meat-packing facilitites. One of the largest stationery plants in the world is located here. The Pony Express museum is a unique tribute to a fearless group of men and their mounts. Mr. Howard's home (assumed name of Jesse JAMES (1847-1882) is open to visitors. The St. Joseph Museum has an unusually complete Indian collection. the Psychiatric Museum covers 17 rooms of displays. There is an annual Jesse James Festival and a Joseph Robidoux Festival.

SAINT LAWRENCE RIVER SYSTEM AND SEAWAY. Although the St. Lawrence is usually considered as an eastern river, it has its farthest source in Minnesota, remote from the East. The ST. LOUIS RIVER is considered the St. Lawrence's official source and is the principal Minnesota river emptying into Lake

SUPERIOR, at the port of DULUTH, Minnesota, and SUPERIOR, Wisconsin. The source river itself is navigable for ships only through the length of the port, but the system it spawns now also is known as the St. Lawrence Seaway, which, through a system of canals and docks, enables large oceangoing vessels to pass through the St. Lawrence River and navigate the entire extent of the GREAT LAKES, bringing ocean commerce as far west as the Duluth-Superior area and to CHICAGO, MILWAUKEE, DETROIT, DAYTON, CLEVELAND and all the other ports of the Great Lakes.

SAINT LOUIS BLUES. Composed in 1914 by blind composer-conductor William Christopher HANDY (1873-1958), the song became the symbol of the city which gave it its name. Handy was one of the first to transcribe the blues in musical notation. This song became the basis for his growing worldwide reputation.

SAINT LOUIS RIVER. Considered the ultimate source of the ST. LAWRENCE RIVER. The St. Louis River arises in northeast Minnesota near the eastern border of St. Louis County. It flows southwest and then southeast to empty into Lake SUPERIOR at DULUTH, Minnesota and SUPERIOR, Wisconsin.

SAINT LOUIS SYMPHONY. Founded in 1880, the symphony of ST. LOUIS, Missouri, has the distinction of being the second oldest in the United States. Among its distinguished conductors was Rudolph Ganz, one of America's most noted music educators, who was also a distinguished composer, as well as conductor. In St. Louis, Ganz introduced concerts for children. *Time* magazine, in its annual evaluation for 1988, described the St. Louis Symphony as second only to the CHICAGO SYMPHONY in musical quality. This distinction has come about mainly through the efforts of its current conductor, Leonard Slatkin, who also is known as a masterful advocate of contemporary American classical composers.

SAINT LOUIS UNIVERSITY. Independent coed Roman Catholic institution, located on a 225-acre campus in ST. LOUIS, Missouri. Founded in 1818, the university is one of the largest American Catholic universities, and was the first university to be founded west of the MISSISSIPPI RIVER. The university has two other campuses, the medical campus, one mile away, and Parks College of Aeronautic Technology, in CAHOKIA, Illinos. Undergraduate colleges include Arts and Sciences, Schools of Nursing and

Allied Health Professions, Social Services, and Business Administration. Undergraduate majors include meteorology, geophysics, anthropology, communicative disorders, and geography. A church-related institution, the university requires all students to take a total of nine hours of theology during their undergraduate tenure. Enrollment: 10,712. Faculty: 2,237.

SAINT LOUIS, MISSOURI

Name: From Louis IX of France who was canonized in 1297, patron saint of Louis XV of France.

Nickname: Gateway City

Area: 61.4 square miles

Elevation: 616 feet

Population:
1984: 429,296
Rank: 29th
Percent change (1980-1984): minus 5.2%
Density (city): 7,427 per sq. mi.
Metropolitan Population: 2,398,000
Percent change (1980-1984): .88%

Racial and Ethnic Makeup (1980):
White: 53.6%
Black: 45.6%
Hispanic origin: 5,380 persons
Indian: 679 persons
Asian: 2,214 persons
Other: 1,034 persons

Age:
18 and under: 26.1%
65 and over: 17.6%

TV Stations: 6

Radio Stations: 35

Hospitals: 65

Sports Teams:
Cardinals (baseball)
Cardinals (football)
Blues (hockey)

Further Information: St. Louis Convention and Visitors Bureau, 500 N. Broadway, St. Louis, MO 63101

SAINT LOUIS, Missouri. Independent city, not in any county, on the MISSISSIPPI RIVER 20 miles downstream from its confluence with the MISSOURI RIVER. One of the great economic centers of the Mississippi basin, St. Louis is the heart of a metropolitan area of 2.3 million Missouri and Illinois residents. It developed as the principal point of departure for Western settlers, and its role as gateway to the West is now commemorated by the 630-foot-high stainless steel Gateway Arch that towers over the downtown riverfront in JEFFERSON NATIONAL EXPANSION MEMORIAL.

The city's origins are French, and they can be traced to a grant in 1764 of exclusive trading rights with the local Indians issued to the New Orleans merchant Pierre LACLEDE (1724?-1778). Laclede immediately traveled upriver to take possession of his grant, and on February 14, 1764, he landed on the present site of the city with a party of 30 men that included his stepson Auguste CHOUTEAU (1749-1829). It was Laclede who named the new settlement after the patron saint of Louis XV of France.

The early history of the settlement is one of shifting colonial allegiances. By the time Laclede arrived, the French had already ceded lands on the east bank of the Mississippi to the British. This brought a migration of French settlers from that region to St. Louis on the river's west bank.

In 1770 the Spanish took control of St. Louis under the terms of the earlier Treaty of Fountainebleu (1762) and made the settlement the governmental center of the Upper Louisiana territory. St. Louis was thus a Spanish possession during the American Revolution and so remained virtually untouched by the war.

St. Louis came under French possession again in 1800 by the terms of the San Ildefonso Treaty, but the French were by that time already negotiating the LOUISIANA PURCHASE with the U.S. The U.S. took formal possession of the Louisiana Territory on March 9, 1804, with St. Louis again serving as the seat of government for the entire territory.

Incorporated in 1808, St. Louis was also the capital of the Missouri Territory (1812-21) until Missouri became a state.

U.S. possession of the area brought a great influx of pioneers from eastern states to St. Louis, which jumped in population from 1,000 in 1800 to 5,600 in 1821. Until that time fur trading was the basis of the economy, but the first river steamboat reached St. Louis in 1817, and, from that point on, its economy was based on shipping and transportation. Steamboat traffic operated on both the Mississippi and Missouri rivers, bringing settlers to the begin-

Saint Louis

Gateway Arch frames St. Louis, Missouri.

ning of the OREGON and SANTA FE trails there.

Another leap in transportation came in 1851, when the Pacific Railroad Company began construction both east and west from St. Louis. The route east to the Atlantic coast was completed in 1863, opening the city to German and Irish immigrants, who by 1870 represented more than one-third of the total population.

The growth of the city was unaffected by the CIVIL WAR, which had a devastating impact on other parts of Missouri.

By the end of the 19th century St. Louis' economic prosperity brought about a cultural renaissance. Its primary intellectual body was the St. Louis Philosophical Society, which was founded in 1866 by William T. Harris and Henry C. Brockmeyer and published *The Journal of Specultive Philosophy* (1867-93). In 1878 Joseph PULITZER (1847-1911) began publicaton of the St. Louis *Post-Dispatch.*

Another indication of the city's cultural atmosphere was the flourishing there of the poets T. S. Eliot, Sara TEASDALE (1884-1933) and Eugene FIELD (1850-1895). By the 20th century, St. Louis was prominent enough to host the LOUISIANA PURCHASE EXHIBITION of 1904, a centennial celebration that was at the time the largest world's fair in history.

Following WORLD WAR II, however, the city underwent a period of urban decline, exacerbated by the flight of its population to the suburbs. The city's population in 1950 was 856,796, but by 1980 it had fallen 47% to 453,085. By 1984 KANSAS CITY had surpassed St. Louis in population. For a time, the St. Louis metropolitan area expanded by this shift, growing 11% in the 1960s, but a further

exurban migration brought about a 2.7% decline in metropolitan population during the 1970s. To counteract the effects of this population shift, the city began a series of bond issues for physical improvements in 1955 and an effort to attract federal funding that has produced significant interstate highway projects.

The city nevertheless remains the principal industrial hub of the Mississippi basin. It is second only to DETROIT in automobile manufacture, is the headquarters of aerospace industries, the home of the world's largest beer brewer, Anheuser-Busch, and the location of numerous food processing plants and textile manufacturers of national importance. It is also the largest inland freight port in the U.S., and the second largest rail center in the country.

St. Louis is the home of WASHINGTON UNIVERSITY, a branch of the University of MISSOURI, and ST. LOUIS UNIVERSITY.

Its principal cultural facilities include the St. Louis Art Museum, the Museum of Science and Natural History, the ST. LOUIS SYMPHONY and St. Louis Opera Theatre. Among the most recent signs of progress, St. Louis has transformed its enormous railroad station into a hotel-shopping center complex which has been praised as one of the finest of its type. There is also a vast modern downtown mall connected to two major department stores, and much additional modernization has helped to maintain civic interest.

The JEFFERSON NATIONAL EXPANSION MEMORIAL with Eero Saarinen's soaring GATEWAY ARCH is the focal point of the huge riverfront area, the west end of Eads Bridge, Laclede's Landing, several dining, dancing and excursion boats, the

Old Courthouse, the Old Cathedral, St. Louis Sports Hall of Fame, the National Bowling Hall of Fame and Museum, St. Louis Cathedral and many other points of interest. Vast Busch Stadium is located near the riverfront.

SAINT MARY'S COLLEGE. Roseland, Indiana, Roman Catholic institution of higher learning for girls. St. Mary's was founded in 1855 as a result of a request from Father Edward SORIN, president and founder of NOTRE DAME. Sister Angela (Eliza Maria Gillespie) led twenty-five nuns from the Bertrand Mission in Bertrand, Michigan, to the present site to form an academy. During the 1985-1986 academic year, St. Mary's enrolled 1,770 students and had 172 faculty members.

SAINT MARYS RIVER (Michigan). International boundary waterway between Lake SUPERIOR and Lake HURON which flows past SAULT STE. MARIE. Because it provides the only water route between Lake Superior, with its wealthy region of minerals and crops, and the lower GREAT LAKES and then through the ST. LAWRENCE SEAWAY to the sea, the St. Marys is considered one of the world's most strategic waterways. Technically, it should be called a strait rather than a river. It has been made navigable between the lakes by the SOO CANAL.

SAINT MARY'S RIVER (Ohio-Indiana). The source of the St. Marys is found near the Ohio town of the same name. It flows north then northwest, crossing the Ohio-Indiana border near Decatur, Indiana. It turns almost directly north to FORT WAYNE, where it joins the ST. JOSEPH to form the MAUMEE, which then flows almost directly eastward, then northeast, to empty into Lake ERIE at TOLEDO.

SAINT OLAF COLLEGE. Privately supported liberal arts college established in NORTH-FIELD, Minnesota, in 1874 and affiliated with the Evangelical Lutheran Church in America. Located on a three-hundred-acre campus with thirty buildings. Approximately sixty percent of the students participate in the overseas programs available through the college. Saint Olaf offers preparation for the Minnesota teaching certificate. Tutoring programs for all students are available. Foreign language and religion classes are required. It is particularly well-known for its music program. During the 1985-1986 academic year Saint Olaf enrolled 3,029 students and had 318 faculty members.

SAINT PAUL, MINNESOTA

Name: For the Christian Apostle Paul "the apostle of nations."

Nickname: Along with Minneapolis, the two are known as the "Twin cities."

Area: 55.4 square miles

Elevation: 687 feet

Population:
1984: 265,903
Rank: 57
Percent change (1980-1984): minus 1.6%
Density (city): 4,800 per sq. mi.
Metropolitan Population: 2,114,256
Percent change (1980-1984): 1%

Racial and Ethnic Makeup (1980):
White: 90%
Black: 5%
Hispanic origin: 7,864 persons
Indian: 2,538 persons
Asian: 5,345 persons
Other: 3,514 persons

Age:
18 and under: 24.1%
65 and over: 15%

TV Stations: 5

Radio Stations: 36

Hospitals: 14

Sports Teams:
Minnesota Twins (baseball)
Minnesota Vikings (football)
Minnesota North Stars (hockey)

Further Information: Chamber of Commerce, 701 North Central Tower, 445 Minnesota Street, Saint Paul, MN 55101

SAINT PAUL, Minnesota. City, capital of Minnesota and seat of Ramsey County, lies on the bluffs of the MISSISSIPPI RIVER, contiguous with MINNEAPOLIS, with which it is generally linked as the Twin Cities. St. Paul lies at a great bend of the river, at the head of navigation, point of debarkation for river traffic and a rail center. The city covers 52.4 square miles in area.

Neighboring communities on the south are South St. Paul and West St. Paul. To the north

Saint Paul

are the suburbs of Maplewood, which pulls its narrow boundaries also along most of the city's west boundary, North St. Paul, and Roseville.

The substantial riverfront and the location of the city have brought massive infusions of industry. Manufacturing includes the largest calendar factory in the world. Along with Minneapolis, St. Paul ranks among the national leaders in electronics and computers. It also is a leader in tape and abrasives production, steel and iron items, chemicals, paper, and furniture. Because of its access to farm products, the city is a center of food processing and brewing.

The city had an unprepossesing beginning in 1838 when Pierre Parrant, nicknamed PIG'S EYE, sold whiskey from a cabin he had built on the present site of St. Paul. First named Pig's Eye, the community was saved from that name by the establishment of a log cabin chapel there in 1841 by Father Lucian Galtier. He dedicated the chapel to St. Paul, and the settlement changed its name.

The village's first store opened in 1842, and a year later an observer wrote, "It [the town] had but three or four log houses, with a population not to exceed twelve white people, and was a mixture of forests, hills, running brooks, ravines, bog mires, lakes, whiskey, mosquitos, snakes, and Indians."

With the coming of the first steamboat in 1823, river traffic accelerated in the region. However, nearby FORT SNELLING and the community of MENDOTA preceded St. Paul as a business center. St. Paul was platted in 1846 and was made the capital of Minnesota Territory in 1849. When Minnesota was admitted as a state in 1858, St. Paul was named the state capital.

The coming of the first railroad in 1862 brought a boom to the area, and the city became headquarters for the railroad empire of James J. HILL (1838-1916). Large numbers of Irish and German Roman Catholics were attracted to the community. Bishop John Ireland came to St. Paul in 1852. Long the beloved leader of the Catholic community, Bishop Ireland's most notable achievement was the building of the great Cathedral of St. Paul.

During this period there was much rivalry between Minneapolis and St. Paul. Census takers were kidnapped to keep one town from outpacing the other in population.

The great new capitol was dedicated in 1905.

In the period between the 1970 census and the count in 1984, the population of St. Paul dropped from 310,000 to 266,000, making it 54th in rank among U.S. cities. It ranks eighth in population among major Midwest cities.

For tourists, one of the principal attractions is the great capitol, designed by famed architect Cass GILBERT (1859-1934). It boasts the world's largest unsupported marble dome, rising to a height of 223 feet. The architect used St. Peters Cathedral in Rome as his model. Over the massive front portico looms a Daniel Chester French sculpture, the dashing gold-leafed chariot of Prosperity, drawn by four horses. French also was the sculptor of the six statues of the virtues above the door. Light shines through the great glass mosaic Star of the North, dramatically placed under the ceiling of the dome.

In addition to the capitol and the Cathedral, one of the most notable buildings is the massive nineteen-story City Hall. Its four-story-high lobby is dominated by the mammoth statue of an Indian by renowned sculptor Carl Milles. This sculpture is considered to represent the god of peace and is known as the Peace Memorial Statue.

The State Historical Society is the oldest organization in the state, and its museum holds a fascinating collection of the region's past. Seven of the city's cultural institutions are grouped at the modern Civic Arts and Science Center. These include the Science Museum, Theatre Guild, Theatre Saint Paul, School and Gallery of Art, Schubert Club, Civic Opera, and Council of Arts and Sciences.

Como park is the site of the city's notable zoo. Indian Mounds Park is another interesting city feature, showing the work of prehistoric peoples of the area. The Capital Centre Redevelopment Project houses one of the world's major indoor shopping areas, covering eight blocks in the heart of the city.

One of the nation's ten most notable annual festivals is St. Paul's Winter Carnival. Its gigantic palace of ice and the widest variety of winter activities make this perhaps the leading winter event in the U.S.

Another annual event is the state fair, housed at the Midway district between the Twin Cities.

St. Paul is home to many notable institutions of higher education, including the College of ST. THOMAS, Hamline University, MACALESTER COLLEGE, College of St. Catherine, William Mitchell College of Law, and several well-known theological seminaries.

Nearby Mendota is the home of one of the state's most notable personalities, Governor H. H. SIBLEY (1811-1891). It was the state's first stone dwelling. The governor used the top floor as a dormitory for his many Indian friends as they passed through the area. Mendota is considered the first permanent European settlement in the state.

SAINT PETER, Minnesota. City (pop. 9,056), south-central Minnesota, east of NEW ULM and north of MANKATO in Le Sueur County, located on the MISSISSIPPI, founded in 1853 by Captain William B. Dodd, builder of the first section of the military road near Traverse des Sioux to MENDOTA. It has been home to five state governors and is the location of GUSTAVUS ADOLPHUS COLLEGE. The city received its name from the MINNESOTA RIVER, which during the 1700s was called Riviere St. Pierre by the French and the St. Peter River by the British. The river's name was changed to the Minnesota in 1852. Belief that Minnesota would be a horizontal state caused many early settlers to think about moving the state capital from ST. PAUL to the more centrally located St. Peter. Land was quickly donated and a bill to move the capital passed both the House and Senate. A man named Joseph Rolette stole the bill and hid with it in a hotel room until the constitutional time limit was passed and St. Peter lost out on its bid. While never directly attacked in the Sioux Uprising, St. Peter was on the edge of a battle in which 500 whites were killed.

SAINT THOMAS COLLEGE. Privately supported Roman Catholic liberal arts college for men in ST. PAUL, Minnesota. Established in 1885, the school granted its first bachelor's degree in 1910. It is accredited by the North Central Association of Colleges and Schools and the American Chemical Society. A coeducational graduate program was added in 1950. The campus occupies forty-five acres. Thirteen buildings include dormitory facilities for 570 men. A three-year pre-engineering program is available for students who will transfer to NOTRE DAME for their senior year. During the 1985-1986 academic year the school enrolled 6,775 students and had 392 faculty members.

SAINTE GENEVIEVE, Missouri. City (pop. 4,481), eastern Missouri on the MISSISSIPPI RIVER, south of ST. LOUIS in Sainte Genevieve County. Sainte Genevieve was the first permanent European settlement in Missouri. It was established in the 18th century when Frenchmen began mining lead in the area. A great flood in 1785 caused the residents to move the town to high ground and it prospered as the chief rival of St. Louis. There are many points of interest in such an historic setting. Bolduc

House, built around 1770, preserves a French home made with heavy upright oak logs. Amoureaux House, constructed in about the same period, is one of the oldest examples of French Creole architecture in existence and is restored with period furniture. The Felix Valle Home State Historic Site is the restored and furnished Federal-style home of one of the area's many fur traders. Demonstrations of colonial crafts and cooking may be seen at the Ribault Living History Museum. A unique triangular fireplace opening into three rooms may be seen in the Green Tree Tavern, used as an inn and tavern soon after the Louisiana Purchase. An annual event is the Jour de Fete a Ste. Genevieve, a tour of historic homes on the second weekend in August.

SANDBURG, Carl. (Galesburg, IL, Jan. 6, 1878—Flat Rock, NC, July 22, 1967). Poet and folklorist. From the age of eleven, Sandburg combined school with work at various jobs in GALESBURG, helping his Swedish immigrant blacksmith father. He saw service in Puerto Rico during the SPANISH AMERICAN WAR. Continuing a combination of work and schooling he graduated from Galesburg's Lombard College in 1902. Heeding the call of the road he became a hobo, sometimes working on newspaper jobs. He recruited for the Social-Democratic party in Wisconsin and became the secretary of Milwaukee's Socialist mayor from 1910 to 1912. Between 1913 and the late 1920s he worked for Chicago newspapers and became feature editor of the Chicago *Daily News* in 1919. His poetry had been published since 1904 but attracted little attention until Chicago's famed *Poetry Magazine*, edited by Harriet MONROE (1860-1936), began to publish his work in 1914. His fame spread with his often quoted "Fog" (1914). Lasting attention came to him with the 1916 publication of his first book, *Chicago Poems*. By 1918 he had won the PULITZER PRIZE for *Cornhuskers*. The success of his Pulitzer Prize biography, *Abraham Lincoln*, six volumes, (1926-1939), allowed him to leave journalism and concentrate on literature. The last volume of that series won another Pulitzer Prize in 1940. Among his best-known poems is "Chicago," published in 1914, which portrayed the brutality he saw in American cities, while paying tribute to the power and energy of modern industry. In *The American Songbag* he presented many ballads and folk songs collected after 1920. Protesting against war, Sandburg wrote, "Grass" in 1918 and "A.E.F." in 1920. His *Complete Poems*, published in 1950, won his third Pulitzer Prize, this for poetry (1951). *Rootabaga Stories, Rootabaga Pigeons,* and *Potato Face* were three volumes of humorous stories Sandburg wrote for children (1922, 1923 and 1930). Although he has been compared to Walt Whitman, Sandburg had a deeper appreciation of the land and its people, gained through his wide travel and depth of experience. He knew the language of the people and used it in his works, in expression ranging from the fragile to the crude. He brought new insight into the life and world of everyday people, and the common things of life. He believed unswervingly in the people's wisdom, and his work provides a sensitive reflection of that belief.

SANDUSKY BAY. The outlet of the Sandusky River in central Ohio, Sandusky Bay is one of the finest harbors on lake ERIE. This body of water is almost landlocked by the protective arms of the Cedar Point and Marblehead peninsulas. It extends inland for eighteen miles and is bridged at its narrowest point. A map published in Amsterdam in 1720 showed a body of water called Lac Sundouske, the present Sandusky Bay.

SANDUSKY, Ohio. City, (pop. 31,360), seat of Erie County, situated on Lake ERIE, in north central Ohio, it occupies a flat slope facing SANDUSKY BAY, where it stretches for six and a half miles. The name was taken from the Wyandotte Indians' "ot-san-doos-tee," which means "at the cold water," referring to the cold springs of the area. Sandusky is the second largest coal shipping port on the GREAT LAKES. Salt, gravel and sand are also extensively shipped. Before pollution damaged the fishing industry of the Great Lakes, the port was one of the major fishing ports, and with the restoration of the lakes, the fishing industry has revived. The Wyandotte and OTTAWA Indians occupied the area for generations. English trader George CROGHAN (1720?-1782) found them there in 1760. The first permanent white settlement was made in 1816. The almost perfect harbor made a natural place for shipping, and the port annually received hundreds of boatloads of products and settlers from both the east and north. Almost every vessel which sailed the Great Lakes stopped at Sandusky. On a single day as many as 285 grain wagons arrived to be loaded on ships at the port, which at one time was one of the leading grain ports of the nation. Sandusky lost out as terminus of the OHIO AND ERIE CANAL, but the

RAILROADS soon arrived. Then in June, 1849, cholera struck, killing more than 400, and half the people fled the city. The city was an important station on the UNDERGROUND RAILROAD before the CIVIL WAR. Fishing developed until 10,000,000 pounds of fish were shipped in a year. Wine making became an important industry. Tourism became another leading enterprise, when resorts began to spring up in the 1880s. Cedar Point is a tourist and recreational attraction, with an amusement park, marina, resort hotel and other features. Boat trips to KELLEYS ISLAND and across the lake to Ontario are popular. Battery Park features a wave-action swimming pool. An unusual natural feature is Blue Hole, an artesian spring ninety feet across, with a sixty-foot depth of clear water.

SANFORD, Maria L. (Old Saybrook, CT, Dec. 19, 1836—Minneapolis, MN, April 21, 1920). Educator. Sanford gained fame as the first American woman to be named as a full professor. Sanford served as a professor of rhetoric and elocution at the University of MINNESOTA from 1880 until 1909. Prior to her appointment to the staff, Sanford had served on the history staff at Swarthmore College in Pennsylvania from 1871 to 1880. She is credited with being one of the most effective instructors in developing a love of literature.

SANGAMON RIVER. Illinois river. The Sangamon flows westward from its source northeast of DECATUR, Illinois, to its mouth at the ILLINOIS RIVER near Browning. The Sangamon forms the border between Menard and Mason counties and flows through Decatur and SPRINGFIELD, Illinois. Abraham LINCOLN's first Illinois home was near Decatur on the Sangamon at a place now preserved as the LINCOLN TRAIL HOMESTEAD PARK. Hopes that the Sangamon would become an important avenue of commerce led to the founding of the town of NEW SALEM. It soon became clear that the river was not deep enough for steamboats and the town was deserted.

SANITARY AND SHIP CANAL. Illinois engineering project. When it was completed in 1900, the work was acclaimed as one of the greatest engineering accomplishments of all time. The project was started when it was realized that sewage from CHICAGO, dumped into the CHICAGO RIVER, was flowing into Lake MICHIGAN near where the city was pumping out its drinking water. To correct the problem, the

South Branch of the Chicago River was deepened so that the water would flow south instead of north and east into the GREAT LAKES. A canal was dug between the Chicago and DES PLAINES rivers and locks installed so that canal boats could travel from one level to another. Locks were also placed at the mouth of the Chicago River to keep Lake Michigan from flowing too rapidly into the river. The canal completed an all water route from the Great Lakes to the Gulf of Mexico and reversed the flow of the Chicago River.

SANTA CLAUS, Indiana. Town (pop. 514), southwest Indiana town in Spencer Coounty, Indiana community platted in 1846. In naming the town, the name of Santa Fe was ruled out because it had been used. As a joke the name of Santa Claus was suggested in 1852 and adopted because it was the Christmas season. Every year thousands of parcels are mailed through Santa Claus to receive its postmark, and more thousands of letters are mailed to the town by children hoping to reach Santa himself, all totalling over a million pieces of mail. Holiday World is a forty-seven acre amusement park featuring Santa Claus Land and other holiday theme areas. Many antique musical instruments are displayed at the House of Mechanical Music Machines at Holly Plaza.

SANTA FE TRAIL. Important route leading from Missouri to New Mexico. The trail was established by the successful commercial venture of William BECKNELL (1796-1865) and a small party of traders who left Franklin, Missouri, in 1821 for the overland trip. From 1822 to the beginning of the CIVIL WAR the Santa Fe Trail was the principal route to the Southwest. Hunters, trappers, and traders traveled the route which, in 1860, saw as many as 3,000 wagons and 9,000 men involved in some form of trade that had an estimated value of $5,000,000. The trail's usefulness ended with the construction of the Atchison, Topeka, and Santa Fe Railroad, between 1868 and 1880.

SAPPINGTON, John. (MD, May 15, 1776—Saline County, MO, Sept. 7, 1856). Physician. Sappington experimented with the use of quinine without the use of bleeding, purging, or vomiting in the treatment of malaria, a common disease on the frontier. Confident in the use of quinine, Sappington began the distribution of Dr. John Sappington's Fever Pills in 1832. His treatment became the standard worldwide. He may also have written the first medical paper produced west of the MISSISSIPPI RIVER. This was entitled *Theory and Treatment of Fevers* (1844).

SAUK CENTRE, Minnesota. Town (pop. 3,709), central Minnesota on the Sauk River; southeast of Alexandria; at the southern end of Big Sauk Lake. Sauk Centre received its name because it was considered the center point between Lake Osakis and Sauk Rapids. Like its neighbor Melrose, Sauk Centre developed near a ford in a river. The town's principal fame came with the birth there of Nobelist Sinclair LEWIS (1885-1951). His 1920 novel, *Main Street* "looked beneath the charm and innocence of life in a small town (Gopher Prairie) like Sauk Center." Many of Sauk Center's residents took the publication of Lewis' book personally and the author was disowned for a time. Attitudes changed after 1930 when Lewis became the first American to win the NOBEL PRIZE for literature. Sauk Center now has a street and center named for Lewis. His boyhood home has been restored and furnished with period furniture. Sinclair Lewis Intrepretative Center features the author. Annually from July 12 to 15 residents participate in Sinclair Lewis Days which includes a golf tournament, canoe race and fishing contests.

SAUK INDIANS. Algonquian tribe (later Sac) whose resistance to removal from their homes in Illinois was known as the BLACK HAWK WAR (1832). The name Sauk, or Sac, is the shortened form of Osakiwug, which was the tribe's name for itself meaning "yellow earth." Culturally and linguistically the Sauk are related to the KICKAPOO and FOX.

The Sauk tribe had two divisions, Oskukh and Kishko, black and white. These two divisions were subdivided into twelve clans. Each person inherited the clan of his father. Members of clans were forbidden to marry within the clan. The tribe was governed by a council of hereditary civil chiefs. The Sauk believed in many deities, of which Wisaka, the founder of the Medicine Dance, was the most important. Other Sauk spirits included the Earth Spirit, the South Wind, and Fire.

The Sauk believed that a dead person's soul followed the Milky Way and, if quick enough, crossed the river on a log and reached the land of the dead. Mourners painted their faces with charcoal. A dead chief's face was painted green.

The Sauk had summer and winter villages. Lodges were made with poles covered with bark and were from forty to sixty feet long.

The earliest Sauk were expelled by the OJIBWAY from their home in eastern Michigan around Saginaw Bay. They settled near GREEN BAY, Wisconsin, where they were visited by French missionaries and explorers in 1667. The men hunted otter, raccoon, beaver, deer, buffalo, muskrat and mink. Sauk men used bow and arrows, spears or lances, and war clubs.

Women cared for the corn fields, along with gardens of melons, pumpkins, beans and squash. Women also gathered berries, nuts, wild rice and maple sugar. Surplus food, after the harvest, was sold to traders or dried, wrapped in bark containers and placed in pits carefully concealed with sod.

The Sauk then migrated to their winter homes which were always close to good hunting grounds. Winter lodges were smaller and more snug than summer ones and were covered with tightly woven reed mats and lined with skins and more mats.

In 1773 the MENOMINEE, Ojibway and French pushed the Sauk and Fox southward where they settled on the banks of the MISSISSIPPI RIVER on lands formerly controlled by the ILLINI. Culturally the tribe remained one based on hunting and cultivating extensive fields of corn.

In 1804 one band of the Sauk ceded the Illinois lands to the United States. The rest of the tribe refused to leave. Pressure from the whites brought on the Black Hawk War. After their defeat in that war, the Sauk and Fox gradually took over the lands of the Sioux in Iowa, but in 1842 ceded these to the United States and accepted a reservation in Kansas. By an 1867 treaty the Sauk were moved to Indian Territory. In the late 1970s the Sauk and Fox tribe of Oklahoma controlled about 800 acres of tribally owned land and governed themselves through a business committee.

SAULT (Soo) SAINTE MARIE, Michigan. City (pop.14,448), seat of Chippewa County, northeastern corner of Michigan's UPPER PENINSULA on the south shore of the ST. MARY'S RIVER, named for the rapids between Lakes HURON and SUPERIOR which were christened in 1641 by Fathers Isaac JOGUES (1607-1646) and Charles Raymbault. Sault Ste. Marie was once described by Henry Clay as the "remotest settlement in the United States, if not in the moon."

It is today the only port of entry between the United States and Canada for a three-hundred-mile stretch of the border. Sault Ste. Marie was the first permanent settlement in Michigan and is the third-oldest surviving U.S. settlement.

The first European to find the site was probably Etienne BRULE (1592?-1632?) who was sent by Samuel de CHAMPLAIN (1567?-1635) to find a Northwest Passage, and landed at "The Soo" in 1618. He named it Sault de Gaston in honor of the King of France, Louis XIII. Other prominent travelers such as Jean NICOLET (1598-1642), Pierre-Esprit RADISSON (1637?-1710?), and Medart de GROSSEILLIERS (1618?-1690) journeyed through the area. The Jesuits in 1668 constructed a mission at Sault Ste. Marie which became the center for the work of Father Jacques MARQUETTE (1637-1675). Sault Ste. Marie was chosen as the site of the PAGEANT OF THE SAULT" by which the French claimed North America in 1671 while impressing the Indians with their fancy clothes and military might.

The Soo continued under French control until 1762, the same year the French fort, Repentigny, was destroyed by fire, and the British took over after the French and Indian War in 1763.

The Treaty of Paris after the Revolution ceded all the lands south of the GREAT LAKES to the United States, but the British continued to trade in the region and refused to leave. In 1820 Michigan Governor Lewis CASS (1782-1866) recklessly carried the American flag into the British region and, though narrowly avoiding a massacre by pro-British Indians, claimed the land for the United States. The construction of Fort Brady in 1823 ended the British influence in the region.

Sault Ste. Marie in 1850 had a population of nearly 500. Cardboard tokens passed as money. In 1855 the State of Michigan, with a land grant from Congress, built a canal and lock at the Soo. The canal was not appreciated by those who earned a living portaging freight around the rapids. When an embankment broke several years later only sailor volunteers worked to repair the damage. The Weitzel Lock was finished in 1881, the year the federal government took over control of the locks.

By the end of the nineteenth century, the population of Sault Ste. Marie had risen to 10,000. The increase in new industry provided work that kept the young people from migrating to the large industrial communities. Rapid growth in population occurred during the 1930s.

It is believed that during WORLD WAR II the Sault Ste. Marie area was the most heavily guarded location in the United States because of the importance of the canal. Today four locks on the United States side and one lock on the Canadian side of the SOO CANAL bypass the twenty-two foot drop of the rapids in the course of the St. Marys River from Lake Superior to Lake Huron. The Soo locks annually handle over ninety-five million tons of freight and are known as the world's busiest.

SAWTEETH MOUNTAINS. Notable highland region just beyond the north shore of Lake SUPERIOR and running parallel to it from Beaver Bay to Grand Marais. The mountains have an abrupt elevation of from five hundred to nine hundred feet above the lake level.

SCARLET FEVER. Indiana physicians George Frederick Dick and his wife, Gladys Dick, were pioneers in the investigation of infections caused by streptococcal germs. They injected minute amounts of scarlet fever toxin into a horse's blood and developed an antitoxin from the animal's blood serum. The Dicks also developed a skin test to indicate sensivity to scarlet fever.

SCHOLTE, Henrik Peter. (Amsterdam, Netherlands, Sept. 25, 1805—Pella, IA, 1868). Dynamic preacher and community developer. Scholte was the spiritual Dominie and temporal leader of a group of wealthy Dutch immigrants to Iowa. When Dominie Scholte and his wife left Holland in 1847, he told his wife he would build her a home in America similar to the lovely one they were leaving and furnish it with their own household goods, shipped across the Atlantic. The settlers bought 18,000 acres of Iowa land, paying for it in gold, and under Scholte's leadership settled the community of PELLA in 1847. One year after he had arrived in Pella, Scholte presented his wife with the handsome home he had promised her, complete with all of their furnishings, except for some more fragile items broken in the long journey from Holland. They made their pioneer Iowa home a center of culture, and he continued to preach vigorous sermons, write and lecture prodigiously and edit Pella's first newspaper. Unlike most of the other staid Dutch women of the group, Mrs. Scholte dressed in the latest Paris fashion and was a talented musician. The Scholtes were the revered principal citizens of Pella until their deaths. Their home has been preserved at Pella as a museum.

SCHOOL OF THE OZARKS. Presbyterian sponsored institution located at Point Lookout, Missouri. It was founded through the efforts of Reverend James Forsyth in 1907 and began with an enrollment of thirty-five students. Many of the present buildings were gifts of

wealthy Missourians. Education at the school began as grade school work only, but, because no high school existed in the adjoining counties, high school work was added in 1915, and college level work soon followed. During the 1985-1986 academic year the college enrolled 1,198 students and had 98 faculty members.

SCHOOLCRAFT LAKE. Small Minnesota lake discovered by Henry SCHOOLCRAFT (1793-1864) in 1832, source of the smaller branch of the upper Mississippi River.

SCHOOLCRAFT, Henry Rowe. (Albany County, NY, Mar. 28, 1793—Washington, DC, December 10, 1864). Explorer, scientist. Schoolcraft, in his day one of the greatest authorities on Indians, discovered Lake ITASCA, the source of the mighty MISSISSIPPI RIVER. This discovery occurred in 1832 while Schoolcraft was on a mission as Indian agent in the Northwest to make peace between the CHIPPEWA and SIOUX Indians. Schoolcraft served as the superintendent of Indian affairs for Michigan from 1836 to 1841 and negotiated several treaties with the Chippewa including one which gave the United States parts of Michigan. Schoolcraft was also responsible for much of the future development of the mineral wealth of the region. As a geologist, Schoolcraft accompanied the expedition in 1820 of Governor Lewis CASS (1782-1866) which established many of the mineral sources. Schoolcraft also collected Indian legends. One told of the formation of SLEEPING BEAR sand dune. Longfellow's "Hiawatha" was based on Schoolcraft's book entitled *Indian Tales.* He produced a six-part work *Historical and Statistical Information Respecting the History, Condition and Prospects of the Indian Tribes of the United States* (1851-1857). This series contained the famed illustrations from paintings by Seth Eastman.

SCHURZ, Carl. (Cologne, Germany, Mar. 2, 1829—New York, NY, May 14, 1906). Politician. Involved in the German uprisings of 1848, he came to the U.S. in 1852 and practiced law in Wisconsin where he became interested in the REPUBLICAN PARTY and supported the Abolitionist cause. During the CIVIL WAR, he commanded a battalion at First Bull Run. Schurz joined the Republican Party and was a devoted supporter of Abraham LINCOLN (1809-1865), who appointed him minister to Spain (1861-62). After the war, President Andrew Johnson asked him to tour the South. In his report Schurz recommended suffrage for the former slaves and promoted civil rights policies, but the report was not accepted by the president. He became a political journalist in ST. LOUIS, Missouri, and was elected as a Republican U.S. Senator from that state (1869-1875). He outspokenlly criticized the corruption of Ulysses S. Grant's administration, opposed the annexation of Santo Domingo and promoted merit-based civil service. President Rutherford B. HAYES (1822-1893) appointed him Secretary of the Interior (1877-1881). In that post he continued to promote merit civil service and was an enlightened administrator of Indian affairs. For the rest of his life he continued his political and editorial activities.

SCIOTO RIVER. Rising west of Kenton, in west central Ohio, the Scioto flows north, then east, passing Kenton. Turning south it passes the state capital of COLUMBUS, past CIRCLEVILLE and CHILLICOTHE to empty into the OHIO RIVER at PORTSMOUTH, 237 miles from its source. Even before portions of the river were developed as a section of the OHIO AND ERIE CANAL, the river was an important shipping artery for Ohio produce.

SEABORG, Glenn Theodore. (Ishpeming, MI, 1912—). Chemist. In 1939 he became an instructor at the University of California at Berkeley. During WORLD WAR II he went to Chicago as one of the principal figures in the development of the atomic bomb in its initial phases at the University of CHICAGO. Returning to Berkeley he became chancellor of the university in 1958. In 1961 President John S. Kennedy asked him to serve as head of the Atomic Energy Commission, a post he retained until 1971. Seaborg was the first scientist to head the AEC. He represented the U.S. at atomic and other scientific conferences, and served on numerous scientific and educational boards. Upon leaving the AEC, returned to the University of California at Berkeley. He shared the 1951 NOBEL PRIZE in chemistry. He is the discoverer of nine elements, an unique achievement for which he received the Enrico Fermi award in 1959.

SEABURY-WESTERN THEOLOGICAL SEMINARY. Privately supported graduate theological seminary in EVANSTON, Illinois. Founded in 1858 as Saint Columba's Mission in Faribault, Minnesota, the theological school also has been known as the Seabury Divinity School. In 1933 Seabury merged with Western Theological Seminary in Evanston. The seminary, under the control of the Episcopal Church, recently enrolled sixty-six students and maintains a faculty of thirteen. The school lies on most of a city block adjacent to the campus of NORTHWESTERN UNIVERSITY.

SEARS TOWER. Tallest building in the world, located in CHICAGO, Illinois. The Sears Tower is exceeded in floor space only by the Pentagon in Washington D.C. The tower has 110 stories, 102 elevators, a cafeteria which occupies two-thirds of an acre and can seat 1,700, and a parking garage for 150 cars. When topped out in 1973, the Tower was meant to house all the office personnel of Sears, Roebuck headquarters. Sears now occupies more than half the Tower with tenants on the other floors.

SEDALIA, Missouri. City (pop. 22,847), seat of Pettis County, in west central Missouri. The city was founded by George R. Smith in 1857, who named it after his daughter. Situated on the Missouri Pacific Railroad, it was used as a federal military post during the CIVIL WAR. Sedalia was incorporated in 1864, and was an important railhead for the Texas cattle drives of 1866. Today the city is a distribution and shipping point for agricultural products, and a diversified manufacturer of glass, textiles, shoes, and housewares. Sedalia has become known as the birthplace of ragtime music. At the turn of the century composer Scott Joplin lived in and studied music in Sedalia and wrote the "Maple Leaf Rag," considered to be the music that launched the ragtime era. The Sedalia Ragtime Archives honors Joplin and ragtime music with memorabilia and piano rolls from the Maple Leaf Club, a local saloon in the late 1800s that catered to railroad men. Exhibits trace the history of Joplin from childhood through his mental decline and to his tragic end in the Manhattan (New York) State Hospital. Sedalia is the home of the Missouri State Fair held annually in August since 1901.

SELBY, Joseph. (—1855?) Joseph Selby was a slave who died in Ohio on the UNDERGROUND RAILROAD. Song writer Benjamin HANBY (1833-1867) was very much interested in the stories of the slaves who came through his father's station on one of the most important routes on the railroad. In 1855, while studying for the ministry, Hanby heard the story of Joe Selby and his desperate flight trying to escape to Canada where he hoped to earn enough money to buy freedom for his sweetheart, Nellie Gray. Hanby wrote a song about the situation, calling it "Darling Nellie Gray" (1861). Before long the entire North was singing the song about Selby and his sweetheart.

SELFRIDGE, Harry Gordon. (Ripon, WI, Jan. 11, 1864—London, England, May 8, 1947). Merchant. Selfridge became a partner in the Marshall Field Company and manager of the retail store in CHICAGO before selling out his interest and retiring in 1904. With several partners he bought the firm of Schlesinger and Mayer and changed the name to H. G. Selfridge and Company. This store was sold to Carson, Pirie, Scott and Company of Chicago in August of 1904. Selfridge traveled to London in 1906 and organized Selfridge and Company Ltd., wholesale and retail merchants, and built one of the largest stores in Europe. He became a naturalized British citizen on June 1, 1937.

SERPENT MOUND. One of the unique EFFIGY MOUNDS built by prehistoric peoples is the almost perfectly preserved Serpent Mound in Adams County, Ohio. This gigantic snake effigy writhes in seven great loops for a total length of more than a quarter of a mile. The mouth seems to be in the act of swallowing a giant egg. The area is now Serpent Mound State Park.

SETTLEMENT. French traders and missionaries were responsible for the first settlements by Europeans in the Midwest. The first permanent European settlement in what is now the Midwest was founded in 1668 at the Soo (SAULT STE. MARIE) in present upper Michigan. CAHOKIA, Illinois, was founded by the French in 1699 and FORT WAYNE in Indiana probably a year later. St. Francis Xavier in present Missouri was founded in 1700 on the site of present ST. LOUIS but did not prove to be permanent. STE. GENEVIEVE, first permanent European settlement in Missouri was founded in 1735. ST. LOUIS was not permanently founded until 1764.

Wisconsin did not have a permanent European settlement until GREEN BAY was founded in 1764. By this time the whole region had changed from French to English hands. The French had not encouraged many permanent settlers in the region. They preferred to keep it as a wilderness to support the vast fur trade of the area. After the English took control, King George III issued the Proclamation of 1763, which forbade settlement west of the Alleghenies, keeping the region as a sanctuary for the Indians and also preserving the wilderness areas for the profitable fur trade.

However, settlers disregarded this law, and, pushed westward by population pressures in the East, they settled in the West. By the time the American Revolution was over, the Midwest was ripe for settlement. At first, this was most easily accomplished by taking whatever means

Spectacular Serpent Mound, Adams County, Ohio.

of travel was available to the OHIO RIVER and floating down the river on flatboats. Thousands followed this course, the first being the founders of MARIETTA, Ohio, in 1788. That same year another group founded CINCINNATI.

DETROIT, Michigan, founded in 1701, is the oldest major city in the Midwest. Most of the others were slow in gaining stature. Not until 1825, when the Erie Canal enabled settlers and commerce to enter the GREAT LAKES by an easy water route, did the sleepy village of CHICAGO begin to grow. It was not incorporated as a city until 1837, with a population then of only 4,000. Iowa and Minnesota were the last states of the Midwest to experience a large influx of settlers.

Although, with the establishment of FORT SNELLING in 1824, MINNEAPOLIS had begun to grow, Minnesota was still mostly unsettled during the time of the CIVIL WAR when the last of the Indian troubles in the state was settled. From that time onward, the entire Midwest was available for the rush of settlement which followed.

SHAEFFER, W.A. (Bloomfield, IA, July 27, 1867—Fort Madison, IA, June, 19, 1946). Inventor, manufacturer. As a jewelry store operater at FORT MADISON, Shaeffer toyed with the idea of a better writing instrument. He devised a means of pulling ink into a rubber container in the handle of the pen, using a lever and suction. This ink was then delivered in a continuous flow to the pen point. This relatively simple 1912 invention revolutionized writing and resulted in the founding of the Shaeffer factory, for its manufacture. The pens have carried the Shaeffer name around the world. One of the largest of its kind, the business has been continued by three generations of Shaeffers, who have managed to keep pace with modern developments in writing instruments of all kinds. The company is known for its profit-sharing and other employee considerations.

SHAW, Henry. (Sheffield, England, July 24, 1800—St. Louis, MO, Aug. 25, 1889). Founder of the Missouri Botanical Garden. Shaw was a retired businessman when he established the Garden in ST. LOUIS in 1857. The original purpose of the Garden was the systematic study of plants, but it was opened to the public around 1860. Shaw left a trust for the maintenance of the Garden and established one of the nation's finest botanical libraries. He endowed the Henry Shaw School of Botany at WASHINGTON UNIVERSITY in St. Louis.

SHAWNEE INDIANS. Of the Algonquian language group, they are thought to have originated in what is now Ohio. The Shawnee were constantly migrating to the South, to the East and then back to the Midwest. Because of their wanderings, they were known as the "Bedouins...of the North American tribes." In the mid-1600s the tribe was attacked by the Cherokee Indians and divided, but finally reunited, again in Ohio, about a century later. Constantly at war with the settlers, they joined in the Creek and Cherokee wars. They were forced by the Treaty of GREEN VILLE (1794) to give up their lands in Ohio and move to Indiana. In the early 1800s, Chief TECUMSEH (1768-1813) and his brother Tenskwatawa (The PROPHET, 1770-1834) tried to form an alliance of the Shawnee and many other tribes and bring about an uprising. William Henry HARRISON (1773-1841) destroyed their principal village at the mouth of the Tippecanoe River, in the Battle of TIPPECANOE (Nov. 7, 1811), crushing Tecumseh's attempt to drive out the white man forever. The tribe was moved to various sites in the West, finally settling on a reservation in Oklahoma.

SHAWNEE NATIONAL FOREST. Reserve in Illinois stretching from the OHIO RIVER across much of extreme southern Illinois to the MISSISSIPPI RIVER. The Shawnee National Forest was placed under the control of the Forest Service of the United States Department of Agriculture in 1933. The Forest Service has promoted multiple use of the more than two hundred thousand acres in the forest. The Service has logged part of the area and given twenty-five percent of the money received to the county, built a lake, and with Southern Illinois Power of Marion restored the Iron Furnace that was used between 1839 and 1863. A demonstration of good land use is provided by the University of ILLINOIS at the Dixon Springs Agricultural Center. More than one million people visit the forest every year to hunt, fish, or camp.

SHAWNEETOWN, Illinois. City (pop. 1,-841), county seat of Gallatin County, gateway to Illinois for pioneers moving along the OHIO RIVER, named for the Indian tribe. Shawnee-town's geographical position on the River continued to benefit the city until the Erie Canal brought thousands of immigrants into Illinois by way of the GREAT LAKES. Shawneetown was a center for salt which was shipped by keelboat to the South. The great flood of 1937 destroyed much of the area, and the city was moved four miles to higher ground. The old city location became the Old Shawneetown State Memorial. Restoration work has preserved several of the remaining original buildings.

SHEBOYGAN, Wisconsin. City (pop. 48,-085), Seat of Sheboygan County, situated in southeast Wisconsin at the mouth of the Sheboygan River, where it empties into Lake MICHIGAN, north of MILWAUKEE. Named from an Algonquin word of unknown meaning, the city is a leading industrial center and renowned fishing port. The NORTHWEST COMPANY opened a trading post there in 1795. In 1835 a sawmill built at present Sheboygan Falls was the nucleus for settlement in the area. Settlement was spotty, however, until 1843 when a country store was built. A year later there was considerable development, including a post office for what was then called "The Mouth," for the mouth of the river. As a port for settlers moving into the northern Midwest, as a winter home for sailors and as a port for a fleet of ships built at The Mouth, the community had a steady growth. Many of the settlers were German immigrants or Hollanders seeking religious freedom. With phenomenal crops in the region, the first of many grain elevators was built in 1849. By 1860 there were twenty flour mills in the county. Manufacturing expanded with furniture factories turning out millions of chairs, and other woodworkers producing wagons, ships and even wooden shoes. By 1875 there were forty-five cheese factories. The Kohler foundry moved to a nearby site now named KOHLER, where it became a world leader in enameled bathroom and kitchen fixtures, along with many other products. The Kohler name is attached to two local attractions, John Michael Kohler Arts Center for all the arts and Terry Andrae-John M. Kohler State Park on Lake Michigan, a magnet for nature and water lovers. Waelderhaus is a reproduction of a chalet and furnishings of the Kohler family home in the Austrian Alps. Lakeland College, founded in 1862, also offers a public museum. The Outdoor Arts Festival is held the third weekend in July, Holland Festival, with wooden-shoe dancing and street scrubbing on the last Friday and Saturday of July and Bratwurst day on the first Saturday of August.

SHEDD AQUARIUM. Chicago, Illinois, exhibit of live fish and aquatic animals. The Shedd Aquarium's exhibits are said to be the largest and most complete of their type in the world. Not content with that record, the aquarium embarked in 1987 on an expansion to more than double its interior space to provide an indoor seaquarium for very large mammals. The aquarium is named for John Shedd, a Marshall Field and Company executive, who gave three million dollars as an endowment in 1924. In 1931, the first year the aquarium was open, nearly five million visitors viewed the exhibits. Special attention is given to duplicating the appearance and conditions found in the natural surroundings of the specimens. The central exhibit is one of the largest indoor reproductions of a coral reef habitat.

SHELBYVILLE, Indiana. City (pop. 14,-989), seat of Shelby County, east central Indiana city southeast of INDIANAPOLIS, located in Indiana's richest corn producing country. Shelbyville, platted in 1822, was the home of Thomas A. Hendricks, former Vice President of the United States and governor of Indiana. Shelbyville was also the home of author Charles Major, whose book *When Knighthood Was in Flower* (1898) became a best-seller. Near Shelbyville is a marker commemorating the completion, on July 4, 1834, of the first railroad track in Indiana. When the owner was unable to find a locomotive, he hired a farmer to pull the single passenger coach with a horse.

SHELLEY, KATE. (Tipperary, Ireland, Sept. 25, 1865—Moingona, IA, Jan. 21, 1912). Heroine. Sixteen-year-old Kate Shelley had no idea on that stormy night outside the hamlet of Moingona, Iowa, that she was about to become a national heroine. Kate's father, a railroad man, was killed in a railroad accident, leaving his wife and Kate, the oldest of several brothers and sisters. They lived close to the railroad bridge over Honey Creek, which was flooding so badly that the bridge went out. Almost immediately they heard the sound of an approaching engine, which was wrecked at the creek. There was no way the family could help the trainmen, who were clinging to trees in the raging waters. Excitedly the family remembered the fast express, which was due in a few minutes. Kate rushed out into the storm. She had to pass over the long bridge crossing the DES MOINES RIVER, not far away. The ties were two and three feet apart, and the bridge swayed with the pressure of the rushing water. One misstep would have sent her into the raging waters. She stumbled on, cut and bleeding from railroad spikes. Reaching the other side, she hurried to town, where she was just in time to stop the passenger express before she collapsed. Rescuers picked up the marooned engineer and fireman near the Shelley house. When the press heard of the incident, reporters swarmed over the Shelley property. Newspapers around the world picked up the story with headlines, calling the Iowa girl a heroine. The railroad company gave her a cash award, a lifetime pass, and made her the station agent at Moingona. The employees gave her a gold watch and chain. She received a gold medal and the thanks of the state from the Iowa legislature. People wrote requesting pieces of her dress, slivers from the bridge or asking for her photograph. At her death, the railroad sent a special train for the funeral. Hundreds of magazine accounts were later written and embroidered with imagination. The new bridge across the Des Moines River was called the Kate Shelley.

SHERIDAN, Philip Henry. (Albany, N.Y., Mar. 6, 1831—Nonquitt, MA, Aug. 5, 1888). Military leader. At the age of one year, Sheridan is generally thought to have been brought by his parents to SOMERSET, Ohio, but he sometimes named Somerset as his birthplace. In any case, he grew up there, then graduated from West Point in 1853 and took part in the Indian wars. At the outbreak of the CIVIL WAR he held a captaincy and quartermaster position in Missouri. Appointed colonel in command of the 2nd Michigan Cavalry, he was so successful in the battle at Booneville, Mississippi, on July 1, 1862, that he received promotion to brigadier general of volunteers. His tactics against Confederate general Rosecrans and a daring charge at Missionary Ridge (November 14, 1863), brought him to Ulysses S. Grant's attention as a rival to take public attention away from daring Confederate cavalry leader, Jeb Stuart. Beginning in August, 1864, Sheridan won great success as Union commander in the Shenandoah Valley. Starting in March, 1865, his maneuvers against Lee at Petersburg, Dinwiddie Courthouse and Five Forks in 1865 eventually resulted in cutting off Lee's retreat and brought the Southern commander's surrender at Appomatox, April 9, 1865. After the war, Sheridan became military governor of Louisiana and Texas, but he was removed because of his harsh administration. Through 1869, Sheridan again took part in the Indian wars and ended his career as successor to Sherman as commanding general of the army. Congress promoted him to general of the army on June 1, 1888, and he died soon after.

SHERMAN, William Tecumseh. (Lancas-

Old photo of William T. Sherman.

ter, OH, Feb. 8, 1820—New York, NY, Feb. 14, 1891). Military leader. Sherman's father was a judge of the Ohio Supreme Court. He died in 1829 and left his widow with eleven children. William and his brother John were then adopted by Thomas Ewing, a family friend. William grew up with the Ewings. He particularly admired his foster father, saying "...a better, nobler more intellectual man never lived."

When Mrs. Ewing brought William to be baptized, the minister asked his name. When he heard it was Tecumseh, he refused to baptize him in the name of the famed Indian warrior, so they added the name William. Eventually, Sherman married the Ewing's daughter, Eleanor Boyle Ewing, who became known as a philanthropist.

Sherman graduated from West Point in 1840 and served in various stations in the South and then in the War with Mexico, beginning in 1846. He wanted active duty but, instead, served in the far west as Adjutant to the commander of the Division of the Pacific. In this position he adminstered California until its civilian organization in 1848.

After that, he was stationed in ST. LOUIS and New Orleans. Resigning from the army in 1853, Sherman became, in turn, a banker in San Francisco and New York, a lawyer in Leavenworth, Kansas, and later was superintendent of the state military academy at Alexandria, Louisiana, the forerunner of Louisiana State University at Baton Rouge.

When the CIVIL WAR came, Sherman took part

in the first Battle of Bull Run (July 21, 1861), then was assigned to Kentucky. As a general of volunteers, he commanded a division at Shiloh with distinction (April 6-7, 1862). In the advance on Vicksburg, he was defeated at Chickasaw Bluffs (December 19, 1962), but he led the 15th Corps to take part in the crucial Union success at Vicksburg.

Made a brigadier general in the regular army in July, 1863, he had other successes and succeeded Grant as commander of the Union armies in the West. In May, 1864, he assembled an army of 100,000 men and began a campaign that was to become celebrated as "Marching Through Georgia."

Sherman was perhaps the first to realize that warfare was being completely changed. He believed that the only way to win over a free people was to break the spirit not only of the armed forces but of the noncombatants, as well. He felt they must be convinced that "War is hell," as he remarked in his famous comment. His nearly total destruction of much of the Georgia countryside clearly exhibited his wartime philosophy.

After burning Atlanta on November 15, 1864, he swept south with 60,000 men, destroying as he went, to capture Savannah on December 21. The next February he started north, bringing even more severe destruction in South Carolina. Southern general Joseph E. Johnston offered to surrender, and Sherman replied with very generous terms. The victor had lived in the South, and he knew more than any other Northern general how much the South had suffered. Johnston surrendered on April 25, 1865. Congress later repudiated some of the political terms of the surrender, leaving much the same terms as Grant had given to Lee.

In 1869 Sherman succeeded Grant as commander of the U.S. Army, and retired in 1884.

When the Republicans tried to nominate him for president that year, he made his noted statement: "If nominated, I will not accept; if elected, I will not serve." Many Civil War authorities consider Sherman to have been the greatest of the Civil War generals.

SHOE OF VENUS. State flower of Minnesota. Familiar name of cypripedium reginae, the scientific name of this exotic plant.

SHOES, WOODEN. HOLLAND, Michigan has the only wooden shoe manufacturing plant in the United States. The De Klomp Wooden Shoe and Delft Factory offers tours of its production facilities.

SHOT. Round lead pellets used in early firearms. Shot was manufactured at several locations along the MISSISSIPPI RIVER including DUBUQUE, Iowa, and Herculaneum, Missouri. Shot was formed from molten lead mixed with an arsenic alloy. The melted material was poured through a copper sieve at the top of a tall shot tower into a cistern located below. Large shot was dropped 140 feet; and small shot was dropped ninety. The action of the air and the revolution of the lead droplets in space provided their round shape. The round pellets were retrieved from the water, where they cooled, and were then polished in a revolving barrel. One man was capable of casting four or five thousand pounds of shot in a day, but it took nine days to polish the same amount. During eighteen months ending in June, 1817, 668,350 pounds of shot, with a value of more than $50,000 was produced in Herculaneum.

SHOWBOATS. A unique form of entertainment, floating palaces based on stern wheel steamboats. The showboats were popular before and after the turn of the century. They brought the theater and music to communities along the major rivers, to places where such entertainment would never otherwise have been seen. Edna Ferber's famous book *Showboat* (1926) dealt with the ornate vessel of her title, and was made into the equally famous and enduring musical of the same name by Jerome Kern. Today such showboats as the *Goldenrod* at ST. LOUIS still present this old-fashioned entertainment on the river.

SIBLEY, Henry Hastings. (Detroit, MI, Feb. 20, 1811—St. Paul, MN, Feb. 18, 1891). Governor of Minnesota. Sibley worked as a clerk for the AMERICAN FUR COMPANY between 1829 and 1834 before becoming a partner in operating a company post near FORT SNELLING, Minnesota, which handled the trade with SIOUX Indians living between Lake PEPIN and the Canadian border. Sibley began his political career as territorial representative in the United States Congress. He served in 1848 and 1849 when it is said his dapper appearance, stately manner and command of parliamentary procedure did much to promote the organization of the Minnesota Territory. Sibley became the Minnesota territorial representative to Congress from the territory and served from 1849 to 1853. He was elected as first governor of Minnesota and held office from 1858 to 1860. Sibley was a regent of Minnesota State University from 1860 to 1869. During this time he led volunteer military forces against Indians in the Sioux Uprising in 1862. During the rest of the CIVIL WAR, Sibley held the rank of brigadier general and fought at the Battle of Wood Lake. In 1863 and again in 1864 he led expeditions against the Sioux in the Dakota area. He was mainly responsible for the defeat of the Indians, although before they went on the warpath he had been one of their most important friends. Sibley was a member of the Minnesota legislature in 1871 and became the president of the Minnesota Historical Society in 1879.

SIKESTON, Missouri. City (pop. 17,341), New Madrid and Scott Counties, in southeastern Missouri. Settled in 1860 and incorporated in 1874, the city is located in an industrial-farming area. Sikeston has cotton gins as well as flour and feed mills, and manufactures include shoes, toys, sporting goods, and building supplies. Farms produce corn, cotton, soybeans, and wheat. The Bootheel Rodeo is held there each August, and Cotton Carnival is held in September.

SILVER DOLLAR CITY. Modern recreational version of an 1880s-style Ozark mining town, built nine miles west of BRANSON, Missouri. Among the attractions is a diving bell, plunging visitors beneath the waters of Lake Silver, a steam train pursued by bandits, and dance halls complete with rollicking music. It features many widely known annual art, craft and other attractions.

SILVER TREASURE CAVE. Reputed cache of Choctaw silver bars near Dover Hill, Indiana. An early settler, Absalom Fields, was reportedly kidnapped and taken to a cave filled with silver. Blindfolded on the trip to and from the mine, Fields was never able to find the silver, nor was an Indian in 1866 who was given landmarks to the cave, but found them missing. Several bars have been found, but the bulk of the treasure is unclaimed.

SINKHOLES. Naturally occurring depressions in the earth, such as those found at ALPENA, Michigan, caused by subterranean streams eroding the limestone crust. Some Midwest sinkholes measure 150 feet in depth.

SIOUX CITY, Iowa. City (pop. 82,003), Woodbury County, western Iowa on the MISSOURI RIVER. Sioux City is one of the largest livestock and grain centers in the United States. Its civic ballet, theaters and symphony orchestra have given it recognition as the Cultural Mecca of the Plains. Historically it is remembered as the place where Sergeant Charles FLOYD (-1804), the only person to die on the LEWIS AND CLARK EXPEDITION (1804-1806), is buried.

Geographically, Sioux City lies along the BIG SIOUX and the Floyd Rivers at the place where they empty into the Missouri. High bluffs give a spectacular view of Iowa's adjoining states of South Dakota and Nebraska. It may have been the bluffs and surrounding beautiful country that inspired George CATLIN (1796-1872), the famous western artist. Catlin sang the praises of the region on his return from a trip in 1832.

In 1848 the community of Thompsonville, now part of Sioux City, was platted. Theophile Bruguier, a French-Canadian trader, arrived in 1849 with his wives, their father, Chief War Eagle, and other SIOUX Indians. Brugier's relationship with the Sioux kept the area peaceful. Joe Leonais, a trapper, paid Bruguier $100 for his claim of 160 acres in 1852. Leonais, in turn, sold the land to Dr. John K. Cook for $3000. Cook's political connections led to the location of a land office and post office in the community in 1855. Missouri river commerce began in 1856 with the arrival of the steamboat *Omaha*. James A. Jackson, a son-in-law of Dr. Cook had a frame store constructed in ST. LOUIS and shipped to Sioux City in pieces ready for assembly.

As settlers set out for the Northwest, Sioux City became an important supply base. The first blacks came there as deckhands on the steamboats. One who stayed was Aunty Wooden whose opossum dinners were so popular that professional and business people bid for an invitation. The arrival of the Illinois Central Railroad in 1870 made Sioux City an important shipping town. The beginning of Sioux City's meat-packing industry dates to the sinking of a boatload of grain in the Missouri River. When recovered the grain was worthless for anything but animal feed. James E. Booge, the owner of the grain, fed the grain to hogs, and since there was no market for live hogs he slaughtered them and sold the meat. Soon Booge hired butchers from St. Louis to keep up with the demand, and a small packing plant was built. Other businessmen furnished feeders to a limited area around Sioux City for farmers to raise on surplus crops. This activity resulted in organization of the Livestock Exchange, 1887.

In 1914 members of the Industrial Workers of the World made their first appearance in

Sioux City. Agitation continued for thirty days, and by April 17th the jails were overcrowded and the city was importing granite blocks for the prisoners to work on as punishment. Wallace M. Short, a local minister, made a campaign issue of the mistreatment of labor and with its support won the mayoral election. Greater problems came in the early 1930s when low prices, drought and grasshoppers created hard times for farmers who united behind the militant Farmers' Holiday Association. Commercial traffic into Sioux City was brought almost to a complete standstill, but as farm and labor conditions improved, the city regained its prosperity.

Artifacts from Sioux City's past are displayed in the Sioux City Public Museum. The Floyd Monument, on the summit of Floyd's Bluff, marks the site of Sergeant Floyd's burial. His death was caused by appendicitis.

SIOUX INDIANS (DACOTAH). Of the Siouian linguistic stock, the Sioux are the dominant branch of seven tribes: Wahpekute, Mdewakanton, Wahpeton, SISSETON (Santee or eastern division), Yankton, Yanktonai and Teton. The first record of their presence in northeastern Minnesota was made in 1640, for they had been driven there earlier by hostile tribes with more modern weapons. In the Midwest, in addition to Minnesota, they occupied parts of Iowa and Wisconsin, where their culture was typically that of the plains, including buffalo hunting and the sun dance. The Sioux became friendly with the British and supported them during the American Revolution and in the WAR OF 1812. Their revolt in Minnesota in 1862 resulted in the massacre of 600 white settlers, leading to the eventual Sioux defeat and their treaty removal to reservations in South Dakota.

SISSETON INDIANS. Branch of the SIOUX INDIANS (Dacotah), the most powerful group of the great Siouian family, which, altogether, comprised the largest and most prevalent group of the plains Indians. The seven groups of the Dacotah were divided into three main subdivisions. The subdivision which lived between the Mississippi and Missouri rivers was the Eastern or Forest division, known as the Santee. One of the branches of this group was the Sisseton. Each of the Dacotah groups, including the Sisseton, was broken into small bands. Each band had its own differing customs and traditions, but all Dacotah people followed basically the same pattern of life as other Plains

Indians. As other Indian bands were driven farther west and as European-style settlement followed, the Plains Indians also were driven westward. The present Sisseton reservation was established in the corner of northeastern South Dakota, on the border of Minnesota. There are presently estimated to be about 2,430 Sisseton descendants.

SIX FLAGS GREAT AMERICA. Amusement park. Near Gurnee, Illinois, this division of the chain of Six flags resorts, has one of the most complete operations of its kind. In that Chicago suburb, Great America experiments with the newest in thrill rides and has continued to add outstanding stage attractions such as the Acrobats of China.

SIX FLAGS OVER MID-AMERICA. Largest amusement park in the Midwest. Six Flags, thirty miles southwest of ST. LOUIS, covers two hundred acres and features among its one hundred rides the "Screaming Eagle," the "Jetscream" rollercoasters and a recreated whitewater rafting trip called "Thunder River."

SKUNK RIVER. The two branches of the Skunk River and the main stream combine to form near Rubio, Iowa, draining one of the largest watersheds in the state. The shorter North Branch begins just west of Melbourne, Iowa, and the longer South Branch forms north of Ellsworth, the first town which it passes in a turbulent course, totalling 264 miles to its mouth on the MISSISSIPPI RIVER south of BURLINGTON, Iowa. From the farthest source to the mouth, the Skunk encompasses a fall of 680 feet and drains 4,325 square miles, including all or parts of twenty Iowa counties. The swift-flowing stream provided ideal waterpower for the early mills of the state.

SKYSCRAPERS. Tall multi-use buildings which originated in the Midwest. Nineteenth-century contractors, faced with increasing land prices and limited space, sought new building techniques to permit tall buildings. Taller buildings required broader bases and thicker walls to hold the increased weight. But William JENNEY (1832-1907) developed a framework of metal beams which took less ground space and allowed buildings, called skyscrapers, to rise higher. The first skyscraper, built by Jenney in 1884, was the Home Insurance Building, CHICAGO, Illinois. Chicago also is home to the world's tallest skyscraper, the Sears Tower, 110 stories.

SLAVERY. Institutionalized and legalized bonded servitude, usually of a labor force, for economic gain. Slavery has existed in various forms since the earliest recorded histories, and it persistently appears as an illicit trade in underdeveloped areas. The single most historically important appearance of institutionalized slavery occurred in the American South, where it became a principal motivation behind the secession movement and as a cause of the American CIVIL WAR.

The Midwest's principal reaction to slavery was, generally, to oppose it in every way possible. The "border" states, Ohio, Indiana, Illinois and Iowa, were in a particularly favorable position to do more than talk about abolition. Some of the most effective stations on the UNDERGROUND RAILROAD operated in the Midwest, especially in Ohio and Indiana. The publication of *Uncle Tom's Cabin* (1852), written by Harriet Beecher STOWE (1811-1896), was one of the most important factors in shaping the northern opposition to slavery. Its author gathered the background material for the story while living in Ohio and visiting with Abolitionists. In Indiana, where there were many underground railroad stations, the Levi COFFIN (1789-1877) house at FOUNTAIN CITY, Indiana, was known as "Central Union Station of the Underground Railroad." He, alone, sheltered more than 2,000 black people in his Quaker home. After he left Indiana, Coffin became a leading figure in the world fight against slavery.

In Iowa, John BROWN drilled some of his Abolitionist followers at TABOR and SPRINGDALE.

When Edward COLES (1876-1878) came to Illinois, he made the symbollic gesture of freeing his slaves at the free state border in the middle of the OHIO RIVER, without waiting to reach the other side. He later became governor and helped to keep slavery from Illinois.

The Fugitive Slave Law of 1850 made it a crime for anyone to assist a slave in pursuit of freedom, and the Kansas-Nebraska Act of 1854 made it possible for new states to vote to be slave. These pro-slavery measures resulted in even more violent action between pro-slave and Abolitionist factions.

In 1854, Wisconsin was the scene of the famous controversy over Joshua GLOVER, who was freed from a MILWAUKEE jail by a mob and escaped to freedom in Canada. Abolitionist newspaper editor Sherman Booth had been considered responsible for the riot and was jailed, set free by the Wisconsin Supreme Court, tried and convicted by the U.S. courts and pardoned by President Buchanan.

Michigan, Wisconsin and Illinois all claim honors as the site of the founding of the REPUBLICAN PARTY (1854-1856), which came about mostly as an anti-slavery movement.

To say that the Civil War was "fought over slavery" is simplistic. But the North and the South both felt strongly about their positions over slavery. In the north slavery was considered a moral outrage and in the South as an economic necessity. Historians are increasingly inclined to feel that the war was brought on by arrogant extremists and blundering politicians on both sides.

Whatever the cause, the war marked the beginning of the end of slavery in the U.S.

On January 1, 1863, Illinois' great Abraham LINCOLN (1809-1865) signed the Emancipation Proclamation. This declared the slaves were free in those areas in rebellion against the Union government. It did not affect the slaves in other U.S. areas.

Legalized slavery throughout the U.S. was ended by the Thirteenth Amendment to the constitution, declared ratified on December 18, 1865. The rights of former slaves were further given legal safeguard by the Fourteenth Amendment, declared ratified on July 21, 1868. This states that, "No State shall make or enforce any law which shall abridge the priviliges or immunities of citizens of the United States..." Legally slavery was over in the U.S. Unfortunately, its effects lingered on for generations.

SLEEPING BEAR DUNES NATIONAL LAKESHORE. Thirty-three miles of Lake MICHIGAN lakeshore north of FRANKFORT, Michigan, and including the MANITOU ISLANDS. The dunes were named from a CHIPPEWA legend that told of a female bear and her cubs swimming across Lake Michigan to escape a fierce forest fire. The mother bear arrived and, as the legend goes, sits today in the form of a hill of sand waiting for her two cubs which perished in the water and became, to the Indians, North and South Manitou Islands. The dunes were produced by several glaciers that occurred as recently as eleven thousand years ago. "Ghost forests," bleached remains of trees trapped by the advancing sand then exposed as the dunes passed by, are visible. Pierce Stocking Scenic Drive provides a seven-mile access to the high dunes, a favorite recreation area. The dunes are noted for their dune buggies and other related recreation facilities.

SLICKER WAR." Vigilante action taken by the residents of WARSAW, Missouri, against outlaws living in the area. The fighting began in 1841 and lasted four years. The citizens of Warsaw and the farmers began by banding together to "slick" the outlaws, meaning the desperadoes were beaten with hickory switches. Soon the outlaws infiltrated the "Slicker" organization and brought its name into disgrace. A group of law-abiding residents began another organization called the "Anti-Slickers" and war broke out. Murder, night raids, and trials were common. Nine people died before the trouble was settled.

SLOAN, Earl Sawyer. (1848—1923). Inventor. Sloan and his brother operated a livery stable in CHILLICOTHE, Missouri, between 1870 and 1872. Sloan developed a liniment to relieve sprains and bruises in horses and found it worked just as well on humans. He returned to Ohio to produce the liniment, and his product, "Sloan's Liniment," became world famous.

SLOCUM, Frances. (Warwick, RI, March 4, 1773—Peru, IN, Mar. 9, 1847). Indian captive known as the "White Rose of the Miamis." Slocum was kidnapped by Indians when she was four years old. Raised as an Indian, she was discovered by George Ewing, an Indian trader, who wrote of his findings in a letter which later resulted in the reuniting of the captive with members of her family. Slocum rejected the idea of returning permanently to her white family, choosing to continue to live where she could be buried near her husband and son.

SMITH, Jean Wilson. (Girvin Farm, Kilpatrick, Scotland, Jan. 30, 1840—Waterloo, IA, July 9, 1919). Educator. As a girl Jean Wilson walked with her family across the Iowa prairies from DAVENPORT to the new family home on the bare prairie near where TRAER, Iowa, now stands. A few years later she graduated from the first class of GRINNELL COLLEGE, GRINNELL, Iowa. After teaching in Traer High School, she joined the staff of the asylum for the blind at VINTON, Iowa. At the time it was thought that the blind must be sheltered and cared for. Jean Smith studied her blind charges and became convinced that they could be educated and lead successful lives. She therefore pioneered in teaching methods for the blind. When the state legislature requested that she come to DES MOINES to demonstrate these methods to them, they were so impressed that they voted money for a school for the blind at Vinton. Jean

Wilson married S.P. Smith in 1873, and the legislature provided a wedding dinner and gifts to the bride. This is considered to have been the only gesture of its kind ever made by lawmakers of any state.

SMITH, Joseph. (Sharon, Windsor County, VT, Dec. 23, 1805—Carthage, IL, June 27, 1844). Mormon prophet and religious leader. At age eleven, Smith moved with his parents to Palmyra, New York. About four years later, in 1820, he claimed to have had visions foretelling that god would give him revelations about Christ and true Christianity. He claimed that one of these visions provided directions to a hill near Manchester, New York. There he found plates of gold, inscribed with what he called the history of the true church in America. By "magical means," Smith transcribed the messages, and these were published in 1830 as *The Book of Mormon*. This was followed on April 6 of that year by the founding by Smith In Feyette, New York, of the Church of Jesus Christ of Latter-Day Saints (generally called Mormon). Immediately some converts were won. The next year Smith and his then small group of MORMONS moved to Kirtland Ohio where the number of converts swelled rapidly. Persecution and dissension then took most of the faithful to Jackson County, Missouri, in 1838. Their success in founding several communities in Missouri led to new persecution, imprisonment of the Mormon officials and sentences of death. Before any sentences could be carried out, in 1839 Smith led his followers to Commerce (renamed NAUVOO), Illinois in 1839. Smith ruled the rapidly growing community as the spiritual, military and civil leader. He was a candidate for President of the United States in 1844, but was arrested following a riot on June 10th. While a prisoner in the CARTHAGE, Illinois, jail he was shot and killed by a mob.

SNELLING, Josiah. (Boston, MA, 1782—Washington, DC, Aug. 20, 1828). Army officer. Snelling was the military commander and constructing engineer of Fort St. Anthony from 1820 to 1828 near the Minnesota cities of MINNEAPOLIS and ST. PAUL. He was later responsible for governing the community. In 1825 the name of the fort was changed by the War Department to FORT SNELLING in his honor. Snelling first gained distinction in the Battle of TIPPECANOE in 1811 and the Battle of Brownstone in 1812.

SNOWSHOES. One of the major contributions made by the Indians of the northern Midwest to present-day culture. Without snowshoes it would have been almost impossible to travel through the deep snows of winter in the area.

SOAP BOX DERBY. The All-American Soap Box Derby is held each year in AKRON, Ohio, where it originated. Boys and girls from the U.S. and abroad compete on a specially built track at Derby Downs, a sloping asphalt strip. Their vehicles are cars without motors, which they have designed and built themselves. The derby was founded to provide greater outlet for young engineering talent. Local competitions in various cities prepare the youngsters for the big event at Akron, competing for the valuable prizes offered to the ones who can glide and guide their cars down the slope in the fastest time.

SOD HOUSES. Type of shelter constructed in prairie regions of the Midwest where timber was scarce and the soil was unbroken. The ground was excavated a few feet deep with a ridge left around the inside for seating. Blocks of prairie sod, made tough by interlaced masses of roots from prairie grass, were stacked up to form the outer walls. Roofs were made by covering poles with grass. Chimneys were made of more sod blocks. There were very few openings in the walls. Some of these structures remain, and a few have been restored and opened to the public.

SOLTI, Georg. (Budapest, Hungary, 1912—). Musical conductor. In 1969 Sir Georg Solti became the conductor of the CHICAGO SYMPHONY ORCHESTRA. His musical career began at the Budapest Opera House, where he served from 1930 to 1939. During WORLD WAR II he lived in Switzerland. Solti accepted a number of important conducting posts in Europe. His career as music director and conductor of the Chicago orchestra has enhanced that body's reputation as perhaps the finest in the world. He has conducted the Chicago orchestra in winning more Grammy awards than any other person or ensemble and is perhaps the single best-known musical personality of the Midwest.

SONS AND DAUGHTERS OF PIONEER RIVERMEN. An organization started at MARIETTA, Ohio, to preserve the memories of the early days of river traffic on the OHIO and other Midwest rivers. A museum was established at Marietta, now the Ohio River Museum State

Memorial, with exhibits on history and development of inland waterways. A steamboat built in 1918 has been restored and moored on the MUSKINGUM RIVER.

SOO (SAULT STE. MARIE) CANALS. Two canals bypassing the rapids in the ST. MARY'S RIVER, outlet of Lake SUPERIOR. A Canadian fur company built the first canal on the Canadian side as early as 1797. But it was inadequate, and the present Canadian canal was completed in 1895. The U.S. canal was constructed in 1853 by the state of Michigan and then taken over by the federal government which reconstructed it to take larger vessels. It has four locks. Although closed during the winter months, the canals are said to be busiest in the world. Because they are of vital need to U.S. shipping and commerce, they were said to be the most closely guarded of any single location during WORLD WAR II. Most ships now use the U.S. canal.

SORIN, Edward. (Ahvelle, France Feb. 6, 1814—Oct. 31, 1893). Clergyman. Fr. Sorin, ordained a Roman Catholic priest in 1838, came to the United States in 1841 to do missionary work in Indiana. He obtained a charter from the Indiana General Assembly to found the University of NOTRE DAME at SOUTH BEND, St. Joseph County, in 1844 and served as president from 1844 to 1865. Fr. Sorin was also the provincial superior in charge of mission posts in northeastern Illinois, northern Indiana, and southern Michigan.

SOUTH AMHERST, Ohio. Town (pop. 1,848), situated in north central Ohio, once was named Podunk, and is principally noted as the location of the world's largest sandstone quarry.

SOUTH BASS ISLAND. Situated in Lake ERIE about fifteen miles north of SANDUSKY, Ohio, South Bass is the largest and most important of the Bass Islands. It is best known for PUT-IN-BAY from which Oliver Hazard PERRY (1785-1819) departed (September 10, 1813) to win the Battle of LAKE ERIE. Nine states and the federal government combined to build the massive monument at Put-in-Bay, which memorializes the victory. Completed in 1915, the granite shaft is the tallest Doric column in the world, 352 feet high. The monument and park around it are now designated as PERRY'S VICTORY AND INTERNATIONAL PEACE MEMORIAL. At one time the island boasted a large colony of wealthy summer residents, who stayed at the grand hotels. Then the hotels burned, and the millionaires bought islands of their own. Today the island remains a popular summer resort.

SOUTH BEND, Indiana. City (pop. 109,-727), seat of St. Joseph county, situated in central Indiana at the great southernmost bend of the ST. JOSEPH RIVER, takes its name from the bend. The city was incorporated in 1865 and occupies an area of 36.4 square miles.

Even before it was incorporated, the city had become a manufacturing center with the coming of the Studebaker company in 1852.

After many decades as a well-known wagon maker, Studebaker made an early venture into the automobile field, and manufactured a popular car until it was discontinued in 1962, ending sixty-three years of automobile production which began at South Bend in 1899, when Studebaker first made bodies for electric automobiles.

Another South Bend industry began in 1855 when James Oliver (1823-1908) commenced manufacture of plows. In 1864 he discovered a method to harden steel by chilling, permitting the steel moldboard on plows to remain sharp for long periods.

Today, the city remains a ranking automotive center with the huge operation of the Bendix Products Company, manufacturers of starters, alternators and other automotive electrical products. Other industries include non-electrical machinery, paint, rubber, plastics, farm equipment and metal products. The city processes many of the agricultural products of the region, which is particularly noted as a center of mint growing.

In late 1679 Robert Cavelier, Sieur de LA SALLE (1643-1687), and his party reached the bottom of the St. Joseph River bend where the city is now located, There they began their portage to the KANKAKEE RIVER, and then proceeded south to the MISSISSIPPI.

An early French mission stood at the site of South Bend when it was founded in 1820, as a post of the AMERICAN FUR COMPANY.

Prior to the CIVIL WAR, the city was an important station on the UNDERGROUND RAILROAD, assisting runaway slaves to safety in Canada.

One of the nation's major universities began life there in 1842 when Brothers of the Holy Cross founded the University of NOTRE DAME DU LAC, now called simply Notre Dame. Despite its noted law school, research facilities in geology, metallurgy, radiation and botany, and its general high-ranking academic programs, Notre Dame has become most famous through its perennially successful football teams and other athletics.

After a long period of cooperation with St. Mary's Academy for Women, Notre Dame merged with the academy in 1971, forming a single coeducational institution. The city also hosts a branch of INDIANA UNIVERSITY.

The campus of Notre Dame, one of the largest in the world, is a particular attraction for parents and tourists to South Bend. The art treasures of the library include paintings by Van Dyck, Tintoretto, Murillo and many others. There also is an outstanding collection of furniture of the Medici and Borgia families, along with other antique and art objects. Many of the noted murals in various university buildings were created by long time head of the Notre Dame art department, Luigi Gregory.

The four-hundred-year-old Council Oak, preserved reminders of an historic agreement between La Salle and the Indians on the present site of South Bend. The trading post of the city's first settler, Pierre Navarre Cabin, and Northern Indiana Historical Society are of more than passing interest.

SOUTHEAST MISSOURI STATE UNIVERSITY. Publicly supported university located in CAPE GIRARDEAU, Missouri. Southeast Missouri State is accredited by the North Central Association of Colleges and Schools, the National Council for the Accreditation of Teacher Education and the National Association of Schools of Music. The university is situated on a two-hundred acre campus with forty-two buildings. Bachelor, Master and Specialist degrees are granted. During the 1985-1986 academic year 9,058 students were enrolled and there were 475 faculty members.

SOUTHERN ILLINOIS UNIVERSITY. State-supported coeducational institution with campuses in Edwardsville and Carbondale, (site of its first campus). The Edwardsville campus opened in 1965. Courses lead to the bachelor's, master's, or doctor's degrees. In 1985-1986 the Carbondale campus enrolled 22,672 students and had 1,478 faculty. The Edwardsville campus enrolled 10,236 students and had 650 faculty. Southern Illinois University experienced tremendous growth under the guidance of Dr. Delyte Morris who in his twenty-two year career as president of the university witnessed the enrollment increase twelvefold. Morris had been at Carbondale only one year when S.I.U. opened a residence center for classes at

Belleville. In 1957 the university took over Shurtleff College and gave instruction there and at EAST ST. LOUIS.

SOUTHWEST MISSOURI STATE UNIVERSITY.
Publicly supported liberal arts and teachers university in SPRINGFIELD, Missouri. Southwest Missouri was established in 1905 for teacher training. As needs of the students changed, course work in sciences, vocational subjects and several preprofessional areas were added. Graduate work leading to the master's degree is now available. The campus is located on a 125-acre campus with twenty-two buildings. Entrance requires accredited high school graduation with a rank in the upper two-thirds of the class. Accreditation for the school comes from the North Central Association of Colleges and Schools and others. During the 1985-1986 academic year 15,511 students were enrolled. The university has 716 faculty members.

SOYBEANS.
Annual plant, also known as soya or soja, which supplies food for animals, humans, and raw materials for industry. Soybeans, one of the world's cheapest sources of protein, contain forty percent of that nutrient compared to eighteen percent found in such other sources as fish or beef. Like other legumes, soybeans obtain nitrogen from the air and so do not require nitrogen fertilizers. Farmers in the United States, producers of two-thirds of the world's supply of soybeans, plant more of this crop than any other, with the exceptions of wheat and corn. Soybean farming in the United States is primarily centered in the Midwestern states. Soybeans, like corn, thrive in fertile, well-drained soil with at least twenty inches of rain annually. Among the states which produce soybeans, Illinois and Iowa alternate first and second in annual value and total production, with Indiana in third place and Missouri in fourth. Forty percent of the crop is exported to Japan and Western European countries. Soybeans are the United States' largest single source of vegetable oil and protein meal for livestock and meat substitutes for humans. Soy flour is used in baby foods, cereals, and low-calorie products. Soy grits are used in processed meats and candy. Soy oil is the basis of candles, soaps, varnishes, adhesive tape and explosives. In its historical development, the soybean was brought to America in the early 20th Century by agents of agricultural secretary Tama Jim WILSON, but lightning growth of the crop did not strike until the 1930s.

SPANISH AMERICAN WAR.
This brief conflict, begun and ended in the single year of 1898, was the only U.S. war fought entirely by volunteers. The various quotas for volunteers were more than filled in each of the Midwest states. Iowa had a special association with the war, and feeling there ran especially high. The U.S. battleship *Maine* was sunk by Spanish forces in the harbor of Havana, Cuba, on February 15, 1898. One of the two officers killed on the battleship was an Iowan, Darwin R. Merritt, of RED OAK, the assistant engineer of the ship. Memorial services were held at RED OAK, and demand for revenge on the "assassins" grew to fever pitch throughout Iowa. War was declared on April 21, 1898. Soon after, when the fifty-first Iowa Regiment of volunteers left for war service in the Philippines, it was the first time that Iowa soldiers had served overseas. Years after the *Maine* was raised, the men's personal property was taken out, and the Iowa Historical Library at DES MOINES has preserved the trinkets taken from Darwin Merritt's locker—a bunch of moldy keys, an old watch case, the rusted hilt of a sword—Midwestern mementoes of the deed which started the Spanish American War. A number of prominent Midwesterners served in the war, including Missouri's John J. PERSHING (1860-1948), later to become the American commander in WORLD WAR I. William MC KINLEY (1843-1901) of Ohio was president during the war, and he established the policies for disposition of the Spanish territories following the war.

SPIEGEL GROVE.
The estate of President Rutherford B. HAYES (1822-1893) at FREMONT, Ohio, is now preserved as a state memorial, known as Hayes Presidential Center. The twenty-five acre wooded tract was owned by the Hayes family. The Hayes House was built in 1859 and was the Hayes home from 1873 to 1893. It is a Victorian structure furnished in the manner of the period. Near the house are the graves of President and Mrs. Hayes. The Hayes property was turned over to the state in 1915. In addition to the house, the property includes the Museum and library.

SPILLVILLE, Iowa.
Town (pop. 415). Situated in northeast Iowa, on the Turkey River. The hamlet basks in its two great claims to fame. J. J. Kovarik, a native of Spillville, was the assistant to the famed Czech composer, Antonin DVORAK (1841-1904), when the composer was writing music and conducting in New York. When the great man indicated he wanted

a summer away from the maddening city, his assistant suggested his own home town. The arrival of the famous family, Dvorak, his wife, six children and the assistant, brought instant fame to the little community, where Dvorak spent a musically profitable summer. The house where the composer lived is still preserved at Spillville. The church where he played the organ is still standing, and the town has erected a monument in his honor. Another tourist attraction, rare for such a small town is the Bily Brothers Museum, said to be the only one of its kind. For many years the brothers spent most of their time fashioning an extraordinarily large number of unusual clock works and cases. Their sometimes strange, always interesting, work may still be seen there.

SPIRIT LAKE MASSACRE. The outlaw Indian, Inkpaduta, has been called the John Dillinger of his time. He and his hundred-odd followers were outcasts from their own tribe. This mob ran a kind of protection racket, shaking down settlers. If a settler refused to pay, he might find one of his cattle slain in the night. If a pioneer family stood up for its treaty rights (The territory was open by treaty to settlement.), they might find their barn in flames during the night. When the gang descended on the cabin of the Gardner family one night in the spring of 1857, Mr. Gardner wanted to bolt the door and sell their lives dearly, but his wife felt that the Indians might return kindness for kindness, so the renegades were let in. They ate all the food in sight, made signs for more, and when Gardner went to get more, they shot him in the back. Then the mother and three of her children were dragged outdoors and their heads bashed against the rocks. Then the howling Indians overran the tiny town of SPIRIT LAKE. Altogether 42 men, women and children of the Spirit Lake-Okiboji region were killed. Three young girls (including Abigail, the only living member of the Gardner family) were taken captive to Minnesota, where they eventually were ransomed by the state of Minnesota. A monument was erected as a memorial to the victims of one of the Midwest's worst massacres.

SPLIT ROCK LIGHTHOUSE. Maritime navigational aid near TWO HARBORS, Minnesota. In the late 1800s the waters around Two Harbors were considered among the most dangerous in the world due to the reefs. Perched on a cliff 168 feet above Lake SUPERIOR, Split

Rock Lighthouse is of great assistance to ships in the vicinity whose compass needles are diverted from their true readings by the magnetic rock formations in the area. Its greatest fame comes as a picturesque landmark, one of the country's favorites with photographers.

SPOON RIVER. Western Illinois river with its source near Kewanee, Illinois. It empties into the ILLINOIS RIVER near Havana. Edgar Lee MASTERS (1869-1950) made the river famous in his *Spoon River Anthology* (1915). Percy Grainger wrote "Spoon River," as a piano solo based on an old folk tune played by fiddlers in 1857.

SPRING GREEN, Wisconsin. Village (pop. 1,265), situated in southwest Wisconsin west of MADISON, the community is principally known for its variety of associations with renowned architect Frank Lloyd WRIGHT (1867-1959), who grew up there, built his home and established the TALIESIN Fellowship for the training of architectural apprentices there. One of the most noted of American dwellings, however, was not designed by Wright. House on the Rock, nine miles from Spring Green, was designed and built by Alexander J. Jordan, who perched it on a towering chimney-like rock 450 feet above the valley. The house and its surroundings have been turned into a museum-entertainment complex, featuring the world's largest merry-go-round. At Spring Green the Taliesin Fellowship summer campus of the Wright Foundation is available for tours from early July through Labor Day. Wright's grave is a much-visited site.

SPRINGDALE, Iowa. Town (pop. 100). A Quaker settlement in Cedar county in east central Iowa, the town was particularly known as a haven on the UNDERGROUND RAILROAD and as one of the drilling and training places for the "troops" which the flaming Abolitionist John BROWN (1800-1859) led on his raids in Kansas. In 1858, in one of his most famous rescues, Brown spirited twelve slaves out of Kansas, by way of Nebraska, and they were given rest at Springdale before going on to safety in Canada.

SPRINGFIELD, Illinois. City (pop. 102,000 1984) capital of Illinois and seat of Sangamon County, situated in central Illinois on the SANGAMON RIVER and bordered by Lake Springfield, incorporated as a city in 1840. The city covers an area of 40.8 square miles. It was named for the springs in the area, which give rise to Spring Creek.

The nearly level countryside surrounds the city, and there are no large hills in the area. However, rolling terrain is found near the Sangamon River and Spring Creek. In the typically continental climate, with cold winters and warm to hot summers, the July temperature average holds in the upper seventies, and the winter average is the upper twenties in January.

As the hub of the state ranked second in the growing of food products, Springfield is one of the major agricultural centers of the region. Food processing, and manufacturing based on the coal of the region are among the leading industries. Much of the commerce of the area thrives on the large-scale operations of government in the city, which is also a medical and insurance center.

In 1818, when Illinois became a state, the Springfield area was still a beautiful valley, swarming with wild turkeys, deer and other game. In that year Elisha Kelly was so impressed with the lush region that he returned to his home in North Carolina and persuaded his father and four brothers to return to his paradise on the Sangamon River. Here the Kellys built a substantial log cabin, and the Kelly establishment became the nucleus of a slowly growing settlement.

Although not yet deserving town status, when Sangamon County was created, Springfield was the only settlement large enough to house county officials, and so the community was chosen as county seat. John Kelly was given the contract to build the county courthouse of "logs twenty feet long... a door and a window cut out..." In 1832 the city was excited by the coming of the first steamboat, but the river proved too small and treacherous for any consistent commerce.

Led by Abraham LINCOLN (1809-1865), in February, 1837, the legislature chose Springfield as the state capital, and Lincoln moved there the following April. For more than two decades the city was his home, and he was there when delegates from the 1860 Republican convention in CHICAGO came to notify him of his nomination for the presidency. In April of 1861, Lincoln boarded the train for Washington. His address to the people from the train is considered one of the finest of all his speeches, and he seemed to sense that he would never return alive. In the speech he said, "To this place and the kindness of its people I owe

Illinois capitol at Springfield.

everything. Here I have lived a quarter of a century, and have passed from a young to an old man..."

In early May, 1865, Lincoln's body was brought home to Springfield where it was laid to rest in Oak Ridge Cemetery. Both the Lincolns had often admired the beauty of that place. In that same year Peoria aspired to become the state capital, but Springfield raised $200,000 to buy the old capitol and provide the seed money for the new building. The cornerstone was laid in 1868. Some state departments moved to the new building in 1875, but the legislature argued over appropriating funds to finish the work, which was not completed until 1887.

After the CIVIL WAR, the GRAND ARMY OF THE REPUBLIC was organized at Springfield in 1866. A local chapter of the Knights of Labor was founded in Springfield in 1877, and the labor movement grew rapidly. An 1883 law barring labor activities was declared unconstitutional in 1900.

In 1924 the city approved an overall plan for developing Springfield in an orderly manner to make and develop a city worthy of the capital of a major state, and work has proceeded sporadically on this project. In 1930 the legislature appropriated funds for the creation of Lake Springfield.

Springfield suffered the kind of decline in population experienced by most of the state's other large cities as shown in the 1980 census. However, by 1984 the population had surpassed the 1980 figure by nearly 10,000.

There are more memories of Lincoln at Springfield than at any other place in Illinois, the Land of Lincoln. At eighth and Jackson is the only house the Emancipator ever owned. Lincoln's son, Robert Todd LINCOLN (1843-1926), donated it to the state in 1887, and it has been maintained as a shrine ever since. A

$4,000,000 refurbishing of the Lincoln home was completed in 1988. The former state capital has been rebuilt exactly as it was when Lincoln made his famous speech there on his nomination for the U.S. Senate in 1858, the famous "house divided against itself" speech. The building now houses the state historical library. Throughout Springfield, plaques, bronze tablets and preserved architecture point to the Lincoln presence. The railroad station where he bade farewell is now the Lincoln Depot Museum. There is an Abraham Lincoln Museum and an Abraham Lincoln Memorial Garden.

Probably the most-visited spot at Springfield is the magnificent tomb where the 16th President and Mrs. Lincoln and three of their four sons are buried. After a drive for funds by Springfield residents, the tomb was started in 1869 and dedicated in 1874. Just two years later, one of the most bizarre epsiodes in American history occurred. Counterfeiter Ben Boyd was in prison, and his gang planned to steal Lincoln's body and hold it for Boyd's freedom, as ransom. The plotters actually had removed the casket from the tomb before they were captured.

The first thing seen by most visitors to Springfield is the 261-foot dome of the capitol. Statues of both Lincoln and Stephen A. DOUGLAS (1813-1861) stand on the nine-acre grounds. The statue of *Illinois Welcoming the World* was brought to the capitol from the Illinois building of the 1893 WORLD'S COLUMBIAN EXPOSITION at Chicago. Other important Springfield buildings are the Centennial Building, Archives Building, Armory, Supreme Court and Governor's Mansion, erected in 1855. The Illinois State Museum of Natural History and Art is one of the finest of its type. Other Springfield museums include the Grand Army of the Republic Memorial Museum, the Springfield Art Association's historic Edwards Place, and the Vachel Lindsay home, featuring exhibits of the poet's original manuscripts and drawings. Ranked as one of the top five among expositions of its type is the Illinois State Fair, which opened modestly in 1853 and is now held in one of the most extensive of all state fairgrounds.

Not far from Springfield is historic New Salem, early home of Lincoln, and Camp Butler National Cemetery. Lake Springfield provides a convenient locale for water sports and lakeside housing.

SPRINGFIELD, Missouri. City (pop. 133,-116), southwest Missouri. Springfield is known as "the Gateway to the Ozarks." Potential settlers of southwestern Missouri were discouraged by the Federal Government's designation of southwestern Missouri as an Indian reservation. Settlers began coming to the Springfield area after 1850 when the tribes were moved west. Locating the land office at the junction of two roads assured Springfield of population as settlers migrated west and stopped to look at the land available.

Today Springfield is an industrial city, dairy center and shipping point. Springfield is the headquarters of the St. Louis-San Francisco Railway.

In August, 1861, Confederate troops seized Springfield in the Battle of WILSON'S CREEK (August 10, 1861). The town was recaptured by the Union a year later, but guerrilla warfare continued. One of the Union scouts was "Wild Bill" Hickok, later a famous marshall. The National Cemetery was established by the federal government in 1869. It is the only cemetery in this country where Confederate and Union soldiers are buried in adjoining ground. Controversy arose when a bill was introduced to make a gateway between the two burial sites. Opponents argued that the soldiers in death, as in life, should be apart, but the bill was passed and the gateway opened.

Drury College, Southwest Missouri State University, Baptist College, Central Bible Institute, and Evangel College are located there, along with the international headquarters of the Assemblies of God Church.

Annually in June some of this country's finest artists participate in Watercolor, U.S.A. Victorian elegance and charm come alive at Bentley House, an eighteen-room Queen Anne-style mansion. Nearby is the restored home of Laura Ingalls Wilder, author of the *Little House on the Prairie* book series.

History is very much a part of the community. Fantastic Caverns, near Springfield, is an electrically-lighted cave with a fascinating past. During Prohibition, the cave was transformed into a speakeasy with dance floor, bar and gambling tables. It served as a meetingplace in the 1930s and a theater in the 1960s. Today, tours by jeep-drawn tram are available.

SPRINGFIELD, Ohio. City (pop. 72,563), seat of Clark County, situated in west central Ohio, bisected by Buck Creek, which empties into the Mad river on the western outskirts. Springfield was settled in 1799 and incorporated as a city in 1850. An early settler, Simon

Kenton, established a gristmill and sawmill where the International Harvester plant now stands, and his wife named the community because of the spring water coming down the cliffs of Buck Creek valley. The great NATIONAL ROAD gave Springfield a boost, as did the nearby MIAMI AND ERIE CANAL, and Springfield became a "jumping off place for the frontier." Railroads came in 1846, further expanding the economy of this community, center of a rich agricultural area. Agricultural machinery was first manufactured there in 1850. A farm journal published in the 1880s provided the start for the mammoth Crowell Publishing Company. International Harvester arrived in the early 1900s, and the national 4-H movement was started at Springfield at about the same time. Wittenburg College at Springfield was founded in 1845 as a Lutheran institution. ANTIOCH COLLEGE is at nearby YELLOW SPRINGS. The local history is preserved by the Clark County Historical Society Museum. Springfield Art Center has a worthwhile collection and operates a fine arts school. The summer arts festival offers a series of music drama and dance performances, along with visual arts displays.

"SQUIRREL HUNTERS." In August, 1862, when it appeared that CINCINNATI, Ohio, might be invaded by Confederate forces during the CIVIL WAR, Governor David Tod called for volunteers, and placed twenty-five-year-old Lew WALLACE (1827-1905) in charge. The amazing total of 15,766 responded. They arrived in such a hurry and so casually dressed that people said they looked like squirrel hunters. Although the Squirrel Hunters dug trenches at Cincinnati and looked formidable, the enemy never arrived. The volunteers were sent home with their expenses paid, and the General Assembly adopted a resolution: "Resolved. that the Governor is authorized...to appropriate out of his contingent fund, a sufficient sum to pay for the printing and lithographing of discharges to the patriotic men of the state...and who will be known in history as the Squirrel Hunters."

STAGECOACH. Vehicle drawn by teams of four or six horses which carried both passengers and freight. Horses were changed at stations along the route. The stations were known as stages. Because of poor road conditions, stagecoaches were not used much in the Midwest until the 19th century. The increased use of stagecoaches encouraged better road construction and maintenance. Passengers in stagecoaches traveled an average of fifteen hours per day during which time forty miles were covered in summer and twenty-five miles in winter. The capacity of a stagecoach ran upward to fourteen passengers plus baggage, mail and the driver. Most of the stagecoach routes to the west originated in Missouri. Railroad construction spelled an end to the need for this type of transportation.

STAGG, Amos Alonzo. (West Orange, NJ, 1862—Stockton, CA, Mar. 17, 1965). "Football's Grand Old Man." Stagg coached football at the University of CHICAGO for forty-one years. After he retired from the Chicago post, at the age of seventy, he coached at the College of the Pacific from 1933 to 1946 and at Susquehanna Pennsylvania University from 1947 to 1952. Stagg developed many new football techniques, including the tackling dummy. He became even more famous as the oldest active coach in the United States and as the coach with the greatest number of coaching seasons.

STARR, Belle. (Carthage, MO, 1846—Canadian River, Indian Territory, 1889). Outlaw. Starr became famous nationwide as one of the West's few female outlaws. However, that reputation is now being questioned. She may have begun outlaw life as a member of William QUANTRILL's guerrilla band after the death of her brother, Edward, who was also one of Quantrill's raiders. She bore a child of outlaw Cole Young (c.1869), then kept a Dallas, Texas, livery stable which often dealt in stolen horses. In 1888 she married Sam Starr, a Cherokee Indian who died in 1887. Starr then settled near present Eufala, Oklahoma, on a ranch on the Canadian River. This ranch became a hideout for outlaws, among them Jesse JAMES. The ranch was reputed to have been headquarters for Starr's own gang which operated under her orders. However, it is now thought that she herself never was the leader of an outlaw band. Starr was killed by Edgar Watson, wanted in Florida for murder. As with other outlaws, she died and was buried with her boots on.

STARVED ROCK STATE PARK. Oldest of the Illinois state parks. Starved Rock, located between OTTAWA and LA SALLE, on the ILLINOIS RIVER, opened in 1912. It is a narrow park running approximately four miles. The main feature of the park, and the source of its name, is the wall of rocky cliffs, which rise one hundred forty feet above the river. The strategic importance of Starved Rock was

Historic Starved Rock, Illinois.

noted, in 1679, by LA SALLE (1643-1687) and de Tonti, who built Fort St. Louis du Rocher on the summit in 1682. The fort was abandoned as a military post in 1702, but was used by French fur traders through 1721, when it was burned by the Indians. The park takes its name from the group of ILLINI INDIANS, said to have taken refuge there when other Indian groups attacked, blaming them for the death of Chief PONTIAC (1720?-1769). They are said to have starved on the high bluff, rather than suffer capture and death at enemy hands. Over fifty points of interest in the park are marked along approximately eighteen miles of trail.

STASSEN, Harold Edward. (St. Paul, MN, 1907—). Former Minnesota governor, candidate for the Republican nomination for president in election years, beginning in 1948, then 1952 and 1964. Continuing to announce his candidacy for nomination, as late as 1988, without much hope of selection, he became known as the "perennial candidate." Stassen was an attorney in Dakota County before being elected governor of Minnesota in 1938. He was re-elected twice and resigned early in his third term to serve in the Navy. While governor, Stassen gained national attention by supporting a labor law which provided a "cooling-off"

period before striking. After service in WORLD WAR II Stassen was a delegate to the conference in San Francisco which founded the United Nations. He was appointed president of the University of Pennsylvania in 1948. He served until 1953 when he resigned to serve as a mutual security administrator and then as a foreign operations administrator in which he controlled American aid to many countries. Stassen attempted to win the nomination for governor of Pennsylvania in 1958, but lost. In 1987, at the age of eighty, Stassen again announced his intention to run for the presidency in 1988 but did not make much headway beyond the announcement.

STATE FAIRS. Statewide events where people gather to present or see exhibits that show how other people live, work or play. The first Illinois state fair was held in 1853. Today as many as one million visitors come to SPRINGFIELD, Illinois, annually in August to the state fair which lasts eleven days and features exhibitions of agricultural products, entertainers, and automobile races. Another state fair is held in DU QUOIN, Illinois, on Labor Day. This is known as the Du Quoin State Fair and Hambletonian Harness Race. The Indiana State Fair is held annually in August in INDIANAPOLIS. The Iowa State Fair, one of the most important annual events in the state and among the best known in the country, is held in DES MOINES during the last week in August. Visitors see the Ohio State Fair in COLUMBUS in late August or early September. Michigan, like Illinois, claims two state fairs with the first, called the Upper Peninsula State Fair, coming in mid-August in the town of ESCANABA, while a second is held in DETROIT in late August. ST. PAUL, Minnesota hosts that state's fair from late August through Labor Day. The Wisconsin State Fair is held during August, in MILWAUKEE.

STEAM AUTOMOBILES. The first crude self-propelled vehicle to be built in the state which would some day gain world automobile leadership was the steam-driven car built during the winter of 1884-1885 in the machine shop of John and Thomas Clegg of Memphis, Michigan. Ransom Olds built the first truly practical steam-driven vehicle in 1893. This type of car was the first American automobile sold abroad, and steam automobiles remained popular for many years. They still retain certain qualities lacking in gasoline powered vehicles, but the steam power source is said to "require an engineer" to master it.

STEAMBOATS. The first steamboat in the Midwest was the *New Orleans*, which puffed down the OHIO and MISSISSIPPI rivers in 1811. The steamboat era has been described as one of the romantic periods in America history. The *Virginia* was the first steamboat on the upper Mississippi. *Walk-in-the-Water* was the first steamboat on the Great Lakes (1818). Soon routes between most of the Great Lakes ports were established.

Steamboats moved settlers down the Ohio River from the East to the succession of new ports established on the river, such as Shawneetown and Cairo, Illinois. Later steamboats moved supplies to St. Joseph and Westport, Missouri, springboards for the great migration westward on the MISSOURI RIVER.

Steamboats were things of terror to the first Indians who witnessed their passage on the major inland waterways. Whites tried to convince the Indians the huge ships were pulled by schools of fish. Guns fired from The *Warrior,* a gunboat, turned Black Hawk's people back into the hands of the whites during the BLACK HAWK WAR (1832), as they attempted to flee across the Mississipi toward the west. The first steamboat to become part of the inland navy of the United States was the *Western Engineer,* which, in 1819, also became the first steamboat to navigate the Missouri River. This ship was specifically designed to frighten Indians. Its bow was made to look like a serpent. Smoke and flames poured from its gaping mouth.

Navigating steamboats was a challenging job. Mississippi river pilots earned upwards of $1000 per month. Certainly the job was no easier on the treacherous Missouri River where it was said that navigating during low water was like putting one of the huge steamers on land and sending a boy ahead with a sprinkling can. Risk-taking was all a part of the job. In addition to meandering channels and sandbars the pilots were often induced to gamble their skill against the seasons. Large prizes awaited the first captain to pilot his ship through the ice jams in the spring to reach ST. PAUL, Minnesota.

Men who later gained fame in other occupations began working on steamboats. James J. HILL (1838-1916) operated a steamboat on the RED RIVER OF THE NORTH before buying the bankrupt St. Paul and Pacific Railroad. Abraham LINCOLN (1809-1965) piloted The *Talisman* to Portland Landing, Illinois. Samuel CLEMENS (1835-1910) gained his Mark Twain nickname on the Mississippi, where the call of "mark twain" announced a certain river depth.

Steamboat manufacturing was a way-of-life for many residents of river port cities. Jeffersonville, Indiana, built two thousand. New Albany, Indiana, boasted its construction of the *Robert E. Lee* and the *Eclipse.* The largest steamboat of all time was the *J.M. White II.* Its side paddles were four stories high. The smokestacks were seventy-five feet tall. Height was one of the problems for steamboats and size was another.

Steamboat traffic on the Great Lakes was severely hampered by the rapids on the ST. MARYS RIVER. To carry cargo from Lake SUPERIOR to Lake HURON the steamers and their freight were moved by rollers. The *Algonquin* took nearly all of the winter of 1839-1840 to make the journey in this manner. The *Independence* and *Julia Palmer* were hauled in 1846 before the SOO CANAL was available.

Of course, many accidents occurred in steamboating. The steamer Seawing capsized in Lake PEPIN and killed ninety-eight passengers. The White Cloud caught fire at the ST. LOUIS levee in 1849. The blaze spread and destroyed twenty-two other ships and fifteen blocks of the city in the Great St. Louis FIRE of 1849. Storms and fires took many a toll on the stormy Great Lakes. Perhaps the worst steamer tragedy occurred at the dock. On July 24, 1915, a happy crowd on the chartered steamer *Eastland* rushed from one side of the boat to the other as it was docked on the CHICAGO RIVER. The boat suddenly capsized, and 812 persons lost their lives.

Despite the occasional tragedy, the steamboat captured the hearts and minds of America. The *Virginia* made the trip from St. Louis to Fort Snelling in twenty days. It was able to travel an uncharted channel only in daylight, and the boat had to stop frequently for the crew to cut wood for fuel. The epic race of the *Grey Eagle* against the *Itasca* in 1858 would still make a classic racing story today. That ship, captained by Daniel Harris, carried a newspaper copy of Queen Victoria's message to President Buchanan congratulating him on the laying of the Atlantic cable. To reach St. Paul first, the *Grey Eagle* had to overtake and pass the *Itasca* which had a sixty-five-mile lead on a course only 265 miles long. The *Grey Eagle* made the run in twenty-four hours and forty minutes, a record for the fastest time ever made by a steamboat, thirteen miles per hour while underway.

Cargoes on steamboats were often as interesting as the passengers. The bodies of the murderers of George Davenport were purchased by a doctor in St. Louis and placed in casks of alcohol on board a steamer. When the steamer docked in St. Louis it was found that someone had discovered the casks and spiked them with a spigot from which, it is assumed, many strangely flavored drinks were poured. Cargoes of livestock added profits as well as peculiar odors. By 1850 it was not unusual for boat owners to load their ships to the water's edge with animals. An 1857 report indicates that the steamboat *W.L. Ewing* was jammed with horses, mules, cattle, sheep, and hogs from central Illinois. Unusual animal cargoes included the 10,830 pound elephant Hannibal, part of the mammoth circus of Herr Dreisbach which also traveled with a rhinoceros, several lions and, as the Midwestern papers reported, "other varmints."

In August, 1861, the steamboat *Key City* struck Dan Rice's circus steamboat nineteen miles below the city of LA CROSSE. The cage containing the "trained rhinoceros" was knocked overboard and feared lost. The relief can be imagined when a few days later the bulky animal was found trying to escape the buoy chain at the wharf in DUBUQUE, Iowa. In 1860 a Minnesota paper reported a new business venture for steamboats, hauling special barges of ice to the "fire-eaters" of the South.

Historians claim the age of the inland waters steamboat ended with the laying of railroad tracks westward. A few of the old time paddlewheelers (now with reciprocating engines) still operate cruises today as a luxurious and nostalgic reminder of a glorious past.

STEEL. A major industry of the upper Midwest region. Iron ore, the basic component of steel, was found in abundance in areas of Minnesota and Michigan. The MESABI RANGE in Minnesota produced more iron than any other region of the United States. Inland Steel opened a plant in East Chicago in 1893. United States Steel Corporation chose Indiana in 1905 as the future site of its greatest mills. The city of GARY, Indiana, was constructed, and thousands of workers were moved in. The Gary Land Company purchased 7,000 acres near the steel plant and platted a future city of 200,000.

The steel industry drew hundreds of related industries to the region. Republic Steel and other smaller steel companies became known as "Little Steel."

In 1918 steel workers, according to the Interchurch World Commission, earned less than a living wage. Unskilled labor often worked twelve hours a day in shifts of 18 to 24

hours. The American Federation of Labor, in attempting to unionize the workers, led a massive strike in 1919 which nearly closed down several of the cities and did not end until January, 1920. The steel companies refused all attempts to compromise or arbitrate. Hunger finally drove the workers back to their jobs. The strike dramatized the evils of long work days, and by September, 1922, the eight-hour day was in effect in Gary and in ninety-seven percent of the other steel plants.

By 1929 steel was the leading industry in Indiana. After the mid-1900s that leadership was threatened by competition from abroad. Imports of German, Japanese and other foreign made steel brought a depression to the steel industry and to much of the Midwest dependent on it. Gary was the worst hit of all. The steelmakers were accused of ignoring modern techniques, of permitting their plants to become obsolete in view of foreign developments. U.S. steel production of 131.5 million tons in 1970 had dropped to 92.5 million tons in 1980. However, during the 1970s and 1980s some progress was made in the midwest steel industry, although experts continue to describe it as "sick." Nevertheless, the Midwest steel producers in Ohio, Indiana, Illinois and Michigan continue to be among the leading U.S. steel companies, and Midwest steel production continues to account for more than a fourth of the U.S. total.

STEINDLER, Arthur. (Vienna, Austria, June 22, 1878—Iowa City, IA, July 21, 1959). Surgical pioneer. One of the pioneer team of medical men who made the Medical Center of the University of IOWA known worldwide for its excellence, Dr. Steindler became one of the world's most distinguished orthopedic specialists. He was responsible for the development of many of the techniques used universally today, including methods of bone care, treatment, straightening, grafting, lengthening and other orthopedic practices.

STEPHENS COLLEGE. Privately supported liberal arts college for women located in Columbia, Missouri. Originally known as Columbia Female Academy, Stephens College was founded by Lucy Wales in 1833. The 325-acre campus is the site of fifty buildings. The chapel is considered one of the most beautiful in the United States. The school holds accreditation from the North Central Association of Colleges and Schools and associate membership in the National Association of Schools of Music.

There are cooperative plans with several universities in the fields of animal science and engineering. During the 1985-1986 academic year, the college enrolled 987 students and had 113 faculty members.

STERLING HEIGHTS, Michigan. City (108,999), situated in Macomb County in southeast Michigan, a suburb of DETROIT, located north of the larger city. It was named in honor of Azariah W. Sterling, an early settler. The city is particularly notable for its remarkable growth during the period of 1970 through 1984. As a popular "bedroom" community, it grew from 61,000 in 1970 to 109,000 in 1984 and ranks 148th in population among all U.S. cities.

STEVENSON, Adlai Ewing. (Christian Co., KY, Oct. 23, 1835—Chicago, IL, June 14, 1914). Lawyer, politician, and Vice President of the United States (1893-1897). Admitted to the bar in 1858, he was elected Illinois state's attorney in 1865. As a staunch Democrat he served twice in the U.S. House of Representatives (1875-1877, 1879-1881) before being appointed first assistant postmaster general under President Grover Cleveland (1885-89). After serving as vice president with Cleveland, he was appointed by President William MC KINLEY (1843-1901) to serve as chairman of a commission sent to Europe to secure international bimetallism. He was an unsuccessful candidate for vice president (1900) and for the Illinois governorship (1908).

STEVENSON, Adlai Ewing II. (Los Angeles, CA, Feb. 5, 1900—London, England, July 14, 1965). Statesman, Illinois governor. After studies at Princeton and Harvard, Stevenson received his law degree from NORTHWESTERN UNIVERSITY. Stevenson's first public office was in the Agricultural Adjustment Administration from 1933 to 1934. During WORLD WAR II he was a special counsel to Secretary of the Navy, Frank Knox. After the war, Stevenson was an alternate delegate to the United Nations. In 1948 he was elected governor of Illinois, his home state, on a reform Democratic ticket, by the largest plurality in the state's history to that point. He is credited with spearheading 78 "clean-up" measures. In 1952 he was drafted as the Democratic candidate for president, despite the fact that he refused to campaign for the nomination. However, as the nominee, he did campaign vigorously, in a manner said to have been "marked by eloquent speeches whose wit and civility were often memorable." He was

defeated then and again in 1956 by Dwight D. Eisenhower. In that campaign he was hampered by what some considered his overly-intellectual approach to national issues as contrasted to Eisenhower's more homey touch. Stevenson served as one of the United States' most notable ambassadors to the United Nations, from 1961 until his death.

STILL, Andrew Taylor. (Jonesville, VA, Aug. 6, 1828—Kirksville, MO, Dec. 12, 1917). Physician, founder of Osteopathy. Beginning his medical practice in 1853 in Kansas and Missouri, he became involved in antislavery work and was elected to the Kansas legislature in 1857. He fought for the North in the CIVIL WAR and was promoted to major. After the death of three of his children due to cerebrospinal meningitis, Still began exploring manipulative means of treating such disease rather than traditional methods. For 25 years he traveled around the country teaching and promoting. He founded the American School of Osteopathy in KIRKSVILLE, Missouri, in 1892.

STILLWATER, Minnesota. City (pop. 12,-290), seat of Washington County, eastern Minnesota near the MISSISSIPPI RIVER, northeast of ST. PAUL, considered the birthplace of the logging industry in Minnesota. John McKusick named it in 1843 because the still waters of Lake ST. CROIX reminded him and his fellow settlers of their homes in Stillwater, Maine. The first townsite was laid out by Joseph Brown in 1839 at the head of Lake St. Croix and named Dahkotah. The Territory of Minnesota was born here in a public meeting known as the "Stillwater Convention of 1848." Henry H. SIBLEY was chosen to represent the territory in Congress. The first sawmill was constructed in Stillwater in 1844. By 1854 the city was a major lumber center and one of the three largest cities in the state, along with ST. ANTHONY and St. Paul. Stillwater continued to be the lumber capital of the state until the mid-1800s when it was surpassed by MINNEAPOLIS. Stillwater was the site of the area's first prison which was constructed in Battle Hollow. Artifacts of early Stillwater, including children's toys, Victorian furniture, and tools, may be seen at the Washington County Historical Society and Warden's Home Museum.

STITES, Benjamin. (—) Major Stites was principally responsible for the early settlement of much of southwest Ohio and the Ohio River valley. He visited the region in the late 1700s and became so convinced of the value of the land that he is said to have walked the entire way to New York City, where he tried to interest capitalists in the land. He said every acre was "worth a silver dollar." Judge John Cleves Symmes of New Jersey was interested and formed a company which petitioned Congress for permission to buy 30,000 acres. This first purchase (1792) was augmented until the company was said to have owned hundreds of thousands of acres. However, they had previously sold the site of present CINCINNATI to three other speculators, and Benjamin Stites led the first settlers to Cincinnati in 1788.

STOCK, Frederick. (Julich, Germany, Nov. 11, 1872—Chicago, IL, Oct. 20, 1942). Orchestra conductor. Stock came to CHICAGO, in 1895, to join the CHICAGO SYMPHONY ORCHESTRA as principal viola. He served as the assistant director for several years and, after the death of principal conductor Theodore THOMAS in 1903, Stock became the musical director and conductor of the Chicago Symphony. Stock, a naturalized citizen of the United States in 1919, conducted several performances of Wagnerian opera for the Civic Opera Company of Chicago in 1923. He was the general music director for Chicago's CENTURY OF PROGRESS EXPOSITION in 1933. Stock's compositions include a symphony, two concert overtures, a tone poem for orchestra and a concerto for violin and orchestra. He is renowned for his support of modern composers, presenting world premieres of works of many composers well known today. In one of the longest tenures as conductor of a major symphony, Stock was the symphony's conductor until his death.

STONE CITY, Iowa. Town (pop 100). Situated north of CEDAR RAPIDS, east central Iowa, the hamlet today is best known for the artist colony founded there by famed Iowa artist Grant WOOD (1891-1942). One of Wood's better known works is titled "Stone City" and represents his view of his favorite village. Wood hoped the colony would be a place where midwesterners could "unselfconsciously paint the things they knew best," the German, Swedish and Indian cultures of the region, the fields and farms, mansions and poor places. He also hoped to include poets and musicians in his flock of artists, who at one time lived in icewagon bunkhouses. Others rented space in the Green Mansion or the Water Tower. At one time the community was larger and more prosperous commercially than at present, busy

with the flourishing limestone industry followed by cement works. Richard's Inn at Stone City is a favorite gathering place for those who come to visit the site made famous by one of the most currently respected artists of his genre.

STONG, Phil. (Pittsburg, IA, Jan. 27, 1899—Washington, CT., Apr. 26, 1957). American author, best known for his novel *State Fair* (1932), from which two popular motion pictures were drawn. The novel did much to enhance the reputation of the Iowa State Fair as one of the country's most notable annual expositions. After his death in Connecticut, Stong's body was returned to his native Pittsburg, Iowa, for burial in the small town in the bend of the lower DES MOINES RIVER.

"STOOL PIGEON." Term derived from a scheme used to lure passenger pigeons for the hunt. A live bird was tied to a stool. When the stool was moved the pigeon would flap its wings and attract other birds which were then killed. The practice gave rise to the slang term, "stool pigeon," for someone who "takes the rap" for another.

STOUT, William Bushnell. (Quincy, IL, Mar. 16, 1880—Phoenix, AZ, Mar. 20, 1956). Aeronautical engineer. Stout sold the Stout Metal Aircraft Company to Ford Motor Company in 1925, but remained as a vice-president and general manager during the development of the Ford trimotor transport plane from a single engine transport. Stout founded the Stout Air Services in 1926, the first company in the U.S. to provide passenger service exclusively. The airline flew between DETROIT and GRAND RAPIDS, Michigan. With the development of the trimotor, Stout moved the airline from Detroit to CLEVELAND in 1927 and added a Detroit to CHICAGO route. Stout opened the Stout Engineering Labs in 1929 for research and development in aeronautics. His company developed and built the all-metal Sky Car, a new type of airplane for private owner use, and under contract to the Pullman Car and Manufacturing Company, developed a high-speed Railplane. Stout's last major invention was a fiberglass automobile with the engine in the rear. This was produced at the Graham-Paige Motors Corporation at Willow Run, Michigan.

STOWE, Harriet Beecher. (Litchfield, CT, June 14, 1811—July 1, 1896. Author, social reformer. In 1832, when her father, Henry

Ward Beecher, came to CINCINNATI, Ohio, to head the Lane Theological Seminary there, Harriet moved to Cincinnati with him and began teaching and writing. In 1836 she married Professor Calvin Ellis Stowe. Cincinnati was a hotbed of anti-slave sentiment, and Harriet's brothers were ardent Abolitionists. She had experienced the effects of slavery in Kentucky and had helped a slave escape. When the Fugitive Slave Act was passed in 1850, Harriet Stowe decided to write a novel about slavery. The story is told that she had visited the home of Abolitionist the Rev. John Rankin, at RIPLEY, Ohio. He operated one of the busiest of all the stations on the UNDERGROUND RAILROAD. Rankin is said to have told Harriet of the escape he witnessed of the slave ELIZA, fleeing across the Ohio River on the ice, carrying a baby in her arms. This incident was "claimed" by several other Ohio River towns. However, it was brought to life in one of the most famous books of all times, Stowe's *Uncle Tom's Cabin* (1852). The book electrified the North in its response against SLAVERY and probably was more responsible than any other single cause for bringing on the CIVIL WAR. Three-hundred-thousand copies were sold. Foreign-language editions were produced, and plays were written based upon the novel. Mrs. Stowe's published output totalled sixteen volumes, but she never achieved another success to equal her first effort.

STRAITS OF MACKINAC. Narrow extension of water between the Upper and Lower peninsulas of Michigan. The first white man to travel through the straits is thought to have been Jean NICOLET (1598-1642), in 1634. The military significance of the straits prompted the French to build FORT MICHILIMACKINAC on the straits in 1715. Today the straits are crossed by the MACKINAC BRIDGE, opened in 1957, the fourth longest suspension bridge in the world and one of Michigan's major tourist attractions.

STRANG, James Jesse. (Scipio, NY, Mar. 21, 1813—MI, July 9, 1856). Leader of a Mormon religious branch. Strang founded the city of St. James on BEAVER ISLAND in Lake MICHIGAN in 1849 and ruled the community as a dictator. He called himself "King" of the island. In 1850 Strang announced a "revelation" claiming the sanctity of plural marriage and the next year he was charged with robbing the mail and counterfeiting. Acquitted of the charges, Strang ran successfully for a seat in the Michigan legislature in 1852 and served until

1854. He was assassinated on July 16, 1856, by Alexander Wentworth. Strang had refused to name a successor, and his church failed.

STRITCH, Samuel Alphonsus. (Nashville, TN, Aug. 17, 1887—Rome, Italy, May 27, 1958). Catholic cardinal. Ordained a Roman Catholic priest in 1910, he served in many official positions in Nashville, Tennessee, Ohio and CHICAGO before being named cardinal in 1946. As head of the Diocese of Chicago, the largest in the country, he became increasingly influential. He was the first American ever to be appointed to the Roman Curia, the principal governing body of the Roman Catholic Church. Shortly before his death, he was appointed head of all Catholic mission work.

STURGEON BAY, Wisconsin. City (pop. 8,847), seat of Door County, situated at the farthest inland position on the bay from which it takes its name, at one time sturgeons were caught and said to be "piled like cordwood along the shore." Its location placed the site on a short portage from the main body of Lake MICHIGAN to GREEN BAY. From the earliest times, explorers, trappers and others had portaged across this narrowest part of the peninsula, which forms DOOR COUNTY. For entrance into Green Bay, this shortcut eliminated a one-hundred mile passage around the point of the peninsula. In 1673 Father Jacques MARQUETTE (1637-1675) was the first European known to have visited the site. Later Henri de Tonti and his men were saved from starvation there by POTAWATOMI chief Onanguisse. Almost two centuries later sawmilling became the main activity of the site, which had not yet become a settlement. In 1878 the limestone separating Green Bay and the main lake was blasted away to form a 6,600-foot canal, and water traffic at last could travel through the peninsula. The canal is large enough to accommodate lake freighters. Today, shipyards and fruit packing provide most of the industry of Sturgeon Bay. Ten million pounds of cherries are canned there every year. One of the main tourist centers of the Midwest, the city offers almost every type of recreation, much of which may be found in the nearby La Salle and Cave Point county parks and Potawatomi State Park. Door County Museum features a country store and old-time fire department, along with other displays of regional history. Sturgeon Bay Marine Museum concentrates on the shipbuilding industry and its history. The annual House and Garden Walk is held on the last Tuesday of

July and the Door County Fair in mid-August.

SUBLETTE, William Lewis (Lincoln Co., KY, c.1799—Pittsburgh, PA, July 23, 1845). Fur trader. He moved with his family to ST. CHARLES, MISSOURI, about 1818. He joined the 1822 expedition of William H. ASHLEY (1778?- 1838) to the Rocky Mountains. After Ashley started Sublette in his own fur trading business, in 1823 his wagons were the first to cross the Rockies. Sublette amassed a fortune in fur trading and later became an important figure in the state politics of Missouri.

SULLIVAN, Louis Henry. (Boston, Massachusetts, September 3, 1856—Chicago, Illinois, April 14, 1924). Architect. Sullivan was considered one of the foremost architects in the United States. His design for the National Farmers' Bank Building in OWATONNA, Minnesota, is said to be one of his most interesting. Sullivan was given complete control of the project despite the concern of the conservative bankers as to what he might have in mind. He contended that outward form should reflect the function of a building. He first attracted national attention with his Transporation Building at the 1893 WORLD'S COLUMBIAN EXPOSITION in CHICAGO, which was renowned for its originality and for heralding a new viewpoint. It contrasted sharply with the classical buildings of the rest of the exposition. Sullivan was especially noted for the elaborate ornamentation which decorated his structures. The Carson Pirie Scott store in Chicago is a particularly fine example of this. His young colleague, Frank Lloyd WRIGHT (1867-1957), gained much of his inspiration from working with the older master.

SULLIVAN, Missouri. City (pop. 5,461), eastern Missouri, southwest of ST. LOUIS, established 1856, named for Stephen Sullivan, who came to the area from Kentucky in 1800 after having made a fortune in tobacco, lead and copper mining. Legend holds that he was executed by Federal troops during the CIVIL WAR after they found he was making gunpowder for the Confederacy. Sullivan was the birthplace of George HEARST (1820-1891) who later became a mining engineer, United States Senator and extremely wealthy California businessman. His son was William Randolph Hearst, the publisher. Near Sullivan, geologists have found unusually white stalagmites and stalactites in Cathedral Cave. Lost River, lying two hundred feet below ground level, continues to eat its way

through the bluffs of the MERAMEC RIVER. Visitors ride on the Lost River in flat-bottomed boats during expeditions through Onondaga Cave located in Onondaga Cave State Park. Personal belongings of the Jesse James gang and a $100,000 gun collection have been displayed at the Jesse James Wax Museum.

SUMMER SCHOOL. Mount Union College at Alliance, Ohio, founded in 1846, is said to have developed the first summer session ever held at the college level.

SUNDAY, William Ashley (Billy). (Ames, IA, Nov. 19, 1863—Winona Lake, IN, Nov., 1935). Evangelist and prohibitionist. Sunday, a minister of the Chicago Presbytery, ordained April 15, 1903, is said to have preached to more people than any other man in Christian history before the age of mass communication. He is further given credit for being the single greatest factor in causing the decline of the saloon in the United States. Between 1904 and 1907 Sunday received from one thousand to five thousand converts per month. He galvanized evangelistic meetings in major cities across the country during which he was known to jump over the pulpit, tear his hair, and occasionally roll on the floor, while still delivering sermons with sincere warmth. Sunday began his life in the Midwest as a very successful professional baseball player from 1883 to 1890 with teams of CHICAGO, Pittsburgh and Philadelphia. He is credited with developing the bunt.

SUPERIOR UPLANDS. Rugged northeastern region of Minnesota, southern portion of the Canadian Shield. The Upland is the region of Minnesota least affected by glacial action. The section of the Uplands just north of Lake SUPERIOR contains the most isolated and roughest part of the state. Prominent features of the Upland include Cook County's Eagle Mountain, the highest point in Minnesota, and the arrowhead shape of the northeastern tip of the region which gives the region its name, Arrowhead Country. Commercially the area contains most of Minnesota's iron ore deposits.

SUPERIOR, LAKE. Westernmost, northernmost, deepest and highest above sea level of the GREAT LAKES. Lake Superior is bordered on the north and east by the Canadian province of Ontario and on the south by Michigan and Wisconsin and on the west by Minnesota. Lake Superior is 350 miles in length and covers an area of 31,800 square miles. Its greatest recorded depth is 1,333 feet. Lake Superior drains an area of 80,100 square miles and ranks as the largest body of fresh water in the world. At its southeast end, it is connected with Lake HURON by the ST. MARYS RIVER. The coastline of Lake Superior tends to be rocky. Sandstone walls, known as the Pictured Rocks, line the shore in Michigan. A famous landmark, SPLIT ROCK LIGHTHOUSE, warns shippers of the reefs in Beaver Bay along the Minnesota shore. The lake contains the mouths of nearly two hundred rivers, the largest of which is the St. LOUIS RIVER, the headwaters of the ST. LAWRENCE RIVER SYSTEM. Jutting into the lake in upper Michigan is the Keweenaw Peninsula, famous for its deposits of copper. Michigan's ISLE ROYALE and Ontario's Ignace and Michipicoten are the lake's largest islands. Shipping on Lake Superior runs from mid-April to December. Although the lake does not freeze over in winter, frozen harbors limit the season. Ships loaded with wheat, lumber, TACONITE, and copper avoid the rapids in the ST. MARYS RIVER by traversing the locks at SAULT STE. MARIE making the connection from Lake Superior to Lake Huron. Among the chief ports on Lake Superior are TWO HARBORS, DULUTH, Taconite Harbor, and GRAND MARAIS, all in Minnesota; MARQUETTE in Michigan; ASHLAND and SUPERIOR, Wisconsin.

SUPERIOR, Wisconsin. City (pop. 29,571, seat of Douglas County, situated at the farthest tip of Lake SUPERIOR, from which it takes its name. The city boasts the finest harbor on the Great Lakes, Superior Bay, which it shares with DULUTH, Minnesota. The harbor is formed by the estuary of the ST. LOUIS RIVER, down the middle of which runs the Wisconsin-Minnesota border. The area was explored by Pierre RADISSON (1636-1710) in 1661 and DULUTH (1710-1769) in 1679. Duluth may have established a trading post on the site. The Hudson's Bay Company the NORTH WEST FUR COMPANY and AMERICAN FUR COMPANY successively managed the fur trade. Principal settlement began as early as 1852. However, the real boom started with the first shipment of ore from the Vermillion Range in Minnesota in 1884. Within five years, the community had achieved the beginnings of most of the industry which supports it today. The port ranks first or second among all the Great Lake ports, depending on the year. The vast grain elevators (including the world's largest) and enormous coal and ore facilities, oil refineries, shipyards and the surrounding dairy industry, all contribute to the Superior economy. The Burlington Northern docks and

TACONITE pellet handling complex are the country's largest, as are the coal-handling facilities of the area. For tourists, the Stockade Site marks the spot where a stockade was raised for protection during the Sioux Uprising. Narrated cruises of the harbor are available. Fairlawn Mansion and Museum offers a 42-room restored Victorian home overlooking Lake Superior. Of interest, also, is the Children's Chapel, part of St. Joseph's Orphanage. The Old Firehouse Museum displays the history of firefighting. The Superior Municipal Forest, Amnicon Falls State Park, Pattison State Park and Brule River State Forest all provide all-season sports of great popularity. The Head-of-the-Lakes Fair is held in late July or early August.

SUPERIOR-QUETICO PRIMITIVE RE-GION. Recreational and wildlife area maintained on both sides of the United States-Canadian border. Accessible in only a few areas by roads, the region is a paradise for those who crave wilderness solitude. Superior is in the United States and Quetico in Canada. Superior National Forest has more than two thousand crystal clear lakes with picturesque islands and rugged shorelines. The Boundary Waters Canoe Area Wilderness is considered the finest canoe country in the United States. The adjacent Quetico Provincial Park is similar to Superior National Forest.

SWAN LAKE NATIONAL WILDLIFE REFUGE. Wintering grounds near Brookfield, Missouri, for one of the largest concentrations of Canada geese in North America. The refuge contains 10,670 acres and annually attracts more than one hundred bald eagles. Waterfowl concentrations are the highest in March through April and October through November. Photographers are welcome and birdwatching is permitted. A self-guided tour and observation tower are open all year.

SWISS VOLKSFEST. One of the best-known villages settled mainly by immigrants from Switzerland is NEW GLARUS, Wisconsin. Today every effort is made to maintain and strengthen the Swiss character of the community. The annual Swiss Volksfest, held there in early August, is the most comprehensive of its type. Held in William Tell Shooting Park, archery competitions, yodeling, Swiss dancing and other attractions herald the birth of the Swiss nation in 1291.

SWISSHELM, Jane Grey Cannon. (Pittsburgh, PA, Dec. 6, 1815—Swissvale, PA, July 22, 1884. Abolitionist, women's rights reformer. She used her newspaper, the ST. CLOUD (Minnesota) *Democrat*, to attack slavery. The operation was destroyed by pro-slavery forces. She established the Pittsburgh *Saturday Visitor* (1847-1857), a weekly advocating temperance, abolition and woman's suffrage. She contributed to the New York *Tribune* and clerked in government offices in Washington, D.C. until dismissed when she began *The Reconstructionist.*

SWOPE, Herbert Bayard. (St. Louis, MO, Jan. 5, 1882—Sands Point, LI, NY, June 20, 1958) Journalist. War correspondent for the New York *World*, Swope was awarded the 1917 Pulitzer prize for reporting. As executive editor of the newspaper, he became renowned for good writing and crusading. Originating the Op-Ed Page, Swope carried the bylines of Heywood Broun, Alexander Woollcott and many other notable writers. During both world wars and on many other occasions he was a valued consultant to government officials and agencies.

T

TABOR, Iowa. Town (Pop. 1,088), situated in Fremont County, in far southwest Iowa. The name, from the Biblical Tabor and the Czech city of Tabor. A key depot on the UNDERGROUND RAILROAD, Abolitionist John BROWN (1800-1859) often trained some of his "troops" and also stored arms there. An older college at Tabor was for a time in the 1950s transformed into one of the new wave experimental institutions but kept the name Tabor College. It specialized in enrolling students who had failed in high school.

TACONITE. A hard rock named for the Taconic Mountains of Vermont and western Massachusetts. Useful taconite contains as little as thirty percent iron, consisting of fine specks of iron oxide. The stone is found in large amounts in the MESABI RANGE in Minnesota which had held the large deposits of high-grade iron ore first mined in the area. The stone is too hard for ordinary drilling. Miners must shoot alternating streams of burning kerosene and cold water at the stone. The kerosene heats the rock to temperatures in excess of four thousand degrees. The blast of cold water cracks the rock which may then be blasted into chunks. A successful method of extracting iron ore from taconite was developed by Professor E.W. Davis at the University of MINNESOTA. Davis converted the small iron content of the magnetic taconite found in the eastern Mesabi into pellets containing sixty percent iron. This process, known as beneficiating, breathed new economic life into northern Minnesota at a time when deposits of high-grade iron ore were becoming

exhausted. The process is increasingly used wherever taconite ore is found.

TAFT, Lorado. (Elmwood, IL, April 20, 1860—Chicago, IL, Oct. 30, 1936). Sculptor. Taft is recognized as one of the Midwest's finest sculptors. Examples of his work are displayed across the United States. His statue of America's great French benefactor, Lafayette, stands in Elliott Hall of Music in PURDUE UNIVERSITY in Indiana. This was Taft's first commission when he arrived in CHICAGO at the age of twenty-six, but even then a recognized genius of his art. Taft was an instructor at the ART INSTITUTE OF CHICAGO from 1886 to 1907 and lectured at the same institution from 1886 to 1929. Other works commissioned from Taft include "Solitude of the Soul" for the Art Institute of Chicago; heroic "Blackhawk" now standing in Oregon, Illinois; the Columbus Memorial Fountain in Washington, D.C.; The "Pioneers" in Elmwood, Illinois; and the "Lincoln" in URBANA, Illinois. Taft was awarded the Designer's Medal at the Chicago WORLD'S COLUMBIAN EXPOSITION in 1893, the silver medal at the Buffalo Exposition in 1901, and the gold medal at the St. Louis LOUISIANA PURCHASE EXPOSITION in 1904.

TAFT, Robert Alphonso. (Cincinnati, OH, Sept. 8, 1889—New York, NY, July 31, 1953). U.S. Senator. Son of William Howard TAFT. Robert Taft practiced law in Ohio and served in the state legislature. He was elected to the U.S. Senate in 1938. A foe of big government, he opposed F.D. Roosevelt in a number of his programs and became the leader of the conservative Republicans. His influence in Congress was so great that he blocked many of President Harry S Truman's Fair Deal measures, turning Truman into an unforgiving foe. Although he was an isolationist before WORLD WAR II, Taft favored the United Nations. He was co-author of the Taft-Hartley Act, regulating labor practices. This is considered his principal legislative accomplishment. Taft opposed U.S. entry into the North Atlantic Treaty Organization (NATO). He considered the Truman administrtion to be soft on Communism and supported the early investigations of Communism of Senator Eugene McCarthy concerning Communist infiltration into government. Taft was so thoroughly in tune with his party's line that he became known as Mr. Republican. He unsuccessfully sought the Republican nomination in 1940 and in 1948. In 1952, he was considered to be the most likely candidate for the Republican nomination for president. However, the candidacy of Dwight D. Eisenhower brought on a long struggle with Taft supporters which almost split the party. After losing the Republican nomination of 1952 to Eisenhower, he loyally supported the Eisenhower candidacy. Taft became the majority leader in the Senate and worked closely as an Eisenhower adviser. Some authorities consider Robert Taft to have been one of the five most influential senators in U.S. history.

TAFT, William Howard. (Cincinnati, OH, Sept. 15, 1857—March 8, 1930). Twenty-seventh President of the United States, Chief Justice of the United States. Upon graduation from Yale in 1878, Taft attended Cincinnati Law School and took a law degree in 1880. He began the practice of law in CINCINNATI and almost immediately took an active part in local Republican politics, holding several minor public offices before being appointed to serve on the superior court of Ohio (1887-1890).

In 1890 his selection by President Benjamin HARRISON (1833-1911) as U.S. Solicitor General brought him into national political prominence. Beginning in 1892, he was presiding judge of the sixth federal circuit court of appeals and spent eight years on that bench. He gained a reputation as serving conservatively but effectively in the post. Although considered anti-labor, his decisions were based on what he thought were the proper limits of labor actions, opposing such practices as secondary boycotts and violence.

In 1900 as president of the U.S. commission to the Phillipines he began at once to organize an efficient civilian government there, continuing his effective administration when he became the first U.S. governor of the Phillipines. He was particularly successful in improving relations between the Philippine people and the United States.

In 1904 President Theodore Roosevelt appointed Taft secretary of war, and they became close friends, with Taft as one of the president's most cherished advisers. He was a prime mover in the organization of the Panama Canal construction.

Personally chosen by Roosevelt as his successor, Taft had little difficulty in the election of 1908 and was inaugurated as president. The parcel post system, the postal savings bank and the Department of Labor were among the innovations of his administration.

The principal accomplishments of his administration were a trade agreement with Canada and arbitration treaties with France and Britain. However, the Senate failed to ratify any of these. His anti-trust actions were more numerous than Roosevelt's, but failed to attract much attention.

He became increasingly more attuned to the conservative wing of the Republican Party. He approved the Payne-Aldrich Tariff Act of 1909, which made few concessions to tariff reduction, because he felt it was the best possible politically. But this angered the Progressive Republicans, and his growing conservatism led him to fall out of favor with Theodore Roosevelt. Roosevelt fought Taft for the Republican presidential nomination in 1912. Failing to get the Republican nod when Taft received the nomination, Roosevelt organized his own PROGRESSIVE PARTY (popularly called the Bull Moose Party) and ran for president. With the Republican Party split, the Democrats won one of the closest elections in American history, and Taft retired to private life, teaching law at Yale University.

In 1921 he was appointed to the post of Chief Justice of the United States by President Warren G. HARDING (1865-1923). He made substantial contributions to the administrative procedures of the Supreme Court, inaugurating methods by which he managed to eliminate the backlog of cases on the docket. In 1925 he was instrumental in the passage of the Judges' Act. This permitted the courts more discrimination in accepting cases.

One of his important opinions came in *Bailey v. Drexel Furniture Co.* (1922). This was the case in which he concurred with the majority that Congress had exceeded its authority to the loss of state sovereignty. In *Adkins v. Children's Hospital* (1923), he demonstrated his more liberal side, upholding a women's minimum wage law in the District of Columbia. His majority opinion in *Myers v. United States* (1926) clarified and extended the power of the president to remove executive officeholders. Taft resigned as Chief Justice early in 1930, due to poor health, and died a month later. William Howard Taft is the only person in U.S. history to have served as both president and chief justice.

William Howard Taft was the seventh of his father's ten children, the second of five children of a second marriage. In Cincinnati, on June 19, 1886, at the age of 28, he married Helen Herron Taft, a native of Cincinnati. They had three children, of whom the most prominent was the oldest, Robert Alphonso TAFT (1889-1953), who became known as "Mr. Republican" for his service in the U.S. Senate. The Tafts were married for a period of 43 years, and Mrs. Taft survived the president for thirteen years, living to the age of 75.

TAHQUAMENON RIVER. Rising in the eastern section of Michigan's UPPER PENINSULA, the Tahquamenon flows almost directly south to McMillan, then turns east past Dollarville. It flows into Whitefish Bay of Lake SUPERIOR at the village of Shelldrake, Michigan.

TALIESIN. The Frank Lloyd WRIGHT (1867-1959) home near SPRING GREEN, Wisconsin, was designed by him to follow the contour of a hill. It was built of brown stucco and limestone, quarried near by. Wright called it "an example of the use of native materials and the play of space relations, the long stretches of low ceilings extending outside over and beyond the windows, related in direction to some feature in the landscape." In later years the structure gave its name to and became a part of Wright's larger activities through his foundation and his Taliesin Fellowships for architectural apprentices.

TAMA, Iowa. City (pop. 2,968), situated in Tama County in south central eastern Iowa, first named Iuka, then changed to Tama, named either for the Fox chief Taimah or for the wife of Chief Poweshiek. The meaning is variously interpreted as sound of thunder, or pleasant, or a bear with a voice that makes the rocks tremble. The city has been an important

railroad and commercial center, connected without interruption to its twin city to the north, TOLEDO. West of Tama is the settlement of the MESQUAKI INDIANS, who returned to their native Iowa and bought 3,600 acres of land near Tama, where about 600 still live. They are often called the Tama Indians.

TAMAROA INDIANS. One of a group of tribes which lived in Illinois at the time of the explorations of MARQUETTE (1637-1675) and JOLLIET (1645-1700). The Tamaroa, Michigamea, Moingwena, Peoria, Cahokia and Kaskaskia referred to themselves as the ILLINI, which meant "the men," because they felt themselves superior to other tribes living in the region.

TANEYCOMO, LAKE. In Taney County, in southwestern Missouri near the Arkansas line. BULL SHOALS LAKE is just to the south and SPRINGFIELD to the north. Taneycomo was created by the construction of Forsyth Dam (1,720 feet), which impounded the WHITE RIVER. This 25-mile lake forms a resort area in the Ozark region.

TARHE THE CRANE (Chief). (—). Chief of the WYANDOTTE Indians, Tarhe remained friendly to the Americans during the WAR OF 1812. He led a group of other friendly Indians in an agreement to stay neutral during the war, relieving much of the pressure on U.S. forces in the Midwest.

TARKINGTON, Newton Booth. (Indianapolis, IN, July 29, 1869—Indianapolis, IN, May 19, 1946). Novelist and dramatist. Tarkington, twice awarded the PULITZER PRIZE for literature, is considered one of the nation's most capable authors in depicting the wholesome aspects of midwestern life. He is best remembered for *Seventeen* (1916), portraying the joys and problems of adolescence. He also presented a cross-section of life in his hometown of INDIANAPOLIS in such works as 1918 Pulitzer Prize winning *The Magnificent Ambersons*. His best work is considered to be *Alice Adams*, which brought his second Pulitzer in 1921. Among his other honors were the gold medal, National Institute of Arts and Sciences and the Theodore Roosevelt Memorial medal. He served in the Indiana House of Representatives from 1902 to 1903.

TARKIO RIVER. Rising in south Iowa, it crosses into northwest Missouri and flows approximately 50 miles to drain into the

MISSOURI RIVER in the Blacksnake Hills. The river passes through a grain production valley and has a migratory waterfowl refuge on its banks.

TAUM SAUK MOUNTAIN. Highest point in Missouri at 1,771.7 feet, in the southeastern part of the state southwest of Iron Mountain and Pilot Knob.

TAYLOR, Maxwell Davenport. (Keytesville, MO, Aug. 26, 1901—). Military officer. A 1922 graduate of the U.S. Military Academy at West Point, N.Y., he helped organize the first army airborne division, the 82nd, in the early years of WORLD WAR II. He was cited for bravery when he chose to cross enemy lines at great personal risk just 24 hours before the Allied invasion of Italy (1943), to discuss with Italian leaders the possible seizure of Roman airfields. He also led the 101st Airborne Division in assaults on Normandy and the Netherlands. In 1953 he served as commanding general of the 8th Army, directed the United Nations forces in Korea, was appointed army chief of staff then chairman of the Joint Chiefs of Staff in 1962, and served as U.S. ambassador to South Vietnam. Urging President Lyndon B. Johnson to increase U.S. participation in the war with North Vietnam, he was one of the most important factors in expanding that unpopular conflict.

TAYLOR, Zachary. (Montebello, VA, Nov. 24, 1784—Washington, DC, July 9, 1850). Twelfth President of the United States. Taylor had several important missions in the Midwest. As an Army officer in 1812, Taylor, with only fifty men, defended FORT HARRISON, Indiana, from Indian attack involving four hundred warriors. Taylor's later military career included campaigns in the BLACK HAWK WAR (1832). On the national scene, as the hero of the MEXICAN WAR, his popularity brought him the Whig presidential nomination in 1848. Because of a split in the Democratic Party, Taylor won the election, although he had very little knowledge of the political process. He advocated the admission of California and New Mexico and opposed many of the interests of the South. In 1850 he was about to reorganize his cabinet because of charges of corruption of some officials when he died following a July 4th celebration.

TAYLORS FALLS, Minnesota. Village (pop. 623), eastern Minnesota, northeast of ST.

PAUL, historic lumbering center, located in an area of interest to geologists who find many fossils among the shale and limestone outcroppings, named for Jesse Taylor who settled in the area in 1838 to establish timber claims. The first frame building in town was constructed in 1851 by William H.C. Folsom, an independent logger and valley historian. In 1854 Folsom built a another home which is maintained today as a museum and example of both Federal and Greek Revival architecture. The growth of the lumber industry and the construction of the Northern Pacific Railroad branch line from Wyoming to Taylors Falls created a boom economy for many years. Today the town is dependent on tourists who come to view the spectacular beauty of the St. Croix Dalles, unusual rock formations and lava cliffs.

TEASDALE, Sara. (St. Louis, MO, Aug. 8, 1884—New York, NY, Jan. 28, 1933). Poet. Excessively sheltered early in life by her parents, Teasdale published, while traveling with a chaperone, *Sonnets to Duse and Other Poems* (1907) and *Helen of Troy and Other Poems* (1911). These brought her some critical attention, and following her marriage in 1914 she broke away from her family to lead a more daring, although never entirely happy, life as a poet. She received the 1918 PULITZER PRIZE for *Love Songs* (1917), and she published several other collections before taking her own life.

TECUMSEH (Chief). (Scioto River Valley, OH, 1765—Moraviantown, Ontario, Canada, Oct. 5, 1813). Indian leader of the NORTHWEST TERRITORY. Tecumseh is remembered as the gifted Indian warrior and leader who worked tirelessly to create an Indian confederacy which would protect Indian lands from white invasion. From his home in Ohio, Tecumseh traveled to nearly every Indian tribe east of the Rocky Mountains to promote his idea of a united Indian front against the white settlers. The cornerstone of his Indian policy was to reject any further land sales to the whites. Tecumseh suffered both a military and political defeat when his brother, the PROPHET (1770-1834), unwisely chose to attack American troops while Tecumseh was away, and the Prophet was defeated at the Battle of TIPPECANOE in 1811. During the WAR OF 1812, Tecumseh, with the rank of British brigadier general, in command of Indian troops, was allied with the British in the last hope of defeating the Americans. He was killed leading his forces in Canada.

Chief Tecumseh.

TERRAPIN RIDGE. Scenic highway. Following a high crest of land running east of GALENA, Illinois, Terrapin Ridge, nearly level at the top, wanders through one of the most scenic areas of the Midwest. U.S. Highway 20 winds along the crest, providing splendid views on both sides for more than twenty miles.

TERRE HAUTE, Indiana. City (pop. 61,-125), seat of Vigo County, major eastern Indiana city on the WABASH RIVER near the Illinois border, commercial and banking center. Terre Haute, "high land" in French for the city's location on a bank 60 feet above the river, was once the home of the WEA Indians. From 1720 until 1763, Terre Haute was on the dividing line between the French colonial provinces of Canada and Louisiana.

In 1811 General William Henry HARRISON (1773-1841) and his troops provided the basis for settlement in the area when the general had FORT HARRISON built on the Wabash River three miles north of the present city. The Terre Haute Town Company bought a tract of land in 1816 and platted the city. By promising to erect public buildings, the developers had Terre Haute designated the seat of government in the county. River traffic made Terre Haute a

terminus, as low water and sand bars made travel farther north too full of risk.

In 1838 the completion of the NATIONAL ROAD from Washington, D.C., to Terre Haute brought stages and wagon trains with more settlers. In 1849 the WABASH AND ERIE CANAL reached the city, giving Terre Haute a direct and low-cost outlet to the Atlantic. Railroad building in the last quarter of the nineteenth century made large-scale coal production practical and further added to Terre Haute's importance with the development of coal mines in its area. Today, in addition to coal, the city produces steel and aluminum fabricated items, communications equipment and phonograph records.

Terre Haute lists among its distinguished citizens Eugene Debs, labor leader; Paul Dresser, song writer; Gilbert Wilson, mural painter; Max Ehrmann, poet; and Claude Bowers, historian and diplomat. Terre Haute is the home of INDIANA STATE UNIVERSITY and St. Mary-of-the-Woods College.

Sheldon Swope Art Gallery displays a collection of 19th and 20th century paintings by American artists and features lectures, concerts, and special exhibits. The Historical Museum of the Wabash Valley re-creates a general store, Victorian-style bedroom, parlor, nursery, bathroom and toy shop. The museum is furnished with local antiques and memorabilia. The Eugene Debs home is open as a memorial to the labor leader. Paul Dresser, composer of "On the Banks of the Wabash Far Away" and popular song writer and publisher in the 1890s, is honored in the Dresser Memorial Park. Antique vehicles featuring classic autos, locomotives and early bicycles, including several European models, are displayed in the Early Wheels Museum. The Farrington's Grove Historical District, an 80-acre site, contains more than one thousand early homes.

TERRITORIES. The Midwest holds a special place in the history and development of the nation. After fighting a war for self government, Americans wanted to retain their hard-won political rights as they moved out into the unorganized areas to the west. In taking the western lands, the government had promised to form new states from them, states which would have the same powers as the original thirteen. Because it provided the pattern for the entry of new states, the NORTHWEST ORDINANCE of 1787 was one of the most important acts of the government under the Articles of Confederation. It set up a three stage procedure under which not more than five states were to be carved from the area. In the first stage a governor, secretary and three judges were named by the Congress to govern the entire Northwest. When the adult male population reached 5,000, the entire territory elected its own legislature. This shared power with a council selected by Congress. The legislature named a non-voting delegate to the national congress. As population increased in a given area, that area was carved out as a smaller territory until a territory reached a population of 60,000. Whenever a proposed area reached 60,000, it could write a constitution and ask Congress to be admitted as a state on an equal basis with the already existing states. This procedure was followed in all but six of the states formed after the original thirteen. Most of the territories had the same names as present day states, but they frequently covered a much greater area than the states which followed. When the Northwest Territory was organized, in 1800 the western portion became Indiana Territory. By 1803, when Ohio became a state, Indiana Territory included the present states of Indiana, Illinois, Michigan, Wisconsin and part of Minnesota. Michigan was split off as a separate territory in 1805, and Indiana was reduced to its present size in 1809. At that time Illinois Territory was created from what was left. After Illinois became a state in 1818, the remainder became part of Michigan Territory. When Michigan became a state in 1837, present Wisconsin, Iowa and Minnesota became part of a vast Wisconsin Territory, extending as far as Montana. Previously, Missouri, Iowa and parts of Minnesota had been part of the Louisiana Territory, formed from the huge LOUISIANA PURCHASE. When Missouri became a state in 1821, Iowa Territory next included present Wisconsin, Iowa and the western portion of present Minnesota. When Iowa reached statehood in 1846 and Wisconsin in 1848, Minnesota Territory was formed, including the eastern portions of the Dakotas. By the time Minnesota became a state in 1858, the entire Midwest had reached its present state boundaries, and the Midwest territories had become history.

THOMAS, Danny. (Deerfield, MI, Jan. 6, 1914—). Nightclub comedian and television star. A television pioneer Thomas had his own television series (1953-1965) for which he received special Emmy awards in 1953 and 1964. He also played many roles in motion pictures. Thomas is renowned for his appearances for charity, especially for his efforts on behalf of St. Jude's Children's hospital. He is the father of actress Marlo Thomas.

THOMAS, Theodore. (Esens, Hanover, Germany, Oct. 11, 1835—Chicago, IL, 1905). Orchestra conductor. Thomas, an inspired solo violinist from the age of ten, is credited with founding the CHICAGO SYMPHONY, now one of the finest in the world. Thomas came to the United States in 1845 and performed as a soloist in New York and on national tours. He inaugurated orchestral concerts in 1864 and founded the Thomas Orchestra three years later. Thomas was elected conductor of the Brooklyn Philharmonic Society in 1862 and the New York Philharmonic Society in 1877, holding the positions until 1891 when he moved to CHICAGO, a move many of his eastern friends and critics incorrectly thought was the end of a promising career. The orchestra's home was the great Auditorium Theater, which Thomas considered too large. His influence in Chicago was so great that he gathered a group of wealthy Chicagoans to support a plan to build Theodore Thomas Orchestra Hall. When the new hall, still the home of the symphony, opened in 1905, Thomas was so appalled by the acoustics, some said that he died of a broken heart.

THOMPSON, James. (Chicago, IL, May 8, 1936—). Illinois governor. Between 1959, when he was admitted to the Illinois bar, and 1977 when he was first elected Illinois governor, James Thompson held a variety of legal positions in the state. He served for five years as an associate professor of law at NORTHWESTERN UNIVERSITY. Thompson was also a member of the Chicago Mayor's Commission on Draft Legislation to Combat Organized Crime and the President's Task Force on Crime. He served as United States District Attorney for Chicago until he took the Illinois governor's seat in 1977. Thompson was reelected three times, the most recent in 1986 when he began his fourth term as governor, an Illinois record. The press frequently has speculated on his aspirations for the national presidency. As governor his principal aim has been to maintain the state's fiscal responsibility.

THORPE, James Francis (Jim). (Prague, OK, May 28, 1888—Lomita, CA, March 28, 1953). Athlete. Ranked as outstanding athlete of the Twentieth Century by the Associated Press poll and by some as the greatest all around male athlete America has produced, Jim Thorpe had several associations with the

Midwest. The most unusual was with the Oorang Dog Kennels at La Rue, Ohio. There, as a promotion, he joined a group of Indian athletes who lived at La Rue in native style and played football in many of the larger cities under the name of the Oorang Indians. Later, Thorpe played professional football with the CANTON, Ohio, Bulldogs and other teams. His statue stands in the FOOTBALL HALL OF FAME at Canton. After his playing career was over, Thorpe became supervisor of recreation for the CHICAGO, Illinois parks. Jim Thorpe, Pennysylvania is named in his honor. As a student at Carlisle Indian School, Carlisle, Pennsylvania, Thorpe led his team to victory over Army, Harvard and other major teams and was named All-American. In the 1912 Olympics at Stockholm, Sweden, Thorpe won both the pentathlon and decathlon, a feat never accomplished before or since. When King Gustav V of Sweden presented his medals, the king called Thorpe the world's greatest athlete. However, Thorpe was stripped of his medals when it was found that he had played semi-professional baseball with the Rocky Mountain, North Carolina, team. He went on to play baseball with the New York Giants before turning to professional football and was the most popular of his time in the game. In later years he fell into bad luck and died in obscurity.

THORPE, Rose Hartwick. (Mishawaka, IN, July 18, 1850—San Diego, CA, July 19, 1939). Author. Thorpe, who attended school in Litchfield, Michigan, set the scene of one of her poems, "Curfew Shall Not Ring Tonight," in the Hillsdale, Michigan, village square, and the phrase has been familiar ever since.

THUMB PENINSULA. If the outline of the state of Wisconsin is considered to be in the form of a rough mitten, the thumb would be formed by the peninsula which juts out into Lake MICHIGAN and separates the lake proper from GREEN BAY. This historic area was one of the first to be explored by Europeans who had ventured that far west on the GREAT LAKES. Today the peninsula is occupied primarily by Door County, Wisconsin, with its many attractive small towns and villages, and offers almost every available variety of recreation both winter and summer.

TIFFIN, Ohio. City (pop. 19,549), seat of Seneca County, situated in northeastern Ohio on the broad SANDUSKY RIVER, it was incorporated in 1835 and takes its name from Edward TIFFIN, first governor of Ohio. The center of a farming community, its industries include heavy machinery, radiators, machine parts, glassware, china, electrical equipment and wire and cable. Erastus Bowe saw the site during an expedition in the WAR OF 1812, and returned in 1817 to build Pan Yan Tavern, which became a stagecoach stop. A town called Oakley sprang up around the tavern on the north side of the river. A rival town was founded on the north side and called Tiffin. There was much rivalry between the two towns until they were united in 1950 under the Tiffin name. The first bridge was built in 1834, but a flood carried it away. The flood of 1883 destroyed four bridges, and the rampaging Sandusky has been a frequent threat to the community. Heidelberg College was opened at Tiffin in 1850. Tiffin University is a business school. Tiffin-Seneca Heritage Festival is held in mid September.

TIPPECANOE BATTLEFIELD STATE MEMORIAL. Park near LAFAYETTE, Indiana, which marks the site of the battle in 1811 in which General William Henry HARRISON (1772-1841) defeated Indians under the leadership of the PROPHET (1770-1834), brother of TECUMSEH (1768-1813). The original sixteen acre park, now enlarged to ninety acres, was encircled by a tall iron fence. A glass encased pictorial map detailed the progress of the battle including points from which the Indians attacked and where casualties occurred. In a memorable tour of the memorial the renowned James Whitcomb RILEY (1849-1916) was asked if he had any questions. In a response typical of the whimsical nature which endeared him to his readers Riley replied, "How in the devil did the Indians get over that fence?"

TIPPECANOE RIVER. Indiana river whose source lies in Tippecanoe Lake in northeast Kosciusko County. Tippecanoe River flows west-northwest initially, turning southwestward through lakes Shafer and Freeman and into the WABASH RIVER near LAFAYETTE, Indiana. The river was the scene of a major battle in 1811 between United States troops and an Indian confederation under Chief TECUMSEH (1768-1813). The name Tippecanoe comes from the Indian word for "place of buffalo fish."

TIPPECANOE, BATTLE OF. Battle fought November 7, 1811 on the site of present-day Battle Ground, Indiana, between forces of General William Henry HARRISON (1773-1841), governor of the Indiana Territory, and an

Indian confederacy organized by Shawnee chief TECUMSEH (1768-1831) and his brother, The PROPHET (1770-1834). The Indians were led by The Prophet while Tecumseh was away, and he attacked foolishly. However, the Indians' nominal defeat in this battle was not as overwhelming as the general would later pretend. Nevertheless, the battle wrapped up his brilliant campaign against the Indians of the time and put an end to the power of the confederacy. With a force of 900 men, Harrison followed the battle by destroying the Indian capital of PROPHETSTOWN on Tippecanoe Creek and ended the threat to westward migration in the Mississippi watershed. The American victory also weakened British efforts to incite the Indians to attack American settlements. Harrison's victory led to the slogan "Tippecanoe and Tyler Too" when presidential candidate Harrison campaigned in the election of 1840.

TOLEDO, Iowa. City, (pop. 2,445), seat of Tama County, situated in east central Iowa, it was named for TOLEDO, Ohio, which took its name from the Toledo in Spain. Founded in 1853, the Iowa community was one of the first of several Midwest cities to pipe centrally heated water to homes and businesses. On two major transcontinental railroads, the city is a center of agricultural shipment and small industry. In 1912, the Wieting family of Toledo, provided the Wieting Theater for community enjoyment. In 1919 Western College in Toledo was taken over by COE COLLEGE in CEDAR RAPIDS, Iowa. Toledo is usually thought of along with its adjoining twin, TAMA, Iowa.

TOLEDO, OHIO.

Name: From the Spanish city of Toledo just south of Madrid.

Nickname: Glass Capital of the World

Area: 84.3 square miles (1984)

Elevation: 630 feet

Population:
1986: 340,680
Rank: 44
Percent change (1980-1986): -3.9%
Density (city): 4,080 per sq. mi.(1984)
Metropolitan Population: 610,824 (1984)
Percent change (1980-1984): -1%

Racial and Ethnic Makeup (1980):
White: 80.1%
Black: 17.4%
Hispanic origin: 10,984 persons
Indian: 989 persons
Asian: 2,005 persons
Other: 5,682 persons

Age:
18 and under: 28.1%
65 and over: 12.5%

TV Stations: 5

Radio Stations: 17

Hospitals: 9

Sports Teams:
Mud Hens (baseball)
Hornets (hockey)

Further Information: Toledo Officer of Tourism and Conventions, 218 Huron, Toledo, OH 43604.

TOLEDO, Ohio. City. Seat of Lucas County, situated in northwest Ohio, on Lake ERIE at the mouth of the MAUMEE RIVER. It is the center of an urban area which includes the communities of Maumee, Perrysburg, Rossford, Oregon and Sylvania. Toledo occupies an area of 84.3 square miles. Toledo was incorporated in 1837. The name comes from Toledo, Spain.

The river mouth provides a splendid harbor, making the city a port of entry and one of the leading ports on the GREAT LAKES. A network of railroads and highways adds to its importance as a shipping center.

In addition to the shipyards, other commercial activities include oil refineries, glass manufacture, machinery, automobile parts, cosmetics, paints, metal stampings, die castings and plastics. The city took an early industrial lead when the Toledo Scales Company was established, making the city's name practically synonymous with weighing equipment. Another name known around the world is the Jeep, originating in the city and produced there for many years.

First settled in 1817 as Port Lawrence. Toledo was consolidated with Vistula in 1833 and took the present name. The city was the center of the "Toledo War" with Michigan over ownership of the area and the location of the Ohio-Michigan boundary. In 1838 Congress settled the dispute in Ohio's favor, and Toledo remained a part of Ohio.

The Erie Canal, in 1825, and various local canals, along with the arrival of railroad lines,

Toledo, University - Tornadoes

development of Ohio coal fields, the tapping of the state's oil and gas in the late 1900s, all strengthened the city's commerce. Particularly noteworthy was the establishment of the Libbey glassworks in 1888.

Needed political reform came in 1897 with the election of Mayor Samuel M. Jones, who died in 1904 and was succeeded by Brand Whitlock.

In 1946 the Toledo plan of labor conciliation was introduced and was widely adopted.

The cost of labor and diminished importance of some industries, the flight of others to the south caused a general decline of urban centers in the Midwest, and Toledo's population followed the general trend. In the period 1970 through 1984, the city's population diminished from 383,000 to 344,000, not quite such a severe loss as some other Ohio metropolises. Black residents comprise 17.4 percent of the population.

Institutions of higher learning include the University of TOLEDO, Medical College of Ohio at Toledo, Mary Manse College and several technical schools.

Notable civic features include the Anthony Wayne suspension bridge, the Toledo Museum of Art, Wolcott Museum Complex, a large zoo and the nearby site of the Battle of FALLEN TIMBERS (August 20, 1794), now a national historic landmark. The city hosts the annual International Festival in mid May.

TOLEDO, UNIVERSITY OF. Considered one of the first municipally sponsored universities in the country, the University of Toledo, at TOLEDO, Ohio, was chartered in 1872 on a tract of land donated by Jessup Scott. It began operations in 1875 and received its first municipal support in 1884. The present name was taken in 1940, and in 1967 the university was transferred to the state. The student body of 20,639 is instructed by a faculty of 1,112.

TOMATO JUICE. Official beverage of the state of Ohio. The state is a leader in tomato production both outdoor and indoor. It produces as much as half of all the hothouse and greenhouse tomatoes grown in the United States.

TORNADOES. Whirling funnel clouds extending downwards from dark clouds. The exact reasons for the formation of tornadoes are still uncertain, but the storm is usually linked to a marked instability in the lower layers of the atmosphere associated with strong cold fronts

and squall lines or with thunderstorms. Winds in tornadoes may exceed three hundred miles per hour. Most tornadoes measure hundreds of yards in diameter and many have caused extensive death and destruction. Most tornadoes last less than one hour. The average duration is four minutes.

In the Northern Hemisphere the winds whirl in a counterclockwise direction and clockwise in the Southern Hemisphere. While tornadoes, also called cyclones and twisters, occur throughout the world most are found in the United States during the months of April, May and June with the greatest number of these occurring in a path, referred to as "Tornado Alley," extending northeasterly from the panhandle region of Texas through Oklahoma, Kansas, and northwest Missouri. This region averages more than two hundred tornadoes annually.

A widespread region surrounding this area and extending into Iowa, Illinois, and Indiana receives an average of one hundred to two hundred tornadoes each year.

Farther north and east of the latter region, Minnesota, Michigan, Wisconsin, and Ohio receive fifty to one hundred, making much of the Midwest in substantial danger of tornadoes.

Annually the United States reports an average of seven hundred tornadoes. According to the United States Weather Bureau between 1916 and 1957 Iowa, with 518, had the fourth highest number of tornadoes in the United States. Illinois had the eleventh highest rank with 289. The other states of the Midwest, in order of largest number to the smallest, were Indiana, Minnesota, Michigan, Wisconsin and lastly, with 154 tornadoes, Ohio.

The greatest loss of life in the Midwest occurred on March 18, 1925, when a tornado ripped through Missouri, Iowa, and Indiana killing 689 people. The path of this storm measured 220 miles and was up to one mile wide. The storm traveled overland at speeds averaging 60 miles per hour. The longest path of a tornado was 293 miles from Louisiana, Missouri, to Jennings County, Indiana.

A tornado's intensity is measured by the Fujita-Pearson Scale, a rating classification from 0-5 based on intensity, wind speed, and the length and width of the storm's path. F5 tornadoes are any with winds of more than 260 miles per hour.

The damage from tornadoes is not caused by the high winds alone. The extremely low atmospheric pressure inside the storm creates an imbalance outside, which makes the high-pressure air inside buildings explode outward.

The power of tornadoes is well recorded. On May 31, 1931, near Moorhead, Minnesota, a tornado hit the Empire Builder train when it was traveling at 60 miles per hour. Five seventy ton cars were lifted from the track, one being carried eighty feet and dumped in a ditch. The coaches had been lifted several inches vertically—the connecting coupling was found still closed. On June 12, 1957, a tornado struck a steel airport hangar in Dallas County, Texas, and pulled the concrete piers from the ground.

TORONTO, Ohio. City (pop. 6,934), situated in east central Ohio on the north/south segment of the OHIO RIVER, the city takes its name from Toronto, Canada, the home town of a man named Dunspaugh, who was influential in developing the clay industry for which the Ohio city is famous. Part of the site was donated by the government to Mike Myers, an Indian fighter and scout, as payment for his services in opening the Ohio country to settlement. Although he often fought with the Indians and was wounded a number of times, Myers died in bed at the age of 107. In addition to the clay industry, the country's first titanium roll and forge plant was opened at Toronto in 1956.

TOURISM. The attractions of the Midwest region range from the bustle of many of the nation's largest cities to the eerie stillness of wilderness areas such as ISLE ROYALE and SUPERIOR-QUETICO PRIMITIVE REGION, from the craggy peaks of the OZARKS to the water wonderlands of Michigan, from the circus world of BARABOO to the world's finest symphony, from the world's tallest building to the humble log cabin home of a great man.

More likely to be thought of as the breadbasket of the world than the recreation center of the country, the Midwest, nevertheless, pulls in over $33,000,000,000 each year in tourist income. Illinois spends the most of any state in the nation to bring in tourists and ranks first in tourist dollars in the Midwest. Despite its many recreation facilities and its high rank as a place to live, Minnesota earns least from tourists.

Illinois. As the land of Lincoln, Illinois promotes its many Abraham LINCOLN (1809-1865) attractions. New Salem, where he matured, is now a completely restored memorial to the great man. His magnificent tomb and the only house he ever owned are in SPRINGFIELD, along with other memories throughout central Illinois. Lincoln never saw the present capitol, but the splendid building attracts a host of tourists. Many downstate Illinois attractions are found in its state parks, ranging from Illinois Beach on Lake Michigan to STARVED ROCK, from historic KASKASKIA Bell to the gigantic remnants left by prehistoric people who built the mounds at CAHOKIA MOUNDS park. Here is the largest primitive earthwork in the world, MONKS MOUND. To the north one of the country's longest chain of lakes and in the far south the rugged outreach of the Ozark Mountains form other contrasts. But for the conventioneers who make Chicago the greatest convention center in the world and for the millions of other tourists, Chicago is Illinois' star attraction. Most obvious are the great skyscrapers, with SEARS TOWER looming higher than any other building in the world. All over the city are the striking buildings by world famous architects which have made Chicago the world center for modern architectural forms. Perhaps nowhere else is there such a contrast and such a variety of museums, with the MUSEUM OF SCIENCE AND INDUSTRY in the forefront, attracting the greatest crowd of any museum worldwide. Not far behind is the FIELD MUSEUM OF NATURAL HISTORY, inventor of the DIORAMA, said by some to be the finest museum of its type anywhere. Ranked as one of the country's five major art museums, the ART INSTITUTE hosts most of the major touring exhibits and boasts the largest collection of French impressionists on display. The SHEDD AQUARIUM offers the largest indoor marine collection anywhere. Museums are to found for almost every special interest including two opened in 1987, the Museum of Broadcasting and the Terra Museum of American Art. Time and again the CHICAGO SYMPHONY has been labeled the finest in the world. In another art form Chicago ranks with Johannesburg, South Africa, in outdoor sculpture, with almost every major modern sculptor represented in such works as Picasso's huge steel woman at the Daley civic Center, Chagall's half-block-long mosaic, Calder's Flamingo and many others. Only Chicago and New York can boast of two major league baseball teams, and the city has top professional teams in all the other major sports.

Indiana. The one-day sporting event which attracts the world's largest crowd, the Indianapolis 500, is a grueling race, every year bringing world attention to INDIANAPOLIS, the capital. Heart of the city is Monument Circle with its soaring Soldiers and Sailors Monument. Down one of the streets radiating from it is the splendid capitol. The World War memorial Plaza honors the dead of the two wars and is notable for the largest bronze statue ever cast in the United States. Childrens museum is a unique attraction, and there is a fine art museum and excellent symphony. Not far southwest is BROWN COUNTY, centered in tiny NASHVILLE, home of many famous artists and galleries. It has been said that there are more galleries, shops and restaurants than residents in Nashville. During the color seasons of spring and fall Brown County roads are bumper to bumper. To the east lies COLUMBUS, which outranks all others of its size for the number and variety of structures created in recent years by some of the world's finest architects, who vie with one another for architectural commissions in Columbus. Parke County is known for its 30 COVERED BRIDGES and annual Covered Bridge Festival. Indiana's three major universities include NOTRE DAME and its renowned teams, PURDUE with the world's largest theater and INDIANA UNIVERSITY, with its outstanding music department. Among the many state parks, one of the most unusual is Johnny Appleseed memorial park at FORT WAYNE, which honors the memory of the beloved eccentric (John CHAP-MAN, 1774-1845) who wandered over much of the Midwest planting apple trees.

Iowa. Dubuque occupies Iowa's most scenic site on a towering bluff overlooking the great MISSISSIPPI RIVER. Unusual for the flat Midwest is the block long cable railroad, taking visitors to the top of the bluff. Up river is an even more dramatic Mississippi panorama, Mc Gregor Heights, overlooking the great mouth of the WISCONSIN RIVER on the opposite side. North of MC GREGOR is EFFIGY MOUNDS NATIONAL MONUMENT, the only national preserve in Iowa. The only president who was an Iowa native, and the first president born west of the Mississippi is memorialized in the HERBERT HOOVER NATIONAL HISTORIC SITE, with its library and homestead, where President and Mrs. Hoover are buried. Not far to the north and west are the seven villages named AMANA, fascinating reminders of the most successful of all the communal settlements so popular in the U.S. during the last half of the 1800s. There the visitor revels in the wines, the native crafts and the home cooked, home served meals. At IOWA CITY the state's old capitol is now administrative headquarters for the University of IOWA. The building is said to be one of the finest examples of its type. DES MOINES is no longer an overgrown village. Few communities of its size have

advanced so dramatically in creating urban advantages of almost every type. The art museum there features one of the finest buildings, housing a collection that would do honor to a city of many times Des Moines' size. The governor's mansion is also well worth a visit. Nearby is the unique attraction of Living History Farms. Fully operating, this center presents farms of three different periods.

Michigan. With frontage on three GREAT LAKES, the largest area of inland fresh water of any of the 48 conterminous states and thousands of miles of inland rivers, Michigan deserves its title of Water Wonderland, with every type of recreation for winter and summer, plus the unique attraction of several hundred miles of Lake MICHIGAN dunes. The gateway to the north, Big Mac, once the world's longest suspension bridge, looms over restored FORT MICHILIMACKINAC. Near the northern end is MACKINAC ISLAND, where no private automobiles are permitted and visitors rock on the long porch of the world's largest summer hotel. To the north a popular tourist attraction is the SOO CANAL, carrying the world's largest volume of canal traffic. The far north brings more intrepid visitors to ISLE ROYALE NATIONAL PARK, where there are no wheeled vehicles and the largest population is that of the magnificent moose. The most popular tourist attraction of Michigan is perhaps the complex founded by Henry FORD at DEARBORN. There at GREENFIELD VILLAGE Henry Ford (1863-1947) imported and assembled homes and structures of famous people from around the country, particularly his favorite, Thomas EDISON (1847-1931). Ford even insisted that the original earth from around the buildings also be brought in to add authenticity. The Ford Museum at Dearborn harbors a vast collection of transportation equipment and memorabilia. DETROIT is the oldest major city in the Midwest. It attracts visitors to the Renaissance Center and BELLE ISLAND Park. The capital at LANSING features the great capitol building which was replete with features much ahead of its time. Lansing is also the home of the Gerald FORD Museum and also Michigan State Police Headquarters, housing the country's second largest collection of fingerprints. One of the Midwest's most attractive annual festivals is Tulip Time at HOLLAND, Michigan.

Minnesota. Of all the nation's twin cities, MINNEAPOLIS and ST. PAUL are the duo which most often come to mind first. These forward-looking communities have been ranked by the Urban Institute of Washington, D.C., as having the best overall quality of life of any metropolitan area in the country. They share many features of the area, including Fort Snelling State Park and Metropolitan Stadium, home of the Minnesota Twins. Minneapolis has defeated its bitter winters by building a complex arrangement of overhead walkways, linking building to building for many blocks. The city has long been a pioneer in the arts, with famed GUTHRIE Theater, The Children's Theater and the Minnesota Symphony Orchestra. St. Paul hosts one of the nation's major annual festivals, the Winter Carnival, founded in 1886. The massive capitol boasts sculpture by several of the leading artists. St. Paul is proud of its Capital Centre redevelopment project encompassing eight city blocks with climate controlled walkways. A unique national preserve in Minnesota is PIPESTONE NATIONAL MONUMENT, where the Indians of countless generations came to carve their pipes of peace from the soft red stone. Indians are the only ones now permitted to work with the pipestone. NIAGARA CAVE is the largest cavern in the Midwest, and a principal landmark of the Mississippi Valley is Sugar Loaf Monolith at WINONA. The largest and most complete health community outside a major urban setting is housed at the modest city of ROCHESTER, where the vast health enterprises were established by the pioneering MAYO family, who made Rochester's name synonymous with medical excellence. The wilderness areas of the north can be traversed only by foot or canoe. DULUTH is known as a City on a Rock, perched high on the rocky bluffs above vast Lake SUPERIOR. One of the nation's most scenic highways follows the lake shore to the Canadian border. In the ore country, visitors find the great open pits from which the world's largest supply of high grade ore was extracted and made into iron and steel. BRAINARD calls itself the home of Paul BUNYAN, the legendary hero who personifies the lumbering epic of the north. Bunyan and his blue ox BABE are represented at Brainard in the world's largest moving statue.

Missouri. ST. LOUIS not only calls itself the gateway to the west it also looks like a gateway, thanks to the enormous GATEWAY ARCH which welcomes visitors to the city through, around and to the top of the nation's tallest monument. St. Louis has been a leader among major cities in renovation and restoration of downtown areas, including the cavernous railroad station, now a hotel and multi-use mall. The ST. LOUIS SYMPHONY consistently ranks as second only to the CHICAGO SYMPHONY in quality, and the city

has notable botanical gardens, the second largest planetarium and other attractions, including Busch Stadium and Bowling Hall of Fame and Museum. The Veiled Prophet Fair is one of the most notable of all Fourth of July celebrations. Across the state, KANSAS CITY belies its packing town reputation with cultural attractions that make it one of the nation's most cosmopolitan centers. It boasts the first major shopping center in the nation, still one of the most attractive, and is particularly proud of the William Rockhill Nelson Gallery of Art, which houses one of the four greatest collections of Oriental art outside the Orient. City Center Square, Bartle Exposition Hall and the twin stadia of Harry S Truman Sports Complex have varied attractions. The American Royal Livestock and Horse show is the outstanding event of its kind. Nearby INDEPENDENCE provides memories of President Harry and Mrs. Truman at the HARRY S TRUMAN NATIONAL HISTORIC SITE, with the Truman library and home. The massive Capitol at JEFFERSON CITY closely resembles the U.S. capitol at Washington. Missouri is noted for its many caves open to tourists and for the vast artificial lakes which provide water resorts for a state where few existed before.

Ohio. As one of the two "mother states" of presidents, Ohio takes particular pride in its sites and structures which preserve their memories. All eight of the presidents associated with Ohio are honored in this way. Perhaps most impressive is the MC KINLEY BIRTHPLACE NATIONAL MEMORIAL at NILES, a splendid marble structure honoring the martyred president. When Moses CLEAVELAND (1754-1806) founded his city on Lake Erie, a printer ran out of type for the letter "A" and dropped it when he spelled the new city's name, and it has, in a sense, been misspelled ever since. Cleveland is noted for its Health Museum, Rockefeller Park, Public Square and its symphony orchestra, among many other attractions. The grand capitol at COLUMBUS was begun in 1839 and not finished until 1861, after the work of five architects under twelve different governors. CINCINNATI, at one time the major city of the Midwest, still in many ways deserves its title as Queen City. In many fields of culture, especially in music, Cincinnati influenced the rest of the region, and its arts flourished when much of the area was still wilderness. Outstanding are the city zoo, natural history and art museums. Riverfront Stadium is home to the first of all professional baseball teams, the Cincinnati Reds, and now houses football's Bengals.

Wisconsin. The Indians called the area

along Lake Michigan malm-a-waukee sape, meaning gathering place by the river, and Wisconsin's largest city presents its own version of that name. Noted for its beers and wonderful German cooking, MILWAUKEE also has a world renowned horticultural building and collection and one of the most up-to-date museums of natural history. The capital, MADISON, is dominated by its two handsome downtown lakes. On the shore of Lake MENDOTA, the great University of WISCONSIN spreads its major campus. The capitol is the only one in the country built in the form of a Greek cross. Madison's radio station WHA is the world's oldest station in continual operation. Two of the Midwest's most elegant centers of summer homes are OCONOMOWOC and Lake GENEVA. A boat trip on Lake Geneva provides a rare view of the estates of the wealthy. Several Wisconsin villages have preserved the aspects of the home villages from which the early immigrants came. NEW GLARUS is noted for its Swiss bell ringers, flag throwers, alpenhorns, yodeling and William Tell Festival. Memories of a different kind are found in southwest Wisconsin where MINERAL POINT was one of the centers of America's first large scale mineral rush to the West. Pioneer lead mining days are preserved in numerous restorations, along with the many elegant homes. WISCONSIN DELLS is one of the country's major tourist villages, bringing in more tourist dollars then some entire states. Its world reputation is built around the dramatic scenery of the upper and lower dells of the surging WISCONSIN RIVER. Indian pow-wows, water shows and attractive shops add to the visitor appeal. Nearby BARABOO features the memorabilia of the days when it was the headquarters of the RINGLING BROTHERS and Barnum and Bailey Circus. The oldest settlement in Wisconsin, GREEN BAY, is the smallest city with a major league football team and the gateway to famed DOOR COUNTY, with its mixture of water, scenery and summer music and theater festivals. Across the state on the Mississippi are the historic communities of LA CROSSE and PRAIRIE DU CHIEN, dog prairie. At Prairie du Chien, the estate of the Midwest's first millionaire, fur trader Hercules DOUSMAN, has been restored to much of its early glamor when it had its own race track, the Midwest's first piano and billiard table and glittering entertainment. Interstate State Park near ST. CROIX FALLS is maintained by both Wisconsin and Minnesota. Far to the north are the APOSTLE ISLANDS, not twelve, but totalling twenty-three. SUPERIOR is still the bustling capital of northern Wisconsin, occupying the

southern half of the finest harbor on the Great Lakes.

TRAER, Iowa. City (pop. 1,703), situated in east central Iowa, cited for the unusual number and quality of its early citizenry for a community of its size and for the quality of its journalism and cultural features. James "Tama Jim" WILSON (1836-1920) made his home in Traer, edited a local newspaper and went on to serve in the cabinet of three presidents, longer than any other person in the history of the cabinet.

Margaret WILSON (1882-1976), Traer native and missionary in India, received the PULITZER PRIZE for her novel, *The Able McLaughlins*, which she said was based on the Traer Community. Jean Wilson SMITH (1840-1919) was a leader in development of teaching methods for the blind and in developing one of the earliest schools for the blind at VINTON, Iowa. Her daughter, Theodosia Smith Carpenter, was a dramatic soprano soloist on the concert stage and formed the Nevin Quartet, an early touring women's group.

One of the leading families of the community, the Moores, had made five trips around the world (sadly, burying a daughter in China) at a time when most of Iowa was still looked upon as a frontier. The Traer *Star-Clipper,* founded and carried on for more than eighty years by the various members of the Taylor family of Traer, is said to have received more national awards for journalism than any other weekly. Barely past pioneer times, the people of Traer built a fine opera house and enjoyed notable music and attracted national figures for speeches. Today, the city has one of the finest community centers of any community of its size in the country and is a thriving center of the world's most productive agricultural area. A leading Iowa writer has claimed that "my relatives in Iowa around Traer, far from being provincial, have the best of both worlds. They have the liberty of a farm community, with their own farm airstrips for quick jaunts to Chicago or Denver, their boats on the Mississippi and their condos in Florida or Scottsdale."

TRANSPORTATION. Because of its central location, the Midwest early became and has remained a focal point of national and international transportation. The OHIO RIVER provides the first great route to the Midwest, bringing the early settlements to Ohio, Indiana and Illinois and continuing through modern times as one of the greatest carriers of freight, first by flatboat, then by paddlewheel steamboat and at last by tugboats and barges.

The NATIONAL ROAD was begun in 1815 and eventually reached from Cumberland, Maryland, to ST. LOUIS, Missouri. It opened the Midwest to land based travel from the East. When the Erie Canal opened in New York in 1825, it immediately gave immigrants and business a much easier route by water to a large part of the present Midwest, and strategically located Midwest villages became cities, as thousands of immigrants flocked in and brought the need for services and merchandise of all kinds. This was particularly true for CHICAGO, which mushroomed, as did most of the other major ports on the GREAT LAKES.

Chicago also quickly became a center for railroads, which radiated away from the city in all directions. Those to the west and southwest were instrumental in opening up vast new areas to settlement and commerce. ST. LOUIS, terminus of the National Road and jumping off place to the great West, had long been the major center for MISSISSIPPI RIVER traffic, as well as for that of the MISSOURI RIVER and much of the OHIO. It soon became a railroad center, second only to Chicago. As westward traffic grew, Iowa lay on the route of the first railroad to cross the continent. KANSAS CITY became a center for much of the Missouri River traffic and a major jumping off place for western travel.

Today every major Midwest city has one or more important airports. As the natural hub of transport, Chicago early became the premiere air destination, with Midway Airport becoming the busiest in the nation and its successor, O'Hare Airport, then taking the busiest title. Today St. Louis and Kansas City are almost equally important air centers.

Perhaps no single factor in the field of transportation has been more important to the Midwest, historically as well as today, as the unequalled opportunities for water transportation. The Midwest practically "owns" the Great Lakes, which early became the quickest and best route for the shipment of grain and later for the ores, coal and other minerals which built the furnaces and factories of the area. Most of the nation's navigable rivers are centered in the Midwest. The Ohio brought thousands of the first settlers to begin the process of growth. The Mississippi-Ohio-Missouri river system continues to be one of the major lifelines of commerce, with barge traffic far surpassing the tonnage of the picturesque earlier forms of river transportation.

Those great rivers, and others, have been improved by series of dams and locks and other additions, including the dredging of much of their channels to a depth of nine feet.

Inland cities, early were eager to reach the rivers and clamored for canals, and in the second quarter of the 1800s these were built through Ohio, Indiana and Illinois. Most of them quickly lost to the railroads, but some have remained vital transportation links, such as the ILLINOIS AND MICHIGAN CANAL, which joined the Great Lakes with the Gulf of Mexico. The world's busiest canal, the SOO, in UPPER MICHIGAN, connects Lake SUPERIOR with the lower GREAT LAKES. Its importance in WORLD WAR II was so great that it became one of the most heavily guarded places in the nation

TRAVERSE CITY, Michigan. City (pop. 15,516), seat of Grand Traverse County, located at the head of the West Arm of Grand Traverse Bay on the northwest side of Michigan's LOWER PENINSULA. The name is from the SIOUX mdeh-dakinyan, meaning "lake lying crosswise." Traverse City had its origins in 1847 when the Boardmans, a father and son, purchased 200 acres of land and constructed a mill at the mouth of Mill Creek. The Boardmans were bought out by three men led by Perry Hannah in 1851. Hannah and his partners built docks to accommodate large lake ships. New mills and several bridges were constructed. Cherry growing became important commercially just as the lumber business began to fade in the region. Traverse City, known as the "Cherry Capital of the World," celebrates its favorite crop every July with a week-long Cherry Festival featuring arts and crafts, parades, and music. Fifteen miles from Traverse City is the internationally recognized INTERLOCHEN Center for the Arts. Annually nearly two thousand talented students gather there to study dance, theater, music and art. In mid-January the city plays host to the Ranch Rudolph Sled Dog Races.

TRAVOIS. A mode of transporting goods, used by the American Indian and other cultures. Two long poles and a platform or net are lashed together with a harness at one end. This is tied to a person or a pack animal which pulls the device over the ground, with the ends dragging on the ground. Before horses were reintroduced to the Americas, dogs often served to drag the Indians' travois.

TREATIES, INDIAN. Countless treaties with the Indians were made in the Midwest, most of them, unfortunately, broken by circumstances often outside the control of either the

Indians or the federal government. One of the earliest and most important in the Midwest was the TREATY OF GREEN VILLE (1795). This came about after a conference of over a thousand Indian leaders, which lasted for two months. The Indians gave up most of their lands in Ohio, and there were no more uprisings in the state. As white settlement moved inexorably westward, Indian lands were occupied in spite of sometimes feeble efforts of the government to intervene. Each time a treaty was made the Indians agreed to give up their lands for cash or for settlement in kind or for new lands or reservations in the West. The BLACK HAWK WAR (1832) came about because Chief BLACK HAWK (1767-1838) believed that his people had been cheated in a treaty. The last Indian troubles in the Midwest, in Minnesota, resulted from white encroachment on Indian lands. Modern times have seen Indian "uprisings" initiated to call attention to unfulfilled promises of the government. In some recent cases, the courts have acknowledged certain injustices as treaty violations and have made rulings of substantial cash settlements to present day Indian groups. In Minnesota the CHIPPEWA laid aside their pipe of peace and sought restoration of their treaty rights through an appeal directly to the United Nations. This challenge brought about the formation of mechanisms to handle appeal of such grievances by the U.S. government, and a number of such cases are now pending in the appropriate jurisidictions.

TRENTON, Missouri.

City (pop. 6,811); seat of Grundy County; northwest Missouri; north of Chillicothe; probably named for Trenton, New Jersey. From 1897 to 1905 Trenton was involved in an unique cooperative experiment in education and business. The property of Avalon College was purchased by Walter Vrooman and a group of socialists. Avalon, which had been closed since 1891, was renamed Ruskin College, as the American branch of England's Ruskin Hall Movement, inspired by the theories of author and lecturer John Ruskin. In 1902 the "Multitude Incorporated" was formed as a trustee for the businesses the group purchased and used to support the college. The project was unpopular from the beginning and soon dissolved because of internal bickering. The twenty seven elm trees planted in 1920 at Soldiers and Sailors Memorial Arch at Moberly Park commemorate twenty-seven men killed in WORLD WAR I and referred to as the "silent victors." Beneath the arch in a sealed box, imbedded in concrete, are the life histories of the men.

TRUMAN, Harry S

(Lamar, MO, May 8, 1884—Independence, MO, Dec. 26, 1972). Senator from Missouri and thirty-third President of the United States. Following graduation from public high school in INDEPENDENCE, Harry Truman, whose middle name, he insisted, was simply S due to an unresolved family debate over whether it should stand for Shippe or Solomon, went to work on his father's farm and pursued a series of odd-job occupations. During WORLD WAR I, he served in the Meuse-Argonne theater, and after the armistice he returned to Missouri to open a haberdashery business that proved unsuccessful.

Truman never received a formal college education and used this fact to garner the support of the common man, but he did attend Kansas City School of Law from 1923 to 1925.

Truman began his political career as an adherent of the Democratic party machine of Kansas City's Thomas J. Prendergast but without acquiring any of the unsavory reputation of the machine. After serving in local offices and judgeships, he was elected to the U.S. Senate in 1934 and reelected in 1940.

As senator, he established a national reputation, heading a committee formed to investigate defense department contracts awarded to private industry.

Picked by President F. D. Roosevelt to be his running mate in the 1944 election, Truman became president when Roosevelt died on April 12, 1945.

His immediate concern was to end WORLD WAR II combat in the Pacific, which he managed by authorizing the world's first atomic bomb drops (1945) on the Japanese cities of Hiroshima and Nagasaki. Despite most predictions, he was reelected to a full term by defeating Thomas E. DEWEY (1902-1971) in 1948.

During his terms, Truman continued the New Deal domestic policies of Roosevelt, but his most important achievements were in foreign policy. At first an advocate of cooperation with Russia, he then formulated the Truman Doctrine (May 15, 1947) to protect Greece and turkey from Communist domination. With United Nations approval he sent U.S. military forces to protect South Korea from invasion by communist North Korea. The first U.S. ground troops arrived there on June 1, 1950. One of his most controversial acts was the removal of General Douglas MacArthur (April 11, 1951) from his Far Eastern command, because Truman contended that MacArthur had failed to heed a presidential directive. This raised a great furor among MacArthur's many supporters. Truman also established the Marshall Plan to assist European recovery from World War II, beginning April 2, 1948. On September 25, 1949, the president signed the NATO pact, forming the North Atlantic Treaty Organization for the defense of North Atlantic countries.

On November 1, 1950, Truman survived an assassination attempt by two Puerto Rican nationalists who tried to shoot their way into Blair House where the President and Mrs. Truman were living during renovation of the White House.

In domestic matters, he proposed the far-reaching reforms which he called the Fair Deal. Some of his proposals were intended to finish the F.D. Roosevelt New Deal programs. The Fair Deal called for measures dealing with civil rights, improvement of schools nationwide and assistance for the disadvantages and the elderly. The Fair Deal was blocked by conservatives of both parties, and Truman failed to overcome this obstacle. However, much of the Truman plan for the Fair Deal was carried out during the Lyndon Baines Johnson period. Although eligible for a second full term, Truman chose to retire in 1952 to his home in Independence.

Harry S Truman was the oldest of a family of three. At the age of 35, he married Bess (Elizabeth Virginia) Wallace Truman at Independence, on June 28, 1919. They had one child, (Mary) Margaret Truman, who attracted considerable attention to her slight career as a concert singer and who later became prominent as a writer of mystery stories. The Trumans were married for 53 years. He was 88 years old when he died; Bess Truman survived him for nine years and died at the age of 97.

TULIP FESTIVAL. Annual event held the third week of May in HOLLAND, Michigan. Activities during the week include traditional street scrubbing, tulip tours, Dutch market, parades, and dancing. The idea of the festival came from a teacher in 1929, as a local expression of pride in Holland's flowers, of which as many as fifty varieties are shown. Annually more than half a million visitors enjoy the pageant.

TUSCARAWAS RIVER. The Tuscarawas rises in northern Tuscarawas County in east central Ohio, very near the crest of the divide which separates the waters of the GREAT LAKES

Harry S Truman birthplace, Lamar, Missouri.

from those of the Ohio-Mississippi watershed. It flows south and west past New Philadelphia, Tuscarawas and Port Washington before joining the MUSKINGUM RIVER at COSHOCTON.

TWO HARBORS, Minnesota. City (4,039), county seat of Lake County, northeastern Minnesota. Two Harbors was originally called Agate Bay, which it overlooks and from whose harbors it received its present name. The first settlement in the region, which was Indian territory until 1855, was named for Thomas Saxon who arrived on Agate Bay in 1856. In 1857 a second village was platted around a sawmill at Burlington Bay. Both communities were ruined in the financial panic of 1857. Two Harbors, then called Agate Bay, was made the Lake Superior terminus of the Duluth and Iron Range Railroad when iron ore was discovered on the Vermilion Range. The dock that received the first iron ore had forty-six pockets each having a capacity of three hundred tons. At one time Dock No. 1 was the largest iron-ore dock in the world. A record was established when twelve thousand tons of ore were loaded in sixteen minutes. The railroad brought a sharp increase in the number of residents including large numbers of Swedes, Norwegians, Canadians, and Danes. The first church, Presbyterian, was organized in 1887, the year the railroad was extended from Two Harbors to DULUTH. In 1888 the county seat was moved from Beaver Bay to Two Harbors which continued to grow as a lakeside community, shipping port for iron ore, and tourist attraction. Two Harbors was designated a city in 1907.

TWO RIVERS, Wisconsin. City (pop. 13,-354), situated in Manitowoc County in east central Wisconsin, takes its name from the Mishicot and Neshoto rivers which unite there to flow into Lake MICHIGAN, where the port was once the busiest in the area. In the 1870s the community lost this distinction to the city of MANITOWOC, its neighbor immediately to the south on the lake. Settlement began when a ten-barrel catch of whitefish in 1836 influenced the influx of French Canadian fishermen in their flat-bottomed craft known as Mackinaw boats. Lumbering and woodworking were the next industries, the latter including chairmaking and pail manufacturing. The Hamilton Manufacturing Company, beginning in 1880, became the largest manufacturer of very large wooden printing type, useful in cases where no metal type was large enough. The aluminum industry was started there by Joseph Koenig. In the days when aluminum was still very much an expensive curiosity, Koenig had been the director of the aluminum exhibit at the 1893 WORLD'S COLUMBIAN EXPOSITION in CHICAGO. With the aid of the city, Koenig made a trip to Chicago to sell his wares and came back with more orders than he could fill in several months. The aluminum industry at Two Rivers expanded to become the Aluminum Goods Manufacturing Company under direction of the Mellon interests. Today, tourists are attracted by the Rogers Street Fishing Village Museum, which depicts the commercial fishing industry of early days. Nuclear energy is explained graphically at the Point Beach Energy Information Center of the Point Beach Nuclear Plant. Point Beach State Forest provides woodlands, sand dunes on Lake Michigan, and sports.

TYPEWRITER. The modern typewriter was introduced in 1869 by Christopher Latham Sholes of KENOSHA, Wisconsin, after he and his assistant, Carlos Glidden, had worked on it for six years. Wisconsin claims the distinction of being the birthplace of the typewriter, but the first instrument was patented in England in 1714. However, the Sholes typewriter was the first practical commercial application of a writing machine. Although it could produce only capital letters, Philo Remington placed this first typewriter on the market in 1874, and the rest was business history.

TYPHA. Fiber from cattails, used in stuffing, upholstering and insulation. The Ness Typha Company, the only typha operation in the United States, is carried on at Holt, Minnesota.

U

UNDERGROUND RAILROAD. Organized system for helping slaves to escape from the slave states, operated by local groups of Abolitionists, both white and free blacks. The railroad terminology became common in the 1840s. Slaves were "passengers," those helping them "conductors" and the places where they were sheltered were called "stations." The highly organized secret operation became successful in its efforts. Because the Midwest offered the longest border between the free and the slave states, the border states from Ohio to Iowa were critically important in the operation. John Rankin's home on the banks of the OHIO RIVER near CINCINNATI, Ohio, was one of the important stations. As many as twelve escaping slaves might be sheltered there during a single night. The story Rankin to told Harriet Beecher STOWE (1818-1896) about one of the slave women escaping across the Ohio became the inflamatory *Uncle Tom's Cabin* (1852). NEWPORT, Indiana, was the site of the activities of Quaker Levi COFFIN (1789-1877), also noted for the number of slaves he sheltered. It is said that he assisted as many as 2,000 on the route to safety in Canada. "Stations" were found in all the major Indiana cities and many of the smaller ones, as well. Both Illinois and Iowa took an active part in hiding escaped slaves by day and shepherding them from station to station during the night. Fiery Abolitionist John BROWN maintained headquarters at SPRINGDALE and TABOR in Iowa.

UNITY SCHOOL OF CHRISTIANITY. Nondenominational religious movement headquartered at Lee's Summit, Missouri. The movement, founded in 1899 by Charles and

"On to Liberty," the Underground Railroad by Theodore Kaufmann

Myrtle Fillmore as a cult for faith healing, related to Christian Science and New Thought. The Unity name was used beginning in 1891. Followers believe that since they are children of God they do not inherit sickness. Unity Farm at Lee's Summit includes 1,200 acres and a school of religious instruction and spiritual healing. The doctrine looks upon the Bible as allegorical and not final, with revelation being a process which continues.

UPPER IOWA UNIVERSITY. Founded in 1857 at Fayette, a privately supported, nonsectarian institution. With a faculty of 47 and a student body of 1,228, Upper Iowa concentrates on individualized instruction in the arts and sciences.

UPPER MISSISSIPPI RESERVOIR SYSTEM. A program begun in the 1880s in Minnesota to control floods and keep water at higher levels during the summer months.

UPPER PENINSULA. Northern and westernmost region of Michigan. The original Territory of Michigan included the LOWER PENINSULA and the eastern Upper Peninsula. In the border dispute between Michigan and Ohio over a strip of land near TOLEDO, Ohio, Congress settled the problem in 1836 by giving the disputed section to Ohio and awarding the

entire Upper Peninsula to Michigan in exchange. Today, mineral resources of Michigan, with the exception of salt and petroleum, are found almost entirely in the Upper Peninsula.

ISLE ROYALE NATIONAL PARK is within the Upper Peninsula's borders. The island, largest in Lake SUPERIOR, is twenty-two miles from the shore. With no roads on the island or wheeled vehicles, the island remains nearly untouched by man. It contains one of the largest herds of great antlered moose in the United States. The animals are thought to have been trapped on the island after having crossed to it during a severe winter in 1912.

Skiing opportunities in the Upper Peninsula are internationally recognized. The art of ski jumping in the United States began in ISHPEMING in 1887, now the site of the National Ski Museum and the National Ski Hall of Fame.

Popular state parks in the area include Fort Wilkins State Park with its old stockade at Cooper Harbor and Porcupine Mountains State Park in Ontonagon County.

Tourists flock every year to the region of the ST. MARYS RIVER and its center, SAULT STE. MARIE, the oldest city of Michigan. The SOO CANAL and Locks are the favorite attraction, featuring the world's busiest canal. A CHIPPEWA museum containing many precolonial relics is housed in the building where Henry SCHOOLCRAFT (1793-

1864) wrote Indian Tales, the basis of Longfellow's "The Song of Hiawatha." Visitors may see a model of Sault Ste. Marie and the locks as they looked in the mid-1850s when the locks were new.

Geographically, the Upper Peninsula has on its eastern portion low-lying lands, some of which are swamps, with the largest of these being along the TAHQUAMENON RIVER. The western half of the Upper Peninsula contains some of Michigan's most scenic areas. Running parallel to the lake are ranges of hills that mark the shore lines of lakes Superior and Michigan. Shores of the Upper Peninsula are generally rocky and picturesque. Rough too are the streams of the Upper Peninsula, which frequently tumble over waterfalls and boulders on their way to the lakes. The Tahquamenon River has perhaps the most impressive falls in the state.

The mean annual temperature of the Upper Peninsula is 39 degrees F. as compared with 48 degrees F. in the Lower Peninsula. The extreme temperature range in the Upper Peninsula is 130 degrees, ten degrees wider than that of the Lower Peninsula. Snowfalls tend to accumulate and usually exceed 100 inches annually. Rainfall in the Upper Peninsula is also heavier.

The swift flowing streams of the Upper Peninsula are favorite spots for the brook, rainbow, or brown trout. Larger streams hold huge walleye and northern pike. Bear are fairly numerous in all of the Upper Peninsula.

UPPER RED CEDAR LAKE. Minnesota lake discovered in February of 1806 by Zebulon PIKE (1779-1813). Both Pike and Governor Lewis CASS (in 1820), mislabeled the lake as the source of the MISSISSIPPI RIVER. The body of water was later renamed CASS LAKE.

URBANA, Illinois. City (pop. 35,978). Seat of Champaign County, in east central Illinois, location of the main campus of the University of ILLINOIS. Urbana was settled in 1822 by Willard Tompkins, and the name comes from the Latin meaning "urban," pertaining to life in a city. In 1854 the Illinois Central Railroad chose to bypass the city. The city continued without the railroad, but attempted to annex a settlement called West Urbana which had developed near the tracks. The annexation failed and the residents of West Urbana incorporated in 1860 under the name of CHAMPAIGN. As it grew, Champaign unsuccessfully attempted to take the county seat from Urbana. The University of Illinois in Urbana gives the region much of its prosperity.

VALPARAISO UNIVERSITY. Valparaiso, Indiana, founded in 1859 as a Methodist school called the Valparaiso Male and Female College. The school closed in 1870 because of financial difficulty, but was soon reopened by Henry Baker Brown, a professor in an Ohio normal school. Brown developed the college into "the poor man's Harvard," known for its excellence. The death of Brown in 1915 and WORLD WAR I hindered the school's development until it was purchased by the Lutheran Church in 1925 and opened to students of all faiths. In the 1985-1986 academic year Valparaiso University enrolled 3,906 students and had 366 faculty members.

VAN ALLEN RADIATION BELTS. Eccentric ellipses which form two bands of intensive radiation at varying distances from the earth were named for Dr. James VAN ALLEN (1914-), of the University of IOWA, who

discovered them by interpreting the findings of the first Explorer Satellite, launched in 1958 as part of the International Geophysical year of 1957-1958. The belts extend from about 400 miles to 40,000 miles above and around the earth in a region known as the magnetosphere, above the earth's atmosphere. The belts are formed by charged particles of high energy electrons and protons, which cluster along the earth's magnetic lines. They are supposed to come from gigantic solar flares, which are trapped by the earth's magnetic field.

VAN ALLEN, James. (Mount Pleasant, IA, Sept. 7, 1914—). Astrophysicist. Dr. Van Allen, head of the Department of Physics and Chemistry at the University of IOWA, discovered the VAN ALLEN RADIATION BELTS around the earth. The belts were named for Dr. Van Allen, who was the first to interpret the findings of the Explorer Satellite, which confirmed the existence of the belts. Dr. Van Allen was responsible for the design of much of the equipment on board the satellite. He is considered to be the only person of modern times to have given his name to the "heavens."

VAN RAALTE, Albertus Christiaan. (Wanneperveen, Netherlands, Oct. 17, 1811—Nov. 7, 1876). Pioneer minister. Reverend Van Raalte arrived in DETROIT, Michigan, in 1846, and after determining a suitable Michigan locale for his people, returned the next year with his wife and several men to western Michigan on February 9, 1847. They started a settlement called HOLLAND, where Reverend Van Raalte served as both the village physician and preacher. He founded Hope College and a theological seminary at Holland. Van Raalte also established *De Hope*, a religious periodical in the Dutch language.

VAN WERT, Ohio. City (pop. 11,035), seat of Van Wert County, situated in northwest Ohio near the Indiana line, it was named for Isaac Van Wert, who captured John Andre during the American Revolution. At one time, the site of an Indian village, the location was selected by James Watson Riley in 1835. He foresaw that the high ridge on which it was situated would be a natural travel and commercial route. Now the center of a rich grain farming area, the city's products include cigars, woodworking machinery, cheese, electronic equipment and fabricated metal products. The community is renowned for its peonies, which seem to grow everywhere, and for its annual Peony Festival in early June, attracting thousands. Peony growing started with Miss Clara Anderson, who was given some peony plants, experimented with them and accidentally developed a spectacular bloom named Jubilee, which is known to peony lovers everywhere. A Victorian mansion of 1890 vintage at Van Wert houses the Van Wert County Historical Society Museum, restored to original decor.

VANDALIA, Illinois. City (pop. 5,338), county seat of Fayette County, western end of the National or Cumberland Road, second capital of Illinois. Beginning in 1819, Vandalia was the center of political power in Illinois for almost twenty years. In 1837, a group of legislators, including Abraham LINCOLN (1809-1865), began efforts to have the capital moved from Vandalia to SPRINGFIELD. Two years later, the over-six-foot legislators, known as the "Long Nine" because of their height, were

Old Statehouse, Vandalia, Illinois

successful. The Vandalia State House, built in 1836, was the fourth capitol of Illinois. Abraham Lincoln served as a member of the House there from 1836 to 1839. The charter for the village of CHICAGO was issued in the Vandalia State House on March 4, 1837. On a corner of the state house lawn stands a monument known as the "MADONNA OF THE TRAIL." Erected, in 1928, by the Daughters of the American Revolution, this monument marks the western end of the NATIONAL ROAD. The present Masonic Hall was once a trading post and station on the UNDERGROUND RAILROAD. A bell, dating from 1830 and said to be the state's oldest Protestant church bell, is housed in the First Presbyterian Church. Modern Vandalia serves as a distributing center for farm products and is a popular tourist center.

VANDER MEER, Johnny. (Prospect Park, NJ, Nov. 2, 1914—). Known as "Double No-Hit" Johnny, Vander Meer spent his professional baseball career in Ohio, first as a pitcher with the Cincinnati Reds from 1937 to 1950. He gained his greatest fame as the only pitcher in the history of professional baseball to hurl two consecutive no-hitters, first against the Boston Braves and second against the Brooklyn Dodgers. After his career in CINCINNATI, he went to CLEVELAND in 1951.

VASA, Minnesota. Typical of the planned communities platted by land speculators. Vasa, founded in 1853, was named in honor of a Swedish king, in order to attract immigrants. The founder, Hans Mattson, was a captain of a company of soldiers largely composed of Swedish immigrants. The 300-acre townsite was located near present-day William O'Brien State Park. Vasa's promoters claimed the town had a sawmill, good steamboat landing and several stores. As early as 1854, Vasa and the Chisago Lake area were centers for the

Lutheran church in Minnesota. The fortunes of the town declined when the sawmill went bankrupt after a partner stole the little money it made. The town's name was changed to Otis when another town named Vasa was organized in Goodhue County. The post office was discontinued in 1860 and Marine residents voted to reannex the area. Today the only buildings in the area of the old town are the Crabtree Kitchen restaurant and the 1875 schoolhouse along Highway 95.

VEBLEN, Thorstein B. (Cato, WI, 1857—Palo Alto, CA, Aug. 3, 1929). Teacher, author, widely recognized economist. Veblen is considered one of the most creative thinkers in American economic history. A Scandinavian American, he studied at CARLETON COLLEGE and took a PhD. in philosphy from Yale in 1884, but could not find a teaching place and so returned home to farm work. Eventually he was accepted at the University of CHICAGO to teach political economy (1892 to 1906). His scholarly and satiric book, *The Theory of the Leisure Class* (1899), attacked false values and social waste and brought him almost instant fame. He advocated a planned economic society in which scientists and engineers would play a significant role. His ideas were so controversial that he was forced to leave the university and spent many years at other schools, sometimes involved in entanglments with women. He is credited with great importance in turning the U.S. from a course which he said would have led to absolute control by business interests. He died at his cabin retreat.

VERMILION RIVER. The Vermilion originates in north central Ohio in Huron County, near Goodrich, Ohio. It flows north and slightly east, past Clarksfield, Wakeman and Florence to empty into Lake ERIE at the community of Vermilion, site of the Great Lakes Historical Society Museum.

VERMILION, Lake. Fifth largest internal Minnesota lake, with 186 miles of shoreline which mark part of the eroded core of the Laurentian Mountains at the center of the Vermilion Iron Range. Vermilion's hunting grounds were bitterly contested in the 1740s by the SIOUX and OJIBWAY. Fur traders established trading posts on it. In a treaty of 1854, known as the "Miners' Treaty," the Indians gave the mineral and lumber rights of most of the North Shore region, known as the Arrowhead, to the whites in exchange for a reservation west of

Cloquet, called Fond du Lac. A rumor in 1865 was circulated that gold had been discovered on the northeastern side of the lake. By May of 1866 nearly three hundred miners were working the area, despite the fact that no trace of gold was ever found. Iron ore was discovered by Henry Eames, a state geologist. In 1865 Eames wrote about finding two, sixty-foot wide veins of iron ore at the mouth of TWO RIVERS on Lake Vermilion. From that time the area became known as the Vermilion Range. The same year a prospector, George Stuntz, discovered the first iron to be mined in Minnesota. The mine was named Breitung and the first ore was shipped in 1884.

VEST, George Graham. (Frankfort, KY, Dec. 6, 1830—Kansas City, MO, 1904). Attorney and United States Senator. Vest served as a member of the Missouri House of Representatives from 1860 to 1861. He was elected to the Confederate Congress where he served in the house for two years and the senate for one year. He became a United States Senator from Missouri in 1879 and served until 1903. Vest is best remembered, however, for his impassioned "Eulogy for a Dog" delivered in the famous Missouri "DOG TRIAL."

VETERANS OF FOREIGN WARS. One of the largest veterans' organizations in the United States. The restored headquarters of the organization is at EATON RAPIDS near LANSING, Michigan. Membership is open to any officer or enlisted man or woman, either on active duty or honorably discharged, who fought in any military campaign outside the U.S. The National Home for Veterans' Orphans is operated by the V.F.W. in Eaton Rapids. In this center care is given to the children of deceased veterans. Family-size homes are available, as are a hospital, gymnasium, community social center, a swimming pool and a nursery.

VEVAY, Indiana. City (pop. 1,343), seat of Switzerland County, located in extreme southeast Indiana on the OHIO RIVER, founded in 1801 by Swiss immigrants. The first Swiss residents of Vevay started vineyards which produced a regionally popular wine. Wine-making gradually gave way to other agriculture, and river traffic created a brief history of furniture factories and woolen mills. The development of railroads in other parts of the state discouraged the further growth of industry. Edward Eggleston, author of *The Hoosier Schoolmaster* (1871,

School-master in this edition), was born in Vevay and used the experiences of his brother, a teacher in Jefferson County, as the basis for the book.

VICTORY, Wisconsin. No longer on the map, the village of Victory, near PRAIRIE DU CHIEN, was named for the Battle of BAD AXE which was fought nearby. The 1832 defeat of Chief BLACK HAWK (1767-1838) and his tribe marked the last battle with the Indians east of the MISSISSIPPI RIVER.

VIGO, Joseph Maria Francesco (Francis). (Mondoni, Piedmont, Italy, Dec. 3, 1747—Vincennes, IN, March 22, 1836). Army officer and fur trader. Vigo, a rich trader at VINCENNES, made a dangerous journey to KASKASKIA, Illinois, to tell George Rogers CLARK (1752-1818) that the British garrison at Vincennes was weak. The British commander, Henry HAMILTON, had dismissed most of his troops, feeling confident that an American attack in winter was impossible. This news encouraged Clark to plan his own daring attack of February, 1779, on the British at Vincennes and resulted in the eventual recapture of the post for the Americans during the American Revolution. Vigo was known for his continuing support of the American cause in the Midwest. Vigo County in Indiana is named in his honor.

VIKINGS. The theory that Vikings or other European explorers, perhaps even the ancient Phoenecians, reached the Western Hemisphere before Columbus has been rather well established, although not thoroughly verified. However, rather compelling evidence has been found that by the mid-1300s Viking explorers had even penetrated the North American continent, as far inland as Minnesota or Oklahoma.

In 1898, Olaf Ohman, a Minnesota farmer, stumbled onto a piece of "evidence" to that effect which has kept scholars arguing ever since. He dug out a slab of graywacke stone from under the roots of a poplar tree on his farm four miles northeast of the village of Kensington. The inscriptions carved on the stone were identified by the Minnesota scholar Hjalmar HOLAND (1872-1963) as the rune inscriptions used in Scandinavia up to the thirteenth century. And the inscribed monolith has been called the KENSINGTON RUNESTONE.

Holand made this translation: "Eight Goths Swedes and twenty-two Norwegians, on a journey of discovery from Vinland westward. We had a camp by two skerries [islands] one day's journey north of this stone. We were out fishing one day. When we returned home, we found ten men red of blood and dead. Ave Virgo Maria, Save us from evil." From the edge of the stone, Holand transcribed the following, "We have ten men by the sea to look after our ships fourteen days' journey from this island. In the year of our Lord 1362."

Holand was an authority on Scandinavian history of the middle ages, and he was convinced that the runestone was an authentic record. The tree roots in which it was entangled must have come from a tree at least seventy years old. If the stone were a hoax it must have been planted at a time when few Europeans were in the area, let alone those with sufficient sophistication to have created such a convincing hoax.

Actual Norse implements of the fourteenth century have been found in Minnesota along the route the Norsemen must have traveled. Two axes, a spear, a firesteel, two ceremonial halberds and thirteen other implements have proven to be over six hundred years old and of medieval Norse origin. Along the same route several holes had been found chiseled into stones on lake shores, now mostly dry land. These holes were identical with those used by the early Norwegians to moor heavy boats. The account refers to "this island." It is thought that the region where the stone was found was once covered by a lake with an island in it.

All of these discoveries indicate that if there was a deception, someone with almost superhuman knowledge and skill had produced a hoax at a period when the region was still a wilderness. However, most scholars continue to feel that it must have been a hoax, despite the evidence.

Perhaps more legendary is the claim that a group of White Indians lived in Indiana as early as the year 1200.

Another carved stone was discovered in 1830 in a ravine near Heavener, Oklahoma, and labeled the Heavener Runestone. The stone was left at the site of its discovery, now Heavener Runestone State Park. Two Similar stones have been found in nearby communities. Such experts as Gloria Farley and Dr. John Denmark feel the relics may be authentic evidence of Scandinavian inland penetration in that southern region.

VILLA LOUIS. The mansion of wealthy PRAIRIE DU CHIEN, Wisconsin, fur trader Hercules L. DOUSMAN has been meticulously restored to the grandeur of the 1840s when it was built on the site of several former forts at Prairie du Chien. The last was called FORT CRAWFORD. The mansion was enlarged and altered by Dousman's son in 1872. Extending to the MISSISSIPPI RIVER, the grounds provided Dousman with room for his own private racetrack on which purebred horses were raced on a cork surface shipped from Ireland. Stocked ponds provided easy fishing for the guests, who were offered such other entertainment as pool on the inlaid ivory table or a recital by Madame Dousman on one of the Midwest's first pianos. Visitors who see the French "casket" bathtubs, the carved rosewood furniture, Audubon plates and private chapel are apt to marvel that all this luxury was possible in the "wilderness" of pioneer Wisconsin. The estate was served by its own dairy, ice house, preserve room, laundry and school. Colonel Dousman had his offices of the AMERICAN FUR COMPANY on the grounds. The Old Coach house is now a museum displaying the history of the community.

VINCENNES, BATTLE OF. British success in stirring up the Indians against the Americans was marked by such violence against isolated American pioneer settlements that 1777 was long remembered as "the bloody year." British posts at such forts as KASKASKIA, Illinois, and VINCENNES, Indiana, were harried by

Hamilton surrenders at Vincennes.

the Indians who had temporarily gained the upper hand. George Rogers CLARK (1752-1818), a militia officer representing the county of Kentucky in Virginia's legislature, had, in 1778, captured Kaskaskia and Vincennes without difficulty, only to lose Vincennes in December of the same year to Governor Henry "Hair Buyer" HAMILTON (-1796), who seized the position with 600 men. Hamilton repaired Fort Sackville but, feeling safe from attack in winter, dismissed most of his men until spring. News of the developments came to Clark in Kaskaskia through the heroic flight from Vincennes by canoe of Francis VIGO (1747-1836), a wealthy Vincennes trader. Clark realized the danger. If the British were allowed to wait until spring, their superior numbers would mean almost certain defeat for the Americans. Despite the nearly impassable nature of the country in winter, Clark did not hesitate. Gathering together 170 French and American volunteers he set out on an epic 240-mile march across icy swamps and through rivers in flood. As they reached Vincennes, a message was sent to the residents warning them of the attack and urging them to remain in their homes. Much to their pleasant surprise, the message was returned by the citizens with supplies of dry powder and other necessities. Clark's men surrounded the fort in darkness. The British were dazed by the turn of events, and when a volley of shots silenced their cannon they surrendered on February 25, 1779. Fort Sackville became Fort Patrick Henry.

VINCENNES, Francois Marie Bissot, Sieur de. (Montreal, Que., Canada, 1700—on the Tombigby River, Mississsippi, 1736). French soldier and official. Son of a famous early explorer of the same surname, he became a cadet under his father until his father's death. His father had won the great respect of the powerful MIAMI INDIANS, whom he had helped in wars with other tribes. The son likewise was most respected by his Indian companions. About 1730 he established a post on the WABASH RIVER, where the French, then the Spanish, had previously established a post. By 1732 Vincennes fortified the already growing town which was named in his honor. The city of VINCENNES which developed from this beginning, claims to be the first European community in Indiana.

VINCENNES, Indiana. City (pop. 20,857), seat of Knox County, located in southwest Indiana at the Illinois border, on the east bank of the WABASH RIVER, within fifteen miles of

Indiana's richest coal fields. It is Indiana's oldest town, capital of the old NORTHWEST TERRITORY. Vincennes was French territory until 1763, British until 1779, and then part of the United States. The earliest French settlement may have been in 1683, and the first fort was built about 1732 under the command of Francois Marie Bissot, sieur de VINCENNES (1700-1736), for whom the community was named. Over the years, Vincennes was known by many names including Au Poste, Poste Ouabache, and Post St. Francis Xavier. Vincennes was finally decided upon in honor of the founder who was captured and killed by Chickasaw Indians in 1736.

Vincennes was ceded to Britain by the Treaty of Paris in 1763. After the start of the Revolution, the British used Vincennes as a place to arm Indians to attack American settlers. George Rogers CLARK (1752-1816) recognized the importance of the town and, with the help of supplies from Virginia, captured the post on February 25, 1779.

The new American government was unable to police the new territory, and Vincennes entered a period of lawlessness which ended with creation of Indiana Territory in 1800, with Vincennes as its capital. For many years Vincennes was populated largely by blacks and Creole descendents of the early French settlers and soldiers. The character of the town changed with marriages between the residents and American settlers and with arrival of large numbers of German immigrants who came to the area after 1840.

The Cincinnati-St. Louis Division of the Ohio and Mississippi Railroad through Vincennes in 1857 brought in large numbers of Irish. The development of the Indianapolis and Vincennes Railroad in 1867 and the opening of the Bicknell coal fields in 1875 established Vincennes as an industrial city. Today's manufactures include wood, paper, glass, plastic products, storage batteries, fertilizers and farm implements.

During the first two decades of the twentieth century Vincennes experienced its most rapid population growth, and it lost the last characteristics of the old city, as sections of the city, once inhabited by specific groups of residents, were blended together with industrial development. The population has remained fairly constant since WORLD WAR I. Historic sites surround the city. Two miles north of Vincennes is the archaeological site of Fort Knox, military outpost from 1803 to 1813. The GEORGE ROGERS CLARK NATIONAL HISTORICAL PARK, with its granite and marble memorial building, commemorates Clark's 1779 campaign during the American Revolution when, with a small group of frontiersmen, he captured Fort Sackville from the British.

The Harrison Mansion was the first brick building in Indiana. Built in 1803 by William Henry HARRISON (1773-1841), ninth President of the United States, the mansion was his home as Governor of the Indiana Territory. The Indiana Territory Capitol State Historic Site includes Indiana Territory's first capitol, built about 1800, and a reconstruction of Elihu Stout's newspaper and printing office. The building in which the office is housed was the birthplace of Maurice Thompson, author of the Revolutionary War novel, *Alice of Old Vincennes* (1900). Old Cathedral, St. Francis Xavier Church, stands on the site of the first log church. Simon Brute Library in Vincennes, with five thousand volumes dating from the 12th to 18th centuries, is the oldest in Indiana. A collection of Indiana artist Louis Bonsib's work is displayed in the historic State Bank-Northwest Territory Art Guild.

Vincennes University, founded in 1806, was the second oldest university in the old Northwest Territory. Presently a two-year college, Vincennes University enrolled 4,780 students and employed 182 faculty members during the 1985-1986 academic year.

Annual civic events include the Spirit of Vincennes Rendezvous and the Clark Battle Reenactment.

VINELAND, Minnesota. Early Minnesota community located on the western shore of Mille Lacs and named after an early Norwegian settlement on the northeast coast of Canada. Located at the mouth of the Rum River, Vineland is today a trading post for a group of OJIBWAY Indians living on the reservation. There is an Ojibway museum with exhibits of the Indian culture.

VINTON, Iowa. City (pop. 5,040), Seat of Benton County, named for Vinton, Ohio, which was named for Ohio congressman Plynn Vinton, who was said to have offered the community fifty dollars to name the town for him. Vinton has a unique and peculiar distinction as the firefly capital of the world. The people of the area collect the insects and provide a third of the total used by a chemical company for medical research. Industry is provided by Krunchy Nuggets, an Iowa corn snack. The community is a center of a large farming area and has small industries. One of the largest private Christmas displays is that of Larry Kersten of rural Vinton, who covers four acres of his homestead with decorations attracting busloads of spectators. The Iowa College for the Blind is located at Vinton.

VIOLET. State flower of Illinois, with the wood violet as the state flower of Wisconsin. The violet has been adopted, also, by two of the eastern states as their state flower. The violet is a member of a family of over 60 branches in the United States alone, and is widely cultivated, in addition to the wild varieties.

VIRGIN PRAIRIE PRESERVES. From the arrival of the early European explorers in the Midwest through the time the early settlers began to take over the land, much of the region consisted of the finest prairies in the world. Millions of acres were covered with lush grasses, some reaching seven feet in height. Nodding among the dozens of varieties of prairie grasses were wild flowers in profusion. Because there were no trees in much of the Midwest, for a long time it was considered to be a desert, by Europeans who associated agriculture only with the once-forested lands. Also, the centuries of prairie root growth had made the surface of the prairies so tough that old-fashioned plows could do little to turn the soil for cultivation. However, once it was discovered that much of this prairie soil was the richest known anywhere and after the invention of the steel plow, the prairies were plowed and cultivated until the wonderful virgin expanses almost disappeared. Only a few scattered acres accidentally remained due to such factors as the care of small tracts by succeeding generations of owners, or even simply by lucky happenstance. Surprisingly, one or two such tracts remain intact in the Chicago area, and conservationists so far have withstood the efforts of builders to destroy them. Also, The Morton Arboretum near Chicago is one of the several institutions dedicated to restoring small acreages to the virgin prairie conditions. Morton is a leader in this with its Prairie Restoration Project. Iowa has perhaps the largest and most successful representation of the lost prairie heritage at the Virgin Prairie Area Preserve in Guthrie County. In this forty-acre sanctuary, visitors may explore a prairie which has not been changed since the early days of settlement.

VIRGINIA MILITARY SURVEY. After the Revolutionary War, several states claimed land west of the Alleghenies, with Virginia claiming the largest share. Finally, Virginia gave up rights to the area but kept 4,500,000 acres of land between the SCIOTO and Little Miami rivers and called this the Virginia Military Survey or Virginia Military District, as it is sometimes known. Portions of this land were given by Virginia to her Revolutionary War veterans to compensate them for wartime services. George WASHINGTON was one of those so compensated, receiving 70,000 acres of this land.

VIRGINIA, Minnesota. City (pop. 11,100), northeastern Minnesota, northeast of HIBBING and CHISHOLM, city in a one-industry region of Minnesota dominated by the fortunes of the iron-mining industry. Lumbering was the principal industry in the early years. By 1893 both iron ore and timber were being shipped out of the region, and Virginia had become one of the main lumbering towns in Minnesota and remained so until 1893 when it was entirely destroyed by a forest fire. A financial panic soon after the fire caused many residents to lose their holdings in the mines. Work stopped and many citizens left, unable to pay their bills. The unbelievable happened seven years later when a second fire, started in the Finlayson Mill, again destroyed what little community remained. The city, which died twice, next rebuilt with stone, concrete and brick with a new economy based on as many as twenty mines working in the area by the early 1900s. Mine View in the Sky observation platform on the south edge of the town provides a panoramic scene. The history of Virginia is displayed through artifacts housed in the Virginia Historical Museum.

VOYAGEURS NATIONAL PARK. At INTERNATIONAL FALLS, Minnesota. Interconnected northern lakes, once the route of the French-Canadian voyageurs, are surrounded by forest. Boaters ply the waters in summer. Snowmobilers and crosscountry skiers travel over the frozen lakes and wooded trails in winter.

VOYAGEURS. Early French-Canadian licensed traders who brought the Indians of the frontier blankets, guns, utensils, ornaments and other trinkets to exchange for furs. The Indians were generally cheated. A tin cup worth less than three dollars would command muskrat skins valued at more than twelve dollars. Muskrats were the most numerous animals trapped by the Indians and became the standard fur after beaver became scarce.

Voyageurs - Wabsh and Erie

"Voyageurs," by Charles Deas.

Voyageurs remained in business in the GREAT LAKES and upper Mississippi regions even after the end of the French empire in North America in 1763. Whether their employer was the Hudson's Bay Company, NORTH WEST COMPANY or the AMERICAN FUR COMPANY was of little concern to these hardy men.

Short and stocky with over-developed shoulders and thin legs (both due to the almost constant canoe paddling), voyageurs were essential to the fur business for any nation which claimed the frontier.

Voyageurs were able to sit day after day in canoes, whether on the rough waters of Lake SUPERIOR or the treacherous rapids of inland streams. Northern canoes, rarely more than twenty-five feet in length, required crews of eight voyageurs, while the huge Montreal canoes, thirty-five to forty feet long, required fourteen. Two men typically portaged the canoe, while the others staggered over the portages with trade goods or furs in bales weighing ninety pounds. The ability to swim was not encouraged by the fur companies which wanted the trappers to stay with their furs if the canoe tipped over.

Few histories assign adequate credit to these bold adventurers. They were the ones who really knew the countryside, who knew the local peoples across wide areas and who knew how to deal with them. The voyageurs for the most part had little interest in or knowledge of formal geography and sociology, but the accounts they gave, the diaries kept by some and other facts they made known to seasoned explorers provided some of the most important background for the later development of the areas where they traveled. Some, of course, became leaders capable of developing their own trading companies and providing other useful services. James BRIDGER (1804-1881) was perhaps the most renowned and accomplished of the frontiersmen. He was a fur trader who "...for 20 years remained in the west...gaining an incomparable knowledge of the country." His skills as a guide for the army, for such trail blazers as John M. Bozeman and others provided the kind of assistance without which much of the opening of the West would have been far more difficult. There were many others of similar skills and contributions whose names are not so well known.

WABASH AND ERIE CANAL. One of the longest canals ever built and claimed to be the longest on the American continents. Construction of the canal proceeded over a period of twenty years (first barge in 1843). It was designed to connect Lake ERIE with the OHIO RIVER, utilizing the historic river route over the MAUMEE and WABASH. It extended for a length of 460 miles. Most of the laborers on the canal were from Ireland. Since about half were from the Protestant Northern Counties and the other half from Ireland proper, the rivalries of the mother country were brought with them to the shores of the canal. The "IRISH WAR" began when about three hundred from each side formed battle lines. The few shots of this "war" were fired just before the militia arrived to enforce the peace. The canal did much to spur the growth of communities along the way. TOLEDO benefitted greatly from it. Business flourished. Grain elevators and warehouses were built, and a solid line of stores prospered on the canal trade. Toledo expanded along the river bank for more than a mile. Mills foundries and factories were attracted by the fine shipping facilities. However, the canal's value was to be short lived. The coming of the railroads in the 1840s and 1850s provided quicker and better transportation.

WABASH RIVER. Principal interior river of Indiana. The Wabash, four hundred seventy-five miles long, flows northwest from its source in Ohio into Indiana where it turns southwest at HUNTINGTON flowing past LOGANSPORT, through LAFAYETTE to Covington where it turns south toward TERRE HAUTE. The Wabash, popularized in many Indiana songs, forms the Indiana-Illinois boundary from Terre Haute to the OHIO RIVER. The WABASH AND ERIE CANAL follows the river from Huntington to Terre Haute.

WABASH, Indiana. City (pop. 36.640), seat of Wabash County, northeast Indiana, on the WABASH RIVER, northwest of MARION, built on an old Indian gathering place called Oubache, "water over white stones." In October, 1826, Wabash was the site of the signing of the Treaty of Paradise Springs which opened the region to white settlement. The WABASH AND ERIE CANAL brought with it not only commerce but also religious strife known as the "IRISH WAR" fought among Irish workers who brought longstanding disputes from the old country. The canal was soon reduced in use by the railroad. Wabash claims to have been the first city in the United States to use electricity for public lighting. Canal Days on the last weekend of July celebrates the historic canal.

WADE HOUSE. Midwest stage stop. Near SHEBOYGAN, Wisconsin, visitors may see an interesting restored example of an early inn and stage stop. Wade House was built by Sylvanus Wade in 1851 at a cost of only $300.00. At one time it was one of the most popular stagecoach stops on what was then the frontier. The restoration was made by the Kohler Foundation under the supervision of Ruth and Marie Kohler.

WAGNER, Robert. (Detroit, MI, Feb. 10, 1930—). Actor. He was discovered by a talent scout while a college student. Wagner is remembered for his starring role in the television series, *It Takes A Thief* (1968-1970) in which he played Alexander Mundy, son of another thief, played by Fred Astaire. In films, Wagner's roles include *The Longest day* (1962), the *Towering Inferno* (1976) and many others.

WAGON TRAINS. Caravan of wagons organized for efficient travel and mutual protection. The first wagon train is believed to have been one organized by the ROCKY MOUNTAIN FUR COMPANY in 1830. Made up of ten wagons, this train left ST. LOUIS, Missouri, for the Wind River country. The most frequently used wagon was the "prairie schooner," a canvas covered wagon pulled by mules, oxen or horses. The wagons traveled well-marked trails starting in ST. JOSEPH or St. Louis. Within eighteen years of the first caravan an estimated 5,500 wagon trains were annually passing into California or Oregon. On an average day a train covered ten to fifteen miles. The construction of the Union Pacific-Central Pacific Railroad and other railroads marked an end to much of the need for wagon travel.

WALK-IN-THE-WATER. First steamboat on the GREAT LAKES. The *Walk-in-the-Water* arrived at DETROIT, Michigan, and other lake ports in 1818, on her maiden voyage and pioneered a revolution in inland TRANSPORTATION.

WALL LAKE, Iowa. Town (pop. 892). Situated in west central Iowa, the community takes its name from Wall Lake. The lake is said to be unique in the formation of its wall. Relatively shallow, the lake freezes to the bottom, pushing up rocks and boulders around its edges, forming a constantly growing wall. The town is the center for one of the most popular wildlife sanctuaries, harboring a large wildlife population.

WALLACE, Henry. (near West Newton, PA, 1836-Des Moines, Iowa, 1916). Agriculturalist. He was founder of a notable Iowa family including three generations of the world's best-known agriculturalists. Known as "Uncle Henry," he was a leader in advocating scientific agriculture. Beginning his life work as a minister at DAVENPORT, Iowa (1863-1876), he resigned for reasons of health and went into farming. Later he became a prominent agricultural writer, went into journalism and, with his son Henry C. WALLACE (1866-1924) founded *Wallace's Farmer* in 1895. It is still a leading farm journal. Along with his close friend, James "Tama Jim" WILSON (1836-1920), Uncle Henry helped reorganize the State College at Ames, placing it on the road to becoming the world's pre-eminent agricultural institution. He served as president of the National Conservation Congress in 1910. He was widely acclaimed on a world-wide tour with Tama Jim, after the latter retired as secretary of agriculture in 1913. Uncle Henry's son, Henry C, and grandson, Henry A. WALLACE (1888-1965), served as secretary of agriculture.

WALLACE, Henry Agard. (Adair County, IA, Oct. 7, 1888—Danbury, CT, Nov. 18, 1965). Agricultural scientist, secretary of agriculture, vice president of the U.S. He graduated from Iowa State College in 1910 and joined the publishing operation founded by his grandfather, Henry "Uncle Henry" WALLACE (1836-1913) and his father Henry C. WALLACE (1866-1924). Henry A. studied farm prices and produced the first hog-ratio charts. He was able to forecast the farm price collapse of 1920. He became a leader in developing hybrid corn, one of the pioneers in the genetic movement which has revolutionized agriculture and may change every aspect of future life. He founded one of the most successful of all the hybrid corn operations, Pioneer Hybrid Corn Company. In 1928 he shifted from the Republican to the Democratic party. Because of his success in practical agriculture and the reputation of the Wallace family, F.D. Roosevelt chose Wallace as his first secretary of agriculture (1933-1940), beginning one of the nation's most controversial public careers. Wallace was the instigator of policies which have been carried on for succeeding generations, including farm subsidies, reduction of crop and livestock production and the killing of hogs to keep prices up. These and other measures have been increasingly under fire over the years. Wallace was elected vice president as Roosevelt's running mate in 1940. Serving in many duties besides the vice president's, he was U.S. goodwill ambassador to Latin America and was chairman of the Board of Economic Warfare (1942-1943) during WORLD WAR II. For the 1944 election, Roosevelt bypassed Wallace for the vice presidency and chose

Harry S TRUMAN (1884-1972). As history unfolded, it appeared that had Wallace been the vice president on Roosevelt's death, he would have become the President of the United States. However, Wallace reluctantly became secretary of commerce under Roosevelt in 1945 and kept the post under Truman but resigned a year later. Embittered by his dismissal and later rebuffs, in 1948 Wallace ran for president on the Progressive Party ticket against Truman, calling for closer Soviet-American relations, U.N. supervision of foreign aid and reduction of armaments. He received no electoral votes despite polling more than a million popular votes.

WALLACE, Henry Cantwell (called Harry). (Rock Island, IL, 1866—Washington, DC, 1924). Secretary of Agriculture. Harry Wallace was a member of America's most famous family of agriculturists, son of Henry "Uncle Henry" WALLACE (1836-1916) and father of Henry A. WALLACE (1888-1965). He graduated in 1892 from Iowa State Agricultural College. Associated with his father in publishing Wallace's Farmer in 1895, he became its editor in 1916. Although his son Henry A. turned to the Democratic party, Harry Wallace remained a Republican, serving as secretary of agriculture under Presidents HARDING (1865-1922) and Coolidge. He died in that office in 1924. As secretary, he emphasized the department's role in adjusting production to consumption. He championed conservation and founded the bureau of agricultural economics and bureau of home economics in the department. He also inaugurated radio market reporting.

WALLACE, Lew(is). (Brookville, IN, Apr. 10, 1827—Crawfordsville, IN, Feb. 15, 1905) Lawyer, soldier, diplomat, author. Known best for his novel *Ben Hur* (1880), Wallace had one of the most unusually varied careers of any American. He began his military career at the age of nineteen in the War with Mexico (1846). His first novel was written in 1853 but not published until much later. As the CIVIL WAR approached, he was one of the few military men who had foresight to prepare. He organized and trained a company at CRAWFORDSVILLE, Indiana. A flashy and colorful group of Zouaves, they gave exhibitions all over the state. In 1862 Wallace was placed in charge of the defenses of CINCINNATI when it appeared that city might by invaded by Confederates. He was made adjutant general of Indiana, then a brigadier general of volunteers and at the age of thirty-four he became the youngest major general. General U.S. GRANT (1822-1885) was displeased with what he thought was Wallace's failure to carry out an order at the Battle of Shiloh, and this clouded Wallace's career, although Grant agreed later he was mistaken. After the war, Wallace was a member of the court which tried those accused of plotting Lincoln's assassination. In a strange twist of activity, immediately after the war Wallace accepted for a short time the title of general in the Mexican army. Between various assignments, he returned to Crawfordsville to practice law. In 1878 he was sent to New Mexico to put down a local dispute known as the Lincoln County War. While governor of New Mexico territory, he finished *Ben Hur,* one of the best-selling novels of all time, a work made into many plays and motion pictures. In 1881 Wallace was appointed by President GARFIELD to be U.S. minister to Turkey. At Constantinople he wrote *The Prince of India* (1893). Another of his works, *The Fair God* (1873), was the story of the conquest of Mexico. He was said to have disliked military life except when needed by his country and his most vital interests were music and literature.

WALLEYE. Official state fish of Minnesota. The walleye, or walleyed pike, is a member of the large perch family. Walleyes may reach a weight of ten pounds and are known as voracious eaters. They are a highly prized game fish.

WAPSIPINICON RIVER. The Wapsipinicon originates in far northeast Iowa, cutting across the entire northeastern sector of the state and emptying into the MISSISSIPPI RIVER at Folletts. It drains an area of rural Iowa, passing no large communities. The river takes its name from legendary Indian lovers, Wapsie, a young Indian brave and Pinicon, a beautiful Indian maiden. Wapsie was said to have been drowned in the river while escaping from his sweetheart's father.

WAR of 1812. Often called "Second War of Independence" between Great Britain and the United States, beginning with President James Madison's declaration of war on June 18, 1812, and ending with the Treaty of Ghent signed on December 24, 1814. In the Midwest the theme

of the war could be called the "British second chance."

Defeated in the Revolution in that area by James Rogers CLARK (1752-1818), the British had continued to stir up the Indians against the Americans at every opportunity, and they retained their hold in some key areas despite the treaty. British weapons were found on the battlefield at TIPPECANOE in 1811.

With the beginning of hostilities, most Indians sided with the British as the last hope of retaining their lands. TECUMSEH (1768-1813) was made an officer in the British army. Forts Harrison and Wayne were besieged (September 1812), but held out. Settlers were constantly under attack. Twenty whites, mostly women and children, were killed at Pigeon Roost in southern Indiana. At the outbreak of the war, General William Henry HARRISON (1773-1841) resigned as governor of Indiana to return to the battlefield and became commander of the regular army of the Northwest. One of his greatest successes was in the Battle of Thames in Canada (October 5, 1813) when he defeated British General Henry Proctor. In the same battle Tecumseh was killed and with him the last great hope of an Indian confederacy.

There were many American losses. On January 22, 1813 a detachment of Kentucky troops was sent to drive the British from Frenchtown near present-day Monroe, Michigan. Defeated in battle, only the healthy Americans were seized by the British as prisoners. The wounded were left to the Indians who massacred them. At DETROIT on 16, 1812, two thousand troops under General William HULL were attacked by British troops under General Sir Issac Brock as they attempted to cross into Canada. The Americans were surrounded and captured along with the city. In 1813 General Harrison recaptured Detroit. After the massacre of the people of FORT DEARBORN (Chicago) August 15, 1812, the British and Indians captured that fort and FORT MICHILIMACKINAC in Michigan Territory. So intent were the British in keeping the Americans out of the northern frontier that they initially demanded the establishment of a huge permanent Indian reservation in the Northwest. These demands were dropped with American military victories in 1814. The war ended formally with the Treaty of Ghent in 1815.

WARD, A. Montgomery. (Chatham, NJ, Feb. 17, 1843—Highland Park, IL, Dec. 7,

1913). Merchant. In the spring of 1872, with less than two thousand dollars raised from his savings, Ward and a partner opened a small dry goods store in Chicago. He bought in large quantities at low prices. This policy enabled him to resell his merchandise to rural consumers at prices they could afford. He also allowed the return of goods, a radically new business approach. Conducted on a cash basis, Ward's business survived the financial panic of 1873. An eight-page catalogue, replacing the single price sheet, had grown to one hundred fifty pages by 1876. The construction of Ward Tower, in 1900, brought national attention to the founder. Ward's company had annual sales of forty million dollars at the time of his death. The unparalleled public lake shore at CHICAGO, Illinois, was made secure by Ward, a man better known for his business success. Ward fought lengthy legal battles to maintain, free from obstruction, the area now known as Grant Part, and his victory in the courts created the open area of Grant Park which makes Chicago so distinctive. In 1923 Ward's widow gave NORTH-WESTERN UNIVERSITY over four million dollars to build a medical and dental school in his memory. Three years later over four million additional dollars were added.

WARREN, Michigan. City (pop. 152,000), situated in Warren County in southeast Michigan, Warren is the largest suburb of DETROIT, lying to the north adjacent to the city. It is the only Detroit suburb in the over-100,000 population classification. It now ranks as the state's third largest city, but it was not incorporated as a city until 1957. Warren occupies an area of 34.4 square miles. Known earlier as a home of many Detroit automobile employees, the city experienced the beginning of its great industrial growth during WORLD WAR II. In its own right, the city has begun to challenge its larger neighbor as an automotive center. All the big three U.S. manufacturers, along with Volkswagen, have manufacturing and assembly plants there. Other metal processing operations and steel and die making are also important. The industrial base is being broadened with electronics and defense contracting. The Detroit Arsenal at Warren manufactures military vehicles. General Motors helps to stimulate automobile advancement with a technical center at Warren. As with other major U.S. automotive centers, Warren has suffered from competition with Japanese manufacturers and the lessened demand for cars due to recent recessions. The pickup in auto sales beginning

in 1983 has helped the local economy. However, as with most industrial cities, the population dropped dramatically during the period from 1970 through 1984, from 179,000 to 152,000. With a black population of fewer than 500, Warren has the smallest number of black residents of any American city of over 100,000 population.

WARSAW, Indiana. City (pop. 10,647), seat of Kosciusko County, northeast Indiana City, south of ELKHART and northwest of FORT WAYNE. Located in the center of Indiana's lake country, Warsaw is primarily a resort town with seasonal residents. Manufacturing has included surgical supplies and cut glass. The northern part of town, now a fine residential area, was once a swamp and rendezvous for counterfeiters and horse thieves. Warsaw's International Palace of Sports Hall of Fame features wax figures of sports celebrities and other items of sports interest. The Mermaid Festival is held the last week of June and the Round Barn Festival occurs the second weekend of July.

WARSAW, Missouri. Town (pop. 1,494), seat of Benton County since 1837, west-central Missouri, northwest of Lebanon. Warsaw became almost immediately an important shipping town because of its location on the OSAGE RIVER and the crossing of the Springfield Road. Freight was shipped as far north as Warsaw for distribution, while pork, hides, tallow and fur were shipped downstream. Law-abiding residents of Warsaw and farmers banded together twice to rid the area of outlaws in what became known as the SLICKER WAR. Beginning in 1841, terror and killing reigned until 1845 when the trouble ended. By the 1870s the river traffic declined and Warsaw eased into the role of a quiet country town until the construction of the Bagnell Dam from 1929 to 1931. Now, with its location at the head of the Lake of the OZARKS, Warsaw is again a booming community with an economy based on tourists and sportsmen. Visitors can hike along part of the Butterfield Overland Trail, an early stagecoach road within the city. Gunstocks are manufactured by the E.C. Bishop and Son company which offers tours of its plant. In June the annual Jubilee Days duplicates the activities of a county fair including contests and appearances by well-known entertainers.

WASHINGTON ISLAND. Lying in Lake MICHIGAN off DOOR COUNTY, Wisconsin, forming an extension of the THUMB PENINSULA. Between the island and the mainland lies treacherous DEATH'S DOOR STRAIT, at one time one of the most feared passages on the lakes and still a peril during its sudden storms. The island was settled by immigrants from Iceland and remains the center of the U.S. Icelandic community. The Scandinavian Festival, with a renowned smorgasbord, is held there the first Friday and Saturday of August. The Washington Island Museum preserves Indian artifacts and fossils. A privately-owned ferry brings visitors to Rock Island State Park on the northeast corner of the island. This was the summer home of electrical tycoon C. H. Thordarson. Its buildings are in Icelandic architectural style. Potawatomi Lighthouse, built in 1863, crowns the island's northern point.

WASHINGTON UNIVERSITY. Independent coed university located on a 200- acre campus in ST. LOUIS, Missouri. The institution was founded in 1853. Washington University has ten schools, five of which are for undergraduates: the School of Engineering and Applied Science, College of Arts and Sciences, School of Architecture, School of Business, and School of Fine Arts. Majors include arts and sciences, linguistics, urban studies, women's studies, anthropology, Jewish studies, Latin American studies, black studies, Chinese, dance, drama, and Japanese. The university has a national student body: 27% North Central, 21% Middle Atlantic, 17% South, 23% West. Some 60% of all students pursue full-time graduate study. Washington University ranks among the nation's top 100 producers of medical school entrants, and in the top 50 for developing business executives. Library: 1,800,-000 volumes, 15,000 journal subscriptions. 23,500 records/ tapes. Faculty of 2,309 provides instruction for an enrollment 8,000.

WASHINGTON, George. (Westmorland County, VA, Feb. 22, 1732—Mount Vernon, VA, Dec. 14, 1799). First president of the United States, general. George Washington was associated with the Midwest in several interesting ways. His half brother had interested him in Ohio lands, and in 1753, at the age of twenty, with the title of adjutant, Washington volunteered to carry a message from Governor Dinwiddie of Virginia to the French who were becoming more and more aggressive, warning them to quit the Ohio country, which was claimed by Virginia. Washington brought back word that the French were rapidly building

their forces, and he was sent back to the West with troops, but he did not reach the Midwest due to his defeat on May 28, 1754, at Fort Necessity in present Pennsylvania. In 1770 Washington explored the Ohio Valley to select the land which he had received for his part in the FRENCH AND INDIAN WAR. At the point where the Little Hocking River enters the OHIO, Washington wrote in his journal that they stopped "opposite the Little Hockhocking the original name which may be distinguished by having a large stone in its mouth." As a result of the trip, Washington took title to about 40,000 acres in present Ohio and West Virginia. After the Revolution, Virginia kept title to 4,500,000 acres of land in Ohio between the Little Miami and Scioto rivers. For his wartime services, Washington was given 70,000 acres of this land, and in 1784 he journeyed west to visit his holdings there. His personal knowledge of the territory was a help in making presidential decisions concerning what was then the West.

WASHINGTON, Harold. (Chicago, IL, 1922—Chicago, IL, Nov. 25, 1987). First black mayor of CHICAGO, Illinois. Washington began his career in public service as a Democrat in the Illinois House of Representatives from 1965 to 1976. He served in the Illinois Senate from 1976 to 1980. Between 1981 and 1983 he represented the First Congressional District of Illinois in the United States House of Representatives. In 1983 he was elected mayor of Chicago and, when re-elected in 1986, became the first Chicago mayor re-elected since Richard Daley. Washington served as an advisor to Operation Breadbasket and PUSH. He died suddenly of a massive heart attack soon after his second term began. Throughout most of his first term, Chicago's political situation was explosive. Mayor Washington had been elected on a dynamic-sounding reform platform. However, a powerful bloc of aldermen opposed almost every measure he proposed and managed to keep the mayor from carrying out most of his proposals. With his second election, he received a majority of the aldermanic vote and had managed to reorganize the council but did not have time to put through his program before his untimely death intervened.

WASHINGTON, Iowa. City (pop. 6,584), seat of Washington County, situated in southeastern Iowa. It takes its name from George Washington, and the county is one of thirty-one in the U.S. to bear his name, a record for counties named for any one personality. The city claims to be the site of the world's largest calendar factory. It is also a center for manufacture of concrete culverts and bridges, and for chain-store operations. Its community center is notable for a town of its size.

WATERLOO, Iowa. City (pop. 76,800), seat of Black Hawk County, east of CEDAR FALLS and northeast of CEDAR RAPIDS. Waterloo has been heavily dependent upon such industries as meat packing and farm equipment. John Deere is a major employer, operating the world's largest tractor plant there. The first whites to visit the area came to cut red cedar trees along the CEDAR RIVER. The logs were then rafted down the rivers to ST. LOUIS and sold.

Charles Dyer was a leading logger, but not a person liked by the others in the area. Loggers stripped bark from a tree, drew a likeness of Dyer on the bark and then riddled the picture with bullets. Dyer took the hint and was never seen again.

The first permanent resident was George Hanna who built a cabin on the west bank of the river, 1845, where the first church service was held two years later. The town's name was chosen by Charles Mullen while thumbing through a list of towns in other states. Mullen found many Waterloos and thought the name was appropriate. The city was platted in 1853, the same year the first school was established.

Many famous people share in the history of Waterloo. William GALLOWAY (1877-1952), a pioneer Waterloo manufacturer, is remembered as one of the prominent developers of mail-order merchandising, which made his farm machinery company a leader for many years. F.L. MAYTAG, (1857-1937) the Newton washing machine tycoon, tried to manufacture automobiles in Waterloo in 1909 and 1910. The first cars featured a two-cylinder engine designed by Maytag and August Duesenberg. Each car cost from $1,250 to $1,750. The cars were successful, so Maytag manufactured a four-cylinder model that proved to be a complete financial failure. The company collapsed and Maytag returned to a business he knew much better.

According to a popular tale, Sinclair LEWIS (1885-1951) had Waterloo in mind for his novel-to-be, *Main Street*. Waterloo residents did not want their city to have that kind of publicity, so they met Lewis at the train station. According to one eyewitness, a series of planned parties resulted in Lewis' drinking enough liquor to ensure he was unable to gather local color for his book. He left Waterloo and evidently by the time he recovered, all thoughts

of Waterloo were forgotten. Lewis returned to his hometown of SAUK CENTER, Minnesota, the account continues, to collect story ideas, and Waterloo escaped. Actually, however, Lewis was a reporter on the Waterloo *Courier* in 1908-1909.

Waterloo is the hometown of Dan Gable, the only man ever to win 100 matches as a collegiate wrestler and a collegiate wrestling coach. Gable's amateur wrestling record was 306-7. He won the 1972 Olympic 149.5 pound championship.

Among the other well-known residents of Waterloo were the Sullivan brothers. George, Eugene, Madison, Albert, and Francis, who ranged in age from 20 to 29 when they enlisted in the U.S. Navy after learning of the death of a good friend at Pearl Harbor. At their request, the five brothers were assigned to the same ship, the cruiser *Juneau*. In November, 1942, the *Juneau* was sunk by the Japanese. Four of the brothers died in the attack, and the fifth died on a life raft before help could arrive. A destroyer was named in their honor and a movie made of their courageous action. Sullivan Memorial Park is located in the neighborhood where the boys grew up.

Another Waterloo native was Lou Henry who became the wife of Herbert HOOVER, (1874-1964) the 31st President of the United States.

Allan Carpenter (1917-), author of 214 books, including 174 supplementary school texts, was born in Waterloo.

An important annual event is the National Dairy Cattle Congress held in September. At one time this fair brought together more blooded animals than any other, including its specialty of heavy Percherons and other draft horses.

WATERTOWN, Wisconsin. City (pop. 18,-113), situated in Jefferson County on the ROCK RIVER in southeast Wisconsin, the city was founded on the basis of the falls of the river, which descended twenty feet in the course of two miles. Beginning in 1836, sawmills and factories used the waterpower to make barrels, wagons and other wood products. The city was notable for its elite German immigrants, university students and professional men known locally as the Latin Farmers, because when they gathered at a local tavern, they often spoke in Latin. They also were known for their failures in farming, in running a brewery and in shoemaking. It was said that "they made shoes which could not be worn and cigars which could not be smoked." The last remnant of their brewery was the 35-gallon copper basin, which became the kettledrum of a Watertown orchestra. A leading figure among the German immigrants was political reformer Carl SCHURZ (1829-1906), who fled Germany and arrived at Watertown in 1855. Most of the German settlers were Democrats, but, hating slavery, Schurz ran for state lieutenant governor as a Republican in 1857 but was defeated. He successfully campaigned for Abraham LINCOLN (1809-1865) in Wisconsin in the campaign with Stephen A. DOUGLAS (1813-1861) and was made minister to Spain and later served as secretary of the interior. Mrs. Schurz (Margaretha Meyer Schurz) made a more lasting contribution by creating at Watertown the first kindergarten in America. Octagon House, where the kindergarten was established, is open to visitors today. The fifty-seven-room mansion is known for its forty-foot spiral cantilever hanging staircase. On the grounds the restored kindergarten is also displayed.

WAUKESHA, Wisconsin. City (pop. 50,-365), seat of Waukesha County, situated just west of MILWAUKEE in southeast Wisconsin, it takes its name from the Little Fox River flowing through it. The POTAWATOMI Indian word "waukesha" means "By the Little Fox River." The Potawatomi had a village there in 1833 when the land was ceded to the federal government. In 1834 a waterpowered sawmill was built. When lumber was exhausted, a gristmill took over. Manufacturing of plows and other products began as early as 1842. Limestone from the nearby quarries was used in many Milwaukee buildings. Waukesha was an important Abolitionist center and a major station on the UNDERGROUND RAILROAD. However, in the later part of the 1800s the community was made most famous as a health resort, based on its mineral waters. In 1869 New Yorker Colonel Richard Dunbar thought he was cured by the waters and became the most ardent sponsor of the "miracle" springwater. The streets were swarming with women in fashionable gowns. Actors performed on the stages of the many significant hotels. When a group of promoters tried to pipe Waukesha waters to the Chicago world's fair, local supporters frightened them off. The health fad soon died out, and the great hotels were razed or turned to other uses. However, Waukesha water continues to make itself widely known as a bottled product. Today the city is an important industrial center. Old World Wisconsin is a cluster of fifty buildings reflecting early Wisconsin ethnic, historical and cultural conditions. All the buildings are authentically furnished and staffed by costumed guides.

WAUSAU, Wisconsin. City (pop. 32,426), seat of Marathon County, situated in north central Wisconsin along the rapids of the WISCONSIN RIVER, the city takes it name from the Indian "wassa," meaning far away place. When it was settled as a lumber camp, it was known as Big Bull Falls after the French "gros taureau." Several sawmills were built, along with a hotel, and the settlement took its present name in 1850. After the saw timber was gone, the community turned to paper mills and paper products, still the main products of the area. The Marathon County Historical Society, at the home of early lumberman Cyrus C. Yawkey, displays lumbering and pioneer life. Art is exhibited at the Leigh Yawkey Woodson Art Museum. Nearby Rib Mountain State Park features the sturdy, ancient granite peak which split the mighty glaciers of the glacial age. From its summit, magnificent views of the river valley are obtained. The Rib Mountain Ski Area is also operated in the park. February finds the community celebrating with Winter Frolic, indoor and outdoor competitions and activities.

WAWASEE, LAKE. Largest natural lake in Indiana. Lake Wawasee, located southeast of GOSHEN, Indiana, in Kosciusko County, has twenty-one miles of shore line. The Wawasee Fish Hatchery, near the southeastern corner of the lake, is one of the oldest state fish hatcheries. Lake Wawasee is one of a chain of three lakes including Papakeechee Lake, an artifically developed and privately owned lake, and Lake Syracuse, a small lake adjoining Lake Wawasee on the north.

WAYNE STATE UNIVERSITY. State supported institution in DETROIT, Michigan. Accredited by the North Central Association of Colleges and Schools and by professional and educational organizations, Wayne State awards degrees of Certificate, Bachelor, Specialist, Master, Professional and Doctorate. During the 1985-1986 academic year Wayne State enrolled 28,424 students and had 1,560 faculty members.

WAYNE, Anthony (Mad Anthony). (Waynesboro, PA, Jan. 1, 1745—Presque Isle, PA, Dec. 15, 1796). Army officer. Wayne was a Revolutionary War hero at such battles as Stony Point, for which he received a medal from Congress. His actions as a military leader were so bold that he became known as "Mad Anthony." He retired from military service and served as a member of the United States House of Representatives from Georgia (1791-1792). He returned to the military and became a major general in command of the U.S. Legion in 1791. Sent to the Ohio country, he built a string of forts, carefully trained his raw troops, and on August 20, 1794, he defeated hostile Indians in the NORTHWEST TERRITORY at the decisive Battle of FALLEN TIMBERS (August 20, 1794) on the MAUMEE RIVER near present-day TOLEDO, Ohio. Wayne was able to bring about a gradual pacification of the Indians. In 1795 he assembled them at the community named in his honor, FORT WAYNE, Indiana, and dictated the terms of the Treaty of GREEN VILLE, which opened a large portion of the Northwest Territory to settlement. His name is remembered in many other communities and institutions in the Midwest.

WELLS, William. (—near Fort Dearborn Chicago, Aug., 1812) Adopted white son of LITTLE TURTLE (1752-1812). Kidnapped as a child in Kentucky, Wells became Indian in almost every way and aided Little Turtle in his victories over Harmar (1790) and ST. CLAIR (1736-1818) in 1791. He asked if he could return to his own people and Little Turtle granted his request. Wells served as the chief scout for General Anthony WAYNE (1745-1796) in 1796), helped build FORT WAYNE and with Little Turtle signed the Treaty of GREEN VILLE (1795) which opened settlement to half of Ohio and a strip of land in Indiana. After the treaty signing, Wells was promoted to Indian agent. Little Turtle and Wells managed to keep the Miamis out of the Shawnee confederacy of TECUMSEH (1768-1813) and the PROPHET (circa 1770-1834?), but was suspected of not being entirely trustworthy on several occasions. Dismissed as Indian agent in 1809 for his failure to deliver $350 in annuities to the Eel River Indians, he may have been involved in agitating the Indians. Governor William Henry HARRISON (1773-1841) managed to convince Wells to spy on Indians at Prophet's Town in 1811 and the resulting report led to the Battle of TIPPECANOE (November, 1811) in which the Indian rebellion was crushed. On July 14, 1812, Little Turtle died at Well's home in Fort Wayne. About one month later Wells was killed at FORT DEARBORN (Chicago) attempting to prevent the massacre of the garrison.

"Mad" Anthony Wayne, by Edward Savage.

WEST ALLIS, Wisconsin. City (pop. 63,-982), suburb of MILWAUKEE, situated west of the major city. The name comes from a plant of the Allis Chalmers manufacturing company, located west of the main plant in Milwaukee. An industrial and "bedroom" community, West Allis experienced a drop in population typical of Midwest cities, from 71,649 in 1970 to 63,982 in the 1980 census.

WEST BEND, Wisconsin. City (pop. 21,-484), seat of Washington County, is situated in southeast Wisconsin on the great bend of the MILWAUKEE RIVER, from which it takes its name. In 1845, Dr. E. B. Wolcott of MILWAUKEE decided that the site would be excellent as a halfway stop between his homes in Milwaukee and FOND DU LAC. Many of the present residents are descendants of the substantial numbers of German immigrants. Today it is known for its manufacture of aluminum utensils, along with machine tools, tools and dies, leather products and washers.

WEST BRANCH, Iowa. City (pop. 1,887), situated in southeast Iowa. West Branch was the birthplace of Herbert HOOVER (1874-1964), first United States president to be born west of the MISSISSIPPI RIVER. President Hoover's birthplace is now a National Historic Site, which includes the cottage where he was born, the Hoover blacksmith shop, the Quaker meeting house and a splendid presidential library. President and Mrs. Hoover are buried at the site.

WEST SALEM, Wisconsin. Town (pop. 3,276), situated in southwest Wisconsin in La

Crosse County, just east of the city of LA CROSSE. The community was founded in 1858 and became a principal center for butter and powdered buttermilk. It is known principally as the home of author Hamlin GARLAND (1860-1940).

WESTERN ENGINEER. River Steamship. The first vessel of the inland navy of the United States. This steamer was designed to frighten the Indians. Its bow was formed to look like a serpent, and from the serpent's mouth smoke and flames poured out. This was the first steam vessel to sail up the MISSOURI RIVER, reaching as far as COUNCIL BLUFFS, Iowa in 1819. Just fifteen years after Meriwether LEWIS (1774-1809) and William CLARK (1770-1838) had struggled up the river. By strange quirk, steamboats did not reach the upper navigable portions of the Mississippi until four years later. This "puffing canoe" had exactly the hoped-for effect on the Indians. Even the strongest braves quailed at the sight of such a monster. However, the tribesmen and women soon became used to steamboats and even to steamboat travel, and the Missouri became accessible to a fleet of sternwheelers which reached into the far interior of the continent.

WESTERN ILLINOIS UNIVERSITY. In Macomb, Illinois. Established in 1899 as Western Illinois State Normal School, the university has seven schools and one graduate school. There are nearly forty buildings on a campus of 750 acres, a farm of 90 acres, and a Life Sciences Station on the MISSISSIPPI RIVER. During the 1985-1986 academic year Western Illinois University enrolled 11,845 students and had 680 faculty members.

WESTERN MICHIGAN UNIVERSITY. Publically supported institution in KALAMAZOO, Michigan. Western Michigan has Schools of Education, Continuing Education, Arts and Sciences, Applied Sciences, Business, Health and Human Services and Graduate Studies. An Honors College provides students of exceptional ability the maximum opportunity for independent study and research in a self-directed environment. The university is accredited by the North Central Association of Colleges and Secondary Schools. The campus consists of seventy acres, with fifteen devoted to physical education and recreation. During the 1985-1986 academic year the university enrolled 20,963 students and employed 891 faculty members.

WESTERN RESERVE. Midwest land claimed by Connecticut. Almost from the time of their founding, Connecticut and Virginia had claimed large areas to the west of their present borders, including much of what is now known as the Midwest. States which did not make such claims refused to recognize the Connecticut and Virginia rights. In 1786 Connecticut ceded its claims to the central government but "reserved" 500,000 acres on the shore of Lake ERIE. Because this area was to be given to Connecticut citizens whose property had been burned in the Revolution, the grants were known as "fire lands." The Connecticut Land Company purchased the remaining lands, and Moses CLEAVELAND (1754-1806) founded the first community in the Western Reserve. This is now the city of CLEVELAND. The term Western Reserve is still used in many ways in the area, which now also includes ten counties of Ohio and parts of four others. Other major cities in Western Reserve territory are AKRON, ASHTABULA, LORAIN, SANDUSKY and YOUNGSTOWN.

WESTERVILLE, Ohio. City (pop. 23,414), situated in central Ohio just north of the capital city of COLUMBUS, named for a prominent farm family. Westerville was most famous in history for its anti-liquor sentiments. It was often referred to as the driest town in the state, if not the nation. The Anti-Saloon League was established permanently in Westerville in 1909. OTTERBEIN COLLEGE was founded at Westerville in 1847 by the United Brethren Church. The community is also known as the home of composer Benjamin HANBY (1833-1867). Hanby prepared for the ministry at Otterbein College and his home at Westerville has been preserved as a shrine to his memory.

WESTMINSTER COLLEGE. Privately supported coeducational liberal arts college in FULTON, Missouri. The college was founded as Fulton College in 1851. The present name was adopted in 1853. Women were admitted as full-time students in the fall of 1979. An overseas program is offered with an Institute of European Studies in Spain, France, England, Germany and Austria. Programs in the United States, but away from the college, include United Nations Semester and Washington Semester. The college is located on a two-hundred acre campus with twenty-three buildings. Library facilities are provided to the students on campus and at nearby William Woods College. To honor Winston Churchill's famed "Iron Curtain" speech at the college

(March 5, 1946), a twelfth-century London church, rebuilt by Christopher Wren in the 1600s, was reconstructed, stone by stone, on the campus and now houses the college chapel and Churchill Museum. During the 1985-1986 academic year 661 students were enrolled. The college has sixty faculty members.

WESTPORT LANDING. Predecessor of present-day KANSAS CITY, Missouri. Westport Landing was established in 1821 as Chouteau's Post, named for Francois Chouteau, an employee of the AMERICAN FUR COMPANY. The site was the steamboat landing used by merchants of Westport, then a flourishing community. Originally the landing was the depot from which the other posts of the American Fur Company were supplied and at which their furs were collected and shipped. The success of the port was due to a precedent set by Ceran St. Vrain and William Bent, famous fur traders on the upper Arkansas River, who hauled their freight directly to the landing in 1845. When farmer Gabriel Prudhomme died, the "Kansas Town Company" bought his land for $4,220 and platted it for a town to be named Kansas. Trade on the SANTA FE TRAIL brought additional business to the new town. As many as six steamboats unloaded their freight at the levee at one time. A cholera epidemic in 1849 caused the economic boom to collapse until 1855 when overland trade was resumed. Residents realized they were in a tough economic competition with Leavenworth and ST. JOSEPH and a board of trade became the Kansas City Chamber of Commerce in 1857. Albert D. Richardson of the New York *Tribune* found Kansas City of 1855 a confusing crowd of nearly two thousand, but a place with much vitality and an unquestioned faith that this was to be the city of the future, and such faith appears to have been well founded.

WESTPORT, BATTLE OF. Battle known as the "Gettysburg of the West." This name was given because of the fierceness of the battle and because it kept the CIVIL WAR from spreading west of the MISSISSIPPI. The battle was fought near WESTPORT, Missouri, on October 23, 1864. Confederate troops under the command of General Sterling Price were defeated in an attempt to recapture Missouri for the South. The defeat of Price marked the end of major fighting in Missouri for the remainder of the Civil War.

WEYERHAEUSER, Frederick. (Neider-saulheim, Germany, Nov. 21, 1834—Pasadena, CA, April 4, 1914). Businessman. He moved to the United States in 1856 and lived in Pennsylvania and Illinois, where he worked for lumber companies and formed a lumber syndicate in 1870. In 1891 he moved the company to ST. PAUL, Minnesota. Adding huge acreages of timber to the company holdings Weyerhaeuser became known as the "Lumber King." With the depletion of timber in the Midwest Weyerhauser and his companies eventually followed the "timber trail" to the West Coast, where the company now has its headquarters. During his lifetime, Weyerhaeuser had acquired two million acres of forest land from Wisconsin to Oregon and made a fortune in the process.

WHIPPLE, Henry Benjamin. (Adams, NY, Feb. 15, 1823—Faribault, MN, 1901). Episcopal bishop of Minnesota, known as the "Apostle to the Indians." Whipple was consecrated the bishop of Minnesota in 1859. He was active in evangelization among the Indians and established missions for both the SIOUX and the CHIPPEWA. Whipple's fair treatment while serving on several commissions which made treaties with the Indians led them to call him, "Straight Tongue." He was a pioneer in working to make the Indians wards of the government to avoid cheating among them. Whipple established the free church system in CHICAGO; held the first Protestant service ever conducted in Havana, Cuba; founded St. Mary's Hall, Shattuck Military School and Seabury Divinity School in FARIBAULT, Minnesota; and served as chaplain of the General Sons of the Revolution.

WHISTLING SWAN. Once thought to be on the road to extinction, the whistling swan has made a substantial comeback. One of the distinctions of GREEN BAY in northern Lake Michigan is the arrival each year of a flock of these birds, said to contain almost every living member of the group. They put down on the great bay on their migration to the north. Residents look forward to their arrival, sometime between March nineteenth and twenty-third, without fail.

WHITE RIVER (Indiana). Flows 255 miles from its source in Madison County near ANDERSON, southwestward through INDIANAPOLIS. It meets with the Eel River near Worthington, Indiana, and continues on toward the WABASH and its mouth near East Mount Carmel.

WHITE RIVER. (Arkansas-Missouri). From its source in the Boston Mountains of Madison County in northwest Arkansas, it flows north into Missouri and then southeast across Arkansas until it empties into the MISSISSIPPI RIVER, a total distance of 690 miles. The White River has been dammed to make several of the largest artificial lakes in the area, including BULL SHOALS, mostly in Missouri.

WHITEWATER CANAL. Indiana's project to improve the WHITEWATER RIVER as a canal link between Cambridge City and the OHIO RIVER. The canal was given precedence over other projects beginning in 1836, and by December, 1838, the Indiana part of the canal was completed twenty miles northwest of West Harrison. All work ceased at this point until 1842 because Indiana's Mammoth Internal Improvement Program had bankrupted the state. A private company took over the canal and completed it to Cambridge City by 1846. Floods in 1847 and 1848, causing $200,000 in damage, proved the canal was impractical. In 1865 the Whitewater Valley Railroad was built parallel to the canal and completely replaced it as a means of transportation. Some portions of the canal were then used for water power.

WHITING, Indiana. City (pop. 5,630), located in extreme northwest Indiana on the shore of Lake MICHIGAN, northwest of GARY. Whiting was for many years a predominately German settlement. It has been known as Whiting's Crossing, Whiting's Station, Whiting's and now Whiting. Whiting's major employer from 1889 was Standard Oil until 1934 when Carbide and Carbon Chemicals Corporation entered the community. It remains largely an oil refining center with one of the largest refineries in the world, covering nearly one thousand acres.

WILCOX, Ella Wheeler. (Johnstown Center, WI, 1850—Branford, CO, Oct. 31, 1919) Poet and Spiritualist. Wilcox grew up in Johnstown Center, Wisconsin. Mrs. Wilcox is said to have written her first novel at the age of nine. She wrote a daily verse for a syndicated newspaper column and published over twenty volumes of verse. Her best known collection is called *Poems of Passion* (1883). Her autobiography *The Worlds and I* (1912) is centered about the posthumous message she said she received from her husband who had promised that "should he precede me to the realm beyond, he would importune God until he was allowed to

communicate with me." Her Poem "Two Glasses" illustrates her lifelong devotion to the temperance cause. It is a dialog between a wine glass and a water glass. In the period of temperance promotion, it was a favorite recitation at school and temperance meetings. She is responsible for one of the most often quoted phrases in English, beginning, "Laugh and the world laughs with you..."

WILD ROSE. Official flower of Iowa, the only Midwestern state to have selected it as official flower. It was designated for the honor by the 26th general assembly in an extraordinary session on May 7, 1897. This modest member of the vast rose family grows in hedgerows and wherever else it has not been forced to make way for agriculture. It shows a slight variation from the prairie rose, official flower of North Dakota.

WILLIAM HOWARD TAFT NATIONAL HISTORIC SITE. At CINCINNATI, Ohio, the birthplace and boyhood home of the only man to serve both as President and Chief Justice of the United States. He was the 27th President, 1909-1913; U.S. Chief Justice, 1921-1930. There are limited Federal facilities.

WILLIAM WOODS COLLEGE. An independent women's college under the direction of the Christian Church, in FULTON, Missouri. William Woods was founded in 1870 at Camden Point, Missouri, as the Orphan's School for Girls of the Christian Church of Missouri. The original building burned, and the church then moved the school to Fulton where it reopened in 1890. The name was changed to Daughter's College and in 1900, after receiving financial assistance from Dr. William S. Woods, a Kansas City banker, it became William Woods College. The school has been the home of the Margaret L. Barber Loan Collection of oil paintings from Mexico, early American and European furniture, and primitive American portraits. During the 1985-1986 academic year the college enrolled seven hundred women and maintained a staff of sixty-five.

WILLIAMS, Charles W. (Chatham, Columbia County, NY, Dec. 4, 1856—Independence, IA, Feb. 18, 1936). Williams brought international racing fame to himself and to his community of INDEPENDENCE, Iowa. He is the only man to develop two horses to win world trotting records. In 1885 Williams, who owned an Independence creamery, bought two colts,

Axtell and Allerton, carefully trained and developed them. Axtell established records for two-year-olds and continued to set records, including a world trotting record for stallions of any age. Williams sold him to a syndicate for $105,000. Allerton, too, gained world fame as the champion stallion and lost only one important race. Williams also brought the racing world to remote Iowa with a new track, said to be the fastest in the world. He built a fancy hotel and financed an electric railroad from downtown Independence to his track. Williams also published an international racing newspaper, the *American Trotter*. With the coming of the depression of 1893, Williams sold his horses, became a traveling evangelist, and Independence's racing fame dwindled.

WILLIAMS, Daniel Hale. (Hollidaysburg, PA, Jan. 18, 1858—Idlewild, MI, Aug. 4, 1931). Surgeon. Williams, graduated from the Chicago Medical Center in 1883. Recognizing the lack of facilities for training blacks as medical practioners, Williams, a black, organized Provident Hospital at CHICAGO. The hospital provided the first nurses' training school for black women. He served on the staff until 1912, interrupted in 1893 when President Cleveland appointed him surgeon-in-chief of the Freedmens' Hospital in Washington. During his five-year tenure, he reorganized that hospital and opened another nurses' training school for black women. Williams returned to Chicago in 1898 and served on the surgical staff of Cook County Hospital from 1900 to 1906. From 1907 until his death he was an associate attending surgeon at St. Lukes Hospital. He performed the first successful surgical closure of a wound of the heart and perfected a suture for hemorrhages from the spleen. He was the only black invited to be a charter member of the American College of Surgeons and was one of the founders of the National Medical Association, a society of black professional men, organized in 1895.

WILLKIE, Wendell Lewis. (Elwood, IN, Feb. 18, 1892—New York, NY Oct. 8, 1944). Lawyer and presidential candidate. Willkie attracted national attention during the Great Depression as president and chief executive officer of the Commonwealth and Southern Corporation, a giant utility holding company, and as a crusader for the League of Nations and against the Ku Klux Klan and the two policies of the New Deal: the Public Utility Holding Company Act and the Tennessee Valley Authority. While acknowledging past abuses in

the management of utilities, Willkie opposed public ownership and excessive federal control. His winning of the Republican presidential nomination in 1940 over better known candidates such as Thomas E. DEWEY (1902-1971) and Robert A. TAFT (1889-1953), was remarkable, considering that many of his best friends never knew that he had changed party affiliation and that he did not actively campaign until May, too late to enter many primaries. His victory was due to his reputation in the business community, his support from several key Republicans, his personal charisma, and his strong stand for aid to England after Germany's easy conquest of the continent. In the election Willkie polled a larger popular vote than any other Republican candidate before Eisenhower, but lost to F.D. Roosevelt by a wide margin. Following the election, Willkie worked to unite the country behind aid to Britain. He supported Roosevelt's Lend-Lease proposal and became the president's good-will ambassador to the Middle East, the Soviet Union and China. His "Report to the People" radio broadcast upon his return to the United States was estimated to have had a larger audience than any speech except Roosevelt's following the attack on Pearl Harbor. His theme became one of encouraging colonial peoples to join the West in a global partnership based on economic, racial, and political justice. Willkie campaigned for the 1944 Republican presidential nomination, but lost in the Wisconsin primary and withdrew from the race. Excluded by Dewey from an active role, Willkie attempted to influence the party with a series of newspaper articles entitled a "Proposed Platform" in which he called for anti-lynching laws, an extension of social security, and a world organization in which the small states would have real power. Campaigning weakened him, and he died after having a series of heart attacks.

WILLSON, Meredith. (Mason City, IA, May 18, 1902—Santa Monica, CA, June 15, 1984). Musician, conductor and composer, best known for his *Music Man* (1957). He studied flute and piano, played in the John Philip Sousa band and in the New York Philharmonic under Arturo Toscanini. He claimed his boyhood in MASON CITY and his later experiences were the basis for his famed musical and that Mason City was the "River City" of the musical. Willson wrote both the words and music of his masterpiece. One of his best known songs was "May the Good Lord Bless and Keep You," which sold half a million copies soon after it was published.

WILMETTE, Illinois. Village (pop. 28,229), residential community on Lake MICHIGAN, north of CHICAGO, with many splendid older homes, named for Antoine Ouilmette, whose Indian wife received 1,280 acres of land under an 1829 treaty between the federal government and the Indians. As the community grew, a section became known as "No Man's Land" where fireworks, illegal in other places, could be purchased. In 1860 there were 293 lives lost when the Lady Elgin was struck by a lumber schooner in Lake Michigan off the community. Wilmette is the United States headquarters of the Baha'i faith. The nine-sided temple, one of the major attractions of the Chicago area, is open to the public and tours are available.

WILSON'S CREEK NATIONAL BATTLEFIELD. Near Republic, Missouri. The Confederate victory here on August 20, 1861, was the first major Civil War engagement west of the MISSISSIPPI. It culminated in severe losses on both sides, yet Union troops were able to retreat and regroup. Major features include "Bloody Hill" and the recently restored 1852 Ray House.

WILSON, James (Tama Jim). (Girvin Farm, Kilpatrick, Ayreshire, Scotland, Aug. 16, 1836—Traer, IA, Aug. 16, 1920). Celebrated in his day as "the man who fed the world," and honored by nations around the world for his contributions to their agriculture, James Wilson of Iowa is hardly remembered today. Yet he served for sixteen years in the cabinets of three presidents, longer than anyone else has ever served in any cabinet post. Brought by his parents to Connecticut in 1851, he again moved with the family to Iowa, near where the town of Traer now stands.

A successful farmer and newspaper publisher, he served in the state legislature, and in Congress for three terms. In his third, his seat was contested by Benjamin T. Frederick, Wilson was sure to win, but the question was not decided until the last day of the session when Wilson gave up his seat in favor of Frederick in order to secure action by the Democratic House on a bill placing Illinois resident and former United States President U.S. GRANT (1822-1885) on the retired list. During his three terms in Congress, Wilson was a member of the committee on agriculture. He was given the nickname "Tama Jim" to distinguish him from "Jefferson Jim" Falconer Wilson from Iowa who had been elected to the Senate.

In 1895 Tama Jim became director of the agricultural experiment station and professor of agriculture at what is now IOWA STATE UNIVERSITY. There he developed the scientific agricultural theories and methods which led President William MC KINLEY (1843-1901) to call him to Washington as secretary of agriculture.

He found a small weak department which he determined to develop for the benefit of farmers throughout the world. Most of the practices in use today were initiated under his direction; among these, the department extended its work by establishing experiment stations in all parts of the nation, farm demonstration work, and co-operative extension work in agriculture and home economics. Wilson initiated the practice of searching the world for products to grow in the U.S., and master-minded the fight against the boll weevil. The millions of copies of practical publications on farming provided a generation of farmers with the best available instruction on farming techniques. He was noted for his unusual success in dealing with Congress. Notable publications of the day declared that he might well have become president if he had been born in the United States.

On leaving office in 1913, Wilson and his friend "Uncle Henry" WALLACE of Iowa, toured widely among nations which had benefitted from Wilson's work. He received honorary doctorates and other honors. He spent the rest of his retirement in Traer, where he is buried.

WILSON, Margaret. (Traer, IA, 1882—London, England, 1976). Author. Margaret Wilson was educated at the University of CHICAGO and went to India as a Presbyterian missionary. She wrote many articles and gave numerous lectures on life in India, especially on the treatment of Indian women. In India she met Douglas Turner, a British criminologist, and they were married. Wilson continued her writing, and in 1924 won the PULITZER PRIZE for fiction for her novel *The Able McLaughlins*, which she claimed was a true account of life in the Traer community where she grew up. Her writing continued with other novels and the nonfiction *The Crime of Punishment*. This was based on her study of the British criminal system of which her husband was the head. The book was widely hailed and as widely critcized for its sharp denunciation of the system.

War Dance of the Winnebago, by Karl Bodmer.

WINNEBAGO INDIANS. A branch of the Sioux nation, they were first found in present eastern Wisconsin by Father Jean NICOLET (1598-1642) in 1634 in their village of Red Bank, near GREEN BAY. The Winnebago hunted buffalo, fished and practiced some agriculture by raising squash and corn. Chiefs, sometimes women, inherited their rank. They lived a generally peaceful life, except for troubles with the ILLINI and the OJIBWAY. They were alligned with the French until the British took over their area, then they fought with the British in both the REVOLUTIONARY WAR and the WAR OF 1812. Some Winnebago lived in a village called Prophetstown, on the ROCK RIVER in Illinois. The town was named for their leader, Wabokieshiek (White Cloud), who was one of several known as the Prophet. The Winnebago ceded their Wisconsin and Illinois lands to the federal government in the 1830s and were moved to Minnesota, South Dakota and finally Nebraska.

WINNEBAGO, LAKE. Nestled in the FOX RIVER Valley, covering 215 square miles, Lake Winnebago is the largest interior lake in Wisconsin, it is both fed and drained by the Fox. Part of the pioneer water route from the GREAT LAKES to the MISSISSIPPI, the lake is now an important center of recreation. The cities of NEENAH and MENASHA lie at the northern entrance to the lake, and FOND DU LAC lives up to its name as the "end" of the lake. Largest city on the lake shore is OSHKOSH.

WINNETKA, Illinois. City (pop. 12,772). Chicago, Illinois, suburb frequently mentioned in surveys as representative of many of the best aspects of middle-class America, name taken from an Indian word meaning, "beautiful place." Large estates have riparian rights and private beaches on Lake MICHIGAN, and there are many splendid inland homes. In 1919 Winnetka schools pioneered an innovative form of education with individualized instruction of the child in a controlled environment. Winnetka-prepared instructional materials were designed to allow the student to progress at his or her own rate under general supervision of the instructor. While regular studies are handled in this manner, students also take part in non-graded group activities.

WINONA, Minnesota. City (pop. 25,075), seat of Winona County, southeastern Minnesota, east of ROCHESTER, early Minnesota lumbering town, A MISSISSIPPI RIVER industrial community with three colleges, the community was named Winona for a local Winnebago woman and was platted in June of 1852 on land known as the Wabasha Prairie for the SIOUX chief who lived in the area. Subject to flooding, the land was never of interest to land speculators until Erwin F. Johnson, hired by Captain Orrin Smith of the steamboat *Nominee,* occupied the site and erected a small cabin. Beginning as a lumbering and wheat-shipping port the town attracted twenty-four factories by 1900 and had eighty-two by 1957. Some of the commercial success of the city came from limestone quarries, but perhaps the most unique employers were two button factories which used Mississippi River clam shells as their raw material. Manufacturing today includes heavy road equipment, metal products, automotive products and flour. Higher education is represented by Winona State College, College of St. Teresa and St. Mary's College. Winona abounds in historical sights, including the Bunnell House, an unusual "Steamboat Gothic" home constructed in the 1850s. The Winona County Historical Society Museum features a country store, barber shop, blacksmith shop, Indian artifacts and logging and lumbering displays. The Rohrer Rose Garden features over two thousand roses of some two hundred varieties. Annual events include the popular Steamboat Days in early July with a carnival, art fair and powerboat races. In mid-October Winona hosts its Victorian Fair in which costumed guides play the roles of early settlers.

WINTERSET, Iowa. City (pop. 4,021), seat of Madison County, situated in south central Iowa, about thirty miles southwest of DES MOINES. The name is thought to have been given by early settlers who arrived by train on a cold day. Winterset is the birthplace of Michael Morrison, who is far better known as movie idol John Wayne. The home where he was born in May, 1907, has been refurbished for visitors. Winterset is also known as the center for the greatest number of covered bridges in Iowa. There is an annual Madison County covered bridge festival, which features not only the bridges, but also art exhibits, craft fairs and other festivities.

WISCONSIN. State, situated in the north central Midwest. Nearly two-thirds of Wisconsin's borders are formed by lakes and rivers. The unusual border with Michigan is delineated in part by Lake SUPERIOR on the north and Lake MICHIGAN on the east. The Brule and Menominee rivers mark the Wisconsin border to the northeast across from the Michigan UPPER PENINSULA. The tiny Montreal river provides a short water border between north central

Wisconsin and Michigan. The ST. CROIX and the MISSISSIPPI rivers form most of the western border between Minnesota and Iowa. A straight border connects the St. Croix with the Cloquet River, at a point just west of SUPERIOR. The other straight border separates Wisconsin from Illinois to the south. The rest of the Wisconsin-Upper Peninsula border is manmade, connecting the Brule and Montreal rivers.

With 10,000 miles of rivers and 8,700 interior lakes, Wisconsin truly deserves its name, derived from the Indian term meaning "Gathering of the Waters." Lake OSHKOSH is the largest of its inland lakes. With access to the two greatest rivers of the eastern U.S., Wisconsin has been a crossroads from time immemorial. Through the ST. LAWRENCE RIVER SYSTEM AND SEAWAY, the state now has access to the Atlantic from both lakes SUPERIOR and Michigan. A portage of only two miles between the FOX and WISCONSIN rivers gives the city of PORTAGE its name, and for early travelers provided the only easy route from Lake Michigan to the Mississippi and from there to the Gulf of Mexico.

With an area of 56,154 square miles, Wisconsin ranks fifth in area, just behind Iowa, among the Midwest states. Most of the surface of Wisconsin is rolling and dotted with lakes. The most spectacular feature is old RIB MOUNTAIN. This extremely aged uplift was so rugged that the ancient glaciers which pushed across Wisconsin could not conquer it. They were forced to go around. This accounts for the unglaciated area of the state's southwest. The glaciers scoured out the basins not only of the many interior lakes but also accounted for the formation of the GREAT LAKES, providing Wisconsin's water heritage.

Shallow lowlands in the southeast are separated by three broad parallel limestone ridges, running north to south, stretching to the northwest. The sandy crescent-shaped Central Plain slopes upward to the Northern Highland, which meets the narrow Lake Superior Lowland plain, completing Wisconsin's topography.

Geologically, a wedge of Precambrian surface pushes into Wisconsin from the north. Around this, on both sides and to the south, is the early Paleozoic area.

Winters, especially in the north, are long and cold, but are tempered in much of the state by the Great Lakes. The short hot summers are also modified by the lakes.

Wisconsin has realized its greatest assets from the soil. The immense forests of early times provided what seemed to be limitless supplies of fine-grade lumber until they were almost worked out. With the forests' comeback of recent years, the state once again has stands of close to thirty billion board feet, second only to Michigan in the Midwest.

The agricultural primacy of the state comes from its dairy farms and dairy products. From its nearly two million cows, the Dairy State produces almost twice the milk of the next leading state. It is world-renowned for its cheese, ranking first among the states, second in butter. Other leading dairy products are condensed, powdered and malted milk. William HORLICK (1846-1936) invented malted milk, and the Horlick plant at RACINE is the largest of its kind. Cattle, corn and hogs are the other leading agricultural products.

Machinery production of various kinds leads the state's industries. Papermaking machinery is particularly important. One BELOIT firm produces more than half of the country's paper-producing machinery. Some of these machines can turn out paper at the rate of a mile a minute. Heavy machinery of other kinds is another specialty. Ever since the equipment manufacturers of Wisconsin began to produce great steam shovels for the Panama Canal, they have been turning out enormous digging machinery. Production of electric generating machinery is Milwaukee's leading industry.

Papermaking ranks third among the state's industries. Pulp to make paper produces greater annual income than dairying. Wisconsin holds third rank in the production of automobiles. In a related field, the state ranks first in internal-combustion engines.

Enamelware, such as bathtubs and lavatories, of the Kohler and Vollrath companies makes Wisconsin a leader in this field. The manufacture of aluminum utensils is concentrated at TWO RIVERS, MANITOWOC and WEST BEND. Food processing, in addition to dairy products, is also important. The state also turns out twenty percent of the nation's canned goods, including forty percent of the canned peas.

With annual manufacturing income of $52,-482,000,000 Wisconsin generally ranks about twelfth among the states.

The port of MILWAUKEE is especially known for its efficiency in loading and unloading world cargoes. SUPERIOR is a leading grain port and the site of the world's largest grain elevator.

Wisconsin's population of 4,775,000 in 1984 showed a thirteen percent increase over the 1980 census. Projections for the year 2000 indicate a population of 5,216,000, showing a consistent increase for the period. Non-white population is less than half of one percent.

COPPER CULTURE Peoples lived in Wisconsin as long as eight thousand years ago. A burial ground near OCONTO contained well-crafted jewelry and copper utensils. Wisconsin peoples, both before and after the Copper Culture, left mounds which they used for different purposes. Among the most interesting of these are the EFFIGY MOUNDS, made to look like snakes, birds, turtles and other creatures. The famed MAN MOUND of BARABOO is about 150 feet tall and 50 feet at the shoulders.

One of the most interesting prehistoric sites in the entire Midwest has been named AZTALAN because it is believed to have been the northernmost settlement of the Aztec civilization. The work of these people in shell, bone, stone and copper sheet is considerably more advanced than that of their Indian neighbors. Apparently they were quite different from the local Indians. Cannibal remains have been found in the village. The people were massacred by the surrounding tribes, apparently in revenge. Aztalan probably survived until only about 200 years before European exploration of the area.

Early European explorers found several ALGONQUIN tribes which had been driven west by the IROQUOIS. These included POTAWATOMI, MAS-COUTEN, CHIPPEWA, HURON, OTTAWA, FOX and MIAMI. Of the Algonquin groups, the MENOMINEE were outstanding. Also in the area were the WINNEBAGO, a SIOUX branch.

One of the most unusual events in the history of exploration occurred in 1634 near the head of GREEN BAY when the first European explorer of Wisconsin, Jean NICOLET (1598-1642), landed there. Nicolet thought he had found the long-sought route to China. He dressed in beautiful embroidered robes and plumes and stepped ashore shooting into the air from pistols in each hand. The astonished Winnebago of the village of Red Banks had been told a strange person would arrive. They soon convinced Nicolet that he was far from China.

Twenty years later, Medart Chouart, known as Sieur de GROSEILLIERS (1618?-1690), came to present Wisconsin. On another visit, accompanied by Pierre Esprit RADISSON (c1636-c1710), Chouart set up the first fur trading operation in what is now the state. Other traders and missionaries (known as Black Robes) arrived in increasing numbers. Best known of the missionaries was Father Pierre MARQUETTE (1637-1675), who along with Louis JOLLIET (1645-1700), made the famous journey across Wisconsin, which resulted in their discovery of the upper reaches of the Mississippi.

Wisconsin

Counties and County Seats

Wisconsin

STATE OF WISCONSIN

Name: Wisconsin for the Wisconsin River which the Ojibway Indians called Wees-kon-san, meaning "the gathering of the waters."

Nickname: The Badger State

Capital: Madison

Motto: Forward

Symbols and Emblems:
Bird: Robin
Flower: Wood Violet
Tree: Sugar Maple
Stone: Red Granite
Animal: Badger
Fish: Muskellunge
Song: "On, Wisconsin!"

Population:
1985: 4,775,000 (1985)
Rank: 16th
Gain or Loss (1970-80): +126,000
Projection (1980-2000): +511,000
Density: 88 per sq. mi. of land (1984)
Percent urban: 64.2% (1980)

Racial and Ethnic Makeup (1980):
White: 94.4%
Black: 3.9%
Hispanic: 62,981 persons
Indian: 29,500 persons
Others: 50,600 persons

Largest City:
Milwaukee (621,000 - 1984)

Other Cities:
Madison (171,000 - 1984)
Green Bay (87,899 - 1980)
Racine (85,725 - 1980)
Kenosha (77,685 - 1980)
West Allis (63,982 - 1980)
Appleton (58,913 - 1980)

Area: 56,153 sq. mi. (145,436 sq. km.)
Rank: 26th

Highest Point: 1,951 ft. Timms Hill

Lowest Point: 581 ft. Lake Michigan

H.S. Completed: 69.6% (1980)

Four Yrs. College Completed: 14.8% (1980)

STATE GOVERNMENT

ELECTED OFFICIALS (4 yr.-terms, expiring Jan. 1991):
GOVERNOR: $75,337 (1986)
LT. GOV.: $41,390 (1986)
SEC. OF STATE: $37,334 (1986)

GENERAL ASSEMBLY:
Meets Annually at Madison
Salary: $27,202 annually plus $45.00 per day expenses (1985)
Senate: 33 members
Assembly: 99 members
Congressional Representatives
Senate: Terms expire 1989, 1993
House of Representatives: Nine members

These early Frenchmen gave France its claims to the whole Great Lakes region and beyond, but few French people came as settlers. After 111 years of trading and missionary work, the first permanent European settlement in Wisconsin was GREEN BAY, established in 1764. As the 19th century opened, there still were only about 200 French settlers in Wisconsin. By this time, of course, the region had changed hands, first going to the British, then to the Americans.

However, the British were not completely driven from their claims until the end of the WAR OF 1812. The only notable episode of that war in Wisconsin was the British capture and burning of Fort McKay, built in 1813 at PRAIRIE DU CHIEN for American protection.

During the lead mining boom in southwestern Wisconsin, the region was as rip-roaring as any mining region of the far west. MINERAL POINT was established in 1829 as the seat of the mining region. Three years later, chief BLACK HAWK (1767-1838) and his fugitive people were driven into Wisconsin during the BLACK HAWK WAR (1832). When they attempted to cross the Mississippi to Iowa, many drowned or were shot during the Battle of BAD AXE, near the now abandoned town of Victory, named ironically by the winning side.

Because all the existing towns were rivals for the capital, an undeveloped site was chosen and named MADISON in honor of the fourth president. Between 1836 and 1848, the population of the state had grown from 22,000 to 250,000, and Wisconsin became the thirtieth state in the latter year. Milwaukee had been founded only two years before.

The inexpensive land attracted many settlers from Europe, including such numbers of Germans to Milwaukee and other parts of the state that Wisconsin became known as a second Germany.

On March 20, 1854, RIPON was the site of a meeting of a new political party, calling itself REPUBLICAN. Wisconsin claims to be the birthplace of the national Republican Party, but this claim is disputed. Two years later, Republicans captured the Wisconsin governor's chair.

Wisconsin Abolitionists were in the forefront of the dispute over slavery. Abolitionist editor Sherman M. Booth became a local hero when he helped a former slave escape to Canada, was jailed, released by the local courts, held by the U.S. courts and finally pardoned by President Buchanan.

In the CIVIL WAR, Wisconsin's EAGLE REGIMENT gained world fame. It took its name from OLD ABE, its eagle mascot. the bird took part in some of the battles and was given so much attention it become the country's most famous bird. In 1862 Louis P. Harvey became governor of Wisconsin. On a trip to assist Wisconsin servicemen, the governor was drowned after only seventy-three days in office. His wife, Cordelia Harvey, became known as the Wisconsin Angel for her part in creating better war hospitals.

On the same day, October 8, 1871, that CHICAGO was devastated by fire and a fire was also raging in Michigan, a forest fire, starting at PESHTIGO, swept across forests and villages and took over 800 lives. This was a far worse toll than in Chicago, which received all the attention.

In 1873 Dr. F. W. Carhart of RACINE pioneered with his steam-powered automobile. In the same period, C. Latham Sholes invented the typewriter and APPLETON was the scene of the first use of waterpower in generating electricity. The turn of the century in 1901 brought Robert M. LA FOLLETTE (1855-1925) to the Wisconsin governor's chair, the first Wisconsin-born man to hold that office. Governor La Follette gained international fame as a political innovator and friend of the common man. With his new PROGRESSIVE REPUBLICAN PARTY, the governor pioneered in proposing the primary election law, pensions for blind, old age assistance, aid to dependent children, child labor laws, minimum wage for women and children, apprenticeship regulations, unemployment compensation and other social legislation. Parts of this "Wisconsin Idea" have been widely adopted in other states.

As a U.S. Senator, La Follette opposed WORLD WAR I but supported the war effort.

The fears of many Wisconson people that because of their German background they might suffer for Germany's part in that war were generally groundless. Many became part of the total of 125,000 in the armed services from Wisconsin. WORLD WAR II called 350,000 from Wisconsin, and Wisconsin men and women served during the Korean War, beginning in 1950.

In a far different event, Milwaukee celebrated when the Braves baseball team made the city their home in 1953; the state went wild when their team won the World Series in 1957.

A still different celebration had more far-reaching implications when Queen Elizabeth of Britain visited Milwaukee in honor of the opening of the ST. LAWRENCE SEAWAY in 1959.

In 1961 the MENOMINEE Indian Reservation

was turned over to its Indian people and Menominee became a Wisconsin county. Indian properties were shared by the people in a corporation. In 1975, a group of Menominee occupied property of the Alexian Brothers and demanded that it be turned over to the Menominee for a hospital. After thirty-five days, the property was turned over to the Indian people.

For the period 1970 through 1987, Wisconsin had the largest population growth of the Midwest states. In the elections of 1980 and 1984 Ronald REAGAN (1911-) took the Wisconsin vote. In the election of 1986 the Republicans also took the governor's chair in the person of Tommy Thompson. Robert E. Kasten, Jr., became one of the few Republicans to capture a U.S. Senate seat in that election year.

Robert M. La Follette rose from a boyhood in a poor family to become one of the most prominent persons in U.S. politics. His first national attention came as a Republican in the U.S. Congress. By 1911 he was dissatisfied with the Republican Party and helped to found the Progressive Republican Party. His reforms gained him further fame. He served in the U.S. Senate from 1906 until his death in 1925. He gained 5 million votes in a futile 1924 run for the presidency, but the effort contributed to his death. His son, Robert, Jr., succeeded him in the Senate.

Another internationally known Wisconsin man was Frank Lloyd WRIGHT (1867-1959), native of Richland Center. He became perhaps the most widely acknowledged architect of all time. His home, TALIESIN, at SPRING GREEN, was also used as an architectural school, and it has become a shrine to Wright.

Other creative Wisconsonites are sculptor Vinnie REAM (1847-1915), authors Zona G A L E (1874-1938), Hamlin GARLAND (1860-1940), Edna FERBER (1885-1968) and Ben HECHT (1893-1964), composer Carrie Jacobs BOND (1862-1946), cartoonist Claire Briggs, baseball record holder Cy YOUNG (1867-1955) and noted Civil War hero Edward S. Bragg.

Scientists and inventors have played an important part in Wisconsin life. After twenty-five tries, Christopher Latham Sholes invented the typewriter. In another field, Increase Allen LAPHAM (1811-1875) was the father of modern weather forecasting. John Appleby invented the grain knotter, and Ole Evenirude was the father of the outboard motor industry. William Hoard became known as the Father of Modern Dairying through his work in improving dairy

herds. Dr. Stephen M. BABCOCK (1843-1931) produced a simple method of testing the richness of butterfat; even more importantly his work in another field led to the discovery of vitamins.

The Menominee name for Wisconsin means "a good place to live." Not only is that true, but the many attractions of the state, particularly its great outdoors, have made tourism the state's second most important source of income, approaching annual revenues of nearly seven billion dollars.

One of the nation's major annual events is Milwaukee's Summmerfest. Since Marquette and Jolliet were the first to visit the site, in 1673, the city has grown to substantial cultural stature. Its natural history museum is one of the newest and best designed in the country. The geodesic domes of the Mitchell Park Horticultural center are landmarks known around the world. The Lake Michigan shore is graced by the County War Memorial and Art Center, as well as Municipal Pier. The city has long been recognized as the best place outside of Germany to enjoy German cuisine.

Milwaukee is a very young city; Green Bay is the oldest in the state. Its most newsworthy feature is its Packers football team, making its home in the smallest city to host a professional ball club. Tank Cottage (1776) is the oldest European style building still standing in Wisconsin. The National Railroad Museum at Green Bay preserves historic equipment, and steam engines still pull passengers around in historic rail cars.

The City of Green Bay is not far from Sturgeon Bay, which stands at the entrance to the playground formed by Lake Michigan's greatest embayment, also named Green Bay. This is the vacation land of DOOR COUNTY. Some of the world's best fishing around WASHINGTON ISLAND and other water sports are enjoyed in Door County, along with the world famed summer music and theater festival at Fish Creek. Egg Harbor is another Door County vacation treasure.

West of SHEBOYGEN is historic WADE HOUSE, a popular stagecoach stop of the mid-1850s. It was restored to the condition of its heyday by the Kohler family.

The capital of Madison has not only one of the leading educational institutions of the country, the University of WISCONSIN, but it also boasts one of the nation's finest state historical societies. Its X-shaped capitol is unique.

LITTLE NORWAY harks back to its Norwegian heritage, and NEW GLARUS holds a noted annual

William Tell festival. Yodelers, bell ringers, flag throwers and a William Tell pageant add to the festive atmosphere.

MONROE, the Swiss cheese center of the nation, and the Spring Green home-school of Frank Lloyd Wright attract many visitors. Memories of a different kind—the mining boom—still enliven MINERAL POINT. At Prairie du Chien, on the Mississippi River, one of the nation's notable historic mansions still stands, thoroughly restored. This was the home of Hercules DOUSMAN, the state's first millionaire, who built a cork-surfaced race track and found many other ways to live a kingly life.

One of the nation's most visited areas is that of WISCONSIN DELLS and BARABOO. The rock-ribbed canyon of the great Wisconsin River is the main attraction at the very door of Wisconsin Dells. Its scenery has been augmented for visitors by water shows and other sports as well as many shops and restaurants. Baraboo remembers its fame as the birthplace of the RINGLING BROTHERS of circus fame. The five Ringling boys started there in 1882. Today visitors at the Circus World Museum are treated to views of circus wagons, a steam calliope, a live menagerie and other mementoes of circus days.

WISCONSIN ALUMNI RESEARCH FOUNDATION. Known familiarly as WARF, the foundation has a history of almost unparalleled accomplishment. The foundation came about through the efforts of Dr. Harry Steenbock, discoverer of vitamin D. Dr. Steenbock turned over to the foundation the rights to this discovery, for which he had been offered $900,000. With the income from this and its many other patents, the foundation continues in work which has already resulted in the development of DICUMAROL, a helpful drug to prevent blood clotting, WARFARIN, a successful rodent poison, a special strain of penicillin, nicotinic acid and a pellagra cure, among many others.

WISCONSIN DELLS, Wisconsin. City (pop. 2,521), situated in Sauk County on the dells of the WISCONSIN RIVER, the city takes its name from the "dalles," meaning waters running rapidly through steep cliffs. However, until 1931, the community was known as Kilbourn. The name was changed in order to attract tourists to the highly scenic area. As a resident remarked, "It worked!" Today Wisconsin Dells is one of the ten most popular small tourist cities in the country. Natural wonders

are still the featured attraction. Boat trips of the upper dells feature a scenic ride between the towering cliffs, landings at Cold Water Canyon, so narrow in some places a few visitors cannot squeeze through, Witches Gulch and Stand Rock. The latter is one of the country's most famous of the many balanced rocks which perch on precariously narrow bases. The Lower Dells tour takes the boaters past an incredible array of rock formations, carved from the rushing waters, a mixture of "the grand, the beautiful and fantastic." Tours by "Duck Boats," amphibious craft, are also popular. Two entertainment parks, Biblical Gardens, Xanadu, a futuristic house, Deer Park and Tommy Bartlett's Water Ski, Sky and Stage Show and Robot World are other attractions. The city itself is a typical small tourist spot, with all of the charm which many people find in such concentrations of souvenir shops and art galleries. The community grew around the railroad, which bridged the mighty river between the upper and lower portions. The Stand Rock Indian Ceremonial is held nightly from June through Labor Day, and the Great Wisconsin Dells Balloon Rally lifts off the weekend after Memorial Day.

WISCONSIN IDEA. The term given to the social concepts of Wisconsin Governor Robert M. LA FOLLETTE, which over the years he managed to put through the Wisconsin legislature. When he became governor in 1901, La Follette considered that governments, generally, did not give enough attention to the ordinary individual. Convinced that the two ensconced political parties were not attentive to those needs, La Follette founded the PROGRESSIVE REPUBLICAN PARTY to further his proposal for greater social consciousness. Over a period of years under his guidance, mostly during his tenure as governor (1900-1906) Wisconsin pioneered in adoption of such social legislation as statewide primary elections, pensions for the blind, old age assistance, aid to dependent children, child labor laws, unemployment compensation, compulsory vocational education for employed children, minimum wage law for women and children and apprenticeship law. Much of the Wisconsin Idea has been adopted and adapted by most states, the national government and many other nations.

WISCONSIN RAPIDS, Wisconsin. City (pop. 17,995), seat of Wood County, it takes its name from the frothy stretch of the WISCONSIN RIVER where the community was founded. Two communities, Centralia on the west bank and Grand Rapids on the east, were united in 1900 as Grand Rapids, and the name was changed in 1920 because of confusion with the Michigan city of the same name. The flood of June, 1880, caused the almost complete destruction of both the towns. Lumbering was the first industry, followed by pulp factories, hardware and woodworking followed. Today's city is a paper manufacturing and cranberry processing center. The vast neighboring cranberry bogs make the area the largest inland cranberry producer in the nation. South Wood County Historical Corporation Museum preserves the lore of the area. Seven million trees a year are distributed from the Griffith State Forestry nursery. Nearby Grotto Shrine and Wonder Cave feature religious tableaux. Self-guided forest tours are popular. Discover Greater Wisconsin Rapids Week in early August features parades, races, arts and crafts and other attractions.

WISCONSIN RIVER. Rising near Wisconsin's northern border with Michigan, in the SUPERIOR UPLANDS region, this major river flows for 430 miles through what were once the greatest conifer forests of North America. The upper river passes Tomahawk, WAUSAU and others, all founded on the basis of the waterpower produced by the river. Continuing southward through the Pettenwell Flowage and Castle Rock Flowage, the river shifts slightly eastward through the WISCONSIN DELLS near the source of the northern FOX RIVER. The Fox and the Wisconsin, with the short portage between them, provided the earliest route from the GREAT LAKES to the MISSISSIPPI, where the Wisconsin River empties in a wide delta near the historic Wisconsin community of PRAIRIE DU CHIEN, with MC GREGOR, Iowa, facing the mouth on the opposite side of the Mississippi.

WISCONSIN, UNIVERSITY OF. Founded at MADISON, Wisconsin, in 1848, almost before the community existed, the university has grown until it boasts twelve other campuses scattered throughout the state. The 45,050 students at the Madison campus, who are taught by a faculty of 2,289, are augmented by almost 100,000 other students in the other twelve branches, with additional faculty numbering over 3,100. The Madison campus spreads picturesquely along the shores of Lake MENDOTA. Its history has been peppered by the disputes over educators Glenn Frank and Alexander Meikelejohn. As president of the University, Frank introduced the university's famous

experimental college and changed the program of agricultural education. He was fired in 1937 by Governor Philip Fox LaFollette. Among the notable facilities are the Geophysical and Polar Research Laboratory, Space Astronomy Laboratory, Numerical Analysis Laboratory and the State Engineering Experiment Station, which includes a solar research laboratory. Unique among universities is the WISCONSIN ALUMNI RESEARCH FOUNDATION, which has contributed many important discoveries to medicine and other science.

WITTENMEYER, Annie Turner. (Sandy Spring County, OH, Aug. 26, 1827—Saratoga, PA, Feb. 12, 1900). During her work in military hospitals in the CIVIL WAR, Annie Wittenmeyer was horrified at the poor, sometimes disgusting, food served to the sick and wounded soldiers. "On a dingy-looking wooden tray," she wrote, "was a tin cup full of black strong coffee; beside it was a leaden looking tin platter, on which was a piece of fried fat bacon, swimming in its own grease, and a slice of bread." Mrs. Wittenmeyer finally persuaded the government to establish special diet kitchens, where two women prepared food for each patient according to the doctors' written orders. She was in charge of the more than one hundred diet kitchens created before the war was over. General U.S. GRANT (1822-1885) said, "No soldier on the firing line gave more heroic service than she rendered." After the war Mrs. Wittenmeyer lobbied for army nurses' pensions, and a law was passed giving 500 nurses $12.00 per month. In 1898, when she was 70, she finally received a pension herself—$25.00 a month.

WOLF RIVER WILD AND SCENIC RIVER SYSTEM. Near Keshena, Wisconsin, noted as one of the most scenic and rugged rivers in the Midwest, the Wolf flows through the MENOMINEE INDIAN reservation.

WORLD WAR I. In proportion to population, the Midwest contributed almost a ten percent more men and women to the armed services during the war than any other of the country's other regions. One of the reasons for this is undoubtedly due to the fact that fewer Midwest residents were found unfit for service, indicating the general health of the region.

Those in the front lines in the fighting took the brunt of some of the most disastrous battles fought until that time. James Gresham of Indiana was one of the first three American men who lost their lives in the war. The

World War II

Supreme Commander of U.S. Expeditionary Forces in Europe was Missouri's own John J. PERSHING (1860-1948). He and the other returning service men and women were hailed as heroes.

The experiences of Midwesterners in Europe and other parts of the U.S. brought a new comprehension of the world to many who may never before have left the farm or small town.

The First World War proved a stimulus to industrialization and farm economy in the Midwest. Farm products, in demand in Europe even before the war, increased in price as the demand for wheat, corn and livestock skyrocketed. The failure of farm prices to keep up with the cost of living, the lowered productivity of soil, and increased farm surpluses, all made farming increasingly expensive for those who remained in the field.

Industrialization, proceeding at a rapid pace before the war, experienced labor shortages as thousands of men joined the military. However, the Midwest poured out military equipment and other needed goods at a rate unequalled in any other region.

Those at home helped put together "comfort kits," made surgical dressings, or knit sweaters and socks. The saving on the home front of food needed by the troops was encouraged by participation in programs under the slogan "Food will win the war." Sales of savings bonds rose, as did the sales of thrift stamps, to help finance the war.

In all branches of service, a total of 1,377,833 men and women came from the Midwest states during the war. Of those, 85,238 were casualties. Illinois sent the most service men and women, 323,741, with 18,264 casualties. Ohio men and women totalled 239,572, with 16,007 casualties. From the other states were 133,215 from Indiana, 5,766 casualties; Iowa, 114,404, 7,311 casualties; Michigan, 163,919, 10,369 casualties; Minnesota, 119,194, 7,323 casualties; Missouri, 162,222, 10,385 casualties; and Wisconsin, 120,663, 9,813 casualties.

WORLD WAR II. The contribution of the Midwest to World War II must be considered in terms of both human and industrial contributions and sacrifices. During that worst of all wars in cost of human life and property, the Midwest was the arsenal of the free world, sometimes credited with turning out more war materiel than the rest of the world combined. Michigan, alone, produced the incredible total of one-eighth of all the war materiel manufactured in the entire United States—the then unbelievable total of twenty-seven billion dollars worth of munitions and equipment.

The Ford Motor Company's WILLOW RUN plant could build an entire B-24 bomber every hour. The Defoe company developed a new method of production which permitted them to complete a fighting boat every week. Michigan school children donated their pennies to build a glider which became the first to land in Normandy in the invasion. The Michigan Red Arrow combat unit set a record of 654 days in combat, more than any other in history.

The appropriate industries in all of the other Midwest states, Illinois in particular, also went all-out in producing for the war effort.

Iowa led all the nation in food production for the U.S. and its allies, and the claim has been made that the Midwest produced more food and fiber during World War II than the rest of the world combined.

Illinois made a unique contribution to the war effort.

In what may have been the greatest secrecy of any major war operation, the scientists at Chicago produced the first workable system for releasing atomic energy, which led very quickly to the atomic destruction in Japan.

Upper Michigan was the site of another kind of unprecedented wartime security. Sabotage of the SOO CANAL would have brought much of the industry of the country to a halt, and it was said that the area of SAULT STE. MARIE was the most heavily guarded in the United States.

The Midwest states produced many heroes of the war, both in and out of service, including Ohio's flying ace Eddie RICKENBACKER and Wisconsin's ace, Richard Bong, who shot down 40 Japanese planes. as well as the wartime atomic contributions of Iowa's F. H. SPEDDING. A wartime hero not in army uniform was famed war correspondent Ernie PYLE 1900-1945) of Indiana, who died of wounds suffered while reporting the war in the Pacific.

There was some concern that the large German populations in such states as Wisconsin might cause a problem, but the Midwest people of German background almost overwhelmingly supported the Allies. All the Midwest states contributed war personnel in numbers out of proportion to their populations. Minnesota fielded 350,000 men and women, of whom 6,000 lost their lives; Iowa, 260,000, 8,398 dead; Wisconsin, 350,000 served; Illinois approximately a million, with 27,000 dead; Indiana, 338,000 in service, 10,000 dead; Michigan, 673,000 served; Ohio, 800,000 served, and Missouri, 350,000 served.

WORLD'S COLUMBIAN EXPOSITION. CHICAGO, Illinois, observance of the 400th anniversary of Christopher Columbus' arrival in the Americas. CHICAGO outbid such cities as Washington, D.C., New York, and ST. LOUIS for the exposition. Chicago business leaders matched the five million dollars raised from the sale of stock, while the federal government contributed one and one-half million dollars. Daniel H. Burnham acted as the Chief of Construction. Held in 1893, one year later than originally planned, the Exposition featured wonders of the time, including the linotype, PULLMAN cars, the original FERRIS WHEEL, and the expansion engine. It used more electricity than the entire city of Chicago. The main buildings shone so white, because of their finish in a plaster composition called "staff," that the fair was nicknamed "The White City." The grounds, covering 666 acres, were the site of construction of the largest exposition building up to that time, the Building of Manufacturers and Liberal Arts. The Palace of Fine Arts, built for the Exposition, now houses Chicago's MUSEUM OF SCIENCE AND INDUSTRY. The effect of the exposition on the Midwest was dramatic. Thousands of people who had never before left their farms and small town homes flocked to the city where the sights of both the exposition and the city were a revelation, an experience never to be forgotten.

WORTHINGTON, Minnesota. City (pop. 10,234), southwestern Minnesota; Nobles County; settled in 1871 by the National Colony Company. In 1873 a cloud of grasshoppers made the first of several destructive visits to the farming areas around Worthington. Appeals went out nationally to help the farmers. Many residents turned to trapping as a means of staying alive. Nearly twenty-eight thousand muskrat skins were shipped from Worthington in the winter of 1874-1875. Worthington has received national attention by maintaining a local polo team with national ratings. The Okabena apple was developed in the area. Geographically the area is important for a series of north-south valleys and ridges which mark the western edge of the Keewatin Glacier during the last ice age. The Coteau des Prairies, a rise of land in southwestern Minnesota, prevented any further expansion of the glacier. These plains are approximately eight hundred feet higher than the central prairie of Minnesota. A typical pioneer settlement with bank, town hall, and church is maintained by the Nobles County Historical Society. Annual events include the Nobles County Fair in mid-August and King Turkey Days and Great Gobbler Gallop in September with its parade, races and food booths.

WORTHINGTON, Thomas. (Near Charleston, WV, 1773—New York, NY, 1827) Sometimes called the "Father of Ohio Statehood," Thomas Worthington served two terms as governor of Ohio (1804-1818) and two terms as U.S. senator from Ohio (1803-1807—1811-1814). In the early days of Ohio settlement, Worthington was a leader of a group of politically active young men at CHILLICOTHE, Ohio. Their main aim was to bring statehood to Ohio. Territorial governor, Arthur ST. CLAIR, was opposed to statehood because it would cost him his position. Tempers grew so strong that a mob broke into his home and was about to lynch the aged governor when Worthington stepped in and saved him, although the two held bitterly opposing positions. Worthington built a magnificent home at Chillicothe. It was designed by famed Washington architect Benjamin Latrobe, and Worthington called it Adena, which means in Hebrew "a place remarkable for the delightfulness of its situation." In the spring of 1803, soon after statehood was achieved, the estate was the scene of an all-night meeting of state leaders. During the meeting they felt they had made great plans for the new state. Going outside to the terrace, they saw the sun rise from behind Mt. Logan. William Creighton, the secretary of state, exclaimed, "The rising sun of a new State!" They were so impressed with the scene that it became the state seal and has been Ohio's state seal ever since. Worthington was noted for his entertaining at Adena. Many notable personages, such as Aaron BURR, visited there. When famed Chief TECUMSEH (1768-1813) visited, he lost his temper and hurled a tomahawk through one of Mrs. Worthington's draperies. Regretting this display of anger, he later presented his tomahawk as a gift to her.

WRIGHT STATE UNIVERSITY. Founded in 1867 at DAYTON, Ohio, Wright State's museum offers one of the largest collections of mementos of the WRIGHT Brothers, who made their headquarters in Dayton. One of the notable Wright State facilities is the university's Garden of the Senses, for the handicapped. The student body of 16,116 is instructed by a faculty numbering 876.

WRIGHT, Frances. (Dundee, Scotland, Sept.

6, 1795—Dec. 13, 1852). Reformer. A free-thinker and heiress of a large fortune, Wright wrote her first book at the age of 18, published in 1822 as *A Few Days in Athens.* She came to America in 1818, toured widely, returned to England and wrote *Views of Society and Manners in America* (1821), an unusual appreciation of the country for Europeans of the time. Visiting Thomas Jefferson and James Madison, she won their approval for her plan of emancipation of slaves. She invested heavily in land at Nashoba, Tennessee, and attempted to demonstrate her emancipation theories. Wright served with Robert Dale OWEN (1801-1877) as the editor of the NEW HARMONY *Gazette.* She frequently lectured on birth control, emancipation of women and slaves, religion and legal obligations of marriage. Unused to women lecturers, the public was shocked by her appearances and her philosophy, but her example of a liberated woman was a helpful one.

WRIGHT, Frank Lloyd. (Richland Center, WI, 1867—Phoenix, AZ, Apr. 9, 1959). Architect. Wright, considered by some as one of America's most imaginative architects, left a wealth of striking architectural forms across the nation, but particularly in his native Midwest. He studied civil engineering at the University of WISCONSIN from 1884 to 1888, when he was apprenticed to CHICAGO architects Louis SULLIVAN (1856-1924) and Dankmar Adler and soon became their chief draftsman.

He left in 1893 to build his own practice, but continued to show Sullivan's influence in attempts to bring harmony to a building's function, form and location. Wright's unique style soon brought him the extremes in praise and scorn usually reserved for politicians. The Unity Temple in OAK PARK, Illinois, was the first public building in the United States to show its concrete construction. Wright planned many Prairie-style houses in and around Chicago. Prairie-style buildings permit the open spaces inside to expand into the outdoors through the use of terraces and porches. Willitts House in Highland Park, Illinois, is shaped like a cross, with rooms arranged so that they seem to flow into each other. The Robie house in Chicago appears to be a series of horizontal layers floating in the air. The Johnson Wax building in RACINE, Wisconsin, gave the same impression of streamlined style as Wright's other products of the late 1930s. The building featured a smooth curved exterior of glass and brick.

One of his most famous buildings was Fallingwater at Mill Run, Pennsylvania. An-other was the Imperial hotel in Tokyo completed in 1922, one of the major buildings to survive the terrible earthquake of the next year. While Wright's influence was felt internationally, he remained a Midwesterner at heart.

In 1932 Wright established the TALIESIN Fellowship where architectural students paid to live and work with Wright in the summer at Taliesin, Wright's home in SPRING GREEN, Wisconsin, and in the winter at Taliesin West, his home in Scottsdale, Arizona. He continued to design controversial buildings such as the Guggenheim Museum in New York city, a daring spiral structure (1959).

WRIGHT, Harold Bell. (Rome, NY, May 4, 1872—Escondido, CA, May 24, 1944). Author. Bell began his literary career while serving as the pastor of the First Lutheran Church in LEBANON, Missouri. Wright had been a painter and decorator from 1887 to 1892 and a landscape painter until 1897 when he began service as a minister in the cities of Pierce City, Missouri; Pittsburg and KANSAS CITY, Missouri; and finally Lebanon. His best known work, and the most popular of his books associated with Missouri, was *Shepherd of the Hills,* which he wrote in 1907.

WRIGHT, Orville and Wilbur. (Orville, Dayton, OH, Aug. 19, 1871—Dayton, Jan. 30, 1948; Wilbur, Millville, IN, Apr. 16, 1867—Dayton, May 30, 1912). Pioneers in man-carrying, powered aircraft. They first became interested in the possibility of man's flight in the 1890s after hearing about the glider flights of the German aviation pioneer Otto Lilienthal. In their DAYTON, Ohio, bicycle repair shop and factory, the Wrights, very able mechanics, were experimenting (most called it tinkering) with kites and gliders and every other aspect of aerodynamics. In their efforts to learn about every discovery having to do with flight, it was said they read every book in the Dayton public library pertaining to aerodynamics. They built a wind tunnel, first in the world, and developed their own science of flying, drawing up valuable tables of wind current and drift and noting other discoveries. They discovered the use of the aileron, probably the single most important discovery they made in preparation for the world's first flight of a heavier-than-air craft at Kitty Hawk, North Carolina (December 17, 1903). They chose Kitty Hawk because their investigations showed the air currents there were probably the best for their purposes. They continued their experiments at Dayton. The record-breaking flights of Wilbur in the United States and Orville in France brought them world fame, as well as orders from government and private organizations. they formed the American Wright Company in 1909. In 1948, the year of Orville's death, their historic Kitty Hawk plane was installed at the Smithsonian Institution. The house where Orville was born and their bicycle shop laboratory were bought by Henry FORD and moved to his GREENFIELD VILLAGE in Michigan, where they were restored and put on public display.

WRIGHT-PATTERSON AIR FORCE BASE. Dayton, Ohio. One of the largest airport installations in the world, Wright-Patterson is the main research and development base for the Air Force, headquarters of the Air Force Logistics Command. It is also the site of the Air Force Institute of Technology, the Air Force Medical Laboratory and the Air Force Museum, which exhibits more than 150 major historic aircraft and missles, spanning the period from the Wright Brothers, who made their headquarters in Dayton, to the space age.

WYANDOTTE (HURON) INDIANS. Descendants of the Huron tribe. Hurons early accepted Christianity and served as agents of the French in stirring up anti-IROQUOIS sentiment in the northeastern region of the United States. For this the Indians were named "Huron," a word in the French language similar to "slob." In 1648 a large group of Seneca and Mohawk attacked the Hurons north of modern Toronto, Canada. While probably fewer than three hundred Hurons were killed, panic caused many to flee into the winter unprepared. Many died of starvation and exposure. Survivors fled, many escaping into the area of present-day Indiana, Ohio and Michigan. They adopted for their name the word they used for their confederacy in the 1600s, Wendat, which became Wyandotte in white literature.

WYANDOTTE CAVE. One of the largest caves in North America. Wyandotte Cave, near White Cloud, Indiana, is a dry cavern with five floor levels and twenty-three miles of explored passages. Many spectacular side caverns exist along a four-hundred foot passage called Washington Avenue. One hundred thirty-five foot tall Monument Mountain is said to be the highest underground mountain in the world, but this is contested by such caverns as MARVEL CAVE in Missouri, 175 feet in height. Indians were known to have lived in the cave, which some scientists believe also shows evidence of prehistoric man.

WYANDOTTE, Michigan. City (pop. 34,-006), Wayne County, southeast Michigan. Wyandotte has been a U.S. steel industry pioneer, introducing the first steel analysis laboratory in 1862 and manufacturing the first Bessemer steel in America in 1864. The site of Wyandotte was first occupied by the WYANDOTTE Indians. Major John Biddle removed the Indians in 1818 and obtained 2,200 acres of land in the area. In 1853 Captain Eber B. Ward purchased the farm Biddle had established and founded the Eureka Iron and Steel Company on the waterfront, the first plant of that type in the DETROIT region. The position of the steel mill between the coal fields of Indiana and Ohio and the ore fields of upper Michigan seemed to assure the city of a bright future. Luck for Wyandotte suddenly changed with the unexpected death of Ward in 1875 and the financial panic of the same year. Ward's partners allowed the mill to fall into ruin. The fortunes of the city seemed bleak until J.B. Ford, a Pittsburgh glassmaker, drilled several experimental wells and established a small salt works. The first product of the works was soda ash, formerly imported from Belgium for the manufacture of plate glass. The city's extensive chemical industry expanded as caustic soda, calcium chloride, bromine, baking soda, and magnesium were also processed from the salt. Other products are automobile parts and barrels.

WYMAN, Jane. (St. Joseph, MO, Jan. 4, 1914—). Leading actress of the forties, divorced from Ronald REAGAN (1911-), and, later, star of television. Wyman's career has developed from playing dumb blondes to parts portraying scheming successful businesswomen. Her movie credits include *The Lost Weekend* (1945), *Johnny Belinda* (1948), for which she won the Academy Award for best actress, and *Magnificent Obsession* (1954). She has had one of the leading roles in the continuing television series *Falcon Crest*.

X-Y-Z

XAVIER UNIVERSITY. Established at CINCINNATI, Ohio, in 1831 as a Catholic Men's College, Xavier now incorporates Edgecliff College. The Emery Art Galleries are open to visitors, and the college operates a seismological observatory. A student body of 6,785 is instructed by a faculty of 343.

YATES, Richard. (Warsaw, KY, Jan. 18, 1815—St. Louis, MO, Nov. 27, 1873). CIVIL WAR governor of Illinois. Richard Yates was one of the state's most popular governors. He served three terms, 1842-1850, in the state legislature and was elected to Congress in 1850 and again in 1852. Yates favored the Homestead Act, opposed the Kansas-Nebraska bill, and supported establishing colleges with federal land grants. As a member of the new REPUBLICAN PARTY (established 1854-1856), he was a conservative supporter of Abraham LINCOLN (1809-1965). Yates served as governor from 1861 to 1865 and so vigorously supported the Civil War that he had to be advised to reduce the number of regiments and discharge the excessive recruits. He gave U. S. GRANT his first Civil War commission. After the war, Yates served one term in the United States Senate from 1865 to 1871. He supported vindictive Radical Republican measures against the South and voted in favor of President Johnson's conviction in the impeachment proceedings.

YEAR OF THE TEN BOATS. Name given to the period of a private, military-like sweep up the MISSISSIPPI RIVER in 1788 in an effort to drive out river PIRATES. The ten boats and their crews carried out the operation which resulted in the removal of the pirates as an obstacle to the rapid growth of such river towns as ST. LOUIS.

YELLOW SPRINGS, Ohio. Town (pop. 4,077), situated in southwest Ohio, near DAYTON, this quiet town took its name from the neighboring iron springs. The yellow discharges of the water attracted many health seekers. The community was founded in 1804. Mainly residential, it is noted particularly as the home of ANTIOCH UNIVERSITY, where the Antioch Plan of cooperative education gave the institution a worldwide reputation. The first president was the renowned educator Horace MANN (1796-1859). He was buried on the campus, and a monument marks the site, although the body was later removed to Rhode Island.

YERKES OBSERVATORY. Operated by the University of CHICAGO on its site at Williams Bay on LAKE GENEVA in southern Wisconsin, the telescope and observatory were the gift of Charles T. Yerkes. The facility was completed in 1897. The 40-inch refractor, largest of its type in the world, has a focal length of sixty-two feet and a weight of over twenty tons. This is considered to be about the limit of size of such a lens due to optical problems beyond that size. The refractor has made important contributions to the study of the heavens, especially in photographing the Milky Way and measuring the distances and spectra of stars and the size of double stars. Two other smaller scopes supplement the work of the larger.

YEWELL, George Henry. (Havre de Grace, MD, June. 20, 1830—Diamond Point, Lake George, NY, Sept. 26, 1923). Artist. Increasingly regarded by some experts as one of the nation's most undervalued artists, George Yewell began the study of art at IOWA CITY, Iowa. Recognizing his talent, his friends made it possible for Yewell to study in New York at an early age. Later his Iowa patron, Judge Charles Mason, paid his expenses for study in Paris. Staying in Paris, Yewell became one of the best known and best liked of the American painting group in the French capital. Painting for a time in Italy, he created one of the best-known works of the day. His "The Interior of St. Marks', Venice," is now a valued treasure of the Metropolitan Museum in New York. A stay in Egypt produced two richly colored "Street Scenes in Cairo," now belonging to the Memorial Union at the University of IOWA. One of his most famous portraits was that of Governor Samuel KIRKWOOD (1813-1894) of Iowa, one of the nine Yewell portraits in the possession of the Iowa State Historical Society. A Master of the National Academy, Yewell was all too familiar with the passing fads of art, which seemed to eclipse his fame. However he continued to produce his luminous works until his death at the age of ninety-two.

YOUNG, Brigham. (Whitingham, VT, June 1, 1801—Salt Lake City, UT, Aug. 29, 1877). Colonizer of Utah and second president of the MORMON Church. Young helped to organize the Mormon settlement of NAUVOO, Illinois, and became the leader of most Mormons after the murder of Joseph SMITH (1805-1844) in Carthage, Illinois, on June 27, 1844. Continued problems with other settlers in Illinois caused Young to leave the Midwest and find a settlement, now Salt Lake City, Utah, where there were no neighbors to interfere with the Mormon religion. Under Young's brilliant guidance, the Mormons built a substantial winter headquarters and spent the winter of 1846 at the present site of COUNCIL BLUFFS, Iowa, then moved on westward under Young's leadership.

YOUNG, Denton True (Cy). (Gilmore, OH, Mar. 29, 1867—Nov. 4, 1955). Professional baseball pitcher. Outstanding pitcher for whom the Best Pitcher of the Year award is named. Young began his career in the National League with Cleveland in 1890 and continued with St. Louis from 1899 to 1900. He went to the American league with Boston, from 1901 to 1908, and ended his playing career with Cleveland from 1909 to 1911. His record of 511 pitching wins still stands. He pitched a perfect game in 1904, and was a 20-game winner sixteen times and 30-game winner fifteen times. He was inducted into the Baseball Hall of Fame in 1937.

YOUNGER, Thomas Coleman (Cole). (Jackson County, MO, Jan 15, 1844—Jackson County, MO, Mar 21, 1916). Outlaw. He was a Confederate guerilla during the CIVIL WAR and later joined the Jesse James gang. In 1876 he and his brothers, James and Robert, were sentenced to life imprisonment after being apprehended in a bank robbery attempt. Robert Younger died in prison, but James was paroled in 1901. Cole was pardoned in 1903 and later joined a Wild West show.

YOUNGSTOWN, Ohio. City (pop. 115,436), seat of Mahoning County, situated in northeastern Ohio near the Pennsylvania border. Incorpated in 1849, it occupies an area of 34.5 square Miles. The city was named for early settler John Young, who moved on west without knowing that one of the great steelmaking cities of the world would be named for him. Despite the decline in U.S. steel production due to foreign competition, Youngstown is still one of the three major Ohio producers. The other extensive manufactures include aluminum extrusions, AUTOMOBILES and automobile parts, sprinkler systems, rubber goods, rolling mill equipment, plant equipment and electric lamps. Operation of the first iron furnace of the city came in 1803, soon after the discovery nearby of all the necessary raw materials for the industry—iron ore, COAL and limestone. Steel making arrived in the late 1800s. The city's growth also was stimulated by the opening of the Ohio Canal in 1839 and by the arrival of the railroad in 1853. Youngstown is the seat of Youngstown State University, founded in 1908 as a part of the operation of the city YMCA.

Butler Art Institute attracts many Youngstown visitors.

YUKON, Missouri. Village near Licking. One of history's minor mysteries began here in 1930 when a mysterious man known as Harry Watson constructed an eighteen-room, cream-colored mansion next to an eighty-foot wooden observation tower. Upon investigation by the Texas County sheriff, the man known as Watson was identified as Harry Getchie, wanted for mail robbery. Getchie was arrested, convicted by a Federal court, and died in prison. His estate remained unoccupied and the proposed use of the tower was never known.

ZANE, Ebenezer. (Moorefield, WV, then VA, 1747—Wheeling WV, Nov. 19, 1812). Ohio pioneer, Zane and his brothers Silas and Jonathan began their westward trek in 1769, founding Wheeling in what is now West Virginia. They became prominent as Indian fighters, defending the Wheeling region from attacks in 1777 and 1782. Their sister, Elizabeth Zane, was noted for her heroism in these attacks. In 1796 Congress gave Zane permission to build a road through Ohio from Wheeling to Maysville, Kentucky. With the help of brother Jonathan and brother-in-law John McIntire, famed Zanes Trace was constructed and the builders established communities along the way, among them ZANESVILLE, Ohio, purchased by Ebenezer, then sold to his brother and son-in-law. The Trace played a key role in opening Ohio and the West. Ebenezer Zane's grandson was Zane GREY (1875-1939), famed author of western tales.

ZANESVILLE, Ohio. City (pop. 28,655), seat of Muskingum County, is situated in east central Ohio on the broad plain and the hills at the confluence of the MUSKINGUM and Licking rivers, which divide the city into three parts. It took its name from founder Ebenezer ZANE (1747-1812). In 1797 Ebenezer Zane surveyed Zane's Trace, for which service he was granted a square mile of territory and chose the site of present Zanesville. He soon sold the land to his brother Jonathan and son-in-law John McIntire. The fine clay of the area provided the first industry, and Zanesville is still known for its pottery. The glass sands in the region provided for the glass industry there. Zane GREY (1875-1939), the noted writer of western tales and grandson of Ebenezer Zane, was born at Zanesville. The Ohio Ceramics Center and Dillon Reservoir State Park are nearby.

ZION, Illinois. City (pop. 17,861), Lake County, northeastern Illinois near the Wisconsin border. Zion was founded by John Alexander Dowie, a Scottish fundamentalist preacher who organized the Christian Catholic Apostolic Church in 1896. Dowie announced on December 31, 1899, that land had been acquired in Lake County on which the city of Zion would be built. The object of the new city was to establish "the rule of God in every department of the government." Dowie preached that "where God rules, man prospers." Crude shacks were hastily built to accommodate the thousands who raced to the new city. A lace factory was established by Dowie who brought in skilled workers from Nottingham, England. Dowie's declaration that he was another Elijah led many to leave, and he died while fighting the division in his church. After Dowie's death, the church was led by Wilbur Glenn Voliva, a man who seriously believed that the earth was flat. Voliva enforced the rules established by Dowie which made the church the owner of all commercial establishments. Among the prohibited businesses were theaters, pharmacies, and offices or residences of practicing surgeons and physicians. Dowie's rules also prohibited playing cards, eating of oysters, clams and rabbit meat and the sale of liquor and tobacco. Bacon was made of beef, as pork was also prohibited. With the city always precariously balanced between prosperity and financial failure, Voliva lost political control in 1939. Reorganization led to individual ownership of real estate and drastic modification of the managed economy. Today Zion is much like any of its neighboring communities. However, in 1987 the city was sued in an attempt to remove a religious content from its city seal, a matter not settled at this writing.

ZOAR, Ohio. Village (pop. 238). Described as a "quaint village," Zoar is situated in northeast Ohio in Tuscarawas County, south of CANTON, Ohio. In 1817-1818 a group of Separatists from southern Germany came to the area seeking religious freedom. They purchased 5,600 acres, which they began farming on an individual basis. However, the number of old and invalid people among them prompted the organization of a communal society, chartered in 1832 as the Separatist Society of Zoar. The town was named for the Biblical city to which Lot fled when he left Sodom. This experiment prospered for eighty years. By 1874 the society had 300 members, had increased the holdings at Zoar to 7,000 acres and had purchased land in Iowa. They also operated numerous industries. After younger members began to demand more individual freedom, in 1898 the society disbanded and divided the property among the members. The King's Palace was built in 1835 and used as a residence by Zoarist leader Joseph Bimeler until his death in 1853. It was turned into a museum of records of the society along with pottery, furniture, musical instruments and other mementos. Among the accomplishments of the Zoarists was the Zoar Garden in the center of the village, planted by the founders in the manner of the New Jerusalem found in the Bible's book of Revelation. Twelve walks were built to radiate from a spruce tree in the center, with the spruce representing the tree of life. The historic site is now operated as the Zoar Village State Museum.

GENERAL

Alsberg, Henry G., ed. *The American Guide*. New York: Hastings, 1949

Andrews, Clarence, Ed. *Growing Up in the Midwest*. Ames: Iowa State Univ., 1981

Banta, Richard E. *The Ohio: A History of the River and the Valley*. New York: Rinehart 1949

Beard, Charles A. and Mary R. *The Rise of American Civilization*, Rev and enl. ed. New York: Macmillan, 1966

Bissell, Richard. *My Life on the Mississippi, Or Why I Am Not Mark Twain*. New York: Little Brown, 1973

Cantor, George. *The Great Lakes Guidebook*. Ann Arbor; Univ. of Michigan, 1973

Dary, David. *True Tales of the Old-Time Plains*. New York: Crown, 1979

Davis, Norah Deakin. *The Father of Waters; A Mississippi River Chronicle*. San Francisco: Sierra Club, 1982

Drury, John. *Midwest Heritage: Short Survey of Midwest History, Illustrated with Old engravings*. New York: Crowell, 1966

Eckert, Allan W. *Gateway to Empire*. New York: Little Brown, 1982

Glazer, Sidney. *The Middle West: A Study of Progress*. New York: Bookman, 1962

Havighurst, Walter. *River to the West: Three Centuries of the Ohio*. Putnam, 1970

Havighurst, Walter. *The Heartland: Ohio, Indiana, Illinois*. New York: Harper, 1962

Laycock, George and Ellen. *The Ohio Valley: Your Guide to America's Heartland*. New York: Doubleday, 1983

Madson, John. *Where the Sky Began: Land of the Tall Grass Prairie*. New York: Houghton, 1982

McLaughlin, Robert. *The Heartland: Illinois, Indiana, Michigan, Ohio, Wisconsin*. New York: Time, 1967

Severin, Timothy. *Explorers of the Mississippi*. New York: Knopf, 1968

Stevens, R. Harry. *The Middle West*. New York: Macmillan, 1958

Waitley, Douglas. *Portrait of the Midwest: An Informal History*. New York: Abelard, 1963

ARCHITECTURE

Brooks, H. Allen. *The Prairie School: F. L. Wright and his Midwest Contemporaries*. Toronto: Univ. of Toronto, 1972

Condit, Carl W. *The Chicago School of Architecture: A History of Commercial and Public Building in the Chicago Area, 1875-1925*. Chicago: Univ. of Chicago, 1964

ART

Heller, Nancy and Julia Williams. *The Regionalists*. Cincinnati: Watson-Guptil, 1976

COMMUNES

Holloway, Mark. *Heavens on Earth: Utopian Communities in America, 1680-1880*. rev. ed. New York: Dover, 1966

CULTURE

Brock, Wallace and B. K. Winer, eds. *Homespun America*. New York: Simon and Schuster, 1958

Lawrence College. *The Culture of the Middle West*. Appleton, Wis.: Lawrence College, 1944

ETHNIC GROUPS

Dinnerstein, Leonard and Frederic C. Jaker, eds. *Aliens: A History of Ethnic Minorities in America*. New York: Appleton, 1970

EXPLORATION

Clark, William and Meriwether Lewis. *History of the Expedition of Captains Lewis and Clark, to the Sources of the Missouri, Thence Across the Rocky Mountains, and Down the River Columbia to the Pacific Ocean*, 2 vols. Philadelphia and New York: 1814

Cox, Isaac J. ed. The Journals of Rene Robert Cavelier, Sieur La Salle, 2 vols. New York: Barnes, 1905

Nicollet, Joseph Nichols. *Journals*. St. Paul: Minn. Historical Society, 1970

Pike, Zebulon M. *An Account of Expeditions...During the Years 1805, 1806 and 1807*. Philadelphia and Baltimore: 1810

FOLKLORE

Dorson, Richard M. *American Folklore*. Chicago: Univ. of Chicago, 1959

HISTORY

Blegen, Theodore C. *The Land Lies Open: History of the Upper Mississippi.* Minneapolis: Univ. of Minnesota, 1949

Bond, Beverly W., Jr. *The Civilization of the Old Northwest...1788-1812.* New York: Macmillan, 1934

Clark, Daniel E. *The Middle West in American History.* New York: Crowell, 1966

Clark, George Rogers. *The Conquest of the Illinois.* Chicago: Donnelley, 1920

Croy, Homer *Corn Country: Folksy History of the Corn Belt.* New York: Duell, 1947

Gilbert, Paul and Charles L. Bryson. *Chicago and its Makers.* Chicago: Mendelsohn, 1929

Havighurst, Walter. *Land of Promise: The Story of the Northwest Territory.* New York: Macmillan, 1946

McDermott, John F., ed. *The French in the Mississippi Valley.* Urbana: Univ. of Illinois, 1965

INDIANS—PREHISTORIC PEOPLES

Hyde, George E. *Indians of the High Plains: From the Prehistoric Period to the Coming of the Europeans.* Norman: Univ. of Oklahoma, 1959

Hyde, George E. *Indians of the Woodlands: From Prehistoric Times to 1725.* Norman: Univ of Oklahoma, 1962

Jackson, Helen Hunt. *A Century of Dishonor: A Sketch of the U.S. Government's Dealing with Some of the Indian Tribes.* New York: Harper, 1881

Kinietz, W. Vernon. *The Indians of the Western Great Lakes: 1615-1760.* Ann Arbor: Univ. of Michigan, 1940

LITERATURE

Kramer, Dale. *Chicago Renaissance: The Literary Life of the Midwest, 1900-1930.* New York: Appleton, 1960

Rusk, Ralph. *The Literature of the Middle Western Frontier,* 2 vols. New York: Columbia Univ., 1925

Stein, Rita. *A Literary Tour Guide to the U.S.: West and Midwest.* New York: Morrow, 1979

POLITICS

Nye, Russell. Midwestern Progressive Politics, 1870-1958. rev. ed. East Lansing: Michigan State Univ., 1959

RELIGION

Obenham, Victor. *The Church and Faith in Middle America.* Philadelphia, Westminster, 1963

SOCIAL LIFE

Aaron, Daniel. *Men of Good Hope: A Story of American Progressives.* New York: Oxford, 1951

Hutton, Graham. *Midwest at Noon.* Chicago: Univ. of Chicago, 1946

STATES

Illinois

Alford, Clarence, ed. *Centennial History of Illinois,* 6 vols. Springfield: Centennial Commission, 1917-1920

Angle, Paul M., ed. *Prairie State: Impressions of Illinois, 1673-1967, by Travelers and Other Observers.* Chicago: Univ. of Chicago, 1968

Carpenter, Allan. *Illinois: Enchantment of America.* Chicago: Childrens Press, 1979

WPA Federal Writers' Project. *Illinois: A Descriptive and Historical Guide,* rev. ed. New York: Hastings House, 1974

Indiana

Atherton, Lewis E. *Main Street in the Middle Border.* Bloomington: Indiana Univ., 1954

Carpenter, Allan. *Indiana: Enchantment of America.* Chicago: Childrens Press, 1978

Wilson, William E. *Indiana: A History.* Bloomington: Indiana Univ., 1966

WPA Federal Writers' Project. *Indiana: A Guide to the Hoosier State.* New York: Oxford Univ. Press, 1941

Iowa

Carpenter, Allan. *Iowa: Enchantment of America.* Chicago: Childrens Press, 1979

Hake, Herbert. *Iowa Inside Out.* Ames: Iowa State Univ., 1968

WPA Federal Writers' Project. *Iowa: A Guide to the Hawkeye State.* New York: Viking, 1938

Michigan

Carpenter, Allan. *Michigan: Enchantment of America.* Chicago: Childrens Press, 1978

WPA Federal Writers' Project. *Michigan: A Guide to the Wolverine State.* New York: Oxford, 1941

Minnesota

Blegen, Theodore C. *Minnesota: A History of the State.* Minneapolis: Univ. of Minnesota, 1963

Carpenter, Allan. *Minnesota: Enchantment of America.* Chicago: Childrens Press, 1978

WPA Federal Writers' Project. *Minnesota: A State Guide,* rev. ed. New York: Hastings, 1954

Missouri

Carpenter, Allan. *Missouri: Enchantment of America.* Chicago: Childrens Press, 1978

March, David. *History of Missouri,* 4 vols. New York: Lewis, 1967

McReynolds, Edwin C. Missouri: A History of the Crossroads State. Norman: Univ. of Oklahoma, 1962

WPA Federal Writers Project. *Missouri: A Guide to the "Show Me" State.* New York: Duell, 1941

Ohio

Carpenter, Allan. *Ohio: Enchantment of America.* Chicago: Childrens Press, 1978

Roseboom, Eugene H. and Francis P. Weisenburger. *A History of Ohio,* 2nd ed. Columbus: Ohio Historical Soc., 1967

WPA Federal Writers' Project. *The Ohio Guide,* 3rd ed. New York: Oxford Univ. Press, 1946

Wisconsin

Austin, H. Russell. *The Wisconsin Story: The Building of a Vanguard State* rev. ed. Milwaukee: Milwaukee Journal, 1957

Carpenter, Allan. *Wisconsin: Enchantment of America* Chicago: Childrens Press, 1978

WPA Federal Writers' Project. *Wisconsin, A Guide to the Badger State,* rev. ed. New York, Hastings House, 1954

A

Index

Index

Index

Index

Index

Index

E

F

Index

H

Index

Index

Index

Index

M

Index

Index

Index

P

Index

T

Index

Index

X

Index

Zoar Village has been restored.